Application-Specific Integrated Circuits

Michael John Sebastian Smith

University of Hawaii
Compass Design Automation

ADDISON-WESLEY

An imprint of Addison Wesley Longman, Inc.

Reading, Massachusetts • Harlow, England • Menlo Park, California • Berkeley, California
Don Mills, Ontario • Sydney • Bonn • Amsterdam • Tokyo • Mexico City

This book is in the Addison-Wesley VLSI Systems Series
Lynn Conway and Charles Seitz, *Consulting Editors*

Sponsoring Editor	Peter Gordon
Associate Editor	Helen Goldstein
Senior Production Supervisor	Juliet Silveri
Copyeditor/Proofreader	Cynthia Benn
Cover Design Supervisor	Simone Payment
Marketing Manager	Tracy Russ
Manufacturing Manager	Roy Logan

Material in Chapters 10–12, Chapter 14, Appendix A, and Appendix B in this book is reprinted from IEEE Std 1149.1-1990, "IEEE Standard Test Access Port and Boundary-Scan Architecture," Copyright © 1990; IEEE Std 1076/INT-1991 "IEEE Standards Interpretations: IEEE Std 1076-1987, IEEE Standard VHDL Language Reference Manual," Copyright © 1991; IEEE Std 1076-1993 "IEEE Standard VHDL Language Reference Manual," Copyright © 1993; IEEE Std 1164-1993 "IEEE Standard Multivalue Logic System for VHDL Model Interoperability (Std_logic_1164)," Copyright © 1993; IEEE Std 1149.1b-1994 "Supplement to IEEE Std 1149.1-1990, IEEE Standard Test Access Port and Boundary-Scan Architecture," Copyright © 1994; IEEE Std 1076.4-1995 "IEEE Standard for VITAL Application-Specific Integerated Circuit (ASIC) Modeling Specification," Copyright © 1995; IEEE Std 1364-1995 "IEEE Standard Description Language Based on the Verilog® Hardware Description Language," Copyright © 1995; and IEEE Std 1076.3-1997 "IEEE Standard for VHDL Synthesis Packages," Copyright © 1997; by the Institute of Electrical and Electronics Engineers, Inc. The IEEE disclaims any responsibility or liability resulting from the placement and use in the described manner. Information is reprinted with the permission of the IEEE. Figures produced by the Compass Design Automation software in Chapters 9–17 are reprinted with permission of Compass Design Automation. Figures describing Xilinx FPGAs in Chapters 4–8 are courtesy of Xilinx, Inc. ©Xilinx, Inc. 1996, 1997. All rights reserved. Figures describing Altera CPLDs in Chapters 4–8 are courtesy of Altera Corporation. Altera is a trademark and service mark of Altera Corporation in the United States and other countries. Altera products are the intellectual property of Altera Corporation and are protected by copyright laws and one or more U.S. and foreign patents and patent applications. Figures describing Actel FPGAs in Chapters 4–8 are courtesy of Actel Corporation.

Library of Congress Cataloging-in-Publication Data

Smith, Michael J. S. (Michael John Sebastian)
   Application-specific integrated circuits / Michael J.S. Smith.
      p.   cm.
   Includes bibliographical references and index.
   ISBN 0-201-50022-1
   1. Application-specific integrated circuits. I. Title.
TK7874.6.S63   1997
621.39'5--dc20   93-32538
                                                          CIP

This book is due for return on or before the last date shown below.

Don Gresswell Ltd., London, N21   Cat. No. 1207

DG 02242/71

PREFACE

In 1988 I began to teach full-custom VLSI design. In 1990 I started teaching ASIC design instead, because my students found it easier to get jobs in this field. I wrote a proposal to The National Science Foundation (NSF) to use electronic distribution of teaching material. Dick Lyon helped me with preparing the first few CD-ROMs at Apple, but Chuck Seitz, Lynn Conway, and others explained to me that I was facing a problem that Carver Mead and Lynn had experienced in trying to get the concept of multichip wafers adopted. It was not until the publication of the Mead–Conway text that people accepted this new idea. It was suggested that I must generate interest using a conventional format before people would use my material in a new one (CD-ROM or the Internet). In 1992 I stopped writing papers and began writing this book—a result of my experiments in computer-based education. I have nearly finished this book twice. The first time was a copy of my notes. The second time was just before the second edition of Weste and Eshragian was published—a hard act to follow. In order to finish in 1997 I had to stop updating and including new ideas and material and now this book consists of three parts: Chapters 1–8 are an introduction to ASICs, 9–14 cover ASIC logical design, and 15–17 cover the physical design of ASICs.

The book is intended for a wide audience. It may be used in an undergraduate or graduate course. It is also intended for those in industry who are involved with ASICs. Another function of this book is an "ASIC Encyclopedia," and therefore I have kept the background material needed to a minimum. The book makes extensive use of industrial tools and examples. The examples in Chapters 2 and 3 use tools and libraries from MicroSim (PSpice), Meta Software (HSPICE), Compass Design Automation (standard-cell and gate-array libraries), and Tanner Research (L-Edit). The programmable ASIC design examples in Chapter 4–8 use tools from Compass, Synopsys, Actel, Altera, and Xilinx. The examples in Chapter 9 (covering low-level design entry) used tools from Exemplar, MINC, AMD, UC Berkeley, Compass, Capilano, Mentor Graphics Corporation, and Cadence Design Automation. The VHDL examples in Chapter 10 were checked using QuickVHDL from Mentor, V-System Plus from Model Technology, and Scout from Compass. The Verilog examples in Chapter 11 were checked using Verilog–XL from Cadence, V-System Plus, and VeriWell from Wellspring Solutions. The logic synthesis examples in

Chapter 12 were checked with the ASIC Synthesizer product family from Compass and tools from Mentor, Synopsys, and UC Berkeley. The simulation examples in Chapter 13 were checked with QuickVHDL, V-System/Plus, PSpice, Verilog-XL, DesignWorks from Capilano Computing, CompassSim, QSim, MixSim, and HSPICE. The test examples in Chapter 14 were checked using test software from Compass, Cadence, Mentor, Synopsys and Capilano's DesignWorks. The physical design examples in Chapters 15–17 were generated and tested using Preview, Gate Ensemble, and Cell Ensemble (Cadence) as well as ChipPlanner, ChipCompiler, and PathFinder (Compass). All these tools are installed at the University of Hawaii.

I wrote the text using FrameMaker. This allows me to project the text and figures using an LCD screen and an overhead projector. I used a succession of Apple Macintosh computers: a PowerBook 145, a 520, and lastly a 3400 with 144 MB of RAM, which made it possible for me to create updates to the index in just under one minute. Equations are "live" in FrameMaker. Thus,

$$\text{book thickness} = \#\text{pages} \times 0.0015 \text{ in./page} \approx (1000)(1.5 \times 10^{-3}) = 1.5 \text{ in.}$$

can be updated in a lecture and the new result displayed. The circuit layouts are color EPS files with enhanced B&W PICT previews created using L-Edit from Tanner Research. All of the Verilog and VHDL code examples, compiler and simulation input/output, and the layout CIF that were used in the final version are included as conditional (hidden) text in the FrameMaker document, which is approximately 200 MB and just over 6,000 pages (my original source material spans fourteen 560 MB optical disks). Software can operate on the hidden text, allowing, for example, a choice of simulators to run the HDL code live in class. I converted draft versions of the VHDL and Verilog LRMs and related standards to FrameMaker and built hypertext links to my text, but copyright problems will have to be solved before this type of material may be published. I drew all the figures using FreeHand. They are "layered" allowing complex drawings to be built-up slowly or animated by turning layers on or off. This is difficult to utilize in book form, but can be done live in the classroom.

A course based on FPGAs can use Chapter 1 and Chapters 4–8. A course using commercial semicustom ASIC design tools may use Chapters 1–2 or Chapters 1–3 and then skip to Chapter 9 if you use schematic entry, Chapter 10 (if you use VHDL), or Chapter 11 (if you use Verilog) together with Chapter 12. All classes can use Chapters 13 and 14. FPGA-based classes may skim Chapters 15–17, but classes in semicustom design should cover these chapters. The chapter dependencies—Y(X) means Chapter Y depends on X—are approximately: 1, 2(1), 3(2), 4(2), 5(4), 6(5), 7(6), 8(7), 9(2), 10(2), 11(2), 12(10 or 11), 13(2), 14(13), 15(2), 16(15), 17(16).

I used the following references to help me with the orthography of complex terms, style, and punctuation while writing: *Merriam-Webster's Collegiate Dictionary,* 10th edition, 1996, Springfield, MA: Merriam-Webster, ISBN 0-87779-709-9, PE1628.M36; *The Chicago Manual of Style,* 14th edition, Chicago: University of

Chicago Press, 1993, ISBN 0-226-10389-7, Z253.U69; and *Merriam-Webster's Standard American Style Manual*, 1985, Springfield, MA: Merriam-Webster, ISBN 0-87779-133-3, PN147.W36. A particularly helpful book on technical writing is *BUGS in Writing* by Lyn Dupré, 1995, Reading, MA: Addison-Wesley, ISBN 0-201-60019-6, PE1408.D85 (this book grew from Lyn Dupré's unpublished work, Style SomeX, which I used).

The bibliography at the end of each chapter provides alternative sources if you cannot find what you are looking for. I have included the International Standard Book Number[1] (ISBN) and Library of Congress (LOC) Call Number for books, and the International Standard Serial Number[2] (ISSN) for journals (see the LOC information system, LOCIS, at `http://www.loc.gov`). I did not include references to material that I could not find myself (except where I have noted in the case of new or as yet unpublished books). The electronic references given in this text have (a last) access date of 4/19/97 and omit enclosing <> if the reference does not include spaces.

I receive a tremendous level of support and cooperation from industry in my work. I thank the following for help with this project: Cynthia Benn and Lyn Dupré for editing; Helen Goldstein, Peter Gordon, Susan London-Payne, Tracy Russ, and Juliet Silveri, all at Addison-Wesley; Matt Bowditch and Kim Arney at Argosy; Richard Lyon, Don North, William Rivard, Glen Stone, the managers of the Newton group, and many others at Apple Computer who provided financial support; Apple for providing support in the form of software and computers; Bill Becker, Fern Forcier, Donna Isidro, Mike Kliment, Paul McLellan, Tom Schaefer, Al Stein, Rich Talburt, Bill Walker, and others at Compass Design Automation and VLSI Technology for providing the opportunity for me to work on this book over many years and allowing me to test material inside these companies and on lecture tours they sponsored; Chuck Seitz at Caltech; Joseph Cavallaro, Bernie Chern, Jerry Dillion, Mike Foster, and Paul Hulina at the NSF; the NSF for financial support with a Presidential Young Investigator Award; Jim Rowson and Doug Fairbairn; Constantine Anagnostopolous, Pin Tschang and members of the ASIC design groups at Kodak for financial support; the disk-drive design group at Digital Equipment Corp. (Massachusetts), Hewlett-Packard, and Sun Microsystems for financial support; Ms. MOSIS and all of the staff at MOSIS who each have helped me at one point or another by providing silicon, technical support, and documentation; Bob Brodersen, Roger Howe, Randy Katz, and Ed Lee of UC Berkeley for help while I was visiting UCB; James Plummer of Stanford, for providing me with access to the Terman Engineering Library as a visiting scholar, as well as Abbas El Gamal and Paul Losleben, also at Stanford, for help on several occasions; Don Bouldin at University of Tennessee; Krzysztof Kozminski at MCNC for providing Uncle lay-

---

[1] A code that uniquely identifies a book, the tenth and last digit is a check digit.

[2] This number uniquely identifies a serial (a magazine, a journal, and so on). It is a seven-digit number with an eighth check digit (which may be the roman numeral X, the value ten).

out software; Gershom Kedem at Duke University for the public domain tools his group has written; Sue Drouin, José De Castro, and others at Mentor Graphics Corporation in Oregon for providing documentation and tools; Vahan Kasardjhan, Gail Grego, Michele Warthen, Steve Gardner, and others at the University Program at Cadence Design Automation in San Jose who helped with tools, documentation, and support; Karen Dorrington and the Cadence group in Massachusetts; Andy Haines, Tom Koppin, Sherri Mieth, Velma Miller, Robert Nalesnik, Mike Sarpa, Telle Whitney, and others at Actel for software, hardware, parts, and documentation; Peter Alfke, Leslie Baxter, Brad Fawcett, Chris Kingsley, Karlton Lau, Rick Mitchell, Scott Nance, and Richard Ravel at Xilinx for support, parts, software, and documentation; Greg Hedmann at NorComp for data on FPGAs; Anna Acevedo, Suzanne Bailey, Antje MacNaughton, Richard Terrell, and Altera for providing software, hardware programmers, parts, and documentation; the documentation group and executive management at LSI Logic for tools, libraries, and documentation; Toshiba, NEC, AT&T/NCR, Lucent, and Hitachi (for documentation); NEC for their visiting scholar program at UH; Fred Furtek, Oscar Naval, and Claire Pinkham at Concurrent Logic, Randy Fish at Crosspoint, and Gary Banta at Plus Logic—all for documentation; Paul Titchener and others at Comdisco (now part of Cadence Design Automation) for providing design tools; John Tanner and his staff at Tanner Research for providing their tools and documentation; Mahendra Jain and Nanci Magoun, who let me debug early prototypes at the IDEA conference organized by ASIC Technology and News; Exemplar for providing documentation on its tools; MINC for providing a copy of its FPGA software and documentation; Claudia Traver and Synopsys for tools and documentation; Mentor Graphics Corporation for providing its complete range of software; Alain Hanover and others at ViewLogic for providing tools; Mary Shepherd and Jerry Walker at IEEE for help with permissions; Meta Software for providing HSPICE; Chris Dewhurst and colleagues at Capilano Computing for its design tools; Greg Seltzer (Model Technology) and Charley Rowley for providing V-System Plus with online documentation prototypes; Farallon and Telebit for the software and hardware I used for early experiments with telelectures. Many research students at the University of Hawaii helped me throughout this project including: Chin Huang, Clem Portmann, Christeen Gray, Karlton Lau, Jon Otaguro, Moe Lwin, Troy Stockstad, Ron Jorgenson, Derwin Mattos, William Rivard, Wendy Ching, Anil Aggrawal, Sudhakar Jilla, Linda Xu, Angshuman Saha, Harish Pareek, Claude van Ham, Wen Huang, Kumar Vadhri, Yan Zhong, Yatin Acharya, and Barana Ranaweera. Each of the classes that used early versions of this text at the University of Hawaii at Manoa have also contributed by finding errors. The remaining errors are mine.

Michael John Sebastian Smith
Palo Alto and Honolulu, 1997

CONTENTS

INTRODUCTION TO ASICs

1

An **ASIC** (pronounced "A-sick"; bold typeface defines a new term) is an **application-specific integrated circuit**—at least that is what the acronym stands for. Before we answer the question of what *that* means we first look at the evolution of the silicon chip or **integrated circuit (IC)**.

Figure 1.1(a) shows an IC package (this is a pin-grid array, or PGA, shown upside down; the pins will go through holes in a printed-circuit board). People often call the package a chip, but, as you can see in Figure 1.1(b), the silicon chip itself (more properly called a **die**) is mounted in the cavity under the sealed lid. A PGA package is usually made from a ceramic material, but plastic packages are also common.

FIGURE 1.1 An integrated circuit (IC). (a) A pin-grid array (PGA) package. (b) The silicon die or chip is under the package lid.

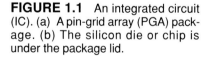
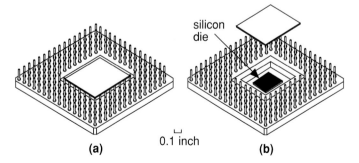

0.1 inch

(a)   **(b)**

1

The physical size of a silicon die varies from a few millimeters on a side to over 1 inch on a side, but instead we often measure the size of an IC by the number of logic gates or the number of transistors that the IC contains. As a unit of measure a **gate equivalent** corresponds to a two-input NAND gate (a circuit that performs the logic function, $F = \overline{A \cdot B}$). Often we just use the term *gates* instead of gate equivalents when we are measuring chip size—not to be confused with the gate terminal of a transistor. For example, a 100 k-gate IC contains the equivalent of 100,000 two-input NAND gates.

The semiconductor industry has evolved from the first ICs of the early 1970s and matured rapidly since then. Early **small-scale integration** (**SSI**) ICs contained a few (1 to 10) logic gates—NAND gates, NOR gates, and so on—amounting to a few tens of transistors. The era of **medium-scale integration** (**MSI**) increased the range of integrated logic available to counters and similar, larger scale, logic functions. The era of **large-scale integration** (**LSI**) packed even larger logic functions, such as the first microprocessors, into a single chip. The era of **very large scale integration** (**VLSI**) now offers 64-bit microprocessors, complete with cache memory and floating-point arithmetic units—well over a million transistors—on a single piece of silicon. As CMOS process technology improves, transistors continue to get smaller and ICs hold more and more transistors. Some people (especially in Japan) use the term **ultra large scale integration** (**ULSI**), but most people stop at the term VLSI; otherwise we have to start inventing new words.

The earliest ICs used **bipolar technology** and the majority of logic ICs used either **transistor–transistor logic** (**TTL**) or emitter-coupled logic (ECL). Although invented before the bipolar transistor, the **metal-oxide-silicon** (**MOS**) transistor was initially difficult to manufacture because of problems with the oxide interface. As these problems were gradually solved, metal-gate *n*-channel MOS (**nMOS** or **NMOS**) technology developed in the 1970s. At that time MOS technology required fewer masking steps, was denser, and consumed less power than equivalent bipolar ICs. This meant that, for a given performance, an MOS IC was cheaper than a bipolar IC and led to investment and growth of the MOS IC market.

By the early 1980s the aluminum gates of the transistors were replaced by polysilicon gates, but the name MOS remained. The introduction of polysilicon as a gate material was a major improvement in CMOS technology, making it easier to make two types of transistors, *n*-channel MOS and *p*-channel MOS transistors, on the same IC—a **complementary MOS** (**CMOS**, never cMOS) technology. The principal advantage of CMOS over NMOS is lower power consumption. Another advantage of a polysilicon gate was a simplification of the fabrication process, allowing devices to be scaled down in size.

There are four CMOS transistors in a two-input NAND gate (and a two-input NOR gate too), so to convert between gates and transistors, you multiply the number of gates by 4 to obtain the number of transistors. We can also measure an IC by the smallest **feature size** (roughly half the length of the smallest transistor) imprinted on the IC. Transistor dimensions are measured in microns (a micron, 1 μm, is a millionth of a meter). Thus we talk about a 0.5 µm IC or say an IC is built in (or with) a 0.5 µm process, meaning that the smallest transistors are 0.5 µm in length. We give a special label, λ or **lambda**, to this smallest feature size. Since lambda is equal to half of the smallest transistor length, $\lambda \approx 0.25$ µm in a 0.5 µm process. Many of the drawings in this book use a scale marked with lambda for the same reason we place a scale on a map.

A modern submicron CMOS process is now just as complicated as a submicron bipolar or BiCMOS (a combination of bipolar and CMOS) process. However, CMOS ICs have established a dominant position, are manufactured in much greater volume than any other technology, and therefore, because of the economy of scale, the cost of CMOS ICs is less than a bipolar or BiCMOS IC for the same function. Bipolar and BiCMOS ICs are still used for special needs. For example, bipolar technology is generally capable of handling higher voltages than CMOS. This makes bipolar and BiCMOS ICs useful in power electronics, cars, telephone circuits, and so on.

Some digital logic ICs and their analog counterparts (analog/digital converters, for example) are **standard parts**, or standard ICs. You can select standard ICs from catalogs and data books and buy them from distributors. Systems manufacturers and designers can use the same standard part in a variety of different **microelectronic systems** (systems that use microelectronics or ICs).

With the advent of VLSI in the 1980s engineers began to realize the advantages of designing an IC that was customized or tailored to a particular system or application rather than using standard ICs alone. Microelectronic system design then becomes a matter of defining the functions that you can implement using standard ICs and then implementing the remaining logic functions (sometimes called **glue logic**) with one or more **custom ICs**. As VLSI became possible you could build a system from a smaller number of components by combining many standard ICs into a few custom ICs. Building a microelectronic system with fewer ICs allows you to reduce cost and improve reliability.

Of course, there are many situations in which it is not appropriate to use a custom IC for each and every part of an microelectronic system. If you need a large amount of memory, for example, it is still best to use standard memory ICs, either **dynamic random-access memory** (**DRAM** or dRAM), or **static RAM** (**SRAM** or sRAM), in conjunction with custom ICs.

One of the first conferences to be devoted to this rapidly emerging segment of the IC industry was the *IEEE Custom Integrated Circuits Conference* (CICC), and the proceedings of this annual conference form a useful reference to the development of custom ICs. As different types of custom ICs began to evolve for different types of applications, these new ICs gave rise to a new term: application-specific IC, or ASIC. Now we have the *IEEE International ASIC Conference*, which tracks advances in ASICs separately from other types of custom ICs. Although the exact definition of an ASIC is difficult, we shall look at some examples to help clarify what people in the IC industry understand by the term.

Examples of ICs that are *not* ASICs include standard parts such as: memory chips sold as a commodity item—ROMs, DRAM, and SRAM; microprocessors; TTL or TTL-equivalent ICs at SSI, MSI, and LSI levels.

Examples of ICs that *are* ASICs include: a chip for a toy bear that talks; a chip for a satellite; a chip designed to handle the interface between memory and a microprocessor for a workstation CPU; and a chip containing a microprocessor as a cell together with other logic.

As a general rule, if you can find it in a data book, then it is probably not an ASIC, but there are some exceptions. For example, two ICs that might or might not be considered ASICs are a controller chip for a PC and a chip for a modem. Both of these examples are specific to an application (shades of an ASIC) but are sold to many different system vendors (shades of a standard part). ASICs such as these are sometimes called **application-specific standard products** (**ASSPs**).

Trying to decide which members of the huge IC family are application-specific is tricky—after all, every IC has an application. For example, people do not usually consider an application-specific microprocessor to be an ASIC. I shall describe how to design an ASIC that may include large cells such as microprocessors, but I shall not describe the design of the microprocessors themselves. Defining an ASIC by looking at the application can be confusing, so we shall look at a different way to categorize the IC family. The easiest way to recognize people is by their faces and physical characteristics: tall, short, thin. The easiest characteristics of ASICs to understand are physical ones too, and we shall look at these next. It is important to understand these differences because they affect such factors as the price of an ASIC and the way you design an ASIC.

1.1   Types of ASICs

ICs are made on a thin (a few hundred microns thick), circular silicon **wafer**, with each wafer holding hundreds of die (sometimes people use dies or dice for the plural of die). The transistors and wiring are made from many layers (usually between 10 and 15 distinct layers) built on top of one another. Each successive **mask layer** has a pattern that is defined using a **mask** similar to a glass photographic slide. The first half-dozen or so layers define the transistors. The last half-dozen or so layers define the metal wires between the transistors (the **interconnect**).

A **full-custom IC** includes some (possibly all) logic cells that are customized and all mask layers that are customized. A microprocessor is an example of a full-custom IC—designers spend many hours squeezing the most out of every last square micron of microprocessor chip space by hand. Customizing all of the IC features in this way allows designers to include analog circuits, optimized memory cells, or mechanical structures on an IC, for example. Full-custom ICs are the most expensive to manufacture and to design. The **manufacturing lead time** (the time it takes just to make an IC—not including design time) is typically eight weeks for a full-custom IC. These specialized full-custom ICs are often intended for a specific application, so we might call some of them full-custom ASICs.

We shall discuss full-custom ASICs briefly next, but the members of the IC family that we are more interested in are **semicustom ASICs**, for which all of the logic cells are predesigned and some (possibly all) of the mask layers are customized. Using predesigned cells from a **cell library** makes our lives as designers much, much easier. There are two types of semicustom ASICs that we shall cover: standard-cell–based ASICs and gate-array–based ASICs. Following this we shall describe the **programmable ASICs**, for which all of the logic cells are predesigned and none of the mask layers are customized. There are two types of programmable ASICs: the programmable logic device and, the newest member of the ASIC family, the field-programmable gate array.

1.1.1 Full-Custom ASICs

In a **full-custom ASIC** an engineer designs some or all of the logic cells, circuits, or layout specifically for one ASIC. This means the designer abandons the approach of using pretested and precharacterized cells for all or part of that design. It makes sense to take this approach only if there are no suitable existing cell libraries available that can be used for the entire design. This might be because existing cell libraries are not fast enough, or the logic cells are not small enough or consume too much power. You may need to use full-custom design if the ASIC technology is new or so specialized that there are no existing cell libraries or because the ASIC is so specialized that some circuits must be custom designed. Fewer and fewer full-custom ICs are being designed because of the problems with these special parts of the ASIC. There is one growing member of this family, though, the mixed analog/digital ASIC, which we shall discuss next.

Bipolar technology has historically been used for precision analog functions. There are some fundamental reasons for this. In all integrated circuits the matching of component characteristics between chips is very poor, while the matching of characteristics between components on the same chip is excellent. Suppose we have transistors T1, T2, and T3 on an analog/digital ASIC. The three transistors are all the same size and are constructed in an identical fashion. Transistors T1 and T2 are located adjacent to each other and have the same orientation. Transistor T3 is the same size as T1 and T2 but is located on the other side of the chip from T1 and T2 and has a different orientation. ICs are made in batches called wafer lots. A **wafer lot** is a group of silicon wafers that are all processed together. Usually there are between 5 and 30 wafers in a lot. Each wafer can contain tens or hundreds of chips depending on the size of the IC and the wafer.

If we were to make measurements of the characteristics of transistors T1, T2, and T3 we would find the following:

- Transistors T1 will have virtually identical characteristics to T2 on the same IC. We say that the transistors **match** well or the **tracking** between devices is excellent.

- Transistor T3 will match transistors T1 and T2 on the same IC very well, but not as closely as T1 matches T2 on the same IC.

- Transistor T1, T2, and T3 will match fairly well with transistors T1, T2, and T3 on a different IC on the same wafer. The matching will depend on how far apart the two ICs are on the wafer.

- Transistors on ICs from different wafers in the same wafer lot will not match very well.

- Transistors on ICs from different wafer lots will match very poorly.

For many analog designs the close matching of transistors is crucial to circuit operation. For these circuit designs pairs of transistors are used, located adjacent to each other. Device physics dictates that a pair of bipolar transistors will always match more precisely than CMOS transistors of a comparable size. Bipolar technology has historically been more widely used for full-custom analog design because of its improved precision. Despite its poorer analog properties, the use of CMOS technology for analog functions is increasing. There are two reasons for this. The first reason is that CMOS is now by far the most widely available IC technology. Many more CMOS ASICs and CMOS standard products are now being manufactured than bipolar ICs. The second reason is that increased levels of integration require mixing analog and digital functions on the same IC: this has forced designers to find ways to use CMOS technology to implement analog functions. Circuit designers, using clever new techniques, have been very successful in finding new ways to design analog CMOS circuits that can approach the accuracy of bipolar analog designs.

1.1.2   Standard-Cell–Based ASICs

A **cell-based ASIC** (cell-based IC, or **CBIC**—a common term in Japan, pronounced "sea-bick") uses predesigned logic cells (AND gates, OR gates, multiplexers, and flip-flops, for example) known as **standard cells**. We could apply the term CBIC to any IC that uses cells, but it is generally accepted that a cell-based ASIC or CBIC means a standard-cell–based ASIC.

The standard-cell areas (also called flexible blocks) in a CBIC are built of rows of standard cells—like a wall built of bricks. The standard-cell areas may be used in combination with larger predesigned cells, perhaps microcontrollers or even microprocessors, known as **megacells**. Megacells are also called megafunctions, full-custom blocks, system-level macros (SLMs), fixed blocks, cores, or Functional Standard Blocks (FSBs).

The ASIC designer defines only the placement of the standard cells and the interconnect in a CBIC. However, the standard cells can be placed anywhere on the silicon; this means that all the mask layers of a CBIC are customized and are unique to a particular customer. The advantage of CBICs is that designers save time, money, and reduce risk by using a predesigned, pretested, and precharacterized **standard-cell library**. In addition each standard cell can be optimized individually. During the design of the cell library each and every transistor in every standard cell can be chosen to maximize speed or minimize area, for example. The disadvantages are the time or expense of designing or buying the standard-cell library and the time needed to fabricate all layers of the ASIC for each new design.

Figure 1.2 shows a CBIC (looking down on the die shown in Figure 1.1b, for example). The important features of this type of ASIC are as follows:

- All mask layers are customized—transistors and interconnect.
- Custom blocks can be embedded.
- Manufacturing lead time is about eight weeks.

FIGURE 1.2 A cell-based ASIC (CBIC) die with a single standard-cell area (a flexible block) together with four fixed blocks. The flexible block contains rows of standard cells. This is what you might see through a low-powered microscope looking down on the die of Figure 1.1(b). The small squares around the edge of the die are bonding pads that are connected to the pins of the ASIC package.

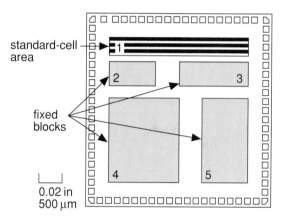

Each standard cell in the library is constructed using full-custom design methods, but you can use these predesigned and precharacterized circuits without having to do any full-custom design yourself. This design style gives you the same performance and flexibility advantages of a full-custom ASIC but reduces design time and reduces risk.

Standard cells are designed to fit together like bricks in a wall. Figure 1.3 shows an example of a simple standard cell (it is simple in the sense it is not maximized for density—but ideal for showing you its internal construction). Power and ground buses (VDD and GND or VSS) run horizontally on metal lines inside the cells.

Standard-cell design allows the automation of the process of assembling an ASIC. Groups of standard cells fit horizontally together to form rows. The rows stack vertically to form flexible rectangular blocks (which you can reshape during

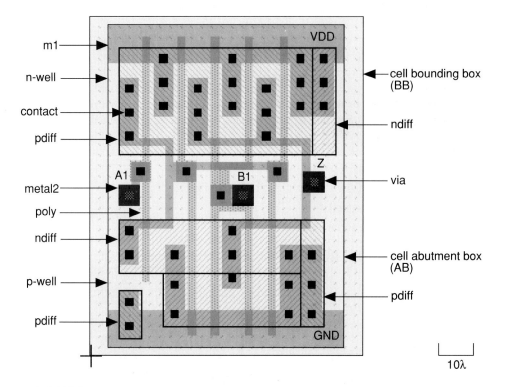

FIGURE 1.3 Looking down on the layout of a standard cell. This cell would be approximately 25 microns wide on an ASIC with λ (lambda) = 0.25 microns (a micron is 10^{-6} m). Standard cells are stacked like bricks in a wall; the abutment box (AB) defines the "edges" of the brick. The difference between the bounding box (BB) and the AB is the area of overlap between the bricks. Power supplies (labeled VDD and GND) run horizontally inside a standard cell on a metal layer that lies above the transistor layers. Each different shaded and labeled pattern represents a different layer. This standard cell has center connectors (the three squares, labeled A1, B1, and Z) that allow the cell to connect to others. The layout was drawn using ROSE, a symbolic layout editor developed by Rockwell and Compass, and then imported into Tanner Research's L-Edit.

design). You may then connect a **flexible block** built from several rows of standard cells to other standard-cell blocks or other full-custom logic blocks. For example, you might want to include a custom interface to a standard, predesigned microcontroller together with some memory. The microcontroller block may be a fixed-size megacell, you might generate the memory using a memory compiler, and the custom logic and memory controller will be built from flexible standard-cell blocks, shaped to fit in the empty spaces on the chip.

Both cell-based and gate-array ASICs use predefined cells, but there is a difference—we can change the transistor sizes in a standard cell to optimize speed and performance, but the device sizes in a gate array are fixed. This results in a trade-off in performance and area in a gate array at the silicon level. The trade-off between area and performance is made at the library level for a standard-cell ASIC.

Modern CMOS ASICs use two, three, or more levels (or layers) of metal for interconnect. This allows wires to cross over different layers in the same way that we use copper traces on different layers on a printed-circuit board. In a two-level metal CMOS technology, connections to the standard-cell inputs and outputs are usually made using the second level of metal (**metal2**, the upper level of metal) at the tops and bottoms of the cells. In a three-level metal technology, connections may be internal to the logic cell (as they are in Figure 1.3). This allows for more sophisticated routing programs to take advantage of the extra metal layer to route interconnect over the top of the logic cells. We shall cover the details of routing ASICs in Chapter 17.

A connection that needs to cross over a row of standard cells uses a feedthrough. The term **feedthrough** can refer either to the piece of metal that is used to pass a signal through a cell or to a space in a cell waiting to be used as a feedthrough—very confusing. Figure 1.4 shows two feedthroughs: one in cell A.14 and one in cell A.23.

In both two-level and three-level metal technology, the power buses (VDD and GND) inside the standard cells normally use the lowest (closest to the transistors) layer of metal (**metal1**). The width of each row of standard cells is adjusted so that they may be aligned using **spacer cells**. The power buses, or rails, are then connected to additional vertical power rails using **row-end cells** at the aligned ends of each standard-cell block. If the rows of standard cells are long, then vertical power rails can also be run in metal2 through the cell rows using special **power cells** that just connect to VDD and GND. Usually the designer manually controls the number and width of the vertical power rails connected to the standard-cell blocks during physical design. A diagram of the power distribution scheme for a CBIC is shown in Figure 1.4.

All the mask layers of a CBIC are customized. This allows megacells (SRAM, a SCSI controller, or an MPEG decoder, for example) to be placed on the same IC with standard cells. Megacells are usually supplied by an ASIC or library company complete with behavioral models and some way to test them (a test strategy). ASIC library companies also supply compilers to generate flexible DRAM, SRAM, and ROM blocks. Since all mask layers on a standard-cell design are customized, memory design is more efficient and denser than for gate arrays.

For logic that operates on multiple signals across a data bus—a **datapath** (**DP**)—the use of standard cells may not be the most efficient ASIC design style. Some ASIC library companies provide a **datapath compiler** that automatically generates **datapath logic**. A **datapath library** typically contains cells such as adders, subtracters, multipliers, and simple **arithmetic and logical units** (**ALUs**). The con-

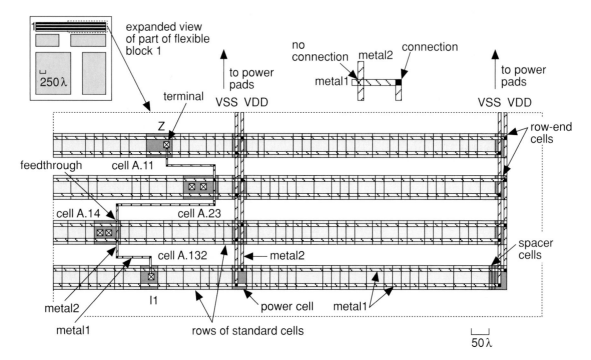

FIGURE 1.4 Routing the CBIC (cell-based IC) shown in Figure 1.2. The use of regularly shaped standard cells, such as the one in Figure 1.3, from a library allows ASICs like this to be designed automatically. This ASIC uses two separate layers of metal interconnect (metal1 and metal2) running at right angles to each other (like traces on a printed-circuit board). Interconnections between logic cells uses spaces (called channels) between the rows of cells. ASICs may have three (or more) layers of metal allowing the cell rows to touch with the interconnect running over the top of the cells.

nectors of datapath library cells are **pitch-matched** to each other so that they fit together. Connecting datapath cells to form a datapath usually, but not always, results in faster and denser layout than using standard cells or a gate array.

Standard-cell and gate-array libraries may contain hundreds of different logic cells, including combinational functions (NAND, NOR, AND, OR gates) with multiple inputs, as well as latches and flip-flops with different combinations of reset, preset and clocking options. The ASIC library company provides designers with a data book in paper or electronic form with all of the functional descriptions and timing information for each library element.

1.1.3   Gate-Array–Based ASICs

In a **gate array** (sometimes abbreviated to GA) or gate-array–based ASIC the transistors are predefined on the silicon wafer. The predefined pattern of transistors on a gate array is the **base array**, and the smallest element that is replicated to make the base array (like an M. C. Escher drawing, or tiles on a floor) is the **base cell** (sometimes called a **primitive cell**). Only the top few layers of metal, which define the interconnect between transistors, are defined by the designer using custom masks. To distinguish this type of gate array from other types of gate array, it is often called a **masked gate array** (**MGA**). The designer chooses from a gate-array library of predesigned and precharacterized logic cells. The logic cells in a gate-array library are often called **macros**. The reason for this is that the base-cell layout is the same for each logic cell, and only the interconnect (inside cells and between cells) is customized, so that there is a similarity between gate-array macros and a software macro. Inside IBM, gate-array macros are known as **books** (so that books are part of a library), but unfortunately this descriptive term is not very widely used outside IBM.

We can complete the diffusion steps that form the transistors and then stockpile wafers (sometimes we call a gate array a **prediffused array** for this reason). Since only the metal interconnections are unique to an MGA, we can use the stockpiled wafers for different customers as needed. Using wafers prefabricated up to the metallization steps reduces the time needed to make an MGA, the **turnaround time**, to a few days or at most a couple of weeks. The costs for all the initial fabrication steps for an MGA are shared for each customer and this reduces the cost of an MGA compared to a full-custom or standard-cell ASIC design.

There are the following different types of MGA or gate-array–based ASICs:

- Channeled gate arrays.
- Channelless gate arrays.
- Structured gate arrays.

The hyphenation of these terms when they are used as adjectives explains their construction. For example, in the term "channeled gate-array architecture," the *gate array* is *channeled*, as will be explained. There are two common ways of arranging (or arraying) the transistors on a MGA: in a channeled gate array we leave space between the rows of transistors for wiring; the routing on a channelless gate array uses rows of unused transistors. The channeled gate array was the first to be developed, but the channelless gate array architecture is now more widely used. A structured (or embedded) gate array can be either channeled or channelless but it includes (or embeds) a custom block.

1.1.4   Channeled Gate Array

Figure 1.5 shows a **channeled gate array**. The important features of this type of MGA are:

- Only the interconnect is customized.
- The interconnect uses predefined spaces between rows of base cells.
- Manufacturing lead time is between two days and two weeks.

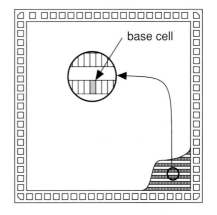

FIGURE 1.5   A channeled gate-array die. The spaces between rows of the base cells are set aside for interconnect.

A channeled gate array is similar to a CBIC—both use rows of cells separated by channels used for interconnect. One difference is that the space for interconnect between rows of cells are fixed in height in a channeled gate array, whereas the space between rows of cells may be adjusted in a CBIC.

1.1.5   Channelless Gate Array

Figure 1.6 shows a **channelless gate array** (also known as a **channel-free gate array**, **sea-of-gates array**, or **SOG** array). The important features of this type of MGA are as follows:

- Only some (the top few) mask layers are customized—the interconnect.
- Manufacturing lead time is between two days and two weeks.

The key difference between a channelless gate array and channeled gate array is that there are no predefined areas set aside for routing between cells on a channelless gate array. Instead we route over the top of the gate-array devices. We can do this because we customize the contact layer that defines the connections between metal1, the first layer of metal, and the transistors. When we use an area of transistors for routing in a channelless array, we do not make any contacts to the devices lying underneath; we simply leave the transistors unused.

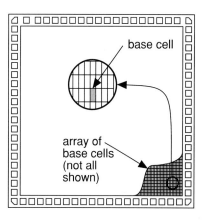

FIGURE 1.6 A channelless-gate-array or sea-of-gates (SOG) array die. The core area of the die is completely filled with an array of base cells (the base array).

The logic density—the amount of logic that can be implemented in a given silicon area—is higher for channelless gate arrays than for channeled gate arrays. This is usually attributed to the difference in structure between the two types of array. In fact, the difference occurs because the contact mask is customized in a channelless gate array, but is not usually customized in a channeled gate array. This leads to denser cells in the channelless architectures. Customizing the contact layer in a channelless gate array allows us to increase the density of gate-array cells because we can route over the top of unused contact sites.

1.1.6   Structured Gate Array

An **embedded gate array** or **structured gate array** (also known as **masterslice** or **masterimage**) combines some of the features of CBICs and MGAs. One of the disadvantages of the MGA is the fixed gate-array base cell. This makes the implementation of memory, for example, difficult and inefficient. In an embedded gate array we set aside some of the IC area and dedicate it to a specific function. This embedded area either can contain a different base cell that is more suitable for building memory cells, or it can contain a complete circuit block, such as a microcontroller.

Figure 1.7 shows an embedded gate array. The important features of this type of MGA are the following:

- Only the interconnect is customized.
- Custom blocks (the same for each design) can be embedded.
- Manufacturing lead time is between two days and two weeks.

An embedded gate array gives the improved area efficiency and increased performance of a CBIC but with the lower cost and faster turnaround of an MGA. One disadvantage of an embedded gate array is that the embedded function is fixed. For example, if an embedded gate array contains an area set aside for a 32 k-bit memory,

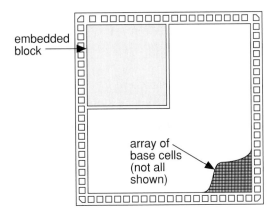

FIGURE 1.7 A structured or embedded gate array die showing an embedded block in the upper left corner (a static random-access memory, for example). The rest of the die is filled with an array of base cells.

but we only need a 16 k-bit memory, then we may have to waste half of the embedded memory function. However, this may still be more efficient and cheaper than implementing a 32 k-bit memory using macros on a SOG array.

ASIC vendors may offer several embedded gate array structures containing different memory types and sizes as well as a variety of embedded functions. ASIC companies wishing to offer a wide range of embedded functions must ensure that enough customers use each different embedded gate array to give the cost advantages over a custom gate array or CBIC (the Sun Microsystems SPARCstation 1 described in Section 1.3 made use of LSI Logic embedded gate arrays—and the 10K and 100K series of embedded gate arrays were two of LSI Logic's most successful products).

1.1.7 Programmable Logic Devices

Programmable logic devices (**PLDs**) are standard ICs that are available in standard configurations from a catalog of parts and are sold in very high volume to many different customers. However, PLDs may be configured or programmed to create a part customized to a specific application, and so they also belong to the family of ASICs. PLDs use different technologies to allow programming of the device. Figure 1.8 shows a PLD and the following important features that all PLDs have in common:

- No customized mask layers or logic cells
- Fast design turnaround
- A single large block of programmable interconnect
- A matrix of logic macrocells that usually consist of programmable array logic followed by a flip-flop or latch

The simplest type of programmable IC is a **read-only memory** (**ROM**). The most common types of ROM use a metal fuse that can be blown permanently (a **programmable ROM** or **PROM**). An **electrically programmable ROM**, or

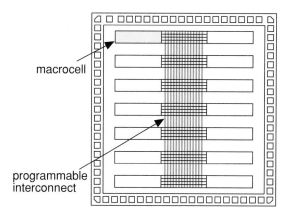

FIGURE 1.8 A programmable logic device (PLD) die. The macrocells typically consist of programmable array logic followed by a flip-flop or latch. The macrocells are connected using a large programmable interconnect block.

EPROM, uses programmable MOS transistors whose characteristics are altered by applying a high voltage. You can erase an EPROM either by using another high voltage (an **electrically erasable PROM**, or **EEPROM**) or by exposing the device to ultraviolet light (**UV-erasable PROM**, or **UVPROM**).

There is another type of ROM that can be placed on any ASIC—a **mask-programmable ROM** (mask-programmed ROM or masked ROM). A masked ROM is a regular array of transistors permanently programmed using custom mask patterns. An embedded masked ROM is thus a large, specialized, logic cell.

The same programmable technologies used to make ROMs can be applied to more flexible logic structures. By using the programmable devices in a large array of AND gates and an array of OR gates, we create a family of flexible and programmable logic devices called **logic arrays**. The company Monolithic Memories (bought by AMD) was the first to produce **Programmable Array Logic** (PAL®, a registered trademark of AMD) devices that you can use, for example, as transition decoders for state machines. A PAL can also include registers (flip-flops) to store the current state information so that you can use a PAL to make a complete state machine.

Just as we have a mask-programmable ROM, we could place a logic array as a cell on a custom ASIC. This type of logic array is called a **programmable logic array** (PLA). There is a difference between a PAL and a PLA: a PLA has a programmable AND logic array, or **AND plane**, followed by a programmable OR logic array, or **OR plane**; a PAL has a programmable AND plane and, in contrast to a PLA, a fixed OR plane.

Depending on how the PLD is programmed, we can have an **erasable PLD** (EPLD), or **mask-programmed PLD** (sometimes called a masked PLD but usually just PLD). The first PALs, PLAs, and PLDs were based on bipolar technology and used programmable fuses or links. CMOS PLDs usually employ floating-gate transistors (see Section 4.3, "EPROM and EEPROM Technology").

1.1.8   Field-Programmable Gate Arrays

A step above the PLD in complexity is the **field-programmable gate array** (**FPGA**). There is very little difference between an FPGA and a PLD—an FPGA is usually just larger and more complex than a PLD. In fact, some companies that manufacture programmable ASICs call their products FPGAs and some call them **complex PLDs**. FPGAs are the newest member of the ASIC family and are rapidly growing in importance, replacing TTL in microelectronic systems. Even though an FPGA is a type of gate array, we do not consider the term gate-array–based ASICs to include FPGAs. This may change as FPGAs and MGAs start to look more alike.

Figure 1.9 illustrates the essential characteristics of an FPGA:

- None of the mask layers are customized.
- A method for programming the basic logic cells and the interconnect.
- The core is a regular array of programmable basic logic cells that can implement combinational as well as sequential logic (flip-flops).
- A matrix of programmable interconnect surrounds the basic logic cells.
- Programmable I/O cells surround the core.
- Design turnaround is a few hours.

We shall examine these features in detail in Chapters 4–8.

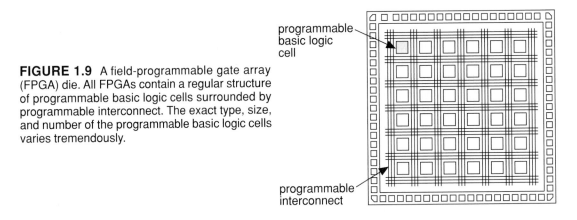

FIGURE 1.9 A field-programmable gate array (FPGA) die. All FPGAs contain a regular structure of programmable basic logic cells surrounded by programmable interconnect. The exact type, size, and number of the programmable basic logic cells varies tremendously.

programmable basic logic cell

programmable interconnect

1.2   Design Flow

Figure 1.10 shows the sequence of steps to design an ASIC; we call this a **design flow**. The steps are listed below (numbered to correspond to the labels in Figure 1.10) with a brief description of the function of each step.

1. *Design entry.* Enter the design into an ASIC design system, either using a **hardware description language** (**HDL**) or *schematic entry.*

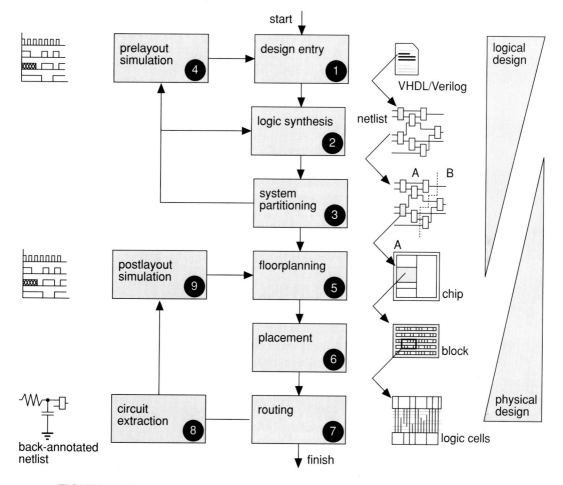

FIGURE 1.10 ASIC design flow.

2. *Logic synthesis*. Use an HDL (VHDL or Verilog) and a logic synthesis tool to produce a **netlist**—a description of the logic cells and their connections.

3. *System partitioning*. Divide a large system into ASIC-sized pieces.

4. *Prelayout simulation*. Check to see if the design functions correctly.

5. *Floorplanning*. Arrange the blocks of the netlist on the chip.

6. *Placement*. Decide the locations of cells in a block.

7. *Routing*. Make the connections between cells and blocks.

8. *Extraction*. Determine the resistance and capacitance of the interconnect.

9. *Postlayout simulation.* Check to see the design still works with the added loads of the interconnect.

Steps 1–4 are part of **logical design**, and steps 5–9 are part of **physical design**. There is some overlap. For example, system partitioning might be considered as either logical or physical design. To put it another way, when we are performing system partitioning we have to consider both logical and physical factors. Chapters 9–14 of this book is largely about logical design and Chapters 15–17 largely about physical design.

1.3   Case Study

Sun Microsystems released the SPARCstation 1 in April 1989. It is now an old design but a very important example because it was one of the first workstations to make extensive use of ASICs to achieve the following:

- Better performance at lower cost
- Compact size, reduced power, and quiet operation
- Reduced number of parts, easier assembly, and improved reliability

The SPARCstation 1 contains about 50 ICs on the system motherboard—excluding the DRAM used for the system memory (standard parts). The SPARCstation 1 designers partitioned the system into the nine ASICs shown in Table 1.1 and wrote specifications for each ASIC—this took about three months.[1] LSI Logic and Fujitsu designed the SPARC **integer unit** (IU) and **floating-point unit** (**FPU**) to these specifications. The clock ASIC is a fairly straightforward design and, of the six remaining ASICs, the video controller/data buffer, the RAM controller, and the **direct memory access** (**DMA**) controller are defined by the 32-bit **system bus** (**SBus**) and the other ASICs that they connect to. The rest of the system is partitioned into three more ASICs: the **cache controller**, **memory-management unit** (MMU), and the data buffer. These three ASICs, with the IU and FPU, have the most critical timing paths and determine the system partitioning. The design of ASICs 3–8 in Table 1.1 took five Sun engineers six months after the specifications were complete. During the design process, the Sun engineers simulated the entire SPARCstation 1—including execution of the Sun operating system (SunOS).

---

[1]Some information in Section 1.3 and Section 15.3 is from the SPARCstation 10 Architecture Guide—May 1992, p. 2 and pp. 27–28 and from two publicity brochures (known as "sparkle sheets"). The first is "Concept to System: How Sun Microsystems Created SPARCstation 1 Using LSI Logic's ASIC System Technology," A. Bechtolsheim, T. Westberg, M. Insley, and J. Ludemann of Sun Microsystems; J-H. Huang and D. Boyle of LSI Logic. This is an LSI Logic publication. The second paper is "SPARCstation 1: Beyond the 3M Horizon," A. Bechtolsheim and E. Frank, a Sun Microsystems publication. I did not include these as references since they are impossible to obtain now, but I would like to give credit to Andy Bechtolsheim and the Sun Microsystems and LSI Logic engineers.

TABLE 1.1   The ASICs in the Sun Microsystems SPARCstation 1.

	SPARCstation 1 ASIC	Gates (k-gates)
1	SPARC integer unit (IU)	20
2	SPARC floating-point unit (FPU)	50
3	Cache controller	9
4	Memory-management unit (MMU)	5
5	Data buffer	3
6	Direct memory access (DMA) controller	9
7	Video controller/data buffer	4
8	RAM controller	1
9	Clock generator	1

Table 1.2 shows the software tools used to design the SPARCstation 1, many of which are now obsolete. The important point to notice, though, is that there is a lot more to microelectronic system design than designing the ASICs—less than one-third of the tools listed in Table 1.2 were ASIC design tools.

TABLE 1.2   The CAD tools used in the design of the Sun Microsystems SPARCstation 1.

Design level	Function	Tool[1]
ASIC design	ASIC physical design	LSI Logic
	ASIC logic synthesis	Internal tools and UC Berkeley tools
	ASIC simulation	LSI Logic
Board design	Schematic capture	Valid Logic
	PCB layout	Valid Logic Allegro
	Timing verification	Quad Design Motive and internal tools
Mechanical design	Case and enclosure	Autocad
	Thermal analysis	Pacific Numerix
	Structural analysis	Cosmos
Management	Scheduling	Suntrac
	Documentation	Interleaf and FrameMaker

[1]Names are trademarks of their respective companies.

The SPARCstation 1 cost about $9000 in 1989 or, since it has an execution rate of approximately 12 million instructions per second (MIPS), $750/MIPS. Using ASIC technology reduces the motherboard to about the size of a piece of paper—8.5 inches by 11 inches—with a power consumption of about 12 W. The SPARCstation 1 "pizza box" is 16 inches across and 3 inches high—smaller than a typical IBM-compatible personal computer in 1989. This speed, power, and size performance is (there are still SPARCstation 1s in use) made possible by using ASICs. We shall return to the SPARCstation 1, to look more closely at the partitioning step, in Section 15.3, "System Partitioning."

1.4 Economics of ASICs

In this section we shall discuss the economics of using ASICs in a product and compare the most popular types of ASICs: an FPGA, an MGA, and a CBIC. To make an economic comparison between these alternatives, we consider the ASIC itself as a product and examine the components of product cost: fixed costs and variable costs. Making cost comparisons is dangerous—costs change rapidly and the semiconductor industry is notorious for keeping its costs, prices, and pricing strategy closely guarded secrets. The figures in the following sections are approximate and used to illustrate the different components of cost.

1.4.1 Comparison Between ASIC Technologies

The most obvious economic factor in making a choice between the different ASIC types is the **part cost**. Part costs vary enormously—you can pay anywhere from a few dollars to several hundreds of dollars for an ASIC. In general, however, FPGAs are more expensive per gate than MGAs, which are, in turn, more expensive than CBICs. For example, a 0.5 μm, 20 k-gate array might cost 0.01–0.02 cents/gate (for more than 10,000 parts) or $2–$4 per part, but an equivalent FPGA might be $20. The price per gate for an FPGA to implement the same function is typically 2–5 times the cost of an MGA or CBIC.

Given that an FPGA is more expensive than an MGA, which is more expensive than a CBIC, when and why does it make sense to choose a more expensive part? Is the increased flexibility of an FPGA worth the extra cost per part? Given that an MGA or CBIC is specially tailored for each customer, there are extra hidden costs associated with this step that we should consider. To make a true comparison between the different ASIC technologies, we shall quantify some of these costs.

1.4.2 Product Cost

The total cost of any product can be separated into **fixed costs** and **variable costs**:

$$\text{total product cost} = \text{fixed product cost} + \text{variable product cost} \times \text{products sold}. \quad (1.1)$$

Fixed costs are independent of **sales volume**—the number of products sold. However, the fixed costs amortized per product sold (fixed costs divided by products sold) decrease as sales volume increases. Variable costs include the cost of the parts used in the product, assembly costs, and other manufacturing costs.

Let us look more closely at the parts in a product. If we want to buy ASICs to assemble our product, the total part cost is

$$\text{total part cost} = \text{fixed part cost} + \text{variable cost per part} \times \text{volume of parts.} \quad (1.2)$$

Our fixed cost when we use an FPGA is low—we just have to buy the software and any programming equipment. The fixed part costs for an MGA or CBIC are higher and include the costs of the masks, simulation, and test program development. We shall discuss these extra costs in more detail in Sections 1.4.3 and 1.4.4. Figure 1.11 shows a **break-even graph** that compares the total part cost for an FPGA, MGA, and a CBIC with the following assumptions:

- FPGA fixed cost is $21,800, part cost is $39.
- MGA fixed cost is $86,000, part cost is $10.
- CBIC fixed cost is $146,000, part cost is $8.

At low volumes, the MGA and the CBIC are more expensive because of their higher fixed costs. The total part costs of two alternative types of ASIC are equal at the **break-even volume**. In Figure 1.11 the break-even volume for the FPGA and the MGA is about 2000 parts. The break-even volume between the FPGA and the CBIC is about 4000 parts. The break-even volume between the MGA and the CBIC is higher—at about 20,000 parts.

We shall describe how to calculate the fixed part costs next. Following that we shall discuss how we came up with cost per part of $39, $10, and $8 for the FPGA, MGA, and CBIC.

1.4.3 ASIC Fixed Costs

Figure 1.12 shows a spreadsheet, "Fixed Costs," that calculates the fixed part costs associated with ASIC design.

The **training cost** includes the cost of the time to learn any new **electronic design automation (EDA)** system. For example, a new FPGA design system might require a few days to learn; a new gate-array or cell-based design system might require taking a course. Figure 1.12 assumes that the cost of an engineer (including overhead, benefits, infrastructure, and so on) is between $100,000 and $200,000 per year or $2000 to $4000 per week (in the United States in 1990s dollars).

Next we consider the **hardware and software cost** for ASIC design. Figure 1.12 shows some typical figures, but you can spend anywhere from $1000 to $1 million (and more) on ASIC design software and the necessary infrastructure.

We try to measure **productivity** of an ASIC designer in gates (or transistors) per day. This is like trying to predict how long it takes to dig a hole, and the number of gates per day an engineer averages varies wildly. ASIC design productivity must

cost of parts

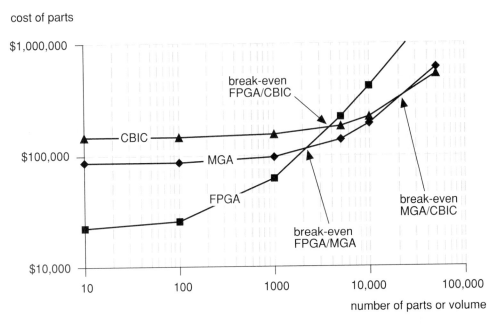

FIGURE 1.11 A break-even analysis for an FPGA, a masked gate array (MGA) and a custom cell-based ASIC (CBIC). The break-even volume between two technologies is the point at which the total cost of parts are equal. These numbers are very approximate.

increase as ASIC sizes increase and will depend on experience, design tools, and the ASIC complexity. If we are using similar design methods, design productivity ought to be independent of the type of ASIC, but FPGA design software is usually available as a complete bundle on a PC. This means that it is often easier to learn and use than semicustom ASIC design tools.

Every ASIC has to pass a **production test** to make sure that it works. With modern test tools the generation of any test circuits on each ASIC that are needed for production testing can be automatic, but it still involves a cost for **design for test**. An FPGA is tested by the manufacturer before it is sold to you and before you program it. You are still paying for testing an FPGA, but it is a hidden cost folded into the part cost of the FPGA. You do have to pay for any **programming costs** for an FPGA, but we can include these in the hardware and software cost.

The **nonrecurring-engineering** (**NRE**) charge includes the cost of work done by the ASIC vendor and the cost of the masks. The production test uses sets of test inputs called **test vectors**, often many thousands of them. Most ASIC vendors require simulation to generate test vectors and test programs for production testing, and will charge for a **test-program development cost**. The number of masks required by an ASIC during fabrication can range from three or four (for a gate array) to 15 or more (for a CBIC). Total mask costs can range from $5000 to

	FPGA		MGA		CBIC	
Training:	$800		$2,000		$2,000	
Days		2		5		5
Cost/day		$400		$400		$400
Hardware	$10,000		$10,000		$10,000	
Software	$1,000		$20,000		$40,000	
Design:	$8,000		$20,000		$20,000	
Size (gates)		10,000		10,000		10,000
Gates/day		500		200		200
Days		20		50		50
Cost/day		$400		$400		$400
Design for test:			$2,000		$2,000	
Days				5		5
Cost/day				$400		$400
NRE:			$30,000		$70,000	
Masks				$10,000		$50,000
Simulation				$10,000		$10,000
Test program				$10,000		$10,000
Second source:	$2,000		$2,000		$2,000	
Days		5		5		5
Cost/day		$400		$400		$400
Total fixed costs	$21,800		$86,000		$146,000	

FIGURE 1.12 A spreadsheet, "Fixed Costs," for a field-programmable gate array (FPGA), a masked gate array (MGA), and a cell-based ASIC (CBIC). These costs can vary wildly.

$50,000 or more. The total NRE charge can range from $10,000 to $300,000 or more and will vary with volume and the size of the ASIC. If you commit to high volumes (above 100,000 parts), the vendor may waive the NRE charge. The NRE charge may also include the costs of software tools, design verification, and prototype samples.

If your design does not work the first time, you have to complete a further design **pass** (**turn** or **spin**) that requires additional NRE charges. Normally you sign a contract (sign off a design) with an ASIC vendor that guarantees first-pass success—this means that if you designed your ASIC according to rules specified by the vendor, then the vendor guarantees that the silicon will perform according to the simulation or you get your money back. This is why the difference between semicustom and full-custom design styles is so important—the ASIC vendor will not (and cannot) guarantee your design will work if you use any full-custom design techniques.

Nowadays it is almost routine to have an ASIC work on the first pass. However, if your design does fail, it is little consolation to have a second pass for free if your company goes bankrupt in the meantime. Figure 1.13 shows a **profit model** that represents the **profit flow** during the **product lifetime**. Using this model, we can estimate the lost profit due to any delay.

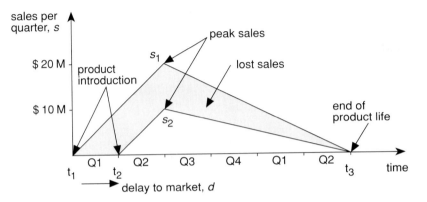

FIGURE 1.13   A profit model. If a product is introduced on time, the total sales are $60 million (the area of the higher triangle). With a three-month (one fiscal quarter) delay the sales decline to $25 million. The difference is shown as the shaded area between the two triangles and amounts to a lost revenue of $35 million.

Suppose we have the following situation:

- The product lifetime is 18 months (6 fiscal quarters).
- The product sales increase (linearly) at $10 million per quarter independently of when the product is introduced (we suppose this is because we can increase production and sales only at a fixed rate).
- The product reaches its peak sales at a point in time that is independent of when we introduce a product (because of external market factors that we cannot control).
- The product declines in sales (linearly) to the end of its life—a point in time that is also independent of when we introduce the product (again due to external market forces).

The simple profit and revenue model of Figure 1.13 shows us that we would lose $35 million in sales in this situation due to a 3-month delay. Despite the obvious problems with such a simple model (how can we introduce the same product twice to compare the performance?), it is widely used in marketing. In the electronics industry product lifetimes continue to shrink. In the PC industry it is not unusual to have a product lifetime of 18 months or less. This means that it is critical to achieve a rapid design time (or high **product velocity**) with no delays.

The last fixed cost shown in Figure 1.12 corresponds to an "insurance policy." When a company buys an ASIC part, it needs to be assured that it will always have a back-up source, or **second source**, in case something happens to its first or primary source. Established FPGA companies have a second source that produces equivalent parts. With a custom ASIC you may have to do some redesign to transfer your ASIC to the second source. However, for all ASIC types, switching production to a second source will involve some cost. Figure 1.12 assumes a second-source cost of $2000 for all types of ASIC (the amount may be substantially more than this).

1.4.4 ASIC Variable Costs

Figure 1.14 shows a spreadsheet, "Variable Costs," that calculates some example part costs. This spreadsheet uses the terms and parameters defined below the figure.

	FPGA	MGA	CBIC	Units
Wafer size	6	6	6	inches
Wafer cost	1,400	1,300	1,500	$
Design	10,000	10,000	10,000	gates
Density	10,000	20,000	25,000	gates/sq.cm
Utilization	60	85	100	%
Die size	1.67	0.59	0.40	sq.cm
Die/wafer	88	248	365	
Defect density	1.10	0.90	1.00	defects/sq.cm
Yield	65	72	80	%
Die cost	25	7	5	$
Profit margin	60	45	50	%
Price/gate	0.39	0.10	0.08	cents
Part cost	$39	$10	$8	

FIGURE 1.14 A spreadsheet, "Variable Costs," to calculate the part cost (that is the variable cost for a product using ASICs) for different ASIC technologies.

- The **wafer size** increases every few years. From 1985 to 1990, 4-inch to 6-inch diameter wafers were common; equipment using 6-inch to 8-inch wafers was introduced between 1990 and 1995; the next step is the 300 cm or 12-inch wafer. The 12-inch wafer will probably take us to 2005.
- The **wafer cost** depends on the equipment costs, process costs, and overhead in the fabrication line. A typical wafer cost is between $1000 and $5000, with $2000 being average; the cost declines slightly during the life of a process and increases only slightly from one process generation to the next.

- **Moore's Law** (after Gordon Moore of Intel) models the observation that the number of transistors on a chip roughly doubles every 18 months. Not all designs follow this law, but a "large" ASIC design seems to grow by a factor of 10 every 5 years (close to Moore's Law). In 1990 a large ASIC design size was 10 k-gate, in 1995 a large design was about 100 k-gate, in 2000 it will be 1 M-gate, in 2005 it will be 10 M-gate.

- The **gate density** is the number of gate equivalents per unit area (remember: a gate equivalent, or gate, corresponds to a two-input NAND gate).

- The **gate utilization** is the percentage of gates that are on a die that we can use (on a gate array we waste some gate space for interconnect).

- The **die size** is determined by the design size (in gates), the gate density, and the utilization of the die.

- The number of **die per wafer** depends on the die size and the wafer size (we have to pack rectangular or square die, together with some test chips, on to a circular wafer so some space is wasted).

- The **defect density** is a measure of the quality of the fabrication process. The smaller the defect density the less likely there is to be a flaw on any one die. A single defect on a die is almost always fatal for that die. Defect density usually increases with the number of steps in a process. A defect density of less than $1 \, \mathrm{cm}^{-2}$ is typical and required for a submicron CMOS process.

- The **yield** of a process is the key to a profitable ASIC company. The yield is the fraction of die on a wafer that are good (expressed as a percentage). Yield depends on the complexity and maturity of a process. A process may start out with a yield of close to zero for complex chips, which then climbs to above 50 percent within the first few months of production. Within a year the yield has to be brought to around 80 percent for the average complexity ASIC for the process to be profitable. Yields of 90 percent or more are not uncommon.

- The **die cost** is determined by wafer cost, number of die per wafer, and the yield. Of these parameters, the most variable and the most critical to control is the yield.

- The **profit margin** (what you sell a product for, less what it costs you to make it, divided by the cost) is determined by the ASIC company's fixed and variable costs. ASIC vendors that make and sell custom ASICs have huge fixed and variable costs associated with building and running fabrication facilities (a fabrication plant is a **fab**). FPGA companies are typically **fabless**—they do not own a fab—they must pass on the costs of the chip manufacture (plus the profit margin of the chip manufacturer) and the development cost of the FPGA structure in the FPGA part cost. The profitability of any company in the ASIC business varies greatly.

- The **price per gate** (usually measured in cents per gate) is determined by die costs and design size. It varies with design size and declines over time.

- The **part cost** is determined by all of the preceding factors. As such it will vary widely with time, process, yield, economic climate, ASIC size and complexity, and many other factors.

As an estimate you can assume that the price per gate for any process technology falls at about 20% per year during its life (the average life of a CMOS process is 2–4 years, and can vary widely). Beyond the life of a process, prices can increase as demand falls and the fabrication equipment becomes harder to maintain. Figure 1.15 shows the price per gate for the different ASICs and process technologies using the following assumptions:

- For any new process technology the price per gate decreases by 40% in the first year, 30% in the second year, and then remains constant.

- A new process technology is introduced approximately every 2 years, with feature size decreasing by a factor of two every 5 years as follows: 2 μm in 1985, 1.5 μm in 1987, 1 μm in 1989, 0.8–0.6 μm in 1991–1993, 0.5–0.35 μm in 1996–1997, 0.25–0.18 μm in 1998–2000.

- CBICs and MGAs are introduced at approximately the same time and price.

- The price of a new process technology is initially 10% above the process that it replaces.

- FPGAs are introduced one year after CBICs that use the same process technology.

- The initial FPGA price (per gate) is 10 percent higher than the initial price for CBICs or MGAs using the same process technology.

From Figure 1.15 you can see that the successive introduction of new process technologies every 2 years drives the price per gate down at a rate close to 30 percent per year. The cost figures that we have used in this section are very approximate and can vary widely (this means they may be off by a factor of 2 but probably are correct within a factor of 10). ASIC companies do use spreadsheet models like these to calculate their costs.

Having decided if, and then which, ASIC technology is appropriate, you need to choose the appropriate cell library. Next we shall discuss the issues surrounding ASIC cell libraries: the different types, their sources, and their contents.

1.5   ASIC Cell Libraries

The cell library is the key part of ASIC design. For a programmable ASIC the FPGA company supplies you with a library of logic cells in the form of a **design kit**, you normally do not have a choice, and the cost is usually a few thousand dollars. For MGAs and CBICs you have three choices: the **ASIC vendor** (the company that will

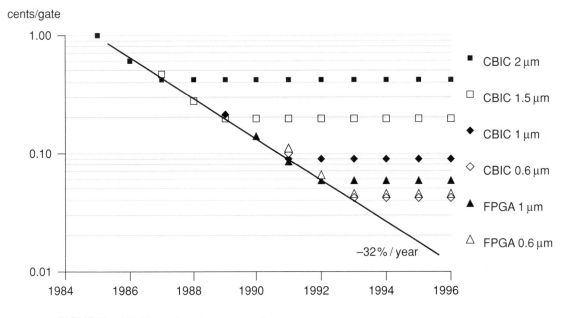

FIGURE 1.15 Example price per gate figures.

build your ASIC) will supply a cell library, or you can buy a cell library from a third-party **library vendor**, or you can build your own cell library.

The first choice, using an **ASIC-vendor library**, requires you to use a set of design tools approved by the ASIC vendor to enter and simulate your design. You have to buy the tools, and the cost of the cell library is folded into the NRE. Some ASIC vendors (especially for MGAs) supply tools that they have developed in-house. For some reason the more common model in Japan is to use tools supplied by the ASIC vendor, but in the United States, Europe, and elsewhere designers want to choose their own tools. Perhaps this has to do with the relationship between customer and supplier being a lot closer in Japan than it is elsewhere.

An ASIC vendor library is normally a **phantom library**—the cells are empty boxes, or **phantoms**, but contain enough information for layout (for example, you would only see the bounding box or abutment box in a phantom version of the cell in Figure 1.3). After you complete layout you **hand off** a netlist to the ASIC vendor, who fills in the empty boxes (**phantom instantiation**) before manufacturing your chip.

The second and third choices require you to make a **buy-or-build decision**. If you complete an ASIC design using a cell library that you bought, you also own the masks (the **tooling**) that are used to manufacture your ASIC. This is called **customer-owned tooling** (**COT**, pronounced "see-oh-tee"). A library vendor normally develops a cell library using information about a process supplied by an **ASIC**

foundry. An ASIC foundry (in contrast to an ASIC vendor) only provides manufacturing, with no design help. If the cell library meets the foundry specifications, we call this a **qualified cell library**. These cell libraries are normally expensive (possibly several hundred thousand dollars), but if a library is qualified at several foundries this allows you to shop around for the most attractive terms. This means that buying an expensive library can be cheaper in the long run than the other solutions for high-volume production.

The third choice is to develop a cell library in-house. Many large computer and electronics companies make this choice. Most of the cell libraries designed today are still developed in-house despite the fact that the process of **library development** is complex and very expensive.

However created, each cell in an ASIC cell library must contain the following:

- A physical layout
- A behavioral model
- A Verilog and/or VHDL model
- A detailed timing model
- A test strategy
- A circuit schematic
- A cell icon
- A wire-load model
- A routing model

For MGA and CBIC cell libraries we need to complete cell design and **cell layout** and shall discuss this in Chapter 2. The ASIC designer may not actually see the layout if it is hidden inside a phantom, but the layout will be needed eventually. In a programmable ASIC the cell layout is part of the programmable ASIC design (see Chapter 4).

The ASIC designer needs a high-level, **behavioral model** for each cell because simulation at the detailed timing level takes too long for a complete ASIC design. For a NAND gate a behavioral model is simple. A multiport RAM model can be very complex. We shall discuss behavioral models when we describe Verilog and VHDL in Chapter 10 and Chapter 11. The designer may require Verilog and VHDL models in addition to the models for a particular logic simulator.

ASIC designers also need a detailed **timing model** for each cell to determine the performance of the critical pieces of an ASIC. It is too difficult, too time-consuming, and too expensive to build every cell in silicon and measure the cell delays. Instead library engineers simulate the delay of each cell, a process known as **characterization**. Characterizing a standard-cell or gate-array library involves **circuit extraction** from the full-custom cell layout for each cell. The extracted schematic includes all the parasitic resistance and capacitance elements. Then library engineers perform a simulation of each cell including the parasitic elements to determine the switching delays. The simulation models for the transistors are derived from measurements on special chips included on a wafer called **process control monitors** (**PCMs**) or **drop-ins**. Library engineers then use the results of the circuit simulation to generate detailed timing models for logic simulation. We shall cover timing models in Chapter 13.

All ASICs need to be production tested (programmable ASICs may be tested by the manufacturer before they are customized, but they still need to be tested). Simple cells in small or medium-size blocks can be tested using automated techniques, but large blocks such as RAM or multipliers need a planned strategy. We shall discuss test in Chapter 14.

The **cell schematic** (a netlist description) describes each cell so that the cell designer can perform simulation for complex cells. You may not need the detailed cell schematic for all cells, but you need enough information to compare what you think is on the silicon (the schematic) with what is actually on the silicon (the layout)—this is a **layout versus schematic** (**LVS**) check.

If the ASIC designer uses schematic entry, each cell needs a **cell icon** together with connector and naming information that can be used by design tools from different vendors. We shall cover ASIC design using schematic entry in Chapter 9. One of the advantages of using **logic synthesis** (Chapter 12) rather than schematic design entry is eliminating the problems with icons, connectors, and cell names. Logic synthesis also makes moving an ASIC between different cell libraries, or **retargeting**, much easier.

In order to estimate the parasitic capacitance of wires before we actually complete any routing, we need a statistical estimate of the capacitance for a net in a given size circuit block. This usually takes the form of a look-up table known as a **wire-load model**. We also need a **routing model** for each cell. Large cells are too complex for the physical design or layout tools to handle directly and we need a simpler representation—a **phantom**—of the physical layout that still contains all the necessary information. The phantom may include information that tells the automated routing tool where it can and cannot place wires over the cell, as well as the location and types of the connections to the cell.

1.6 Summary

In this chapter we have looked at the difference between full-custom ASICs, semicustom ASICs, and programmable ASICs. Table 1.3 summarizes their different features. ASICs use a library of predesigned and precharacterized logic cells. In fact, we could define an ASIC as a design style that uses a cell library rather than in terms of what an ASIC is or what an ASIC does.

You can think of ICs like pizza. A full-custom pizza is built from scratch. You can customize all the layers of a CBIC pizza, but from a predefined selection, and it takes a while to cook. An MGA pizza uses precooked crusts with fixed sizes and you choose only from a few different standard types on a menu. This makes MGA pizza

TABLE 1.3   Types of ASIC.

ASIC type	Family member	Custom mask layers	Custom logic cells
Full-custom	Analog/digital	All	Some
Semicustom	Cell-based (CBIC)	All	None
	Masked gate array (MGA)	Some	None
Programmable	Field-programmable gate array (FPGA)	None	None
	Programmable logic device (PLD)	None	None

a little faster to cook and a little cheaper. An FPGA is rather like a frozen pizza—you buy it at the supermarket in a limited selection of sizes and types, but you can put it in the microwave at home and it will be ready in a few minutes.

In each chapter we shall indicate the key concepts. In this chapter they are

- The difference between full-custom and semicustom ASICs
- The difference between standard-cell, gate-array, and programmable ASICs
- The ASIC design flow
- Design economics including part cost, NRE, and breakeven volume
- The contents and use of an ASIC cell library

Next, in Chapter 2, we shall take a closer look at the semicustom ASICs that were introduced in this chapter.

1.7   Problems

1.1 (Break-even volumes, 60 min.) You need a spreadsheet program (such as Microsoft Excel) for this problem.

- **a.** Build a spreadsheet, "Break-even Analysis," to generate Figure 1.11.
- **b.** Derive equations for the break-even volumes (there are three: FPGA/MGA, FPGA/CBIC, and MGA/CBIC) and calculate their values.
- **c.** Increase the FPGA part cost by $10 and use your spreadsheet to produce the new break-even graph. *Hint:* (For users of Excel-like spreadsheets) use the XY scatter plot option. Use the first column for the *x*-axis data.
- **d.** Find the new break-even volumes (change the volume until the cost becomes the same for two technologies).
- **e.** Program your spreadsheet to automatically find the break-even volumes. Now graph the break-even volume (for a choice between FPGA and CBIC) for

values of FPGA part costs ranging from \$10–\$50 and CBIC costs ranging from \$2–\$10 (do not change the fixed costs from Figure 1.12).

f. Calculate the sensitivity of the break-even volumes to changes in the part costs and fixed costs. There are three break-even volumes and each of these is sensitive to two part costs and two fixed costs. Express your answers in two ways: in equation form and as numbers (for the values in Section 1.4.2 and Figure 1.11).

g. The costs in Figure 1.11 are not unrealistic. What can you say from your answers if you are a defense contractor, primarily selling products in volumes of less than 1000 parts? What if you are a PC board vendor selling between 10,000 and 100,000 parts?

1.2 (Design productivity, 10 min.) Given the figures for the SPARCstation 1 ASICs described in Section 1.3 what was the productivity measured in transistors/day? and measured in gates/day? Compare your answers with the figures for productivity in Section 1.4.3 and explain any differences. How accurate do you think productivity estimates are?

1.3 (ASIC package size, 30 min.) Assuming, for this problem, a gate density of $1.0 \, \text{gate/mil}^{-2}$ (see Section 15.4, "Estimating ASIC Size," for a detailed explanation of this figure), the maximum number of gates you can put in a package is determined by the maximum die size for each of the packages shown in Table 1.4. The maximum die size is determined by the package cavity size; these are **package-limited** ASICs. Calculate the maximum number of I/O pads that can be placed on a die for each package if the pad spacing is: (i) 5 mil, and (ii) 10 mil. Compare your answers with the maximum numbers of pins (or leads) on each package and comment. Now calculate the minimum number of gates that you can put in each package determined by the minimum die size.

1.4 (ASIC vendor costs, 30 min.) There is a well-known saying in the ASIC business: "We lose money on every part—but we make it up in volume." This has a serious side. Suppose Sumo Silicon currently has two customers: Mr. Big, who currently buys 10,000 parts per week, and Ms. Smart, who currently buys 4800 parts per week. A new customer, Ms. Teeny (who is growing fast), wants to buy 1200 parts per week. Sumo's costs are

$$\text{wafer cost} = \$500 + (\$250,000/W),$$

where W is the number of wafer starts per week. Assume each wafer carries 200 chips (parts), all parts are identical, and the yield is

$$\text{yield} = 70 + 0.2 \times (W - 80) \% \tag{1.1}$$

Currently Sumo has a profit margin of 35 percent. Sumo is currently running at 100 wafer starts per week for Mr. Big and Ms. Smart. Sumo thinks they can get 50 cents more out of Mr. Big for his chips, but Ms. Smart won't pay any more. We

TABLE 1.4   Die size limits for ASIC packages.

Package[1]	Number of pins or leads	Maximum die size[2] (mil^2)	Minimum die size[3] (mil^2)
PLCC	44	320 × 320	94 × 94
PLCC	68	420 × 420	154 × 154
PLCC	84	395 × 395	171 × 171
PQFP	100	338 × 338	124 × 124
PQFP	144	350 × 350	266 × 266
PQFP	160	429 × 429	248 × 248
PQFP	208	501 × 501	427 × 427
CPGA	68	480 × 480	200 × 200
CPGA	84	370 × 370	200 × 200
CPGA	120	480 × 480	175 × 175
CPGA	144	470 × 470	250 × 250
CPGA	223	590 × 590	290 × 290
CPGA	299	590 × 590	470 × 470
PPGA	64	230 × 230	120 × 120
PPGA	84	380 × 380	150 × 150
PPGA	100	395 × 395	150 × 150
PPGA	120	395 × 395	190 × 190
PPGA	144	660 × 655	230 × 230
PPGA	180	540 × 540	330 × 330
PPGA	208	500 × 500	395 × 395

[1]PLCC = plastic leaded chip carrier, PQFP = plastic quad flat pack,
 CPGA = ceramic pin-grid array, PPGA = plastic pin-grid array.
[2]Maximum die size is not standard and varies between manufacturers.
[3]Minimum die size is an estimate based on bond length restrictions.

can calculate how much Sumo can afford to lose per chip if they want Ms. Teeny's business really badly.

a. What is Sumo's current yield?

b. How many good parts is Sumo currently producing per week? (*Hint:* Is this enough to supply Mr. Big and Ms. Smart?)

c. Calculate how many extra wafer starts per week we need to supply Ms. Teeny (the yield will change—what is the new yield?). Think when you give this answer.

d. What is Sumo's increase in costs to supply Ms. Teeny?

e. Multiply your answer to part d by 1.35 (to account for Sumo's profit). This is the increase in revenue we need to cover our increased costs to supply Ms. Teeny.

f. Now suppose we charge Mr. Big 50 cents more per part. How much extra revenue does that generate?

g. How much does Ms. Teeny's extra business reduce the wafer cost?

h. How much can Sumo Silicon afford to lose on each of Ms. Teeny's parts, cover its costs, and still make a 35 percent profit?

1.5 (Silicon, 20 min.) How much does a 6-inch silicon wafer weigh? a 12-inch wafer? How much does a carrier (called a boat) that holds twenty 12-inch wafers weigh? What implications does this have for manufacturing?

a. How many die that are 1-inch on a side does a 12-inch wafer hold? If each die is worth $100, how much is a 20-wafer boat worth? If a factory is processing 10 of these boats in different furnaces when the power is interrupted and those wafers have to be scrapped, how much money is lost?

b. The size of silicon factories (fabs or foundries) is measured in wafer starts per week. If a factory is capable of 5000 12-inch wafer starts per week, with an average die of 500 mil on a side that sells for $20 and 90 percent yield, what is the value in dollars/year of the factory production? What fraction of the current gross national (or domestic) product (GNP/GDP) of your country is that? If the yield suddenly drops from 90 percent to 40 percent (a yield bust) how much revenue is the company losing per day? If the company has a cash reserve of $100 million and this revenue loss drops "straight to the bottom line," how long does it take for the company to go out of business?

c. TSMC produced 2 million 6-inch wafers in 1996, how many 500 mil die is that? TSMC's $500 million Camas fab in Washington is scheduled to produce 30,000 8-inch wafers per month by the year 2000 using a 0.35 μm process. If a 1 Mb SRAM yields 1500 good die per 8-inch wafer and there are 1700 gross die per wafer, what is the yield? What is the die size? If the SRAM cell size is 7 μm^2, what fraction of the die is used by the cells? What is TSMC's cost per bit for SRAM if the wafer cost is $2000? If a 16Mb DRAM on the same fab line uses a 16 mm^2 die, what is the cost per bit for DRAM assuming the same yield?

1.6 (Simulation time, 30 min.) "…The system-level simulation used approximately 4000 lines of SPARC assembly language…each simulation clock was simulated in three real time seconds" (Sun Technology article).

a. With a 20 MHz clock how much slower is simulated time than real time?

b. How long would it take to simulate all 4000 lines of test code? (Assume one line of assembly code per cycle—a good approximation compared to the others we are making.)

The article continues: "the entire system was simulated, running actual code, including several milliseconds of SunOS execution. Four days after power-up, SPARCstation 1 booted SunOS and announced: 'hello world'."

c. How long would it take to simulate 5 ms of code?

d. Find out how long it takes to boot a UNIX workstation in real time. How many clock cycles is this?

e. The machine is not executing boot code all this time; you have to wait for disk drives to spin-up, file systems checks to complete, and so on. Make some estimates as to how much code is required to boot an operating system (OS) and how many clock cycles this would take to execute.

The number of clock cycles you need to simulate to boot a system is somewhere between your answers to parts d and e.

f. From your answers make an estimate of how long it takes to simulate booting the OS. Does this seem reasonable?

g. Could the engineers have simulated a complete boot sequence?

h. Do you think the engineers expected the system to boot on first silicon, given the complexity of the system and how long they would have to wait to simulate a complete boot sequence? Explain.

1.7 (Price per gate, 5 min.) Given the assumptions of Section 1.4.4 on the price per gate of different ASIC technologies, what has to change for the price per gate for an FPGA to be less than that for an MGA or CBIC—if all three use the same process?

1.8 (Pentiums, 20 min.) Read the online tour of the Pentium Pro at http://www.intel.com (adapted from a paper presented at the 1995 International Solid-State Circuits Conference). This is not an ASIC design; notice the section on full-custom circuit design. Notice also the comments on the use of 'assert' statements in the HDL code that described the circuits. Find out the approximate cost of the Intel Pentium (3.3 million transistors) and Pentium Pro (5.5 million transistors) microprocessors.

a. Assuming there a four transistors per gate equivalent, what is the price per gate?

b. Find out the cost of a 1 Mb, 4 Mb, 8 Mb, or 16 Mb DRAM. Assuming one transistor per memory bit, what is the price per gate of DRAM?

c. Considering that both have roughly the same die size, are just as complex to design and to manufacture, why is there such a huge difference in price per gate between microprocessors and DRAM?

1.9 (Inverse embedded arrays, 10 min.) A relatively new cousin of the embedded gate array, the **inverse-embedded gate array**, is a cell-based ASIC that contains an embedded gate-array megacell. List the features as well as the advantages and disadvantages of this type of ASIC in the same way as for the other members of the ASIC family in Section 1.1.

1.10 (0.5-gate design, 60 min.) It is a good idea to complete a 0.5-gate ASIC design (an inverter connected between an input pad and an output pad) in the first week (day) of class. Capture the commands in a report that shows all the steps taken to create your chip starting from an empty directory—`halfgate`.

1.11 (Filenames, 30 min.) Start a list of filename extensions used in ASIC design. Table 1.5 shows an example. Expand this list as you use more tools.

TABLE 1.5   CAD tool filename extensions.

Extension	Description	From	To
`.ini`	Viewlogic startup file, library search paths, etc.	Viewlogic/Viewdraw	Internal tools use other Viewlogic tools
`.wir`	Schematic file		

1.8   Bibliography

The Addison-Wesley VLSI Design Series covers all aspects of VLSI design. Mead and Conway [1980] is an introduction to VLSI design. Glasser and Dobberpuhl [1985] deal primarily with NMOS technology, but their book is still a valuable circuit design reference. Bakoglu's book [1990] concentrates on system interconnect issues. Both editions of Weste and Eshraghian [1993] describe full-custom VLSI design.

Other books on CMOS design include books by Kang and Leblebici [1996], Wolf [1994], Price [1994], Hurst [1992], and Shoji [1988]. Alvarez [1993] covers BiCMOS, but concentrates more on technology than design. Embabi, Bellaouar, and Elmasry [1993] also cover BiCMOS design from a similar perspective. Elmasry's book [1994] contains a collection of papers on BiCMOS design. Einspruch and Hilbert [1991]; Huber and Rosneck [1991]; and Veendrick [1992] are introductions to ASIC design for nontechnical readers. Long and Butner [1990] cover gallium arsenide (GaAs) IC design. Most books on CMOS and ASIC design are classified in the TK7874 section of the Library of Congress catalog (T is for technology).

Several journals and magazines publish articles on ASICs and ASIC design. The *IEEE Transactions on Very Large Scale Integration (VLSI) Systems* (ISSN 1063-8210, TK7874.I3273, 1993–) is dedicated to VLSI design. The *IEEE Custom Integrated Circuits Conference* (ISSN 0886-5930, TK7874.C865, 1979–) and the *IEEE International ASIC Conference* (TK7874.6.I34a, 1988–1991; TK7874.6.I35,

ISSN 1063-0988, 1991–) both cover the design and use of ASICs. *EE Times* (ISSN 0192-1541, `http://techweb.cmp.com/eet`) is a newsletter that includes a wide-ranging coverage of system design, ASICs, and ASIC design. *Integrated System Design* (ISSN 1080-2797), formerly *ASIC & EDA*) is a monthly publication that includes ASIC design topics. *High Performance Systems* (ISSN 0887-9664), formerly *VLSI Design* (ISSN 0279-2834), deals with system design including the use of ASICs. *EDN* (ISSN 0012-7515, `http://www.ednmag.com`) has broader coverage of the electronics industry, including articles on VLSI and systems design. *Computer Design* (ISSN 0010-4566) is targeted at systems-level design but includes coverage of ASICs (for example, a special issue in August 1996 was devoted to ASIC design).

The Electronic Industries Association (EIA) has produced a standard, JESD12-1B, "Terms and definitions for gate arrays and cell-based digital integrated circuits," to define terms and definitions.

University Video Communication (`http://www.uvc.com`) produces several videotapes on computer science and engineering topics including ASIC design. Maly's book [1987] is a picture book containing drawings and cross-sections of devices, and shows how a transistor is fabricated.

It is difficult to obtain detailed technical information from ASIC companies and vendors apart from the glossy brochures (**sparkle sheets**). It used to be possible to obtain data books on cell libraries (now these are large and difficult to produce, and are often only available in electronic form) as well as design guidelines and handbooks. Fortunately there are now many resources available on the World Wide Web, which are, of course, constantly changing. EDAC (Electronic Design Automation Companies) has a Web page (`http://www.edac.org`) with links to most of the EDA companies. The Electrical Engineering page on the World Wide Web (E2W3) (`http://www.e2w3.com`) contains links to many ASIC related areas, including distributors, ASIC companies, and semiconductor companies. SEMATECH (Semiconductor Manufacturing Technology) is a nonprofit consortium of U.S. semiconductor companies and has a Web page (`http://www.sematech.org`) that includes links to major semiconductor manufacturers. The MIT Semiconductor Subway (`http://www-mtl.mit.edu`) is more oriented toward devices, processes, and materials but contains links to other VLSI industrial and academic areas. There is a list of EDA companies at `http://www.yahoo.com` under `Business_and_Economy` in `Companies/Computers/Software/Graphics/CAD/IC_Design`.

The MOS Implementation Service (MOSIS), located at the Information Sciences Institute (ISI) at the University of Southern California (USC), is a "silicon broker" for universities in the United States and also provides commercial access to fabrication facilities (`http://www.isi.edu`). Professor Don Bouldin maintains The Microelectronic Systems Newsletter, formerly the MOSIS Users Group (MUG) Newsletter, at `http://www-ece.engr.utk.edu/ece`.

NASA (`http://nppp.jpl.nasa.gov/dmg/jpl/loc/asic`) has an extensive online ASIC guide, developed by the Office of Safety and Mission Assurance, that covers ASIC management, vendor evaluation, design, and part acceptance.

1.9   References

Alvarez, A. R. (Ed.). 1993. *BiCMOS Technology and Applications.* Norwell, MA: Kluwer. ISBN 0-7923-9384-8. TK7871.99.M44.

Bakoglu, H. B. 1990. *Circuits, Interconnections, and Packaging for VLSI.* Reading, MA: Addison-Wesley, 527 p. ISBN 0-86341-165-7. TK7874.B345. Based on a Stanford Ph.D. thesis and contains chapters on: devices and interconnections, packaging, transmission lines, cross talk, clocking of high-speed systems, system level performance.

Einspruch N. G., and J. L. Hilbert (Eds.). 1991. *Application Specific Integrated Circuit (ASIC) Technology.* San Diego, CA: Academic Press. ISBN 0122341236. TK7874.V56 vol. 23. Includes: "Introduction to ASIC technology," Hilbert; "Market dynamics of the ASIC revolution," Collett; "Marketing ASICs," Chakraverty; "Design and architecture of ASIC products," Hickman et al.; "Model and library development," Lubhan; "Computer-aided design tools and systems," Rowson; "ASIC manufacturing," Montalbo; "Test and testability of ASICs," Rosqvist; "Electronic packaging for ASICs," Herrell and Prokop; "Application and selection of ASICs," Mitchell; "Designing with ASICs," Wilkerson; "Quality and reliability," Young.

Elmasry, M. I. 1994. *BiCMOS Integrated Circuit Design: with Analog, Digital, and Smart Power Applications.* New York: IEEE Press, ISBN 0780304306. TK7871.99.M44.B53.

Embabi, S. H. K., A. Bellaouar, and M. I. Elmasry. 1993. *Digital BiCMOS Integrated Circuit Design.* Norwell: MA: Kluwer, 398 p. ISBN 0-7923-9276-0. TK7874.E52.

Glasser, L. A., and D. W. Dobberpuhl. 1985. *The Design and Analysis of VLSI Circuits.* Reading, MA: Addison-Wesley, 473 p. ISBN 0-201-12580-3. TK7874.G573. Detailed analysis of circuits, but largely nMOS.

Huber, J. P., and M. W. Rosneck. 1991. *Successful ASIC Design the First Time Through.* New York: Van Nostrand Reinhold, 200 p. ISBN 0-442-00312-9. TK7874.H83.

Hurst, S. L. 1992. *Custom VLSI Microelectronics.* Englewood Cliffs, NJ: Prentice-Hall, 466 p. ISBN 0-13-194416-9. TK7874.H883.

Kang, S-M, and Y. Leblebici. 1996. *CMOS Digital Integrated Circuits: Analysis and Design.* New York: McGraw-Hill, 614 p. ISBN 0070380465.

Long, S. I., and S. E. Butner. 1990. *Gallium Arsenide Digital Integrated Circuit Design.* New York: McGraw-Hill, 486 p. ISBN 0-07-038687-0. TK7874.L66.

Maly, W. 1987. *Atlas of IC Technologies: An Introduction to VLSI Processes.* Menlo Park, CA: Benjamin-Cummings, 340 p. ISBN 0-8053-6850-7. TK7874.M254. Cross-sectional drawings showing construction of nMOS and CMOS processes.

Mead, C. A., and L. A. Conway. 1980. *Introduction to VLSI Systems.* Reading, MA: Addison-Wesley, 396 p. ISBN 0-201-04358-0. TK7874.M37.

Price, T. E. 1994. *Introduction to VLSI Technology.* Englewood Cliffs, NJ: Prentice-Hall, 280 p. ISBN 0-13-500422-5. TK7874.P736.

Shoji, M. 1988. *CMOS Digital Circuit Technology.* Englewood Cliffs, NJ: Prentice-Hall, 434 p. ISBN 0131388436. TK7871.99.M44. See also Shoji, M., *High Speed Digital Circuits,* Reading, MA: Addison-Wesley, 1996, 360 p., ISBN 0-201-63483-X, TK7874.65.S56

Weste, N. H. E., and K. Eshraghian. 1993. *Principles of CMOS VLSI Design: A Systems Perspective.* 2nd ed. Reading, MA: Addison-Wesley, 713 p. ISBN 0-201-53376-6. TK7874.W46. Concentrates on full-custom design.

Wolf, W. H. 1994. *Modern VLSI Design: A Systems Approach.* Englewood Cliffs, NJ: Prentice-Hall, 468 p. ISBN 0-13-588377-6. TK7874.65.W65.

Veendrick, H. J. M. 1992. *MOS ICs from Basics to ASICs.* New York: VCH, ISBN 1-56081197-8. TK7874.V397.

CMOS LOGIC

A **CMOS transistor** (or device) has four terminals: **gate**, **source**, **drain**, and a fourth terminal that we shall ignore until the next section. A CMOS transistor is a switch. The switch must be conducting or *on* to allow current to flow between the source and drain terminals (using open and closed for switches is confusing—for the same reason we say a tap is *on* and not that it is *closed*). The transistor source and drain terminals are equivalent as far as digital signals are concerned—we do not worry about labeling an electrical switch with two terminals.

- V_{AB} is the potential difference, or voltage, between nodes A and B in a circuit; V_{AB} is positive if node A is more positive than node B.

- Italics denote variables; constants are set in roman (upright) type. Uppercase letters denote DC, large-signal, or steady-state voltages.

- For TTL the positive power supply is called VCC (V_{CC} or V_{CC}). The 'C' denotes that the supply is connected indirectly to the collectors of the *npn* bipolar transistors (a bipolar transistor has a collector, base, and emitter— corresponding roughly to the drain, gate, and source of an MOS transistor).

- Following the example of TTL we used VDD (V_{DD} or V_{DD}) to denote the positive supply in an NMOS chip where the devices are all *n*-channel transistors and the drains of these devices are connected indirectly to the positive supply. The supply nomenclature for NMOS chips has stuck for CMOS.

- VDD is the name of the power supply node or net; V_{DD} represents the value (uppercase since V_{DD} is a DC quantity). Since V_{DD} is a variable, it is italic (words and multiletter abbreviations use roman—thus it is V_{DD}, but V_{drain}).
- Logic designers often call the CMOS negative supply VSS or V_{SS} even if it is actually ground or GND. I shall use VSS for the node and V_{SS} for the value.
- CMOS uses **positive logic**—VDD is logic '1' and VSS is logic '0'.

We turn a transistor on or off using the gate terminal. There are two kinds of CMOS transistors: *n*-channel transistors and *p*-channel transistors. An *n*-channel transistor requires a logic '1' (from now on I'll just say a '1') on the gate to make the switch conducting (to turn the transistor *on*). A *p*-channel transistor requires a logic '0' (again from now on, I'll just say a '0') on the gate to make the switch nonconducting (to turn the transistor *off*). The *p*-channel transistor symbol has a bubble on its gate to remind us that the gate has to be a '0' to turn the transistor *on*. All this is shown in Figure 2.1(a) and (b).

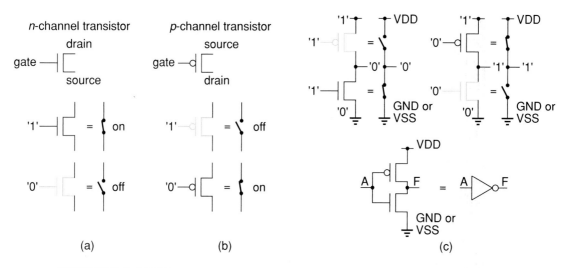

(a)   (b)   (c)

FIGURE 2.1 CMOS transistors as switches. (a) An *n*-channel transistor. (b) A *p*-channel transistor. (c) A CMOS inverter and its symbol (an *equilateral* triangle and a *circle*).

If we connect an *n*-channel transistor in series with a *p*-channel transistor, as shown in Figure 2.1(c), we form an **inverter**. With four transistors we can form a two-input **NAND gate** (Figure 2.2a). We can also make a two-input **NOR gate** (Figure 2.2b). Logic designers normally use the terms NAND gate and logic gate (or just gate), but I shall try to use the terms NAND **cell** and **logic cell** rather than NAND gate or logic gate in this chapter to avoid any possible confusion with the gate terminal of a transistor.

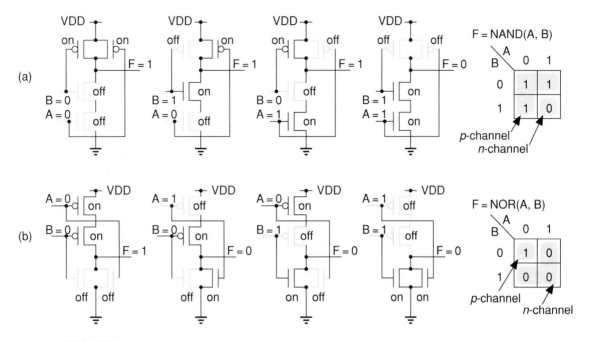

FIGURE 2.2 CMOS logic. (a) A two-input NAND logic cell. (b) A two-input NOR logic cell. The *n*-channel and *p*-channel transistor switches implement the '1's and '0's of a Karnaugh map.

2.1 CMOS Transistors

Figure 2.3 illustrates how electrons and holes abandon their dopant atoms leaving a **depletion region** around a transistor's source and drain. The region between source and drain is normally nonconducting. To make an *n*-channel transistor conducting, we must apply a positive voltage V_{GS} (the gate voltage with respect to the source) that is greater than the *n*-channel transistor **threshold voltage**, V_{tn} (a typical value is 0.5 V and, as far as we are presently concerned, is a constant). This establishes a thin (≈ 50 Å) conducting channel of electrons under the gate. MOS transistors can carry a very small current (the **subthreshold current**—a few microamperes or less) with $V_{GS} < V_{tn}$, but we shall ignore this. A transistor can be conducting ($V_{GS} > V_{tn}$) without any current flowing. To make current flow in an *n*-channel transistor we must also apply a positive voltage, V_{DS}, to the drain with respect to the source. Figure 2.3 shows these connections and the connection to the fourth terminal of an MOS transistor—the **bulk** (**well**, **tub**, or **substrate**) terminal. For an *n*-channel transistor we must connect the bulk to the most negative potential, GND or VSS, to reverse bias the bulk-to-drain and bulk-to-source *pn*-diodes. The arrow in the four-terminal *n*-channel transistor symbol in Figure 2.3 reflects the polarity of these *pn*-diodes.

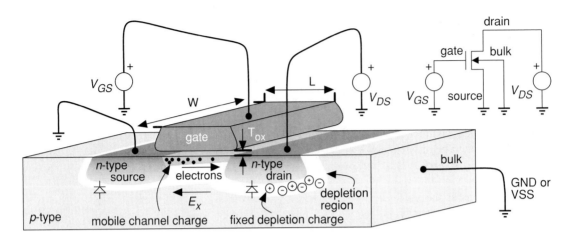

FIGURE 2.3 An *n*-channel MOS transistor. The gate-oxide thickness, T_{OX}, is approximately 100 angstroms (0.01 µm). A typical transistor length, $L = 2\lambda$. The bulk may be either the substrate or a well. The diodes represent *pn*-junctions that must be reverse-biased.

The current flowing in the transistor is

$$\text{current (amperes)} = \text{charge (coulombs) per unit time (second)}. \qquad (2.1)$$

We can express the current in terms of the total charge in the channel, Q (imagine taking a picture and counting the number of electrons in the channel at that instant). If t_f (for **time of flight**—sometimes called the **transit time**) is the time that it takes an electron to cross between source and drain, the drain-to-source current, I_{DSn}, is

$$I_{DSn} = \frac{Q}{t_f}. \qquad (2.2)$$

We need to find Q and t_f. The velocity of the electrons **v** (a vector) is given by the equation that forms the basis of Ohm's law:

$$\mathbf{v} = -\mu_n \mathbf{E}, \qquad (2.3)$$

where μ_n is the **electron mobility** (μ_p is the **hole mobility**) and **E** is the electric field (with units Vm^{-1}).

Typical **carrier mobility** values are $\mu_n = 500$–$1000 \text{ cm}^2 V^{-1} s^{-1}$ and $\mu_p = 100$–$400 \text{ cm}^2 V^{-1} s^{-1}$. Equation 2.3 is a vector equation, but we shall ignore the vertical electric field and concentrate on the horizontal electric field, E_x, that moves the electrons between source and drain. The horizontal component of the electric field is $E_x = -V_{DS}/L$, directed from the drain to the source, where L is the channel length (see Figure 2.3). The electrons travel a distance L with horizontal velocity $v_x = -\mu_n E_x$, so that

$$t_f = \frac{L}{v_x} = \frac{L^2}{\mu_n V_{DS}}.$$ (2.4)

Next we find the channel charge, Q. The channel and the gate form the plates of a capacitor, separated by an insulator—the gate oxide. We know that the charge on a linear capacitor, C, is $Q = CV$. Our lower plate, the channel, is not a linear conductor. Charge only appears on the lower plate when the voltage between the gate and the channel, V_{GC}, exceeds the n-channel threshold voltage. For our nonlinear capacitor we need to modify the equation for a linear capacitor to the following:

$$Q = C(V_{GC} - V_{tn}).$$ (2.5)

The lower plate of our capacitor is resistive and conducting current, so that the potential in the channel, V_{GC}, varies. In fact, $V_{GC} = V_{GS}$ at the source and $V_{GC} = V_{GS} - V_{DS}$ at the drain. What we really should do is find an expression for the channel charge as a function of channel voltage and sum (integrate) the charge all the way across the channel, from $x = 0$ (at the source) to $x = L$ (at the drain). Instead we shall assume that the channel voltage, $V_{GC}(x)$, is a linear function of distance from the source and take the average value of the charge, which is thus

$$Q = C\left[(V_{GS} - V_{tn}) - \frac{1}{2}V_{DS}\right].$$ (2.6)

The gate capacitance, C, is given by the formula for a parallel-plate capacitor with length L, width W, and plate separation equal to the gate-oxide thickness, T_{ox}. Thus the gate capacitance is

$$C = \frac{WL\varepsilon_{ox}}{T_{ox}} = WLC_{ox},$$ (2.7)

where ε_{ox} is the gate-oxide dielectric permittivity. For silicon dioxide, SiO_2, $\varepsilon_{ox} \approx 3.45 \times 10^{-11}\,\mathrm{Fm^{-1}}$, so that, for a typical gate-oxide thickness of 100 Å (1 Å = 1 angstrom = 0.1 nm), the gate capacitance per unit area, $C_{ox} \approx 3\,\mathrm{fF\mu m^{-2}}$.

Now we can express the channel charge in terms of the transistor parameters,

$$Q = WLC_{ox}\left[(V_{GS} - V_{tn}) - \frac{1}{2}V_{DS}\right].$$ (2.8)

Finally, the drain–source current is

$$I_{DSn} = \frac{Q}{t_f} = \frac{W}{L}\mu_n C_{ox}\left[(V_{GS} - V_{tn}) - \frac{1}{2}V_{DS}\right]V_{DS}$$

$$= \frac{W}{L}k'_n\left[(V_{GS} - V_{tn}) - \frac{1}{2}V_{DS}\right]V_{DS}. \tag{2.9}$$

The constant k'_n is the process transconductance parameter (or **intrinsic transconductance**):

$$k'_n = \mu_n C_{ox}. \tag{2.10}$$

We also define β_n, the **transistor gain factor** (or just **gain factor**) as

$$\beta_n = k'_n\frac{W}{L}. \tag{2.11}$$

The factor W/L (transistor width divided by length) is the transistor **shape factor**.

Equation 2.9 describes the **linear region** (or triode region) of operation. This equation is valid until $V_{DS} = V_{GS} - V_{tn}$ and then predicts that I_{DS} decreases with increasing V_{DS}, which does not make physical sense. At $V_{DS} = V_{GS} - V_{tn} = V_{DS(sat)}$ (the **saturation voltage**) there is no longer enough voltage between the gate and the channel to support any channel charge. Clearly a small amount of charge remains or the current would go to zero, but with very little free charge the channel resistance in a small region close to the drain increases rapidly and any further increase in V_{DS} is dropped over this region. Thus for $V_{DS} > V_{GS} - V_{tn}$ (the **saturation region**, or pentode region, of operation) the drain current I_{DS} remains approximately constant at the **saturation current**, $I_{DSn(sat)}$, where

$$I_{DSn(sat)} = \frac{\beta_n}{2}(V_{GS} - V_{tn})^2; \quad V_{DS} > V_{GS} - V_{tn}. \tag{2.12}$$

Figure 2.4 shows the *n*-channel transistor I_{DS}–V_{DS} characteristics for a generic 0.5 µm CMOS process that we shall call **G5**. We can fit Eq. 2.12 to the long-channel transistor characteristics (W = 60 µm, L = 6 µm) in Figure 2.4(a). If $I_{DSn(sat)} = 2.5$ mA (with $V_{DS} = 3.0$ V, $V_{GS} = 3.0$ V, $V_{tn} = 0.65$ V, $T_{ox} = 100$ Å), the intrinsic transconductance is

$$k'_n = \frac{2(L/W)I_{DSnsat}}{(V_{GS} - V_{tn})^2} = \frac{2(6/60)(2.5\times10^{-3})}{(3.0 - 0.65)^2} = 9.05\times10^{-5}\,AV^{-2}, \tag{2.13}$$

or approximately 90 µAV^{-2}. This value of k'_n, calculated in the saturation region, will be different (typically lower by a factor of 2 or more) from the value of k'_n measured in the linear region. We assumed the mobility, μ_n, and the threshold voltage, V_{tn}, are constants—neither of which is true, as we shall see in Section 2.1.2.

For the p-channel transistor in the G5 process, $I_{DSp(sat)} = -850\,\mu\text{A}$ ($V_{DS} = -3.0\,\text{V}, V_{GS} = -3.0\,\text{V}, V_{tp} = -0.85\,\text{V}, W = 60\,\mu\text{m}, L = 6\,\mu\text{m}$). Then

$$k_p' = \frac{2\,(L/W)\,(-I_{DSp\,(sat)})}{(V_{GS} - V_{tp})^2} = \frac{2\,(6/60)\,(850\times10^{-6})}{(-3.0 - (-0.85))^2} = 3.68\times10^{-5}\,\text{AV}^{-2}. \quad (2.14)$$

The next section explains the signs in Eq. 2.14.

2.1.1   P-Channel Transistors

The source and drain of CMOS transistors look identical; we have to know which way the current is flowing to distinguish them. The source of an n-channel transistor is lower in potential than the drain and vice-versa for a p-channel transistor. In an n-channel transistor the threshold voltage, V_{tn}, is normally positive, and the terminal voltages V_{DS} and V_{GS} are also usually positive. In a p-channel transistor V_{tp} is normally negative and we have a choice: We can write everything in terms of the magnitudes of the voltages and currents or we can use negative signs in a consistent fashion.

Here are the equations for a p-channel transistor using negative signs:

$$I_{DS} = -k_p' \frac{W}{L} \left[(V_{GS} - V_{tp}) - \frac{1}{2} V_{DS} \right] V_{DS} \qquad V_{DS} > V_{GS} - V_{tp}$$

$$I_{DSp\,(sat)} = \frac{-\beta_p}{2} (V_{GS} - V_{tp})^2 \qquad V_{DS} < V_{GS} - V_{tp} \qquad (2.15)$$

In these two equations V_{tp} is negative, and the terminal voltages V_{DS} and V_{GS} are also normally negative (and $-3\,\text{V} < -2\,\text{V}$, for example). The current I_{DSp} is then negative, corresponding to conventional current flowing from source to drain of a p-channel transistor (and hence the negative sign for $I_{DSp(sat)}$ in Eq. 2.14).

2.1.2   Velocity Saturation

For a deep submicron transistor, Eq. 2.12 may overestimate the drain–source current by a factor of 2 or more. There are three reasons for this error. First, the threshold voltage is not constant. Second, the actual length of the channel (the electrical or effective length, often written as L_{eff}) is less than the drawn (mask) length. The third reason is that Eq. 2.3 is not valid for high electric fields. The electrons cannot move any faster than about $v_{maxn} = 10^5\,\text{ms}^{-1}$ when the electric field is above $10^6\,\text{Vm}^{-1}$ (reached when $1\,\text{V}$ is dropped across $1\,\mu\text{m}$); the electrons become **velocity saturated**. In this case $t_f = L_{eff}/v_{maxn}$, the drain–source saturation current is independent of the transistor length, and Eq. 2.12 becomes

$$I_{DSn\,(sat)} = W v_{maxn} C_{ox} (V_{GS} - V_{tn}); V_{DS} > V_{DS\,(sat)} \quad \text{(velocity saturated).} \quad (2.16)$$

We can see this behavior for the short-channel transistor characteristics in Figure 2.4(a) and (c).

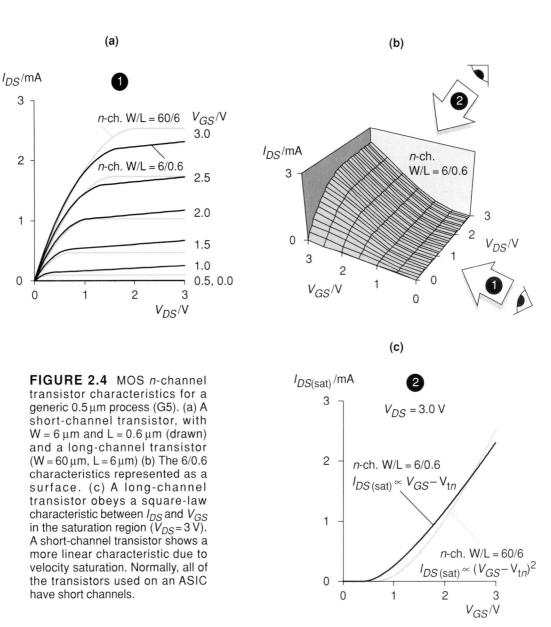

FIGURE 2.4 MOS n-channel transistor characteristics for a generic 0.5 μm process (G5). (a) A short-channel transistor, with W = 6 μm and L = 0.6 μm (drawn) and a long-channel transistor (W = 60 μm, L = 6 μm) (b) The 6/0.6 characteristics represented as a surface. (c) A long-channel transistor obeys a square-law characteristic between I_{DS} and V_{GS} in the saturation region ($V_{DS} = 3$ V). A short-channel transistor shows a more linear characteristic due to velocity saturation. Normally, all of the transistors used on an ASIC have short channels.

Transistor current is often specified per micron of gate width because of the form of Eq. 2.16. As an example, suppose $I_{DSn(\text{sat})}/W = 300\ \mu\text{A}\mu\text{m}^{-1}$ for the n-channel transistors in our G5 process (with $V_{DS} = 3.0$ V, $V_{GS} = 3.0$ V, $V_{tn} = 0.65$ V, $L_{\text{eff}} = 0.5\ \mu\text{m}$ and $T_{\text{ox}} = 100\ \text{Å}$). Then $E_x \approx (3 - 0.65)\ \text{V}/0.5\ \mu\text{m} \approx 5\ \text{V}\mu\text{m}^{-1}$,

$$v_{maxn} = \frac{I_{DSn\,(sat)}/W}{C_{ox}(V_{GS} - V_{tn})} = \frac{(300 \times 10^{-6})\,(1 \times 10^6)}{(3.45 \times 10^{-3})\,(3 - 0.65)} = 37,000\ ms^{-1}, \quad (2.17)$$

and $t_f \approx 0.5\ \mu m/37,000\,ms^{-1} \approx 13$ ps.

The value for v_{maxn} is lower than the $10^5\ ms^{-1}$ we expected because the carrier velocity is also lowered by **mobility degradation** due the vertical electric field—which we have ignored. This vertical field forces the carriers to keep "bumping" in to the interface between the silicon and the gate oxide, slowing them down.

2.1.3   SPICE Models

The simulation program **SPICE** (which stands for **Simulation Program with Integrated Circuit Emphasis**) is often used to characterize logic cells. Table 2.1 shows a typical set of model parameters for our G5 process. The SPICE parameter KP (given in μAV^{-2}) corresponds to k_n' (and k_p'). SPICE parameters VT0 and TOX correspond to V_{tn} (and V_{tp}), and T_{ox}. SPICE parameter U0 (given in $cm^2V^{-1}s^{-1}$) corresponds to the ideal **bulk mobility** values, μ_n (and μ_p). Many of the other parameters model velocity saturation and mobility degradation (and thus the effective value of k_n' and k_p').

TABLE 2.1   SPICE parameters for a generic 0.5 μm process, G5 (0.6 μm drawn gate length). The n-channel transistor characteristics are shown in Figure 2.4.

```
.MODEL CMOSN NMOS LEVEL=3 PHI=0.7 TOX=10E-09 XJ=0.2U TPG=1 VTO=0.65 DELTA=0.7
+ LD=5E-08 KP=2E-04 UO=550 THETA=0.27 RSH=2 GAMMA=0.6 NSUB=1.4E+17 NFS=6E+11
+ VMAX=2E+05 ETA=3.7E-02 KAPPA=2.9E-02 CGDO=3.0E-10 CGSO=3.0E-10 CGBO=4.0E-10
+ CJ=5.6E-04 MJ=0.56 CJSW=5E-11 MJSW=0.52 PB=1
.MODEL CMOSP PMOS LEVEL=3 PHI=0.7 TOX=10E-09 XJ=0.2U TPG=-1 VTO=-0.92 DELTA=0.29
+ LD=3.5E-08 KP=4.9E-05 UO=135 THETA=0.18 RSH=2 GAMMA=0.47 NSUB=8.5E+16 NFS=6.5E+11
+ VMAX=2.5E+05 ETA=2.45E-02 KAPPA=7.96 CGDO=2.4E-10 CGSO=2.4E-10 CGBO=3.8E-10
+ CJ=9.3E-04 MJ=0.47 CJSW=2.9E-10 MJSW=0.505 PB=1
```

2.1.4   Logic Levels

Figure 2.5 shows how to use transistors as logic switches. The bulk connection for the *n*-channel transistor in Figure 2.5(a–b) is a *p*-well. The bulk connection for the *p*-channel transistor is an *n*-well. The remaining connections show what happens when we try and pass a logic signal between the drain and source terminals.

In Figure 2.5(a) we apply a logic '1' (or V_{DD}—I shall use these interchangeably) to the gate and a logic '0' (V_{SS}) to the source (we know it is the source since electrons must flow from this point, since V_{SS} is the lowest voltage on the chip). The application of these voltages makes the *n*-channel transistor conduct current, and electrons flow from source to drain.

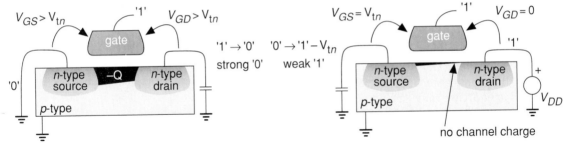

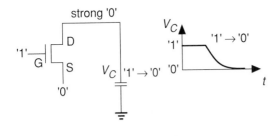

(a)

(b)

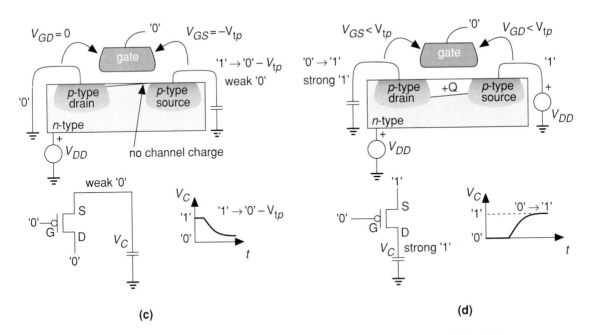

(c)

(d)

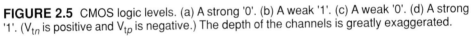

FIGURE 2.5 CMOS logic levels. (a) A strong '0'. (b) A weak '1'. (c) A weak '0'. (d) A strong '1'. (V_{tn} is positive and V_{tp} is negative.) The depth of the channels is greatly exaggerated.

Suppose the drain is initially at logic '1'; then the n-channel transistor will begin to discharge any capacitance that is connected to its drain (due to another logic cell, for example). This will continue until the drain terminal reaches a logic '0', and at that time V_{GD} and V_{GS} are both equal to V_{DD}, a full logic '1'. The transistor is strongly conducting now (with a large channel charge, Q, but there is no current flowing since $V_{DS} = 0\,\text{V}$). The transistor will strongly object to attempts to change its drain terminal from a logic '0'. We say that the **logic level** at the drain is a **strong** '0'.

In Figure 2.5(b) we apply a logic '1' to the drain (it must now be the drain since electrons have to flow toward a logic '1'). The situation is now quite different—the transistor is still on but V_{GS} is decreasing as the source voltage approaches its final value. In fact, the source terminal never gets to a logic '1'—the source will stop increasing in voltage when V_{GS} reaches V_{tn}. At this point the transistor is very nearly off and the source voltage creeps slowly up to $V_{DD} - V_{tn}$. Because the transistor is very nearly off, it would be easy for a logic cell connected to the source to change the potential there, since there is so little channel charge. The logic level at the source is a **weak** '1'. Figure 2.5(c–d) show the state of affairs for a p-channel transistor is the exact reverse or complement of the n-channel transistor situation.

In summary, we have the following logic levels:

- An n-channel transistor provides a strong '0', but a weak '1'.

- A p-channel transistor provides a strong '1', but a weak '0'.

Sometimes we refer to the weak versions of '0' and '1' as **degraded logic levels**. In CMOS technology we can use both types of transistor together to produce strong '0' logic levels as well as strong '1' logic levels.

2.2 The CMOS Process

Figure 2.6 outlines the steps to create an integrated circuit. The starting material is silicon, Si, refined from quartzite (with less than 1 impurity in 10^{10} silicon atoms). We draw a single-crystal silicon **boule** (or ingot) from a crucible containing a melt at approximately 1500 °C (the melting point of silicon at 1 atm. pressure is 1414 °C). This method is known as Czochralski growth. Acceptor (p-type) or donor (n-type) dopants may be introduced into the melt to alter the type of silicon grown.

The boule is sawn to form thin circular wafers (6, 8, or 12 inches in diameter, and typically 600 µm thick), and a flat is ground (the primary flat), perpendicular to the <110> crystal axis—as a "this edge down" indication. The boule is drawn so that the wafer surface is either in the (111) or (100) crystal planes. A smaller secondary flat indicates the wafer crystalline orientation and doping type. A typical submicron CMOS processes uses p-type (100) wafers with a resistivity of approximately 10 Ωcm—this type of wafer has two flats, 90° apart. Wafers are made by chemical companies and sold to the IC manufacturers. A blank 8-inch wafer costs about $100.

To begin IC fabrication we place a batch of wafers (a **wafer lot**) on a **boat** and grow a layer (typically a few thousand angstroms) of **silicon dioxide**, SiO_2, using a furnace. Silicon is used in the semiconductor industry not so much for the properties of silicon, but because of the physical, chemical, and electrical properties of its native oxide, SiO_2. An IC fabrication **process** contains a series of masking steps (that in turn contain other steps) to create the layers that define the transistors and metal interconnect.

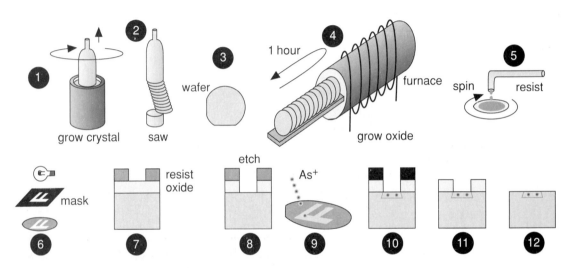

FIGURE 2.6 IC fabrication. Grow crystalline silicon (1); make a wafer (2–3); grow a silicon dioxide (oxide) layer in a furnace (4); apply liquid photoresist (resist) (5); mask exposure (6); a cross-section through a wafer showing the developed resist (7); etch the oxide layer (8); ion implantation (9–10); strip the resist (11); strip the oxide (12). Steps similar to 4–12 are repeated for each layer (typically 12–20 times for a CMOS process).

Each masking step starts by spinning a thin layer (approximately 1 μm) of liquid photoresist (**resist**) onto each wafer. The wafers are baked at about 100 °C to remove the solvent and harden the resist before being exposed to ultraviolet (UV) light (typically less than 200 nm wavelength) through a **mask**. The UV light alters the structure of the resist, allowing it to be removed by developing. The exposed oxide may then be **etched** (removed). Dry **plasma etching** etches in the vertical direction much faster than it does horizontally (an **anisotropic** etch). Wet etch techniques are usually **isotropic**. The resist functions as a mask during the etch step and transfers the desired pattern to the oxide layer.

Dopant ions are then introduced into the exposed silicon areas. Figure 2.6 illustrates the use of **ion implantation**. An **ion implanter is** a cross between a TV and a mass spectrometer and fires dopant ions into the silicon wafer. Ions can only penetrate materials to a depth (the **range**, normally a few microns) that depends on the closely controlled **implant energy** (measured in keV—usually between 10 and 100 keV; an electron volt, 1 eV, is 1.6×10^{-19} J). By using layers of resist, oxide, and polysilicon we can prevent dopant ions from reaching the silicon surface and thus block the silicon from receiving an **implant**. We control the doping level by counting the number of ions we implant (by integrating the ion-beam current). The **implant dose** is measured in atoms/cm^2 (typical doses are from 10^{13} to 10^{15} cm^{-2}). As an alternative to ion implantation we may instead strip the resist and introduce dopants by diffusion from a gaseous source in a furnace.

Once we have completed the transistor diffusion layers we can deposit layers of other materials. Layers of polycrystalline silicon (polysilicon or **poly**), SiO$_2$, and silicon nitride (Si$_3$N$_4$), for example, may be deposited using **chemical vapor deposition (CVD)**. Metal layers can be deposited using **sputtering**. All these layers are patterned using masks and similar **photolithography** steps to those shown in Figure 2.6.

TABLE 2.2   CMOS process layers.

Mask/layer name	Derivation from drawn layers	Alternative names for mask/layer	MOSIS mask label
n-well	= nwell[1]	bulk, substrate, tub, n-tub, moat	CWN
p-well	= pwell[1]	bulk, substrate, tub, p-tub, moat	CWP
active	= pdiff + ndiff	thin-oxide, thinox, island, gate-oxide	CAA
polysilicon	= poly	poly, gate	CPG
n-diffusion implant[2]	= grow (ndiff)	ndiff, n-select, nplus, n+	CSN
p-diffusion implant[2]	= grow (pdiff)	pdiff, p-select, pplus, p+	CSP
contact	= contact	contact cut, poly contact, diffusion contact	CCP and CCA[3]
metal1	= m1	first-level metal	CMF
metal2	= m2	second-level metal	CMS
via2	= via2	metal2/metal3 via, m2/m3 via	CVS
metal3	= m3	third-level metal	CMT
glass	= glass	passivation, overglass, pad	COG

[1]If only one well layer is drawn, the other mask may be derived from the drawn layer. For example, p-well (mask) = not (nwell (drawn)). A single-well process requires only one well mask.
[2]The implant masks may be derived or drawn.
[3]Largely for historical reasons the contacts to poly and contacts to active have different layer names. In the past this allowed a different sizing or process bias to be applied to each contact type when the mask was made.

Table 2.2 shows the mask layers (and their relation to the drawn layers) for a submicron, silicon-gate, three-level metal, self-aligned, CMOS **process**. A process in which the effective gate length is less than 1 μm is referred to as a **submicron process**. Gate lengths below 0.35 μm are considered in the **deep submicron** regime.

Figure 2.7 shows the layers that we draw to define the masks for the logic cell of Figure 1.3. Potential confusion arises because we like to keep layout simple but maintain a "what you see is what you get" (WYSIWYG) approach. This means that the drawn layers do not correspond directly to the masks in all cases.

We can construct wells in a CMOS process in several ways. In an **n-well process**, the substrate is p-type (the wafer itself) and we use an n-well mask to build the n-well. We do not need a p-well mask because there are no p-wells in an n-well process—the n-channel transistors all sit in the substrate (the wafer)—but we often draw the p-well layer as though it existed. In a **p-well process** we use a p-well mask to make the p-wells and the n-wells are the substrate. In a **twin-tub** (or **twin-well**) process, we create individual wells for both types of transistors, and neither well is the substrate (which may be either n-type or p-type). There are even **triple-well** processes used to achieve even more control over the transistor performance. Whatever process that we use we must connect all the n-wells to the most positive potential on the chip, normally VDD, and all the p-wells to VSS; otherwise we may forward bias the bulk to source/drain pn-junctions. The bulk connections for CMOS transistors are not usually drawn in digital circuit schematics, but these **substrate contacts** (**well contacts** or **tub ties**) are very important. After we make the well(s), we grow a layer (approximately 1500 Å) of Si_3N_4 over the wafer. The **active** mask (CAA) leaves this nitride layer only in the active areas that will later become transistors or substrate contacts. Thus

$$CAA \text{ (mask)} = ndiff \text{ (drawn)} \vee pdiff \text{ (drawn)}, \tag{2.18}$$

the $\vee$ symbol represents OR (union) of the two drawn layers, ndiff and pdiff. Everything outside the active areas is known as the field region, or just **field**.

Next we implant the substrate to prevent unwanted transistors from forming in the field region—this is the **field implant** or **channel-stop implant**. The nitride over the active areas acts as an implant mask and we may use another field-implant mask at this step also. Following this we grow a thick (approximately 5000 Å) layer of SiO_2, the **field oxide** (**FOX**). The FOX will not grow over the nitride areas. When we strip the nitride we are left with FOX in the areas we do *not* want to dope the silicon. Following this we deposit, dope, mask, and etch the poly gate material, CPG (mask) = poly (drawn). Next we create the doped regions that form the sources, drains, and substrate contacts using ion implantation. The poly gate functions like masking tape in these steps. One implant (using phosphorous or arsenic ions) forms the n-type source/drain for the n-channel transistors and n-type substrate contacts

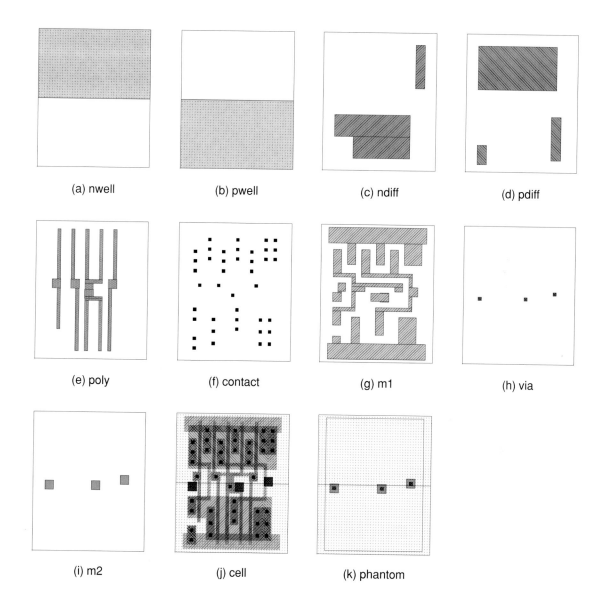

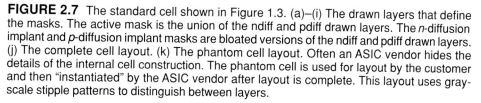

FIGURE 2.7 The standard cell shown in Figure 1.3. (a)–(i) The drawn layers that define the masks. The active mask is the union of the ndiff and pdiff drawn layers. The *n*-diffusion implant and *p*-diffusion implant masks are bloated versions of the ndiff and pdiff drawn layers. (j) The complete cell layout. (k) The phantom cell layout. Often an ASIC vendor hides the details of the internal cell construction. The phantom cell is used for layout by the customer and then "instantiated" by the ASIC vendor after layout is complete. This layout uses grayscale stipple patterns to distinguish between layers.

(CSN). A second implant (using boron ions) forms the p-type source/drain for the p-channel transistors and p-type substrate contacts (CSP). These implants are masked as follows

$$\text{CSN (mask)} = \text{grow (ndiff (drawn))}, \qquad (2.19)$$

$$\text{CSP (mask)} = \text{grow (pdiff (drawn))}, \qquad (2.20)$$

where "grow" means that we expand or **bloat** the drawn ndiff and drawn pdiff layers slightly (usually by a few λ).

During implantation the **dopant** ions are blocked by the resist pattern defined by the CSN and CSP masks. The CSN mask thus prevents the n-type regions being implanted with p-type dopants (and vice-versa for the CSP mask). As we shall see, the CSN and CSP masks are not intended to define the edges of the n-type and p-type regions. Instead these two masks function more like newspaper that prevents paint from spraying everywhere. The dopant ions are also blocked from reaching the silicon surface by the poly gates and this aligns the edge of the source and drain regions to the edges of the gates (we call this a **self-aligned process**). In addition, the implants are blocked by the FOX and this defines the outside edges of the source, drain, and substrate contact regions.

The only areas of the silicon surface that are doped n-type are

$$n\text{-diffusion (silicon)} = (\text{CAA (mask)} \wedge \text{CSN (mask)}) \wedge (\neg \text{CPG (mask)}); \qquad (2.21)$$

where the $\wedge$ symbol represents AND (the intersection of two layers); and the $\neg$ symbol represents NOT.

Similarly, the only regions that are doped p-type are

$$p\text{-diffusion (silicon)} = (\text{CAA (mask)} \wedge \text{CSP (mask)}) \wedge (\neg \text{CPG (mask)}). \qquad (2.22)$$

If the CSN and CSP masks do not overlap, it is possible to save a mask by using one implant mask (CSN or CSP) for the other type (CSP or CSN). We can do this by using a **positive resist** (the pattern of resist remaining after developing is the same as the dark areas on the mask) for one implant step and a **negative resist** (vice-versa) for the other step. However, because of the poor resolution of negative resist and because of difficulties in generating the implant masks automatically from the drawn diffusions (especially when opposite diffusion types are drawn close to each other or touching), it is now common to draw both implant masks as well as the two diffusion layers.

It is important to remember that, even though poly is above diffusion, the polysilicon is deposited first and acts like masking tape. It is rather like air-brushing a stripe—you use masking tape and spray everywhere without worrying about making straight lines. The edges of the pattern will align to the edge of the tape. Here the analogy ends because the poly is left in place. Thus,

$$n\text{-diffusion (silicon)} = (\text{ndiff (drawn)}) \wedge (\neg \text{poly (drawn)}) \quad \text{and} \qquad (2.23)$$

$$p\text{-diffusion (silicon)} = (\text{pdiff (drawn)}) \wedge (\neg \text{poly (drawn)}). \qquad (2.24)$$

In the ASIC industry the names nplus, *n+*, and *n*-diffusion (as well as the *p*-type equivalents) are used in various ways. These names may refer to either the drawn diffusion layer (that we call ndiff), the mask (CSN), or the doped region on the silicon (the intersection of the active and implant mask that we call *n*-diffusion)—very confusing.

The source and drain are often formed from two separate implants. The first is a light implant close to the edge of the gate, the second a heavier implant that forms the rest of the source or drain region. The separate diffusions reduce the electric field near the drain end of the channel. Tailoring the device characteristics in this fashion is known as **drain engineering** and a process including these steps is referred to as an **LDD process**, for **lightly doped drain**; the first light implant is known as an **LDD diffusion** or LDD implant.

FIGURE 2.8 Drawn layers and an example set of black-and-white stipple patterns for a CMOS process. On top are the patterns as they appear in layout. Underneath are the magnified 8 by 8 pixel patterns. If we are trying to simplify layout we may use solid black or white for contact and vias. If we have contacts and vias placed on top of one another we may use stipple patterns or other means to help distinguish between them. Each stipple pattern is transparent, so that black shows through from underneath when layers are superimposed. There are no standards for these patterns.

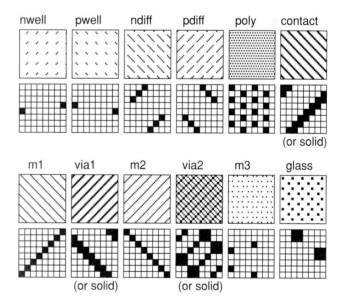

Figure 2.8 shows a **stipple-pattern** matrix for a CMOS process. When we draw layout you can see through the layers—all the stipple patterns are OR'ed together. Figure 2.9 shows the transistor layers as they appear in layout (drawn using the patterns from Figure 2.8) and as they appear on the silicon. Figure 2.10 shows the same thing for the interconnect layers.

2.2.1   Sheet Resistance

Tables 2.3 and 2.4 show the sheet resistance for each conducting layer (in decreasing order of resistance) for two different generations of CMOS process.

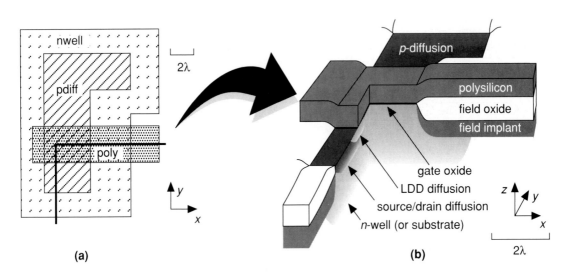

FIGURE 2.9 The transistor layers. (a) A *p*-channel transistor as drawn in layout. (b) The corresponding silicon cross section (the heavy lines in part a show the cuts). This is how a *p*-channel transistor would look just after completing the source and drain implant steps.

FIGURE 2.10 The interconnect layers. (a) Metal layers as drawn in layout. (b) The corresponding structure (as it might appear in a scanning-electron micrograph). The insulating layers between the metal layers are not shown. Contact is made to the underlying silicon through a platinum barrier layer. Each via consists of a tungsten plug. Each metal layer consists of a titanium–tungsten and aluminum–copper sandwich. Most deep submicron CMOS processes use metal structures similar to this. The scale, rounding, and irregularity of the features are realistic.

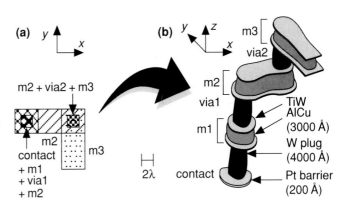

The **diffusion** layers, *n*-diffusion and *p*-diffusion, both have a high resistivity—typically from 1–100 Ω/square. We measure resistance in Ω/**square** (ohms per square) because for a fixed thickness of material it does not matter what the size of a square is—the resistance is the same. Thus the resistance of a rectangular shape of a sheet of material may be calculated from the number of squares it contains times the **sheet resistance** in Ω/square. We can use diffusion for very short connections inside a logic cell, but not for interconnect between logic cells. Poly has the next highest

TABLE 2.3   Sheet resistance (1 μm CMOS).

Layer	Sheet resistance	Units
n-well	1.15 ± 0.25	kΩ/square
poly	3.5 ± 2.0	Ω/square
n-diffusion	75 ± 20	Ω/square
p-diffusion	140 ± 40	Ω/square
m1/2	70 ± 6	mΩ/square
m3	30 ± 3	mΩ/square

TABLE 2.4   Sheet resistance (0.35 μm CMOS).

Layer	Sheet resistance	Units
n-well	1 ± 0.4	kΩ/square
poly	10 ± 4.0	Ω/square
n-diffusion	3.5 ± 2.0	Ω/square
p-diffusion	2.5 ± 1.5	Ω/square
m1/2/3	60 ± 6	mΩ/square
metal4	30 ± 3	mΩ/square

resistance to diffusion. Most submicron CMOS processes use a **silicide** material (a metallic compound of silicon) that has much lower resistivity (at several Ω/square) than the poly or diffusion layers alone. Examples are tantalum silicide, TaSi; tungsten silicide, WSi; or titanium silicide, TiSi. The **stoichiometry** of these deposited silicides varies. For example, for tungsten silicide W:Si ≈ 1:2.6.

There are two types of silicide process. In a silicide process only the gate is silicided. This reduces the poly sheet resistance, but not that of the source–drain. In a self-aligned silicide (**salicide**) process, both the gate and the source–drain regions are silicided. In some processes silicide can be used to connect adjacent poly and diffusion (we call this feature **LI**, white metal, local interconnect, metal0, or m0). LI is useful to reduce the area of ASIC RAM cells, for example.

Interconnect uses metal layers with resistivities of tens of mΩ/square, several orders of magnitude less than the other layers. There are usually several layers of metal in a CMOS ASIC process, each separated by an insulating layer. The metal layer above the poly gate layer is the first-level metal (**m1** or metal1), the next is the second-level metal (**m2** or metal2), and so on. We can make connections from m1 to diffusion using **diffusion contacts** or to the poly using **polysilicon contacts**.

After we etch the contact holes a thin **barrier metal** (typically platinum) is deposited over the silicon and poly. Next we form **contact plugs** (**via plugs** for connections between metal layers) to reduce contact resistance and the likelihood of breaks in the contacts. Tungsten is commonly used for these plugs. Following this we form the metal layers as sandwiches. The middle of the sandwich is a layer (usually from 3000 Å to 10,000 Å) of aluminum and copper. The top and bottom layers are normally titanium–tungsten (TiW, pronounced "tie-tungsten"). Submicron processes use **chemical–mechanical polishing** (**CMP**) to smooth the wafers flat before each metal deposition step to help with step coverage.

An insulating glass, often sputtered quartz (SiO_2), though other materials are also used, is deposited between metal layers to help create a smooth surface for the deposition of the metal. Design rules may refer to this insulator as an **intermetal** oxide (**IMO**) whether they are in fact oxides or not, or **interlevel dielectric (ILD)**. The IMO may be a spin-on polymer; boron-doped phosphosilicate glass (BPSG); Si_3N_4; or sandwiches of these materials (oxynitrides, for example).

We make the connections between m1 and m2 using **metal vias**, **cuts**, or just **vias**. We cannot connect m2 directly to diffusion or poly; instead we must make these connections through m1 using a via. Most processes allow contacts and vias to be placed directly above each other without restriction, arrangements known as **stacked vias** and **stacked contacts**. We call a process with m1 and m2 a **two-level metal (2LM)** technology. A **3LM** process includes a third-level metal layer (**m3** or metal3), and some processes include more metal layers. In this case a connection between m1 and m2 will use an m1/m2 via, or **via1**; a connection between m2 and m3 will use an m2/m3 via, or **via2**, and so on.

The minimum spacing of interconnects, the **metal pitch**, may increase with successive metal layers. The minimum metal pitch is the minimum spacing between the centers of adjacent interconnects and is equal to the minimum metal width plus the minimum metal spacing.

Aluminum interconnect tends to break when carrying a high current density. Collisions between high-energy electrons and atoms move the metal atoms over a long period of time in a process known as **electromigration**. Copper is added to the aluminum to help reduce the problem. The other solution is to reduce the current density by using wider than minimum-width metal lines.

Tables 2.5 and 2.6 show maximum specified **contact resistance** and **via resistance** for two generations of CMOS processes. Notice that a m1 contact in either process is equal in resistance to several hundred squares of metal.

TABLE 2.5   Contact resistance (1 μm CMOS).

Contact/via type	Resistance (maximum)
m2/m3 via (via2)	$5\,\Omega$
m1/m2 via (via1)	$2\,\Omega$
m1/p-diffusion contact	$20\,\Omega$
m1/n-diffusion contact	$20\,\Omega$
m1/poly contact	$20\,\Omega$

TABLE 2.6   Contact resistance (0.35 μm CMOS).

Contact/via type	Resistance (maximum)
m2/m3 via (via2)	$6\,\Omega$
m1/m2 via (via1)	$6\,\Omega$
m1/p-diffusion contact	$20\,\Omega$
m1/n-diffusion contact	$20\,\Omega$
m1/poly contact	$20\,\Omega$

2.3   CMOS Design Rules

Figure 2.11 defines the **design rules** for a CMOS process using pictures. Arrows between objects denote a minimum spacing, and arrows showing the size of an

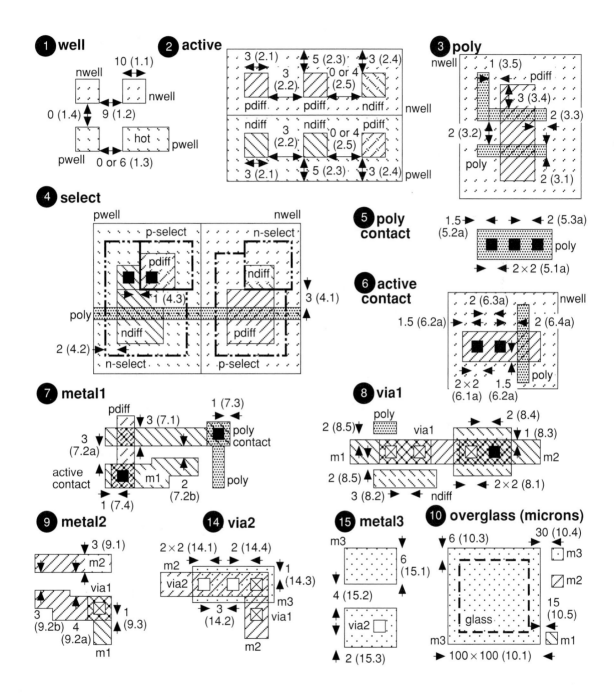

FIGURE 2.11 The MOSIS scalable CMOS design rules (rev. 7). Dimensions are in λ. Rule numbers are in parentheses (missing rule sets 11–13 are extensions to this basic process).

object denote a minimum width. Rule 3.1, for example, is the minimum width of poly (2λ). Each of the rule numbers may have different values for different manufacturers—there are no standards for design rules. Tables 2.7–2.9 show the MOSIS scalable CMOS rules. Table 2.7 shows the layer rules for the **process front end**, which is the front end of the line (as in production line) or **FEOL**. Table 2.8 shows the rules for the process back end (**BEOL**), the metal interconnect, and Table 2.9 shows the rules for the pad layer and glass layer.

The rules in Table 2.7 and Table 2.8 are given as multiples of λ. If we use **lambda-based rules** we can move between successive process generations just by changing the value of λ. For example, we can scale 0.5 μm layouts ($\lambda = 0.25$ μm) by a factor of 0.175/0.25 for a 0.35 μm process ($\lambda = 0.175$ μm)—at least in theory. You may get an inkling of the practical problems from the fact that the values for pad dimensions and spacing in Table 2.9 are given in microns and not in λ. This is because bonding to the pads is an operation that does not scale well. Often companies have two sets of design rules: one in λ (with fractional λ rules) and the other in microns. Ideally we would like to express all of the design rules in integer multiples of λ. This was true for revisions 4–6, but not revision 7 of the MOSIS rules. In revision 7 rules 5.2a/6.2a are noninteger. The original Mead/Conway NMOS rules include a noninteger 1.5λ rule for the implant layer.

2.4   Combinational Logic Cells

The AND-OR-INVERT (AOI) and the OR-AND-INVERT (OAI) logic cells are particularly efficient in CMOS. Figure 2.12 shows an AOI221 and an OAI321 logic cell (the logic symbols in Figure 2.12 are not standards, but are widely used). All indices (the indices are the numbers after AOI or OAI) in the logic cell name greater than 1 correspond to the inputs to the first "level" or stage—the AND gate(s) in an AOI cell, for example. An index of '1' corresponds to a direct input to the second-stage cell. We write indices in descending order; so it is AOI221 and not AOI122 (but both are equivalent cells), and AOI32 not AOI23. If we have more than one direct input to the second stage we repeat the '1'; thus an AOI211 cell performs the function $Z = (A.B + C + D)'$. A three-input NAND cell is an OAI111, but calling it that would be very confusing. These rules are not standard, but form a convention that we shall adopt and one that is widely used in the ASIC industry.

There are many ways to represent the logical operator, AND. I shall use the **middle dot** and write $A \cdot B$ (rather than AB, A.B, or $A \wedge B$); occasionally I may use AND(A, B). Similarly I shall write $A + B$ as well as OR(A, B). I shall use an apostrophe like this, A', to denote the complement of A rather than $\overline{A}$ since sometimes it is difficult or inappropriate to use an overbar (*vinculum*) or diacritical mark (macron). It is possible to misinterpret AB' as $A\overline{B}$ rather than $\overline{AB}$ (but the former alternative would be $A \cdot B'$ in my convention). I shall be careful in these situations.

TABLE 2.7   MOSIS scalable CMOS rules version 7—the process front end.

Layer	Rule	Explanation	Value / λ
well (CWN, CWP)	1.1	minimum width	10
	1.2	minimum space (different potential, a hot well)	9
	1.3	minimum space (same potential)	0 or 6
	1.4	minimum space (different well type)	0
active (CAA)	2.1/2.2	minimum width/space	3
	2.3	source/drain active to well edge space	5
	2.4	substrate/well contact active to well edge space	3
	2.5	minimum space between active (different implant type)	0 or 4
poly (CPG)	3.1/3.2	minimum width/space	2
	3.3	minimum gate extension of active	2
	3.4	minimum active extension of poly	3
	3.5	minimum field poly to active space	1
select (CSN, CSP)	4.1	minimum select spacing to channel of transistor[1]	3
	4.2	minimum select overlap of active	2
	4.3	minimum select overlap of contact	1
	4.4	minimum select width and spacing [2]	2
poly contact (CCP)	5.1.a	exact contact size	2×2
	5.2.a	minimum poly overlap	1.5
	5.3.a	minimum contact spacing	2
active contact (CCA)	6.1.a	exact contact size	2×2
	6.2.a	minimum active overlap	1.5
	6.3.a	minimum contact spacing	2
	6.4.a	minimum space to gate of transistor	2

[1]To ensure source and drain width.
[2]Different select types may touch but not overlap.

TABLE 2.8   MOSIS scalable CMOS rules version 7—the process back end.

Layer	Rule	Explanation	Value/λ
metal1 (CMF)	7.1	minimum width	3
	7.2.a	minimum space	3
	7.2.b	minimum space (for minimum-width wires only)	2
	7.3	minimum overlap of poly contact	1
	7.4	minimum overlap of active contact	1
via1 (CVA)	8.1	exact size	2×2
	8.2	minimum via spacing	3
	8.3	minimum overlap by metal1	1
	8.4	minimum spacing to contact	2
	8.5	minimum spacing to poly or active edge	2
metal2 (CMS)	9.1	minimum width	3
	9.2.a	minimum space	4
	9.2.b	minimum space (for minimum-width wires only)	3
	9.3	minimum overlap of via1	1
via2 (CVS)	14.1	exact size	2×2
	14.2	minimum space	3
	14.3	minimum overlap by metal2	1
	14.4	minimum spacing to via1	2
metal3 (CMT)	15.1	minimum width	6
	15.2	minimum space	4
	15.3	minimum overlap of via2	2

TABLE 2.9   MOSIS scalable CMOS rules version 7—the pads and overglass (passivation).

Layer	Rule	Explanation	Value
glass (COG)	10.1	minimum bonding-pad width	100μm×100μm
	10.2	minimum probe-pad width	75μm×75μm
	10.3	pad overlap of glass opening	6μm
	10.4	minimum pad spacing to unrelated metal2 (or metal3)	30μm
	10.5	minimum pad spacing to unrelated metal1, poly, or active	15μm

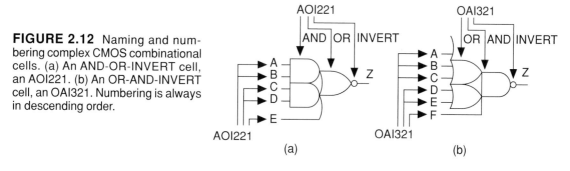

FIGURE 2.12 Naming and numbering complex CMOS combinational cells. (a) An AND-OR-INVERT cell, an AOI221. (b) An OR-AND-INVERT cell, an OAI321. Numbering is always in descending order.

We can express the function of the AOI221 cell in Figure 2.12(a) as

$$Z = (A \cdot B + C \cdot D + E)'. \tag{2.25}$$

We can also write this equation unambiguously as $Z = OAI221(A, B, C, D, E)$, just as we might write $X = NAND(I, J, K)$ to describe the logic function $X = (I \cdot J \cdot K)'$.

This notation is useful because, for example, if we write OAI321(P, Q, R, S, T, U) we immediately know that U (the sixth input) is the (only) direct input connected to the second stage. Sometimes we need to refer to particular inputs without listing them all. We can adopt another convention that letters of the input names change with the index position. Now we can refer to input B2 of an AOI321 cell, for example, and know which input we are talking about without writing

$$Z = AOI321(A1, A2, A3, B1, B2, C). \tag{2.26}$$

Table 2.10 shows the **AOI family** of logic cells with three indices (with branches in the family for AOI, OAI, AO, and OA cells). There are 5 types and 14 separate members of each branch of this family. There are thus $4 \times 14 = 56$ cells of the type $Xabc$ where $X = \{OAI, AOI, OA, AO\}$ and each of the indexes a, b, and c can range from 1 to 3. We form the AND-OR (AO) and OR-AND (OA) cells by adding an inverter to the output of an AOI or OAI cell.

2.4.1   Pushing Bubbles

The AOI and OAI logic cells can be built using a single stage in CMOS using series–parallel networks of transistors called **stacks**. Figure 2.13 illustrates the procedure to build the n-channel and p-channel stacks, using the AOI221 cell as an example.

Here are the steps to construct any single-stage combinational CMOS logic cell:

1. Draw a schematic icon with an inversion (bubble) on the last cell (the bubble-out schematic). Use **de Morgan's theorems**—"A NAND is an OR with inverted inputs and a NOR is an AND with inverted inputs"—to push the output bubble back to the inputs (this the dual icon or bubble-in schematic).

TABLE 2.10   The AOI family of cells with three index numbers or less.

Cell type[1]	Cells	Number of unique cells
Xa1	X21, X31	2
Xa11	X211, X311	2
Xab	X22, X33, X32	3
Xab1	X221, X331, X321	3
Xabc	X222, X333, X332, X322	4
Total		14

[1]Xabc: X = {AOI, AO, OAI, OA}; a, b, c = {2, 3}; {} means "choose one."

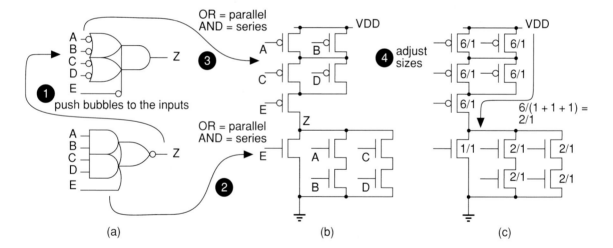

(a)   (b)   (c)

FIGURE 2.13 Constructing a CMOS logic cell—an AOI221. (a) First build the dual icon by using de Morgan's theorem to "push" inversion bubbles to the inputs. (b) Next build the n-channel and p-channel stacks from series and parallel combinations of transistors. (c) Adjust transistor sizes so that the n-channel and p-channel stacks have equal strengths.

2. Form the n-channel stack working from the inputs on the bubble-out schematic: OR translates to a parallel connection, AND translates to a series connection. If you have a bubble at an input, you need an inverter.

3. Form the p-channel stack using the bubble-in schematic (ignore the inversions at the inputs—the bubbles on the gate terminals of the p-channel transistors

take care of these). If you do not have a bubble at the input gate terminals, you need an inverter (these will be the same input gate terminals that had bubbles in the bubble-out schematic).

The two stacks are **network duals** (they can be derived from each other by swapping series connections for parallel, and parallel for series connections). The n-channel stack implements the strong '0's of the function and the p-channel stack provides the strong '1's. The final step is to adjust the drive strength of the logic cell by sizing the transistors.

2.4.2 Drive Strength

Normally we **ratio** the sizes of the n-channel and p-channel transistors in an inverter so that both types of transistors have the same resistance, or **drive strength**. That is, we make $\beta_n = \beta_p$. At low dopant concentrations and low electric fields μ_n is about twice μ_p. To compensate we make the shape factor, W/L, of the p-channel transistor in an inverter about twice that of the n-channel transistor (we say the logic has a ratio of 2). Since the transistor lengths are normally equal to the minimum poly width for both types of transistors, the ratio of the transistor widths is also equal to 2. With the high dopant concentrations and high electric fields in submicron transistors the difference in mobilities is less—typically between 1 and 1.5.

Logic cells in a library have a range of drive strengths. We normally call the minimum-size inverter a 1X inverter. The drive strength of a logic cell is often used as a suffix; thus a 1X inverter has a cell name such as INVX1 or INVD1. An inverter with transistors that are twice the size will be an INVX2. Drive strengths are normally scaled in a geometric ratio, so we have 1X, 2X, 4X, and (sometimes) 8X or even higher, drive-strength cells. We can size a logic cell using these basic rules:

- Any string of transistors connected between a power supply and the output in a cell with 1X drive should have the same resistance as the n-channel transistor in a 1X inverter.

- A transistor with shape factor W_1/L_1 has a resistance proportional to L_1/W_1 (so the larger W_1 is, the smaller the resistance).

- Two transistors in parallel with shape factors W_1/L_1 and W_2/L_2 are equivalent to a single transistor $(W_1/L_1 + W_2/L_2)/1$. For example, a 2/1 in parallel with a 3/1 is a 5/1.

- Two transistors, with shape factors W_1/L_2 and W_2/L_2, in series are equivalent to a single $1/(L_1/W_1 + L_2/W_2)$ transistor.

For example, a transistor with shape factor 3/1 (we shall call this "a 3/1") in series with another 3/1 is equivalent to a $1/((1/3) + (1/3))$ or a 3/2. We can use the following method to calculate equivalent transistor sizes:

- To add transistors in parallel, make all the lengths 1 and add the widths.

- To add transistors in series, make all the widths 1 and add the lengths.

We have to be careful to keep W and L reasonable. For example, a 3/1 in series with a 2/1 is equivalent to a $1/((1/3)+(1/2))$ or 1/0.83. Since we cannot make a device 2λ wide and 1.66λ long, a 1/0.83 is more naturally written as 3/2.5. We like to keep both W and L as integer multiples of 0.5 (equivalent to making W and L integer multiples of λ), but W and L must be greater than 1.

In Figure 2.13(c) the transistors in the AOI221 cell are sized so that any string through the p-channel stack has a drive strength equivalent to a 2/1 p-channel transistor (we choose the worst case, if more than one transistor in parallel is conducting then the drive strength will be higher). The n-channel stack is sized so that it has a drive strength of a 1/1 n-channel transistor. The ratio in this library is thus 2.

If we were to use four drive strengths for each of the AOI family of cells shown in Table 2.10, we would have a total of 224 combinational library cells—just for the AOI family. The synthesis tools can handle this number of cells, but we may not be able to design this many cells in a reasonable amount of time. Section 3.3, "Logical Effort," will help us choose the most logically efficient cells.

2.4.3   Transmission Gates

Figure 2.14(a) and (b) shows a CMOS **transmission gate** (**TG**, TX gate, pass gate, coupler). We connect a p-channel transistor (to transmit a strong '1') in parallel with an n-channel transistor (to transmit a strong '0').

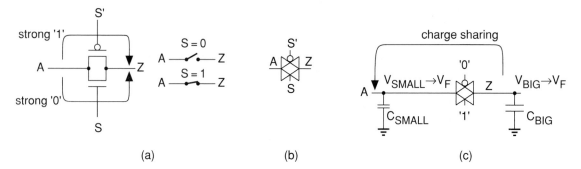

(a)   (b)   (c)

FIGURE 2.14 CMOS transmission gate (TG). (a) An n-channel and p-channel transistor in parallel form a TG. (b) A common symbol for a TG. (c) The charge-sharing problem.

We can express the function of a TG as

$$Z = TG(A, S), \tag{2.27}$$

but this is ambiguous—if we write TG(X, Y), how do we know if X is connected to the gates or sources/drains of the TG? We shall always define TG(X, Y) when we use it. It is tempting to write $TG(A, S) = A \cdot S$, but what is the value of Z when S = '0' in Figure 2.14(a), since Z is then left floating? A TG is a switch, not an AND logic cell.

There is a potential problem if we use a TG as a switch connecting a node Z that has a large capacitance, C_{BIG}, to an input node A that has only a small capacitance C_{SMALL} (see Figure 2.14c). If the initial voltage at A is V_{SMALL} and the initial voltage at Z is V_{BIG}, when we close the TG (by setting S = '1') the final voltage on both nodes A and Z is

$$V_F = \frac{C_{BIG} V_{BIG} + C_{SMALL} V_{SMALL}}{C_{BIG} + C_{SMALL}}. \tag{2.28}$$

Imagine we want to drive a '0' onto node Z from node A. Suppose $C_{BIG} = 0.2$ pF (about 10 standard loads in a 0.5 μm process) and $C_{SMALL} = 0.02$ pF, $V_{BIG} = 0$ V and $V_{SMALL} = 5$ V; then

$$V_F = \frac{(0.2 \times 10^{-12}) 0 + (0.02 \times 10^{-12}) 5}{(0.2 \times 10^{-12}) + (0.02 \times 10^{-12})} = 0.45 \text{ V}. \tag{2.29}$$

This is not what we want at all, the "big" capacitor has forced node A to a voltage close to a '0'. This type of problem is known as **charge sharing**. We should make sure that either (1) node A is strong enough to overcome the big capacitor, or (2) insulate node A from node Z by including a **buffer** (an inverter, for example) between node A and node Z. We must not use charge to drive another logic cell—only a logic cell can drive a logic cell.

If we omit one of the transistors in a TG (usually the p-channel transistor) we have a **pass transistor**. There is a branch of full-custom VLSI design that uses pass-transistor logic. Much of this is based on relay-based logic, since a single transistor switch looks like a relay contact. There are many problems associated with pass-transistor logic related to charge sharing, reduced noise margins, and the difficulty of predicting delays. Though pass transistors may appear in an ASIC cell inside a library, they are not used by ASIC designers.

We can use two TGs to form a **multiplexer** (or multiplex*or*—people use both orthographies) as shown in Figure 2.15(a). We often shorten multiplexer to **MUX**. The MUX function for two data inputs, A and B, with a select signal S, is

$$Z = TG(A, S') + TG(B, S). \tag{2.30}$$

We can write this as $Z = A \cdot S' + B \cdot S$, since node Z is always connected to one or other of the inputs (and we assume both are driven). This is a two-input MUX (2-to-1 MUX or 2:1 MUX). Unfortunately, we can also write the MUX function as $Z = A \cdot S + B \cdot S'$, so it is difficult to write the MUX function unambiguously as $Z = MUX(X, Y, Z)$. For example, is the select input X, Y, or Z? We shall define the function MUX(X, Y, Z) each time we use it. We must also be careful to label a MUX if we use the symbol shown in Figure 2.15(b). Symbols for a MUX are shown in Figure 2.15(b–d). In the IEEE notation 'G' specifies an AND dependency. Thus, in Figure 2.15(c), G = '1' selects the input labeled '1'. Figure 2.15(d) uses the **common control block** symbol (the notched rectangle). Here, G1 = '1' selects the input '1',

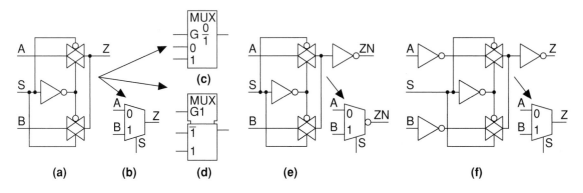

FIGURE 2.15 The CMOS multiplexer (MUX). (a) A noninverting 2:1 MUX using transmission gates without buffering. (b) A symbol for a MUX (note how the inputs are labeled). (c) An IEEE standard symbol for a MUX. (d) A nonstandard, but very common, IEEE symbol for a MUX. (e) An inverting MUX with output buffer. (f) A noninverting buffered MUX.

and G1 = '0' selects the input '1̄'. Strictly this form of IEEE symbol should be used only for elements with more than one section controlled by common signals, but the symbol of Figure 2.15(d) is used often for a 2:1 MUX.

The MUX shown in Figure 2.15(a) works, but there is a potential charge-sharing problem if we cascade MUXes (connect them in series). Instead most ASIC libraries use MUX cells built with a more conservative approach. We could buffer the output using an inverter (Figure 2.15e), but then the MUX becomes inverting. To build a safe, noninverting MUX we can buffer the inputs and output (Figure 2.15f)—requiring 12 transistors, or 3 gate equivalents (only the gate equivalent counts are shown from now on).

Figure 2.16 shows how to use an OAI22 logic cell (and an inverter) to implement an inverting MUX. The implementation in equation form (2.5 gates) is

$$ZN = A' \cdot S' + B' \cdot S = [(A' \cdot S')' \cdot (B' \cdot S)']' = [(A + S) \cdot (B + S')]'$$

$$= OAI22[A, S, B, NOT(S)]. \tag{2.31}$$

(both A' and NOT(A) represent an inverter, depending on which representation is most convenient—they are equivalent). I often use an equation to describe a cell implementation.

The following factors will determine which MUX implementation is best:

1. Do we want to minimize the delay between the select input and the output or between the data inputs and the output?

2. Do we want an inverting or noninverting MUX?

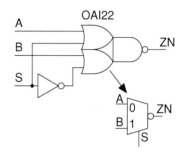

FIGURE 2.16 An inverting 2:1 MUX based on an OAI22 cell.

3. Do we object to having any logic cell inputs tied directly to the source/drain diffusions of a transmission gate? (Some companies forbid such **transmission-gate inputs**—since some simulation tools cannot handle them.)

4. Do we object to any logic cell outputs being tied to the source/drain of a transmission gate? (Some companies will not allow this because of the dangers of charge sharing.)

5. What drive strength do we require (and is size or speed more important)?

A minimum-size TG is a little slower than a minimum-size inverter, so there is not much difference between the implementations shown in Figure 2.15 and Figure 2.16, but the difference can become important for 4:1 and larger MUXes.

2.4.4   Exclusive-OR Cell

The two-input **exclusive-OR** (**XOR**, EXOR, not-equivalence, ring-OR) function is

$$A1 \oplus A2 = XOR(A1, A2) = A1 \cdot A2' + A1' \cdot A2. \tag{2.32}$$

We are now using multiletter symbols, but there should be no doubt that $A1'$ means anything other than NOT($A1$). We can implement a two-input XOR using a MUX and an inverter as follows (2 gates):

$$XOR(A1, A2) = MUX[NOT(A1), A1, A2], \tag{2.33}$$

where

$$MUX(A, B, S) = A \cdot S + B \cdot S'. \tag{2.34}$$

This implementation only buffers one input and does not buffer the MUX output. We can use inverter buffers (3.5 gates total) or an inverting MUX so that the XOR cell does not have any external connections to source/drain diffusions as follows (3 gates total):

$$XOR(A1, A2) = NOT[MUX(NOT[NOT(A1)], NOT(A1), A2)]. \tag{2.35}$$

We can also implement a two-input XOR using an AOI21 (and a NOR cell), since

$$\text{XOR}(A1, A2) = A1 \cdot A2' + A1' \cdot A2 = [\,(A1 \cdot A2) + (A1 + A2)'\,]'$$

$$= \text{AOI21}[A1, A2, \text{NOR}(A1, A2)], \tag{2.36}$$

(2.5 gates). Similarly we can implement an **exclusive-NOR** (XNOR, equivalence) logic cell using an inverting MUX (and two inverters, total 3.5 gates) or an OAI21 logic cell (and a NAND cell, total 2.5 gates) as follows (using the MUX function of Eq. 2.34):

$$\text{XNOR}(A1, A2) = A1 \cdot A2 + \text{NOT}(A1) \cdot \text{NOT}(A2)$$

$$= \text{NOT}[\text{NOT}[\text{MUX}(A1, \text{NOT}(A1), A2]]$$

$$= \text{OAI21}[A1, A2, \text{NAND}(A1, A2)] \tag{2.37}$$

2.5 Sequential Logic Cells

There are the two main approaches to clocking in VLSI design: **multiphase clocks** or a single clock and **synchronous design**. The second approach has the following key advantages: (1) it allows automated design, (2) it is safe, and (3) it permits vendor signoff (a guarantee that the ASIC will work as simulated). These advantages of synchronous design (especially the last one) usually outweigh every other consideration in the choice of a clocking scheme. The vast majority of ASICs use a rigid synchronous design style.

2.5.1 Latch

Figure 2.17(a) shows a sequential logic cell—a **latch**. The internal clock signals, CLKN (N for negative) and CLKP (P for positive), are generated from the system clock, CLK, by two inverters (I4 and I5) that are part of every latch cell—it is usually too dangerous to have these signals supplied externally, even though it would save space.

To emphasize the difference between a latch and flip-flop, sometimes people refer to the clock input of a latch as an **enable**. This makes sense when we look at Figure 2.17(b), which shows the operation of a latch. When the clock input is high, the latch is **transparent**—changes at the D input appear at the output Q (quite different from a flip-flop as we shall see). When the enable (clock) goes low (Figure 2.17c), inverters I2 and I3 are connected together, forming a storage loop that holds the last value on D until the enable goes high again. The storage loop will hold its state as long as power is on; we call this a **static** latch. A **sequential logic cell** is different from a combinational cell because it has this feature of storage or memory.

Notice that the output Q is unbuffered and connected directly to the output of I2 (and the input of I3), which is a storage node. In an ASIC library we are conservative and add an inverter to buffer the output, isolate the sensitive storage node, and

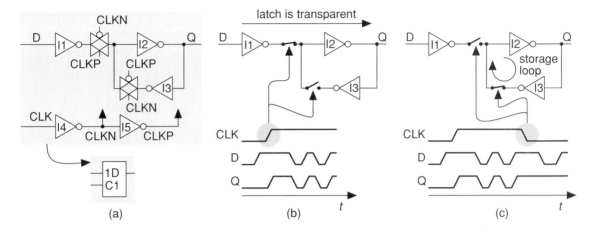

FIGURE 2.17 CMOS latch. (a) A positive-enable latch using transmission gates without output buffering, the enable (clock) signal is buffered inside the latch. (b) A positive-enable latch is transparent while the enable is high. (c) The latch stores the last value at D when the enable goes low.

thus invert the sense of Q. If we want both Q and QN we have to add two inverters to the circuit of Figure 2.17(a). This means that a latch requires seven inverters and two TGs (4.5 gates).

The latch of Figure 2.17(a) is a positive-enable D latch, active-high D latch, or transparent-high D latch (sometimes people also call this a D-type latch). A negative-enable (active-low) D latch can be built by inverting all the clock polarities in Figure 2.17(a) (swap CLKN for CLKP and vice-versa).

2.5.2 Flip-Flop

Figure 2.18(a) shows a **flip-flop** constructed from two D latches: a **master latch** (the first one) and a **slave latch**. This flip-flop contains a total of nine inverters and four TGs, or 6.5 gates. In this flip-flop design the storage node S is buffered and the clock-to-Q delay will be one inverter delay less than the clock-to-QN delay.

In Figure 2.18(b) the clock input is high, the master latch is transparent, and node M (for master) will follow the D input. Meanwhile the slave latch is disconnected from the master latch and is storing whatever the previous value of Q was. As the clock goes low (the negative edge) the slave latch is enabled and will update its state (and the output Q) to the value of node M at the negative edge of the clock. The slave latch will then keep this value of M at the output Q, despite any changes at the D input while the clock is low (Figure 2.18c). When the clock goes high again, the slave latch will store the captured value of M (and we are back where we started our explanation).

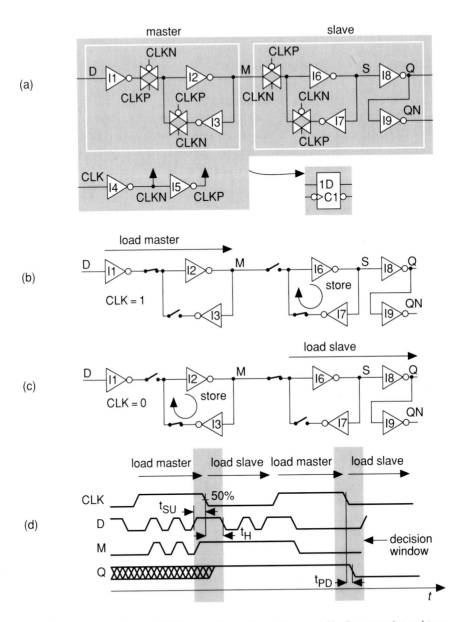

FIGURE 2.18 CMOS flip-flop. (a) This negative-edge–triggered flip-flop consists of two latches: master and slave. (b) While the clock is high, the master latch is loaded. (c) As the clock goes low, the slave latch loads the value of the master latch. (d) Waveforms illustrating the definition of the flip-flop setup time t_{SU}, hold time t_H, and propagation delay from clock to Q, t_{PD}.

The combination of the master and slave latches acts to capture or sample the D input at the negative clock edge, the **active clock edge**. This type of flip-flop is a **negative-edge–triggered flip-flop** and its behavior is quite different from a latch. The behavior is shown on the IEEE symbol by using a triangular "notch" to denote an edge-sensitive input. A bubble shows the input is sensitive to the negative edge. To build a positive-edge–triggered flip-flop we invert the polarity of all the clocks— as we did for a latch.

The waveforms in Figure 2.18(d) show the operation of the flip-flop as we have described it, and illustrate the definition of **setup time** (t_{SU}), **hold time** (t_H), and clock-to-Q propagation delay (t_{PD}). We must keep the data stable (a fixed logic '1' or '0') for a time t_{SU} prior to the active clock edge, and stable for a time t_H after the active clock edge (during the decision window shown).

In Figure 2.18(d) times are measured from the points at which the waveforms cross 50 percent of V_{DD}. We say the **trip point** is 50 percent or 0.5. Common choices are 0.5 or 0.65/0.35 (a signal has to reach $0.65V_{DD}$ to be a '1', and reach $0.35V_{DD}$ to be a '0'), or 0.1/0.9 (there is no standard way to write a trip point). Some vendors use different trip points for the input and output waveforms (especially in I/O cells).

The flip-flop in Figure 2.18(a) is a D flip-flop and is by far the most widely used type of flip-flop in ASIC design. There are other types of flip-flops—J-K, T (toggle), and S-R flip-flops—that are provided in some ASIC cell libraries mainly for compatibility with TTL design. Some people use the term **register** to mean an array (more than one) of flip-flops or latches (on a data bus, for example), but some people use register to mean a single flip-flop or a latch. This is confusing since flip-flops and latches are quite different in their behavior. When I am talking about logic cells, I use the term *register* to mean more than one flip-flop.

To add an **asynchronous set** (Q to '1') or **asynchronous reset** (Q to '0') to the flip-flop of Figure 2.18(a), we replace one inverter in both the master and slave latches with two-input NAND cells. Thus, for an active-low set, we replace I2 and I7 with two-input NAND cells, and, for an active-low reset, we replace I3 and I6. For both set and reset we replace all four inverters: I2, I3, I6, and I7. Some TTL flip-flops have **dominant reset** or **dominant set**, but this is difficult (and dangerous) to do in ASIC design. An input that forces Q to '1' is sometimes also called **preset**. The IEEE logic symbols use 'P' to denote an input with a presetting action. An input that forces Q to '0' is often also called **clear**. The IEEE symbols use 'R' to denote an input with a resetting action.

2.5.3   Clocked Inverter

Figure 2.19 shows how we can derive the structure of a **clocked inverter** from the series combination of an inverter and a TG. The arrows in Figure 2.19(b) represent the flow of current when the inverter is charging (I_R) or discharging (I_F) a load capacitance through the TG. We can break the connection between the inverter cells and use the circuit of Figure 2.19(c) without substantially affecting the operation of the circuit. The symbol for the clocked inverter shown in Figure 2.19(d) is common, but by no means a standard.

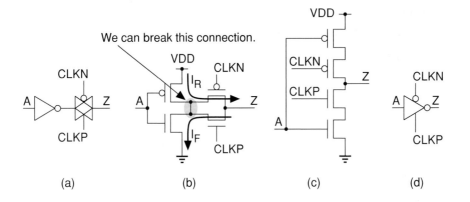

FIGURE 2.19 Clocked inverter. (a) An inverter plus transmission gate (TG). (b) The current flow in the inverter and TG allows us to break the connection between the transistors in the inverter. (c) Breaking the connection forms a clocked inverter. (d) A common symbol.

We can use the clocked inverter to replace the inverter/TG pairs in latches and flip-flops. For example, we can replace one or both of the inverters I1 and I3 (together with the TGs that follow them) in Figure 2.17(a) by clocked inverters. There is not much to choose between the different implementations in this case, except that layout may be easier for the clocked inverter versions (since there is one less connection to make).

More interesting is the flip-flop design: We can only replace inverters I1, I3, and I7 (and the TGs that follow them) in Figure 2.18(a) by clocked inverters. We cannot replace inverter I6 because it is not directly connected to a TG. We can replace the TG attached to node M with a clocked inverter, and this will invert the sense of the output Q, which thus becomes QN. Now the clock-to-Q delay will be slower than clock-to-QN, since Q (which was QN) now comes one inverter later than QN.

If we wish to build a flip-flop with a fast clock-to-QN delay it may be better to build it using clocked inverters and use inverters with TGs for a flip-flop with a fast clock-to-Q delay. In fact, since we do not always use both Q and QN outputs of a flip-flop, some libraries include Q only or QN only flip-flops that are slightly smaller than those with both polarity outputs. It is slightly easier to layout clocked inverters than an inverter plus a TG, so flip-flops in commercial libraries include a mixture of clocked-inverter and TG implementations.

2.6   Datapath Logic Cells

Suppose we wish to build an *n*-bit adder (that adds two *n*-bit numbers) and to exploit the regularity of this function in the layout. We can do so using a *datapath* structure.

The following two functions, SUM and COUT, implement the sum and carry out for a **full adder** (**FA**) with two data inputs (A, B) and a carry in, CIN:

$$SUM = A \oplus B \oplus CIN = SUM(A, B, CIN) = PARITY(A, B, CIN), \tag{2.38}$$

$$COUT = A \cdot B + A \cdot CIN + B \cdot CIN = MAJ(A, B, CIN). \tag{2.39}$$

The sum uses the **parity function** ('1' if there are an odd numbers of '1's in the inputs). The carry out, COUT, uses the 2-of-3 **majority function** ('1' if the majority of the inputs are '1'). We can combine these two functions in a single FA logic cell, ADD(A[*i*], B[*i*], CIN, S[*i*], COUT), shown in Figure 2.20(a), where

$$S[i] = SUM(A[i], B[i], CIN), \tag{2.40}$$

$$COUT = MAJ(A[i], B[i], CIN). \tag{2.41}$$

Now we can build a 4-bit **ripple-carry adder** (**RCA**) by connecting four of these ADD cells together as shown in Figure 2.20(b). The *i*th ADD cell is arranged with the following: two bus inputs A[*i*], B[*i*]; one bus output S[*i*]; an input, CIN, that is the carry in from stage $(i-1)$ below and is also passed up to the cell above as an output; and an output, COUT, that is the carry out to stage $(i+1)$ above. In the 4-bit adder shown in Figure 2.20(b) we connect the carry input, CIN[0], to VSS and use COUT[3] and COUT[2] to indicate arithmetic overflow (in Section 2.6.1 we shall see why we may need both signals). Notice that we build the ADD cell so that COUT[2] is available at the top of the datapath when we need it.

Figure 2.20(c) shows a layout of the ADD cell. The A inputs, B inputs, and S outputs all use m1 interconnect running in the horizontal direction—we call these **data** signals. Other signals can enter or exit from the top or bottom and run vertically across the datapath in m2—we call these **control** signals. We can also use m1 for control and m2 for data, but we normally do not mix these approaches in the same structure. Control signals are typically clocks and other signals common to elements. For example, in Figure 2.20(c) the carry signals, CIN and COUT, run vertically in m2 between cells. To build a 4-bit adder we stack four ADD cells creating the array structure shown in Figure 2.20(d). In this case the A and B data bus inputs enter from the left and bus S, the sum, exits at the right, but we can connect A, B, and S to either side if we want.

The layout of buswide logic that operates on data signals in this fashion is called a **datapath**. The module ADD is a **datapath cell** or **datapath element**. Just as we do for standard cells we make all the datapath cells in a library the same height so we can abut other datapath cells on either side of the adder to create a more complex datapath. When people talk about a datapath they always assume that it is oriented so that increasing the size in bits makes the datapath grow in height, upwards in the vertical direction, and adding different datapath elements to increase the function makes the datapath grow in width, in the horizontal direction—but we can rotate and position a completed datapath in any direction we want on a chip.

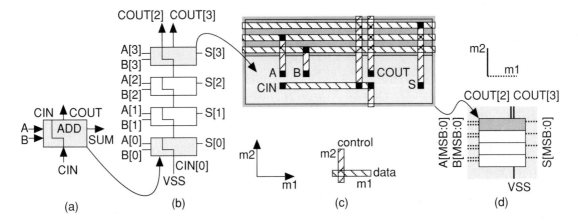

FIGURE 2.20 A datapath adder. (a) A full-adder (FA) cell with inputs (A and B), a carry in, CIN, sum output, S, and carry out, COUT. (b) A 4-bit adder. (c) The layout, using two-level metal, with data in m1 and control in m2. In this example the wiring is completed outside the cell; it is also possible to design the datapath cells to contain the wiring. Using three levels of metal, it is possible to wire over the top of the datapath cells. (d) The datapath layout.

What is the difference between using a datapath, standard cells, or gate arrays? Cells are placed together in rows on a CBIC or an MGA, but there is no generally no regularity to the arrangement of the cells within the rows—we let software arrange the cells and complete the interconnect. Datapath layout automatically takes care of most of the interconnect between the cells with the following advantages:

- Regular layout produces predictable and equal delay for each bit.
- Interconnect between cells can be built into each cell.

There are some disadvantages of using a datapath:

- The overhead (buffering and routing the control signals, for example) can make a narrow (small number of bits) datapath larger and slower than a standard-cell (or even gate-array) implementation.
- Datapath cells have to be predesigned (otherwise we are using full-custom design) for use in a wide range of datapath sizes. Datapath cell design can be harder than designing gate-array macros or standard cells.
- Software to assemble a datapath is more complex and not as widely used as software for assembling standard cells or gate arrays.

There are some newer standard-cell and gate-array tools that can take advantage of regularity in a design and position cells carefully. The problem is in finding the regularity if it is not specified. Using a datapath is one way to specify regularity to ASIC design tools.

2.6.1 Datapath Elements

Figure 2.21 shows some typical datapath symbols for an adder (people rarely use the IEEE standards in ASIC datapath libraries). I use heavy lines (they are 1.5 point wide) with a stroke to denote a data bus (that flows in the horizontal direction in a datapath), and regular lines (0.5 point) to denote the control signals (that flow vertically in a datapath). At the risk of adding confusion where there is none, this stroke to indicate a data bus has nothing to do with mixed-logic conventions. For a bus, A[31:0] denotes a 32-bit bus with A[31] as the leftmost or **most-significant bit** or **MSB**, and A[0] as the **least-significant bit** or **LSB**. Sometimes we shall use A[MSB] or A[LSB] to refer to these bits. Notice that if we have an n-bit bus and LSB = 0, then MSB = $n-1$. Also, for example, A[4] is the fifth bit on the bus (from the LSB). We use a 'Σ' or 'ADD' inside the symbol to denote an adder instead of '+', so we can attach '–' or '+/–' to the inputs for a subtracter or adder/subtracter.

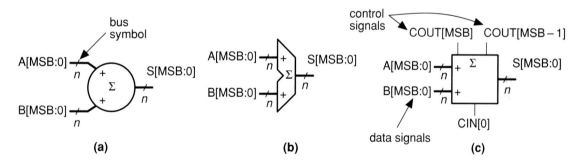

FIGURE 2.21 Symbols for a datapath adder. (a) A data bus is shown by a heavy line (1.5 point) and a bus symbol. If the bus is n-bits wide then MSB = $n-1$. (b) An alternative symbol for an adder. (c) Control signals are shown as lightweight (0.5 point) lines.

Some schematic datapath symbols include only data signals and omit the control signals—but we must not forget them. In Figure 2.21, for example, we may need to explicitly tie CIN[0] to VSS and use COUT[MSB] and COUT[MSB – 1] to detect overflow. Why might we need both of these control signals? Table 2.11 shows the process of simple arithmetic for the different binary number representations, including unsigned, signed magnitude, ones' complement, and two's complement.

TABLE 2.11   Binary arithmetic.

	Binary Number Representation			
Operation	**Unsigned**	**Signed magnitude**	**Ones' complement**	**Two's complement**
	no change	**if** positive **then** MSB = 0 **else** MSB = 1	**if** negative **then** flip bits	**if** negative **then** {flip bits; add 1}
3 =	0011	0011	0011	0011
−3 =	NA	1011	1100	1101
zero =	0000	0000 or 1000	1111 or 0000	0000
max. positive =	1111 = 15	0111 = 7	0111 = 7	0111 = 7
max. negative =	0000 = 0	1111 = −7	1000 = −7	1000 = −8
addition = $S = A + B$ = addend + augend $SG(A)$ = sign of A	$S = A + B$	**if** SG(A) = SG(B) **then** $S = A + B$ **else** {**if** B < A **then** S = A − B **else** S = B − A}	$S =$ $A + B + COUT[MSB]$ COUT is carry out	$S = A + B$
addition result: OV = overflow, OR = out of range	OR = COUT[MSB] COUT is carry out	**if** SG(A) = SG(B) **then** OV = COUT[MSB] **else** OV = 0 (impossible)	OV = XOR(COUT[MSB], COUT[MSB−1])	OV = XOR(COUT[MSB], COUT[MSB − 1])
SG(S) = sign of S $S = A + B$	NA	**if** SG(A) = SG(B) **then** SG(S) = SG(A) **else** {**if** B < A **then** SG(S) = SG(A) **else** SG(S) = SG(B)}	NA	NA
subtraction = $D = A − B$ = minuend − subtrahend	D = A − B	SG(B) = NOT(SG(B)); D = A + B	Z = −B (negate); D = A + Z	Z = −B (negate); D = A + Z
subtraction result: OV = overflow, OR = out of range	OR = BOUT[MSB] BOUT is borrow out	as in addition	as in addition	as in addition
negation: $Z = −A$ (negate)	NA	Z = A; SG(Z) = NOT(SG(A))	Z = NOT(A)	Z = NOT(A) + 1

2.6.2   Adders

We can view addition in terms of **generate**, $G[i]$, and **propagate**, $P[i]$, signals.

method 1

method 2

$$G[i] = A[i] \cdot B[i] \qquad\qquad G[i] = A[i] \cdot B[i] \qquad\qquad (2.42)$$

$$P[i] = A[i] \oplus B[i] \qquad\qquad P[i] = A[i] + B[i] \qquad\qquad (2.43)$$

$$C[i] = G[i] + P[i] \cdot C[i-1] \quad C[i] = G[i] + P[i] \cdot C[i-1] \qquad (2.44)$$

$$S[i] = P[i] \oplus C[i-1] \qquad S[i] = A[i] \oplus B[i] \oplus C[i-1] \qquad (2.45)$$

where $C[i]$ is the carry-out signal from stage i, equal to the carry in of stage $(i+1)$. Thus, $C[i] = \text{COUT}[i] = \text{CIN}[i+1]$. We need to be careful because $C[0]$ might represent either the carry in or the carry out of the LSB stage. For an adder we set the carry in to the first stage (stage zero), $C[-1]$ or $\text{CIN}[0]$, to '0'. Some people use **delete** (D) or **kill** (K) in various ways for the complements of $G[i]$ and $P[i]$, but unfortunately others use C for COUT and D for CIN—so I avoid using any of these. Do not confuse the two different methods (both of which are used) in Eqs. 2.42–2.45 when forming the sum, since the propagate signal, $P[i]$, is different for each method.

Figure 2.22(a) shows a conventional RCA. The delay of an n-bit RCA is proportional to n and is limited by the propagation of the carry signal through all of the stages. We can reduce delay by using pairs of "go-faster" bubbles to change AND and OR gates to fast two-input NAND gates as shown in Figure 2.22(a). Alternatively, we can write the equations for the carry signal in two different ways:

either $\qquad C[i] = A[i] \cdot B[i] + P[i] \cdot C[i-1] \qquad\qquad (2.46)$

or $\qquad C[i] = (A[i] + B[i]) \cdot (P[i]' + C[i-1]), \qquad\qquad (2.47)$

where $P[i]' = \text{NOT}(P[i])$. Equations 2.46 and 2.47 allow us to build the carry chain from two-input NAND gates, one per cell, using different logic in even and odd stages (Figure 2.22b):

even stages

odd stages

$$C1[i]' = P[i] \cdot C3[i-1] \cdot C4[i-1] \quad C3[i]' = P[i] \cdot C1[i-1] \cdot C2[i-1] \quad (2.48)$$

$$C2[i] = A[i] + B[i] \qquad\qquad C4[i]' = A[i] \cdot B[i] \qquad\qquad (2.49)$$

$$C[i] = C1[i] \cdot C2[i] \qquad\qquad C[i] = C3[i]' + C4[i]' \qquad\qquad (2.50)$$

(the carry inputs to stage zero are $C3[-1] = C4[-1] = '0'$). We can use the RCA of Figure 2.22(b) in a datapath, with standard cells, or on a gate array.

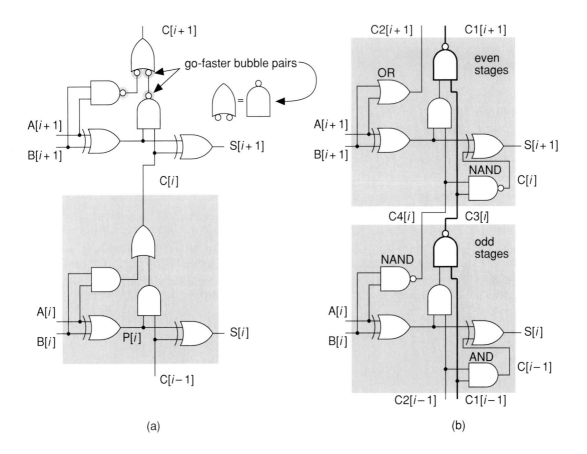

FIGURE 2.22 The ripple-carry adder (RCA). (a) A conventional RCA. The delay may be reduced slightly by adding pairs of bubbles as shown to use two-input NAND gates. (b) An alternative RCA circuit topology using different cells for odd and even stages and an extra connection between cells. The carry chain is a fast string of NAND gates (shown in bold).

Instead of propagating the carries through each stage of an RCA, Figure 2.23 shows a different approach. A **carry-save adder** (**CSA**) cell CSA(A1[i], A2[i], A3[i], CIN, S1[i], S2[i], COUT) has three outputs:

$$S1[i] = CIN \tag{2.51}$$

$$S2[i] = A1[i] \oplus A2[i] \oplus A3[i] = PARITY(A1[i], A2[i], A3[i]) \tag{2.52}$$

$$COUT = A1[i] \cdot A2[i] + [(A1[i] + A2[i]) \cdot A3[i]] = MAJ(A1[i], A2[i], A3[i]) \tag{2.53}$$

The inputs, A1, A2, and A3; and outputs, S1 and S2, are buses. The input, CIN, is the carry from stage $(i-1)$. The carry in, CIN, is connected directly to the output bus S1—indicated by the schematic symbol (Figure 2.23a). We connect CIN[0] to VSS. The output, COUT, is the carry out to stage $(i+1)$.

A 4-bit CSA is shown in Figure 2.23(b). The arithmetic overflow signal for ones' complement or two's complement arithmetic, OV, is XOR(COUT[MSB], COUT[MSB − 1]) as shown in Figure 2.23(c). In a CSA the carries are "saved" at each stage and shifted left onto the bus S1. There is thus no carry propagation and the delay of a CSA is constant. At the output of a CSA we still need to add the S1 bus (all the saved carries) and the S2 bus (all the sums) to get an n-bit result using a final stage that is not shown in Figure 2.23(c). We might regard the n-bit sum as being encoded in the two buses, S1 and S2, in the form of the parity and majority functions.

We can use a CSA to add multiple inputs—as an example, an adder with four 4-bit inputs is shown in Figure 2.23(d). The last stage sums two input buses using a **carry-propagate adder** (CPA). We have used an RCA as the CPA in Figure 2.23(d) and (e), but we can use any type of adder. Notice in Figure 2.23(e) how the two CSA cells and the RCA cell abut together horizontally to form a **bit slice** (or slice) and then the slices are stacked vertically to form the datapath.

We can register the CSA stages by adding vectors of flip-flops as shown in Figure 2.23(f). This reduces the adder delay to that of the slowest adder stage, usually the CPA. By using registers between stages of combinational logic we use **pipelining** to increase the speed and pay a price of increased area (for the registers) and introduce **latency**. It takes a few clock cycles (the latency, equal to n clock cycles for an n-stage pipeline) to fill the pipeline, but once it is filled, the answers emerge every clock cycle. Ferris wheels work much the same way. When the fair opens it takes a while (latency) to fill the wheel, but once it is full the people can get on and off every few seconds. (We can also pipeline the RCA of Figure 2.20. We add i registers on the A and B inputs before ADD[i] and add $(n-i)$ registers after the output S[i], with a single register before each C[i].)

The problem with an RCA is that every stage has to wait to make its carry decision, C[i], until the previous stage has calculated C[$i-1$]. If we examine the propagate signals we can bypass this critical path. Thus, for example, to bypass the carries for bits 4–7 (stages 5–8) of an adder we can compute BYPASS = P[4].P[5].P[6].P[7] and then use a MUX as follows:

$$C[7] = (G[7] + P[7] \cdot C[6]) \cdot BYPASS' + C[3] \cdot BYPASS. \qquad (2.54)$$

Adders based on this principle are called **carry-bypass adders** (CBA) [Sato et al., 1992]. Large, custom adders employ **Manchester-carry chains** to compute the carries and the bypass operation using TGs or just pass transistors [Weste and Eshraghian, 1993, pp. 530–531]. These types of carry chains may be part of a predesigned ASIC adder cell, but are not used by ASIC designers.

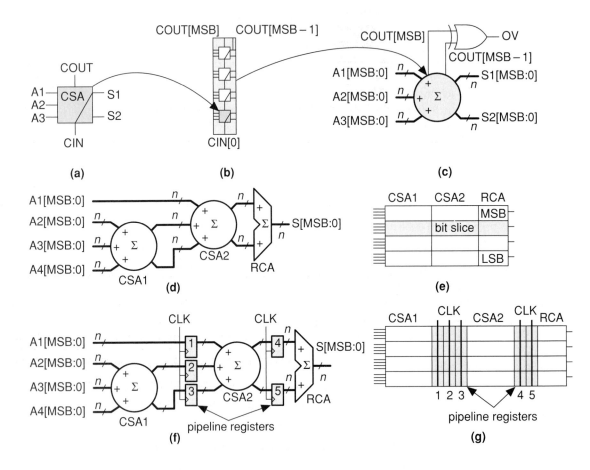

FIGURE 2.23 The carry-save adder (CSA). (a) A CSA cell. (b) A 4-bit CSA. (c) Symbol for a CSA. (d) A four-input CSA. (e) The datapath for a four-input, 4-bit adder using CSAs with a ripple-carry adder (RCA) as the final stage. (f) A pipelined adder. (g) The datapath for the pipelined version showing the pipeline registers as well as the clock control lines that use m2.

Instead of checking the propagate signals we can check the inputs. For example we can compute $SKIP = (A[i-1] \oplus B[i-1]) + (A[i] \oplus B[i])$ and then use a 2:1 MUX to select $C[i]$. Thus,

$$CSKIP[i] = (G[i] + P[i] \cdot C[i-1]) \cdot SKIP' + C[i-2] \cdot SKIP. \qquad (2.55)$$

This is a **carry-skip adder** [Keutzer, Malik, and Saldanha, 1991; Lehman, 1961]. Carry-bypass and carry-skip adders may include redundant logic (since the carry is computed in two different ways—we just take the first signal to arrive). We must be careful that the redundant logic is not optimized away during logic synthesis.

If we evaluate Eq. 2.44 recursively for $i = 1$, we get the following:

$$C[1] = G[1] + P[1] \cdot C[0] = G[1] + P[1] \cdot (G[0] + P[1] \cdot C[-1])$$

$$= G[1] + P[1] \cdot G[0]. \tag{2.56}$$

This result means that we can "look ahead" by two stages and calculate the carry into the third stage (bit 2), which is $C[1]$, using only the first-stage inputs (to calculate $G[0]$) and the second-stage inputs. This is a **carry-lookahead adder** (**CLA**) [MacSorley, 1961]. If we continue expanding Eq. 2.44, we find:

$$C[2] = G[2] + P[2] \cdot G[1] + P[2] \cdot P[1] \cdot G[0],$$

$$C[3] = G[3] + P[2] \cdot G[2] + P[2] \cdot P[1] \cdot G[1] + P[3] \cdot P[2] \cdot P[1] \cdot G[0]. \tag{2.57}$$

As we look ahead further these equations become more complex, take longer to calculate, and the logic becomes less regular when implemented using cells with a limited number of inputs. Datapath layout must fit in a bit slice, so the physical and logical structure of each bit must be similar. In a standard cell or gate array we are not so concerned about a regular physical structure, but a regular logical structure simplifies design. The **Brent–Kung adder** reduces the delay and increases the regularity of the carry-lookahead scheme [Brent and Kung, 1982]. Figure 2.24(a) shows a regular 4-bit CLA, using the carry-lookahead generator cell (CLG) shown in Figure 2.24(b).

In a **carry-select adder** we duplicate two small adders (usually 4-bit or 8-bit adders—often CLAs) for the cases CIN = '0' and CIN = '1' and then use a MUX to select the case that we need—wasteful, but fast [Bedrij, 1962]. A carry-select adder is often used as the fast adder in a datapath library because its layout is regular.

We can use the carry-select, carry-bypass, and carry-skip architectures to split a 12-bit adder, for example, into three blocks. The delay of the adder is then partly dependent on the delays of the MUX between each block. Suppose the delay due to 1-bit in an adder block (we shall call this a bit delay) is approximately equal to the MUX delay. In this case may be faster to make the blocks 3, 4, and 5-bits long instead of being equal in size. Now the delays into the final MUX are equal—3 bit-delays plus 2 MUX delays for the carry signal from bits 0–6 and 5 bit-delays for the carry from bits 7–11. Adjusting the block size reduces the delay of large adders (more than 16 bits).

We can extend the idea behind a carry-select adder as follows. Suppose we have an n-bit adder that generates two sums: One sum assumes a carry-in condition of '0', the other sum assumes a carry-in condition of '1'. We can split this n-bit adder into an i-bit adder for the i LSBs and an $(n-i)$-bit adder for the $n-i$ MSBs. Both of the smaller adders generate two conditional sums as well as true and complement carry signals. The two (true and complement) carry signals from the LSB adder are used to select between the two $(n-i+1)$-bit conditional sums from the MSB adder using $2(n-i+1)$ two-input MUXes. This is a **conditional-sum adder** (also often abbreviated to CSA) [Sklansky, 1960]. We can recursively apply this technique. For example, we can split a 16-bit adder using $i = 8$ and $n = 8$; then we can split one or both 8–bit adders again—and so on.

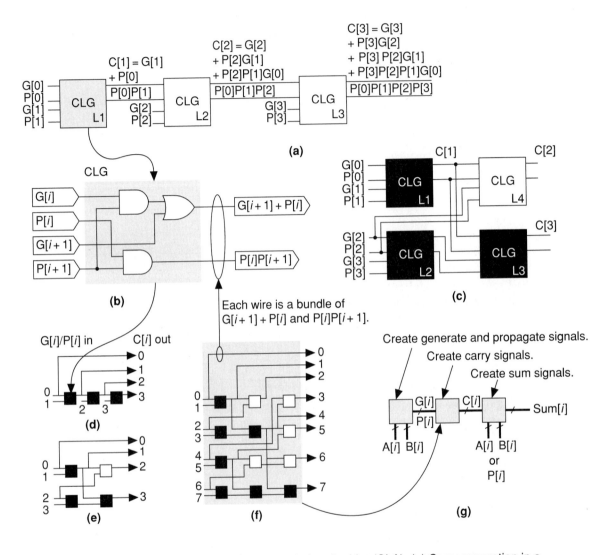

FIGURE 2.24 The Brent–Kung carry-lookahead adder (CLA). (a) Carry generation in a 4-bit CLA. (b) A cell to generate the lookahead terms, C[0]–C[3]. (c) Cells L1, L2, and L3 are rearranged into a tree that has less delay. Cell L4 is added to calculate C[2] that is lost in the translation. (d) and (e) Simplified representations of parts a and c. (f) The lookahead logic for an 8-bit adder. The inputs, 0–7, are the propagate and carry terms formed from the inputs to the adder. (g) An 8-bit Brent–Kung CLA. The outputs of the lookahead logic are the carry bits that (together with the inputs) form the sum. One advantage of this adder is that delays from the inputs to the outputs are more nearly equal than in other adders. This tends to reduce the number of unwanted and unnecessary switching events and thus reduces power dissipation.

Figure 2.25 shows the simplest form of an *n*-bit conditional-sum adder that uses *n* single-bit conditional adders, H (each with four outputs: two conditional sums, true carry, and complement carry), together with a tree of 2:1 MUXes (Qi_j). The conditional-sum adder is usually the fastest of all the adders we have discussed (it is the fastest when logic cell delay increases with the number of inputs—this is true for all ASICs except FPGAs).

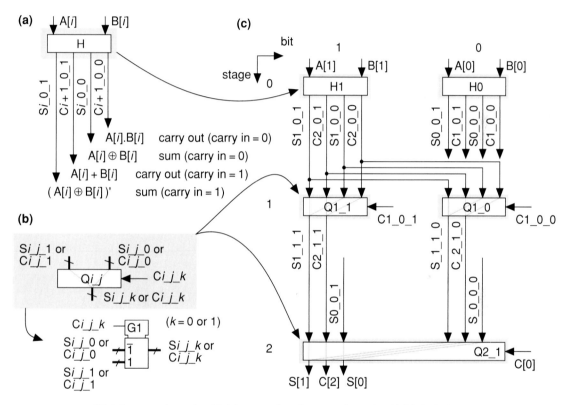

Ci_j_k = carry in to the *i*th bit assuming the carry in to the *j*th bit is k (k = 0 or 1)
Si_j_k = sum at the *i*th bit assuming the carry in to the *j*th bit is k (k = 0 or 1)

FIGURE 2.25 The conditional-sum adder. (a) A 1-bit conditional adder that calculates the sum and carry out assuming the carry in is either '1' or '0'. (b) The multiplexer that selects between sums and carries. (c) A 4-bit conditional-sum adder with carry input, C[0].

2.6.3   A Simple Example

How do we make and use datapath elements? What does a design look like? We may use predesigned cells from a library or build the elements ourselves from logic cells using a schematic or a design language. Table 2.12 shows an 8-bit conditional-sum adder intended for an FPGA. This Verilog implementation uses the same structure as Figure 2.25, but the equations are collapsed to use four or five variables. A basic logic cell in certain Xilinx FPGAs, for example, can implement two equations of the same four variables or one equation with five variables. The equations shown in Table 2.12 requires three levels of FPGA logic cells (so, for example, if each FPGA logic cell has a 5ns delay, the 8-bit conditional-sum adder delay is 15ns).

TABLE 2.12   An 8-bit conditional-sum adder (the notation is described in Figure 2.25).

```
module m8bitCSum (C0, a, b, s, C8); // Verilog conditional-sum adder for an FPGA   //1
input [7:0] C0, a, b; output [7:0] s; output C8;                                    //2
wire A7,A6,A5,A4,A3,A2,A1,A0,B7,B6,B5,B4,B3,B2,B1,B0,S8,S7,S6,S5,S4,S3,S2,S1,S0;    //3
wire C0, C2, C4_2_0, C4_2_1, S5_4_0, S5_4_1, C6, C6_4_0, C6_4_1, C8;                //4
assign {A7,A6,A5,A4,A3,A2,A1,A0} = a; assign {B7,B6,B5,B4,B3,B2,B1,B0} = b;         //5
assign s = { S7,S6,S5,S4,S3,S2,S1,S0 };                                             //6
assign S0 = A0^B0^C0 ; // start of level 1: & = AND, ^ = XOR, | = OR, ! = NOT       //7
assign S1 = A1^B1^(A0&B0|(A0|B0)&C0) ;                                              //8
assign C2 = A1&B1|(A1|B1)&(A0&B0|(A0|B0)&C0) ;                                      //9
assign C4_2_0 = A3&B3|(A3|B3)&(A2&B2) ; assign  C4_2_1 = A3&B3|(A3|B3)&(A2|B2) ;    //10
assign S5_4_0 = A5^B5^(A4&B4) ; assign S5_4_1 = A5^B5^(A4|B4) ;                     //11
assign C6_4_0 = A5&B5|(A5|B5)&(A4&B4) ; assign C6_4_1 = A5&B5|(A5|B5)&(A4|B4) ;     //12
assign S2 = A2^B2^C2 ; // start of level 2                                          //13
assign S3 = A3^B3^(A2&B2|(A2|B2)&C2) ;                                              //14
assign S4 = A4^B4^(C4_2_0|C4_2_1&C2) ;                                              //15
assign S5 = S5_4_0& !(C4_2_0|C4_2_1&C2)|S5_4_1&(C4_2_0|C4_2_1&C2) ;                 //16
assign C6 = C6_4_0|C6_4_1&(C4_2_0|C4_2_1&C2) ;                                      //17
assign S6 = A6^B6^C6 ; // start of level 3                                          //18
assign S7 = A7^B7^(A6&B6|(A6|B6)&C6) ;                                              //19
assign C8 = A7&B7|(A7|B7s)&(A6&B6|(A6|B6)&C6) ;                                     //20
endmodule                                                                          //21
```

Source: R. Halversen, University of Hawaii.

Figure 2.26 shows the normalized delay and area figures for a set of predesigned datapath adders. The data in Figure 2.26 is from a series of ASIC datapath cell libraries (Compass Passport) that may be synthesized together with test vectors and simulation models. We can combine the different adder techniques, but the adders then lose regularity and become less suited to a datapath implementation.

There are other adders that are not used in datapaths, but are occasionally useful in ASIC design. A **serial adder** is smaller but slower than the **parallel adders** we have described [Denyer and Renshaw, 1985]. The **carry-completion adder** is a variable delay adder and rarely used in synchronous designs [Sklansky, 1960].

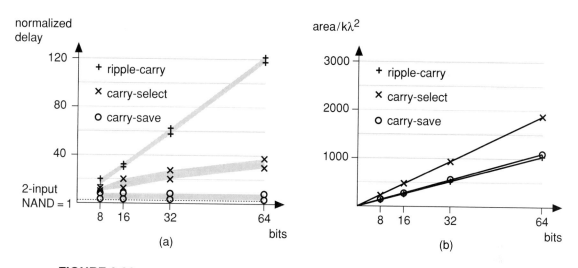

FIGURE 2.26 Datapath adders. This data is from a series of submicron datapath libraries. (a) Delay normalized to a two-input NAND logic cell delay (approximately equal to 250 ps in a 0.5 µm process). For example, a 64-bit ripple-carry adder (RCA) has a delay of approximately 30 ns in a 0.5 µm process. The spread in delay is due to variation in delays between different inputs and outputs. An n-bit RCA has a delay proportional to n. The delay of an n-bit carry-select adder is approximately proportional to $\log_2 n$. The carry-save adder delay is constant (but requires a carry-propagate adder to complete an addition). (b) In a datapath library the area of all adders are proportional to the bit size.

2.6.4   Multipliers

Figure 2.27 shows a symmetric 6-bit array **multiplier** (an n-bit multiplier multiplies two n-bit numbers; we shall use n-bit by m-bit multiplier if the lengths are different). Adders a0–f0 may be eliminated, which then eliminates adders a1–a6, leaving an asymmetric CSA array of 30 (5×6) adders (including one half adder). An n-bit array multiplier has a delay proportional to n plus the delay of the CPA (adders b6–f6 in Figure 2.27). There are two items we can attack to improve the performance of a multiplier: the number of partial products and the addition of the partial products.

Suppose we wish to multiply 15 (the **multiplicand**) by 19 (the **multiplier**) mentally. It is easier to calculate 15×20 and subtract 15. In effect we complete the multiplication as $15 \times (20 - 1)$ and we could write this as $15 \times 2\bar{1}$, with the overbar representing a minus sign. Now suppose we wish to multiply an 8-bit binary number, A, by B = 00010111 (decimal $16 + 4 + 2 + 1 = 23$). It is easier to multiply A by the canonical signed-digit vector (**CSD vector**) D = $0010\bar{1}001$ (decimal $32 - 8 + 1 = 23$) since this requires only three add or subtract operations (and a sub-

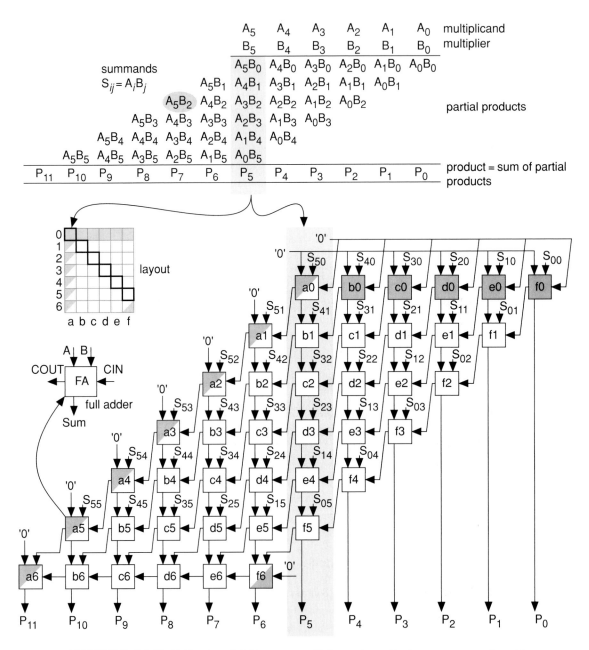

FIGURE 2.27 Multiplication. A 6-bit array multiplier using a final carry-propagate adder (full-adder cells a6–f6, a ripple-carry adder). Apart from the generation of the summands this multiplier uses the same structure as the carry-save adder of Figure 2.23(d).

traction is as easy as an addition). We say B has a **weight** of 4 and D has a weight of 3. By using D instead of B we have reduced the number of partial products by 1 ($=4-3$).

We can **recode** (or encode) any binary number, B, as a CSD vector, D, as follows (canonical means there is only one CSD vector for any number):

$$D_i = B_i + C_i - 2C_{i+1}, \tag{2.58}$$

where C_{i+1} is the carry from the sum of $B_{i+1} + B_i + C_i$ (we start with $C_0 = 0$).

As another example, if $B = 011$ ($B_2 = 0$, $B_1 = 1$, $B_0 = 1$; decimal 3), then, using Eq. 2.58,

$$D_0 = B_0 + C_0 - 2C_1 = 1 + 0 - 2 = \bar{1},$$

$$D_1 = B_1 + C_1 - 2C_2 = 1 + 1 - 2 = 0,$$

$$D_2 = B_2 + C_2 - 2C_3 = 0 + 1 - 0 = 1, \tag{2.59}$$

so that $D = 10\bar{1}$ (decimal $4 - 1 = 3$). CSD vectors are useful to represent fixed coefficients in digital filters, for example.

We can recode using a **radix** other than 2. Suppose B is an $(n+1)$-digit two's complement number,

$$B = B_0 + B_1 2 + B_2 2^2 + \ldots + B_i 2^i + \ldots + B_{n-1} 2^{n-1} - B_n 2^n. \tag{2.60}$$

We can rewrite the expression for B using the following sleight-of-hand:

$$2B - B = B = -B_0 + (B_0 - B_1)2 + \ldots + (B_{i-1} - B_i)2^i + \ldots + B_{n-1}2^{n-1} - B_n 2^n$$

$$= (-2B_1 + B_0)2^0 + (-2B_3 + B_2 + B_1)2^2 + \ldots$$

$$+ (-2B_i + B_{i-1} + B_{i-2})2^{i-1} + (-2B_{i+2} + B_{i+1} + B_i)2^{i+1} + \ldots$$

$$+ (-2B_n + B_{i-1} + B_{i-2})2^{n-1}. \tag{2.61}$$

This is very useful. Consider $B = 101001$ (decimal $9 - 32 = -23$, $n = 5$),

$$B = 101001 = (-2B_1 + B_0)2^0 + (-2B_3 + B_2 + B_1)2^2 + (-2B_5 + B_4 + B_3)2^4$$

$$= ((-2 \times 0) + 1)2^0 + ((-2 \times 1) + 0 + 0)2^2 + ((-2 \times 1) + 0 + 1)2^4. \tag{2.62}$$

Equation 2.61 tells us how to encode B as a radix-4 signed digit, $E = \bar{1}\bar{2}1$ (decimal $-16 - 8 + 1 = -23$). To multiply by B encoded as E we only have to perform a multiplication by 2 (a shift) and three add/subtract operations.

Using Eq. 2.61 we can encode any number by taking groups of three bits at a time and calculating

$$E_j = -2B_i + B_{i-1} + B_{i-2}, \quad E_{j+1} = -2B_{i+2} + B_{i+1} + B_i, \quad \ldots, \qquad (2.63)$$

where each 3-bit group overlaps by one bit. We pad B with a zero, $B_n \ldots B_1 B_0 0$, to match the first term in Eq. 2.61. If B has an odd number of bits, then we extend the sign: $B_n B_n \ldots B_1 B_0 0$. For example, B = 01011 (eleven), encodes to $E = 1\bar{1}\bar{1}$ ($16 - 4 - 1$); and B = 101 is $E = \bar{1}1$. This is called **Booth encoding** and reduces the number of partial products by a factor of two and thus considerably reduces the area as well as increasing the speed of our multiplier [Booth, 1951].

Next we turn our attention to improving the speed of addition in the CSA array. Figure 2.28(a) shows a section of the 6-bit array multiplier from Figure 2.27. We can collapse the chain of adders a0–f5 (5 adder delays) to the **Wallace tree** consisting of adders 5.1–5.4 (4 adder delays) shown in Figure 2.28(b).

Figure 2.28(c) pictorially represents multiplication as a sort of golf course. Each link corresponds to an adder. The holes or dots are the outputs of one stage (and the inputs of the next). At each stage we have the following three choices: (1) sum three outputs using a full adder (denoted by a box enclosing three dots); (2) sum two outputs using a half adder (a box with two dots); (3) pass the outputs directly to the next stage. The two outputs of an adder are joined by a diagonal line (full adders use black dots, half adders white dots). The object of the game is to choose (1), (2), or (3) at each stage to maximize the performance of the multiplier. In **tree-based multipliers** there are two ways to do this—working forward and working backward.

In a **Wallace-tree multiplier** we work forward from the multiplier inputs, compressing the number of signals to be added at each stage [Wallace, 1960]. We can view an FA as a **3:2 compressor** or **(3, 2) counter**—it counts the number of '1's on the inputs. Thus, for example, an input of '101' (two '1's) results in an output '10' (2). A half adder is a **(2, 2) counter**. To form P_5 in Figure 2.29 we must add 6 summands (S_{05}, S_{14}, S_{23}, S_{32}, S_{41}, and S_{50}) and 4 carries from the P_4 column. We add these in stages 1–7, compressing from 6:3:2:2:3:1:1. Notice that we wait until stage 5 to add the last carry from column P_4, and this means we expand (rather than compress) the number of signals (from 2 to 3) between stages 3 and 5. The maximum delay through the CSA array of Figure 2.29 is 6 adder delays. To this we must add the delay of the 4-bit (9 inputs) CPA (stage 7). There are 26 adders (6 half adders) plus the 4 adders in the CPA.

In a **Dadda multiplier** (Figure 2.30) we work backward from the final product [Dadda, 1965]. Each stage has a maximum of 2, 3, 4, 6, 9, 13, 19, ... outputs (each successive stage is 3/2 times larger—rounded down to an integer). Thus, for example, in Figure 2.28(d) we require 3 stages (with 3 adder delays—plus the delay of a 10-bit output CPA) for a 6-bit Dadda multiplier. There are 19 adders (4 half adders) in the CSA plus the 10 adders (2 half adders) in the CPA. A Dadda multiplier is usually faster and smaller than a Wallace-tree multiplier.

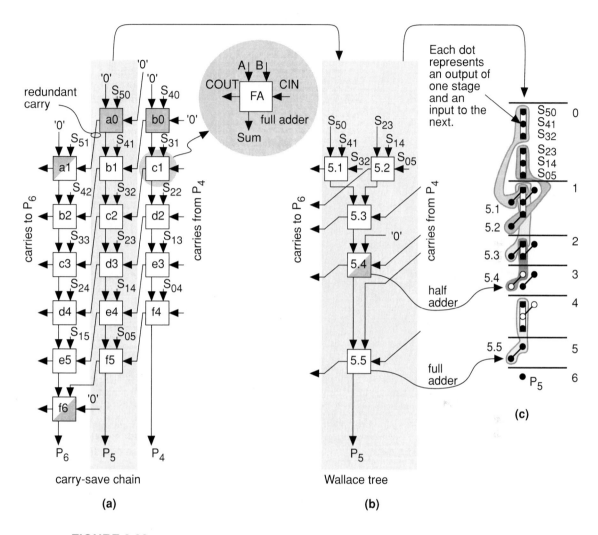

FIGURE 2.28 Tree-based multiplication. (a) The portion of Figure 2.27 that calculates the sum bit, P_5, using a chain of adders (cells a0–f5). (b) We can collapse this chain to a Wallace tree (cells 5.1–5.5). (c) The stages of multiplication.

In general, the number of stages and thus delay (in units of an FA delay—excluding the CPA) for an n-bit tree-based multiplier using (3, 2) counters is

$$\log_{1.5} n = \log_{10} n / \log_{10} 1.5 = \log_{10} n / 0.176. \qquad (2.64)$$

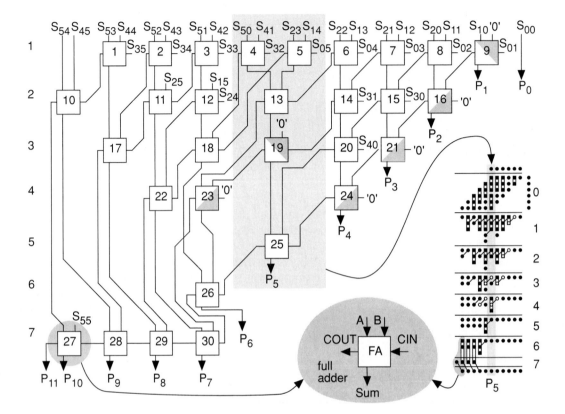

FIGURE 2.29 A 6-bit Wallace-tree multiplier. The carry-save adder (CSA) requires 26 adders (cells 1–26, six are half adders). The final carry-propagate adder (CPA) consists of 4 adder cells (27–30). The delay of the CSA is 6 adders. The delay of the CPA is 4 adders.

Figure 2.31(a) shows how the partial product array is constructed in a conventional 4-bit multiplier. The **Ferrari–Stefanelli multiplier** (Figure 2.31b) "nests" multipliers—the 2-bit submultipliers reduce the number of partial products [Ferrari and Stefanelli, 1969].

There are several issues in deciding between parallel multiplier architectures:

1. Since it is easier to fold triangles rather than trapezoids into squares, a Wallace-tree multiplier is more suited to full-custom layout, but is slightly larger, than a Dadda multiplier—both are less regular than an array multiplier. For cell-based ASICs, a Dadda multiplier is smaller than a Wallace-tree multiplier.

2. The overall multiplier speed does depend on the size and architecture of the final CPA, but this may be optimized independently of the CSA array. This means a Dadda multiplier is always at least as fast as the Wallace-tree version.

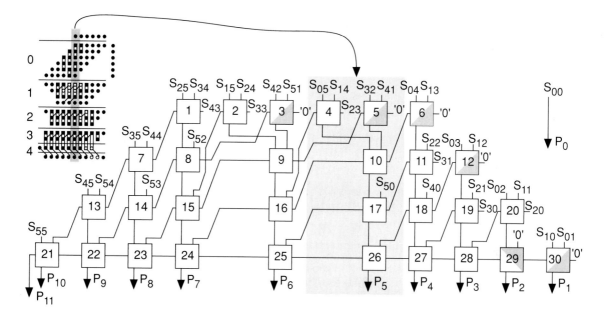

FIGURE 2.30 The 6-bit Dadda multiplier. The carry-save adder (CSA) requires 20 adders (cells 1–20, four are half adders). The carry-propagate adder (CPA, cells 21–30) is a ripple-carry adder (RCA). The CSA is smaller (20 versus 26 adders), faster (3 adder delays versus 6 adder delays), and more regular than the Wallace-tree CSA of Figure 2.29. The overall speed of this implementation is approximately the same as the Wallace-tree multiplier of Figure 2.29; however, the speed may be increased by substituting a faster CPA.

3. The low-order bits of any parallel multiplier settle first and can be added in the CPA before the remaining bits settle. This allows multiplication and the final addition to be overlapped in time.

4. Any of the parallel multiplier architectures may be pipelined. We may also use a **variably pipelined** approach that tailors the register locations to the size of the multiplier.

5. Using (4, 2), (5, 3), (7, 3), or (15, 4) counters increases the stage compression and permits the size of the stages to be tuned. Some ASIC cell libraries contain a (7, 3) counter—a **2-bit full-adder**. A (15, 4) counter is a 3-bit full adder. There is a trade-off in using these counters between the speed and size of the logic cells and the delay as well as area of the interconnect.

6. Power dissipation is reduced by the tree-based structures. The simplified carry-save logic produces fewer signal transitions and the tree structures produce fewer glitches than a chain.

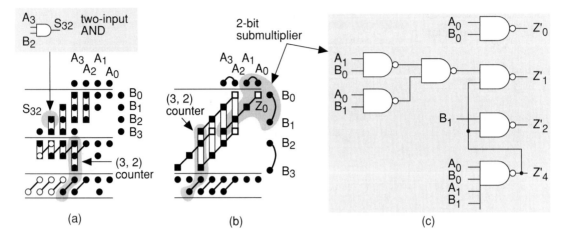

(a)   (b)   (c)

FIGURE 2.31 Ferrari–Stefanelli multiplier. (a) A conventional 4-bit array multiplier using AND gates to calculate the summands with (2, 2) and (3, 2) counters to sum the partial products. (b) A 4-bit Ferrari–Stefanelli multiplier using 2-bit submultipliers to construct the partial product array. (c) A circuit implementation for an inverting 2-bit submultiplier.

7. None of the multiplier structures we have discussed take into account the possibility of staggered arrival times for different bits of the multiplicand or the multiplier. Optimization then requires a logic synthesis tool.

2.6.5   Other Arithmetic Systems

There are other schemes for addition and multiplication that are useful in special circumstances. Addition of numbers using **redundant binary encoding** avoids carry propagation and is thus potentially very fast. Table 2.13 shows the rules for addition using an intermediate carry and sum that are added without the need for carry. For example,

binary	decimal	redundant binary	CSD vector	
1010111	87	$10\bar{1}0\bar{1}00\bar{1}$	$10\bar{1}0\bar{1}00\bar{1}$	addend
+ 1100101	101	+ $1\bar{1}10011\bar{1}$	+ 01100101	augend
= 10011100	= 188	$0100\bar{1}\bar{1}10$	$\bar{1}\bar{1}00\bar{1}100$	intermediate sum
		$1\bar{1}00010\bar{1}$	11000000	intermediate carry
		= $1\bar{1}1000\bar{1}00$	= $10\bar{1}00\bar{1}100$	sum

TABLE 2.13   Redundant binary addition.

A[*i*]	B[*i*]	A[*i*−1]	B[*i*−1]	Intermediate sum	Intermediate carry
$\bar{1}$	$\bar{1}$	x	x	0	$\bar{1}$
$\bar{1}$	0	A[i−1]=0/1 and B[i−1]=0/1		$\bar{1}$	0
0	$\bar{1}$	A[i−1]=$\bar{1}$ or B[i−1]=$\bar{1}$		1	$\bar{1}$
$\bar{1}$	1	x	x	0	0
1	$\bar{1}$	x	x	0	0
0	0	x	x	0	0
0	1	A[i−1]=0/1 and B[i−1]=0/1		$\bar{1}$	1
1	0	A[i−1]=$\bar{1}$ or B[i−1]=$\bar{1}$		1	0
1	1	x	x	0	1

The redundant binary representation is not unique. We can represent 101 (decimal), for example, by 1100101 (binary and CSD vector) or $1\bar{1}10011\bar{1}$. As another example, 188 (decimal) can be represented by 10011100 (binary), $1\bar{1}1000\bar{1}00$, $10\bar{1}00\bar{1}100$, or $10\bar{1}000\bar{1}00$ (CSD vector). Redundant binary addition of binary, redundant binary, or CSD vectors does not result in a unique sum, and addition of two CSD vectors does not result in a CSD vector. Each *n*-bit redundant binary number requires a rather wasteful 2*n*-bit binary number for storage. Thus $10\bar{1}$ is represented as 010010, for example (using sign magnitude). The other disadvantage of redundant binary arithmetic is the need to convert to and from binary representation.

Table 2.14 shows the (5, 3) **residue number system**. As an example, 11 (decimal) is represented as [1, 2] residue (5, 3) since $11R_5 = 11$ mod 5 = 1 and $11R_3 = 11$ mod 3 = 2. The size of this system is thus $3 \times 5 = 15$. We add, subtract, or multiply residue numbers using the modulus of each bit position—without any carry. Thus:

```
    4      [4, 1]        12      [2, 0]          3       [3, 0]
 +  7    + [2, 1]      -  4    - [4, 1]       ×  4     × [4, 1]
 = 11    = [1, 2]      =  8    = [3, 2]       = 12     = [2, 0]
```

The choice of moduli determines the system size and the computing complexity. The most useful choices are relative primes (such as 3 and 5). With *p* prime, numbers of the form 2^p and $2^p - 1$ are particularly useful ($2^p - 1$ are **Mersenne's numbers**) [Waser and Flynn, 1982].

2.6.6   Other Datapath Operators

Figure 2.32 shows symbols for some other datapath elements. The combinational datapath cells, NAND, NOR, and so on, and sequential datapath cells (flip-flops and latches) have standard-cell equivalents and function identically. I use a bold outline

TABLE 2.14   The 5, 3 residue number system.

n	residue 5	residue 3	n	residue 5	residue 3	n	residue 5	residue 3
0	0	0	5	0	2	10	0	1
1	1	1	6	1	0	11	1	2
2	2	2	7	2	1	12	2	0
3	3	0	8	3	2	13	3	1
4	4	1	9	4	0	14	4	2

(1 point) for datapath cells instead of the regular (0.5 point) line I use for scalar symbols. We call a set of identical cells a **vector** of datapath elements in the same way that a bold symbol, **A**, represents a vector and A represents a scalar.

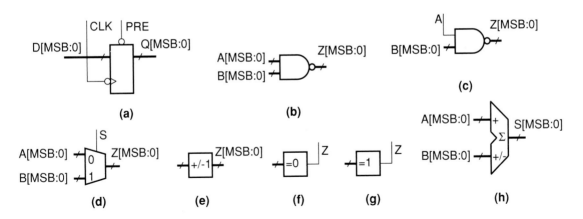

FIGURE 2.32 Symbols for datapath elements. (a) An array or vector of flip-flops (a register). (b) A two-input NAND cell with databus inputs. (c) A two-input NAND cell with a control input. (d) A buswide MUX. (e) An incrementer/decrementer. (f) An all-zeros detector. (g) An all-ones detector. (h) An adder/subtracter.

A **subtracter** is similar to an adder, except in a **full subtracter** we have a borrow-in signal, BIN; a borrow-out signal, BOUT; and a difference signal, DIFF:

$$\text{DIFF} = A \oplus \text{NOT}(B) \oplus \text{NOT}(\text{BIN}) = \text{SUM}(A, \text{NOT}(B), \text{NOT}(\text{BIN})) \quad (2.65)$$

$$\text{NOT}(\text{BOUT}) = A \cdot \text{NOT}(B) + A \cdot \text{NOT}(\text{BIN}) + \text{NOT}(B) \cdot \text{NOT}(\text{BIN})$$

$$= \text{MAJ}(\text{NOT}(A), B, \text{NOT}(\text{BIN})) \quad (2.66)$$

These equations are the same as those for the FA (Eqs. 2.38 and 2.39) except that the B input is inverted and the sense of the carry chain is inverted. To build a subtracter that calculates $(A - B)$ we invert the entire B input bus and connect the BIN[0] input to VDD (not to VSS as we did for CIN[0] in an adder). As an example, to subtract B = '0011' from A = '1001' we calculate '1001' + '1100' + '1' = '0110'. As with an adder, the true overflow is XOR(BOUT[MSB], BOUT[MSB − 1]).

We can build a ripple-borrow subtracter (a type of borrow-propagate subtracter), a borrow-save subtracter, and a borrow-select subtracter in the same way we built these adder architectures. An **adder/subtracter** has a control signal that gates the A input with an exclusive-OR cell (forming a programmable inversion) to switch between an adder or subtracter. Some adder/subtracters gate both inputs to allow us to compute $(-A - B)$. We must be careful to connect the input to the LSB of the carry chain (CIN[0] or BIN[0]) when changing between addition (connect to VSS) and subtraction (connect to VDD).

A **barrel shifter** rotates or shifts an input bus by a specified amount. For example if we have an eight-input barrel shifter with input '1111 0000' and we specify a shift of '0001 0000' (3, coded by bit position) the right-shifted 8-bit output is '0001 1110'. A barrel shifter may rotate left or right (or switch between the two under a separate control). A barrel shifter may also have an output width that is smaller than the input. To use a simple example, we may have an 8-bit input and a 4-bit output. This situation is equivalent to having a barrel shifter with two 4-bit inputs and a 4-bit output. Barrel shifters are used extensively in floating-point arithmetic to align (we call this **normalize** and **denormalize**) floating-point numbers (with sign, exponent, and mantissa).

A **leading-one detector** is used with a normalizing (left-shift) barrel shifter to align mantissas in floating-point numbers. The input is an n-bit bus A, the output is an n-bit bus, S, with a single '1' in the bit position corresponding to the most significant '1' in the input. Thus, for example, if the input is A = '0000 0101' the leading-one detector output is S = '0000 0100', indicating the leading one in A is in bit position 2 (bit 7 is the MSB, bit zero is the LSB). If we feed the output, S, of the leading-one detector to the shift select input of a normalizing (left-shift) barrel shifter, the shifter will normalize the input A. In our example, with an input of A = '0000 0101', and a left-shift of S = '0000 0100', the barrel shifter will shift A left by five bits and the output of the shifter is Z = '1010 0000'. Now that Z is aligned (with the MSB equal to '1') we can multiply Z with another normalized number.

The output of a **priority encoder** is the binary-encoded position of the leading one in an input. For example, with an input A = '0000 0101' the leading 1 is in bit position 3 (MSB is bit position 7) so the output of a 4-bit priority encoder would be Z = '0011' (3). In some cell libraries the encoding is reversed so that the MSB has an output code of zero, in this case Z = '0101' (5). This second, reversed, encoding scheme is useful in floating-point arithmetic. If A is a mantissa and we normalize A to '1010 0000' we have to subtract 5 from the exponent, this **exponent correction** is equal to the output of the priority encoder.

An **accumulator** is an adder/subtracter and a register. Sometimes these are combined with a multiplier to form a **multiplier–accumulator** (**MAC**). An **incrementer** adds 1 to the input bus, $Z = A + 1$, so we can use this function, together with a register, to negate a two's complement number for example. The implementation is $Z[i] = \text{XOR}(A[i], \text{CIN}[i])$, and $\text{COUT}[i] = \text{AND}(A[i], \text{CIN}[i])$. The carry-in control input, $\text{CIN}[0]$, thus acts as an enable: If it is set to '0' the output is the same as the input.

The implementation of arithmetic cells is often a little more complicated than we have explained. CMOS logic is naturally inverting, so that it is faster to implement an incrementer as

$$Z[i(\text{even})] = \text{XOR}(A[i], \text{CIN}[i]) \quad \text{and} \quad \text{COUT}[i(\text{even})] = \text{NAND}(A[i], \text{CIN}[i]).$$

This inverts COUT, so that in the following stage we must invert it again. If we push an inverting bubble to the input CIN we find that:

$$Z[i(\text{odd})] = \text{XNOR}(A[i], \text{CIN}[i]) \quad \text{and} \quad \text{COUT}[i(\text{even})] = \text{NOR}(\text{NOT}(A[i]), \text{CIN}[i]).$$

In many datapath implementations all odd-bit cells operate on inverted carry signals, and thus the odd-bit and even-bit datapath elements are different. In fact, *all* the adder and subtracter datapath elements we have described may use this technique. Normally this is completely hidden from the designer in the datapath assembly and any output control signals are inverted, if necessary, by inserting buffers.

A **decrementer** subtracts 1 from the input bus, the logical implementation is $Z[i] = \text{XOR}(A[i], \text{CIN}[i])$ and $\text{COUT}[i] = \text{AND}(\text{NOT}(A[i]), \text{CIN}[i])$. The implementation may invert the odd carry signals, with $\text{CIN}[0]$ again acting as an enable.

An **incrementer/decrementer** has a second control input that gates the input, inverting the input to the carry chain. This has the effect of selecting either the increment or decrement function.

Using the **all-zeros detectors** and **all-ones detectors**, remember that, for a 4-bit number, for example, zero in ones' complement arithmetic is '1111' or '0000', and that zero in signed magnitude arithmetic is '1000' or '0000'.

A **register file** (or scratchpad memory) is a bank of flip-flops arranged across the bus; sometimes these have the option of multiple ports (multiport register files) for read and write. Normally these register files are the densest logic and hardest to fit in a datapath. For large register files it may be more appropriate to use a multiport memory. We can add control logic to a register file to create a **first-in first-out register** (**FIFO**), or **last-in first-out register** (**LIFO**).

In Section 2.5 we saw that the standard-cell version and gate-array macro version of the sequential cells (latches and flip-flops) each contain their own clock buffers. The reason for this is that (without intelligent placement software) we do not know where a standard cell or a gate-array macro will be placed on a chip. We also have no idea of the condition of the clock signal coming into a sequential cell. The ability to place the clock buffers outside the sequential cells in a datapath gives us more flexibility and saves space. For example, we can place the clock buffers for all the clocked elements at the top of the datapath (together with the buffers for the control signals) and **river route** (in river routing the interconnect lines all flow in the same direction on the same layer) the connections to the clock lines. This saves space and allows us to guarantee the clock skew and timing. It may mean, however, that there is a fixed overhead associated with a datapath. For example, it might make no sense to build a 4-bit datapath if the clock and control buffers take up twice the space of the datapath logic. Some tools allow us to design logic using a **portable netlist**. After we complete the design we can decide whether to implement the portable netlist in a datapath, standard cells, or even a gate array, based on area, speed, or power considerations.

2.7   I/O Cells

Figure 2.33 shows a three-state bidirectional output buffer (Tri-State® is a registered trademark of National Semiconductor). When the output enable (OE) signal is high, the circuit functions as a noninverting buffer driving the value of DATAin onto the I/O pad. When OE is low, the output transistors or **drivers**, M1 and M2, are disconnected. This allows multiple drivers to be connected on a bus. It is up to the designer to make sure that a bus never has two drivers—a problem known as **contention**.

In order to prevent the problem opposite to contention—a bus floating to an intermediate voltage when there are no bus drivers—we can use a **bus keeper** or **bus-hold** cell (TI calls this Bus-Friendly logic). A bus keeper normally acts like two weak (low drive-strength) cross-coupled inverters that act as a latch to retain the last logic state on the bus, but the latch is weak enough that it may be driven easily to the opposite state. Even though bus keepers act like latches, and will simulate like latches, they should not be used as latches, since their drive strength is weak.

Transistors M1 and M2 in Figure 2.33 have to drive large off-chip loads. If we wish to change the voltage on a $C = 200\,\text{pF}$ load by 5 V in 5 ns (a **slew rate** of $1\,\text{Vns}^{-1}$) we will require a current in the output transistors of

$$I_{DS} = C\,(dV/dt) = (200 \times 10^{-12})\,(5/5 \times 10^{-9}) = 0.2\,\text{A} \quad \text{or} \quad 200\,\text{mA}.$$

Such large currents flowing in the output transistors must also flow in the power supply bus and can cause problems. There is always some inductance in series with the power supply, between the point at which the supply enters the ASIC package and reaches the power bus on the chip. The inductance is due to the bond wire, lead frame, and package pin. If we have a power-supply inductance of 2 nH and a current changing from zero to 1 A (32 I/O cells on a bus switching at 30 mA each) in 5 ns, we will have a voltage spike on the power supply (called **power-supply bounce**) of $L(dI/dt) = (2 \times 10^{-9})(1/(5 \times 10^{-9})) = 0.4\,\text{V}$.

We do several things to alleviate this problem: We can limit the number of **simultaneously switching outputs** (SSOs), we can limit the number of I/O drivers that can be attached to any one VDD and GND pad, and we can design the output buffer to limit the slew rate of the output (we call these slew-rate limited I/O pads).

Quiet-I/O cells also use two separate power supplies and two sets of I/O drivers: an AC supply (clean or quiet supply) with small AC drivers for the I/O circuits that start and stop the output slewing at the beginning and end of a output transition, and a DC supply (noisy or dirty supply) for the transistors that handle large currents as they slew the output.

The three-state buffer allows us to employ the same pad for input and output— **bidirectional I/O**. When we want to use the pad as an input, we set OE low and take the data from DATAin. Of course, it is not necessary to have all these features on every pad: We can build output-only or input-only pads.

FIGURE 2.33 A three-state bidirectional output buffer. When the output enable, OE, is '1' the output section is enabled and drives the I/O pad. When OE is '0' the output buffer is placed in a high-impedance state.

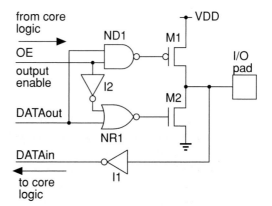

We can also use many of these output cell features for input cells that have to drive large on-chip loads (a clock pad cell, for example). Some gate arrays simply turn an output buffer around to drive a grid of interconnect that supplies a clock signal internally. With a typical interconnect capacitance of $0.2\,\text{pFcm}^{-1}$, a grid of 100 cm (consisting of 10 by 10 lines running all the way across a 1 cm chip) presents a load of 20 pF to the clock buffer.

Some libraries include I/O cells that have passive pull-ups or pull-downs (resistors) instead of the transistors, M1 and M2 (the resistors are normally still constructed from transistors with long gate lengths). We can also omit one of the driver transistors, M1 or M2, to form **open-drain** outputs that require an external pull-up or pull-down. We can design the output driver to produce TTL output levels rather than CMOS logic levels. We may also add input hysteresis (using a Schmitt trigger) to the input buffer, I1 in Figure 2.33, to accept input data signals that contain glitches (from bouncing switch contacts, for example) or that are slow rising. The input buffer can also include a **level shifter** to accept TTL input levels and shift the input signal to CMOS levels.

The gate oxide in CMOS transistors is extremely thin (100 Å or less). This leaves the gate oxide of the I/O cell input transistors susceptible to breakdown from static electricity (**electrostatic discharge**, or **ESD**). ESD arises when we or machines handle the package leads (like the shock I sometimes get when I touch a doorknob after walking across the carpet at work). Sometimes this problem is called **electrical overstress** (EOS) since most ESD-related failures are caused not by gate-oxide breakdown, but by the thermal stress (melting) that occurs when the n-channel transistor in an output driver overheats (melts) due to the large current that can flow in the drain diffusion connected to a pad during an ESD event.

To protect the I/O cells from ESD, the input pads are normally tied to device structures that clamp the input voltage to below the gate breakdown voltage (which can be as low as 10 V with a 100 Å gate oxide). Some I/O cells use transistors with a special **ESD implant** that increases breakdown voltage and provides protection. I/O driver transistors can also use elongated drain structures (ladder structures) and large drain-to-gate spacing to help limit current, but in a salicide process that lowers the drain resistance this is difficult. One solution is to mask the I/O cells during the salicide step. Another solution is to use *pnpn* and *npnp* diffusion structures called silicon-controlled rectifiers (SCRs) to clamp voltages and divert current to protect the I/O circuits from ESD.

There are several ways to model the capability of an I/O cell to withstand EOS. The **human-body model** (**HBM**) represents ESD by a 100 pF capacitor discharging through a 1.5 kΩ resistor (this is an International Electrotechnical Committee, IEC, specification). Typical voltages generated by the human body are in the range of 2–4 kV, and we often see an I/O pad cell rated by the voltage it can withstand using the HBM. The **machine model** (**MM**) represents an ESD event generated by automated machine handlers. Typical MM parameters use a 200 pF capacitor (typically charged to 200 V) discharged through a 25 Ω resistor, corresponding to a peak initial current of nearly 10 A. The **charge-device model** (**CDM**, also called device charge–discharge) represents the problem when an IC package is charged, in a shipping tube for example, and then grounded. If the maximum charge on a package is 3 nC (a typical measured figure) and the package capacitance to ground is 1.5 pF, we can simulate this event by charging a 1.5 pF capacitor to 2 kV and discharging it through a 1 Ω resistor.

If the diffusion structures in the I/O cells are not designed with care, it is possible to construct an SCR structure unwittingly, and instead of protecting the transistors the SCR can enter a mode where it is latched on and conducting large enough currents to destroy the chip. This failure mode is called **latch-up**. Latch-up can occur if the *pn*-diodes on a chip become forward-biased and inject minority carriers (electrons in *p*-type material, holes in *n*-type material) into the substrate. The source–substrate and drain–substrate diodes can become forward-biased due to power-supply bounce or output **undershoot** (the cell outputs fall below V_{SS}) or **overshoot** (outputs rise to greater than V_{DD}) for example. These injected minority carriers can travel fairly large distances and interact with nearby transistors causing latch-up. I/O cells normally surround the I/O transistors with **guard rings** (a continuous ring of *n*-diffusion in an *n*-well connected to VDD, and a ring of *p*-diffusion in a *p*-well connected to VSS) to collect these minority carriers. This is a problem that can also occur in the logic core and this is one reason that we normally include substrate and well connections to the power supplies in every cell.

2.8 Cell Compilers

The process of hand crafting circuits and layout for a full-custom IC is a tedious, time-consuming, and error-prone task. There are two types of automated layout assembly tools, often known as a **silicon compilers**. The first type produces a specific kind of circuit, a **RAM compiler** or **multiplier compiler**, for example. The second type of compiler is more flexible, usually providing a programming language that assembles or tiles layout from an input command file, but this is full-custom IC design.

We can build a register file from latches or flip-flops, but, at 4.5–6.5 gates (18–26 transistors) per bit, this is an expensive way to build memory. Dynamic RAM (DRAM) can use a cell with only one transistor, storing charge on a capacitor that has to be periodically refreshed as the charge leaks away. ASIC RAM is invariably static (SRAM), so we do not need to refresh the bits. When we refer to RAM in an ASIC environment we almost always mean SRAM. Most ASIC RAMs use a six-transistor cell (four transistors to form two cross-coupled inverters that form the storage loop, and two more transistors to allow us to read from and write to the cell). RAM compilers are available that produce **single-port RAM** (a single shared bus for read and write) as well as **dual-port RAMs**, and **multiport RAMs**. In a multiport RAM the compiler may or may not handle the problem of **address contention** (attempts to read and write to the same RAM address simultaneously). RAM can be **asynchronous** (the read and write cycles are triggered by control and/or address transitions asynchronous to a clock) or **synchronous** (using the system clock).

In addition to producing layout we also need a **model compiler** so that we can verify the circuit at the behavioral level, and we need a netlist from a **netlist compiler** so that we can simulate the circuit and verify that it works correctly at the structural level. Silicon compilers are thus complex pieces of software. We assume that a silicon compiler will produce working silicon even if every configuration has not been tested. This is still ASIC design, but now we are relying on the fact that the tool works correctly and therefore the compiled blocks are **correct by construction**.

2.9 Summary

The most important concepts that we covered in this chapter are the following:

- The use of transistors as switches
- The difference between flip-flop and a latch
- The meaning of set-up time and hold time
- Pipelines and latency
- The difference between datapath, standard-cell, and gate-array logic cells
- Strong and weak logic levels

- Pushing bubbles
- Ratio of logic
- Resistance per square of layers and their relative values in CMOS
- Design rules and λ

2.10 Problems

$*$ = Difficult, $**$ = Very difficult, $***$ = Extremely difficult

2.1 (Switches, 20 min.) **(a)** Draw a circuit schematic for a two-way light switch: flipping the switch at the top or bottom of the stairs reverses the state of two light bulbs, one at the top and one at the bottom of the stairs. Your schematic should show and label all the cables, switches, and bulbs. **(b)** Repeat the problem for three switches and one light in a warehouse.

2.2 (Logic, 10 min.) The queen wished to choose her successor wisely. She blindfolded and then placed a crown on each of her three children, explaining that there were three red and two blue crowns, and they must deduce the color of their own crown. With blindfolds removed the children could see the two other crowns, but not their own. After a while Anne said: "My crown is red." How did she know?

2.3 (Minus signs, 20 min.) The channel charge in an n-channel transistor is negative. **(a)** Should there not be a minus sign in Eq. 2.5 to account for this? **(b)** If so, then where in the derivation of Section 2.1 does the minus sign disappear to arrive at Eq. 2.9 for the current in an n-channel transistor? **(c)** The equations for the current in a p-channel transistor (Eq. 2.15) have the opposite sign to those for an n-channel transistor. Where in the derivation in Section 2.1 does the extra minus sign arise?

FIGURE 2.34 Transistor characteristics for a $0.3\,\mu\text{m}$ process (Problem 2.4).

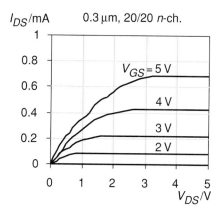

2.4 (Transistor curves, 20 min.) Figure 2.34 shows the measured I_{DS}–V_{DS} characteristics for a 20/20 n-channel transistor in a 0.3 μm (effective gate length) process from an ASIC foundry. Derive as much information as you can from this figure.

2.5 (Body effect, 20 min). The equations for the drain-source current (2.9, 2.12, and 2.15) do not contain V_{SB}, the source voltage with respect to the bulk, because we assumed that it was zero. This is not true for the n-channel transistor whose drain is connected to the output in a two-input NAND gate, for example. A reverse **substrate-bias** (or back-gate bias; $V_{SB} > 0$ for an n-channel transistor) makes the bulk act like a second gate (the back gate) and modifies an n-channel transistor threshold voltage as follows:

$$V_{tn} = V_{t0n} + \gamma \left(\sqrt{\phi_0 + V_{SB}} - \sqrt{\phi_0} \right) , \tag{2.67}$$

where V_{t0n} is measured with $V_{SB} = 0$ V; ϕ_0 is called the surface potential; and γ (gamma) is the **body-effect coefficient** (back-gate bias coefficient),

$$\gamma = \frac{\sqrt{2q\varepsilon_{Si}N_A}}{C_{ox}}. \tag{2.68}$$

There are several alternative names and symbols for ϕ_0 ("phi," a positive quantity for an n-channel transistor, typically between 0.6–0.7 V)—you may also see ϕ_b (for bulk potential) or $2\phi_F$ (twice the Fermi potential, a negative quantity). In Eq. 2.68, $\varepsilon_{Si} = \varepsilon_0 \varepsilon_r = 1.053 \times 10^{-10}$ Fm^{-1} is the **permittivity of silicon** (the permittivity of a vacuum $\varepsilon_0 = 8.85 \times 10^{-12}$ Fm^{-1} and the relative permittivity of silicon is $\varepsilon_r = 11.7$); N_A is the acceptor doping concentration in the bulk (for p-type substrate or well—N_D for the donor concentration in an n-type substrate or well); and C_{ox} is the gate capacitance per unit area given by

$$C_{ox} = \frac{\varepsilon_{ox}}{T_{ox}}. \tag{2.69}$$

a. Calculate the theoretical value of γ for $N_A = 10^{16}$ cm^{-3}, $T_{ox} = 100$ Å.

b. Calculate and plot V_{tn} for V_{SB} ranging from 0 V to 5 V in increments of 1 V assuming values of $\gamma = 0.5$, $\phi_0 = 0.6$ V, and $V_{t0n} = 0.5$ V obtained from transistor characteristics.

c. Fit a linear approximation to V_{tn}.

d. Recognizing $V_{SB} \leq 0$, rewrite Eq. 2.67 for a p-channel device.

e. (Harder) What effect does the back-gate bias effect have on CMOS logic circuits?

Answer: (a) 0.17 (b) 0.50–1.3 V.

2.6 (Sizing layout, 10 min.) Stating clearly whatever assumptions you make and describing the tools and methods you use, estimate the size (in λ) of the standard cell shown in Figure 1.3. Estimate the size of each of the transistors, giving their channel lengths and widths (stating clearly which is which).

2.7 (CMOS process) (20 min.) Table 2.15 shows the major steps involved in a typical deep submicron CMOS process. There are approximately 100 major steps in the process.

a. If each major step has a yield of 0.9, what is the overall process yield?

b. If the process yield is 90% (not uncommon), what is the average yield at each major step?

c. If each of the major steps in Table 2.15 consists of an average of five other microtasks, what is the average yield of each of the 500 microtasks.

d. Suppose, for example, an operator loads and unloads a furnace five times a day as a microtask, how many days must the operator work without making a mistake to achieve this microtask yield?

e. Does this seem reasonable? What is wrong with our model?

f. (**60 min.) Draw the process cross-section showing, in particular, the poly, FOX, gate oxide, IMOs and metal layers. You may have to make some assumptions about the meanings and functions of the various steps and layers. Assume all layers are deposited on top of each other according to the thicknesses shown (do not attempt to correct for the silicon consumed during oxidation—even if you understand what this means). The abbreviations in Table 2.15 are as follows: dep. = deposition; LPCVD = low-pressure chemical vapor deposition (for growing oxide and poly); LDD = lightly doped drain (a way to improve transistor characteristics); SOG = silicon overglass (a deposited quartz to help with step coverage between metal layers).

Answer: (a) Zero. (b) 0.999. (c) 0.9998. (d) 3 years.

2.8 (Stipple patterns, 30 min.)

a. Check the stipple patterns in Figure 2.9. Using ruled paper draw 8-by-8 stipple patterns for all the combinations of layers shown.

b. Repeat part a for Figure 2.10.

2.9 (Select, 20 min.) Can you draw a design-rule correct (according to the design rules in Tables 2.7–2.9) layout with a piece of select that has a minimum width of 2λ (rule 4.4)?

2.10 (*Inverter layout, 60 min.) Using 1/4-inch ruled paper (or similar) draw a minimum-size inverter (W/L = 1 for both p-channel and n-channel transistors). Use a scale of one square to 2λ and the design rules in Table 2.7–Table 2.9. Do not use m2 or m3—only m1. Draw the nwell, pwell, ndiff, and pdiff layers, but not the implant layers or the active layer. Include connections to the input, output, VDD, and VSS in m1. There must be at least one well connection to each well (n-well to VDD, and p-well to VSS). Minimize the size of your cell BB. Draw the BB outline and write its size in λ^2 on your drawing. Use green diagonal stripes for ndiff, brown diagonal stripes for pdiff, red diagonal stripes for poly, blue diagonal stripes for m1, solid black for contact). Include a key on your drawing, and clearly label the input, output, VDD, and VSS contacts.

TABLE 2.15 CMOS process steps (Problem 2.7).[1]

Step	Depth	Step	Depth	Step	Depth
1 substrate		32 resist strip		63 m1 mask	
2 oxide 1 dep.	500	33 WSi anneal		64 m1 etch	
3 nitride 1 dep.	1500	34 nLDD mask		65 resist strip	
4 *n*-well mask		35 nLDD implant		66 base oxide dep.	6000
5 *n*-well etch		36 resist strip		67 SOG coat1/2	3000
6 *n*-well implant		37 pLDD mask		68 SOG cure/etch	−4000
7 resist strip		38 pLDD implant		69 cap oxide dep.	4000
8 blocking oxide dep.	2000	39 resist strip		70 via1 mask	
9 nitride 1 strip		40 spacer oxide dep.	3000	71 via1 etch	−2500
10 *p*-well implant		41 WSi anneal		72 resist strip	
11 *p*-well drive		42 SD oxide dep	200	73 TiW dep.	2000
12 active oxide dep.	250	43 n+ mask		74 AlCu/TiW dep.	4000
13 nitride 2 dep.	1500	44 n+ implant		75 m2 mask	
14 active mask		45 resist strip		76 m2 etch	
15 active etch		46 ESD mask		77 resist strip	
16 resist strip		47 ESD implant		78 base oxide dep.	6000
17 field mask		48 resist strip		79 SOG coat 1/2	3000
18 field implant		49 p+ mask		80 SOG cure/etch	−4000
19 resist strip		50 p+ implant		81 cap oxide dep.	4000
20 field oxide dep.	5000	51 resist strip		82 via2 mask	
21 nitride 2 strip		52 implant anneal		83 via2 etch	−2500
22 sacrificial oxide dep.	300	53 LPCVD oxide dep.	1500	84 resist strip	
23 Vt adjust implant		54 BPSG dep./densify	4000	85 TiW dep.	2000
24 gate oxide dep.	80	55 contact mask		86 AlCu/TiW dep.	4000
25 LPCVD poly dep.	1500	56 contact etch	−2500	87 m3 mask	
26 deglaze		57 resist strip		88 m3 etch	
27 WSi dep.	1500	58 Pt dep.	200	89 resist strip	
28 LPCVD oxide dep.	750	59 Pt sinter		90 oxide dep.	4000
29 poly mask		60 Pt strip		92 nitride dep.	10,000
30 oxide etch		61 TiW dep.	2000	93 pad mask	
31 polycide etch		62 AlCu/TiW dep.	4000	94 pad etch	

[1]Depths of layers are in angstroms (negative values are etch depths). For abbreviations used, see Problem 2.7.

2.11 (*AOI221 Layout, 120 min.) Layout the AOI221 shown in Figure 2.13 with the design rules of Tables 2.7–2.9 and using Figure 1.3 as a guide. Label clearly the m1 corresponding to the inputs, output, VDD bus, and GND (VSS) bus. Remember to include substrate contacts. What is the size of your BB in λ^2?

2.12 (Resistance, 20 min.)

a. Using the values for sheet resistance shown in Table 2.3, calculate the resistance of a 200λ long (in the direction of current flow) by 3λ wide piece of each of the layers.

b. Estimate the resistance of an 8-inch, $10\,\Omega\,\mathrm{cm}$, p-type, <100> wafer, measured (i) from edge to edge across a diameter and (ii) from face center to the face center on the other side.

2.13 (*Layout graphics, 120 min.) Write a tutorial for capturing layout. As an example:

To capture EPSF (encapsulated PostScript format) from Tanner Research's L-Edit for documentation, Macintosh version... Create a black-and-white technology file, use Setup, Layers..., in L-Edit. The method described here does not work well for grayscale or color. Use File, Print..., Destination check button File to print from L-Edit to an EPS (encapsulated PostScript) file. After you choose Save, a dialog box appears. Select Format: EPS Enhanced Mac Preview, ASCII, Level 1 Compatible, Font Inclusion: None. Save the file. Switch to Frame. Create an Anchored Frame. Use File, Import, File... to bring up a dialog box. Check button Copy into Document, select Format: EPSF. Import the EPS file that will appear as a "page image". Grab the graphic inside the Anchored Frame and move the "page image" around. There will be a footer with text on the "page image" that you may want to hide by using the Anchored Frame edges to crop the image.

Your instructions should be precise, concise, assume nothing, and use the names of menu items, buttons and so on exactly as they appear to the user. Most of the layout figures in this book were created using L-Edit running on a Macintosh, with labels added in FrameMaker. Most of the layouts use the Compass layout editor.

2.14 (Transistor resistance, 20 min.) Calculate I_{DS} and the resistance (the DC value V_{DS}/I_{DS} as well as the AC value $\partial V_{DS}/\partial I_{DS}$ as appropriate) of long-channel transistors with the following parameters, under the specified conditions. In each case state whether the transistor is in the saturation region, linear region, or off:

(i) n-channel: $V_{tn} = 0.5\mathrm{V}$, $\beta_n = 40\,\mu\mathrm{AV}^{-2}$:

$V_{GS} = 3.3\mathrm{V}$:   **a.** $V_{DS} = 3.3\,\mathrm{V}$ **b.** $V_{DS} = 0.0\,\mathrm{V}$ **c.** $V_{GS} = 0.0\mathrm{V}$, $V_{DS} = 3.3\,\mathrm{V}$

(ii) p-channel: $V_{tp} = -0.6\mathrm{V}$, $\beta_p = 20\,\mu\mathrm{A/V}^{-2}$:

$V_{GS} = 0.0\,\mathrm{V}$:   **a.** $V_{DS} = 0.0\,\mathrm{V}$ **b.** $V_{DS} = -5.0\,\mathrm{V}$ **c.** $V_{GS} = -5.0\,\mathrm{V}$, $V_{DS} = -5.0\,\mathrm{V}$

2.15 (Circuit theory, 15 min.) You accidentally created the "inverter" shown in Figure 2.35 on a full-custom ASIC currently being fabricated. Will it work? Your manager wants a yes or no answer. Your group is a little more understanding: You are to make a presentation to them to explain the problems ahead. Prepare two foils as well as a one page list of alternatives and recommendations.

FIGURE 2.35 A CMOS "inverter" with *n*-channel and *p*-channel transistors swapped (Problem 2.15).

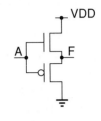

2.16 (Mask resolution, 10 min.) People use LaserWriters to make printed-circuit boards all the time.

a. Do you think it is possible to make an IC mask using a 600 dpi (dots per inch) LaserWriter and a transparency?

b. What would λ be?

c. (Harder) See if you can use a microscope to look at the dot and the rectangular bars (serifs) of a letter 'i' from the output of a LaserWriter on paper (most are 300 dpi or 600 dpi). Estimate λ. What is causing the problem? Why is there no rush to generate 1200 dpi LaserWriters for paper? Put a page of this textbook under the microscope: can you see the difference? What are the similar problems printing patterns on a wafer?

2.17 (Lambda, 10 min.) Estimate λ

a. for your TV screen,

b. for your computer monitor,

c. (harder) a photograph.

2.18 (Pass-transistor logic, 10 min.)

a. In Figure 2.36 suppose we set A = B = C = D = '1', what is the value of F?

b. What is the logic strength of the signal at F?

c. If $V_{DD} = 5$ V and $V_{tn} = 0.6$ V, what would the voltage at the source and drain terminals of M1, M2, and M3 be?

d. Will this circuit still work if $V_{DD} = 3$ V?

e. At what point does it stop working?

FIGURE 2.36 A pass transistor chain (Problem 2.18).

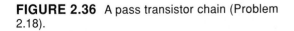
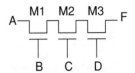

2.19 (Transistor parameters, 20 min.) Calculate the (a) electron and (b) hole mobility for the transistor parameters given in Section 2.1 if $k'_n = 80\,\mu AV^{-2}$ and $k'_p = 40\,\mu AV^{-2}$.

Answer: (a) $0.023\,m^2V^{-1}s^{-1}$.

2.20 (Quantum behavior, 10 min.) The average thermal energy of an electron is approximately kT, where $k = 1.38 \times 10^{-23}\,JK^{-1}$ is Boltzmann's constant and T is the absolute temperature in kelvin.

a. The kinetic energy of an electron is $(1/2)mv^2$, where v is due to random thermal motion, and $m = 9.11 \times 10^{-31}$ kg is the rest mass. What is v at 300 K?

b. The electron wavelength $l = h/p$, where $h = 6.62 \times 10^{-34}$ Js is the Planck constant, and $p = mv$ is the electron momentum. What is l at 25 °C?

c. Compare the thermal velocity with the saturation velocity.

d. Compare the electron wavelength with the MOS channel length and with the gate-oxide thickness in a 0.25 μm process and a 0.1 μm process.

2.21 (Gallium arsenide, 5 min.) The electron mobility in GaAs is about $8500\,cm^2V^{-1}s^{-1}$; the hole mobility is about $400\,cm^2V^{-1}s^{-1}$. If we could make complementary *n*-channel and *p*-channel GaAs transistors (the same way that we do in a CMOS process) what would the ratio of a GaAs inverter be to equalize rise and fall times? About how much faster would you expect GaAs transistors to be than silicon for the same transistor sizes?

2.22 (Margaret of Anjou, 5 min.)

a. Why is it ones' complement but two's complement?

b. Why Queen's College, Belfast but Queens' College, Cambridge?

2.23 (Logic cell equations, 5 min.) Show that Eq. 2.31, 2.36, and 2.37 are correct.

2.24 (Carry-lookahead equations, 10 min.)

a. Derive the carry-lookahead equations for $i = 8$. Write them in the same form as Eq. 2.56.

b. Derive the equations for the Brent–Kung structure for $i = 8$.

2.25 (OAI cells, 20 min.) Draw a circuit schematic, including transistor sizes, for (a) an OAI321 cell, (b) an AOI321 cell. (c) Which do you think will be larger?

2.26 (**Making stipple patterns) Construct a set of black-and-white, transparent, 8-by-8 stipple patterns for a CMOS process in which we draw both well layers, the active layer, poly, and both diffusion implant layers separately. Consider only the layers up to m1 (but include m1 and the contact layer). One useful tool is the Apple Macintosh Control Panel, 'General Controls,' that changes the Mac desktop pattern.

a. (60 min.) Create a set of patterns with which you can detect any errors (for example, *n*-well and *p*-well overlap, or *n*-implant and *p*-implant overlap).

b. (60 min.+) Using a layout of an inverter as an example, find a set of patterns that allows you to trace transistors and connections (a very qualitative goal).

c. (Days+) Find a set of grayscale stipple patterns that allow you to produce layouts that "look nice" in a report (much, much harder than it sounds).

2.27 (AOI and OAI cells, 10 min.). Draw the circuit schematics for an AOI22 and an OAI22 cell. Clearly label each transistor as on or off for each cell for an input vector of (A1, A2, B1, B2) = (0101).

2.28 (Flip-flops and latches, 10 min.) In no more than 20 words describe the difference between a flip-flop and a latch.

2.29 (**An old argument) Should setup and hold times appear under maximum, minimum, or typical in a data sheet? (From Peter Alfke.)

2.30 (***Setup, 20 min.) "There is no such thing as a setup and hold time, just two setup times—for a '1' and for a '0'." Comment. (From Clemenz Portmann.)

2.31 (Subtracter, 20 min.) Show that you can rewrite the equations for a full subtracter (Eqs. 2.65–2.66) to be the same as a full adder—except that A is inverted in the borrow out equation, as follows:

$$DIFF = A \oplus B \oplus BIN = SUM(A, B, BIN) \tag{2.70}$$

$$BOUT = NOT(A) \cdot B + NOT(A) \cdot BIN + B \cdot BIN = MAJ(NOT(A), B, CIN) \tag{2.71}$$

Explain very carefully why we need to connect BIN[0] to VSS. Show that for a subtracter implemented by inverting the B input of an adder and setting CIN[0] = '1', the true overflow for ones' complement or two's complement representations is XOR(CIN[MSB], CIN[MSB – 1]). Does this hold for the above subtracter?

2.32 (Complex CMOS cells) Logic synthesis has completely changed the nature of combinational logic design. Synthesis tools like to see a huge selection of cells from which to choose in order to optimize speed or area.

a. (20 min.) How many AOI*nnnn* cells are there, if the maximum value of $n = 4$?

b. (30 min.) Consider cells of the form AOI*nnnn* where *n* can be negative—indicating a set of inputs are inverted. Thus, an AOI-22 (where the hyphen '-' indicates the following input is inverted) is a NOR(NOR(A, B), AND(C, D)), for example. How many logically different cells of the AOI*xxxx* family are there if *x* can be '-2', '-1', '1', or '2' with no more than four inputs? Remember the AOI family includes OAI, AO, and OA cells as well as just AOI. List them using an extension to the notation for a cell with mixed-sign inputs: for example, an AO(1-1)1 cell is NOT(NOR(AND(A, NOT(B)), C)). *Hint:* Be very careful because some cells with negative inputs are logically equivalent to others with positive inputs.

c. (10 min.) If we include NAND and NOR cells with inverting inputs in a library, how many different cells in the NAND family are there with four or fewer inputs (the NAND family includes NOR, AND, and OR cells)?

d. (30 min.) How many cells in the AOI and NAND families are there with four inputs or less that use fewer than eight transistors? Include cells that are logically equivalent but have different physical implementations. For example, a NAND1-1 cell, requiring six transistors, is logically equivalent to an OR1-1 cell that requires eight transistors. The OR1-1 implementation may be useful because the output inverter can easily be sized to produce an OR1-1 cell with higher drive.

e. (**60 min.) How many cells are there with fewer than four inputs that do not fit into the AOI or NAND families? *Hint:* There is an inverter, a buffer, a half-adder, and the three-input majority function, for example.

f. (***) Recommend a better, user-friendly, naming system (which is also CAD tool compatible) for combinational cells.

2.33 (**Design rules, 60 min.) A typical set of deep submicron CMOS design rules is shown in Table 2.16. Design rules are often confusing and use the following "buzz-words," perhaps to prevent others from understanding them.

The **end cap** is the extension of poly gate beyond the active or diffusion.

Overlap. Normally one material is completely contained within the other, overlap is then the amount of the "surround."

Extension refers to the extension of diffusion beyond the poly gate.

Same (in a spacing rule) means the space to the same type of diffusion or implant.

Opposite refers to the space to the opposite type of diffusion or implant.

A **dogbone** is the area surrounding a contact. Often the spacing to a dogbone contact is allowed be slightly less than to an isolated line.

Field is the area outside the active regions. The field oxide (sandwiched between the diffusion layers and the poly or m1 layers) is thicker than the gate oxide and separates transistors.

Exact refers to contacts that are all the same size to simplify fabrication.

A **butting contact** consists of two adjacent diffusions of the opposite type (connected with metal). This occurs when a well contact is placed next to a source contact.

Fat metal. Some design rules use different spacing for metal lines that are wider than a certain amount.

a. Draw a copy of the MOSIS rules as shown in Figure 2.11, but using the rule numbers and values in microns and λ from Table 2.16.

b. How compatible are the two sets of rules?

2.34 (ESD, 10 min.)

a. Explain carefully why a CMOS device can withstand a 2000 V ESD event when the gate breakdown voltage is only 5–10 V, but that shorting a device pin to a 10 V supply can destroy it.

b. Explain why an electric shock from a 240 VAC supply can kill you, but an 3000 VDC shock from a static charge (walking across a nylon carpet and touching a metal doorknob) only gives you a surprise.

2.35 (*Stacks in CMOS cells, 60 min.)

a. Given a CMOS cell of the form AOI*ijk* or OAI*ijk* ($i, j, k > 0$) derive an equation for the height (the number of transistors in series) and the width (the number of transistor in parallel) of the *n*-channel and *p*-channel stacks.

b. Suppose we increase the number of indices to four, i.e. AOI*ijkl*. How do your equations change?

TABLE 2.16   ASIC design rules (Problem 2.33). Absolute values in microns are given for $\lambda = 0.2\,\mu m$.

Layer	Rule[1]	μm	λ	Layer	Rule	μm	λ
nwell	N.1 width	2	10	implant	I.1 width	0.6	3
	N.2 sp. (same)	1	5		I.2 sp. (same)	0.6	3
diff	D.1 width	0.5	2.5		I.3 sp. to diff (same)	0.55	2.75
	D.2 transistor width	0.6	3		I.4 sp. to butting diff	0	0
	D.3 sp. (same)	0.6	3		I.4 ov. of diff	0.25	1.25
	D.4 sp. (opposite)	0.8	4		I.5 sp. to poly on active	0.5	2.5
	D.5 p+ (nwell) to n+ (pwell)	2.4	12		I.6 sp. (opposite)	0.3	1.5
	D.6 nwell ov. of n+	0.6	3		I.7 sp. to butting implant	0	0
	D.7 nwell sp. to p+	0.6	3	contact	C.1 size (exact)	0.4	2
	D.8 extension over gate	0.6	3		C.2 sp.	0.6	3
	D.9 nwell ov. of p+	1.2	6		C.3 poly ov.	0.3	1.5
	D.10 nwell sp. to p+	1.2	6		C.4 diff ov. (2 sides/others)	0.25/0.35	1.25/1.75
poly	P.1 width	0.4	2		C.5 metal ov.	0.25	1.25
	P.2 gate	0.4	2		C.6 sp. to poly	0.3	1.5
	P.3 sp. (over active)	0.6	3		C.7 poly contact to diff	0.5	2.5
	P.4 sp. (over field)	0.5	2.5	m1	Mn.1 width	0.6/0.7/1.0	3/3.5/4
	P.5 short sp. (dogbone)	0.45	2.25	+ m2/m3	Mn.2 sp. (fat > 25λ is 5λ)	0.6/0.7/1.0	3/3.5/4
	P.6 end cap	0.45	2.25		Mn.3 sp. (dogbone)	0.5	2.5
	P.7 sp. to diffusion	0.2	1	v1	Vn.1 size (exact)	0.4	2
				+v2/v3	Vn.2 sp.	0.8	4
					Vn.3 metal ov.	0.25	1.25

[1]sp. = space; ov. = overlap; same = same diffusion or implant type; opposite = opposite implant or diffusion type; diff = p+ or n+; p+ = p+ diffusion; n+ = n+ diffusion; implant = p+ or n+ implant select.

      c. If the stack height cannot be greater than three, which three-index AOI*ijk* and OAI*ijk* cells are illegal? Often limiting the stack height to three or four is a design rule for **radiation-hard** libraries—useful for satellites.

    2.36 (Duals, 20 min.) Draw the *n*-channel stack (including device sizes, assuming a ratio of 2) that complements the *p*-channel stack shown in Figure 2.37.

      2.37 (***FPGA conditional-sum adder, days+) A Xilinx application-note (M. Klein, "Conditional sum adder adds 16 bits in 33 ns," Xilinx Application Brief, Xilinx data book, 1992, p. 6-26) describes a 16-bit conditional-sum adder using 41 CLBs in three stages of addition; see also [Sklansky, 1960]. A Xilinx XC3000 or

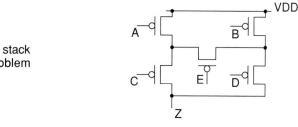

FIGURE 2.37 A *p*-channel stack using a bridge device, E (Problem 2.36).

XC4000 CLB can perform any logic function of five variables, or two functions of (the same) four variables. Can you find a solution with fewer CLBs in three stages? *Hint:* R. P. Halverson of the University of Hawaii produced a solution with 36 CLBs.

2.38 (Encoding, 10 min.) Booth's algorithm was suggested by a shortcut used by operators of decimal calculating machines that required turning a handle. To multiply 5 by 23 you set the levers to 5 and turned the handle three times, change gears and turn twice more.

a. What is the equivalent of $1\bar{4}\bar{2}\bar{3}4\bar{3}$?

b. How many turns do we save using the shortcut?

2.39 (CSD, 20 min.)

a. Show how to convert 1010111 (decimal 87) to the CSD vector $10\bar{1}0\bar{1}00\bar{1}$.

b. Convert 1000101 to the CSD vector.

c. How do you know that $1\bar{1}10011\bar{1}$ (decimal 101) is not the CSD vector representation of 1100101 (decimal 101)?

2.11   Bibliography

The topics of this chapter are covered in more detail in Weste and Eshraghian [1993]. The simulator SPICE was developed at UC Berkeley and now has many commercial derivatives including Meta Software's HSPICE and Microsim's PSpice. Mead [1989] gives a description of MOS transistor operation in the subthreshold region of operation. Muller and Kamins provide an introduction to device physics [1977 and 1986]. Sze [1988]; Chang and Sze [1996]; and Campbell [1996] cover process technology in detail at an advanced level. Rabaey [1996] describes full-custom CMOS datapath circuit design, Chandrakasan and Brodersen [1995] describe low-power datapath design. Books by Brodersen [1992] and Gajski [1988] cover silicon compilers. Mukherjee [1986] covers CMOS process and fabrication issues at an introductory level. Texts on analog ASIC design include Haskard and May [1988], and Trontelj [1989]. J. Y. Chen [1990] and Uyemura [1992] provide an analysis of combinational and sequential logic design. The book by Diaz [1995] contains hard to find material on I/O cell design for ESD protection. The patent literature is the only source for often proprietary high-speed and quiet I/O design. Wakerly [1994] and Katz [1994] are basic references for CMOS logic design (including sequential logic and binary arithmetic) though they emphasize PLDs rather than ASICs. Advanced material on computer arithmetic can be found in books by Hwang [1979]; Waser and Flynn [1982]; Cavanagh [1984]; and C. H. Chen [1992].

A large number of papers on digital arithmetic were published in the 1960s. In ASIC design we work at the architectural level and not at the transistor level and so this early work is useful. Many of these early papers appeared in the *IRE Transactions on Computers* that changed to *IRE Transactions on Electronic Computers* (ISSN 0367-7508, 1963–67) and then to the *IEEE Transactions on Computers* (ISSN 0018-9340, 1967–). A series of important papers on multipliers appeared in *Alta Frequenza* (ISSN 0002-6557, 1932–89; ISSN 1120-1908, 1989–) [Dadda, 1965; Dadda and Ferrari, 1968]. Copies of these papers may be obtained through interlibrary loans (in the United States from Texas A&M library, for example). The two volumes by Swartzlander [1990] contain reprints of some of these articles. Ranganathan [1993] contains reprints of more recent articles. Papers on CMOS logic and arithmetic may be found in the reports of the following conferences: *Proceedings of the Symposium on Computer Arithmetic* (QA76.9.C62.S95a, ISSN 1063-6889), *IEEE International Conference on Computer Design* (TK7888.4.I35a, ISSN 1063-6404), and the *IEEE International Solid-State Circuits Conference* (TK7870.I58; ISSN 0074-8587, 1960-68; ISSN 0193-6530, 1969–). Papers on arithmetic and algorithms that are more theoretical in nature can be found in the *Journal of the Association of Computing Machinery*. Online ACM journal articles can be found at http://www.acm.org.

2.12 References

Page numbers in brackets after a reference indicate its location in the chapter body.

Bedrij, O. 1962. "Carry select adder." *IRE Transactions on Electronic Computers,* vol. 11, pp. 340–346. Original reference to carry-select adder. See also [Weste, 1993] p. 532. [p. 83]

Booth, A. 1951. "A signed binary multiplication technique." *Quarterly Journal of Mechanics and Applied Mathematics,* vol. 4, pt. 2, pp. 236–240. Original reference for the Booth-encoded multiplier. See also Swartzlander [1990] and Weste [1993, pp. 547–554]. [p. 90]

Brent, R., and H. T. Kung. 1982. "A regular layout for parallel adders." *IEEE Transactions on Computers,* vol. 31, no. 3, pp. 260–264. Describes a regular carry-lookahead adder. [p. 83]

Brodersen, R. (Ed.). 1992. *Anatomy of a Silicon Compiler.* Boston: Kluwer, 362 p. ISBN 0-7923-9249-3. TK7874.A59.

Campbell, S. 1996. *The Science and Engineering of Microelectronic Fabrication.* New York: Oxford University Press, 536 p. ISBN 0-19-510508-7. TK7871.85.C25. [p. 113]

Cavanagh, J. J. F. 1984. *Digital Computer Arithmetic Design and Implementation.* New York: McGraw-Hill, 468 p. QA76.9.C62.C38. ISBN 0070102821.

Chandrakasan A. P., and R. Brodersen. 1995. *Low Power Digital CMOS Design.* Boston: Kluwer, 424 p. ISBN 0-7923-9576-X. TK7871.99.M44C43.

Chang, C. Y., and S. M. Sze. 1996. *ULSI Technology.* New York: McGraw-Hill, 726 p. ISBN 0070630623.

Chen, C. H. (Ed.). 1992. *Computer Engineering Handbook.* New York: McGraw-Hill. ISBN 0-07-010924-9. TK7888.3.C652. Chapter 4, "Computer arithmetic," by E. E. Swartzlander, pp. 20, contains descriptions of adder, multiplier, and divider architectures.

Chen, J. Y. 1990. *CMOS Devices and Technology for VLSI.* Englewood Cliffs, NJ: Prentice-Hall, 348 p. ISBN 0-13-138082-6. TK7874.C523.

Dadda, L. 1965. "Some schemes for parallel multipliers."*Alta Frequenza,* vol. 34, pp. 349–356. The original reference to the Dadda multiplier. This paper contains some errors in the diagrams for the multipliers; some remain in the reprint in Swartzlander [1990, vol. 1]. See also sequel papers: L. Dadda and D. Ferrari, "Digital multipliers: a unified approach,"*Alta Frequenza,* vol. 37, pp. 1079–1086, 1968; and L. Dadda, "On parallel digital multipliers,"*Alta Frequenza,* vol. 45, pp. 574–580, 1976. [p. 90]

Denyer, P. B., and D. Renshaw. 1985. *VLSI Signal Processing: A Bit-Serial Approach.* Reading, MA: Addison-Wesley, 312 p. ISBN 0201144042. TK7874.D46. See also P. B. Denyer and S. G. Smith, *Serial-Data Computation.* Boston: Kluwer, 1988, 239 p. ISBN 089838253X. TK7874.S623. [p. 86]

Diaz, C. H., et al. 1995. *Modeling of Electrical Overstress in Integrated Circuits.* Norwell, MA: Kluwer Academic, 148 p. ISBN 0-7923-9505-0. TK7874.D498. Includes 101 references. Introduction to ESD problems and models.

Ferrari, D., and R. Stefanelli. 1969. "Some new schemes for parallel multipliers." *Alta Frequenza,* vol. 38, pp. 843–852. The original reference for the Ferrari–Stefanelli multiplier. Describes the use of 2-bit and 3-bit submultipliers to generate the product array. Contains tables showing the number of stages and delay for different configurations. [p. 92]

Gajski, D. D. (Ed.). 1988. *Silicon Compilation.* Reading, MA: Addison-Wesley, 450 p. ISBN 0-201-109915-2. TK7874.S52.

Goldberg, D. 1990. "Computer arithmetic." In D. A. Patterson and J. L. Hennessy,*Computer Architecture: A Quantitative Approach.* San Mateo, CA: Morgan Kaufmann, 2nd ed., 1995. QA76.9.A73. P377. ISBN 1-55860-329-8. See also the first edition of this book (1990).

Haskard, M. R., and I. C. May. 1988. *Analog VLSI Design: nMOS and CMOS.* Englewood Cliffs, NJ: Prentice-Hall, 243 p. ISBN 0-13-032640-2. TK7874.H392.

Hwang, K. 1979. *Computer Arithmetic: Principles, Architecture, and Design.* New York: Wiley, 423 p. ISBN 0471034967. TK7888.3.H9.

Katz, R. H., 1994. *Contemporary Logic Design.* Reading, MA: Addison-Wesley, 699 p. ISBN 0-8053-2703-7.

Keutzer, K., S. Malik, and A. Saldanha. 1991. "Is redundancy necessary to reduce delay?"*IEEE Transactions on Computer-Aided Design,* vol. 10, no. 4, pp. 427–435. Describes the carry-skip adder. The paper describes the redundant logic that is added in a carry-skip adder and how to remove it without changing the function or delay of the circuit. [p. 82]

Lehman, M., and N. Burla. 1961. "Skip techniques for high-speed carry-propagation in binary arithmetic units." *IRE Transactions on Electronic Computers,* vol. 10, pp. 691–698. Original reference to carry-skip adder. [p. 82]

MacSorley, O. L. 1961. "High speed arithmetic in binary computers."*IRE Proceedings,* vol. 49, pp. 67–91. Early reference to carry-lookahead adder. Reprinted in Swartzlander [1990, vol. 1]. See also Weste [1993, pp. 526–529]. [p. 83]

Mead, C. A. 1989. *Analog VLSI and Neural Systems.* Reading, MA: Addison-Wesley, p.371. ISBN 0-201-05992-4. QA76.5.M39. Includes a description of MOS device operation.

Muller, R. S., and T. I. Kamins. 1977. *Device Electronics for Integrated Circuits.* New York: Wiley, p. 404. ISBN 0-471-62364-4. TK7871.85.M86. See also the second edition of this book (1986).

Mukherjee, A. 1986. *Introduction to nMOS and CMOS VLSI Systems Design.* Englewood Cliffs, NJ: Prentice-Hall, 370 p. ISBN 0-13-490947-X. TK7874.M86.

Rabaey, J. 1996. *Digital Integrated Circuits: A Design Perspective.* Englewood Cliffs, NJ: Prentice-Hall, pp. 700. ISBN 0-13-178609-1. TK7874.65.R33. Chapters 4 and 7 describe the design of full-custom CMOS datapath circuits.

Ranganathan, N. (Ed.). 1993. *VLSI Algorithms and Architectures: Fundamentals.* New York: IEEE Press, 305 p. ISBN 0-8186-4390-0. TK7874.V5554. See also N. Ranganathan (Ed.), 1993. *VLSI Algorithms and Architectures: Advanced Concepts.* New York: IEEE Press, 303 p. ISBN 0-8186-4400-1. TK7874.V555. Collections of articles mostly from *Computer* and *IEEE Transactions on Computers.*

Sato, T., et al. 1992. "An 8.5 ns 112-b transmission gate adder with a conflict-free bypass circuit." *IEEE Journal of Solid-State Circuits,* vol. 27, no. 4, pp. 657–659. Describes an implementation of a carry-bypass adder. [p. 81]

Sklansky, J. 1960. "Conditional-sum addition logic." *IRE Transactions on Electronic Computers,* vol. 9, pp. 226–231. Original reference to conditional-sum adder. Several texts have propagated an error in the spelling of Sklansky (two k's). See also [Weste, 1993] pp. 532–533; A. Rothermel et al., "Realization of transmission-gate conditional (TGCS) adders with low latency time," *IEEE Journal of Solid-State Circuits,* vol. 24, no. 3, 1989, pp. 558–561; each of these are examples of adders based on Sklansky's design. [p. 83]

Swartzlander, E. E., Jr. 1990. *Computer Arithmetic.* Los Alamitos, CA: IEEE Computer Society Press, vols. 1 and 2. ISBN 0818689315 (vol. 1). QA76.6.C633. Volume 1 is a reprint (originally published: Stroudsberg, PA: Dowden, Hutchinson & Ross). Volume 2 is a sequel. Contains reprints of many of the early (1960–1970) journal articles on adder and multiplier architectures.

Sze, S. (Ed.). 1988. *VLSI Technology.* New York: McGraw-Hill, 676 p. ISBN 0-07-062735-5. TK7874.V566. Edited book on fabrication technology.

Trontelj, J., et al. 1989. *Analog Digital ASIC Design.* New York: McGraw-Hill, 249 p. ISBN 0-07-707300-2. TK7874.T76.

Uyemura, J. P. 1992. *Circuit Design for CMOS VLSI.* Boston: Kluwer, 450 p. ISBN 0-7923-9184-5. TK7874.U93. See also: J. P. Uyemura, 1988, *Fundamentals of MOS Digital Integrated Circuits,* Reading, MA: Addison-Wesley, 624 p. ISBN 0-201-13318-0. TK7874.U94. Includes basic circuit equations related to NMOS and CMOS logic design.

Wakerly, J. F. 1994. *Digital Design: Principles and Practices.* 2nd ed. Englewood Cliffs, NJ: Prentice-Hall, 840 p. ISBN 0-13-211459-3. TK7874.65.W34. Undergraduate level introduction to logic design covering: binary arithmetic, CMOS and TTL, combinational logic, PLDs, sequential logic, memory, and the IEEE standard logic symbols.

Wallace, C. S. 1960. "A suggestion for a fast multiplier." *IEEE Transactions on Electronic Computers,* vol. 13, pp. 14–17. Original reference to Wallace-tree multiplier. Reprinted in Swartzlander [1990, vol. 1]. [p. 90]

Waser, S., and M. J. Flynn. 1982. *Introduction to Arithmetic for Digital Systems Designers.* New York: Holt, Rinehart, and Winston, 308 p. ISBN 0030605717. TK7895.A65.W37. [p. 114]

Weste, N. H. E., and K. Eshraghian. 1993. *Principles of CMOS VLSI Design: A Systems Perspective.* 2nd ed. Reading, MA: Addison-Wesley, 713 p. ISBN 0-201-53376-6. TK7874.W46. Chapter 5 covers CMOS logic gate design. Chapter 8 covers datapath elements. See also the first edition of this book. [p. 81]

ASIC LIBRARY DESIGN

Once we have decided to use an ASIC design style—using predefined and precharacterized cells from a library—we need to design or buy a cell library. Even though it is not necessary a knowledge of ASIC library design makes it easier to use library cells effectively.

3.1   Transistors as Resistors

In Section 2.1, "CMOS Transistors," we modeled transistors using ideal switches. If this model were accurate, logic cells would have no delay.

The ramp input, v(in1), to the inverter in Figure 3.1(a) rises quickly from zero to V_{DD}. In response the output, v(out1), falls from V_{DD} to zero. In Figure 3.1(b) we measure the **propagation delay** of the inverter, t_{PD}, using an input trip point of 0.5 and output trip points of 0.35 (falling, t_{PDf}) and 0.65 (rising, t_{PDr}). Initially the n-channel transistor, m1, is *off*. As the input rises, m1 turns *on* in the saturation region ($V_{DS} > V_{GS} - V_{tn}$) before entering the linear region ($V_{DS} < V_{GS} - V_{tn}$). We model transistor m1 with a resistor, R_{pd} (Figure 3.1c); this is the **pull-down resistance**. The equivalent resistance of m2 is the **pull-up resistance**, R_{pu}.

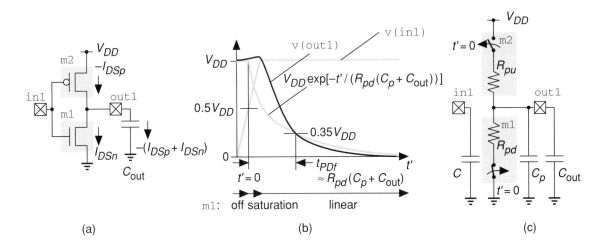

FIGURE 3.1 A model for CMOS logic delay. (a) A CMOS inverter with a load capacitance, C_{out}. (b) Input, v(in1), and output, v(out1), waveforms showing the definition of the falling propagation delay, t_{PDf}. In this case delay is measured from the input trip point of 0.5. The output trip points are 0.35 (falling) and 0.65 (rising). The model predicts $t_{PDf} \approx R_{pd}(C_p + C_{out})$. (c) The model for the inverter includes: the input capacitance, C; the pull-up resistance (R_{pu}) and pull-down resistance (R_{pd}); and the parasitic output capacitance, C_p.

Delay is created by the pull-up and pull-down resistances, R_{pd} and R_{pu}, together with the parasitic capacitance at the output of the cell, C_p (the **intrinsic output capacitance**) and the **load capacitance** (or **extrinsic output capacitance**), C_{out} (Figure 3.1c). If we assume a constant value for R_{pd}, the output reaches a lower trip point of 0.35 when (Figure 3.1b),

$$0.35V_{DD} = V_{DD}\exp\left[\frac{-t_{PDf}}{R_{pd}(C_{out} + C_p)}\right]. \tag{3.1}$$

An output trip point of 0.35 is convenient because $\ln(1/0.35) = 1.04 \approx 1$ and thus

$$t_{PDf} = R_{pd}(C_{out} + C_p)\ln\left(\frac{1}{0.35}\right) \approx R_{pd}(C_{out} + C_p). \tag{3.2}$$

The expression for the rising delay (with a 0.65 output trip point) is identical in form. Delay thus increases linearly with the load capacitance. We often measure load capacitance in terms of a **standard load**—the input capacitance presented by a particular cell (often an inverter or two-input NAND cell).

We may adjust the delay for different trip points. For example, for output trip points of 0.1/0.9 we multiply Eq. 3.2 by $-\ln(0.1) = 2.3$, because $\exp(-2.3) = 0.100$.

Figure 3.2 shows the DC characteristics of a CMOS inverter. To form Figure 3.2(b) we take the n-channel transistor surface (Figure 2.4b) and add that for a p-channel transistor (rotated to account for the connections). Seen from above, the intersection of the two surfaces is the static transfer curve of Figure 3.2(a)—along this path the transistor currents are equal and there is no output current to change the output voltage. Seen from one side, the intersection is the curve of Figure 3.2(c).

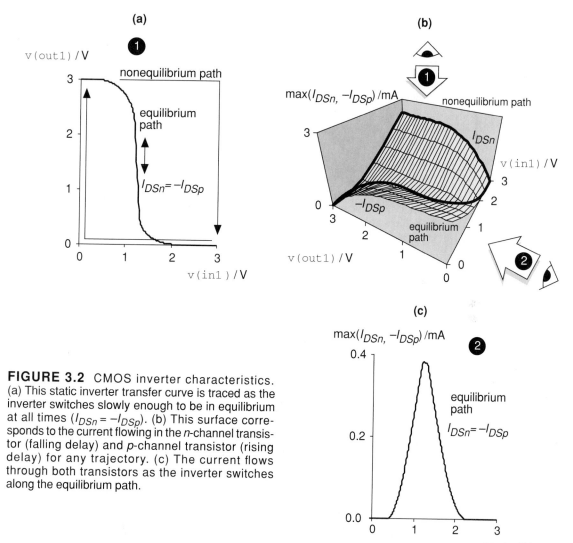

FIGURE 3.2 CMOS inverter characteristics. (a) This static inverter transfer curve is traced as the inverter switches slowly enough to be in equilibrium at all times ($I_{DSn} = -I_{DSp}$). (b) This surface corresponds to the current flowing in the n-channel transistor (falling delay) and p-channel transistor (rising delay) for any trajectory. (c) The current flows through both transistors as the inverter switches along the equilibrium path.

The input waveform, v(in1), and the output load (which determines the transistor currents) dictate the path we take on the surface of Figure 3.2(b) as the inverter switches. We can thus see that the currents through the transistors (and thus the pull-up and pull-down resistance values) will vary in a nonlinear way during switching. Deriving theoretical values for the pull-up and pull-down resistance values is difficult—instead we work the problem backward by picking the trip points, simulating the propagation delays, and then calculating resistance values that fit the model.

Figure 3.3 shows a simulation experiment (using the G5 process SPICE parameters from Table 2.1). From the results in Figure 3.3(c) we can see that $R_{pd} = 817\,\Omega$ and $R_{pu} = 1281\,\Omega$ for this inverter (with shape factors of 6/0.6 for the n-channel transistor and 12/0.6 for the p-channel) using 0.5 (input) and 0.35/0.65 (output) trip points. Changing the trip points would give different resistance values.

We can check that $817\,\Omega$ is a reasonable value for the pull-down resistance. In the saturation region $I_{DS(sat)}$ is (to first order) independent of V_{DS}. For an n-channel transistor from our generic 0.5 µm process (G5 from Section 2.1) with shape factor $W/L = 6/0.6$, $I_{DSn(sat)} = 2.5\,\text{mA}$ (at $V_{GS} = 3V$ and $V_{DS} = 3V$). The pull-down resistance, R_1, that would give the same drain–source current is

$$R_1 = 3.0\text{V}/(2.5 \times 10^{-3}\text{A}) = 1200\,\Omega. \qquad (3.3)$$

This value is greater than, but not too different from, our measured pull-down resistance of $817\,\Omega$. We might expect this result since Figure 3.2b shows that the pull-down resistance reaches its maximum value at $V_{GS} = 3V$, $V_{DS} = 3V$. We could adjust the ratio of the logic so that the rising and falling delays were equal; then $R = R_{pd} = R_{pu}$ is the **pull resistance**.

Next, we check our model against the simulation results. The model predicts

$$\text{v(out1)} \approx V_{DD}\exp\frac{-t'}{R_{pd}(C_{out} + C_p)} \quad \text{for } t' > 0 \qquad (3.4)$$

(t' is measured from the point at which the input crosses the 0.5 trip point, $t' = 0$ at $t = 20\,\text{ps}$). With $C_p = 4$ standard loads $= 4 \times 0.034\,\text{pF} = 0.136\,\text{pF}$,

$$R_{pd}(C_{out} + C_p) = (38 + 817(0.136))\,\text{ps} = 149.112\,\text{ps}. \qquad (3.5)$$

To make a comparison with the simulation we need to use $\ln(1/0.35) = 1.04$ and not approximately 1 as we have assumed, so that (with all times in ps)

$$\text{v(out1)} \approx 3.0\exp\left[\frac{-t'}{149.112/1.04}\right]\text{V} = 3.0\exp\left[\frac{-(t-20)}{143.4}\right]\text{V} \quad \text{for } t > 20\,\text{ps}. \qquad (3.6)$$

Equation 3.6 is plotted in Figure 3.3(d). For v(out1) = 1.05 V (equal to the 0.35 output trip point), Eq. 3.6 predicts $t = 20 + 149.112 \approx 169\,\text{ps}$ and agrees with Figure 3.3(b)—it should because we derived the model from these results!

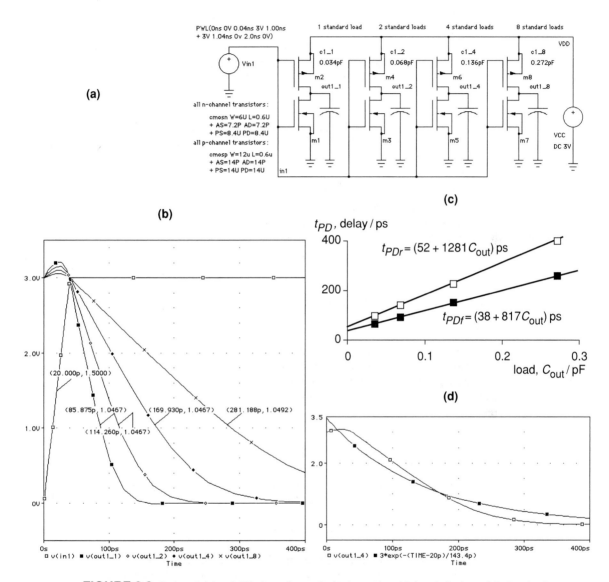

FIGURE 3.3 Delay. (a) LogicWorks schematic for inverters driving 1, 2, 4, and 8 standard loads (1 standard load = 0.034 pF in this case). (b) Transient response (falling delay only) from PSpice. The postprocessor Probe was used to mark each waveform as it crosses its trip point (0.5 for the input, 0.35 for the outputs). For example $v(out1\_4)$ (4 standard loads) crosses 1.0467 V ($\approx 0.35 V_{DD}$) at $t = 169.93$ ps. (c) Falling and rising delays as a function of load. The slopes in pspF^{-1} corresponds to the pull-up resistance (1281 Ω) and pull-down resistance (817 Ω). (d) Comparison of the delay model (valid for $t > 20$ ps) and simulation (4 standard loads). Both are equal at the 0.35 trip point.

Now we find C_p. From Figure 3.3(c) and Eq. 3.2

$$t_{PDr} = (52 + 1281C_{out}) \, \text{ps} \Rightarrow C_{pr} = 52/1281 = 0.041 \, \text{pF} \qquad \text{(rising)}$$

$$t_{PDf} = (38 + 817C_{out}) \, \text{ps} \Rightarrow C_{pf} = 38/817 = 0.047 \, \text{pF} \qquad \text{(falling)} \qquad (3.7)$$

These intrinsic parasitic capacitance values depend on the choice of output trip points, even though $C_{pf}R_{pdf}$ and $C_{pr}R_{pdr}$ are constant for a given input trip point and waveform, because the pull-up and pull-down resistances depend on the choice of output trip points. We take a closer look at parasitic capacitance next.

3.2   Transistor Parasitic Capacitance

Logic cell delay results from transistor resistance, transistor (intrinsic) parasitic capacitance, and load (extrinsic) capacitance. When one logic cell drives another, the parasitic input capacitance of the driven cell becomes the load capacitance of the driving cell and this will determine the delay of the driving cell.

Figure 3.4 shows the components of transistor parasitic capacitance. SPICE prints all of the MOS parameter values for each transistor at the DC operating point. The following values were printed by PSpice (v5.4) for the simulation of Figure 3.3:

NAME	m1	m2
MODEL	CMOSN	CMOSP
ID	7.49E-11	-7.49E-11
VGS	0.00E+00	-3.00E+00
VDS	3.00E+00	-4.40E-08
VBS	0.00E+00	0.00E+00
VTH	4.14E-01	-8.96E-01
VDSAT	3.51E-02	-1.78E+00
GM	1.75E-09	2.52E-11
GDS	1.24E-10	1.72E-03
GMB	6.02E-10	7.02E-12
CBD	2.06E-15	1.71E-14
CBS	4.45E-15	1.71E-14
CGSOV	1.80E-15	2.88E-15
CGDOV	1.80E-15	2.88E-15
CGBOV	2.00E-16	2.01E-16
CGS	0.00E+00	1.10E-14
CGD	0.00E+00	1.10E-14
CGB	3.88E-15	0.00E+00

The parameters ID (I_{DS}), VGS, VDS, VBS, VTH (V_t), and VDSAT ($V_{DS(sat)}$) are DC parameters. The parameters GM, GDS, and GMB are small-signal conductances (corresponding to $\partial I_{DS}/\partial V_{GS}$, $\partial I_{DS}/\partial V_{DS}$, and $\partial I_{DS}/\partial V_{BS}$, respectively). The

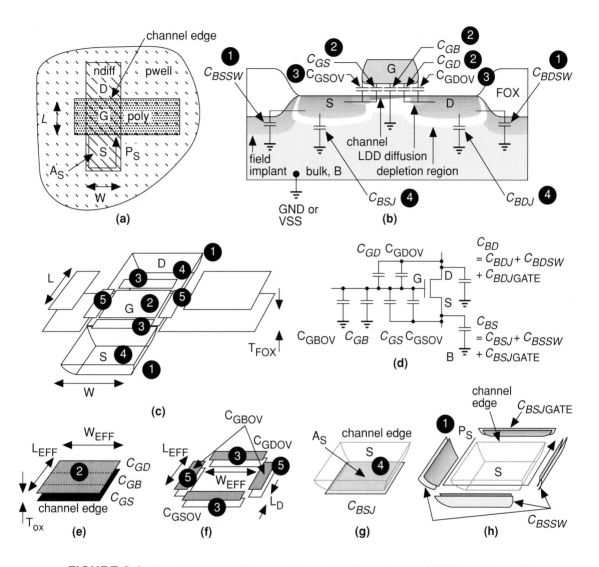

FIGURE 3.4 Transistor parasitic capacitance. (a) An *n*-channel MOS transistor with (drawn) gate length L and width W. (b) The gate capacitance is split into: the constant overlap capacitances C_{GSOV}, C_{GDOV}, and C_{GBOV} and the variable capacitances C_{GS}, C_{GB}, and C_{GD}, which depend on the operating region. (c) A view showing how the different capacitances are approximated by planar components (T_{FOX} is the field-oxide thickness). (d) C_{BS} and C_{BD} are the sum of the area (C_{BSJ}, C_{BDJ}), sidewall (C_{BSSW}, C_{BDSW}), and channel edge ($C_{BSJGATE}$, $C_{BDJGATE}$) capacitances. (e)–(f) The dimensions of the gate, overlap, and sidewall capacitances (L_D is the lateral diffusion).

remaining parameters are the parasitic capacitances. Table 3.1 shows the calculation of these capacitance values for the n-channel transistor m1 (with $W = 6\,\mu m$ and $L = 0.6\,\mu m$) in Figure 3.3(a).

3.2.1   Junction Capacitance

The junction capacitances, C_{BD} and C_{BS}, consist of two parts: junction area and sidewall; both have different physical characteristics with parameters: CJ and MJ for the junction, CJSW and MJSW for the sidewall, and PB is common. These capacitances depend on the voltage across the junction (V_{DB} and V_{SB}). The calculations in Table 3.1 assume both source and drain regions are $6\,\mu m \times 1.2\,\mu m$ rectangles, so that $A_D = A_S = 7.2\,(\mu m)^2$, and the perimeters (excluding the $1.2\,\mu m$ channel edge) are $P_D = P_S = 6 + 1.2 + 1.2 = 8.4\,\mu m$. We exclude the channel edge because the sidewalls facing the channel (corresponding to $C_{BSJGATE}$ and $C_{BDJGATE}$ in Figure 3.4) are different from the sidewalls that face the field. There is no standard method to allow for this. It is a mistake to exclude the gate edge assuming it is accounted for in the rest of the model—it is not. A pessimistic simulation includes the channel edge in P_D and P_S (but a true worst-case analysis would use more accurate models and worst-case model parameters). In HSPICE there is a separate mechanism to account for the channel edge capacitance (using parameters ACM and CJGATE). In Table 3.1 we have neglected C_{JGATE}.

For the p-channel transistor m2 ($W = 12\,\mu m$ and $L = 0.6\,\mu m$) the source and drain regions are $12\,\mu m \times 1.2\,\mu m$ rectangles, so that $A_D = A_S \approx 14\,(\mu m)^2$, and the perimeters are $P_D = P_S = 12 + 1.2 + 1.2 \approx 14\,\mu m$ (these parameters are rounded to two significant figures solely to simplify the figures and tables).

In passing, notice that a $1.2\,\mu m$ strip of diffusion in a $0.6\,\mu m$ process ($\lambda = 0.3\,\mu m$) is only 4λ wide—wide enough to place a contact only with aggressive spacing rules. The conservative rules in Figure 2.11 would require a diffusion width of at least 2 (rule 6.4a) + 2 (rule 6.3a) + 1.5 (rule 6.2a) = 5.5λ.

3.2.2   Overlap Capacitance

The overlap capacitance calculations for C_{GSOV} and C_{GDOV} in Table 3.1 account for lateral diffusion (the amount the source and drain extend under the gate) using SPICE parameter LD = 5E-08 or $L_D = 0.05\,\mu m$. Not all versions of SPICE use the equivalent parameter for width reduction, WD (assumed zero in Table 3.1), in calculating C_{GDOV} and not all versions subtract W_D to form W_{EFF}.

3.2.3   Gate Capacitance

The gate capacitance calculations in Table 3.1 depend on the operating region. The gate–source capacitance C_{GS} varies from zero when the transistor is off to $0.5C_O$ ($0.5 \times 1.035 \times 10^{-15} = 5.18 \times 10^{-16}\,F$) in the linear region to $(2/3)C_O$ in the saturation region ($6.9 \times 10^{-16}\,F$). The gate–drain capacitance C_{GD} varies from zero (off) to $0.5C_O$ (linear region) and back to zero (saturation region).

TABLE 3.1 Calculations of parasitic capacitances for an n-channel MOS transistor.

PSpice	Equation	Values[1] for $V_{GS} = 0V$, $V_{DS} = 3V$, $V_{SB} = 0V$
CBD	$C_{BD} = C_{BDJ} + C_{BDSW}$	$C_{BD} = 1.855 \times 10^{-15} + 2.04 \times 10^{-16} = 2.06 \times 10^{-15} F$
	$C_{BDJ} = A_D C_J (1 + V_{DB}/\phi_B)^{-m_J}$ $(\phi_B = \text{PB})$	$C_{BDJ} = (4.032 \times 10^{-15}) (1 + (3/1))^{-0.56}$ $= 1.8550983 \times 10^{-15} F$
	$C_{BDSW} = P_D C_{JSW} (1 + V_{DB}/\phi_B)^{-m_{JSW}}$ (P_D may or may not include channel edge)	$C_{BDSW} = (4.2 \times 10^{-16}) (1 + (3/1))^{-0.52}$ $= 2.0425754 \times 10^{-16} F$
CBS	$C_{BS} = C_{BSJ} + C_{BSSW}$	$C_{BS} = 4.032 \times 10^{-15} + 4.2 \times 10^{-16} = 4.452 \times 10^{-15} F$
	$C_{BSJ} = A_S C_J (1 + V_{SB}/\phi_B)^{-m_J}$	$A_S C_J = (7.2 \times 10^{-12}) (5.6 \times 10^{-4}) = 4.032 \times 10^{-15} F$
	$C_{BSSW} = P_S C_{JSW} (1 + V_{SB}/\phi_B)^{-m_{JSW}}$	$P_S C_{JSW} = (8.4 \times 10^{-6}) (5 \times 10^{-11}) = 4.2 \times 10^{-16} F$
CGSOV	$C_{GSOV} = W_{EFF} C_{GSO}$; $W_{EFF} = W - 2W_D$	$C_{GSOV} = (6 \times 10^{-6}) (3 \times 10^{-10}) = 1.8 \times 10^{-16} F$
CGDOV	$C_{GDOV} = W_{EFF} C_{GSO}$	$C_{GDOV} = (6 \times 10^{-6}) (3 \times 10^{-10}) = 1.8 \times 10^{-15} F$
CGBOV	$C_{GBOV} = L_{EFF} C_{GBO}$; $L_{EFF} = L - 2L_D$	$C_{GBOV} = (0.5 \times 10^{-6}) (4 \times 10^{-10}) = 2 \times 10^{-16} F$
CGS	$C_{GS}/C_O = 0 \text{ (off)}, 0.5 \text{ (lin.)}, 0.66 \text{ (sat.)}$ $C_O \text{(oxide capacitance)} = \dfrac{W_{EFF} L_{EFF} \varepsilon_{ox}}{T_{ox}}$	$C_O = (6 \times 10^{-6}) (0.5 \times 10^{-6}) (0.00345)$ $= 1.035 \times 10^{-14} F.$ $C_{GS} = 0.0F$
CGD	$C_{GD}/C_O = 0 \text{ (off)}, 0.5 \text{ (lin.)}, \approx 0 \text{ (sat.)}$	$C_{GD} = 0.0F$
CGB	$C_{GB} = 0 \text{ (on)}, \approx C_O \text{ in series with } C_S \text{ (off)}$	$C_{GB} = 3.88 \times 10^{-15} F$, $C_S = \text{depletion capacitance}$

[1]Input
```
.MODEL CMOSN NMOS LEVEL=3 PHI=0.7 TOX=10E-09 XJ=0.2U TPG=1 VTO=0.65 DELTA=0.7
+ LD=5E-08 KP=2E-04 UO=550 THETA=0.27 RSH=2 GAMMA=0.6 NSUB=1.4E+17 NFS=6E+11
+ VMAX=2E+05 ETA=3.7E-02 KAPPA=2.9E-02 CGDO=3.0E-10 CGSO=3.0E-10 CGBO=4.0E-10
+ CJ=5.6E-04 MJ=0.56 CJSW=5E-11 MJSW=0.52 PB=1
m1  out1 in1 0 0 cmosn W=6U L=0.6U AS=7.2P AD=7.2P PS=8.4U PD=8.4U
```

The gate–bulk capacitance C_{GB} may be viewed as two capacitors in series: the fixed gate-oxide capacitance, $C_O = W_{EFF} L_{EFF} \varepsilon_{ox} / T_{ox}$, and the variable depletion capacitance, $C_S = W_{EFF} L_{EFF} \varepsilon_{Si} / x_d$, formed by the depletion region that extends under the gate (with varying depth x_d). As the transistor turns on the conducting channel appears and shields the bulk from the gate—and at this point C_{GB} falls to zero. Even with $V_{GS} = 0$ V, the depletion width under the gate is finite and thus $C_{GB} \approx 4 \times 10^{-15}$ F is less than $C_O \approx 10^{-16}$ F. In fact, since $C_{GB} \approx 0.5\, C_O$, we can tell that at $V_{GS} = 0$ V, $C_S \approx C_O$.

Figure 3.5 shows the variation of the parasitic capacitance values.

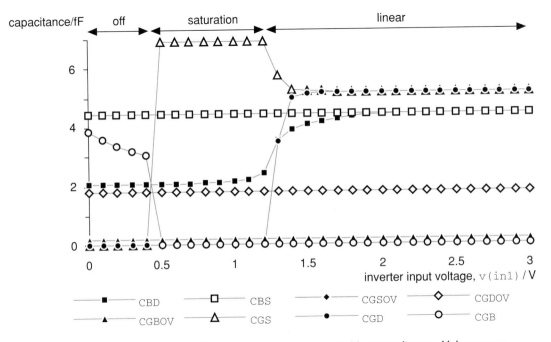

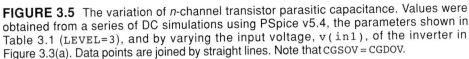

FIGURE 3.5 The variation of n-channel transistor parasitic capacitance. Values were obtained from a series of DC simulations using PSpice v5.4, the parameters shown in Table 3.1 (LEVEL=3), and by varying the input voltage, v(in1), of the inverter in Figure 3.3(a). Data points are joined by straight lines. Note that CGSOV = CGDOV.

3.2.4 Input Slew Rate

Figure 3.6 shows an experiment to monitor the input capacitance of an inverter as it switches. We have introduced another variable—the delay of the input ramp or the slew rate of the input.

In Figure 3.6(b) the input ramp is 40 ps long with a slew rate of 3 V/40 ps or 75 GVs^{-1}—as in our previous experiments—and the output of the inverter hardly moves before the input has changed. The input capacitance varies from 20 to 40 fF with an average value of approximately 34 fF for both transitions—we can measure the average value in Probe by plotting AVG(-i(Vin)).

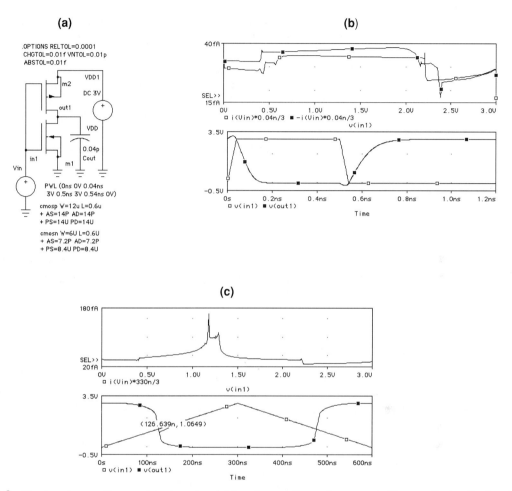

FIGURE 3.6 The input capacitance of an inverter. (a) Input capacitance is measured by monitoring the input current to the inverter, i(Vin). (b) Very fast switching. The current, i(Vin), is multiplied by the input ramp delay ($\Delta t = 0.04$ ns) and divided by the voltage swing ($\Delta V = V_{DD} = 3$ V) to give the equivalent input capacitance, $C = i\Delta t/\Delta V$. Thus an adjusted input current of 40 fA corresponds to an input capacitance of 40 fF. The current, i(Vin), is positive for the rising edge of the input and negative for the falling edge. (c) Very slow switching. The input capacitance is now equal for both transitions.

In Figure 3.6(c) the input ramp is slow enough (300 ns) that we are switching under almost equilibrium conditions—at each voltage we allow the output to find its level on the static transfer curve of Figure 3.2(a). The switching waveforms are quite different. The average input capacitance is now approximately 0.04 pF (a 20 percent difference). The propagation delay (using an input trip point of 0.5 and an output trip point of 0.35) is negative and approximately $150 - 127 = -23$ ns. By changing the input slew rate we have broken our model. For the moment we shall ignore this problem and proceed.

The calculations in Table 3.1 and behavior of Figures 3.5 and 3.6 are very complex. How can we find the value of the parasitic capacitance, C, to fit the model of Figure 3.1? Once again, as we did for pull resistance and the intrinsic output capacitance, instead of trying to derive a theoretical value for C, we adjust the value to fit the model. Before we formulate another experiment we should bear in mind the following questions that the experiment of Figure 3.6 raises: Is it valid to replace the nonlinear input capacitance with a linear component? Is it valid to use a linear input ramp when the normal waveforms are so nonlinear?

Figure 3.7 shows an experiment crafted to answer these questions. The experiment has the following two steps:

1. Adjust c2 to model the input capacitance of m5/6; then $C = c2 = 0.0335$ pF.

2. Remove all the parasitic capacitances for inverter m9/10—except for the gate capacitances C_{GS}, C_{GD}, and C_{GB}—and then adjust c3 (0.01 pF) and c4 (0.025 pF) to model the effect of these missing parasitics.

We can summarize our findings from this and previous experiments as follows:

1. Since the waveforms in Figure 3.7 match, we can model the input capacitance of a logic cell with a linear capacitor. However, we know the input capacitance may vary (by up to 20 percent in our example) with the input slew rate.

2. The input waveform to the inverter m3/m4 in Figure 3.7 is from another inverter—not a linear ramp. The difference in slew rate causes an error. The measured delay is 85 ps (0.085 ns), whereas our model (Eq. 3.7) predicts

$$t_{PDr} = (38 + 817C_{out}) \, \text{ps} = (38 + (817)(0.0335)) \, \text{ps} = 65 \, \text{ps} . \qquad (3.8)$$

3. The total gate-oxide capacitance in our inverter with $T_{ox} = 100$Å is

$$\begin{aligned}
C_O &= (W_n L_n + W_p L_p) \varepsilon_{ox} T_{ox} \\
&= (34.5 \times 10^{-4}) ((6)(0.6) + (12)(0.6)) \, \text{pF} = 0.037 \, \text{pF}.
\end{aligned} \qquad (3.9)$$

4. All the transistor parasitic capacitances excluding the gate capacitance contribute 0.01 pF of the 0.035 pF input capacitance—about 30 percent. The gate capacitances contribute the rest—0.025 pF (about 70 percent).

The last two observations are useful. Since the gate capacitances are nonlinear, we only see about 0.025/0.037 or 70 percent of the 0.037 pF gate-oxide capacitance, C_O, in the input capacitance, C. This means that it happens by chance that the total gate-oxide capacitance is also a rough estimate of the gate input capacitance, $C \approx C_O$. Using L and W rather than L_{EFF} and W_{EFF} in Eq. 3.9 helps this estimate. The accuracy of this estimate depends on the fact that the junction capacitances are approximately one-third of the gate-oxide capacitance—which happens to be true for many CMOS processes for the shapes of transistors that normally occur in logic cells. In the next section we shall use this estimate to help us design logic cells.

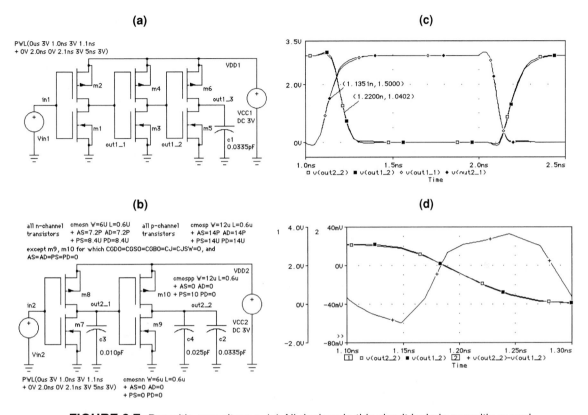

FIGURE 3.7 Parasitic capacitance. (a) All devices in this circuit include parasitic capacitance. (b) This circuit uses linear capacitors to model the parasitic capacitance of m9 / 10. The load formed by the inverter (m5 and m6) is modeled by a 0.0335 pF capacitor (c2); the parasitic capacitance due to the overlap of the gates of m3 and m4 with their source, drain, and bulk terminals is modeled by a 0.01 pF capacitor (c3); and the effect of the parasitic capacitance at the drain terminals of m3 and m4 is modeled by a 0.025 pF capacitor (c4). (c) The two circuits compared. The delay shown (1.22 − 1.135 = 0.085 ns) is equal to t_{PDf} for the inverter m3 / 4. (d) An exact match would have both waveforms equal at the 0.35 trip point (1.05 V).

3.3   Logical Effort

In this section we explore a delay model based on *logical effort*, a term coined by Ivan Sutherland and Robert Sproull [1991], that has as its basis the time-constant analysis of Carver Mead, Chuck Seitz, and others.

We add a "catch all" nonideal component of delay, t_q, to Eq. 3.2 that includes: (1) delay due to internal parasitic capacitance; (2) the time for the input to reach the switching threshold of the cell; and (3) the dependence of the delay on the slew rate of the input waveform. With these assumptions we can express the delay as follows:

$$t_{PD} = R(C_{out} + C_p) + t_q. \tag{3.10}$$

(The input capacitance of the logic cell is C, but we do not need it yet.)

We will use a standard-cell library for a 3.3 V, 0.5 μm (0.6 μm drawn) technology (from Compass) to illustrate our model. We call this technology **C5**; it is almost identical to the G5 process from Section 2.1 (the Compass library uses a more accurate and more complicated SPICE model than the generic process). The equation for the delay of a 1X drive, two-input NAND cell is in the form of Eq. 3.10 (C_{out} is in pF):

$$t_{PD} = (0.07 + 1.46C_{out} + 0.15) \text{ ns}. \tag{3.11}$$

The delay due to the intrinsic output capacitance (0.07 ns, equal to RC_p) and the nonideal delay ($t_q = 0.15$ ns) are specified separately. The nonideal delay is a considerable fraction of the total delay, so we may hardly ignore it. If data books do not specify these components of delay separately, we have to estimate the fractions of the constant part of a delay equation to assign to RC_p and t_q (here the ratio RC_p/t_q is approximately 2).

The data book tells us the input trip point is 0.5 and the output trip points are 0.35 and 0.65. We can use Eq. 3.11 to estimate the pull resistance for this cell as $R \approx 1.46$ nspF^{-1} or about 1.5 kΩ. Equation 3.11 is for the falling delay; the data book equation for the rising delay gives slightly different values (but within 10 percent of the falling delay values).

We can **scale** any logic cell by a scaling factor s (transistor gates become s times wider, but the gate lengths stay the same), and as a result the pull resistance R will decrease to R/s and the parasitic capacitance C_p will increase to sC_p. Since t_q is nonideal, by definition it is hard to predict how it will scale. We shall assume that t_q scales linearly with s for all cells. The total cell delay then scales as follows:

$$t_{PD} = \frac{R}{s}(C_{out} + sC_p) + st_q. \tag{3.12}$$

For example, the delay equation for a 2X drive ($s = 2$), two-input NAND cell is

$$t_{PD} = (0.03 + 0.75C_{out} + 0.51) \text{ ns}. \tag{3.13}$$

Compared to the 1X version (Eq. 3.11), the output parasitic delay has decreased to 0.03 ns (from 0.07 ns), whereas we predicted it would remain constant (the difference is because of the layout); the pull resistance has decreased by a factor of 2 from 1.5 kΩ to 0.75 kΩ, as we would expect; and the nonideal delay has increased to 0.51 ns (from 0.15 ns). The differences between our predictions and the actual values give us a measure of the model accuracy.

We rewrite Eq. 3.12 using the input capacitance of the scaled logic cell, $C_{in} = sC$,

$$t_{PD} = RC \left(\frac{C_{out}}{C_{in}} \right) + RC_p + st_q. \tag{3.14}$$

Finally we normalize the delay using the time constant formed from the pull resistance R_{inv} and the input capacitance C_{inv} of a minimum-size inverter:

$$d = \frac{(RC) \left(\dfrac{C_{out}}{C_{in}} \right) + RC_p + st_q}{\tau} = f + p + q. \tag{3.15}$$

The time constant **tau**,

$$\tau = R_{inv} C_{inv}, \tag{3.16}$$

is a basic property of any CMOS technology. We shall measure delays in terms of τ.

The delay equation for a 1X (minimum-size) inverter in the C5 library is

$$t_{PD} = (0.06 + 1.60 C_{out} + 0.10) \text{ ns}. \tag{3.17}$$

Thus $t_{qinv} = 0.1$ ns and $R_{inv} = 1.60$ kΩ. The input capacitance of the 1X inverter (the standard load for this library) is specified in the data book as $C_{inv} = 0.036$ pF; thus $\tau = (0.036 \text{ pF})(1.60 \text{ k}\Omega) = 0.06$ ns for the C5 technology.

The use of logical effort consists of rearranging and understanding the meaning of the various terms in Eq. 3.15. The delay equation is the sum of three terms,

$$d = f + p + q. \tag{3.18}$$

We give these terms special names as follows:

$$\text{delay} = \text{effort delay} + \text{parasitic delay} + \text{nonideal delay}. \tag{3.19}$$

The **effort delay** f we write as a product of logical effort, g, and electrical effort, h:

$$f = gh. \tag{3.20}$$

So we can further partition delay into the following terms:

$$\text{delay} = \text{logical effort} \times \text{electrical effort} + \text{parasitic delay} + \text{nonideal delay}. \tag{3.21}$$

The **logical effort** g is a function of the type of logic cell,

$$g = \frac{RC}{\tau}. \tag{3.22}$$

What size of logic cell do the R and C refer to? It does not matter because the R and C will change as we scale a logic cell, but the RC product stays the same—the logical effort is independent of the size of a logic cell. We can find the logical effort by scaling down the logic cell so that it has the same drive capability as the 1X minimum-size inverter. Then the logical effort, g, is the ratio of the input capacitance, C_{in}, of the 1X version of the logic cell to C_{inv} (see Figure 3.8).

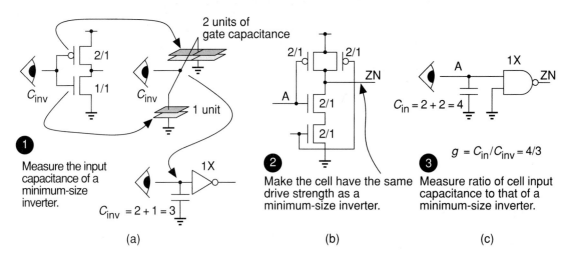

FIGURE 3.8 Logical effort. (a) The input capacitance, C_{inv}, looking into the input of a minimum-size inverter in terms of the gate capacitance of a minimum-size device. (b) Sizing a logic cell to have the same drive strength as a minimum-size inverter (assuming a logic ratio of 2). The input capacitance looking into one of the logic-cell terminals is then C_{in}. (c) The logical effort of a cell is C_{in}/C_{inv}. For a two-input NAND cell, the logical effort, $g = 4/3$.

The **electrical effort** h depends only on the load capacitance C_{out} connected to the output of the logic cell and the input capacitance of the logic cell, C_{in}; thus

$$h = \frac{C_{out}}{C_{in}}. \qquad (3.23)$$

The **parasitic delay** p depends on the intrinsic parasitic capacitance C_p of the logic cell, so that

$$p = \frac{RC_p}{\tau}. \qquad (3.24)$$

Table 3.2 shows the logical efforts for single-stage logic cells. Suppose the minimum-size inverter has an n-channel transistor with $W/L = 1$ and a p-channel transistor with $W/L = 2$ (logic ratio, r, of 2). Then each two-input NAND logic cell input is connected to an n-channel transistor with $W/L = 2$ and a p-channel transistor with $W/L = 2$. The input capacitance of the two-input NAND logic cell divided by that of the inverter is thus 4/3. This is the logical effort of a two-input NAND when $r = 2$. Logical effort depends on the ratio of the logic. For an n-input NAND cell

---

TABLE 3.2   Cell effort, parasitic delay, and nonideal delay (in units of τ) for single-stage CMOS cells.

Cell	Cell effort (logic ratio = 2)	Cell effort (logic ratio = r)	Parasitic delay/τ	Nonideal delay/τ
inverter	1 (by definition)	1 (by definition)	p_{inv} (by definition)[1]	q_{inv} (by definition)[1]
n-input NAND	$(n+2)/3$	$(n+r)/(r+1)$	$n\,p_{inv}$	$n\,q_{inv}$
n-input NOR	$(2n+1)/3$	$(nr+1)/(r+1)$	$n\,p_{inv}$	$n\,q_{inv}$

[1]For the Compass 0.5 µm technology (C5): $p_{inv} = 1.0$, $q_{inv} = 1.7$, $R_{inv} = 1.5\,k\Omega$, $C_{inv} = 0.036\,pF$.

---

with ratio r, the p-channel transistors are W/L = $r/1$, and the n-channel transistors are W/L = $n/1$. For a NOR cell the n-channel transistors are $1/1$ and the p-channel transistors are $nr/1$.

The parasitic delay arises from parasitic capacitance at the output node of a single-stage logic cell and most (but not all) of this is due to the source and drain capacitance. The parasitic delay of a minimum-size inverter is

$$p_{inv} = \frac{C_p}{C_{inv}}. \tag{3.25}$$

The parasitic delay is a constant, for any technology. For our C5 technology we know $RC_p = 0.06$ ns and, using Eq. 3.17 for a minimum-size inverter, we can calculate $p_{inv} = RC_p/\tau = 0.06/0.06 = 1$ (this is purely a coincidence). Thus C_p is about equal to C_{inv} and is approximately 0.036 pF. There is a large error in calculating p_{inv} from extracted delay values that are so small. Often we can calculate p_{inv} more accurately from estimating the parasitic capacitance from layout.

Because RC_p is constant, the parasitic delay is equal to the ratio of parasitic capacitance of a logic cell to the parasitic capacitance of a minimum-size inverter. In practice this ratio is very difficult to calculate—it depends on the layout. We can approximate the parasitic delay by assuming it is proportional to the sum of the widths of the n-channel and p-channel transistors connected to the output. Table 3.2 shows the parasitic delay for different cells in terms of p_{inv}.

The **nonideal delay** q is hard to predict and depends mainly on the physical size of the logic cell (proportional to the cell area in general, or width in the case of a standard cell or a gate-array macro),

$$q = \frac{st_q}{\tau}. \tag{3.26}$$

We define q_{inv} in the same way we defined p_{inv}. An n-input cell is approximately n times larger than an inverter, giving the values for nonideal delay shown in Table 3.2. For our C5 technology, from Eq. 3.17, $q_{inv} = t_{qinv}/\tau = 0.1\,\text{ns}/0.06\,\text{ns} = 1.7$.

3.3.1   Predicting Delay

As an example, let us predict the delay of a three-input NOR logic cell with 2X drive, driving a net with a fanout of four, with a total load capacitance (comprising the input capacitance of the four cells we are driving plus the interconnect) of 0.3 pF.

From Table 3.2 we see $p = 3p_{inv}$ and $q = 3q_{inv}$ for this cell. We can calculate C_{in} from the fact that the input gate capacitance of a 1X drive, three-input NOR logic cell is equal to gC_{inv}, and for a 2X logic cell, $C_{in} = 2gC_{inv}$. Thus,

$$gh = g\frac{C_{out}}{C_{in}} = \frac{g\,(0.3\text{pF})}{2g\,(C_{inv})} = \frac{(0.3\text{pF})}{2\,(0.036\text{pF})}. \tag{3.27}$$

(Notice that g cancels out in this equation, we shall discuss this in the next section.)
The delay of the NOR logic cell, in units of τ, is thus

$$d = gh + p + q = \frac{(0.3 \times 10^{-12})}{(2)\,(0.036 \times 10^{-12})} + (3)\,(1) + (3)\,(1.7) \tag{3.28}$$

$$= (4.1666667 + 3 + 5.1)$$

$$= 12.266667\tau,$$

equivalent to an absolute delay, $t_{PD} \approx 12.3 \times 0.06\,\text{ns} = 0.74\,\text{ns}$.
The delay for a 2X drive, three-input NOR logic cell in the C5 library is

$$t_{PD} = (0.03 + 0.72C_{out} + 0.60)\,\text{ns}. \tag{3.29}$$

With $C_{out} = 0.3$ pF,

$$t_{PD} = 0.03 + 0.72\,(0.3) + 0.60 = 0.846\text{ns}, \tag{3.30}$$

compared to our prediction of 0.74 ns. Almost all of the error here comes from the inaccuracy in predicting the nonideal delay. Logical effort gives us a method to examine relative delays and not accurately calculate absolute delays. More important is that logical effort gives us an insight into why logic has the delay it does.

3.3.2   Logical Area and Logical Efficiency

Figure 3.9 shows a single-stage OR-AND-INVERT cell that has different logical efforts at each input. The logical effort for the OAI221 is the **logical-effort vector** $g = (7/3, 7/3, 5/3)$. For example, the first element of this vector, 7/3, is the logical effort of inputs A and B in Figure 3.9.

FIGURE 3.9 An OAI221 logic cell with different logical efforts at each input. In this case $g = (7/3, 7/3, 5/3)$. The logical effort for inputs A and B is 7/3, the logical effort for inputs C and D is also 7/3, and for input E the logical effort is 5/3. The logical area is the sum of the transistor areas, 33 logical squares.

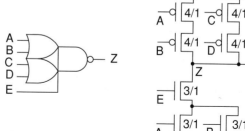

We can calculate the area of the transistors in a logic cell (ignoring the routing area, drain area, and source area) in units of a minimum-size n-channel transistor—we call these units **logical squares**. We call the transistor area the **logical area**. For example, the logical area of a 1X drive cell, OAI221X1, is calculated as follows:

- n-channel transistor sizes: $3/1 + 4 \times (3/1)$
- p-channel transistor sizes: $2/1 + 4 \times (4/1)$
- total logical area $= 2 + (4 \times 4) + (5 \times 3) = 33$ logical squares

Figure 3.10 shows a single-stage AOI221 cell, with $g = (8/3, 8/3, 6/3)$. The calculation of the logical area (for a AOI221X1) is as follows:

- n-channel transistor sizes: $1/1 + 4 \times (2/1)$
- p-channel transistor sizes: $6/1 + 4 \times (6/1)$
- logical area $= 1 + (4 \times 2) + (5 \times 6) = 39$ logical squares

These calculations show us that the single-stage AOI221, with an area of 33 logical squares and logical effort of $(7/3, 7/3, 5/3)$, is more **logically efficient** than the single-stage OAI221 logic cell with a larger area of 39 logical squares and larger logical effort of $(8/3, 8/3, 6/3)$.

3.3.3   Logical Paths

When we calculated the delay of the NOR logic cell in Section 3.3.1, the answer did not depend on the logical effort of the cell, g (it cancelled out in Eqs. 3.27 and 3.28). This is because g is a measure of the input capacitance of a 1X drive logic cell. Since we were not driving the NOR logic cell with another logic cell, the input capacitance of the NOR logic cell had no effect on the delay. This is what we do in a data book—we measure logic-cell delay using an ideal input waveform that is the

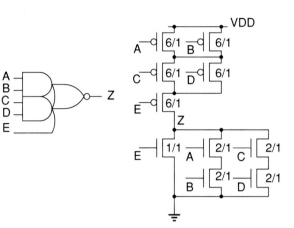

FIGURE 3.10 An AND-OR-INVERT cell, an AOI221, with logical-effort vector, $g = (8/3, 8/3, 7/3)$. The logical area is 39 logical squares.

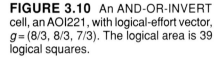

same no matter what the input capacitance of the cell. Instead let us calculate the delay of a logic cell when it is driven by a minimum-size inverter. To do this we need to extend the notion of logical effort.

So far we have only considered a single-stage logic cell, but we can extend the idea of logical effort to a chain of logic cells or **logical path**. Consider the logic path when we use a minimum-size inverter ($g_0 = 1$, $p_0 = 1$, $q_0 = 1.7$) to drive one input of a 2X drive, three-input NOR logic cell with $g_1 = (nr + 1)/(r + 1)$, $p_1 = 3$, $q_1 = 3$, and a load equal to four standard loads. If the logic ratio is $r = 1.5$, then $g_1 = 5.5/2.5 = 2.2$.

The delay of the inverter is

$$d_0 = g_0 h_0 + p_0 + q_0 = (1) \left(\frac{2 g_1 C_{inv}}{C_{inv}} \right) + 1 + 1.7$$

$$= (1)(2)(2.2) + 1 + 1.7$$

$$= 7.1. \tag{3.31}$$

Of this 7.1τ delay we can attribute 4.4τ to the loading of the NOR logic cell input capacitance, which is $2 g_1 C_{inv}$. The delay of the NOR logic cell is, as before, $d_1 = g_1 h_1 + p_1 + q_1 = 12.3$, making the total delay $7.1 + 12.3 = 19.4$, so the absolute delay is $(19.4)(0.06 \text{ ns}) = 1.164 \text{ ns}$, or about 1.2 ns.

We can see that the **path delay** D is the sum of the logical effort, parasitic delay, and nonideal delay at each stage. In general, we can write the path delay as

$$D = \sum_{i \in \text{path}} g_i h_i + \sum_{i \in \text{path}} (p_i + q_i). \tag{3.32}$$

3.3.4   Multistage Cells

Consider the following function (a multistage AOI221 logic cell):

$$ZN(A1, A2, B1, B2, C) = NOT(NAND(NAND(A1, A2), AOI21(B1, B2, C)))$$

$$= (((A1 \cdot A2)' \cdot (B1 \cdot B2 + C)')')' = (A1 \cdot A2 + B1 \cdot B2 + C)'$$

$$= AOI221(A1, A2, B1, B2, C). \tag{3.33}$$

Figure 3.11(a) shows this implementation with each input driven by a minimum-size inverter so we can measure the effect of the cell input capacitance.

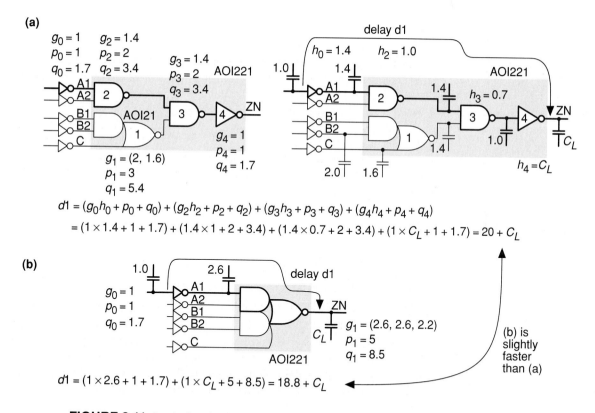

FIGURE 3.11 Logical paths. (a) An AOI221 logic cell constructed as a multistage cell from smaller cells. (b) A single-stage AOI221 logic cell.

The logical efforts of each of the logic cells in Figure 3.11(a) are as follows:

$$g_0 = g_4 = g(\text{NOT}) = 1,$$

$$g_1 = g\,(\text{AOI21}) = (2, (2r+1)/(r+1)) = (2, 4/2.5) = (2, 1.6),$$

$$g_2 = g_3 = g(\text{NAND2}) = (r+2)/(r+1) = (3.5)/(2.5) = 1.4. \qquad (3.34)$$

Each of the logic cells in Figure 3.11 has a 1X drive strength. This means that the input capacitance of each logic cell is given, as shown in the figure, by gC_{inv}.

Using Eq. 3.32 we can calculate the delay from the input of the inverter driving A1 to the output ZN as

$$
\begin{aligned}
d1 &= (1)\,(1.4) + 1 + 1.7 + 1.4\,(1) + 2 + 3.4 \\
&\quad + (1.4)\,(0.7) + 2 + 3.4 + (1)\,C_L + 1 + 1.7 \\
&= (20 + C_L).
\end{aligned}
\qquad (3.35)
$$

In Eq. 3.35 we have normalized the output load, C_L, by dividing it by a standard load (equal to C_{inv}). We can calculate the delays of the other paths similarly.

More interesting is to compare the multistage implementation with the single-stage version. In our C5 technology, with a logic ratio, $r = 1.5$, we can calculate the logical effort for a single-stage AOI221 logic cell as

$$
\begin{aligned}
g(\text{AOI221}) &= ((3r+2)/(r+1), (3r+2)/(r+1), (3r+1)/(r+1)) \\
&= (6.5/2.5, 6.5/2.5, 5.5/2.5) = (2.6, 2.6, 2.2).
\end{aligned}
\qquad (3.36)
$$

This gives the delay from an inverter driving the A input to the output ZN of the single-stage logic cell as

$$d1 = (\,(1)\,(2.6) + 1 + 1.7 + (1)C_L + 5 + 8.5) = (18.8 + C_L). \qquad (3.37)$$

The single-stage delay is very close to the delay for the multistage version of this logic cell. In some ASIC libraries the AOI221 is implemented as a multistage logic cell instead of using a single stage. It raises the question: Can we make the multistage logic cell any faster by adjusting the scale of the intermediate logic cells?

3.3.5   Optimum Delay

Before we can attack the question of how to optimize delay in a logic path, we shall need some more definitions. The **path logical effort** G is the product of logical efforts on a path:

$$G = \prod_{i\,\in\,\text{path}} g_i. \qquad (3.38)$$

The **path electrical effort** H is the product of the electrical efforts on the path,

$$H = \prod_{i \in \text{path}} h_i = \frac{C_{\text{out}}}{C_{\text{in}}}, \tag{3.39}$$

where C_{out} is the last output capacitance on the path (the load) and C_{in} is the first input capacitance on the path.

The **path effort** F is the product of the path electrical effort and logical efforts,

$$F = GH. \tag{3.40}$$

The optimum effort delay for each stage is found by minimizing the path delay D by varying the electrical efforts of each stage h_i, while keeping H, the path electrical effort fixed. The optimum effort delay is achieved when each stage operates with equal effort,

$$\hat{f}_i = g_i h_i = F^{1/N}. \tag{3.41}$$

This a useful result. The optimum path delay is then

$$\hat{D} = NF^{1/N} + P + Q = N(GH)^{1/N} + P + Q, \tag{3.42}$$

where $P + Q$ is the sum of path parasitic delay and nonideal delay,

$$P + Q = \sum_{i \in \text{path}} p_i + q_i. \tag{3.43}$$

We can use these results to improve the AOI221 multistage implementation of Figure 3.11(a). Assume that we need a 1X cell, so the output inverter (cell 4) must have 1X drive strength. This fixes the capacitance we must drive as $C_{\text{out}} = C_{\text{inv}}$ (the capacitance at the input of this inverter). The input inverters are included to measure the effect of the cell input capacitance, so we cannot cheat by altering these. This fixes the input capacitance as $C_{\text{in}} = C_{\text{inv}}$. In this case $H = 1$.

The logic cells that we can scale on the path from the A input to the output are NAND logic cells labeled as 2 and 3. In this case

$$G = g_0 \times g_2 \times g_3 = 1 \times 1.4 \times 1.4 = 1.95. \tag{3.44}$$

Thus $F = GH = 1.95$ and the optimum stage effort is $1.95^{(1/3)} = 1.25$, so that the optimum delay $NF^{1/N} = 3.75$. From Figure 3.11(a) we see that

$$g_0 h_0 + g_2 h_2 + g_3 h_3 = 1.4 + 1.4 + 1 = 3.8. \tag{3.45}$$

This means that even if we scale the sizes of the cells to their optimum values, we only save a fraction of a τ ($3.8 - 3.75 = 0.05$). This is a useful result (and one that is true in general)—the delay is not very sensitive to the scale of the cells. In this case it means that we can reduce the size of the two NAND cells in the multicell implementation of an AOI221 without sacrificing speed. We can use logical effort to predict what the change in delay will be for any given cell sizes.

We can use logical effort in the design of logic cells and in the design of logic that uses logic cells. If we do have the flexibility to continuously size each logic cell (which in ASIC design we normally do not, we usually have to choose from 1X, 2X, 4X drive strengths), each logic stage can be sized using the equation for the individual stage electrical efforts,

$$\hat{h}_i = \frac{F^{1/N}}{g_i}. \tag{3.46}$$

For example, even though we know that it will not improve the delay by much, let us size the cells in Figure 3.11(a). We shall work backward starting at the fixed load capacitance at the input of the last inverter.

For NAND cell 3, $gh = 1.25$; thus (since $g = 1.4$), $h = C_{out}/C_{in} = 0.893$. The output capacitance, C_{out}, for this NAND cell is the input capacitance of the inverter—fixed as 1 standard load, C_{inv}. This fixes the input capacitance, C_{in}, of NAND cell 3 at $1/0.893 = 1.12$ standard loads. Thus, the scale of NAND cell 3 is $1.12/1.4$ or 0.8X.

Now for NAND cell 2, $gh = 1.25$; C_{out} for NAND cell 2 is the C_{in} of NAND cell 3. Thus C_{in} for NAND cell 2 is $1.12/0.893 = 1.254$ standard loads. This means the scale of NAND cell 2 is $1.254/1.4$ or 0.9X.

The optimum sizes of the NAND cells are not very different from 1X in this case because $H = 1$ and we are only driving a load no bigger than the input capacitance. This raises the question: What is the optimum stage effort if we have to drive a large load, $H \gg 1$? Notice that, so far, we have only calculated the optimum stage effort when we have a fixed number of stages, N. We have said nothing about the situation in which we are free to choose, N, the number of stages.

3.3.6   Optimum Number of Stages

Suppose we have a chain of N inverters each with equal stage effort, $f = gh$. Neglecting parasitic and nonideal delay, the total path delay is $Nf = Ngh = Nh$, since $g = 1$ for an inverter. Suppose we need to drive a path electrical effort H; then $h^N = H$, or $N \ln h = \ln H$. Thus the delay, $Nh = h \ln H / \ln h$. Since $\ln H$ is fixed, we can only vary $h/\ln (h)$. Figure 3.12 shows that this is a very shallow function with a minimum at $h = e \approx 2.718$. At this point $\ln h = 1$ and the total delay is $Ne = e \ln H$. This result is particularly useful in driving large loads either on-chip (the clock, for example) or off-chip (I/O pad drivers, for example).

Figure 3.12 shows us how to minimize delay regardless of area or power and neglecting parasitic and nonideal delays. More complicated equations can be derived, including nonideal effects, when we wish to trade off delay for smaller area or reduced power.

FIGURE 3.12 Stage effort.

h	h/(ln h)
1.5	3.7
2	2.9
2.7	2.7
3	2.7
4	2.9
5	3.1
10	4.3

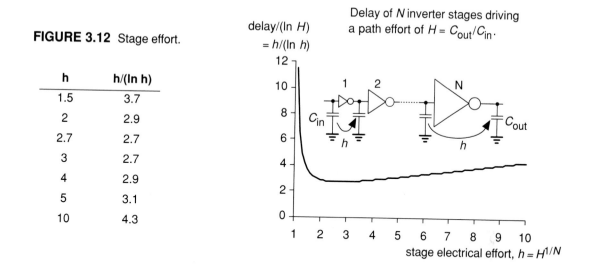

$$\text{delay}/(\ln H)$$
$$= h/(\ln h)$$

Delay of N inverter stages driving a path effort of $H = C_{out}/C_{in}$.

stage electrical effort, $h = H^{1/N}$

3.4 Library-Cell Design

The optimum cell layout for each process generation changes because the design rules for each ASIC vendor's process are always slightly different—even for the same generation of technology. For example, two companies may have very similar 0.35 μm CMOS process technologies, but the third-level metal spacing might be slightly different. If a cell library is to be used with both processes, we could construct the library by adopting the most stringent rules from each process. A library constructed in this fashion may not be competitive with one that is constructed specifically for each process. Even though ASIC vendors prize their design rules as secret, it turns out that they are similar—except for a few details. Unfortunately, it is the details that stop us moving designs from one process to another. Unless we are a very large customer it is difficult to have an ASIC vendor change or **waive** design rules for us. We would like all vendors to agree on a common set of design rules. This is, in fact, easier than it sounds. The reason that most vendors have similar rules is because most vendors use the same manufacturing equipment and a similar process. It is possible to construct a highest common denominator library that extracts the most from the current manufacturing capability. Some library companies and the large Japanese ASIC vendors are adopting this approach.

Layout of library cells is either hand-crafted or uses some form of **symbolic layout**. Symbolic layout is usually performed in one of two ways: using either interactive graphics or a text layout language. Shapes are represented by simple lines or rectangles, known as **sticks** or **logs**, in symbolic layout. The actual dimensions of the sticks or logs are determined after layout is completed in a postprocessing step.

An alternative to graphical symbolic layout uses a text layout language, similar to a programming language such as C, that directs a program to assemble layout. The spacing and dimensions of the layout shapes are defined in terms of variables rather than constants. These variables can be changed after symbolic layout is complete to adjust the layout spacing to a specific process.

Mapping symbolic layout to a specific process technology uses 10–20 percent more area than hand-crafted layout (though this can then be further reduced to 5–10 percent with compaction). Most symbolic layout systems do not allow 45° layout and this introduces a further area penalty (my experience shows this is about 5–15 percent). As libraries get larger, and the capability to quickly move libraries and ASIC designs between different generations of process technologies becomes more important, the advantages of symbolic layout may outweigh the disadvantages.

3.5   Library Architecture

Figure 3.13(a) shows cell use data from over 150 CMOS gate array designs. These results are remarkably similar to that from other ASIC designs using different libraries and different technologies and show that typically 80 percent of an ASIC uses less than 20 percent of the cell library.

We can use the data in Figure 3.13(a) to derive some useful conclusions about the number and types of cells to be included in a library. Before we do this, a few words of caution are in order. First, the data shown in Figure 3.13(a) tells us about cells that are included a library. This data cannot tell us anything about cells that are not (and perhaps should be) included in a library. Second, the type of design entry we use—and the type of ASIC we are designing—can dramatically affect the profile of the use of different cell types. For example, if we use a high-level design language, together with logic synthesis, to enter an ASIC design, this will favor the use of the complex combinational cells (cells of the AOI family that are particularly area efficient in CMOS, but are difficult to work with when we design by hand).

Figure 3.13(a) tells us which cells we use most often, but does not take into account the cell area. What we really want to know are which cells are most important in determining the area of an ASIC. Figure 3.13(b) shows the area of the cells—normalized to the area of a minimum-size inverter. If we take the data in Figure 3.13(a) and multiply by the cell areas, we can derive a new measure of the contribution of each cell in a library (Figure 3.13c). This new measure, **cell importance,** is a measure of how much area each cell in a library contributes to a typical ASIC. For example, we can see from Figure 3.13(c) that a D flip-flop (with a cell importance of 3.5) contributes 3.5 times as much area on a typical ASIC than does an inverter (with a cell importance of 1).

Figure 3.13(c) shows cell importance ordered by the cell frequency of use and normalized to an inverter. We can rearrange this data in terms of cell importance, as

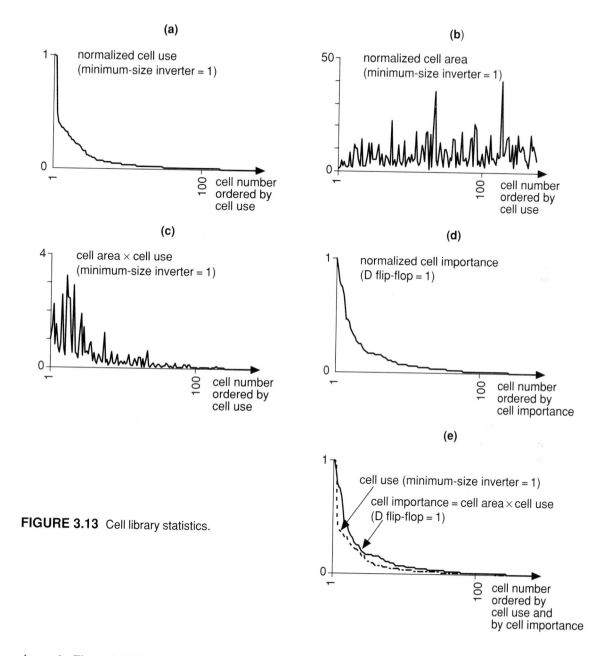

FIGURE 3.13 Cell library statistics.

shown in Figure 3.13(d), and normalized so that now the most important cell, a D flip-flop, has a cell importance of 1. Figure 3.13(e) includes the cell use data on the same scale as the cell importance data. Both show roughly the same shape, reflecting that both measures obey an 80–20 rule. Roughly 20 percent of the cells in a library correspond to 80 percent of the ASIC area and 80 percent of the cells we use (but not the same 20 percent—that is why cell importance is useful).

Figure 3.13(e) shows us that the most important cells, measured by their contribution to the area of an ASIC, are not necessarily the cells that we use most often. If we wish to build or buy a dense library, we must concentrate on the area of those cells that have the highest cell importance—not the most common cells.

3.6   Gate-Array Design

Each logic cell or macro in a gate-array library is predesigned using fixed tiles of transistors known as the **gate-array base cell** (or just **base cell**). We call the arrangement of base cells across a whole chip in a complete gate array the **gate-array base** (or just **base**). ASIC vendors offer a selection of bases, with a different total numbers of transistors on each base. For example, if our ASIC design uses 48k equivalent gates and the ASIC vendor offers gate arrays bases with 50k-, 75k-, and 100k-gates, we will probably have to use the 75k-gate base (because it is unlikely that we can use 48/50 or 96 percent of the transistors on the 50k-gate base).

We isolate the transistors on a gate array from one another either with thick field oxide (in the case of oxide-isolated gate arrays) or by using other transistors that are wired permanently off (in gate-isolated gate arrays). Channeled and channelless gate arrays may use either gate isolation or oxide isolation.

Figure 3.14(a) shows a base cell for a **gate-isolated gate array**. This base cell has two transistors: one p-channel and one n-channel. When these base cells are placed next to each other, the n-diffusion and p-diffusion layers form continuous strips that run across the entire chip broken only at the poly gates that cross at regularly spaced intervals (Figure 3.14b). The metal interconnect spacing determines the separation of the transistors. The metal spacing is determined by the design rules for the metal and contacts. In Figure 3.14(c) we have shown all possible locations for a contact in the base cell. There is room for 21 contacts in this cell and thus room for 21 interconnect lines running in a horizontal direction (we use m1 running horizontally). We say that there are 21 **horizontal tracks** in this cell or that the cell is 21 tracks high. In a similar fashion the space that we need for a vertical interconnect (m2) is called a **vertical track**. The horizontal and vertical track widths are not necessarily equal, because the design rules for m1 and m2 are not always equal.

We isolate logic cells from each other in gate-isolated gate arrays by connecting transistor gates to the supply bus—hence the name, **gate isolation**. If we connect the gate of an n-channel transistor to V_{SS}, we isolate the regions of n-diffusion on each side of that transistor (we call this an **isolator transistor** or device, or just isolator). Similarly if we connect the gate of a p-channel transistor to V_{DD}, we isolate adjacent p-diffusion regions.

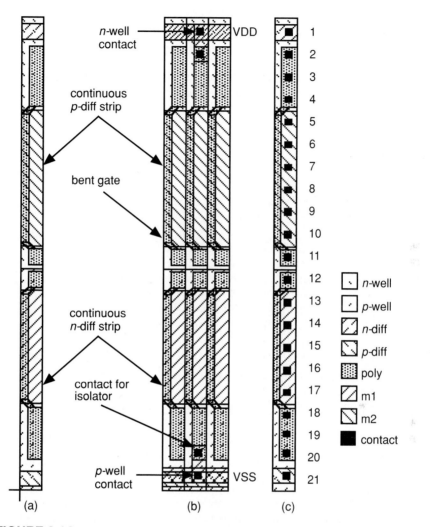

FIGURE 3.14 The construction of a gate-isolated gate array. (a) The one-track-wide base cell containing one *p*-channel and one *n*-channel transistor. (b) Three base cells: the center base cell is being used to isolate the base cells on either side from each other. (c) A base cell including all possible contact positions (there is room for 21 contacts in the vertical direction, showing the base cell has a height of 21 tracks).

Oxide-isolated gate arrays often contain four transistors in the base cell: the two *n*-channel transistors share an *n*-diffusion strip and the two *p*-channel transistors share a *p*-diffusion strip. This means that the two *n*-channel transistors in each base cell are electrically connected in series, as are the *p*-channel transistors. The base cells are isolated from each other using **oxide isolation**. During the fabrication process a layer of the thick field oxide is left in place between each base cell and this separates the *p*-diffusion and *n*-diffusion regions of adjacent base cells.

Figure 3.15 shows an **oxide-isolated gate array**. This cell contains eight transistors (which occupy six vertical tracks) plus one-half of a single track that contains the well contacts and substrate connections that we can consider to be shared by each base cell.

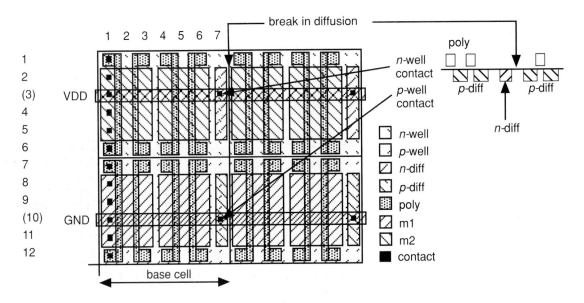

FIGURE 3.15 An oxide-isolated gate-array base cell. The figure shows two base cells, each containing eight transistors and two well contacts. The *p*-channel and *n*-channel transistors are each 4 tracks high (corresponding to the width of the transistor). The leftmost vertical track of the left base cell includes all 12 possible contact positions (the height of the cell is 12 tracks). As outlined here, the base cell is 7 tracks wide (we could also consider the base cell to be half this width).

Figure 3.16 shows a base cell in which the gates of the *n*-channel and *p*-channel transistors are connected on the polysilicon layer. Connecting the gates in poly saves contacts and a metal interconnect in the center of the cell where interconnect is most congested. The drawback of the preconnected gates is a loss in flexibility in cell design. Implementing memory and logic based on transmission gates will be less efficient using this type of base cell, for example.

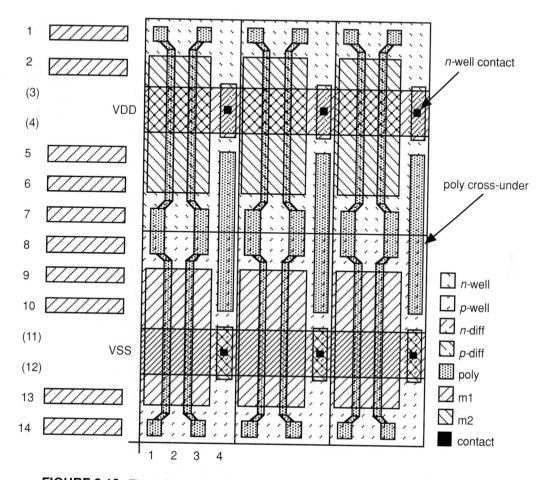

FIGURE 3.16 This oxide- isolated gate-array base cell is 14 tracks high and 4 tracks wide. VDD (tracks 3 and 4) and GND (tracks 11 and 12) are each 2 tracks wide. The metal lines to the left of the cell indicate the 10 horizontal routing tracks (tracks 1, 2, 5–10, 13, 14). Notice that the *p*-channel and *n*-channel polysilicon gates are tied together in the center of the cell. The well contacts are short, leaving room for a poly cross-under in each base cell.

Figure 3.17 shows the metal **personalization** for a D flip-flop macro in a gate-isolated gate array using a base cell similar to that shown in Figure 3.14(a). This macro uses 20 base cells, for a total of 40 transistors, equivalent to 10 gates.

The gates of the base cells shown in Figures 3.14–3.16 are bent. The **bent gate** allows contacts to the gates to be placed on the same grid as the contacts to diffusion. The polysilicon gates run in the space between adjacent metal interconnect lines. This saves space and also simplifies the routing software.

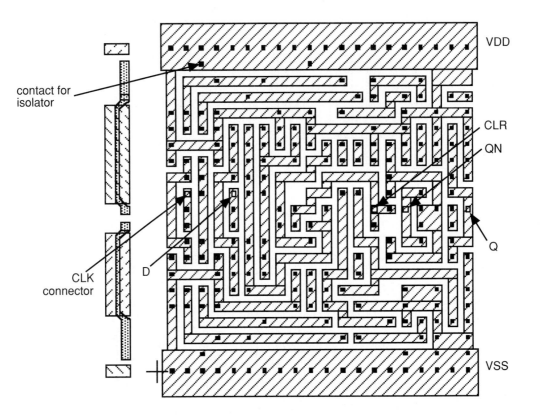

FIGURE 3.17 An example of a flip-flop macro in a gate-isolated gate-array library. Only the first-level metallization and contact pattern (the personalization) is shown on the right, but this is enough information to derive the schematic. The base cell is shown on the left. This macro is 20 tracks wide.

There are many trade-offs that determine the gate-array base cell height. One factor is the number of wires that can be run horizontally through the base cell. This will determine the capacity of the routing channel formed from an unused row of base cells. The base cell height also determines how easy it is to wire the logic macros since it determines how much space for wiring is available inside the macros.

There are other factors that determine the width of the base-cell transistors. The widths of the *p*-channel and *n*-channel transistors are slightly different in Figure 3.14(a). The *p*-channel transistors are 6 tracks wide and the *n*-channel transistors are 5 tracks wide. The ratio for this gate-array library is thus approximately 1.2. Most gate-array libraries are approaching a ratio of 1.

ASIC designers are using ever-increasing amounts of RAM on gate arrays. It is inefficient to use the normal base cell for a static RAM cell and the size of RAM on an embedded gate array is fixed. As an alternative we can change the design of the base cell. A base cell designed for use as RAM has extra transistors (either four— two *n*-channel and two *p*-channel—or two *n*-channel; usually minimum width) allowing a six-transistor RAM cell to be built using one base cell instead of the two or three that we would normally need. This is one of the advantages of the **CBA** (cell-based array) base cell shown in Figure 3.18.

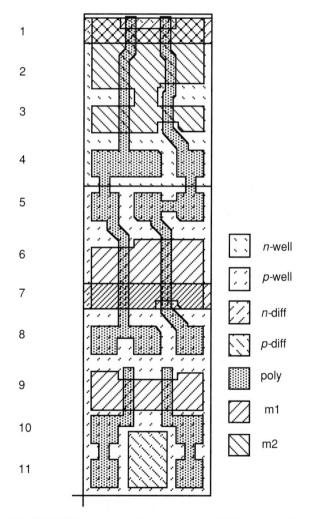

FIGURE 3.18   The SiARC/Synopsys cell-based array (CBA) basic cell.

3.7 Standard-Cell Design

Figure 3.19 shows the components of the standard cell from Figure 1.3. Each standard cell in a library is rectangular with the same height but different widths. The **bounding box** (**BB**) of a logic cell is the smallest rectangle that encloses all of the geometry of the cell. The cell BB is normally determined by the well layers. Cell connectors or terminals (the **logical connectors**) must be placed on the cell **abutment box** (**AB**). The **physical connector** (the piece of metal to which we connect wires) must normally overlap the abutment box slightly, usually by at least 1λ, to assure connection without leaving a tiny space between the ends of two wires. The standard cells are constructed so they can all be placed next to each other horizontally with the cell ABs touching (we **abut** two cells).

A standard cell (a D flip-flop with clear) is shown in Figure 3.20 and illustrates the following features of standard-cell layout:

- Layout using 45° angles. This can save 10%–20% in area compared to a cell that uses only Manhattan or 90° geometry. Some ASIC vendors do not allow transistors with 45° angles; others do not allow 45° angles at all.

- Connectors are at the top and bottom of the cell on m2 on a routing grid equal to the vertical (m2) track spacing. This is a double-entry cell intended for a two-level metal process. A standard cell designed for a three-level metal process has connectors in the center of the cell.

- Transistor sizes vary to optimize the area and performance but maintain a fixed ratio to balance rise times and fall times.

- The cell height is 64λ (all cells in the library are the same height) with a horizontal (m1) track spacing of 8λ. This is close to the minimum height that can accommodate the most complex cells in a library.

- The power rails are placed at the top and bottom, maintaining a certain width inside the cell and abut with the power rails in adjacent cells.

- The well contacts (substrate connections) are placed inside the cell at regular intervals. Additional well contacts may be placed in spacers between cells.

- In this case both wells are drawn. Some libraries minimize the well or moat area to reduce leakage and parasitic capacitance.

- Most commercial standard cells use m1 for the power rails, m1 for internal connections, and avoid using m2 where possible except for cell connectors.

When a library developer creates a gate-array, standard-cell, or datapath library, there is a trade-off between using wide, high-drive transistors that result in large cells with high-speed performance and using smaller transistors that result in smaller cells that consume less power. A **performance-optimized library** with large cells might be used for ASICs in a high-performance workstation, for example. An **area-optimized library** might be used in an ASIC for a battery-powered portable computer.

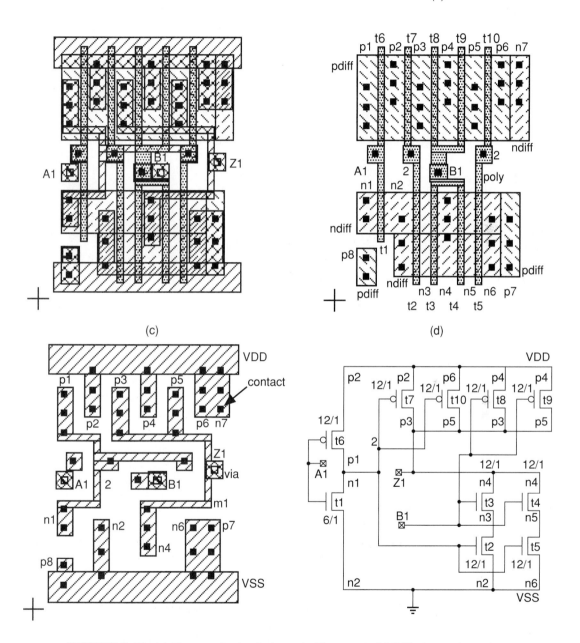

FIGURE 3.19 (a) The standard cell shown in Figure 1.3. (b) Diffusion, poly, and contact layers. (c) m1 and contact layers. (d) The equivalent schematic.

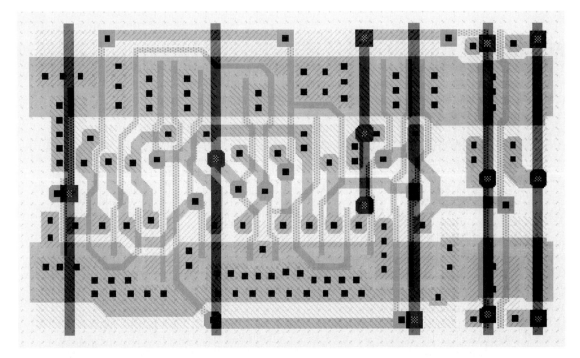

FIGURE 3.20 A D flip-flop standard cell. The wide power buses and transistors show this is a performance-optimized cell. This double-entry cell is intended for a two-level metal process and channel routing. The five connectors run vertically through the cell on m2 (the extra short vertical metal line is an internal crossover).

3.8   Datapath-Cell Design

Figure 3.21 shows a datapath flip-flop. The primary, thicker, power buses run vertically on m2 with thinner, internal power running horizontally on m1. The control signals (clock in this case) run vertically through the cell on m2. The control signals that are common to the cells above and below are connected directly in m2. The other signals (data, q, and qbar in this example) are brought out to the wiring channel between the rows of datapath cells.

Figure 3.22 is the schematic for Figure 3.21. This flip-flop uses a pair of cross-coupled inverters for storage in both the master and slave latches. This leads to a smaller and potentially faster layout than the flip-flop circuits that we use in gate-array and standard-cell ASIC libraries. The device sizes of the inverters in the datapath flip-flops are adjusted so that the state of the latches may be changed. Normally using this type of circuit is dangerous in an uncontrolled environment. However,

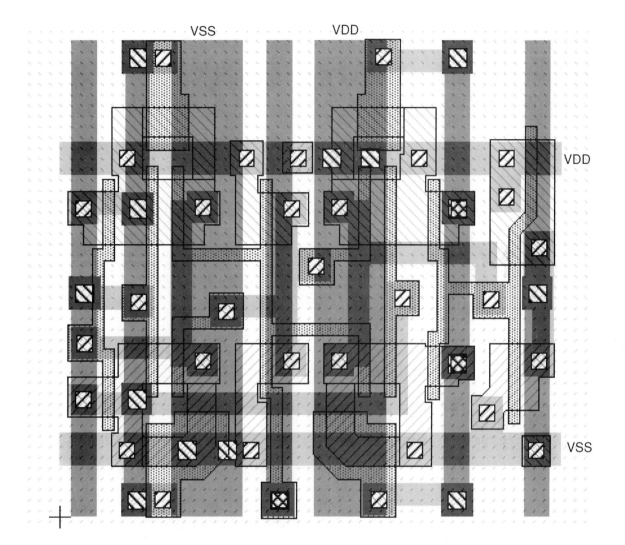

FIGURE 3.21 A datapath D flip-flop cell.

because the datapath structure is regular and known, the parasitic capacitances that affect the operation of the logic cell are also known. This is another advantage of the datapath structure.

Figure 3.23 shows an example of a datapath. Figure 3.23(a) depicts a two-level metal version showing the space between rows or slices of the datapath. In this case there are many connections to be brought out to the right of the datapath, and this causes the routing channel to be larger than normal and thus easily seen.

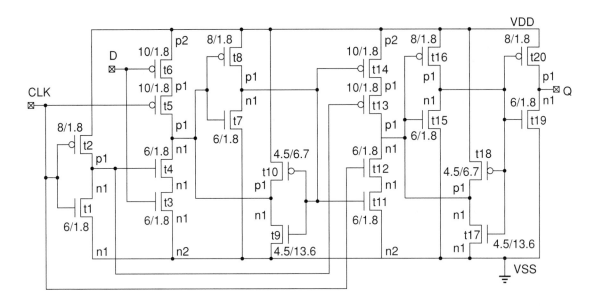

FIGURE 3.22 The schematic of the datapath D flip-flop cell shown in Figure 3.21.

Figure 3.23(b) shows a three-level metal version of the same datapath. In this case more of the routing is completed over the top of the datapath slices, reducing the size of the routing channel.

(a)

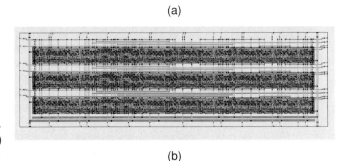

FIGURE 3.23 A datapath. (a) Implemented in a two-level metal process. (b) Implemented in a three-level metal process.

(b)

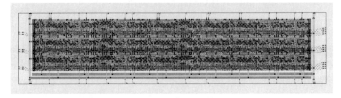

3.9 Summary

In this chapter we covered ASIC libraries: cell design, layout, and characterization. The most important concepts that we covered in this chapter were

- Tau, logical effort, and the prediction of delay
- Sizes of cells, and their drive strengths
- Cell importance
- The difference between gate-array macros, standard cells, and datapath cells

3.10 Problems

$*$ = difficult, $**$ = very difficult, $***$ = extremely difficult

3.1 (Pull resistance, 10 min.)

a. Show that, for small V_{DS}, an n-channel transistor looks like a resistor, $R = 1 / (\beta_n (V_{DD} - V_{tn}))$.

b. If $V_{GS} = V_{DD}$, $V_{DS} = 0$, and $k_n' = 200 \, \mu AV^{-2}$ (equal to the n-channel transistor SPICE parameter KP in Table 2.1), find the pull resistance, R, for a 6/0.6 transistor in the linear region.

Answer: (b) 213 Ω.

3.2 (Inversion layer depth, 15 min.) In the absence of surface charge, Gauss's law demands continuity of the electric displacement vector, $\mathbf{D} = \epsilon \mathbf{E}$, at the silicon surface, so that $\epsilon_{ox} E_{ox} = \epsilon_{Si} E_{Si}$, where $\epsilon_{ox} = 3.9$, $\epsilon_{Si} = 11.7$.

a. Assuming the potential at the surface is $V_{GS} - V_t = 2.5V$, calculate E_{ox} and E_{Si} if $T_{ox} = 100 \, \text{Å}$.

b. Assume that carrier density $\propto \exp(-q\phi/kT)$, where ϕ is the potential; calculate the distance below the surface at which the inversion charge density falls to 10 percent of its value at the surface.

c. Comment on the accuracy of your answers.

Answer: (a) $2.5 \times 10^8 \, \text{Vm}^{-1}$, $0.833 \times 10^8 \, \text{Vm}^{-1}$. (b) 7.16 Å.

3.3 (Depletion layer depth, 15 min.) The depth of the depletion region under the gate is given by $x_d = \sqrt{(2\epsilon_{Si}\phi_s) / (qN_A)}$, where $\phi_s = 2V_T \ln (N_A/n_i)$ is the surface potential at strong inversion. Calculate ϕ_s and x_d assuming: $\epsilon_{Si} = 1.0359 \times 10^{-10} \, \text{Fm}^{-1}$, the substrate doping, $N_A = 1.4 \times 10^{17} \, \text{cm}^{-3}$, the **intrinsic carrier concentration** $n_i = 1.45 \times 10^{10} \, \text{cm}^{-3}$ (at room temperature), and the thermal voltage $V_T = kT/q = 25.9 \, \text{mV}$.

Answer: 0.833 V, 900 Å.

3.4 (Logical effort, 45 min.) Calculate the logical effort at each input of an AOI122 cell. Find an expression that allows you to calculate the logical effort for each input of an AOI*nnnn* cell for $n = 1, 2, 3$.

3.5 (Gate-array macro design, 120 min.) Draw a 1X drive, two-input NAND cell using the gate-array base cells shown in Figures 3.14(a)–3.16 (lay a piece of thin paper over the figures and draw the contacts and metal personalization only). Label the inputs and outputs. Lay out a 1X drive, four-input NAND cell using the same base array cells. Now lay out a 2X drive, four-input NAND cell (think about this one). Make sure that you size your transistors properly to balance rise times and fall times.

3.6 (Flip-flop library, 20 min.) Suppose we wish to build a library of flip-flops. We want to have flops with: positive-edge and negative-edge triggering: clear, preset (either, both, or neither); synchronous or asynchronous reset and preset controls if present (but not mixed on the same flip-flop); all flip-flops with or without scan as an option; flip-flops with Q and Qbar (either or both). How many flip-flops is that? (***) How would you attempt to prioritize which flip-flops to include in a library?

3.7 (AOI and OAI cell ratios, 30 min.) In Figure 2.13(c) we adjusted the sizes of the transistors assuming that there was only one path through the *n*-channel and *p*-channel stacks. Suppose that *p*-channel transistors A, B, C, and D are all on and *p*-channel transistor E turns on. What is the equivalent resistance of the *p*-channel stack in this case?

3.8 (**Eight-input AND, 60 min.) This question is an example in the paper by Sutherland and Sproull [1991] on logical effort. Figure 3.24 shows three different ways to design an eight-input AND cell, using NAND and NOR cells.

   a. Find the logical effort at each input for A, B, C. Assume a logic ratio of 2.

   b. Find the parasitic delay for A, B, C. Assume the parasitic delay of an inverter is 0.6.

   c. Show that the path delays are given by the following equations where H is the path electrical effort, if we ignore the nonideal delays:

   (i) $2(3.33H)^{0.5} + 5.4$ (alternative A)
   (ii) $2(3.33H)^{0.5} + 3.6$ (alternative B)
   (iii) $4(2.96H)^{0.25} + 4.2$ (alternative C)

   d. Use these equations to determine the best alternative for $H = 2$ and $H = 32$.

3.9 (Special logic cells, 30 min.) Many ASIC cell libraries contain "special" logic cells. For example the Compass libraries contain a two-input NAND cell with an inverted input, FN01 = (A + B'). This saves routing area, is faster than using two separate cells, and is useful because the combination of a two-input NAND gate with one inverted input is heavily used by synthesis tools. Other "special" cells include:

- FN02 = MAJ3 = (A·B + A·C + B·C)'

- FN03 = AOI2-2 = ((A'·B') + (C·D))' = (A + B)(C' + D') = OA2-2

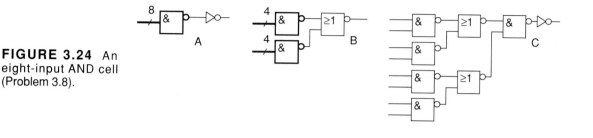

FIGURE 3.24 An eight-input AND cell (Problem 3.8).

- FN04 = OAI2-2
- FN05 = A·B' = (A' + B)'

a. Draw schematics for these cells.

b. Calculate the logical effort and logical area for each cell.

c. Can you explain where and why these cells might be useful?

3.10 (Euler paths, 60 min.) There are several ways to arrange the stacks in the AOI211 cell shown in Figure 3.25. For example, the *n*-channel transistor A can be below B without altering the function. Which arrangement would you predict gives a faster delay from A to Z and why? The *p*-channel transistors A and B can be above or below transistors C and D. How many distinct ways of arranging the transistors are there for this cell? What effect do the different arrangements have on layout? What effects do these different arrangements have on the cell performance?

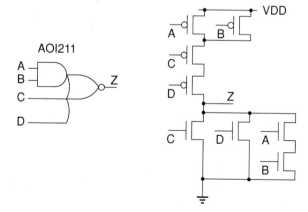

FIGURE 3.25 There are several ways to arrange the transistors in this AOI211 cell (Problem 3.10).

3.11 (*AOI and OAI cell efficiency, 60 min.) A standard-cell library data book contains the following data:

- AOI221: $t_R = 1.06–1.15$ns; $t_F = 1.09–1.55$ns; $C_{in} = 0.21–0.28$pF; $W_C = 28.8\,\mu m$
- OAI221: $t_R = 0.77–1.05$ns; $t_F = 0.81–0.96$ns; $C_{in} = 0.25–0.39$pF; $W_C = 22.4\,\mu m$

(W_C is the cell width, the cell height is $25.6\,\mu m$.) Calculate the **(a)** logical effort and **(b)** logical area for the AOI221 and OAI221 cells.

The implementation of the OAI221 in this library uses a single stage,

$$OAI221 = OAI221(a1, a2, b1, b2, c),$$

whereas the AOI221 uses the following multistage implementation:

$$AOI221 = NOT(NAND(NAND(a1, a2), AOI21(b1, b2, c))).$$

(c) What are the alternative implementations for these two cells? **(d)** From your answers attempt to explain the implementations chosen.

3.12 (**Logical efficiency, 60 min.) Extending Problem 3.11, let us compare an AOI33 with an OAI33 cell. **(a)** Calculate the logical effort and **(b)** logical areas for these cells.

The AOI33 uses a single-stage implementation as follows:

$$AOI33 = AOI33(a1, a2, a3, b1, b2, b3).$$

The OAI33 uses the following multistage implementation:

$$OAI33 = NOT[NOR[NOR(a1, a2, a3), NOR(b1, b2, b3)]].$$

(c) Calculate the path delay, D, as a function of path electrical effort, H, for both of these implementations ignoring parasitic and nonideal delays. **(d)** Use Eq. 3.42 to calculate the optimum path delay for these cells. **(e)** Compare and explain the differences between your answers to parts d. and e. for $H = 1, 2, 4$, and 8.

The timing data from the data book is as follows (the cell height is $25.6\,\mu m$):

- AOI33: $t_R = 0.70–1.06$ ns; $t_F = 0.72–1.15$ns; $C_{in} = 0.21–0.28$pF; $W_C = 35.2\,\mu m$
- OAI33: $t_R = 1.06–1.70$ns; $t_F = 1.42–1.98$ns; $C_{in} = 0.31–0.36$pF; $W_C = 48\,\mu m$

(f) How does this data compare with your theoretical analysis?

3.13 (EXOR cells and logical effort, 60 min.) Show how to implement a two-input EXOR cell using an AOI22 and two inverters. Using logical effort, compare this with an implementation using an AOI21 cell and a NOR cell.

3.14 (***XNOR cells, 60 min.) Table 3.3 shows the implementation of XNOR cells in a standard-cell library. Analyze this data using the concept of logical effort.

3.15 (***Extensions to logical effort, 60 min.) The **path branching effort** B is the product of branching efforts:

$$B = \prod_{i \in \text{path}} b_i. \tag{3.47}$$

TABLE 3.3 Implementations of XNOR cells in CMOS (Problem 3.14).

Cell	Implementation
Library 1: XNOR2D1	NAND[OR(a1,a2),NAND(a1,a2)]
Library 2: XNOR2D1	NOT[NOT[MUX[a1, NOT(a1),a2)]]
Library 1: XNOR2D2	NOT[NOT[MUX(a1,NOT(a1),a2)]]
Library 2: XNOR2D2	NAND[OR(a1,a2),NAND(a1,a2)]
Library 1: XNOR3D1	NOT[NOT[MUX(a1, NOT(a1), NOT(MUX(a3, NOT(a3),a2)))]]
Library 1: XNOR3D2	NOT[NOT[MUX(a1, NOT(a1), NOT(MUX(a3, NOT(a3),a2)))]]

The **branching effort** is the ratio of the on-path plus off-path capacitance to the on-path capacitance. The **path effort** F becomes the product of the path electrical effort, path branching effort, and path logical effort:

$$F = GBH. \tag{3.48}$$

Show that the path delay D is

$$D = \sum_{i \in \text{path}} g_i b_i h_i + \sum_{i \in \text{path}} p_i. \tag{3.49}$$

(***) Show that the optimum path delay is then

$$\hat{D} = NF^{1/N} + P = N(GBH)^{1/N} + P. \tag{3.50}$$

3.16 (*Circuits from layout, 120 min.) Figure 3.26 shows a D flip-flop with clear from a 1.0 μm standard-cell library. Figure 3.27 shows two layout views of this D flip-flop. Construct the circuit diagram for this flip-flop, labeling the nodes and transistors as shown. Include the transistor sizes—use estimates for transistors with 45° gates—you only need W/L values, you can assume the gate lengths are all $L = 2\lambda$, equal to the minimum feature size. Label the inputs and outputs to the cell and identify their functions.

3.17 (Flip-flop circuits, 30 min.) Draw the circuit schematic for a positive-edge–triggered D flip-flop with active-high set and reset (base your schematic on Figure 2.18a, a negative-edge–triggered D flip-flop). Describe the problem when both SET and RESET are high.

If we want an active-high set or reset we can: (1) use an inverter on the set or reset signal or (2) we can substitute NOR cells. Since NOR cells are slower than NAND cells, which we do depends on whether we want to optimize for speed or area.

Thus, the largest flip-flop would be one with both Q and QN outputs, active high set and reset—requiring four TX gates, three inverters (four of the seven we

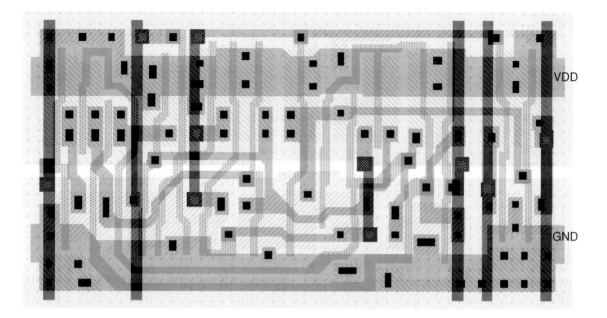

FIGURE 3.26 A D flip-flop from a 1.0 µm standard-cell library (Problem 3.16).

normally need are replaced with NAND cells), four NAND cells, and two inverters to invert the set and reset, making a total of 34 transistors, or 8.5 gates.

3.18 (Set and reset, 10 min.) Show how to add a **synchronous set** or a **synchronous reset** to the flip-flop of Figure 2.18(a) using a two-input MUX.

3.19 (Clocked inverters, 45 min.) Using PSpice compare the delay of an inverter with transmission gate with that of a clocked inverter using the G5 process SPICE parameters from Table 2.1.

3.20 (S-R, T, J-K flip-flops, 30 min.) The **characteristic equation** for a D flip-flop is $Q_{t+1} = D$. The characteristic equation for a J-K flip-flop is $Q_{t+1} = J(Q_t)' + K'Q_t$.

a. Show how you can build a J-K flip-flop using a D flip-flop.

b. The characteristic equation for a T flip-flop (toggle flip-flop) is $Q_{t+1} = (Q_t)'$. Show how to build a T flip-flop using a D flip-flop.

c. The characteristic equation does not show the timing behavior of a sequential element—the characteristic equation for a D latch is the same as that for a D flip-flop. The characteristic equation for an S-R latch and an S-R flip-flop is $Q_{t+1} = S + R'Q_t$. An S-R flip-flop is sometimes called a pulse-triggered flip-flop. Find out the behavior of an S-R latch and an S-R flip-flop and describe the differences between these elements and a D latch and a D flip-flop.

d. Explain why it is probably not a good idea to use an S-R flip-flop in an ASIC design.

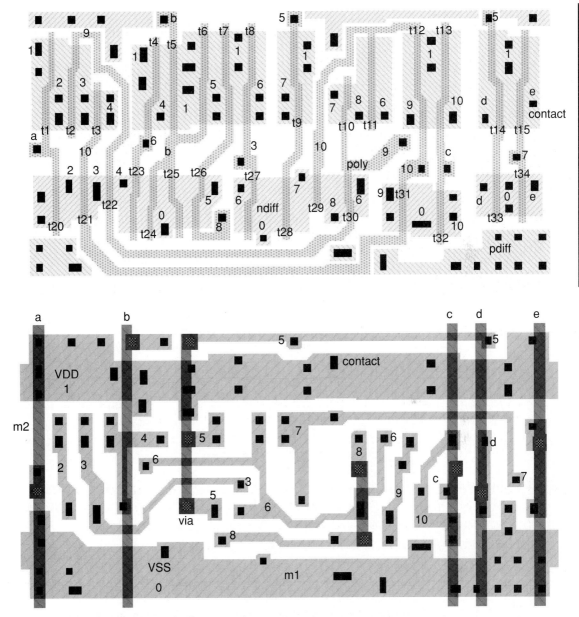

FIGURE 3.27 (Top) A standard cell showing the diffusion (*n*-diffusion and *p*-diffusion), poly, and contact layers (the *n*-well and *p*-well are not shown). (Bottom) Shows the m1, contact, m2, and via layers. Problem 3.16 traces this circuit for this cell.

3.21 (**Optimum logic, 60 min.) Suppose we have a fixed logic path of length n_1. We want to know how many (if any) buffer stages we should add at the output of this path to optimize the total path delay given the output load capacitance.

a. If the total number of stages is N (logic path of length n_1 plus $N - n_1$ inverters), show that the total path delay is

$$\hat{D} = NF^{1/N} + \sum_{i=1}^{n_1} (p_i + q_i) + (N - n_1)(p_{inv} + q_{inv}) \,. \tag{3.51}$$

The optimum number of stages is given by the solution to the following equation:

$$\frac{\partial \hat{D}}{\partial N} = \frac{\partial}{\partial N}(NF^{1/N} + (N - n_1)(p_{inv} + q_{inv})) = 0 \,. \tag{3.52}$$

b. Show that the solutions to this equation can be written in terms of $F^{1/\hat{N}}$ (the optimum stage effort) where $\hat{N}$ is the optimum number of stages:

$$F^{1/\hat{N}}(1 - \ln F^{1/\hat{N}}) + (p_{inv} + q_{inv}) = 0 \,. \tag{3.53}$$

3.22 (XOR and XNOR cells, 60 min.) Table 3.4 shows the implementations of two- and three-input XOR cells in an ASIC standard-cell library (D1 are the 1X drive cells, and D2 are the 2X drive versions). Can you explain the choices for the two-input XOR cell and complete the table for the three-input XOR cell?

TABLE 3.4   Implementations of XOR cells (Problem 3.22).

Cell	Actual implementation[1]	Alternative implementation(s)
XOR2D1	AOI21[a1, a2, NOR(a1,a2)]	NOT[MUX(a1, NOT(a1), a2)]
		AOI22(a1, a2, NOT(a1), NOT(a2))
XOR2D2	NOT[MUX(a1, NOT(a1), a2)]	AOI21[a1, a2, NOR(a1, a2)]
		AOI22(a1, a2, NOT(a1), NOT(a2))
XOR3D1	NOT[MUX[a1, NOT(a1), NOT(MUX(a3, NOT(a3), a2))]]	?
XOR3D2	NOT[MUX[a1, NOT(a1), NOT(MUX(a3, NOT(a3), a2))]]	?

[1]MUX(a, b, c) = a·c + b·c'

3.23 (Library density, 10 min.) Derive an upper limit on cell density as follows: Assume a chip consists only of two-input NAND cells with no routing channels between rows (often achievable in a 3LM process with over-the-cell routing).

a. Explain how many vertical tracks you need to connect to a two-input NAND cell, assuming each connection requires a separate track.

b. If the NAND cell is 64λ high with a vertical track width of 8λ, calculate the NAND cell area, carefully explaining any assumptions.

c. Calculate the cell density (in gate/mil^2) for a $0.35\,\mu m$ process, $\lambda = 0.175\,\mu m$.

Answer: 3 tracks, $47\,\mu m^2$, 13.7 gates/mil^2 or 21×10^3 gates mm^{-2}.

3.24 (Gate-array density, 20 min.) The LSI Logic 10k and 100k gate arrays use a four-transistor base cell, equivalent to 1 gate, that is 12 tracks high and 3 tracks wide.

a. If a metal track is 8λ, where $\lambda = 0.75\,\mu m$ for a $1.5\mu m$ technology, calculate the area of the LSI Logic base cell A_L in mil^2.

b. If we could use every base cell in the gate array, the cell density would be $D_G = 1/A_L$. Assume that, because of routing area and inefficiency of the gate array, we can use only 50 percent of the base cells for logic. What is D_G for the LSI Logic $1.5\,\mu m$ array?

c. Chip cell density D_G is about 1.0 gate/mil^2 for a $1\,\mu m$ technology (a two-input NAND cell occupies an area $25\,\mu m$ on a side in a technology whose transistors are $1\,\mu m$ long). This can change by a factor of 2 or more for a gate-array/standard-cell ASIC or high-density/high-performance library. Assume that cell density D_G scales ideally with technology. If the minimum feature size of a technology is 2λ, then $D_G \propto 1/\lambda^2$. Thus, for example, a $1.5\,\mu m$ technology should have a cell density of roughly $(1/1.5)^2$ gates/mil^2. How does this agree with your estimate for the LSI Logic array?

3.25 (SiArc RAM, 10 min.) Suppose we need 16 k-bit of SRAM and 20 k-gate of random logic on a channelless gate array. Assume a base cell with four transistors and that we can build a RAM cell using two of these base cells. The RAM bits will require 32k base cells and the random logic will require 20k base cells. Suppose the base cell area is 12 tracks high, 3 tracks wide, and the horizontal and vertical track spacing is equal at 8λ.

a. Calculate the total area of the base cells we need. Now suppose we redesign the gate-array base cell so that we can build a RAM bit cell using a single base cell that is 20 tracks high, 3 tracks wide, and has 4 logic cell transistors and 4 RAM cell transistors. Assume that since the base cell now contains 8 transistors we only need 12 k base cells to implement 20 k-gate of random logic (the new base cell is less efficient than the old cell for implementing random logic).

b. Calculate the base cell area using the new base cell design.

c. Comment.

Answer: $1.2 \times 10^8\ \lambda^2$, $1.1 \times 10^8\ \lambda^2$.

3.26 (***Gate-array base cell, 60 min.) Figure 3.28 shows a simple gate-array base cell. Use the design rules shown in Table 2.16 (Problem 2.33) to calculate the minimum size of this base cell. Do this by determining which design rules apply to the labels shown adjacent to each space or width in the figure. In most cases each of the spaces is determined by a single rule related to the region labeled, for example, the contact width labeled 'cc' is 2λ determined by rule C.1, the exact contact size. There is one exception, shown in the figure. Space 'aa' (bounding box, BB, to edge of pdiff) and width 'bb' (edge of pdiff to edge of contact) are determined by the minimum space labeled 'xx' (bounding box, BB, to poly edge) and width 'yy' (edge of poly to edge of contact). Space 'xx' is one half of the poly to poly spacing over field (rule P.4) because two base cells abut as shown in the figure. Width 'yy' is equal to the minimum poly overlap of contact (rule C.3). The distance 'aa + bb' is thus determined by the minimum distance 'xx + yy', as shown. The other distances are more straightforward to determine.

Answer: 40λ high by 26.25λ wide.

3.27 (CIF, 15 min.) Here is the part of the CIF for a standard cell that describes the *n*-well (CWN) and *p*-well (CWP) structure. The statement B length height xCenter, yCenter is CIF for a box (CIF dimensions are in centimicrons, 0.01 μm):

```
DS1;LCWN;B6000
1560 13600,3660;B2480 60 11840,2850;B2320 60 15440,2850;LCWP;B680 60
13740,2730;B6000 1380 13600,2010;
```

    a. Draw the wells and BB. Label the dimensions in microns and λ (λ = 0.4 μm).

    b. This is a double-entry cell with m2 connectors at top and bottom. For this cell library the cell AB is 3λ (120 centimicrons, determined by the well rules) inside the cell BB on all sides. What is the size of the cell AB in microns and λ?

    c. The vertical (m2) routing pitch (the distance between centers of adjacent vertical m2 interconnect lines) is equal to the vertical track spacing and is 8λ (320 centimicrons). How many vertical tracks are there in this cell?

3.28 (CIF, 60 min.) Figure 3.29 shows an example of CIF that describes a single rectangle (box) of m1 with an accompanying label.

The CIF code has the following meaning:

- Lines 1–5 are CIF comments.

- Line 6 is a **definition start** for symbol 1 and marks the beginning of a **symbol definition** (a symbol is a piece of layout, symbol numbers are unique identifiers). The integers 2 and 8 define a **scaling factor** 2/8 (= 0.25) to be applied to distance measurements (the CIF unit, after scaling, is a **centimicron** or 0.01 μm).

- Line 7 is a **user extension** or expansion (all extensions begin with a digit). L-Edit uses user extension 9 for cell names (Cell0 in this case).

- Line 8 is a user extension for a **cell label** located on layer CM (first-level metal in this technology) located at *x* = 60 units, *y* = 180 units (60, 180).

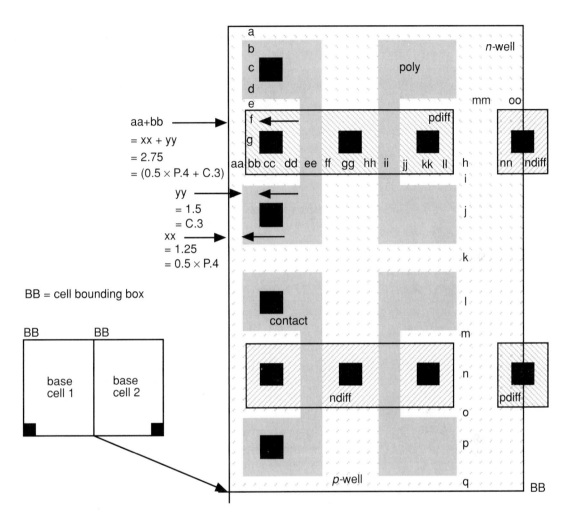

FIGURE 3.28 A simple gate-array base cell (Problem 3.26).

Applying the scaling factor of 0.25, this translates to (15, 45) in centimicrons or (0.5, 1.5) in lambda.

- Line 9 is a **layer specification** or command (begins with L).
- Line 10 is a **box command** and describes a box with (in order) length, L, of 240 units; width, W, of 120 units; and center at $x = 120$ units and $y = 300$ units. Applying the DS scaling factor of 0.25 gives L = 60, W = 30, center = (30, 75)(centimicrons) or L = 2, W = 1, center = (1, 2.5) in lambda.
- Line 11 is the **definition finish** (DS and DF must be paired).
- Line 12 is the **end command**.

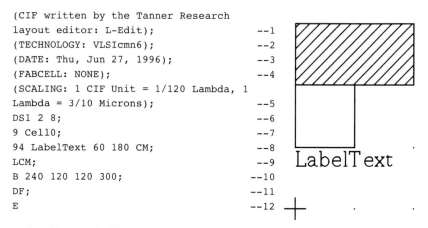

```
(CIF written by the Tanner Research
layout editor: L-Edit);                 --1
(TECHNOLOGY: VLSIcmn6);                  --2
(DATE: Thu, Jun 27, 1996);              --3
(FABCELL: NONE);                        --4
(SCALING: 1 CIF Unit = 1/120 Lambda, 1
Lambda = 3/10 Microns);                 --5
DS1 2 8;                                --6
9 Cell0;                                --7
94 LabelText 60 180 CM;                 --8
LCM;                                    --9
B 240 120 120 300;                      --10
DF;                                     --11
E                                       --12
```

FIGURE 3.29 A simple CIF example (Problem 3.28).

3.29 (CIF conversion, 60 min.+) You receive a CIF file whose mask layer names are different from the technology file you are using. The mapping between layer names is shown in Table 3.5.

a. Write an awk/sed script (or use another automated editing technique) to change the layer names. At this point you realize that there are several layer names (LTRAN, LESD) in the input file that are not required (or recognized) by your layout software (these particular examples are for software to recognize unused transistors in a gate array, and for an ESD implant in I/O devices).

b. (**) Enhance your script to completely remove an unwanted layer from the CIF file. There are some comments and CIF constructs that are not supported by your editor. Here is one example:

```
(BB: 39.2,82.6 72.8,122.5 in lambda);
```

Comments in this format specify the AB and BB for the cell. Other CIF user extensions, not recognized by your software, are used for labels for power supplies and connectors:

```
4A 1680 3360 2800 4844;
4M a 1 2292 4028 2356 4092 CM2;
4M z 4 2639 4090 2703 4154 CM2;
4X vdd 2 2800 4774 180 * * metal;
```

c. (**) Add code to remove all these constructs from the CIF file.

TABLE 3.5   Mapping CIF layer names (Problem 3.29).[1]

Input mask label	MOSIS mask label	Input mask label	MOSIS mask label	Input mask label	MOSIS mask label
LCNW	CWN	LCND[2]	CSN	LCM2	CMS
LCPW	CWP	LCPD[2]	CSP	LCC2	CVS
none[3]	CAA	LCC[4]	CCA	LCM3	CMT
LCP	CPG	LCM	CMF	none	COG

[1]This mapping is for input to a layout editor; the CIF may have to be modified again when written out from the layout editor.
[2]Map the input diffusion layers to the implant select layers. On output from the layout editor these layers should be sized up to generate the "real" implant select layers.
[3]There is no active layer in the input. Instead use the diffusion layers.
[4]There is only one contact layer in the input; map all contacts to CAA. There is no easy way to generate the MOSIS CCP layer. This prevents handling of poly and diffusion contacts separately.

3.11   Bibliography

The first part of this chapter is covered in greater detail in Weste and Eshraghian [1993]. The experiments presented in this chapter may be reproduced using PSpice and Probe from MicroSim (http://www.microsim.com). A free CD-ROM is available from MicroSim containing PC versions of their software together with reference manuals in Adobe Acrobat format that are readable on all platforms. Other PSpice and Probe versions are available online including the Apple Macintosh version used in this book (which requires a math coprocessor). Mukherjee [1986] covers CMOS process and fabrication issues. Analog ASIC design is covered by Haskard and May [1988] and Trontelj et al. [1989]. Chen [1990] and Uyemura [1992] provide more depth on analysis of combinational and sequential logic design. The book by Diaz [1995] includes material on I/O cell design for ESD protection that is hard to find. The patent literature is the best reference for high-speed and quiet I/O design. Wakerly's book [1994] on digital design is an excellent reference for logic design in general (including sequential logic, metastability, and binary arithmetic), though it emphasizes PLDs rather than ASICs.

3.12   References

Chen, J. Y. 1990. *CMOS Devices and Technology for VLSI.* Englewood Cliffs, NJ: Prentice-Hall, 348 p. ISBN 0-13-138082-6. TK7874.C523.

Diaz, C. H., et al. 1995. *Modeling of Electrical Overstress in Integrated Circuits.* Norwell, MA: Kluwer Academic, 148 p. ISBN 0-7923-9505-0. TK7874.D498. Includes 101 references. Good introduction to ESD problems and models. Most of the book deals with thermal analysis and thermal stress modeling.

Haskard, M. R., and I. C. May. 1988. *Analog VLSI Design: nMOS and CMOS.* Englewood Cliffs, NJ: Prentice-Hall, 243 p. ISBN 0-13-032640-2. TK7874.H392.

Mukherjee, A. 1986. *Introduction to nMOS and CMOS VLSI Systems Design.* Englewood Cliffs, NJ: Prentice-Hall, 370 p. ISBN 0-13-490947-X. TK7874.M86.

Sutherland, I. E., and R. F. Sproull. 1991. "Logical effort: designing for speed on the back of an envelope." In *Proceedings of the Advanced Research in VLSI,* Santa Cruz, CA, pp. 1–16. This reference may be hard to find, but similar treatments (without the terminology of logical effort) are given in Mead and Conway, or Weste and Eshraghian.

Trontelj, J., et al. 1989. *Analog Digital ASIC Design.* New York: McGraw-Hill, 249 p. ISBN 0-07-707300-2. TK7874.T76.

Uyemura, J. P. 1992. *Circuit Design for CMOS VLSI.* Boston: Kluwer Academic Publishers, 450 p. ISBN 0-7923-9184-5. TK7874.U93. See also: J. P. Uyemura, *Fundamentals of MOS Digital Integrated Circuits,* Reading, MA: Addison-Wesley, 1988, 624 p. ISBN 0-201-13318-0. TK7874.U94. Reference for basic circuit equations related to NMOS and CMOS logic design.

Wakerly, J. F. 1994. *Digital Design: Principles and Practices.* 2nd ed. Englewood Cliffs, NJ: Prentice-Hall, 840 p. ISBN 0-13-211459-3. TK7874.65.W34. Introduction to logic design covering: binary arithmetic, CMOS and TTL, combinational logic, PLDs, sequential logic, memory, and the IEEE standard logic symbols.

Weste, N. H. E., and K. Eshraghian. 1993. *Principles of CMOS VLSI Design: A Systems Perspective.* 2nd ed. Reading, MA: Addison-Wesley, 713 p. ISBN 0-201-53376-6. TK7874.W46. See also the first edition of this book.

PROGRAMMABLE ASICs

There are two types of programmable ASICs: programmable logic devices (PLDs) and field-programmable gate arrays (FPGAs). The distinction between the two is blurred. The only real difference is their heritage. PLDs started as small devices that could replace a handful of TTL parts, and they have grown to look very much like their younger relations, the FPGAs. We shall group both types of programmable ASICs together as FPGAs.

An FPGA is a chip that you, as a systems designer, can program yourself. An IC foundry produces FPGAs with some connections missing. You perform design entry and simulation. Next, special software creates a string of bits describing the extra connections required to make your design—the **configuration file**. You then connect a computer to the chip and program the chip to make the necessary connections according to the configuration file. There is no customization of any mask level for an FPGA, allowing the FPGA to be manufactured as a standard part in high volume.

FPGAs are popular with microsystems designers because they fill a gap between TTL and PLD design and modern, complex, and often expensive ASICs. FPGAs are ideal for prototyping systems or for low-volume production. FPGA vendors do not need an IC fabrication facility to produce the chips; instead they contract IC foundries to produce their parts. Being fabless relieves the FPGA vendors of the huge burden of building and running a fabrication plant (a new submicron fab costs hundreds of millions of dollars). Instead FPGA companies put their effort into the FPGA architecture and the software, where it is much easier to make a profit than building chips. They often sell the chips through distributors, but sell design software and any necessary programming hardware directly.

All FPGAs have certain key elements in common. All FPGAs have a regular array of basic logic cells that are configured using a **programming technology**. The chip inputs and outputs use special I/O logic cells that are different from the basic logic cells. A programmable interconnect scheme forms the wiring between the two types of logic cells. Finally, the designer uses custom software, tailored to each programming technology and FPGA architecture, to design and implement the programmable connections. The programming technology in an FPGA determines the type of basic logic cell and the interconnect scheme. The logic cells and interconnection scheme, in turn, determine the design of the input and output circuits as well as the programming scheme.

The programming technology may or may not be permanent. You cannot undo the permanent programming in **one-time programmable** (**OTP**) FPGAs. Reprogrammable or erasable devices may be reused many times. We shall discuss the different programming technologies in the following sections.

4.1   The Antifuse

An **antifuse** is the opposite of a regular fuse—an antifuse is normally an open circuit until you force a **programming current** through it (about 5 mA). In a poly–diffusion antifuse the high current density causes a large power dissipation in a small area, which melts a thin insulating dielectric between polysilicon and diffusion electrodes and forms a thin (about 20 nm in diameter), permanent, and resistive silicon **link**. The programming process also drives dopant atoms from the poly and diffusion electrodes into the link, and the final level of doping determines the resistance value of the link. Actel calls its antifuse a programmable low-impedance circuit element (**PLICE**™).

Figure 4.1 shows a poly–diffusion antifuse with an **oxide–nitride–oxide** (**ONO**) dielectric sandwich of: silicon dioxide (SiO_2) grown over the n-type antifuse diffusion, a silicon nitride (Si_3N_4) layer, and another thin SiO_2 layer. The layered ONO dielectric results in a tighter spread of blown antifuse resistance values than using a single-oxide dielectric. The effective electrical thickness is equivalent to 10 nm of SiO_2 (Si_3N_4 has a higher dielectric constant than SiO_2, so the actual thickness is less than 10 nm). Sometimes this device is called a fuse even though it is an *anti*fuse, and both terms are often used interchangeably.

The fabrication process and the programming current control the average resistance of a blown antifuse, but values vary as shown in Figure 4.2. In a particular technology a programming current of 5 mA may result in an average blown antifuse resistance of about 500 Ω. Increasing the programming current to 15 mA might reduce the average antifuse resistance to 100 Ω. Antifuses separate interconnect

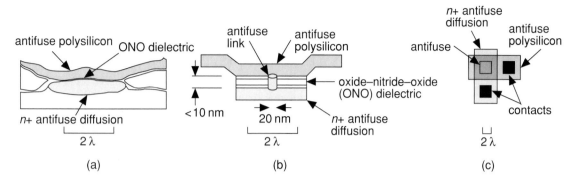

FIGURE 4.1 Actel antifuse. (a) A cross section. (b) A simplified drawing. The ONO (oxide–nitride–oxide) dielectric is less than 10 nm thick, so this diagram is not to scale. (c) From above, an antifuse is approximately the same size as a contact.

wires on the FPGA chip and the programmer blows an antifuse to make a permanent connection. Once an antifuse is programmed, the process cannot be reversed. This is an OTP technology (and radiation hard). An Actel 1010, for example, contains 112,000 antifuses (see Table 4.1), but we typically only need to program about 2 percent of the fuses on an Actel chip.

TABLE 4.1 Number of antifuses on Actel FPGAs.

Device	Antifuses
A1010	112,000
A1020	186,000
A1225	250,000
A1240	400,000
A1280	750,000

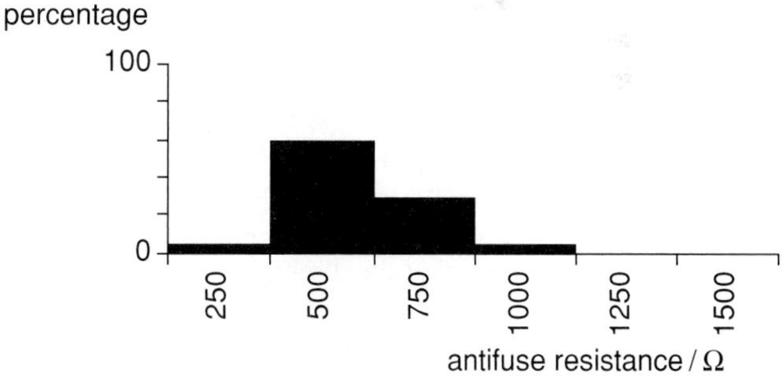

FIGURE 4.2 The resistance of blown Actel antifuses. The average antifuse resistance depends on the programming current. The resistance values shown here are typical for a programming current of 5 mA.

To design and program an Actel FPGA, designers iterate between design entry and simulation. When they are satisfied the design is correct they plug the chip into a socket on a special programming box, called an **Activator**, that generates the programming voltage. A PC downloads the configuration file to the Activator instructing it to blow the necessary antifuses on the chip. When the chip is programmed it may be removed from the Activator without harming the configuration data and the chip assembled into a system. One disadvantage of this procedure is that modern packages with hundreds of thin metal leads are susceptible to damage when they are inserted and removed from sockets. The advantage of other programming technologies is that chips may be programmed after they have been assembled on a printed-circuit board—a feature known as **in-system programming** (**ISP**).

The Actel antifuse technology uses a modified CMOS process. A double-metal, single-poly CMOS process typically uses about 12 masks—the Actel process requires an additional three masks. The n-type antifuse diffusion and antifuse polysilicon require an extra two masks and a 40 nm (thicker than normal) gate oxide (for the high-voltage transistors that handle 18 V to program the antifuses) uses one more masking step. Actel and Data General performed the initial experiments to develop the PLICE technology and Actel has licensed the technology to Texas Instruments (TI).

The programming time for an ACT 1 device is 5 to 10 minutes. Improvements in programming make the programming time for the ACT 2 and ACT 3 devices about the same as the ACT 1. A 5-day work week, with 8-hour days, contains about 2400 minutes. This is enough time to program 240 to 480 Actel parts per week with 100 percent efficiency and no hardware down time. A production schedule of more than 1000 parts per month requires multiple or gang programmers.

4.1.1   Metal–Metal Antifuse

Figure 4.3 shows a QuickLogic **metal–metal antifuse** (**ViaLink**™). The link is an alloy of tungsten, titanium, and silicon with a bulk resistance of about 500 $\mu\Omega$cm.

There are two advantages of a metal–metal antifuse over a poly–diffusion antifuse. The first is that connections to a metal–metal antifuse are direct to metal—the wiring layers. Connections from a poly–diffusion antifuse to the wiring layers require extra space and create additional parasitic capacitance. The second advantage is that the direct connection to the low-resistance metal layers makes it easier to use larger programming currents to reduce the antifuse resistance. For example, the antifuse resistance $R \approx 0.8/I$, with the programming current I in mA and R in Ω, for the QuickLogic antifuse. Figure 4.4 shows that the average QuickLogic metal–metal antifuse resistance is approximately 50 Ω (with a standard deviation of 4 Ω) using a programming current of 15 mA as opposed to an average antifuse resistance of 500 Ω (with a programming current of 5 mA) for a poly–diffusion antifuse.

The size of an antifuse is limited by the resolution of the lithography equipment used to makes ICs. The Actel antifuse connects diffusion and polysilicon, and both these materials are too resistive for use as signal interconnects. To connect the antifuse to the metal layers requires contacts that take up more space than the antifuse itself, reducing the advantage of the small antifuse size. However, the antifuse is so

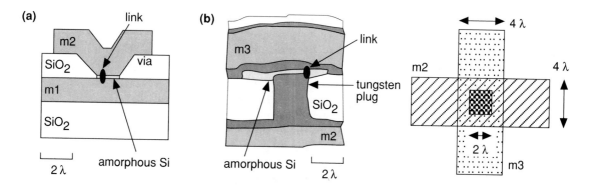

FIGURE 4.3 Metal–metal antifuse. (a) An idealized (but to scale) cross section of a QuickLogic metal–metal antifuse in a two-level metal process. (b) A metal–metal antifuse in a three-level metal process that uses contact plugs. The conductive link usually forms at the corner of the via where the electric field is highest during programming.

FIGURE 4.4 Resistance values for the QuickLogic metal–metal antifuse. A higher programming current (about 15 mA), made possible partly by the direct connections to metal, has reduced the antifuse resistance from the poly–diffusion antifuse resistance values shown in Figure 4.2.

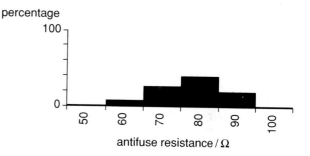

small that it is normally the contact and metal spacing design rules that limit how closely the antifuses may be packed rather than the size of the antifuse itself.

An antifuse is resistive and the addition of contacts adds parasitic capacitance. The intrinsic parasitic capacitance of an antifuse is small (approximately 1–2 fF in a 1 µm CMOS process), but to this we must add the extrinsic parasitic capacitance that includes the capacitance of the diffusion and poly electrodes (in a poly–diffusion antifuse) and connecting metal wires (approximately 10 fF). These unwanted parasitic elements can add considerable RC interconnect delay if the number of antifuses connected in series is not kept to an absolute minimum. Clever routing techniques are therefore crucial to antifuse-based FPGAs.

The long-term reliability of antifuses is an important issue since there is a tendency for the antifuse properties to change over time. There have been some problems in this area, but as a result we now know an enormous amount about this failure mechanism. There are many failure mechanisms in ICs—electromigration is a classic example—and engineers have learned to deal with these problems. Engineers design the circuits to keep the failure rate below acceptable limits and systems designers accept the statistics. All the FPGA vendors that use antifuse technology have extensive information on long-term reliability in their data books.

4.2   Static RAM

An example of **static RAM (SRAM)** programming technology is shown in Figure 4.5. This Xilinx SRAM configuration cell is constructed from two cross-coupled inverters and uses a standard CMOS process. The configuration cell drives the gates of other transistors on the chip—either turning pass transistors or transmission gates *on* to make a connection or *off* to break a connection.

FIGURE 4.5 The Xilinx SRAM (static RAM) configuration cell. The outputs of the cross-coupled inverter (configuration control) are connected to the gates of pass transistors or transmission gates. The cell is programmed using the WRITE and DATA lines.

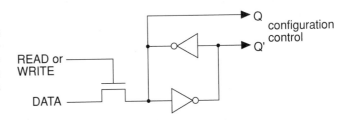

The advantages of SRAM programming technology are that designers can reuse chips during prototyping and a system can be manufactured using ISP. This programming technology is also useful for upgrades—a customer can be sent a new configuration file to reprogram a chip, not a new chip. Designers can also update or change a system on the fly in **reconfigurable hardware**.

The disadvantage of using SRAM programming technology is that you need to keep power supplied to the programmable ASIC (at a low level) for the volatile SRAM to retain the connection information. Alternatively you can load the configuration data from a permanently programmed memory (typically a **programmable read-only memory** or **PROM**) every time you turn the system on. The total size of an SRAM configuration cell plus the transistor switch that the SRAM cell drives is also larger than the programming devices used in the antifuse technologies.

4.3   EPROM and EEPROM Technology

Altera MAX 5k EPLDs and Xilinx EPLDs both use UV-erasable **electrically programmable read-only memory (EPROM)** cells as their programming technology. Altera's EPROM cell is shown in Figure 4.6. The EPROM cell is almost as small as an antifuse. An EPROM transistor looks like a normal MOS transistor except it has a second, floating, gate (gate1 in Figure 4.6). Applying a programming voltage V_{PP} (usually greater than 12 V) to the drain of the n-channel EPROM transistor programs the EPROM cell. A high electric field causes electrons flowing toward the drain to move so fast they "jump" across the insulating gate oxide where they are trapped on the bottom, floating, gate. We say these energetic electrons are *hot* and the effect is known as **hot-electron injection** or **avalanche injection**. EPROM technology is sometimes called **floating-gate avalanche MOS (FAMOS)**.

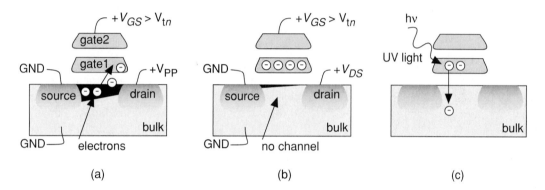

FIGURE 4.6   An EPROM transistor. (a) With a high (> 12 V) programming voltage, V_{PP}, applied to the drain, electrons gain enough energy to "jump" onto the floating gate (gate1). (b) Electrons stuck on gate1 raise the threshold voltage so that the transistor is always off for normal operating voltages. (c) Ultraviolet light provides enough energy for the electrons stuck on gate1 to "jump" back to the bulk, allowing the transistor to operate normally.

Electrons trapped on the floating gate raise the threshold voltage of the n-channel EPROM transistor (Figure 4.6b). Once programmed, an n-channel EPROM device remains *off* even with V_{DD} applied to the top gate. An unprogrammed n-channel device will turn *on* as normal with a top-gate voltage of V_{DD}. The programming voltage is applied either from a special programming box or by using on-chip charge pumps. Exposure to an ultraviolet (UV) lamp will erase the EPROM cell (Figure 4.6c). An absorbed light quantum gives an electron enough energy to jump from the floating gate. To erase a part we place it under a UV lamp (Xilinx specifies one hour within 1 inch of a $12,000\,\mu Wcm^{-2}$ source for its EPLDs). The manufacturer provides a software program that checks to see if a part is erased. You can buy an EPLD part in a windowed package for development, erase it, and use it again, or buy it in a nonwindowed package and program (or burn) the part once only for production. The packages get hot while they are being erased, so that windowed option is available with only ceramic packages, which are more expensive than plastic packages.

Programming an EEPROM transistor is similar to programming an UV-erasable EPROM transistor, but the erase mechanism is different. In an EEPROM transistor an electric field is also used to remove electrons from the floating gate of a programmed transistor. This is faster than using a UV lamp and the chip does not have to be removed from the system. If the part contains circuits to generate both program and erase voltages, they may use ISP.

4.4   Practical Issues

System companies often select an ASIC technology first, which narrows the choice of software design tools. The software then influences the choice of computer. Most **computer-aided engineering (CAE)** software for FPGA design uses some type of security. For workstations this usually means floating licenses (any of *n* users on a network can use the tools) or node-locked licenses (only *n* particular computers can use the tools) using the hostid (or host I.D., a serial number unique to each computer) in the boot EPROM (a chip containing start-up instructions). For PCs this is a hardware key, similar to the Viewlogic key illustrated in Figure 4.7. Some keys use the serial port (requiring extra cables and adapters); most now use the parallel port. There are often conflicts between keys and other hardware/software. For example, for a while some security keys did not work with the serial-port driver on Intel motherboards—users had to buy another serial-port I/O card.

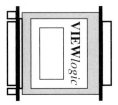

FIGURE 4.7 CAE companies use hardware security keys that fit at the back of a PC (this one is shown at about half the real size). Each piece of software requires a separate key, so that a typical design system may have a half dozen or more keys daisy-chained on one socket. This presents both mechanical and software conflict problems. Software will not run without a key, so it is easily possible to have $60,000 worth of keys attached to a single PC.

Most FPGA vendors offer software on multiple platforms. The performance difference between workstations and PCs is becoming blurred, but the time taken for the place-and-route step for Actel and Xilinx designs seems to remain constant—typically taking tens of minutes to over an hour for a large design—bounded by designers' tolerances.

A great deal of time during FPGA design is spent in schematic entry, editing files, and documentation. This often requires moving between programs and this is difficult on IBM-compatible PC platforms. Currently most large CAD and CAE programs completely take over the PC; for example you cannot always run third-party design entry and the FPGA vendor design systems simultaneously.

There are many other factors to be considered in choosing hardware:

- Software packages are normally less expensive on a PC.
- Peripherals are less expensive and easier to configure on a PC.
- Maintenance contracts are usually necessary and expensive for workstations.
- There is a much larger network of users to provide support for PC users.
- It is easier to upgrade a PC than a workstation.

4.4.1 FPGAs in Use

I once placed an order for a small number of FPGAs for prototyping and received a sales receipt with a scheduled shipping date three months away. Apparently, two customers had recently disrupted the vendor's product planning by placing large orders. Companies buying parts from suppliers often keep an **inventory** to cover emergencies such as a defective lot or manufacturing problems. For example, assume that a company keeps two months of inventory to ensure that it has parts in case of unforeseen problems. This **risk inventory** or safety supply, at a sales volume of 2000 parts per month, is 4000 parts, which, at an ASIC price of $5 per part, costs the company $20,000. FPGAs are normally sold through distributors, and, instead of keeping a risk inventory, a company can order parts as it needs them using a **just-in-time** (**JIT**) inventory system. This means that the distributors rather than the customer carry inventory (though the distributors wish to minimize inventory as well). The downside is that other customers may change their demands, causing unpredictable supply difficulties.

There are no standards for FPGAs equivalent to those in the TTL and PLD worlds; there are no standard pin assignments for VDD or GND, and each FPGA vendor uses different power and signal I/O pin arrangements. Most FPGA packages are intended for surface-mount **printed-circuit boards** (**PCBs**). However, surface mounting requires more expensive PCB test equipment and vapor soldering rather than bed-of-nails testers and surface-wave soldering. An alternative is to use socketed parts. Several FPGA vendors publish socket-reliability tests in their data books.

Using sockets raises its own set of problems. First, it is difficult to find wire-wrap sockets for surface-mount parts. Second, sockets may change the pin configuration. For example, when you use an FPGA in a PLCC package and plug it into a socket that has a PGA footprint, the resulting arrangement of pins is different from the same FPGA in a PGA package. This means you cannot use the same board layout for a prototype PCB (which uses the socketed PLCC part) as for the production PCB (which uses the PGA part). The same problem occurs when you use through-hole mounted parts for prototyping and surface-mount parts for production. To deal with this you can add a small piece to your prototype board that you use as a converter. This can be sawn off on the production boards—saving a board iteration.

Pin assignment can also cause a problem if you plan to convert an FPGA design to an MGA or CBIC. In most cases it is desirable to keep the same pin assignment as the FPGA (this is known as **pin locking** or **I/O locking**), so that the same PCB can be used in production for both types of devices. There are often restrictions for custom gate arrays on the number and location of power pads and package pins. Systems designers must consider these problems before designing the FPGA and PCB.

4.5 Specifications

All FPGA manufactures are continually improving their products to increase performance and reduce price. Often this means changing the design of an FPGA or moving a part from one process generation to the next without changing the part number (and often without changing the specifications).

FPGA companies usually explain their part history in their data books.[1] The following history of Actel FPGA ACT 1 part numbers illustrates changes typical throughout the IC industry as products develop and mature:

- The Actel ACT 1 A1010/A1020 used a 2 μm process.
- The Actel A1010A/A1020A used a 1.2 μm process.
- The Actel A1020B was a die revision (including a shrink to a 1.0 μm process). At this time the A1020, A1020A, and A1020B all had different speeds.
- Actel graded parts into three speed bins as they phased in new processes, dropping the distinction between the different die suffixes.
- At the same time as the transition to die rev. 'B', Actel began specifying timing at worst-case commercial conditions rather than at typical conditions.

From this history we can see that it is often possible to have parts from the same family that use different circuit designs, processes, and die sizes, are manufactured in different locations, and operate at very different speeds. FPGA companies ensure that their products always meet the current published worst-case specifications, but there is no guarantee that the average performance follows the typical specifications, and there are usually no best-case specifications.

There are also situations in which two parts with identical part numbers can have different performance—when different ASIC foundries produce the same parts. Since FPGA companies are fabless, second sourcing is very common. For example, TI began making the TPC1010A/1020A to be equivalent to the original Actel ACT 1 parts produced elsewhere. The TI timing information for the TPC1010A/1020A was the same as the 2 μm Actel specifications, but TI used a faster 1.2 μm process. This meant that "equivalent" parts with the same part numbers were *much* faster than a designer expected. Often this type of information can only be obtained by large customers in the form of a **qualification kit** from FPGA vendors.

---

[1]See, for example, p.1-8 of the Xilinx 1994 data book.

A similar situation arises when the FPGA manufacturer adjusts its product mix by selling fast parts under a slower part number in a procedure known as **down-binning**. This is not a problem for synchronous designs that always work when parts are faster than expected, but is another reason to avoid asynchronous designs that may not always work when parts are much faster than expected.

4.6 PREP Benchmarks

Which type of FPGA is best? This is an impossible question to answer. The **Programmable Electronics Performance Company (PREP)** is a nonprofit organization that organized a series of benchmarks for programmable ASICs. The nine PREP benchmark circuits in the version 1.3 suite are:

1. An 8-bit datapath consisting of 4:1 MUX, register, and shift-register
2. An 8-bit timer–counter consisting of two registers, a 4:1 MUX, a counter and a comparator
3. A small state machine (8 states, 8 inputs, and 8 outputs)
4. A larger state machine (16 states, 8 inputs, and 8 outputs)
5. An ALU consisting of a 4×4 multiplier, an 8-bit adder, and an 8-bit register
6. A 16-bit accumulator
7. A 16-bit counter with synchronous load and enable
8. A 16-bit prescaled counter with load and enable
9. A 16-bit address decoder

The data for these benchmarks is archived at http://www.prep.org. PREP's online information includes Verilog and VHDL source code and test benches (provided by Synplicity) as well as additional synthesis benchmarks including a bit-slice processor, multiplier, and R4000 MIPS RISC microprocessor.

One problem with the FPGA benchmark suite is that the examples are small, allowing FPGA vendors to replicate multiple instances of the same circuit on an FPGA. This does not reflect the way an FPGA is used in practice. Another problem is that the FPGA vendors badly misused the results. PREP made the data available in a spreadsheet form and thus inadvertently challenged the marketing department of each FPGA vendor to find a way that company could claim to win the benchmarks (usually by manipulating the data using a complicated weighting scheme). The PREP benchmarks do demonstrate the large variation in performance between different FPGA architectures that results from differences in the type and mix of logic. This shows that designers should be careful in evaluating others' results and performing their own experiments.

4.7 FPGA Economics

FPGA vendors offer a wide variety of packaging, speed, and qualification (military, industrial, or commercial) options in each family. For example, there are several hundred possible part combinations for the Xilinx LCA series. Figure 4.8 shows the Xilinx part-naming convention, which is similar to that used by other FPGA vendors.

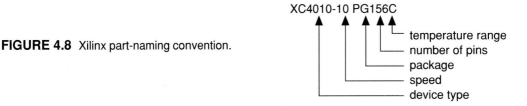

FIGURE 4.8 Xilinx part-naming convention.

Table 4.2 shows the various codes used by manufacturers in their FPGA part numbers. Not all possible part combinations are available, not all packaging combinations are available, and not all I/O options are available in all packages. For example, it is quite common for an FPGA vendor to offer a chip that has more I/O cells than pins on the package. This allows the use of cheaper plastic packages without having to produce separate chip designs for each different package. Thus a customer can buy an Actel A1020 that has 69 I/O cells in an inexpensive 44-pin PLCC package but uses only 34 pins for I/O—the other 10 (=44 − 34) pins are required for programming and power: three for GND, four for VDD, one for MODE (a pin that controls four other multifunction pins), and one for VPP (the programming voltage). A designer who needs all 69 IOs can buy the A1020 in a bigger package. Tables in the FPGA manufacturers' data books show the availability, and these matrices change constantly.

4.7.1 FPGA Pricing

Asking "How much do FPGAs cost?" is rather like asking "How much does a car cost?" Prices of cars are published, but pricing schemes used by semiconductor manufactures are closely guarded secrets. Many FPGA companies use a pricing strategy based on a cost model that uses a series of multipliers or adders for each part option to calculate the suggested price for their distributors. Although the FPGA companies will not divulge their methods, it is possible to reverse engineer these factors to create a pricing matrix.

Many FPGA vendors sell parts through distributors. This can introduce some problems for the designer. For example, in 1992 the Xilinx XC3000 series offered the following part options:

- Five different size parts: XC30{20, 30, 42, 64, 90}
- Three different speed grades or bins: {50, 70, 100}

TABLE 4.2   Programmable ASIC part codes.

Item	Code	Description	Code	Description
Manufacturer's code	A	Actel	ATT	AT&T (Lucent)
	XC	Xilinx	isp	Lattice Logic
	EPM	Altera MAX	M5	AMD MACH 5 is on the device
	EPF	Altera FLEX	QL	QuickLogic
	CY7C	Cypress		
Package type	PL or PC	plastic J-leaded chip carrier, PLCC	VQ	very thin quad flatpack, VQFP
	PQ	plastic quad flatpack, PQFP	TQ	thin plastic flatpack, TQFP
	CQ or CB	ceramic quad flatpack, CQFP	PP	plastic pin-grid array, PPGA
	PG	ceramic pin-grid array, PGA	WB, PB	ball-grid array, BGA
Application	C	commercial	B	MIL-STD-883
	I	industrial	E	extended
	M	military		

TABLE 4.3   1992 base Actel FPGA prices.

Actel part	1H92 base price
A1010A-PL44C	$23.25
A1020A-PL44C	$43.30
A1225-PQ100C	$105.00
A1240-PQ144C	$175.00
A1280-PQ160C	$305.00

TABLE 4.4   1992 base Xilinx XC3000 FPGA prices.

Xilinx part	1H92 base price
XC3020-50PC68C	$26.00
XC3030-50PC44C	$34.20
XC3042-50PC84C	$52.00
XC3064-50PC84C	$87.00
XC3090-50PC84C	$133.30

- Ten different packages: {PC68, PC84, PG84, PQ100, CQ100, PP132, PG132, CQ184, PP175, PG175}
- Four application ranges or qualification types: {C, I, M, B}

where { } means "Choose one."

This range of options gave a total of 600 possible XC3000 products, of which 127 were actually available from Xilinx, each with a different part code. If a designer is uncertain as to exact size, speed, or package required, then they might easily need price information on several dozen different part numbers. Distributors know the price information—it is given to each distributor by the FPGA vendors. Sometimes the distributors are reluctant to give pricing information out—for the

TABLE 4.5   Actel price adjustment factors.

Purchase quantity, all types

(1–9)	(10–99)	(100–999)
100 %	96 %	84 %

Purchase time, in (100–999) quantity

1H92	2H92	93
100 %	80–95 %	60–80 %

Qualification type, same package

Commercial	Industrial	Military	883-B
100 %	120 %	150 %	230–300 %

Speed bin[1]

ACT 1-Std	ACT 1-1	ACT 1-2	ACT 2-Std	ACT 2-1
100 %	115 %	140 %	100 %	120 %

Package type

A1010:	PL44, 64, 84	PQ100	PG84		
	100 %	125 %	400 %		
A1020:	PL44, 64, 84	PQ100	JQ44, 68, 84	PG84	CQ84
	100 %	125 %	270 %	275 %	400 %
A1225:	PQ100	PG100			
	100 %	175 %			
A1240:	PQ144	PG132			
	100 %	140 %			
A1280:	PQ160	PG176	CQ172		
	100 %	145 %	160 %		

[1]Actel speed bins are: Std = standard speed grade; 1 = medium speed grade; 2 = fastest speed grade.

same reason car salespeople do not always like to advertise the pricing scheme for cars. However, pricing of the components of a microelectronics system is a vital factor in making decisions such as whether to use FPGAs or some alternative technology. Designers would like to know how FPGAs are priced and how prices may change.

4.7.2   Pricing Examples

Table 4.3 shows the prices of the least-expensive version of the Actel ACT 1 and ACT 2 FPGA families, the **base prices**, in the first half of 1992 (1H92). Table 4.4 shows the 1H92 base prices for the Xilinx XC3000 FPGA family. Current FPGA prices are much lower. As an example, the least-expensive XC3000 part, the XC3020A-7PC68C, was $13.75 in 1996—nearly half the 1992 price.

Using historical prices helps prevent accusations of bias or distortion, but still realistically illustrates the pricing schemes that are used. We shall use these base prices to illustrate how to estimate the sticker price of an FPGA by adding options— as we might for a car. To estimate the price of any part, multiply the base prices by the **adjustment factors** (shown in Table 4.5 for the Actel parts).

The adjustment factors in Table 4.5 were calculated by taking averages across a matrix of prices. Not all combinations of product types are available (for example, there was no military version of an A1280-1 in 1H92). The dependence of price over time is especially variable. An example price calculation for an Actel part is shown in Table 4.6. Many FPGA vendors use similar pricing models.

TABLE 4.6   Example Actel part-price calculation using the base prices of Table 4.3 and the adjustment factors of Table 4.5.

Example: A1020A-2-PQ100I in (100–999) quantity, purchased 1H92.

Factor	Example	Value
Base price	A1020A	$43.30
Quantity	100–999	84%
Time	1H92	100%
Qualification type	Industrial (I)	120%
Speed bin[1]	2	140%
Package	PQ100	125%
Estimated price (1H92)		$76.38
Actual Actel price (1H92)		$75.60

[1]The speed bin is a manufacturer's code (usually a number) that follows the family part number and indicates the maximum operating speed of the device.

Some distributors now include FPGA prices and availability online (for example, Marshall at `http://marshall.com` for Xilinx parts) so that is possible to complete an up-to-date analysis at any time. Most distributors carry only one FPGA vendor; not all of the distributors publish prices; and not all FPGA vendors sell through distributors. Currently Hamilton-Avnet, at `http://www.hh.avnet.com`, carries Xilinx; and Wyle, at `http://www.wyle.com`, carries Actel and Altera.

4.8   Summary

In this chapter we have covered FPGA programming technologies including antifuse, SRAM, and EPROM technologies; the programming technology is linked to all the other aspects of a programmable ASIC. Table 4.7 summarizes the programming technologies and the fabrication processes used by programmable ASIC vendors.

TABLE 4.7   Programmable ASIC technologies.

	Actel	Xilinx LCA[1]	Altera EPLD	Xilinx EPLD
Programming technology	Poly–diffusion antifuse, PLICE	Erasable SRAM ISP	UV-erasable EPROM (MAX 5k) EEPROM (MAX 7/9k)	UV-erasable EPROM
Size of programming element	Small but requires contacts to metal	Two inverters plus pass and switch devices. Largest.	One n-channel EPROM device. Medium.	One n-channel EPROM device. Medium.
Process	Special: CMOS plus three extra masks.	Standard CMOS	Standard EPROM and EEPROM	Standard EPROM
Programming method	Special hardware	PC card, PROM, or serial port	ISP (MAX 9k) or EPROM programmer	EPROM programmer

	QuickLogic	Crosspoint	Atmel	Altera FLEX
Programming technology	Metal–metal antifuse, ViaLink	Metal–polysilicon antifuse	Erasable SRAM. ISP.	Erasable SRAM. ISP.
Size of programming element	Smallest	Small	Two inverters plus pass and switch devices. Largest.	Two inverters plus pass and switch devices. Largest.
Process	Special, CMOS plus ViaLink	Special, CMOS plus antifuse	Standard CMOS	Standard CMOS
Programming method	Special hardware	Special hardware	PC card, PROM, or serial port	PC card, PROM, or serial port

[1]Lucent (formerly AT&T) FPGAs have almost identical properties to the Xilinx LCA family.

All FPGAs have the following key elements:

- The programming technology
- The basic logic cells
- The I/O logic cells
- Programmable interconnect
- Software to design and program the FPGA

4.9   Problems

* = Difficult, ** = Very difficult, *** = Extremely difficult

4.1 (Antifuse properties, 20 min.) In this problem we examine some of the physical and electrical features of the antifuse programming process.

a. If the programming current of an antifuse is 5 mA and the link diameter that is formed is 20 nm, what is the current density during programming?

b. If the average antifuse resistance is 500 Ω after programming is complete and the programming current is 5 mA, what is the voltage across the antifuse at completion of programming?

c. What power is dissipated in the antifuse link at the end of programming?

d. Suppose we wish to reduce the antifuse resistance from 500 Ω to 50 Ω. If the antifuse link is a tall, thin cylinder, what is the diameter of a 50 Ω antifuse?

e. Assume we need to keep the power dissipated per unit volume of the antifuse link the same at the end of the programming process for both 500 Ω and 50 Ω antifuses. What current density is required to program a 50 Ω antifuse?

f. With these assumptions what is the required programming current for a 50 Ω antifuse? Comment on your answer and the assumptions that you have made.

4.2 (Actel antifuse programming, 20 min.) In this problem we examine the time taken to program an antifuse-based FPGA.

a. We have stated that it takes about 5 to 10 minutes to program an Actel part. Given the number of antifuses on the smallest Actel part, and the number of antifuses that need to be blown on average, work out the equivalent time it takes to blow one antifuse. Does this seem reasonable?

b. Because of a failure process known as electromigration, the current density in a metal wire on a chip is limited to about 50 kAcm^{-2}. You can exceed this current for a short time as long as the time average does not exceed the limit. Suppose we want to use a minimum metal width to connect the programming transistors: Would these facts help explain your answer to part a?

c. What other factors might be involved in the process of blowing antifuses that may help explain your answer to part a?

4.3 (*Xilinx cell) Estimate the area components of a Xilinx cell as follows:

a. (30 min.) Assume the two inverters in the cross-coupled SRAM cell are minimum size (they are not, the *p*-channels—or *n*-channels—in one inverter need to be weak—long and narrow—but ignore this). Assume the read–write device is minimum size. Estimate the size of the SRAM cell including an allowance for wiring (state your assumptions clearly).

b. (15 min.) Assume a single *n*-channel pass transistor is connected to the SRAM cell and has an on-resistance of $500\,\Omega$ (equal to the average Actel ACT 1 antifuse resistance for comparison; the actual Xilinx pass transistors have closer to $1\,k\Omega$ on-resistance). Estimate the transistor size. Assume the gate voltage of the pass transistor is at 5 V, and the source and drain voltages are both at 0 V (the best case). *Hint:* Use the parameters from Section 3.1, "Transistors as Resistors."

c. (15 min.) Compare your total area estimates of the cell with other FPGA technologies. Explain why the assumptions you made may be too simple, and suggest ways to make more accurate estimates.

4.4 (FPGA vendors, 60 min.) Update the information shown in Table 4.7 using the online information provided by FPGA vendors.

4.5 (Prices) Adjustment factors, calculated from averages across the Xilinx price matrix, are shown in Table 4.8 (the adjustment factors for the Xilinx military and MIL-STD parts vary so wildly that it is not possible to use a simple model to predict these prices).

a. (5 min.) Estimate the price of a XC3042-70PG132I in 100+ quantity, purchased in 1H92.

b. (30 min.) Use the 1992 prices in Figure 4.9 to derive as much of the information shown in Table 4.8 as you can, explaining your methods.

3042	(1–24)	(25–99)	(100+)
50PC84C	$52.00	$47.30	$40.05
50PC84I	$67.30	$61.25	$51.80
70PC84C	$56.50	$51.40	$43.50
70PC84I	$73.30	$66.70	$56.45
100PC84C	$67.70	$61.60	$52.15
125PC84C	$114.00	$103.75	$87.80
50PP132C	$124.50	$113.30	$95.85
50PQ100C	$60.40		
50PG84C	$161.50		
50CQ100C	$194.50		
50PG132C	$191.20		

FIGURE 4.9 Xilinx XC3042 prices (1992). Problem 4.5 reconstructs part of Table 4.8 from this data.

TABLE 4.8 **Xilinx price adjustment factors (1992) for Problem 4.5**

Purchase quantity, all types

(1–24)	(25–99)	(100+)	(5000+)
100%	91%	77%	70%

Purchase time, in (100–999) quantity

1H92	+18 months
100%	60%

Qualification type, same package

Commercial	Industrial	Military	883-B
100%	130%	varies	varies

Speed bin

50	70	100	125
100%	110%	130%	220%

Package type

3020:	PC68	PC84	PQ100	PG84	CQ100	
	100%	106%	127%	340%	490%	
3030:	PC44	PC68	PC84	PQ100	PG84	
	100%	107%	113%	135%	330%	
3042:	PC84	PQ100	PP132	PG84	PG132	CQ100
	100%	175%	240%	310%	370%	375%
3064:	PC84	PQ160	PP132	PG132		
	100%	150%	190%	260%		
3090:	PC84	PQ160	PP175	PG175	CQ164	
	100%	130%	150%	230%	240%	

c. (Hours) Construct a table (using the format of Table 4.8) for a current FPGA family. You may have to be creative in capturing the HTML and filtering it into a spreadsheet. *Hint:* In Microsoft Word 5.0 you can select columns of text by holding down the Option key.

Answer: (a) $211.85 (the actual Xilinx price was $210.20).

4.6 (PREP benchmarks, 60 min.) Download the PREP 1.3 benchmark results as spreadsheets from `http://www.prep.org`. Split the participating companies among groups and challenge each group to produce an averaging or analysis scheme that shows the group's assigned company as a "winner." For hints on this problem, consult advertisements in past issues of *EE Times*.

4.7 (FPGA patents) Patents are a good place to find information on FPGAs.

a. Find U.S. Patent 5,440,245, Galbraith et al. "Logic module with configurable combinational and sequential blocks." Find and explain a method to paste the figures into a report.

b. Conduct a patent search on FPGAs. Good places to start are the **U.S. Patent and Trademark Office (PTO)** at `http://www.uspto.gov` and the IBM patent resource at `http://patent.womplex.ibm.com`. Until 1996 the full text of recent U.S. patents was available at `http://www.town.hall.org/patent`; this is still a good site to visit for references to other locations. Table 4.9 lists the patents awarded to the major FPGA companies up until 1996 (in the case of Actel and Altera the list includes only patents issued after 1990, corresponding roughly to patent numbers greater than number 5,000,000, which was issued in March 1990).

4.8 (**Maskworks, days) If you really want to find out about FPGA technology you tear chips apart. There is another way. Most U.S. companies register their chips as a type of copyright called a **Maskwork**. You will often see a little circle containing an "M" on a chip in the same way that a copyright sign is a circle surrounding the letter "C". Companies that require a Maskwork are required to deposit plots and samples of the chips with a branch of the Library of Congress. These plots are open for public inspection in Washington, D.C. It is perfectly legal to use this information. You have to sign a visitors' book, and most of the names in the book are Japanese. Research Maskworks and write a summary of its implications, the protection it provides, and (if you can find them) the rules for the materials that must be deposited with the authorities.

TABLE 4.9 FPGA Patents (U.S.).

QuickLogic	Xilinx	5,329,181	4,713,557	5,308,795	5,008,855	5,280,203
5,416,367	5,436,575	5,329,174	4,706,216	5,304,871		5,274,581
5,397,939	5,432,719	5,329,181	4,695,740	5,299,150	**Altera**	5,272,368
5,396,127	5,430,687	5,321,704	4,642,487	5,286,992	5,477,474	5,268,598
5,362,676	5,430,390	5,319,254		5,272,388	5,473,266	5,260,611
5,319,238	5,426,379	5,319,252	**Actel**	5,272,101	5,463,328	5,260,610
5,302,546	5,426,378	5,302,866	5,479,113	5,266,829	5,444,394	5,258,668
5,220,213	5,422,833	5,295,090	5,477,165	5,254,886	5,438,295	5,247,478
5,196,724	5,414,377	5,291,079	5,469,396	5,223,792	5,436,575	5,247,477
	5,410,194	5,245,277	5,464,790	5,208,530	5,436,574	5,243,233
Intel	5,410,189	5,224,056	5,457,644	5,198,705	5,434,514	5,241,224
4,543,594[1]	5,399,925	5,166,858	5,451,887	5,194,759	5,432,467	5,237,219
	5,399,924	5,155,432	5,449,947	5,191,241	5,414,312	5,220,533
Crosspoint	5,394,104	5,148,390	5,448,185	5,187,393	5,399,922	5,220,214
5,440,453	5,386,154	5,068,603	5,440,245	5,181,096	5,384,499	5,200,920
5,394,103	5,367,207	5,047,710	5,432,441	5,172,014	5,376,844	5,166,604
5,384,481	5,365,125	5,028,821	5,414,364	5,171,715	5,371,422	5,162,680
5,322,812	5,362,999	5,023,606	5,412,244	5,163,180	5,369,314	5,144,167
5,313,119	5,361,229	5,012,135	5,411,917	5,134,457	5,359,243	5,138,576
5,233,217	5,360,747	4,967,107	5,404,029	5,132,571	5,359,242	5,128,565
5,221,865	5,359,536	4,940,909	5,391,942	5,130,777	5,353,248	5,121,006
	5,349,691	4,902,910	5,387,812	5,126,282	5,352,940	5,111,423
Concurrent	5,349,250	4,870,302	5,373,169	5,111,262	5,350,954	5,097,208
5,218,240	5,349,249	4,855,669	5,371,414	5,107,146	5,349,255	5,091,661
5,144,166	5,349,248	4,855,619	5,369,054	5,095,228	5,341,308	5,066,873
5,089,973	5,343,406	4,847,612	5,367,208	5,087,958	5,341,048	5,045,772
	5,337,255	4,835,418	5,365,165	5,083,083	5,341,044	
Plus Logic	5,349,248	4,821,233	5,341,092	5,073,729	5,329,487	
5,028,821	5,343,406	4,820,937	5,341,043	5,070,384	5,317,210	
5,023,606	5,337,255	4,783,607	5,341,030	5,057,451	5,315,172	
5,012,135	5,332,929	4,758,985	5,317,698	5,055,718	5,301,416	
4,967,107	5,331,226	4,750,155	5,316,971	5,017,813	5,294,975	
4,940,909	5,331,220	4,746,822	5,309,091	5,015,885	5,285,153	

[1]Mohsen's patent on the antifuse structure.

4.10   Bibliography

Books by Ukeiley [1993], Chan [1994], and Trimberger [1994] are dedicated to FPGAs and their uses. The *International Workshop on Field-Programmable Logic and Applications* describes the latest developments and applications of FPGAs [Grünbacher and Hartenstein, 1992; Hartenstein and Servit, 1994; Moore and Luk, 1995]; Hartenstein and Glesner [1996]. Many of the FPGA vendors have Web sites that include white papers and technical documentation. The annual *IEEE International Electron Devices Meeting* (IEDM, ISSN 0163-1918, TK 7801.I53) is a forum for presenting new device and IC technology including new FPGA programming technologies. The *IEEE Transaction on Electron Devices* (ISSN 0018-9383) is the archival source for developments in device technology.

There is a large U.S. patent literature on FPGAs (see Table 4.9). Sometimes the FPGA vendors hide the basic low-level structures from the user to simplify their description or to prevent the competition from understanding their secrets. Patents have to explain the details of operation (otherwise they will not be awarded or cannot be enforced), so sometimes it can be useful to at least know where to look. One place to start is the front or back of the data book, which often contains a list of the manufacturer's patents.

4.11   References

Chan, P. K., and S. Mourad. 1994. *Digital Design Using Field Programmable Gate Arrays.* Englewood Cliffs, NJ: Prentice-Hall, 233 p. ISBN 0-13-319021-8. TK7888.4.C43.

Grünbacher, H., and R. W. Hartenstein. (Eds.). 1993. *International Workshop on Field-Programmable Logic and Applications* (2nd: 1992: Vienna). Berlin; New York: Springer-Verlag. ISBN 0387570918. TK7895.G36.I48.

Hartenstein, R. W., and M. Glesner (Eds.). 1996. *International Workshop on Field-Programmable Logic and Applications* (6th: 1996: Darmstadt). Berlin; New York: Springer-Verlag. ISBN 3540617302. TK7868.L6.I56.

Hartenstein, R. W., and M. Z. Servit. (Eds.). 1994. *International Workshop on Field-Programmable Logic and Applications* (4th: 1994: Prague). Berlin; New York: Springer-Verlag. ISBN 0387584196. TK7868.L6.I56.

Moore, W., and W. Luk. (Eds.). 1995. *International Workshop on Field-Programmable Logic and Applications* (5th: 1995: Oxford). Berlin; New York: Springer-Verlag. ISBN 3540602941. TK7895.G36.I48.

Trimberger, S. M. (Ed.). 1994. *Field-Programmable Gate Array Technology.* Boston: Kluwer Academic Publishers. ISBN 0-7923-9419-4. TK7895.G36.F54.

Ukeiley, R. L. 1993. *Field Programmable Gate Arrays (FPGAs): The 3000 Series.* Englewood Cliffs, NJ: Prentice-Hall, 173 p. ISBN 0-13-319468-X. TK7895.G36.U44.

PROGRAMMABLE ASIC LOGIC CELLS

5

All programmable ASICs or FPGAs contain a **basic logic cell** replicated in a regular array across the chip (analogous to a base cell in an MGA). There are the following three different types of basic logic cells: (1) multiplexer based, (2) look-up table based, and (3) programmable array logic. The choice among these depends on the programming technology. We shall see examples of each in this chapter.

5.1   Actel ACT

The basic logic cells in the Actel ACT family of FPGAs are called **Logic Modules**. The ACT 1 family uses just one type of Logic Module and the ACT 2 and ACT 3 FPGA families both use two different types of Logic Module.

5.1.1   ACT 1 Logic Module

The functional behavior of the Actel ACT 1 Logic Module is shown in Figure 5.1(a). Figure 5.1(b) represents a possible circuit-level implementation. We can build a logic function using an Actel Logic Module by connecting logic signals to some or all of the Logic Module inputs, and by connecting any remaining Logic Module inputs to VDD or GND. As an example, Figure 5.1(c) shows the connections to implement the function $F = A \cdot B + B' \cdot C + D$. How did we know what connections to make? To understand how the Actel Logic Module works, we take a detour via multiplexer logic and some theory.

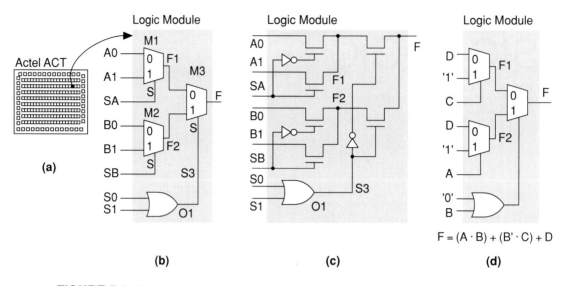

FIGURE 5.1 The Actel ACT architecture. (a) Organization of the basic logic cells. (b) The ACT 1 Logic Module. (c) An implementation using pass transistors (without any buffering). (d) An example logic macro. (*Source*: Actel.)

5.1.2 Shannon's Expansion Theorem

In logic design we often have to deal with functions of many variables. We need a method to break down these large functions into smaller pieces. Using the **Shannon expansion theorem,** we can **expand** a Boolean logic function F in terms of (or with respect to) a Boolean variable A,

$$F = A \cdot F(A = '1') + A' \cdot F(A = '0'), \tag{5.1}$$

where $F(A = 1)$ represents the function F evaluated with A set equal to '1'.

For example, we can expand the following function F with respect to (I shall use the abbreviation *wrt*) A,

$$F = A' \cdot B + A \cdot B \cdot C' + A' \cdot B' \cdot C$$

$$= A \cdot (B \cdot C') + A' \cdot (B + B' \cdot C). \tag{5.2}$$

We have split F into two smaller functions. We call $F(A = '1') = B \cdot C'$ the **cofactor** of F *wrt* A in Eq. 5.2. I shall sometimes write the cofactor of F *wrt* A as F_A (the cofactor of F *wrt* A' is $F_{A'}$). We may expand a function *wrt* any of its variables. For example, if we expand F *wrt* B instead of A,

$$F = A' \cdot B + A \cdot B \cdot C' + A' \cdot B' \cdot C$$

$$= B \cdot (A' + A \cdot C') + B' \cdot (A' \cdot C). \tag{5.3}$$

We can continue to expand a function as many times as it has variables until we reach the **canonical form** (a unique representation for any Boolean function that uses only minterms. A **minterm** is a product term that contains all the variables of F—such as $A \cdot B' \cdot C$). Expanding Eq. 5.3 again, this time *wrt* C, gives

$$F = C \cdot (A' \cdot B + A' \cdot B') + C' \cdot (A \cdot B + A' \cdot B). \qquad (5.4)$$

As another example, we will use the Shannon expansion theorem to implement the following function using the ACT 1 Logic Module:

$$F = (A \cdot B) + (B' \cdot C) + D. \qquad (5.5)$$

First we expand F *wrt* B:

$$F = B \cdot (A + D) + B' \cdot (C + D)$$
$$= B \cdot F2 + B' \cdot F1. \qquad (5.6)$$

Equation 5.6 describes a 2:1 MUX, with B selecting between two inputs: $F(A = '1')$ and $F(A = '0')$. In fact Eq. 5.6 also describes the output of the ACT 1 Logic Module in Figure 5.1! Now we need to split up F1 and F2 in Eq. 5.6. Suppose we expand $F2 = F_B$ *wrt* A, and $F1 = F_{B'}$ *wrt* C:

$$F2 = A + D = (A \cdot 1) + (A' \cdot D), \qquad (5.7)$$

$$F1 = C + D = (C \cdot 1) + (C' \cdot D). \qquad (5.8)$$

From Eqs. 5.6–5.8 we see that we may implement F by arranging for A, B, C to appear on the select lines and '1' and D to be the data inputs of the MUXes in the ACT 1 Logic Module. This is the implementation shown in Figure 5.1(d), with connections: A0 = D, A1 = '1', B0 = D, B1 = '1', SA = C, SB = A, S0 = '0', and S1 = B.

Now that we know that we can implement Boolean functions using MUXes, how do we know which functions we can implement and how to implement them?

5.1.3 Multiplexer Logic as Function Generators

Figure 5.2 illustrates the 16 different ways to arrange '1's on a Karnaugh map corresponding to the 16 logic functions, $F(A, B)$, of two variables. Two of these functions are not very interesting ($F = '0'$, and $F = '1'$). Of the 16 functions, Table 5.1 shows the 10 that we can implement using just one 2:1 MUX. Of these 10 functions, the following six are useful:

- INV. The MUX acts as an inverter for one input only.
- BUF. The MUX just passes one of the MUX inputs directly to the output.
- AND. A two-input AND.
- OR. A two-input OR.
- AND1–1. A two-input AND gate with inverted input, equivalent to an NOR–11.
- NOR1–1. A two-input NOR gate with inverted input, equivalent to an AND–11.

FIGURE 5.2 The logic functions of two variables.

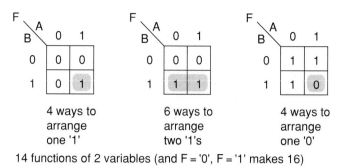

4 ways to arrange one '1'

6 ways to arrange two '1's

4 ways to arrange one '0'

14 functions of 2 variables (and F = '0', F = '1' makes 16)

TABLE 5.1   Boolean functions using a 2:1 MUX.

	Function, F	F =	Canonical form	Minterms[1]	Minterm code[2]	Function number[3]	M1[4] AO	A1	SA
1	'0'	'0'	'0'	none	0000	0	0	0	0
2	NOR1-1(A, B)	(A + B')'	A' · B	1	0010	2	B	0	A
3	NOT(A)	A'	A' · B' + A' · B	0, 1	0011	3	0	1	A
4	AND1-1(A, B)	A · B'	A · B'	2	0100	4	A	0	B
5	NOT(B)	B'	A' · B' + A · B'	0, 2	0101	5	0	1	B
6	BUF(B)	B	A' · B + A · B	1, 3	1010	6	0	B	1
7	AND(A, B)	A · B	A · B	3	1000	8	0	B	A
8	BUF(A)	A	A · B' + A · B	2, 3	1100	9	0	A	1
9	OR(A, B)	A + B	A' · B + A · B' + A · B	1, 2, 3	1110	13	B	1	A
10	'1'	'1'	A' · B' + A' · B + A · B' + A · B	0, 1, 2, 3	1111	15	1	1	1

[1]The minterm numbers are formed from the product terms of the canonical form. For example, A · B' = 10 = 2.
[2]The minterm code is formed from the minterms. A '1' denotes the presence of that minterm.
[3]The function number is the decimal version of the minterm code.
[4]Connections to a two-input MUX: A0 and A1 are the data inputs and SA is the select input (see Eq. 5.11).

Figure 5.3(a) shows how we might view a 2:1 MUX as a **function wheel**, a three-input black box that can generate any one of the six functions of two-input variables: BUF, INV, AND-11, AND1-1, OR, AND. We can write the output of a function wheel as

$$F1 = WHEEL1 \ (A, B). \tag{5.9}$$

where I define the wheel function as follows:

$$\text{WHEEL1 (A, B)} = \text{MUX (A0, A1, SA)}. \qquad (5.10)$$

The MUX function is not unique; we shall define it as

$$\text{MUX (A0, A1, SA)} = \text{A0} \cdot \text{SA'} + \text{A1} \cdot \text{SA}. \qquad (5.11)$$

The inputs (A0, A1, SA) are described using the notation

$$\text{A0, A1, SA} = \{\text{A, B, '0', '1'}\} \qquad (5.12)$$

to mean that each of the inputs (A0, A1, and SA) may be any of the values: A, B, '0', or '1'. I chose the name of the wheel function because it is rather like a dial that you set to your choice of function. Figure 5.3(b) shows that the ACT 1 Logic Module is a function generator built from two function wheels, a 2:1 MUX, and a two-input OR gate.

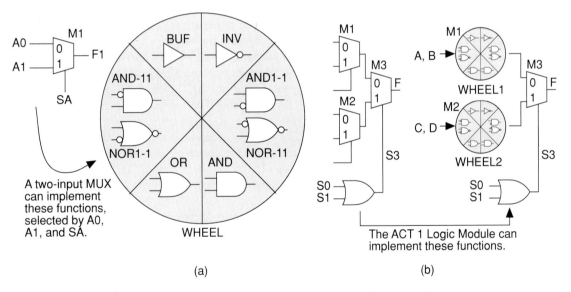

FIGURE 5.3 The ACT 1 Logic Module as a Boolean function generator. (a) A 2:1 MUX viewed as a function wheel. (b) The ACT 1 Logic Module viewed as two function wheels, an OR gate, and a 2:1 MUX.

We can describe the ACT 1 Logic Module in terms of two WHEEL functions:

$$\text{F} = \text{MUX [WHEEL1, WHEEL2, OR (S0, S1)]} \qquad (5.13)$$

Now, for example, to implement a two-input NAND gate, $F = \text{NAND}(A, B) = (A \cdot B)'$, using an ACT 1 Logic Module we first express F as the output of a 2:1 MUX. To split up F we expand it *wrt* A (or *wrt* B; since F is symmetric in A and B):

$$F = A \cdot (B') + A' \cdot ('1') \tag{5.14}$$

Thus to make a two-input NAND gate we assign WHEEL1 to implement INV(B), and WHEEL2 to implement '1'. We must also set the select input to the MUX connecting WHEEL1 and WHEEL2, $S0 + S1 = A$—we can do this with $S0 = A$, $S1 = '1'$.

Before we get too carried away, we need to realize that we do not have to worry about how to use Logic Modules to construct combinational logic functions—this has already been done for us. For example, if we need a two-input NAND gate, we just use a NAND gate symbol and software takes care of connecting the inputs in the right way to the Logic Module.

How did Actel design its Logic Modules? One of Actel's engineers wrote a program that calculates how many functions of two, three, and four variables a given circuit would provide. The engineers tested many different circuits and chose the best one: a small, logically efficient circuit that implemented many functions. For example, the ACT 1 Logic Module can implement all two-input functions, most functions with three inputs, and many with four inputs.

Apart from being able to implement a wide variety of combinational logic functions, the ACT 1 module can implement sequential logic cells in a flexible and efficient manner. For example, you can use one ACT 1 Logic Module for a transparent latch or two Logic Modules for a flip-flop. The use of latches rather than flip-flops does require a shift to a two-phase clocking scheme using two nonoverlapping clocks and two clock trees. Two-phase synchronous design using latches is efficient and fast but, to handle the timing complexities of two clocks requires changes to synthesis and simulation software that have not occurred. This means that most people still use flip-flops in their designs, and these require two Logic Modules.

5.1.4   ACT 2 and ACT 3 Logic Modules

Using two ACT 1 Logic Modules for a flip-flop also requires added interconnect and associated parasitic capacitance to connect the two Logic Modules. To produce an efficient two-module flip-flop macro we could use extra antifuses in the Logic Module to cut down on the parasitic connections. However, the extra antifuses would have an adverse impact on the performance of the Logic Module in other macros. The alternative is to use a separate flip-flop module, reducing flexibility and increasing layout complexity. In the ACT 1 family Actel chose to use just one type of Logic Module. The ACT 2 and ACT 3 architectures use two different types of Logic Modules, and one of them does include the equivalent of a D flip-flop.

Figure 5.4 shows the ACT 2 and ACT 3 Logic Modules. The ACT 2 **C-Module** is similar to the ACT 1 Logic Module but is capable of implementing five-input logic functions. Actel calls its C-module a *combinatorial* module even though the module implements *combinational* logic. John Wakerly blames MMI for the introduction of the term combinatorial [Wakerly, 1994, p. 404].

The use of MUXes in the Actel Logic Modules (and in other places) can cause confusion in using and creating logic macros. For the Actel library, setting $S = '0'$ selects input A of a two-input MUX. For other libraries setting $S = '1'$ selects input A. This can lead to some very hard to find errors when moving schematics between libraries. Similar problems arise in flip-flops and latches with MUX inputs. A safer way to label the inputs of a two-input MUX is with '0' and '1', corresponding to the input selected when the select input is '1' or '0'. This notation can be extended to bigger MUXes, but in Figure 5.4, does the input combination $S0 = '1'$ and $S1 = '0'$ select input D10 or input D01? These problems are not caused by Actel, but by failure to use the IEEE standard symbols in this area.

The **S-Module** (**sequential module**) contains the same combinational function capability as the C-Module together with a **sequential element** that can be configured as a flip-flop. Figure 5.4(d) shows the sequential element implementation in the ACT 2 and ACT 3 architectures.

5.1.5 Timing Model and Critical Path

Figure 5.5(a) shows the **timing model** for the ACT family.[1] This is a simple timing model since it deals only with logic buried inside a chip and allows us only to estimate delays. We cannot predict the exact delays on an Actel chip until we have performed the place-and-route step and know how much delay is contributed by the interconnect. Since we cannot determine the exact delay before physical layout is complete, we call the Actel architecture **nondeterministic**.

Even though we cannot determine the preroute delays exactly, it is still important to estimate the delay on a logic path. For example, Figure 5.5(a) shows a typical situation deep inside an ASIC. Internal signal I1 may be from the output of a register (flip-flop). We then pass through some combinational logic, C1, through a register, S1, and then another register, S2. The register-to-register delay consists of a clock–Q delay, plus any combinational delay between registers, and the setup time for the next flip-flop. The speed of our system will depend on the slowest register–register delay or **critical path** between registers. We cannot make our clock period any longer than this or the signal will not reach the second register in time to be clocked.

Figure 5.5(a) shows an internal logic signal, I1, that is an input to a C-module, C1. C1 is drawn in Figure 5.5(a) as a box with a symbol comprising the overlapping letters "C" and "L" (borrowed from carpenters who use this symbol to mark the centerline on a piece of wood). We use this symbol to describe combinational logic.

---

[1]1994 data book, p. 1-101.

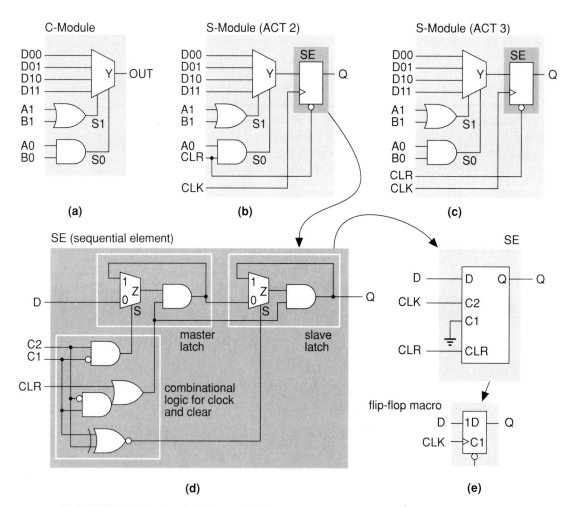

FIGURE 5.4 The Actel ACT 2 and ACT 3 Logic Modules. (a) The C-Module for combinational logic. (b) The ACT 2 S-Module. (c) The ACT 3 S-Module. (d) The equivalent circuit (without buffering) of the SE (sequential element). (e) The sequential element configured as a positive-edge–triggered D flip-flop. (*Source:* Actel.)

For the standard-speed grade ACT 3 (we shall look at speed grading in Section 5.1.6) the delay between the input of a C-module and the output is specified in the data book as a parameter, t_{PD}, with a maximum value of 3.0 ns.

The output of C1 is an input to an S-Module, S1, configured to implement combinational logic and a D flip-flop. The Actel data book specifies the minimum setup time for this D flip-flop as $t_{SUD} = 0.8$ ns. This means we need to get the data to the input of S1 at least 0.8 ns before the rising clock edge (for a positive-edge–triggered flip-flop). If we do this, then there is still enough time for the data to go through the combinational logic inside S1 and reach the input of the flip-flop inside S1 in time to be clocked. We can guarantee that this will work because the combinational logic delay inside S1 is fixed.

The S-Module seems like good value—we get all the combinational logic functions of a C-module (with delay t_{PD} of 3 ns) as well as the setup time for a flip-flop for only 0.8 ns? ...not really. Next I will explain why not.

Figure 5.5(b) shows what is happening *inside* an S-Module. The setup and hold times, as measured *inside* (not outside) the S-Module, of the flip-flop are t'_{SUD} and t'_H (a prime denotes parameters that are measured inside the S-Module). The clock–Q propagation delay is t'_{CO}. The parameters t'_{SUD}, t'_H, and t'_{CO} are measured using the *internal* clock signal CLKi. The propagation delay of the combinational logic *inside* the S-Module is t'_{PD}. The delay of the combinational logic that drives the flip-flop clock signal (Figure 5.4d) is t'_{CLKD}.

From *outside* the S-Module, with reference to the outside clock signal CLK1:

$$t_{SUD} = t'_{SUD} + (t'_{PD} - t'_{CLKD}),$$

$$t_H = t'_H + (t'_{PD} - t'_{CLKD}),$$

$$t_{CO} = t'_{CO} + t'_{CLKD}. \tag{5.15}$$

Figure 5.5(c) shows an example of flip-flop timing. We have no way of knowing what the *internal* flip-flop parameters t'_{SUD}, t'_H, and t'_{CO} actually are, but we can assume some reasonable values (just for illustration purposes):

$$t'_{SUD} = 0.4 \text{ ns}, \quad t'_H = 0.1 \text{ ns}, \quad t'_{CO} = 0.4 \text{ ns}. \tag{5.16}$$

We do know the delay, t'_{PD}, of the combinational logic inside the S-Module. It is exactly the same as the C-Module delay, so $t'_{PD} = 3$ ns for the ACT 3. We do not know t'_{CLKD}; we shall assume a reasonable value of $t'_{CLKD} = 2.6$ ns (the exact value does not matter in the following argument).

Next we calculate the *external* S-Module parameters from Eq. 5.15 as follows:

$$t_{SUD} = 0.8 \text{ ns}, \quad t_H = 0.5 \text{ ns}, \quad t_{CO} = 3.0 \text{ ns}. \tag{5.17}$$

These are the same as the ACT 3 S-Module parameters shown in Figure 5.5(a), and I chose t'_{CLKD} and the values in Eq. 5.16 so that they would be the same. So now we see where the combinational logic delay of 3.0 ns has gone: 0.4 ns went into increasing the setup time and 2.6 ns went into increasing the clock–output delay, t_{CO}.

From the outside we can say that the combinational logic delay is *buried* in the flip-flop setup time. FPGA vendors will point this out as an advantage that they have. Of course, we are not getting something for nothing here. It is like borrowing money—you have to pay it back.

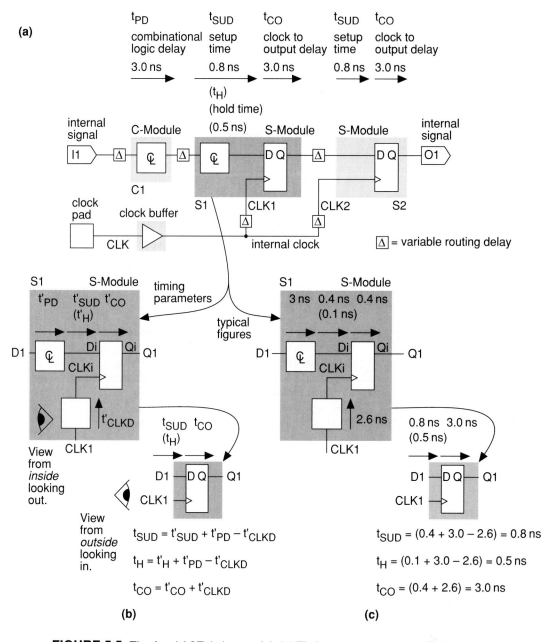

FIGURE 5.5 The Actel ACT timing model. (a) Timing parameters for a 'Std' speed grade ACT 3. (*Source*: Actel.) (b) Flip-flop timing. (c) An example of flip-flop timing based on ACT 3 parameters.

5.1.6 Speed Grading

Most FPGA vendors sort chips according to their speed (the sorting is known as **speed grading** or **speed binning**, because parts are automatically sorted into plastic bins by the production tester). You pay more for the faster parts. In the case of ACT family of FPGAs, Actel measures performance with a special **binning circuit**, included on every chip, that consists of an input buffer driving a string of buffers or inverters followed by an output buffer. The parts are sorted from measurements on the binning circuit according to Logic Module propagation delay. The propagation delay, t_{PD}, is defined as the average of the rising (t_{PLH}) and falling (t_{PHL}) propagation delays of a Logic Module

$$t_{PD} = (t_{PLH} + t_{PHL}) / 2. \tag{5.18}$$

Since the transistor properties match so well across a chip, measurements on the binning circuit closely correlate with the speed of the rest of the Logic Modules on the die. Since the speeds of die on the same wafer also match well, most of the good die on a wafer fall into the same speed bin. Actel speed grades are: a 'Std' speed grade, a '1' speed grade that is approximately 15 percent faster, a '2' speed grade that is approximately 25 percent faster than 'Std', and a '3' speed grade that is approximately 35 percent faster than 'Std'.

5.1.7 Worst-Case Timing

If you use fully synchronous design techniques you only have to worry about how slow your circuit may be—not how fast. Designers thus need to know the maximum delays they may encounter, which we call the **worst-case timing**. Maximum delays in CMOS logic occur when operating under minimum voltage, maximum temperature, and slow–slow process conditions. (A slow–slow process refers to a process variation, or **process corner**, which results in slow p-channel transistors and slow n-channel transistors—we can also have fast–fast, slow–fast, and fast–slow process corners.)

Electronic equipment has to survive in a variety of environments and ASIC manufacturers offer several classes of qualification for different applications:

- Commercial. $V_{DD} = 5\,\text{V} \pm 5\%$, T_A (ambient) = 0 to +70 °C.
- Industrial. $V_{DD} = 5\,\text{V} \pm 10\%$, T_A (ambient) = –40 to +85 °C.
- Military: $V_{DD} = 5\,\text{V} \pm 10\%$, T_C (case) = –55 to +125 °C.
- Military: Standard MIL-STD-883C Class B.
- Military extended: Unmanned spacecraft.

ASICs for commercial application are cheapest; ASICs for the Cruise missile are very, very expensive. Notice that commercial and industrial application parts are specified with respect to the **ambient temperature T_A** (room temperature or the temperature inside the box containing the ASIC). Military specifications are relative to the package **case temperature, T_C**. What is really important is the temperature of the transistors on the chip, the **junction temperature, T_J**, which is always higher than T_A (unless we dissipate zero power). For most applications that dissipate a few hundred mW, T_J is only 5–10 °C higher than T_A. To calculate the value of T_J we need to know the power dissipated by the chip and the thermal properties of the package—we shall return to this in Section 6.6.1, "Power Dissipation."

Manufacturers have to specify their operating conditions with respect to T_J and not T_A, since they have no idea how much power purchasers will dissipate in their designs or which package they will use. Actel used to specify timing under nominal operating conditions: $V_{DD} = 5.0$ V, and $T_J = 25$ °C. Actel and most other manufacturers now specify parameters under **worst-case commercial** conditions: $V_{DD} = 4.75$ V, and $T_J = +70$ °C.

Table 5.2 shows the ACT 3 commercial worst-case timing.[2] In this table Actel has included some estimates of the variable routing delay shown in Figure 5.5(a). These delay estimates depend on the number of gates connected to a gate output (the fanout).

When you design microelectronic systems (or design *anything*) you must use worst-case figures (just as you would design a bridge for the worst-case load). To convert nominal or typical timing figures to the worst case (or best case), we use measured, or empirically derived, constants called **derating factors** that are expressed either as a table or a graph. For example, Table 5.3 shows the ACT 3 derating factors from commercial worst-case to industrial worst-case and military worst-case conditions (assuming $T_J = T_A$). The ACT 1 and ACT 2 derating factors are approximately the same.[3]

TABLE 5.2   ACT 3 timing parameters.[1]

		Fanout				
Family	Delay[2]	1	2	3	4	8
ACT 3-3 (data book)	t_{PD}	2.9	3.2	3.4	3.7	4.8
ACT3-2 (calculated)	$t_{PD}/0.85$	3.41	3.76	4.00	4.35	5.65
ACT3-1 (calculated)	$t_{PD}/0.75$	3.87	4.27	4.53	4.93	6.40
ACT3-Std (calculated)	$t_{PD}/0.65$	4.46	4.92	5.23	5.69	7.38

Source: Actel.

[1] $V_{DD} = 4.75$ V, T_J (junction) $= 70$ °C. Logic module plus routing delay. All propagation delays in nanoseconds.
[2] The Actel '1' speed grade is 15 % faster than 'Std'; '2' is 25 % faster than 'Std'; '3' is 35 % faster than 'Std'.

[2] ACT 3: May 1995 data sheet, p. 1-173. ACT 2: 1994 data book, p. 1-51.
[3] 1994 data book, p. 1-12 (ACT 1), p. 1-52 (ACT 2), May 1995 data sheet, p. 1-174 (ACT 3).

TABLE 5.3   ACT 3 derating factors.[1]

V_{DD}/V	Temperature T_J (junction)/°C						
	−55	−40	0	25	70	85	125
4.5	0.72	0.76	0.85	0.90	1.04	1.07	1.17
4.75	0.70	0.73	0.82	0.87	1.00	1.03	1.12
5.00	0.68	0.71	0.79	0.84	0.97	1.00	1.09
5.25	0.66	0.69	0.77	0.82	0.94	0.97	1.06
5.5	0.63	0.66	0.74	0.79	0.90	0.93	1.01

Source: Actel.

[1]Worst-case commercial: V_{DD} = 4.75V, T_A (ambient) = +70 °C. Commercial: V_{DD} = 5V±5 %, T_A (ambient) = 0 to +70 °C. Industrial: V_{DD} = 5V±10%, T_A (ambient) = −40 to +85 °C. Military V_{DD} = 5V±10 %, T_C (case) = −55 to +125 °C.

As an example of a timing calculation, suppose we have a Logic Module on a 'Std' speed grade A1415A (an ACT 3 part) that drives four other Logic Modules and we wish to estimate the delay under worst-case industrial conditions. From the data in Table 5.2 we see that the Logic Module delay for an ACT 3 'Std' part with a fanout of four is t_{PD} = 5.7 ns (commercial worst-case conditions, assuming $T_J = T_A$).

If this were the slowest path between flip-flops (very unlikely since we have only one stage of combinational logic in this path), our estimated **critical path delay between registers, t_{CRIT}**, would be the combinational logic delay plus the flip-flop setup time plus the clock–output delay:

$$t_{CRIT} \text{ (w-c commercial)} = t_{PD} + t_{SUD} + t_{CO}$$

$$= 5.7 \text{ ns} + 0.8 \text{ ns} + 3.0 \text{ ns} = 9.5 \text{ ns}. \qquad (5.19)$$

(I use w-c as an abbreviation for worst-case.) Next we need to adjust the timing to worst-case industrial conditions. The appropriate derating factor is 1.07 (from Table 5.3); so the estimated delay is

$$t_{CRIT} \text{ (w-c industrial)} = 1.07 \times 9.5 \text{ ns} = 10.2 \text{ ns.} \qquad (5.20)$$

Let us jump ahead a little and assume that we can calculate that $T_J = T_A + 20 °C = 105 °C$ in our application. To find the derating factor at 105 °C we linearly interpolate between the values for 85 °C (1.07) and 125 °C (1.17) from Table 5.3). The interpolated derating factor is 1.12 and thus

$$t_{CRIT} \text{ (w-c industrial, } T_J = 105 °C) = 1.12 \times 9.5 \text{ ns} = 10.6 \text{ ns,} \qquad (5.21)$$

giving us an operating frequency of just less than 100 MHz.

It may seem unfair to calculate the worst-case performance for the slowest speed grade under the harshest industrial conditions—but the examples in the data books are always for the fastest speed grades under less stringent commercial conditions. If we want to illustrate the use of derating, then the delays can only get worse than the data book values! The ultimate word on logic delays for all FPGAs is the timing analysis provided by the FPGA design tools. However, you should be able to calculate whether or not the answer that you get from such a tool is reasonable.

5.1.8   Actel Logic Module Analysis

The sizes of the ACT family Logic Modules are close to the size of the base cell of an MGA. We say that the Actel ACT FPGAs use a **fine-grain architecture**. An advantage of a fine-grain architecture is that, whatever the mix of combinational logic to flip-flops in your application, you can probably still use 90 percent of an Actel FPGA. Another advantage is that synthesis software has an easier time mapping logic efficiently to the simple Actel modules.

The physical symmetry of the ACT Logic Modules greatly simplifies the place-and-route step. In many cases the router can swap equivalent pins on opposite sides of the module to ease channel routing. The design of the Actel Logic Modules is a balance between efficiency of implementation and efficiency of utilization. A simple Logic Module may reduce performance in some areas—as I have pointed out—but allows the use of fast and robust place-and-route software. Fast, robust routing is an important part of Actel FPGAs (see Section 7.1, "Actel ACT").

5.2   Xilinx LCA

Xilinx LCA (a trademark, denoting logic cell array) basic logic cells, **configurable logic blocks** or **CLBs**, are bigger and more complex than the Actel or QuickLogic cells. The Xilinx LCA basic logic cell is an example of a **coarse-grain architecture**. The Xilinx CLBs contain both combinational logic and flip-flops.

5.2.1   XC3000 CLB

The XC3000 CLB, shown in Figure 5.6, has five logic inputs (A–E), a common clock input (K), an asynchronous direct-reset input (RD), and an enable (EC). Using programmable MUXes connected to the SRAM programming cells, you can independently connect each of the two CLB outputs (X and Y) to the output of the flip-flops (QX and QY) or to the output of the combinational logic (F and G).

A 32-bit **look-up table** (LUT), stored in 32 bits of SRAM, provides the ability to implement combinational logic. Suppose you need to implement the function $F = A \cdot B \cdot C \cdot D \cdot E$ (a five-input AND). You set the contents of LUT cell number 31 (with address '11111') in the 32-bit SRAM to a '1'; all the other SRAM cells are set to '0'. When you apply the input variables as an address to the 32-bit SRAM, only

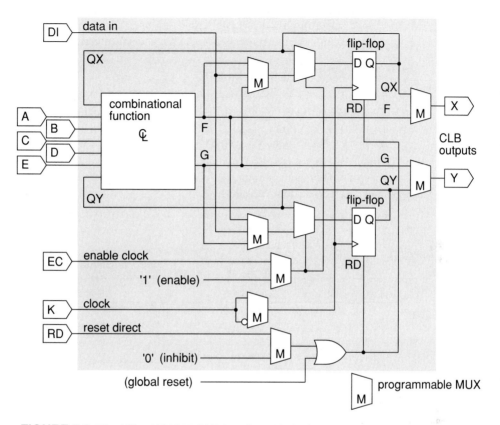

FIGURE 5.6 The Xilinx XC3000 CLB (configurable logic block). (*Source:* Xilinx.)

when ABCDE = '11111' will the output F be a '1'. This means that the CLB propagation delay is fixed, equal to the LUT access time, and independent of the logic function you implement.

There are seven inputs for the combinational logic in the XC3000 CLB: the five CLB inputs (A–E), and the flip-flop outputs (QX and QY). There are two outputs from the LUT (F and G). Since a 32-bit LUT requires only five variables to form a unique address ($32 = 2^5$), there are several ways to use the LUT:

- You can use five of the seven possible inputs (A–E, QX, QY) with the entire 32-bit LUT. The CLB outputs (F and G) are then identical.

- You can split the 32-bit LUT in half to implement two functions of four variables each. You can choose four input variables from the seven inputs (A–E, QX, QY). You have to choose two of the inputs from the five CLB inputs (A–E); then one function output connects to F and the other output connects to G.

- You can split the 32-bit LUT in half, using one of the seven input variables as a select input to a 2:1 MUX that switches between F and G. This allows you to implement some functions of six and seven variables.

5.2.2   XC4000 Logic Block

Figure 5.7 shows the CLB used in the XC4000 series of Xilinx FPGAs. This is a fairly complicated basic logic cell containing 2 four-input LUTs that feed a three-input LUT. The XC4000 CLB also has special fast carry logic hard-wired between CLBs. MUX control logic maps four control inputs (C1–C4) into the four inputs: LUT input H1, direct in (DIN), enable clock (EC), and a set/reset control (S/R) for the flip-flops. The control inputs (C1–C4) can also be used to control the use of the F' and G' LUTs as 32 bits of SRAM.

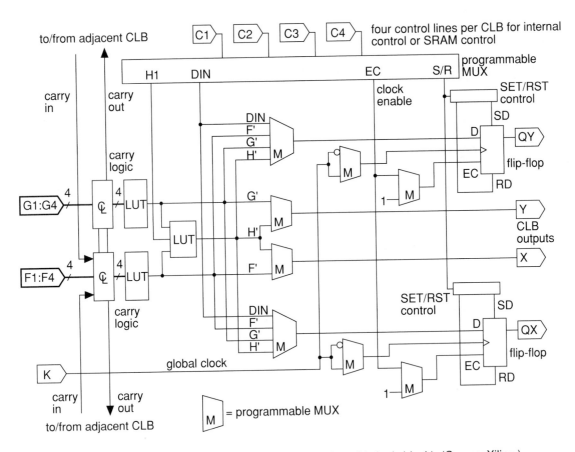

FIGURE 5.7 The Xilinx XC4000 family CLB (configurable logic block). (*Source:* Xilinx.)

5.2.3   XC5200 Logic Block

Figure 5.8 shows the basic logic cell, a **Logic Cell** or LC, used in the XC5200 family of Xilinx LCA FPGAs.[4] The LC is similar to the CLBs in the XC2000/3000/4000 CLBs, but simpler. Xilinx retained the term CLB in the XC5200 to mean a group of four LCs (LC0–LC3).

The XC5200 LC contains a four-input LUT, a flip-flop, and MUXes to handle signal switching. The arithmetic carry logic is separate from the LUTs. A limited capability to cascade functions is provided (using the MUX labeled F5_MUX in logic cells LC0 and LC2 in Figure 5.8) to gang two LCs in parallel to provide the equivalent of a five-input LUT.

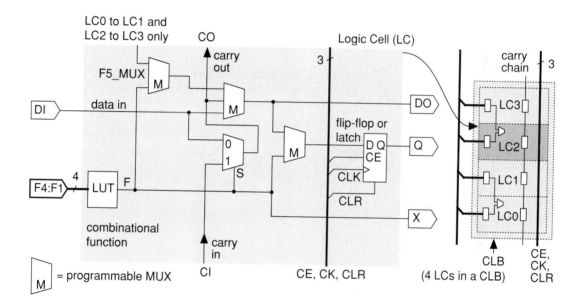

FIGURE 5.8 The Xilinx XC5200 family LC (Logic Cell) and CLB (configurable logic block). (*Source:* Xilinx.)

5.2.4   Xilinx CLB Analysis

The use of a LUT in a Xilinx CLB to implement combinational logic is both an advantage and a disadvantage. It means, for example, that an inverter is as slow as a five-input NAND. On the other hand a LUT simplifies timing of synchronous logic,

---

[4] Xilinx decided to use Logic Cell as a trademark in 1995 rather as if IBM were to use Computer as a trademark today. Thus we should now only talk of a Xilinx Logic Cell (with capital letters) and not Xilinx logic cells.

simplifies the basic logic cell, and matches the Xilinx SRAM programming technology well. A LUT also provides the possibility, used in the XC4000, of using the LUT directly as SRAM. You can configure the XC4000 CLB as a memory—either two 16×1 SRAMs or a 32×1 SRAM, but this is expensive RAM.

Figure 5.9 shows the timing model for Xilinx LCA FPGAs.[5] Xilinx uses two speed-grade systems. The first uses the maximum guaranteed toggle rate of a CLB flip-flop measured in MHz as a suffix—so higher is faster. For example a Xilinx XC3020-125 has a toggle frequency of 125 MHz. The other Xilinx naming system (which supersedes the old scheme, since toggle frequency is rather meaningless) uses the approximate delay time of the combinational logic in a CLB in nanoseconds—so lower is faster in this case. Thus, for example, an XC4010-6 has $t_{ILO} = 6.0$ ns (the correspondence between speed grade and t_{ILO} is fairly accurate for the XC2000, XC4000, and XC5200 but is less accurate for the XC3000).

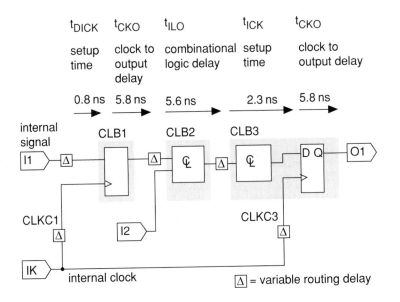

FIGURE 5.9 The Xilinx LCA timing model. The paths show different uses of CLBs (configurable logic blocks). The parameters shown are for an XC5210-6. (*Source:* Xilinx.)

The inclusion of flip-flops and combinational logic inside the basic logic cell leads to efficient implementation of state machines, for example. The coarse-grain architecture of the Xilinx CLBs maximizes performance given the size of the SRAM programming technology element. As a result of the increased complexity of the basic logic cell we shall see (in Section 7.2, "Xilinx LCA") that the routing between cells is more complex than other FPGAs that use a simpler basic logic cell.

---

[5]October 1995 (Version 3.0) data sheet.

5.3 Altera FLEX

Figure 5.10 shows the basic logic cell, a **Logic Element** (LE), that Altera uses in its FLEX 8000 series of FPGAs. Apart from the cascade logic (which is slightly simpler in the FLEX LE) the FLEX cell resembles the XC5200 LC architecture shown in Figure 5.8. This is not surprising since both architectures are based on the same SRAM programming technology. The FLEX LE uses a four-input LUT, a flip-flop, cascade logic, and carry logic. Eight LEs are stacked to form a Logic Array Block (the same term as used in the MAX series, but with a different meaning).

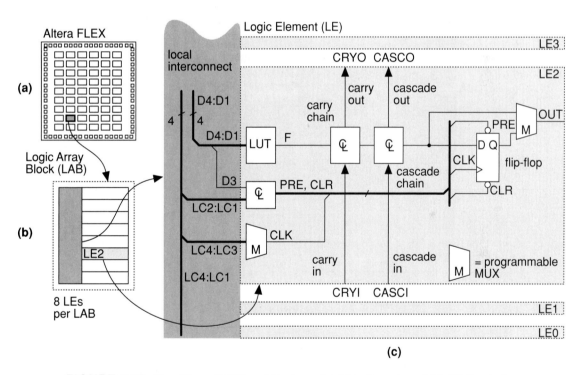

FIGURE 5.10 The Altera FLEX architecture. (a) Chip floorplan. (b) LAB (Logic Array Block). (c) Details of the LE (Logic Element). (*Source:* Altera (adapted with permission).)

5.4 Altera MAX

Suppose we have a simple two-level logic circuit that implements a sum of products as shown in Figure 5.11(a). We may redraw any two-level circuit using a regular structure (Figure 5.11b): a vector of buffers, followed by a vector of AND gates

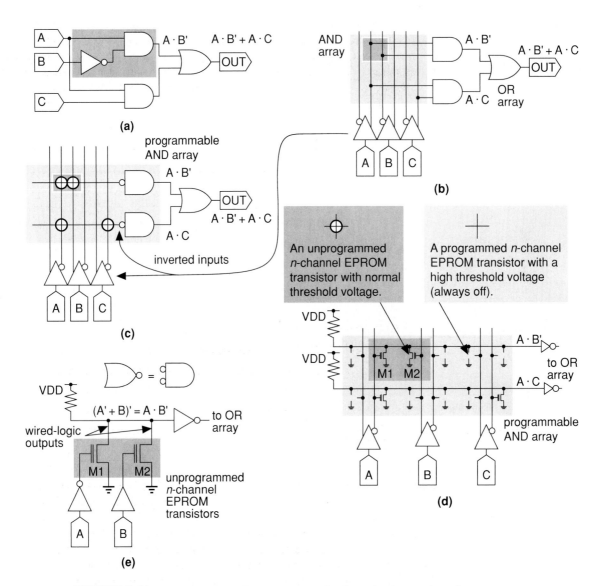

FIGURE 5.11 Logic arrays. (a) Two-level logic. (b) Organized sum of products. (c) A programmable-AND plane. (d) EPROM logic array. (e) Wired logic.

(which construct the product terms) that feed OR gates (which form the sums of the product terms). We can simplify this representation still further (Figure 5.11c), by drawing the input lines to a multiple-input AND gate as if they were one horizontal wire, which we call a **product-term line**. A structure such as Figure 5.11(c) is called **programmable array logic**, first introduced by Monolithic Memories as the PAL series of devices.

Because the arrangement of Figure 5.11(c) is very similar to a ROM, we sometimes call a horizontal product-term line, which would be the bit output from a ROM, the **bit line**. The vertical input line is the **word line**. Figure 5.11(d) and (e) show how to build the **programmable-AND array** (or product-term array) from EPROM transistors. The horizontal product-term lines connect to the vertical input lines using the EPROM transistors as pull-downs at each possible connection. Applying a '1' to the gate of an unprogrammed EPROM transistor pulls the product-term line low to a '0'. A programmed n-channel transistor has a threshold voltage higher than V_{DD} and is therefore always *off*. Thus a programmed transistor has no effect on the product-term line.

Notice that connecting the n-channel EPROM transistors to a **pull-up resistor** as shown in Figure 5.11(e) produces a **wired-logic** function—the output is high only if all of the outputs are high, resulting in a **wired-AND** function of the outputs. The product-term line is low when any of the inputs are high. Thus, to convert the wired-logic array into a programmable-AND array, we need to invert the sense of the inputs. We often conveniently omit these details when we draw the schematics of logic arrays, usually implemented as NOR–NOR arrays (so we need to invert the outputs as well). They are not minor details when you implement the layout, however.

Figure 5.12 shows how a programmable-AND array can be combined with other logic into a **macrocell** that contains a flip-flop. For example, the widely used **22V10** PLD, also called a registered PAL, essentially contains 10 of the macrocells shown in Figure 5.12. The part number, 22V10, denotes that there are 22 inputs (44 vertical input lines for both true and complement forms of the inputs) to the programmable AND array and 10 macrocells. The PLD or registered PAL shown in Figure 5.12 has an $2i \times jk$ programmable-AND array.

5.4.1   Logic Expanders

The basic logic cell for the Altera MAX architecture, a macrocell, is a descendant of the PAL. Using the **logic expander**, shown in Figure 5.13 to generate extra logic terms, it is possible to implement functions that require more product terms than are

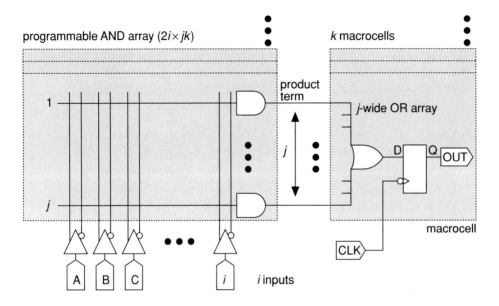

FIGURE 5.12 A registered PAL with i inputs, j product terms, and k macrocells.

available in a simple PAL macrocell. As an example, consider the following function:

$$F = A' \cdot C \cdot D + B' \cdot C \cdot D + A \cdot B + B \cdot C'. \qquad (5.22)$$

This function has four product terms and thus we cannot implement F using a macrocell that has only a three-wide OR array (such as the one shown in Figure 5.13). If we rewrite F as a "sum of (products of products)" like this:

$$F = (A' + B') \cdot C \cdot D + (A + C') \cdot B$$

$$= (A \cdot B)' (C \cdot D) + (A' \cdot C)' \cdot B ; \qquad (5.23)$$

we can use logic expanders to form the **expander terms** $(A \cdot B)'$ and $(A' \cdot C)'$ (see Figure 5.13). We can even share these extra product terms with other macrocells if we need to. We call the extra logic gates that form these shareable product terms a **shared logic expander**, or just **shared expander**.

The disadvantage of the shared expanders is the extra logic delay incurred because of the second pass that you need to take through the product-term array. We usually do not know before the logic tools assign logic to macrocells (**logic assignment**) whether we need to use the logic expanders. Since we cannot predict the exact timing the Altera MAX architecture is not strictly **deterministic**. However,

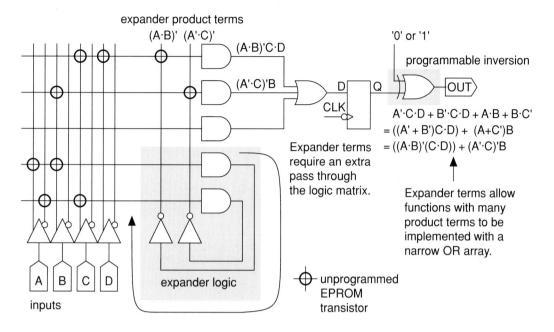

FIGURE 5.13 Expander logic and programmable inversion. An expander increases the number of product terms available and programmable inversion allows you to reduce the number of product terms you need.

once we do know whether a signal has to go through the array once or twice, we can simply and accurately predict the delay. This is a very important and useful feature of the Altera MAX architecture.

The expander terms are sometimes called **helper terms** when you use a PAL. If you use helper terms in a 22V10, for example, you have to go out to the chip I/O pad and then back into the programmable array again, using **two-pass logic**.

Another common feature in complex PLDs, also used in some PLDs, is shown in Figure 5.13. Programming one input of the XOR gate at the macrocell output allows you to choose whether or not to invert the output (a '1' for inversion or to a '0' for no inversion). This **programmable inversion** can reduce the required number of product terms by using a de Morgan equivalent representation instead of a conventional sum-of-products form, as shown in Figure 5.14.

As an example of using programmable inversion, consider the function

$$F = A \cdot B' + A \cdot C' + A \cdot D' + A' \cdot C \cdot D , \qquad (5.24)$$

which requires four product terms—one too many for a three-wide OR array.

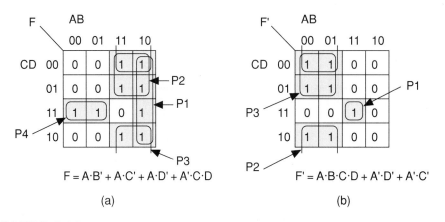

FIGURE 5.14 Use of programmed inversion to simplify logic: (a) The function $F = A \cdot B' + A \cdot C' + A \cdot D' + A' \cdot C \cdot D$ requires four product terms (P1–P4) to implement while (b) the complement, $F' = A \cdot B \cdot C \cdot D + A' \cdot D' + A' \cdot C'$ requires only three product terms (P1–P3).

If we generate the complement of F instead,

$$F' = A \cdot B \cdot C \cdot D + A' \cdot D' + A' \cdot C' , \qquad (5.25)$$

this has only three product terms. To create F we invert F', using programmable inversion.

Figure 5.15 shows an Altera MAX macrocell and illustrates the architectures of several different product families. The implementation details vary among the families, but the basic features: wide programmable-AND array, narrow fixed-OR array, logic expanders, and programmable inversion—are very similar.[6] Each family has the following individual characteristics:

- A typical MAX 5000 chip has: 8 dedicated inputs (with both true and complement forms); 24 inputs from the chipwide interconnect (true and complement); and either 32 or 64 shared expander terms (single polarity). The MAX 5000 LAB looks like a 32V16 PLD (ignoring the expander terms).

- The MAX 7000 LAB has 36 inputs from the chipwide interconnect and 16 shared expander terms; the MAX 7000 LAB looks like a 36V16 PLD.

- The MAX 9000 LAB has 33 inputs from the chipwide interconnect and 16 local feedback inputs (as well as 16 shared expander terms); the MAX 9000 LAB looks like a 49V16 PLD.

---

[6]1995 data book p. 274 (5000), p. 160 (7000), p. 126 (9000).

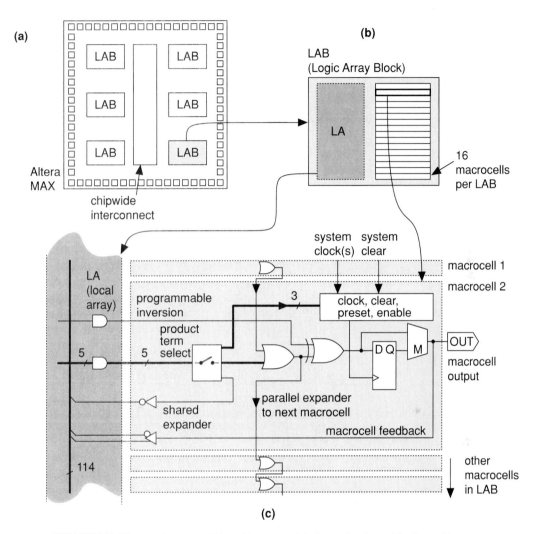

FIGURE 5.15 The Altera MAX architecture. (a) Organization of logic and interconnect. (b) A MAX family LAB (Logic Array Block). (c) A MAX family macrocell. The macrocell details vary between the MAX families—the functions shown here are closest to those of the MAX 9000 family macrocells.

5.4.2 Timing Model

Figure 5.16 shows the Altera MAX timing model for local signals.[7] For example, in Figure 5.16(a) an internal signal, I1, enters the local array (the LAB interconnect with a fixed delay $t_1 = t_{LOCAL} = 0.5$ ns), passes through the AND array (delay

---

[7] March 1995 data sheet, v2.

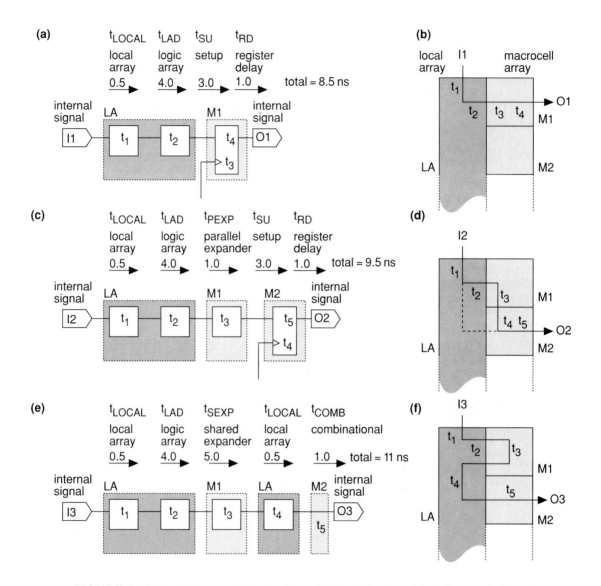

FIGURE 5.16 The timing model for the Altera MAX architecture. (a) A direct path through the logic array and a register. (b) Timing for the direct path. (c) Using a parallel expander. (d) Parallel expander timing. (e) Making two passes through the logic array to use a shared expander. (f) Timing for the shared expander (there is no register in this path). All timing values are in nanoseconds for the MAX 9000 series, '15' speed grade. (*Source:* Altera.)

$t_2 = t_{LAD} = 4.0$ ns), and to the macrocell flip-flop (with setup time, $t_3 = t_{SU} = 3.0$ ns, and clock–Q or **register delay**, $t_4 = t_{RD} = 1.0$ ns). The path delay is thus: $0.5 + 4 + 3 + 1 = 8.5$ ns.

Figure 5.16(c) illustrates the use of a **parallel logic expander**. This is different from the case of the *shared* expander (Figure 5.13), which required two passes in series through the product-term array. Using a parallel logic expander, the extra product term is generated in an adjacent macrocell in parallel with other product terms (not in series—as in a shared expander).

We can illustrate the difference between a parallel expander and a shared expander using an example function that we have used before (Eq. 5.22),

$$F = A' \cdot C \cdot D + B' \cdot C \cdot D + A \cdot B + B \cdot C. \tag{5.26}$$

This time we shall use macrocell M1 in Figure 5.16(d) to implement F1 equal to the sum of the first three product terms in Eq. 5.26. We use F1 (using the parallel expander connection between adjacent macrocells shown in Figure 5.15) as an input to macrocell M2. Now we can form $F = F1 + B \cdot C'$ without using more than three inputs of an OR gate (the MAX 5000 has a three-wide OR array in the macrocell, the MAX 9000, as shown in Figure 5.15, is capable of handling five product terms in one macrocell—but the principle is the same). The total delay is the same as before, except that we add the delay of a parallel expander, $t_{PEXP} = 1.0$ ns. Total delay is then $8.5 + 1 = 9.5$ ns.

Figure 5.16(e) and (f) shows the use of a shared expander—similar to Figure 5.13.

The Altera MAX macrocell is more like a PLD than the other FPGA architectures discussed here; that is why Altera calls the MAX architecture a complex PLD. This means that the MAX architecture works well in applications for which PLDs are most useful: simple, fast logic with many inputs or variables.

5.4.3 Power Dissipation in Complex PLDs

A programmable-AND array in any PLD built using EPROM or EEPROM transistors uses a passive pull-up (a resistor or current source), and these macrocells consume **static power**. Altera uses a switch called the **Turbo Bit** to control the current in the programmable-AND array in each macrocell. For the MAX 7000, static current varies between 1.4 mA and 2.2 mA per macrocell in high-power mode (the current depends on the part—generally, but not always, the larger 7000 parts have lower operating currents) and between 0.6 mA and 0.8 mA in low-power mode. For the MAX 9000, the static current is 0.6 mA per macrocell in high-current mode and 0.3 mA in low-power mode, independent of the part size.[8] Since there are 16 macrocells in a LAB and up to 35 LABs on the largest MAX 9000 chip ($16 \times 35 = 560$ macrocells), just the static power dissipation in low-power mode can be substantial

---

[8] 1995 data book, p. 1-47.

$(560 \times 0.3 \, \text{mA} \times 5 \, \text{V} = 840 \, \text{mW})$. If all the macrocells are in high-power mode, the static power will double. This is the price you pay for having an (up to) 114-wide AND gate delay of a few nanoseconds ($t_{LAD} = 4.0 \, \text{ns}$) in the MAX 9000. For any MAX 9000 macrocell in the low-power mode it is necessary to add a delay of between 15 ns and 20 ns to any signal path through the local interconnect and logic array (including t_{LAD} and t_{PEXP}).

5.5   Summary

Table 5.4 is a look-up table to Tables 5.5–5.9, which summarize the features of the logic cells used by the various FPGA vendors.

TABLE 5.4   Logic cell tables.

Programmable ASIC family		Programmable ASIC family	
Table 5.5	Actel (ACT 1) Xilinx (XC3000) Actel (ACT 2) Xilinx (XC4000)	Table 5.8	Actel (ACT 3) Xilinx LCA (XC5200) Altera FLEX (8000/10k)
Table 5.6	Altera MAX (EPM 5000) Xilinx EPLD (XC7200/7300) QuickLogic (pASIC 1)	Table 5.9	AMD MACH 5 Actel 3200DX Altera MAX (EPM 9000)
Table 5.7	Crosspoint (CP20K) Altera MAX (EPM 7000) Atmel (AT6000)		

The key points in this chapter are:

- The use of multiplexers, look-up tables, and programmable logic arrays
- The difference between fine-grain and coarse-grain FPGA architectures
- Worst-case timing design
- Flip-flop timing
- Timing models
- Components of power dissipation in programmable ASICs
- Deterministic and nondeterministic FPGA architectures

Next, in Chapter 6, we shall examine the I/O cells used by the various programmable ASIC families.

TABLE 5.5 Logic cells used by programmable ASICs.

	Actel ACT 1	Xilinx XC3000	Actel ACT 2	Xilinx XC4000
Basic logic cell	Logic module (LM)	CLB (Configurable Logic Block)	C-Module (combinatorial-module) and S-Module (sequential module)	CLB (Configurable Logic Block)
Logic cell contents	Three 2:1MUXes plus OR gate	32-bit LUT, 2 D flip-flops, 9 MUXes	C-Module: 4:1 MUX, 2-input OR, 2-input AND S-Module: 4-input MUX, 2-input OR, latch or D flip-flop	32-bit LUT, 2 D flip-flops, 10 MUXes, including fast carry logic E-suffix parts contain dual-port RAM.
Logic path delay	Fixed	Fixed with ability to bypass FF	Fixed	Fixed with ability to bypass FF
Combinational logic functions	Most 3-input, many 4-input functions (total 702 macros)	All 5-input functions plus 2 D flip-flops	Most 3- and 4-input functions (total 766 macros)	Two 4-input LUTs plus combiner with ninth input CLB as 32-bit SRAM (except D-suffix parts)
Flip-flop (FF) implementation	1 LM required for latch, 2 LMs required for flip-flops	2 D-flip-flops per CLB, latches can be built from pre-FF logic.	1 S-Module per D flip-flop; some FFs require 2 modules.	2 D flip-flops per CLB
Basic logic cells in each chip	LMs: A1010: 352 (8R×44C) = 295 + 57 I/O A1020: 616 (14 R×44C) = 547 + 69 I/O	64 (XC3020/A/L, XC3120/A) 100 (XC3030/A/L, XC3130/A) 144 (XC3042/A/L, XC3142/A) 224 (XC3064/A/L, XC3164/A) 320 (XC3090/A/L, XC3190/A) 484 (XC3195/A)	A1225: 451 = 231 S + 220 C A1240: 684 = 348 S + 336 C A1280: 1232 = 624 S + 608 C	64 (XC4002A) 100 (XC4003/A/E/H) 144 (XC4004A) 196 (XC4005/A/E/H) 256 (XC4006/E) 324 (XC4008/E) 400 (XC4010/D/E) 576 (XC4013/D/E) 784 (XC4020/E) 1024 (XC4025/E)

TABLE 5.6   Logic cells used by programmable ASICs.

	Altera MAX 5000	Xilinx XC7200/7300	QuickLogic pASIC 1
Basic logic cell	16 macrocells in a LAB (Logic Array Block) except EPM5032, which has 32 macrocells in a single LAB	9 macrocells within a FB (Functional Block), fast FBs (FFBs) omit ALU	Logic Cell (LC)
Logic cell contents	Macrocell: 64-106 wide-AND, 3-wide OR array, 1 flip-flop, 2 MUXes, programmable inversion. 32–64 shared logic expander OR terms. LAB looks like a 32V16 PLD.	Macrocell: 21-wide AND, 16-wide OR array, 1 flip-flop, 1 ALU FB looks like 21V9 PLD.	Four 2-input and two 6-input AND, three 2:1 MUXes and one D flip-flop
Logic path delay	Fixed (unless using shared logic expanders)	Fixed	Fixed
Combinational logic functions per logic cell	Wide input functions with ability to share product terms	Wide input functions with added 2-input ALU	All 3-input functions
Flip-flop (FF) implementation	1 D flip-flop or latch per macrocell. More can be constructed in arrays.	1 D flip-flop or latch per macrocell	1 D flip-flop per LC. LCs for other flip-flops not specified.
Basic logic cells in each chip	LABs: 32 (EPM5032) 64 (EPM5064) 128 (EPM5128) 128 (EPM5130) 192 (EPM5192)	FBs: 4 (XC7236A) 8 (XC7272A) 2 (XC7318) 4 (XC7336) 6 (XC7354) 8 (XC7372) 12 (XC73108) 16 (XC73144)	48 (QL6X8) 96 (QL8X12) 192 (QL12X16) 384 (QL16X24)

TABLE 5.7 Logic cells used by programmable ASICs.

	Crosspoint CP20K	Altera MAX 7k	Atmel AT6000
Basic logic cell	Transistor-pair tile (TPT), RAM-logic Tile (RLT)	16 macrocells in a LAB (Logic Array Block)	Cell
Logic cell contents	TPT: 2 transistors (0.5 gate). RLT: 3 inverters, two 3-input NANDs, 2-input NAND, 2-input AND.	Macrocell: wide AND, 5-wide OR array, 1 flip-flop, 3 MUXes, programmable inversion. 16 shared logic expander OR terms, plus parallel logic expander. LAB looks like a 36V16 PLD.	Two 5:1 MUXes, two 4:1 MUXes, 3:1 MUX, three 2:1 MUXes, 6 pass gates, four 2-input gates, 1 D flip-flop
Logic path delay	Variable	Fixed (unless using shared logic expanders)	Variable
Combinational functions per logic cell	TPT is smaller than a gate, approx. 2 TPTs = 1 gate.	Wide input functions with ability to share product terms	1-, 2-, and 3-input combinational configurations: 44 logical states and 72 physical states
Flip-flop (FF) implementation	D flip-flop requires 2 RLTs and 9 TPTs	1 D flip-flop or latch per macrocell. More can be constructed in arrays.	1 D flip-flop per cell

Basic logic cells in each chip	TPTs:
	  1760 (20220)
	  15,876 (22000)
	
	RLTs:
	  440 (20220)
	  3969 (22000)
		Macrocells:
		  32 (EPM7032/V)
		  64 (EPM7064)
		  96 (EPM7096)
		  128 (EPM70128E)
		  160 (EPM70160E)
		  192 (EPM70192E)
		  256 (EPM70256E)
			1024 (AT6002)
			1600 (AT6003)
			3136 (AT6005)
			6400 (AT6010)

TABLE 5.8   Logic cells used by programmable ASICs.

	Actel ACT 3	Xilinx XC5200	Altera FLEX 8000/10k
Basic logic cell	2 types of Logic Module: C-Module and S-Module (similar but not identical to ACT 2)	4 Logic Cells (LC) in a CLB (Configurable Logic Block)	8 Logic Elements (LE) in a Logic Array Block (LAB)
Logic cell contents (LUT = look-up table)	C-Module: 4:1 MUX, 2-input OR, 2-input AND. S-Module: 4:1 MUX, 2-input OR, latch or D flip-flop.	LC has 16-bit LUT, 1 flip-flop (or latch), 4 MUXes	16-bit LUT, 1 programmable flip-flop or latch, MUX logic for control, carry logic, cascade logic
Logic path delay	Fixed	Fixed	Fixed with ability to bypass FF
Combinational functions per logic cell	Most 3- and 4-input functions (total 766 macros)	One 4-input LUT per LC may be combined with adjacent LC to form 5-input LUT	4-input LUT may be cascaded with adjacent LE
Flip-flop (FF) implementation	1 D flip-flop (or latch) per S-Module; some FFs require 2 modules.	1 D flip-flop (or latch) per LC (4 per CLB)	1 D flip-flop (or latch) per LE

Basic logic cells in each chip	A1415: 104 S + 96 C
	A1425: 160 S + 150 C
	A1440: 288 S + 276 C
	A1460: 432 S + 416 C
	A14100: 697 S + 680 C
		64 CLB (XC5202)
		120 CLB (XC5204)
		196 CLB (XC5206)
		324 CLB (XC5210)
		484 CLB (XC5215)
			LEs:
			    208 (EPF8282/V/A /AV)
			    336 (EPF8452/A)
			    504 (EPF8636A)
			    672 (EPF8820/A)
			    1008 (EPF81188/A)
			    1296 (EPF81500/A)
			
			    576 (EPF10K10)
			    1152 (EPF10K20)
			    1728 (EPF10K30)
			    2304 (EPF10K40)
			    2880 (EPF10K50)
			    3744 (EPF10K70)
			    4992 (EPF10K100)

TABLE 5.9 Logic cells used by programmable ASICs.

	AMD MACH 5	Actel 3200DX	Altera MAX 9000
Basic logic cell	4 PAL Blocks in a Segment, 16 macrocells in a PAL Block	Based on ACT 2T, plus D-module (decode) and dual-port SRAM	16 macrocells in a LAB (Logic Array Block)
Logic cell contents	20-bit to 32-bit wide OR array, switching logic, XOR gate, programmable flip-flop	C-Module: 4:1 MUX, 2-input OR, 2-input AND S-Module: 4-input MUX, 2-input OR, latch or D flip-flop D-module: 7-input AND, 2-input XOR	Macrocell: 114-wide AND, 5-wide OR array, 1 flip-flop, 5 MUXes, program-mable inversion. 16 shared logic expander OR terms, plus parallel logic expander. LAB looks like a 49V16 PLD.
Logic path delay	Fixed	Fixed	Fixed (unless using expanders)
Combinational functions per logic cell	Wide input functions	Most 3- and 4-input functions (total 766 macros)	Wide input functions with ability to share product terms
Flip-flop (FF) implementation	1 D flip-flop or latch per macrocell	1 D flip-flop or latch per S-Module; some FFs require 2 modules.	1 D flip-flop or latch per macrocell. More can be constructed in arrays.
Basic logic cells in each chip	128 (M5-128) 192 (M5-192) 256 (M5-256) 320 (M5-320) 384 (M5-384) 512 (M5-512)	A3265DX: 510 S + 475 C + 20 D A32100DX: 700 S + 662 C + 20 D + 2 kSRAM A32140D): 954 S + 912 C + 24 D A32200DX: 1 230 S + 1 184 C + 24 D + 2.5 kSRAM A32300DX: 1 888 S + 1 833 C + 28 D + 3kSRAM A32400DX: 2 526 S + 2 466 C + 28 D + 4 kSRAM	Macrocells: 320 (EPM9320) 4×5 LABs 400 (EPM9400) 5×5 LABs 480 (EPM9480) 6×5 LABs 560 (EPM9560) 7×5 LABs

5.6 Problems

* = Difficult, ** = Very difficult, *** = Extremely difficult

5.1 (Using the ACT 1 Logic Module, 30 min.) Consider the Actel ACT 1 Logic Module shown in Figure 5.1. Show how to implement: **(a)** a three-input NOR gate, **(b)** a three-input majority function gate, **(c)** a 2:1 MUX, **(d)** a half adder, **(e)** a three-input XOR gate, and **(f)** a four-input MUX.

5.2 (Worst-case and best-case timing, 10 min.) Seasoned digital CMOS designers do not worry too much when their designs stop working when they get too hot or when they reduce the supply voltage, but an ASIC that stops working either when increasing the supply voltage above normal or when it gets cold causes panic. Why?

5.3 (Typical to worst-case variation, 10 min.) The 1994 Actel data book (p. 1-5) remarks that: "the total derating factor from typical to worst-case for a standard ACT 1 array is only 1.19:1, compared to 2:1 for a masked gate array."

  a. Can you explain why this is when the basic ACT 1 CMOS process is identical to a CMOS process for masked gate arrays?

  b. There is a price to pay for the reduced spread in timing delays from typical to worst-case in an ACT 1 array. What is this disadvantage of the ACT 1 array over a masked gate array?

5.4 (ACT 2/3 sequential element, 30 min.). Show how the Actel ACT 2 and ACT 3 sequential element of Figure 5.4 (used in the S-Module) can be wired to implement:

  a. a positive-edge–triggered flip-flop with clear,

  b. a negative-edge–triggered flip-flop with clear,

  c. a transparent-high latch,

  d. a transparent-low latch, and

  e. how it can be made totally transparent.

5.5 (*ACT 1 logic functions, 40 min.+)

  a. How many different combinational functions of four logic variables are there?

  b. of n variables? *Hint*: Consider the truth table.

  c. The ACT 1 module can implement 213 of the 256 functions with three variables. How many of the 43 three-input functions that it cannot implement can you find?

  d. (harder) Show that if you have access to both the true and complement form of the input variables you can implement all 256 logic functions of three variables with the ACT 1 Logic Module.

5.6 (Actel and Xilinx, 10 min.) The Actel Logic Modules (ACT 1, ACT 2, and ACT 3) have eight inputs and can implement most three-input logic functions and a few logic functions with four input variables. In contrast, the Xilinx XC5200 CLB, for example, has only four inputs but can implement all logic functions with four or fewer variables. Why would Actel choose these logic cell designs and how can they be competitive with the Xilinx FPGA (which they are)?

5.7 (Actel address decoders, 10 min.) The maximum number of inputs that the ACT 1 Logic Module can handle is four. The ACT 2/ACT 3 C-module increases this to five.

    a. How many ACT 1 Logic Modules do you need to implement a 32-bit wide address decoder (a 32-input AND gate)?

    b. How many ACT 2/ACT 3 C-modules do you need?

5.8 (Altera shared logic expanders, 30 min.) Consider an Altera MAX 5000 logic array with three product-term lines. You cannot directly implement the function $Z = A \cdot B \cdot C + A \cdot B' \cdot C' + A' \cdot B \cdot C' + A' \cdot B' \cdot C$ with a programmable array logic macrocell that has only three product-term lines, since Z has four product terms.

    a. How many Boolean functions of three variables are there that cannot be implemented with a programmable array logic macrocell that has only three product terms? *Hint:* Use a Karnaugh map to consider how many Boolean functions of three variables have more than three product terms in their sum-of-products representation.

    b. Show how to use shared logic expanders that feed terms back into the product-term array to implement the function Z using a macrocell with three product terms.

    c. How many shared expander lines do you need to add to be able to implement all the Boolean functions of three variables?

    d. What is the largest number of product terms that you need to implement a Boolean function with n variables?

5.9 (Splitting the XC3000 CLB, 20 min.) In Section 5.2.1 we noted "You can split the (XC3000) 32-bit LUT in half, using one of the seven input variables to switch between the F and G outputs. This technique can implement some functions of six and seven variables."

    a. Show which functions of six and seven variables can, and

    b. which functions cannot, be implemented using this method.

5.10 (Programmable inversion, 20 min.) Section 5.4 described how the Altera MAX series logic cells can use programmable inversion to reduce the number of product terms needed to implement a function. Give another example of a function of four variables that requires four product terms. Is there a way to tell how many product terms a function may require?

5.11 (Table look-up mapping, 20 min.) Consider a four-input LUT (used in the CLB in the Xilinx XC2000, the first generation of Xilinx FPGAs, and in the XC5200 LE). This CLB can implement any Boolean function of four variables. Consider the function

$$Z = (A \cdot (B + C)) + (B \cdot D) + (E \cdot F \cdot G \cdot H \cdot I) . \tag{5.27}$$

We can use four CLBs to implement Z as follows:

$$\text{CLB1: } Z = Z1 + (B \cdot D) + Z3,$$

$$\text{CLB2: } Z1 = A \cdot (B + C),$$

$$\text{CLB3: } Z3 = E \cdot F \cdot G \cdot Z5,$$

$$\text{CLB4: } Z5 = H \cdot I. \tag{5.28}$$

What is the length of the critical path? Find a better assignment in terms of area and critical path.

5.12 (Multiplexer mapping, 10 min.) Consider the function:

$$F = (A \cdot B) + (B' \cdot C) + D. \tag{5.29}$$

Use Shannon's expansion theorem to expand F *wrt* B:

$$F = B \cdot F1 + B' \cdot F2. \tag{5.30}$$

In other words express F in terms of B, B', F1, and F2 (*Hint*: F1 is a function of A and D only, F2 is a function of C and D only). Now expand F1 *wrt* A, and F2 *wrt* C. Using your answer, implement F using a single ACT 1 Logic Module.

5.13 (*Xilinx hazards, 10 min.) Explain why the outputs of the Xilinx CLBs are hazard-free for input changes in only one variable. Is this important?

5.14 (**Actel S-Modules, 10 min.) Notice that CLR is tied to the input corresponding to B0 of the C-module in the ACT 2 S-Module but the CLR input is separate from the B0 input in the ACT 3 version. Why?

5.15 (**Timing estimates, 60 min.) Using data book values for an FPGA architecture that you choose, and explaining your calculations carefully, estimate the (worst-case commercial) delay for the following functions: **(a)** 16-bit address decoder, **(b)** 8-bit ripple-carry adder, **(c)** 8-bit ripple-carry counter. Give your answers in terms of the data book symbols, and using actual parameters, for a speed grade that you specify, give an example calculation with the delay in ns.

5.16 (Actel logic. 30 min.) Table 5.10 shows how to use the Actel ACT 1 Logic Module to implement some of the 16 functions of two input variables. Complete this table.

5.17 (ACT 1 module implementation, 120 min.)

a. Show that the circuit shown in Figure 5.17, with buffered inputs and outputs, is equivalent to the one shown in Figure 5.1.

b. Show that the circuit for the ACT 1 Logic Module shown in Figure 5.18 is also the same.

c. Convert the circuit of Figure 5.18 to one that uses more efficient CMOS gates: inverters, AOI, and NAND gates.

d. (harder) Assume that the ACT 1 Logic Module has the equivalent of a 2X drive and the logic ratio is close to one. Compare your answer to part c against Figure 5.17 in terms of logical efficiency and logical area.

TABLE 5.10   Boolean functions using the ACT 1 Logic Module (Problem 5.16).

	Function, F	F =	Canonical form	Min-terms	M1			M2			OR1	
					A0	A1	SA	B0	B1	SB	S0	S1
1	0	0	0	—	0	0	0					
2	AND(A, B)	A · B	A · B	3	0	B	A					
3	AND1-1(A, B)	A · B'	A · B'	2	A	0	B					
4	NOR(A, B)	A + B	A' · B'	0								
5	NOR1-1(A, B)	A + B'	A' · B	1	B	0	A					
6	A	A	A · B' + A · B	2, 3	0	A	1					
7	B	B	A' · B + A · B	1, 3	0	B	1					
8	NOT(A)	A'	A' · B' + A' · B	0, 1	0	1	A					
9	NOT(B)	B'	A' · B' + A · B'	0, 2	0	1	B					
10	EXOR(A, B)	A ⊕ B	A' · B + A · B'	1, 2								
11	EXNOR(A, B)	(A ⊕ B)'	A' · B' + A · B	0, 3								
12	OR(A, B)	A + B	A' · B + A · B' + A · B	1, 2, 3	B	1	A					
13	OR1-1(A, B)	A + B'	A' · B' + A · B' + A · B	0, 2, 3								
14	NAND(A, B)	(A · B)'	A' · B' + A' · B + A · B'	0, 1, 2								
15	NAND1-1(A, B)	(A · B')'	A' · B' + A' · B + A · B	0, 1, 3								
16	1	1	A' · B' + A' · B + A · B' + A · B	0, 1, 2, 3	1	1	1					

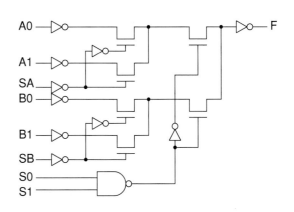

FIGURE 5.17   An alternative implementation of the ACT 1 Logic Module shown in Figure 5.1 (Problem 5.17).

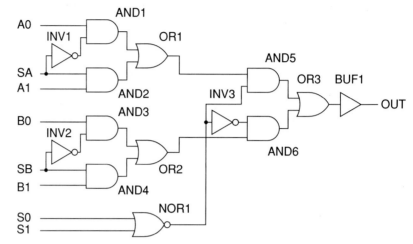

FIGURE 5.18 A schematic equivalent of the Actel ACT 1 Logic Module using a two-input AND/OR gate and a NOR gate (Problem 5.17).

5.18 (**Xilinx CLB analysis, 60 min.) Table 5.11 shows some information derived from a die photo in the AT&T ATT3000 series data book that shows the eight by eight CLB matrix on an ATT3020 (equivalent to a XC3020) clearly. By measuring the die size in the photo and knowing the actual die size we can calculate the size of a CLB **matrix element** (ME) that includes a single XC3000 CLB as approximately 277 mil^2. The ME includes interconnect, SRAM, programming, and other resources as well as a CLB.

TABLE 5.11   ATT3020 die information (Problem 5.18).[1]

Parameter	Data book	Die photo	Calculated
3020 die width	183.5 mil	4.1 cm	—
3020 die height	219.3 mil	4.9 cm	—
3000 ME width	—	0.325 cm	14.55 mil = 370 μm
3000 ME height	—	0.425 cm	19.02 mil = 483 μm
3000 ME area	—	—	277 mil^2
3020 pad pitch	—	1.6 mm/pad	7.21 mil/pad

[1]Data from AT&T data book, July 1992, p. 3-76, MN92-024FPGA

a. The minimum feature size in the AT&T Holmdel twin-tub V process used for the ATT3000 family is 0.9 μm. Using a value of $\lambda = 0.45$ μm, calculate the Xilinx XC3000 ME size in λ^2.

b. Estimate, explaining your assumptions, the area of the XC4000 ME, and the XC5200 ME (both in λ^2).

c. Table 5.12 shows the ATT3000 die information. Using a value of 277 mil^2 for the ATT/XC3000 ME area, complete this table.

TABLE 5.12   ATT3000 die information (Problem 5.18).[1]

Die	Die height mil	Die width mil	Die area mil^2	Die area cm^2	CLBs	ME area mil^2	ME area cm^2
3020	219.3	183.5	40,242	0.26	8 x 8		
3030	259.8	215.0	55,857	0.36	10 x 10		
3042	295.3	242.5	71,610	0.46	12 x 12		
3064	270.9	366.5	99,285	0.64	16 x 14		
3090	437.0	299.2	130,750	0.84	16 x 20		

[1] Data from AT&T data book, July 1992, p. 3-75, MN92-024FPGA. 1 mil^2 = 10^{-6} in^2 = 2.54^2 x 10^{-6} cm^2 = 6.452 x 10^{-6} cm^2

5.7 Bibliography

The book by Brown et al. [1992] on FPGAs deals with commercially available FPGAs and logic block architecture. There are several easily readable articles on FPGAs in the July 1993 issue of the *IEEE Proceedings* including articles by Rose et al. [1993] and Greene et al. [1993]. Greene's article is a good place to start digging deeper into the Actel FPGA architecture and gives an idea of the very complex problem of programming antifuses, something we have not discussed. Trimberger, who works at Xilinx, has edited a book on FPGAs [1994]. For those wishing to understand even more about the trade-offs in the different programmable ASIC architectures, a student of Stanford Professor Abbas El Gamal (one of the cofounders of Actel) has completed a Ph.D. on this topic [Kouloheris, 1993]. The best resources for information on FPGAs and their logic cells are the manufacturer's data sheets, data books, and application notes. The data books change every year or so as new products are released, so it is difficult to give specific references, but Xilinx, Actel, and Altera currently produce huge volumes complete with excellent design guides and application notes—you should obtain each of these even if you are not currently using that particular technology. Many of these are also online in Adobe Acrobat and PostScript format as well as in CD-ROM format (see also the bibliography in Chapter 4).

5.8   References

Brown, S. D., et al. 1992. *Field-Programmable Gate Arrays.* Norwell, MA: Kluwer Academic. 206 p. ISBN 0-7923-9248-5. TK7872.L64F54. Introduction to FPGAs, Commercially Available FPGAs, Technology Mapping for FPGAs, Logic Block Architecture, Routing for FPGAs, Flexibility of FPGA Routing Resources, A Theoretical Model for FPGA Routing. Includes an introduction to commercially available FPGAs. The rest of the book covers research on logic synthesis for FPGAs and FPGA architectures, concentrating on LUT-based architectures.

Greene, J., et al. 1993. "Antifuse field programmable gate arrays." *Proceedings of the IEEE*, vol. 81, no. 7, pp. 1042–1056. Review article describing the Actel FPGAs. (Included in the Actel 1994 data book.)

Kouloheris, J. L. 1993. "Empirical study of the effect of cell granularity on FPGA density and performance." Ph.D. Thesis, Stanford, CA. 114 p. Detailed research study of the different FPGA architectures concentrating on structures similar to the Actel and Altera FPGAs.

Rose, J., et al. 1993. "A classification and survey of field-programmable gate array architectures." *Proceedings of the IEEE*, vol. 81, no. 7.

Trimberger, S. M. (Ed.). 1994. *Field-Programmable Gate Array Technology.* Boston: Kluwer Academic Publishers. ISBN 0-7923-9419-4. TK7895.G36.F54.

PROGRAMMABLE ASIC I/O CELLS

6

All programmable ASICs contain some type of **input/output cell** (**I/O cell**). These I/O cells handle driving logic signals off-chip, receiving and conditioning external inputs, as well as handling such things as electrostatic protection. This chapter explains the different types of I/O cells that are used in programmable ASICs and their functions.

The following are different types of I/O requirements.

- *DC output*. Driving a resistive load at DC or low frequency (less than 1 MHz). Example loads are light-emitting diodes (LEDs), relays, small motors, and such. Can we supply an output signal with enough voltage, current, power, or energy?

- *AC output*. Driving a capacitive load with a high-speed (greater than 1 MHz) logic signal off-chip. Example loads are other logic chips, a data or address bus, ribbon cable. Can we supply a valid signal fast enough?

- *DC input*. Example sources are a switch, sensor, or another logic chip. Can we correctly interpret the digital value of the input?

- *AC input*. Example sources are high-speed logic signals (higher than 1 MHz) from another chip. Can we correctly interpret the input quickly enough?

- *Clock input.* Examples are system clocks or signals on a synchronous bus. Can we transfer the timing information from the input to the appropriate places on the chip correctly and quickly enough?

- *Power input.* We need to supply power to the I/O cells and the logic in the core, without introducing voltage drops or noise. We may also need a separate power supply to program the chip.

These issues are common to all FPGAs (and all ICs) so that the design of FPGA I/O cells is driven by the I/O requirements as well as the programming technology.

6.1   DC Output

Figure 6.1 shows a robot arm driven by three small motors together with switches to control the motors. The motor armature current varies between 50 mA and nearly 0.5 A when the motor is stalled. Can we replace the switches with an FPGA and drive the motors directly?

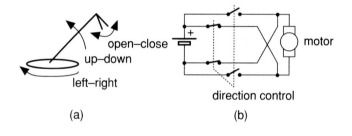

FIGURE 6.1 A robot arm. (a) Three small DC motors drive the arm. (b) Switches control each motor.

Figure 6.2 shows a CMOS complementary output buffer used in many FPGA I/O cells and its DC characteristics. Data books typically specify the output characteristics at two points, A (V_{OHmin}, I_{OHmax}) and B (V_{OLmax}, I_{OLmax}), as shown in Figure 6.2(d). As an example, values for the Xilinx XC5200 are as follows[1]:

- $V_{OLmax} = 0.4$ V, **low-level output voltage** at $I_{OLmax} = 8.0$ mA.

- $V_{OHmin} = 4.0$ V, **high-level output voltage** at $I_{OHmax} = -8.0$ mA.

By convention the **output current**, I_O, is positive if it flows into the output. Input currents, if there are any, are positive if they flow into the inputs. The Xilinx XC5200 specifications show that the output buffer can force the output pad to 0.4 V or lower and **sink** no more than 8 mA if the load requires it. CMOS logic inputs that may be connected to the pad draw minute amounts of current, but bipolar TTL inputs can require several milliamperes. Similarly, when the output is 4 V, the buffer

---

[1]XC5200 data sheet, October 1995 (v. 3.0).

can **source** 8 mA. It is common to say that $V_{OLmax} = 0.4$ V and $V_{OHmin} = 4.0$ V for a technology—without referring to the current values at which these are measured—strictly this is incorrect.

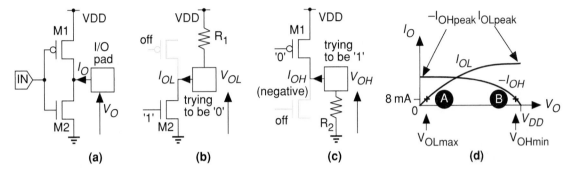

FIGURE 6.2 (a) A CMOS complementary output buffer. (b) Pull-down transistor M2 (M1 is off) sinks (to GND) a current I_{OL} through a pull-up resistor, R_1. (c) Pull-up transistor M1 (M2 is off) sources (from VDD) current $-I_{OH}$ (I_{OH} is negative) through a pull-down resistor, R_2. (d) Output characteristics.

If we force the **output voltage**, V_O, of an output buffer, using a voltage supply, and measure the output current, I_O, that results, we find that a buffer is capable of sourcing and sinking far more than the specified I_{OHmax} and I_{OLmax} values. Most vendors do not specify output characteristics because they are difficult to measure in production. Thus we normally do not know the value of I_{OLpeak} or I_{OHpeak}; typical values range from 50 to 200 mA.

Can we drive the motors by connecting several output buffers in parallel to reach a peak drive current of 0.5 A? Some FPGA vendors do specifically allow you to connect adjacent output cells in parallel to increase the output drive. If the output cells are not adjacent or are on different chips, there is a risk of contention. Contention will occur if, due to delays in the signal arriving at two output cells, one output buffer tries to drive an output high while the other output buffer is trying to drive the same output low. If this happens we essentially short VDD to GND for a brief period. Although contention for short periods may not be destructive, it increases power dissipation and should be avoided.[2]

It is thus possible to parallel outputs to increase the DC drive capability, but it is not a good idea to do so because we may damage or destroy the chip (by exceeding the maximum metal electromigration limits). Figure 6.3 shows an alternative—a

[2]Actel specifies a maximum I/O current of ± 20 mA for ACT3 family (1994 data book, p. 1-93) and its ES family. Altera specifies the maximum DC output current per pin, for example ± 25 mA for the FLEX 10k (July 1995, v. 1 data sheet, p. 42).

simple circuit to boost the drive capability of the output buffers. If we need more power we could use two operational amplifiers (**op-amps**) connected as voltage followers in a bridge configuration. For even more power we could use discrete power MOSFETs or power op-amps.

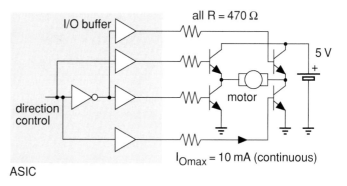

FIGURE 6.3 A circuit to drive a small electric motor (0.5 A) using ASIC I/O buffers. Any *npn* transistors with a reasonable gain ($\beta \approx 100$) that are capable of handling the peak current (0.5 A) will work with an output buffer that is capable of sourcing more than 5 mA. The 470 Ω resistors drop up to 5 V if an output buffer current approaches 10 mA, reducing the drive to the output transistors.

6.1.1   Totem-Pole Output

Figure 6.4(a) and (b) shows a **totem-pole** output buffer and its DC characteristics. It is similar to the TTL totem-pole output from which it gets its name (the totem-pole

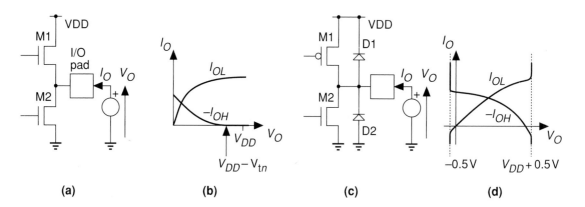

FIGURE 6.4 Output buffer characteristics. (a) A CMOS totem-pole output stage (both M1 and M2 are *n*-channel transistors). (b) Totem-pole output characteristics. (c) Clamp diodes, D1 and D2, in an output buffer (these diodes are present in all output buffers—totem-pole or complementary). (d) The clamp diodes start to conduct as the output voltage exceeds the supply voltage bounds.

circuit has two stacked transistors of the same type, whereas a complementary output uses transistors of opposite types). The high-level voltage, V_{OHmin}, for a totem pole is lower than V_{DD}. Typically V_{OHmin} is in the range of 3.5 V to 4.0 V (with $V_{DD} = 5$ V), which makes rising and falling delays more symmetrical and more closely matches TTL voltage levels. The disadvantage is that the totem pole will typically only drive the output as high as 3–4 V; so this would not be a good choice of FPGA output buffer to work with the circuit shown in Figure 6.3.

6.1.2   Clamp Diodes

Figure 6.4(c) show the connection of **clamp diodes** (D1 and D2) that prevent the I/O pad from voltage excursions greater than V_{DD} and less than V_{SS}. Figure 6.4(d) shows the resulting characteristics.

6.2   AC Output

Figure 6.5 shows an example of an off-chip three-state bus. Chips that have inputs and outputs connected to a bus are called **bus transceivers**. Can we use FPGAs to perform the role of bus transceivers? We will focus on one bit, B1, on bus BUSA, and we shall call it BUSA.B1. We need unique names to refer to signals on each chip; thus CHIP1.OE means the signal OE inside CHIP1. Notice that CHIP1.OE is not connected to CHIP2.OE.

Figure 6.6 shows the timing of part of a **bus transaction** (a sequence of signals on a bus):

1. Initially CHIP2 drives BUSA.B1 high (CHIP2.D1 is '1' and CHIP2.OE is '1').

2. The buffer output enable on CHIP2 (CHIP2.OE) goes low, **floating** the bus. The bus will stay high because we have a bus keeper, BK1.

3. The buffer output enable on CHIP3 (CHIP3.OE) goes high and the buffer drives a low onto the bus (CHIP3.D1 is '0').

We wish to calculate the delays involved in driving the off-chip bus in Figure 6.6. In order to find t_{float}, we need to understand how Actel specifies the delays for its I/O cells. Figure 6.7(a) shows the circuit used for measuring I/O delays for the ACT FPGAs. These measurements do not use the same trip points that are used to characterize the internal logic (Actel uses input and output trip points of 0.5 for internal logic delays).

Notice in Figure 6.7(a) that when the output enable E is '0' the output is **three-stated** (**high-impedance** or **hi-Z**). Different companies use different polarity and naming conventions for the "output enable" signal on a three-state buffer. To

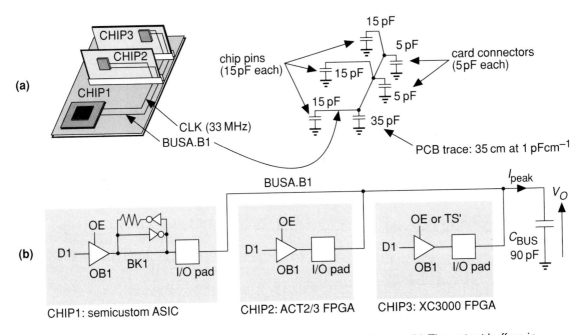

(a)

(b)

FIGURE 6.5 A three-state bus. (a) Bus parasitic capacitance. (b) The output buffers in each chip. The ASIC CHIP1 contains a bus keeper, BK1.

FIGURE 6.6 Three-state bus timing for Figure 6.5. The on-chip delays, t_{2OE} and t_{3OE}, for the logic that generates signals CHIP2.E1 and CHIP3.E1 are derived from the timing models described in Chapter 5 (the minimum values for each chip would be the clock-to-Q delay times).

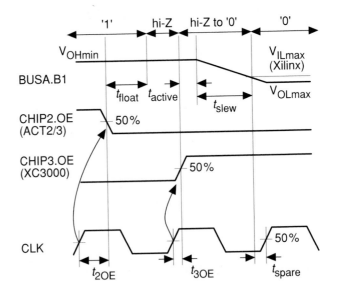

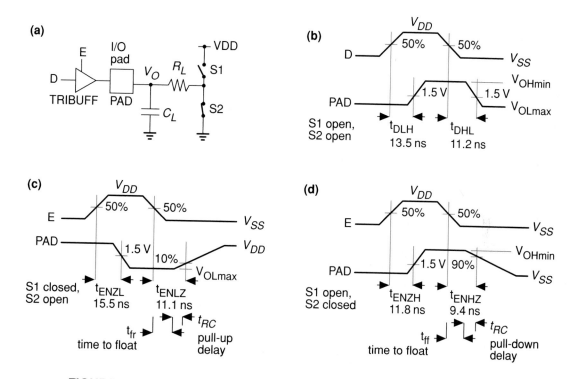

FIGURE 6.7 (a) The test circuit for characterizing the ACT 2 and ACT 3 I/O delay parameters. (b) Output buffer propagation delays from the data input to PAD (output enable, E, is high). (c) Three-state delay with D low. (d) Three-state delay with D high. Delays are shown for ACT 2 'Std' speed grade, worst-case commercial conditions ($R_L = 1\ k\Omega$, $C_L = 50$ pF, $V_{OHmin} = 2.4$ V, $V_{OLmax} = 0.5$ V). (The Actel three-state buffer is named TRIBUFF, an input buffer INBUF, and the output buffer, OUTBUF.)

measure the buffer delay (measured from the change in the enable signal, E) Actel uses a resistor load ($R_L = 1\ k\Omega$ for ACT 2). The resistor pulls the buffer output high or low depending on whether we are measuring:

- t_{ENZL}, when the output switches from hi-Z to '0'.
- t_{ENLZ}, when the output switches from '0' to hi-Z.
- t_{ENZH}, when the output switches from hi-Z to '1'.
- t_{ENHZ}, when the output switches from '1' to hi-Z.

Other vendors specify the **time to float** a three-state output buffer directly (t_{fr} and t_{ff} in Figure 6.7c and d). This delay time has different names (and definitions): **disable time**, **time to begin hi-Z**, or **time to turn off**.

Actel does not specify the time to float but, since $R_LC_L = 50$ ns, we know $t_{RC} = -R_LC_L \ln 0.9$ or approximately 5.3 ns. Now we can estimate that

$$t_{fr} = t_{ENLZ} - t_{RC} = 11.1 - 5.3 = 5.8 \text{ ns}, \qquad \text{and} \qquad t_{ff} = 9.4 - 5.3 = 4.1 \text{ ns},$$

and thus the Actel buffer can float the bus in $t_{float} = 4.1$ ns (Figure 6.6).

The Xilinx FPGA is responsible for the second part of the bus transaction. The time to make the buffer CHIP2.B1 active is t_{active}. Once the buffer is active, the output transistors turn on, conducting a current I_{peak}. The output voltage V_O across the load capacitance, C_{BUS}, will **slew** or change at a steady rate, $dV_O/dt = I_{peak}/C_{BUS}$; thus $t_{slew} = C_{BUS}\Delta V_O/I_{peak}$, where ΔV_O is the change in output voltage.

Vendors do not always provide enough information to calculate t_{active} and t_{slew} separately, but we can usually estimate their sum. Xilinx specifies the time from the three-state input switching to the time the "pad is active and valid" for an XC3000-125 switching with a 50 pF load, to be $t_{active} = t_{TSON} = 11$ ns (fast option), and 27 ns (slew-rate limited option).[3] If we need to drive the bus in less than one clock cycle (30 ns), we will definitely need to use the fast option.

A supplement to the XC3000 timing data specifies the additional fall delay for switching large capacitive loads (above 50 pF) as $R_{fall} = 0.06$ nspF^{-1} (falling) and $R_{rise} = 0.12$ nspF^{-1} (rising) using the fast output option.[4] We can thus estimate that

$$I_{peak} \approx (5 \text{ V})/(-0.06 \times 10^3 \text{ sF}^{-1}) \approx -84 \text{ mA} \qquad \text{(falling)}$$

and

$$I_{peak} \approx (5 \text{ V})/(0.12 \times 10^3 \text{ sF}^{-1}) \approx 42 \text{ mA} \qquad \text{(rising)}.$$

Now we can calculate,

$$t_{slew} = R_{fall}(C_{BUS} - 50 \text{ pF}) = (90 \text{ pF} - 50 \text{ pF})(0.06 \text{ nspF}^{-1}) \qquad \text{or 2.4 ns,}$$

for a total falling delay of $11 + 2.4 = 13.4$ ns. The rising delay is slower at $11 + (40 \text{ pF})(0.12 \text{ nspF}^{-1})$ or 15.8 ns. This leaves $(30 - 15.8)$ ns, or about 14 ns worst-case, to generate the output enable signal CHIP2.OE (t_{3OE} in Figure 6.6) and still leave time t_{spare} before the bus data is latched on the next clock edge. We can thus probably use a XC3000 part for a 30 MHz bus transceiver, but only if we use the fast slew-rate option.

An aside: Our example looks a little like the PCI bus used on Pentium and PowerPC systems, but the bus transactions are simplified. PCI buses use a **sustained three-state** system (**s/t/s**). On the PCI bus an s/t/s driver must drive the bus high for at least one clock cycle before letting it float. A new driver may not start driving the bus until a clock edge after the previous driver floats it. After such a **turnaround cycle** a new driver will always find the bus parked high.

---

[3]1994 data book, p. 2-159.

[4]Application Note XAPP 024.000, Additional XC3000 Data, 1994 data book p. 8-15.

6.2.1 Supply Bounce

Figure 6.8(a) shows an *n*-channel transistor, M1, that is part of an output buffer driving an output pad, OUT1; M2 and M3 form an inverter connected to an input pad, IN1; and M4 and M5 are part of another output buffer connected to an output pad, OUT2. As M1 sinks current pulling OUT1 low (V_{o1} in Figure 6.8b), a substantial current I_{OL} may flow in the resistance, R_S, and inductance, L_S, that are between the on-chip GND net and the off-chip, external ground connection.

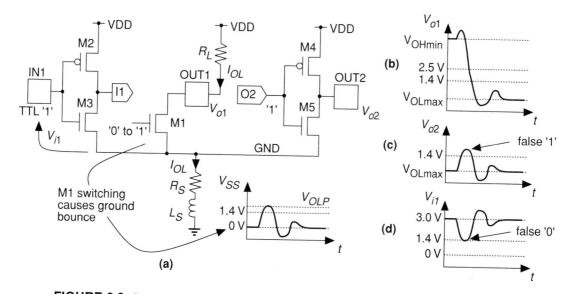

FIGURE 6.8 Supply bounce. (a) As the pull-down device, M1, switches, it causes the GND net (value V_{SS}) to bounce. (b) The supply bounce is dependent on the output slew rate. (c) Ground bounce can cause other output buffers to generate a logic glitch. (d) Bounce can also cause errors on other inputs.

The voltage drop across R_S and L_S causes a spike (or transient) on the GND net, changing the value of V_{SS}, leading to a problem known as **supply bounce**. The situation is illustrated in Figure 6.8(a), with V_{SS} bouncing to a maximum of V_{OLP}. This **ground bounce** causes the voltage at the output, V_{o2}, to bounce also. If the threshold of the gate that OUT2 is driving is a TTL level at 1.4 V, for example, a ground bounce of more than 1.4 V will cause a logic high **glitch** (a momentary transition from one logic level to the opposite logic level and back again).

Ground bounce may also cause problems at chip inputs. Suppose the inverter M2/M3 is set to have a TTL threshold of 1.4 V and the input, IN1, is at a fixed voltage equal to 3 V (a respectable logic high for bipolar TTL). In this case a ground bounce of greater than 1.6 V will cause the input, IN1, to see a logic low instead of a high and a glitch will be generated on the inverter output, I1. Supply bounce can also occur on the VDD net, but this is usually less severe because the pull-up transistors in an output buffer are usually weaker than the pull-down transistors. The risk of generating a glitch is also greater at the low logic level for TTL-threshold inputs and TTL-level outputs because the low-level noise margins are smaller than the high-level noise margins in TTL.

Sixteen SSOs, with each output driving 150 pF on a bus, can generate a ground bounce of 1.5 V or more. We cannot simulate this problem easily with FPGAs because we are not normally given the characteristics of the output devices. As a rule of thumb we wish to keep ground bounce below 1 V. To help do this we can limit the maximum number of SSOs, and we can limit the number of I/O buffers that share GND and VDD pads.

To further reduce the problem, FPGAs now provide options to limit the current flowing in the output buffers, reducing the slew rate and slowing them down. Some FPGAs also have quiet I/O circuits that sense when the input to an output buffer changes. The quiet I/O then starts to change the output using small transistors; shortly afterwards the large output transistors "drop-in." As the output approaches its final value, the large transistors "kick-out," reducing the supply bounce.

6.2.2   Transmission Lines

Most of the problems with driving large capacitive loads at high speed occur on a bus, and in this case we may have to consider the bus as a transmission line. Figure 6.9(a) shows how a transmission line appears to a driver, D1, and receiver, R1, as a constant impedance, the **characteristic impedance** of the line, Z_0. For a typical PCB trace, Z_0 is between 50 Ω and 100 Ω.

The voltages on a transmission line are determined by the value of the driver source resistance, R_0, and the way that we terminate the end of the transmission line. In Figure 6.9(a) the termination is just the capacitance of the receiver, C_{in}. As the driver switches between 5 V and 0 V, it launches a voltage wave down the line, as shown in Figure 6.9(b). The wave will be $Z_0 / (R_0 + Z_0)$ times 5 V in magnitude, so that if R_0 is equal to Z_0, the wave will be 2.5 V.

Notice that it does not matter what is at the far end of the line. The bus driver sees only Z_0 and not C_{in}. Imagine the transmission line as a tunnel; all the bus driver can see at the entrance is a little way into the tunnel—it could be 500 m or 5 km long. To find out, we have to go with the wave to the end, turn around, come back, and tell the bus driver. The final result will be the same whether the transmission line is there or not, but with a transmission line it takes a little longer for the voltages and currents to settle down. This is rather like the difference between having a conversation by telephone or by post.

The propagation delay (or time of flight), t_f, for a typical PCB trace is approximately 1 ns for every 15 cm of trace (the signal velocity is about one-half the speed of light). A voltage wave launched on a transmission line takes a time t_f to get to the end of the line, where it finds the load capacitance, C_{in}. Since no current can flow at

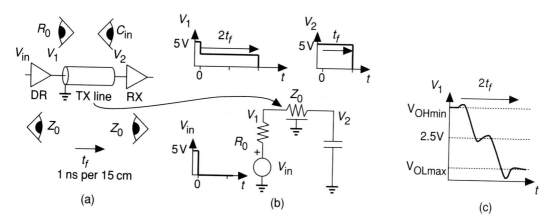

FIGURE 6.9 Transmission lines. (a) A printed-circuit board (PCB) trace is a transmission (TX) line. (b) A driver launches an incident wave, which is reflected at the end of the line. (c) A connection starts to look like a transmission line when the signal rise time is about equal to twice the line delay ($2t_f$).

this point, there must be a reflection that exactly cancels the incident wave so that the voltage at the input to the receiver, at V_2, becomes exactly zero at time t_f. The reflected wave travels back down the line and finally causes the voltage at the output of the driver, at V_1, to be exactly zero at time $2t_f$. In practice the nonidealities of the driver and the line cause the waves to have finite rise times. We start to see transmission line behavior if the rise time of the driver is less than $2t_f$, as shown in Figure 6.9(c).

There are several ways to terminate a transmission line. Figure 6.10 illustrates the following methods:

- *Open-circuit or capacitive termination.* The bus termination is the input capacitance of the receivers (usually less than 20 pF). The PCI bus uses this method.

- *Parallel resistive termination.* This requires substantial DC current (5 V / 100 Ω = 50 mA for a 100 Ω line). It is used by bipolar logic, for example emitter-coupled logic (ECL), where we typically do not care how much power we use.

- *Thévenin termination.* Connecting 300 Ω in parallel with 150 Ω across a 5 V supply is equivalent to a 100 Ω termination connected to a 1.6 V source. This reduces the DC current drain on the drivers but adds a resistance directly across the supply.

- *Series termination at the source.* Adding a resistor in series with the driver so that the sum of the driver source resistance (which is usually 50 Ω or even less) and the termination resistor matches the line impedance (usually around

100 Ω). The disadvantage is that it generates reflections that may be close to the switching threshold.

- *Parallel termination with a voltage bias.* This is awkward because it requires a third supply and is normally used only for a specialized high-speed bus.
- *Parallel termination with a series capacitance.* This removes the requirement for DC current but introduces other problems.

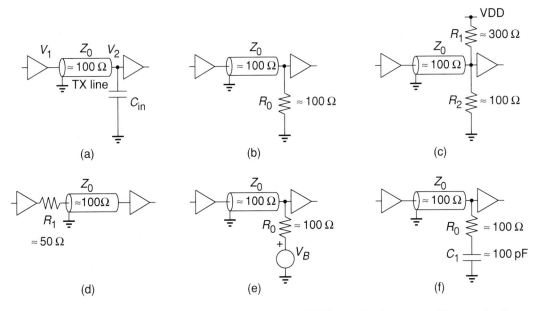

FIGURE 6.10 Transmission line termination. (a) Open-circuit or capacitive termination. (b) Parallel resistive termination. (c) Thévenin termination. (d) Series termination at the source. (e) Parallel termination using a voltage bias. (f) Parallel termination with a series capacitor.

Until recently most bus protocols required strong bipolar or BiCMOS output buffers capable of driving all the way between logic levels. The PCI standard uses weaker CMOS drivers that rely on reflection from the end of the bus to allow the intermediate receivers to see the full logic value. Many FPGA vendors now offer complete PCI functions that the ASIC designer can "drop in" to an FPGA [PCI, 1995].

An alternative to using a transmission line that operates across the full swing of the supply voltage is to use current-mode signaling or differential signals with low-voltage swings. These and other techniques are used in specialized bus structures and in high-speed DRAM. Examples are Rambus, and **Gunning transistor logic (GTL)**. These are analog rather than digital circuits, but ASIC methods apply if the interface circuits are available as cells, hiding some of the complexity from the designer. For example, Rambus offers a **Rambus access cell (RAC)** for standard-cell design (but not yet for an FPGA). Directions to more information on these topics are in the bibliography at the end of this chapter.

6.3   DC Input

Suppose we have a pushbutton switch connected to the input of an FPGA as shown in Figure 6.11(a). Most FPGA input pads are directly connected to a buffer. We need to ensure that the input of this buffer never floats to a voltage between valid logic levels (which could cause both n-channel and p-channel transistors in the buffer to turn on, leading to oscillation or excessive power dissipation) and so we use the optional pull-up resistor (usually about $100 \, k\Omega$) that is available on many FPGAs (we could also connect a $1 \, k\Omega$ pull-up or pull-down resistor externally).

Contacts may bounce as a switch is operated (Figure 6.11b). In the case of a Xilinx XC4000 the effective pull-up resistance is 5–$50 \, k\Omega$ (since the specified pull-up current is between 0.2 and 2.0 mA) and forms an RC time constant with the parasitic capacitance of the input pad and the external circuit. This time constant (typically hundreds of nanoseconds) will normally be much less than the time over which the contacts bounce (typically many milliseconds). The buffer output may thus be a series of pulses extending for several milliseconds. It is up to you to deal with this in your logic. For example, you may want to **debounce** the waveform in Figure 6.11(b) using an SR flip-flop.

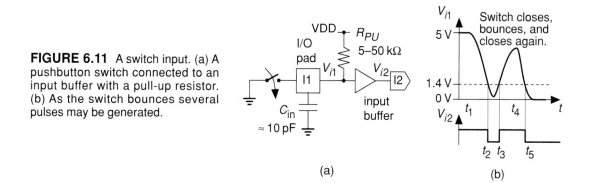

FIGURE 6.11 A switch input. (a) A pushbutton switch connected to an input buffer with a pull-up resistor. (b) As the switch bounces several pulses may be generated.

A bouncing switch may create a noisy waveform in the time domain, we may also have noise in the voltage level of our input signal. The **Schmitt-trigger** inverter in Figure 6.12(a) has a lower switching threshold of 2 V and an upper switching threshold of 3 V. The difference between these thresholds is the **hysteresis**, equal to 1 V in this case. If we apply the noisy waveform shown in Figure 6.12(b) to an inverter with no hysteresis, there will be a glitch at the output, as shown in Figure 6.12(c). As long as the noise on the waveform does not exceed the hysteresis, the Schmitt-trigger inverter will produce the glitch-free output of Figure 6.12(d).

Most FPGA input buffers have a small hysteresis (the 200 mV that Xilinx uses is a typical figure) centered around 1.4 V (for compatibility with TTL), as shown in Figure 6.12(e). Notice that the drawing inside the symbol for a Schmitt trigger looks like the transfer characteristic for a buffer, but is backward for an inverter. Hysteresis in the input buffer also helps prevent oscillation and noise problems with inputs that have slow rise times, though most FPGA manufacturers still have a restriction that input signals must have a rise time faster than several hundred nanoseconds.

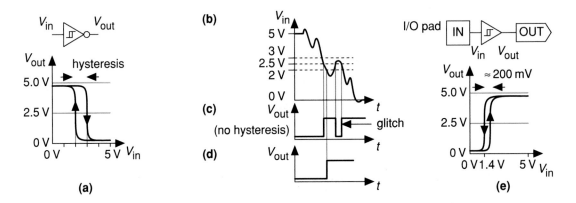

FIGURE 6.12 DC input. (a) A Schmitt-trigger inverter. (b) A noisy input signal. (c) Output from an inverter with no hysteresis. (d) Hysteresis helps prevent glitches. (e) A typical FPGA input buffer with a hysteresis of 200 mV centered around a threshold of 1.4 V.

6.3.1 Noise Margins

Figure 6.13(a) and (b) show the worst-case DC transfer characteristics of a CMOS inverter. Figure 6.13(a) shows a situation in which the process and device sizes create the lowest possible switching threshold. We define the maximum voltage that will be recognized as a '0' as the point at which the gain (V_{out}/V_{in}) of the inverter is -1. This point is $V_{ILmax} = 1V$ in the example shown in Figure 6.13(a). This means that any input voltage that is lower than 1V will definitely be recognized as a '0', even with the most unfavorable inverter characteristics. At the other worst-case extreme we define the minimum voltage that will be recognized as a '1' as $V_{IHmin} = 3.5V$ (for the example in Figure 6.13b).

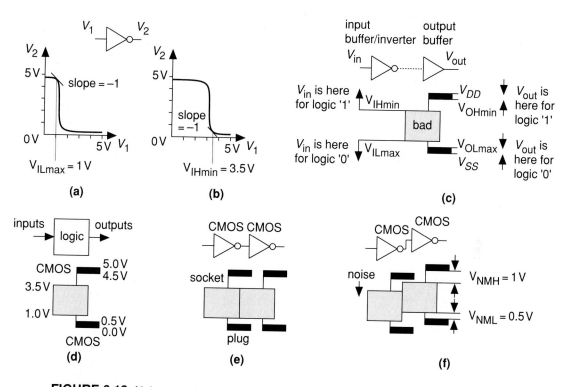

FIGURE 6.13 Noise margins. (a) Transfer characteristics of a CMOS inverter with the lowest switching threshold. (b) The highest switching threshold. (c) A graphical representation of CMOS logic thresholds. (d) Logic thresholds at the inputs and outputs of a logic gate or an ASIC. (e) The switching thresholds viewed as a plug and socket. (f) CMOS plugs fit CMOS sockets and the clearances are the noise margins.

Figure 6.13(c) depicts the following relationships between the various voltage levels at the inputs and outputs of a logic gate:

- A logic '1' output must be between V_{OHmin} and V_{DD}.
- A logic '0' output must be between V_{SS} and V_{OLmax}.
- A logic '1' input must be above the **high-level input voltage, V_{IHmin}**.
- A logic '0' input must be below the **low-level input voltage, V_{ILmax}**.
- Clamp diodes prevent an input exceeding V_{DD} or going lower than V_{SS}.

The voltages, V_{OHmin}, V_{OLmax}, V_{IHmin}, and V_{ILmax}, are the **logic thresholds** for a technology. A logic signal outside the areas bounded by these logic thresholds is "bad"—an unrecognizable logic level in an electronic no-man's land. Figure 6.13(d) shows typical logic thresholds for a CMOS-compatible FPGA. The V_{IHmin} and V_{ILmax} logic thresholds come from measurements in Figure 6.13(a) and (b) and V_{OHmin} and V_{OLmax} come from the measurements shown in Figure 6.2(c).

Figure 6.13(d) illustrates how logic thresholds form a plug and socket for any gate, group of gates, or even a chip. If a plug fits a socket, we can connect the two components together and they will have compatible logic levels. For example, Figure 6.13(e) shows that we can connect two CMOS gates or chips together.

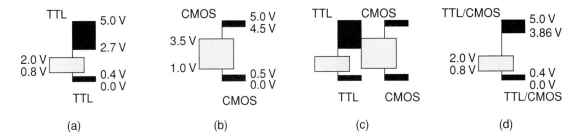

FIGURE 6.14 TTL and CMOS logic thresholds. (a) TTL logic thresholds. (b) Typical CMOS logic thresholds. (c) A TTL plug will not fit in a CMOS socket. (d) Raising V_{OHmin} solves the problem.

Figure 6.13(f) shows that we can even add some noise that shifts the input levels and the plug will still fit into the socket. In fact, we can shift the plug down by exactly $V_{OHmin} - V_{IHmin}$ (4.5 − 3.5 = 1 V) and still maintain a valid '1'. We can shift the plug up by $V_{ILmax} - V_{OLmax}$ (1.0 − 0.5 = 0.5 V) and still maintain a valid '0'. These clearances between plug and socket are the **noise margins**:

$$V_{NMH} = V_{OHmin} - V_{IHmin} \quad \text{and} \quad V_{NML} = V_{ILmax} - V_{OLmax}. \tag{6.1}$$

For two logic systems to be compatible, the plug must fit the socket. This requires both the **high-level noise margin (V_{NMH})** and the **low-level noise margin (V_{NML})** to be positive. We also want both noise margins to be as large as possible to give us maximum immunity from noise and other problems at an interface.

Figure 6.14(a) and (b) show the logic thresholds for TTL together with typical CMOS logic thresholds. Figure 6.14(c) shows the problem with trying to plug a TTL chip into a CMOS input level—the lowest permissible TTL output level, $V_{OHmin} = 2.7$ V, is too low to be recognized as a logic '1' by the CMOS input. This is fixed by most FPGA manufacturers by raising V_{OHmin} to around 3.8–4.0V (Figure 6.14d). Table 6.1 lists the logic thresholds for several FPGAs.

6.3.2   Mixed-Voltage Systems

To reduce power consumption and allow CMOS logic to be scaled below 0.5 μm it is necessary to reduce the power supply voltage below 5 V. The JEDEC 8 [JEDEC

I/O] series of standards sets the next lower supply voltage as 3.3 ± 0.3 V. Figure 6.15(a) and (b) shows that the 3 V CMOS I/O logic-thresholds can be made compatible with 5 V systems. Some FPGAs can operate on both 3 V and 5 V supplies, typically using one voltage for internal (or core) logic, V_{DDint} and another for the I/O circuits, $V_{DDI/O}$ (Figure 6.15c).

TABLE 6.1 FPGA logic thresholds.

	I/O options		Input levels		Output levels (high current)				Output levels (low current)			
	Input	Output	V_{IH} (min)	V_{IL} (max)	V_{OH} (min)	I_{OH} (max)	V_{OL} (max)	I_{OL} (max)	V_{OH} (min)	I_{OH} (max)	V_{OL} (max)	I_{OL} (max)
XC3000[1]	TTL		2.0	0.8	3.86	−4.0	0.40	4.0				
	CMOS		3.85[2]	0.9[3]	3.86	−4.0	0.40	4.0				
XC3000L			2.0	0.8	2.40	−4.0	0.40	4.0	2.80[4]	−0.1	0.2	0.1
XC4000[5]			2.0	0.8	2.40	−4.0	0.40	12.0				
XC4000H[6]	TTL	TTL	2.0	0.8	2.40	−4.0	0.50	24.0				
	CMOS	CMOS	3.85[2]	0.9[3]	4.00[7]	−1.0	0.50	24.0				
XC8100[8]	TTL	R	2.0	0.8	3.86	−4.0	0.50	24.0				
	CMOS	C	3.85[2]	0.9[3]	3.86	−4.0	0.40	4.0				
ACT 2/3			2.0	0.8	2.4	−8.0	0.50	12.0	3.84	−4.0	0.33	6.0
FLEX10k[9]		3V/5V	2.0	0.8	2.4	−4.0	0.45	12.0				

[1]XC2000, XC3000/A have identical thresholds. XC3100/A thresholds are identical to XC3000 except for ±8mA source–sink current. XC5200 thresholds are identical to XC3100A.
[2]Defined as $0.7 V_{DD}$, calculated with $V_{DDmax} = 5.5$ V.
[3]Defined as $0.2 V_{DD}$, calculated with $V_{DDmin} = 4.5$ V.
[4]Defined as $V_{DD} - 0.2$ V, calculated with $V_{DDmin} = 3.0$ V.
[5]XC4000, XC4000A have identical I/O thresholds except XC4000A has −24 mA sink current.
[6]XC4000H/E have identical I/O thresholds except XC4000E has −12 mA sink current. Options are independent.
[7]Defined as $V_{DD} - 0.5$ V, calculated with $V_{DDmin} = 4.5$ V.
[8]Input and output options are independent.
[9]MAX 9000 has identical thresholds to FLEX 10k.
Note: All voltages in volts, all currents in milliamperes.

There is one problem when we mix 3 V and 5 V supplies that is shown in Figure 6.15(d). If we apply a voltage to a chip input that exceeds the power supply of a chip, it is possible to power a chip inadvertently through the clamp diodes. In the worst case this may cause a voltage as high as 2.5 V (= 5.5 V − 3.0 V) to appear across the clamp diode, which will cause a very large current (several hundred milliamperes) to flow. One way to prevent damage is to include a series resistor between the chips, typically around 1 kΩ. This solution does not work for all chips in all systems. A difficult problem in ASIC I/O design is constructing **5 V-tolerant I/O**. Most solutions may never surface (there is little point in patenting a solution to a problem that will go away before the patent is granted).

Similar problems can arise in several other situations:

- when you connect two ASICs with "different" 5 V supplies;

- when you power down one ASIC in a system but not another, or one ASIC powers down faster than another;

- on system power-up or system reset.

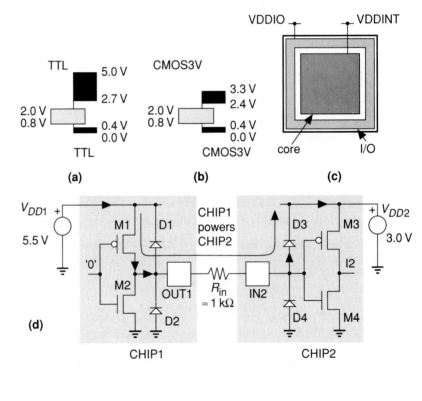

FIGURE 6.15 Mixed-voltage systems. (a) TTL levels. (b) Low-voltage CMOS levels. (c) A mixed-voltage ASIC. (d) A problem when connecting two chips with different supply voltages—caused by the input clamp diodes.

6.4   AC Input

Suppose we wish to connect an input bus containing sampled data from an **analog-to-digital converter** (**A/D**) that is running at a clock frequency of 100 kHz to an FPGA that is running from a system clock on a bus at 10 MHz (a NuBus). We are to perform some filtering and calculations on the sampled data before placing it on the

NuBus. We cannot just connect the A/D output bus to our FPGA, because we have no idea when the A/D data will change. Even though the A/D data rate (a sample every 10 μs or every 100 NuBus clock cycles) is much lower than the NuBus clock, if the data happens to arrive just before we are due to place an output on the NuBus, we have no time to perform any calculations. Instead we want to register the data at the input to give us a whole NuBus clock cycle (100 ns) to perform the calculations. We know that we should have the A/D data at the flip-flop input for at least the flip-flop setup time before the NuBus clock edge. Unfortunately there is no way to guarantee this; the A/D converter clock and the NuBus clock are completely independent. Thus it is entirely possible that every now and again the A/D data will change just before the NuBus clock edge.

6.4.1 Metastability

If we change the data input to a flip-flop (or a latch) too close to the clock edge (called a setup or hold-time **violation**), we run into a problem called **metastability**, illustrated in Figure 6.16. In this situation the flip-flop cannot decide whether its out-

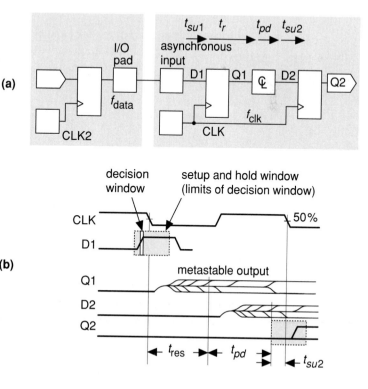

FIGURE 6.16 Metastability. (a) Data coming from one system is an asynchronous input to another. (b) A flip-flop has a very narrow decision window bounded by the setup and hold times. If the data input changes inside this decision window, the output may be metastable—neither '1' or '0'.

put should be a '1' or a '0' for a long time. If the flip-flop makes a decision, at a time t_r after the clock edge, as to whether its output is a '1' or a '0', there is a small, but finite, probability that the flip-flop will decide the output is a '1' when it should have been a '0' or vice-versa. This situation, called an **upset**, can happen when the data is coming from the outside world and the flip-slop can't determine when it will arrive; this is an **asynchronous signal**, because it is not synchronized to the chip clock.

Experimentally we find that the **probability of upset, p,** is

$$p = T_0 \exp \frac{-t_r}{\tau_c}, \tag{6.2}$$

where t_r is the time a **sampler** (flip-flop or latch) has to **resolve** the sampler output; T_0 and τ_c are constants of the sampler circuit design. Let us see how serious this problem is in practice. If $t_r = 5$ ns, $\tau_c = 0.1$ ns, and $T_0 = 0.1$ s, Eq. 6.2 gives the upset probability as

$$p = 0.1 \exp \frac{(-5 \times 10^{-9})}{(0.1 \times 10^{-9})} = 2 \times 10^{-23}, \tag{6.3}$$

which is very small, but the data and clock may be running at several MHz, causing the sampler plenty of opportunities for upset.

The **mean time between upsets** (**MTBU**, similar to MTBF—mean time between failures) is

$$\text{MTBU} = \frac{1}{pf_{\text{clock}}f_{\text{data}}} = \frac{\exp \dfrac{t_r}{\tau_c}}{T_0 f_{\text{clock}} f_{\text{data}}}, \tag{6.4}$$

where f_{clock} is the clock frequency and f_{data} is the data frequency.

If $t_r = 5$ ns, $\tau_c = 0.1$ ns, $T_0 = 0.1$ s (as in the previous example), $f_{\text{clock}} = 100$ MHz, and $f_{\text{data}} = 1$ MHz, then

$$\text{MTBU} = \frac{\exp \left(\dfrac{5 \times 10^{-9}}{0.1 \times 10^{-9}} \right)}{(100 \times 10^6)(1 \times 10^6)(0.1)} = 5.2 \times 10^8 \text{ sec}, \tag{6.5}$$

or about 16 years (10^8 seconds is three years, and a day is 10^5 sec). An MTBU of 16 years may seem safe, but suppose we have a 64-bit input bus using 64 flip-flops. If each flip-flop has an MTBU of 16 years, our system-level MTBF is three months. If we ship 1000 systems we would have an average of 10 systems failing every day. What can we do?

The parameter τ_c is the inverse of the **gain-bandwidth product, GB,** of the sampler at the instant of sampling. It is a constant that is independent of whether we are sampling a positive or negative data edge. It may be determined by a small-signal analysis of the sampler at the sampling instant or by measurement. It cannot be determined by simulating the transient response of the flip-flop to a metastable event since the gain and bandwidth both normally change as a function of time. We cannot change τ_c.

The parameter T_0 (units of time) is a function of the process technology and the circuit design. It may be different for sampling a positive or negative data edge, but normally only one value of T_0 is given. Attempts have been made to calculate T_0 and to relate it to a physical quantity. The best method is by measurement or simulation of metastable events. We cannot change T_0.

Given a good flip-flop or latch design, τ_c and T_0 should be similar for comparable CMOS processes (so, for example, all $0.5\,\mu m$ processes should have approximately the same τ_c and T_0). The only parameter we can change when using a flip-flop or latch from a cell library is t_r, and we should allow as much resolution time as

TABLE 6.2 Metastability parameters for FPGA flip-flops. These figures are not guaranteed by the vendors.

FPGA	T_0/s	τ_c/s
Actel ACT 1	1.0E–09	2.17E–10
Xilinx XC3020-70	1.5E–10	2.71E–10
QuickLogic QL12x16-0	2.94E–11	2.91E–10
QuickLogic QL12x16-1	8.38E–11	2.09E–10
QuickLogic QL12x16-2	1.23E–10	1.85E–10
Xilinx XC8100	2.15E-12	4.65E–10
Xilinx XC8100 synchronizer	1.59E-17	2.07E–10
Altera MAX 7000	2.98E-17	2.00E–10
Altera FLEX 8000	1.01E–13	7.89E–11

Sources: Actel April 1992 data book, p. 5-1, gives $C1 = T_0 = 10^{-9} Hz^{-1}$, $C2 = 1/\tau_c = 4.6052\,ns^{-1}$, or $\tau_c = 2.17E{-}10\,s$ and $T_0 = 1.0E{-}09\,s$. Xilinx gives $K1 = T_0 = 1.5E{-}10\,s$ and $K2 = 1/\tau_c = 3.69E9\,s^{-1}$, $\tau_c = 2.71E{-}10\,s$, for the XC3020-70 (p. 8-20 of 1994 data book). QuickLogic pASIC 1 QL12X16: $\tau_c = 0.2\,ns$ to $0.3\,ns$, $T_0 = 0.3E{-}10\,s$ to $1.2E{-}10\,s$ (1994 data book, p. 5-25, Fig. 2). Xilinx XC8100 data, $\tau_c = 4.65E{-}10\,s$ and $T_0 = 2.15E{-}12\,s$, is from October 1995 (v. 1.0) data sheet, Fig. 17 (the XC8100 was discontinued in August 1996). Altera 1995 data book p. 437, Table 1.

we can after the output of a *latch* before the signal is clocked again. If we use a *flip-flop* constructed from two latches in series (a master–slave design), then we are sampling the data twice. The resolution time for the first sample t_r is fixed, it is half the clock cycle (if the clock is high and low for equal times—we say the clock has a 50 percent **duty cycle**, or equal **mark–space ratio**). Using such a flip-flop we need to allow as much time as we can before we clock the second sample by connecting two flip-flops in series, without any combinational logic between them, if possible. If you are really in trouble, the next step is to divide the clock so you can extend the resolution time even further.

Table 6.2 shows flip-flop metastability parameters and Figure 6.17 graphs the metastability data for $f_{\text{clock}} = 10$ MHz and $f_{\text{data}} = 1$ MHz. From this graph we can see the enormous variation in MTBF caused by small variations in τ_c. For example, in the QuickLogic pASIC 1 series the range of T_0 from 0.3 to 1.2×10^{-10}s is 4:1, but it is the range of $\tau_c = 0.2 - 0.3$ ns (a variation of only 1:1.5) that is responsible for the enormous variation in MTBF (nearly four orders of magnitude at $t_r = 5$ ns). The variation in τ_c is caused by the variation in *GB* between the QuickLogic speed grades. Variation in the other vendors' parts will be similar, but most vendors do not show this information. To be safe, build a large safety margin for MTBF into any design— it is not unreasonable to use a margin of four orders of magnitude.

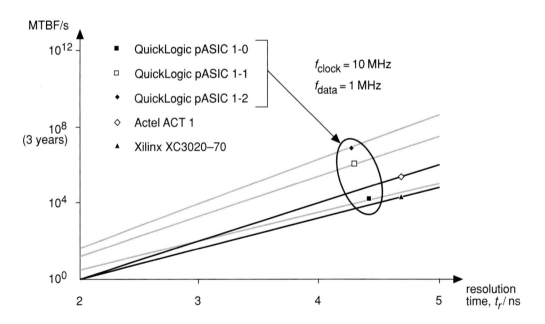

FIGURE 6.17   Mean time between failures (MTBF) as a function of resolution time. The data is from FPGA vendors' data books for a single flip-flop with clock frequency of 10 MHz and a data input frequency of 1 MHz (see Table 6.2).

Some cell libraries include a **synchronizer**, built from two flip-flops in cascade, that greatly reduces the effective values of τ_c and T_0 over a single flip-flop. The penalty is an extra clock cycle of latency.

To compare discrete TTL parts with ASIC flip-flops, the 74AS4374 TTL **metastable-hardened dual flip-flops**, from TI, have $\tau_c = 0.42$ ns and $T_0 = 4$ ns. The parameter T_0 ranges from about 10 s for the 74LS74 (a regular flip-flop) to 4 ns for the 74AS4374 (over nine orders of magnitude different); τ_c only varies from 0.42 ns (74AS374) to 1.3 ns (74LS74), but this small variation in τ_c is just as important.

6.5 Clock Input

When we bring the clock signal onto a chip, we may need to adjust the logic level (clock signals are often driven by TTL drivers with a high current output capability) and then we need to distribute the clock signal around the chip as it is needed. FPGAs normally provide special clock buffers and clock networks. We need to minimize the clock delay (or latency), but we also need to minimize the clock skew.

6.5.1 Registered Inputs

Some FPGAs provide a flip-flop or latch that you can use as part of the I/O circuit (registered I/O). For other FPGAs you have to use a flip-flop or latch using the basic logic cell in the core. In either case the important parameter is the input setup time. We can measure the setup with respect to the clock signal at the flip-flop or the clock signal at the clock input pad. The difference between these two parameters is the clock delay.

Figure 6.18 shows part of the I/O timing model for a Xilinx XC40005-6.[5]

- t_{PICK} is the fixed setup time for a flip-flop relative to the flip-flop clock.
- t_{skew} is the variable **clock skew**, the signed delay between two clock edges.
- t_{PG} is the variable clock delay or **latency**.

To calculate the flip-flop setup time ($t_{PSUFmin}$) relative to the clock pad (which is the parameter system designers need to know), we subtract the clock delay, so that

$$t_{PSUF} = t_{PICK} - t_{PG}. \tag{6.6}$$

The problem is that we cannot easily calculate t_{PG}, since it depends on the clock distribution scheme and where the flip-flop is on the chip. Instead Xilinx specifies

[5]The Xilinx XC4005-6 timing parameters are from the 1994 data book p. 2-50 to p. 2-53.

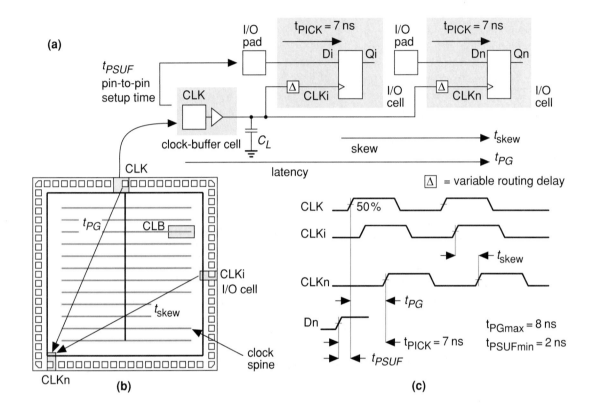

FIGURE 6.18 Clock input. (a) Timing model with values for a Xilinx XC4005-6. (b) A simplified view of clock distribution. (c) Timing diagram. Xilinx eliminates the variable internal delay t_{PG}, by specifying a pin-to-pin setup time, $t_{PSUFmin} = 2$ ns.

$t_{PSUFmin}$ directly, measured from the data pad to the clock pad; this time is called a **pin-to-pin timing parameter**. Notice $t_{PSUFmin} = 2$ ns $\neq t_{PICK} - t_{PGmax} = -1$ ns.

Figure 6.19 shows that the hold time for a XC4005-6 flip-flop (t_{CKI}) with respect to the flip-flop clock is zero. However, the pin-to-pin hold time including the clock delay is $t_{PHF} = 5.5$ ns. We can remove this inconvenient hold-time restriction by delaying the input signal. Including a programmable delay allows Xilinx to guarantee the pin-to-pin hold time (t_{PH}) as zero. The penalty is an increase in the pin-to-pin setup time (t_{PSU}) to 21 ns (from 2 ns) for the XC4005-6, for example.

We also have to account for clock delay when we register an output. Figure 6.20 shows the timing model diagram for the clock-to-output delay.

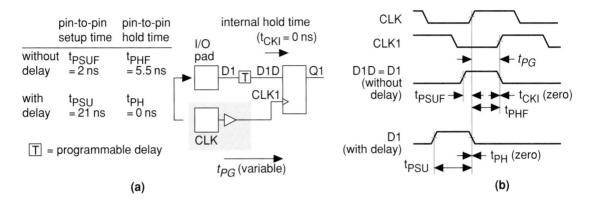

FIGURE 6.19 Programmable input delay. (a) Pin-to-pin timing model with values from an XC4005-6. (b) Timing diagrams with and without programmable delay.

FIGURE 6.20 Registered output. (a) Timing model with values for an XC4005-6 programmed with the fast slew-rate option. (b) Timing diagram.

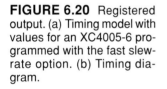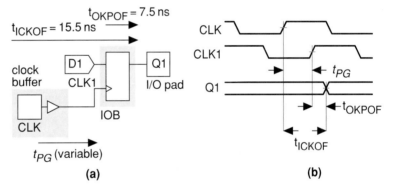

6.6 Power Input

The last item that we need to bring onto an FPGA is the power. We may need multiple VDD and GND power pads to reduce supply bounce or separate VDD pads for mixed-voltage supplies. We may also need to provide power for on-chip programming (in the case of antifuse or EPROM programming technology). The package type and number of pins will determine the number of power pins, which, in turn, affects the number of SSOs you can have in a design.

6.6.1   Power Dissipation

As a general rule a plastic package can dissipate about 1 W, and more expensive ceramic packages can dissipate up to about 2 W. Table 6.3 shows the thermal characteristics of common packages. In a high-speed (high-power) design the ASIC power

TABLE 6.3   Thermal characteristics of ASIC packages.

Package[1]	Pin count	Max. power P_{max}/W	θ_{JA}/°CW^{-1} (still air)[2,3]	θ_{JA}/°CW^{-1} (still air)[4]
CPGA	84		33	32–38
CPGA	100		35	
CPGA	132		30	
CPGA	175		25	16
CPGA	207		22	
CPGA	257		15	
CQFP	84		40	
CQFP	172		25	
PQFP	100	1.0	55	56–75
PQFP	160	1.75	33	30–33
PQFP	208	2.0	33	27-32
VQFP	80		68	
PLCC	44		52	44
PLCC	68		45	28–35
PLCC	84	1.5	44	
PPGA	132			33–34

[1]CPGA = ceramic pin-grid array; CQFP = ceramic quad flatpack; PQFP = plastic quad flatpack; VQFP = very thin quad flatpack; PLCC = plastic leaded chip carrier; PPGA = plastic pin-grid array.
[2] θ_{JA} varies with die size.
[3]Data from Actel 1994 data book p. 1-9, p. 1-45, and p. 1-94.
[4]Data from Xilinx 1994 data book p. 4-26 and p. 4-27.

consumption may dictate your choice of packages. Actel provides a formula for calculating typical dynamic chip power consumption of their FPGAs. The formula for the ACT 2 and ACT 3 FPGAs are complex; therefore we shall use the simpler formula for the ACT 1 FPGAs as an example[6]:

---

[6]1994 data book, p.1-9

Total chip power $= 0.2\,(N \times F1) + 0.085\,(M \times F2) + 0.8\,(P \times F3)$ mW   (6.7)

where

F1 = average logic module switching rate in MHz

F2 = average clock pin switching rate in MHz

F3 = average I/O switching rate in MHz

M = number of logic modules connected to the clock pin

N = number of logic modules used on the chip

P = number of I/O pairs used (input + output), with 50 pF load

As an example of a power-dissipation calculation, consider an Actel 1020B-2 with a 20 MHz clock. We shall initially assume 100 percent utilization of the 547 Logic Modules and assume that each switches at an average speed of 5 MHz. We shall also initially assume that we use all of the 69 I/O Modules and that each switches at an average speed of 5 MHz. Using Eq. 6.7, the Logic Modules dissipate

$$P_{LM} = (0.2)\,(547)\,(5) = 547 \text{ mW}, \qquad (6.8)$$

and the I/O Module dissipation is

$$P_{IO} = (0.8)\,(69)\,(5) = 276 \text{ mW}. \qquad (6.9)$$

If we assume the clock buffer drives 20 percent of the Logic Modules, then the additional power dissipation due to the clock buffer is

$$P_{CLK} = (0.085)\,(547)\,(0.2)\,(5) = 46.495 \text{ mW}. \qquad (6.10)$$

The total power dissipation is thus

$$P_D = (547 + 276 + 46.5) = 869.5 \text{ mW}, \qquad (6.11)$$

or about 900 mW (with an accuracy of certainly no better than $\pm$ 100 mW).

Suppose we intend to use a **very thin quad flatpack (VQFP)** with no cooling (because we are trying to save area and board height). From Table 6.3 the thermal resistance, θ_{JA}, is approximately $68\,°CW^{-1}$ for an 80-pin VQFP. Thus the maximum junction temperature under industrial worst-case conditions ($T_A = 85\,°C$) will be

$$T_J = (85 + (0.87)(68)) = 144.16\,°C, \tag{6.12}$$

(with an accuracy of no better than $10\,°C$). Actel specifies the maximum junction temperature for its devices as $T_{Jmax} = 150\,°C$ (T_{Jmax} for Altera is also $150\,°C$, for Xilinx $T_{Jmax} = 125°C$). Our calculated value is much too close to the rated maximum for comfort; therefore we need to go back and check our assumptions for power dissipation. At or near 100 percent module utilization is not unreasonable for an Actel device, but more questionable is that all nodes and I/Os switch at 5 MHz.

Our real mistake is trying to use a VQFP package with a high θ_{JA} for a high-speed design. Suppose we use an 84-pin PLCC package instead. From Table 6.3 the thermal resistance, θ_{JA}, for this alternative package is approximately $44\,°CW^{-1}$. Now the worst-case junction temperature will be a more reasonable

$$T_J = (85 + (0.87)(44)) = 123.28\,°C. \tag{6.13}$$

It is possible to estimate the power dissipation of the Actel architecture because the routing is regular and the interconnect capacitance is well controlled (it has to be since we must minimize the number of series antifuses we use). For most other architectures it is much more difficult to estimate power dissipation. The exception, as we saw in Section 5.4 "Altera MAX," are the programmable ASICs based on programmable logic arrays with passive pull-ups where a substantial part of the power dissipation is static.

6.6.2 Power-On Reset

Each FPGA has its own power-on reset sequence. For example, a Xilinx FPGA configures all flip-flops (in either the CLBs or IOBs) as either SET or RESET. After chip programming is complete, the global SET/RESET signal forces all flip-flops on the chip to a known state. This is important since it may determine the initial state of a state machine, for example.

6.7 Xilinx I/O Block

The Xilinx I/O cell is the **input/output block (IOB)**. Figure 6.21 shows the Xilinx XC4000 IOB, which is similar to the IOB in the XC2000, XC3000, and XC5200 but performs a superset of the options in these other Xilinx FPGAs.

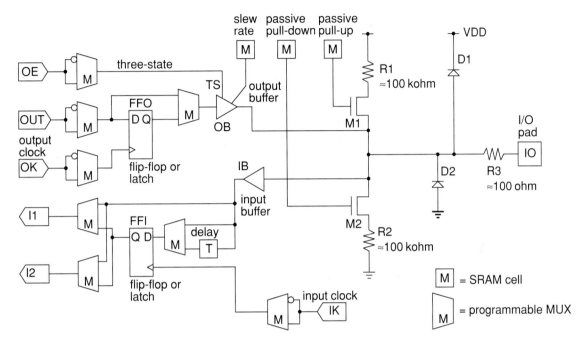

FIGURE 6.21 The Xilinx XC4000 family IOB (input/output block). (*Source:* Xilinx.)

The outputs contain features that allow you to do the following:

- Switch between a totem-pole and a complementary output (XC4000H).
- Include a passive pull-up or pull-down (both *n*-channel devices) with a typical resistance of about 50 kΩ.
- Invert the three-state control (output enable OE or three-state, TS).
- Include a flip-flop, or latch, or a direct connection in the output path.
- Control the slew rate of the output.

The features on the inputs allow you to do the following:

- Configure the input buffer with TTL or CMOS thresholds.
- Include a flip-flop, or latch, or a direct connection in the input path.
- Switch in a delay to eliminate an input hold time.

Figure 6.22 shows the timing model for the XC5200 family.[7] It is similar to the timing model for all the other Xilinx LCA FPGAs with one exception—the XC5200 does not have registers in the I/O cell; you go directly to the core CLBs to include a flip-flop or latch on an input or output.

---

[7]October 1995 (v. 3.0) data sheet.

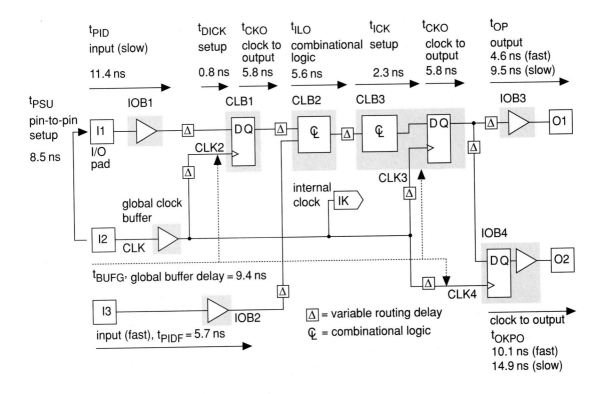

FIGURE 6.22 The Xilinx LCA (Logic Cell Array) timing model. The paths show different uses of CLBs (Configurable Logic Blocks) and IOBs (Input/Output Blocks). The parameters shown are for an XC5210-6. (*Source:* Xilinx.)

6.7.1   Boundary Scan

Testing PCBs can be done using a bed-of-nails tester. This approach becomes very difficult with closer IC pin spacing and more sophisticated assembly methods using surface-mount technology and multilayer boards. The IEEE implemented boundary-scan standard 1149.1 to simplify the problem of testing at the board level. The Joint Test Action Group (JTAG) developed the standard; thus the terms JTAG boundary scan or just JTAG are commonly used.

Many FPGAs contain a standard boundary-scan test logic structure with a four-pin interface. By using these four signals, you can program the chip using ISP, as well as serially load commands and data into the chips to control the outputs and check the inputs. This is a great improvement over bed-of-nails testing. We shall cover boundary scan in detail in Section 14.6, "Scan Test."

6.8   Other I/O Cells

The Altera MAX 5000 and 7000 use the **I/O Control Block** (IOC) shown in
Figure 6.23. In the MAX 5000, all inputs pass through the chipwide interconnect.
The MAX 7000E has special fast inputs that are connected directly to macrocell reg-
isters in order to reduce the setup time for registered inputs.

FIGURE 6.23 A simplified block
diagram of the Altera I/O Control
Block (IOC) used in the MAX 5000
and MAX 7000 series. The I/O pin
feedback allows the I/O pad to be
isolated from the macrocell. It is
thus possible to use a LAB without
using up an I/O pad (as you often
have to do using a PLD such as a
22V10). The PIA is the chipwide
interconnect.

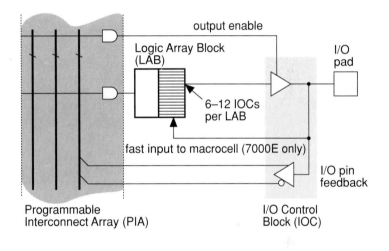

The FLEX 8000 and 10k use the **I/O Element** (IOE) shown in Figure 6.24 (the
MAX 9000 IOC is similar). The interface to the IOE is directly to the chipwide
interconnect rather than the core logic. There is a separate bus, the **Peripheral Control Bus**, for the IOE control signals: clock, preset, clear, and output enable.

The AMD MACH 5 family has some I/O features not currently found on other
programmable ASICs. The MACH 5 family has 3.3 V and 5 V versions that are both
suitable for mixed-voltage designs. The 3 V versions accept 5 V inputs, and the outputs of the 3 V versions do not drive above 3.3 V. You can apply a voltage up to
5.5 V to device inputs before you connect VDD (this is known as **hot insertion** or
hot switching, allowing you to swap cards with power still applied without causing
latch-up). During power-up and power-down, all I/Os are three-state, and there is no
I/O current during power-down, allowing power-down while connected to an active
bus. All MACH 5 devices in the same package have the same pin configuration, so
you can increase or reduce the size of device after completing the board layout.

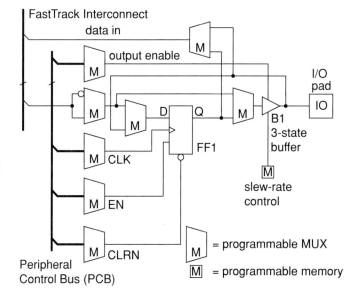

FIGURE 6.24 A simplified block diagram of the Altera I/O Element (IOE), used in the FLEX 8000 and 10k series. The MAX 9000 IOC (I/O Cell) is similar. The FastTrack Interconnect bus is the chipwide interconnect. The PCB is used for control signals common to each IOE.

6.9   Summary

Among the options available in I/O cells are: different drive strengths, TTL-compatibility, registered or direct inputs, registered or direct outputs, pull-up resistors, over-voltage protection, slew-rate control, and boundary-scan. Table 6.4 shows a list of features. Interfacing an ASIC with a system starts at the outputs where you check the voltage levels first, then the current levels. Table 6.5 is a look-up table for Tables 6.6 and 6.7, which show the I/O resources present in each type of programmable ASIC (using the abbreviations of Table 6.4).

Important points that we covered in this chapter are the following:

- Outputs can typically source or sink 5–10 mA continuously into a DC load, and 50–200 mA transiently into an AC load.
- Input buffers can be CMOS (threshold at $0.5V_{DD}$) or TTL (1.4 V).
- Input buffers normally have a small hysteresis (100–200 mV).
- CMOS inputs must never be left floating.
- Clamp diodes to GND and VDD are present on every pin.
- Inputs and outputs can be registered or direct.
- I/O registers can be in the I/O cell or in the core.
- Metastability is a problem when working with asynchronous inputs.

TABLE 6.4   I/O options for programmable ASICs.

Code[1]	I/O Option	Function
IT/C	TTL/CMOS input	Programmable input buffer threshold
OT/C	TTL/CMOS output	Complementary or totem-pole output
nSNK	Sink capability	Maximum current sink ability (e.g., 12SNK is $I_0 = 12\,mA$ sink)
nSRC	Source capability	Maximum current source ability (e.g., 12SRC is $I_0 = -12\,mA$ source)
5/3	5V/3V	Separate I/O and core voltage supplies
OD	Open drain/collector	Programmable open-drain at the output buffer
TS	Three-state	Output buffer with three-state control
SR	Slew-rate control	Fast or slew-rate limited output buffer to reduce ground bounce
PD	Pull-down	Programmable pull-down device or resistor at the I/O pad
PU	Pull-up	Programmable pull-up device or resistor at the I/O pad
EP	Enable polarity	Driver control can be positive (three-state) or negative (enable).
RI	Registered input	Inputs may be registered in I/O cell.
RO	Registered output	Outputs may be registered in I/O cell.
RIO	Registered I/O	Both inputs and outputs may be registered in I/O cell.
ID	Input delay	Input delay to eliminate input hold time
JTAG	JTAG	Boundary-scan test
SCH	Schmitt trigger	Schmitt trigger or input hysteresis
HOT	Hot insertion	Inputs protected from hot insertion
PCI	PCI compliant	Output buffer characteristics comply with PCI specifications.

[1]These codes are used in Tables 6.6 and 6.7.

6.10   Problems

* = Difficult, ** = Very difficult, *** = Extremely difficult

6.1 (I/O resources, 60 min.) Obtain the specifications for the latest version of your choice of FPGA vendor from a data book or online data sheet and complete a table in the same format as Tables 6.6 and 6.7.

6.2 (I/O timing, 60 min.) On-chip delays are only half the battle in a typical design. Using data book parameters for an FPGA that you choose, estimate (worst-case commercial) how long it takes to bring a signal on-chip; through an input regis-

TABLE 6.5   I/O Cell Tables.

Programmable ASIC family	Table	Programmable ASIC family	Table
Actel (ACT 1)		Actel (ACT 3)	
Xilinx (XC3000)		Xilinx LCA (XC5200)	
Actel (ACT 2)		Altera FLEX (8000/10k)	
Altera MAX (EPM 5k)		AMD MACH 5	
Xilinx EPLD (XC7200/7300)	Table 6.6	Actel 3200DX	Table 6.7
QuickLogic (pASIC 1)		Altera MAX (EPM 9000)	
Crosspoint (CP20K)		Xilinx (XC8100)	
Altera MAX (EPM 7000)		AT&T ORCA (2C)	
Atmel (AT6000)		Xilinx (XC4000)	

ter (a flip-flop); through a combinational function (assume an inverter); and back off chip again through another (flip-flop) register. Give your answer in three parts:

a. The delay from a CMOS-level pad input (trip-point of 0.5) to the D input of the input register plus the flip-flop setup time.

b. The delay (measured from the clock, so include the clock-to-Q delay) through the inverter to the output register plus the setup time.

c. The delay from the output register (measured from the clock edge) to the output pad (trip point of 0.5) with a 50 pF load.

In each case give your answers: (i) Using data book symbols (specify which symbols and where in the data books you found them); and (ii) as calculated values, in nanoseconds, using a speed grade that you specify. State and explain very clearly any assumptions that you need to make about the clock to determine the setup times.

6.3 (Clock timing, 30 min.) When we calculate FPGA timing we need to include the time it takes to bring the clock onto the chip. For an FPGA you choose, estimate (worst-case commercial) the delay from the clock pad (0.5 trip-point) to the clock pin of an internal flip-flop

a. in terms of data book symbols (specify which and where you found them— t_{AB} on p. 2-32 of the ABC 1994 data book, for example), and

b. as calculated values in nanoseconds.

6.4 (**Bipolar drivers, 60 min.) The circuit in Figure 6.3 uses *npn* transistors.

a. Design a similar circuit that uses *pnp* transistors.

b. The *pnp* circuit may work better, why?

c. Design an even better circuit that uses *npn* and *pnp* transistors.

d. Explain why your circuit is even better.

e. Draw a diagram for a controller using op-amps instead of bipolar transistors.

TABLE 6.6   Programmable ASIC I/O logic resources.

	Actel (ACT 1)	Xilinx (XC3000)	Actel (ACT 2)
I/O cell name	I/O module	IOB (Input/Output Block)	I/O module
I/O cell functions[1]	TS, 10SRC, 10SNK	TS, RIO, IT/C, PU, 4SRC, 4SNK, 8SRC (3100), 8SNK (3100)	TS, (RIO)[2], 10SRC, 10SNK
Number of I/O cells	Max. I/O: 57 (1010) 69 (1020)	Max. I/O: 64 (3020) 144 (3090)	Max. I/O: 83 (1225) 140 (1280)

	Altera MAX 5000	Xilinx EPLD	QuickLogic (pASIC 1)
I/O cell name	I/O control block	I/O block	Bidirectional input/output cell & dedicated input cell
I/O cell functions	TS, 4SRC, 8SNK	(TS), (RI)[3], 5/3, 4SRC, 12SNK	TS
Number of I/O cells	8 (5016) −64 (5192)	38 (7336)–156 (73144) 36 (7236) −72 (7272)	32 (QL6X8)[4] −104 (QL16X24)

	Crosspoint (CP20K)	Altera MAX 7000	Atmel (AT6000)
I/O cell name	I/O cell	IOC (I/O Control Block)	Entrance and exit cells
I/O cell functions	TS, SR, IC/T , JTAG, SCH	TS, SR, 5/3, PCI, 4SRC, 12SNK	TS, SR, PU, OD, IT/C, 16SRC, 16SNK
Number of I/O cells	91 (20220) −270 (22000)	36 (7032) −164 (7256)	96 (6002) −160 (6010)

[1]Code definitions are listed in Table 6.4.
[2]ACT 2 I/O Module is separate from the I/O Pad Driver.
[3]Xilinx EPLD uses a mixture of I/O blocks, input-only blocks, and output-only blocks. The I/O blocks and input only blocks contain the equivalent of a D flip-flop (configured to be a flip-flop or latch).
[4]8 I/O are dedicated inputs on all parts.

6.5 (Xilinx output buffers, 15 min.) For the Xilinx XC2000 and XC3000 series[8]: $I_{OLpeak} = 120 \, mA$ and $I_{OHpeak} = 80 \, mA$; for the XC4000 family: $I_{OLpeak} = 160 \, mA$ and $I_{OHpeak} = 130 \, mA$; and for the XC7300 series: $I_{OLpeak} = 100 \, mA$ and $I_{OHpeak} = 65 \, mA$. For a typical 0.8–1.0 μm process:

---

[8]1994 databook, p. 8-15 and p. 9-23.

TABLE 6.7   Programmable ASIC I/O logic resources (contd.).

	Actel (ACT 3)	Xilinx LCA (XC5200)	Altera FLEX (8000/10k)
I/O cell name	I/O Module	IOB (I/O Block)	IOE (I/O Element)
I/O cell functions[1]	TS, SR, (RIO)[2], 8SRC, 12SNK	TS, PU, PD, JTAG	TS, SR, RI or RO, JTAG, PCI(8k), 4SRC, 12SNK
Number of I/O cells	80 (1415) –228 (14100)	84 (5202) –244 (5215)	78 (8282)–208 (81500) 150 (10K10) –406 (10K100)

	AMD MACH 5	Actel 3200DX	Altera MAX (EPM 9000)
I/O cell name	I/O Cell	I/O Module	IOE (I/O Element)
I/O cell functions	TS, 3.2SRC, 16SNK, PCI	Same as ACT 2	TS, SR, 5/3, PCI, JTAG, 4SRC, 8SNK
Number of I/O cells	120 (M5-128) –256 (M5-512)	126 (A3265DX) –292 (A32400DX)	168 (9320) –216 (9560)

	Xilinx (XC8100)[3]	AT&T ORCA 2C	Xilinx (XC4000)
I/O cell name	I/O Cell	PIC (Programmable input/output cells)	IOB (I/O Block)
I/O cell functions	TS, PU, IT/C (global), JTAG, PCI, 4SRC, 4/24SNK[4]	TS, IT/C, ID, PU, PD, OD, JTAG, PCI, (6SRC and 12SNK) or (3SRC and 6SNK), SCH	TS, RIO, JTAG, ID, IT/C, OT/C, PU, PD, 4SRC, 12SNK, 24SNK (4000A/H)
Number of I/O cells	32 (8100) –208 (8109)	160 (2C04) –480 (2C40)	80 (4003) –256 (4025)

[1] Code definitions are listed in Table 6.4.
[2] ACT 3 I/O Module is separate from the I/O Pad Driver.
[3] Discontinued August 1986.
[4] Two output modes: Capacitive (4SNK) and Resistive (24SNK).

$$p\text{-channel } (20/1): I_{DS} = 3.0\text{--}5.0 \text{ mA} \quad \text{with } V_{DS} = -5 \text{ V}, V_{GS} = -5 \text{ V}$$
$$n\text{-channel } (20/1): I_{DS} = 7.5\text{--}10.0 \text{ mA} \quad \text{with } V_{DS} = 5 \text{ V}, V_{GS} = 5 \text{ V}$$

a. Calculate the effective sizes of the transistors in the Xilinx output buffer.

b. Why might these only be "effective" sizes?

c. The Xilinx data book gives values for "source current and output high impedance" shown in Table 6.8. Graph the buffer characteristics when sourcing current.

d. Explain which parts in Table 6.8 use complementary output buffers and which use totem-pole outputs and explain how you can tell.

e. Can you explain how Xilinx arrived at the figures for impedance?

f. Comment on the method that Xilinx used.

g. Suggest and calculate a better measure of impedance.

TABLE 6.8   Xilinx output buffer characteristics.

| Part | V_O (output voltage)[1]/V | | | Impedance/Ω |
	4	3	2	
I_O (2018)	−30	−52	−60	30
I_O (3020)	−35	−60	−75	30
I_O (4005)	0	−12	−50	25
I_O (73108)	0	−10	−26	40

[1]Currents in milliamperes.

6.6 (Xilinx logic levels, 10 min.) Most manufacturers measure V_{OLmax} with V_{DD} set to its minimum value, Xilinx measures V_{OLmax} at V_{DDmax}. For example, for the Xilinx XC4000[9]: $V_{OLmax} = 0.4$ V at $I_{OLmax} = 12$ mA and V_{DDmax}. A footnote also explains that V_{OLmax} is measured with "50 % of the outputs simultaneously sinking 12 mA."

a. Can you explain why Xilinx measures V_{OLmax} this way?

b. What information do you need to know to estimate V_{OLmax} if all the other outputs were *not* sourcing or sinking any current.

6.7 (Output levels, 10 min.) In Figure 6.7(b–d) the PAD signal is labeled with different levels: In Figure 6.7(b) the PAD high and low levels are V_{OHmin} and V_{OLmax} respectively, in Figure 6.7(c) they are V_{DD} and V_{OLmax}, and in Figure 6.7(c) they are V_{OHmin} and V_{SS}.

a. Explain why this is.

b. In no more than 20 words explain the difference between V_{DD} and V_{OHmin} as well as the difference between V_{OLmax} and V_{SS}.

6.8 (TTL and CMOS outputs, 10 min.) The ACT 2 figures for t_{DLH} and t_{DHL} in Figure 6.7 are for the CMOS levels. For TTL levels the figures are (with the CMOS figures in parentheses): $t_{DLH} = 10.6$ ns (13.5 ns), and $t_{DHL} = 13.4$ ns (11.2 ns). The output buffer is the same in both cases, but the delays are measured using different levels. Explain the differences in these delays quantitatively.

---

[9] Xilinx 1994 data book, p. 2-48.

6.9 (Bus-keeper contention, 30 min.) Figure 6.25 shows a three-state bus, similar to Figure 6.5, that has a bus keeper on CHIP1 and a pull-up resistor that is part of a Xilinx IOB on CHIP2—we have a type of bus-keeper contention. For the XC3000 the **pull-up current** is 0.02–0.17 mA and thus RL1 is between 5 and 50 kΩ (1994 data book, p. 2-155).

a. Explain what might happen when both the bus drivers turn off.

b. Have you considered all possibilities?

c. Is bus-keeper contention a problem?

d. In the PCI specification control signals are required to be sustained three-state. A driver must deassert a control signal to the inactive state (high for the PCI control signals) for at least one clock cycle before three-stating the line. This means that a driver has to "put the signal back where it found it." Does this affect your answers?

e. Suggest a "fix" that stops you having to worry about any potential problems.

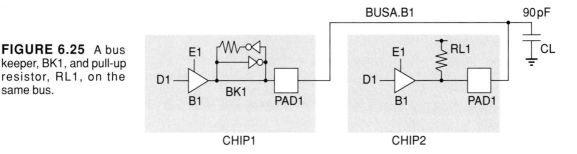

FIGURE 6.25 A bus keeper, BK1, and pull-up resistor, RL1, on the same bus.

6.10 (Short-circuit, 10 min.) What happens if you short-circuit the output of a complementary output buffer to **(a)** GND and **(b)** VDD? **(c)** What difference does it make if the output buffer is complementary or a totem-pole?

6.11 (Transmission line bias, 10 min.)

a. Why do we adjust the resistors in Figure 6.10(c) so that the Thévenin equivalent voltage source is 1.6 V?

b. What current does a driver have to sink if we want $V_{OLmax} = 0.4$ V?

c. What current does a driver have to source if we want $V_{OHmin} = 2.4$ V?

6.12 (Ground resistance, 10 min.) Calculate the resistance of an aluminum GND net that is 0.5 mm long and 10 μm wide.

6.13 (*Temperature) **(a)** (30 min.) You are about to ship a product and you have a problem with an FPGA. A high case temperature is causing it to be slower than you thought. You calculated the power dissipation, but you forgot that the InLet microprocessor is toasting the next door FPGA. You have no easy way to calculate T_J now, so we need to measure it in order to redesign the FPGA with fixed I/O locations. You remember that a diode forward voltage has a temperature coefficient of about $-2\,\text{mV}°\text{C}^{-1}$ and there are clamp diodes on the FPGA I/O. Explain, using circuit diagrams, how to measure the T_J of an FPGA in-circuit using: a voltage supply, DVM, thermometer, resistors, spoon, and a coffee maker. **(b)** (**120 min.) Try it.

6.14 (Delay measurement, 10 min.) Sumo Silicon has a new process ready before we do and Sumo's data book timing figures are much better than ours. Explain how to reduce our logic delays by changing our measurement circuits and trip points.

6.15 (Data sheets, 10 min.) In the 1994 data book Xilinx specifies $V_{\text{ILmin}} = 0.3\,\text{V}$ (and $V_{\text{ILmax}} = 0.8\,\text{V}$) for the XC2000L. Why does this surprise you and what do you think the value for V_{ILmin} really is? FPGA vendors produce thousands of pages of data every year with virtually no errors. It is important to have the confidence to question a potential error.

6.16 (GTL, 60 min.) Find the original reference to Gunning transistor logic. Write a one-page summary of its uses and how it works.

6.17 (Thresholds, 10 min.) With some FPGAs it is possible to configure an output at TTL thresholds and an input (on the same pad) at CMOS thresholds. Can you think of a reason why you might want to do this?

6.18 (Input levels, 10 min.) When we define $V_{\text{IHmin}} = 0.7V_{DD}$, why do we calculate the *minimum* value of V_{IH} using $V_{\text{DDmax}} = 5.5\,\text{V}$?

6.19 (Metastability equations, 30 min.)

a. From Eq. 6.4 show that if we make two measurements of t_r and MTBF then:

$$\tau_c = \frac{t_{r1} - t_{r2}}{\ln\text{MTBF}_1 - \ln\text{MTBF}_2},\tag{6.14}$$

$$T_0 = \frac{\exp\dfrac{t_{r1}}{\tau_c}}{\text{MTBF}_1 f_c f_d}.\tag{6.15}$$

b. MTBU is extremely sensitive to variations in τ_c, show that:

$$\frac{d}{d\tau_c}\text{MTBU} = \frac{-t_r}{\tau_c^2}.\tag{6.16}$$

c. Show that the variation in MTBU is related to the variation in τ_c by the following expression:

$$\left(\frac{\Delta\text{MTBU}}{\text{MTBU}}\right) = \frac{-t_r}{\tau_c}\left(\frac{\Delta\tau_c}{\tau_c}\right).\tag{6.17}$$

6.20 (***Alternative metastability solutions, 120 min.) Write a minitutorial on metastability solutions. The best sources for this type of information are usually application notes written by FPGA and TTL manufacturers, many of which are available on the Web (TI is a good source on this topic).

6.21 (Altera 8000 I/O, 10 min) Figure 6.26 shows the Altera FLEX 8000 I/O characteristics. Determine as much as you are able to from these figures.

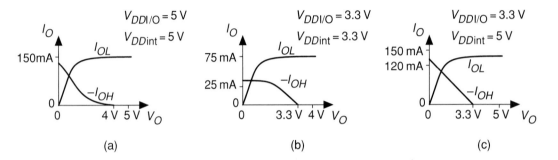

FIGURE 6.26 (a) Altera FLEX 8000 I/O characteristics operating at 5 V. (b) EPF8282V I/O operating at 3.3 V. (c) Characteristics with mixed 5V and 3.3 V I/O operation.

6.22 (Power calculation, 60 min.) Suppose we wish to limit power dissipation on an ACT 1 A1020 chip to below 1 W for a 44-pin PLCC package.

a. Derive an equation for the number of logic modules, number of I/O modules, number of modules connected to the clock and system clock frequency in terms of the package parameters and the worst-case T_A.

b. Assume:

> 100 percent utilization of I/Os,
> 50 percent are outputs connected to a 50 pF load,
> 100 percent utilization of logic modules,
> 10 percent of the logic modules are connected to the clock,
> 20 percent of the logic modules toggle every clock cycle,
> 20 percent of the I/Os toggle every clock cycle.

Determine an upper limit on clock frequency.

c. Next vary each of the assumptions you made in part b. Draw graphs showing the variation of clock frequency as you vary each of the above parameters, including the power dissipation limit (a spreadsheet will help).

d. Can you draw any conclusions from this exercise?

6.23 (Switch debounce, 30 min) Design a logic circuit to "debounce" the output from a buffer whose input is connected to a bounce-prone switch. Your system operates at a clock frequency of 1 MHz.

6.24 (Plugs and sockets, 30 min.) Draw the plugs and sockets (to scale) for the technologies in Table 6.9.

TABLE 6.9   TTL-compatible CMOS logic thresholds (Problems 6.24 and 6.25).[1]

| Family | Input levels | | Output levels driving TTL | | | | Output levels driving CMOS[2] | | | |
	V_{IHmin}	V_{ILmax}	V_{OHmin}	I_{OHmax}	V_{OLmax}	I_{OLmax}	V_{OHmin}	I_{OHmax}	V_{OLmax}	I_{OLmax}
74HCT	2.0	0.8	3.84	−4.0	0.33	4.0	4.4	−0.02	0.1	0.02
74HC	3.85	1.35	3.84	−4.0	0.33	4.0	4.4	−0.02	0.1	0.02
74ACT	2.0	0.8	3.76	−24.0	0.37	24.0	4.4	−0.05	0.1	0.05
74AC	3.85	1.35	3.76	−24.0	0.37	24.0	4.4	−0.05	0.1	0.05

[1]All voltages in volts, all currents in milliamperes.
[2]$I_{IHmax} = \pm0.001$ mA, $I_{ILmax} = \pm0.001$ mA for all families.

6.25 (TTL compatibility, 30 min.) Explain very carefully, giving an example using actual figures from the tables, how you would determine the compatibility between the TTL and CMOS logic thresholds shown in Table 6.9 and Table 6.10 and the FPGA logic thresholds in Table 6.1.

TABLE 6.10   TTL logic thresholds (Problem 6.25).[1]

TTL Family[2]	V_{IHmin}	V_{ILmax}	V_{OHmin}	I_{OHmax}	V_{OLmax}	I_{OLmax}	I_{IHmax}	I_{ILmax}
74S	2.0	0.8	2.7	−1.0	0.5	20.0	0.05	−2.0
74LS	2.0	0.8	2.7	−0.4	0.5	8.0	0.02	−0.4
74ALS	2.0	0.8	2.7	−0.4	0.5	8.0	0.02	−0.2
74AS	2.0	0.8	2.7	−2.0	0.5	20.0	0.02	−0.5
74F	2.0	0.8	2.7	−1.0	0.5	20.0	0.02	−0.6
74FCT	2.0	0.8	2.4	−15.0	0.5	48.0	±0.005	±0.005
74FCT-T	2.0	0.8	2.4	−8.0	0.5	48.0	±0.005	±0.005

[1]All voltages in volts, all currents in milliamperes
[2]Other (older) TTL and CMOS logic families include 4000, 74, 74H, and 74L

6.26 (ECL, 30 min.) Emitter-coupled logic (ECL) uses a positive supply, $V_{CC} = 0$ V, and a negative supply, $V_{EE} = -5.2$ V. The highest logic voltage allowed is -0.81 V and the lowest is -1.85 V. Table 6.11 shows the ECL 10K thresholds.

a. Calculate the high-level and low-level noise margins.

b. Find out the 100K thresholds and

c. calculate the 100K noise margins.

TABLE 6.11   ECL logic thresholds (Problem 6.26).

	V_{IHmin}/V	V_{ILmax}/V	V_{OHmin}/V	V_{OLmax}/V
ECL10K	-1.105	-1.475	-0.980	-1.630
ECL100K				

6.27 (Schmitt trigger, 30 min.) Find out the typical hysteresis for a TTL Schmitt trigger. What are the advantages and disadvantages of changing the hysteresis?

6.28 (Hysteresis, 20 min.)

a. Draw the transfer curve for an inverting buffer with very high gain that has a switching threshold centered at 2.2 V and 300 mV hysteresis.

b. If the center of the characteristic shifts by -0.3 V and $+0.4$ V and the hysteresis varies from 260 mV to 350 mV, calculate V_{IHmin} and V_{ILmax}.

6.29 (Driving an LED, 30 min.) Find out the typical current and voltage drive required by an LED and design a circuit to drive it. List your sources of information.

6.30 (**Driving TTL, 60 min.) Find out the input current requirements of different TTL families and write a minitutorial on the I/O requirements (in particular the current) when driving high and low levels onto a bus.

6.11   Bibliography

Wakerly's [1994] book describes TTL and CMOS logic thresholds as well as noise margins. The specification of digital I/O interfaces (voltage and current levels) is defined by the JEDEC (part of the Electronic Industries Association, EIA) JC-16 committee standards [JEDEC I/O]. Standards for ESD measurement are not as well defined; companies use a range of specifications: MIL-STD-883, EIAJ, a published model used by AT&T (see, for example, p. 5-13 to p. 5-19 in the AT&T 1995 FPGA data book) as well as JEDEC and ANSI/IEEE standards [JEDEC I/O, JEDEC ESD,

ANSI/IEEE ESD]. You are not likely to find any of these standards at the library, but they are available through specialist technical document distributors (typical 1996 costs were about $25 for the JEDEC documents; catalogs are generally free of charge). These standards are not technical reports, most only contain a few pages, but they are the source of the parameters that you see in data sheets.

6.12 References

Page numbers in brackets after a reference indicate its location in the chapter body.

[JEDEC I/O] [p. 246] In numerical (not chronological) order the relevant JEDEC standards for I/O are:

JESD8-A. Interface Standard for Nominal 3 V/3.3 V Supply Digital Integrated Circuits (June 1994). This standard replaces JEDEC Standards 8, 8-1, and 8-1-A and defines the DC interface parameters for digital circuits operating from a power supply of nominal 3 V/3.3 V.

JESD8-2. Standard for Operating Voltages and Interface Levels for Low Voltage Emitter-Coupled Logic (ECL) Integrated Circuits (March 1993). Describes 300K ECL (voltage and temperature compensated, with threshold levels compatible with 100K ECL).

JESD8-3. Gunning Transceiver Logic (GTL) Low-Level, High-Speed Interface Standard for Digital Integrated Circuits (Nov. 1993). Defines the DC input and output specifications for a low-level, high-speed interface for integrated circuits.

JESD8-4. Center-Tap-Terminated (CTT) Low-Level, High-Speed Interface Standard for Digital Integrated Circuits (Nov. 1993). Defines the DC I/O specifications for a low-level, high-speed interface for integrated circuits that can be a superset of LVCMOS and LVTTL.

JESD8-5. 2.5 V +/– 0.2 V (Normal Range), and 1.8 V–2.7 V (Wide Range) Power Supply Voltage and Interface Standard for Nonterminated Digital Integrated Circuit (Oct. 1995). Defines power supply voltage ranges, DC interface parameters for a high-speed, low-voltage family of nonterminated digital circuits.

JESD8-6. High Speed Transceiver Logic (HSTL): A 1.5 V Output Buffer Supply Voltage Based Interface Standard for Digital Integrated Circuits (Aug. 1995). Describes a 1.5 V high-performance CMOS interface suitable for high I/O count CMOS and BiCMOS devices operating at over 200 MHz.

JESD12-6. Interface Standard for Semicustom Integrated Circuits (March 1991). Defines logic interface levels for CMOS, TTL, and ECL inputs and outputs for 5 V operation.

[JEDEC ESD, ANSI/IEEE ESD] The JEDEC and IEEE standards for ESD are:

JESD22-C101. Field Induced Charged Device Model Test Method for Electrostatic Discharge Withstand Thresholds of Microelectronic Components (May 1995). Describes Charged Device Model that simulates charging/discharging events that occur in production equipment and processes. Potential for CDM ESD events occur with metal-to-metal contact in manufacturing.

ANSI/EOS/ESD S5.1-1993. Electrostatic Discharge (ESD) Sensitivity Testing, Human Body Model (HBM), Component Level.

ANSI/IEEE C62.47-1992. Guide on Electrostatic Discharge (ESD): Characterization of the ESD Environment.

ANSI/IEEE 1181-1991. Latchup Test Methods for CMOS and BiCMOS Integrated Circuit Process Characterization.

PCI Local Bus Specification, Revision 2.1, June 1, 1995. Available from PCI Special Interest Group, PO Box 14070, Portland OR 97214. (800) 433-5177 (U.S.), (503)797-4207 (International). 282 p. Detailed description of the electrical and mechanical requirements for the PCI Bus written for engineers who already understand the basic operation of the bus protocol. [p. 242]

Wakerly, J. F. 1994. *Digital Design: Principles and Practices.* 2nd ed. Englewood Cliffs, NJ: Prentice-Hall, 840 p. ISBN 0-13-211459-3. TK7874.65.W34. [p. 272]

PROGRAMMABLE ASIC INTERCONNECT

7

All FPGAs contain some type of **programmable interconnect**. The structure and complexity of the interconnect is largely determined by the programming technology and the architecture of the basic logic cell. The raw material that we have to work with in building the interconnect is aluminum-based metallization, which has a sheet resistance of approximately $50\,\text{m}\Omega$/square and a line capacitance of $0.2\,\text{pFcm}^{-1}$. The first programmable ASICs were constructed using two layers of metal; newer programmable ASICs use three or more layers of metal interconnect.

7.1   Actel ACT

The Actel ACT family interconnect scheme shown in Figure 7.1 is similar to a channeled gate array. The channel routing uses dedicated rectangular areas of fixed size within the chip called **wiring channels** (or just **channels**). The **horizontal channels** run across the chip in the horizontal direction. In the vertical direction there are similar **vertical channels** that run over the top of the basic logic cells, the Logic Modules. Within the horizontal or vertical channels wires run horizontally or vertically, respectively, within **tracks**. Each track holds one wire. The **capacity** of a fixed wiring channel is equal to the number of tracks it contains. Figure 7.2 shows a detailed view of the channel and the connections to each Logic Module—the **input stubs** and **output stubs**.

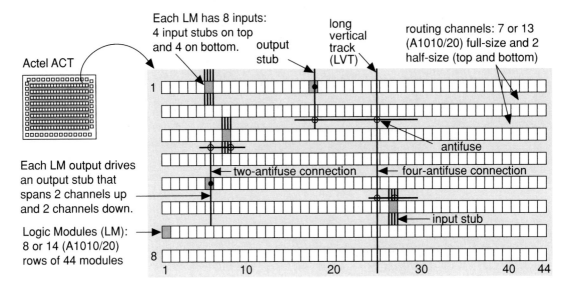

FIGURE 7.1 The interconnect architecture used in an Actel ACT family FPGA. (*Source:* Actel.)

In a channeled gate array the designer decides the location and length of the interconnect within a channel. In an FPGA the interconnect is fixed at the time of manufacture. To allow programming of the interconnect, Actel divides the fixed interconnect wires within each channel into various lengths or **wire segments**. We call this **segmented channel routing**, a variation on channel routing. Antifuses join the wire segments. The designer then programs the interconnections by blowing antifuses and making connections between wire segments; unwanted connections are left unprogrammed. A statistical analysis of many different layouts determines the optimum number and the lengths of the wire segments.

7.1.1   Routing Resources

The ACT 1 interconnection architecture uses 22 horizontal tracks per channel for signal routing with three tracks dedicated to VDD, GND, and the global clock (GCLK), making a total of 25 tracks per channel. Horizontal segments vary in length from four columns of Logic Modules to the entire row of modules (Actel calls these long segments **long lines**).

Four Logic Module inputs are available to the channel below the Logic Module and four inputs to the channel above the Logic Module. Thus eight vertical tracks per Logic Module are available for inputs (four from the Logic Module above the channel and four from the Logic Module below). These connections are the **input stubs**.

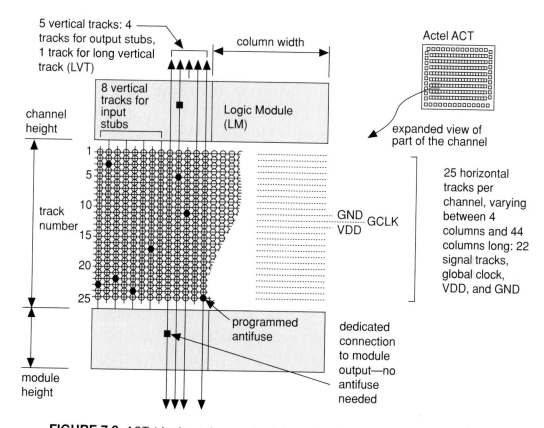

FIGURE 7.2 ACT 1 horizontal and vertical channel architecture. (*Source:* Actel.)

The single Logic Module output connects to a vertical track that extends across the two channels above the module and across the two channels below the module. This is the **output stub**. Thus module outputs use four vertical tracks per module (counting two tracks from the modules below, and two tracks from the modules above each channel). One vertical track per column is a **long vertical track** (**LVT**) that spans the entire height of the chip (the 1020 contains some segmented LVTs). There are thus a total of 13 vertical tracks per column in the ACT 1 architecture (eight for inputs, four for outputs, and one for an LVT).

Table 7.1 shows the routing resources for both the ACT 1 and ACT 2 families. The last two columns show the total number of antifuses (including antifuses in the I/O cells) on each chip and the total number of antifuses assuming the wiring channels are **fully populated** with antifuses (an antifuse at every horizontal and vertical interconnect intersection). The ACT 1 devices are very nearly fully populated.

TABLE 7.1   Actel FPGA routing resources.

	Horizontal tracks per channel, H	Vertical tracks per column, V	Rows, R	Columns, C	Total antifuses on each chip	H×V×R×C
A1010	22	13	8	44	112,000	100,672
A1020	22	13	14	44	186,000	176,176
A1225A	36	15	13	46	250,000	322,920
A1240A	36	15	14	62	400,000	468,720
A1280A	36	15	18	82	750,000	797,040

If the Logic Module at the end of a net is less than two rows away from the driver module, a connection requires two antifuses, a vertical track, and two horizontal segments. If the modules are more than two rows apart, a connection between them will require a long vertical track together with another vertical track (the output stub) and two horizontal tracks. To connect these tracks will require a total of four antifuses in series and this will add delay due to the resistance of the antifuses. To examine the extent of this delay problem we need some help from the analysis of RC networks.

7.1.2   Elmore's Constant

Figure 7.3 shows an **RC tree**—representing a net with a **fanout** of two. We shall assume that all nodes are initially charged to $V_{DD} = 1$ V, and that we short node 0 to ground, so $V_0 = 0$ V, at time $t = 0$ sec. We need to find the node voltages, V_1 to V_4, as a function of time. A similar problem arose in the design of wideband vacuum tube distributed amplifiers in the 1940s. Elmore found a measure of delay that we can use today [Rubenstein, Penfield, and Horowitz, 1983].

The current in branch k of the network is

$$i_k = -C_k \frac{dV_k}{dt}. \tag{7.1}$$

The linear superposition of the branch currents gives the voltage at node i as

$$V_i = -\sum_{k=1}^{n} R_{ki} C_k \frac{dV_k}{dt}, \tag{7.2}$$

where R_{ki} is the resistance of the path to V_0 (ground in this case) shared by node k and node i. So, for example, $R_{24} = R_1$, $R_{22} = R_1 + R_2$, and $R_{31} = R_1$.

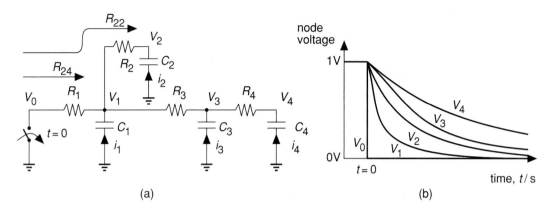

FIGURE 7.3 Measuring the delay of a net. (a) An RC tree. (b) The waveforms as a result of closing the switch at $t = 0$.

Unfortunately, Eq. 7.2 is a complicated set of coupled equations that we cannot easily solve. We know the node voltages have different values at each point in time, but, since the waveforms are similar, let us assume the slopes (the time derivatives) of the waveforms are related to each other. Suppose we express the slope of node voltage V_k as a constant, a_k, times the slope of V_i,

$$\frac{dV_k}{dt} = a_k \frac{V_i}{dt}.$$ (7.3)

Consider the following measure of the error, **E**, of our approximation:

$$E = \sum_{k=1}^{n} R_{ki} C_k \int_{0}^{\infty} \left| a_k \frac{dV_i}{dt} - \frac{dV_k}{dt} \right| dt.$$ (7.4)

The error, E, is a minimum when $a_k = 1$ since initially $V_i(t=0) = V_k(t=0) = 1$ V (we normalized the voltages) and $V_i(t=\infty) = V_k(t=\infty) = 0$.

Now we can rewrite Eq. 7.2, setting $a_k = 1$, as follows:

$$V_i = -\sum_{k=1}^{n} R_{ki} C_k \frac{dV_i}{dt}.$$ (7.5)

This is a linear first-order differential equation with the following solution:

$$V_i(t) = e^{-t/\tau_{Di}}; \quad \tau_{Di} = \sum_{k=1}^{n} R_{ki} C_k.$$ (7.6)

The time constant τ_{Di} is often called the **Elmore delay** and is different for each node. We shall refer to τ_{Di} as the **Elmore time constant** to remind us that, if we approximate V_i by an exponential waveform, the delay of the RC tree using 0.35/0.65 trip points is approximately τ_{Di} seconds.

7.1.3   RC Delay in Antifuse Connections

Suppose a single antifuse, with resistance R_1, connects to a wire segment with parasitic capacitance C_1. Then a connection employing a single antifuse will delay the signal passing along that connection by approximately one time constant, or R_1C_1 seconds. If we have more than one antifuse, we need to use the Elmore time constant to estimate the interconnect delay.

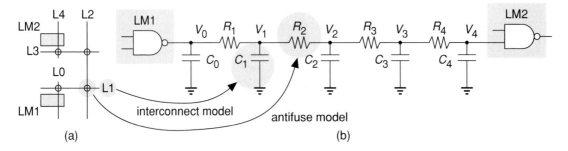

FIGURE 7.4 Actel routing model. (a) A four-antifuse connection. L0 is an output stub, L1 and L3 are horizontal tracks, L2 is a long vertical track (LVT), and L4 is an input stub. (b) An RC-tree model. Each antifuse is modeled by a resistance and each interconnect segment is modeled by a capacitance.

For example, suppose we have the four-antifuse connection shown in Figure 7.4. Then, from Eq. 7.6,

$$V_4(t) = R_{14}C_1 + R_{24}C_2 + R_{34}C_3 + R_{44}C_4$$
$$= (R_1 + R_2 + R_3 + R_4)C_4 + (R_1 + R_2 + R_3)C_3 + (R_1 + R_2)C_2 + R_1C_1.$$

If all the antifuse resistances are approximately equal (a reasonably good assumption) and the antifuse resistance is much larger than the resistance of any of the metal lines, L1–L5, shown in Figure 7.4 (a very good assumption) then $R_1 = R_2 = R_3 = R_4 = R$, and the Elmore time constant is

$$\tau_{D4} = 4RC_4 + 3RC_3 + 2RC_2 + RC_1. \tag{7.7}$$

Suppose now that the capacitance of each interconnect segment (including all the antifuses and programming transistors that may be attached) is approximately constant, and equal to C. A connection with two antifuses will generate a $3RC$ time constant, a connection with three antifuses a $6RC$ time constant, and a connection with four antifuses gives a $10RC$ time constant. This analysis is disturbing—it says that the interconnect delay grows quadratically ($\propto n^2$) as we increase the interconnect length and the number of antifuses, n. The situation is worse when the intermediate wire segments have larger capacitance than that of the short input stubs and output stubs. Unfortunately, this is the situation in an Actel FPGA where the horizontal and vertical segments in a connection may be quite long.

7.1.4 Antifuse Parasitic Capacitance

We can determine the number of antifuses connected to the horizontal and vertical lines for the Actel architecture. Each column contains 13 vertical signal tracks and each channel contains 25 horizontal tracks (22 of these are used for signals). Thus, assuming the channels are fully populated with antifuses,

- An input stub (1 channel) connects to 25 antifuses.
- An output stub (4 channels) connects to 100 (25×4) antifuses.
- An LVT (1010, 8 channels) connects to 200 (25×8) antifuses.
- An LVT (1020, 14 channels) connects to 350 (25×14) antifuses.
- A four-column horizontal track connects to 52 (13×4) antifuses.
- A 44-column horizontal track connects to 572 (13×44) antifuses.

A connection to the diffusion of an Actel antifuse has a parasitic capacitance due to the diffusion junction. The polysilicon of the antifuse has a parasitic capacitance due to the thin oxide. These capacitances are approximately equal. For a $2\,\mu m$ CMOS process the capacitance to ground of the diffusion is 200 to $300\,aF\mu m^{-2}$ (area component) and 400 to $550\,aF\mu m^{-1}$ (perimeter component). Thus, including both area and perimeter effects, a $16\,\mu m^2$ diffusion contact (consisting of a $2\,\mu m$ by $2\,\mu m$ opening plus the required overlap) has a parasitic capacitance of 10–14 fF. If we assume an antifuse has a parasitic capacitance of approximately 10 fF in a 1.0 or $1.2\,\mu m$ process, we can calculate the parasitic capacitances shown in Table 7.2.

We can use the figures from Table 7.2 to estimate the interconnect delays. First we calculate the following resistance and capacitance values:

1. The antifuse resistance is assumed to be $R = 0.5\,k\Omega$.

2. $C_0 = 1.2\,pF$ is the sum of the gate output capacitance (which we shall neglect) and the output stub capacitance (1.0 pF due to antifuses, 0.2 pF due to metal). The contribution from this term is zero in our calculation because we have neglected the pull resistance of the driving gate.

3. $C_1 = C_3 = 0.59\,pF$ (0.52 pF due to antifuses, 0.07 pF due to metal) corresponding to a minimum-length horizontal track.

TABLE 7.2   Actel interconnect parameters.

Parameter	A1010/A1020	A1010B/A1020B
Technology	2.0 µm, λ = 1.0 µm	1.2 µm, λ = 0.6 µm
Die height (A1010)	240 mil	144 mil
Die width (A1010)	360 mil	216 mil
Die area (A1010)	86,400 mil^2 = 56 Mλ^2	31,104 mil^2 = 56 Mλ^2
Logic Module (LM) height (Y1)	180 µm = 180 λ	108 µm = 180 λ
LM width (X)	150 µm = 150 λ	90 µm = 150 λ
LM area (X×Y1)	27,000 µm^2 = 27 kλ^2	9,720 µm^2 = 27 kλ^2
Channel height (Y2)	25 tracks = 287 µm	25 tracks = 170 µm
Channel area per LM (X×Y2)	43,050 µm^2 = 43 kλ^2	15,300 µm^2 = 43 kλ^2
LM and routing area (X×Y1 + X×Y2)	70,000 µm^2 = 70 kλ^2	25,000 µm^2 = 70 kλ^2
Antifuse capacitance	—	10 fF
Metal capacitance	0.2 pFmm^{-1}	0.2 pFmm^{-1}
Output stub length (spans 3 LMs + 4 channels)	4 channels = 1688 µm	4 channels = 1012 µm
Output stub metal capacitance	0.34 pF	0.20 pF
Output stub antifuse connections	100	100
Output stub antifuse capacitance	—	1.0 pF
Horiz. track length	4–44 cols. = 600–6600 µm	4–44 cols. = 360–3960 µm
Horiz. track metal capacitance	0.1–1.3 pF	0.07–0.8 pF
Horiz. track antifuse connections	52–572 antifuses	52–572 antifuses
Horiz. track antifuse capacitance	—	0.52–5.72 pF
Long vertical track (LVT)	8–14 channels = 3760–6580 µm	8–14 channels = 2240–3920 µm
LVT metal capacitance	0.08–0.13 pF	0.45–0.8 pF
LVT track antifuse connections	200–350 antifuses	200–350 antifuses
LVT track antifuse capacitance		2–3.5 pF
Antifuse resistance (ACT 1)		0.5 kΩ (typ.), 0.7 kΩ (max.)

4. C_2 = 4.3 pF (3.5 pF due to antifuses, 0.8 pF due to metal) corresponding to a LVT in a 1020B.

5. The estimated input capacitance of a gate is C_4 = 0.02 pF (the exact value will depend on which input of a Logic Module we connect to).

From Eq. 7.7, the Elmore time constant for a four-antifuse connection is

$$\tau_{D4} = (4) (0.5) (0.02) + (3) (0.5) (0.59) + (2) (0.5) (4.3) + (0.5) (0.59)$$
$$= 5.52\text{ns}. \tag{7.8}$$

This matches delays obtained from the Actel delay calculator. For example, an LVT adds between 5–10 ns delay in an ACT 1 FPGA (6–12 ns for ACT 2, and 4–14 ns for ACT 3). The LVT connection is about the slowest connection that we can make in an ACT array. Normally less than 10 percent of all connections need to use an LVT and we see why Actel takes great care to make sure that this is the case.

7.1.5   ACT 2 and ACT 3 Interconnect

The ACT 1 architecture uses two antifuses for routing nearby modules, three antifuses to join horizontal segments, and four antifuses to use a horizontal or vertical long track. The ACT 2 and ACT 3 architectures use increased interconnect resources over the ACT 1 device that we have described. This reduces further the number of connections that need more than two antifuses. Delay is also reduced by decreasing the population of antifuses in the channels, and by decreasing the antifuse resistance of certain critical antifuses (by increasing the programming current).

The **channel density** is the absolute minimum number of tracks needed in a channel to make a given set of connections (see Section 17.2.2, "Measurement of Channel Density"). Software to route connections using channeled routing is so efficient that, given complete freedom in location of wires, a channel router can usually complete the connections with the number of tracks equal or close to the theoretical minimum, the channel density. Actel's studies on segmented channel routing have shown that increasing the number of horizontal tracks slightly (by approximately 10 percent) above density can lead to very high routing completion rates.

The ACT 2 devices have 36 horizontal tracks per channel rather than the 22 available in the ACT 1 architecture. Horizontal track segments in an ACT 3 device range from a module pair to the full channel length. Vertical tracks are: input (with a two channel span: one up, one down); output (with a four-channel span: two up, two down); and long (LVT). Four LVTs are shared by each column pair. The ACT 2/3 Logic Modules can accept five inputs, rather than four inputs for the ACT 1 modules, and thus the ACT 2/3 Logic Modules need an extra two vertical tracks per channel. The number of tracks per column thus increases from 13 to 15 in the ACT 2/3 architecture.

The greatest challenge facing the Actel FPGA architects is the resistance of the polysilicon-diffusion antifuse. The nominal antifuse resistance in the ACT 1/2 1–2 μm processes (with a 5 mA programming current) is approximately 500 Ω and, in the worst case, may be as high as 700 Ω. The high resistance severely limits the number of antifuses in a connection. The ACT 2/3 devices assign a special antifuse to each output allowing a direct connection to an LVT. This reduces the number of antifuses in a connection using an LVT to three. This type of antifuse (a **fast fuse**) is blown at a higher current than the other antifuses to give them about half the nominal resistance (about 0.25 kΩ for ACT 2) of a normal antifuse. The nominal antifuse resistance is reduced further in the ACT 3 (using a 0.8 μm process) to 200 Ω (Actel does not state whether this value is for a normal or fast fuse). However, it is the worst-case antifuse resistance that will determine the worst-case performance.

7.2   Xilinx LCA

Figure 7.5 shows the hierarchical Xilinx LCA interconnect architecture.

- The **vertical lines** and **horizontal lines** run between CLBs.
- The **general-purpose interconnect** joins **switch boxes** (also known as **magic boxes** or **switching matrices**).
- The **long lines** run across the entire chip. It is possible to form internal buses using long lines and the three-state buffers that are next to each CLB.
- The **direct connections** (not used on the XC4000) bypass the switch matrices and directly connect adjacent CLBs.
- The **Programmable Interconnection Points** (**PIPs**) are programmable pass transistors that connect the CLB inputs and outputs to the routing network.
- The **bidirectional (BIDI) interconnect buffers** restore the logic level and logic strength on long interconnect paths.

Table 7.3 shows the interconnect data for an XC3020, a typical Xilinx LCA FPGA, that uses two-level metal interconnect. Figure 7.6 shows the switching matrix. Programming a switch matrix allows a number of different connections between the general-purpose interconnect.

In Figure 7.6 (d), (g), and (h):

- $C_1 = 3C_{P1} + 3C_{P2} + 0.5C_{LX}$ is the parasitic capacitance due to the switch matrix and PIPs (F4, C4, G4) for CLB1, and half of the line capacitance for the double-length line adjacent to CLB1.
- C_{P1} and R_{P1} are the switching-matrix parasitic capacitance and resistance.
- C_{P2} and R_{P2} are the parasitic capacitance and resistance for the PIP connecting YQ of CLB1 and F4 of CLB3.
- $C_2 = 0.5C_{LX} + C_{LX}$ accounts for half of the line adjacent to CLB1 and the line adjacent to CLB2.
- $C_3 = 0.5C_{LX}$ accounts for half of the line adjacent to CLB3.
- $C_4 = 0.5C_{LX} + 3C_{P2} + C_{LX} + 3C_{P1}$ accounts for half of the line adjacent to CLB3, the PIPs of CLB3 (C4, G4, YQ), and the rest of the line and switch matrix capacitance following CLB3.

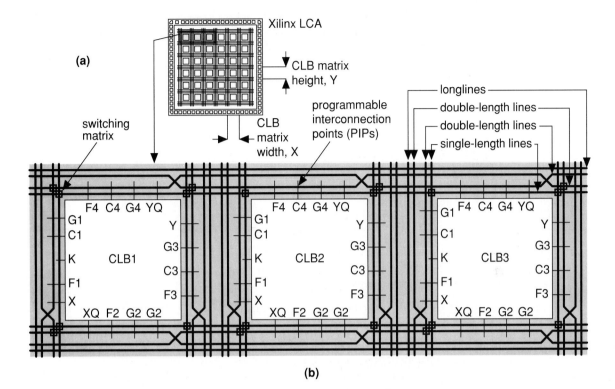

FIGURE 7.5 Xilinx LCA interconnect. (a) The LCA architecture (notice the matrix element size is larger than a CLB). (b) A simplified representation of the interconnect resources. Each of the lines is a bus.

We can determine Elmore's time constant for the connection shown in Figure 7.6 as

$$\tau_D = R_{P2}(C_{P2} + C_2 + 3C_{P1}) + (R_{P2} + R_{P1})(3C_{P1} + C_3 + C_{P2})$$
$$+ (2R_{P2} + R_{P1})(C_{P2} + C_4). \tag{7.9}$$

If $R_{P1} = R_{P2}$, and $C_{P1} = C_{P2}$, then

$$\tau_D = (15 + 21)R_P C_P + (1.5 + 1 + 4.5)R_P C_{LX}. \tag{7.10}$$

We need to know the pass-transistor resistance R_P. For example, suppose $R_P = 1 k\Omega$. If $k_n' = 50 \mu AV^{-2}$, then (with $V_{tn} = 0.65$ V and $V_{DD} = 3.3$ V)

$$W/L = \frac{1}{k_n' R_P (V_{DD} - V_{tn})} = \frac{1}{(50 \times 10^{-6})(1 \times 10^3)(3.3 - 0.65)} = 7.5. \tag{7.11}$$

TABLE 7.3   XC3000 interconnect parameters.

Parameter	XC3020
Technology	$1.0\,\mu m$, $\lambda = 0.5\,\mu m$
Die height	220 mil
Die width	180 mil
Die area	$39{,}600\,mil^2 = 102\,M\lambda^2$
CLB matrix height (Y)	$480\,\mu m = 960\,\lambda$
CLB matrix width (X)	$370\,\mu m = 740\,\lambda$
CLB matrix area (X×Y)	$17{,}600\,\mu m^2 = 710\,k\lambda^2$
Matrix transistor resistance, R_{P1}	$0.5–1\,k\Omega$
Matrix transistor parasitic capacitance, C_{P1}	0.01–0.02 pF
PIP transistor resistance, R_{P2}	$0.5–1\,k\Omega$
PIP transistor parasitic capacitance, C_{P2}	0.01-0.02 pF
Single-length line (X, Y)	$370\,\mu m$, $480\,\mu m$
Single-length line capacitance: C_{LX}, C_{LY}	0.075 pF, 0.1 pF
Horizontal Longline (8X)	8 cols. $= 2960\,\mu m$
Horizontal Longline metal capacitance, C_{LL}	0.6 pF

If $L = 1\,\mu m$, both source and drain areas are $7.5\,\mu m$ long and approximately $3\,\mu m$ wide (determined by diffusion overlap of contact, contact width, and contact-to-gate spacing, rules $6.1a + 6.2a + 6.4a = 5.5\,\lambda$ in Table 2.7). Both drain and source areas are thus $23\,\mu m^2$ and the sidewall perimeters are $14\,\mu m$ (excluding the sidewall facing the channel). If we have a diffusion capacitance of $140\,aF\mu m^{-2}$ (area) and $500\,aF\mu m^{-1}$ (perimeter), typical values for a $1.0\,\mu m$ process, the parasitic source and drain capacitance is

$$C_P = (140 \times 10^{-18})\,(23) + (500 \times 10^{-18})\,(14) = 1.022 \times 10^{-14}\,F. \qquad (7.12)$$

If we assume $C_P = 0.01$ pF and $C_{LX} = 0.075$ pF (Table 7.3),

$$\tau_D = (36)\,(1)\,(0.01) + (7)\,(1)\,(0.075) = 0.885\ \text{ns}. \qquad (7.13)$$

A delay of approximately 1 ns agrees with the typical values from the XACT delay calculator and is about the fastest connection we can make between two CLBs.

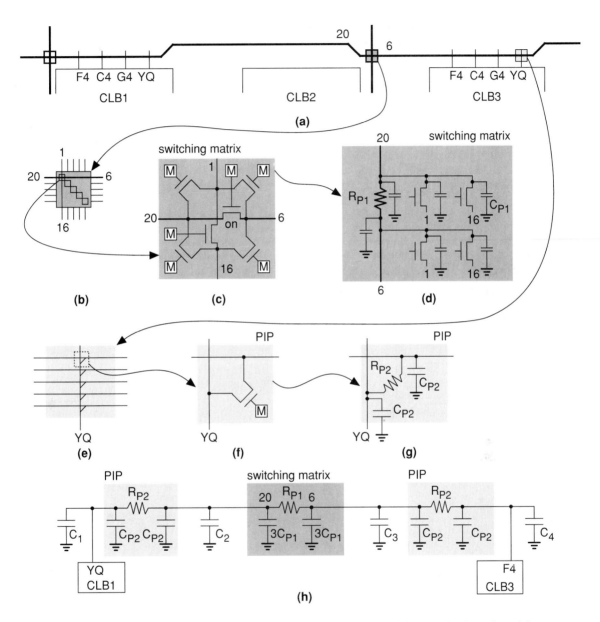

FIGURE 7.6 Components of interconnect delay in a Xilinx LCA array. (a) A portion of the interconnect around the CLBs. (b) A switching matrix. (c) A detailed view inside the switching matrix showing the pass-transistor arrangement. (d) The equivalent circuit for the connection between nets 6 and 20 using the matrix. (e) A view of the interconnect at a Programmable Interconnection Point (PIP). (f) and (g) The equivalent schematic of a PIP connection. (h) The complete RC delay path.

7.3   Xilinx EPLD

The Xilinx EPLD family uses an interconnect bus known as **Universal Interconnection Module** (**UIM**) to distribute signals within the FPGA. The UIM, shown in Figure 7.7, is a programmable AND array with constant delay from any input to any output. In Figure 7.7:

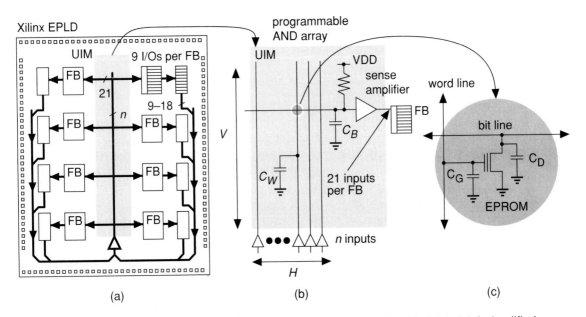

FIGURE 7.7 The Xilinx EPLD UIM (Universal Interconnection Module). (a) A simplified block diagram of the UIM. The UIM bus width, *n*, varies from 68 (XC7236) to 198 (XC73108). (b) The UIM is actually a large programmable AND array. (c) The parasitic capacitance of the EPROM cell.

- C_G is the fixed gate capacitance of the EPROM device.
- C_D is the fixed drain parasitic capacitance of the EPROM device.
- C_B is the variable horizontal bus ("bit" line) capacitance.
- C_W is the variable vertical bus ("word" line) capacitance.

Figure 7.7 shows the UIM has 21 output connections to each FB.[1] Thus the XC7272 UIM (with a 4×2 array of eight FBs as shown in Figure 7.7) has 168 (8×21) output connections. Most (but not all) of the nine I/O cells attached to each FB have two input connections to the UIM, one from a chip input and one feedback

---

[1] 1994 data book p. 3-62 and p. 3-78.

from the macrocell output. For example, the XC7272 has 18 I/O cells that are out-puts only and thus have only one connection to the UIM, so $n = (18 \times 8) - 18 = 126$ input connections. Now we can calculate the number of tracks in the UIM: the XC7272, for example, has $H = 126$ tracks and $V = 168/2 = 84$ tracks. The actual physical height, V, of the UIM is determined by the size of the FBs, and is close to the die height.

The UIM ranges in size with the number of FBs. For the smallest XC7236 (with a 2×2 array of four FBs), the UIM has $n = 68$ inputs and 84 outputs. For the XC73108 (with a 6×2 array of 12 FBs), the UIM has $n = 198$ inputs. The UIM is a large array with large parasitic capacitance; it employs a highly optimized structure that uses EPROM devices and a **sense amplifier** at each output. The signal swing on the UIM uses less than the full $V_{DD} = 5$ V to reduce the interconnect delay.

7.4   Altera MAX 5000 and 7000

Altera MAX 5000 devices (except the EPM5032, which has only one LAB) and all MAX 7000 devices use a **Programmable Interconnect Array** (**PIA**), shown in Figure 7.8. The PIA is a cross-point switch for logic signals traveling between LABs. The advantages of this architecture (which uses a fixed number of connections) over programmable interconnection schemes (which use a variable number of

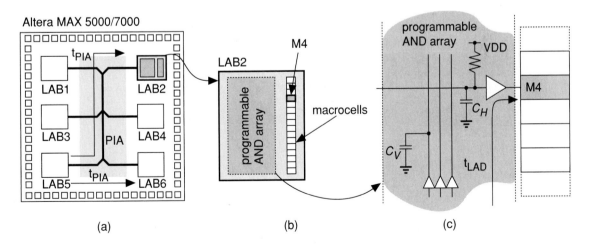

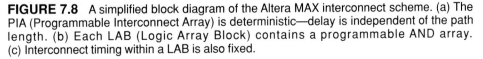

FIGURE 7.8 A simplified block diagram of the Altera MAX interconnect scheme. (a) The PIA (Programmable Interconnect Array) is deterministic—delay is independent of the path length. (b) Each LAB (Logic Array Block) contains a programmable AND array. (c) Interconnect timing within a LAB is also fixed.

connections) is the fixed routing delay. An additional benefit of the simpler nature of a large regular interconnect structure is the simplification and improved speed of the placement and routing software.

Figure 7.8(a) illustrates that the delay between any two LABs, t_{PIA}, is fixed. The delay between LAB1 and LAB2 (which are adjacent) is the same as the delay between LAB1 and LAB6 (on opposite corners of the die). It may seem rather strange to slow down all connections to the speed of the longest possible connection—a large penalty to pay to achieve a deterministic architecture. However, it gives Altera the opportunity to highly optimize all of the connections since they are completely fixed.

7.5   Altera MAX 9000

Figure 7.9 shows the Altera MAX 9000 interconnect architecture. The size of the MAX 9000 LAB arrays varies between 4×5 (rows $\times$ columns) for the EPM9320 and 7×5 for the EPM9560. The MAX 9000 is an extremely coarse-grained architecture, typical of complex PLDs, but the LABs themselves have a finer structure. Sometimes we say that complex PLDs with arrays (LABs in the Altera MAX family) that are themselves arrays (of macrocells) have a **dual-grain architecture**.

FIGURE 7.9 The Altera MAX 9000 interconnect scheme. (a) A 4 × 5 array of Logic Array Blocks (LABs), the same size as the EMP9400 chip. (b) A simplified block diagram of the interconnect architecture showing the connection of the FastTrack buses to a LAB.

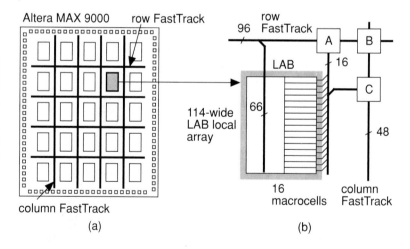

In Figure 7.9(b), boxes A, B, and C represent the interconnection between the FastTrack buses and the 16 macrocells in each LAB:

- Box A connects a macrocell to one row channel.
- Box B connects three column channels to two row channels.
- Box C connects a macrocell to three column channels.

7.6 Altera FLEX

Figure 7.10 shows the interconnect used in the Altera FLEX family of complex PLDs. Altera refers to the FLEX interconnect and MAX 9000 interconnect by the same name, FastTrack, but the two are different because the granularity of the logic cell arrays is different. The FLEX architecture is of finer grain than the MAX arrays—because of the difference in programming technology. The FLEX horizontal interconnect is much denser (at 168 channels per row) than the vertical interconnect (16 channels per column), creating an aspect ratio for the interconnect of over 10:1 (168:16). This imbalance is partly due to the aspect ratio of the die, the array, and the aspect ratio of the basic logic cell, the LAB.

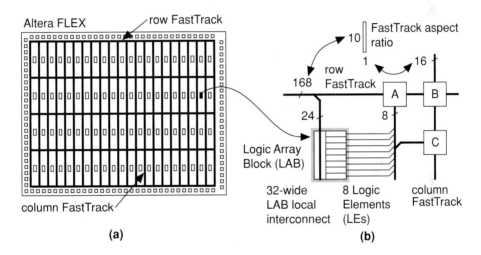

FIGURE 7.10 The Altera FLEX interconnect scheme. (a) The row and column FastTrack interconnect. The chip shown, with 4 rows × 21 columns, is the same size as the EPF8820. (b) A simplified diagram of the interconnect architecture showing the connections between the FastTrack buses and a LAB. Boxes A, B, and C represent the bus-to-bus connections.

As an example, the EPF8820 has 4 rows and 21 columns of LABs (Figure 7.10a). Ignoring, for simplicity's sake, what happens at the edge of the die we can total the routing channels as follows:

- Horizontal channels = 4 rows × 168 channels/row = 672 channels.
- Vertical channels = 21 rows × 16 channels/row = 336 channels.

It appears that there is still approximately twice (672:336) as much interconnect capacity in the horizontal direction as the vertical. If we look inside the boxes A, B, and C in Figure 7.10(b) we see that for individual lines on each bus:

- Box A connects an LE to two row channels.
- Box B connects two column channels to a row channel.
- Box C connects an LE to two column channels.

There is some dependence between boxes A and B since they contain MUXes rather than direct connections, but essentially there are twice as many connections to the column FastTrack as the row FastTrack, thus restoring the balance in interconnect capacity.

7.7 Summary

The RC product of the parasitic elements of an antifuse and a pass transistor are not too different. However, an SRAM cell is much larger than an antifuse which leads to coarser interconnect architectures for SRAM-based programmable ASICs. The EPROM device lends itself to large wired-logic structures. These differences in programming technology lead to different architectures:

- The antifuse FPGA architectures are dense and regular.
- The SRAM architectures contain nested structures of interconnect resources.
- The complex PLD architectures use long interconnect lines but achieve deterministic routing.

Table 7.4 is a look-up table for Tables 7.5 and 7.6, which summarize the features of the logic cells used by the various FPGA vendors.

TABLE 7.4   I/O Cell Tables.

Table	Programmable ASIC family	Table	Programmable ASIC family
Table 7.5	Actel (ACT 1)	Table 7.6	Xilinx (XC8100)
	Xilinx (XC3000)		Lucent ORCA (2C)
	Actel (ACT 2)		Altera FLEX (8000/10k)
	Xilinx (XC4000)		AMD MACH 5
	Altera MAX (EPM 5000)		Actel 3200DX
	Xilinx EPLD (XC7200/7300)		Altera MAX (EPM 9000)
	Actel (ACT 3)		
	QuickLogic (pASIC 1)		
	Crosspoint (CP20K)		
	Altera MAX (EPM 7000)		
	Atmel (AT6000)		
	Xilinx LCA (XC5200)		

TABLE 7.5 Programmable ASIC interconnect.

	Actel (ACT 1)	Xilinx (XC3000)	Actel (ACT 2)	Xilinx (XC4000)
Interconnect between logic cells (tracks = trks)	Channeled array with segmented routing, long lines: 25 trks/ch. (horiz.); 13 trks/ch. (vert.); < 4 antifuses/path	Switch box, PIPs (Programmable Interconnect Points), 3-state internal bus, and long lines	Channeled array with segmented routing, long lines: 36 trks/ch. (horiz.); 15 trks/ch. (vert.); < 4 antifuses/path	Switch box, PIPs (Programmable Interconnect Points), 3-state internal bus, and long lines
Interconnect delay	Variable	Variable	Variable	Variable
Interconnect inside logic cells	Poly–diffusion antifuse	32-bit SRAM LUT	Poly–diffusion antifuse	32-bit SRAM LUT

	Altera (MAX 5000)	Xilinx EPLD	QuickLogic (pASIC 1)	Actel (ACT 3)
Interconnect between logic cells	Cross-bar PIA (Programmable Interconnect Architecture) using EPROM programmable-AND array	UIM (Universal Interconnect Matrix) using EPROM programmable-AND array	Programmable fully populated antifuse matrix	Channeled array with segmented routing, long lines: <4 antifuses/path
Interconnect delay	Fixed	Fixed	Variable	Variable
Interconnect inside logic cells	EPROM	EPROM	Metal–metal antifuse	Poly–diffusion antifuse

	Crosspoint (CP20K)	Altera MAX (MAX 7000)	Atmel (AT6000)	Xilinx LCA (XC5200)
Interconnect between logic cells	Programmable highly interconnected matrix	Fixed cross-bar PIA (Programmable Interconnect Architecture)	Programmable regular, local, and express bus scheme with line repeaters	Switch box, PIPs (Programmable Interconnect Points), 3-state internal bus, and long lines
Interconnect delay	Variable	Fixed	Variable	Variable
Interconnect inside logic cells	Metal–metal antifuse	EEPROM	SRAM	16-bit SRAM LUT

TABLE 7.6 Programmable ASIC interconnect (continued).

	Xilinx (XC8100)	Lucent ORCA 2C	Altera FLEX 8000/10k
Interconnect between logic cells	Channeled array with segmented routing, long lines. Programmable fully populated antifuse matrix.	Switch box, SRAM programmable interconnect, 3-state internal bus, and long lines	Row and column FastTrack between LABs
Interconnect delay	Variable	Variable	Fixed with small variation in delay in row FastTrack
Interconnect inside logic cells	Antifuse	SRAM LUTs and MUXs	LAB local interconnect between LEs. 16-bit SRAM LUT in LE.

	AMD MACH 5	Actel 3200DX	Altera MAX 9000
Interconnect between logic cells	EPROM programmable array	Channeled gate array with segmented routing, long lines	Row and column FastTrack between LABs
Interconnect delay	Fixed	Variable	Fixed
Interconnect inside logic cells	EPROM	Poly–diffusion antifuse	Programmable AND array inside LAB, EEPROM MUXes

The key points covered in this chapter are:

- The difference between deterministic and nondeterministic interconnect
- Estimating interconnect delay
- Elmore's constant

Next, in Chapter 8, we shall cover the software you need to design with the various FPGA families and explain how FPGAs are programmed.

7.8   Problems

* = Difficult, ** = Very difficult, *** = Extremely difficult

7.1 (*Xilinx interconnect, 120 min.)

a. Write a minitutorial (one or two pages) explaining what you need to know to run and use the XACT delay calculator. Explain how to choose the part, set the display preferences, make connections to CLBs and the interconnect, and obtain timing figures.

b. Use the XACT editor to determine typical delays using the longlines, a switch matrix, the PIPs, and BIDI buffers (see the Xilinx data book for more detailed explanations of the interconnect structure). Draw six different typical paths using these elements and show the components of delay. Include screen shots showing the layout of the paths and cells with detailed explanations of the figures.

c. Construct a path using the TBUFs, the three-state buffers, driving a longline (do not forget the pull-up). Show the XACT calculated delay for your path and explain the number from data book parameters (list them and the page number from the data book).

d. Extend one simple path to the I/O and explain the input and output timing, again using the data book.

e. Include screen shots from the layout editor showing you example paths.

f. Bury all the ASCII (but not binary) files you used and the tools produced inside your report using "Hidden Text." Include explanations as to what these files are and which parts of the report they go with. This includes any schematic files, netlist files, and all files produced by the Xilinx tools. Use a separate directory for this problem and make a list in your report of all files (binary and ASCII) with explanations of what each file is.

7.2 (*Actel interconnect, 120 min.) Use the Actel chip editor to explore the properties of the interconnect scheme in a similar fashion to Problem 7.1 with the following changes: in part b make at least six different paths using various antifuse connections and explain the numbers from the delay calculator. Omit part c.

7.3 (*Altera MAX interconnect, 120 min.) Use the Altera tools to determine the properties of the MAX or FLEX interconnect in a similar fashion to Problem 7.1 with the following changes: In parts b and c construct at least six example circuits that show the various paths through the FastTrack or PIA chip-level interconnect, the local LAB array, the LAB, and the macrocells.

7.4 (**Custom ASICs, 120 min.)

a. Write a minitutorial (one or two pages) explaining how to run an ASIC tool (Compass/Mentor/Cadence/Tanner). Enter a simple circuit (using schematic entry or synthesis and cells from a cell library) and obtain a delay estimate.

b. Construct at least six example circuits that show various logic paths using various logic cells (for example: an inverter, a full adder).

c. Perform a timing simulation (either using a static timing verifier or using a logic simulator). Compare your results with those from a data book.

d. Extract the circuit to include the parasitic capacitances from layout in your circuit netlist and run a simulation to predict the delays.

e. Compare the results that include routing capacitance with the data book values for the logic cell delays and with the values predicted before routing.

f. Extend one simple path to the outputs of the chip by including I/O pads in your circuit and explain the input and output timing predictions.

g. Bury the ASCII files you used and the tools produced inside your report.

7.5 (**Actel stubs, 60 min.)

a. Which metal layers do you think Actel assigns to the horizontal and vertical interconnect in the ACT 1/2/3 architectures and why?

b. Why do the ACT 1/2/3 input stubs not extend over more than two channels above and below the Logic Modules, since this would reduce the need for LVTs?

c. The ACT 2 data sheet describes the output stubs as "twisted" (or interwoven) so that they occupy only four tracks. Show that the stubs occupy four vertical tracks whether they are twisted or not.

d. Suggest the real reason for the twisted stubs.

7.6 (A three-input NAND in ACT 1, 30 min.) The macros that require two ACT 1 modules include the three-input NAND (others include four-input NAND, AND, NOR).

a. What is the problem with trying to implement a three-input NAND gate using the Actel ACT 1 Logic Module?

b. Suggest a modification to the ACT 1 Logic Module that would allow the implementation of a three-input NAND using one of your new Logic Modules.

c. Can you think of a reason why Actel did not use your modification to its Logic Module design? *Hint*: The modification has to do with routing, and not the logic itself.

7.7 (*Actel architecture, 60 min.) This is a long but relatively straightforward problem that "reverse-engineers" the Actel architecture. If you measured the chip photo on the front of the April 1990 Actel data book, you would find the following:

1. Die height (scribe to scribe) = 170 mm.

2. Channel height = 8 mm (there are 7 full-height and 2 half-height channels).

3. Logic Module height = 5 mm (there are 8 rows of Logic Modules).

4. Column (Logic Module) width = 4.2 mm.

(The **scribe line** is an area at the edge of a die where a cut is made by a diamond saw when the dice are separated.) An Actel 1010 die in 2 μm technology is 240 mil high by 360 mil wide (p. 4-17 in the 1990 data book). Assuming these data book dimensions are scribe to scribe, calculate **(a)** the Logic Module height, **(b)** the channel height, and **(c)** the column (Logic Module) width.

Given that there are 25 tracks per horizontal channel, and 13 tracks per column in the vertical direction, calculate **(d)** the horizontal channel track spacing and **(e)** the vertical channel track spacing. **(f)** Using the fact that each output stub spans two channels above and below the Logic Module, calculate the height of the output stub.

We can now estimate the capacitance of the Logic Module stubs and interconnect. Assume the interconnect capacitance is $0.2\,\mathrm{pFmm}^{-1}$. (**g**) Calculate the capacitance of an output stub and an input stub. (**h**) Calculate the width and thus the capacitance of the horizontal tracks that are from four columns to 44 columns long.

You should not have to make any other assumptions to calculate these figures, but if you do, state them clearly. The figures you have calculated are summarized in Table 7.2.

7.8 (Xilinx bank shots, 20 min.) Figure 7.11 shows a magic box. Explain how to use a "bank shot" to enter one side of the box, bounce off another, and exit on a third side. What is the delay involved in this maneuver?

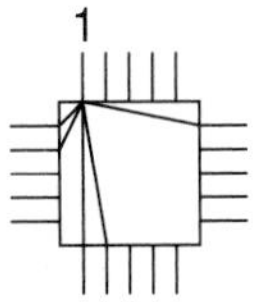

FIGURE 7.11 A Xilinx magic box showing one set of connections from connection 1 (Problem 7.8).

7.9 Bibliography

The paper by Greene et al. [1993] (reprinted in the 1994 Actel data book) is a good description of the Actel interconnect. The 1995 AT&T data book contains a very detailed account of the routing for the ORCA series of FPGAs, which is similar to the Xilinx LCA interconnect. You can learn a great deal about the details of the Lucent and Xilinx interconnect architecture from the AT&T data book. The Xilinx data book gives a good high-level overview of SRAM-based FPGA interconnect. The best way to learn about any FPGA interconnect is to use the software tools provided by the vendor. The Xilinx XACT editor that shows point-to-point routing delays on a graphical representation of the chip layout is an easy way to become familiar with the interconnect properties. The book by Brown et al. [1992] covers FPGA interconnect from a theoretical point of view, concentrating on routing for LUT based FPGAs, and also describes specialized routing algorithms for FPGAs.

7.10 References

Brown, S. D., et al. 1992. *Field-Programmable Gate Arrays*. Norwell, MA: Kluwer Academic, 206 p. ISBN 0-7923-9248-5. TK7872.L64F54. Contents: Introduction to FPGAs, Commercially Available FPGAs, Technology Mapping for FPGAs, Logic Block Architecture, Routing for FPGAs, Flexibility of FPGA Routing Resources, A Theoretical Model for FPGA Routing. Includes an introduction to commercially available FPGAs. The rest of the book covers research on logic synthesis for FPGAs and FPGA architectures, concentrating on LUT-based architectures.

Greene, J., et al. 1993. "Antifuse field programmable gate arrays." *Proceedings of the IEEE,* vol. 81, no. 7, pp. 1042–1056, 1993. Review article describing the Actel FPGAs. (Included in the Actel 1994 data book.)

Rubenstein, J., P. Penfield, and M. A. Horowitz. 1983. "Signal delay in RC tree networks." *IEEE Transactions on CAD,* vol. CAD-2, no. 3, July 1983, pp. 202–211. Derives bounds for the response of RC networks excited by an input step voltage.

PROGRAMMABLE ASIC DESIGN SOFTWARE

There are five components of a programmable ASIC or FPGA: (1) the programming technology, (2) the basic logic cell, (3) the I/O cell, (4) the interconnect, and (5) the design software that allows you to program the ASIC. The design software is much more closely tied to the FPGA architecture than is the case for other types of ASICs.

8.1 Design Systems

The sequence of steps for FPGA design is similar to the sequence discussed in Section 1.2, "Design Flow." As for any ASIC a designer needs design-entry software, a cell library, and physical-design software. Each of the FPGA vendors sells **design kits** that include all the software and hardware that a designer needs. Many of these kits use design-entry software produced by a different company. Often designers buy that software from the FPGA vendor. This is called an **original equipment manufacturer** (**OEM**) arrangement—similar to buying a car with a stereo manufactured by an electronics company but labeled with the automobile company's name. Design entry uses cell libraries that are unique to each FPGA vendor. All of the FPGA vendors produce their own physical-design software so they can tune the algorithms to their own architecture.

Unfortunately, there are no standards in FPGA design. Thus, for example, Xilinx calls its 2:1 MUX an M2_1 with inputs labeled D0, D1, and S0 with output O. Actel calls a 2:1 MUX an MX2 with inputs A, B, and S with output Y. This problem is not peculiar to Xilinx and Actel; each ASIC vendor names its logic cells, buffers, pads, and so on in a different manner. Consequently designers may not be able to transfer a netlist using one ASIC vendor library to another. Worse than this, designers may not even be able to transfer a design between two FPGA families made by the same FPGA vendor!

One solution to the lack of standards for cell libraries is to use a **generic cell library**, independent from any particular FPGA vendor. For example, most of the FPGA libraries include symbols that are equivalent to TTL 7400 logic series parts. The FPGA vendor's own software automatically handles the conversion from schematic symbols to the logic cells of the FPGA.

Schematic entry is not the only method of design entry for FPGAs. Some designers are happier describing control logic and state machines in terms of state diagrams and logic equations. A solution to some of the problems with schematic entry for FPGA design is to use one of several **hardware description languages** (**HDLs**) for which there are some standards. There are two sets of languages in common use. One set has evolved from the design of programmable logic devices (PLDs). The **ABEL** (pronounced "able"), **CUPL** ("cupple"), and **PALASM** ("pal-azzam") languages are simple and easy to learn. These languages are useful for describing state machines and combinational logic. The other set of HDLs includes **VHDL** and **Verilog**, which are higher-level and are more complex but are capable of describing complete ASICs and systems.

After completing design entry and generating a netlist, the next step is simulation. Two types of simulators are normally used for FPGA design. The first is a **logic simulator** for behavioral, functional, and timing simulation. This tool can catch any design errors. The designer provides input waveforms to the simulator and checks to see that the outputs are as expected. At this point, using a nondeterministic architecture, logic path delays are only estimates, since the wiring delays will not be known until after physical design (place-and-route) is complete. Designers then add or **back-annotate** the **postlayout timing information** to the **postlayout netlist** (also called a **back-annotated netlist**). This is followed by a **postlayout timing simulation**.

The second type of simulator, the type most often used in FPGA design, is a **timing-analysis** tool. A timing analyzer is a static simulator and removes the need for input waveforms. Instead the timing analyzer checks for critical paths that limit the speed of operation—signal paths that have large delays caused, say, by a high fanout net. Designers can set a certain delay restriction on a net or path as a **timing constraint**; if the actual delay is longer, this is a **timing violation**. In most design systems we can return to design entry and tag critical paths with attributes before completing the place-and-route step again. The next time we use the place-and-route software it will pay special attention to those signals we have labeled as critical in order to minimize the routing delays associated with those signals. The problem is that this iterative process can be lengthy and sometimes nonconvergent. Each time timing violations are fixed, others appear. This is especially a problem with place-and-route software that uses random algorithms (and forms a chaotic system). More complex (and expensive) logic synthesizers can automate this iterative stage of the design process. The critical path information is calculated in the logic synthesizer, and timing constraints are created in a feedforward path (this is called **forward-annotation**) to direct the place-and-route software.

Although some FPGAs are reprogrammable, it is not a good idea to rely on this fact. It is very tempting to program the FPGA, test it, make changes to the netlist, and then keep programming the device until it works. This process is much more time consuming and much less reliable than performing thorough simulation. It is quite possible, for example, to get a chip working in an experimental fashion without really knowing why. The danger here is that the design may fail under some other set of operating conditions or circumstances. Simulation is the proper way to catch and correct these potential disasters.

8.1.1   Xilinx

Figure 8.1 shows the Xilinx design system. Using third-party design-entry software, the designer creates a netlist that forms the input to the Xilinx software. Utility software (`pin2xnf` for FutureNet DASH and `wir2xnf` for Viewlogic, for example) translate the netlist into a **Xilinx netlist format** (**XNF**) file. In the next step the Xilinx program `xnfmap` takes the XNF netlist and **maps** the logic into the Xilinx **Logic Cell Array** (**LCA**) architecture. The output from the mapping step is a MAP file. The schematic MAP file may then be **merged** with other MAP files using `xnfmerge`. This technique is useful to merge different pieces of a design, some created using schematic entry and others created, for example, using logic synthesis. A translator program `map2lca` translates from the logic gates (NAND gates, NOR gates, and so on) to the required CLB configurations and produces an unrouted LCA file. The Xilinx place-and-route software (`apr` or `ppr`) takes the unrouted LCA file and performs the allocation of CLBs and completes the routing. The result is a routed LCA file. A control program `xmake` (that works like the `make` program in C) can automatically handle the mapping, merging, and place-and-route steps. Following the place-and-route step, the logic and wiring delays are known and the postlayout netlist may be generated. After a postlayout simulation the **download file** or BIT file used to program the FPGA (or a PROM that will load the FPGA) is generated using the Xilinx `makebits` program.

Xilinx also provides a software program (Xilinx design editor, XDE) that permits manual control over the placement and routing of a Xilinx FPGA. The designer views a graphical representation of the FPGA, showing all the CLBs and interconnect, and can make or alter connections by pointing and clicking. This program is useful to check an automatically generated layout, or to explore critical routing paths, or to change and hand tune a critical connection, for example.

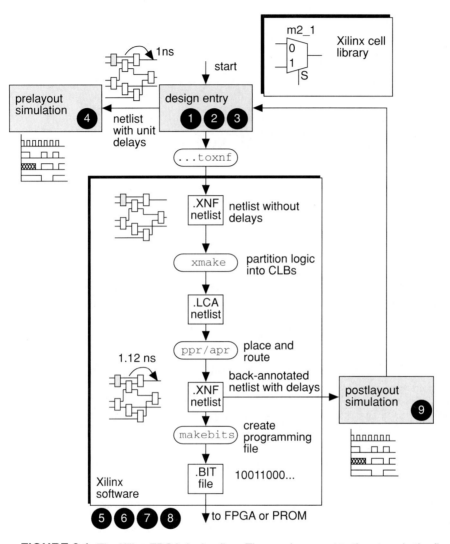

FIGURE 8.1 The Xilinx FPGA design flow. The numbers next to the steps in the flow correspond to those in the general ASIC design flow of Figure 1.10.

Xilinx uses a system called X-BLOX for creating regular structures such as vectored instances and datapaths. This system works with the Xilinx XNF netlist format. Other vendors, notably Actel and Altera, use a standard called **Relationally Placed Modules** (**RPM**), based on the EDIF standard, that ensures that the pieces of an 8-bit adder, for example, are treated as a macro and stay together during placement.

8.1.2   Actel

Actel FPGA design uses third-party design entry and simulators. After creating a netlist, a designer uses the Actel software for the place-and-route step. The Actel design software, like other FPGA and ASIC design systems, employs a large number of file formats with associated filename extensions. Table 8.1 shows some of the Actel file extensions and their meanings.

TABLE 8.1   File types used by Actel design software.

ADL	Main design netlist
IPF	Partial or complete pin assignment for the design
CRT	Net criticality
VALIDATED	Audit information
COB	List of macros removed from design
VLD	Information, warning, and error messages
PIN	Complete pin assignment for the design
DFR	Information about routability and I/O assignment quality
LOC	Placement of non-I/O macros, pin swapping, and freeway assignment
PLI	Feedback from placement step
SEG	Assignment of horizontal routing segments
STF	Back-annotation timing
RTI	Feedback from routing step
FUS	Fuse coordinates (column-track, row-track)
DEL	Delays for input pins, nets, and I/O modules
AVI	Fuse programming times and currents for last chip programmed

Actel software can also map hardware description files from other programmable logic design software into the Actel FPGA architecture. As an example, Table 8.2 shows a text description of a state machine using an HDL from a company called LOG/iC. You can then convert the LOG/iC code to the PALASM code shown in Table 8.2. The Actel software can take the PALASM code and merge it with other PALASM files or netlists.

8.1.3   Altera

Altera uses a self-contained design system for its complex PLDs that performs design entry, simulation, and programming of the parts. Altera also provides an input and output interface to EDIF so that designers may use third-party schematic entry or a logic

TABLE 8.2   FPGA state-machine language.

LOG/iC state-machine language	PALASM version
| ```
*IDENTIFICATION
sequence detector
LOG/iC code
*X-NAMES
X; !input
*Y-NAMES
D; !output, D = 1 when three 1's appear on X
*FLOW-TABLE
;State, X input, Y output,   next state
  S1,    X1,       Y0,        F2;
  S1,    X0,       Y0,        F1;
  S2,    X1,       Y0,        F3;
  S2,    X0,       Y0,        F1;
  S3,    X1,       Y0,        F4;
  S3,    X0,       Y0,        F1;
  S4,    X1,       Y1,        F4;
  S4,    X0,       Y0,        F1;
*STATE-ASSIGNMENT
BINARY;
*RUN-CONTROL
PROGFORMAT = P-EQUATIONS;
*END
``` | ```
TITLE sequence detector
CHIP MEALY USER
CLK Z QQ2 QQ1 X
EQUATIONS
Z = X * QQ2 * QQ1
QQ2 := X * QQ1 + X * QQ2
QQ1 := X * QQ2 + X * /QQ1
``` |

synthesizer. We have seen that the interconnect scheme in the Altera complex PLDs is nearly deterministic, simplifying the physical-design software as well as eliminating the need for back-annotation and a postlayout simulation. As Altera FPGAs become larger and more complex, there are some exceptions to this rule. Some special cases require signals to make more than one pass through the routing structures or travel large distances across the Altera FastTrack interconnect. It is possible to tell if this will be the case only by trying to place and route an Altera device.

8.2   Logic Synthesis

Designers are increasingly using logic synthesis as a replacement for schematic entry. As microelectronic systems and their ASICs become more complex, the use of schematics becomes less practical. For example, a complex ASIC that contains over 10,000 gates might require hundreds of pages of schematics at the gate level. As another example, it is easier to write $A = B + C$ than to draw a schematic for a 32-bit adder at the gate level.

The term *logic synthesis* is used to cover a broad range of software and software capabilities. Many logic synthesizers are based on **logic minimization**. Logic minimization is usually performed in one of two ways, either using a set of rules or using algorithms. Early logic-minimization software was designed using algorithms for two-level logic minimization and developed into multilevel logic-optimization software. Two-level and multilevel logic minimization is well suited to random logic that is to be implemented using a CBIC, MGA, or PLD. In these technologies, two-level logic can be implemented very efficiently. Logic minimization for FPGAs, including complex PLDs, is more difficult than other types of ASICs, because of the complex basic logic cells in FPGAs.

There are two ways to use logic synthesis in the design of FPGAs. The first and simplest method takes a hardware description, optimizes the logic, and then produces a netlist. The netlist is then passed to software that **maps** the netlist to an FPGA architecture. The disadvantage of this method is the inefficiency of decoupling the logic optimization from the mapping step. The second, more complicated, but more efficient method, takes the hardware description and directly optimizes the logic for a specific FPGA architecture.

Some logic synthesizers produce files in PALASM, ABEL, or CUPL formats. Software provided by the FPGA vendor then take these files and maps the logic to the FPGA architecture. The FPGA mapping software requires detailed knowledge of the FPGA architecture. This makes it difficult for third-party companies to create logic synthesis software that can map directly to the FPGA.

A problem with design-entry systems is the difficulty of moving netlists between different FPGA vendors. Once you have completed a design using an FPGA cell library, for example, you are committed to using that type of FPGA unless you repeat design entry using a different cell library. ASIC designers do not like this approach since it exposes them to the mercy of a single ASIC vendor. Logic synthesizers offer a degree of independence from FPGA vendors (universally referred to as **vendor independence**, but this should, perhaps, be designer independence) by delaying the point in the design cycle at which designers need to make a decision on which FPGA to use. Of course, now designers become dependent on the synthesis software company.

8.2.1   FPGA Synthesis

For low-level logic synthesis, PALASM is a de facto standard as the lowest-common-denominator interchange format. Most FPGA design systems are capable of converting their own native formats into a PALASM file. The most common programmable logic design systems are ABEL from Data I/O, CUPL from P-CAD, LOG/iC from IsData, PALASM2 from AMD, and PGA-Designer from Minc. At a higher level, CAD companies (Cadence, Compass, Mentor, and Synopsys are examples) support most FPGA cell libraries. This allows you to map from a VHDL or Verilog description to an EDIF netlist that is compatible with FPGA design software. Sometimes you have to buy the cell library from the software company, sometimes from the FPGA vendor.

TABLE 8.3   The VHDL code for the sequence detector of Table 8.2.

```
entity detector is port (X, CLK: in BIT; Z : out BIT); end;
architecture behave of SEQDET is
   type STATES is (S1, S2, S3, S4);
   signal current, next: STATES;
begin
   combinational: process begin
      case current is
         when S1 =>
            if X = '1' then Z <= '0'; next <= S3; else Z <= '0'; next <= S1; end if;
         when S2 =>
            if X = '1' then Z <= '0'; next <= S2; else Z <= '0'; next <= S1; end if;
         when S3 =>
            if X = '1' then Z <= '0'; next <= S2; else Z <= '0'; next <= S1; end if;
         when S4 =>
            if X = '1' then Z <= '1'; next <= S4; else Z <= '0'; next <= S1; end if
      end case;
   end process
   sequential: process begin
      wait until CLK'event and CLK = '1'; current <= next ;
   end process;
end behave;
```

As an example, Table 8.3 shows a VHDL model for a pattern detector to check for a sequence of three '1's (excluding the code for the I/O pads). Table 8.4 shows a **script** or **command file** that runs the Synopsys software to generate an EDIF netlist from this VHDL that **targets** the TI version of the Actel FPGA parts. A script is a recipe that tells the software what to do. If we wanted to **retarget** this design to another type of FPGA or an MGA or CBIC ASIC, for example, we may only need a new set of cell libraries and to change the script (if we are lucky). In practice, we shall probably find we need to make a few changes in the VHDL code (in the areas of I/O pads, for example, that are different for each kind of ASIC). We now have a **portable design** and a measure of vendor independence. We have also introduced some dependence on the Synopsys software since the code in Table 8.3 might be portable, but the script (which is just as important a part of the design) in Table 8.4 may only be used with the Synopsys software. Nevertheless, using logic synthesis results in a more portable design than using schematic entry.

TABLE 8.4   The Synopsys script for the VHDL code of Table 8.3.

```
/design checking/                              report_design > detector.rpt
search_path = .                                /optimize for area/
/use the TI cell libraries/                    max_area 0.0
link_library = tpc10.db                        compile
target_library = tpc10.db                      write -h -f db -o detector_opt.db
symbol_library = tpc10.sdb                     report -area -cell -timing > detector.rpt
read -f vhdl detector.vhd                       free -all
current_design = detector                      /write EDIF netlist/
write -n -f db -hierarchy -0 detector.db       write -h -f edif -0
check_design > detector.rpt                    exit
```

8.3   The Halfgate ASIC

This section illustrates FPGA design using a very simple ASIC—a single inverter. The hidden details of the design and construction of this "halfgate FPGA" are quite complicated. Fortunately, most of the inner workings of the design software are normally hidden from the designer. However, when software breaks, as it sometimes does, it is important to know how things work in order to fix the problem. The formats, filenames, and flow will change, but the information needed at each stage and the order in which it is conveyed will stay much the same.

8.3.1   Xilinx

Table 8.5 shows an FPGA design flow using Compass and Xilinx software. On the left of Table 8.5 is a script for the Compass programs—scripts for Cadence, Mentor, and Synopsys software are similar, but not all design software has the capability to be run on autopilot using scripts and a command language. The diagrams in Table 8.5 illustrate what is happening at each of the design steps. The following numbered comments, corresponding to the labels in Table 8.5, highlight the important steps:

1. The Verilog code, in `halfgate.v`, describes a single inverter.

2. The script runs the logic synthesizer that converts the Verilog description to an inverter (using elements from the Xilinx XC4000 library) and saves the result in a netlist, `halfgate_p.nls` (a Compass internal format).

3. The script next runs the logic optimizer for FPGAs. This program also adds the I/O pads. In this case, logic optimization implements the inverter by using an inverting output pad. The software writes out the netlist as `halfgate_p.xnf`.

4. A timing simulation is run on the netlist `halfgate_p.nls` (the Compass format netlist). This netlist uses the default delays—every gate has a delay of 1 ns.

TABLE 8.5 Design flow for the Xilinx implementation of the halfgate ASIC.

Script	Design flow

``
# halfgate.xilinx.inp 	
shell setdef
   path working xc4000d xblox cmosch000x
quit
asic
   open [v]halfgate
   synthesize
   save [nls]halfgate_p
quit
fpga
   set tag xc4000
   set opt area
   optimize [nls]halfgate_p
quit
qtv
   open [nls]halfgate_p
   trace critical
   print trace [txt]halfgate_p
quit
shell vuterm
   exec xnfmerge -p 4003PC84 halfgate_p > /dev/null
   exec xnfprep halfgate_p > /dev/null
   exec ppr halfgate_p > /dev/null
   exec makebits -w halfgate_p > /dev/null
   exec lca2xnf -g -v halfgate_p halfgate_b > /dev/null
quit
manager notice
utility netlist
   open [xnf]halfgate_b
   save [nls]halfgate_b
   save [edf]halfgate_b
quit
qtv
   open [nls]halfgate_b
   trace critical
   print trace [txt]halfgate_b
quit
``
 	
	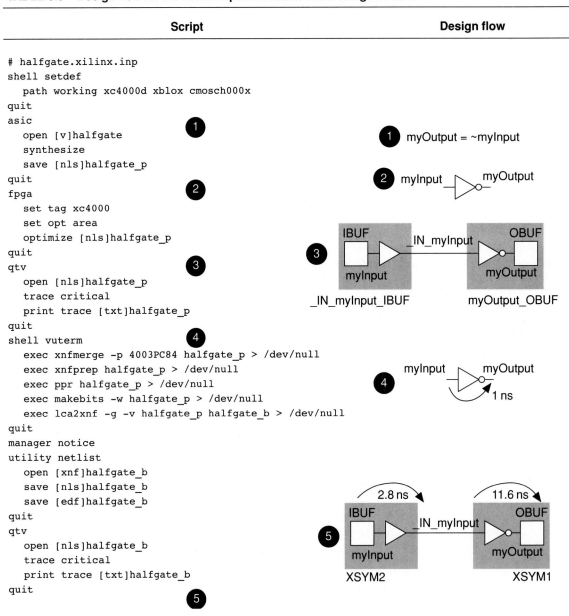

TABLE 8.6   The Xilinx files for the halfgate ASIC.

Verilog file (`halfgate.v`)

```
module halfgate(myInput, myOutput); input myInput; output myOutput; wire myOutput;
   assign myOutput = ~myInput;
endmodule
```

Preroute XNF file (`halfgate_p.xnf`)

```
LCANET, 5                                         PIN, O, O, _IN_myInput,
USER, FPGA-Optimizer, 4.1, Date:960710 ,             END
Option: Area                                      EXT, myInput, I,
PROG, FPGA-Optimizer, 4.1, "Lib=4000"             SYM, myOutput_obuf,OBUF,LIBVER=2.0.0,
PART,  4010PG191                                  PIN, I, I, _IN_myInput,, INV
PWR, 0, GND                                       PIN, O, O, myOutput,
PWR, 1, VCC                                        END
SYM, _IN_myInput_IBUF, IBUF, LIBVER=2.0.0         EXT,  myOutput, O,
PIN, I, I, myInput,                               EOF
```

LCA file (`halfgate_p.lca`)

```
;: halfgate_p.lca (4003PC84-4), makebits         Config INFF: I1: I2:I O: OUT: PAD: TRI:
5.2.0, Tue Jul 16 20:09:43 1996                   Endblk
Version 2                                         Editblk PAD1
Design 4003PC84 4 0                               Base IO
Speed -4                                          Config INFF: I1: I2: O: OUT:O:NOT PAD:
Addnet PAD_myInput PAD61.I2 PAD1.O                TRI:
Netdelay PAD_myInput PAD1.O 3.1                   Endblk
Program PAD_myInput {65G521} {65G287}             Nameblk PAD61 myInput
{65G50} {63G50} {52G50} {45G50}                   Nameblk PAD1 myOutput
NProgram PAD_myInput col.B.long.3:PAD1.O          Intnet myOutput PAD myOutput
col.B.long.3:row.G.local.1                        Intnet myInput PAD myInput
col.B.long.3:row.M.local.5-s MB.                  System FGG 0 VERS 2 !
40.1.14 MB.40.1.35 row.M.local.5:PAD61.I2         System FGG 1 GD0 0 !
Editblk PAD61
Base IO
```

Postroute XNF file (`halfgate_b.xnf`)

```
LCANET, 4                                         END
PROG, LCA2XNF, 5.2.0, "COMMAND = -g -v            SYM, XSYM2, IBUF
halfgate_p halfgate_b  TIME = Tue Jul 16             PIN, O, O, _IN_myInput, 2.8
21:53:31 1996"                                      PIN, I, I, myInput
PART, 4003PC84-4                                   END
SYM, XSYM1, OBUF, SLOW                             EXT, myOutput, O, 10
   PIN, O, O, myOutput, 3.0                        EXT, myInput, I, 29
   PIN, I, I, _IN_myInput, 8.6, INV                EOF
```

5. At this point the script has run all of the Xilinx programs required to complete the place-and-route step. The Xilinx programs have created several files, the most important of which is `halfgate_p.lca`, which describes the FPGA layout. This postroute netlist is converted to `halfgate_b.nls` (the added suffix `'b'` stands for back-annotation). Next a timing simulation is performed on the postroute netlist, which now includes delays, to find the delay from the input (`myInput`) to the output (`myOutput`). This is the critical—and only—path. The simulation (not shown) reveals that the delay is 2.8 ns (for the input buffer) plus 11.6 ns (for the output buffer), for a total delay of 14.4 ns (this is for a XC4003 in a PC84 package, and default speed grade '4').

Table 8.6 shows the key Xilinx files that are created. The preroute file, `halfgate_p.xnf`, describes the IBUF and OBUF library cells but does not contain any delays. The LCA file, `halfgate_p.lca`, contains all the physical design information, including the locations of the pads and I/O cells on the FPGA (`PAD61` for `myInput` and `PAD1` for `myOutput`), as well as the details of the programmable connections between these I/O Cells. The postroute file, `halfgate_b.xnf`, is similar to the preroute version except that now the delays are included. Xilinx assigns delays to a pin (connector or terminal of a cell). In this case 2.8 ns is assigned to the output of the input buffer, 8.6 ns is assigned to the input of the output buffer, and finally 3.0 ns is assigned to the output of the output buffer.

8.3.2   Actel

The key Actel files for the halfgate design are the netlist file, `halfgate_io.adl`, and the STF delay file for back-annotation, `halfgate_io.stf`. Both of these files are shown in Table 8.7 (the STF file is large and only the last few lines, which contain the delay information, are shown in the table).

8.3.3   Altera

Because Altera complex PLDs use a deterministic routing structure, they can be designed more easily using a self-contained software package—an "all-in-one" software package using a single interface. We shall assume that we can generate a netlist that the Altera software can accept using Cadence, Mentor, or Compass software with an Altera design kit (the most convenient format is EDIF).

Table 8.8 shows the EDIF preroute netlist in a format that the Altera software can accept. This netlist file describes a single inverter (the line `'cellRef not'`). The majority of the EDIF code in Table 8.8 is a standard template to pass information about how the VDD and VSS nodes are named, which libraries are used, the name of the design, and so on. We shall cover EDIF in Chapter 9.

Table 8.9 shows a small part of the reports generated by the Altera software after completion of the place-and-route step. This report tells us how the software has used the basic logic cells, interconnect, and I/O cells to implement our design. With practice it is possible to read the information from reports such as Table 8.9

TABLE 8.7   The Actel files for the halfgate ASIC.

ADL file	STF file
; HEADER	; HEADER
; FILEID ADL ./halfgate_io.adl 85e8053b	; FILEID STF ./halfgate_io.stf c96ef4d8
; CHECKSUM 85e8053b	
; PROGRAM certify	... lines omitted ... (126 lines total)
; VERSION 23/1	
; ALSMAJORREV 2	DEF halfgate_io.
; ALSMINORREV 3	USE ; INBUF_2/U0;
; ALSPATCHREV .1	TPADH:'11:26:37',
; NODEID 72705192	TPADL:'13:30:41',
; VAR FAMILY 1400	TPADE:'12:29:41',
; ENDHEADER	TPADD:'20:48:70',
DEF halfgate_io; myInput, myOutput.	TYH:'8:20:27',
USE ADLIB:INBUF; INBUF_2.	TYL:'12:28:39'.
USE ADLIB:OUTBUF; OUTBUF_3.	PIN u2:A;
USE ADLIB:INV; u2.	RDEL:'13:31:42',
NET DEF_NET_8; u2:A, INBUF_2:Y.	FDEL:'11:26:37'.
NET DEF_NET_9; myInput, INBUF_2:PAD.	USE ; OUTBUF_3/U0;
NET DEF_NET_11; OUTBUF_3:D, u2:Y.	TPADH:'11:26:37',
NET DEF_NET_12; myOutput, OUTBUF_3:PAD.	TPADL:'13:30:41',
END.	TPADE:'12:29:41',
	TPADD:'20:48:70',
	TYH:'8:20:27',
	TYL:'12:28:39'.
	PIN OUTBUF_3/U0:D;
	RDEL:'14:32:45',
	FDEL:'11:26:37'.
	END.

directly, but it is a little easier if we also look at the netlist. The EDIF version of
postroute netlist for this example is large. Fortunately, the Altera software can also
generate a Verilog version of the postroute netlist. Here is the generated Verilog postroute netlist, halfgate_p.vo (not '.v'), for the halfgate design:

```
// halfgate_p (EPM7032LC44) MAX+plus II Version 5.1 RC6 10/03/94
// Wed Jul 17 04:07:10 1996
`timescale 100 ps / 100 ps
module TRI_halfgate_p( IN, OE, OUT ); input IN; input OE; output OUT;
bufif1 ( OUT, IN, OE );
  specify
    specparam TTRI = 40; specparam TTXZ = 60; specparam TTZX = 60;
    (IN => OUT) = (TTRI,TTRI);
```

TABLE 8.8   EDIF netlist in Altera format for the halfgate ASIC.

```
(edif halfgate_p
(edifVersion 2 0 0)
(edifLevel 0)
(keywordMap
 (keywordLevel 0))
(status
 (written
  (timeStamp 1996 7 10 23
55 8)
  (program "COMPASS Design
Automation -- EDIF Interface"
   (version "v9r1.2 last
updated 26-Mar-96"))
  (author "mikes")))
(library flex8kd
 (edifLevel 0)
 (technology
  (numberDefinition )
  (simulationInfo
   (logicValue  H)
   (logicValue  L)))
 (cell not
  (cellType GENERIC)
  (view COMPASS_mde_view
   (viewType NETLIST)
   (interface
    (port IN
```

```
     (direction INPUT))
    (port OUT
     (direction OUTPUT))
    (designator
"@@Label")))))
(library working
 (edifLevel 0)
 (technology
  (numberDefinition )
  (simulationInfo
   (logicValue  H)
   (logicValue  L)))
 (cell halfgate_p
  (cellType GENERIC)
  (view COMPASS_nls_view
   (viewType NETLIST)
   (interface
    (port myInput
     (direction INPUT))
    (port myOutput
     (direction OUTPUT))
    (designator "@@Label"))
   (contents
    (instance B1_i1
     (viewRef
COMPASS_mde_view
      (cellRef not
```

```
       (libraryRef
flex8kd))))
    (net myInput
     (joined
      (portRef myInput)
      (portRef IN
       (instanceRef
B1_i1))))
    (net myOutput
     (joined
      (portRef myOutput)
      (portRef OUT
       (instanceRef
B1_i1))))
    (net VDD
     (joined )
     (property global
      (string "vcc")))
    (net VSS
     (joined )
     (property global
      (string "gnd"))))))))
(design halfgate_p
 (cellRef halfgate_p
  (libraryRef working))))
```

```
        (OE => OUT) = (0,0, TTXZ, TTZX, TTXZ, TTZX);
      endspecify
    endmodule

    module halfgate_p (myInput, myOutput);
      input myInput; output myOutput; supply0 gnd; supply1 vcc;
      wire B1_i1, myInput, myOutput, N_8, N_10, N_11, N_12, N_14;
      TRI_halfgate_p tri_2 ( .OUT(myOutput), .IN(N_8), .OE(vcc) );
      TRANSPORT transport_3 ( N_8, N_8_A );
      defparam transport_3.DELAY = 10;
      and delay_3 ( N_8_A, B1_i1 );
      xor xor2_4 ( B1_i1, N_10, N_14 );
      or or1_5 ( N_10, N_11 );
      TRANSPORT transport_6 ( N_11, N_11_A );
```

TABLE 8.9   Report for the halfgate ASIC fitted to an Altera MAX 7000 complex PLD.

```
** INPUTS **
                              Shareable
                              Expanders     Fan-In      Fan-Out
   Pin    LC LAB  Primitive   Code  Total Shared n/a INP  FBK  OUT  FBK  Name
   43      -  -     INPUT            0      0    0   0    0    0    1  myInput
** OUTPUTS **
                              Shareable
                              Expanders     Fan-In      Fan-Out
   Pin    LC LAB  Primitive   Code  Total Shared n/a INP  FBK  OUT  FBK  Name
   41     17  B    OUTPUT      t     0      0    0   1    0    0    0  myOutput
** LOGIC CELL INTERCONNECTIONS **
Logic Array Block 'B':
        +- LC17 myOutput
        |
LC      |  | A B | Name

Pin
43   -> *  | - * | myInput


* = The logic cell or pin is an input to the logic cell (or LAB) through the PIA.
- = The logic cell or pin is not an input to the logic cell (or LAB).
```

```verilog
   defparam transport_6.DELAY = 60;
   and and1_6 ( N_11_A, N_12 );
   TRANSPORT transport_7 ( N_12, N_12_A );
   defparam transport_7.DELAY = 40;
   not not_7 ( N_12_A, myInput );
   TRANSPORT transport_8 ( N_14, N_14_A );
   defparam transport_8.DELAY = 60;
   and and1_8 ( N_14_A, gnd );
endmodule
```

The Verilog model for our ASIC, halfgate_p, is written in terms of other models: and, xor, or, not, TRI_halfgate_p, TRANSPORT. The first four of these are **primitive models** for basic logic cells and are built into the Verilog simulator. The model for TRI_halfgate_p is generated together with the rest of the code. We also need the following model for TRANSPORT, which contains the delay information for the Altera MAX complex PLD. This code is part of a file (alt_max2.vo) that is generated automatically.

```verilog
// MAX+plus II Version 5.1 RC6 10/03/94 Wed Jul 17 04:07:10 1996
`timescale 100 ps / 100 ps
module TRANSPORT( OUT, IN ); input IN; output OUT; reg OUTR;
```

```verilog
wire OUT = OUTR; parameter DELAY = 0;
`ifdef ZeroDelaySim
   always @IN OUTR <= IN;
`else
   always @IN OUTR <= #DELAY IN;
`endif
`ifdef Silos
   initial #0 OUTR = IN;
`endif
endmodule
```

The Altera software can also write the following VHDL postroute netlist:

```vhdl
-- halfgate_p (EPM7032LC44) MAX+plus II Version 5.1 RC6 10/03/94
-- Wed Jul 17 04:07:10 1996
LIBRARY IEEE; USE IEEE.std_logic_1164.all;
ENTITY n_tri_halfgate_p IS
GENERIC (ttri: TIME := 1 ns; ttxz: TIME := 1 ns; ttzx: TIME := 1 ns);
PORT (in0 : IN X01Z; oe  : IN X01Z; out0: OUT X01Z);
END n_tri_halfgate_p;

ARCHITECTURE behavior OF n_tri_halfgate_p IS
BEGIN
PROCESS (in0, oe) BEGIN
   IF oe'EVENT THEN
      IF oe = '0' THEN out0 <= TRANSPORT 'Z' AFTER ttxz;
      ELSIF oe = '1' THEN out0 <= TRANSPORT in0 AFTER ttzx;
      END IF;
   ELSIF oe = '1' THEN out0 <= TRANSPORT in0 AFTER ttri;
   END IF;
END PROCESS;
END behavior;

LIBRARY IEEE; USE IEEE.std_logic_1164.all; USE work.n_tri_halfgate_p;
ENTITY n_halfgate_p IS
   PORT ( myInput : IN X01Z; myOutput : OUT X01Z);
END n_halfgate_p;

ARCHITECTURE EPM7032LC44 OF n_halfgate_p IS
SIGNAL gnd : X01Z := '0'; SIGNAL vcc : X01Z := '1';
SIGNAL n_8, B1_i1, n_10, n_11, n_12, n_14 : X01Z;
COMPONENT n_tri_halfgate_p
   GENERIC (ttri, ttxz, ttzx: TIME);
   PORT (in0, oe  : IN X01Z; out0 : OUT X01Z);
END COMPONENT;
BEGIN
PROCESS(myInput) BEGIN ASSERT myInput /= 'X' OR Now = 0 ns
   REPORT "Unknown value on myInput" SEVERITY Warning;
END PROCESS;
n_tri_2: n_tri_halfgate_p
```

```
   GENERIC MAP (ttri => 4 ns, ttxz => 6 ns, ttzx => 6 ns)
   PORT MAP (in0 => n_8, oe => vcc, out0 => myOutput);
n_delay_3: n_8 <= TRANSPORT B1_i1 AFTER 1 ns;
n_xor_4: B1_i1 <= n_10 XOR n_14;
n_or_5: n_10 <= n_11;
n_and_6: n_11 <= TRANSPORT n_12 AFTER 6 ns;
n_not_7: n_12 <= TRANSPORT NOT myInput AFTER 4 ns;
n_and_8: n_14 <= TRANSPORT gnd AFTER 6 ns;
END EPM7032LC44;

LIBRARY IEEE; USE IEEE.std_logic_1164.all; USE work.n_halfgate_p;
ENTITY halfgate_p IS
   PORT ( myInput : IN std_logic; myOutput : OUT std_logic);
END halfgate_p;
ARCHITECTURE EPM7032LC44 OF halfgate_p IS
COMPONENT n_halfgate_p PORT (myInput : IN X01Z; myOutput : OUT X01Z);
END COMPONENT;
BEGIN
   n_0: n_halfgate_p
   PORT MAP ( myInput => TO_X01Z(myInput), myOutput => myOutput);
END EPM7032LC44;
```

The VHDL is a little harder to decipher than the Verilog, so the schematic for the VHDL postroute netlist is shown in Figure 8.2. This VHDL netlist is identical in function to the Verilog netlist, but the net names and component names are different. Compare Figure 8.2 with Figure 5.15(c) in Section 5.4, "Altera MAX," which shows the Altera basic logic cell and Figure 6.23 in Section 6.8, "Other I/O Cells," which describes the Altera I/O cell. The software has fixed the inputs to the various elements in the Altera MAX device to implement a single inverter.

8.3.4   Comparison

The halfgate ASIC design illustrates the differences between a nondeterministic coarse-grained FPGA (Xilinx XC4000), a nondeterministic fine-grained FPGA (Actel ACT 3), and a deterministic complex PLD (Altera MAX 7000). These differences, summarized as follows, were apparent even in the halfgate design:

1. The Xilinx LCA architecture does not permit an accurate timing analysis until after place and route. This is because of the coarse-grained nondeterministic architecture.

2. The Actel ACT architecture is nondeterministic, but the fine-grained structure allows fairly accurate preroute timing prediction.

3. The Altera MAX complex PLD requires logic to be fitted to the product steering and programmable array logic. The Altera MAX 7000 has an almost deterministic architecture, which allows accurate preroute timing.

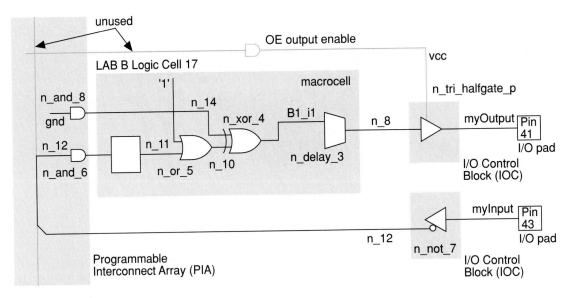

FIGURE 8.2 The VHDL version of the postroute Altera MAX 7000 schematic for the half-gate ASIC. Compare this with Figure 5.15(c) and Figure 6.23.

8.4   Summary

The important concepts covered in this chapter are:

- FPGA design flow: design entry, simulation, physical design, and programming
- Schematic entry, hardware design languages, logic synthesis
- PALASM as a common low-level hardware description
- EDIF, Verilog, and VHDL as vendor-independent netlist standards

8.5   Problems

* = Difficult, ** = Very difficult, *** = Extremely difficult

8.1 (Files, 60 min.) Create a version of Table 8.1 for your design system.

8.2 (Scripts, 60 min.) Create a version of Table 8.5 for your design system.

8.3 (Halfgate, 60 min.)

a. Using an FPGA of your choice, estimate the preroute delay of a single inverter (including I/O delays).

b. Complete a halfgate design and explain the postroute delays (make sure you know what conditions are being used—worst-case commercial, for example).

8.4 (***Xilinx die analysis, 120 min.) The data in Table 8.10 shows some information derived from a die photo of an ATT3020 (equivalent to a Xilinx 3020) in the AT&T data book. The die photo shows the CLBs clearly enough that we can measure their size. Then, knowing the actual die size, we can calculate the CLB size and other parameters. From your knowledge of the contents of the XC3020 CLB, as well as the programming and interconnect structures, make an estimate (showing all of your approximations and explaining all of your assumptions) of the CLB area and compare this to the value of 277 mils^2 shown in Table 8.10. You will need to calculate the number of logic gates in each CLB including the LUT resources. Estimate how many pass transistors and memory elements are required as well as calculate how much routing resources are assigned to each CLB. *Hint:* You may need to use the Xilinx software, look at the Xilinx data books, or even the AT&T (Lucent) Orca documentation.

TABLE 8.10   ATT3020 die information (Problem 8.4).

Parameter	Specified in data book	Measured on die photo	Calculated from die photo
3020 die width	183.5 mil	4.1 cm	—
3020 die height	219.3 mil	4.9 cm	—
3000 CLB width	—	0.325 cm	14.55 mil = 370 µm
3000 CLB height	—	0.425 cm	19.02 mil = 483 µm
3000 CLB area	—	—	277 mils^2
3020 pad pitch	—	1.61 mm/pad	7.21 mil/pad

Source: AT&T Data Book, July 1992, p. 3-76, MN92-024FPGA.

8.5 (***FPGA process, 120 min.) Table 8.11 describes AT&T's 0.9 µm twin-tub V CMOS process, with 0.75 µm minimum design rules and 0.6 µm effective channel length and silicided (TiS$_2$) poly, source, and drain. This is the process used by AT&T to second-source the Xilinx XC3000 family of FPGAs. Calculate the parasitic resistance and capacitance parameters for the interconnect.

8.6 (Xilinx die costs, 10 min.) Table 8.12 shows the AT&T ATT3000 series die information. Assume a 6-inch wafer that costs $2000 to fabricate and has a 90 percent yield. **(a)** What are the die costs? **(b)** Compare these figures to the costs of XC3020 parts in 1992 and comment.

TABLE 8.11   ATT3000 0.9 μm twin-tub V CMOS process (Problem 8.5).

Parameter	Value
Die thickness, t_{die}	21 mil
Wafer diameter, W_D	5 inch
Wafer thickness, W_t	25 mil
Minimum feature size, 2λ	0.75 μm
Effective gate length, L_{eff} (*n*-channel and *p*-channel)	0.6 μm
First-level metal, m1	Ti/AlCuSi
Second-level metal, m2	AlCuSi
m1 width	0.9 μm
m2 width	1.2 μm
m1 thickness	0.5 μm
m2 thickness	1.0 μm
m1 spacing	1.0 μm
m2 spacing	1.3 μm
D1 dielectric thickness, boron/phosphorus doped glass	3500 Å
D2 dielectric thickness, undoped glass	9000 Å
Minimum contact size	1.0 μm
Minimum via size	1.2 μm
Isolation oxide, FOX	3500 Å
Gate oxide	150 Å

Source: AT&T Data Book, July 1992, p. 2-37 and p. 3-76, MN92-024FPGA.

TABLE 8.12   ATT3000 die information (Problem 8.6).

Die	Die height /mils	Die width /mils	Die area /mils^2	Die area /cm^2	CLBs	Die perimeter /mils	I/O pads
3020	219.3	183.5	40,242	0.26	8×8	806	74
3030	259.8	215.0	55,857	0.36	10×10	950	98
3042	295.3	242.5	71,610	0.46	12×12	1076	118
3064	270.9	366.5	99,285	0.64	16×14	1275	142
3090	437.0	299.2	130,750	0.84	16×20	1472	166

Source: AT&T Data Book, July 1992, p. 3-75, MN92-024FPGA. 1 mil^2 = $2.54^2 \times 10^{-6}$ cm^2 = 6.452×10^{-6} cm^2.

8.7 (Pad density) Table 8.12 shows the number of pads on each of the AT&T 3000 (equivalent to the Xilinx XC3000) die. Calculate the pad densities in mil/pad for each part and compare with the figure for the ATT3020 in Table 8.10.

8.8 (Xilinx HardWire, 10 min.) Xilinx manufactures nonprogrammable versions of its LCA family of FPGAs. These **HardWire** chips are useful when a customer wishes to convert to high-volume production. The Xilinx 1996 Product overview (p. 16) shows two die photographs: one, an XC3090 (with the four quadrants of 8×10 CLB matrices visible), which is $32\,\text{mm} \times 47\,\text{mm}$; the other shows the HardWire version ($24\,\text{mm} \times 29\,\text{mm}$). Estimate the die size of the HardWire version from the data in Table 8.12 and estimate the percentage of a Xilinx LCA that is taken up by SRAM.

Answer: $60{,}500\,\text{mils}^2$; 50 %.

8.9 (Xilinx XDE, 10 min.) During his yearly appraisal Dewey explains to you how he improved three Xilinx designs last year and managed to use 100 percent of the CLBs on these LCA chips by means of the XDE manual place-and-route program. As Dewey's boss, rank Dewey from 1 (bad) to 5 (outstanding) and explain your ranking in a space that has room for no more than 20 words.

8.10 (Clocks, 60 min) (From a discussion on an Internet newsgroup including comments from Peter Alfke of Xilinx) "Xilinx guarantees that the minimum value for any delay parameter is always more than 25 % of the maximum value for that same parameter, as published for the fastest speed grade offered at any time. Many parameters have been reduced significantly over the years, but the clock delay has not. For example, comparing the fastest available XC3020-70 in 1988 with the fastest available XC3020A-6 (1996):

- logic delay (t_{ILO}) decreased from 9 ns to 4.1 ns
- output-to-pad delay decreased from 10 ns to 5 ns
- internal-clock-to-output pad delay decreased from 13 ns to 7 ns

The internal speed has more than doubled, but the worst-case clock distribution delay specification has only changed from 6.0 ns (1988) to 5.7 ns (1996)."

Comment on the reasons for these changes and their repercussions.

8.11 (State-machine design)

a. (10 min.) Draw the state diagram for the LOG/iC code in Table 8.2.

b. (10 min.) Show, using an example input sequence, that the detector works.

c. (10 min.) Show that the state equations and the encoding for the PALASM code in Table 8.2 correctly describe the sequence detector state machine.

d. (30 min.) Convert this design to a different format of your choice: schematic, low-level design language, or HDL.

e. (30 min.) Simulate and test your design.

8.12 (FPGA software, 60 min.) Write a minitutorial (less than 2 pages) on using your FPGA design system. An example set of instructions for the Altera MAX PLUS II software on a Unix system are shown below:

Setup:

1. Copy `~altera/M+2/maxplus2.ini` into `~you/yourDirectory` (call this the working directory).

2. Edit `maxplus2.ini` and point the `DESIGN_NAME` to your design

3. Copy `~altera/M+2/compass.lmf` and `~altera/M+2/compass.edc` into your working directory.

4. Copy `~altera/M+2/foo.acf` into your working directory and rename it `mydesign.acf` if your design name is `mydesign.edf`.

5. Set the environment as follows:

```
setenv LM_LICENSE_FILE ~altera/maxplus2/adm/license.altera
set path=($path ~altera/maxplus5.1/bin)
```

and run the programs in batch mode: `maxplus2 -c mydesign.edf`. Add to this information on any peculiarities of the system you are using (handling of overwriting of files, filename extensions and when they are created, arguments required to run the programs, and so on).

8.13 (Help, 20 min.) Print the "help" for the key programs in your FPGA system and form it into a condensed "cheat-sheet." Most programs echo help instruction when called with a `'-help'` or `'?'` argument (this ought to be a standard). For example, in the Actel system the key programs are `edn2adl`, `adl2edn`, and `als` (in newer versions `adl2edn` is now an option to `als`). *Hint:* Actel does not use `'-help'` argument, but you can get instructions on the syntax for each option individually. Table 8.13 shows an example for the Xilinx `xdelay` program.

8.6 Bibliography

There are few books on FPGA design software. Skahill's book [1996] covers PLD and FPGA design with Cypress FPGAs and the Cypress Warp design system. Connor has written two articles in EDN describing a complete FPGA design project [1992]. Most of the information on design software is available from the software companies themselves—increasingly in online form. There is still some material that is only available through the BBS or from a **file-transfer protocol (ftp)** site. There is also a great deal of valuable material available in data books printed between 1990 and 1995, prior to the explosion of the use of the Internet in the late-1990s. I have included pointers to these sources in the following sections.

TABLE 8.13 Xilinx xdelay **arguments.**

```
usage: xdelay [<options>] [<lcafile> ..]
where <options> are:
  -help                    Print this help.
  -timespec                Do timespec based delay analysis.
  -s                       Write short xdelay report.
  -x                       Write long xdelay report.
  -t <template file>       Read <template file>.
  -r                       Use two letter style block names in output.
  -o <file>                Send output to file.
  -w                       Write design file, after retiming net delays.
  -u <speed>               Use the <speed> speed grade.
  -d                       Don't trace delay paths.
  -convert <input .lca file> <new part type> <output .lca file>
                              Convert the input design to a new part type.
Specify no arguments to run xdelay in interactive mode.

        To Select Report          Specify Option
        ------------------------   --------------------------
        TimeSpec summary           -timespec
        Short path details         -s
        Long path details          -x
        Analyze summary            none of -s, -x or -timespec

A template file can be specified with the -t option to further filter the selected
report. Only those template commands relevant to the selected report will be used.

Using -w and -d options together will insert delay information into the design file(s),
without tracing any paths.

The -convert option may not be used with any other options.
```

8.6.1 FPGA Vendors

Actel (http://www.actel.com) has a Frequently Asked Questions (FAQ) guide
that is an indication of the most common problems with FPGA design:

- Software versions, installation, and security, and not having enough computer memory

- X11, Motif, and OpenWindows—problems with paths and fonts. Compatibility problems with Windows 95 and NT

- Including I/O pads in a design using schematic entry and logic synthesis—problems with the commands and the exact syntax to use

- Using third-party software for schematic entry or logic synthesis and libraries—problems with versions and paths
- EDIF netlist issues

It seems most of these problems never go away—they just keep resurfacing. If you design a halfgate ASIC, an inverter, start-to-finish, as soon as you get a new set of software, this will alert you to most of the problems you are likely to encounter.

The May 1989 Actel data book contains details of the early antifuse experiments. The Actel April 1990 data book has a chip photo of the Actel 1010 on the cover (from which some useful information may be derived). Reliability reports and article reprints are now included in the data books (see, for example, [Actel, 1996]). There is PowerPoint presentation on FPGAs (`architec.exe`) and the Actel FPGA architecture at its Web site.

The Xilinx data book (see, for example, [Xilinx, 1996]) contains several hundred pages of information on LCA parts. Xilinx produced a separate *User Guide and Tutorials* book that contains over 600 pages of application notes, guides, and tutorials on designing with FPGAs and Xilinx FPGAs in particular. XCELL is the quarterly *Xilinx Newsletter*, first published in 1988. It is available online and contains useful tips and pointers to new application notes. There is an extensive set of Xilinx Application Notes at `http://www.xilinx.com/apps`. A 250-page guide to using the Synopsys software (`hdl_dg.pdf`) covers many of the problems users experience in using any logic synthesizer for FPGA design.

Xilinx provides design kits for its EPLD FPGAs for third-party software such as the Viewlogic design entry and simulation programs. The interconnect architecture in the Xilinx EPLD FPGA is deterministic and so postlayout timing results are close to prelayout estimates.

AMD, before it sold its stake in Xilinx, published the 1989/1990 Programmable Data Array Book, which was distinct from the Xilinx data book. The AMD data book contains useful information and code for programs to download configuration files to Xilinx FPGAs from a PC that are still useful.

Altera publishes a series of loose-leaf application notes on a variety of topics, some of them are in the data book (see, for example [Altera, 1996]), but some are not. Most of these application notes are available as the AN series of documents at `http://www.altera.com/html/literature`. This includes guides on using Cadence, Mentor, Viewlogic, and Synopsys software. The 100-page Synopsys guide (`as_sig.pdf`) explains many of the limitations of logic synthesizers for FPGA design and includes the complete VHDL source code for a voice-mail machine as an example.

Atmel has a series of data sheets and application notes for its PLD logic at `http://www.atmel.com`. Some of the data sheets (for the ATV2500, for example, available as `doc156.pdf`) also include examples of the use of CUPL and ABEL. An application note in Atmel's data book (available as `doc168.pdf`) includes the ABEL source code for a video frame grabber and a description of the NTSC video format. Atmel offers a review of its links to third-party software in a section "PLD Software

Tools Overview" in its data book (available online as `doc150.pdf` at `http:www.atmel.com/atmel/products`). Atmel uses an IBM-compatible PC-based system based on the Viewlogic software. Schematic entry uses Viewdraw and simulation uses Viewsim. Atmel provides a separate program, a **fitter**, to optimize a schematic for its FPGA architecture. The output from this software generates an optimized schematic. The place-and-route software then works with this new schematic. Atmel provides an interactive editor similar to the Xilinx design editor that allows the designer to perform placement manually. Atmel also supports PLD design software such as Synario from Data I/O.

The QuickLogic design kit uses the ECS (Engineering Capture System) developed by the CAD/CAM Group and now part of DATA I/O. Simulation uses X-SIM, a product of Silicon Automation Systems.

Cypress has a low-cost design system (for QuickLogic and its own series of complex PLDs) called Warp that uses VHDL for design entry.

8.6.2 Third-Party Software

There is a bewildering array of software and software companies that make, sell, and develop products for PLD and FPGA design. These are referred to as **third-party vendors**. In the remainder of this section we shall describe (in alphabetical order) some of the available third-party software. This list changes frequently and for more information you might search the EE sites from the Bibliography in Chapter 1.

Accel (`http://www.edac.org/EDAC/Companies`) produces Tango and P-CAD (which used to belong to Personal CAD Systems) that are a low-cost and popular schematic-entry and PCB layout software for PCs. Currently there are no FPGA vendors that support P-CAD or Tango directly. The missing ingredient is a set of libraries with the appropriate schematic symbols for the logic macros and cells used by the FPGA vendor.

AMD (`http://www.amd.com`) produces the Mach series of PLDs and is also the owner of PALASM. All of the FPGA vendors use the PALASM and PALASM2 languages as interchange formats. Using PALASM is an easy way to incorporate a PLD into an FPGA.

Antares (`http://www.anteresco.com`) is a spin-off from Mentor Corporation formed from Exemplar Logic, a company specializing in synthesis software for PLDs and FPGAs, and Model Technology, who produce a VHDL and Verilog simulator using a common kernel.

Cadence (`http://www.cadence.com`) is one of the largest EDA companies. They offer design kits for PLD and FPGA design with its schematic-entry (Composer) and logic-synthesis (Concept) software. The Cadence Web site has some pictures of ASIC and FPGA design flow in its third-party support area. To find these, search for "FPGA" from the main menu.

Compass Design Automation (http://www.compass-da.com) is a spin-off from VLSI Technology that specializes in ASIC design software and cell libraries. As part of its system design software, this vendor includes compilers and libraries for Xilinx, Actel, and Altera FPGAs.

Data I/O (http://www.data-io.com) makes the FutureNet DASH schematic-entry program primarily for IBM-compatible PCs. Version 5 also has an EDIF 2 0 0 netlist writer, and an optional program PLDlinx to convert designs to ABEL. Data I/O's ABEL is a very widely used PLD design standard. Most FPGA software allows the merging of ABEL files with netlists from schematic-entry programs. Usually you have to translate ABEL to PALASM first and then merge the PALASM file with any netlists that you created from schematics. ABEL is available on SUN workstations, IBM-compatible PC-DOS, and Macintosh platforms. The Macintosh version is available through Capilano Computing, using its DesignWorks program. Data I/O has extended its ABEL language for use with FPGA design. ABEL-FPGA is a set of software that can accept hardware descriptions in ABEL-HDL. ABEL-HDL is an extension of the ABEL language which is optimized for programmable logic. One of the features of ABEL-HDL is a set of naming extensions, **dot extensions**, which allow the designer to specify how certain signals will be mapped into an FPGA.

Data I/O also makes a number of programmers. For example, the Unisite PROM programmer can be used to program Actel, Altera MAX, and Xilinx EPLD devices.

Data I/O has recently launched a separate division called Synario Design Automation (http://www.synario.com) that has taken over ABEL and produces a new series of PLD and FPGA design software under the Synario banner.

Exemplar, now part of Antares, writes many of the software modules for logic synthesis used by other companies in their FPGA synthesis software. Exemplar provides a software package that allows you to enter hardware descriptions in ABEL, PALASM, CUPL, or Minc formats.

ISDATA produces a system called LOG/iC that can be used for FPGA design. LOG/iC produces **JEDEC fusemap** files, which can be converted and merged with netlists created with other vendors' software. An evaluation diskette contains LOG/iC software that programs the Lattice GAL16V8. ISDATA also makes a program called STATE/view for design using state diagrams and flow charts and works with LOG/iC and ABEL. HINT is a program that accepts a subset of VHDL and compiles to the LOG/iC language.

Logical Devices (http://www.logicaldevices.com) acquired **CUPL**, a widely used programming language for PLDs, from Personal CAD Systems in 1987. Most FPGA vendors allow you to use files in CUPL format indirectly. Usually you translate to the PALASM format first in order to incorporate any logic you design with CUPL. Logical Devices also sells EPROM programming hardware. They manufacture programmers for FPGAs.

Mentor Graphics Corporation (http://www.mentorg.com) is a large EDA company. Mentor produces schematic-entry and logic-synthesis software, IDEA Station and FPGA Station, that interface to the major FPGA vendors (see also Antares).

Minc's PLDesigner software allows the entry of PLD designs using a mixture of truth tables, waveforms, Minc's Design Synthesis Language (DSL), schematic entry, or a netlist (in EDIF format). Another Minc program PGADesigner includes the ability to target FPGAs as well as PLDs. This program is compatible with the OrCAD, P-CAD, and FutureNet DASH schematic-entry programs.

OrCAD (http://www.orcad.com) is a popular low-cost PC schematic-entry program supported directly by a number of FPGA vendors.

Simucad (http://www.simucad.com) produces PC-SILOS, a low-cost logic-simulation program for PCs machines. Xilinx used to bundle Simucad with FutureNet DASH in its least expensive, entry-level design kit.

Synopsys (http://www.synopsys.com) sells logic-synthesis software. There are two main products: the Design Compiler for ASIC design and the FPGA Compiler for FPGA design. FPGA Express is a PC-based FPGA logic synthesizer. There is an extensive on-line help system available for Synopsys customers.

Tanner Research (http://www.tanner.com) offers a variety of ASIC design software and a "burning service"; you send them the download files to program the FPGAs and Tanner Research programs the parts and ships them to you. Tanner Research also offers an Actel schematic library for its schematic-entry program S-Edit.

Texas Instruments (TI) and Minc produces mapping software between TI's gate arrays and FPGAs (TI's relationship with Actel is somewhere between a second-source and a partner). Mapping software allows designers to design for a TI gate array, for example, but prototype in FPGAs. Alternatively you could take an existing FPGA design and map it into a TI gate array. This type of design flow is popular with vendors such as AT&T (Lucent), TI, and Motorola who would like you to prototype with their FPGAs before transferring any high-volume products to their ASICs.

Viewlogic (http://www.viewlogic.com) produces the Workview and PRODesigner systems that are sets of ASIC design programs available on a variety of platforms. The Workview software consists of a schematic-entry program Viewdraw; two simulators: Viewsim and Viewfault; a synthesis tool, Viewgen; Viewplace for layout interface; Viewtrace for simulation analysis; and Viewwave for graphical display. There is also a package, Viewbase, that is a set of software routines enabling programmers to access Viewlogic's database in order to create EDIF, VHDL, and CFI (CAD Framework Initiative) interfaces. Most of the FPGA vendors have a means to incorporate Viewlogic's schematic netlists using Viewlogic's WIR netlist format. Viewlogic provides a number of applications notes (TECHniques) and includes a list of bug fixes, software limitations, and workarounds online.

8.7 References

Page numbers in brackets after a reference indicate its location in the chapter body.

Actel. 1996. *FPGA Data Book and Design Guide*. No catalog information. Available from Actel Corporation, 955 East Arques Avenue, Sunnyvale, CA 94086-4533, (408) 739-1010. Contains design guides and applications notes, including: Estimating Capacity and Performance for ACT 2 FPGA Designs (describes circuits to connect FPGAs to PALs); Binning Circuit of Actel FPGAs (describes circuits and data for performance measurement); Global Clock Networks (describes clock distribution schemes); Fast On and Off Chip Delays with ACT 2 I/O Latches (describes techniques to improve I/O performance); Board Level Considerations for Actel FPGAs (describes ground bounce and SSO problems); A Power-On Reset (POR) Circuit for Actel Devices (describes problems caused by slowly rising supply voltage); Implementing Load (*sic*) Latency Fast Counters with ACT 2 FPGAs; Oscillators for Actel FPGAs (describes crystal and RC oscillators); Designing a DRAM Controller Using Language-Based Synthesis (a detailed Verilog description of a 4 MB DRAM controller including refresh). See also the Actel Web site. [p. 322]

Altera. 1996. *Data Book*. No catalog information. Available from Altera Corporation, 2610 Orchard Parkway, San Jose, CA 95134-2020, (408) 944-0952. Contains information on the FLEX 10k and 8000 complex PLDs; MAX 9000, 7000, and 5000 complex PLDs; FLASH-logic; and EPLDs. A limited number of application notes are also included. More information may be found at the Altera Web site. [p. 322]

Connor, D. 1992. "Taking the first steps." *EDN*, April 9, p. 98. ISSN 0012-7515. The second part of this article, "Migrating to FPGAs: Any designer can do it," was published in *EDN*, April 23, 1992, p. 120. See also http://www.ednmag.com. Both articles are reprinted in the 1994 Actel Data Book. A description of designing, simulating, and testing a voicemail system using Viewlogic software. [p. 320]

Skahill, K. 1996. *VHDL for Programmable Logic*. Menlo Park, CA: Addison-Wesley, 593 p. ISBN 0-201-89573-0. TK7885.7.S55. Covers VHDL design for PLDs using Cypress Warp design system. [p. 320]

Xilinx. 1996. *The Programmable Logic Data Book*. No catalog information. Available from Xilinx Corporation, 2100 Logic Drive, San Jose, CA 95124-3400, (408) 559-7778. Contains details of XC9500, XC7300, and XC7200 CPLDs; XC5200, XC4000, XC3000 LCA FPGAs; and XC6200 sea-of-gates FPGAs. Earlier editions of this data book (the 1994 edition, for example) contained a section titled "Best of XCELL" that contained extremely useful design information. Much of this design material is now only available online, at the Xilinx Web site. [p. 322]

LOW-LEVEL DESIGN ENTRY

9

The purpose of **design entry** is to describe a microelectronic system to a set of **electronic-design automation (EDA)** tools. Electronic systems used to be, and many still are, constructed from off-the-shelf components, such as TTL ICs. Design entry for these systems now usually consists of drawing a picture, a **schematic**. The schematic shows how all the components are connected together, the **connectivity** of an ASIC. This type of design-entry process is called **schematic entry**, or **schematic capture**. A circuit schematic describes an ASIC in the same way an architect's plan describes a building.

The circuit schematic is a picture, an easy format for us to understand and use, but computers need to work with an ASCII or binary version of the schematic that we call a **netlist**. The output of a schematic-entry tool is thus a netlist file that contains a description of all the components in a design and their interconnections.

Not all the design information may be conveyed in a circuit schematic or netlist, because not all of the functions of an ASIC are described by the connectivity information. For example, suppose we use a programmable ASIC for some random logic functions. Part of the ASIC might be designed using a text language. In this case design entry also includes writing the code. What if an ASIC in our system contains a programmable memory (PROM)? Is the PROM microcode, the '1's and '0's, part of design entry? The operation of our system is certainly dependent on the correct programming of the PROM. So perhaps the PROM code ought to be considered part of design entry. On the other hand nobody would consider the operating-system code that is loaded into a RAM on an ASIC to be a part of design entry. Obviously, then, there are several different forms of design entry. In each case it is important to make sure that you have completely specified the system—not only so that it can be correctly constructed, but so that someone else can understand how the system is put together. Design entry is thus an important part of **documentation**.

Until recently most ASIC design entry used schematic entry. As ASICs have become more complex, other design-entry methods are becoming common. Alternative design-entry methods can use graphical methods, such as a schematic, or text files, such as a programming language. Using a **hardware description language** (**HDL**) for design entry allows us to generate netlists directly using **logic synthesis**. We will concentrate on **low-level design-entry** methods together with their advantages and disadvantages in this chapter.

9.1   Schematic Entry

Schematic entry is the most common method of design entry for ASICs and is likely to be useful in one form or another for some time. HDLs are replacing conventional gate-level schematic entry, but new graphical tools based on schematic entry are now being used to create large amounts of HDL code.

Circuit schematics are drawn on **schematic sheets**. Standard schematic sheet sizes (Table 9.1) are ANSI A–E (more common in the United States) and ISO A4–A0 (more common in Europe). Usually a **frame** or **border** is drawn around the schematic containing boxes that list the name and number of the schematic page, the designer, the date of the drawing, and a list of any modifications or changes.

TABLE 9.1   ANSI (American National Standards Institute) and ISO (International Standards Organization) schematic sheet sizes.

ANSI sheet	Size (inches)	ISO sheet	Size (cm)
A	8.5×11	A5	21.0×14.8
B	11×17	A4	29.7×21.0
C	17×22	A3	42.0×29.7
D	22×34	A2	59.4×42.0
E	34×44	A1	84.0×59.4
		A0	118.9×84.0

Figure 9.1 shows the "spades" and "shovels," the recognized symbols for AND, NAND, OR, and NOR gates. One of the problems with these recommendations is that the corner points of the shapes do not always lie on a grid point (using a reasonable grid size).

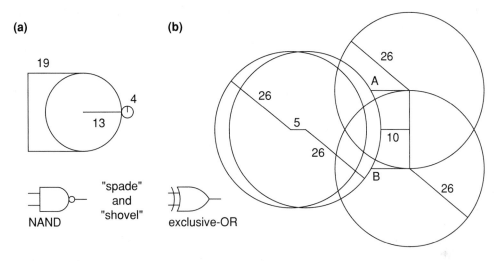

FIGURE 9.1   IEEE-recommended dimensions and their construction for logic-gate symbols. (a) NAND gate (b) exclusive-OR gate (an OR gate is a subset).

Figure 9.2 shows some pictorial definitions of objects you can use in a simple schematic. We shall discuss the different types of objects that might appear in an ASIC schematic first and then discuss the different types of connections.

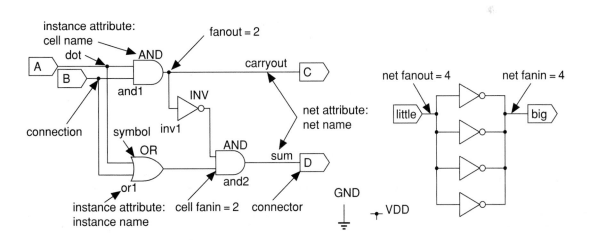

FIGURE 9.2   Terms used in circuit schematics.

Schematic-entry tools for ASIC design are similar to those for printed-circuit board (PCB) design. The basic object on a PCB schematic is a **component** or **device**—a TTL IC or resistor, for example. There may be several hundred components on a typical PCB. If we think of a logic gate on an ASIC as being equivalent to a component on a PCB, then a large ASIC contains hundreds of thousands of components. We can normally draw every component on a few schematic sheets for a PCB, but drawing every component on an ASIC schematic is impractical.

9.1.1   Hierarchical Design

Hierarchy reduces the size and complexity of a schematic. Suppose a building has 10 floors and contains several hundred offices but only three different basic office plans. Furthermore, suppose each of the floors above the ground floor that contains the lobby is identical. Then the plans for the whole building need only show detailed plans for the ground floor and one of the upper floors. The plans for the upper floor need only show the locations of each office and the office type. We can then use a separate set of three detailed plans for each of the different office types. All these different plans together form a nested structure that is a **hierarchical design**. The plan for the whole building is the top-level plan. The plans for the individual offices are the lowest level. To clarify the relationship between different levels of hierarchy we say that a **subschematic** (an office) is a **child** of the **parent** schematic (the floor containing offices). An electrical schematic can contain subschematics. The subschematic, in turn, may contain other subschematics. Figure 9.3 illustrates the principles of schematic hierarchical design.

The alternative to hierarchical design is to draw all of the ASIC components on one giant schematic, with no hierarchy, in a **flat design**. For a modern ASIC containing thousands or more logic gates using a flat design or a flat schematic would be hopelessly impractical. Sometimes we do use **flat netlists** though.

9.1.2   The Cell Library

Components in an ASIC schematic are chosen from a library of cells. Library elements for all types of ASICs are sometimes also known as **modules**. Unfortunately the term *module* will have a very specific meaning when we come to discuss hardware description languages. To avoid any chance of confusion I use the term *cell* to mean either a cell, a module, a macro, or a book from an ASIC library. Library cells are equivalent to the offices in our office building.

Most ASIC companies provide a **schematic library** of primitive gates to be used for schematic entry. The first problem with ASIC schematic libraries is that there are no naming conventions. For example, a primitive two-input NAND gate in a Xilinx FPGA library does not have the same name as the two-input NAND gate in an LSI Logic gate-array library. This means that you cannot take a schematic that you used to create a prototype product using a Xilinx FPGA and use that schematic to create an LSI Logic gate array for production (something you might very likely want to do). As soon as you start entering a schematic using a library from an ASIC

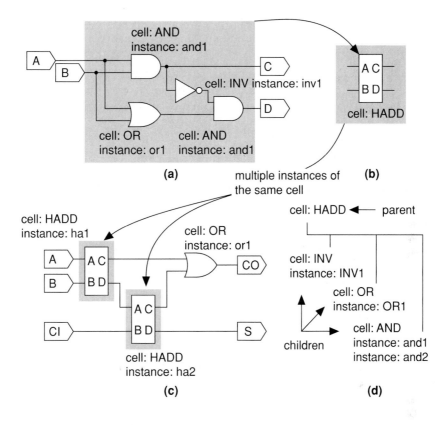

FIGURE 9.3 Schematic example showing hierarchical design. (a) The schematic of a half-adder, the subschematic of cell HADD. (b) A schematic symbol for the half adder. (c) A schematic that uses the half-adder cell. (d) The hierarchy of cell HADD.

vendor, you are, to some extent, making a commitment to use that vendor's ASIC. Most ASIC designers are much happier maintaining a large degree of vendor independence.

A second problem with ASIC schematic libraries is that there are no standards for cell behavior. For example, a two-input MUX in an Actel library operates so that the input labeled A is selected when the MUX select input S = '0'. A two-input MUX in a VLSI Technology library operates in the reverse fashion, so that the input labeled B is selected when S = '0'. These types of differences can cause hard-to-find problems when trying to convert a schematic from one vendor to another by hand. These problems make changing or **retargeting** schematics from one vendor to another difficult. This process is sometimes known as **porting** a design.

Library cells that represent basic logic gates, such as a NAND gate, are known as **primitive cells**, usually referred to just as *cells*. In a hierarchical ASIC design a cell may be a NAND gate, a flip-flop, a multiplier, or even a microprocessor, for example. To use the office building analogy again, each of the three basic office types is a primitive cell. However, the plan for the second floor is also a cell. The second-floor cell is a subschematic of the schematic for the whole building. Now we see why the commonly accepted use of the term *cell* in schematic entry can be so confusing. The term *cell* is used to represent both primitive cells and subschematics. These are two different, but closely related, things.

There are two types of macros for MGAs and programmable ASICs. The most common type of macro is a **hard macro** that includes placement information. A hard macro can change in position and orientation, but the relative location of the transistors, other layout, and wiring inside the macro is fixed. A **soft macro** contains only connection information (between transistors for a gate array or between logic cells for a programmable ASIC). Thus the placement and wiring for a soft macro can vary. This means that the timing parameters for a soft macro can only be determined after you complete the place-and-route step. For this reason the basic library elements for MGAs and programmable ASICs, such as NAND gates, flip-flops, and so on, are hard macros.

A standard cell contains layout information on all mask levels. An MGA hard macro contains layout information on just the metal, contact, and via layers. An MGA soft macro or programmable ASIC macro does not contain any layout information at all, just the details of connections to be made inside the macro.

We can stretch the office building analogy to explain the difference between hard and soft macros. A hard macro would be an office with fixed walls in which you are not allowed to move the furniture. A soft macro would be an office with partitions in which you can move the furniture around and you can also change the shape of your office by moving the partitions.

9.1.3 Names

Each of the cells, primitive or not, that you place on an ASIC schematic has a **cell name**. Each use of a cell is a different **instance** of that cell, and we give each instance a unique **instance name**. A cell instance is somewhere between a copy and a reference to a cell in a library. An analogy would be the pictures of hamburgers on the wall in a fast-food restaurant. The pictures are somewhere between a copy and a reference to a real hamburger.

We represent each cell instance by a picture or **icon**, also known as a **symbol**. We can represent primitive cells, such as NAND and NOR gates, with familiar icons that look like spades and shovels. Some schematic editors offer the option of switching between these familiar icons and using the rectangular IEEE standard symbols for logic gates. Unfortunately the term *icon* is also often used to refer to any of the pictures on a schematic, including those that represent subschematics. There is no accepted way to differentiate between an icon that represents a primitive cell and one that represents a subschematic that may be in turn a collection of primitive cells. In fact, there is usually no easy way to tell by looking at a schematic which icons represent primitive cells and which represent subschematics.

We will have three different icons for each of the three different primitive offices in the imaginary office building example of Section 9.1.1. We also will have icons to represent the ground floor and the plan for the other floors. We shall call the common plan for the second through tenth floors, `Floor`. Then we say that the second floor is an instance of the cell name `Floor`. The third through tenth floors are also instances of the cell name `Floor`. The same icon will be used to represent the second through tenth floors, but each will have a unique instance name. We shall give them instance names: `FloorTwo`, `FloorThree`, ..., `FloorTen`. We say that `FloorTwo` through `FloorTen` are unique instance names of the cell name `Floor`.

At the risk of further confusion I should point out that, strictly speaking, the definition of a primitive cell depends on the type of library being used. Schematic-entry libraries for the ASIC designer stop at the level of NAND gates and other similar low-level logic gates. Then, as far as the ASIC designer is concerned, the primitive cells are these logic gates. However, from the view of the library designer there is another level of hierarchy below the level of logic gates. The library designer needs to work with libraries that contain schematics of the gates themselves, and so at this level the primitive cells are transistors.

Let us look at the building analogy again to understand the subtleties of primitive cells. A building contractor need only concern himself with the plans for our office building down to the level of the offices. To the building contractor the primitive cells are the offices. Suppose that the first of the three different office types is a corner office, the second office type has a window, and a third office type is without a window. We shall call these office cells: `CornerOffice`, `WindowOffice`, and `NoWindowOffice`. These cells are primitive cells as far as the contractor is concerned. However, when discussing the plans with a client, the architect of our building will also need to see how each offices is furnished. The architect needs to see a level of detail of each office that is more complicated than needed by the building contractor. The architect needs to see the cells that represent the tables, chairs, and desks that make up each type of office. To the architect the primitive cells are a library containing cells such as `chair`, `table`, and `desk`.

9.1.4 Schematic Icons and Symbols

Most schematic-entry programs allow the designer to draw special or custom icons. In addition, the schematic-entry tool will also usually create an icon automatically for a subschematic that is used in a higher-level schematic. This is a **derived icon**, or **derived symbol**. The external connections of the subschematic are automatically attached to the icon, usually a rectangle.

Figure 9.4(c) shows what a derived icon for a cell, `DLAT`, might look like (we could also have drawn this by hand). The subschematic for `DLAT` is shown in Figure 9.4(b). We say that the inverter with the instance name `inv1` in the subschematic is a **subcell** (or submodule) of the cell DLAT. Alternatively we say that cell instance inv1 is a child of the cell DLAT, and cell DLAT is a parent of cell instance inv1.

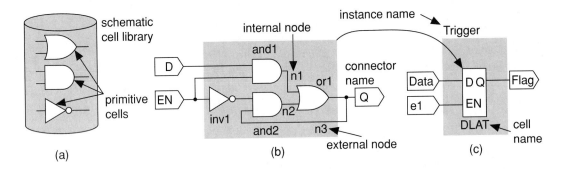

FIGURE 9.4 A cell and its subschematic. (a) A schematic library containing icons for the primitive cells. (b) A subschematic for a cell, DLAT, showing the instance names for the primitive cells. (c) A symbol for cell DLAT.

Figure 9.5(a) shows a more complex subschematic for a 4-bit latch. Each primitive cell instance in this schematic must have a unique name. This can get very tiresome for large circuits. Instead of creating complex, but repetitive, subschematics for complex cells we can use hierarchy.

Figure 9.5(b) shows a hierarchical subschematic for a cell FourBit, which in turn uses four instances of the cell DLAT. The four instances of DLAT in Figure 9.5(b) have different instance names: L1, L2, L3, and L4. Notice that we cannot use just one name for the four instances of DLAT to indicate that they are all the same cell. If we did, we could not differentiate between L1 and L2, for example.

The vertical row of instances in Figure 9.5(b) looks like a vector of elements. Figure 9.5(c) shows a **vectored instance** representing four copies of the DLAT cell. We say the **cardinality** of this instance is 4. Tools normally use bold lines or some other distinguishing feature to represent a vectored instance. The cardinality information is often shown as a vector. Thus L[1:4] represents four instances: L[1], L[2], L[3], L[4]. This is convenient because now we can see that all subcells are identical copies of L, but we have a unique name for each.

Finally, as shown in Figure 9.5(d) we can create a new symbol for the 4-bit latch, FourBit. The symbol for FourBit has a 4-bit-wide input bus for the four D inputs, and a 4-bit wide output bus for the four Q outputs. The subschematic for FourBit could be either Figure 9.5(a), (b), or (c) (though the exact naming of the inputs and outputs and their attachment to the buses may be different in each case).

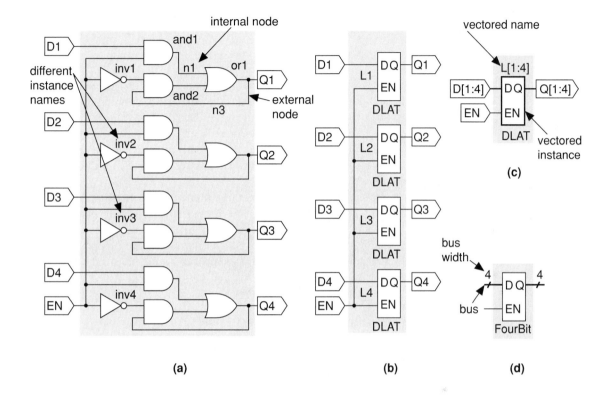

FIGURE 9.5 A 4-bit latch: (a) drawn as a flat schematic from gate-level primitives, (b) drawn as four instances of the cell symbol DLAT, (c) drawn using a vectored instance of the DLAT cell symbol with cardinality of 4, (d) drawn using a new cell symbol with cell name FourBit.

We need a convention to distinguish, for example, between the inverter subcells, inv1, which are children of the cell DLAT, which are in turn children of the cell FourBit. Most schematic-entry tools do this by combining the instance names of the subcells in a hierarchical manner using a special character as a delimiter. For example, if we drew the subschematic as in Figure 9.5(b), the four inverters in FourBit might be named L1.inv1, L2.inv1, L3.inv1, and L4.inv1. Once again this makes it clear that the inverters, inv1, are identical in all four subcells.

In our office building example, the offices are subcells of the cell Floor. Suppose you and I both have corner offices. Mine is on the second floor and yours is above mine on the third floor. My office is 211 and your office is 311. Another way to name our offices on a building plan might be FloorTwo.11 for my office and FloorThree.11 for your office. This shows that FloorTwo.11 is a subcell of

`FloorTwo` and also makes it clear that, apart from being on different floors, your office and mine are identical. Both our offices have instance names `11` and are instances of cell name `Corner`.

9.1.5 Nets

The schematics shown in Figure 9.4 contain both **local nets** and **external nets**. An example of a local net in Figure 9.4(b) is `n1`, the connection between the output terminal of the `AND` cell `and1` to the `OR` cell `or1`. When the four copies of this circuit are placed in the parent cell `FourBit` in Figure 9.5(d), four copies of net `n1` are created. Since the four nets named `n1` are not actually electrically connected, even though they have the same name at the lowest hierarchical level, we must somehow find a way to uniquely identify each net.

The usual convention for naming nets in a hierarchical schematic uses the parent cell instance name as a prefix to the local net name. A special character (`':'` `'/'` `'$'` `'#'` for example) that is not allowed to appear in names is used as a **delimiter** to separate the net name from the cell instance name. Supposing that we drew the subschematic for cell `FourBit` as shown in Figure 9.5(b), the four different nets labeled `n1` might then become:

> `FourBit.L1:n1`   `FourBit.L2:n1`   `FourBit.L3:n1`   `FourBit.L4:n1`

This naming is usually done automatically by the schematic-entry tool.

The schematic `DLAT` also contains three external nets: `D`, `EN`, and `Q`. The terminals on the symbol `DLAT` connect these nets to other nets in the hierarchical level above. For example, the signal `Trigger:flag` in Figure 9.4(c) is also `Trigger.DLAT:Q`. Each schematic tool handles this situation differently, and life becomes especially difficult when we need to refer to these nodes from a simulator outside the schematic tool, for example. HDLs such as VHDL and Verilog have a very precise and well-defined standard for naming nets in hierarchical structures.

9.1.6 Schematic Entry for ASICs and PCBs

A symbol on a schematic may represent a **component**, which may contain **component parts**. You are more likely to come across the use of components in a PCB schematic. A component is slightly different from an ASIC library cell. A simple example of a component would be a TTL gate, an SN74LS00N, that contains four 2-input NAND gates. We call an SN74LS00N a component and each of the individual NAND gates inside is a component part. Another common example of a component would be a resistor pack—a single package that contains several identical resistors.

In PCB design language a component label or name is a **reference designator**. A reference designator is a unique name attribute, such as `R99`, attached to each component. A reference designator, such as `R99`, has two pieces: an alpha prefix `R` and a numerical suffix `99`. To understand the difference between reference designators and instance names, we need to look at the special requirements of PCB design.

PCBs usually contain packaged ASICs and other ICs that have pins that are soldered to a board. For rectangular, dual-in-line (DIP) packages the pins are numbered counterclockwise from the upper-left corner looking down on the package.

IC symbols have a **pin number** for each part in the package. For example, the TTL 74174 hex D flip-flop with clear, contains six parts: six identical D flip-flops. The IC symbol representing this device has six PinNumber attribute entries for the D input corresponding to the six possible input pins. They are pins 3, 4, 6, 11, 13, and 14.

When we need a flip-flop in our design, we use a symbol for a 74174 from a schematic library, suppose the symbol name is dffClr. We shall assign a unique instance name to the symbol, CarryFF. Now suppose we need another, identical, flip-flop and we call this BitFF. We do not mind which of the six flip-flop parts in a 74174 we use for CarryFF and BitFF. In fact they do not even have to be in the same package. We shall delay the choice of assigning CarryFF and BitFF to specific packages until we get to the PCB routing step. So at this point on our schematic we do not even know the pin numbers for CarryFF and BitFF. For example the D input to CarryFF could be pin 3, 4, 6, 11, 13, or 14.

The number of wire crossings on a PCB is minimized by careful assignment of components to packages and choice of parts within a package. So the placement-and-routing software may decide which part of which package to use for CarryFF and BitFF depending on which is easier to route. Then, only after the placement and routing is complete, are unique reference designators assigned to the component parts. Only at this point do we know where CarryFF is actually located on the PCB by referring to the reference designator, which points to a specific part in a specific package. Thus CarryFF might be located in IC4 on our PCB. At this point we also know which pins are used for each symbol. So we now know, for example, that the D-input to CarryFF is pin 3 of IC4.

There is no process in ASIC design directly equivalent to the process of **part assignment** described above and thus no need to use reference designators. The reference-designator naming convention quickly becomes unwieldy if there are a large number of components in a design. For example, how will we find a NAND gate named X3146 in an ASIC schematic with 100 pages? Instead, for ASICs, we use a naming scheme based on hierarchy.

In large hierarchical ASIC designs it is difficult to provide a unique reference designator to each element. For this reason ASIC designs use instance names to identify the individual components. Meaningful names can be assigned to low-level components and also the symbols that represent hierarchy. We derive the component names by joining all of the higher level cell names together. A special character is used as a delimiter and separates each level.

Examples of hierarchical instance names are:

```
cpu.alu.adder.and01
MotherBoard:Cache:RAM4:ReadBit4:Inverter2
```

9.1.7   Connections

Cell instances have **terminals** that are the inputs and outputs of the cell. Terminals are also known as **pins**, **connectors**, or **signals**. The term *pin* is widely used, but we shall try to use terminal, and reserve the term *pin* for the metal leads on an ASIC package. The term *pin* is used in schematic entry and routing programs that are primarily intended for PCB design.

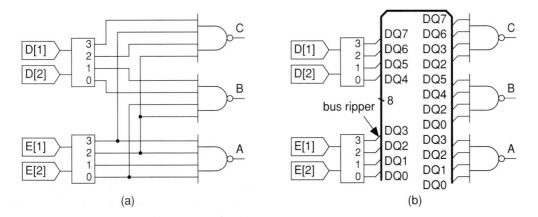

FIGURE 9.6 An example of the use of a bus to simplify a schematic. (a) An address decoder without using a bus. (b) A bus with bus rippers simplifies the schematic and reduces the possibility of making a mistake in creating and reading the schematic.

Electrical connections between cell instances use **wire segments** or **nets**. We can group closely related nets, such as the 32 bits of a 32-bit digital word, together into a **bus** or into **buses** (not busses). If signals on a bus are not closely related, we usually use the term **bundle** or **array** instead of bus. An example of a bundle might be a bus for a SCSI disk system, containing not only data bits but handshake and control signals too. Figure 9.6 shows an example of a bus in a schematic. If we need to access individual nets in a bus or a bundle, we use a **breakout** (also known as a **ripper**, an EDIF term, or **extractor**). For example, a breakout is used to access bits 0–7 of a 32-bit bus. If we need to rearrange bits on a bus, some schematic editors offer something called a **swizzle**. For example, we might use a swizzle to reorder the bits on an 8-bit bus so that the MSB becomes the LSB and so on down to the LSB, which now becomes the MSB. Swizzles can be useful. For example, we can multiply or divide a number by 2 by swizzling all the bits up or down one place on a bus.

9.1.8   Vectored Instances and Buses

So far the naming conventions are fairly standard and easy to follow. However, when we start to use vectored instances and buses (as is now common in large

ASICs), there are potential areas of difficulty and confusion. Figure 9.7(a) shows a schematic for a 16-bit latch that uses multiple copies of the cell FourBit. The buses are labeled with the appropriate bits. Figure 9.7(b) shows a new cell symbol for the 16-bit latch with 16-bit wide buses for the inputs, D, and outputs, Q.

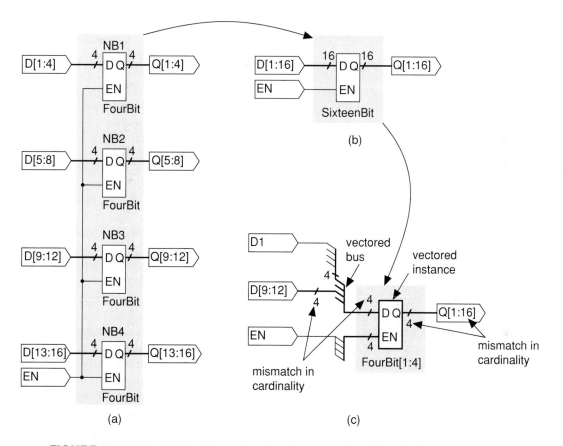

FIGURE 9.7 A 16-bit latch: (a) drawn as four instances of cell FourBit; (b) drawn as a cell named SixteenBit; (c) drawn as four multiple instances of cell FourBit.

Figure 9.7(c) shows an alternative representation of the 16-bit latch using a vectored instance of FourBit with cardinality 4. Suppose we wish to make a connection to expressly one bit, D1 (we have used D1 as the first bit rather than the more conventional D0 so that numbering is easier to follow). We also wish to make a connection to bits D9–D12, represented as D[9:12]. We do this using a bus ripper. Now we have the rather awkward situation of bus naming shown in Figure 9.7(c). Problems arise when we have "buses of buses" because the numbers for the bus widths do not match on either side of a ripper. For this reason it is best to use the single-bus approach shown in Figure 9.7(b) rather than the vectored-bus approach of Figure 9.7(c).

9.1.9   Edit-in-Place

Figure 9.7(b) shows a symbol SixteenBit, which uses the subschematic shown in Figure 9.7(a) containing four copies of FourBit, named NB1, NB2, NB3, and NB4 (the NB stands for nibble, which is half of a word; a nibble is 4 bits for 8-bit words). Suppose we use the schematic-entry program to edit the subcell NB1.L1, which is an instance of DLAT inside NB1. Perhaps we wish to change the D latch to a D latch with a reset, for example. If the schematic editor supports **edit-in-place**, we can edit a cell instance directly. After we edit the cell, the program will update all the DLAT subcells in the cell that is currently loaded to reflect the changes that have been made.

To see how edit-in-place works, consider our office building again. Suppose we wish to change some of the offices on each floor from offices without windows to offices with windows. We select the cell instance FloorTwo—that is, an instance of cell Floor. Now we choose the edit mode in the schematic-entry program. But wait! Do we want to edit the cell Floor, or do we want to edit the cell *instance* FloorTwo? If we edit the cell Floor, we will be making changes to all of the floors that use cell name Floor—that is, instances FloorTwo through FloorTen. If we edit the cell instance FloorTwo, then the second floor will become different from all the other floors. It will no longer be an instance of cell name Floor and we will have to create another cell name for the cell used by instance FloorTwo. This is like the difference between ordering just one hamburger without pickles and changing the picture on the wall that will change all future hamburgers.

Using edit-in-place we can edit the cell Floor. Suppose we change some of the cell instances of cell name NoWindowOffice to instances of cell name WindowOffice. When we finish editing and save the cell Floor, we have effectively changed all of the floors that contain instances of this cell.

Instead of editing a cell in place, you may really want to edit just one instance of a cell and leave any other instances unchanged. In this case you must create a new cell with a new symbol and new, unique cell name. It might also be wise to change the instance name of the new cell to avoid any confusion.

For example, we might change the third-floor plan of our office to be different from the other upper floors. Suppose the third floor is now an instance of cell name FloorVIP instead of Floor. We could continue to call the third floor cell instance FloorThree, but it would be better to rename the instance differently, FloorSpecial for example, to make it clear that it is different from all the other floors.

Some tools have the ability to **alias** nets. Aliasing creates a net name from the highest level in the design. Local names are net names at the lowest level such as D, and Q in a flip-flop cell. These local names are automatically replaced by the appropriate top-level names such as Clock1, or Data2, using a **dictionary**. This greatly speeds tracing of signals through a design containing many levels of hierarchy.

9.1.10   Attributes

You can attach a **name**, also known as an **identifier** or **label**, to a component, cell instance, net, terminal, or connector. You can also attach an **attribute**, or **property**, which describes some aspect of the component, cell instance, net, or connector. Each attribute has a name, and some attributes also have values. The most common problems in working with schematics and netlists, especially when you try to exchange schematic information between different tools, are problems in naming.

Since cells and their contents have to be stored in a database, a cell name frequently corresponds (or is mapped to) a filename. This then raises the problems of naming conventions including: case sensitivity, name-collision resolution, dictionaries, handling of "common" special characters (such as embedded blanks or underscores), other special characters (such as characters in foreign alphabets), first-character restrictions, name-length problems (only 28 characters are permitted on an NFS compatible filename), and so on.

9.1.11   Netlist Screener

A surprising number of problems can be found by checking a schematic for obviously fatal errors. A program that analyzes a schematic netlist for simple errors is sometimes called a **schematic screener** or **netlist screener**. Errors that can be found by a netlist screener include:

- unconnected cell inputs,
- unconnected cell outputs,
- nets not driven by any cells,
- too many nets driven by one cell,
- nets driven by more than one cell.

The screener can work continuously as the designer is creating the schematic or can be run as a separate program independently from schematic entry. Usually the designer provides attributes that give the screener the information necessary to perform the checks. A few of the typical attributes that schematic-entry programs use are described next.

A screener usually generates a list of errors together with the locations of the problem on the schematic where appropriate. Some editors associate an identifier, or **handle**, to every piece of a schematic, including comments and every net. Normally there is some convention to the assigned names such as a grid on a schematic. This works like the locator codes on a map, so that a net with A1 as part of the name is in the upper-left-hand corner, for example. This allows you to quickly and uniquely find any problems found by a screener. The term *handle* is a computer programming term that is used in referring to a location in memory. Each piece of information on a schematic is stored in lists in memory. This technique breaks down completely when we move to HDLs.

Most schematic-entry programs work on a grid. The designer can control the size of the grid and whether it is visible or not. When you place components or wires you can instruct the editor to force your drawing to **snap to grid**. This means that drawing a schematic is like drawing on graph paper. You can only locate symbols, wires, and connections on grid points. This simplifies the internal mechanics of the schematic-entry program. It also makes the transfer of schematics between different EDA systems more manageable. Finally, it allows the designer to produce schematic diagrams that are cleaner in appearance and thus easier to read.

Most schematic-entry programs allow you to find components by instance name or cell name. The editor may either jump to the component location and center the graphic window on the component or highlight the component. More sophisticated options allow more complex searches, perhaps using **wildcard** matching. For example, to find all three-input NAND gates (primitive cell name ND3) or three-input NOR gates (primitive cell name NO3), you could search for cell name N*3, where * is a wildcard symbol standing for any character. The editor may generate a list of components, perhaps with page number and coordinate locations. Extensive find features are useful for large schematics where it quickly becomes impossible to find individual components.

Some schematic editors can complete **automatic naming** of reference designators or instance names to the schematic symbols either as the editor is running or as a postprocessing step. A component attribute, called a prefix, defines the prefix for the name for each type of component. For example, the prefix for all resistor component types may be R. Each time a prefix is found or a new instance is placed, the number in the reference designator or name is automatically incremented. Thus if the last resistor component type you placed was R99, the next time you place a resistor it would automatically be named R100.

For large schematics it is useful to be able to generate a report on the used and unused reference designators. An example would be:

```
Reference designator prefix: R
Unused reference designator numbers: 153, 154
Last used reference designator number: 180
```

If you need this feature, you probably are not using enough hierarchy to simplify your design.

During schematic entry of an ASIC design you will frequently need multiple copies of components. This often occurs during **datapath** design, where operations are carried out across multiple signals on a bus. A common example would be multiple copies of a latch, one for each signal on a bus. It is tedious and inefficient to have to draw and label the same cell many times on a schematic. To simplify this task, most editors allow you to place a special **vectored cell instance** of a cell. A vectored cell instance, or **vectored instance** for short, uses the same icon for a single instance but with a special attribute, the **cell cardinality**, that denotes the number of copies of the cell. Connections between signals on a bus and vectored instances should be handled automatically. The width or **cardinality** of the bus and the cell cardinality must match, and the design-entry tool should issue a warning if this is not the case.

A schematic-entry program can use a terminal attribute to determine which cell terminals are output terminals and which terminals are input terminals. This attribute is usually called **terminal polarity** or **terminal direction**. Possible values for terminal polarity might be: `input`, `output`, and `bidirectional`. Checking the terminal polarity of the terminals on a net can help find problems such as a net with all input terminals or all output terminals.

The **fanout** of a cell measures the driving capability of an output terminal. The **fanin** of a cell measures the number of input terminals. Fanout is normally measured using a standard load. A **standard load** is the load presented by one input of a primitive cell, usually a two-input NAND. For example, a library cell `Counter` may have an input terminal, `Clock`, that is connected to the input terminals of five primitive cells. The loading at this terminal is then five standard loads. We say that the fanout of `Clock` is five. In a similar fashion, we say that if a cell `Buffer` is capable of driving the inputs of three primitive cells, the fanout of `Buffer` is three. Using the fanin and fanout attributes a netlist screener can check to see if the fanout driving a net is greater than the sum of all loads on that net. (See Figure 9.2 on page 329.)

9.1.12 Schematic-Entry tools

Some editors offer **icon edit-in-place** in a similar fashion as schematic edit-in-place for cells. Often you have to toggle editing modes in the schematic-entry program to switch between editing cells and editing cell icons. A schematic-entry program must keep track of when cells are edited. Normally this is done by using a **timestamp** or **datestamp** for each cell. This is a text field within the data file for each cell that holds the date and time that the cell was last modified. When a new schematic or cell is loaded, the program needs to compare its timestamp with the timestamps of any subcells. If any of the subcell timestamps are more recent, then the designer needs to be alerted. Usually a message appears to inform you that changes have been made to subcells since the last time the cell currently loaded was saved. This may be what you expect or it may be a warning that somehow a subcell has been changed inadvertently (perhaps someone else changed it) since you last loaded that cell.

Normally the primitive cells in a library are locked and cannot be edited. If you can edit a primitive cell, you have to make a copy, edit the copy, and rename it. Normally the ASIC designer cannot do this and does not want to. For example, to edit a primitive NAND gate stored in an ASIC schematic library would require that the subschematic of the primitive cell be available (usually not the case) and also that the next lower level primitives (symbols for the transistors making up the NAND gate) also be available to the designer (also usually not the case).

What do you do if somehow changes were made to a cell by mistake, perhaps by someone else, and you don't want the new cell, you want the old version? Most schematic-entry and other EDA tools keep old versions of files as a back-up in case this kind of problem occurs. Most EDA software automatically keeps track of the different **versions** of a file by appending a **version number** to each file. Usually this is transparent to the designer. Thus when you edit a cell named Floor, the file on disk might be called Floor.6. When you save the changes, the software will not overwrite Floor.6, but write out a new file and automatically name it Floor.7.

Some design-entry tools are more sophisticated and allow users to create their own libraries as they complete an ASIC design. Designers can then control access to libraries and the cells that they build during a design. This normally requires that a schematic editor, for example, be part of a larger EDA system or framework rather than work as a stand-alone tool. Sometimes the process of library control operates as a separate tool, as a **design manager** or **library manager**. Often there is a program similar to the UNIX make command that keeps track of all files, their dependencies, and the tools that are necessary to create and update each file.

You can normally set the number of back-up versions of files that EDA software keeps. The **version history** controls the number of files the software will keep. If you accidentally update, overwrite, or delete a file, there is usually an option to select and revert to an earlier version. More advanced systems have **check-out** services (which work just as in source control systems in computer programming databases) that prevent these kinds of problems when many people are working on the same design. Whenever possible, the management of design files and different versions should be left under software control because the process can become very complicated. Reverting to an earlier version of a cell can have drastic consequences for other cells that reference the cell you are working with. Attempts to manually edit files by changing version numbers and timestamps can quickly lead to chaos.

Most schematic-entry programs allow you to **undo** commands. This feature may be restricted to simply undoing the last command that you entered, or may be an unlimited undo and redo, allowing you to back up as many commands as you want in the current editing session.

You can spend a lot of time in a schematic editor placing components and drawing the connections between them. Features that simplify initial entry and allow modifications to be made easily can make an enormous difference to the efficiency of the schematic-entry process.

Most schematic editors allow you to make connections by dragging the cursor with the wire following behind, in a process known as **rubber banding**. The connection snaps to a right angle when the connection is completed. For wire connections that require more than two line segments, an automatic wiring feature is useful. This allows you to define the wire path roughly using mouse clicks and have the editor complete the connection.

It is exceedingly painful to move components if you have to rewire connections each time. Most schematic editors allow you to move the components and drag any wires along with them.

One of the most annoying problems that can arise in schematic entry is to think that you have joined two wires on a schematic but find that in reality they do not quite meet. This error can be almost impossible to find. A good editing program will have a way of avoiding this problem. Some editors provide a visual (flash) or audible (beep) feedback when the designer draws a wire that makes an electrical connection with another. Some editors will also automatically insert a dot at a "T" connection to show that an electrical connection is present. Other editors refuse to allow four-way connections to be made, so there can be no ambiguity when wires cross each other if an electrical connection is present or not.

A cell library or a collection of libraries is a key part of the schematic-entry process. The ability to handle and control these libraries is an important feature of any schematic editor. It should be easy to select components from the library to be placed on a schematic.

In large schematics it is necessary to continue large nets and signals across several pages of schematics. Signals such as power and ground, VDD and GND, can be connected using **global nets** or special **connectors**. Global nets allow the designer to label a net with the same name at different places on a schematic page or on different pages without having to draw a connection explicitly. The schematic editor treats these nets as though they were electrically connected. Special connector symbols can be used for connections that cross schematic pages. An **off-page connector** or **multipage connector** is a special symbol that will show and label a connection to different schematic pages. More sophisticated editors can automatically label these connectors with the page numbers of the destination connectors.

9.1.13 Back-Annotation

After you enter a schematic you simulate the design to make sure it works as expected. This completes the logical design. Next you move to ASIC physical design and complete the layout. Only after you complete the layout do you know the parasitic capacitance and therefore the delay associated with the interconnect. This postroute delay information must be returned to the schematic in a process known as **back-annotation**. Then you can complete a final, postlayout simulation to make sure that the specifications for the ASIC are met. Chapter 13 covers simulation, and the physical design steps are covered in Chapters 15 to 17.

9.2 Low-Level Design Languages

Schematics can be a very effective way to convey design information because pictures are such a powerful medium. There are two major problems with schematic entry, however. The first problem is that making changes to a schematic can be difficult. When you need to include an extra few gates in the middle of a schematic sheet, you may have to redraw the whole sheet. The second problem is that for many years there were no standards on how symbols should be drawn or how the schematic information should be stored in a netlist. These problems led to the development of design-entry tools based on text rather than graphics. As TTL gave way to PLDs, these text-based design tools became increasingly popular as de facto standards began to emerge for the format of the design files.

PLDs are closely related to FPGAs. The major advantage of PLD tools is their low cost, their ease of use, and the tremendous amount of knowledge and number of designs, application notes, textbooks, and examples that have been built up over years of their use. It is natural then that designers would want to use PLD development systems and languages to design FPGAs and other ASICs. For example, there is a tremendous amount of PLD design expertise and working designs that can be reused.

In the case of ASIC design it is important to use the right tool for the job. This may mean that you need to convert from a low-level design medium you have used for PLD design to one more appropriate for ASIC design. Often this is because you are merging several PLDs into a single, much larger, ASIC. The reason for covering the PLD design languages here is not to try and teach you how to use them, but to allow you to read and understand a PLD language and, if necessary, convert it to a form that you can use in another ASIC design system.

9.2.1   ABEL

ABEL is a PLD programming language from Data I/O. Table 9.2 shows some examples of the ABEL statements. The following example code describes a 4:1 MUX (equivalent to the LS153 TTL part):

```
module MUX4
title '4:1 MUX'
MyDevice device 'P16L8' ;
@ALTERNATE
"inputs
A, B, /P1G1, /P1G2 pin 17,18,1,6 "LS153 pins 14,2,1,15
P1C0, P1C1, P1C2, P1C3 pin 2,3,4,5 "LS153 pins 6,5,4,3
P2C0, P2C1, P2C2, P2C3 pin 7,8,9,11 "LS153 pins 10,11,12,13
"outputs
P1Y, P2Y pin 19, 12 "LS153 pins 7,9
equations
   P1Y = P1G*(/B*/A*P1C0 + /B*A*P1C1 + B*/A*P1C2 + B*A*P1C3);
   P1Y = P1G*(/B*/A*P1C0 + /B*A*P1C1 + B*/A*P1C2 + B*A*P1C3);
end MUX4
```

TABLE 9.2   ABEL.

Statement	Example	Comment
Module	`module MyModule`	You can have multiple modules.
Title	`title 'Title in a String'`	A string is a character series between quotes.
Device	`MYDEV device '22V10' ;`	`MYDEV` is Device ID for documentation. `22V10` is checked by the compiler.
Comment	`"comments go between double quotes"` `"end of line is end of comment`	The end of a line signifies the end of a comment; there is no need for an end quote.
`@ALTERNATE`	`@ALTERNATE "use alternate symbols`	

operator	alternate	default
AND	`*`	`&`
OR	`+`	`#`
NOT	`/`	`!`
XOR	`:+:`	`$`
XNOR	`:*:`	`!$`

Statement	Example	Comment
Pin declaration	`MYINPUT pin 2; I3, I4 pin 3, 4 ;` `/MYOUTPUT pin 22; IO3,IO4 pin 21,20 ;`	Pin 22 is the IO for input on pin 2 for a 22V10. `MYOUTPUT` is active-low at the chip pin. Signal names must start with a letter.
Equations	`equations` `IO4 = HELPER ; HELPER = /I4 ;`	Defines combinational logic. Two-pass logic
Assignments	`MYOUTPUT = /MYINPUT ;` `IO3 := I4 ;`	Equals `'='` is unlocked assignment. Clocked assignment operator (registered IO)
Signal sets	`D = [D0, D1, D2, D3] ;` `Q = [Q0, Q1, Q2, Q3];`	A signal set, an ABEL bus
Suffix	`Q := D ;` `MYOUTPUT.RE = CLR ;` `MYOUTPUT.PR = PRE ;`	4-bit-wide register Register reset Register preset
Addition	`COUNT = [D0, D1, D2];` `COUNT := COUNT + 1;`	Can't use `@ALTERNATE` if you use `'+'` to add.
Enable	`ENABLE IO3 = IO2;` `IO3 = MYINPUT;`	Three-state enable (`ENABLE` is a keyword). `IO3` must be a three-state pin.
Constants	`K = [1, 0, 1] ;`	K is 5.
Relational	`IO# = D == K5 ;`	Operators: `==    !=    <    >    <=    >=`
End	`end MyModule`	Last statement in module

9.2.2   CUPL

CUPL is a PLD design language from Logical Devices. We shall review the CUPL 4.0 language here. The following code is a simple CUPL example describing sequential logic:

```
SEQUENCE BayBridgeTollPlaza {
   PRESENT red
      IF car NEXT green OUT go;      /* conditional synchronous output */
      DEFAULT NEXT red;             /* default next state */
   PRESENT green
      NEXT red; }                   /* unconditional next state */
```

This code describes a state machine with two states. Table 9.3 shows the different state machine assignment statements.

TABLE 9.3   CUPL statements for state-machine entry.

Statement			Description
IF	NEXT		Conditional next state transition
IF	NEXT	OUT	Conditional next state transition with synchronous output
	NEXT		Unconditional next state transition
	NEXT	OUT	Unconditional next state transition with asynchronous output
		OUT	Unconditional asynchronous output
IF		OUT	Conditional asynchronous output
DEFAULT	NEXT		Default next state transition
DEFAULT		OUT	Default asynchronous output
DEFAULT	NEXT	OUT	Default next state transition with synchronous output

You may also encode state machines as truth tables in CUPL. Here is another simple example:

```
FIELD input = [in1..0];
FIELD output = [out3..0];
TABLE input => output {00 => 01; 01 => 02; 10 => 04; 11 => 08; }
```

The advantage of the CUPL language, and text-based PLD languages in general, is now apparent. First, we do not have to enter the detailed logic for the state decoding ourselves—the software does it for us. Second, to make changes only requires simple text editing—fast and convenient.

Table 9.4 shows some examples of CUPL statements. In CUPL Boolean equations may use variables that contain a suffix, or an **extension**, as in the following example:

```
output.ext = (Boolean expression);
```

TABLE 9.4   CUPL.

Statement	Example	Comment
Boolean expression	`A = !B;`	Logical negation
	`A = B & C;`	Logical AND
	`A = B # C;`	Logical OR
	`A = B $ C;`	Logical exclusive-OR
Comment	`A = B & C /* comment */`	
Pin declaration	`PIN 1 = CLK;`	Device dependent
	`PIN = CLK;`	Device independent
Node declaration	`NODE A;`	Number automatically assigned
	`NODE [B0..7];`	Array of buried nodes
Pinnode declaration	`PINNODE 99 = A;`	Node assigned by designer
	`PINNODE [10..17] = [B0..7];`	Array of pinnodes
Bit-field declaration	`FIELD Address = [B0..7];`	8-bit address field
Bit-field operations	`add_one = Address:FF;`	True if Address = 0xFF
	`add_zero = !(Address:&);`	True if Address = 0x00
	`add_range = Address:[0F..FF];`	True if 0F.LE.Address.LE.FF

The extensions steer the software, known as a **fitter**, in assigning the logic. For example, a signal-name suffix of `.OE` marks that signal as an output enable.

Here is an example of a CUPL file for a 4-bit counter placed in an ATMEL PLD part that illustrates the use of some common extensions:

```
Name 4BIT; Device V2500B;
/* inputs */
pin 1 = CLK; pin 3 = LD_; pin 17 = RST_;
pin [18,19,20,21] = [I0,I1,I2,I3];
/*  outputs  */
pin [4,5,6,7] = [Q0,Q1,Q2,Q3];
field CNT = [Q3,Q2,Q1,Q0];
/* equations */
Q3.T = (!Q2 & !Q1 & !Q0) & LD_ & RST_ /* count down */
```

```
        # Q3 & !RST_ /* ReSeT */
        # (Q3 $ I3) & !LD_; /* LoaD*/
Q2.T = (!Q1 & !Q0) & LD_ & RST_ # Q2 & !RST_ # (Q2 $ I2) & !LD_;
Q1.T = !Q0 & LD_ & RST_ # Q1 & !RST_ # (Q1 $ I1) & !LD_;
Q0.T = LD_ & RST_ # Q0 & !RST_ # (Q0 $ I0) & !LD_;
CNT.CK = CLK; CNT.OE = 'h'F; CNT.AR = 'h'0; CNT.SP = 'h'0;
```

In this example the suffix extensions have the following effects: .CK marks the clock; .T configures sequential logic as T flip-flops; .OE (wired high) is the output enable; .AR (wired low) is the asynchronous reset; and .SP (wired low) is the synchronous preset. Table 9.5 shows the different CUPL extensions.

The 4-bit counter is a very simple example of the use of the Atmel ATV2500B. This PLD is quite complex and has many extra "buried" features. In order to use these features in CUPL (and ABEL) you need to refer to special pin numbers and node numbers that are given in tables in the manufacturer's data sheets. You may need the pin-number tables to reverse engineer or convert a complicated CUPL (or ABEL) design from one format to another.

Atmel also gives skeleton headers and pin declarations for their parts in their data sheets. Table 9.6 shows the headers and pin declarations in ABEL and CUPL format for the ATMEL ATV2500B.

9.2.3   PALASM

PALASM is a PLD design language from AMD/MMI. Table 9.7 shows the format of PALASM statements. The following simple example (a video shift register) shows the most basic features of the PALASM 2 language:

```
TITLE video ; shift register
CHIP video PAL20X8
CK /LD D0 D1 D2 D3 D4 D5 D6 D7 CURS GND NC REV Q7 Q6 Q5 Q4 Q3 Q2 Q1 Q0
/RST VCC
STRING Load 'LD*/REV*/CURS*RST' ; load data
STRING LoadInv 'LD*REV*/CURS*RST' ; load inverted of data
STRING Shift '/LD*/CURS*/RST' ; shift data from MSB to LSB
EQUATIONS
/Q0 := /D0*Load+D0*LoadInv:+:/Q1*Shift+RST
/Q1 := /D1*Load+D1*LoadInv:+:/Q2*Shift+RST
/Q2 := /D2*Load+D2*LoadInv:+:/Q3*Shift+RST
/Q3 := /D3*Load+D3*LoadInv:+:/Q4*Shift+RST
/Q4 := /D4*Load+D4*LoadInv:+:/Q5*Shift+RST
/Q5 := /D5*Load+D5*LoadInv:+:/Q6*Shift+RST
/Q6 := /D6*Load+D6*LoadInv:+:/Q7*Shift+RST
/Q7 := /D7*Load+D7*LoadInv:+:Shift+RST;
```

TABLE 9.5 CUPL 4.0 extensions.

Extension[1]		Explanation	Extension		Explanation
D	L	D input to a D register	DFB	R	D register feedback of combinational output
L	L	L input to a latch	LFB	R	Latched feedback of combinational output
J, K	L	J-K-input to a J-K register	TFB	R	T register feedback of combinational output
S, R	L	S-R input to an S-R register	INT	R	Internal feedback
T	L	T input to a T register	IO	R	Pin feedback of registered output
DQ	R	D output of an input D register	IOD/T	R	D/T register on pin feedback path selection
LQ	R	Q output of an input latch	IOL	R	Latch on pin feedback path selection
AP, AR	L	Asynchronous preset/reset	IOAP, IOAR	L	Asynchronous preset/reset of register on feedback path
SP, SR	L	Synchronous preset/reset	IOSP, IOSR	L	Synchronous preset/reset of register on feedback path
CK	L	Product clock term (async.)	IOCK	L	Clock for pin feedback register
OE	L	Product-term output enable	APMUX, ARMUX	L	Asynchronous preset/reset multiplexor selection
CA	L	Complement array	CKMUX	L	Clock multiplexor selector
PR	L	Programmable preload	LEMUX	L	Latch enable multiplexor selector
CE	L	CE input of a D-CE register	OEMUX	L	Output enable multiplexor selector
LE	L	Product-term latch enable	IMUX	L	Input multiplexor selector of two pins
OBS	L	Programmable observability of buried nodes	TEC	L	Technology-dependent fuse selection
BYP	L	Programmable register bypass	T1	L	T1 input of 2-T register

[1] L means that the extension is used only on the LHS of an equation; R means that the extension is used only on the RHS of an equation.

TABLE 9.6   ABEL and CUPL pin declarations for an ATMEL ATV2500B.

ABEL	CUPL
`device_id device 'P2500B';`	`device V2500B;`
`"device_id used for JEDEC filename`	`pin [1,2,3,17,18] = [I1,I2,I3,I17,I18];`
`I1,I2,I3,I17,I18 pin 1,2,3,17,18;`	`pin [7,6,5,4] = [O7,O6,O5,O4];`
`O4,O5 pin 4,5 istype 'reg_d,buffer';`	`pinnode [41,65,44] = [O4Q2,O4Q1,O7Q2];`
`O6,O7 pin 6,7 istype 'com';`	`pinnode [43,68] = [O6Q2,O7Q1];`
`O4Q2,O7Q2 node 41,44 istype 'reg_d';`	
`O6F2 node 43 istype 'com';`	
`O7Q1 node 220 istype 'reg_d';`	

TABLE 9.7   PALASM 2.

Statement	Example	Comment
Chip	`CHIP abc 22V10`	Specific PAL type
	`CHIP xyz USER`	Free-form equation entry
Pinlist	`CLK /LD D0 D1 D2 D3 D4 GND NC` `Q4 Q3 Q2 Q1 Q0 /RST VCC`	Part of `CHIP` statement; PAL pins in numerical order starting with pin 1
String	`STRING string_name 'text'`	Before `EQUATIONS` statement
Equations	`EQUATIONS`	After `CHIP` statement
	`A = /B`	Logical negation
	`A = B * C`	Logical AND
	`A = B + C`	Logical OR
	`A = B :+: C`	Logical exclusive-OR
	`A = B :*: C`	Logical exclusive-NOR
Polarity inversion	`/A = /(B + C)`	Same as `A = B + C`
Assignment	`A = B + C`	Combinational assignment
	`A := B + C`	Registered assignment
Comment	`A = B + C ; comment`	Comment
Functional equation	`name.TRST`	Output enable control
	`name.CLKF`	Register clock control
	`name.RSTF`	Register reset control
	`name.SETF`	Register set control

The order of the pin numbers in the previous example is important; the order must correspond to the order of pins for the DEVICE. This means that you probably need the device data sheet in order to be able to translate a design from PALASM to another format by hand. The alternative is to use utilities that many PLD and FPGA companies offer that automatically translate from PALASM to their own formats.

9.3   PLA Tools

We shall use the Berkeley PLA tools to illustrate logic minimization using an example to minimize the logic required to implement the following three logic functions:

F1 = A|B|!C;   F2 = !B&C;   F3 = A&B|C;

These equations are in eqntott input format. The eqntott (for "equation to truth table") program converts the input equations into a tabular format. Table 9.8 shows the truth table and eqntott output for functions F1, F2, and F3 that use the six minterms: A, B, !C, !B&C, A&B, C.

TABLE 9.8   A PLA tools example.

Input (6 minterms): F1 = A|B|!C; F2 = !B&C; F3 = A&B|C;

A	B	C	F1	F2	F3	eqntott output	espresso output
0	0	0	1	0	0	.i 3	.i 3
0	0	1	0	1	1	.o 3	.o 3
0	1	0	1	0	0	.p 6	.p 6
						--0 100	1-- 100
0	1	1	1	0	1	--1 001	11- 001
1	0	0	1	0	0	-01 010	--0 100
						-1- 100	-01 011
1	0	1	1	1	1	1-- 100	-11 101
1	1	0	1	0	1	11- 001	.e
						.e	
1	1	1	1	0	1		

Output (5 minterms): F1 = A|!C|(B&C); F2 = !B&C; F3 = A&B|(!B&C)|(B&C);

This eqntott output is not really a truth table since each line corresponds to a min-term. The output forms the input to the espresso logic-minimization program. Table 9.9 shows the format for espresso input and output files. Table 9.10 explains the format of the input and output planes of the espresso input and output files. The espresso output in Table 9.8 corresponds to the eqntott logic equations on the next page.

TABLE 9.9   The format of the input and output files used by the PLA design tool espresso.

Expression	Explanation
# comment	# must be first character on a line.
[d]	Decimal number
[s]	Character string
.i [d]	Number of input variables
.o [d]	Number of output variables
.p [d]	Number of product terms
.ilb [s1] [s2]... [sn]	Names of the binary-valued variables must be after .i and .o.
.ob [s1] [s2]... [sn]	Names of the output functions must be after .i and .o.
.type f	Following table describes the ON set; DC set is empty.
.type fd	Following table describes the ON set and DC set.
.type fr	Following table describes the ON set and OFF set.
.type fdr	Following table describes the ON set, OFF set, and DC set.
.e	Optional, marks the end of the PLA description.

TABLE 9.10   The format of the plane part of the input and output files for espresso.

Plane	Character	Explanation
I	1	The input literal appears in the product term.
I	0	The input literal appears complemented in the product term.
I	–	The input literal does not appear in the product term.
O	1 or 4	This product term appears in the ON set.
O	0	This product term appears in the OFF set.
O	2 or –	This product term appears in the don't care set.
O	3 or ~	No meaning for the value of this function.

```
F1 = A|!C|(B&C);    F2 = !B&C;    F3 = A&B|(!B&C)|(B&C);
```

We see that `espresso` reduced the original six minterms to these five: A, A&B, !C, !B&C, B&C.

The Berkeley PLA tools were widely used in the 1980s. They were important stepping stones to modern logic synthesis tools. There are so many testbenches, examples, and old designs that used these tools that we occasionally need to convert files in the Berkeley PLA format to formats used in new tools.

9.4 EDIF

An ASIC designer spends an increasing amount of time forcing different tools to communicate. One standard for exchanging information between EDA tools is the **electronic design interchange format** (**EDIF**). We will describe EDIF version 2 0 0. The most important features added in EDIF 3 0 0 were to handle buses, bus rippers, and buses across schematic pages. EDIF 4 0 0 includes new extensions for PCB and multichip module (MCM) data. The **Library of Parameterized Modules** (LPM) standard is also based on EDIF. The newer versions of EDIF have a richer feature set, but the ASIC industry seems to have standardized on EDIF 2 0 0. Most EDA companies now support EDIF. The FPGA companies Altera and Actel use EDIF as their netlist format, and Xilinx has announced its intention to switch from its own XNF format to EDIF. We only have room for a brief description of the EDIF format here. A complete description of the EDIF standard is contained in the **Electronic Industries Association** (**EIA**) publication, Electronic Design Interchange Format Version 2 0 0 (ANSI/EIA Standard 548-1988) [EDIF, 1988].

9.4.1 EDIF Syntax

The structure of EDIF is similar to the Lisp programming language or the Postscript printer language. This makes EDIF a very hard language to read and almost impossible to write by hand. EDIF is intended as an exchange format between tools, not as a design-entry language. Since EDIF is so flexible each company reads and writes different "flavors" of EDIF. Inevitably EDIF from one company does not quite work when we try and use it with a tool from another company, though this situation is improving with the gradual adoption of EDIF 3 0 0. We need to know just enough about EDIF to be able to fix these problems.

Figure 9.8 illustrates the hierarchy of the EDIF file. Within an EDIF file are one or more libraries of cell descriptions. Each library contains technology information that is used in describing the characteristics of the cells it contains. Each cell description contains one or more user-named views of the cell. Each view is defined as a particular `viewType` and contains an `interface` description that identifies where the cell may be connected to and, possibly, a `contents` description that identifies the components and related interconnections that make up the cell.

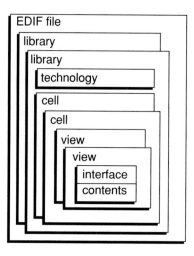

FIGURE 9.8 The hierarchical nature of an EDIF file.

The EDIF syntax consists of a series of statements in the following format:

```
(keywordName {form})
```

A left parenthesis (round bracket) is always followed by a **keyword name**, followed by one or more EDIF **forms** (a form is a sequence of identifiers, primitive data, symbolic constants, or EDIF statements), ending with a right parenthesis. If you have programmed in Lisp or Postscript, you may understand that EDIF uses a "define it before you use it" approach and why there are so many parentheses in an EDIF file.

The semantics of EDIF are defined by the **EDIF keywords**. Keywords are the only types of name that can immediately follow a left parenthesis. Case is not significant in keywords.

An **EDIF identifier** represents the name of an object or group of data. Identifiers are used for name definition, name reference, keywords, and symbolic constants. Valid EDIF identifiers consist of alphanumeric or underscore characters and must be preceded by an ampersand (&) if the first character is not alphabetic. The ampersand is not considered part of the name. The length of an identifier is from 1 to 255 characters and case is not significant. Thus &clock, Clock, and clock all represent the same EDIF name (very confusing).

Numbers in EDIF are 32-bit signed integers. Real numbers use a special EDIF format. For example, the real number 1.4 is represented as (e 14 -1). The e form requires a mantissa (14) and an exponent (-1). Reals are restricted to the range $\pm 1 \times 10^{\pm 35}$. Numbers in EDIF are dimensionless and the units are determined according to where the number occurs in the file. Coordinates and line widths are units of distance and must be related to meters. Each coordinate value is converted to meters by applying a **scale factor**. Each EDIF library has a `technology` section that contains a required `numberDefinition`. The `scale` keyword is used with the `numberDefinition` to relate EDIF numbers to physical units.

Valid EDIF strings consist of sequences of ASCII characters enclosed in double quotes. Any alphanumeric character is allowed as well as any of the following characters: `! # $ & ' () * + , -   . / : ; < = > ? @ [ \ ] ^ _ ` { | } ~.` Special characters, such as `"` and `%` are entered as escape sequences: `%number%`, where number is the integer value of the ASCII character. For example, `"A quote is % 34 %"` is a string with an embedded double-quote character. Blank, tab, line feed, and carriage-return characters (white space) are used as delimiters in EDIF. Blank and tab characters are also significant when they appear in strings.

The `rename` keyword can be used to create a new EDIF identifier as follows:

```
(cell (rename TEST_1 "test$1") ...
```

In this example the EDIF string contains the original name, `test$1`, and a new name, `TEST_1`, is created as an EDIF identifier.

9.4.2   An EDIF Netlist Example

Table 9.11 shows an EDIF netlist. This EDIF description corresponds to the halfgate example in Chapter 8 and describes an inverter. We shall explain the functions of the EDIF in Table 9.11 by showing a piece of the code at a time followed by an explanation.

```
(edif halfgate_p
   (edifVersion 2 0 0) (edifLevel 0) (keywordMap (keywordLevel 0))
(status (written (timeStamp 1996 7 10 22 5 10)
(program "COMPASS Design Automation -- EDIF Interface"
(version "v9r1.2 last updated 26-Mar-96")) (author "mikes")))
```

Every EDIF file must have an `edif` form. The `edif` form must have a `name`, an `edifVersion`, an `edifLevel`, and a `keywordMap`. The `edifVersion` consists of three integers describing the **major** (first number) and **minor version** of EDIF. The `keywordMap` must have a `keywordLevel`. The optional `status` can contain a `written` form that must have a `timeStamp` and, optionally, `author` or `program` forms.

```
(library xc4000d (edifLevel 0) (technology
```

(The unbalanced parentheses are deliberate since we are showing segments of the EDIF code.) The `library` form must have a `name`, `edifLevel` and `technology`. The `edifLevel` is normally 0. The `xc4000d` library contains the cells we are using in our schematic.

TABLE 9.11   EDIF file for the `halfgate` **netlist from Chapter 8.**

```
(edif halfgate_p                (viewType NETLIST)           (contents
(edifVersion 2 0 0)             (interface                     (instance B1_i1
(edifLevel 0)                     (port I                        (viewRef
(keywordMap                         (direction INPUT))      COMPASS_mde_view
  (keywordLevel 0))               (port O                          (cellRef INV
(status                             (direction OUTPUT))            (libraryRef
  (written                        (designator "@@Label")))))  xc4000d))))
    (timeStamp 1996 7 10 22   (library working                 (net myInput
5 10)                           (edifLevel 0)                    (joined
    (program "COMPASS Design   (technology                        (portRef myInput)
Automation -- EDIF Interface"    (numberDefinition )              (portRef I
    (version "v9r1.2 last        (simulationInfo                    (instanceRef
updated 26-Mar-96"))               (logicValue  H)          B1_i1))))
    (author "mikes")))             (logicValue  L)))              (net myOutput
  (library xc4000d              (cell                              (joined
    (edifLevel 0)                 (rename HALFGATE_P                 (portRef myOutput)
    (technology                "halfgate_p")                        (portRef O
      (numberDefinition )         (cellType GENERIC)                 (instanceRef
      (simulationInfo            (view COMPASS_nls_view       B1_i1))))
        (logicValue  H)            (viewType NETLIST)             (net VDD
        (logicValue  L)))         (interface                       (joined ))
    (cell                          (port myInput                  (net VSS
      (rename INV "inv")             (direction INPUT))             (joined ))))))
      (cellType GENERIC)           (port myOutput              (design HALFGATE_P
      (view COMPASS_mde_view         (direction OUTPUT))         (cellRef HALFGATE_P
                                   (designator "@@Label"))       (libraryRef working))))
```

```
(numberDefinition ) (simulationInfo (logicValue  H) (logicValue  L)))
```

The `simulationInfo` form is used by simulation tools; we do not need that information for netlist purposes for this cell. We shall discuss `numberDefinition` in the next example. It is not needed in a netlist.

```
(cell (rename INV "inv") (cellType GENERIC)
```

This `cell` form defines the name and type of a cell `inv` that we are going to use in the schematic.

```
(view COMPASS_mde_view (viewType NETLIST)
(interface (port I (direction INPUT)) (port O (direction OUTPUT))
(designator "@@Label")))))
```

The NETLIST view of this inverter cell has an input port I and an output port O. There is also a place holder "@@Label" for the instance name of the cell.

```
(library working...
```
This begins the description of our schematic that is in our library working. The lines that follow this library form are similar to the preamble for the cell library xc4000d that we just explained.

```
(cell (rename HALFGATE_P "halfgate_p")(cellType GENERIC)
   (view COMPASS_nls_view (viewType NETLIST)
```
This cell form is for our schematic named halfgate_p.

```
(interface (port myInput (direction INPUT))
   (port myOutput (direction OUTPUT))
```
The interface form defines the names of the ports that were used in our schematic, myInput and myOutput. At this point we have not associated these ports with the ports of the cell INV in the cell library.

```
(designator "@@Label")) (contents (instance B1_i1
```
This gives an instance name B1_i1 to the cell in our schematic.

```
(viewRef COMPASS_mde_view (cellRef INV (libraryRef xc4000d))))
```
The cellRef form links the cell instance name B1_i1 in our schematic to the cell INV in the library xc4000d.

```
(net myInput (joined (portRef myInput)
   (portRef I (instanceRef B1_i1))))
```
The net form for myInput (and the one that follows it for myOutput) ties the net names in our schematic to the ports I and O of the library cell INV.

```
(net VDD (joined )) (net VSS (joined ))))))
```
These forms for the global VDD and VSS nets are often handled differently by different tools (one company might call the negative supply GND instead of VSS, for example). This section is where you most often have to edit the EDIF.

```
(design HALFGATE_P (cellRef HALFGATE_P (libraryRef working))))
```
The design form names and places our design in library working, and completes the EDIF description.

9.4.3   An EDIF Schematic Icon

EDIF is capable of handling many different representations. The next EDIF example is another view of an inverter that describes how to draw the icon (the picture that appears on the printed schematic or on the screen) shown in Figure 9.9. We shall examine the EDIF created by the CAD/CAM Group's Engineering Capture System (ECS) schematic editor.

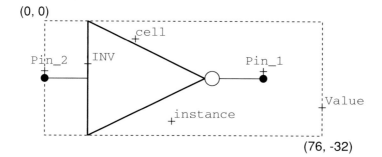

FIGURE 9.9 An EDIF view of an inverter icon. The coordinates shown are in EDIF units. The crosses that show the text location origins and the dotted bounding box do not print as part of the icon.

This time we shall give more detailed explanations after each piece of EDIF code. We shall also maintain balanced parentheses to make the structure easier to follow. To shorten the often lengthy EDIF code, we shall use an ellipsis (...) to indicate any code that has been left out.

```
(edif ECS
   (edifVersion 2 0 0)
   (edifLevel 0)
   (keywordMap (keywordLevel 0))
   (status
      (written
         (timeStamp 1987 8 20 0 50 23)
         (program "CAD/CAM Group, Inc. ECS" (Version "1"))))
   (library USER ...
   )
   ...
)
```

This preamble is virtually identical to the previous netlist example (and demonstrates that EDIF is useful to store design information as software tools come and go over many years). The first line of the file defines the name of the file. This is followed by lines that identify the version of EDIF being used and the highest EDIF level used in the file (each library may use its own level up to this maximum). EDIF level 0 supports only literal constants and basic constructs. Higher EDIF levels support parameters, expressions, and flow control constructs. EDIF keywords may be mapped to aliases, and keyword macros may be defined within the `keywordMap` form. These features are not often used in ASIC design because of a lack of standardization. The `keywordLevel` 0 indicates these capabilities are not used here. The status construct is used for administration: when the file was created, the software used to create the file, and so on. Following this preamble is the main section of the file, which contains design information.

```
(library USER (edifLevel 0)
  (technology
    (numberDefinition
      (scale 4 (e 254 -5) (unit distance)))
    (figureGroup NORMAL
      (pathWidth 0) (borderWidth 0)
      (textHeight 5))
    (figureGroup WIDE
      (pathWidth 1) (borderWidth 1)
      (textHeight 5)))
  (cell 7404 ...
  )
)
```

The `technology` form has a `numberDefinition` that defines the scaling information (we did not use this form for a netlist, but the form must be present). The first `numberValue` after `scale` represents EDIF numbers and the second `numberValue` represents the units specified by the `unit` form. The EDIF unit for distance is the meter. The `numberValue` can be an integer or an exponential number. The `e` form has a mantissa and an exponent. In this example, within the USER library, a distance of 4 EDIF units equals 254×10^{-5} meters (or 4 EDIF units equals 0.1 inch).

After the `numberDefinition` in the `technology` form there are one or more `figureGroup` definitions. A `figureGroup` defines drawing information such as `pathWidth`, `borderWidth`, `color`, `fillPattern`, `borderPattern`, and `textHeight`. The `figureGroup` form must have a name, which will be used later in the library to refer back to these definitions. In this example the USER library has one `figureGroup` (NORMAL) for lines and paths of zero width (the actual width will be implementation dependent) and another `figureGroup` (WIDE) that will be used for buses with a wider width (for bold lines). The `borderWidth` is used for drawing filled areas such as rectangles, circles, and polygons. The `pathWidth` is used for open figures such as lines (paths) and open arcs.

Following the `technology` section the `cell` forms each represent a symbol. The `cell` form has a name that will appear in the names of any files produced. The `cellType` form GENERIC type is required by this schematic editor. The `property` form is used to list properties of the cell.

```
(cell 7404 (cellType GENERIC)
  (property SymbolType (string "GATE"))
  (view PCB_Symbol (viewType SCHEMATIC)
```

```
        (interface ...
        )
    )
)
```

The `SymbolType` property is used to distinguish between purely graphical symbols that do not occur in the parts list (a ground connection, for example), gate or component symbols, and block or cell symbols (for hierarchical schematics). The `SymbolType` property is a `string` that may be COMPONENT, GATE, CELL, BLOCK, or GRAPHIC. Each cell may contain `view` forms and each `view` must have a name. Following the name of the `view` must be a `viewType` that is either GRAPHIC or SCHEMATIC. Following the `viewType` is the `interface` form, which contains the symbol and terminal information. The `interface` form contains the actual symbol data.

```
(interface
  (port Pin_1
    (designator "2")
    (direction OUTPUT)
    (dcMaxFanout 50))
  (port Pin_2
    (designator "1")
    (direction INPUT)
    (dcFanoutLoad 8)
    (property Cap
      (string "22")))
  (property Value
    (string "45"))
  (symbol ...
  )
```

If the symbol has terminals, they are listed before the `symbol` form. The `port` form defines each terminal. The required `port` name is used later in the `symbol` form to refer back to the port. Since this example is from a PCB design, the terminals have pin numbers that correspond to the IC package leads. The pin numbers are defined in the `designator` form with the pin number as a string. The polarity of the pin is indicated by the `direction` form, which may be INPUT, OUTPUT, or INOUT. If the pin is an output pin, its `Drive` can be represented by dcMaxFanout and if it is an input pin its `Load` can be represented by dcFanoutLoad. The `port` form can also contain forms unused, dcMaxFanin, dcFaninLoad, acLoad, and portDelay. All other attributes for pins besides `PinNumber`, `Polarity`, `Load`, and `Drive` are contained in the `property` form.

An attribute string follows the name of the property in the `string` form. In this example port Pin_2 has a property Cap whose value is 22. This is the input capacitance of the inverter, but the interpretation and use of this value depends on the tools. In ASIC design pins do not have pin numbers, so `designator` is not used.

Instead, the pin names use the property form. So (property NetName (string "1")) would replace the (designator "1") in this example on Pin_2. The interface form may also contain attributes of the symbol.

Symbol attributes are similar to pin attributes. In this example the property name Value has an attribute string "45". The names occurring in the property form may be referenced later in the interface under the symbol form to refer back to the property.

```
(symbol
  (boundingBox (rectangle (pt 0 0) (pt 76 -32)))
  (portImplementation Pin_1
    (connectLocation (figure NORMAL (dot (pt 60 -16)))))
    (keywordDisplay designator
      (display NORMAL
        (justify LOWERCENTER) (origin (pt 60 -14)))))
  (portImplementation Pin_2
    (connectLocation (figure NORMAL (dot (pt 0 -16)))))
    (keywordDisplay designator
      (display NORMAL
        (justify LOWERCENTER) (origin (pt 0 -14)))))
  (keywordDisplay cell
    (display NORMAL (justify CENTERLEFT) (origin (pt 25 -5))))
  (keywordDisplay instance
    (display NORMAL
      (justify CENTERLEFT) (origin (pt 36 -28))))
  (keywordDisplay designator
    (display (figureGroupOverride NORMAL (textHeight 7))
      (justify CENTERLEFT) (origin (pt 13 -16))))
  (propertyDisplay Value
    (display (figureGroupOverride NORMAL (textHeight 9))
      (justify CENTERRIGHT) (origin (pt 76 -24))))
  (figure ... )
)
```

The interface contains a symbol that contains the pin locations and graphical information about the icon. The optional boundingBox form encloses all the graphical data. The x- and y-locations of two opposite corners of the bounding rectangle use the pt form. The scale section of the numberDefinition from the technology section of the library determines the units of these coordinates. The pt construct is used to specify coordinate locations in EDIF. The keyword pt must be followed by the x-location and the y-location. For example: (pt 100 200) is at $x=100, y=200$.

- Each pin in the symbol is given a location using a portImplementation.
- The portImplementation refers back to the port defined in the interface.
- The connectLocation defines the point to connect to the pin.

- The `connectLocation` is specified as a `figure`, a dot with a single `pt` for its location.

```
(symbol
  ( ...
    (figure WIDE
      (path (pointList (pt 12 0) (pt 12 -32)))
      (path (pointList (pt 12 -32) (pt 44 -16)))
      (path (pointList (pt 12 0) (pt 44 -16))))
    (figure NORMAL
      (path (pointList (pt 48 -16) (pt 60 -16)))
      (circle (pt 44 -16) (pt 48 -16))
      (path (pointList (pt 0 -16) (pt 12 -16))))
    (annotate
      (stringDisplay "INV"
        (display NORMAL
          (justify CENTERLEFT) (origin (pt 12 -12)))))
  )
```

The `figure` form has either a name, previously defined as a `figureGroup` in the `technology` section, or a `figureGroupOverride` form. The `figure` has all the attributes (`pathWidth`, `borderWidth`, and so on) that were defined in the `figureGroup` unless they are specifically overridden with a `figureGroupOverride`.

Other objects that may appear in a `figure` are: `circle`, `openShape`, `path`, `polygon`, `rectangle`, and `shape`. Most schematic editors use a grid, and the pins are only allowed to occur **on grid**.

A `portImplementation` can contain a `keywordDisplay` or a `propertyDisplay` for the location to display the pin number or pin name. For a `GATE` or `COMPONENT`, `keywordDisplay` will display the `designator` (pin number), and `designator` is the only keyword that can be displayed. For a `BLOCK` or `CELL`, `propertyDisplay` will display the `NetName`. The `display` form displays text in the same way that the `figure` displays graphics. The `display` must have either a name previously defined as a `figureGroup` in the `technology` section or a `figureGroupOverride` form. The `display` will have all the attributes (`textHeight` for example) defined in the `figureGroup` unless they are overridden with a `figureGroupOverride`.

A **symbolic constant** is an EDIF name with a predefined meaning. For example, `LOWERLEFT` is used to specify text justification. The `display` form can contain a `justify` to override the default `LOWERLEFT`. The `display` can also contain an `orientation` that overrides the default `R0` (zero rotation). The choices for orientation are rotations (`R0`, `R90`, `R180`, `R270`), mirror about axis (`MX`, `MY`), and mirror with rotation (`MXR90`, `MYR90`). The `display` can contain an `origin` to override the default (`pt 0 0`).

The symbol itself can have either `keywordDisplay` or `propertyDisplay` forms such as the ones in the `portImplementation`. The choices for `keywordDisplay` are: `cell` for attribute `Type`, `instance` for attribute `InstName`, and `designator` for attribute `RefDes`. In the preceding example an attribute window currently mapped to attribute `Value` is displayed at location (76, –24) using right-justified text, and a font size is set with (`textHeight 9`).

The graphical data in the symbol are contained in `figure` forms. The `path` form must contain `pointList` with two or more points. The `figure` may also contain a `rectangle` or `circle`. Two points in a `rectangle` define the opposite corners. Two points in a `circle` represent opposite ends of the diameter. In this example a `figure` from `figureGroup WIDE` has three lines representing the triangle of the inverter symbol.

Arcs use the `openShape` form. The `openShape` must contain a curve that contains an arc with three points. The three points in an arc correspond to the starting point, any point on the arc, and the end point. For example, (`openShape (curve (arc (pt - 5 0) (pt 0 5 ) (pt 5 0))))`) is an arc with a radius of 5, centered at the origin. Arcs and lines use the `pathWidth` from the `figureGroup` or `figureGroupOverride`; circles and rectangles use `borderWidth`.

The fixed text for a symbol uses `annotate` forms. The `stringDisplay` in `annotate` contains the text as a string. The `stringDisplay` contains a `display` with the `textHeight`, `justification`, and `location`. The `symbol` form can contain multiple `figure` and `annotate` forms.

9.4.4 An EDIF Example

In this section we shall illustrate the use of EDIF in translating a cell library from one set of tools to another—from a Compass Design Automation cell library to the Cadence schematic-entry tools. The code in Table 9.12 shows the EDIF description of the symbol for a two-input AND gate, an02d1, from the Compass cell library.

The Cadence schematic tools do contain a procedure, EDIFIN, that reads the Compass EDIF files. This procedure works, but, as we shall see, results in some problems when you use the icons in the Cadence schematic-entry tool. Instead we shall make some changes to the original files before we use EDIFIN to transfer the information to the Cadence database, `cdba`.

The original Compass EDIF file contains a `figureGroup` for each of the following four EDIF cell symbols:

connector_FG   icon_FG   instance_FG   net_FG bus_FG

The EDIFIN application translates each `figureGroup` to a Cadence layer–purpose pair definition that must be defined in the Cadence technology file associated with the library. If we use the original EDIF file with EDIFIN this results in the automatic modification of the Cadence technology file to define layer names, purposes, and the required properties to enable use of the `figureGroup` names. This results in non-Cadence layer names in the Cadence database.

TABLE 9.12   EDIF file for a Compass standard-cell schematic icon.

```
(edif pvsc370d
 (edifVersion 2 0 0)
 (edifLevel 0)
 (keywordMap
  (keywordLevel 0))
 (status
  (written
   (timeStamp 1993 2 9 22 38 36)
   (program "COMPASS"
    (version "v8"))
   (author "mikes")))
 (library pvsc370d
  (edifLevel 0)
  (technology
   (numberDefinition )
   (figureGroup connector_FG
    (color 100 100 100)
    (textHeight 30)
    (visible
     (true )))
   (figureGroup icon_FG
    (color 100 100 100)
    (textHeight 30)
    (visible
     (true )))
   (figureGroup instance_FG
    (color 100 100 100)
    (textHeight 30)
    (visible
     (true )))
   (figureGroup net_FG
    (color 100 100 100)
    (textHeight 30)
    (visible
     (true )))
   (figureGroup bus_FG
    (color 100 100 100)
    (textHeight 30)
    (visible
     (true ))
    (pathWidth 4)))
  (cell an02d1
   (cellType GENERIC)
   (view Icon_view
    (viewType SCHEMATIC)
    (interface
```

```
   (port A2
    (direction INPUT))
   (port A1
    (direction INPUT))
   (port Z
    (direction OUTPUT))
   (property label
    (string ""))
   (symbol
    (portImplementation
     (name A2
      (display connector_FG
       (origin
        (pt -5 1))))
      (connectLocation
       (figure connector_FG
        (dot
         (pt 0 0)))))
    (portImplementation
     (name A1
      (display connector_FG
       (origin
        (pt -5 21))))
      (connectLocation
       (figure connector_FG
        (dot
         (pt 0 20)))))
    (portImplementation
     (name Z
      (display connector_FG
       (origin
        (pt 60 15))))
      (connectLocation
       (figure connector_FG
        (dot
         (pt 60 10)))))
    (figure icon_FG
     (path
      (pointList
       (pt 0 20)
       (pt 10 20)))
     (path
      (pointList
       (pt 0 0)
       (pt 10 0)))
     (path
```

```
    (pointList
     (pt 10 -5)
     (pt 10 25)))
   (path
    (pointList
     (pt 10 -5)
     (pt 30 -5)))
   (path
    (pointList
     (pt 10 25)
     (pt 30 25)))
   (path
    (pointList
     (pt 45 10)
     (pt 60 10)))
   (openShape
    (curve
     (arc
      (pt 30 -5)
      (pt 45 10)
      (pt 30 25)))))
 (boundingBox
  (rectangle
   (pt -15 -28)
   (pt 134 27)))
 (keywordDisplay instance
  (display icon_FG
   (origin
    (pt 20 29))))
 (propertyDisplay label
  (display icon_FG
   (origin
    (pt 20 -1))))
 (keywordDisplay cell
  (display icon_FG
   (origin
    (pt 20 -10))))
 (commentGraphics
  (annotate
   (stringDisplay "1x"
    (display icon_FG
     (origin
      (pt 20 10)))))))))))))
```

First then, we need to modify the EDIF file to use the standard Cadence layer names shown in Table 9.13. These layer names and their associated purposes and properties are defined in the default Cadence technology file, `default.tf`. There is one more layer name in the Compass files (`bus_FG` figureGroup), but since this is not used in the library we can remove this definition from the EDIF input file.

TABLE 9.13 Compass and corresponding Cadence `figureGroup` names.

Compass name	Cadence name	Compass name	Cadence name
connector_FG	pin	net_FG	wire
icon_FG	device	bus_FG	not used
instance_FG	instance		

Internal scaling differences lead to giant characters in the Cadence tools if we use the `textHeight` of 30 defined in the EDIF file. Reducing the `textHeight` to 5 results in a reasonable text height.

The EDIF `numberDefinition` construct, together with the `scale` construct, defines measurement scaling in an EDIF file. In a Cadence schematic EDIF file the `numberDefinition` and `scale` construct is determined by an entry in the associated library technology file that defines the `edifUnit` to `userUnit` ratio. This ratio affects the printed size of an icon.

For example, the distance defined by the following `path` construct is 10 EDIF units:

```
(path (pointlist (pt 0 0) (pt 0 10)))
```

What is the length of 10 EDIF units? The `numberDefinition` and `scale` construct associates EDIF units with a physical dimension. The following construct

```
(numberDefinition (scale 100 (e 25400 -6) unit DISTANCE))
```

specifies that 100 EDIF units equal 25400×10^{-6} m or approximately 1 inch. Cadence defines schematic measurements in inches by defining the `userUnit` property of the affected `viewType` or `viewName` as inch in the Cadence technology file. The Compass EDIF files do not provide values for the `numberDefinition` and `scale` construct, and the Cadence tools default to a value of 160 EDIF units to 1 user unit. We thus need to add a `numberDefinition` and `scale` construct to the Compass EDIF file to control the printed size of icons.

The EDIF file defines blank label placeholders for each cell using the EDIF `property` construct. Cadence EDIFIN does recognize and translate EDIF properties, but to attach a label property to a `cellview` object it must be defined (not blank) and identified as a property using the EDIF `owner` construct in the EDIF file. Since the intent of a placeholder is to hold an empty spot for later use and since

Cadence Composer (the schematic-entry tool) supports label additions to instantiated icons, we can remove the EDIF `label` property construct in each cell and the associated `propertyDisplay` construct from the Compass file.

There is a problem that we need to resolve with naming. This is a problem that sooner or later everyone must tackle in ASIC design—**case sensitivity**.

In EDIF, input and output pins are called ports and they are identified using `portImplementation` constructs. In order that the ports of a particular cell `icon_view` are correctly associated with the ports in the related functional, layout, and abstract views, they must all have the same name. The Cadence tools are case sensitive in this respect. The Verilog and CIF files corresponding to each cell in the Compass library use lowercase names for each port of a given cell, whereas the EDIF file uses uppercase. The EDIFIN translator allows the case of cell, view, and port names to be automatically changed on translation. Thus pin names such as `'A1'` become `'a1'` and the original view name `'Icon_view'` becomes `'icon_view'`.

The `boundingBox` construct defines a bounding box around a symbol (icon). Schematic-capture tools use this to implement various functions. The Cadence Composer tool, for example, uses the bounding box to control the wiring between cells and as a highlight box when selecting components of a schematic. Compass uses a large `boundingBox` definition for the cells to allow space for long hierarchical names. Figure 9.10(a) shows the original `an02d1` cell bounding box that is larger than the cell icon.

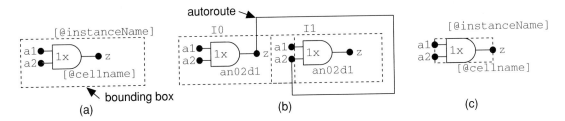

FIGURE 9.10 The bounding box problem. (a) The original bounding box for the an02d1 icon. (b) Problems in Cadence Composer due to overlapping bounding boxes. (c) A "shrink-wrapped" bounding box created using SKILL.

Icons with large bounding boxes create two problems in Composer. Highlighting all or part of a complex design consisting of many closely spaced cells results in a confusion of overlapped highlight boxes. Also, large boxes force strange wiring patterns between cells that are placed too closely together when Composer's automatic routing algorithm is used. Figure 9.10(b) shows an example of this problem.

There are two solutions to the bounding-box problem. We could modify each `boundingBox` definition in the original EDIF file before translation to conform to the outline of the icon. This involves identifying the outline of each icon in the

EDIF file and is difficult. A simpler approach is to use the Cadence tool programming language, SKILL. SKILL provides direct access to the Cadence database, cdba, in order to modify and create objects. Using SKILL you can use a batch file to call functions normally accessed interactively. The solution to the bounding box problem is:

1. Use EDIFIN to create the views in the Cadence database, cdba.
2. Use the schCreateInstBox() command on each icon_view object to eliminate the original bounding box and create a new, minimum-sized, bounding box that is "shrink-wrapped" to each icon.

Figure 9.10(c) shows the results of this process. This modification fixes the problems with highlighting and wiring in Cadence Composer.

This completes the steps required to translate the schematic icons from one set of tools to another. The process can be automated in three ways:

- Write UNIX sed and awk scripts to make the changes to the EDIF file before using EDIFIN and SKILL.
- Write custom C programs to make the changes to the EDIF file and then proceed as in 1.
- Perform all the work using SKILL.

The last approach is the most elegant and most easily maintained but is the most difficult to implement (mostly because of the time required to learn SKILL). The whole project took several weeks (including the time it took to learn how to use each of the tools). This is typical of the problems you face when trying to convert data from one system to another.

9.5   CFI Design Representation

The **CAD Framework Initiative (CFI)** is an independent nonprofit organization working on the creation of standards for the electronic CAD industry. One of the areas in which CFI is working is the definition of standards for **design representation (DR)**. The CFI 1.0 standard [CFI, 1992] has tackled the problems of ambiguity in the area of definitions and terms for schematics by defining an **information model (IM)** for electrical connectivity information.

What this means is that a group of engineers got together and proposed a standard way of using the terms and definitions that we have discussed. There are good things and bad things about standards, and one aspect of the CFI 1.0 DR standard illustrates this point. A good thing about the CFI 1.0 DR standard is that it precisely defines what we mean by terms and definitions in schematics, for example. A bad thing about the CFI DR standard is that in order to be precise it introduces yet more terms that are difficult to understand. A very brief discussion of the CFI 1.0 DR standard is included here, at the end of this chapter, for several reasons:

- It helps to solidify the concepts of the terms and definitions such as cell, net, and instance that we have already discussed. However, there are additional new concepts and terms to define in order to present the standard model, so this is not a good way to introduce schematic terminology.

- The ASIC design engineer is becoming more of a programmer and less of a circuit designer. This trend shows no sign of stopping as ASICs grow larger and systems more complex. A precise understanding of how tools operate and interact is becoming increasingly important.

9.5.1   CFI Connectivity Model

The CFI connectivity model is defined using the **EXPRESS language** and its graphical equivalent **EXPRESS-G**. EXPRESS is an International Standards Organization (ISO) standard [EXPRESS, 1991]. EDIF 3 0 0 and higher also use EXPRESS as the internal formal description of the language. EXPRESS is used to define objects and their relationships. Figure 9.11 shows some simple examples of the EXPRESS-G notation.

The following EXPRESS code (a **schema**) is equivalent to the EXPRESS-G family model shown in Figure 9.11(c):

```
SCHEMA family_model;
   ENTITY person
      ABSTRACT SUPERTYPE OF (ONEOF (man, woman, child));
      name: STRING;
      date of birth: STRING;
   END_ENTITY;

   ENTITY man
      SUBTYPE OF (person);
      wife: SET[0:1] OF woman;
      children: SET[0:?] OF child;
   END_ENTITY;

   ENTITY woman
      SUBTYPE OF (person);
      husband: SET[0:1] OF man;
      children: SET[0:?] OF child;
   END_ENTITY;

   ENTITY child
      SUBTYPE OF (person);
      father: man;
      mother: woman;
```

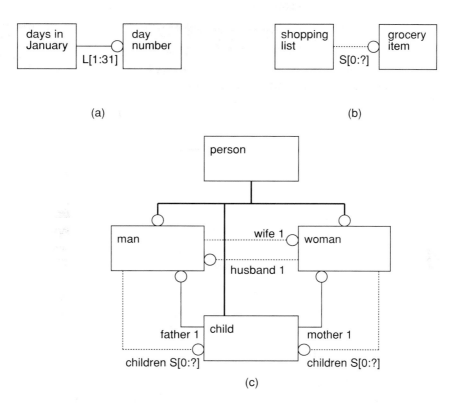

FIGURE 9.11 Examples of EXPRESS-G. (a) Each day in January has a number from 1 to 31. (b) A shopping list may contain a list of items. (c) An EXPRESS-G model for a family.

```
    END_ENTITY;
END_SCHEMA;
```

This **EXPRESS** description is a formal way of saying the following:

- "Men, women, and children are people."
- "A man can have one woman as a wife, but does not have to."
- "A wife can have one man as a husband, but does not have to."
- "A man or a woman can have several children."
- "A child has one father and one mother."

Computers can deal more easily with the formal language version of these statements. The formal language and graphical forms are more precise for very complex models.

Figure 9.12 shows the basic structure of the CFI 1.0.0 **Base Connectivity Model (BCM)**. The actual EXPRESS-G diagram for the BCM defined in the CFI 1.0.0 standard is only a little more complicated than Figure 9.12 (containing 21 boxes or types rather than just six). The extra types are used for bundles (a group of nets) and different views of cells (other than the netlist view).

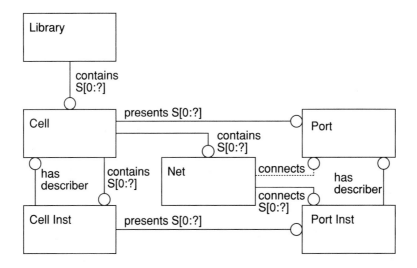

FIGURE 9.12 The original "five-box" model of electrical connectivity. There are actually six boxes or types in this figure; the Library type was added later.

Figure 9.12 says the following ("presents" as used in Figure 9.12 is the Express jargon for "have"):

- "A library contains cells."
- "Cells have ports, contain nets, and can contain other cells."
- "Cell instances are copies of a cell and have port instances."
- "A port instance is a copy of the port in the library cell."
- "You connect to a port using a net."
- "Nets connect port instances together."

Once you understand Figure 9.12 you will see that it replaces the first half of this chapter. Unfortunately you have to read the first half of this chapter to understand Figure 9.12.

9.6 Summary

The important concepts that we covered in this chapter are:

- Schematic entry using a cell library
- Cells and cell instances, nets and ports
- Bus naming, vectored instances in datapath
- Hierarchy
- Editing cells
- PLD languages: ABEL, PALASM, and CUPL
- Logic minimization
- The functions of EDIF
- CFI representation of design information

9.7 Problems

9.1 (EDIF description)

a. (5 min.) Write an EDIF description for an icon for an inverter (just the input and output wires, a triangle, and a bubble). What problems do you face and what assumptions did you make?

b. (30 min.+) Try and import your symbol into your schematic-entry tool. If you fail (as you might) explain what the problem is and suggest a direction of attack. *Hint:* If you can, try Problem 9.2 first.

9.2 (EDIF inverter, 15 min.) If you have access to a tool that generates EDIF for the icons, write out the EDIF for an inverter icon. Explain the code.

9.3 (EDIF netlist, 20 min.) Starting with an empty directory and using a schematic editor (such as Viewlogic) draw a schematic with a single inverter (from any cell library).

a. List the files that are created in the directory.

b. Print each one (check first to make sure it is ASCII, not binary).

c. Try and explain the contents.

9.4 (Minitutorial, 60 min.) Write a minitutorial (no more than five pages) that explains how to set up your system (location and nature of any start-up files such as .ini files for Viewlogic and so on); how to choose or change a library (for cell icons); how to choose cells, instantiate, label, and connect them; how to select, copy and delete symbols; and how to save a schematic. Use a single inverter connected to an input and output pad as an example.

9.5 (Icons, 30 min.) With an example show how to edit and create a symbol icon. Make a triangular icon (the same size as an inverter in your library but without a bubble) for a series connection of two inverters and call it `myBuffer`.

9.6 (Buses, 30 min.)

a. Create an example of a 16-bit bus: connect 8 inverters to bit zero (the MSB or leftmost bit) and bits 10–16 (as if we were taking the sign bit, bit zero, and the seven least-significant bits from a 16-bit signed number). Name the inverter connected to the sign bit, `SIGN`. Name the other inverters `BIT0` through `BIT7`.

b. Write the netlist as an EDIF file, number the lines, and explain the contents by referencing line numbers.

9.7 (VDD and VSS, 30 min.) Using a simple example of two inverters (one with input connected to VDD, the other with input connected to VSS or GND) explain how your schematic-entry system handles global power and ground nets and their connection to cell pins. Can you connect VDD or VSS to an output pin in your system? If your schematic software has a netlist screener, try it on this example.

9.8 (Hierarchy, 30 min.) Create a very simple hierarchical cell. The lowest level, named `bottom`, contains a single inverter (named `invB`). The highest level, called `top`, contains another inverter, `invT`, whose input is connected to the output of cell `bottom`. Write out the netlist (in internal and EDIF format) and explain how the tool labels a hierarchical cell.

9.9 (Vectored instances, 30 min.) Create a vectored instance of eight inverters, `inv0` through `inv7`. Write the netlist in internal and EDIF form and explain the contents.

9.10 (Dangling wires, 30 min.) Create a cell, `dangle1`, containing two inverters, `inv1` and `inv2`. Connect the input of `inv1` to an external connector, `in1`, and the output of `inv2` to an external connector `out2`. Write the netlist and explain what happens to the unlabeled and unused nets. If you have a netlist screener, run it on this example.

9.11 (PLD languages, 60 min.) Conduct a Web search on ABEL, CUPL, or PALASM (start by searching for "Logical Devices" not "ABEL"). Try and find examples of these files and write an explanation of their function using the descriptions of these languages in this chapter.

9.12 (EDIF 3 0 0, 10 min.) Download the EDIF 3 0 0 example schematic file from `http://www.edif.org/edif/workshop.edf` and see if your EDIF reader will accept it. What is it?

9.13 (EXPRESS-G, 15 min.) Draw an EXPRESS-G diagram for the government of your country. For example, in the United States you would start with the president and the White House and work down through the House and Senate, showing the senators and congressional representatives. In the United Kingdom you would draw the prime minister, the House of Commons, and House of Lords with the various MPs.

9.14 (ABEL PCI Target) (10 min.) Download the Xilinx Application Note, Designing Flexible PCI Interfaces with Xilinx EPLDs, January 1995 (pci_epld.pdf at www.xilinx.com). The Appendix of this App. Note contains the ABEL source code for a PCI Bus Interface Target. The code is long but straightforward; most of it describes the next-state transitions for the bus-controller state machine. Extract the ABEL source code using Adobe Acrobat. *Hint:* This is not easy; Acrobat does a poor job of selecting text; you will lose many semicolons at the end of lines that you will have to add by hand. Use Replace... to search for end-of-line, "^p", and replace by " ; ^p" in Word. (60 min.+) Try to convert this code to a system where you can compile it. You may need conversion utilities to do this. For example Altera (www.altera.com) has utilities (EAU018.EXE and EAU019.EXE located at ftp.altera.com/pub) to convert from ABEL 4.0 to AHDL.

9.15 (CUPL, 60 min.) Download and install the CUPL demonstration package from http://www.protel.com/download.htm. Write a two-page help sheet on what you did, where the software is installed, and how to run it.

9.16 (PALASM) (30 min.) Download and install PALASM4 v1.5 from the AMD Web site at ftp://ftp.amd.com/pub/pld/software/palasm.

9.17 (CUPL)

a. (15 min.) Check the equations in the CUPL code for the 4-bit counter in Section 9.2.

b. (10 min.) Add a count-enable signal to the code.

c. (30 min.) If you have access to CUPL, compile your answer.

9.18 (EDIF)

a. (30 min.) Using the syntax definitions below and the example schematic icon shown in Table 9.12 to help you, "stitch" back together the EDIF definition for the 7404 inverter symbol used as an example in Section 9.4.3.

b. (60 min.+) Try to import the EDIF into your schematic entry system. Comment on any problems and how you attempted to resolve them (including failures).

The **EDIF Reference Manual** [EDIF, 1988] uses the following metasyntax rules:

```
[optional] <at most once> {may be repeated zero or more times}
{this|that} indicates any number of this or that in any order
syntactic names are italic
literal words are bold
SYMBOLIC constants are uppercase
IdentifierNameDef means the name is being defined
IdentifierNameRef means the name is being referenced
```

The syntax definitions of the most common EDIF constructs for schematics are as follows:

```
(edif edifFileNameDef
  edifVersion
```

```
        edifLevel
        keywordMap
        {<status>|external|library|design|comment|userdata} )
(library libraryNameDef
        edifLevel
        technology
        {<status>|cell|comment|userdata} )
(technology numberDefinition
        {figureGroup|fabricate|
        <simulationInfos>|<physicalDesignRule>|comment|userdata} )
(cell cellNameDef
        cellType
        {<status>|view|<viewMap>|property|comment|userdata} )
(view viewNameDef
        viewType
        interface
        {<status>|<contents>|comment|property|userdata} )
(interface
        {port|portBundle|<symbol>|<protectionFrame>|
<arrayRelatedInfo>|parameter|joined|mustJoin|weakJoined|
permutable|timing|simulate|<designator>|property|comment|userdata} )
(contents
        {instance|offPageConnector|figure|section|
net|netBundle|page|commentGraphics|portImplementation|
timing|simulate|when|follow|logicPort|<boundingBox>|
comment|userdata} )
(viewMap
        {portMap|portBackAnnotate|instanceMap|instanceBackAnnotate|
netMap|netBackAnnotate|comment|userdata} )
```

9.8 Bibliography

The data books from AMD, Atmel, and other PLD manufacturers are excellent sources of tutorials, examples, and information on PLD design. The EDIF tutorials produced by the EIA [EDIF, 1988, 1989] are hard to find, but there are few other texts or sources that explain EDIF. EDIF does have a World Wide Web site at http://www.edif.org. The EDIF Technical Centre at the University of Manchester (http://www.cs.man.ac.uk/cad, I shall refer to this as ~EDIF) serves as a resource center for EDIF, including the formal information models of the EDIF language in EXPRESS format and the BNF definitions of the language syntax. There is a hypertext version of an EDIF 3 0 0 schematic file with hypertext links at ~EDIF/EDIFTechnicalCenter/software. CFI has a home page and links to other sites at http://www.cfi.org.

PALASM4 v1.5 is available as "freeware" from AMD at `ftp://ftp.amd.com/pub/pld/software/palasm` The Data I/O home page at `http://www.data-io.com` is devoted mainly to Synario. The Viewlogic home page is `http://www.viewlogic.com`. Capilano Computing has a Web page at `http://www.capilano.com` with DesignWorks and MacABEL software. Protel (`http://www.protel.com/download.htm`) has Windows-based schematic-entry tools for FPGAs and a CUPL demonstration package. Logical Devices has a site at `http://www.logicaldevices.com`. Atmel has several demonstration and code examples for ABEL and CUPL at `ftp://www.atmel.com/pub/atmel`.

9.9 References

Page numbers in brackets after a reference indicate its location in the chapter body.

CFI Standards for Electronic Design Automation Release 1.0. 1992. CFI published a four-volume set in 1992, ISBN 1-882750-00-4 (set). The first volume, ISBN 1-882750-01-2, is approximately 300 pages and contains a brief introduction (approximately 10 pages) and the Electrical Connectivity model. Unfortunately two of the volumes were labeled as volume three. The (first) third volume is the Tool Encapsulation Specification, ISBN 1-882750-03-09 (approximately 100 pages). The (second) third volume, ISBN 1-882750-02-0, covers the Inter-Tool Communication Programming Interface (approximately 150 pages). The fourth volume, ISBN 1-882750-04-7, is approximately 100 pages long and covers the Computing Environment Services requirement [p. 369].

EDIF is maintained by the EIA, EIA Standards Sales Office, 2001 Pennsylvania Ave., N.W., Washington, DC 20006, (202) 457-4966 [p. 355]:

EDIF Steering Committee. 1988. EDIF Reference Manual Version 2.0.0. Washington, DC: Electronic Industries Association. ISBN 0-7908-0000-4.

EDIF Steering Committee. 1988. Introduction to EDIF. Washington, DC: Electronic Industries Association. ISBN 0-7908-0001-2.

EDIF Steering Committee. 1989. EDIF Connectivity. Washington, DC: Electronic Industries Association. ISBN 0-7908-0002-0.

EDIF Schematic Technical Subcommittee. 1989. Using EDIF 2.0.0 for Schematic Transfer. Washington, DC: Electronic Industries Association.

EXPRESS Language Reference Manual. ISO TC184/SC4/WG5 Document N14, March 29, 1991 [p. 370].

VHDL

The U.S. Department of Defense (DoD) supported the development of **VHDL** (**VHSIC hardware description language**) as part of the **VHSIC (very high-speed IC**) program in the early 1980s. The companies in the VHSIC program found they needed something more than schematic entry to describe large ASICs, and proposed the creation of a hardware description language. VHDL was then handed over to the Institute of Electrical and Electronics Engineers (IEEE) in order to develop and approve the IEEE Standard 1076-1987.[1] As part of its standardization process the DoD has specified the use of VHDL as the documentation, simulation, and verification medium for ASICs (MIL-STD-454). Partly for this reason VHDL has gained

---

[1]Some of the material in this chapter is reprinted with permission from IEEE Std 1076-1993, © 1993 IEEE. All rights reserved.

rapid acceptance, initially for description and documentation, and then for design entry, simulation, and synthesis as well.

The first revision of the 1076 standard was approved in 1993. References to the VHDL **Language Reference Manual** (**LRM**) in this chapter—[VHDL 87LRM2.1, 93LRM2.2] for example—point to the 1987 and 1993 versions of the LRM [IEEE, 1076-1987 and 1076-1993]. The prefixes 87 and 93 are omitted if the references are the same in both editions. Technically 1076-1987 (known as VHDL-87) is now obsolete and replaced by 1076-1993 (known as VHDL-93). Except for code that is marked 'VHDL-93 only' the examples in this chapter can be **analyzed** (the VHDL word for "compiled") and simulated using both VHDL-87 and VHDL-93 systems.

10.1 A Counter

The following VHDL model describes an electrical "black box" that contains a 50 MHz clock generator and a counter. The counter increments on the negative edge of the clock, counting from zero to seven, and then begins at zero again. The model contains separate *processes* that execute at the same time as each other. Modeling concurrent execution is the major difference between HDLs and computer programming languages such as C.

```
entity Counter_1 is end; -- declare a "black box" called Counter_1
library STD; use STD.TEXTIO.all; -- we need this library to print
architecture Behave_1 of Counter_1 is -- describe the "black box"
-- declare a signal for the clock, type BIT, initial value '0'
    signal Clock : BIT := '0';
-- declare a signal for the count, type INTEGER, initial value 0
    signal Count : INTEGER := 0;
begin
    process begin -- process to generate the clock
        wait for 10 ns; -- a delay of 10 ns is half the clock cycle
        Clock <= not Clock;
        if (now > 340 ns) then wait; end if; -- stop after 340 ns
    end process;
-- process to do the counting, runs concurrently with other processes
    process begin
-- wait here until the clock goes from 1 to 0
        wait until (Clock = '0');
-- now handle the counting
        if (Count = 7) then Count <= 0;
        else Count <= Count + 1;
        end if;
    end process;
    process (Count) variable L: LINE; begin -- process to print
        write(L, now); write(L, STRING'(" Count="));
        write(L, Count); writeline(output, L);
    end process;
end;
```

Throughout this book VHDL **keywords** (reserved words that are part of the language) are shown in bold type in code examples (but not in the text). The code examples use the bold keywords to improve readability. VHDL code is often lengthy and the code in this book is always complete wherever possible. In order to save space many of the code examples do not use the conventional spacing and formatting that is normally considered good practice. So "Do as I say and not as I do."

The steps to simulate the model and the printed results for `Counter_1` using the Model Technology V-System/Plus common-kernel simulator are as follows:

```
> vlib work
> vcom Counter_1.vhd
Model Technology VCOM V-System VHDL/Verilog 4.5b
-- Loading package standard
-- Compiling entity counter_1
-- Loading package textio
-- Compiling architecture behave_1 of counter_1
> vsim -c counter_1
# Loading /../std.standard
# Loading /../std.textio(body)
# Loading work.counter_1(behave_1)
VSIM 1> run 500
# 0 ns Count=0
# 20 ns Count=1
(...15 lines omitted...)
# 340 ns Count=1
VSIM 2> quit
>
```

10.2   A 4-bit Multiplier

This section presents a more complex VHDL example to motivate the study of the syntax and semantics of VHDL in the rest of this chapter.

10.2.1   An 8-bit Adder

Table 10.1 shows a VHDL model for the full adder that we described in Section 2.6, "Datapath Logic Cells." Table 10.2 shows a VHDL model for an 8-bit ripple-carry adder that uses eight instances of the full adder.

10.2.2   A Register Accumulator

Table 10.3 shows a VHDL model for a positive-edge–triggered D flip-flop with an active-high asynchronous clear. Table 10.4 shows an 8-bit register that uses this D flip-flop model (this model only provides the Q output from the register and leaves the QN flip-flop outputs unconnected).

TABLE 10.1 A full adder.

```
entity Full_Adder is                                          --1
   generic (TS : TIME := 0.11 ns; TC : TIME := 0.1 ns);       --2
   port (X, Y, Cin: in BIT; Cout, Sum: out  BIT);             --3
end Full_Adder;                                               --4

architecture Behave of Full_Adder is                          --5
begin                                                         --6
Sum  <= X xor Y xor Cin after TS;                             --7
Cout <= (X and Y) or (X and Cin) or (Y and Cin) after TC;     --8
end;                                                          --9
```

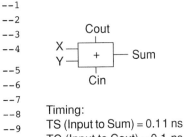

Timing:
TS (Input to Sum) = 0.11 ns
TC (Input to Cout) = 0.1 ns

TABLE 10.2 An 8-bit ripple-carry adder.

```
entity Adder8 is                                          --1
   port (A, B: in BIT_VECTOR(7 downto 0);                 --2
   Cin: in BIT; Cout: out BIT;                            --3
   Sum: out BIT_VECTOR(7 downto 0));                      --4
end Adder8;                                               --5

architecture Structure of Adder8 is                       --6
component Full_Adder                                      --7
port (X, Y, Cin: in BIT; Cout, Sum: out BIT);            --8
end component;                                            --9
signal C: BIT_VECTOR(7 downto 0);                        --10
begin                                                     --11
Stages: for i in 7 downto 0 generate                      --12
   LowBit: if i = 0 generate                              --13
   FA:Full_Adder port map (A(0),B(0),Cin,C(0),Sum(0));    --14
   end generate;                                          --15
   OtherBits: if i /= 0 generate                          --16
   FA:Full_Adder port map                                 --17
     (A(i),B(i),C(i-1),C(i),Sum(i));                      --18
   end generate;                                          --19
end generate;                                             --20
Cout <= C(7);                                             --21
end;                                                      --22
```

TABLE 10.3   Positive-edge–triggered D flip-flop with asynchronous clear.

```
entity DFFClr is                                      --1
   generic(TRQ : TIME := 2 ns; TCQ : TIME := 2 ns);   --2
   port (CLR, CLK, D : in BIT; Q, QB : out BIT);      --3
end;                                                  --4

architecture Behave of DFFClr is                      --5
signal Qi : BIT;                                      --6
begin QB <= not Qi; Q <= Qi;                          --7
process (CLR, CLK) begin                              --8
   if CLR = '1' then Qi <= '0' after TRQ;             --9
   elsif CLK'EVENT and CLK = '1'                      --10
      then Qi <= D after TCQ;                         --11
   end if;                                            --12
end process;                                          --13
end;                                                  --14
```

Timing:
TRQ (CLR to Q/QN) = 2 ns
TCQ (CLK to Q/QN) = 2 ns

TABLE 10.4   An 8-bit register.

```
entity Register8 is                                   --1
   port (D : in BIT_VECTOR(7 downto 0);               --2
   Clk, Clr: in BIT ; Q : out BIT_VECTOR(7 downto 0));--3
end;                                                  --4

architecture Structure of Register8 is                --5
   component DFFClr                                   --6
      port (Clr, Clk, D : in BIT; Q, QB : out BIT);   --7
   end component;                                      --8
   begin                                              --9
      STAGES: for i in 7 downto 0 generate            --10
      FF: DFFClr port map (Clr, Clk, D(i), Q(i), open);--11
      end generate;                                    --12
end;                                                  --13
```

8-bit register. Uses DFFClr positive edge-triggered flip-flop model.

Table 10.5 shows a model for a datapath multiplexer that consists of eight 2:1 multiplexers with a common select input (this select signal would normally be a control signal in a datapath). The multiplier will use the register and multiplexer components to implement a register accumulator.

10.2.3   Zero Detector

Table 10.6 shows a model for a variable-width zero detector that accepts a bus of any width and will produce a single-bit output of '1' if all input bits are zero.

TABLE 10.5   An 8-bit multiplexer.

```
entity Mux8 is                                              --1
  generic (TPD : TIME := 1 ns);                             --2
  port (A, B : in BIT_VECTOR (7 downto 0);                 --3
  Sel : in BIT := '0'; Y : out BIT_VECTOR (7 downto 0));   --4
end;                                                        --5

architecture Behave of Mux8 is                             --6
begin                                                       --7
  Y <= A after TPD when Sel = '1' else B after TPD;        --8
end;                                                        --9
```

Eight 2:1 MUXs with single select input.
Timing:
TPD(input to Y)=1 ns

TABLE 10.6   A zero detector.

```
entity AllZero is                                          --1
  generic (TPD : TIME := 1 ns);                            --2
  port (X : BIT_VECTOR; F : out BIT );                     --3
end;                                                       --4

architecture Behave of AllZero is                          --5
begin process (X) begin F <= '1' after TPD;                --6
  for j in X'RANGE loop                                    --7
    if X(j) = '1' then F <= '0' after TPD; end if;         --8
  end loop;                                                --9
end process;                                               --10
end;                                                       --11
```

Variable-width zero detector.
Timing:
TPD(X to F) =1 ns

10.2.4   A Shift Register

Table 10.7 shows a variable-width shift register that shifts (left or right under input control, DIR) on the positive edge of the clock, CLK, gated by a shift enable, SH. The parallel load, LD, is synchronous and aligns the input LSB to the LSB of the output, filling unused MSBs with zero. Bits vacated during shifts are zero filled. The clear, CLR, is asynchronous.

10.2.5   A State Machine

To multiply two binary numbers A and B, we can use the following algorithm:

1. If the LSB of A is '1', then add B into an accumulator.
2. Shift A one bit to the right and B one bit to the left.
3. Stop when all bits of A are zero.

TABLE 10.7   A variable-width shift register.

```
entity ShiftN is                                              --1
  generic (TCQ : TIME := 0.3 ns; TLQ : TIME := 0.5 ns;        --2
    TSQ : TIME := 0.7 ns);                                    --3
  port(CLK, CLR, LD, SH, DIR: in BIT;                         --4
    D: in BIT_VECTOR; Q: out BIT_VECTOR);                     --5
  begin assert (D'LENGTH <= Q'LENGTH)                         --6
    report "D wider than output Q" severity Failure;          --7
end ShiftN;                                                   --8

architecture Behave of ShiftN is                              --9
  begin Shift: process (CLR, CLK)                             --10
  subtype InB  is NATURAL range D'LENGTH-1 downto 0;          --11
  subtype OutB is NATURAL range Q'LENGTH-1 downto 0;          --12
  variable St: BIT_VECTOR(OutB);                              --13
  begin                                                       --14
    if CLR = '1' then                                         --15
      St := (others => '0'); Q <= St after TCQ;               --16
    elsif CLK'EVENT and CLK='1' then                          --17
      if LD = '1' then                                        --18
        St := (others => '0');                                --19
        St(InB) := D;                                         --20
        Q <= St after TLQ;                                    --21
      elsif SH = '1' then                                     --22
        case DIR is                                           --23
        when '0' => St := '0' & St(St'LEFT downto 1);         --24
        when '1' => St := St(St'LEFT-1 downto 0) & '0';       --25
        end case;                                             --26
        Q <= St after TSQ;                                    --27
      end if;                                                 --28
    end if;                                                   --29
  end process;                                                --30
end;                                                          --31
```

D ─/─┐ n   m ┌─/─ Q
LD ───┤   │
SH ───┤   │
DIR───┤   │
CLK──▷┤   │
      └──────────────┘
         │CLR

CLK	Clock
CLR	Clear, active high
LD	Load, active high
SH	Shift, active high
DIR	Direction, 1 = left
D	Data in
Q	Data out

Variable-width shift register. Input width must be less than output width. Output is left-shifted or right-shifted under control of DIR. Unused MSBs are zero-padded during load. Clear is asynchronous. Load is synchronous.

Timing:
T_{CQ} (CLR to Q) = 0.3ns
T_{LQ} (LD to Q) = 0.5ns
T_{SQ} (SH to Q) = 0. 7ns

Table 10.8 shows the VHDL model for a Moore (outputs depend only on the state) finite-state machine for the multiplier, together with its state diagram.

10.2.6   A Multiplier

Table 10.9 shows a schematic and the VHDL code that describes the interconnection of all the components for the multiplier. Notice that the schematic comprises two halves: an 8-bit-wide datapath section (consisting of the registers, adder, multiplexer,

TABLE 10.8   A Moore state machine for the multiplier.

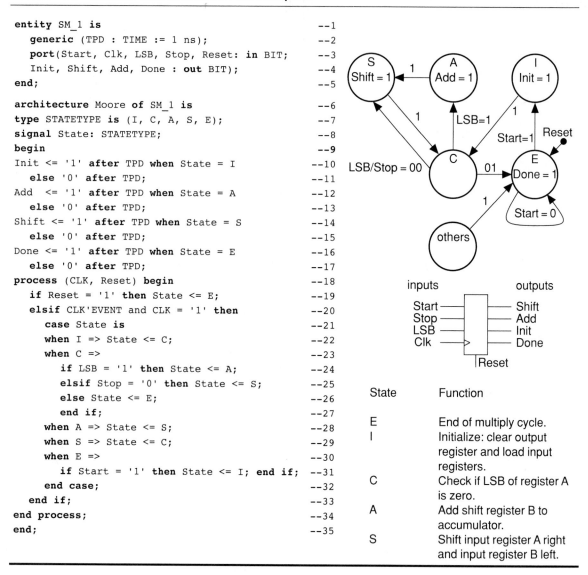

```
entity SM_1 is                                    --1
   generic (TPD : TIME := 1 ns);                  --2
   port(Start, Clk, LSB, Stop, Reset: in BIT;     --3
   Init, Shift, Add, Done : out BIT);             --4
end;                                              --5

architecture Moore of SM_1 is                     --6
type STATETYPE is (I, C, A, S, E);                --7
signal State: STATETYPE;                          --8
begin                                             --9
Init <= '1' after TPD when State = I              --10
   else '0' after TPD;                            --11
Add  <= '1' after TPD when State = A              --12
   else '0' after TPD;                            --13
Shift <= '1' after TPD when State = S             --14
   else '0' after TPD;                            --15
Done <= '1' after TPD when State = E              --16
   else '0' after TPD;                            --17
process (CLK, Reset) begin                        --18
   if Reset = '1' then State <= E;                --19
   elsif CLK'EVENT and CLK = '1' then             --20
      case State is                               --21
      when I => State <= C;                       --22
      when C =>                                   --23
         if LSB = '1' then State <= A;            --24
         elsif Stop = '0' then State <= S;        --25
         else State <= E;                         --26
         end if;                                  --27
      when A => State <= S;                        --28
      when S => State <= C;                        --29
      when E =>                                    --30
         if Start = '1' then State <= I; end if;  --31
      end case;                                    --32
   end if;                                         --33
end process;                                       --34
end;                                               --35
```

State	Function
E	End of multiply cycle.
I	Initialize: clear output register and load input registers.
C	Check if LSB of register A is zero.
A	Add shift register B to accumulator.
S	Shift input register A right and input register B left.

and zero detector) and a control section (the finite-state machine). The arrows in the schematic denote the inputs and outputs of each component. As we shall see in Section 10.7, VHDL has strict rules about the direction of connections.

TABLE 10.9   A 4-bit by 4-bit multiplier.

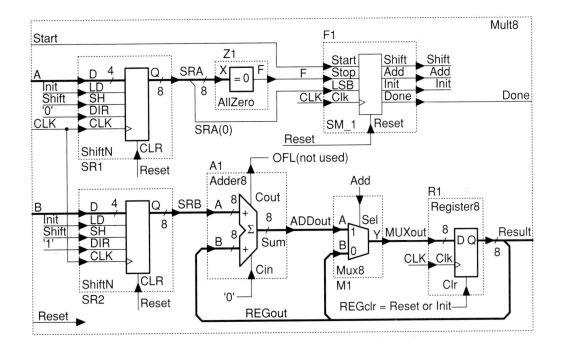

```
entity Mult8 is                                                                        --1
port (A, B: in BIT_VECTOR(3 downto 0); Start, CLK, Reset: in BIT;                       --2
Result: out BIT_VECTOR(7 downto 0); Done: out BIT); end Mult8;                          --3

architecture Structure of Mult8 is use work.Mult_Components.all;                        --4
signal SRA, SRB, ADDout, MUXout, REGout: BIT_VECTOR(7 downto 0);                        --5
signal Zero, Init, Shift, Add, Low: BIT := '0'; signal High: BIT := '1';                --6
signal F, OFL, REGclr: BIT;                                                             --7
begin                                                                                  --8
REGclr <= Init or Reset; Result  <= REGout;                                            --9
SR1 : ShiftN port map(CLK=>CLK,CLR=>Reset,LD=>Init,SH=>Shift,DIR=>Low ,D=>A,Q=>SRA);   --10
SR2 : ShiftN port map(CLK=>CLK,CLR=>Reset,LD=>Init,SH=>Shift,DIR=>High,D=>B,Q=>SRB);   --11
Z1 : AllZero port map(X=>SRA,F=>Zero);                                                  --12
A1 : Adder8  port map(A=>SRB,B=>REGout,Cin=>Low,Cout=>OFL,Sum=>ADDout);                 --13
M1 : Mux8    port map(A=>ADDout,B=>REGout,Sel=>Add,Y=>MUXout);                          --14
R1 : Register8 port map(D=>MUXout,Q=>REGout,Clk=>CLK,Clr=>REGclr);                      --15
F1 : SM_1    port map(Start,CLK,SRA(0),Zero,Reset,Init,Shift,Add,Done);                 --16
end;                                                                                    --17
```

10.2.7   Packages and Testbench

To complete and test the multiplier design we need a few more items. First we need the following "components list" for the items in Table 10.9:

```
package Mult_Components is                                        --1
component Mux8 port (A,B:BIT_VECTOR(7 downto 0);                  --2
  Sel:BIT;Y:out BIT_VECTOR(7 downto 0));end component;           --3
component AllZero port (X : BIT_VECTOR;                           --4
  F:out BIT );end component;                                      --5
component Adder8 port (A,B:BIT_VECTOR(7 downto 0);Cin:BIT;        --6
  Cout:out BIT;Sum:out BIT_VECTOR(7 downto 0));end component;     --7
component Register8 port (D:BIT_VECTOR(7 downto 0);               --8
  Clk,Clr:BIT; Q:out BIT_VECTOR(7 downto 0));end component;       --9
component ShiftN port (CLK,CLR,LD,SH,DIR:BIT;D:BIT_VECTOR;        --10
  Q:out BIT_VECTOR);end component;                                --11
component SM_1 port (Start,CLK,LSB,Stop,Reset:BIT;                --12
  Init,Shift,Add,Done:out BIT);end component;                    --13
end;                                                              --14
```

Next we need some utility code to help test the multiplier. The following VHDL generates a clock with programmable "high" time (HT) and "low" time (LT):

```
package Clock_Utils is                                           --1
procedure Clock (signal C: out Bit; HT, LT:TIME);                --2
end Clock_Utils;                                                 --3

package body Clock_Utils is                                      --4
procedure Clock (signal C: out Bit; HT, LT:TIME) is             --5
begin                                                           --6
  loop C<='1' after LT, '0' after LT + HT; wait for LT + HT;    --7
  end loop;                                                     --8
end;                                                            --9
end Clock_Utils;                                                --10
```

Finally, the following code defines two functions that we shall also use for testing—the functions convert an array of bits to a number and vice-versa:

```
package Utils is                                                 --1
  function Convert (N,L: NATURAL) return BIT_VECTOR;            --2
  function Convert (B: BIT_VECTOR) return NATURAL;              --3
end Utils;                                                       --4

package body Utils is                                            --5
  function Convert (N,L: NATURAL) return BIT_VECTOR is          --6
    variable T:BIT_VECTOR(L-1 downto 0);                        --7
    variable V:NATURAL:= N;                                     --8
    begin for i in T'RIGHT to T'LEFT loop                      --9
      T(i) := BIT'VAL(V mod 2); V:= V/2;                       --10
    end loop; return T;                                         --11
  end;                                                          --12
```

```
function Convert (B: BIT_VECTOR) return NATURAL is          --13
  variable T:BIT_VECTOR(B'LENGTH-1 downto 0) := B;          --14
  variable V:NATURAL:= 0;                                    --15
  begin for i in T'RIGHT to T'LEFT loop                      --16
    if T(i) = '1' then V:= V + (2**i); end if;              --17
    end loop; return V;                                      --18
  end;                                                       --19
end Utils;                                                   --20
```

The following code tests the multiplier model. This is a **testbench** (this simple example is not a comprehensive test). First we reset the logic (line 17) and then apply a series of values to the inputs, A and B. The clock generator (line 14) supplies a clock with a 20 ns period. The inputs are changed 1 ns after a positive clock edge, and remain stable for 20 ns through the next positive clock edge.

```
entity Test_Mult8_1 is end; -- runs forever, use break!!      --1
architecture Structure of Test_Mult8_1 is                     --2
use Work.Utils.all; use Work.Clock_Utils.all;                 --3
  component Mult8 port                                        --4
    (A, B : BIT_VECTOR(3 downto 0); Start, CLK, Reset : BIT;  --5
    Result : out BIT_VECTOR(7 downto 0); Done : out BIT);    --6
  end component;                                              --7
signal A, B : BIT_VECTOR(3 downto 0);                        --8
signal Start, Done : BIT := '0';                             --9
signal CLK, Reset : BIT;                                     --10
signal Result : BIT_VECTOR(7 downto 0);                      --11
signal DA, DB, DR : INTEGER range 0 to 255;                 --12
begin                                                        --13
C: Clock(CLK, 10 ns, 10 ns);                                --14
UUT: Mult8 port map (A, B, Start, CLK, Reset, Result, Done); --15
DR <= Convert(Result);                                       --16
Reset  <= '1', '0' after 1 ns;                              --17
process begin                                                --18
  for i in 1 to 3 loop for j in 4 to 7 loop                 --19
    DA <= i; DB <= j;                                        --20
    A<=Convert(i,A'Length);B<=Convert(j,B'Length);          --21
    wait until CLK'EVENT and CLK='1'; wait for 1 ns;        --22
    Start <= '1', '0' after 20 ns; wait until Done = '1';   --23
    wait until CLK'EVENT and CLK='1';                       --24
  end loop; end loop;                                        --25
  for i in 0 to 1 loop for j in 0 to 15 loop                --26
    DA <= i; DB <= j;                                        --27
    A<=Convert(i,A'Length);B<=Convert(j,B'Length);          --28
    wait until CLK'EVENT and CLK='1'; wait for 1 ns;        --29
    Start <= '1', '0' after 20 ns; wait until Done = '1';   --30
    wait until CLK'EVENT and CLK='1';                       --31
  end loop; end loop;                                        --32
  wait;                                                      --33
```

```
end process;                                                    --34
end;                                                           --35
```

Here is the signal trace output from the Compass Scout simulator:

```
    Time(fs) + Cycle            da            db            dr
----------------------    ------------  ------------  ------------
              0+  0:          0             0             0
              0+  1: *        1 *           4 *           0
...
       92000000+  3:          1             4 *           4
...
      150000000+  1: *        1 *           5             4
...
      193000000+  3:          1             5 *           0
...
      252000000+  3:          1             5 *           5
...
      310000000+  1: *        1 *           6             5
...
      353000000+  3:          1             6 *           0
...
      412000000+  3:          1             6 *           6
```

Positive clock edges occur at 10, 30, 50, 70, 90, ... ns. You can see that the output (dr) changes from '0' to '4' at 92 ns, after five clock edges (with a 2 ns delay due to the output register, R1).

10.3   Syntax and Semantics of VHDL

We might define the **syntax** of a very small subset of the English language in **Backus–Naur form** (**BNF**) using **constructs** as follows:

```
sentence  ::= subject verb object.
subject   ::= The|A noun
object    ::= [article] noun {, and article noun}
article   ::= the|a
noun      ::= man|shark|house|food
verb      ::= eats|paints

::= means "can be replaced by"
|   means "or"
[]  means "contents optional"
{}  means "contents can be left out, used once, or repeated"
```

The following two English sentences are correct according to these syntax rules:

```
A shark eats food.
The house paints the shark, and the house, and a man.
```

We need **semantic rules** to tell us that the second sentence does not make much sense. Most of the VHDL LRM is dedicated to the definition of the language semantics. Appendix A of the LRM (which is not officially part of the standard) explains the complete VHDL syntax using BNF.

The rules that determine the characters you can use (the "alphabet" of VHDL), where you can put spaces, and so on are **lexical rules** [VHDL LRM13]. Any VHDL description may be written using a subset of the VHDL character set:

```
basic_character ::= upper_case_letter|digit|special_character
   |space_character|format_effector
```

The two space characters are: space (`SP`) and the nonbreaking space (`NBSP`). The five format effectors are: horizontal tabulation (`HT`), vertical tabulation (`VT`), carriage return (`CR`), line feed (`LF`), and form feed (`FF`). The characters that are legal in VHDL constructs are defined as the following subsets of the complete character set:

```
graphic_character ::=                                          [10.1]
    upper_case_letter|digit|special_character|space_character
   |lower_case_letter|other_special_character
```

```
special_character ::= " # & ' () * + , - . / : ; < = > [ ] _ |   [10.2]
```

The 11 other special characters are: ! $ % @ ? \ ^ ` { } ~, and (in VHDL-93 only) 34 other characters from the ISO Latin-1 set [ISO, 1987]. If you edit code using a word processor, you either need to turn smart quotes off or override this feature (use Tools... Preferences... General in MS Word; and use `CTRL-'` and `CTRL-"` in Frame).

When you learn a language it is difficult to understand how to use a noun without using it in a sentence. Strictly this means that we ought to define a sentence before we define a noun and so on. In this chapter I shall often break the "Define it before you use it" rule and use code examples and BNF definitions that contain VHDL constructs that we have not yet defined. This is often frustrating. You can use the book index and the table of important VHDL constructs at the end of this chapter (Table 10.28) to help find definitions if you need them.

We shall occasionally refer to the VHDL BNF syntax definitions in this chapter using references—BNF [10.1], for example. Only the most important BNF constructs for VHDL are included here in this chapter, but a complete description of the VHDL language syntax is contained in Appendix A.

10.4 Identifiers and Literals

Names (the "nouns" of VHDL) are known as **identifiers** [VHDL 87LRM6.2, 93LRM13.3]. The correct "spelling" of an identifier is defined in BNF as follows:

```
identifier ::=                                              [10.3]
    letter {[underline] letter_or_digit}
    |\graphic_character{graphic_character}\
```

In this book an underline in VHDL BNF marks items that are new or that have changed in VHDL-93 from VHDL-87. The following are examples of identifiers:

```
s -- a simple name
S -- a simple name, the same as s. VHDL is not case sensitive.
a_name -- imbedded underscores are OK
-- successive underscores are illegal in names: Ill__egal
-- names can't start with underscore: _Illegal
-- names can't end with underscore: Illegal_
Too_Good -- names must start with a letter
-- names can't start with a number: 2_Bad
\74LS00\ -- extended identifier to break rules (VHDL-93 only)
VHDL \vhdl\ \VHDL\ -- three different names (VHDL-93 only)
s_array(0) -- a static indexed name (known at analysis time)
s_array(i) -- a non-static indexed name, if i is a variable
```

You may not use a reserved word as a declared identifier, and it is wise not to use units, special characters, and function names: `ns`, `ms`, `FF`, `read`, `write`, and so on. You may attach qualifiers to names as follows:

```
CMOS.all -- a selected or expanded name, all units in library CMOS
Data'LEFT(1) -- an attribute name, LEFT is the attribute designator
Data(24 downto 1) -- a slice name, part of array: Data(31 downto 0)
Data(1) -- an indexed name, one element of an array
```

Comments follow two hyphens '`--`' and instruct the analyzer to ignore the rest of the line. There are no multiline comments in VHDL. Tabs improve readability, but it is best not to rely on a tab as a space in case the tabs are lost or deleted in conversion. You should thus write code that is still legal if all tabs are deleted.

There are various forms of **literals** (fixed-value items) in VHDL [VHDL LRM13.4–13.7]. The following code shows some examples:

```
entity Literals_1 is end;
architecture Behave of Literals_1 is
begin process
    variable I1 : integer; variable R1 : real;
    variable C1 : CHARACTER; variable S16 : STRING(1 to 16);
    variable BV4: BIT_VECTOR(0 to 3);
    variable BV12 : BIT_VECTOR(0 to 11);
    variable BV16 : BIT_VECTOR(0 to 15);
```

```
  begin
-- Abstract literals are decimal or based literals.
-- Decimal literals are integer or real literals.
-- Integer literal examples (each of these is the same):
    I1 := 120000; Int := 12e4; Int := 120_000;
-- Based literal examples (each of these is the same):
    I1 := 2#1111_1111#; I1 := 16#FFFF#;
-- Base must be an integer from 2 to 16:
    I1 := 16:FFFF:; -- you may use a : if you don't have #
-- Real literal examples (each of these is the same):
    R1 := 120000.0; R1 := 1.2e5; R1 := 12.0E4;
-- Character literal must be one of the 191 graphic characters.
-- 65 of the 256 ISO Latin-1 set are non-printing control characters
    C1 := 'A'; C1 := 'a'; -- different from each other
-- String literal examples:
    S16 := "  string" & " literal";     -- concatenate long strings
    S16 := """Hello,"" I said!";         -- doubled quotes
    S16 := %  string literal%;           -- can use % instead of "
    S16 := %Sale: 50%% off!!!%;          -- doubled %
-- Bit-string literal examples:
    BV4  := B"1100";     -- binary bit-string literal
    BV12 := O"7777";     -- octal  bit-string literal
    BV16 := X"FFFF";     -- hex    bit-string literal
wait; end process; -- the wait prevents an endless loop
end;
```

10.5 Entities and Architectures

The highest-level VHDL construct is the **design file** [VHDL LRM11.1]. A design file contains **design units** that contain one or more **library units**. Library units in turn contain: entity, configuration, and package declarations (**primary units**); and architecture and package bodies (**secondary units**).

```
design_file ::=                                                    [10.4]
   {library_clause|use_clause} library_unit
   {{library_clause|use_clause} library_unit}

library_unit ::= primary_unit|secondary_unit

primary_unit ::=                                                   [10.5]
   entity_declaration|configuration_declaration|package_declaration

secondary_unit ::= architecture_body|package_body                 [10.6]
```

Using the written language analogy: a VHDL library unit is a "book," a VHDL design file is a "bookshelf," and a VHDL library is a collection of bookshelves. A

VHDL primary unit is a little like the chapter title and contents that appear on the first page of each chapter in this book and a VHDL secondary unit is like the chapter contents (though this is stretching our analogy a little far).

I shall describe the very important concepts of entities and architectures in this section and then cover libraries, packages, and package bodies. You define an entity, a black box, using an **entity declaration** [VHDL LRM1.1]. This is the BNF definition:

```
entity_declaration ::=                                          [10.7]
entity identifier is
    [generic (formal_generic_interface_list);]
    [port (formal_port_interface_list);]
    {entity_declarative_item}
  [begin
    {[label:] [postponed] assertion ;
    |[label:] [postponed] passive_procedure_call ;
    |passive_process_statement}]
end [entity] [entity_identifier] ;
```

The following is an example of an entity declaration for a black box with two inputs and an output:

```
entity Half_Adder is
  port (X, Y : in BIT := '0'; Sum, Cout : out BIT); -- formals
end;
```

Matching the parts of this code with the constructs in BNF [10.7] you can see that the `identifier` is `Half_Adder` and that `(X, Y: in BIT := '0'; Sum, Cout: out BIT)` corresponds to `(port_interface_list)` in the BNF. The ports `X`, `Y`, `Sum`, and `Cout` are **formal ports** or **formals**. This particular entity `Half_Adder` does not use any of the other optional constructs that are legal in an entity declaration.

The **architecture body** [VHDL LRM1.2] describes what an entity does, or the contents of the black box (it is architecture body and not architecture declaration).

```
architecture_body ::=                                           [10.8]
    architecture identifier of entity_name is
      {block_declarative_item}
        begin
        {concurrent_statement}
    end [architecture] [architecture_identifier] ;
```

For example, the following architecture body (I shall just call it an architecture from now on) describes the contents of the entity `Half_Adder`:

```
architecture Behave of Half_Adder is
  begin Sum <= X xor Y; Cout <= X and Y;
end Behave;
```

We use the same signal names (the formals: Sum, X, Y, and Cout) in the architecture as we use in the entity (we say the signals of the "parent" entity are **visible** inside the architecture "child"). An architecture can refer to other entity/architecture pairs—so we can nest black boxes. We shall often refer to an entity/architecture pair as entity(architecture). For example, the architecture Behave of the entity Half_Adder is Half_Adder(Behave).

Why would we want to describe the outside of a black box (an entity) separately from the description of its contents (its architecture)? Separating the two makes it easier to move between different architectures for an entity (there must be at least one). For example, one architecture may model an entity at a behavioral level, while another architecture may be a structural model.

A structural model that uses an entity in an architecture must declare that entity and its interface using a **component declaration** as follows [VHDL LRM4.5]:

```
component_declaration ::=                                          [10.9]
   component identifier [is]
     [generic (local_generic_interface_list);]
     [port (local_port_interface_list);]
   end component [component_identifier];
```

For example, the following architecture, Netlist, is a structural version of the behavioral architecture, Behave:

```
architecture Netlist of Half_Adder is
component MyXor port (A_Xor,B_Xor : in BIT; Z_Xor : out BIT);
end component; -- component with locals
component MyAnd port (A_And,B_And : in BIT; Z_And : out BIT);
end component; -- component with locals
begin
   Xor1: MyXor port map (X, Y, Sum);    -- instance with actuals
   And1 : MyAnd port map (X, Y, Cout);  -- instance with actuals
end;
```

Notice that:

- We declare the components: MyAnd, MyXor and their **local ports** (or **locals**): A_Xor, B_Xor, Z_Xor, A_And, B_And, Z_And.

- We instantiate the components with **instance names**: And1 and Xor1.

- We connect instances using **actual ports** (or **actuals**): X, Y, Sum, Cout.

Next we define the entities and architectures that we shall use for the components MyAnd and MyXor. You can think of an entity–architecture pair (and its formal ports) as a data-book specification for a logic cell; the component (and its local ports) corresponds to a software model for the logic cell; and an instance (and its actual ports) is the logic cell.

We do not need to write VHDL code for MyAnd and MyXor; the code is provided as a **technology library** (also called an **ASIC vendor library** because it is often sold or distributed by the ASIC company that will manufacture the chip—the ASIC vendor—and not the software company):

```
-- These definitions are part of a technology library:
entity AndGate is
   port (And_in_1, And_in_2 : in BIT; And_out : out BIT); -- formals
end;

architecture Simple of AndGate is
   begin And_out <= And_in_1 and And_in_2;
end;

entity XorGate is
   port (Xor_in_1, Xor_in_2 : in BIT; Xor_out : out BIT); -- formals
end;

architecture Simple of XorGate is
   begin Xor_out <= Xor_in_1 xor Xor_in_2;
end;
```

If we keep the description of a circuit's interface (the entity) separate from its contents (the architecture), we need a way to link or **bind** them together. A **configuration declaration** [VHDL LRM1.3] binds entities and architectures.

```
configuration_declaration ::=                                    [10.10]
   configuration identifier of entity_name is
      {use_clause|attribute_specification|group_declaration}
      block_configuration
   end [configuration] [configuration_identifier] ;
```

An entity/architecture pair is a **design entity**. The following configuration declaration defines which design entities we wish to use and associates the formal ports (from the entity declaration) with the local ports (from the component declaration):

```
configuration Simplest of Half_Adder is
use work.all;
   for Netlist
      for And1 : MyAnd use entity AndGate(Simple)
         port map -- association: formals => locals
            (And_in_1 => A_And, And_in_2 => B_And, And_out => Z_And);
      end for;
      for Xor1 : MyXor use entity XorGate(Simple)
         port map
            (Xor_in_1 => A_Xor, Xor_in_2 => B_Xor, Xor_out => Z_Xor);
      end for;
   end for;
end;
```

Figure 10.1 diagrams the use of entities, architectures, components, and configurations. This figure seems very complicated, but there are two reasons that VHDL works this way:

- Separating the entity, architecture, component, and configuration makes it easier to reuse code and change libraries. All we have to do is change names in the port maps and configuration declaration.
- We only have to alter and reanalyze the configuration declaration to change which architectures we use in a model—giving us a fast debug cycle.

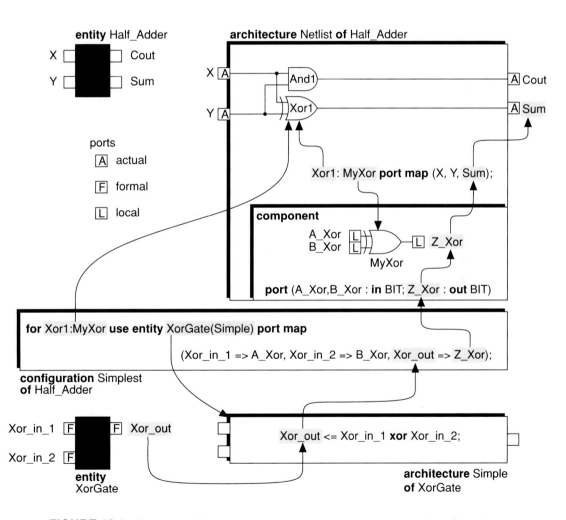

FIGURE 10.1   Entities, architectures, components, ports, port maps, and configurations.

You can think of design units, the analyzed entity/architecture pairs, as compiled object-code modules. The configuration then determines which object-code modules are linked together to form executable binary code.

You may also think of an entity as a block diagram, an architecture for an entity a more detailed circuit schematic for the block diagram, and a configuration as a parts list of the circuit components with their part numbers and manufacturers (also known as a **BOM** for **bill of materials,** rather like a shopping list). Most manufacturers (including the U.S. DoD) use schematics and BOMs as control documents for electronic systems. This is part of the rationale behind the structure of VHDL.

10.6 Packages and Libraries

After the VHDL tool has analyzed entities, architectures, and configurations, it stores the resulting design units in a library. Much of the power of VHDL comes from the use of predefined libraries and packages. A VHDL **design library** [VHDL LRM11.2] is either the current working library (things we are currently analyzing) or a predefined resource library (something we did yesterday, or we bought, or that came with the tool). The **working library** is named work and is the place where the code currently being analyzed is stored. Architectures must be in the same library (but they do not have to be in the same physical file on disk) as their parent entities.

You can use a VHDL **package** [VHDL LRM2.5–2.6] to define subprograms (procedures and functions), declare special types, modify the behavior of operators, or to hide complex code. Here is the BNF for a package declaration:

```
package_declaration ::=                                              [10.11]
package identifier is
{subprogram_declaration    | type_declaration    | subtype_declaration
  | constant_declaration    | signal_declaration    | file_declaration
  | alias_declaration       | component_declaration
  | attribute_declaration   | attribute_specification
  | disconnection_specification | use_clause
  | shared variable declaration | group_declaration
  | group_template_declaration}
  end [package] [package_identifier] ;
```

You need a **package body** if you declare any subprograms in the package declaration (a package declaration and its body do not have to be in the same file):

```
package_body ::=
  package body package_identifier is
{subprogram_declaration    | subprogram_body
  | type_declaration        | subtype_declaration
  | constant_declaration    | file_declaration    | alias_declaration
  | use_clause
```

```
    | shared variable declaration | group declaration
    | group_template_declaration}
end [package body] [package_identifier] ;
```

To make a package **visible** (or accessible, so you can see and use the package and its contents), you must include a **library clause** before a design unit and a **use clause** either before a design unit or inside a unit, like this:

```
library MyLib; -- library clause
use MyLib.MyPackage.all; -- use clause
-- design unit (entity + architecture, etc.) follows:
```

The STD and WORK libraries and the STANDARD package are always visible. Things that are visible to an entity are visible to its architecture bodies.

10.6.1   Standard Package

The VHDL **STANDARD package** [VHDL LRM14.2] is defined in the LRM and implicitly declares the following implementation dependent types: TIME, INTEGER, REAL. We shall use uppercase for types defined in an IEEE standard package. Here is part of the STANDARD package showing the explicit type and subtype declarations:

```
package Part_STANDARD is
type BOOLEAN is (FALSE, TRUE); type BIT is ('0', '1');
type SEVERITY_LEVEL is (NOTE, WARNING, ERROR, FAILURE);
subtype NATURAL is INTEGER range 0 to INTEGER'HIGH;
subtype POSITIVE is INTEGER range 1 to INTEGER'HIGH;
type BIT_VECTOR is array (NATURAL range <>) of BIT;
type STRING is array (POSITIVE range <>) of CHARACTER;
-- the following declarations are VHDL-93 only:
attribute FOREIGN: STRING; -- for links to other languages
subtype DELAY_LENGTH is TIME range 0 fs to TIME'HIGH;
type FILE_OPEN_KIND is (READ_MODE,WRITE_MODE,APPEND_MODE);
type FILE_OPEN_STATUS is
(OPEN_OK,STATUS_ERROR,NAME_ERROR,MODE_ERROR);
end Part_STANDARD;
```

Notice that a STRING array must have a positive index. The type TIME is declared in the STANDARD package as follows:

```
type TIME is range implementation_defined -- and varies with software
  units fs; ps = 1000 fs; ns = 1000 ps; us = 1000 ns; ms = 1000 us;
  sec = 1000 ms; min = 60 sec; hr = 60 min; end units;
```

The STANDARD package also declares the function now that returns the current simulation time (with type TIME in VHDL-87 and subtype DELAY_LENGTH in VHDL-93).

In VHDL-93 the CHARACTER type declaration extends the VHDL-87 declaration (the 128 ASCII characters):

```
type Part_CHARACTER is ( -- 128 ASCII characters in VHDL-87
NUL, SOH, STX, ETX, EOT, ENQ, ACK, BEL, -- 33 control characters
 BS,  HT,  LF,  VT,  FF,  CR,  SO,  SI, -- including:
DLE, DC1, DC2, DC3, DC4, NAK, SYN, ETB, -- format effectors:
CAN,  EM, SUB, ESC, FSP, GSP, RSP, USP, -- horizontal tab = HT
' ', '!', '"', '#', '$', '%', '&', ''', -- line feed = LF
'(', ')', '*', '+', ',', '-', '.', '/', -- vertical tab = VT
'0', '1', '2', '3', '4', '5', '6', '7', -- form feed = FF
'8', '9', ':', ';', '<', '=', '>', '?', -- carriage return = CR
'@', 'A', 'B', 'C', 'D', 'E', 'F', 'G', -- and others:
'H', 'I', 'J', 'K', 'L', 'M', 'N', 'O', -- FSP, GSP, RSP, USP use P
'P', 'Q', 'R', 'S', 'T', 'U', 'V', 'W', -- suffix to avoid conflict
'X', 'Y', 'Z', '[', '\', ']', '^', '_', -- with TIME units
'`', 'a', 'b', 'c', 'd', 'e', 'f', 'g',
'h', 'i', 'j', 'k', 'l', 'm', 'n', 'o',
'p', 'q', 'r', 's', 't', 'u', 'v', 'w',
'x', 'y', 'z', '{', '|', '}', '~', DEL  -- delete = DEL
-- VHDL-93 includes 96 more Latin-1 characters, like ¥ (Yen) and
-- 32 more control characters, better not to use any of them.
);
```

The VHDL-87 character set is the 7-bit coded **ISO 646-1983** standard known as the **ASCII character set**. Each of the printable ASCII graphic **character codes** (there are 33 nonprintable control codes, like DEL for delete) is represented by a **graphic symbol** (the shapes of letters on the keyboard, on the display, and that actually print). VHDL-93 uses the 8-bit coded character set **ISO 8859-1:1987(E)**, known as ISO **Latin-1**. The first 128 characters of the 256 characters in ISO Latin-1 correspond to the 128-character ASCII code. The graphic symbols for the printable ASCII characters are well defined, but not part of the standard (for example, the shape of the graphic symbol that represents 'lowercase a' is recognizable on every keyboard, display, and font). However, the graphic symbols that represent the printable characters from other 128-character codes of the ISO 8-bit character set are different in various fonts, languages, and computer systems. For example, a pound sterling sign in a U.K. character set looks like this–'£', but in some fonts the same character code prints as '#' (known as number sign, hash, or pound). If you use such characters and want to share your models with people in different countries, this can cause problems (you can see all 256 characters in a character set by using Insert... Symbol in MS Word).

10.6.2   Std_logic_1164 Package

VHDL does not have a built-in logic-value system. The STANDARD package predefines the type BIT with two logic values, '0' and '1', but we normally need at least two more values: 'X' (unknown) and 'Z' (high-impedance). Unknown is a **metalogical value** because it does not exist in real hardware but is needed for simulation purposes. We could define our own logic value system with four logic values:

```
type MVL4 is ('X', '0', '1', 'Z'); -- a four-value logic system
```

The proliferation of VHDL logic value systems prompted the creation of the **Std_logic_1164 package** (defined in IEEE Std 1164-1993) that includes functions to perform logical, shift, resolution, and conversion functions for types defined in the Std_logic_1164 system. To use this package in a design unit, you must include the following library clause (before each design unit) and a use clause (either before or inside the unit):

```
library IEEE; use IEEE.std_logic_1164.all;
```

This Std_Logic_1164 package contains definitions for a nine-value logic system. The following code and comments show the definitions and use of the most important parts of the package[2]:

```
package Part_STD_LOGIC_1164 is                                    --1
type STD_ULOGIC is                                               --2
( 'U', -- Uninitialized                                          --3
  'X', -- Forcing Unknown                                        --4
  '0', -- Forcing 0                                              --5
  '1', -- Forcing 1                                              --6
  'Z', -- High Impedance                                         --7
  'W', -- Weak Unknown                                           --8
  'L', -- Weak 0                                                 --9
  'H', -- Weak 1                                                 --10
  '-'  -- Don't Care);                                           --11
type STD_ULOGIC_VECTOR is array (NATURAL range <>) of STD_ULOGIC; --12
function resolved (s : STD_ULOGIC_VECTOR) return STD_ULOGIC;     --13
subtype STD_LOGIC is resolved STD_ULOGIC;                        --14
type STD_LOGIC_VECTOR is array (NATURAL range <>) of STD_LOGIC;  --15
subtype X01  is resolved STD_ULOGIC range 'X' to '1';           --16
subtype X01Z is resolved STD_ULOGIC range 'X' to 'Z';           --17
subtype UX01 is resolved STD_ULOGIC range 'U' to '1';           --18
subtype UX01Z is resolved STD_ULOGIC range 'U' to 'Z';          --19

-- vectorized overloaded logical operators...                    --20
function "and"  (L : STD_ULOGIC; R : STD_ULOGIC) return UX01;    --21
-- logical operators not, and, nand, or, nor, xor, xnor (VHDL-93) --22
-- overloaded for STD_ULOGIC STD_ULOGIC_VECTOR STD_LOGIC_VECTOR  --23

-- strength strippers and type conversion functions...           --24
-- function To_T (X : F) return T;                                --25
-- defined for types, T and F, where                             --26
-- F=BIT BIT_VECTOR STD_ULOGIC STD_ULOGIC_VECTOR STD_LOGIC_VECTOR --27
-- T=types F plus types X01 X01Z UX01 (but not type UX01Z)        --28
```

---

[2]The code in this section is adapted with permission from IEEE Std 1164-1993, © Copyright IEEE. All rights reserved.

```
-- exclude _'s in T in name: TO_STDULOGIC not TO_STD_ULOGIC       --29
-- To_X01 : L->0, H->1 others->X                                  --30
-- To_X01Z: Z->Z, others as To_X01                                --31
-- To_UX01: U->U, others as To_X01                                --32

-- edge detection functions:                                      --33
function rising_edge  (signal s: STD_ULOGIC) return BOOLEAN;      --34
function falling_edge (signal s: STD_ULOGIC) return BOOLEAN;      --35

-- unknown detection (returns true if s = U, X, Z, W)             --36
-- function Is_X (s : T) return BOOLEAN;                          --37
-- defined for T = STD_ULOGIC STD_ULOGIC_VECTOR STD_LOGIC_VECTOR  --38

end Part_STD_LOGIC_1164;                                          --39
```

Notice:

- The type STD_ULOGIC has nine logic values. For this reason IEEE Std 1164 is sometimes referred to as MVL9—multivalued logic nine. There are simpler, but nonstandard, MVL4 and MVL7 packages, as well as packages with more than nine logic values, available. Values 'U', 'X', and 'W' are all metalogical values.

- There are weak and forcing logic value strengths. If more than one logic gate drives a node (there is more than one **driver**) as in wired-OR logic or a three-state bus, for example, the simulator checks the driver strengths to **resolve** the actual logic value of the node using the **resolution function**, resolved, defined in the package.

- The subtype STD_LOGIC is the **resolved** version of the **unresolved** type STD_ULOGIC. Since subtypes are **compatible** with types (you can assign one to the other) you can use either STD_LOGIC or STD_ULOGIC for a signal with a single driver, but it is generally safer to use STD_LOGIC.

- The type STD_LOGIC_VECTOR is the resolved version of unresolved type STD_ULOGIC_VECTOR. Since these are two different types and are not compatible, you should use STD_LOGIC_VECTOR. That way you will not run into a problem when you try to connect a STD_LOGIC_VECTOR to a STD_ULOGIC_VECTOR.

- The don't care logic value '-' (hyphen), is principally for use by synthesis tools. The value '-' is almost always treated the same as 'X'.

- The 1164 standard defines (or **overloads**) the logical operators for the STD_LOGIC types but not the arithmetic operators (see Section 10.12).

10.6.3   TEXTIO Package

You can use the **TEXTIO** package, which is part of the library STD, for text input and output [VHDL LRM14.3]. The following code is a part of the TEXTIO package header and, together with the comments, shows the declarations of types, subtypes, and the use of the procedures in the package:

```
package Part_TEXTIO is -- VHDL-93 version
type LINE is access STRING; -- LINE is a pointer to a STRING value
type TEXT is file of STRING; -- file of ASCII records
type SIDE is (RIGHT, LEFT); -- for justifying output data
subtype WIDTH is NATURAL; -- for specifying widths of output fields
file INPUT : TEXT open READ_MODE is "STD_INPUT"; -- default input file
file OUTPUT : TEXT open WRITE_MODE is "STD_OUTPUT"; -- default output

-- the following procedures are defined for types, T, where
-- T = BIT BIT_VECTOR BOOLEAN CHARACTER INTEGER REAL TIME STRING
-- procedure READLINE(file F : TEXT; L : out LINE);
-- procedure READ(L : inout LINE; VALUE : out T);
-- procedure READ(L : inout LINE; VALUE : out T; GOOD: out BOOLEAN);
-- procedure WRITELINE(F : out TEXT; L : inout LINE);
-- procedure WRITE(
--    L : inout LINE;
--    VALUE : in T;
--    JUSTIFIED : in SIDE:= RIGHT;
--    FIELD:in WIDTH := 0;
--    DIGITS:in NATURAL := 0; -- for T = REAL only
--    UNIT:in TIME:= ns); -- for T = TIME only
-- function ENDFILE(F : in TEXT) return BOOLEAN;

end Part_TEXTIO;
```

Here is an example that illustrates how to write to the screen (STD_OUTPUT):

```
library std; use std.textio.all; entity Text is end;
architecture Behave of Text is signal count : INTEGER := 0;
begin count <= 1 after 10 ns, 2 after 20 ns, 3 after 30 ns;
process (count) variable L: LINE; begin
if (count > 0) then
   write(L, now); -- write time
   write(L, STRING'(" count=")); -- STRING' is a type qualification
   write(L, count); writeline(output, L);
end if; end process; end;

10 ns count=1
20 ns count=2
30 ns count=3
```

10.6.4 Other Packages

VHDL does not predefine arithmetic operators on types that hold bits. Many VHDL simulators provide one or more **arithmetic packages** that allow you to perform arithmetic operations on std_logic_1164 types. Some companies also provide one or more **math packages** that contain functions for floating-point algebra, trigonome-try, complex algebra, queueing, and statistics (see also [IEEE 1076.2, 1996]).

Synthesis tool companies often provide a special version of an arithmetic pack-age, a **synthesis package**, that allows you to synthesize VHDL that includes arith-metic operators. This type of package may contain special instructions (normally comments that are recognized by the synthesis software) that map common func-tions (adders, subtracters, multipliers, shift registers, counters, and so on) to ASIC library cells. I shall introduce the IEEE synthesis package in Section 10.12.

Synthesis companies may also provide **component packages** for such cells as power and ground pads, I/O buffers, clock drivers, three-state pads, and bus keepers. These components may be technology-independent (generic) and are mapped to primitives from technology-dependent libraries after synthesis.

10.6.5   Creating Packages

It is often useful to define constants in one central place rather than using literals wherever you need a specific value in your code. One way to do this is by using VHDL **packaged constants** [VHDL LRM4.3.1.1] that you define in a package. Packages that you define are initially part of the working library, work. Here are two example packages:

```
package Adder_Pkg is -- a package declaration
   constant BUSWIDTH : INTEGER := 16;
end Adder_Pkg;

use work.Adder_Pkg.all; -- a use clause
entity Adder is end Adder;
architecture Flexible of Adder is -- work.Adder_Pkg is visible here
   begin process begin
      MyLoop : for j in 0 to BUSWIDTH loop -- adder code goes here
         end loop; wait; -- the wait prevents an endless cycle
   end process;
end Flexible;

package GLOBALS is
   constant HI : BIT := '1'; constant LO: BIT := '0';
end GLOBALS;
```

Here is a package that declares a function and thus requires a package body:

```
package Add_Pkg_Fn is
function add(a, b, c : BIT_VECTOR(3 downto 0)) return BIT_VECTOR;
end Add_Pkg_Fn;

package body Add_Pkg_Fn is
function add(a, b, c : BIT_VECTOR(3 downto 0)) return BIT_VECTOR is
   begin return a xor b xor c; end;
end Add_Pkg_Fn;
```

The following example is similar to the **VITAL (VHDL Initiative Toward ASIC Libraries)** package that provides two alternative methods (procedures or functions) to model primitive gates (I shall describe functions and procedures in more detail in Section 10.9.2):

```
package And_Pkg is
   procedure V_And(a, b : BIT; signal c : out BIT);
   function V_And(a, b : BIT) return BIT;
end;

package body And_Pkg is
   procedure V_And(a, b : BIT; signal c : out BIT) is
     begin c <= a and b; end;
   function V_And(a, b : BIT) return BIT is
     begin return a and b; end;
end And_Pkg;
```

The software determines where it stores the design units that we analyze. Suppose the package Add_Pkg_Fn is in library MyLib. Then we need a library clause (before each design unit) and use clause with a selected name to use the package:

```
library MyLib; -- use MyLib.Add_Pkg.all; -- use all the package
use MyLib.Add_Pkg_Fn.add; -- just function 'add' from the package

entity Lib_1 is port (s : out BIT_VECTOR(3 downto 0) := "0000"); end;
architecture Behave of Lib_1 is begin process
begin s <= add ("0001", "0010", "1000"); wait; end process; end;
```

The VHDL software dictates how you create the library MyLib from the library work and the actual name and directory location for the physical file or directory on the disk that holds the library. The mechanism to create the links between the file and directory names in the computer world and the library names in the VHDL world depends on the software. There are three common methods:

- Use a UNIX environment variable (SETENV MyLib ~/MyDirectory/MyLibFile, for example).
- Create a separate file that establishes the links between the filename known to the operating system and the library name known to the VHDL software.
- Include the links in an initialization file (often with an '.ini' suffix).

10.7 Interface Declarations

An **interface declaration** declares **interface objects** that may be interface constants, signals, variables, or files [VHDL 87LRM4.3.3, 93LRM4.3.2]. **Interface constants** are generics of a design entity, a component, or a block, or parameters of subprograms. **Interface signals** are ports of a design entity, component, or block, and parameters of subprograms. **Interface variables** and **interface files** are parameters of subprograms.

Each interface object has a **mode** that indicates the direction of information flow. The most common modes are in (the default), out, inout, and buffer (a fifth mode, linkage, is used to communicate with other languages and is infrequently used in ASIC design). The restrictions on the use of objects with these modes are listed in Table 10.10. An interface object is **read** when you use it on the RHS of an assignment statement, for example, or when the object is associated with another interface object of modes in, inout (or linkage). An interface object is **updated** when you use it on the LHS side of an assignment statement or when the object is associated with another interface object of mode out, buffer, inout (or linkage). The restrictions on reading and updating objects generate the diagram at the bottom of Table 10.10 that shows the 10 allowed types of interconnections (these rules for modes buffer and inout are the same). The interface objects (Inside and Outside) in the example in this table are ports (and thus interface signals), but remember that interface objects may also be interface constants, variables, and files.

There are other special case rules for reading and updating interface signals, constants, variables, and files that I shall cover in the following sections. The situation is like the spelling rule, "i before e except after c." Table 10.10 corresponds to the rule "i before e."

10.7.1 Port Declaration

Interface objects that are signals are called **ports** [93LRM 1.1.1.2]. You may think of ports as "connectors" and you must declare them as follows:

port (*port_interface_list*)

interface_list ::=   [10.12]
    port_interface_declaration {; *port_interface_declaration*}

A **port interface declaration** is a list of ports that are the inputs and outputs of an entity, a block, or a component declaration:

interface_declaration ::=   [10.13]
    [**signal**]
        identifier {, identifier}:[**in**|**out**|**inout**|**buffer**|**linkage**]
        subtype_indication [**bus**] [:= *static*_expression]

Each port forms an **implicit signal declaration** and has a **port mode**. I shall discuss bus, which is a **signal kind**, in Section 10.13.1. Here is an example of an entity declaration that has five ports:

```
entity Association_1 is
    port (signal X, Y : in BIT := '0'; Z1, Z2, Z3 : out BIT);
end;
```

TABLE 10.10   Modes of interface objects and their properties.

```
entity E1 is port (Inside : in BIT); end; architecture Behave of E1 is begin end;
entity E2 is port (Outside : inout BIT := '1'); end; architecture Behave of E2 is
component E1 port (Inside: in BIT); end component; signal UpdateMe : BIT; begin
I1 : E1 port map (Inside => Outside);   -- formal/local (mode in) => actual (mode inout)
UpdateMe <= Outside;                    -- OK to read Outside (mode inout)
Outside  <= '0' after 10 ns;            -- and OK to update Outside (mode inout)
end;
```

	in (default)	out	inout	buffer
Possible modes of interface object, Outside	in (default)	out	inout	buffer
Can you read Outside (RHS of assignment)?	Yes	No	Yes	Yes
Can you update Outside (LHS of assignment)?	No	Yes	Yes	Yes
Modes of Inside that Outside may connect to (see below)[1]	in	out	any	any

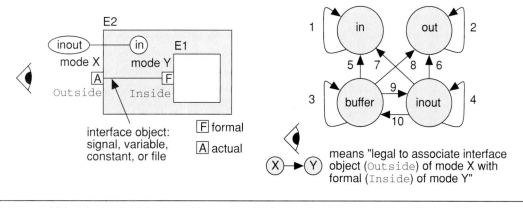

[1]There are additional rules for interface objects that are signals (ports)—see Tables 10.11 and 10.12.

In the preceding declaration the keyword signal is redundant (because all ports are signals) and may be omitted. You may also omit the port mode in because it is the default mode. In this example, the input ports X and Y are driven by a **default value** (in general a **default expression**) of '0' if (and only if) the ports are left unconnected or **open**. If you do leave an input port open, the port must have a default expression.

You use a **port map** and either **positional association** or **named association** to connect the formals of an entity with the locals of a component. Port maps also associate (connect) the locals of a component with the actuals of an instance. For an example of formal, local, and actual ports, and explanation of their function, see Section 10.5, where we declared an entity AndGate. The following example shows how to bind a component to the entity AndGate (in this case we use the **default binding**) and associate the ports. Notice that if we mix positional and named association then all positional associations must come first.

```
use work.all; -- makes analyzed design entity AndGate(Simple) visible
architecture Netlist of Association_1 is
-- the formal port clause for entity AndGate looks like this:
-- port (And_in_1, And_in_2: in BIT; And_out : out BIT); -- formals
component AndGate port
   (And_in_1, And_in_2 : in BIT; And_out : out BIT); -- locals
end component;
begin
-- The component and entity have the same names: AndGate
-- The port names are also the same: And_in_1, And_in_2, And_out
-- so we can use default binding without a configuration
-- The last (and only) architecture for AndGate will be used: Simple
A1:AndGate port map (X, Y, Z1); -- positional association
A2:AndGate port map (And_in_2=>Y, And_out=>Z2, And_in_1=>X); -- named
A3:AndGate port map (X, And_out => Z3, And_in_2 => Y); -- both
end;
```

The interface object rules of Table 10.10 apply to ports. The rule that forbids updating an interface object of mode in prevents modifying an input port (by placing the input signal on the left-hand side of an assignment statement, for example). Less obviously, you cannot read a port of mode out (that is you cannot place an output signal on the right-hand side of an assignment statement). This stops you from accidentally reading an output signal that may be connected to a net with multiple drivers. In this case the value you would read (the unresolved output signal) might not be the same as the resolved signal value. For example, in the following code, since Clock is a port of mode out, you cannot read Clock directly. Instead you can transfer Clock to an intermediate variable and read the intermediate variable instead:

```
entity ClockGen_1 is port (Clock : out BIT); end;
architecture Behave of ClockGen_1 is
begin process variable Temp : BIT := '1';
   begin
-- Clock <= not Clock;    -- illegal, you cannot read Clock (mode out)
   Temp := not Temp;       -- use a temporary variable instead
   Clock <= Temp after 10 ns; wait for 10 ns;
   if (now > 100 ns) then wait; end if; end process;
end;
```

Table 10.10 lists the restrictions on reading and updating interface objects including interface signals that form ports. Table 10.11 lists additional special rules for reading and updating the attributes of interface signals.

TABLE 10.11   Properties of ports.

Example entity declaration:
entity E **is port** (F_1:BIT; F_2:**out** BIT; F_3:**inout** BIT; F_4:**buffer** BIT); **end**;   -- formals

Example component declaration:
component C **port** (L_1:BIT; L_2:**out** BIT; L_3:**inout** BIT; L_4:**buffer** BIT); -- locals
end component;

Example component instantiation:
I1 : C **port map**
(L_1 => A_1, L_2 => A_2, L_3 => A_3, L_4 => A_4); -- locals => actuals

Example configuration:
for I1 : C **use entity** E(Behave) **port map**
(F_1 => L_1, F_2 => L_2, F_3 => L_3, F_4 => L_4); -- formals => locals

Interface object, port F	F_1	F_2	F_3	F_4
Mode of F	**in** (default)	**out**	**inout**	**buffer**
Can you read attributes of F? [LRM 4.3.2]	Yes, but not the attributes: 'STABLE 'QUIET 'DELAYED 'TRANSACTION	Yes, but not the attributes: 'STABLE 'QUIET 'DELAYED 'TRANSACTION 'EVENT 'ACTIVE 'LAST_EVENT 'LAST_ACTIVE 'LAST_VALUE	Yes, but not the attributes: 'STABLE 'QUIET 'DELAYED 'TRANSACTION	Yes

There is one more set of rules that apply to port connections [LRM 1.1.1.2]. If design entity E2 contains an instance, I1, of design entity E1, then the formals (of design entity E1) are associated with actuals (of instance I1). The actuals (of instance I1) are themselves formal ports (of design entity E2). The restrictions illustrated in Table 10.12 apply to the modes of the port connections from E1 to E2 (looking from the inside to the outside).

Notice that the allowed connections diagrammed in Table 10.12 (looking from inside to the outside) are a superset of those of Table 10.10 (looking from the outside to the inside). Only the seven types of connections shown in Table 10.12 are allowed between the ports of nested design entities. The additional rule that ports of mode buffer may only have one source, together with the restrictions on port mode interconnections, limits the use of ports of mode buffer.

TABLE 10.12 Connection rules for port modes.

```
entity E1 is port (Inside : in BIT); end; architecture Behave of E1 is begin end;
entity E2 is port (Outside : inout BIT := '1'); end; architecture Behave of E2 is
component E1 port (Inside : in BIT); end component; begin
I1 : E1 port map (Inside => Outside);   -- formal/local (mode in) => actual (mode inout)
end;
```

Possible modes of interface object, `Inside`	**in** (default)	**out**	inout	buffer
Modes of `Outside` that `Inside` may connect to (see below)	**in inout** **buffer**	**out** **inout**	**inout**[1]	**buffer**[2]

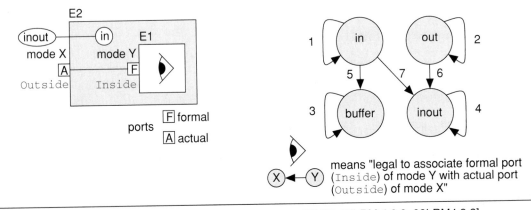

F formal
A actual
ports

means "legal to associate formal port (`Inside`) of mode Y with actual port (`Outside`) of mode X"

[1]A signal of mode inout can be updated by any number of sources [VHDL 87LRM 4.3.3, 93LRM4.3.2].
[2]A signal of mode buffer can be updated by at most one source [VHDL LRM1.1.1.2].

10.7.2 Generics

Ports are signals that carry changing information between entities. A **generic** is similar to a port, except generics carry constant, static information. A generic is an interface constant that, unlike normal VHDL constants, may be given a value in a component instantiation statement or in a configuration specification. You declare generics in an entity declaration and you use generics in a similar fashion to ports. The following example uses a generic parameter to alter the size of a gate:

```
entity AndGateNWide is
    generic (N : NATURAL := 2);
    port (Inputs : BIT_VECTOR(1 to N); Result : out BIT);
end;
```

Notice that the **generic interface list** precedes the port interface list. Generics are useful to carry timing (delay) information, as in the next example:

```
entity AndT is
    generic (TPD : TIME := 1 ns);
    port (a, b : BIT := '0'; q: out BIT);
```

```
end;
architecture Behave of AndT is
   begin q <= a and b after TPD;
end;

entity AndT_Test_1 is end;
architecture Netlist_1 of AndT_Test_1 is
   component MyAnd
      port (a, b : BIT; q : out BIT);
   end component;
   signal a1, b1, q1 : BIT := '1';
   begin
      And1 : MyAnd port map (a1, b1, q1);
end Netlist_1;

configuration Simplest_1 of AndT_Test_1 is use work.all;
   for Netlist_1 for And1 : MyAnd
      use entity AndT(Behave) generic map (2 ns);
   end for; end for;
end Simplest_1;
```

The configuration declaration, Simplest_1, changes the default delay (equal to 1 ns, declared as a default expression in the entity) to 2 ns. Techniques based on this method are useful in ASIC design. Prelayout simulation uses the default timing values. Back-annotation alters the delay in the configuration for postlayout simulation. When we change the delay we only need to reanalyze the configuration, not the rest of the ASIC model.

There was initially no standard in VHDL for how timing generics should be used, and the lack of a standard was a major problem for ASIC designers. The IEEE 1076.4 VITAL standard addresses this problem (see Section 13.5.5).

10.8 Type Declarations

In some programming languages you must declare objects to be integer, real, Boolean, and so on. VHDL (and ADA, the DoD programming language to which VHDL is related) goes further: You must declare the **type** of an object, and there are strict rules on mixing objects of different types. We say VHDL is strongly typed. For example, you can use one type for temperatures in Centigrade and a different type for Fahrenheit, even though both types are real numbers. If you try to add a temperature in Centigrade to a temperature in Fahrenheit, VHDL catches your error and tells you that you have a type mismatch.

This is the formal (expanded) BNF definition of a **type declaration**:

```
type_declaration ::=                                    [10.14]
   type identifier ;
 | type identifier is
```

```
(identifier|'graphic_character' {, identifier|'graphic_character'}) ;
| range_constraint ;          | physical_type_definition ;
| record_type_definition ;    | access subtype_indication ;
| file of type_name ;         | file of subtype_name ;
| array index_constraint of element_subtype_indication ;
| array
  (type_name|subtype_name range <>
    {, type_name|subtype_name range <>}) of
    element_subtype_indication ;
```

There are four **type classes** in VHDL [VHDL LRM3]: **scalar types**, **composite types**, **access types**, and **file types**. The scalar types are: **integer type**, **floating-point type**, **physical type**, and **enumeration type**. Integer and enumeration types are **discrete types**. Integer, floating-point, and physical types are **numeric types**. The **range** of an integer is implementation dependent but is guaranteed to include −2147483647 to +2147483647. Notice the integer range is symmetric and equal to −(2^{31}−1) to (2^{31}−1). Floating-point size is implementation dependent, but the range includes the bounds −1.0E38 and +1.0E38, and must include a minimum of six decimal digits of precision. Physical types correspond to time, voltage, current, and so on and have dimensions—a unit of measure (seconds, for example). Access types are pointers, useful in abstract data structures, but less so in ASIC design. File types are used for file I/O.

You may also declare a subset of an existing type, known as a **subtype**, in a **subtype declaration**. We shall discuss the different treatment of types and subtypes in expressions in Section 10.12.

Here are some examples of scalar type and subtype declarations:

```
entity Declaration_1 is end; architecture Behave of Declaration_1 is
type F is range 32 to 212; -- integer type, ascending range
type C is range 0 to 100; -- range 0 to 100 is the range constraint
subtype G is INTEGER range 9 to 0; -- base type INTEGER, descending
-- this is illegal: type Bad100 is INTEGER range 0 to 100;
-- don't use INTEGER in declaration of type (OK in subtype)
type Rainbow is (R, O, Y, G, B, I, V); -- an enumeration type
-- enumeration types always have an ascending range
type MVL4 is ('X', '0', '1', 'Z');
-- Note that 'X' and 'x' are different character literals.
-- The default initial value is MVL4'LEFT = 'X'.
-- We say '0' and '1' (already enumeration literals
-- for predefined type BIT) are overloaded.
-- illegal enumeration type: type Bad4 is ("X", "0", "1", "Z");
-- enumeration literals must be character literals or identifiers
begin end;
```

The most common composite type is the **array type**. The following examples illustrate the semantics of array declarations:

```
entity Arrays_1 is end; architecture Behave of Arrays_1 is
type Word is array (0 to 31) of BIT; -- a 32-bit array, ascending
type Byte is array (NATURAL range 7 downto 0) of BIT; -- descending
type BigBit is array (NATURAL range <>) of BIT;
-- We call <> a box, it means the range is undefined for now.
-- We call BigBit an unconstrained array.
-- This is OK, we constrain the range of an object that uses
-- type BigBit when we declare the object, like this:
subtype Nibble is BigBit(3 downto 0);
type T1 is array (POSITIVE range 1 to 32) of BIT;
-- T1, a constrained array declaration, is equivalent to a type T2
-- with the following three declarations:
subtype index_subtype is POSITIVE range 1 to 32;
type array_type is array (index_subtype range <>) of BIT;
subtype T2 is array_type (index_subtype);
-- We refer to index_subtype and array_type as being
-- anonymous subtypes of T1 (since they don't really exist).
begin end;
```

You can assign values to an array using **aggregate notation**. For example:

```
entity Aggregate_1 is end; architecture Behave of Aggregate_1 is
type D is array (0 to 3) of BIT; type Mask is array (1 to 2) of BIT;
signal MyData : D := ('0', others => '1'); -- positional aggregate
signal MyMask : Mask := (2 => '0', 1 => '1'); -- named aggregate
begin end;
```

The other composite type is the **record type** that groups elements together:

```
entity Record_2 is end; architecture Behave of Record_2 is
type Complex is record real : INTEGER; imag : INTEGER; end record;
signal s1 : Complex := (0, others => 1); signal s2: Complex;
begin s2 <= (imag => 2, real => 1); end;
```

10.9 Other Declarations

A declaration is one of the following:

```
declaration ::=                                              [10.15]
  type_declaration      | subtype_declaration | object_declaration
| interface_declaration | alias_declaration   | attribute_declaration
| component_declaration | entity_declaration
| configuration_declaration | subprogram_declaration
| package_declaration
| group_template_declaration | group_declaration
```

I discussed entity, configuration, component, package, interface, type, and subtype declarations in Sections 10.5–10.8. Next I shall discuss the other types of declarations (except for groups or group templates, new to VHDL-93, that are not often used in ASIC design).

10.9.1 Object Declarations

There are four **object classes** in VHDL: **constant**, **variable**, **signal**, and **file** [VHDL LRM 4.3.1.1-4.3.1.3]. You use a **constant declaration**, **signal declaration**, **variable declaration**, or **file declaration** together with a type. Signals can only be declared in the **declarative region** (before the first begin) of an architecture or block, or in a package (not in a package body). Variables can only be declared in the declarative region of a process or subprogram (before the first begin). You can think of signals as representing real wires in hardware. You can think of variables as memory locations in the computer. Variables are more efficient than signals because they require less overhead.

You may assign an (explicit) **initial value** when you declare a type. If you do not provide initial values, the (implicit) **default initial value** of a type or subtype T is T'LEFT (the leftmost item in the range of the type). For example:

```
entity Initial_1 is end; architecture Behave of Initial_1 is
type Fahrenheit is range 32 to 212; -- default initial value is 32
type Rainbow is (R, O, Y, G, B, I, V); -- default initial value is R
type MVL4 is ('X', '0', '1', 'Z'); -- MVL4'LEFT = 'X'
begin end;
```

The details of initialization and assignment of initial values are important—it is difficult to implement the assignment of initial values in hardware—instead it is better to mimic the hardware and use explicit reset signals.

Here are the formal definitions of constant and signal declarations:

```
constant_declaration ::= constant                              [10.16]
identifier {, identifier}:subtype_indication [:= expression] ;

signal_declaration ::= signal                                  [10.17]
identifier {, identifier}:subtype_indication [register|bus] [:=expression];
```

I shall explain the use of signals of kind register or bus in Section 10.13.1. Signal declarations are **explicit signal declarations** (ports declared in an interface declaration are implicit signal declarations). Here is an example that uses a constant and several signal declarations:

```
entity Constant_2 is end;
library IEEE; use IEEE.STD_LOGIC_1164.all;
architecture Behave of Constant_2 is
constant Pi : REAL := 3.14159; -- a constant declaration
signal B : BOOLEAN; signal s1, s2: BIT;
signal sum : INTEGER range 0 to 15; -- not a new type
signal SmallBus : BIT_VECTOR (15 downto 0); -- 16-bit bus
```

```
signal GBus : STD_LOGIC_VECTOR (31 downto 0); bus; -- guarded signal
begin end;
```

Here is the formal definition of a variable declaration:

```
variable_declaration ::= [shared] variable                    [10.18]
identifier {, identifier}:subtype_indication [:= expression] ;
```

A **shared variable** can be used to model a varying quantity that is common across several parts of a model, temperature, for example, but shared variables are rarely used in ASIC design. The following examples show that variable declarations belong inside a process statement, after the keyword process and before the first appearance of the keyword begin inside a process:

```
library IEEE; use IEEE.STD_LOGIC_1164.all; entity Variables_1 is end;
architecture Behave of Variables_1 is begin process
   variable i : INTEGER range 1 to 10 := 10; -- initial value = 10
   variable v : STD_LOGIC_VECTOR (0 to 31) := (others => '0');
   begin wait; end process; -- the wait stops an endless cycle
end;
```

10.9.2   Subprogram Declarations

VHDL code that you use several times can be declared and specified as **subprograms** (functions or procedures) [VHDL LRM2.1]. A **function** is a form of expression, may only use parameters of mode in, and may not contain delays or sequence events during simulation (no wait statements, for example). Functions are useful to model combinational logic. A **procedure** is a form of statement and allows you to control the scheduling of simulation events without incurring the overhead of defining several separate design entities. There are thus two forms of **subprogram declaration**: a **function declaration** or a **procedure declaration**.

```
subprogram_declaration ::= subprogram_specification ; ::=      [10.19]
 procedure
   identifier|string_literal [(parameter_interface_list)]
| [pure|impure] function
   identifier|string_literal [(parameter_interface_list)]
return type_name|subtype_name;
```

Here are a function and a procedure declaration that illustrate the difference:

```
function add(a, b, c : BIT_VECTOR(3 downto 0)) return BIT_VECTOR is
-- a function declaration, a function can't modify a, b, or c

procedure Is_A_Eq_B (signal A, B : BIT; signal Y : out BIT);
-- a procedure declaration, a procedure can change Y
```

Parameter names in subprogram declarations are called **formal parameters** (or formals). During a call to a subprogram, known as **subprogram invocation**, the passed values are **actual parameters** (or actuals). An **impure** function, such as the function now or a function that writes to or reads from a file, may return different values each time it is called (even with the same actuals). A **pure** function (the default) returns the same value if it is given the same actuals. You may call subprograms recursively. Table 10.13 shows the properties of subprogram parameters.

TABLE 10.13   Properties of subprogram parameters.

Example subprogram declarations:
```
function my_function(Ff) return BIT is -- formal function  parameter, Ff.
procedure my_procedure(Fp); -- formal procedure parameter, Fp.
```

Example subprogram calls :
```
my_result := my_function(Af); -- calling a function  with an actual parameter, Af.
MY_LABEL:my_procedure(Ap); -- using   a procedure with an actual parameter, Ap.
```

Mode of `Ff` or `Fp` (formals)	`in`	`out`	`inout`	No mode
Permissible classes for `Af` (function actual parameter)	`constant` (default) `signal`	Not allowed	Not allowed	`file`
Permissible classes for `Ap` (procedure actual parameter)	`constant` (default) `variable` `signal`	`constant` `variable` (default) `signal`	`constant` `variable` (default) `signal`	`file`
Can you read attributes of `Ff` or `Fp` (formals)?	Yes, except: `'STABLE` `'QUIET` `'DELAYED` `'TRANSACTION` of a signal	Yes, except: `'STABLE` `'QUIET` `'DELAYED` `'TRANSACTION` `'EVENT` `'ACTIVE` `'LAST_EVENT` `'LAST_ACTIVE` `'LAST_VALUE` of a signal	Yes, except: `'STABLE` `'QUIET` `'DELAYED` `'TRANSACTION` of a signal	

A subprogram declaration is optional, but a **subprogram specification** must be included in the **subprogram body** (and must be identical in syntax to the subprogram declaration—see BNF [10.19]):

```
subprogram_body ::=                                              [10.20]
    subprogram_specification is
    {subprogram_declaration|subprogram_body
    |type_declaration|subtype_declaration
    |constant_declaration|variable_declaration|file_declaration
```

```
|alias_declaration|attribute_declaration|attribute_specification
|use_clause|group_template_declaration|group_declaration}
begin
   {sequential_statement}
end [procedure|function] [identifier|string_literal] ;
```

You can include a subprogram declaration or subprogram body in a package or package body (see Section 10.6) or in the declarative region of an entity or process statement. The following is an example of a function declaration and its body:

```
function subset0(sout0 : in BIT) return BIT_VECTOR -- declaration

-- declaration can be separate from the body

function subset0(sout0 : in BIT) return BIT_VECTOR is -- body
variable y : BIT_VECTOR(2 downto 0);
begin
if (sout0 = '0') then y := "000"; else y := "100"; end if;
return result;
end;

procedure clockGen (clk : out BIT)                    -- declaration

procedure clockGen (clk : out BIT) is                 -- specification
begin -- careful this process runs forever :
   process begin wait for 10 ns; clk <= not clk; end process;
end;
```

One reason for having the optional (and seemingly redundant) subprogram declaration is to allow companies to show the subprogram declarations (to document the interface) in a package declaration, but to hide the subprogram bodies (the actual code) in the package body. If a separate subprogram declaration is present, it must **conform** to the specification in the subprogram body. This means the specification and declaration must be almost identical; the safest method is to copy and paste. If you define common procedures and functions in packages (instead of in each entity or architecture, for example), it will be easier to reuse subprograms. In order to make a subprogram included in a package body visible outside the package, you must declare the subprogram in the package declaration (otherwise the subprogram is **private**).

You may call a function from any expression, as follows:

```
entity F_1 is port (s : out BIT_VECTOR(3 downto 0) := "0000"); end;
architecture Behave of F_1 is begin process
function add(a, b, c : BIT_VECTOR(3 downto 0)) return BIT_VECTOR is
begin return a xor b xor c; end;
begin s <= add("0001", "0010", "1000"); wait; end process; end;

package And_Pkg is
   procedure V_And(a, b : BIT; signal c : out BIT);
   function V_And(a, b : BIT) return BIT;
```

```
end;
package body And_Pkg is
   procedure V_And(a,b : BIT; signal c : out BIT) is
      begin c <= a and b; end;
   function V_And(a,b : BIT) return BIT is
      begin return a and b; end;
end And_Pkg;

entity F_2 is port (s: out BIT := '0'); end;
use work.And_Pkg.all; -- use package already analyzed
architecture Behave of F_2 is begin process begin
s <= V_And('1', '1'); wait; end process; end;
```

I shall discuss the two different ways to call a procedure in Sections 10.10.4 and 10.13.3.

10.9.3   Alias and Attribute Declarations

An **alias declaration** [VHDL 87LRM4.3.4, 93LRM4.3.3] names parts of a type:

```
alias_declaration ::=                                    [10.21]
alias
   identifier|character_literal|operator_symbol [ :subtype_indication]
   is name [signature];
```

(the subtype indication is required in VHDL-87, but not in VHDL-93).

Here is an example of alias declarations for parts of a floating-point number:

```
entity Alias_1 is end; architecture Behave of Alias_1 is
begin process variable Nmbr: BIT_VECTOR (31 downto 0);
-- alias declarations to split Nmbr into 3 pieces :
alias Sign :        BIT is Nmbr(31);
alias Mantissa :    BIT_VECTOR (23 downto 0) is Nmbr (30 downto 7);
alias Exponent :    BIT_VECTOR ( 6 downto 0) is Nmbr ( 6 downto 0);
begin wait; end process; end; -- the wait prevents an endless cycle
```

An **attribute declaration** [VHDL LRM4.4] defines attribute properties:

```
attribute_declaration ::=                                [10.22]
   attribute identifier:type_name ; | attribute identifier:subtype_name ;
```

Here is an example:

```
entity Attribute_1 is end; architecture Behave of Attribute_1 is
begin process type COORD is record X, Y : INTEGER; end record;
attribute LOCATION : COORD; -- the attribute declaration
begin wait ; -- the wait prevents an endless cycle
end process; end;
```

You define the attribute properties in an **attribute specification** (the following example specifies an attribute of a component label). You probably will not need to use your own attributes very much in ASIC design.

```
attribute LOCATION of adder1 : label is (10,15);
```

You can then refer to your attribute as follows:

```
positionOfComponent := adder1'LOCATION;
```

10.9.4   Predefined Attributes

The predefined attributes for scalar and array types in VHDL-93 are shown in Table 10.14 [VHDL LRM8]. There are two attributes, 'STRUCTURE and 'BEHAVIOR, that are present in VHDL-87, but removed in VHDL-93. Both of these attributes apply to architecture bodies. The attribute name A'behavior is TRUE if the architecture A does not contain component instantiations. The attribute name A'structure is TRUE if the architecture A contains only passive processes (those with no assignments to signals) and component instantiations. These two attributes were not widely used. The attributes shown in Table 10.14, however, are used extensively to create packages and functions for type conversion and overloading operators, but should not be needed by an ASIC designer. Many of the attributes do not correspond to "real" hardware and cannot be implemented by a synthesis tool.

The attribute 'LEFT is important because it determines the default initial value of a type. For example, the default initial value for type BIT is BIT'LEFT, which is '0'. The predefined attributes of signals are listed in Table 10.15. The most important signal attribute is 'EVENT, which is frequently used to detect a clock edge. Notice that Clock'EVENT, for example, is a function that returns a value of type BOOLEAN, whereas the otherwise equivalent not(Clock'STABLE), is a signal. The difference is subtle but important when these attributes are used in the wait statement that treats signals and values differently.

10.10 Sequential Statements

A **sequential statement** [VHDL LRM8] is defined as follows:

```
sequential_statement ::=                                    [10.23]
  wait_statement      | assertion_statement
| signal_assignment_statement
| variable_assignment_statement      | procedure_call_statement
| if_statement         | case_statement | loop_statement
| next_statement       | exit_statement
| return_statement     | null_statement | report_statement
```

TABLE 10.14   Predefined attributes for scalar and array types.

Attribute	Kind[1]	Prefix T, A, E[2]	Parameter X or N[3]	Result type[3]	Result
T'BASE	T	any		base(T)	base(T), use only with other attribute
T'LEFT	V	scalar		T	Left bound of T
T'RIGHT	V	scalar		T	Right bound of T
T'HIGH	V	scalar		T	Upper bound of T
T'LOW	V	scalar		T	Lower bound of T
T'ASCENDING	V	scalar		BOOLEAN	True if range of T is ascending[4]
T'IMAGE(X)	F	scalar	base(T)	STRING	String representation of X in T[4]
T'VALUE(X)	F	scalar	STRING	base(T)	Value in T with representation X[4]
T'POS(X)	F	discrete	base(T)	UI	Position number of X in T (starts at 0)
T'VAL(X)	F	discrete	UI	base(T)	Value of position X in T
T'SUCC(X)	F	discrete	base(T)	base(T)	Value of position X in T plus one
T'PRED(X)	F	discrete	base(T)	base(T)	Value of position X in T minus one
T'LEFTOF(X)	F	discrete	base(T)	base(T)	Value to the left of X in T
T'RIGHTOF(X)	F	discrete	base(T)	base(T)	Value to the right of X in T
A'LEFT[(N)]	F	array	UI	T(Result)	Left bound of index N of array A
A'RIGHT[(N)]	F	array	UI	T(Result)	Right bound of index N of array A
A'HIGH[(N)]	F	array	UI	T(Result)	Upper bound of index N of array A
A'LOW[(N)]	F	array	UI	T(Result)	Lower bound of index N of array A
A'RANGE[(N)]	R	array	UI	T(Result)	Range A'LEFT(N) to A'RIGHT(N)[5]
A'REVERSE_RANGE[(N)]	R	array	UI	T(Result)	Opposite range to A'RANGE[(N)]
A'LENGTH[(N)]	V	array	UI	UI	Number of values in index N of array A
A'ASCENDING[(N)]	V	array	UI	BOOLEAN	True if index N of A is ascending[4]
E'SIMPLE_NAME	V	name		STRING	Simple name of E[4]
E'INSTANCE_NAME	V	name		STRING	Path includes instantiated entities[4]
E'PATH_NAME	V	name		STRING	Path excludes instantiated entities[4]

[1]T=Type, F=Function, V=Value, R=Range.
[2]any=any type or subtype, scalar=scalar type or subtype, discrete=discrete or physical type or subtype, name=entity name=identifier, character literal, or operator symbol.
[3]base(T)=base type of T, T=type of T, UI= universal_integer,T(Result)=type of object described in result column.
[4]Only available in VHDL-93. For 'ASCENDING all enumeration types are ascending.
[5]Or reverse for descending ranges.

TABLE 10.15   Predefined attributes for signals.

Attribute	Kind[1]	Parameter T[2]	Result type[3]	Result/restrictions
S'DELAYED [(T)]	S	TIME	base(S)	S delayed by time T
S'STABLE [(T)]	S	TIME	BOOLEAN	TRUE if no event on S for time T
S'QUIET [(T)]	S	TIME	BOOLEAN	TRUE if S is quiet for time T
S'TRANSACTION	S		BIT	Toggles each cycle if S becomes active
S'EVENT	F		BOOLEAN	TRUE when event occurs on S
S'ACTIVE	F		BOOLEAN	TRUE if S is active
S'LAST_EVENT	F		TIME	Elapsed time since the last event on S
S'LAST_ACTIVE	F		TIME	Elapsed time since S was active
S'LAST_VALUE	F		base(S)	Previous value of S, before last event[4]
S'DRIVING	F		BOOLEAN	TRUE if every element of S is driven[5]
S'DRIVING_VALUE	F		base(S)	Value of the driver for S in the current process[5]

[1] F=function, S=signal.
[2]Time T≥0 ns. The default, if T is not present, is T=0 ns.
[3]base(S)=base type of S.
[4]VHDL-93 returns last value of each signal in array separately as an aggregate, VHDL-87 returns the last value of the composite signal.
[5]VHDL-93 only.

Sequential statements may only appear in processes and subprograms. In the following sections I shall describe each of these different types of sequential statements in turn.

10.10.1 Wait Statement

The **wait statement** is central to VHDL, here are the BNF definitions:

```
wait_statement ::= [label:] wait [sensitivity_clause]          [10.24]
   [condition_clause] [timeout_clause] ;
sensitivity_clause ::= on sensitivity_list
sensitivity_list ::= signal_name { , signal_name }
condition_clause ::= until condition
condition ::= boolean_expression
timeout_clause ::= for time_expression
```

A wait statement **suspends** (stops) a process or procedure (you cannot use a wait statement in a function). The **wait** statement may be made sensitive to events (changes) on **static** signals (the value of the signal must be known at analysis time) that appear in the **sensitivity list** after the keyword on. These signals form the **sensitivity set** of a wait statement. The process will **resume** (restart) when an event occurs on any signal (and only signals) in the sensitivity set.

A wait statement may also contain a condition to be met before the process resumes. If there is no **sensitivity clause** (there is no keyword on) the sensitivity set is made from signals (and only signals) from the **condition clause** that appears after the keyword until (the rules are quite complicated [VHDL 93LRM8.1]).

Finally a wait statement may also contain a **timeout** (following the keyword for) after which the process will resume. Here is the expanded BNF definition, which makes the structure of the wait statement easier to see (but we lose the definitions of the clauses and the sensitivity list):

```
wait_statement ::= [label:] wait
  [on signal_name {, signal_name}]
  [until boolean_expression]
  [for time_expression] ;
```

For example, the statement, **wait on** light, makes you wait until a traffic light changes (any change). The statement, **wait until** light = green, makes you wait (even at a green light) until the traffic signal changes to green. The statement,

```
if light = (red or yellow) then wait until light = green; end if;
```

accurately describes the basic rules at a traffic intersection.

The most common use of the wait statement is to describe synchronous logic, as in the following model of a D flip-flop:

```
entity DFF is port (CLK, D : BIT; Q : out BIT); end;            --1
architecture Behave of DFF is                                   --2
process begin wait until Clk = '1'; Q <= D ; end process;       --3
end;                                                            --4
```

Notice that the statement in line 3 above, **wait until** Clk = '1', is equivalent to **wait on** Clk **until** Clk = '1', and detects a clock edge and not the clock level. Here are some more complex examples of the use of the wait statement:

```
entity Wait_1 is port (Clk, s1, s2 :in BIT); end;
architecture Behave of Wait_1 is
signal x : BIT_VECTOR (0 to 15);
  begin process variable v : BIT; begin
  wait; -- wait forever, stops simulation
  wait on s1 until s2 = '1';
  -- The above is legal, but s1, s2 are signals so...
  -- s1 is in sensitivity list, s2 is not in the sensitivity set
  -- sensitivity set is s1 and process will not resume at event on s2
  wait on s1, s2; -- process resumes at event on signal s1 or s2
  wait on s1 for 10 ns; -- resumes at event on s1 or after 10 ns
  wait on x; -- resumes when any element of array x has an event
```

```
-- wait on x(1 to v); -- illegal, nonstatic name, v is variable...
end process;
end;

entity Wait_2 is port (Clk, s1, s2:in BIT); end;
architecture Behave of Wait_2 is
  begin process variable v : BIT; begin
  wait on Clk; -- resumes when Clk has an event: rising or falling
  wait until Clk = '1'; -- resumes on rising edge
  wait on Clk until Clk = '1'; -- equivalent to the last statement
  wait on Clk until v = '1';
  -- The above is legal, but v is a variable so
  -- Clk is in sensitivity list, v is not in the sensitivity set.
  -- Sensitivity set is Clk and process will not resume at event on v.
  wait on Clk until s1 = '1';
  -- The above is legal, but s1 is a signal so
  -- Clk is in sensitivity list, s1 is not in the sensitivity set.
  -- Sensitivity set is Clk, process will not resume at event on s1.
  end process;
end;
```

You may only use interface signals that may be read (port modes in, inout, and buffer—see Section 10.7) in the sensitivity list of a wait statement.

10.10.2 Assertion and Report Statements

You can use an **assertion statement** to conditionally issue warnings. The **report statement** (VHDL-93 only) prints an expression and is useful for debugging.

```
assertion_statement ::= [label:] assert                        [10.25]
boolean_expression [report expression] [severity expression] ;

report_statement
::= [label:] report expression [severity expression] ;
```

Here is an example of an assertion statement:

```
entity Assert_1 is port (I:INTEGER:=0); end;
architecture Behave of Assert_1 is
  begin process begin
  assert (I > 0) report "I is negative or zero"; wait;
  end process;
end;
```

The expression after the keyword report must be of type STRING (the default is "Assertion violation" for the assertion statement), and the expression after the keyword severity must be of type SEVERITY_LEVEL (default ERROR for the assertion statement, and NOTE for the report statement) defined in the STANDARD package. The assertion statement prints if the assertion condition (after the keyword assert) is FALSE. Simulation normally halts for severity of ERROR or FAILURE (you can normally control this threshold in the simulator).

10.10.3 Assignment Statements

There are two sorts of VHDL assignment statements: one for signals and one for variables. The difference is in the timing of the update of the LHS.

A **variable assignment statement** is the closest equivalent to the assignment statement in a computer programming language. Variable assignment statements are always sequential statements and the LHS of a variable assignment statement is always updated immediately. Here is the BNF definition and an example:

```
variable_assignment_statement ::=                                    [10.26]
    [label:] name|aggregate := expression ;
```

```
entity Var_Assignment is end;
architecture Behave of Var_Assignment is
  signal s1 : INTEGER := 0;
  begin process variable v1,v2 : INTEGER := 0; begin
  assert (v1/=0) report "v1 is 0" severity note ; -- this prints
  v1 := v1 + 1; -- after this statement v1 is 1
  assert (v1=0) report "v1 isn't 0" severity note ; -- this prints
  v2 := v2 + s1; -- signal and variable types must match
  wait;
  end process;
end;
```

This is the output from Cadence Leapfrog for example (10.26):

```
ASSERT/NOTE (time 0 FS) from :$PROCESS_000 (design unit
WORK.VAR_ASSIGNMENT:BEHAVE) v1 is 0
ASSERT/NOTE (time 0 FS) from :$PROCESS_000 (design unit
WORK.VAR_ASSIGNMENT:BEHAVE) v1 isn't 0
```

A **signal assignment statement** schedules a future assignment to a signal:

```
signal_assignment_statement::=                                       [10.27]
    [label:] target <=
    [transport | [ reject time expression ] inertial] waveform ;
```

The following example shows that, even with no delay, a signal is updated at the end of a simulation cycle after all the other assignments have been scheduled, just before simulation time is advanced:

```
entity Sig_Assignment_1 is end;
architecture Behave of Sig_Assignment_1 is
  signal s1,s2,s3 : INTEGER := 0;
  begin process variable v1 : INTEGER := 1; begin
  assert (s1 /= 0) report "s1 is 0" severity note ; -- this prints
```

```
s1 <= s1 + 1; -- after this statement s1 is still 0
assert (s1 /= 0) report "s1 still 0" severity note ; -- this prints
wait;
end process;
end;
```

```
ASSERT/NOTE (time 0 FS) from :$PROCESS_000 (design unit
WORK.SIG_ASSIGNMENT_1:BEHAVE) s1 is 0
ASSERT/NOTE (time 0 FS) from :$PROCESS_000 (design unit
WORK.SIG_ASSIGNMENT_1:BEHAVE) s1 still 0
```

Here is an another example to illustrate how time is handled:

```
entity Sig_Assignment_2 is end;
architecture Behave of Sig_Assignment_2 is
  signal s1, s2, s3 :INTEGER := 0;
  begin process variable v1 : INTEGER := 1; begin
  -- s1, s2, s3 are initially 0; now consider the following:
  s1 <= 1 ; -- schedules updates to s1 at end of 0 ns cycle
  s2 <= s1; -- s2 is 0, not 1
  wait for 1 ns;
  s3 <= s1; -- now s3 will be 1 at 1 ns
  wait;
  end process;
end;
```

The Compass simulator produces the following trace file for this example:

Time(fs) + Cycle	s1	s2	s3
0+ 0:	0	0	0
0+ 1: *	1 *	0	0
...			
1000000+ 1:	1	0 *	1

Time is indicated in femtoseconds for each **simulation cycle** plus the number of **delta cycles** (we call this **delta time**, measured in units of **delta**, δ) needed to calculate all transactions on signals. A transaction consists of a new value for a signal (which may be the same as the old value) and the time delay for the value to take effect. An asterisk '*' before a value in the preceding trace indicates that a transaction has occurred and the corresponding signal updated at that time. A transaction that does result in a change in value is an **event**. In the preceding simulation trace for Sig_Assignment_2:Behave

- At 0 ns+ 0δ: all signals are 0.
- At 0 ns+ 1δ: s1 is updated to 1, s2 is updated to 0 (not to 1).
- At 1 ns+ 1δ: s3 is updated to a 1.

The following example shows the behavior of the different **delay models**: **transport** and **inertial** (the default):

```
entity Transport_1 is end;
architecture Behave of Transport_1 is
signal s1, SLOW, FAST, WIRE : BIT := '0';
  begin process begin
  s1 <= '1' after 1 ns, '0' after 2 ns, '1' after 3 ns ;
  -- schedules s1 to be '1' at t+1 ns, '0' at t+2 ns,'1' at t+3 ns
  wait; end process;
-- inertial delay: SLOW rejects pulsewidths less than 5ns:
process (s1) begin SLOW <= s1 after 5 ns ; end process;
-- inertial delay: FAST rejects pulsewidths less than 0.5ns:
process (s1) begin FAST <= s1 after 0.5 ns ; end process;
-- transport delay: WIRE passes all pulsewidths...
process (s1) begin WIRE <= transport s1 after 5 ns ; end process;
end;
```

Here is the trace file from the Compass simulator:

```
    Time(fs) + Cycle    s1 slow fast wire
---------------------   ---- ---- ---- ----
             0+ 0:     '0'  '0'  '0'  '0'
        500000+ 0:     '0'  '0' *'0'  '0'
       1000000+ 0:    *'1'  '0'  '0'  '0'
       1500000+ 0:     '1'  '0' *'1'  '0'
       2000000+ 0:    *'0'  '0'  '1'  '0'
       2500000+ 0:     '0'  '0' *'0'  '0'
       3000000+ 0:    *'1'  '0'  '0'  '0'
       3500000+ 0:     '1'  '0' *'1'  '0'
       5000000+ 0:     '1'  '0'  '1' *'0'
       6000000+ 0:     '1'  '0'  '1' *'1'
       7000000+ 0:     '1'  '0'  '1' *'0'
       8000000+ 0:     '1' *'1'  '1' *'1'
```

Inertial delay mimics the behavior of real logic gates, whereas transport delay more closely models the behavior of wires. In VHDL-93 you can also add a separate **pulse rejection limit** for the inertial delay model as in the following example:

```
process (s1) begin RJCT <= reject 2 ns s1 after 0.5 ns ; end process;
```

10.10.4 Procedure Call

A **procedure call** in VHDL corresponds to calling a subroutine in a conventional programming language. The parameters in a procedure call statement are the actual procedure parameters (or actuals); the parameters in the procedure definition are the formal procedure parameters (or formals). The two are linked using an association list, which may use either positional or named association (association works just as it does for ports—see Section 10.7.1):

```
procedure_call_statement ::=                                    [10.28]
    [label:] procedure_name [(parameter_association_list)];
```

Here is an example:

```
package And_Pkg is
   procedure V_And(a, b : BIT; signal c : out BIT);
   function V_And(a, b : BIT) return BIT;
end;

package body And_Pkg is
   procedure V_And(a, b : BIT; signal c: out BIT) is
      begin c <= a and b; end;
   function V_And(a, b: BIT) return BIT is
      begin return a and b; end;
end And_Pkg;

use work.And_Pkg.all; entity Proc_Call_1 is end;
architecture Behave of Proc_Call_1 is signal A, B, Y: BIT := '0';
   begin process begin V_And (A, B, Y); wait; end process;
end;
```

Table 10.13 on page 416 explains the rules for formal procedure parameters. There is one other way to call procedures, which we shall cover in Section 10.13.3.

10.10.5 If Statement

An **if statement** evaluates one or more Boolean expressions and conditionally executes a corresponding sequence of statements.

```
if_statement ::=                                               [10.29]
    [if_label:] if boolean_expression then {sequential_statement}
      {elsif boolean_expression then {sequential_statement}}
      [else {sequential_statement}]
   end if [if_label];
```

The simplest form of an `if` statement is thus:

```
if boolean_expression then {sequential_statement} end if;
```

Here are some examples of the `if` statement:

```
entity If_Then_Else_1 is end;
architecture Behave of If_Then_Else_1 is signal a, b, c: BIT:='1';
   begin process begin
      if c = '1' then c <= a ; else c <= b; end if; wait;
   end process;
end;
```

```
entity If_Then_1 is end;
architecture Behave of If_Then_1 is signal A, B, Y : BIT:='1';
  begin process begin
    if A = B then Y <= A; end if; wait;
  end process;
end;
```

10.10.6 Case Statement

A **case statement** is a multiway decision statement that selects a sequence of state-ments by matching an expression with a list of (locally static) choices.

```
case_statement ::=                                          [10.30]
[case_label:] case expression is
    when choice {| choice} => {sequential_statement}
    {when choice {| choice} => {sequential_statement}}
end case [case_label];
```

Case statements are useful to model state machines. Here is an example of a Mealy state machine with an asynchronous reset:

```
library IEEE; use IEEE.STD_LOGIC_1164.all;                                --1
entity sm_mealy is                                                        --2
  port (reset, clock , i1, i2 : STD_LOGIC; o1, o2 : out STD_LOGIC);       --3
end sm_mealy;                                                             --4
architecture Behave of sm_mealy is                                       --5
type STATES is (s0, s1, s2, s3); signal current, new : STATES;           --6
begin                                                                    --7
synchronous : process (clock, reset) begin                               --8
  if To_X01(reset) = '0' then current <= s0;                             --9
  elsif rising_edge(clock) then current <= new; end if;                  --10
end process;                                                             --11
combinational : process (current, i1, i2) begin                          --12
case current is                                                          --13
  when s0 =>                                                             --14
    if To_X01(i1) = '1' then o2 <='0'; o1 <='0'; new <= s2;              --15
    else o2 <= '1'; o1 <= '1'; new <= s1; end if;                        --16
  when s1 =>                                                             --17
    if To_X01(i2) = '1' then o2 <='1'; o1 <='0'; new <= s1;              --18
    else o2 <='0'; o1 <='1'; new <= s3; end if;                          --19
  when s2 =>                                                             --20
    if To_X01(i2) = '1' then o2 <='0'; o1 <='1'; new <= s2;              --21
    else o2 <= '1'; o1 <= '0'; new <= s0; end if;                        --22
  when s3 => o2 <= '0'; o1 <= '0'; new <= s0;                            --23
  when others => o2 <= '0'; o1 <= '0'; new <= s0;                        --24
end case;                                                                --25
end process;                                                             --26
end Behave;                                                              --27
```

Each possible value of the case expression must be present once, and once only, in the list of choices (or arms) of the case statement (the list must be **exhaustive**). You can use `'|'` (that means 'or') or `'to'` to denote a range in the expression for choice. You may also use the keyword others as the last, default choice (even if the list is already exhaustive, as in the preceding example).

10.10.7 Other Sequential Control Statements

A **loop statement** repeats execution of a series of sequential statements:

```
loop_statement ::=                                        [10.31]
[loop_label:]
[while boolean_expression|for identifier in discrete_range]
loop
   {sequential_statement}
end loop [loop_label];
```

If the **loop variable** (after the keyword for) is used, it is only visible inside the loop. A while loop evaluates the Boolean expression before each execution of the sequence of statements; if the expression is TRUE, the statements are executed. In a for loop the sequence of statements is executed once for each value of the discrete range.

```
package And_Pkg is function V_And(a, b : BIT) return BIT; end;

package body And_Pkg is function V_And(a,b : BIT) return BIT is
   begin return a and b; end; end And_Pkg;

entity Loop_1 is port (x, y : in BIT := '1'; s : out BIT := '0'); end;
use work.And_Pkg.all;
architecture Behave of Loop_1 is
   begin loop
      s <= V_And(x, y); wait on x, y;
   end loop;
end;
```

The **next statement** forces completion of the current iteration of a loop (the containing loop unless another loop label is specified). Completion is forced if the condition following the keyword then is TRUE (or if there is no condition).

```
next_statement ::=                                        [10.32]
[label:] next [loop_label] [when boolean_expression];
```

An **exit statement** forces an exit from a loop.

```
exit_statement ::=
    [label:] exit [loop_label] [when condition] ;
```
[10.33]

As an example:

```
loop wait on Clk; exit when Clk = '0'; end loop;
-- equivalent to: wait until Clk = '0';
```

The **return statement** completes execution of a procedure or function.

```
return_statement ::= [label:] return [expression];
```
[10.34]

A **null statement** does nothing (but is useful in a case statement where all choices must be covered, but for some of the choices you do not want to do anything).

```
null_statement ::= [label:] null;
```
[10.35]

10.11 Operators

Table 10.16 shows the predefined VHDL **operators**, listed by their (increasing) order of precedence [LRM 7.2]. The shift operators and the xnor operator were added in VHDL-93.

TABLE 10.16   VHDL predefined operators (listed by increasing order of precedence).[1]

logical_operator[2] ::=	and | or | nand | nor | xor | xnor
relational_operator ::=	= | /= | < | <= | > | >=
shift_operator[2] ::=	sll | srl | sla | sra | rol | ror
adding_operator ::=	+ | − | &
sign ::=	+ | −
multiplying_operator ::=	* | / | mod | rem
miscellaneous_operator ::=	** | abs | not

[1]The not operator is a logical operator but has the precedence of a miscellaneous operator.
[2]Underline means "new to VHDL-93."

The binary **logical operators** (and, or, nand, nor, xor, xnor) and the unary not logical operator are predefined for types BIT or BOOLEAN and one-dimensional arrays whose element type is BIT or BOOLEAN. The operands must be of the same base type for the binary logical operators and the same length if they are arrays.

Both operands of **relational operators** must be of the same type and the result type is BOOLEAN. The equality operator and inequality operator (= and /=) are defined for all types (other than file types). The remaining relational operators, ordering operators, are predefined for any scalar type, and for any one-dimensional array whose elements are of a discrete type (enumeration or integer type).

The left operand of the **shift operators** (VHDL-93 only) is a one-dimensional array with element type of BIT or BOOLEAN; the right operand must be INTEGER.

The **adding operators** (+ and −) are predefined for any numeric type. You cannot use the adding operators on BIT or BIT_VECTOR without overloading. The **concatenation operator** & is predefined for any one-dimensional array type. The **signs** (+ and −) are defined for any numeric type.

The **multiplying operators** are: *, /, mod, and rem. The operators * and / are predefined for any integer or floating-point type, and the operands and the result are of the same type. The operators mod and rem are predefined for any integer type, and the operands and the result are of the same type. In addition, you can multiply an INTEGER or REAL by any physical type and the result is the physical type. You can also divide a physical type by REAL or INTEGER and the result is the physical type. If you divide a physical type by the same physical type, the result is an INTEGER (actually type UNIVERSAL_INTEGER, which is a predefined anonymous type). Once again—you cannot use the multiplying operators on BIT or BIT_VECTOR types without overloading the operators.

The **exponentiating operator**, **, is predefined for integer and floating-point types. The right operand, the exponent, is type INTEGER. You can only use a negative exponent with a left operand that is a floating-point type, and the result is the same type as the left operand. The unary operator abs (**absolute value**) is predefined for any numeric type and the result is the same type. The operators abs, **, and not are grouped as **miscellaneous operators**.

Here are some examples of the use of VHDL operators:

```
entity Operator_1 is end; architecture Behave of Operator_1 is      --1
begin process                                                       --2
variable b : BOOLEAN; variable bt : BIT := '1'; variable i : INTEGER;--3
variable pi : REAL := 3.14; variable epsilon : REAL := 0.01;        --4
variable bv4 : BIT_VECTOR (3 downto 0) := "0001";                   --5
variable bv8 : BIT_VECTOR (0 to 7);                                 --6
begin                                                               --7

b   := "0000" < bv4;   -- b is TRUE, "0000" treated as BIT_VECTOR   --8
b   := 'f' > 'g';      -- b is FALSE, 'dictionary' comparison       --9
bt  := '0' and bt;     -- bt is '0', analyzer knows '0' is BIT      --10
bv4 := not bv4;        -- bv4 is "1110"                             --11
i   := 1 + 2;          -- addition, must be compatible types        --12
```

```
i   := 2 ** 3;        -- exponentiation, exponent must be integer   --13
i   := 7/3;           -- division, L/R rounded towards zero, i=2     --14
i   := 12 rem 7;      -- remainder, i=5, in general:                 --15
                      -- L rem R = L-((L/R)*R)                       --16
i   := 12 mod 7;      -- modulus, i=5, in general:                   --17
                      -- L mod R = L-(R*N) for an integer N          --18
-- shift := sll | srl | sla | sra | rol | ror (VHDL-93 only)        --19
bv4 := "1001" srl 2;   -- shift right logical, bv4="0100"            --20
-- logical shift fills with T'LEFT.                                  --21
bv4 := "1001" sra 2;   -- shift right arithmetic, bv4="0111"         --22
-- arithmetic shift fills with element at end being vacated.         --23
bv4 := "1001" ror 2; -- rotate right,           bv4="0110"          --24
-- rotate wraps around.                                              --25
-- integer argument to any shift operator may be negative or zero    --26
if (pi*2.718)/2.718 = 3.14 then wait; end if; -- unreliable          --27
if (abs(((pi*2.718)/2.718)-3.14)<epsilon) then wait; end if;         --28
bv8 := bv8(1 to 7) & bv8(0); -- concatenation, a left rotation       --29
wait; end process;                                                   --30
end;                                                                 --31
```

10.12 Arithmetic

The following example illustrates **type checking** and **type conversion** in VHDL arithmetic operations:

```
entity Arithmetic_1 is end;architecture Behave of Arithmetic_1 is   --1
   begin process
   variable i : INTEGER := 1; variable r : REAL := 3.33;            --2
   variable b : BIT := '1';                                         --3
   variable bv4 : BIT_VECTOR (3 downto 0) := "0001";                --4
   variable bv8 : BIT_VECTOR (7 downto 0) := B"1000_0000";          --5
   begin                                                            --6

--   i := r;            -- can't assign REAL to INTEGER             --7
--   bv4 := bv4 + 2;    -- can't add BIT_VECTOR and INTEGER;        --8
--   bv4 := '1';        -- can't assign BIT to BIT_VECTOR           --9
--   bv8 := bv4;        -- error, arrays are different size         --10

r   := REAL(i);        -- type conversion                           --11
i   := INTEGER(r);     -- 0.5 rounds up or down                     --12
bv4 := "001" & '1';    -- OK, can mix array and scalar              --13
bv8 := "0001" & bv4;   -- OK, correct lengths                       --14
wait; end process; end;
```

The next example shows arithmetic operations between types and subtypes, and also illustrates **range checking** during analysis and simulation:

```
entity Arithmetic_2 is end; architecture Behave of Arithmetic_2 is   --1
type TC is range 0 to 100; -- type INTEGER                            --2
type TF is range 32 to 212;                                          --3
subtype STC is INTEGER range 0 to 100; -- subtype                     --4
subtype STF is INTEGER range 32 to 212; -- base type is INTEGER       --5
begin process                                                         --6
variable t1 : TC := 25; variable t2 : TF := 32;                       --7
variable st1 : STC := 25; variable st2 : STF := 32;                   --8
begin                                                                 --9
--    t1    := t2;        -- illegal, different type                  --10
--    t1    := st1;       -- illegal, different types and subtypes    --11
      st2   := st1;       -- OK, same base type                       --12
      st2   := st1 + 1;   -- OK, subtype and base type                --13
--    st2   := 213;       -- error, outside range at analysis time    --14
--    st2   := 212 + 1;   -- error, outside range at analysis time    --15
      st1   := st1 + 100; -- error, outside range at initialization   --16
wait; end process; end;
```

The MTI simulator, for example, gives the following informative error message during simulation of the preceding model:

```
# ** Fatal: Value 25 is out of range 32 to 212
#    Time: 0 ns  Iteration: 0  Instance:/
# Stopped at Arithmetic_2.vhd line 12
# Fatal error at Arithmetic_2.vhd line 12
```

The assignment st2 := st1 causes this error (since st1 is initialized to 25).

Operations between array types and subtypes are a little more complicated as the following example illustrates:

```
entity Arithmetic_3 is end; architecture Behave of Arithmetic_3 is   --1
type TYPE_1 is array (INTEGER range 3 downto 0) of BIT;               --2
type TYPE_2 is array (INTEGER range 3 downto 0) of BIT;               --3
subtype SUBTYPE_1 is BIT_VECTOR (3 downto 0);                         --4
subtype SUBTYPE_2 is BIT_VECTOR (3 downto 0);                         --5
begin process                                                         --6
variable bv4 : BIT_VECTOR (3 downto 0) := "0001";                     --7
variable st1 : SUBTYPE_1 := "0001";variable t1 : TYPE_1 := "0001";    --8
variable st2 : SUBTYPE_2 := "0001";variable t2 : TYPE_2 := "0001";    --9
begin                                                                 --10
      bv4 := st1;         -- compatible type and subtype              --11
--    bv4 := t1;          -- illegal, different types                 --12
      bv4 := BIT_VECTOR(t1); -- type conversion                       --13
      st1 := bv4;         -- compatible subtype and base type         --14
--    st1 := t1;          -- illegal, different types                 --15
      st1 := SUBTYPE_1(t1); -- type conversion                        --16
```

```
--    t1   := st1;              -- illegal, different types        --17
--    t1   := bv4;              -- illegal, different types        --18
      t1   := TYPE_1(bv4);      -- type conversion                 --19
--    t1   := t2;               -- illegal, different types        --20
      t1   := TYPE_1(t2);       -- type conversion                 --21
      st1  := st2;              -- compatible subtypes             --22
wait; end process; end;                                            --23
```

The preceding example uses BIT and BIT_VECTOR types, but exactly the same considerations apply to STD_LOGIC and STD_LOGIC_VECTOR types or other arrays. Notice the use of **type conversion**, written as type_mark'(expression), to convert between **closely related types**. Two types are closely related if they are abstract numeric types (integer or floating-point) or arrays with the same dimension, each index type is the same (or are themselves closely related), and each element has the same type [93LRM7.3.5].

10.12.1 IEEE Synthesis Packages

The IEEE 1076.3 standard synthesis packages allow you to perform arithmetic on arrays of the type BIT and STD_LOGIC.[3] The NUMERIC_BIT package defines all of the operators in Table 10.16 (except for the exponentiating operator '**') for arrays of type BIT. Here is part of the package header, showing the declaration of the two types UNSIGNED and SIGNED, and an example of one of the function declarations that overloads the addition operator '+' for UNSIGNED arguments:

```
package Part_NUMERIC_BIT is
type UNSIGNED is array (NATURAL range <> ) of BIT;
type SIGNED is array (NATURAL range <> ) of BIT;
function "+" (L, R : UNSIGNED) return UNSIGNED;
-- other function definitions that overload +, -, = , >, and so on.
end Part_NUMERIC_BIT;
```

The package bodies included in the 1076.3 standard define the functionality of the packages. Companies may implement the functions in any way they wish—as long as the results are the same as those defined by the standard. Here is an example of the parts of the NUMERIC_BIT package body that overload the addition operator '+' for two arguments of type UNSIGNED (even with added comments the code is rather dense and terse, but remember this is code that we normally never see or need to understand):

```
package body Part_NUMERIC_BIT is
constant NAU:UNSIGNED(0 downto 1):=(others =>'0'); -- null array
```

---

[3]IEEE Std 1076.3-1997 was approved by the IEEE Standards Board on 20 March 1997. The synthesis package code on the following pages is reprinted with permission from IEEE Std 1076.3-1997, Copyright © 1997 IEEE. All rights reserved.

```
constant NAS : SIGNED(0 downto 1):=(others => '0'); -- null array
constant NO_WARNING : BOOLEAN := FALSE; -- default to emit warnings

function MAX (LEFT, RIGHT : INTEGER) return INTEGER is
begin -- internal function used to find longest of two inputs...
if LEFT > RIGHT then return LEFT; else return RIGHT; end if; end MAX;

function ADD_UNSIGNED (L, R : UNSIGNED; C: BIT) return UNSIGNED is
constant L_LEFT : INTEGER := L'LENGTH-1; -- L, R must be same length.
alias XL : UNSIGNED(L_LEFT downto 0) is L; -- descending alias,
alias XR : UNSIGNED(L_LEFT downto 0) is R; -- aligns left ends
variable RESULT : UNSIGNED(L_LEFT downto 0); variable CBIT: BIT := C;
begin for I in 0 to L_LEFT loop -- descending alias allows loop
RESULT(I) := CBIT xor XL(I) xor XR(I); -- CBIT = carry, initially = C
CBIT := (CBIT and XL(I)) or (CBIT and XR(I)) or (XL(I) and XR(I));
end loop; return RESULT; end ADD_UNSIGNED;

function RESIZE (ARG : UNSIGNED; NEW_SIZE : NATURAL) return UNSIGNED is
constant ARG_LEFT : INTEGER := ARG'LENGTH-1;
alias XARG : UNSIGNED(ARG_LEFT downto 0) is ARG; -- descending range
variable RESULT : UNSIGNED(NEW_SIZE-1 downto 0) := (others => '0');
begin -- resize the input ARG to length NEW_SIZE
  if (NEW_SIZE < 1) then return NAU; end if; -- return null array
  if XARG'LENGTH = 0 then return RESULT; end if; -- null to empty
  if (RESULT'LENGTH < ARG'LENGTH) then -- check lengths
    RESULT(RESULT'LEFT downto 0) := XARG(RESULT'LEFT downto 0);
  else -- need to pad the result with some '0's
    RESULT(RESULT'LEFT downto XARG'LEFT + 1) := (others => '0');
    RESULT(XARG'LEFT downto 0) := XARG;
  end if; return RESULT;
end RESIZE;

function "+" (L, R : UNSIGNED) return UNSIGNED is -- overloaded '+'
constant SIZE : NATURAL := MAX(L'LENGTH, R'LENGTH);
begin -- if length of L or R < 1 return a null array
if ((L'LENGTH < 1) or (R'LENGTH < 1)) then return NAU; end if;
return ADD_UNSIGNED(RESIZE(L, SIZE), RESIZE(R, SIZE), '0'); end "+";

end Part_NUMERIC_BIT;
```

The following conversion functions are also part of the NUMERIC_BIT package:

```
function TO_INTEGER (ARG : UNSIGNED) return NATURAL;
function TO_INTEGER (ARG : SIGNED) return INTEGER;
function TO_UNSIGNED (ARG, SIZE : NATURAL) return UNSIGNED;
function TO_SIGNED (ARG : INTEGER; SIZE : NATURAL) return SIGNED;
function RESIZE (ARG : SIGNED; NEW_SIZE : NATURAL) return SIGNED;
function RESIZE (ARG : UNSIGNED; NEW_SIZE : NATURAL) return UNSIGNED;
-- set XMAP to convert unknown values, default is 'X'->'0'
function TO_01(S : UNSIGNED; XMAP : STD_LOGIC := '0') return UNSIGNED;
function TO_01(S : SIGNED; XMAP : STD_LOGIC := '0') return SIGNED;
```

The NUMERIC_STD package is almost identical to the NUMERIC_BIT package except that the UNSIGNED and SIGNED types are declared in terms of the STD_LOGIC type from the Std_Logic_1164 package as follows:

```
library IEEE; use IEEE.STD_LOGIC_1164.all;
package Part_NUMERIC_STD is
type UNSIGNED is array (NATURAL range <>) of STD_LOGIC;
type SIGNED is array (NATURAL range <>) of STD_LOGIC;
end Part_NUMERIC_STD;
```

The NUMERIC_STD package body is similar to NUMERIC_BIT with the addition of a comparison function called STD_MATCH, illustrated by the following:

```
-- function STD_MATCH (L, R: T) return BOOLEAN;
-- T = STD_ULOGIC UNSIGNED SIGNED STD_LOGIC_VECTOR STD_ULOGIC_VECTOR
```

The STD_MATCH function uses the following table to compare logic values:

```
type BOOLEAN_TABLE is array(STD_ULOGIC, STD_ULOGIC) of BOOLEAN;
constant MATCH_TABLE : BOOLEAN_TABLE := (
-----------------------------------------------------------------
--  U     X     0     1     Z     W     L     H     -
-----------------------------------------------------------------
(FALSE,FALSE,FALSE,FALSE,FALSE,FALSE,FALSE,FALSE, TRUE), --  | U |
(FALSE,FALSE,FALSE,FALSE,FALSE,FALSE,FALSE,FALSE, TRUE), --  | X |
(FALSE,FALSE, TRUE,FALSE,FALSE,FALSE, TRUE,FALSE, TRUE), --  | 0 |
(FALSE,FALSE,FALSE, TRUE,FALSE,FALSE,FALSE, TRUE, TRUE), --  | 1 |
(FALSE,FALSE,FALSE,FALSE,FALSE,FALSE,FALSE,FALSE, TRUE), --  | Z |
(FALSE,FALSE,FALSE,FALSE,FALSE,FALSE,FALSE,FALSE, TRUE), --  | W |
(FALSE,FALSE, TRUE,FALSE,FALSE,FALSE, TRUE,FALSE, TRUE), --  | L |
(FALSE,FALSE,FALSE, TRUE,FALSE,FALSE,FALSE, TRUE, TRUE), --  | H |
( TRUE, TRUE, TRUE, TRUE, TRUE, TRUE, TRUE, TRUE, TRUE));-- | - |
```

Thus, for example (notice we need type conversions):

```
IM_TRUE = STD_MATCH(STD_LOGIC_VECTOR    ("10HLXWZ-"),
                    STD_LOGIC_VECTOR    ("HL10----"))   -- is TRUE
```

The following code is similar to the first simple example of Section 10.1, but illustrates the use of the Std_Logic_1164 and NUMERIC_STD packages:

```
entity Counter_1 is end;                                         --1
   library STD; use STD.TEXTIO.all;                              --2
   library IEEE; use IEEE.STD_LOGIC_1164.all;                    --3
use work.NUMERIC_STD.all;                                        --4
architecture Behave_2 of Counter_1 is                            --5
   signal Clock : STD_LOGIC := '0';                              --6
   signal Count : UNSIGNED (2 downto 0) := "000";                --7
   begin                                                         --8
   process begin                                                 --9
     wait for 10 ns; Clock <= not Clock;                         --10
```

```
    if (now > 340 ns) then wait;                      --11
    end if;                                           --12
  end process;                                        --13
  process begin                                       --14
    wait until (Clock = '0');                         --15
    if (Count = 7)                                    --16
      then Count <= "000";                            --17
      else Count <= Count + 1;                        --18
    end if;                                           --19
  end process;                                        --20
  process (Count) variable L: LINE; begin write(L, now);  --21
  write(L, STRING'(" Count=")); write(L, TO_INTEGER(Count));  --22
  writeline(output, L);                               --23
  end process;                                        --24
end;                                                  --25
```

The preceding code looks similar to the code in Section 10.1 (and the output is identical), but there is more going on here:

- Line 3 is a library clause and a use clause for the std_logic_1164 package, so you can use the STD_LOGIC type and the NUMERIC_BIT package.
- Line 4 is a use clause for NUMERIC_BIT package that was previously analyzed into the library work. If the package is instead analyzed into the library IEEE, you would use the name IEEE.NUMERIC_BIT.all here. The NUMERIC_BIT package allows you to use the type UNSIGNED.
- Line 6 declares Clock to be type STD_LOGIC and initializes it to '0', instead of the default initial value STD_LOGIC'LEFT (which is 'U').
- Line 7 declares Count to be a 3-bit array of type UNSIGNED from NUMERIC_BIT and initializes it using a bit-string literal.
- Line 10 uses the overloaded 'not' operator from std_logic_1164.
- Line 15 uses the overloaded '=' operator from std_logic_1164.
- Line 16 uses the overloaded '=' operator from NUMERIC_BIT.
- Line 17 requires a bit-string literal, you cannot use Count <= 0 here.
- Line 18 uses the overloaded '+' operator from NUMERIC_BIT.
- Line 22 converts Count, type UNSIGNED, to type INTEGER.

10.13 Concurrent Statements

A **concurrent statement** [VHDL LRM9] is one of the following statements:

```
concurrent_statement ::=                              [10.36]
  block_statement
  | process_statement
```

```
| [ label : ] [ postponed ] procedure_call ;
| [ label : ] [ postponed ] assertion ;
| [ label : ] [ postponed ] conditional_signal_assignment
| [ label : ] [ postponed ] selected_signal_assignment
| component_instantiation_statement
| generate_statement
```

The following sections describe each of these statements in turn.

10.13.1 Block Statement

A **block statement** has the following format:

```
block_statement ::=                                        [10.37]
    block_label: block [(guard_expression)] [is]
      [generic (generic_interface_list);
      [generic map (generic_association_list);]]
      [port (port_interface_list);
      [port map (port_association_list);]]
        {block_declarative_item}
        begin
        {concurrent_statement}
    end block [block_label] ;
```

Blocks may have their own ports and generics and may be used to split an architecture into several hierarchical parts (blocks can also be nested). As a very general rule, for the same reason that it is better to split a computer program into separate small modules, it is usually better to split a large architecture into smaller separate entity/architecture pairs rather than several nested blocks.

A block does have a unique feature: It is possible to specify a **guard expression** for a block. This creates a special signal, GUARD, that you can use within the block to control execution [VHDL LRM9.5]. It also allows you to model three-state buses by declaring **guarded signals** (signal kinds **register** and **bus**).

When you make an assignment statement to a signal, you define a **driver** for that signal. If you make assignments to guarded signals in a block, the driver for that signal is turned off, or **disconnected**, when the GUARD signal is FALSE. The use of guarded signals and guarded blocks can become quite complicated, and not all synthesis tools support these VHDL features.

The following example shows two drivers, A and B, on a three-state bus TSTATE, enabled by signals OEA and OEB. The drivers are enabled by declaring a guard expression after the block declaration and using the keyword guarded in the assignment statements. A **disconnect** statement models the driver delay from driving the bus to the high-impedance state (time to "float").

```
library ieee; use ieee.std_logic_1164.all;
entity bus_drivers is end;

architecture Structure_1 of bus_drivers is
signal TSTATE: STD_LOGIC bus; signal A, B, OEA, OEB : STD_LOGIC:= '0';
begin
process begin OEA <= '1' after 100 ns, '0' after 200 ns;
OEB <= '1' after 300 ns; wait; end process;
B1 : block (OEA = '1')
disconnect all : STD_LOGIC after 5 ns; -- only needed for float time
begin TSTATE <= guarded not A after 3 ns; end block;
B2 : block (OEB = '1')
disconnect all : STD_LOGIC after 5 ns; -- float time = 5 ns
begin TSTATE <= guarded not B after 3 ns; end block;
end;
```

| | | 1 | 2 | 3 | 4 | 5 | 6 | 7 |
Time(fs) + Cycle		tstate	a	b	oea	oeb	b1.GUARD	b2.GUARD
0+ 0:		'U'	'0'	'0'	'0'	'0'	FALSE	FALSE
0+ 1:	*	'Z'	'0'	'0'	'0'	'0'	FALSE	FALSE
100000000+ 0:		'Z'	'0'	'0'	*'1'	'0' *	TRUE	FALSE
103000000+ 0:	*	'1'	'0'	'0'	'1'	'0'	TRUE	FALSE
200000000+ 0:		'1'	'0'	'0'	*'0'	'0' *	FALSE	FALSE
200000000+ 1:	*	'Z'	'0'	'0'	'0'	'0'	FALSE	FALSE
300000000+ 0:		'Z'	'0'	'0'	'0'	*'1'	FALSE *	TRUE
303000000+ 0:	*	'1'	'0'	'0'	'0'	'1'	FALSE	TRUE

Notice the creation of implicit guard signals b1.GUARD and b2.GUARD for each guarded block. There is another, equivalent, method that uses the high-impedance value explicitly as in the following example:

```
architecture Structure_2 of bus_drivers is
signal TSTATE : STD_LOGIC; signal A, B, OEA, OEB : STD_LOGIC := '0';
begin
process begin
OEA <= '1' after 100 ns, '0' after 200 ns; OEB <= '1' after 300 ns;
wait; end process;
process(OEA, OEB, A, B) begin
  if    (OEA = '1') then TSTATE <= not A after 3 ns;
  elsif (OEB = '1') then TSTATE <= not B after 3 ns;
  else TSTATE <= 'Z' after 5 ns;
```

```
      end if;
end process;
end;
```

This last method is more widely used than the first, and what is more important, more widely accepted by synthesis tools. Most synthesis tools are capable of recognizing the value 'Z' on the RHS of an assignment statement as a cue to synthesize a three-state driver. It is up to you to make sure that multiple drivers are never enabled simultaneously to cause contention.

10.13.2 Process Statement

A **process statement** has the following format:

[10.38]

```
process_statement ::=
[process_label:]
[postponed] process  [(signal_name {, signal_name})]
[is] {subprogram_declaration     | subprogram_body
    | type_declaration           | subtype_declaration
    | constant_declaration        | variable_declaration
    | file_declaration            | alias_declaration
    | attribute_declaration       | attribute_specification
    | use_clause
    | group_declaration           | group_template_declaration}
begin
  {sequential_statement}
end [postponed] process [process_label];
```

The following process models a 2:1 MUX (combinational logic):

```
entity Mux_1 is port (i0, i1, sel : in BIT := '0'; y : out BIT); end;
architecture Behave of Mux_1 is
  begin process (i0, i1, sel) begin -- i0, i1, sel = sensitivity set
  case sel is when '0' => y <= i0; when '1' => y <= i1; end case;
end process; end;
```

This process executes whenever an event occurs on any of the signals in the process **sensitivity set** (i0, i1, sel). The execution of a process occurs during a simulation cycle—a delta cycle. Assignment statements to signals may trigger further delta cycles. Time advances when all transactions for the current time step are complete and all signals updated.

The following code models a two-input AND gate (combinational logic):

```
entity And_1 is port (a, b : in BIT := '0'; y : out BIT); end;
architecture Behave of And_1 is
begin process (a, b) begin y <= a and b; end process; end;
```

The next example models a D flip-flop (sequential logic). The `process` statement is executed whenever there is an event on clk. The if statement updates the output q with the input d on the rising edge of the signal clk. If the if statement condition is false (as it is on the falling edge of clk), then the assignment statement q <= d will not be executed, and q will keep its previous value. The process thus requires the value of q to be stored between successive process executions, and this implies sequential logic.

```
entity FF_1 is port (clk, d: in BIT := '0'; q : out BIT); end;
architecture Behave of FF_1 is
begin process (clk) begin
   if clk'EVENT and clk = '1' then q <= d; end if;
end process; end;
```

The behavior of the next example is identical to the previous model. Notice that the wait statement is at the end of the equivalent process with the signals in the sensitivity set (in this case just one signal, clk) included in the sensitivity list (that follows the keyword on).

```
entity FF_2 is port (clk, d: in BIT := '0'; q : out BIT); end;
architecture Behave of FF_2 is
begin process begin -- equivalent process has wait at end...
    if clk'event and clk = '1' then q <= d; end if; wait on clk;
end process; end;
```

If we use a wait statement in a process statement, then we may not use a process sensitivity set (the reverse is true: If we do not have a sensitivity set for a process, we must include a wait statement or the process will execute endlessly):

```
entity FF_3 is port (clk, d: in BIT := '0'; q : out BIT); end;
architecture Behave of FF_3 is
begin process begin -- no sensitivity set with a wait statement
   wait until clk = '1'; q <= d;
end process; end;
```

If you include ports (interface signals) in the sensitivity set of a process statement, they must be ports that can be read (they must be of mode in, inout, or buffer, see Section 10.7).

10.13.3 Concurrent Procedure Call

A **concurrent procedure call** appears outside a process statement. The concurrent procedure call is a shorthand way of writing an equivalent process statement that contains a procedure call (Section 10.10.4). Here is an example:

```
package And_Pkg is procedure V_And(a,b:BIT; signal c:out BIT); end;

package body And_Pkg is procedure V_And(a,b:BIT; signal c:out BIT) is
   begin c <= a and b; end; end And_Pkg;

use work.And_Pkg.all; entity Proc_Call_2 is end;
architecture Behave of Proc_Call_2 is signal A, B, Y : BIT := '0';
   begin V_And (A, B, Y); -- concurrent procedure call
```

```
process begin wait; end process; -- extra process to stop.
end;
```

10.13.4 Concurrent Signal Assignment

There are two forms of **concurrent signal assignment statement**. A **selected signal assignment statement** is equivalent to a case statement inside a process statement:

```
selected_signal_assignment ::=                                    [10.39]
  with expression select
    name|aggregate <= [guarded]
      [transport|[reject time_expression] inertial]
        waveform when choice {| choice}
          {, waveform when choice {| choice} } ;
```

The following design unit, Selected_1, uses a selected signal assignment. The equivalent unit, Selected_2, uses a case statement inside a process statement.

```
entity Selected_1 is end; architecture Behave of Selected_1 is
signal y,i1,i2 : INTEGER; signal sel : INTEGER range 0 to 1;
begin with sel select y <= i1 when 0, i2 when 1; end;

entity Selected_2 is end; architecture Behave of Selected_2 is
signal i1,i2,y : INTEGER; signal sel : INTEGER range 0 to 1;
begin process begin
  case sel is when 0 => y <= i1; when 1 => y <= i2; end case;
  wait on i1, i2;
end process; end;
```

The other form of concurrent signal assignment is a **conditional signal assignment statement** that, in its most general form, is equivalent to an if statement inside a process statement:

```
conditional_signal_assignment ::=                                 [10.40]
    name|aggregate <= [guarded]
  [transport|[reject time_expression] inertial]
      {waveform when boolean_expression else}
        waveform [when boolean_expression];
```

Notice that in VHDL-93 the else clause is optional. Here is an example of a conditional signal assignment, followed by a model using the equivalent process with an if statement:

```
entity Conditional_1 is end; architecture Behave of Conditional_1 is
signal y,i,j : INTEGER; signal clk : BIT;
begin y <= i when clk = '1' else j; -- conditional signal assignment
end;

entity Conditional_2 is end; architecture Behave of Conditional_2 is
signal y,i : INTEGER; signal clk : BIT;
begin process begin
```

```
     if clk = '1' then y <= i; else y <= y ; end if; wait on clk;
end process; end;
```

A concurrent signal assignment statement can look just like a sequential signal assignment statement, as in the following example:

```
entity Assign_1 is end; architecture Behave of Assign_1 is
signal Target, Source : INTEGER;
  begin Target <= Source after 1 ns; -- looks like signal assignment
end;
```

However, outside a **process** statement, this statement is a concurrent signal assignment and has its own equivalent **process** statement. Here is the equivalent process for the example:

```
entity Assign_2 is end; architecture Behave of Assign_2 is
signal Target, Source : INTEGER;
begin process begin
  Target <= Source after 1 ns; wait on Source;
end process; end;
```

Every process is executed once during initialization. In the previous example, an initial value will be scheduled to be assigned to `Target` even though there is no event on `Source`. If, for some reason, you do not want this to happen, you need to rewrite the concurrent assignment statement as a `process` statement with a `wait` statement before the assignment statement:

```
entity Assign_3 is end; architecture Behave of Assign_3 is
signal Target, Source : INTEGER; begin process begin
  wait on Source; Target <= Source after 1 ns;
end process; end;
```

10.13.5 Concurrent Assertion Statement

A **concurrent assertion statement** is equivalent to a passive `process` statement (without a sensitivity list) that contains an `assertion` statement followed by a `wait` statement.

```
concurrent_assertion_statement                                    [10.41]
::= [ label : ] [ postponed ] assertion ;
```

If the assertion condition contains a signal, then the equivalent `process` statement will include a final `wait` statement with a sensitivity clause. A concurrent assertion statement with a condition that is static expression is equivalent to a `process` statement that ends in a `wait` statement that has no sensitivity clause. The equivalent process will execute once, at the beginning of simulation, and then wait indefinitely.

10.13.6 Component Instantiation

A **component instantiation statement** in VHDL is similar to placement of a component in a schematic—an instantiated component is somewhere between a copy of the component and a reference to the component. Here is an example:

```
component_instantiation_statement ::=                          [10.42]
instantiation_label:
 [component] component_name
|entity entity_name [(architecture_identifier)]
|configuration configuration_name
   [generic map (generic_association_list)]
   [port map (port_association_list)] ;
```

We examined component instantiation using a *component*_name in Section 10.5. If we instantiate a component in this way we must declare the component (see BNF [10.9]). To bind a component to an entity/architecture pair we can use a configuration, as illustrated in Figure 10.1, or we can use the default binding as described in Section 10.7. In VHDL-93 we have another alternative—we can directly instantiate an entity or configuration. For example:

```
entity And_2 is port (i1, i2 : in BIT; y : out BIT); end;
architecture Behave of And_2 is begin y <= i1 and i2; end;
entity Xor_2 is port (i1, i2 : in BIT; y : out BIT); end;
architecture Behave of Xor_2 is begin y <= i1 xor i2; end;

entity Half_Adder_2 is port (a,b : BIT := '0'; sum, cry : out BIT); end;
architecture Netlist_2 of Half_Adder_2 is
use work.all; -- need this to see the entities Xor_2 and And_2
begin
   X1 : entity Xor_2(Behave) port map (a, b, sum); -- VHDL-93 only
   A1 : entity And_2(Behave) port map (a, b, cry); -- VHDL-93 only
end;
```

10.13.7 Generate Statement

A **generate statement** simplifies repetitive code (the label is required):

```
generate_statement ::=                                         [10.43]
generate_label:   for generate_parameter_specification
                  |if boolean_expression
generate [{block_declarative_item} begin]
   {concurrent_statement}
end generate [generate_label] ;
```

Here is an example:

```
entity Full_Adder is port (X, Y, Cin : BIT; Cout, Sum: out BIT); end;
architecture Behave of Full_Adder is begin Sum <= X xor Y xor Cin;
Cout <= (X and Y) or (X and Cin) or (Y and Cin); end;
```

```
entity Adder_1 is
    port (A, B : in BIT_VECTOR (7 downto 0) := (others => '0');
    Cin : in BIT := '0'; Sum : out BIT_VECTOR (7 downto 0);
    Cout : out BIT);
end;

architecture Structure of Adder_1 is use work.all;

component Full_Adder port (X, Y, Cin: BIT; Cout, Sum: out BIT);
end component;
signal C : BIT_VECTOR(7 downto 0);
begin AllBits : for i in 7 downto 0 generate
    LowBit : if i = 0 generate
        FA : Full_Adder port map (A(0), B(0), Cin, C(0), Sum(0));
    end generate;
    OtherBits : if i /= 0 generate
        FA : Full_Adder port map (A(i), B(i), C(i-1), C(i), Sum(i));
    end generate;
end generate;
Cout <= C(7);
end;
```

The instance names within a generate loop include the generate parameter. For example for i=6, FA'INSTANCE_NAME is

```
:adder_1(structure):allbits(6):otherbits:fa:
```

10.14 Execution

Two successive statements may execute in either a concurrent or sequential fashion depending on where the statements appear.

```
statement 1; statement 2;
```

In **sequential execution,** statement 1 in this sequence is always evaluated before statement 2. In **concurrent execution,** statement 1 and statement 2 are evaluated at the same time (as far as we are concerned—obviously on most computers exactly parallel execution is not possible). Concurrent execution is the most important difference between VHDL and a computer programming language. Suppose we have two signal assignment statements inside a process statement. In this case statement 1 and statement 2 are sequential assignment statements:

```
entity Sequential_1 is end; architecture Behave of Sequential_1 is
signal s1, s2 : INTEGER := 0;
begin
    process begin
        s1 <= 1;              -- sequential signal assignment 1
        s2 <= s1 + 1;         -- sequential signal assignment 2
        wait on s1, s2 ;
```

```
    end process;
end;
```

```
    Time(fs) + Cycle                 s1              s2
------------------------       ------------    ------------
                0+ 0:                0               0
                0+ 1: *              1 *             1
                0+ 2: *              1 *             2
                0+ 3: *              1 *             2
```

If the two statements are outside a process statement they are concurrent assignment statements, as in the following example:

```
entity Concurrent_1 is end; architecture Behave of Concurrent_1 is
signal s1, s2 : INTEGER := 0; begin
  L1 : s1 <= 1;          -- concurrent signal assignment 1
  L2 : s2 <= s1 + 1;  -- concurrent signal assignment 2
end;
```

```
    Time(fs) + Cycle                 s1              s2
------------------------       ------------    ------------
                0+ 0:                0               0
                0+ 1: *              1 *             1
                0+ 2:                1 *             2
```

The two concurrent signal assignment statements in the previous example are equivalent to the two processes, labeled as P1 and P2, in the following model.

```
entity Concurrent_2 is end; architecture Behave of Concurrent_2 is
signal s1, s2 : INTEGER := 0; begin
  P1 : process begin s1 <= 1;      wait on s2 ; end process;
  P2 : process begin s2 <= s1 + 1; wait on s1 ; end process;
end;
```

```
    Time(fs) + Cycle                 s1              s2
------------------------       ------------    ------------
                0+ 0:                0               0
                0+ 1: *              1 *             1
                0+ 2: *              1 *             2
                0+ 3: *              1               2
```

Notice that the results are the same (though the trace files are slightly different) for the architectures Sequential_1, Concurrent_1, and Concurrent_2. Updates to signals occur at the end of the simulation cycle, so the values used will always be the old values. So far things seem fairly simple: We have sequential execution or concurrent execution. However, variables are updated immediately, so the variable values that are used are always the new values. The examples in Table 10.17 illustrate this very important difference.

The various concurrent and sequential statements in VHDL are summarized in Table 10.18.

TABLE 10.17   Variables and signals in VHDL.

Variables	Signals
`entity Execute_1 is end;`	`entity Execute_2 is end;`
`architecture Behave of Execute_1 is`	`architecture Behave of Execute_2 is`
`begin`	`signal s1 : INTEGER := 1;`
`  process`	`signal s2 : INTEGER := 2;`
`  variable v1 : INTEGER := 1;`	`begin`
`  variable v2 : INTEGER := 2;`	`  process`
`  begin`	`  begin`
`    v1 := v2; -- before: v1 = 1, v2 = 2`	`    s1 <= s2; -- before: s1 = 1, s2 = 2`
`    v2 := v1; -- after:  v1 = 2, v2 = 2`	`    s2 <= s1; -- after:  s1 = 2, s2 = 1`
`    wait;`	`    wait;`
`  end process;`	`  end process;`
`end;`	`end;`

TABLE 10.18   Concurrent and sequential statements in VHDL.

Concurrent [VHDL LRM9]	Sequential [VHDL LRM8]	
`block`	`wait`	`case`
`process`	`assertion`	`loop`
`concurrent_procedure_call`	`signal_assignment`	`next`
`concurrent_assertion`	`variable_assignment`	`exit`
`concurrent_signal_assignment`	`procedure_call`	`return`
`component_instantiation`	`if`	`null`
`generate`		

10.15 Configurations and Specifications

The difference between, the interaction, and the use of component/configuration declarations and specifications is probably the most confusing aspect of VHDL. Fortunately this aspect of VHDL is not normally important for ASIC design. The syntax of component/configuration declarations and specifications is shown in Table 10.19.

- A *configuration declaration* defines a configuration—it is a library unit and is one of the basic units of VHDL code.
- A *block configuration* defines the configuration of a block statement or a design entity. A block configuration appears inside a configuration declaration, a component configuration, or nested in another block configuration.

TABLE 10.19   VHDL binding.

configuration declaration[1]	**configuration** identifier **of** *entity*_name **is** 　　　　{use_clause|attribute_specification|group_declaration} 　　　　block_configuration **end** [**configuration**] [*configuration*_identifier];
block configuration	**for** *architecture*_name 　　　　|*block_statement*_label 　　　　|*generate_statement*_label [(index_specification)] {**use** selected_name {, selected_name};} {block_configuration|component_configuration} **end for** ;
configuration specification	**for** 　　　　*instantiation*_label{,*instantiation*_label}:*component*_name 　　　　|**others**:*component*_name 　　　　|**all**:*component*_name 　[**use** 　　　　**entity** *entity*_name [(*architecture*_identifier)] 　　　　|**configuration** *configuration*_name 　　　　|**open**] [**generic map** (*generic*_association_list)] [**port map** (*port*_association_list)];
component declaration[1]	**component** identifier [**is**] 　　　　[**generic** (*local_generic*_interface_list);] 　　　　[**port** (*local_port*_interface_list);] **end component** [*component*_identifier];
component configuration[1]	**for** *instantiation*_label {, *instantiation*_label}:*component*_name |**others**:*component*_name |**all**:*component*_name [[**use** 　　　　**entity** *entity*_name [(*architecture*_identifier)] 　　　　|**configuration** *configuration*_name 　　　　|**open**] 　　　　　　[**generic map** (*generic*_association_list)] 　　　　　　[**port map** (*port*_association_list)];] [block_configuration] **end for**;

[1]Underline means "new to VHDL-93".

- A *configuration specification* may appear in the declarative region of a generate statement, block statement, or architecture body.
- A *component declaration* may appear in the declarative region of a generate statement, block statement, architecture body, or package.
- A *component configuration* defines the configuration of a component and appears in a block configuration.

Table 10.20 shows a simple example (identical in structure to the example of Section 10.5) that illustrates the use of each of the preceding constructs.

TABLE 10.20   VHDL binding examples.

	`entity AD2 is port (A1, A2: in BIT; Y: out BIT); end;`
	`architecture B of AD2 is begin Y <= A1 and A2; end;`
	`entity XR2 is port (X1, X2: in BIT; Y: out BIT); end;`
	`architecture B of XR2 is begin Y <= X1 xor X2; end;`

component
declaration
  configuration
  specification
	`entity Half_Adder is port (X, Y: BIT; Sum, Cout: out BIT); end;`
	`architecture Netlist of Half_Adder is use work.all;`
	`component MX port (A, B: BIT; Z :out BIT);end component;`
	`component MA port (A, B: BIT; Z :out BIT);end component;`
	`for G1:MX use entity XR2(B) port map(X1 => A,X2 => B,Y => Z);`
	`begin`
	   `G1:MX port map(X, Y, Sum); G2:MA port map(X, Y, Cout);`
	`end;`

configuration
declaration
  block
  configuration
  component
  configuration
	`configuration C1 of Half_Adder is`
	`use work.all;`
	  `for Netlist`
	    `for G2:MA`
	      `use entity AD2(B) port map(A1 => A,A2 => B,Y => Z);`
	    `end for;`
	  `end for;`
	`end;`

10.16 An Engine Controller

This section describes part of a controller for an automobile engine. Table 10.21 shows a temperature converter that converts digitized temperature readings from a sensor from degrees Centigrade to degrees Fahrenheit.

To save area the temperature conversion is approximate. Instead of multiplying by 9/5 and adding 32 (so 0°C becomes 32°F and 100°C becomes 212°F) we multiply by 1.75 and add 32 (so 100°C becomes 207°F). Since 1.75 = 1 + 0.5 + 0.25, we can multiply by 1.75 using shifts (for divide by 2, and divide by 4) together with a very simple constant addition (since 32=`"100000"`). Using shift to multiply and divide by powers of 2 is free in hardware (we just change connections to a bus). For

---

TABLE 10.21   A temperature converter.

```
library IEEE;
use IEEE.STD_LOGIC_1164.all; -- type STD_LOGIC, rising_edge
use IEEE.NUMERIC_STD.all ; -- type UNSIGNED, "+", "/"
entity tconv is generic TPD : TIME:= 1 ns;
   port (T_in : in UNSIGNED(11 downto 0);
   clk, rst : in STD_LOGIC; T_out : out UNSIGNED(11 downto 0));
end;
architecture rtl of tconv is
signal T : UNSIGNED(7 downto 0);
constant T2  : UNSIGNED(1 downto 0) := "10" ;
constant T4  : UNSIGNED(2 downto 0) := "100" ;
constant T32 : UNSIGNED(5 downto 0) := "100000" ;
begin
   process(T) begin T_out <= T + T/T2 + T/T4 + T32 after TPD;
   end process;
end rtl;
```

T_in = temperature in °C

T_out = temperature in °F

The conversion formula from Centigrade to Fahrenheit is:
$T(°F) = (9/5) \times T(°C) + 32$

This converter uses the approximation:
$9/5 \approx 1.75 = 1 + 0.5 + 0.25$

---

large temperatures the error approaches 0.05/1.8 or approximately 3 percent. We play these kinds of tricks often in hardware computation. Notice also that temperatures measured in °C and °F are defined as unsigned integers of the same width. We could have defined these as separate types to take advantage of VHDL's type checking.

Table 10.22 describes a digital filter to compute a "moving average" over four successive samples in time (i(0), i(1), i(2), and i(3), with i(0) being the first sample).

The filter uses the following formula:

```
T_out <= ( i(0) + i(1) + i(2) + i(3) )/T4
```

Division by T4="100" is free in hardware. If instead, we performed the divisions before the additions, this would reduce the number of bits to be added for two of the additions and saves us worrying about overflow. The drawback to this approach is round-off errors. We can use the register shown in Table 10.23 to register the inputs.

Table 10.24 shows a **first-in, first-out** stack (**FIFO**). This allows us to buffer the signals coming from the sensor until the microprocessor has a chance to read them. The depth of the FIFO will depend on the maximum amount of time that can pass without the microcontroller being able to read from the bus. We have to determine this with statistical simulations taking into account other traffic on the bus.

TABLE 10.22   A digital filter.

```
library IEEE;
use IEEE.STD_LOGIC_1164.all; -- STD_LOGIC type, rising_edge
use IEEE.NUMERIC_STD.all; -- UNSIGNED type, "+" and "/"
entity filter is
   generic TPD : TIME := 1 ns;
   port (T_in : in UNSIGNED(11 downto 0);
   rst, clk : in STD_LOGIC;
   T_out: out UNSIGNED(11 downto 0));
end;
architecture rtl of filter is
type arr is array (0 to 3) of UNSIGNED(11 downto 0);
signal i : arr ;
constant T4 : UNSIGNED(2 downto 0) := "100";
begin
   process(rst, clk) begin
      if (rst = '1') then
         for n in 0 to 3 loop i(n) <= (others =>'0') after TPD;
         end loop;
      else
         if(rising_edge(clk)) then
         i(0) <= T_in after TPD;i(1) <= i(0) after TPD;
         i(2) <= i(1) after TPD;i(3) <= i(2) after TPD;
         end if;
      end if;
   end process;
   process(i) begin
      T_out <= ( i(0) + i(1) + i(2) + i(3) )/T4 after TPD;
   end process;
end rtl;
```

The filter computes a moving average over four successive samples in time.

Notice
i(0) i(1) i(2) i(3)
are each 12 bits wide.

Then the sum
i(0) + i(1) + i(2) + i(3)
is 14 bits wide, and the average

(i(0) + i(1) + i(2) + i(3))/T4

is 12 bits wide.

All delays are generic TPD.

The FIFO has flags, empty and full, that signify its state. It uses a function to increment two circular pointers. One pointer keeps track of the address to write to next, the other pointer tracks the address to read from. The FIFO memory may be implemented in a number of ways in hardware. We shall assume for the moment that it will be synthesized as a bank of flip-flops.

Table 10.25 shows a controller for the two FIFOs. The controller handles the reading and writing to the FIFO. The microcontroller attached to the bus signals which of the FIFOs it wishes to read from. The controller then places the appropriate data on the bus. The microcontroller can also ask for the FIFO flags to be placed in the low-order bits of the bus on a read cycle. If none of these actions are requested by the microcontroller, the FIFO controller three-states its output drivers.

TABLE 10.23   The input register.

```
library IEEE;
use IEEE.STD_LOGIC_1164.all; -- type STD_LOGIC, rising_edge
use IEEE.NUMERIC_STD.all ; -- type UNSIGNED
entity register_in is
generic ( TPD : TIME := 1 ns);
port (T_in : in UNSIGNED(11 downto 0);
clk, rst : in STD_LOGIC; T_out : out UNSIGNED(11 downto 0)); end;
architecture rtl of register_in is
begin
   process(clk, rst) begin
      if (rst = '1') then T_out <= (others => '0') after TPD;
      else
      if (rising_edge(clk)) then T_out <= T_in after TPD; end if;
      end if;
   end process;
end rtl ;
```

12-bit-wide register for the temperature input signals.

If the input is asynchronous (from an A/D converter with a separate clock, for example), we would need to worry about metastability.

All delays are generic TPD.

Table 10.25 shows the top level of the controller. To complete our model we shall use a package for the component declarations:

```
package TC_Components is
component register_in generic (TPD : TIME := 1 ns);
port (T_in : in UNSIGNED(11 downto 0);
clk, rst : in STD_LOGIC; T_out : out UNSIGNED(11 downto 0));
end component;
component tconv generic (TPD : TIME := 1 ns);
port (T_in : in UNSIGNED (7 downto 0);
   clk, rst : in STD_LOGIC; T_out : out UNSIGNED(7 downto 0));
end component;
component filter generic (TPD : TIME := 1 ns);
port (T_in : in UNSIGNED (7 downto 0);
   rst, clk : in STD_LOGIC; T_out : out UNSIGNED(7 downto 0));
end component;
component fifo generic (width:INTEGER := 12; depth : INTEGER := 16);
   port (clk, rst, push, pop  :  STD_LOGIC;
      Di :  UNSIGNED (width-1 downto 0);
      Do : out UNSIGNED (width-1 downto 0);
      empty, full : out STD_LOGIC);
end component;
component fifo_control generic (TPD:TIME := 1 ns);
   port (D_1, D_2 : in UNSIGNED(7 downto 0);
      select : in UNSIGNED(1 downto 0); read, f1, f2, e1, e2 : in STD_LOGIC;
      r1, r2, w12 : out STD_LOGIC; D : out UNSIGNED(7 downto 0)) ;
```

TABLE 10.24   A first-in, first-out stack (FIFO).

```
library IEEE; use IEEE.NUMERIC_STD.ALL ; -- UNSIGNED type
use ieee.std_logic_1164.all; -- STD_LOGIC type, rising_edge
entity fifo is
   generic (width : INTEGER := 12; depth : INTEGER := 16);
   port (clk, rst, push, pop : STD_LOGIC;
   Di : in UNSIGNED (width-1 downto 0);
   Do : out UNSIGNED (width-1 downto 0);
   empty, full : out STD_LOGIC);
end fifo;
architecture rtl of fifo is
subtype ptype is INTEGER range 0 to (depth-1);
signal diff, Ai, Ao : ptype; signal  f, e : STD_LOGIC;
type a is array (ptype) of UNSIGNED(width-1 downto 0);
signal mem : a ;
function bump(signal ptr : INTEGER range 0 to (depth-1))
return INTEGER is begin
   if (ptr = (depth-1)) then return 0;
   else return (ptr + 1);
   end if;
end;
begin
   process(f,e) begin full <= f ; empty <= e; end process;
   process(diff) begin
   if (diff = depth -1) then f <= '1'; else f <= '0'; end if;
   if (diff = 0) then e <= '1'; else e <= '0'; end if;
   end process;
   process(clk, Ai, Ao, Di, mem, push, pop, e, f) begin
   if(rising_edge(clk)) then
   if(push='0')and(pop='1')and(e = '0') then Do <= mem(Ao); end if;
   if(push='1')and(pop='0')and(f = '0') then mem(Ai) <= Di; end if;
   end if ;
   end process;
   process(rst, clk)  begin
      if(rst = '1') then Ai <= 0; Ao <= 0; diff <= 0;
      else if(rising_edge(clk)) then
         if (push = '1') and (f = '0') and (pop = '0') then
            Ai <= bump(Ai); diff <= diff + 1;
         elsif (pop = '1') and (e = '0') and (push = '0') then
            Ao <= bump(Ao); diff <= diff - 1;
         end if;
      end if;
      end if;
   end process;
end;
```

FIFO (first-in, first-out) register

Reads (pop = 1) and writes (push = 1) are synchronous to the rising edge of the clock. Read and write should not occur at the same time. The width (number of bits in each word) and depth (number of words) are generics.

External signals:
clk, clock
rst, reset active-high
push, write to FIFO
pop, read from FIFO
Di, data in
Do, data out
empty, FIFO flag
full, FIFO flag

Internal signals:
diff, difference pointer
Ai, input address
Ao, output address
f, full flag
e, empty flag

No delays in this model.

TABLE 10.25   A FIFO controller.

<pre>library IEEE;use IEEE.STD_LOGIC_1164.all;use IEEE.NUMERIC_STD.all;
entity fifo_control is generic TPD : TIME := 1 ns;
port(D_1, D_2 : in UNSIGNED(11 downto 0);
sel : in UNSIGNED(1 downto 0) ;
read , f1, f2, e1, e2 : in STD_LOGIC;
r1, r2, w12 : out STD_LOGIC; D : out UNSIGNED(11 downto 0)) ;
end;
architecture rtl of fifo_control is
begin process
(read, sel, D_1, D_2, f1, f2, e1, e2)
begin
r1 <= '0' after TPD; r2 <= '0' after TPD;
if (read = '1') then
w12 <= '0' after TPD;
case sel is
when "01" =>   D <= D_1 after TPD; r1 <= '1' after TPD;
when "10" =>   D <= D_2 after TPD; r2 <= '1' after TPD;
when "00" =>   D(3) <= f1 after TPD; D(2) <= f2 after TPD;
D(1) <= e1 after TPD; D(0) <= e2 after TPD;
when others => D <= "ZZZZZZZZZZZZ" after TPD;
end case;
elsif (read = '0') then
D <= "ZZZZZZZZZZZZ" after TPD; w12 <= '1' after TPD;
else D <= "ZZZZZZZZZZZZ" after TPD;
end if;
end process;
end rtl;</pre>	This handles the reading and writing to the FIFOs under control of the processor (mpu). The mpu can ask for data from either FIFO or for status flags to be placed on the bus. Inputs: D_1 Data in from FIFO1 D_2 Data in from FIFO2 sel FIFO select from mpu read FIFO read from mpu f1,f2,e1,e2 flags from FIFOs Outputs: r1, r2 read enables for FIFOs w12 write enable for FIFOs D data out to mpu bus

```
      end component;
      end;
```

The following testbench completes a set of reads and writes to the FIFOs:

```
library IEEE;
use IEEE.std_logic_1164.all; -- type STD_LOGIC
use IEEE.numeric_std.all; -- type UNSIGNED
entity test_TC is end;
architecture testbench of test_TC is
component T_Control port (T_1, T_2 : in UNSIGNED(11 downto 0);
   clk : in STD_LOGIC; sensor: in UNSIGNED( 1 downto 0) ;
   read : in STD_LOGIC; rst : in STD_LOGIC;
   D : out UNSIGNED(7 downto 0)); end component;
signal T_1, T_2 : UNSIGNED(11 downto 0);
```

TABLE 10.26   Top level of temperature controller.

```
library IEEE; use IEEE.STD_LOGIC_1164.all; use IEEE.NUMERIC_STD.all;
entity T_Control is port (T_in1, T_in2 : in UNSIGNED (11 downto 0);
   sensor: in UNSIGNED(1 downto 0);
   clk, RD, rst : in STD_LOGIC; D : out UNSIGNED(11 downto 0));
end;
architecture structure of T_Control is use work.TC_Components.all;
signal F, E : UNSIGNED (2 downto 1);
signal T_out1, T_out2, R_out1, R_out2, F1, F2, FIFO1, FIFO2 : UNSIGNED(11 downto 0);
signal RD1, RD2, WR: STD_LOGIC ;
begin
RG1 : register_in generic map (1ns) port map (T_in1,clk,rst,R_out1);
RG2 : register_in generic map (1ns) port map (T_in2,clk,rst,R_out2);
TC1 : tconv generic map (1ns) port map (R_out1, T_out1);
TC2 : tconv generic map (1ns) port map (R_out2, T_out2);
TF1 : filter generic map (1ns) port map (T_out1, rst, clk, F1);
TF2 : filter generic map (1ns) port map (T_out2, rst, clk, F2);
FI1 : fifo generic map (12,16) port map (clk, rst, WR, RD1, F1, FIFO1, E(1), F(1));
FI2 : fifo generic map (12,16) port map (clk, rst, WR, RD2, F2, FIFO2, E(2), F(2));
FC1 : fifo_control port map
(FIFO1, FIFO2, sensor, RD, F(1), F(2), E(1), E(2), RD1, RD2, WR, D);
end structure;
```

```
signal clk, read, rst : STD_LOGIC;
signal sensor : UNSIGNED(1 downto 0);
signal D : UNSIGNED(7 downto 0);
begin TT1 : T_Control port map (T_1, T_2, clk, sensor, read, rst, D);
process begin
rst <= '0'; clk <= '0';
wait for 5 ns; rst <= '1'; wait for 5 ns; rst <= '0';
T_in1 <= "000000000011"; T_in2 <= "000000000111"; read <= '0';
   for i in 0 to 15 loop -- fill the FIFOs
   clk <= '0'; wait for 5ns; clk <= '1'; wait for 5 ns;
   end loop;
   assert (false) report "FIFOs full" severity NOTE;
   clk <= '0'; wait for 5ns; clk <= '1'; wait for 5 ns;
read <= '1'; sensor <= "01";
   for i in 0 to 15 loop -- empty the FIFOs
   clk <= '0'; wait for 5ns; clk <= '1'; wait for 5 ns;
   end loop;
   assert (false) report "FIFOs empty" severity NOTE;
   clk <= '0'; wait for 5ns; clk <= '1'; wait;
end process;
end;
```

10.17 Summary

Table 10.27 shows the essential elements of the VHDL language. Table 10.28 shows the most important BNF definitions and their locations in this chapter. The key points covered in this chapter are as follows:

- The use of an `entity` and an `architecture`
- The use of a `configuration` to bind entities and their architectures
- The compile, elaboration, initialization, and simulation steps
- Types, subtypes, and their use in expressions
- The logic systems based on `BIT` and `Std_Logic_1164` types
- The use of the IEEE synthesis packages for `BIT` arithmetic
- Ports and port modes
- Initial values and the difference between simulation and hardware
- The difference between a `signal` and a `variable`
- The different assignment statements and the timing of updates
- The `process` and `wait` statements

VHDL is a "wordy" language. The examples in this chapter are complete rather than code fragments. To write VHDL "nicely," with indentation and nesting of constructs, requires a large amount of space. Some of the VHDL code examples in this chapter are deliberately dense (with reduced indentation and nesting), but the bold keywords help you to see the code structure. Most of the time, of course, we do not have the luxury of bold fonts (or color) to highlight code. In this case, you should add additional space, indentation, nesting, and comments.

TABLE 10.27 VHDL summary.

VHDL feature	Example	Book	93LRM
Comments	`-- this is a comment`	10.3	13.8

Literals (fixed-value items)	`12   1.0E6   '1'   "110"   'Z'`
	`2#1111_1111#   "Hello world"`
	`STRING'("110")`
		10.4	13.4

Identifiers (case-insensitive, start with letter)	`a_good_name   Same   same` `2_Bad   bad_   _bad   very__bad`	10.4	13.3
Several basic units of code	`entity   architecture   configuration`	10.5	1.1-1.3
Connections made through ports	`port (signal in i : BIT; out o : BIT);`	10.7	4.3
Default expression	`port (i : BIT := '1');` `-- i='1' if left open`	10.7	4.3
No built-in logic value system... BIT and BIT_VECTOR (STD)	`type BIT is ('0', '1'); -- predefined` `signal myArray: BIT_VECTOR (7 downto 0);`	10.8	14.2
Arrays	`myArray(1 downto 0) <= ('0', '1');`	10.8	3.2.1
Two basic types of logic signals	a `signal` corresponds to a real wire a `variable` is a memory location in RAM	10.9	4.3.1.2 4.3.1.3
Types and explicit initial/default value	`signal ONE : BIT := '1' ;`	10.9	4.3.2
Implicit initial/default value	`BIT'LEFT = '0'`	10.9	4.3.2
Predefined attributes	`clk'EVENT, clk'STABLE`	10.9.4	14.1

Sequential statements inside processes model things that happen one after another and repeat	`process begin`
	`wait until alarm = ring;`
	`eat; work; sleep;`
	`end process;`
		10.10	8

Timing with wait statement	`wait for 1 ns; -- not wait 1 ns` `wait on light until light = green;`	10.10.1	8.1
Update to signals occurs at the end of a simulation cycle	`signal <= 1; -- delta time delay` `signal <= variable1 after 2 ns;`	10.10.3	8.3
Update to variables is immediate	`variable := 1; -- immediate update`	10.10.3	8.4

Processes and concurrent statements model things that happen at the same time	`process begin rain ; end process;`
	`process begin sing ; end process;`
	`process begin dance; end process;`
		10.13	9.2

IEEE Std_Logic_1164
(defines logic operators on 1164 types)
	`STD_ULOGIC, STD_LOGIC,`
	`STD_ULOGIC_VECTOR, and STD_LOGIC_VECTOR`
	`type STD_ULOGIC is`
	`('U','X','0','1','Z','W','L','H','-');`
		10.6	—

IEEE Numeric_Bit and Numeric_Std
(defines arithmetic operators on BIT and 1164 types)
	`UNSIGNED` and `SIGNED`
	`X <= "10" * "01"`
	`-- OK with numeric pkgs.`
		10.12	—

TABLE 10.28 VHDL definitions.

Structure	Page	BNF	Structure	Page	BNF
alias declaration	418	10.21	next statement	429	10.32
architecture body	394	10.8	null statement	430	10.35
assertion statement	423	10.25	package declaration	398	10.11
attribute declaration	418	10.22	port interface declaration	406	10.13
block statement	438	10.37	port interface list	406	10.12
case statement	428	10.30	primary unit	393	10.5
component declaration	395	10.9	procedure call statement	427	10.28
component instantiation	444	10.42	process statement	440	10.38
concurrent statement	437	10.36	return statement	430	10.34
conditional signal assignment	442	10.40	secondary unit	393	10.6
configuration declaration	396	10.10	selected signal assignment	442	10.39
constant declaration	414	10.16	sequential statement	419	10.23
declaration	413	10.15	signal assignment statement	424	10.27
design file	393	10.4	signal declaration	414	10.17
entity declaration	394	10.7	special character	391	10.2
exit statement	430	10.33	subprogram body	416	10.20
generate statement	444	10.43	subprogram declaration	415	10.19
graphic character	391	10.1	type declaration	411	10.14
identifier	392	10.3	variable assignment statement	424	10.26
if statement	427	10.29	variable declaration	415	10.18
loop statement	429	10.31	wait statement	421	10.24

10.18 Problems

*=Difficult **=Very difficult ***=Extremely difficult

10.1 (Hello World, 10 min.) Set up a new, empty, directory (use `mkdir VHDL`, for example) to run your VHDL simulator (the exact details will depend on your computer and simulator). Copy the code below a file called `hw_1.vhd` in your VHDL directory (leave out the comments to save typing). *Hint:* Use the `vi` editor (`i` inserts text, `x` deletes text, `dd` deletes a line, `ESC :w` writes the file, `ESC :q` quits) or use `cat > hw_1.vhd` and type in the code (use `CTRL-D` to end typing) on a UNIX machine. Remember to save in 'Text Only' mode (Frame or MS Word) on an IBM PC or Apple Macintosh.

Analyze, elaborate, and simulate your model (include the output in your answer). Comment on how easy or hard it was to follow the instructions to use the software and suggest improvements.

```
entity HW_1 is end; architecture Behave of HW_1 is
constant M : STRING := "hello, world"; signal Ch : CHARACTER := ' ';
begin process begin
  for i in M'RANGE loop Ch <= M(i); wait for 1 ns; end loop; wait; end
process; end;
```

10.2 (Running a VHDL simulation, 20 min.) Copy the example from Section 10.1 into a file called `Counter1.vhd` in your VHDL directory (leave out the comments to save typing). Complete the compile (analyze), elaborate (build), and execute (initialize and simulate) or other equivalent steps for your simulator. After each step list the contents of your directory VHDL and any subdirectories and files that are created (use `ls -alR` on a UNIX system).

10.3 (Simulator commands, 10 min.) Make a "cheat sheet" for your simulator, listing the commands that can be used to control simulation.

10.4 (BNF addresses, 10 min.) Create a BNF description of a name including: optional title (Prof., Dr., Mrs., Mr., Miss, or Ms.), optional first name and middle initials (allow up to two), and last name (including unusual hyphenated and foreign names, such as Miss A-S. de La Salle, and Prof. John T. P. McTavish-Fiennes). The lowest level constructs are `letter ::=` a-z, `'.'` (period) and `'-'` (hyphen). Add BNF productions for a postal address in the form: company name, mail stop, street address, address lines (1 to 4), and country.

10.5 (BNF e-mail, 10 min.) Create a BNF description of a valid internet e-mail address in terms of letters, `'@'`, `'.'`, `'gov'`, `'com'`, `'org'`, and `'edu'`. Create a state diagram that "parses" an e-mail address for validity.

10.6 (BNF equivalence) Are the following BNF productions exactly equivalent? If they are not, produce a counterexample that shows a difference.

```
term ::= factor { multiplying_operator factor }
term ::= factor | term multiplying_operator factor
```

10.7 (Environment, 20 min.) Write a simple VHDL model to check and demonstrate that you can get to the IEEE library and have the environment variables, library statements, and such correctly set up for your simulator.

10.8 (Work, 20 min.) Write simple VHDL models to demonstrate that you can retrieve and use previously analyzed design units from the library `work` and that you can also remove design units from `work`. Explain how your models prove that access to `work` is functioning correctly.

10.9 (Packages, 60 min.) Write a simple package (use filename `PackH.vhd`) and package body (filename `PackB.vhd`). Demonstrate that you can store your package (call it `MyPackage`) in the library `work`. Then store, move, or rename (the details will depend on your software) your package to a library called `MyLibrary` in a directory called `MyDir`, and use its contents with a library clause (`library MyLibrary`) and a use clause (`use MyLibrary.MyPackage.all`) in a test bench called `PackTest` (filename `PackT.vhd`) in another directory `MyWork`. You may or may not be amazed at how complicated this can be and how poorly most software companies document this process.

10.10 (***IEEE Std 1164, 60 min.) Prior to VHDL-93 the `xnor` function was not available, and therefore older versions of the `std_logic_1164` library did not provide the `xnor` function for `STD_LOGIC` types either (it was actually included but commented out). Write a simple model that checks to see if you have the newer version of `std_logic_1164`. Can you do this without crashing the simulator?

You are an engineer on a very large project and find that your design fails to compile because your design must use the `xnor` function and the library setup on your company's system still points to the old IEEE `std_logic_1164` library, even though the new library was installed. You are apparently the first person to realize the problem. Your company has a policy that any time a library is changed all design units that use that library must be rebuilt from source. This might require days or weeks of work. Explain in detail, using code, the alternative solutions. What will you recommend to your manager?

10.11 (**VHDL-93 test, 20 min.) Write a simple test to check if your simulator is a VHDL-87 or VHDL-93 environment—without crashing the simulator.

10.12 (Declarations, 10 min.) Analyze the following changes to the code in Section 10.8 and include the simulator output in your answers:

a. Uncomment the declarations for `Bad100` and `Bad4` in `Declaration_1`.

b. Add the following to `Constant_2`:

```
signal wacky : wackytype (31 downto 0); -- wacky
```

c. Remove the library and use clause in `Constant_2`.

10.13 (`STRING` type, 10 min.) Replace the `write` statement that prints the string `" count="` in `Text(Behave)` in Section 10.6.3 with the following, compile it, and explain the result:

```
write(L, " count=" ); -- no type qualification...
```

10.14 (Sequential statements, 10 min.) Uncomment the following line in Wait_1(Behave) in Section 10.10, analyze the code, and explain the result:

```
wait on x(1 to v); -- v is variable
```

10.15 (VHDL logical operators, 10 min.)

a. Explain the problem with the following VHDL statement:

```
Z <= A nand B nand C;
```

b. Explain why this problem does not occur with this statement:

```
Z <= A and B and C;
```

c. What can you say about the logical operators: and, or, nand, nor, xnor, xor?

d. Is the following code legal?

```
Z <= A and B or C;
```

10.16 (*Initialization, 45 min.) Consider the following code:

```
entity DFF_Plain is port (Clk, D : in BIT; Q : out BIT); end;
architecture Bad of DFF_Plain is begin process (Clk) begin
   if Clk = '0' and Clk'EVENT then Q <= D after 1 ns; end if;
end process; end;
```

a. Analyze and simulate this model using a testbench.

b. Rewrite architecture Bad using an equivalent process including a wait statement. Simulate this equivalent model and confirm the behaviors are identical.

c. What is the behavior of the output Q during initial execution of the process?

d. Why does this happen?

e. Why does this not happen with the following code:

```
architecture Good of DFF_Plain is
begin process begin wait until Clk = '0'; Q <= D after 1 ns;
end process; end;
```

10.17 (Initial and default values, 20 min.) Use code examples to explain the difference between: default expression, default value, implicit default value, initial value, initial value expression, and default initial value.

10.18 (Enumeration types, 20 min.) Explain the analysis results for the following:

```
type MVL4 is ('X', '0', '1', 'Z'); signal test : MVL4;
process begin
   test <= 1; test <= Z; test <= z; test <= '1'; test <= 'Z';
end process;
```

Alter the type declaration to the following, analyze your code again, and comment:

```
type Mixed4 is (X , '0', '1', Z);
```

10.19 (Type declarations, 10 min.) Correct these declarations:

```
type BadArray is array (0 to 7) of BIT_VECTOR;
type Byte is array (NATURAL range 7 downto 0) of BIT;
subtype BadNibble is Byte(3 downto 0);
type BadByte is array (range 7 downto 0) of BIT;
```

10.20 (Procedure parameters, 10 min.) Analyze the following package; explain and correct the error. Finally, build a testbench to check your solution.

```
package And_Pkg_Bad is procedure V_And(a, b : BIT; c: out BIT); end;
package body And_Pkg_Bad is
procedure V_And(a,b : BIT;c : out BIT) is begin c <= a and b;end;
end And_Pkg_Bad;
```

10.21 (Type checking, 20 min.) Test the following code and explain the results:

```
type T is INTEGER range 0 to 32; variable a: T;
a := (16 + 17) - 12; a := 16 - 12 + 17; a := 16 + (17 - 12);
```

10.22 (Debugging VHDL code, 30 min.) Find and correct the errors in the following code. Create a testbench for your code to check that it works correctly.

```
entity UpDownCount_Bad is
port(clock, reset, up: STD_LOGIC; D: STD_LOGIC_VECTOR (7 to 0));
end UpDownCount_Bad;

architecture Behave of UpDownCount_Bad is
begin process (clock, reset, up); begin
if (reset = '0') then D <= '0000000';
elseif (rising_edge(clock)) then
if (up = 1) D <= D+1; else D <= D-1; end if;
end if; end process; end Behave;
```

10.23 (Subprograms, 20 min.) Write and test subprograms for these declarations:

```
function Is_X_Zero (signal X : in BIT) return BIT;

procedure Is_A_Eq_B (signal A, B : BIT; signal Y : out BIT);
```

10.24 (Simulator error messages, 10 min.) Analyze and attempt to simulate `Arithmetic_2(Behave)` from Section 10.12 and compare the error message you receive with that from the MTI simulator (not all simulators are as informative). There are no standards for error messages.

10.25 (Exhaustive property of case statement, 30 min.) Write and simulate a testbench for the state machine of Table 10.8 and include your results. Is every state transition tested by your program and is every transition covered by an assignment statement in the code? (*Hint:* Think very carefully.) Repeat this exercise for the state machine in Section 10.10.6.

10.26 (Default values for inputs, 20 min.) Replace the interface declaration for entity Half_Adder in Section 10.5 with the following (to remove the default values):

```
port (X, Y: in BIT ; Sum, Cout: out BIT);
```

Attempt to compile, elaborate, and simulate configuration Simplest (the other entities needed, AndGate and XorGate, must already be in work or in the same file). You should get an error at some stage (different systems find this error at different points—just because an entity compiles, that does not mean it is error-free).

The LRM says "... A port of mode in may be unconnected ...only if its declaration includes a **default expression**..." [93LRM1.1.1.2].

We face a dilemma here. If we do not drive inputs with test signals and leave an input port unconnected, we can compile the model (since it is syntactically correct) but the model is not semantically correct. On the other hand, if we give the inputs default values, we might accidentally forget to make a connection and not notice.

10.27 (Adder generation, 10 min.) Draw the schematic for Adder_1(Structure) of Section 10.13.7, labeling each instance with the VHDL instance name.

10.28 (Generate statement, 20 min.) Draw a schematic corresponding to the following code (label the cells with their instance names):

```
B1: block begin L1 : C port map (T, B, A(0), B(0)) ;
L2: for i in 1 to 3 generate L3 : for j in 1 to 3 generate
L4: if i+j > 4 generate L5: C port map (A(i−1), B(j−1), A(i), B(j)) ;
end generate; end generate; end generate;
L6: for i in 1 to 3 generate L7: for j in 1 to 3 generate
L8: if i+j < 4 generate L9: C port map (A(i+1), B(j+1), A(i), B(j)) ;
end generate; end generate; end generate;
end block B1;
```

Rewrite the code without **generate** statements. How would you prove that your code really is exactly equivalent to the original?

10.29 (Case statement, 20 min.) Create a package (my_equal) that overloads the equality operator so that 'X'='0' and 'X'='1' are both TRUE. Test your package. Simulate the following design unit and explain the result.

```
entity Case_1 is end; architecture Behave of Case_1 is
signal r : BIT; use work.my_equal.all;
begin process variable twobit:STD_LOGIC_VECTOR(1 to 2); begin
   twobit := "X0";
   case twobit is
     when "10" => r <= '1';
     when "00" => r <= '1';
     when others => r <= '0';
   end case; wait;
end process; end;
```

10.30 (State machine) Create a testbench for the state machine of Section 10.2.5.

10.31 (Mealy state machine, 60 min.) Rewrite the state machine of Section 10.2.5 as a Mealy state machine (the outputs depend on the inputs and on the current state).

10.32 (Gate-Level D flip-flop, 30 min.) Draw the schematic for the following D flip-flop model. Create a testbench (check for correct operation with combinations of clear, preset, clock, and data). Have you covered all possible modes of operation? Justify your answer of yes or no.

```
architecture RTL of DFF_To_Test is
signal A, B, C, D, QI, QBarI : BIT; begin
A <= not (Preset and D and B) after 1 ns;
B <= not (A and Clear and Clock) after 1 ns;
C <= not (B and Clock and D) after 1 ns;
D <= not (C and Clear and Data) after 1 ns;
QI <= not (Preset and B and QBarI) after 1 ns;
QBarI <= not (QI and Clear and C) after 1 ns;
Q <= QI; QBar <= QBarI;
end;
```

10.33 (Flip-flop model, 20 min.) Add an asynchronous active-low preset to the D flip-flop model of Table 10.3. Generate a testbench that includes interaction of the preset and clear inputs. What issue do you face and how did you solve it?

10.34 (Register, 45 min.) Design a testbench for the register of Table 10.4. Adapt the 8-bit register design to a 4-bit version with the following interface declaration:

```
entity Reg4 is port (D : in  STD_LOGIC_VECTOR(7 downto 0);
Clk,Pre,Clr : in STD_LOGIC;Q,QB : out STD_LOGIC_VECTOR(7 downto 0));
end Reg8;
```

Create a testbench for your 4-bit register with the following component declaration:

```
component DFF
port(Preset,Clear,Clock,Data:STD_LOGIC;Q,QBar:out STD_LOGIC_VECTOR);
end component;
```

10.35 (*Conversion functions, 30 min.) Write a conversion function from NATURAL to STD_LOGIC_VECTOR using the following declaration:

```
function Convert (N, L: NATURAL) return STD_LOGIC_VECTOR;
-- N is NATURAL, L is length of STD_LOGIC_VECTOR
```

Write a similar conversion function from STD_LOGIC_VECTOR to NATURAL:

```
function Convert (B: STD_LOGIC_VECTOR) return NATURAL;
```

Create a testbench to test your functions by including them in a package.

10.36 (Clock procedure, 20 min.) Design a clock procedure for a two-phase clock (C1, C2) with variable high times (HT1, HT2) and low times (LT1, LT2) and the following interface. Include your procedure in a package and write a model to test it.

```
procedure Clock (C1, C2 : out STD_LOGIC; HT1, HT2, LT1, LT2 : TIME);
```

10.37 (Random number, 20 min.) Design a testbench for the following procedure:

```
procedure uniform (seed : inout INTEGER range 0 to 15) is
  variable x : INTEGER;
  begin x := (seed*11) + 7; seed := x mod 16;
end uniform;
```

10.38 (Full-adder, 30 min.) Design and test a behavioral model of a full adder with the following interface:

```
entity FA is port (X, Y, Cin : STD_LOGIC; Cout, Sum : out STD_LOGIC);
end;
```

Repeat the exercise for inputs and outputs of type UNSIGNED.

10.39 (8-bit adder testbench, 60 min.) Write out the code corresponding to the generate statements of Adder_1 (Structure) in Section 10.13.7. Write a testbench to check your adder. What problems do you encounter? How thorough do you believe your tests are?

10.40 (Shift-register testbench, 60 min.) Design a testbench for the shift register of Table 10.4. Convert this model to use STD_LOGIC types with the following interface:

```
entity ShiftN is
port (CLK, CLR, LD, SH, DIR : STD_LOGIC;
  D : STD_LOGIC_VECTOR; Q : out STD_LOGIC_VECTOR);
end;
```

10.41 (Multiplier, 60 min.) Design and test a multiplier with the following interface:

```
entity Mult8 is
port (A, B : STD_LOGIC_VECTOR(3 downto 0);
Start, CLK, Reset : in STD_LOGIC;
Result : out STD_LOGIC_VECTOR(7 downto 0); Done : out BIT);
end;
```

a. Create testbench code to check your model.

b. Catalog each compile step with the syntax errors as you debug your code.

c. Include a listing of the first code you write together with the final version.

An interesting class project is to collect statistics from other students working on this problem and create a table showing the types and frequency of syntax errors made with each compile step, and the number of compile steps required. Does this information suggest ways that you could improve the compiler, or suggest a new type of tool to use when writing VHDL?

10.42 (Port maps, 5 min.) What is wrong with this VHDL statement?

```
U1 : nand2 port map (a <= set, b <= qb, c <= q);
```

10.43 (DRIVING_VALUE, 15 min.) Use the VHDL-93 attribute Clock'DRIVING_VALUE to rewrite the following clock generator model without using a temporary variable.

```
entity ClockGen_2 is port (Clock : out BIT); end;
architecture Behave of ClockGen_2 is
begin process variable Temp : BIT := '1'; begin
   Temp := not Temp ; Clock <= Temp after 10 ns; wait for 10 ns;
   if (now > 100 ns) then wait; end if; end process;
end;
```

10.44 (Records, 15 min.) Write an architecture (based on the following skeleton) that uses the record structure shown:

```
entity Test_Record_1 is end; architecture Behave of Test_Record_1 is
begin process type Coordinate is record X, Y : INTEGER; end record;
-- a record declaration for an attribute declaration:
attribute Location:Coordinate; -- an attribute declaration
begin wait; end process; end Behave;
```

10.45 (**Communication between processes, 30 min.) Explain and correct the problem with the following skeleton code:

```
variable v1 : INTEGER := 1; process begin v1 := v1+3; wait; end process;
process variable v2 : INTEGER := 2; begin v2 := v1  ; wait; end process;
```

10.46 (*Resolution, 30 min.) Explain and correct the problems with the following:

```
entity R_Bad_1 is port (i : in BIT; o out BIT); end;
architecture Behave of R_Bad_1 is
begin o <= not i after 1 ns; o <= i after 2 ns; end;
```

10.47 (*Inputs, 30 min.) Analyze the following and explain the result:

```
entity And2 is port (A1, A2: in BIT; ZN: out BIT); end;
architecture Simple of And2 is begin ZN <= A1 and A2; end;

entity Input_Bad_1 is end; architecture Netlist of Input_Bad_1 is
component And2 port (A1, A2 : in BIT; ZN : out BIT); end component;
signal X, Z : BIT begin G1 : And2 port map (X, X, Z); end;
```

10.48 (Association, 15 min.) Analyze the following and explain the problem:

```
entity And2 is port (A1, A2 : in BIT; ZN : out BIT); end;
architecture Simple of And2 is begin ZN <= A1 and A2; end;

entity Assoc_Bad_1 is port (signal X, Y : in BIT; Z : out BIT); end;
architecture Netlist of Assoc_Bad_1 is
component And2 port (A1, A2 : in BIT; ZN : out BIT); end component;
```

```
begin
G1: And2 port map (X, Y, Z);
G2: And2 port map (A2 => Y, ZN => Z, A1 => X);
G3: And2 port map (X, ZN => Z, A2 => Y);
end;
```

10.49 (Modes, 30 min.) Analyze and explain the errors in the following:

```
entity And2 is port (A1, A2 : in BIT; ZN : out BIT); end;
architecture Simple of And2 is begin ZN <= A1 and A2; end;

entity Mode_Bad_1 is port (X : in BIT; Y : out BIT; Z : inout BIT); end;
architecture Netlist of Mode_Bad_1 is
component And2 port (A1, A2 : in BIT; ZN : out BIT); end component;
begin G1 : And2 port map (X, Y, Z); end;

entity Mode_Bad_2 is port (X : in BIT; Y : out BIT; Z : inout BIT); end;
architecture Netlist of Mode_Bad_1 is
component And2 port (A1, A2 : in BIT; ZN : inout BIT); end component;
begin G1 : And2 port map (X, Y, Z); end;
```

10.50 (*Mode association, 60 min.) Analyze and explain the errors in the following code. The number of errors, types of error, and the information in the error messages given by different simulators vary tremendously in this area.

```
entity Allmode is port
(I : in BIT; O : out BIT; IO : inout BIT; B : buffer BIT);
end;
architecture Simple of Allmode is begin O<=I; IO<=I; B<=I;end;

entity Mode_1 is port
(I : in BIT; O : out BIT; IO : inout BIT; B : buffer BIT);
end;
architecture Netlist of Mode_1 is
component Allmode port
(I : in BIT; O : out BIT; IO : inout BIT; B : buffer BIT); end
component;
begin
G1:Allmode port map (I , O , IO, B );
G2:Allmode port map (O , IO, B , I );
G3:Allmode port map (IO, B , I , O );
G4:Allmode port map (B , I , O , IO);
end;
```

10.51 (**Declarations, 60 min.) Write a tutorial (approximately two pages of text, five pages with code) with examples explaining the difference between: a component declaration, a component configuration, a configuration declaration, a configuration specification, and a block configuration.

10.52 (**Guards and guarded signals, 60 min.) Write some simple models to illustrate the use of guards, guarded signals, and the disconnect statement. Include an experiment that shows and explains the use of the implicit signal GUARD in assignment statements.

10.53 (**`std_logic_1164`, 120 min.) Write a short (two pages of text) tutorial, with (tested) code examples, explaining the `std_logic_1164` types, their default values, the difference between the `'ulogic'` and `'logic'` types, and their vector forms. Include an example that shows and explains the problem of connecting a `std_logic_vector` to a `std_ulogic_vector`.

10.54 (Data swap, 20 min.) Consider the following code:

```
library ieee; use ieee.std_logic_1164.all;
package config is
type type1 is record
f1 : std_logic_vector(31 downto 0); f2 : std_logic_vector(3 downto 0);
end record;
type type2 is record
f1 : std_logic_vector(31 downto 0); f2 : std_logic_vector(3 downto 0);
end record;
end config;
library ieee; use ieee.STD_LOGIC_1164.all; use work.config.all;
entity Swap_1 is
port (Data1 : type1; Data2 : type2; sel : STD_LOGIC;
Data1Swap : out type1; Data2Swap : out type2); end Swap_1;

architecture Behave of Swap_1 is begin
Swap: process (Data1, Data2, sel) begin case sel is
when '0' => Data1Swap <= Data1; Data2Swap <= Data2;
when others => Data1Swap <= Data2; Data2Swap <= Data1;
end case; end process Swap; end Behave;
```

Compile this code. What is the problem? Suggest a fix. Now write a testbench and test your code. Have you considered all possibilities?

10.55 (*****RTL**, 30 min.) "**RTL** stands for **register-transfer level**. ...when referencing VHDL, the term means that the description includes only concurrent signal assignment statements and possibly block statements. In particular, VHDL data flow descriptions explicitly do not contain either process statements (which describe behavior) or component instantiation statements (which describe structure)" (Dr. VHDL from VHDL International).

a. With your knowledge of process statements and components, comment on Dr. VHDL's explanation.

b. In less than 100 words offer your own definition of the difference between RTL, data flow, behavioral, and structural models.

10.56 (*Operators `mod` and `rem`, 20 min.) Confirm and explain the following:

```
i1 := (-12) rem 7;        -- i1 = -5
i2 := 12    rem (-7);     -- i2 =  5
i3 := (12)  rem (-7);     -- i3 = -5
i4 := 12    mod 7;        -- i4 =  5
i5 := (-12) mod 7;        -- i5 =  2
i6 := 12    mod (-7);     -- i6 = -2
i7 := (12)  mod (-7);     -- i7 = -5
```

Evaluate -5 rem 2 and explain the result.

10.57 (***Event and stable, 60 min.) Investigate the differences between clk'EVENT and clk'STABLE. Write a minitutorial (in the form of a "cheat sheet") with examples showing the differences and potential dangers of using clk'STABLE.

10.58 (PREP benchmark #2, 60 min.) The following code models a benchmark circuit used by **PREP** to measure the capacity of FPGAs. Rewrite the concurrent signal assignment statements (labeled mux and comparator) as equivalent processes. Draw a datapath schematic corresponding to PREP2(Behave_1). Write a testbench for the model. Finally (for extra credit) rewrite the model and testbench to use STD_LOGIC instead of BIT types.

```
library ieee; use ieee.STD_LOGIC_1164.all;
use ieee.NUMERIC_BIT.all; use ieee.NUMERIC_STD.all;
entity PREP2 is
port(CLK,Reset,Sel,Ldli,Ldhi : BIT; D1,D2 : STD_LOGIC_VECTOR(7 downto 0);
   DQ:out STD_LOGIC_VECTOR(7 downto 0));
end;

architecture Behave_1 of PREP2 is
signal EQ : BIT; signal y,lo,hi,Q_i : STD_LOGIC_VECTOR(7 downto 0);
begin
outputDriver: Q <= Q_i;
mux: with Sel select y <= hi when '0', D1 when '1';
comparator: EQ <= '1' when Q_i = lo else '0';
register: process(Reset, CLK) begin
    if Reset = '1' then hi <= "00000000"; lo <= "00000000";
    elsif CLK = '1' and CLK'EVENT then
      if Ldhi='1' then hi<=D2;end if;if Ldlo='1' then lo<=D2;end if;
    end if;
end process register;
counter: process(Reset, CLK) begin
    if Reset = '1' then Q_i <= "00000000";
    elsif CLK = '1' and CLK'EVENT then
      if EQ = '1' then Q_i <= y;
      elsif EQ = '0' then Q_i  <= Q_i + "00000001";
      end if;
    end if;
  end process counter;
  end;
```

10.59 (PREP #3, state machine) Draw the state diagram for the following PREP benchmark (see Problem 10.58). Is this a Mealy or Moore machine? Write a testbench and test this code.

```
library ieee; use ieee.STD_LOGIC_1164.all;
entity prep3_1 is port(Clk, Reset: STD_LOGIC;
   I : STD_LOGIC_VECTOR(7 downto 0); O : out STD_LOGIC_VECTOR(7 downto 0));
end prep3_1;
architecture Behave of prep3_1 is
```

```
type STATE_TYPE is (sX,s0,sa,sb,sc,sd,se,sf,sg);
signal state : STATE_TYPE; signal Oi : STD_LOGIC_VECTOR(7 downto 0);
begin
  O <= Oi;
  process (Reset, Clk) begin
    if (Reset = '1') then state <= s0; Oi <= (others => '0');
    elsif rising_edge(Clk) then
      case state is
        when s0 =>
          if (I = X"3c") then state <= sa; Oi <= X"82";
          else state <= s0; Oi <= (others => '0');
          end if;
        when sa =>
          if (I = X"2A") then state <= sc; Oi <= X"40";
          elsif (I = X"1F") then state <= sb; Oi <= X"20";
          else state <= sa; Oi <= X"04";
          end if;
        when sb =>
          if (I = X"AA") then state <= se; Oi <= X"11";
          else state <= sf; Oi <= X"30";
          end if;
        when sc => state <= sd; Oi <= X"08";
        when sd => state <= sg; Oi <= X"80";
        when se => state <= s0; Oi <= X"40";
        when sf => state <= sg; Oi <= X"02";
        when sg => state <= s0; Oi <= X"01";
        when others => state <= sX; Oi <= (others => 'X');
      end case;
    end if;
  end process;
end;
```

10.60 (Edge detection, 30 min) Explain the construction of the IEEE 1164 function to detect the rising edge of a signal, `rising_edge(s)`. List all the changes in signal s that correspond to a rising edge.

```
function rising_edge (signal s : STD_ULOGIC) return BOOLEAN is
  begin return
  (s'EVENT and (To_X01(s) = '1') and (To_X01(s'LAST_VALUE) = '0'));
end;
```

10.61 (*Real, 10 min.) Determine the smallest real in your VHDL environment.

10.62 (*Stop, 30 min.) How many ways are there to stop a VHDL simulator?

10.63 (*Arithmetic package, 60 min.) Write a function for an arithmetic package to subtract two's complement numbers. Create a test bench to check your function. Your declarations in the package header should look like this:

```
type TC is array (INTEGER range <>) of STD_LOGIC;
function "-"(L : TC; R : TC) return TC;
```

10.64 (***Reading documentation, hours) There are a few gray areas in the interpretation of the VHDL-87 LRM some of which were clarified in the VHDL-93 revision. One VHDL system has a "**compatibility mode**" that allows alternative interpretations. For each of the following "issues" taken from the actual tool documentation try to interpret what was meant, determine the interpretation taken by your own software, and then rewrite the explanation clearly using examples.

a. * "Unassociated variable and signal parameters. Compatibility mode allows variable and signal parameters to subprograms to be unassociated if they have a default value. Otherwise, an error is generated."

Example answer: Consider the following code:

```
package Util_2 is
procedure C(signal Clk : out BIT; signal P : TIME := 10 ns);
end Util_2;
package body Util_2 is
procedure C(signal Clk : out BIT; signal P : TIME := 10 ns) is
begin loop Clk <= '1' after P/2, '0' after P;
wait for P; end loop; end; end Util_2;
entity Test_Compatibility_1 is end; use work.Util_2.all;
architecture Behave of Test_Compatibility_1 is
signal v,w,x,y,z : BIT; signal s : TIME := 5 ns;
begin process variable v : TIME := 5 ns; begin
C(v, s);       -- parameter s is OK since P is declared as signal
-- C(w, v);    -- would be OK if P is declared as variable instead
-- C(x, 5 ns); -- would be OK if P is declared as constant instead
-- C(y);       -- unassociated, an error if P is signal or variable
-- C(z,open);  -- open, an error if P is signal or variable
end process; end;
```

The Compass Scout simulator (which does not have a compatibility mode) generates an error during analysis if a signal or variable subprogram parameter is open or unassociated (a constant subprogram parameter may be unassociated or open).

b. * "Allow others in an aggregate within a record aggregate. The LRM [7.3.2.2] defines nine situations where others may appear in an aggregate. In compatibility mode, a tenth case is added. In this case, others is allowed in an aggregate that appears as an element association in a record element."

c. * "BIT'('1') parsed as BIT ' ('1'). The tick (') character is being used twice in this example. In the first case as an attribute indicator, in the second case, to form a character literal. Without the compatibility option, the analyzer adopts a strict interpretation of the LRM, and without white space around the first tick, the fragment is parsed as BIT '('1'), that is, the left parenthesis ('(') is the character literal."

d. ** "Generate statement declarative region. Generate statements form their own declarative region. In compatibility mode, configuration specifications will apply to items being instantiated within a generate statement."

e. ** "Allow type conversion functions on open parameters. If a parameter is specified as open, it indicates a parameter without an explicit association. In such cases, the presence of a type conversion function is meaningless. Compatibility mode allows the type conversion functions."

f. *** "Entity class flexibility. Section [3.1.2] of the LRM defines the process of creating a new integer type. The type name given is actually assigned to a subtype name, related to an anonymous base type. This implies that the entity class used during an attribute specification [LRM 5.1] should indicate subtype, rather than type. Because the supplied declaration was type rather than subtype, compatibility mode allows type."

g. *** "Allowing declarations beyond an all/others specification. Section [5.1] of the LRM states that the first occurrence of the reserved word `all` or `others` in an attribute specification terminates the declaration of the related entity class. The LRM declares that the entity/architecture and package/package body library units form single declaration regions [LRM 10.1] that are the concatenation of the two individual library declarative regions. For example, if a signal attribute specification with `all` or `others` was specified in the entity, it would be impossible to declare a signal in the architecture. In compatibility mode, this LRM limitation is removed."

h. *** "User-defined attributes on overloaded functions. In compatibility mode, user-defined attributes are allowed to be associated with overloaded functions. Note: Even in compatibility mode, there is no way to retrieve the different attributes."

10.65 (*1076 interpretations, 30 min.) In a DAC paper, the author writes: 'It was experienced that (company R) might have interpreted IEEE 1076 differently than (company S) did, e.g. concatenations (&) are not allowed in "case selector" expressions for (company S).' Can you use concatenation in your VHDL tool for either the `expression` or `choices` for a `case` statement?

10.66 (**Interface declarations, 15 min.) Analyze the following and comment:

```
entity Interface_1 is
    generic (I : INTEGER; J : INTEGER := I; K, L : INTEGER);
    port (A : BIT_VECTOR; B : BIT_VECTOR(A'RANGE); C : BIT_VECTOR (K to L));
    procedure X(P, Q : INTEGER; R : INTEGER range P to Q);
    procedure Y(S : INTEGER range K to L);
end Interface_1;
```

10.67 (**Wait statement, 10 min.) Construct the sensitivity set and thus the sensitivity list for the following `wait` statement (that is, rewrite the `wait` statement in the form `wait on sensitivity_list until condition`).

```
entity Complex_Wait is end;                          --1
architecture Behave of Complex_Wait is               --2
    type A is array (1 to 5) of BOOLEAN;             --3
```

```
function F (P : BOOLEAN) return BOOLEAN;                    --4
signal S : A; signal i, j : INTEGER range 1 to 5;          --5
begin process begin                                        --6
  wait until F(S(3)) and (S(i) or S(j));                   --7
end process;                                               --8
end;                                                       --9
```

10.68 (**Shared variables, 20 min.) Investigate the following code and comment:

```
architecture Behave of Shared_1 is
subtype S is INTEGER range 0 to 1; shared variable C : S := 0; begin
process begin C := C + 1; wait; end process;
process begin C := C - 1; wait; end process;
end;
```

10.69 (Undocumented code and ranges, 20 min.) Explain the purpose of the following function (part of a package from a well-known synthesis company) with a parameter of type SIGNED. Write a testbench to check your explanation. Investigate what happens when you call this function with a string-literal argument, for example with the statement X <= IM("11100"). What is the problem and why does it happen? Rewrite the code, including documentation, to avoid this problem.

```
type SIGNED is array (NATURAL range <> ) of BIT;

function IM (L : SIGNED) return INTEGER is variable M : INTEGER;
begin M := L'RIGHT-1;
  for i in L'LEFT-1 downto L'RIGHT loop
    if (L(i) = (not L(L'LEFT))) then M := i; exit; end if;
  end loop; return M;
end;
```

10.70 (Timing parameters, 20 min.) Write a model and a testbench for a two-input AND gate with separate rising (tpLH) and falling (tpHL) delays using the following interface:

```
entity And_Process is
generic (tpLH, tpHL : TIME); port (a, b : BIT; z : out BIT) end;
```

10.71 (Passive code in entities, 30 min.) Write a procedure (CheckTiming, part of a package Timing_Pkg) to check that two timing parameters (tPLH and tPHL) are both greater than zero. Include this procedure in a two-input AND gate model (And_Process). Write a testbench to show your procedure and gate model both work. Rewrite the entity for And_Process to include the timing check as part of the entity declaration. You are allowed to include **passive code** (no assignments to signals and so on) directly in each entity. This avoids having to include the timing checks in each architecture.

10.72 (Buried code, 30 min.) Some companies bury instructions to the software within their packages. Here is an example of part of the arithmetic package from an imaginary company called SissyN:

```
function UN_plus(A, B : UN) return UN is                          --1
variable CRY : STD_ULOGIC; variable X,SUM : UN (A'LEFT downto 0); --2
-- pragma map_to_operator ADD_UNS_OP                              --3
-- pragma type_function LEFT_UN_ARG                               --4
-- pragma return_port_name Z                                      --5
begin                                                            --6
-- sissyn synthesis_off                                          --7
if (A(A'LEFT) = 'X' or B(B'LEFT) = 'X') then SUM := (others => 'X'); --8
return(SUM);                                                     --9
end if;                                                          --10
-- sissyn synthesis_on                                           --11
CRY := '0'; X := B;                                              --12
for i in 0 to A'LEFT loop                                        --13
SUM(i) := A(i) xor X(i) xor carry;                              --14
CRY := (A(i) and X(i)) or (A(i) and CRY) or (CRY and X(i));     --15
end loop; return SUM;                                            --16
end;                                                             --17
```

Explain what this function does. Can you now hazard a guess at what each of the comments means? What are the repercussions of using comments in this fashion?

10.73 (*Deferred constants, 15 min.) "If the assignment symbol `':='` followed by an expression is not present in a constant declaration, then the declaration declares a **deferred constant**. Such a constant declaration may only appear in a package declaration. The corresponding full constant declaration, which defines the value of the constant, must appear in the body of the package" [93LRM 4.3.1.1].

```
package Constant is constant s1, s2 : BIT_VECTOR; end Constant;

package body Constant is
constant s0 : BIT_VECTOR := "00"; constant s1 : BIT_VECTOR := "01";
end Constant;
```

It is tempting to use deferred constants to hide information. However, there are problems with this approach. Analyze the following code, explain the results, and correct the problems:

```
entity Deferred_1 is end; architecture Behave of Deferred_1 is
use work.all; signal y,i1,i2 : INTEGER; signal sel : INTEGER range 0 to 1;
begin with sel select y <= i1 when s0, i2 when s1; end;
```

10.74 (***Viterbi code, days) Convert the Verilog model of the Viterbi decoder in Chapter 11 to VHDL. This problem is tedious without the help of some sort of **Verilog to VHDL conversion** process. There are two main approaches to this problem. The first uses a synthesis tool to read the behavioral Verilog and write structural VHDL (the Compass ASIC Synthesizer can do this, for example). The second approach uses conversion programs (Alternative System Concepts Inc. at http://www.ascinc.com is one source). Some of these companies allow you to e-mail code to them and they will automatically return a translated version.

10.75 (*Wait statement, 30 min.) Rewrite the code below using a single `wait` statement and write a testbench to prove that both approaches are exactly equivalent:

```
entity Wait_Exit is port (Clk : in BIT); end;
architecture Behave of Wait_Exit is
  begin process begin
     loop wait on Clk; exit when Clk = '1'; end loop;
  end process;
end;
```

10.76 (Expressions, 10 min.) Explain and correct the problems with the following:

```
variable b : BOOLEAN; b := "00" < "11";                          --1
variable bv8 : BIT_VECTOR (7 downto 0) := "1000_0000";           --2
```

10.77 (Combinational logic using `case` statement, 10 min.) A Verilog user suggests the following method to model combinational logic. What are the problems with this approach? Can you get it to work?

```
entity AndCase is port (a, b : BIT; y : out BIT); end;
architecture Behave of AndCase is begin process (a , b) begin
  case a & b is
    when '1'&'1' => y <= '1'; when others => y <= '0';
  end case;
end process; end;
```

10.78 (*Generics and back-annotation, 60 min.)

a. Construct design entities `And_3(Behave)`, a two-input AND gate, and `Xor_3(Behave)`, a two-input XOR gate. Include generic constants to model the propagation delay from each input to the output separately. Use the following entity declaration for `And_3`:

```
entity And_3 is port (I1, I2 : BIT; O : out BIT);
  generic (I1toO, I2toO : DELAY_LENGTH := 0.4 ns); end;
```

b. Create and test a package, `P_1`, that contains `And_3` and `Xor_3` as components.

c. Create and test a design entity `Half_Adder_3(Structure_3)` that uses `P_1`, with the following interface:

```
entity Half_Adder_3 is port (X, Y : BIT; Sum, Carry : out BIT); end;
```

d. Modify and test the architecture `Structure_3` for `Half_Adder_3` so that you can use the following configuration:

```
configuration Structure_3 of Half_Adder_3 is
for Structure_3
for L1 : XOR generic map (0.66 ns,0.69 ns); end for;
for L2 : AND generic map (0.5 ns, 0.6 ns) port map (I2 => HI); end for;
end for; end;
```

10.79 (SNUG'95, *60 min.) In 1995 John Cooley organized a contest between VHDL and Verilog for ASIC designers. The goal was to design the fastest 9-bit counter in under one hour using Synopsys synthesis tools and an LSI Logic vendor technology library. The VHDL interface is as follows:

```
library ieee; use ieee.std_logic_1164.all;
-- use ieee.std_logic_arith.all; -- substitute your package here
entity counter is port (
data_in     : in std_logic_vector(8 downto 0);
up          : in std_logic;
down        : in std_logic;
clock       : in std_logic;
count_out   : inout std_logic_vector(8 downto 0);
carry_out   : out std_logic;
borrow_out  : out std_logic;
parity_out  : out std_logic ); end counter;
architecture example of counter is begin
-- insert your design here
end example;
```

The counter is positive-edge triggered, counts up with `up` = `'1'` and down with `down` = `'1'`. The contestants had the advantage of a predefined testbench with a set of test vectors, you do not. Design a model for the counter and a testbench. How confident are you that you have thoroughly tested your model? (In the real contest none of the VHDL contestants managed to even complete a working design in under one hour. In addition, the VHDL experts that had designed the testbench omitted a test case for one of the design specifications.)

10.80 (*A test procedure, 45 min.) Write a procedure `all` (for a package `test`) that serially generates all possible input values for a signal spaced in time by a delay, `dly`. Use the following interface:

```
library ieee; use ieee.std_logic_1164.all; package test is
procedure all (signal SLV : out STD_LOGIC_VECTOR; dly : in TIME);
end package test ;
```

10.81 (Direct instantiation, 20 min.) Write an architecture for a full-adder, entity `Full_Adder_2`, that directly instantiates units `And_2(Behave)` and `Xor_2(Behave)`. This is only possible in a VHDL-93 environment.

```
entity And_2 is port (i1, i2 : BIT; y : out BIT); end;
entity Xor_2 is port (i1, i2 : BIT; y : out BIT); end;
entity Full_Adder_2 is port (a, b, c : BIT ; sum, cout : out BIT); end;
```

10.82 (**Shift operators for 1164, 60 min.) Write a package body to implement the VHDL-93 shift operators, `sll` and `srl`, for the type `STD_LOGIC_VECTOR`. Use the following package header:

```
package 1164_shift is
function "sll"(x : STD_LOGIC_VECTOR; n : INTEGER)
   return STD_LOGIC_VECTOR;
```

```
function "srl"(x : STD_LOGIC_VECTOR; n : INTEGER)
  return STD_LOGIC_VECTOR;
end package 1164_shift;
```

10.83 (**VHDL wait statement, 60 min.) What is the problem with the following VHDL code? *Hint:* You may need to consult the VHDL LRM.

```
procedure p is begin wait on b; end;
process (a) is begin procedure p; end process;
```

10.84 (**Null range, 45 min.) A range such as 1 **to** −1 or 0 **downto** 1 is a **null range** (0 **to** 0 is a legal range). Write a one-page summary on null ranges, including code examples. Is a null range treated as an ascending or descending range?

10.85 (**Loops, 45 min.) Investigate the following issues with loops, including code examples and the results of analysis and simulation:

a. Try to alter the loop parameter within a loop. What happens?

b. What is the type of the loop parameter?

c. Can the condition inside a loop depend on a loop parameter?

d. What happens in a **for** loop if the range is null?

e. Can you pass a loop parameter out of a procedure as a procedure parameter?

10.86 (Signals and variables, 30 min.) Write a summary on signals and variables, including code examples.

10.87 (Type conversion, 60 min.) There are some very subtle rules involving type conversion, [93LRM7.3.5]. Does the following work? Explain the type conversion rules.

```
BV <= BIT_VECTOR("1111");
```

10.19 Bibliography

The definitive reference guide to VHDL is the IEEE VHDL LRM [IEEE, 1076-1993]. The LRM is initially difficult to read because it is concise and precise (the LRM is intended for tool builders and experienced tool users, not as a tutorial). The LRM does form a useful reference—as does a dictionary for serious users of any language. You might think of the LRM as a legal contract between you and the company that sells you software that is compliant with the standard. VHDL software uses the terminology of the LRM for error messages, so it is necessary to understand the terms and definitions of the LRM. The WAVES standard [IEEE 1029.1-1991] deals with the problems of interfacing VHDL testbenches to testers.

VHDL International maintains VIUF (VHDL International Users' Forum) Internet Services (`http:/www.vhdl.org`) and links to other groups working on VHDL including the IEEE synthesis packages, IEEE WAVES packages, and IEEE VITAL packages (see also Appendix A).

The frequently asked questions (FAQ) list for the VHDL newsgroup `comp.lang.vhdl` is a useful starting point (the list is archived at `gopher://kona.ee.pitt.edu/h0/NewsGroupArchives`). Information on character sets and the problems of exchanging information across national boundaries can be found at `ftp://watsun.cc.columbia.edu/kermit/charsets`.

10.20 References

Page numbers in brackets after the reference indicate the location in the chapter body.

IEEE 1029.1-1991. 1991. IEEE Standard for Waveform and Vector Exchange (WAVES). IEEE Std 1029.1-1991. The Institute of Electrical and Electronics Engineers, Inc., New York. Available from The Institute of Electrical and Electronics Engineers, Inc., 345 East 47th Street, New York, NY 10017 USA.

IEEE 1076-1993. 1993. VHDL. The Institute of Electrical and Electronics Engineers, Inc., New York. Available from The Institute of Electrical and Electronics Engineers, Inc., 345 East 47th Street, New York, NY 10017 USA. [p. 380]

IEEE 1076.2-1996. *Standard VHDL Language Mathematical Packages.* IEEE Ref. AD129-NYF. Approved by IEEE Standards Board on 19 September 1996. [p. 404].

ISO 8859-1. 1987 (E). Information Processing—8-bit single-byte coded graphic character sets—Part 1: Latin Alphabet No. 1. American National Standards Institute, Hackensack, NJ; 1987. Available from Sales Department, American National Standards Institute, 105-111 South State Street, Hackensack, NJ 07601 USA. [p. 391]

VERILOG HDL

In this chapter we look at the **Verilog** hardware description language. Gateway Design Automation developed Verilog as a simulation language. The use of the Verilog-XL simulator is discussed in more detail in Chapter 13. Cadence purchased Gateway in 1989 and, after some study, placed the Verilog language in the public domain. Open Verilog International (OVI) was created to develop the Verilog language as an IEEE standard. The definitive reference guide to the Verilog language is now the Verilog LRM, IEEE Std 1364-1995 [1995].[1] This does not mean that all Verilog simulators and tools adhere strictly to the IEEE Standard—we must abide by the reference manual for the software we are using. Verilog is a fairly simple language to learn, especially if you are familiar with the C programming language. In this chapter we shall concentrate on the features of Verilog applied to high-level design entry and synthesis for ASICs.

---

[1]Some of the material in this chapter is reprinted with permission from IEEE Std 1364-1995, © Copyright 1995 IEEE. All rights reserved.

11.1   A Counter

The following Verilog code models a "black box" that contains a 50 MHz clock (period 20 ns), counts from 0 to 7, resets, and then begins counting at 0 again:

```
`timescale 1ns/1ns                                              //1
module counter;                                                 //2
   reg clock;         // declare reg data type for the clock    //3
   integer count;     // declare integer data type for the count //4
initial // initialize things - this executes once at start      //5
   begin                                                        //6
      clock = 0; count = 0;     // initialize signals           //7
      #340 $finish;             // finish after 340 time ticks  //8
   end                                                          //9
/* an always statement to generate the clock, only one statement
follows the always so we don't need a begin and an end */       //10
                                                                //11
always                                                          //11
   #10 clock = ~ clock; // delay is set to half the clock cycle //12
/* an always statement to do the counting, runs at the same time
(concurrently) as the other always statement */                //13
always                                                          //14
   begin                                                        //15
      // wait here until the clock goes from 1 to 0             //16
      @ (negedge clock);                                        //17
      // now handle the counting                               //18
      if (count == 7)                                           //19
         count = 0;                                             //20
      else                                                      //21
         count = count + 1;                                     //22
      $display("time = ",$time," count = ", count);             //23
   end                                                          //24
endmodule                                                       //25
```

Verilog **keywords** (reserved words that are part of the Verilog language) are shown in bold type in the code listings (but not in the text). References in this chapter such as [Verilog LRM 1.1] refer you to the IEEE Verilog LRM.

The following output is from the Cadence Verilog-XL simulator. This example includes the system input so you can see how the tool is run and when it is finished. Some of the banner information is omitted in the listing that follows to save space (we can use "quiet" mode using a '-q' flag, but then the version and other useful information is also suppressed):

```
> verilog counter.v
VERILOG-XL 2.2.1  Apr 17, 1996  11:48:18
     ... Banner information omitted here...
Compiling source file "counter.v"
Highest level modules:
```

```
counter


time =                    20 count =           1
time =                    40 count =           2
(... 12 lines omitted...)
time =                   300 count =           7
time =                   320 count =           0
L10 "counter.v": $finish at simulation time 340
223 simulation events
CPU time: 0.6 secs to compile + 0.2 secs to link + 0.0 secs in
simulation
End of VERILOG-XL 2.2.1   Apr 17, 1996  11:48:20
>
```

Here is the output of the VeriWell simulator from the console window (future examples do not show all of the compiler output— just the model output):

```
Veriwell -k VeriWell.key -l VeriWell.log -s :counter.v
... banner information omitted ....
Memory Available: 0
Entering Phase I...
Compiling source file : :counter.v
The size of this model is [1%, 1%] of the capacity of the free version


Entering Phase II...
Entering Phase III...
No errors in compilation
Top-level modules:
    counter


C1> .
time =                    20 count =           1
time =                    40 count =           2
(... 12 lines omitted...)
time =                   300 count =           7
time =                   320 count =           0
Exiting VeriWell for Macintosh at time 340
0 Errors, 0 Warnings, Memory Used: 29468
Compile time = 0.6, Load time = 0.7, Simulation time = 4.7


Normal exit
Thank you for using VeriWell for Macintosh
```

11.2 Basics of the Verilog Language

A Verilog **identifier**, including the names of variables, may contain any sequence of letters, digits, a dollar sign '$', and the underscore '_' symbol. The first character of an identifier must be a letter or underscore; it cannot be a dollar sign '$', for example. We cannot use characters such as '-' (hyphen), brackets, or '#' (for active-low signals) in Verilog names (escaped identifiers are an exception). The following is a shorthand way of saying the same thing:

```
identifier ::= simple_identifier | escaped_identifier
simple_identifier ::= [a-zA-Z][a-zA-Z_$]
escaped_identifier ::=
    \ {Any_ASCII_character_except_white_space} white_space
white_space ::= space | tab | newline
```

If we think of '::=' as an equal sign, then the preceding "equation" defines the syntax of an identifier. Usually we use the Backus-Naur form (BNF) to write these equations. We also use the BNF to describe the syntax of VHDL. There is an explanation of the BNF in Appendix A. Verilog syntax definitions are given in Appendix B. In Verilog all names, including keywords and identifiers, are case-sensitive. Special commands for the simulator (a system task or a system function) begin with a dollar sign '$' [Verilog LRM 2.7]. Here are some examples of Verilog identifiers:

```
module identifiers;                                                  //1
/* multiline comments in Verilog                                     //2
   look like C comments and // is OK in here */                      //3
// single-line comment in Verilog                                    //4
reg legal_identifier,two__underscores;                               //5
reg _OK,OK_,OK_$,OK_123,CASE_SENSITIVE, case_sensitive;              //6
reg \/clock ,\a*b ;        // white_space after escaped identifier   //7
//reg $_BAD,123_BAD;       // bad names even if we declare them!     //8
initial begin                                                        //9
legal_identifier = 0;      // embedded underscores are OK            //10
two__underscores = 0;      // even two underscores in a row          //11
_OK = 0;                   // identifiers can start with underscore  //12
OK_ = 0;                   // and end with underscore                //13
OK$ = 0;                   // $ sign is OK: beware foreign keyboards  //14
OK_123 =0;                 // embedded digits are OK                 //15
CASE_SENSITIVE = 0;        // Verilog is case-sensitive              //16
case_sensitive = 1;                                                  //17
\/clock = 0;               // escaped identifier with \ breaks rules //18
\a*b = 0;                  // but be careful! watch the spaces       //19
$display("Variable CASE_SENSITIVE= %d",CASE_SENSITIVE);             //20
$display("Variable case_sensitive= %d",case_sensitive);             //21
$display("Variable \/clock = %d",\/clock );                         //22
$display("Variable \\a*b = %d",\a*b );                              //23
```

```
end                                                              //24
endmodule                                                        //25
```

The following is the output from this model (future examples in this chapter list the simulator output directly after the Verilog code).

```
Variable CASE_SENSITIVE= 0
Variable case_sensitive= 1
Variable /clock = 0
Variable \a*b = 0
```

11.2.1   Verilog Logic Values

Verilog has a predefined logic-value system or **value set** [Verilog LRM 3.1] that uses four logic values: `'0'`, `'1'`, `'x'`, and `'z'` (lowercase `'x'` and lowercase `'z'`). The value `'x'` represents an uninitialized or an unknown logic value—an unknown value is either `'1'`, `'0'`, `'z'`, or a value that is in a state of change. The logic value `'z'` represents a high-impedance value, which is usually treated as an `'x'` value. Verilog uses a more complicated internal logic-value system in order to resolve conflicts between different drivers on the same node. This hidden logic-value system is useful for switch-level simulation, but for most ASIC simulation and synthesis purposes we do not need to worry about the internal logic-value system.

11.2.2   Verilog Data Types

There are several **data types** in Verilog—all except one need to be declared before we can use them. The two main data types are **nets** and **registers** [Verilog LRM 3.2]. Nets are further divided into several net types. The most common and important net types are: **wire** and **tri** (which are identical); **supply1** and **supply0** (which are equivalent to the positive and negative power supplies respectively). The `wire` data type (which we shall refer to as just `wire` from now on) is analogous to a wire in an ASIC. A `wire` cannot store or hold a value. A `wire` must be continuously driven by an assignment statement (see Section 11.5). The default initial value for a `wire` is `'z'`. There are also **integer**, **time**, **event**, and **real** data types.

```
module declarations_1;                                           //1
wire pwr_good, pwr_on, pwr_stable; // Explicitly declare wires   //2
integer i;         // 32-bit, signed (2's complement)            //3
time t;            // 64-bit, unsigned, behaves like a 64-bit reg //4
event e;           // Declare an event data type                 //5
real r;            // Real data type of implementation defined size //6
// assign statement continuously drives a wire:                  //7
assign pwr_stable = 1'b1; assign pwr_on = 1; // 1 or 1'b1        //8
assign pwr_good = pwr_on & pwr_stable;                           //9
initial begin                                                    //10
i = 123.456;       // There must be a digit on either side       //11
r = 123456e-3;     // of the decimal point if it is present.     //12
```

```
t = 123456e-3;    // Time is rounded to 1 second by default.       //13
$display("i=%0g",i," t=%6.2f",t," r=%f",r);                        //14
#2 $display("TIME=%0d",$time," ON=",pwr_on,                        //15
   " STABLE=",pwr_stable," GOOD=",pwr_good);                       //16
$finish; end                                                       //17
endmodule                                                          //18
```

```
i=123 t=123.00 r=123.456000
TIME=2 ON=1 STABLE=1 GOOD=1
```

A **register** data type is declared using the keyword `reg` and is comparable to a variable in a programming language. On the LHS of an assignment a register data type (which we shall refer to as just `reg` from now on) is updated immediately and holds its value until changed again. The default initial value for a `reg` is `'x'`. We can transfer information directly from a `wire` to a `reg` as shown in the following code:

```
module declarations_2;                                             //1
reg Q, Clk; wire D;                                                //2
// drive the wire (D)                                              //3
assign D = 1;                                                      //4
// at +ve clock edge assign the value of wire D to the reg Q:      //5
always @(posedge Clk) Q = D;                                       //6
initial Clk = 0; always #10 Clk = ~ Clk;                           //7
initial begin #50; $finish; end                                    //8
always begin                                                       //9
$display("T=%2g", $time," D=",D," Clk=",Clk," Q=",Q); #10; end     //10
endmodule                                                          //11
```

```
T= 0 D=z Clk=0 Q=x
T=10 D=1 Clk=1 Q=x
T=20 D=1 Clk=0 Q=1
T=30 D=1 Clk=1 Q=1
T=40 D=1 Clk=0 Q=1
```

We shall discuss assignment statements in Section 11.5. For now, it is important to recognize that a `reg` is not always equivalent to a hardware register, flip-flop, or latch. For example, the following code describes purely combinational logic:

```
module declarations_3;                                             //1
reg a,b,c,d,e;                                                     //2
initial begin                                                      //3
   #10; a = 0;b = 0;c = 0;d = 0; #10; a = 0;b = 1;c = 1;d = 0;     //4
   #10; a = 0;b = 0;c = 1;d = 1; #10; $stop;                       //5
end                                                                //6
always begin                                                       //7
   @(a or b or c or d) e = (a|b)&(c|d);                            //8
   $display("T=%0g",$time," e=",e);                                //9
end                                                                //10
endmodule                                                          //11
```

```
T=10 e=0
```

```
T=20 e=1
T=30 e=0
```

A single-bit `wire` or `reg` is a **scalar** (the default). We may also declare a `wire` or `reg` as a **vector** with a **range** of bits [Verilog LRM 3.3]. In some situations we may use implicit declaration for a scalar `wire`; it is the only data type we do not always need to declare. We must use explicit declaration for a vector `wire` or any `reg`. We may access (or **expand**) the range of bits in a vector one at a time, using a **bit-select**, or as a contiguous subgroup of bits (a continuous sequence of numbers— like a straight in poker) using a **part-select** [Verilog LRM 4.2]. The following code shows some examples:

```
module declarations_4;                                          //1
wire Data;                    // a scalar net of type wire       //2
wire [31:0] ABus, DBus;       // two 32-bit-wide vector wires:   //3
// DBus[31] = leftmost = most-significant bit = msb              //4
// DBus[0] = rightmost = least-significant bit = lsb             //5
// Notice the size declaration precedes the names               //6
// wire [31:0] TheBus, [15:0] BigBus; // illegal                 //7
reg [3:0] vector;             // a 4-bit vector register         //8
reg [4:7] nibble;             // msb index < lsb index           //9
integer i;                                                       //10
initial begin                                                    //11
i = 1;                                                           //12
vector = 'b1010;              // vector without an index         //13
nibble = vector;              // this is OK too                  //14
#1; $display("T=%0g",$time," vector=", vector," nibble=", nibble); //15
#2; $display("T=%0g",$time," Bus=%b",DBus[15:0]);                //16
end                                                             //17
assign DBus [1] = 1;          // this is a bit-select            //18
assign DBus [3:0] = 'b1111;   // this is a part-select           //19
// assign DBus [0:3] = 'b1111;   // illegal : wrong direction    //20
endmodule                                                        //21
```

```
T=1 vector=10 nibble=10
T=3 Bus=zzzzzzzzzzzz1111
```

There are no multidimensional arrays in Verilog, but we may declare a **memory** data type as an **array** of registers [Verilog LRM 3.8]:

```
module declarations_5;                                          //1
reg [31:0] VideoRam [7:0]; // a 8-word by 32-bit wide memory     //2
initial begin                                                    //3
VideoRam[1] = 'bxz; // must specify an index for a memory        //4
VideoRam[2] = 1;                                                 //5
VideoRam[7] = VideoRam[VideoRam[2]]; // need 2 clock cycles for this //6
VideoRam[8] = 1; // careful! the compiler won't complain!        //7
// Verify what we entered:                                       //8
```

```
$display("VideoRam[0] is %b",VideoRam[0]);                         //9
$display("VideoRam[1] is %b",VideoRam[1]);                         //10
$display("VideoRam[2] is %b",VideoRam[2]);                         //11
$display("VideoRam[7] is %b",VideoRam[7]);                         //12
end                                                                //13
endmodule                                                          //14

VideoRam[0] is xxxxxxxxxxxxxxxxxxxxxxxxxxxxxxxx
VideoRam[1] is xxxxxxxxxxxxxxxxxxxxxxxxxxxxxxxz
VideoRam[2] is 00000000000000000000000000000001
VideoRam[7] is xxxxxxxxxxxxxxxxxxxxxxxxxxxxxxxz
```

We may also declare an **integer array** or **time array** in the same way as an array of reg, but there are no real arrays [Verilog LRM 3.9]:

```
module declarations_6;                                             //1
integer Number [1:100];     // Notice that size follows name       //2
time Time_Log [1:1000];     // - as in array of reg                //3
// real Illegal [1:10];     // ***no real arrays***                //4
endmodule                                                          //5
```

11.2.3   Other Wire Types

There are the following other Verilog wire types (rarely used in ASIC design) [Verilog LRM 3.7.2]:

- wand, wor, triand, and trior model wired logic. Wiring, or dotting, the outputs of two gates generates a logic function (in emitter-coupled logic, ECL, or in an EPROM, for example). This is one area in which the logic values 'z' and 'x' are treated differently.

- tri0 and tri1 model resistive connections to VSS or VDD.

- trireg is like a wire but associates some capacitance with the net, so it can model charge storage.

There are also other keywords that may appear in declarations:

- scalared and vectored are properties of vectors [Verilog LRM 3.3.2].

- small, medium, and large model the charge strength of trireg connections [Verilog LRM 7].

11.2.4   Numbers

Constant numbers are integer or real constants [Verilog LRM 2.5]. **Integer constant**s are written as

$$width'radix\ value$$

where width and radix are optional. The **radix** (or base) indicates the type of number: **decimal** (d or D), **hex** (h or H), **octal** (o or O), or **binary** (b or B). A number may be **sized** or **unsized**. The length of an unsized number is implementation dependent.

We can use '1' and '0' as numbers since they cannot be identifiers, but we must write 1'bx and 1'bz for 'x' and 'z'. A number may be declared as a **parameter** [Verilog LRM 3.10]. A parameter assignment belongs inside a module declaration and has **local scope**. **Real constants** are written using decimal (100.0) or scientific notation (1e2) and follow IEEE Std 754-1985 for double-precision floating-point numbers. Reals are rounded to the nearest integer, ties (numbers that end in .5) round away from zero [Verilog LRM 3.9.2], but not all implementations follow this rule (the output from the following code is from VeriWell, which rounds ties toward zero for negative integers).

```
module constants;                                                //1
parameter H12_UNSIZED = 'h 12;      // unsized hex 12 = decimal 18  //2
parameter H12_SIZED = 6'h 12;       // sized hex 12 = decimal 18    //3
// Notice that a space between base and value is OK               //4
/* '' (single apostrophes) are not the same as the ' character */ //5
parameter D42 = 8'B0010_1010;        // bin 101010 = dec 42         //6
// ...we can use underscores to increase readability.             //7
parameter D123 = 123;               // unsized decimal (default)   //8
parameter D63 = 8'o 77;             // sized octal, decimal 63     //9
// parameter ILLEGAL = 1'o9;        // no 9's in octal numbers!    //10
/* A = 'hx and B = 'ox assume a 32 bit width */                  //11
parameter A = 'h x, B = 'o x, C = 8'b x, D = 'h z, E = 16'h ????; //12
// ...we can use ? instead of z, same as E = 16'h zzzz            //13
// ...note automatic extension to 16 bits                         //14
reg [3:0] B0011,Bxxx1,Bzzz1; real R1,R2,R3; integer I1,I3,I_3;    //15
parameter BXZ = 8'b1x0x1z0z;                                      //16
initial begin                                                     //17
B0011 = 4'b11; Bxxx1 = 4'bx1; Bzzz1 = 4'bz1;    // left padded    //18
R1 = 0.1e1; R2 = 2.0; R3 = 30E-01;       // real numbers          //19
I1 = 1.1; I3 = 2.5; I_3 = -2.5;          // IEEE rounds away from 0 //20
end                                                               //21
initial begin #1;                                                 //22
$display                                                          //23
("H12_UNSIZED, H12_SIZED (hex) = %h, %h",H12_UNSIZED, H12_SIZED); //24
$display("D42 (bin) = %b",D42," (dec) = %d",D42);                 //25
$display("D123 (hex) = %h",D123," (dec) = %d",D123);             //26
$display("D63 (oct) = %o",D63);                                   //27
$display("A (hex) = %h",A," B (hex) = %h",B);                     //28
$display("C (hex) = %h",C," D (hex) = %h",D," E (hex) = %h",E);   //29
$display("BXZ (bin) = %b",BXZ," (hex) = %h",BXZ);                 //30
$display("B0011, Bxxx1, Bzzz1 (bin) = %b, %b, %b",B0011,Bxxx1,Bzzz1);//31
$display("R1, R2, R3 (e, f, g) = %e, %f, %g", R1, R2, R3);        //32
$display("I1, I3, I_3 (d) = %d, %d, %d", I1, I3, I_3);            //33
end                                                               //34
endmodule                                                         //35

H12_UNSIZED, H12_SIZED (hex) = 00000012, 12
D42 (bin) = 00101010 (dec) =   42
D123 (hex) = 0000007b (dec) =            123
```

```
D63 (oct) = 077
A (hex) = xxxxxxxx B (hex) = xxxxxxxx
C (hex) = xx D (hex) = zzzzzzzz E (hex) = zzzz
BXZ (bin) = 1x0x1z0z (hex) = XZ
B0011, Bxxx1, Bzzz1 (bin) = 0011, xxx1, zzz1
R1, R2, R3 (e, f, g) = 1.000000e+00, 2.000000, 3
I1, I3, I_3 (d) =              1,           3,          -2
```

11.2.5   Negative Numbers

Integer numbers are **signed** (two's complement) or **unsigned**. The following
example illustrates the handling of negative constants [Verilog LRM 3.2.2, 4.1.3]:

```
module negative_numbers;                                           //1
parameter PA = -12, PB = -'d12, PC = -32'd12, PD = -4'd12;         //2
integer IA , IB , IC , ID ; reg [31:0] RA , RB , RC , RD ;         //3
initial begin #1;                                                  //4
IA = -12; IB = -'d12; IC = -32'd12; ID = -4'd12;                   //5
RA = -12; RB = -'d12; RC = -32'd12; RD = -4'd12; #1;               //6
$display("           parameter   integer   reg[31:0]");            //7
$display ("-12      =",PA,IA,,,RA);                                //8
$displayh("             ",,,,PA,,,,IA,,,,,RA);                     //9
$display ("-'d12    =",,PB,IB,,,RB);                               //10
$displayh("             ",,,,PB,,,,IB,,,,,RB);                     //11
$display ("-32'd12 =",,PC,IC,,,RC);                                //12
$displayh("             ",,,,PC,,,,IC,,,,,RC);                     //13
$display ("-4'd12  =",,,,,,,,,,PD,ID,,,RD);                        //14
$displayh("             ",,,,,,,,,,PD,,,,ID,,,,,RD);               //15
end                                                                //16
endmodule                                                          //17
```

```
            parameter    integer    reg[31:0]
-12      =        -12         -12   4294967284
             ffffffff4    ffffffff4    ffffffff4
-'d12    = 4294967284         -12   4294967284
             ffffffff4    ffffffff4    ffffffff4
-32'd12  = 4294967284         -12   4294967284
             ffffffff4    ffffffff4    ffffffff4
-4'd12   =          4         -12   4294967284
                     4    ffffffff4    ffffffff4
```

Verilog only "keeps track" of the sign of a negative constant if it is (1) assigned
to an integer or (2) assigned to a parameter without using a base (essentially the
same thing). In other cases (even though the bit representations may be identical to
the signed number—hex ffffffff4 in the previous example), a negative constant is
treated as an unsigned number. Once Verilog "loses" the sign, keeping track of
signed numbers becomes your responsibility.

11.2.6   Strings

The code listings in this book use `Courier` font. The ISO/ANSI standard for the ASCII code defines the characters, but not the appearance of the graphic symbol in any particular font. The confusing characters are the quote and accent characters:

```
module characters; /*                                          //1
" is ASCII 34 (hex 22), double quote                           //2
' is ASCII 39 (hex 27), tick or apostrophe                     //3
/ is ASCII 47 (hex 2F), forward slash                          //4
\ is ASCII 92 (hex 5C), back slash                             //5
` is ASCII 96 (hex 60), accent grave                           //6
| is ASCII 124 (hex 7C), vertical bar                          //7
no standards for the graphic symbols for codes above 128...    //8
´ is 171 (hex AB), accent acute in almost all fonts            //9
" is 210 (hex D2), open  double quote, like 66 (some fonts)    //10
" is 211 (hex D3), close double quote, like 99 (some fonts)    //11
' is 212 (hex D4), open  single quote, like  6 (some fonts)    //12
' is 213 (hex D5), close single quote, like  9 (some fonts)    //13
*/ endmodule                                                   //14
```

Here is an example showing the use of **string constants** [Verilog LRM 2.6]:

```
module text;                                                   //1
parameter A_String = "abc"; // string constant, must be on one line //2
parameter Say = "Say \"Hey!\"";                                //3
// use escape quote \" for an embedded quote                   //4
parameter Tab = "\t";              // tab character            //5
parameter NewLine = "\n";          // newline character        //6
parameter BackSlash = "\\";        // back slash               //7
parameter Tick = "\047";           // ASCII code for tick in octal //8
// parameter Illegal = "\500";     // illegal - no such ASCII code //9
initial begin                                                  //10
$display("A_String(str) = %s ",A_String," (hex) = %h ",A_String); //11
$display("Say = %s ",Say," Say \"Hey!\"");                     //12
$display("NewLine(str) = %s ",NewLine," (hex) = %h ",NewLine); //13
$display("\(str) = %s ",BackSlash," (hex) = %h ",BackSlash);   //14
$display("Tab(str) = %s ",Tab," (hex) = %h ",Tab,"1 newline..."); //15
$display("\n");                                                //16
$display("Tick(str) = %s ",Tick," (hex) = %h ",Tick);         //17
#1.23; $display("Time is %t", $time);                          //18
end                                                            //19
endmodule                                                      //20
```

```
A_String(str) = abc  (hex) = 616263
Say = Say \"Hey!\"  Say "Hey!"
NewLine(str) = \n  (hex) = 0a
(str) = \\  (hex) = 5c
```

```
Tab(str) = \t   (hex) = 09 1 newline...


Tick(str) = '   (hex) = 27
Time is                        1
```

Instead of parameters you may use a **define directive** that is a **compiler directive**, and not a statement [Verilog LRM 16]. The define directive has **global scope**:

```
module define;                                                          //1
`define G_BUSWIDTH 32 // bus width parameter (G_ for global)            //2
/* Note: there is no semicolon at end of a compiler directive. The
character ` is ASCII 96 (hex 60), accent grave, it slopes down from
left to right. It is not the tick or apostrophe character ' (ASCII 39
or hex 27)*/                                                            //3
wire [`G_BUSWIDTH:0]MyBus; // 32-bit bus                                //4
endmodule                                                              //5
```

11.3   Operators

An expression uses any of the three types of operators: unary operators, binary operators, and a single ternary operator [Verilog LRM 4.1]. The Verilog operators are similar to those in the C programming language—except there is no autoincrement (++) or autodecrement (--) in Verilog. Table 11.1 shows the operators in their (increasing) order of precedence and Table 11.2 shows the unary operators. Here is an example that illustrates the use of the Verilog operators:

```
module operators;                                                       //1
parameter A10xz = {1'b1,1'b0,1'bx,1'bz};    // concatenation            //2
parameter A01010101 = {4{2'b01}};           // replication              //3
// arithmetic operators: +, -, *, /, and modulus %                      //4
parameter A1 = (3+2) %2; // result of % takes sign of argument #1       //5
// logical shift operators: << (left), >> (right)                       //6
parameter A2 = 4 >> 1; parameter A4 = 1 << 2;    // zero fill           //7
// relational operators: <, <=, >, >=                                   //8
initial if (1 > 2) $stop;                                               //9
// logical operators: ! (negation), && (and), || (or)                  //10
parameter B0 = !12; parameter B1 = 1 && 2;                             //11
reg [2:0] A00x; initial begin A00x = 'b111; A00x = !2'bx1; end         //12
parameter C1 = 1 || (1/0); /* this may or may not cause an             //13
error: the short-circuit behavior of && and || is undefined. An       //14
evaluation including && or || may stop when an expression is known     //15
to be true or false */                                                 //16
// == (logical equality), != (logical inequality)                      //17
```

TABLE 11.1 Verilog operators (in increasing order of precedence).

?: (conditional) a ternary operator, a special form of <expression>

|| (logical or)

&& (logical and)

| (bitwise or) ~| (bitwise nor)

^ (bitwise xor) ^~ ~^ (bitwise xnor, equivalence)

& (bitwise and) ~& (bitwise nand)

== (logical equality) != (logical inequality) === (case equality) !== (case inequality)

< (less than) <= (less than or equal) > (greater than) >= (greater than or equal)

<< (shift left) >> (shift right)

+ (addition) - (subtraction)

* (multiply) / (divide) % (modulus)

Unary operators: ! ~ & ~& | ~| ^ ~^ ^~ + -

TABLE 11.2 Verilog unary operators.

Operator	Name	Examples
!	logical negation	!123 is 'b0
~	bitwise unary negation	~1'b10xz is 1'b01xx
&	unary reduction and	& 4'b1111 is 1'b1, & 2'bx1 is 1'bx, & 2'bz1 is 1'bx
~&	unary reduction nand	~& 4'b1111 is 1'b0, ~& 2'bx1 is 1'bx
		unary reduction or	
~|	unary reduction nor	
^	unary reduction xor	
~^ ^~	unary reduction xnor	
+	unary plus	+2'bxz is +2'bxz
-	unary minus	-2'bxz is x

```
parameter Ax = (1==1'bx); parameter Bx = (1'bx!=1'bz);        //18
parameter D0 = (1==0); parameter D1 = (1==1);                 //19
// === case equality, !== (case inequality)                   //20
// case operators only return true or false                   //21
parameter E0 = (1===1'bx); parameter E1 = 4'b01xz === 4'b01xz; //22
parameter F1 = (4'bxxxx === 4'bxxxx);                         //23
```

```
// bitwise logical:                                          //24
// ~ (negation), & (and), | (inclusive or),                 //25
// ^ (exclusive or), ~^ or ^~ (equivalence)                 //26
parameter A00 = 2'b01 & 2'b10;                              //27
// unary logical reduction:                                 //28
// & (and), ~& (nand), | (or), ~| (nor),                    //29
// ^ (xor), ~^ or ^~ (xnor)                                 //30
parameter G1= & 4'b1111;                                    //31
// conditional expression  x = a ? b : c                    //32
// if (a) then x = b else x = c                             //33
reg H0, a, b, c; initial begin a=1; b=0; c=1; H0=a?b:c; end //34
reg[2:0] J01x, Jxxx, J01z, J011;                            //35
initial begin Jxxx = 3'bxxx; J01z = 3'b01z; J011 = 3'b011;  //36
J01x = Jxxx ? J01z : J011; end     // bitwise result        //37
initial begin #1;                                           //38
$display("A10xz=%b",A10xz,"   A01010101=%b",A01010101);     //39
$display("A1=%0d",A1,"   A2=%0d",A2,"   A4=%0d",A4);        //40
$display("B1=%b",B1,"   B0=%b",B0,"   A00x=%b",A00x);       //41
$display("C1=%b",C1,"   Ax=%b",Ax,"   Bx=%b",Bx);          //42
$display("D0=%b",D0,"   D1=%b",D1);                        //43
$display("E0=%b",E0,"   E1=%b",E1,"   F1=%b",F1);          //44
$display("A00=%b",A00,"   G1=%b",G1,"   H0=%b",H0);        //45
$display("J01x=%b",J01x); end                              //46
endmodule                                                   //47
```

```
A10xz=10xz   A01010101=01010101
A1=1   A2=2   A4=4
B1=1   B0=0   A00x=00x
C1=1   Ax=x   Bx=x
D0=0   D1=1
E0=0   E1=1   F1=1
A00=00   G1=1   H0=0
J01x=01x
```

11.3.1   Arithmetic

Arithmetic operations on n-bit objects are performed modulo 2^n in Verilog,

```
module modulo; reg [2:0] Seven;                             //1
initial begin                                               //2
#1 Seven = 7; #1 $display("Before=", Seven);               //3
#1 Seven = Seven + 1; #1 $display("After =", Seven);        //4
end                                                         //5
endmodule                                                   //6
```

```
Before=7
After =0
```

Arithmetic operations in Verilog (addition, subtraction, comparison, and so on) on vectors (reg or wire) are predefined. This is a very important difference for ASIC designers from the situation in VHDL.

There are some subtleties with Verilog arithmetic and negative numbers that are illustrated by the following example (based on an example in the LRM):

```
module LRM_arithmetic;                                              //1
integer IA, IB, IC, ID, IE; reg [15:0] RA, RB, RC;                 //2
initial begin                                                      //3
IA = -4'd12;              RA =  IA / 3;                             //4
RB = -4'd12;             IB =  RB / 3;                              //5
IC = -4'd12 / 3;         RC = -12 / 3;                             //6
ID =    -12 / 3;         IE =  IA / 3;                             //7
end                                                                //8
initial begin #1;                                                  //9
$display("                      hex     default");                //10
$display("IA = -4'd12       = %h%d",IA,IA);                       //11
$display("RA = IA / 3       =    %h     %d",RA,RA);               //12
$display("RB = -4'd12       =    %h     %d",RB,RB);               //13
$display("IB = RB / 3       = %h%d",IB,IB);                       //14
$display("IC = -4'd12 / 3 = %h%d",IC,IC);                         //15
$display("RC = -12 / 3      =    %h     %d",RC,RC);               //16
$display("ID = -12 / 3      = %h%d",ID,ID);                       //17
$display("IE =  IA / 3      = %h%d",IE,IE);                       //18
end                                                                //19
endmodule                                                          //20
```

```
                    hex     default
IA = -4'd12       = fffffff4      -12
RA = IA / 3       =     fffc    65532
RB = -4'd12       =     fff4    65524
IB = RB / 3       = 00005551    21841
IC = -4'd12 / 3 = 55555551 1431655761
RC = -12 / 3      =     fffc    65532
ID = -12 / 3      = fffffffc       -4
IE =  IA / 3      = fffffffc       -4
```

We might expect the results of all these divisions to be $-4 = -12/3$. For integer assignments, the results are correctly signed (ID and IE). Hex fffc (decimal 65532) is the 16-bit two's complement of -4, so RA and RC are also correct if we keep track of the signs ourselves. The integer result IB is incorrect because Verilog treats RB as an unsigned number. Verilog also treats -4'd12 as an unsigned number in the calculation of IC. Once Verilog "loses" a sign, it cannot get it back.

11.4 Hierarchy

The **module** is the basic unit of code in the Verilog language [Verilog LRM 12.1],

```
module holiday_1(sat, sun, weekend);                              //1
   input sat, sun; output weekend;                                //2
   assign weekend = sat | sun;                                    //3
endmodule                                                         //4
```

We do not have to explicitly declare the scalar wires: saturday, sunday, weekend because, since these wires appear in the module interface, they must be declared in an input, output, or inout statement and are thus implicitly declared. The **module interface** provides the means to interconnect two Verilog modules using **ports** [Verilog LRM 12.3]. Each port must be explicitly declared as one of **input**, **output**, or **inout**. Table 11.3 shows the characteristics of ports. Notice that a reg cannot be an input port or an inout port. This is to stop us trying to connect a reg to another reg that may hold a different value.

TABLE 11.3 Verilog ports.

Verilog port	input	output	inout
Characteristics	wire (or other net)	reg or wire (or other net) We *can* read an output port inside a module	wire (or other net)

Within a module we may **instantiate** other modules, but we cannot declare other modules. Ports are linked using **named association** or **positional association**,

```
`timescale 100s/1s // units are 100 seconds with precision of 1s   //1
module life; wire [3:0] n; integer days;                            //2
   wire wake_7am, wake_8am; // wake at 7 on weekdays else at 8      //3
   assign n = 1 + (days % 7); // n is day of the week (1-6)         //4
always@(wake_8am or wake_7am)                                       //5
   $display("Day=",n," hours=%0d ",($time/36)%24,"  8am = ",        //6
     wake_8am,"  7am = ",wake_7am,"  m2.weekday = ", m2.weekday);   //7
   initial days = 0;                                                //8
   initial begin #(24*36*10);$finish; end // run for 10 days        //9
   always #(24*36) days = days + 1; // bump day every 24hrs        //10
   rest m1(n, wake_8am); // module instantiation                   //11
// creates a copy of module rest with instance name m1             //12
// ports are linked using positional notation                      //13
   work m2(.weekday(wake_7am), .day(n));                           //14
// creates a copy of module work with instance name m2             //15
```

```
// ports are linked using named association              //16
endmodule                                                //17

module rest(day, weekend); // module definition           //1
// notice the port names are different from the parent    //2
   input [3:0] day; output weekend; reg weekend;          //3
   always begin #36 weekend = day > 5; end // need delay  //4
endmodule                                                 //5

module work(day, weekday);                                //1
   input [3:0] day; output weekday; reg weekday;          //2
   always begin #36 weekday = day < 6; end // need delay  //3
endmodule                                                 //4

Day= 1 hours=0   8am = 0   7am = 0   m2.weekday = 0
Day= 1 hours=1   8am = 0   7am = 1   m2.weekday = 1
Day= 6 hours=1   8am = 1   7am = 0   m2.weekday = 0
Day= 1 hours=1   8am = 0   7am = 1   m2.weekday = 1
```

The port names in a module definition and the port names in the parent module may be different. We can **associate** (link or map) ports using the same order in the instantiating statement as we use in the module definition—such as instance m1 in module life. Alternatively we can associate the ports by naming them—such as instance m2 in module life (using a period '.' before the port name that we declared in the module definition). Identifiers in a module have local scope. If we want to refer to an identifier outside a module, we use a **hierarchical name** such as m1.weekend or m2.weekday (as in module life), for example. The compiler will first search downward (or inward) then upward (outward) to resolve a hierarchical name [Verilog LRM 12.4].

11.5 Procedures and Assignments

A Verilog **procedure** [Verilog LRM 9.9] is an always or initial statement, a task, or a function. The statements within a sequential block (statements that appear between a begin and an end) that is part of a procedure execute sequentially in the order in which they appear, but the procedure executes concurrently with other procedures. This is a fundamental difference from computer programming languages. Think of each procedure as a microprocessor running on its own and at the same time as all the other microprocessors (procedures). Before I discuss procedures in more detail, I shall discuss the two different types of assignment statements:

- *continuous assignments* that appear outside procedures
- *procedural assignments* that appear inside procedures

To illustrate the difference between these two types of assignments, consider again the example used in Section 11.4:

```
module holiday_1(sat, sun, weekend);                                  //1
   input sat, sun; output weekend;                                    //2
   assign weekend = sat | sun; // outside a procedure                 //3
endmodule                                                             //4
```

We can change `weekend` to a `reg` instead of a `wire`, but then we must declare weekend and use a procedural assignment (inside a procedure—an `always` statement, for example) instead of a continuous assignment. We also need to add some delay (one time tick in the example that follows); otherwise the computer will never be able to get out of the `always` procedure to execute any other procedures:

```
module holiday_2(sat, sun, weekend);                                 //1
   input sat, sun; output weekend; reg weekend;                      //2
   always #1 weekend = sat | sun; // inside a procedure              //3
endmodule                                                            //4
```

We shall cover the continuous assignment statement in the next section, which is followed by an explanation of sequential blocks and procedural assignment statements. Here is some skeleton code that illustrates where we may use these assignment statements:

```
module assignments                                                   //1
//... continuous assignments...                                      //2
always // beginning of a procedure                                   //3
   begin // beginning of sequential block                            //4
   //... procedural assignments...                                   //5
   end                                                               //6
endmodule                                                            //7
```

Table 11.4 at the end of Section 11.6 summarizes assignment statements, including two more forms of assignment—you may want to look at this table now.

11.5.1   Continuous Assignment Statement

A **continuous assignment statement** [Verilog LRM 6.1] assigns a value to a wire in a similar way that a real logic gate drives a real wire,

```
module assignment_1();                                               //1
wire pwr_good,pwr_on,pwr_stable; reg Ok,Fire;                        //2
assign pwr_stable = Ok & (!Fire);                                    //3
assign pwr_on = 1;                                                   //4
assign pwr_good = pwr_on & pwr_stable;                               //5
initial begin Ok = 0;Fire = 0; #1 Ok = 1; #5 Fire = 1;end           //6
initial begin $monitor("TIME=%0d",$time," ON=",pwr_on, " STABLE=",  //7
     pwr_stable," OK=",Ok," FIRE=",Fire," GOOD=",pwr_good);         //8
```

```
          #10 $finish; end                                       //9
endmodule                                                        //10
```

```
TIME=0 ON=1 STABLE=0 OK=0 FIRE=0 GOOD=0
TIME=1 ON=1 STABLE=1 OK=1 FIRE=0 GOOD=1
TIME=6 ON=1 STABLE=0 OK=1 FIRE=1 GOOD=0
```

The assignment statement in this next example models a three-state bus:

```
module assignment_2; reg Enable; wire [31:0] Data;             //1
/* the following single statement is equivalent to a declaration and
continuous assignment */                                        //2
wire [31:0] DataBus = Enable ? Data : 32'bz;                    //3
assign Data = 32'b10101101101011101111000010100001;            //4
   initial begin                                                //5
      $monitor("Enable=%b DataBus=%b ", Enable, DataBus);       //6
      Enable = 0; #1; Enable = 1; #1; end                       //7
endmodule                                                       //8
```

```
Enable = 0 DataBus =zzzzzzzzzzzzzzzzzzzzzzzzzzzzzzzz
Enable = 1 DataBus =10101101101011101111000010100001
```

11.5.2   Sequential Block

A **sequential block** [Verilog LRM 9.8] is a group of statements between a **begin** and an **end**. We may declare new variables within a sequential block, but then we must name the block. A sequential block is considered a statement, so that we may nest sequential blocks.

A sequential block may appear in an **always statement**, in which case the block executes repeatedly. In contrast, an **initial statement** executes only once, so a sequential block within an initial statement only executes once—at the beginning of a simulation. It does not matter where the initial statement appears—it still execute first. Here is an example:

```
module always_1; reg Y, Clk;                                    //1
always // statements in an always statement execute repeatedly: //2
begin: my_block               // start of sequential block       //3
   @(posedge Clk) #5 Y = 1;   // at +ve edge set Y=1             //4
   @(posedge Clk) #5 Y = 0;   // at the NEXT +ve edge set Y=0    //5
end                           // end of sequential block         //6
always #10 Clk = ~ Clk;       // We need a clock.                //7
initial Y = 0;                // These initial statements execute //8
initial Clk = 0;              // only once, but first.           //9
initial $monitor("T=%2g",$time,"  Clk=",Clk,"  Y=",Y);          //10
initial #70 $finish;                                            //11
endmodule                                                       //12
```

```
T= 0  Clk=0  Y=0
T=10  Clk=1  Y=0
T=15  Clk=1  Y=1
```

```
T=20   Clk=0   Y=1
T=30   Clk=1   Y=1
T=35   Clk=1   Y=0
T=40   Clk=0   Y=0
T=50   Clk=1   Y=0
T=55   Clk=1   Y=1
T=60   Clk=0   Y=1
```

11.5.3   Procedural Assignments

A **procedural assignment** [Verilog LRM 9.2] is similar to an assignment statement in a computer programming language such as C. In Verilog the value of an expression on the RHS of an assignment within a procedure (a procedural assignment) updates a `reg` (or memory element) on the LHS. In the absence of any *timing controls* (see in Section 11.6), the `reg` is updated immediately when the statement executes. The `reg` holds its value until changed by another procedural assignment. Here is the BNF definition:

```
blocking_assignment ::= reg-lvalue = [delay_or_event_control] expression
```

(Notice this BNF definition is for a *blocking* assignment—a type of procedural assignment—see Section 11.6.4.) Here is an example of a procedural assignment (notice that a `wire` can only appear on the RHS of a procedural assignment):

```
module procedural_assign; reg Y, A;                                      //1
always @(A)                                                              //2
  Y = A; // procedural assignment                                       //3
initial begin A=0; #5; A=1; #5; A=0; #5; $finish; end                   //4
initial $monitor("T=%2g",$time,,"A=",A,,,"Y=",Y);                       //5
endmodule                                                               //6
```

```
T= 0 A=0   Y=0
T= 5 A=1   Y=1
T=10 A=0   Y=0
```

11.6   Timing Controls and Delay

The statements within a sequential block are executed in order, but, in the absence of any delay, they all execute at the same simulation time—the current **time step**. In reality there are delays that are modeled using a timing control.

11.6.1   Timing Control

A **timing control** is either a delay control or an event control [Verilog LRM 9.7]. A **delay control** delays an assignment by a specified amount of time. A **timescale com-**

piler directive is used to specify the units of time followed by the precision used to calculate time expressions,

```
`timescale 1ns/10ps // time units are ns, round times to 10 ps
```

Time units may only be s, ns, ps, or fs and the multiplier must be 1, 10, or 100. We can delay an assignment in two different ways:

- Sample the RHS immediately and then delay the assignment to the LHS.
- Wait for a specified time and then assign the value of the LHS to the RHS.

Here is an example of the first alternative (an **intra-assignment delay**):

```
x = #1 y;        // intra-assignment
```

The second alternative is **delayed assignment**:

```
#1 x = y;        // delayed assignment
```

These two alternatives are not the same. The intra-assignment delay is equivalent to the following code:

```
begin            // Equivalent to intra-assignment delay.
  hold = y;      // Sample and hold y immediately.
  #1;            // Delay.
  x = hold;      // Assignment to x. Overall same as x = #1 y.
end
```

In contrast, the delayed assignment is equivalent to a delay followed by an assignment as follows:

```
begin            // Equivalent to delayed assignment.
  #1;            // Delay
  x = y;         // Assign y to x. Overall same as #1 x = y
end
```

The other type of timing control, an **event control**, delays an assignment until a specified event occurs. Here is the formal definition:

```
event_control ::= @ event_identifier 1 @ (event_expression)
```

```
event_expression ::= expression | event_identifier
  | posedge expression | negedge expression
  | event_expression or event_expression
```

(Notice there are two different uses of 'or' in this simplified BNF definition—the last one, in bold, is part of the Verilog language, a keyword.) A positive edge (denoted by the keyword posedge) is a transition from '0' to '1' or 'x', or a transition from 'x' to '1'. A negative edge (negedge) is a transition from '1' to '0' or 'x', or a transition from 'x' to '0'. Transitions to or from 'z' do not count. Here are examples of event controls:

```
module delay_controls; reg X,Y,Clk,Dummy;                          //1
always #1 Dummy=!Dummy; // dummy clock, just for graphics          //2
// examples of delay controls:                                     //3
always begin #25 X=1;#10 X=0;#5; end                               //4
// an event control:                                               //5
always @(posedge Clk) Y=X; // wait for +ve clock edge              //6
always #10 Clk = !Clk; // the real clock                           //7
initial begin Clk = 0;                                             //8
  $display("T   Clk X Y");                                         //9
  $monitor("%2g",$time,,,Clk,,,,X,,Y);                             //10
  $dumpvars;#100 $finish; end                                      //11
endmodule                                                          //12
```

```
T    Clk X Y
 0    0   x x
10    1   x x
20    0   x x
25    0   1 x
30    1   1 1
35    1   0 1
40    0   0 1
50    1   0 0
60    0   0 0
65    0   1 0
70    1   1 1
75    1   0 1
80    0   0 1
90    1   0 0
```

The dummy clock in `delay_controls` helps in the graphical waveform display of the results (it provides a one-time-tick timing grid when we zoom in, for example). Figure 11.1 shows the graphical output from the Waves viewer in VeriWell (white is used to represent the initial unknown values). The assignment statements to 'X' in the always statement repeat (every 25 + 10 + 5 = 40 time ticks).

FIGURE 11.1 Output from the module delay_controls.

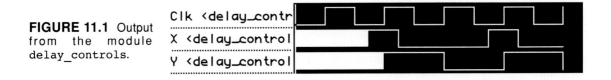

Events can be declared (as **named events**), triggered, and detected as follows:

```
module show_event;                                              //1
reg clock;                                                      //2
event event_1, event_2; // declare two named events            //3
always @(posedge clock) -> event_1; // trigger event_1         //4
always @ event_1                                               //5
begin $display("Strike 1!!"); -> event_2; end // trigger event_2  //6
always @ event_2 begin $display("Strike 2!!");                 //7
$finish; end // stop on detection of event_2                   //8
always #10 clock = ~ clock; // we need a clock                 //9
initial clock = 0;                                            //10
endmodule                                                     //11
```

```
Strike 1!!
Strike 2!!
```

11.6.2 Data Slip

Consider this model for a shift register and the simulation output that follows:

```
module data_slip_1 (); reg Clk,D,Q1,Q2;                        //1
/************ bad sequential logic below *************/        //2
always @(posedge Clk)  Q1 = D;                                 //3
always @(posedge Clk)  Q2 = Q1; // data slips here!            //4
/************ bad sequential logic above *************/        //5
initial begin Clk = 0; D = 1; end always #50 Clk = ~Clk;       //6
initial begin $display("t   Clk D Q1 Q2");                     //7
$monitor("%3g",$time,,Clk,,,,D,,Q1,,,Q2); end                 //8
initial #400 $finish; // run for 8 cycles                      //9
initial $dumpvars;                                            //10
endmodule                                                     //11
```

```
t   Clk D Q1 Q2
  0 0   1 x  x
 50 1   1 1  1
100 0   1 1  1
150 1   1 1  1
200 0   1 1  1
250 1   1 1  1
300 0   1 1  1
350 1   1 1  1
```

The first clock edge at `t = 50` causes `Q1` to be updated to the value of `D` at the clock edge (a '1'), and at the same time `Q2` is updated to this new value of `Q1`. The data, `D`, has passed through both `always` statements. We call this problem **data slip**.

If we include delays in the `always` statements (labeled 3 and 4) in the preceding example, like this—

```
always @(posedge Clk)  Q1 = #1 D;  // delays                          //1
always @(posedge Clk)  Q2 = #1 Q1; // fix data slip                   //2
```

—we obtain the correct output:

```
t    Clk D Q1 Q2
  0 0   1 x  x
 50 1   1 x  x
 51 1   1 1  x
100 0   1 1  x
150 1   1 1  x
151 1   1 1  1
200 0   1 1  1
250 1   1 1  1
300 0   1 1  1
350 1   1 1  1
```

11.6.3   Wait Statement

The **wait statement** suspends a procedure until a condition becomes true. There must be another concurrent procedure that alters the condition (in this case the variable `Done`—in general the condition is an expression) in the following `wait` statement; otherwise we are placed on "infinite hold":

```
wait (Done) $stop; // wait until Done = 1 then stop
```

Notice that the Verilog `wait` statement does not look for an event or a change in the condition; instead it is level-sensitive—it only cares that the condition is true.

```
module test_dff_wait;                                                 //1
reg D,Clock,Reset; dff_wait u1(D,Q,Clock,Reset);                      //2
initial begin D=1;Clock=0;Reset=1'b1;#15 Reset=1'b0;#20 D=0;end       //3
always #10 Clock = !Clock;                                            //4
initial begin $display("T  Clk D Q Reset");                           //5
   $monitor("%2g",$time,,Clock,,,,D,,Q,,Reset); #50 $finish; end      //6
endmodule                                                             //7
```

```
module dff_wait(D,Q,Clock,Reset);                                     //1
output Q; input D,Clock,Reset; reg Q; wire D;                         //2
always @(posedge Clock) if (Reset !== 1) Q=D;                         //3
always begin wait (Reset == 1) Q = 0; wait (Reset !== 1); end         //4
endmodule                                                             //5
```

```
T  Clk D Q Reset
  0 0   1 0 1
 10 1   1 0 1
 15 1   1 0 0
 20 0   1 0 0
```

```
30 1   1 1 0
35 1   0 1 0
40 0   0 1 0
```

We must include `wait` statements in module `dff_wait` above to wait for both `Reset==1` and `Reset==0`. If we were to omit the `wait` statement for `Reset==0`, as in the following code:

```
module dff_wait(D,Q,Clock,Reset);                                  //1
output Q; input D,Clock,Reset; reg Q; wire D;                      //2
always @(posedge Clock) if (Reset !== 1) Q = D;                    //3
// we need another wait statement here or we shall spin forever    //4
always begin wait (Reset == 1) Q = 0; end                          //5
endmodule                                                          //6
```

the simulator would cycle endlessly, and we would need to press the `'Stop'` button or `'CTRL-C'` to halt the simulator. Here is the console window in VeriWell:

```
Cl> .
T  Clk D Q Reset       <- at this point nothing happens, so press CTRL-C
Interrupt at time 0
Cl>
```

11.6.4 Blocking and Nonblocking Assignments

If a procedural assignment in a sequential block contains a timing control, then the execution of the following statement is delayed or **blocked**. For this reason a procedural assignment statement is also known as a **blocking procedural assignment statement** [Verilog LRM 9.2]. We covered this type of statement in Section 11.5.3. The **nonblocking procedural assignment statement** allows execution in a sequential block to continue and registers are all updated together at the end of the current time step. Both types of procedural assignment may contain timing controls. Here is an artificially complicated example that illustrates the different types of assignment:

```
module delay;                                                      //1
reg a,b,c,d,e,f,g,bds,bsd;                                         //2
initial begin                                                      //3
a = 1; b = 0;    // no delay                                       //4
#1 b = 1;        // delayed assignment                             //5
c = #1 1;        // intra-assignment delay                         //6
#1;              //                                                //7
d = 1;           //                                                //8
e <= #1 1;       // intra-assignment, nonblocking                  //9
#1 f <= 1;       // delayed nonblocking                            //10
g <= 1;          // nonblocking                                    //11
end                                                               //12
initial begin #1 bds = b; end // delay then sample (ds)           //13
initial begin bsd = #1 b; end // sample then delay (sd)           //14
initial begin $display("t a b c d e f g bds bsd");               //15
```

```
$monitor("%g",$time,,a,,b,,c,,d,,e,,f,,g,,bds,,,,bsd); end      //16
endmodule                                                       //17
```

```
t a b c d e f g bds bsd
0 1 0 x x x x x x    x
1 1 1 x x x x x 1    0
2 1 1 1 x x x x 1    0
3 1 1 1 1 x x x 1    0
4 1 1 1 1 1 1 1 1    0
```

Many synthesis tools will not allow us to use blocking and nonblocking procedural assignments to the same `reg` within the same sequential block.

11.6.5   Procedural Continuous Assignment

A **procedural continuous assignment statement** [Verilog LRM 9.3] (sometimes called a quasicontinuous assignment statement) is a special form of the `assign` statement that we use within a sequential block. For example, the following flip-flop model assigns to q depending on the clear, `clr_`, and preset, `pre_`, inputs (in general it is considered very bad form to use a trailing underscore to signify active-low signals as I have done to save space; you might use "_n" instead).

```
module dff_procedural_assign;                                         //1
reg d,clr_,pre_,clk; wire q; dff_clr_pre dff_1(q,d,clr_,pre_,clk);    //2
always #10 clk = ~clk;                                                //3
initial begin clk = 0; clr_ = 1; pre_ = 1; d = 1;                     //4
   #20; d = 0; #20; pre_ = 0; #20; pre_ = 1; #20; clr_ = 0;           //5
   #20; clr_ = 1; #20; d = 1; #20; $finish; end                       //6
initial begin                                                         //7
   $display("T  CLK PRE_ CLR_ D Q");                                  //8
   $monitor("%3g",$time,,,clk,,,,pre_,,,,clr_,,,,d,,q); end           //9
endmodule                                                             //10
```

```
module dff_clr_pre(q,d,clear_,preset_,clock);                //1
output q; input d,clear_,preset_,clock; reg q;               //2
always @(clear_ or preset_)                                  //3
   if (!clear_) assign q = 0; // active-low clear            //4
   else if(!preset_) assign q = 1; // active-low preset      //5
   else deassign q;                                          //6
always @(posedge clock) q = d;                               //7
endmodule                                                    //8
```

```
T  CLK PRE_ CLR_ D Q
 0  0   1    1   1 x
10  1   1    1   1 1
20  0   1    1   0 1
30  1   1    1   0 0
40  0   0    1   0 1
50  1   0    1   0 1
```

```
 60  0   1   1    0 1
 70  1   1   1    0 0
 80  0   1   0    0 0
 90  1   1   0    0 0
100  0   1   1    0 0
110  1   1   1    0 0
120  0   1   1    1 0
130  1   1   1    1 1
```

We have now seen all of the different forms of Verilog assignment statements. The following skeleton code shows where each type of statement belongs:

```
module all_assignments                              //1
//... continuous assignments.                       //2
always // beginning of procedure                    //3
  begin // beginning of sequential block            //4
  //... blocking procedural assignments.            //5
  //... non-blocking procedural assignments.        //6
  //... procedural continuous assignments.          //7
  end                                               //8
endmodule                                           //9
```

Table 11.4 summarizes the different types of assignments.

TABLE 11.4   Verilog assignment statements.

Type of Verilog assignment	Continuous assignment statement	Procedural assignment statement	Nonblocking procedural assignment statement	Procedural continuous assignment statement
Where it can occur	outside an `always` or `initial` statement, task, or function	inside an `always` or `initial` statement, task, or function	inside an `always` or `initial` statement, task, or function	`always` or `initial` statement, task, or function
Example	`wire [31:0]` `DataBus;` `assign DataBus` `= Enable ? Data` `:  32'bz`	`reg Y;` `always` `  @(posedge` `clock) Y = 1;`	`reg Y;` `always` `Y <= 1;`	`always @(Enable)` `if(Enable)` `assign Q = D;` `else deassign Q;`
Valid LHS of assignment	net	register or memory element	register or memory element	net
Valid RHS of assignment	<expression> net, reg or memory element	<expression> net, reg or memory element	<expression> net, reg or memory element	<expression> net, reg or memory element
Book	11.5.1	11.5.3	11.6.4	11.6.5
Verilog LRM	6.1	9.2	9.2.2	9.3

11.7   Tasks and Functions

A **task** [Verilog LRM 10.2] is a type of procedure, called from another procedure. A task has both inputs and outputs but does not return a value. A task may call other tasks and functions. A **function** [Verilog LRM 10.3] is a procedure used in any expression, has at least one input, no outputs, and returns a single value. A function may not call a task. In Section 11.5 we covered all of the different Verilog procedures except for tasks and functions. Now that we have covered timing controls, we can explain the difference between tasks and functions: Tasks may contain timing controls but functions may not. The following two statements help illustrate the difference between a function and a task:

```
Call_A_Task_And_Wait (Input1, Input2, Output);
Result_Immediate = Call_A_Function (All_Inputs);
```

Functions are useful to model combinational logic (rather like a subroutine):

```
module F_subset_decode; reg [2:0]A, B, C, D, E, F;        //1
initial begin A = 1; B = 0; D = 2; E = 3;                 //2
  C = subset_decode(A, B); F = subset_decode(D,E);        //3
  $display("A B C D E F"); $display(A,,B,,C,,D,,E,,F); end //4
function [2:0] subset_decode; input [2:0] a, b;           //5
  begin if (a <= b) subset_decode = a; else subset_decode = b; end //6
endfunction                                               //7
endmodule                                                 //8

A B C D E F
1 0 0 2 3 2
```

11.8   Control Statements

In this section we shall discuss the Verilog if, case, loop, disable, fork, and join statements that control the flow of code execution.

11.8.1   Case and If Statement

An **if statement** [Verilog LRM 9.4] represents a two-way branch. In the following example, switch has to be true to execute 'Y = 1'; otherwise 'Y = 0' is executed:

```
if(switch) Y = 1; else Y = 0;
```

The **case statement** [Verilog LRM 9.5] represents a multiway branch. A **controlling expression** is matched with **case expressions** in each of the **case items** (or arms) to determine a match,

```
module test_mux; reg a, b, select; wire out;             //1
mux mux_1(a, b, out, select);                            //2
```

```
initial begin #2; select = 0; a = 0; b = 1;                          //3
   #2; select = 1'bx; #2; select = 1'bz; #2; select = 1; end         //4
initial $monitor("T=%2g",$time,"  Select=",select,"  Out=",out);     //5
initial #10 $finish;                                                 //6
endmodule                                                            //7

module mux(a, b, mux_output, mux_select); input a, b, mux_select;    //1
output mux_output; reg mux_output;                                   //2
always begin                                                         //3
case(mux_select)                                                     //4
   0: mux_output = a;                                                //5
   1: mux_output = b;                                                //6
   default mux_output = 1'bx; // if select = x or z set output to x  //7
endcase                                                              //8
#1; // need some delay, otherwise we'll spin forever                 //9
end                                                                  //10
endmodule                                                            //11
```

```
T= 0  Select=x  Out=x
T= 2  Select=0  Out=x
T= 3  Select=0  Out=0
T= 4  Select=x  Out=0
T= 5  Select=x  Out=x
T= 6  Select=z  Out=x
T= 8  Select=1  Out=x
T= 9  Select=1  Out=1
```

Notice that the case statement must be inside a sequential block (inside an always statement). Because the case statement is inside an always statement, it needs some delay; otherwise the simulation runs forever without advancing simulation time. The **casex statement** handles both 'z' and 'x' as don't care (so that they match any bit value), the **casez statement** handles 'z' bits, and only 'z' bits, as don't care. Bits in case expressions may be set to '?' representing don't care values, as follows:

```
casex (instruction_register[31:29])
   3b'??1 : add;
   3b'?1? : subtract;
   3b'1?? : branch;
endcase
```

11.8.2   Loop Statement

A **loop statement** [Verilog LRM 9.6] is a **for**, **while**, **repeat**, or **forever** statement. Here are four examples, one for each different type of loop statement, each of which performs the same function. The comments with each type of loop statement illustrate how the controls work:

```
module loop_1;                                                       //1
integer i; reg [31:0] DataBus; initial DataBus = 0;                  //2
```

```
initial begin                                                      //3
/************** insert loop code after here ******************/
/* for(execute this <assignment> once before starting loop; exit loop
if this <expression> is false; execute this <assignment> at end of loop
before the check for end of loop) */
for(i = 0; i <= 15; i = i+1) DataBus[i] = 1;                       //4
/************** insert loop code before here ***************/
end                                                                //5
initial begin                                                      //6
$display("DataBus = %b",DataBus);                                  //7
#2; $display("DataBus = %b",DataBus); $finish;                     //8
end                                                                //9
endmodule                                                          //10
```

Here is the while statement code (to replace line 4 in module loop_1):

```
i = 0;
/* while(execute next statement while this expression is true) */
while(i <= 15) begin DataBus[i] = 1; i = i+1; end                 //4
```

Here is the repeat statement code (to replace line 4 in module loop_1):

```
i = 0;
/* repeat(execute next statement the number of times corresponding to
the evaluation of this expression at the beginning of the loop) */
repeat(16) begin DataBus[i] = 1; i = i+1; end                     //4
```

Here is the forever statement code (to replace line 4 in module loop_1):

```
i = 0;
/* forever loops continuously */
forever begin : my_loop
  DataBus[i] = 1;
  if (i == 15) #1 disable my_loop; // need to let time advance to exit
  i = i+1;
end                                                                //4
```

The output for all four forms of looping statement is the same:

```
DataBus = 00000000000000000000000000000000
DataBus = 00000000000000001111111111111111
```

11.8.3   Disable

The **disable statement** [Verilog LRM 11] stops the execution of a labeled sequential block and skips to the end of the block:

```
forever
begin: microprocessor_block // labeled sequential block
  @(posedge clock)
  if (reset) disable microprocessor_block; // skip to end of block
```

```
    else Execute_code;
end
```

Use the `disable` statement with caution in ASIC design. It is difficult to implement directly in hardware.

11.8.4 Fork and Join

The **fork statement** and **join statement** [Verilog LRM 9.8.2] allows the execution of two or more parallel threads in a **parallel block**:

```
module fork_1                                              //1
event eat_breakfast, read_paper;                           //2
initial begin                                              //3
  fork                                                     //4
  @eat_breakfast; @read_paper;                             //5
  join                                                     //6
end                                                        //7
endmodule                                                  //8
```

This is another Verilog language feature that should be used with care in ASIC design, because it is difficult to implement in hardware.

11.9 Logic-Gate Modeling

Verilog has a set of built-in logic models and you may also define your own models.

11.9.1 Built-in Logic Models

Verilog's built-in logic models are the following **primitives**:

> and, nand, nor, or, xor, xnor

You may use these primitives as you use modules. For example:

```
module primitive;                                          //1
nand (strong0, strong1) #2.2                               //2
  Nand_1(n001, n004, n005),                                //3
  Nand_2(n003, n001, n005, n002);                          //4
nand (n006, n005, n002);                                   //5
endmodule                                                  //6
```

This module models three NAND gates (Figure 11.2). The first gate (line 3) is a two-input gate named `Nand_1`; the second gate (line 4) is a three-input gate named `Nand_2`; the third gate (line 5) is unnamed. The first two gates have strong drive strengths (these are the defaults anyway) and 2.2 ns delay; the third gate takes the default values for drive strength (strong) and delay (zero). The first port of a primitive gate is always the output port. The remaining ports for a primitive gate (any number of them) are the input ports.

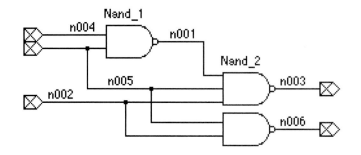

FIGURE 11.2 An example schematic (drawn with Capilano's DesignWorks) to illustrate the use of Verilog primitive gates.

Table 11.5 shows the definition of the and gate primitive (I use lowercase 'and' as the name of the Verilog primitive, rather than 'AND', since Verilog is case-sensitive). Notice that if one input to the primitive 'and' gate is zero, the output is zero, no matter what the other input is.

TABLE 11.5   Definition of the Verilog primitive 'and' gate.

'and'	0	1	x	z
0	0	0	0	0
1	0	1	x	x
x	0	x	x	x
z	0	x	x	x

11.9.2   User-Defined Primitives

We can define our own primitive gates (a **user-defined primitive** or **UDP**) using a truth-table specification. The first port of a UDP must be an output port, and this must be the only output port (we may not use vector or inout ports):

```
primitive Adder(Sum, InA, InB);                          //1
output Sum; input Ina, InB;                               //2
table                                                    //3
// inputs : output                                       //4
00 : 0;                                                  //5
01 : 1;                                                  //6
10 : 1;                                                  //7
```

```
11 : 0;                                                              //8
endtable                                                             //9
endprimitive                                                         //10
```

We may only specify the values '0', '1', and 'x' as inputs in a **UDP truth table**. Any 'z' input is treated as an 'x'. If there is no entry in a UDP truth table that exactly matches a set of inputs, the output is 'x' (unknown).

We can construct a UDP model for sequential logic by including a state in the UDP truth-table definition. The state goes between an input and an output in the table and the output then represents the next state. The following sequential UDP model also illustrates the use of shorthand notation in a UDP truth table:

```
primitive DLatch(Q, Clock, Data);                                    //1
output Q; reg Q; input Clock, Data;                                  //2
table                                                                //3
//inputs : present state : output (next state)                       //4
1 0 : ? : 0; // ? represents 0,1, or x input                         //5
1 1 : b : 1; // b represents 0 or 1 input                            //6
1 1 : x : 1; // could have combined this with previous line          //7
0 1 : ? : -; // - represents no change in an output                  //8
endtable                                                             //9
endprimitive                                                         //10
```

Be careful not to confuse the '?' in a UDP table (shorthand for '0', '1', or 'x') with the '?' in a constant that represents an extension to 'z' (Section 11.2.4) or the '?' in a case statement that represents don't care values (Section 11.8.1).

For sequential UDP models that need to detect edge transitions on inputs, there is another special truth-table notation (ab) that represents a change in logic value from a to b. For example, (01) represents a rising edge. There are also shorthand notations for various edges:

- * is (??)
- r is (01)
- f is (10)
- p is (01), (0x), or (x1)
- n is (10), (1x), or (x0)

```
primitive DFlipFlop(Q, Clock, Data);                                 //1
output Q; reg Q; input Clock, Data;                                  //2
table                                                                //3
//inputs : present state : output (next state)                       //4
r    0 : ? : 0 ; // rising edge, next state = output = 0             //5
r    1 : ? : 1 ; // rising edge, next state = output = 1             //6
(0x) 0 : 0 : 0 ; // rising edge, next state = output = 0             //7
(0x) 1 : 1 : 1 ; // rising edge, next state = output = 1             //8
(?0) ? : ? : - ; // falling edge, no change in output               //9
? (??) : ? : - ; // no clock edge, no change in output              //10
```

```
endtable                                                    //11
endprimitive                                                //12
```

11.10 Modeling Delay

Verilog has a set of built-in methods to define delays. This is very important in ASIC physical design. Before we start layout, we can use ASIC cell library models written in Verilog that include logic delays as a function of fanout and estimated wiring loads. After we have completed layout, we can extract the wiring capacitance, allowing us to calculate the exact delay values. Using the techniques described in this section, we can then back-annotate our Verilog netlist with postlayout delays and complete a postlayout simulation.

We can complete this back-annotation process in a standard fashion since delay specification is part of the Verilog language. This makes working with an ASIC cell library and the ASIC foundry that will fabricate our ASIC much easier. Typically an ASIC library company might sell us a cell library complete with Verilog models that include all the minimum, typical, and maximum delays as well as the different values for rising and falling transitions. The ASIC foundry will provide us with a delay calculator that calculates the net delays (this is usually proprietary technology) from the layout. These delays are held in a separate file (the **Standard Delay Format**, **SDF**, is widely used) and then mapped to parameters in the Verilog models. If we complete back-annotation and a postlayout simulation using an approved cell library, the ASIC foundry will "sign off" on our design. This is basically a guarantee that our chip will work according to the simulation. This ability to design sign-off quality ASIC cell libraries is very important in the ASIC design process.

11.10.1 Net and Gate Delay

We saw how to specify a delay control for any statement in Section 11.6. In fact, Verilog allows us to specify minimum, typical, and maximum values for the delay as follows:

```
#(1.1:1.3:1.7) assign delay_a = a; // min/typ/max
```

We can also specify the delay properties of a `wire` in a similar fashion:

```
wire #(1.1:1.3:1.7) a_delay; // min/typ/max
```

We can specify delay in a `wire` declaration together with a continuous assignment as in the following example:

```
wire #(1.1:1.3:1.7) a_delay = a; // min/typ/max
```

but in this case the delay is associated with the driver and not with the `wire`,

In Section 11.9.1 we explained that we can specify a delay for a logic primitive. We can also specify minimum, typical, and maximum delays as well as separate delays for rising and falling transitions for primitives as follows:

```
nand #3.0 nd01(c, a, b);
nand #(2.6:3.0:3.4) nd02(d, a, b; // min:typ:max
nand #(2.8:3.2:3.4, 2.6:2.8:2.9) nd03(e, a, b);
// #(rising, falling) delay
```

The first NAND gate, nd01, has a delay of 3 ns (assuming we specified nanoseconds as the timescale) for both rising and falling delays. The NAND gate nd02 has a triplet for the delay; this corresponds to a minimum (2.6 ns), typical (3.0 ns), and a maximum delay (3.4 ns). The NAND gate nd03 has two triplets for the delay: The first triplet specifies the min/typ/max rising delay ('0' or 'x' or 'z' to '1'), and the second triplet specifies the min/typ/max falling delay ('1' or 'x' or 'z' to '0').

Some primitives can produce a high-impedance output, 'z'. In this case we can specify a triplet of delay values corresponding to rising transition, falling transition, and the delay to transition to 'z' (from '0' or '1' to 'z'—this is usually the delay for a three-state driver to turn off or float). We can do the same thing for net types,

```
wire #(0.5,0.6,0.7) a_z = a; // rise/fall/float delays
```

11.10.2 Pin-to-Pin Delay

The **specify block** is a special construct in Verilog that allows defining the **pin-to-pin delays** across a module [Verilog LRM 13]. The use of a specify block can include the use of built-in system functions to check setup and hold times, for example. The following example illustrates how to specify pin-to-pin timing for a D flip-flop. We declare the timing parameters first followed by the paths. This example uses the UDP from Section 11.9.2, which does not include preset and clear (so only part of the flip-flop function is modeled), but includes the timing for preset and clear for illustration purposes.

```
module DFF_Spec; reg D, clk;                                    //1
DFF_Part DFF1 (Q, clk, D, pre, clr);                            //2
initial begin D = 0; clk = 0; #1; clk = 1; end                 //3
initial $monitor("T=%2g", $time," clk=", clk," Q=", Q);        //4
endmodule                                                       //5

module DFF_Part(Q, clk, D, pre, clr);                           //1
   input clk, D, pre, clr; output Q;                            //2
   DFlipFlop(Q, clk, D); // no preset or clear in this UDP      //3
   specify                                                      //4
      specparam                                                 //5
      tPLH_clk_Q = 3, tPHL_clk_Q = 2.9,                         //6
      tPLH_set_Q = 1.2, tPHL_set_Q = 1.1;                       //7
   (clk => Q) = (tPLH_clk_Q, tPHL_clk_Q);                       //8
   (pre, clr *> Q) = (tPLH_set_Q, tPHL_set_Q);                  //9
```

```
        endspecify                                                      //10
        endmodule                                                       //11

T= 0 clk=0 Q=x
T= 1 clk=1 Q=x
T= 4 clk=1 Q=0
```

There are the following two ways to specify paths (module `DFF_part` above uses both):

- `x => y` specifies a **parallel connection** (or parallel path) between x and y (x and y must have the same number of bits).

- `x *> y` specifies a **full connection** (or full path) between x and y (every bit in x is connected to y). In this case x and y may be different sizes.

The delay of some logic cells depends on the state of the inputs. This can be modeled using a **state-dependent path delay**. Here is an example:

```
`timescale 1 ns / 100 fs                                               //1
module M_Spec; reg A1, A2, B; M M1 (Z, A1, A2, B);                     //2
initial begin A1=0;A2=1;B=1;#5;B=0;#5;A1=1;A2=0;B=1;#5;B=0; end        //3
initial                                                                //4
    $monitor("T=%4g",$realtime," A1=",A1," A2=",A2," B=",B," Z=",Z);   //5
endmodule                                                              //6

`timescale 100 ps / 10 fs                                              //1
module M(Z, A1, A2, B); input A1, A2, B; output Z;                     //2
or (Z1, A1, A2); nand (Z, Z1, B); // OAI21                             //3
/*A1 A2 B Z   delay=10*100 ps unless shown below:                      //4
  0  0  0 1                                                            //5
  0  0  1 1                                                            //6
  0  1  0 1  B:0->1 Z:1->0 delay=t2                                    //7
  0  1  1 0  B:1->0 Z:0->1 delay=t1                                    //8
  1  0  0 1  B:0->1 Z:1->0 delay=t4                                    //9
  1  0  1 0  B:1->0 Z:0->1 delay=t3                                    //10
  1  1  0 1                                                            //11
  1  1  1 0 */                                                         //12
specify specparam t1 = 11,t2 = 12; specparam t3 = 13,t4 = 14;         //13
    (A1 => Z) = 10; (A2 => Z) = 10;                                    //14
    if (~A1) (B => Z) = (t1, t2); if (A1) (B => Z) = (t3, t4);         //15
endspecify                                                             //16
endmodule                                                              //17

T=   0 A1=0 A2=1 B=1 Z=x
T=   1 A1=0 A2=1 B=1 Z=0
T=   5 A1=0 A2=1 B=0 Z=0
T= 6.1 A1=0 A2=1 B=0 Z=1
T=  10 A1=1 A2=0 B=1 Z=1
T=  11 A1=1 A2=0 B=1 Z=0
T=  15 A1=1 A2=0 B=0 Z=0
T=16.3 A1=1 A2=0 B=0 Z=1
```

11.11 Altering Parameters

Here is an example of a module that uses a parameter:

```
module Vector_And(Z, A, B);                         //1
  parameter CARDINALITY = 1;                         //2
  input [CARDINALITY-1:0] A, B;                      //3
  output [CARDINALITY-1:0] Z;                        //4
  wire [CARDINALITY-1:0] Z = A & B;                  //5
endmodule                                            //6
```

We can override this parameter when we instantiate the module as follows:

```
module Four_And_Gates(OutBus, InBusA, InBusB);                  //1
  input [3:0] InBusA, InBusB; output [3:0] OutBus;              //2
  Vector_And #(4) My_AND(OutBus, InBusA, InBusB); // 4 AND gates //3
endmodule                                                       //4
```

The parameters of a module have local scope, but we may override them using a **defparam** statement and a hierarchical name, as in the following example:

```
module And_Gates(OutBus, InBusA, InBusB);                        //1
  parameter WIDTH = 1;                                           //2
  input [WIDTH-1:0] InBusA, InBusB; output [WIDTH-1:0] OutBus;   //3
  Vector_And #(WIDTH) My_And(OutBus, InBusA, InBusB);           //4
endmodule                                                        //5

module Super_Size; defparam And_Gates.WIDTH = 4; endmodule       //1
```

11.12 A Viterbi Decoder

This section describes an ASIC design for a Viterbi decoder using Verilog. Christeen Gray completed the original design as her MS thesis at the University of Hawaii (UH) working with VLSI Technology, using the Compass ASIC Synthesizer and a VLSI Technology cell library. The design was mapped from VLSI Technology design rules to Hewlett-Packard design rules; prototypes were fabricated by Hewlett-Packard (through Mosis) and tested at UH.

11.12.1 Viterbi Encoder

Viterbi encoding is widely used for satellite and other noisy **communications channels**. There are two important components of a channel using Viterbi encoding: the **Viterbi encoder** (at the transmitter) and the **Viterbi decoder** (at the receiver). A

Viterbi encoder includes extra information in the transmitted signal to reduce the probability of errors in the received signal that may be corrupted by noise.

I shall describe an encoder in which every two bits of a data stream are encoded into three bits for transmission. The ratio of input to output information in an encoder is the **rate** of the encoder; this is a rate 2/3 encoder. The following equations relate the three encoder output bits (Y_n^2, Y_n^1, and Y_n^0) to the two encoder input bits (X_n^2 and X_n^1) at a time nT:

$$Y_n^2 = X_n^2$$
$$Y_n^1 = X_n^1 \oplus X_{n-2}^1 \qquad\qquad (11.1)$$
$$Y_n^0 = X_{n-1}^1$$

We can write the input bits as a single number. Thus, for example, if $X_n^2 = 1$ and $X_n^1 = 0$, we can write $X_n = 2$. Equation 11.1 defines a state machine with two memory elements for the two last input values for X_n^1: X_{n-1}^1 and X_{n-2}^1. These two state variables define four states: $\{X_{n-1}^1, X_{n-2}^1\}$, with $S_0 = \{0, 0\}$, $S_1 = \{1, 0\}$, $S_2 = \{0, 1\}$, and $S_3 = \{1, 1\}$. The 3-bit output Y_n is a function of the state and current 2-bit input X_n.

The following Verilog code describes the rate 2/3 encoder. This model uses two D flip-flops as the state register. When reset (using active-high input signal res) the encoder starts in state S_0. In Verilog I represent Y_n^2 by Y2N, for example.

```
/********************************************************/
/* module viterbi_encode                               */
/********************************************************/
/* This is the encoder. X2N (msb) and X1N form the 2-bit input
message, XN. Example: if X2N=1, X1N=0, then XN=2. Y2N (msb), Y1N, and
Y0N form the 3-bit encoded signal, YN (for a total constellation of 8
PSK signals that will be transmitted). The encoder uses a state
machine with four states to generate the 3-bit output, YN, from the
2-bit input, XN. Example: the repeated input sequence XN = (X2N, X1N)
= 0, 1, 2, 3 produces the repeated output sequence YN = (Y2N, Y1N,
Y0N) = 1, 0, 5, 4. */
module viterbi_encode(X2N,X1N,Y2N,Y1N,Y0N,clk,res);
input X2N,X1N,clk,res; output Y2N,Y1N,Y0N;
wire X1N_1,X1N_2,Y2N,Y1N,Y0N;
dff dff_1(X1N,X1N_1,clk,res); dff dff_2(X1N_1,X1N_2,clk,res);
assign Y2N=X2N; assign Y1N=X1N ^ X1N_2; assign Y0N=X1N_1;
endmodule
```

Figure 11.3 shows the state diagram for this encoder. The first four rows of Table 11.6 show the four different transitions that can be made from state S_0. For example, if we reset the encoder and the input is $X_n = 3$ ($X_n^2 = 1$ and $X_n^1 = 1$), then the output will be $Y_n = 6$ ($Y_n^2 = 1$, $Y_n^1 = 1$, $Y_n^0 = 0$) and the next state will be S_1.

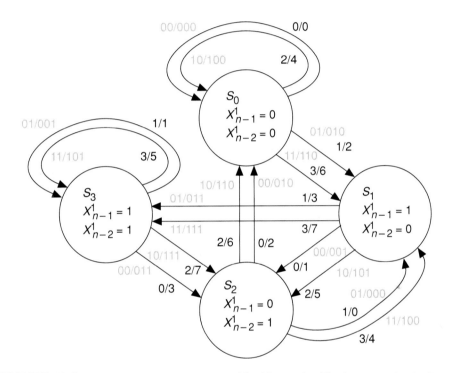

FIGURE 11.3 A state diagram for a rate 2/3 Viterbi encoder. The inputs and outputs are shown in binary as $X_n^2 X_n^1 / Y_n^2 Y_n^1 Y_n^0$, and in decimal as X_n / Y_n .

As an example, the repeated encoder input sequence $X_n = 0, 1, 2, 3, \ldots$ produces the encoder output sequence $Y_n = 1, 0, 5, 4, \ldots$ repeated. Table 11.7 shows the state transitions for this sequence, including the initialization steps.

Next we transmit the eight possible encoder outputs ($Y_n = 0\text{--}7$) as **signals** over our noisy communications channel (perhaps a microwave signal to a satellite) using the **signal constellation** shown in Figure 11.4. Typically this is done using **phase-shift keying** (**PSK**) with each signal position corresponding to a different phase shift in the transmitted carrier signal.

TABLE 11.6   State table for the rate 2/3 Viterbi encoder.

Present state	Inputs X^2_n	X^1_n	State variables X^1_{n-1}	X^1_{n-2}	Outputs $Y^2_n = X^2_n$	$Y^1_n = X^1_n \oplus X^1_{n-2}$	$Y^0_n = X^1_{n-1}$	Next state $\{X^1_{n-1}, X^1_{n-2}\}$	
S_0	0	0	0	0	0	0	0	00	S_0
S_0	0	1	0	0	0	1	0	10	S_1
S_0	1	0	0	0	1	0	0	00	S_0
S_0	1	1	0	0	1	1	0	10	S_1
S_1	0	0	1	0	0	0	1	01	S_2
S_1	0	1	1	0	0	1	1	11	S_3
S_1	1	0	1	0	1	0	1	01	S_2
S_1	1	1	1	0	1	1	1	11	S_3
S_2	0	0	0	1	0	1	0	00	S_0
S_2	0	1	0	1	0	0	0	10	S_1
S_2	1	0	0	1	1	1	0	00	S_0
S_2	1	1	0	1	1	0	0	10	S_1
S_3	0	0	1	1	0	1	1	01	S_2
S_3	0	1	1	1	0	0	1	11	S_3
S_3	1	0	1	1	1	1	1	01	S_2
S_3	1	1	1	1	1	0	1	11	S_3

FIGURE 11.4 The signal constellation for an 8PSK (phase-shift keyed) code.

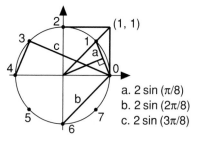

a. $2 \sin (\pi/8)$
b. $2 \sin (2\pi/8)$
c. $2 \sin (3\pi/8)$

TABLE 11.7   A sequence of transmitted signals for the rate 2/3 Viterbi encoder

Time ns	Inputs		State variables		Outputs			Present state	Next state
	X_n^2	X_n^1	X_{n-1}^1	X_{n-2}^1	Y_n^2	Y_n^1	Y_n^0		
0	1	1	x	x	1	x	x	$S_?$	$S_?$
10	1	1	0	0	1	1	0	S_0	S_1
50	0	0	1	0	0	0	1	S_1	S_2
150	0	1	0	1	0	0	0	S_2	S_1
250	1	0	1	0	1	0	1	S_1	S_2
350	1	1	0	1	1	0	0	S_2	S_1
450	0	0	1	0	0	0	1	S_1	S_2
550	0	1	0	1	0	0	0	S_2	S_1
650	1	0	1	0	1	0	1	S_1	S_2
750	1	1	0	1	1	0	0	S_2	S_1
850	0	0	1	0	0	0	1	S_1	S_2
950	0	1	0	1	0	0	0	S_2	S_1

11.12.2   The Received Signal

The noisy signal enters the receiver. It is now our task to discover which of the eight possible signals were transmitted at each time step. First we calculate the distance of each received signal from each of the known eight positions in the signal constellation. Table 11.8 shows the distances between signals in the 8PSK constellation. We are going to assume that there is no noise in the channel to illustrate the operation of the Viterbi decoder, so that the distances in Table 11.8 represent the possible distance measures of our received signal from the 8PSK signals.

The distances, X, in the first column of Table 11.8 are the geometric or algebraic distances. We measure the **Euclidean distance**, $E = X^2$ shown as B (the binary quantized value of E) in Table 11.8. The rounding errors that result from conversion to fixed-width binary are **quantization errors** and are important in any practical implementation of the Viterbi decoder. The effect of the quantization error is to add a form of noise to the received signal.

The following code models the receiver section that digitizes the noisy analog received signal and computes the binary distance measures. Eight binary-distance measures, in0-in7, are generated each time a signal is received. Since each of the distance measures is 3 bits wide, there are a total of 24 bits (8 × 3) that form the digital inputs to the Viterbi decoder.

TABLE 11.8   Distance measures for Viterbi encoding (8PSK).

Signal	Algebraic distance from signal 0	$X=$ Distance from signal 0	Euclidean distance $E=X^2$	$B=$ binary quantized value of E	$D=$ decimal value of B	Quantization error $Q=D-1.75E$
0	$2\sin(0\pi/8)$	0.00	0.00	000	0	0
1	$2\sin(1\pi/8)$	0.77	0.59	001	1	-0.0325
2	$2\sin(2\pi/8)$	1.41	2.00	100	4	0.5
3	$2\sin(3\pi/8)$	1.85	3.41	110	6	0.0325
4	$2\sin(4\pi/8)$	2.00	4.00	111	7	0
5	$2\sin(5\pi/8)$	1.85	3.41	110	6	0.0325
6	$2\sin(6\pi/8)$	1.41	2.00	100	4	0.5
7	$2\sin(7\pi/8)$	0.77	0.59	001	1	-0.0325

```
/********************************************************/
/* module viterbi_distances                            */
/********************************************************/
/* This module simulates the front end of a receiver. Normally the
received analog signal (with noise) is converted into a series of
distance measures from the known eight possible transmitted PSK
signals: s1,...s7. We are not simulating the analog part or noise in
this version, so we just take the digitally encoded 3-bit signal, Y,
from the encoder and convert it directly to the distance measures.
d[N] is the distance from signal = N to signal = 0
d[N] = (2*sin(N*PI/8))**2 in 3-bit binary (on the scale 2=100)
Example: d[3] = 1.85**2 = 3.41 = 110
inN is the distance from signal = N to encoder signal.
Example: in3 is the distance from signal = 3 to encoder signal.
d[N] is the distance from signal = N to encoder signal = 0.
If encoder signal = J, shift the distances by 8-J positions.
Example: if signal = 2, in0 is d[6], in1 is D[7], in2 is D[0], etc. */
module viterbi_distances
    (Y2N,Y1N,Y0N,clk,res,in0,in1,in2,in3,in4,in5,in6,in7);
input clk,res,Y2N,Y1N,Y0N; output in0,in1,in2,in3,in4,in5,in6,in7;
reg [2:0] J,in0,in1,in2,in3,in4,in5,in6,in7; reg [2:0] d [7:0];
initial begin d[0]='b000;d[1]='b001;d[2]='b100;d[3]='b110;
d[4]='b111;d[5]='b110;d[6]='b100;d[7]='b001; end
always @(Y2N or Y1N or Y0N) begin
J[0]=Y0N;J[1]=Y1N;J[2]=Y2N;
J=8-J;in0=d[J];J=J+1;in1=d[J];J=J+1;in2=d[J];J=J+1;in3=d[J];
J=J+1;in4=d[J];J=J+1;in5=d[J];J=J+1;in6=d[J];J=J+1;in7=d[J];
end endmodule
```

As an example, Table 11.9 shows the distance measures for the transmitted encoder output sequence Y_n = 1, 0, 5, 4, ... (repeated) corresponding to an encoder input of X_n = 0, 1, 2, 3, ... (repeated).

TABLE 11.9   Receiver distance measures for an example transmission sequence.

Time ns	Input X_n	Output Y_n	Present state	Next state	in0	in1	in2	in3	in4	in5	in6	in7
0	3	x	$S_?$	$S_?$	x	x	x	x	x	x	x	x
10	3	6	S_0	S_1	4	6	7	6	4	1	0	1
50	0	1	S_1	S_2	1	0	1	4	6	7	6	4
150	1	0	S_2	S_1	0	1	4	6	7	6	4	1
250	2	5	S_1	S_2	6	7	6	4	1	0	1	4
350	3	4	S_2	S_1	7	6	4	1	0	1	4	6
450	0	1	S_1	S_2	1	0	1	4	6	7	6	4
550	1	0	S_2	S_1	0	1	4	6	7	6	4	1
650	2	5	S_1	S_2	6	7	6	4	1	0	1	4
750	3	4	S_2	S_1	7	6	4	1	0	1	4	6
850	0	1	S_1	S_2	1	0	1	4	6	7	6	4
950	1	0	S_2	S_1	0	1	4	6	7	6	4	1

11.12.3 Testing the System

Here is a testbench for the entire system: encoder, receiver front end, and decoder:

```
/*****************************************************/
/* module viterbi_test_CDD                          */
/*****************************************************/
/* This is the top-level module, viterbi_test_CDD, that models the
communications link. It contains three modules: viterbi_encode,
viterbi_distances, and viterbi. There is no analog and no noise in
this version. The 2-bit message, X, is encoded to a 3-bit signal, Y.
In this module the message X is generated using a simple counter.
The digital 3-bit signal Y is transmitted, received with noise as an
analog signal (not modeled here), and converted to a set of eight
3-bit distance measures, in0, ..., in7. The distance measures form
the input to the Viterbi decoder that reconstructs the transmitted
signal Y, with an error signal if the measures are inconsistent.
CDD = counter input, digital transmission, digital reception */
module viterbi_test_CDD;
```

```
wire Error;                   // decoder out
wire [2:0] Y,Out;             // encoder out, decoder out
reg [1:0] X;                  // encoder inputs
reg Clk, Res;                 // clock and reset
wire [2:0] in0,in1,in2,in3,in4,in5,in6,in7;
always #500 $display("t   Clk X Y Out Error");
initial $monitor("%4g",$time,,Clk,,,,X,,Y,,Out,,,,Error);
initial $dumpvars; initial #3000 $finish;
always #50 Clk = ~Clk; initial begin Clk = 0;
X = 3;                        // no special reason to start at 3
#60 Res = 1;#10 Res = 0;end // hit reset after inputs are stable
always @(posedge Clk) #1 X = X + 1; // drive input with counter
viterbi_encode v_1
   (X[1],X[0],Y[2],Y[1],Y[0],Clk,Res);
viterbi_distances v_2
   (Y[2],Y[1],Y[0],Clk,Res,in0,in1,in2,in3,in4,in5,in6,in7);
viterbi v_3
   (in0,in1,in2,in3,in4,in5,in6,in7,Out,Clk,Res,Error);
endmodule
```

The Viterbi decoder takes the distance measures and calculates the most likely transmitted signal. It does this by keeping a running history of the previously received signals in a **path memory**. The path-memory length of this decoder is 12. By keeping a history of possible sequences and using the knowledge that the signals were generated by a state machine, it is possible to select the most likely sequences.

TABLE 11.10   Output from the Viterbi testbench

t	Clk	X	Y	Out	Error	t	Clk	X	Y	Out	Error
0	0	3	x	x	0	1351	1	1	0	0	0
50	1	3	x	x	0	1400	0	1	0	0	0
51	1	0	x	x	0	1450	1	1	0	0	0
60	1	0	0	0	0	1451	1	2	5	2	0
100	0	0	0	0	0	1500	0	2	5	2	0
150	1	0	0	0	0	1550	1	2	5	2	0
151	1	1	2	0	0	1551	1	3	4	5	0

Table 11.10 shows part of the simulation results from the testbench, viterbi_test_CDD, in tabular form. Figure 11.5 shows the Verilog simulator output from the testbench (displayed using VeriWell from Wellspring).

The system input or message, X[1:0], is driven by a counter that repeats the sequence 0, 1, 2, 3, ... incrementing by 1 at each positive clock edge (with a delay of one time unit), starting with X equal to 3 at $t = 0$. The active-high reset signal, Res, is asserted at $t = 60$ for 10 time units. The encoder output, Y[2:0], changes at $t = 151$, which is one time unit (the positive-edge–triggered D flip-flop model contains a

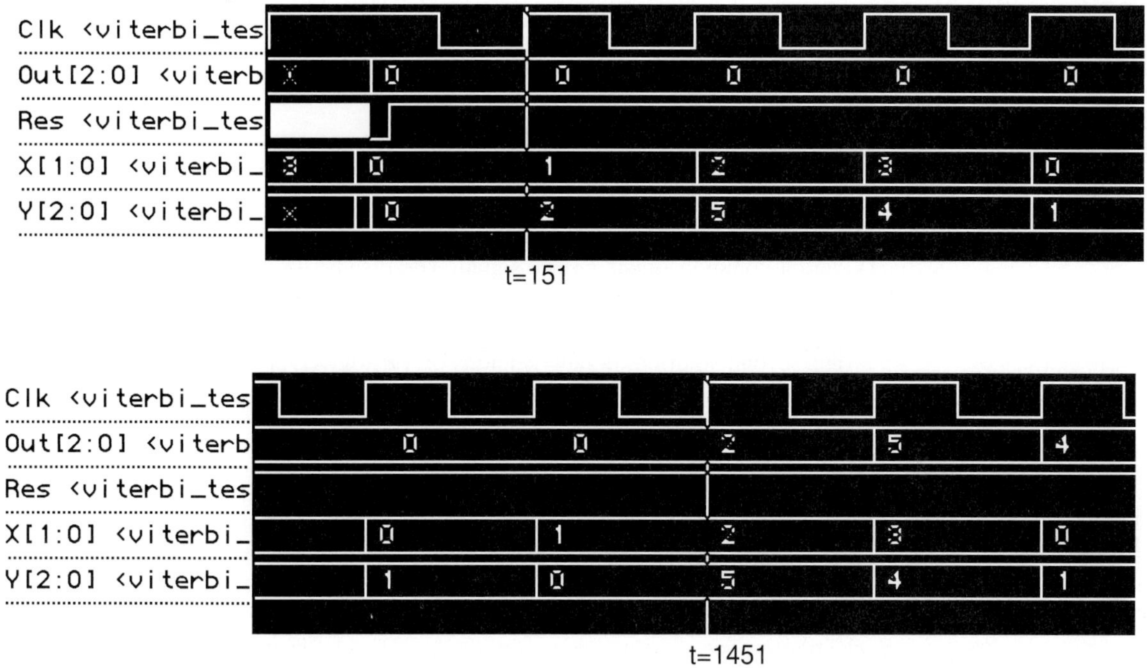

FIGURE 11.5 Viterbi encoder testbench simulation results. (Top) Initialization and the start of the encoder output sequence 2, 5, 4, 1, 0, ... on Y[2:0] at *t* = 151. (Bottom) The appearance of the same encoder output sequence at the output of the decoder, Out[2:0], at *t* = 1451, 1300 time units (13 positive clock edges) later.

one-time-unit delay) after the first positive clock edge (at *t* = 150) following the deassertion of the reset at *t* = 70. The encoder output sequence beginning at *t* = 151 is 2, 5, 4, 1, 0, ... and then the sequence 5, 4, 1, 0, ... repeats. This encoder output sequence is then imagined to be transmitted and received. The receiver module calculates the distance measures and passes them to the decoder. After 13 positive clock-edges (1300 time ticks) the transmitted sequence appears at the output, Out[2:0], beginning at *t* = 1451 with 2, 5, 4, 1, 0, ..., exactly the same as the encoder output.

11.12.4 Verilog Decoder Model

The Viterbi decoder model presented in this section is written for both simulation and synthesis. The Viterbi decoder makes extensive use of vector D flip-flops (registers). Early versions of Verilog-XL did not support vector instantiations of modules. In addition the inputs of UDPs may not be vectors and there are no primitive D flip-flops in Verilog. This makes instantiation of a register difficult other than by writing a separate module instance for each flip-flop.

The first solution to this problem is to use flip-flop models supplied with the synthesis tool such as the following:

```
asDff #(3) subout0(in0, sub0, clk, reset);
```

The asDff is a model in the Compass ASIC Synthesizer standard component library. This statement triggers the synthesis of three D flip-flops, with an input vector ina (with a range of three) connected to the D inputs, an output vector sub0 (also with a range of three) connected to the Q flip-flop outputs, a common scalar clock signal, clk, and a common scalar reset signal. The disadvantage of this approach is that the names, functional behavior, and interfaces of the standard components are different for every software system.

The second solution, in new versions of Verilog-XL and other tools that support the IEEE standard, is to use vector instantiation as follows [LRM 7.5.1, 12.1.2]:

```
myDff subout0[0:2] (in0, sub0, clk, reset);
```

This instantiates three copies of a user-defined module or UDP called myDff. The disadvantage of this approach is that not all simulators and synthesizers support vector instantiation.

The third solution (which is used in the Viterbi decoder model) is to write a model that supports vector inputs and outputs. Here is an example D flip-flop model:

```
/******************************************************/
/*    module dff                                      */
/******************************************************/
/* A D flip-flop module. */

module dff(D,Q,Clock,Reset); // N.B. reset is active-low
output Q; input D,Clock,Reset;
parameter CARDINALITY = 1; reg [CARDINALITY-1:0] Q;
wire [CARDINALITY-1:0] D;
always @(posedge Clock) if (Reset !== 0) #1 Q = D;
always begin wait (Reset == 0); Q = 0; wait (Reset == 1); end
endmodule
```

We use this model by defining a parameter that specifies the bus width as follows:

```
dff #(3) subout0(in0, sub0, clk, reset);
```

The code that models the entire Viterbi decoder is listed below. Notice the following:

- Comments explain the function of each module.
- Each module is about a page or less of code.

- Each module can be tested by itself.
- The code is as simple as possible avoiding clever coding techniques.

The code is not flexible, because bit widths are fixed rather than using parameters. A model with parameters for rate, signal constellation, distance measure resolution, and path memory length is considerably more complex.

We shall use this Viterbi decoder design again when we discuss floorplanning and placement in Chapter 16 and routing in Chapter 17.

```verilog
/* Verilog code for a Viterbi decoder. The decoder assumes a rate
2/3 encoder, 8 PSK modulation, and trellis coding. The viterbi module
contains eight submodules: subset_decode, metric, compute_metric,
compare_select, reduce, pathin, path_memory, and output_decision.
   The decoder accepts eight 3-bit measures of ||r-si||**2 and, after
an initial delay of twelve clock cycles, the output is the best
estimate of the signal transmitted. The distance measures are the
Euclidean distances between the received signal r (with noise) and
each of the (in this case eight) possible transmitted signals s0 to s7.
   Original by Christeen Gray, University of Hawaii. Heavily modified
by MJSS; any errors are mine. Use freely. */
/****************************************************/
/*    module viterbi                              */
/****************************************************/
/* This is the top level of the Viterbi decoder. The eight input
signals {in0,...,in7} represent the distance measures, ||r-si||**2.
The other input signals are clk and reset. The output signals are
out and error. */

module viterbi
     (in0,in1,in2,in3,in4,in5,in6,in7,
     out,clk,reset,error);
input [2:0] in0,in1,in2,in3,in4,in5,in6,in7;
output [2:0] out; input clk,reset; output error;
wire sout0,sout1,sout2,sout3;
wire [2:0] s0,s1,s2,s3;
wire [4:0] m_in0,m_in1,m_in2,m_in3;
wire [4:0] m_out0,m_out1,m_out2,m_out3;
wire [4:0] p0_0,p2_0,p0_1,p2_1,p1_2,p3_2,p1_3,p3_3;
wire ACS0,ACS1,ACS2,ACS3;
wire [4:0] out0,out1,out2,out3;
wire [1:0] control;
wire [2:0] p0,p1,p2,p3;
wire [11:0] path0;

  subset_decode u1(in0,in1,in2,in3,in4,in5,in6,in7,
    s0,s1,s2,s3,sout0,sout1,sout2,sout3,clk,reset);
  metric u2(m_in0,m_in1,m_in2,m_in3,m_out0,
    m_out1,m_out2,m_out3,clk,reset);
  compute_metric u3(m_out0,m_out1,m_out2,m_out3,s0,s1,s2,s3,
```

```
          p0_0,p2_0,p0_1,p2_1,p1_2,p3_2,p1_3,p3_3,error);
      compare_select u4(p0_0,p2_0,p0_1,p2_1,p1_2,p3_2,p1_3,p3_3,
          out0,out1,out2,out3,ACS0,ACS1,ACS2,ACS3);
      reduce u5(out0,out1,out2,out3,
          m_in0,m_in1,m_in2,m_in3,control);
      pathin u6(sout0,sout1,sout2,sout3,
          ACS0,ACS1,ACS2,ACS3,path0,clk,reset);
      path_memory u7(p0,p1,p2,p3,path0,clk,reset,
          ACS0,ACS1,ACS2,ACS3);
      output_decision u8(p0,p1,p2,p3,control,out);
endmodule


/******************************************************/
/* module subset_decode                               */
/******************************************************/
/* This module chooses the signal corresponding to the smallest of
each set {||r-s0||**2,||r-s4||**2}, {||r-s1||**2, ||r-s5||**2},
{||r-s2||**2,||r-s6||**2}, {||r-s3||**2,||r-s7||**2}. Therefore
there are eight input signals and four output signals for the
distance measures. The signals sout0, ..., sout3 are used to control
the path memory. The statement dff #(3) instantiates a vector array
of 3 D flip-flops. */
module subset_decode
      (in0,in1,in2,in3,in4,in5,in6,in7,
      s0,s1,s2,s3,
      sout0,sout1,sout2,sout3,
      clk,reset);
input [2:0] in0,in1,in2,in3,in4,in5,in6,in7;
output [2:0] s0,s1,s2,s3;
output sout0,sout1,sout2,sout3;
input clk,reset;
wire [2:0] sub0,sub1,sub2,sub3,sub4,sub5,sub6,sub7;

    dff #(3) subout0(in0, sub0, clk, reset);
    dff #(3) subout1(in1, sub1, clk, reset);
    dff #(3) subout2(in2, sub2, clk, reset);
    dff #(3) subout3(in3, sub3, clk, reset);
    dff #(3) subout4(in4, sub4, clk, reset);
    dff #(3) subout5(in5, sub5, clk, reset);
    dff #(3) subout6(in6, sub6, clk, reset);
    dff #(3) subout7(in7, sub7, clk, reset);

    function [2:0] subset_decode; input [2:0] a,b;
      begin
        subset_decode = 0;
        if (a<=b) subset_decode = a; else subset_decode = b;
      end
    endfunction
```

```
   function set_control; input [2:0] a,b;
      begin
         if (a<=b) set_control = 0; else set_control = 1;
      end
   endfunction

assign s0 = subset_decode (sub0,sub4);
assign s1 = subset_decode (sub1,sub5);
assign s2 = subset_decode (sub2,sub6);
assign s3 = subset_decode (sub3,sub7);
assign sout0 = set_control(sub0,sub4);
assign sout1 = set_control(sub1,sub5);
assign sout2 = set_control(sub2,sub6);
assign sout3 = set_control(sub3,sub7);
endmodule


/******************************************************/
/*   module compute_metric                          */
/******************************************************/
/* This module computes the sum of path memory and the distance for
each path entering a state of the trellis. For the four states,
there are two paths entering it; therefore eight sums are computed
in this module. The path metrics and output sums are 5 bits wide.
The output sum is bounded and should never be greater than 5 bits
for a valid input signal. The overflow from the sum is the error
output and indicates an invalid input signal.*/
module compute_metric
      (m_out0,m_out1,m_out2,m_out3,
      s0,s1,s2,s3,p0_0,p2_0,
      p0_1,p2_1,p1_2,p3_2,p1_3,p3_3,
      error);
   input [4:0] m_out0,m_out1,m_out2,m_out3;
   input [2:0] s0,s1,s2,s3;
   output [4:0] p0_0,p2_0,p0_1,p2_1,p1_2,p3_2,p1_3,p3_3;
   output error;

   assign
      p0_0 = m_out0 + s0,
      p2_0 = m_out2 + s2,
      p0_1 = m_out0 + s2,
      p2_1 = m_out2 + s0,
      p1_2 = m_out1 + s1,
      p3_2 = m_out3 + s3,
      p1_3 = m_out1 + s3,
      p3_3 = m_out3 + s1;

   function is_error; input x1,x2,x3,x4,x5,x6,x7,x8;
   begin
      if (x1||x2||x3||x4||x5||x6||x7||x8) is_error = 1;
```

```
        else is_error = 0;
    end
    endfunction

    assign error = is_error(p0_0[4],p2_0[4],p0_1[4],p2_1[4],
        p1_2[4],p3_2[4],p1_3[4],p3_3[4]);
endmodule

/*****************************************************/
/*   module compare_select                         */
/*****************************************************/
/* This module compares the summations from the compute_metric
module and selects the metric and path with the lowest value. The
output of this module is saved as the new path metric for each
state. The ACS output signals are used to control the path memory of
the decoder. */
module compare_select
    (p0_0,p2_0,p0_1,p2_1,p1_2,p3_2,p1_3,p3_3,
    out0,out1,out2,out3,
    ACS0,ACS1,ACS2,ACS3);
  input [4:0] p0_0,p2_0,p0_1,p2_1,p1_2,p3_2,p1_3,p3_3;
  output [4:0] out0,out1,out2,out3;
  output ACS0,ACS1,ACS2,ACS3;

    function [4:0] find_min_metric; input [4:0] a,b;
      begin
        if (a <= b) find_min_metric = a; else find_min_metric = b;
      end
    endfunction

    function set_control; input [4:0] a,b;
      begin
        if (a<=b) set_control=0; else set_control=1;
      end
    endfunction

assign out0 = find_min_metric(p0_0,p2_0);
assign out1 = find_min_metric(p0_1,p2_1);
assign out2 = find_min_metric(p1_2,p3_2);
assign out3 = find_min_metric(p1_3,p3_3);
assign ACS0 = set_control (p0_0,p2_0);
assign ACS1 = set_control (p0_1,p2_1);
assign ACS2 = set_control (p1_2,p3_2);
assign ACS3 = set_control (p1_3,p3_3);
endmodule

/*****************************************************/
/*   module path                                   */
/*****************************************************/
/* This is the basic unit for the path memory of the Viterbi
```

decoder. It consists of four 3-bit D flip-flops in parallel. There
is a 2:1 mux at each D flip-flop input. The statement dff #(12)
instantiates a vector array of 12 flip-flops. */

```
module path(in,out,clk,reset,ACS0,ACS1,ACS2,ACS3);
input [11:0] in; output [11:0] out;
input clk,reset,ACS0,ACS1,ACS2,ACS3; wire [11:0] p_in;

dff #(12) path0(p_in,out,clk,reset);

   function [2:0] shift_path; input [2:0] a,b; input control;
      begin
         if (control == 0) shift_path = a; else shift_path = b;
      end
   endfunction

assign p_in[11:9] = shift_path(in[11:9],in[5:3],ACS0);
assign p_in[ 8:6] = shift_path(in[11:9],in[5:3],ACS1);
assign p_in[ 5:3] = shift_path(in[8: 6],in[2:0],ACS2);
assign p_in[ 2:0] = shift_path(in[8: 6],in[2:0],ACS3);
endmodule


/****************************************************/
/*    module path_memory                            */
/****************************************************/
/* This module consists of an array of memory elements (D
flip-flops) that store and shift the path memory as new signals are
added to the four paths (or four most likely sequences of signals).
This module instantiates 11 instances of the path module. */
module path_memory
     (p0,p1,p2,p3,
     path0,clk,reset,
     ACS0,ACS1,ACS2,ACS3);
output [2:0] p0,p1,p2,p3; input [11:0] path0;
input clk,reset,ACS0,ACS1,ACS2,ACS3;
wire [11:0]out1,out2,out3,out4,out5,out6,out7,out8,out9,out10,out11;
     path x1 (path0,out1 ,clk,reset,ACS0,ACS1,ACS2,ACS3),
          x2 (out1, out2 ,clk,reset,ACS0,ACS1,ACS2,ACS3),
          x3 (out2, out3 ,clk,reset,ACS0,ACS1,ACS2,ACS3),
          x4 (out3, out4 ,clk,reset,ACS0,ACS1,ACS2,ACS3),
          x5 (out4, out5 ,clk,reset,ACS0,ACS1,ACS2,ACS3),
          x6 (out5, out6 ,clk,reset,ACS0,ACS1,ACS2,ACS3),
          x7 (out6, out7 ,clk,reset,ACS0,ACS1,ACS2,ACS3),
          x8 (out7, out8 ,clk,reset,ACS0,ACS1,ACS2,ACS3),
          x9 (out8, out9 ,clk,reset,ACS0,ACS1,ACS2,ACS3),
          x10(out9, out10,clk,reset,ACS0,ACS1,ACS2,ACS3),
          x11(out10,out11,clk,reset,ACS0,ACS1,ACS2,ACS3);
assign p0 = out11[11:9];
assign p1 = out11[ 8:6];
assign p2 = out11[ 5:3];
```

```verilog
      assign p3 = out11[ 2:0];
      endmodule


      /*****************************************************/
      /*    module pathin                                */
      /*****************************************************/
      /* This module determines the input signal to the path for each of
      the four paths. Control signals from the subset decoder and compare
      select modules are used to store the correct signal. The statement
      dff #(12) instantiates a vector array of 12 flip-flops. */
      module pathin
           (sout0,sout1,sout2,sout3,
           ACS0,ACS1,ACS2,ACS3,
           path0,clk,reset);
         input sout0,sout1,sout2,sout3,ACS0,ACS1,ACS2,ACS3;
         input clk,reset; output [11:0] path0;
         wire [2:0] sig0,sig1,sig2,sig3; wire [11:0] path_in;

         dff #(12) firstpath(path_in,path0,clk,reset);

         function [2:0] subset0; input sout0;
           begin
             if(sout0 == 0) subset0 = 0; else subset0 = 4;
           end
         endfunction

         function [2:0] subset1; input sout1;
           begin
             if(sout1 == 0) subset1 = 1; else subset1 = 5;
           end
         endfunction

         function [2:0] subset2; input sout2;
           begin
             if(sout2 == 0) subset2 = 2; else subset2 = 6;
           end
         endfunction

         function [2:0] subset3; input sout3;
           begin
             if(sout3 == 0) subset3 = 3; else subset3 = 7;
           end
         endfunction

         function [2:0] find_path; input [2:0] a,b; input control;
           begin
             if(control==0) find_path = a; else find_path = b;
           end
         endfunction

      assign sig0 = subset0(sout0);
```

```
assign sig1 = subset1(sout1);
assign sig2 = subset2(sout2);
assign sig3 = subset3(sout3);
assign path_in[11:9] = find_path(sig0,sig2,ACS0);
assign path_in[ 8:6] = find_path(sig2,sig0,ACS1);
assign path_in[ 5:3] = find_path(sig1,sig3,ACS2);
assign path_in[ 2:0] = find_path(sig3,sig1,ACS3);
endmodule


/****************************************************/
/*    module metric                                 */
/****************************************************/
/* The registers created in this module (using D flip-flops) store
the four path metrics. Each register is 5 bits wide. The statement
dff #(5) instantiates a vector array of 5 flip-flops. */
module metric
     (m_in0,m_in1,m_in2,m_in3,
      m_out0,m_out1,m_out2,m_out3,
      clk,reset);
input [4:0] m_in0,m_in1,m_in2,m_in3;
output [4:0] m_out0,m_out1,m_out2,m_out3;
input clk,reset;
   dff #(5) metric3(m_in3, m_out3, clk, reset);
   dff #(5) metric2(m_in2, m_out2, clk, reset);
   dff #(5) metric1(m_in1, m_out1, clk, reset);
   dff #(5) metric0(m_in0, m_out0, clk, reset);
endmodule


/****************************************************/
/*    module output_decision                        */
/****************************************************/
/* This module decides the output signal based on the path that
corresponds to the smallest metric. The control signal comes from
the reduce module. */

module output_decision(p0,p1,p2,p3,control,out);
   input [2:0] p0,p1,p2,p3; input [1:0] control; output [2:0] out;
   function [2:0] decide;
   input [2:0] p0,p1,p2,p3; input [1:0] control;
   begin
     if(control == 0) decide = p0;
     else if(control == 1) decide = p1;
     else if(control == 2) decide = p2;
     else decide = p3;
     end
   endfunction

assign out = decide(p0,p1,p2,p3,control);
endmodule
```

```
/******************************************************/
/*    module reduce                                  */
/******************************************************/
/* This module reduces the metrics after the addition and compare
operations. This algorithm selects the smallest metric and subtracts
it from the other three metrics. */

module reduce
     (in0,in1,in2,in3,
     m_in0,m_in1,m_in2,m_in3,
     control);
   input [4:0] in0,in1,in2,in3;
   output [4:0] m_in0,m_in1,m_in2,m_in3;
   output [1:0] control; wire [4:0] smallest;

   function [4:0] find_smallest;
      input [4:0] in0,in1,in2,in3; reg [4:0] a,b;
         begin
            if(in0 <= in1) a = in0; else a = in1;
            if(in2 <= in3) b = in2; else b = in3;
            if(a <= b) find_smallest = a;
            else find_smallest = b;
         end
   endfunction

   function [1:0] smallest_no;
   input [4:0] in0,in1,in2,in3,smallest;
      begin
         if(smallest == in0) smallest_no = 0;
         else if (smallest == in1) smallest_no = 1;
         else if (smallest == in2) smallest_no = 2;
         else smallest_no = 3;
      end
   endfunction

assign smallest = find_smallest(in0,in1,in2,in3);
assign m_in0 = in0 - smallest;
assign m_in1 = in1 - smallest;
assign m_in2 = in2 - smallest;
assign m_in3 = in3 - smallest;
assign control = smallest_no(in0,in1,in2,in3,smallest);
endmodule
```

11.13 Other Verilog Features

This section covers some of the more advanced Verilog features. **System tasks** and functions are defined as part of the IEEE Verilog standard.

11.13.1 Display Tasks

The following code illustrates the **display system tasks** [Verilog LRM 14.1]:

```
module test_display; // display system tasks:
initial begin $display ("string, variables, or expression");
/* format specifications work like printf in C:
        %d=decimal %b=binary %s=string %h=hex %o=octal
        %c=character %m=hierarchical name %v=strength %t=time format
        %e=scientific %f=decimal %g=shortest
examples: %d uses default width %0d uses minimum width
        %7.3g uses 7 spaces with 3 digits after decimal point */
// $displayb, $displayh, $displayo print in b, h, o formats
// $write, $strobe, $monitor also have b, h, o versions

$write("write"); // as $display, but without newline at end of line

$strobe("strobe"); // as $display, values at end of simulation cycle

$monitor(v); // disp. @change of v (except v= $time,$stime,$realtime)
$monitoron; $monitoroff; // toggle monitor mode on/off

end endmodule
```

11.13.2 File I/O Tasks

The following example illustrates the **file I/O system tasks** [Verilog LRM 14.2]:

```
module file_1; integer f1, ch; initial begin f1 = $fopen("f1.out");
if(f1==0) $stop(2); if(f1==2)$display("f1 open");
ch = f1|1; $fdisplay(ch,"Hello"); $fclose(f1); end endmodule
```

```
> vlog file_1.v
> vsim -c file_1
# Loading work.file_1
VSIM 1> run 10
# f1 open
# Hello
VSIM 2> q
> more f1.out
Hello
>
```

The $fopen system task returns a 32-bit unsigned integer called a **multichannel descriptor** (f1 in this example) unique to each file. The multichannel descriptor contains 32 flags, one for each of 32 possible channels or files (subject to limitations of the operating system). Channel 0 is the standard output (normally the screen), which is always open. The first call to $fopen opens channel 1 and sets bit 1 of the multichannel descriptor. Subsequent calls set higher bits. The file I/O system tasks: $fdisplay, $fwrite, $fmonitor, and $fstrobe; correspond to their display counterparts. The first parameter for the file system tasks is a multichannel descriptor that may have multiple bits set. Thus, the preceding example writes the string "Hello" to the screen and to file1.out. The task $fclose closes a file and allows the channel to be reused.

The file I/O tasks $readmemb and $readmemh read a text file into a memory. The file may contain only spaces, new lines, tabs, form feeds, comments, addresses, and binary (for $readmemb) or hex (for $readmemh) numbers, as in the following example:

```
mem.dat
@2 1010_1111 @4 0101_1111 1010_1111 // @address in hex
x1x1_zzzz 1111_0000 /* x or z is OK */

module load; reg [7:0] mem[0:7]; integer i; initial begin
$readmemb("mem.dat", mem, 1, 6); // start_address=1, end_address=6
for (i= 0; i<8; i=i+1) $display("mem[%0d] %b", i, mem[i]);
end endmodule

> vsim -c load
# Loading work.load
VSIM 1> run 10
# ** Warning: $readmem (memory mem) file mem.dat line 2:
#    More patterns than index range (hex 1:6)
#    Time: 0 ns  Iteration: 0  Instance:/
# mem[0] xxxxxxxx
# mem[1] xxxxxxxx
# mem[2] 10101111
# mem[3] xxxxxxxx
# mem[4] 01011111
# mem[5] 10101111
# mem[6] x1x1zzzz
# mem[7] xxxxxxxx
VSIM 2> q
>
```

11.13.3 Timescale, Simulation, and Timing-Check Tasks

There are two **timescale tasks**, $printtimescale and $timeformat [Verilog LRM 14.3]. The $timeformat specifies the %t format specification for the display and file I/O system tasks as well as the time unit for delays entered interactively and from files. Here are examples of the timescale tasks:

```
// timescale tasks:
module a; initial $printtimescale(b.c1); endmodule
module b; c c1 (); endmodule
`timescale 10 ns / 1 fs
module c_dat; endmodule

`timescale 1 ms / 1 ns
module Ttime; initial $timeformat(-9, 5, " ns", 10); endmodule
/* $timeformat [ ( n, p, suffix , min_field_width ) ] ;
```

```
units = 1 second ** (-n), n = 0->15, e.g. for n = 9, units = ns
p = digits after decimal point for %t e.g. p = 5 gives 0.00000
suffix for %t (despite timescale directive)
min_field_width is number of character positions for %t */
```

The **simulation control tasks** are $stop and $finish [Verilog LRM 14.4]:

```
module test_simulation_control; // simulation control system tasks:
initial begin $stop; // enter interactive mode (default parameter 1)
$finish(2); // graceful exit with optional parameter as follows:
// 0 = nothing 1 = time and location 2 = time, location, and statistics
end endmodule
```

The **timing-check tasks** [Verilog LRM 14.5] are used in specify blocks. The following code and comments illustrate the definitions and use of timing-check system tasks. The arguments to the tasks are defined and explained in Table 11.11.

TABLE 11.11   Timing-check system task parameters.

Timing task argument	Description of argument	Type of argument
reference_event	to establish reference time	module input or inout (scalar or vector net)
data_event	signal to check against reference_event	module input or inout (scalar or vector net)
limit	time limit to detect timing violation on data_event	constant expression or specparam
threshold	largest pulse width ignored by timing check $width	constant expression or specparam
notifier	flags a timing violation (before -> after): x->0, 0->1, 1->0, z->z	register

```
module timing_checks (data, clock, clock_1,clock_2);              //1
input data,clock,clock_1,clock_2;reg tSU,tH,tHIGH,tP,tSK,tR;      //2
specify // timing check system tasks:                            //3
/* $setup (data_event, reference_event, limit [, notifier]);     //4
violation = (T_reference_event)-(T_data_event) < limit */        //5
$setup(data, posedge clock, tSU);                                //6
/* $hold (reference_event, data_event, limit [, notifier]);      //7
violation =                                                      //8
  (time_of_data_event)-(time_of_reference_event) < limit */      //9
$hold(posedge clock, data, tH);                                  //10
/* $setuphold (reference_event, data_event, setup_limit,         //11
    hold_limit [, notifier]);                                    //12
parameter_restriction = setup_limit + hold_limit > 0 */          //13
```

```
$setuphold(posedge clock, data, tSU, tH);                          //14
/* $width (reference_event, limit, threshold [, notifier]);        //15
violation =                                                        //16
   threshold < (T_data_event) - (T_reference_event) < limit        //17
reference_event = edge                                             //18
data_event = opposite_edge_of_reference_event */                  //19
$width(posedge clock, tHIGH);                                     //20
/* $period (reference_event, limit [, notifier]);                  //21
violation = (T_data_event) - (T_reference_event) < limit          //22
reference_event = edge                                             //23
data_event = same_edge_of_reference event */                      //24
$period(posedge clock, tP);                                       //25
/* $skew (reference_event, data_event, limit [, notifier]);        //26
violation = (T_data_event) - (T_reference_event) > limit */       //27
$skew(posedge clock_1, posedge clock_2, tSK);                     //28
/* $recovery (reference_event, data_event, limit, [, notifier]);   //29
violation = (T_data_event) - (T_reference_event) < limit */       //30
$recovery(posedge clock, posedge clock_2, tR);                    //31
/* $nochange (reference_event, data_event, start_edge_offset,      //32
   end_edge_offset [, notifier]);                                  //33
reference_event = posedge | negedge                               //34
violation = change while reference high (posedge)/low (negedge)   //35
+ve start_edge_offset moves start of window later                 //36
+ve end_edge_offset moves end of window later */                  //37
$nochange (posedge clock, data, 0, 0);                            //38
endspecify endmodule                                              //39
```

You can use **edge specifiers** as parameters for the timing-check events (except for the reference event in $nochange):

```
edge_control_specifier ::= edge [edge_descriptor {, edge_descriptor}]
edge_descriptor ::= 01 | 0x | 10 | 1x | x0 | x1
```

For example, 'edge [01, 0x, x1] clock' is equivalent to 'posedge clock'. Edge transitions with 'z' are treated the same as transitions with 'x'.

Here is a D flip-flop model that uses timing checks and a **notifier register**. The register, notifier, is changed when a timing-check task detects a violation and the last entry in the table then sets the flip-flop output to unknown.

```
primitive dff_udp(q, clock, data, notifier);
output q; reg q; input clock, data, notifier;
table //clock data notifier:state:q
       r    0     ?    :  ?  :0 ;
       r    1     ?    :  ?  :1 ;
       n    ?     ?    :  ?  :- ;
       ?    *     ?    :  ?  :- ;
       ?    ?     *    :  ?  :x ; endtable // notifier
```

```
endprimitive
`timescale 100 fs / 1 fs
module dff(q, clock, data);output q; input clock, data; reg notifier;
dff_udp(q1, clock, data, notifier); buf(q, q1);
specify
    specparam tSU = 5, tH = 1, tPW = 20, tPLH = 4:5:6, tPHL = 4:5:6;
      (clock *> q) = (tPLH, tPHL);
    $setup(data, posedge clock, tSU, notifier); // setup: data to clock
    $hold(posedge clock, data, tH, notifier); // hold: clock to data
    $period(posedge clock, tPW, notifier); // clock: period
endspecify
endmodule
```

11.13.4 PLA Tasks

The **PLA modeling tasks** model two-level logic [Verilog LRM 14.6]. As an example, the following eqntott logic equations can be implemented using a PLA:

```
b1 = a1 & a2; b2 = a3 & a4 & a5 ; b3 = a5 & a6 & a7;
```

The following module loads a PLA model for the equations above (in AND logic) using the **array format** (the array format allows only '1' or '0' in the PLA memory, or **personality array**). The file array.dat is similar to the espresso input plane format.

```
array.dat
1100000
0011100
0000111

module pla_1 (a1,a2,a3,a4,a5,a6,a7,b1,b2,b3);
input a1, a2, a3, a4, a5, a6, a7 ; output b1, b2, b3;
reg [1:7] mem[1:3]; reg b1, b2, b3;
initial begin
    $readmemb("array.dat", mem);
    #1; b1=1; b2=1; b3=1;
    $async$and$array(mem,{a1,a2,a3,a4,a5,a6,a7},{b1,b2,b3});
end
initial $monitor("%4g",$time,,b1,,b2,,b3);
endmodule
```

The next example illustrates the use of the **plane format**, which allows '1', '0', as well as '?' or 'z' (either may be used for don't care) in the personality array.

```
b1 = a1 & !a2; b2 = a3; b3 = !a1 & !a3; b4 = 1;

module pla_2; reg [1:3] a, mem[1:4]; reg [1:4] b;
initial begin
    $async$and$plane(mem,{a[1],a[2],a[3]},{b[1],b[2],b[3],b[4]});
    mem[1] = 3'b10?; mem[2] = 3'b??1; mem[3] = 3'b0?0; mem[4] = 3'b???;
```

```
    #10 a = 3'b111; #10 $displayb(a, " -> ", b);
    #10 a = 3'b000; #10 $displayb(a, " -> ", b);
    #10 a = 3'bxxx; #10 $displayb(a, " -> ", b);
    #10 a = 3'b101; #10 $displayb(a, " -> ", b);
end endmodule

111 -> 0101
000 -> 0011
xxx -> xxx1
101 -> 1101
```

11.13.5 Stochastic Analysis Tasks

The **stochastic analysis tasks** model queues [Verilog LRM 14.7]. Each of the tasks
return a status as shown in Table 11.12.

TABLE 11.12   Status values for the stochastic analysis tasks.

Status value	Meaning
0	OK
1	queue full, cannot add
2	undefined q_id
3	queue empty, cannot remove
4	unsupported q_type, cannot create queue
5	max_length <= 0, cannot create queue
6	duplicate q_id, cannot create queue
7	not enough memory, cannot create queue

The following module illustrates the interface and parameters for these tasks:

```
module stochastic; initial begin // stochastic analysis system tasks:

/* $q_initialize (q_id, q_type, max_length, status) ;
q_id is an integer that uniquely identifies the queue
q_type 1=FIFO 2=LIFO
max_length is an integer defining the maximum number of entries */
$q_initialize (q_id, q_type, max_length, status) ;

/* $q_add (q_id, job_id, inform_id, status) ;
job_id = integer input
inform_id = user-defined integer input for queue entry */
$q_add (q_id, job_id, inform_id, status) ;

/* $q_remove (q_id, job_id, inform_id, status) ; */
$q_remove (q_id, job_id, inform_id, status) ;
```

```
/* $q_full (q_id, status) ;
status = 0 = queue is not full, status = 1 = queue full */
$q_full (q_id, status) ;

/* $q_exam (q_id, q_stat_code, q_stat_value, status) ;
q_stat_code is input request as follows:
1=current queue length 2=mean inter-arrival time 3=max. queue length
4=shortest wait time ever
5=longest wait time for jobs still in queue 6=ave. wait time in queue
q_stat_value is output containing requested value */
$q_exam (q_id, q_stat_code, q_stat_value, status) ;

end endmodule
```

11.13.6 Simulation Time Functions

The **simulation time functions** are as follows [Verilog LRM 14.8]:

```
module test_time; initial begin // simulation time system functions:
$time ;
// returns 64-bit integer scaled to timescale unit of invoking module

$stime ;
// returns 32-bit integer scaled to timescale unit of invoking module

$realtime ;
// returns real scaled to timescale unit of invoking module

end endmodule
```

11.13.7 Conversion Functions

The **conversion functions for reals** are as follows [Verilog LRM 14.9]:

```
module test_convert; // conversion functions for reals:
integer i; real r; reg [63:0] bits;
initial begin #1 r=256;#1 i = $rtoi(r);
#1; r = $itor(2 * i) ; #1 bits = $realtobits(2.0 * r) ;
#1; r = $bitstoreal(bits) ; end
initial $monitor("%3f",$time,,i,,r,,bits); /*
$rtoi converts reals to integers w/truncation e.g. 123.45 -> 123
$itor converts integers to reals e.g. 123 -> 123.0
$realtobits converts reals to 64-bit vector
$bitstoreal converts bit pattern to real
Real numbers in these functions conform to IEEE Std 754. Conversion
rounds to the nearest valid number. */
endmodule
# 0.000000          x 0                  x
# 1.000000          x 256                    x
# 2.000000          256 256                  x
# 3.000000          256 512                  x
```

```
# 4.000000        256 512    4652218415073722368
# 5.000000        256 1024   4652218415073722368
```

Here is an example using the conversion functions in port connections:

```
module test_real;wire [63:0]a; driver d (a); receiver r (a);
initial $monitor("%3g",$time,,a,,d.r1,,r.r2); endmodule

module driver (real_net);
output real_net; real r1; wire [64:1] real_net = $realtobits(r1);
initial #1 r1 = 123.456; endmodule

module receiver (real_net);
input real_net; wire [64:1] real_net; real r2;
initial assign r2 = $bitstoreal(real_net);
endmodule
```

```
# 0                      0 0 0
# 1   4638387860618067575 123.456 123.456
```

11.13.8 Probability Distribution Functions

The probability distribution functions are as follows [Verilog LRM 14.10]:

```
module probability; // probability distribution functions:        //1
/* $random [(seed)] returns random 32-bit signed integer          //2
seed = register, integer, or time */                              //3
reg [23:0] r1,r2; integer r3,r4,r5,r6,r7,r8,r9;                    //4
integer seed, start, \end , mean, standard_deviation;             //5
integer degree_of_freedom, k_stage;                               //6
initial begin seed=1; start=0; \end =6; mean=5;                   //7
standard_deviation=2; degree_of_freedom=2; k_stage=1; #1;         //8
r1 = $random % 60; // random -59 to 59                            //9
r2 = {$random} % 60; // positive value 0-59                       //10
r3=$dist_uniform (seed, start, \end ) ;                           //11
r4=$dist_normal (seed, mean, standard_deviation) ;               //12
r5=$dist_exponential (seed, mean) ;                               //13
r6=$dist_poisson (seed, mean) ;                                   //14
r7=$dist_chi_square (seed, degree_of_freedom) ;                   //15
r8=$dist_t (seed, degree_of_freedom) ;                            //16
r9=$dist_erlang (seed, k_stage, mean) ; end                       //17
initial #2 $display ("%3f",$time,,r1,,r2,,r3,,r4,,r5);            //18
initial begin #3; $display ("%3f",$time,,r6,,r7,,r8,,r9); end     //19
/* All parameters are integer values.                             //20
Each function returns a pseudo-random number                      //21
e.g. $dist_uniform returns uniformly distributed random numbers   //22
mean, degree_of_freedom, k_stage                                  //23
(exponential, poisson, chi-square, t, erlang) > 0.                //24
seed = inout integer initialized by user, updated by function     //25
```

```
start, end ($dist_uniform) = integer bounding return values */     //26
endmodule                                                          //27
```

```
2.000000        8       57          0           4           9
3.000000            7           3           0           2
```

11.13.9 Programming Language Interface

The C language **Programming Language Interface** (**PLI**) allows you to access the internal Verilog data structure [Verilog LRM17-23, A-E]. For example, you can use the PLI to implement the following extensions to a Verilog simulator:

- C language delay calculator for a cell library
- C language interface to a Verilog-based or other logic or fault simulator
- Graphical waveform display and debugging
- C language simulation models
- Hardware interfaces

There are three generations of PLI routines:

- Task/function (TF) routines (or utility routines), the first generation of the PLI, start with `'tf_'`.
- Access (ACC) routines, the second generation of the PLI, start with the characters `'acc_'` and access delay and logic values. There is some overlap between the ACC routines and TF routines.
- Verilog Procedural Interface (VPI) routines, the third generation of the PLI, start with the characters `'vpi_'` and are a superset of the TF and ACC routines.

11.14 Summary

Table 11.13 lists the key features of Verilog HDL. The most important concepts covered in this chapter are:

- Concurrent processes and sequential execution
- Difference between a `reg` and a `wire`, and between a scalar and a vector
- Arithmetic operations on `reg` and `wire`
- Data slip
- Delays and events

TABLE 11.13   Verilog on one page.

Verilog feature	Example

Comments	```a = 0; // comment ends with newline```
	```/* This is a multiline or block```
	```comment */```

Constants: string and numeric	```parameter BW = 32 // local, use BW```
	`` `define G_BUS 32 // global, use `G_BUS``
	```4'b2 1'bx```

Names (case-sensitive, start with letter or '_')	```_12name A_name $BAD NotSame notsame```
Two basic types of logic signals: wire and reg	```wire myWire; reg myReg;```
Use a continuous assignment statement with wire	```assign myWire = 1;```
Use a procedural assignment statement with reg	```always myReg = myWire;```
Buses and vectors use square brackets	```reg [31:0] DBus; DBus[12] = 1'bx;```
We can perform arithmetic on bit vectors	```reg [31:0] DBus; DBus = DBus + 2;```
Arithmetic is performed modulo 2^n	```reg [2:0] R; R = 7 + 1; // now R = 0```
Operators: as in C (but not ++ or --)	
Fixed logic value system	```1, 0, x (unknown), z (high-impedance)```

Basic unit of code is the module	```module bake (chips, dough, cookies);```
	```input chips, dough; output cookies;```
	```assign cookies = chips & dough;```
	```endmodule```

Ports	input or input/output ports are `wire` output ports are `wire` or `reg`

Procedures model things that happen at the same time and may be sensitive to an edge, **posedge**, **negedge**, or to a level.	```always @rain sing; always @rain dance;```
	```always @(posedge clock) D = Q; // flop```
	```always @(a or b) c = a & b; // and gate```

Sequential blocks model repeating things:
always: executes forever
initial: executes once only at start of simulation
	```initial born;```
	```always @alarm_clock begin : a_day```
	```metro=commute; bulot=work; dodo=sleep;```
	```end```

Functions and tasks	```function ... endfunction``` ```task ... endtask```
Output	```$display("a=%f",a);$dumpvars;$monitor(a)```
Control simulation	```$stop; $finish // sudden or gentle halt```
Compiler directives	`` `timescale 1ns/1ps // units/resolution``

Delay	```#1 a = b; // delay then sample b```
	```a = #1 b; // sample b then delay```

11.15 Problems

*=Difficult, **=Very difficult, ***=Extremely difficult

11.1 (Counter, 30 min.) Download the VeriWell simulator from `http://www.`
`wellspring.com` and simulate the counter from Section 11.1 (exclude the comments to save typing). Include the complete input and output listings in your report.

11.2 (Simulator, 30 min.) Build a "cheat sheet" for your simulator, listing the commands for running the simulator and using it in interactive mode.

11.3 (Verilog examples, 10 min.) The Cadence Verilog-XL simulator comes with a directory `examples`. Make a list of the examples from the `README` files in the various directories.

11.4 (Gotchas, 60 min.) Build a "most common Verilog mistakes" file. Start with:

- Extra or missing semicolon ';'
- Forgetting to declare a `reg`
- Using a `reg` instead of a `wire` for an `input` or `inout` port
- Bad declarations: `reg bus[0:31]` instead of `reg [31:0]bus`
- Mixing vector declarations: `wire [31:0]BusA, [15:0]BusB`
- The case-sensitivity of Verilog
- No delay in an `always` statement (simulator loops forever)
- Mixing up ` (accent grave) for `` `define `` and ' (tick or apostrophe) for `1'b1` with ´ (accent acute) or ' (open single quote) or ' (close single quote)
- Mixing " (double quote) with " (open quotes) or " (close quotes)

11.5 (Sensitivity, 10 min.) Explore and explain what happens if you write this:
```
always @(a or b or c) e = (a|b)&(c|d);
```

11.6 (Verilog `if` statement, 10 min.) Build test code to simulate the following Verilog fragment. Explain what is wrong and fix the problem.
```
if (i > 0)
  if (i < 2) $display ("i is 1");
else $display ("i is less than 0");
```

11.7 (Effect of delay, 30 min.). Write code to test the four different code fragments shown in Table 11.14 and print the value of `'a'` at time = 0 and time = 1 for each case. Explain the differences in your simulation results.

11.8 (Verilog events, 10 min.). Simulate the following and explain the results:
```
event event_1, event_2;
always @ event_1 -> event_2;
initial @event_2 $stop;
initial -> event_1;
```

TABLE 11.14 Code fragments for Problem 11.7.

	(a)	(b)	(c)	(d)

Code fragment	```reg a;```
	```initial```
	```begin```
	```a = 0;```
	```a = a + 1;```
	```end```
		```reg a;```
		```initial```
		```begin```
		```#0 a = 0;```
		```#0 a = a + 1;```
		```end```
			```reg a;```
			```initial```
			```begin```
			```a <= 0;```
			```a <= a + 1;```
			```end```
				```reg a;```
				```initial```
				```begin```
				```#1 a = 0;```
				```#1 a = a + 1;```
				```end```

11.9 (Blocking and nonblocking assignment statements, 30 min.). Write code to test the different code fragments shown in Table 11.15 and print the value of 'outp' at time = 0 and time = 10 for each case. Explain the difference in simulation results.

TABLE 11.15 Code fragments for Problem 11.9.

	(a)	(b)	(c)	(d)

Code fragment	```reg outp;```
	```always```
	```begin```
	```#10 outp = 0;```
	```#10 outp = 1;```
	```end```
		```reg outp;```
		```always```
		```begin```
		```outp <= #10 1;```
		```outp <= #10 0;```
		```end```
			```reg outp;```
			```always```
			```begin```
			```#10 outp = 0;```
			```#10 outp <= 1;```
			```end```
				```reg outp;```
				```always```
				```begin```
				```#10 outp <= 0;```
				```#10 outp = 1;```
				```end```

11.10 (Verilog UDPs, 20 min.). Use this primitive to build a half adder:

```
primitive Adder(Sum, InA, InB); output Sum; input Ina, InB;
table 00 : 0; 01 : 1; 10 : 1; 11 : 0; endtable
endprimitive
```

Apply unknowns to the inputs. What is the output?

11.11 (Verilog UDPs, 30 min.). Use the following primitive model for a D latch:

```
primitive DLatch(Q, Clock, Data); output Q; reg Q; input Clock, Data;
table 1 0 : ? : 0; 1 1 : ? : 1; 0 1 : ? : -; endtable
endprimitive
```

Check to see what happens when you apply unknown inputs (including clock transitions to unknown). What happens if you apply high-impedance values to the inputs (again including transitions)?

11.12 (Propagation of unknowns in primitives, 45 min.) Use the following primitive model for a D flip-flop:

```
primitive DFF(Q, Clock, Data); output Q; reg Q; input Clock, Data;
```

```
table
r    0 : ? : 0 ;
r    1 : ? : 1 ;
(0x) 0 : 0 : 0 ;
(0x) 1 : 1 : 1 ;
(?0) ? : ? : - ;
? (??) : ? : - ;
endtable
endprimitive
```

Check to see what happens when you apply unknown inputs (including a clock transition to an unknown value). What happens if you apply high-impedance values to the inputs (again including transitions)?

11.13 (D flip-flop UDP, 60 min.) Table 11.16 shows a UDP for a D flip-flop with QN output and asynchronous reset and set.

TABLE 11.16   D flip-flop UDP for Problem 11.13.

```
primitive DFlipFlop2(QN, Data, Clock, Res, Set);
output QN; reg QN; input Data, Clock, Res, Set;
table
//      Data    Clock   Res     Set     :state  :next state
        1       (01)    0       0       :?      :0;     // line 1
        1       (01)    0       x       :?      :0;
        ?       ?       0       x       :0      :0;
        0       (01)    0       0       :?      :1;
        0       (01)    x       0       :?      :1;
        ?       ?       x       0       :1      :1;
        1       (x1)    0       0       :0      :0;
        0       (x1)    0       0       :1      :1;
        1       (0x)    0       0       :0      :0;
        0       (0x)    0       0       :1      :1;
        ?       ?       1       ?       :?      :1;
        ?       ?       0       1       :?      :0;
        ?       n       0       0       :?      :-;
        *       ?       ?       ?       :?      :-;
        ?       ?       (?0)    ?       :?      :-;
        ?       ?       ?       (?0)    :?      :-;
        ?       ?       ?       ?       :?      :x;     // line 17
endtable
endprimitive
```

---

a. Explain the purpose of each line in the truth table.

b. Write a module to test each line of the UDP.

c. Can you find any errors, omissions, or other problems in this UDP?

11.14 (JK flip-flop, 30 min.) Test the following model for a JK flip-flop:

```
module JKFF (Q, J, K, Clk, Rst);
parameter width = 1, reset_value = 0;
input [width-1:0] J, K; output [width-1:0] Q; reg [width-1:0] Q;
input Clk, Rst; initial Q = {width{1'bx}};
always @ (posedge Clk or negedge Rst )
if (Rst==0 ) Q <= #1 reset_value;
else Q <= #1 (J & ~K) | (J & K & ~Q) | (~J & ~K & Q);
endmodule
```

11.15 (Overriding Verilog parameters, 20 min.) The following module has a parameter specification that allows you to change the number of AND gates that it models (the cardinality or width):

```
module Vector_AND(Z, A, B);
  parameter card = 2; input [card-1:0] A,B; output [card-1:0] Z;
  wire [card-1:0] Z = A & B;
endmodule
```

The next module changes the parameter value by specifying an overriding value in the module instantiation:

```
module Four_AND_Gates(OutBus, InBusA, InBusB);
  input [3:0] InBusA, InBusB; output [3:0] OutBus;
  Vector_AND #(4) My_AND(OutBus, InBusA, InBusB);
endmodule
```

These next two modules change the parameter value by using a `defparam` statement, which overrides the declared parameter value:

```
module X_AND_Gates(OutBus, InBusA, InBusB);
  parameter X = 2;input [X-1:0] InBusA, InBusB;output [X-1:0] OutBus;
  Vector_AND #(X) My_AND(OutBus, InBusA, InBusB);
endmodule

module size; defparam X_AND_Gates.X = 4; endmodule
```

  a. Check that the two alternative methods of specifying parameters are equivalent by instantiating the modules `Four_AND_Gates` and `X_AND_Gates` in another module and simulating.

  b. List and comment on the advantages and disadvantages of both methods.

11.16 (Default Verilog delays, 10 min.). Demonstrate, using simulation, that the following NAND gates have the delays you expect:

```
nand (strong0, strong1) #1
  Nand_1(n001, n004, n005),
  Nand_2(n003, n001, n005, n002);
nand (n006, n005, n002);
```

11.17 (Arrays of modules, 30 min.) Newer versions of Verilog allow the instantiating of **arrays of modules** (in this book we usually call this a vector since we are only allowed one row). You specify the number in the array by using a **range** after the instance name as follows:

```
nand #2 nand_array[0:7](zn, a, b);
```

Create and test a model for an 8-bit register using an array of flip-flops.

11.18 (Assigning Verilog real to integer data types, 10 min.). What is the value of `ImInteger` in the following code?

```
real ImReal; integer ImInteger;
initial begin ImReal = -1.5; ImInteger = ImReal; end
```

11.19 (BNF syntax, 10 min.) Use the BNF syntax definitions in Appendix B to answer the following questions. In each case explain how you arrive at the answer:

a. What is the highest-level construct?

b. What is the lowest-level construct?

c. Can you nest `begin` and `end` statements?

d. Where is a legal place for a `case` statement?

e. Is the following code legal: `reg [31:0] rega, [32:1] regb;`

f. Where is it legal to include sequential statements?

11.20 (Old syntax definitions, 10 min.) Prior to the IEEE LRM, Verilog BNF was expressed using a different notation. For example, an event expression was defined as follows:

```
<event_expression> ::= <expression>
  or <<posedge or negedge> <SCALAR_EVENT_EXPRESSION>>
  or <<event_expression> or <event_expression>>
```

Notice that we are using 'or' as part of the BNF to mean "alternatively" and also 'or' as a Verilog keyword. The keyword 'or' is in bold—the difference is fairly obvious. Here is an alternative definition for an event expression:

```
<event_expression> ::= <expression>
||= posedge <SCALAR_EVENT_EXPRESSION>
||= negedge <SCALAR_EVENT_EXPRESSION>
||= <event_expression> <or <event_expression>>*
```

Are these definitions equivalent (given, of course, that we replaced `||=` with `or` in the simplified syntax)? Explain carefully how you would attempt to prove that they are the same.

11.21 (Operators, 20 min.) Explain Table 11.17 (see next page).

11.22 (Unary reduction, 10 min.) Complete Table 11.18 (see next page).

11.23 (Coerced ports, 20 min.) Perform some experiments to test the behavior of your Verilog simulator in the following situation: "NOTE—A port that is declared as input (output) but used as an output (input) or inout may be coerced to inout. If not coerced to inout, a warning must be issued" [Verilog LRM 12.3.6].

TABLE 11.17   Unary operators (Problem 11.21).

	(a)	(b)	(c)	(d)

Code	`module unary;`
	`reg [4:0] u;`
	`initial u=!'b011z;`
	`initial`
	`$display("%b",u);`
	`endmodule`
		`module unary;`
		`wire u;`
		`assign u=!'b011z;`
		`initial`
		`$display("%b",u);`
		`endmodule`
			`module unary;`
			`wire u;`
			`assign u=!'b011z;`
			`initial`
			`#1 $display("%b",u);`
			`endmodule`
				`module unary;`
				`wire u;`
				`assign u=&'b1;`
				`initial`
				`#1 $display("%b",u);`
				`endmodule`

Output	0000x	z	x	0

TABLE 11.18   Unary reduction (Problem 11.22).

Operand	&	~&	|	~|	^	~^
4'b0000						
4'b1111						
4'b01x0						
4'bz000						

11.24 (*Difficult delay code, 20 min.) Perform some experiments to explain what this difficult to interpret statement does:

```
#2 a <= repeat(2) @(posedge clk) d;
```

11.25 (Fork–join, 20 min.) Write some test code to compare the behavior of the code fragments shown in Table 11.19.

TABLE 11.19   Fork-and-join examples for Problem 11.25.

	(a)	(b)	(c)	(d)

Code fragment	`fork`
	`a = b;`
	`b = a;`
	`join`
		`fork`
		`a <= b;`
		`b <= a;`
		`join`
			`fork`
			`#1 a = b;`
			`#1 b = a;`
			`join`
				`fork`
				`a = #1 b;`
				`b = #1 a;`
				`join`

11.26 (Blocking and nonblocking assignments, 20 min.) Simulate the following code and explain the results:

```
module nonblocking; reg Y;
    always begin Y <= #10 1;Y <= #20 0;#10; end
    always begin $display($time,,"Y=",Y); #10; end
```

```
      initial #100 $finish;
endmodule
```

11.27 (*Flip-flop code, 10 min.) Explain why this flip-flop does not work:

```
module Dff_Res_Bad(D,Q,Clock,Reset);
output Q; input D,Clock,Reset; reg Q; wire D;
always @(posedge Clock) if (Reset !== 1) Q = D; always if (Reset == 1)
Q = 0;
end endmodule
```

11.28 (D flip-flop, 10 min.) Test the following D flip-flop model:

```
module DFF (D, Q, Clk, Rst);
parameter width = 1,  reset_value = 0;
input [width-1:0] D; output [width-1:0] Q; reg [width-1:0] Q;
input Clk,Rst;
initial Q = {width{1'bx}};
always @ ( posedge Clk or negedge Rst )
if ( Rst == 0 ) Q <= #1 reset_value; else Q <= #1 D;
endmodule
```

11.29 (D flip-flop with scan, 10 min.) Explain the following model:

```
module DFFSCAN (D, Q, Clk, Rst, ScEn, ScIn, ScOut);
parameter width = 1,  reset_value = 0;
input [width-1:0] D; output [width-1:0] Q; reg [width-1:0] Q;
input Clk,Rst,ScEn,ScIn; output ScOut;
initial Q = {width{1'bx}};
always @ ( posedge Clk or negedge Rst ) begin
   if ( Rst == 0 )       Q <= #1 reset_value;
   else if (ScEn)        Q <= #1 {Q,ScIn};
   else                  Q <= #1 D;
end
assign ScOut=Q[width-1];
endmodule
```

11.30 (Pads, 30 min.) Test the following model for a bidirectional I/O pad:

```
module PadBidir (C, Pad, I, Oen); // active low enable
parameter width=1, pinNumbers="", \strength =1, level="CMOS",
pull="none", externalVdd=5;
output [width-1:0] C; inout  [width-1:0] Pad; input  [width-1:0] I;
input Oen;
assign #1 Pad = Oen ? {width{1'bz}} : I;
assign #1 C = Pad;
endmodule
```

Construct and test a model for a three-state pad from the above.

11.31 (Loops, 15 min.) Explain and correct the problem in the following code:

```
module Loop_Bad; reg [3:0] i; reg [31:0] DBus;
initial DBus = 0;
```

```
initial begin #1; for (i=0; i<=15; i=i+1) DBus[i]=1; end
initial begin
$display("DBus = %b",DBus); #2; $display("DBus = %b",DBus); $stop;
end endmodule
```

11.32 (Arithmetic, 10 min.) Explain the following:

```
integer IntA;
IntA = -12 / 3; // result is -4
IntA = -'d 12 / 3; // result is 1431655761
```

Determine and explain the values of `intA` and `regA` after each assignment statement in the following code:

```
integer intA; reg [15:0] regA;
intA = -4'd12; regA = intA/3; regA = -4'd12;
intA = regA/3; intA = -4'd12/3; regA = -12/3;
```

11.33 (Arithmetic overflow, 30 min.) Consider the following:

```
reg [7:0] a, b, sum; sum = (a + b) >> 1;
```

The intent is to add a and b, which may cause an overflow, and then shift `sum` to keep the carry bit. However, because all operands in the expression are of an 8-bit width, the expression `(a + b)` is only 8 bits wide, and we lose the carry bit before the shift. One solution forces the expression `(a + b)` to use at least 9 bits. For example, adding an integer value of 0 to the expression will cause the evaluation to be performed using the bit size of integers [LRM 4.4.2]. Check to see if the following alternatives produce the intended result:

```
sum = (a + b + 0) >> 1;
```

```
sum = {0,a} + {0,b} >> 1;
```

11.34 (*Data slip, 60 min.) Table 11.20 shows several different ways to model the connection of a 2-bit shift register. Determine which of these models suffer from data slip. In each case show your simulation results.

11.35 (**Timing, 30 min.) What does a simulator display for the following?

```
assign p = q; initial begin q = 0; #1 q = 1; $display(p); end
```

What is the problem here? Conduct some experiments to illustrate your answer.

11.36 (Port connections, 10 min.) Explain the following declaration:

```
module test (.a(c), .b(c));
```

11.37 (**Functions and tasks, 30 min.) Experiment to determine whether invocation of a function (or task) behaves as a blocking or nonblocking assignment.

11.38 (Nonblocking assignments, 10 min.) Predict the output of the following model:

```
module e1; reg a, b, c;
initial begin a = 0; b = 1; c = 0; end
always c = #5 ~c; always @(posedge c) begin a <= b; b <= a; end
endmodule
```

TABLE 11.20 Data slip (Problem 11.34).

Alternative	Data slip?
1 `always @(posedge Clk) begin Q2 = Q1; Q1 = D1; end`	
2 `always @(posedge Clk) begin Q1 = D1; Q2 = Q1; end`	
3 `always @(posedge Clk) begin Q1 <= #1 D1; Q2 <= #1 Q1; end`	
4 `always @(posedge Clk) Q1 = D1; always @(posedge Clk) Q2 = Q1;`	Y
5 `always @(posedge Clk) Q1 = #1 D1; always @(posedge Clk) Q2 = #1 Q1;`	N
6 `always @(posedge Clk) #1 Q1 = D1; always @(posedge Clk) #1 Q2 = Q1;`	
7 `always @(posedge Clk) Q1 <= D1; always @(posedge Clk) Q2 <= Q1;`	
8 `module FF_1 (Clk, D1, Q1); always @(posedge Clk) Q1 = D1; endmodule` `module FF_2 (Clk, Q1, Q2); always @(posedge Clk) Q2 = Q1; endmodule`	
9 `module FF_1 (Clk, D1, Q1); always @(posedge Clk) Q1 <= D1; endmodule` `module FF_2 (Clk, Q1, Q2); always @(posedge Clk) Q2 <= Q1; endmodule`	

11.39 (Assignment timing, 20 min.) Predict the output of the following module and explain the timing of the assignments:

```
module e2; reg a, b, c, d, e, f;
initial begin a = #10 1; b = #2 0; c = #4 1; end
initial begin d <= #10 1; e <= #2 0; f <= #4 1; end
endmodule
```

11.40 (Swap, 10 min.) Explain carefully what happens in the following code:

```
module e3; reg a, b;
initial begin a = 0; b = 1; a <= b; b <= a; end
endmodule
```

11.41 (*Overwriting, 30 min.) Explain the problem in the following code, determine what happens, and conduct some experiments to explore the problem further:

```
module m1; reg a;
initial a = 1;
initial begin a <= #4 0; a <= #4 1; end
endmodule
```

11.42 (*Multiple assignments, 30 min.) Explain what happens in the following:

```
module m2; reg r1; reg [2:0] i;
initial begin
r1 = 0; for (i = 0; i <= 5; i = i+1) r1 <= # (i*10) i[0]; end
endmodule
```

11.43 (Timing, 30 min) Write a model to mimic the behavior of a traffic light signal. The clock input is 1 MHz. You are to drive the lights as follows (times that the lights are on are shown in parentheses): green (60 s), yellow (1 s), red (60 s).

11.44 (Port declarations, 30 min.) The rules for port declarations are as follows: "The port expression in the port definition can be one of the following:

- a simple identifier
- a bit-select of a vector declared within the module
- a part-select of a vector declared within the module
- a concatenation of any of the above

Each port listed in the module definition's list of ports shall be declared in the body of the module as an input, output, or inout (bidirectional). This is in addition to any other declaration for a particular port—for example, a reg, or wire. A port can be declared in both a port declaration and a net or register declaration. If a port is declared as a vector, the range specification between the two declarations of a port shall be identical" [Verilog LRM 12.3.2].

Compile the following and comment (you may be surprised at the results):

```
module stop (); initial #1 $finish; endmodule
module Outs_1 (a); output [3:0] a; reg [3:0] a;
initial a <= 4'b10xz; endmodule
module Outs_2 (a); output [2:0] a; reg [3:0] a;
initial a <= 4'b10xz; endmodule
module Outs_3 (a); output [3:0] a; reg [2:0] a;
initial a <= 4'b10xz; endmodule
module Outs_4 (a); output [2:0] a; reg [2:0] a;
initial a <= 4'b10xz; endmodule
module Outs_5 (a); output a; reg [3:0] a;
initial a <= 4'b10xz; endmodule
module Outs_6 (a[2:0]); output [3:0] a; reg [3:0] a;
initial a <= 4'b10xz; endmodule
module Outs_7 (a[1]); output [3:0] a; reg [3:0] a;
initial a <= 4'b10xz; endmodule
module Outs_8 (a[1]); output a; reg [3:0] a;
always a <= 4'b10xz; endmodule
```

11.45 (Specify blocks, 30 min.)

a. Describe the pin-to-pin timing of the following module. Build a testbench to demonstrate your explanation.

```
module XOR_spec (a, b, z); input a, b: output z; xor x1 (z, a, b);
specify
   specparam tnr = 1, tnf = 2 specparam tir = 3, tif = 4;
   if ( a)(b => z) = (tir, tif); if ( b)(a => z) = (tir, tif);
   if (~a)(b => z) = (tnr, tnf); if (~b)(a => z) = (tnr, tnf);
endspecify
endmodule
```

b. Write and test a module for a 2:1 MUX with inputs A0, A1, and sel; output z; and the following delays: A0 to z: 0.3 ns (rise) and 0.4 ns (fall); A1 to z: 0.2 ns (rise) and 0.3 ns (fall); sel to z = 0.5 ns.

11.46 (Design contest, **60 min.) In 1995 John Cooley organized a contest between VHDL and Verilog for ASIC designers. The goal was to design the fastest 9-bit counter in under one hour using Synopsys synthesis tools and an LSI Logic vendor technology library. The Verilog interface is as follows:

```
module counter (data_in, up, down, clock,
   count_out, carry_out, borrow_out, parity_out);
output [8:0]  count_out;
output carry_out, borrow_out, parity_out;
input  [8:0]  data_in; input clock, up, down;
reg    [8:0]  count_out; reg carry_out,  borrow_out, parity_out;
// insert your design here
endmodule
```

The counter is positive-edge triggered, counts up with up='1' and down with down='1'. The contestants had the advantage of a predefined testbench with a set of test vectors; you do not. Design a model for the counter and a testbench.

11.47 (Timing checks, ***60 min.+) Flip-flops with preset and clear require more complex timing-check constructs than those described in Section 11.13.3. The following BNF defines a **controlled timing-check event**:

```
controlled_timing_check_event ::= timing_check_event_control
specify_terminal_descriptor [ &&& timing_check_condition ]

timing_check_condition ::=
  scalar_expression | ~scalar_expression
| scalar_expression == scalar_constant
| scalar_expression === scalar_constant
| scalar_expression != scalar_constant
| scalar_expression !== scalar_constant
```

The scalar expression that forms the conditioning signal must be a scalar net, or else the least significant bit of a vector net or a multibit expression value is used. The comparisons in the timing check condition may be **deterministic** (using ===, !==, ~, or no operator) or **nondeterministic** (using == or !=). For deterministic comparisons, an 'x' result disables the timing check. For nondeterministic comparisons, an 'x' result enables the timing check.

As an example the following **unconditioned timing check**,

```
$setup(data, posedge clock, 10);
```

performs a setup timing check on every positive edge of clock, as was explained in Section 11.13.3. The following controlled timing check is enabled only when clear is high, which is what is required in a flip-flop model, for example.

```
$setup(data, posedge clock &&& clear, 10);
```

The next example shows two alternative ways to enable a timing check only when clear is low. The second method uses a nondeterministic operator.

```
$setup(data,posedge clock &&&(~clear),10); // clear=x disables check
$setup(data,posedge clock &&&(clear==0),10); // clear=x enables check
```

To perform the setup check only when `clear` and `preset` signals are high, you can add a gate outside the specify block, as follows:

```
and g1(clear_and_preset, clear, set);
```

A controlled timing check event can then use this `clear_and_preset` signal:

```
$setup(data, posedge clock && clear_and_preset, 10);
```

Use the preceding techniques to expand the D flip-flop model, `dff_udp`, from Section 11.13.3 to include asynchronous active-low preset and clear signals as well as an output, qbar. Use the following module interface:

```
module dff(q, qbar, clock, data, preset, clear);
```

11.48 (Verilog BNF, 30 min.) Here is the "old" BNF definition of a sequential block (used in the Verilog reference manuals and the OVI LRM). Are there any differences from the "new" version?

```
<sequential_block> ::=
    begin <statement>* end
    or
    begin: <block_IDENTIFIER> <block_declaration>*
      <statement>*
    end

<block_declaration> ::= parameter <list_of_param_assignment>;
    or reg <range>? <attribute_decl>*
      <list_of_register_variable>;
    or integer <attribute_decl>* <list_of_register_variable>;
    or real <attribute_decl>* <list_of_variable_IDENTIFIER>;
    or time <attribute_decl>* <list_of_register_variable>;
    or event <attribute_decl>* <list_of_event_IDENTIFIER>;

<statement> ::=
    <blocking_assignment>;
    or <non-blocking_assignment>;
    or if(<expression>) <statement_or_null>
      <else <statement_or_null> >?
    or <case or casez or casex>
      (<expression>) <case item>+ endcase
    or forever <statement>
    or repeat(<expression>) <statement>
    or while(<expression>) <statement>
    or for(<assignment>;
      <expression>; <assignment>) <statement>
    or wait(<expression>) <statement_or_null>
    or disable <task_IDENTIFIER>;
    or disable <block_IDENTIFIER>;
    or force <assignment>; or release <value>;
    or <timing_control> <statement_or_null>
    or -> <event_IDENTIFIER>;
```

```
    or <sequential_block> or <parallel_block>
    or <task_enable> or <system_task_enable>
```

11.49 (Conditional compiler directives, 30 min.) The conditional compiler directives: `` `define``, `` `ifdef``, `` `else``, `` `endif``, and `` `undef``; work much as in C. Write and compile a module that models an AND gate as `'z = a&b'` if the variable behavioral is defined. If behavioral is not defined, then model the AND gate as `'and a1 (z, a, b)'`.

11.50 (*Macros, 30 min.) According to the IEEE Verilog LRM [16.3.1] you can create a **macro** with parameters using `` `define``, as the following example illustrates. This is a particularly difficult area of compliance. Does your software allow the following? You may have to experiment considerably to get this to work. *Hint:* Check to see if your software is substituting for the macro text literally or if it does in fact substitute for parameters.

```
`define M_MAX(a, b)((a) > (b) ? (a) : (b))
`define M_ADD(a,b) (a+b)
module macro;
reg m1, m2, m3, s0, s1;
`define var_nand(delay) nand #delay
`var_nand (2) g121 (q21, n10, n11);
`var_nand (3) g122 (q22, n10, n11);
initial begin s0=0; s1=1;
m1 = `M_MAX (s0, s1); m2 = `M_ADD (s0,s1); m3 = s0 > s1 ? s0 : s1;
end
initial #1 $display(" m1=",m1," m2=",m2," m3=",m3);
endmodule
```

11.51 (**Verilog hazards, 30 min.) The MTI simulator, VSIM, is capable of detecting the following kinds of Verilog hazards:

1. WRITE/WRITE: Two processes writing to the same variable at the same time.

2. READ/WRITE: One process reading a variable at the same time it is being written to by another process. VSIM calls this a READ/WRITE hazard if it executed the read first.

3. WRITE/READ: Same as a READ/WRITE hazard except that VSIM executed the write first.

For example, the following log shows how to simulate Verilog code in hazard mode for the example in Section 11.6.2:

```
> vlib work
> vlog -hazards data_slip_1.v
    > vsim -c -hazards data_slip_1
...(lines omitted)...
# 100 0   1 1   x
# ** Error: Write/Read hazard detected on Q1 (ALWAYS 3 followed by
ALWAYS 4)
#    Time: 150 ns  Iteration: 1  Instance:/
```

```
# 150 1   1 1   1
...(lines omitted)...
```

There are a total of five hazards in the module `data_slip_1`, four are on `Q1`, but there is another. If you correct the code as suggested in Section 11.6.2 and run VSIM, you will find this fifth hazard. If you do not have access to MTI's simulator, can you spot this additional read/write hazard? *Hint*: It occurs at time zero on `Clk`. Explain.

11.15.1 The Viterbi Decoder

11.52 (Understanding, 20 min.) Calculate the values shown in Table 11.8 if we use 4 bits for the distance measures instead of 3.

11.53 (Testbenches)

a. (30 min.) Write a testbench for the encoder, `viterbi_encode`, in Section 11.12 and reproduce the results of Table 11.7.

b. (30 min.) Write a testbench for the receiver front-end `viterbi_distances` and reproduce the results of Table 11.9 (you can write this stand-alone or use the answer to part a to generate the input). *Hint:* You will need a model for a D flip-flop. The sequence of results is more important than the exact timing. If you do have timing differences, explain them carefully.

11.54 (Things go wrong, 60 min.) Things do not always go as smoothly as the examples in this book might indicate. Suppose you accidentally invert the sense of the reset for the D flip-flops in the encoder. Simulate the output of the faulty encoder with an input sequence $X_n = 0, 1, 2, 3, ...$ (in other words run the encoder with the flip-flops being reset continually). The output sequence looks reasonable (you should find that it is $Y_n = 0, 2, 4, 6, ...$). Explain this result using the state diagram of Figure 11.3. If you had constructed a testbench for the entire decoder and did not check the intermediate signals against expected values you would probably never find this error.

11.55 (Subset decoder) Table 11.21 shows the inputs and outputs from the first-stage of the Viterbi decoder, the subset decoder. Calculate the expected output and then confirm your predictions using simulation.

TABLE 11.21   Subset decoder (Problem 11.55).

input	in0	in1	in2	in3	in4	in5	in6	in7	s0	s1	s3	s4	sout0	sout1	sout2	sout3
5	6	7	6	4	1	0	1	4	1	0	1	4				
4	7	6	4	1	0	1	4	6	0	1	4	1				
1	1	0	1	4	6	7	6	4	1	0	1	4				
0	0	1	4	6	7	6	4	1	0	1	4	1				

11.16 Bibliography

The IEEE Verilog LRM [1995] is less intimidating than the IEEE VHDL LRM, because it is based on the OVI LRM, which in turn was based on the Verilog-XL simulator reference manual. Thus it has more of a "User's Guide" flavor and is required reading for serious Verilog users. It is the only source for detailed information on the PLI.

Phil Moorby was one of the original architects of the Verilog language. The Thomas and Moorby text is a good introduction to Verilog [1991]. The code examples from this book can be obtained from the World Wide Web. Palnitkar's book includes an example of the use of the PLI routines [1996].

Open Verilog International (OVI) has a Web site maintained by Chronologic (`http://www.chronologic.com/ovi`) with membership information and addresses and an ftp site maintained by META-Software (`ftp://ftp.metasw.com` in `/pub/OVI/`). OVI sells reference material, including proceedings from the International Verilog HDL Conference.

The newsgroup `comp.lang.verilog` (with a FAQ—frequently asked questions) is accessible from a number of online sources. The FAQ includes a list of reference materials and book reviews. Cray Research maintained an archive for `comp.lang.verilog` going back to 1993 but this was lost in January 1997 and is still currently unavailable. Cadence has a discussion group at `talkverilog@cadence.com`. Wellspring Solutions offers VeriWell, a no-cost, limited capability, Verilog simulator for UNIX, PC, and Macintosh platforms.

There is a free, "copylefted" Verilog simulator, `vbs`, written by Jimen Ching and Lay Hoon Tho as part of their Master's theses at the University of Hawaii, which is part of the `comp.lang.verilog` archive. The package includes explanations of the mechanics of a digital event-driven simulator, including event queues and time wheels.

More technical references are included as part of Appendix B.

11.17 References

IEEE Std 1364-95, Verilog LRM. 1995. The Institute of Electrical and Electronics Engineers. Available from The Institute of Electrical and Electronics Engineers, Inc., 345 East 47th Street, New York, NY 10017 USA. [cited on p. 479]

Palnitkar, S. 1996. *Verilog HDL: A Guide to Digital Design and Synthesis.* Upper Saddle River, NJ: Prentice-Hall, 396 p. ISBN 0-13-451675-3.

Thomas, D. E., and P. Moorby. 1991. *The Verilog Hardware Description Language.* 1st ed. Dordrecht, Netherlands: Kluwer, 223 p. ISBN 0-7923-9126-8, TK7885.7.T48 (1st ed.). ISBN 0-7923-9523-9 (2nd ed.).

LOGIC SYNTHESIS

Logic synthesis provides a link between an HDL (Verilog or VHDL) and a netlist similarly to the way that a C compiler provides a link between C code and machine language. However, the parallel is not exact. C was developed for use with compilers, but HDLs were not developed for use with logic-synthesis tools. Verilog was designed as a simulation language and VHDL was designed as a documentation and description language. Both Verilog and VHDL were developed in the early 1980s, well before the introduction of commercial logic-synthesis software. Because these HDLs are now being used for purposes for which they were not intended, the state of the art in logic synthesis falls far short of that for computer-language compilers. Logic synthesis forces designers to use a subset of both Verilog and VHDL. This makes using logic synthesis more difficult rather than less difficult. The current state of synthesis software is rather like learning a foreign language, and then having to talk to a five-year-old. When talking to a logic-synthesis tool using an HDL, it is necessary to think like hardware, anticipating the netlist that logic synthesis will produce. This situation should improve in the next five years, as logic synthesizers mature.

Designers use graphic or text design entry to create an HDL **behavioral model**, which does not contain any references to logic cells. State diagrams, graphical data-path descriptions, truth tables, RAM/ROM templates, and gate-level schematics may be used together with an HDL description. Once a behavioral HDL model is complete, two items are required to proceed: a **logic synthesizer** (software and documentation) and a cell library (the logic cells—NAND gates and such) that is called the **target library**. Most synthesis software companies produce only software. Most ASIC vendors produce only cell libraries. The behavioral model is simulated to check that the design meets the specifications and then the logic synthesizer is used to generate a netlist, a **structural model**, which contains only references to logic cells. There is no standard format for the netlists that logic synthesis produces, but EDIF is widely used. Some logic-synthesis tools can also create structural HDL (Verilog, VHDL, or both). Following logic synthesis the design is simulated again, and the results are compared with the earlier behavioral simulation. Layout for any type of ASIC may be generated from the structural model produced by logic synthesis.

12.1   A Logic-Synthesis Example

As an example of logic synthesis, we will compare two implementations of the Viterbi decoder described in Chapter 11. Both versions used logic cells from a VLSI Technology cell library. The first ASIC was designed by hand using schematic entry and a data book. The second version of the ASIC (the one that was fabricated) used Verilog for design entry and a logic synthesizer. Table 12.1 compares the two versions. The synthesized ASIC is 16 percent smaller and 13 percent faster than the hand-designed version.

How does logic synthesis generate smaller and faster circuits? Figure 12.1 shows the schematic for a hand-designed comparator and MUX used in the Viterbi decoder ASIC, called here the comparator/MUX example. The Verilog code and the

TABLE 12.1   A comparison of hand design with synthesis (using a 1.0µm VLSI Technology cell library).

	Path delay/ ns[1]	No. of standard cells	No. of transistors	Chip area/ mils[2][2]
Hand design	41.6	1,359	16,545	21,877
Synthesized design	36.3	1,493	11,946	18,322

[1]These delays are under nominal operating conditions with no wiring capacitance. This is the only stage at which a comparison could be made because the hand design was not completed.

[2]Both figures are initial layout estimates using default power-bus and signal routing widths.

schematic in Figure 12.1 describe the same function. The comparison, in Table 12.2, of the two design approaches shows that the synthesized version is smaller and faster than the hand design, even though the synthesized design uses more cells.

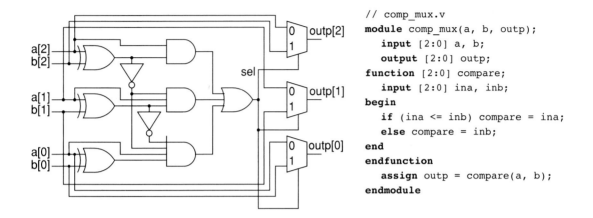

```
// comp_mux.v
module comp_mux(a, b, outp);
    input [2:0] a, b;
    output [2:0] outp;
function [2:0] compare;
    input [2:0] ina, inb;
begin
    if (ina <= inb) compare = ina;
    else compare = inb;
end
endfunction
    assign outp = compare(a, b);
endmodule
```

FIGURE 12.1 Schematic and HDL design entry.

TABLE 12.2   Comparison of the comparator/MUX designs using a 1.0μm standard-cell library.

	Delay /ns	No. of standard cells	No. of transistors	Area /mils^2
Hand design	4.3	12	116	68.68
Synthesized	2.9	15	66	46.43

12.2 A Comparator/MUX

With the Verilog behavioral model of Figure 12.1 as the input, logic-synthesis software generates logic that performs the same function as the Verilog. The software then optimizes the logic to produce a structural model, which references logic cells from the cell library and details their connections.

Before running a logic synthesizer, it is necessary to set up paths and startup files (synopsys_dc.setup, compass.boo, view.ini, or similar). These files set the target library and directory locations. Normally it is easier to run logic synthesis in text mode using a script. A **script** is a text file that directs a software tool to execute a

```
`timescale lns / 10ps
module comp_mux_u (a, b, outp);
input  [2:0] a; input  [2:0] b;
output [2:0] outp;
supply1 VDD; supply0 VSS;

in01d0 u2 (.I(b[1]), .ZN(u2_ZN));
nd02d0 u3 (.A1(a[1]), .A2(u2_ZN), .ZN(u3_ZN));
in01d0 u4 (.I(a[1]), .ZN(u4_ZN));
nd02d0 u5 (.A1(u4_ZN), .A2(b[1]), .ZN(u5_ZN));
in01d0 u6 (.I(a[0]), .ZN(u6_ZN));
nd02d0 u7 (.A1(u6_ZN), .A2(u3_ZN), .ZN(u7_ZN));
nd02d0 u8 (.A1(b[0]), .A2(u3_ZN), .ZN(u8_ZN));
nd03d0 u9 (.A1(u5_ZN), .A2(u7_ZN), .A3(u8_ZN),
.ZN(u9_ZN));
in01d0 u10 (.I(a[2]), .ZN(u10_ZN));
nd02d0 u11 (.A1(u10_ZN), .A2(u9_ZN), .ZN(u11_ZN));
nd02d0 u12 (.A1(b[2]), .A2(u9_ZN), .ZN(u12_ZN));
nd02d0 u13 (.A1(u10_ZN), .A2(b[2]), .ZN(u13_ZN));
nd03d0 u14 (.A1(u11_ZN), .A2(u12_ZN), .A3(u13_ZN),
.ZN(u14_ZN));
nd02d0 u15 (.A1(a[2]), .A2(u14_ZN), .ZN(u15_ZN));
in01d0 u16 (.I(u14_ZN), .ZN(u16_ZN));
nd02d0 u17 (.A1(b[2]), .A2(u16_ZN), .ZN(u17_ZN));
nd02d0 u18 (.A1(u15_ZN), .A2(u17_ZN), .ZN(outp[2]));
nd02d0 u19 (.A1(a[1]), .A2(u14_ZN), .ZN(u19_ZN));
nd02d0 u20 (.A1(b[1]), .A2(u16_ZN), .ZN(u20_ZN));
nd02d0 u21 (.A1(u19_ZN), .A2(u20_ZN), .ZN(outp[1]));
nd02d0 u22 (.A1(a[0]), .A2(u14_ZN), .ZN(u22_ZN));
nd02d0 u23 (.A1(b[0]), .A2(u16_ZN), .ZN(u23_ZN));
nd02d0 u24 (.A1(u22_ZN), .A2(u23_ZN), .ZN(outp[0]));

endmodule
```

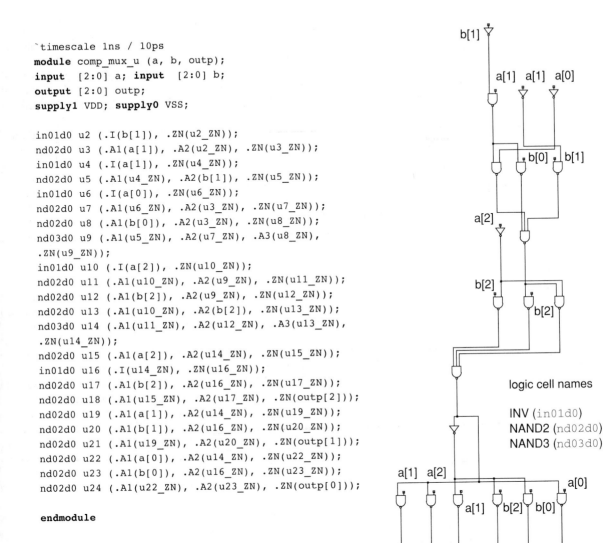

FIGURE 12.2 The comparator/MUX after logic synthesis, but before logic optimization. This figure shows the structural netlist, comp_mux_u.v, and its derived schematic.

series of synthesis commands (we call this a **synthesis run**). Figure 12.2 shows a structural netlist, comp_mux_u.v, and the derived schematic after logic synthesis, but before any logic optimization. A **derived schematic** is created by software from a

```
`timescale 1ns / 10ps
module comp_mux_o (a, b, outp);
input  [2:0] a; input  [2:0] b;
output [2:0] outp;
supply1 VDD; supply0 VSS;

in01d0 B1_i1 (.I(a[2]),
.ZN(B1_i1_ZN));
in01d0 B1_i2 (.I(b[1]),
.ZN(B1_i2_ZN));
oa01d1 B1_i3 (.A1(a[0]),
.A2(B1_i4_ZN), .B1(B1_i2_ZN),
.B2(a[1]), .ZN(B1_i3_Z;
fn05d1 B1_i4 (.A1(a[1]),
.B1(b[1]), .ZN(B1_i4_ZN));
fn02d1 B1_i5 (.A(B1_i3_ZN),
.B(B1_i1_ZN), .C(b[2]),
.ZN(B1_i5_ZN));
mx21d1 B1_i6 (.I0(a[0]),
.I1(b[0]), .S(B1_i5_ZN),
.Z(outp[0]));
mx21d1 B1_i7 (.I0(a[1]),
.I1(b[1]), .S(B1_i5_ZN),
.Z(outp[1]));
mx21d1 B1_i8 (.I0(a[2]),
.I1(b[2]), .S(B1_i5_ZN),
.Z(outp[2]));

endmodule
```

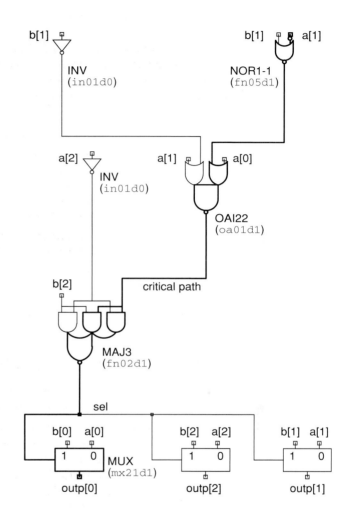

FIGURE 12.3 The comparator/MUX after logic synthesis and logic optimization with the default settings. This figure shows the structural netlist, comp_mux_o.v, and its derived schematic.

structural netlist (as opposed to a schematic drawn by hand). Figure 12.3 shows the structural netlist, comp_mux_o.v, and the derived schematic after logic optimization is performed (with the default settings). Figures 12.2 and 12.3 show the results of the two separate steps: logic synthesis and logic optimization. Confusingly, the whole process, which includes synthesis and optimization (and other steps as well), is referred to as logic synthesis. We also refer to the software that performs all of these steps (even if the software consists of more than one program) as a logic synthesizer.

Logic synthesis parses (in a process sometimes called **analysis**) and translates (sometimes called **elaboration**) the input HDL to a data structure. This data structure is then converted to a network of generic logic cells. For example, the network in Figure 12.2 uses NAND gates (each with three or fewer inputs in this case) and inverters. This network of generic logic cells is technology-independent since cell libraries in any technology normally contain NAND gates and inverters. The next step, **logic optimization**, attempts to improve this technology-independent network under the controls of the designer. The output of the optimization step is an optimized, but still technology-independent, network. Finally, in the **logic-mapping** step, the synthesizer maps the optimized logic to a specified technology-dependent target cell library. Figure 12.3 shows the results of using a standard-cell library as the target.

Text reports such as the one shown in Table 12.3 may be the only output that the designer sees from the logic-synthesis tool. Often, synthesized ASIC netlists and the derived schematics containing thousands of logic cells are far too large to follow. To make things even more difficult, the net names and instance names in synthesized netlists are automatically generated. This makes it hard to see which lines of code in the HDL generated which logic cells in the synthesized netlist or derived schematic.

In the comparator/MUX example the derived schematics are simple enough that, with hindsight, it is clear that the XOR logic cell used in the hand design is logically inefficient. Using XOR logic cells does, however, result in the simple schematic of Figure 12.1. The synthesized version of the comparator/MUX in Figure 12.3 uses complex combinational logic cells that are logically efficient, but the schematic is not as easy to read. Of course, the computer does not care about this—and neither do we since we usually never see the schematic.

Which version is best—the hand-designed or the synthesized version? Table 12.3 shows statistics generated by the logic synthesizer for the comparator/MUX. To calculate the performance of each circuit that it evaluates during synthesis, there is a **timing-analysis** tool (also known as a **timing engine**) built into the logic synthesizer. The timing-analysis tool reports that the critical path in the optimized comparator/MUX is 2.43 ns. This critical path is highlighted on the derived schematic of Figure 12.3 and consists of the following delays:

- 0.33 ns due to cell fn05d1, instance name B1_i4, a two-input NOR cell with an inverted input. We might call this a NOR1-1 or $(A + B')'$ logic cell.
- 0.39 ns due to cell oa01d1, instance name B1_i3, an OAI22 logic cell.
- 1.03 ns due to logic cell fn02d1, instance name B1_i5, a three-input majority function, MAJ3 (A, B, C).
- 0.68 ns due to logic cell mx21d1, instance name B1_i6, a 2:1 MUX.

(In this cell library the 'd1' suffix indicates normal drive strength.)

TABLE 12.3 Reports from the logic synthesizer for the Verilog version of the comparator/MUX.

Command	Synthesizer output[1]				
> synthesize	Cell Name	Num Insts	Gate Count Per Cell	Tot Gate Count	Width Per Cell	Total Width
	---------	-----	----------	--------	--------	--------
	in01d0	5	.8	3.8	7.2	36.0
	nd02d0	16	1.0	16.0	9.6	153.6
	nd03d0	2	1.3	2.5	12.0	24.0
	---------	-----	----------	--------	--------	--------
	Totals:	23		22.2		213.6

Command		Num Insts	Gate Count Per Cell	Tot Gate Count	Width Per Cell	Total Width
> optimize	Cell Name					
	---------	-----	----------	--------	--------	--------
	fn02d1	1	1.8	1.8	16.8	16.8
	fn05d1	1	1.3	1.3	12.0	12.0
	in01d0	2	.8	1.5	7.2	14.4
	mx21d1	3	2.2	6.8	21.6	64.8
	oa01d1	1	1.5	1.5	14.4	14.4
	---------	-----	----------	--------	--------	--------
	Totals:	8		12.8		122.4

> report timing	instance name inPin --> outPin	incr (ns)	arrival (ns)	trs	rampDel (ns)	cap (pf)	cell
	a[1] B1_i4	.00	.00	R	.00	.04	comp_m...
	A1 --> ZN B1_i3	.33	.33	R	.17	.03	fn05d1
	A2 --> ZN B1_i5	.39	.72	F	.33	.06	oa01d1
	A --> ZN B1_i6	1.03	1.75	R	.67	.11	fn02d1
	S --> Z	.68	2.43	R	.09	.02	mx21d1

[1]Cell Name = cell name from the ASIC library (Compass Passport, 0.6 µm high-density, 5 V standard-cell library, cb60hd230); Num Insts = number of cell instances; Gate Count Per Cell = equivalent gates with two-input NAND = 1 gate (with number of transistors ≈ equivalent gates × 4); Width Per Cell = width in µm (cell height in this library is 72 λ or 21.6 µm); incr = incremental delay time due to logic cell delay; trs = transition; R = rising; F = falling; rampDel = ramp delay; cap = capacitance at node or cell output pin.

TABLE 12.4   Logic cell comparisons between the two comparator/MUX designs.

Cell type	Library cell name[1]	[2]t_{PLH} /ns	t_{PHL} /ns	Gate equivalents in cell[3]	Cells used in hand design	Cells used in synthesized design	Gate equivalents used by hand design	Gate equivalents used in synthesized design	Width of cell[4]/μm	Width used by hand design /μm	Width of synthesized design /μm
Inverter	in01d0	0.37	0.36	0.8	2	2	1.6	1.6	7.2	14.4	14.4
2-input XOR	xo02d1	0.93	0.62	1.8	3	—	5.3	—	16.8	50.4	—
2-input AND	an02d1	0.34	0.46	1.3	1	—	1.3	—	12.0	12.0	—
3-input AND	an03d1	0.38	0.52	1.5	1	—	1.5	—	14.4	14.4	—
4-input AND	an04d1	0.41	0.98	1.8	1	—	1.8	—	16.8	16.8	—
3-input OR	or03d1	0.60	0.44	1.8	1	—	1.8	—	16.8	16.8	—
2-input MUX	mx21d1	0.69	0.68	2.2	3	3	6.6	6.6	21.6	64.8	64.8
AOI22	oa01d1	0.51	0.42	1.5	—	1	—	1.5	14.4	—	14.4
MAJ3	fn02d1	0.84	0.81	1.8	—	1	—	1.8	16.8	—	16.8
NOR1–1= (A' + B)'	fn05d1[5]	0.42	0.46	1.3	—	1	—	1.3	12.0	—	12.0
Totals					12	8	19.8	12.8		189.6	122.4

[1]0.6 μm, 5 V, high-density Compass standard-cell library, cb60hd230.
[2]Average over all inputs with load capacitance equal to two standard loads (one standard load = 0.016 pF).
[3] 2-input NAND = 1 gate equivalent.
[4]Cell height is 72 λ (21.6 μm).
[5]Rise and fall delays are different for the two inputs, A and B, of this cell: t_{PLHA} = 0.48 ns; t_{PLHB} = 0.36 ns; t_{PHLA} = 0.59 ns; t_{PHLB} = 0.33 ns.

Table 12.4 lists the name, type, the number of transistors, the area, and the delay of each logic cell used in the hand-designed and synthesized comparator/MUX. We could have performed this analysis by hand using the cell-library data book and a calculator or spreadsheet, but it would have been tedious work—especially calculating the delays. The computer is excellent at this type of bookkeeping. We can think of the timing engine of a logic synthesizer as a logic calculator.

We see from Table 12.4 that the sum of the widths of all the cells used in the synthesized design (122.4 μm) is less than for the hand design (189.6 μm). All the standard cells in a library are the same height, 72 λ or 21.6 μm, in this case. Thus the synthesized design is smaller. We could estimate the critical path of the hand design using the information from the cell-library data book (summarized in Table 12.4). Instead we will use the timing engine in the logic synthesizer as a logic calculator to extract the critical path for the hand-designed comparator/MUX.

Table 12.5 shows a timing analysis obtained by loading the hand-designed schematic netlist into the logic synthesizer. Table 12.5 shows that the hand-designed (critical path 2.42 ns) and synthesized versions (critical path 2.43 ns) of the comparator/MUX are approximately the same speed. Remember, though, that we used the default settings during logic optimization. Section 12.11 shows that the logic synthesizer can do much better.

TABLE 12.5 Timing report for the hand-designed version of the comparator/MUX using the logic synthesizer to calculate the critical path (compare with Table 12.3).

Command	Synthesizer output[1]						
> report	instance name						
timing	inPin --> outPin	incr	arrival	trs	rampDel	cap	cell
		(ns)	(ns)		(ns)	(pf)	
	a[1]	.00	.00	F	.00	.04	comp_mux
	B1_i4						
	A1 --> ZN	.61	.61	F	.14	.03	xo02d1
	B1_i3						
	A2 --> ZN	.85	1.46	F	.19	.05	an04d1
	B1_i5						
	A --> ZN	.42	1.88	F	.23	.09	or03d1
	B1_i6						
	S --> Z	.54	2.42	R	.09	.02	mx21d1
	outp[0]	.00	2.42	R	.00	.00	comp_mux

[1]See footnote 1 in Table 12.3 for explanations of the abbreviations used in this table.

12.2.1 An Actel Version of the Comparator/MUX

Figure 12.4 shows the results of targeting the comparator/MUX design to the Actel ACT 2/3 FPGA architecture. (The EDIF converter prefixes all internal nodes in this netlist with 'block_0_DEF_NET_'. This prefix was replaced with 'n_' in the Verilog file, comp_mux_actel_o_adl_e.v, derived from the .adl netlist.) As can be seen by comparing the netlists and schematics in Figures 12.3 and 12.4, the results are very different between a standard-cell library and the Actel library. Each of the symbols in the schematic in Figure 12.4 represents the eight-input ACT 2/3 C-Module (see Figure 5.4a). The logic synthesizer, during the technology-mapping step, has decided which connections should be made to the inputs to the combinational logic

```
`timescale 1 ns/100 ps
module comp_mux_actel_o (a, b, outp);
input [2:0] a, b; output [2:0] outp;
wire n_13, n_17, n_19, n_21, n_23, n_27, n_29,
n_31, n_62;

CM8 I_5_CM8(.D0(n_31), .D1(n_62), .D2(a[0]),
.D3(n_62), .S00(n_62), .S01(n_13), .S10(n_23),
.S11(n_21), .Y(outp[0]));
CM8 I_2_CM8(.D0(n_31), .D1(n_19), .D2(n_62),
.D3(n_62), .S00(n_62), .S01(b[1]), .S10(n_31),
.S11(n_17), .Y(outp[1]));
CM8 I_1_CM8(.D0(n_31), .D1(n_31), .D2(b[2]),
.D3(n_31), .S00(n_62), .S01(n_31), .S10(n_31),
.S11(a[2]), .Y(outp[2]));
VCC VCC_I(.Y(n_62));
CM8 I_4_CM8(.D0(a[2]), .D1(n_31), .D2(n_62),
.D3(n_62), .S00(n_62), .S01(b[2]), .S10(n_31),
.S11(a[1]), .Y(n_19));
CM8 I_7_CM8(.D0(b[1]), .D1(b[2]), .D2(n_31),
.D3(n_31), .S00(a[2]), .S01(b[1]), .S10(n_31),
.S11(a[1]), .Y(n_23));
CM8 I_9_CM8(.D0(n_31), .D1(n_31), .D2(a[1]),
.D3(n_31), .S00(n_62), .S01(b[1]), .S10(n_31),
.S11(b[0]), .Y(n_27));
CM8 I_8_CM8(.D0(n_29), .D1(n_62), .D2(n_31),
.D3(a[2]), .S00(n_62), .S01(n_27), .S10(n_31),
.S11(b[2]), .Y(n_13));
CM8 I_3_CM8(.D0(n_31), .D1(n_31), .D2(a[1]),
.D3(n_31), .S00(n_62), .S01(a[2]), .S10(n_31),
.S11(b[2]), .Y(n_17));
CM8 I_6_CM8(.D0(b[2]), .D1(n_31), .D2(n_62),
.D3(n_62), .S00(n_62), .S01(a[2]), .S10(n_31),
.S11(b[0]), .Y(n_21));
CM8 I_10_CM8(.D0(n_31), .D1(n_31), .D2(b[0]),
.D3(n_31), .S00(n_62), .S01(n_31), .S10(n_31),
.S11(a[2]), .Y(n_29));
GND GND_I(.Y(n_31));
endmodule
```

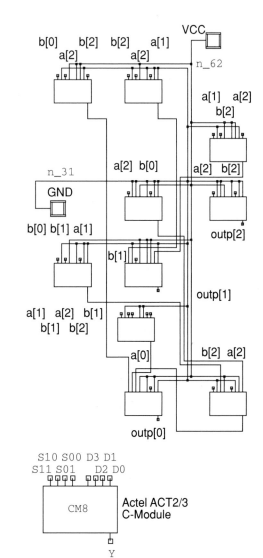

FIGURE 12.4 The Actel version of the comparator/MUX after logic optimization. This figure shows the structural netlist, `comp_mux_actel_o_adl_e.v`, and its derived schematic.

macro, `CM8`. The `CM8` names and the ACT2/3 C-Module names (in parentheses) correspond as follows: `S00(A0)`, `S01(B0)`, `S10(A1)`, `S11(A2)`, `D0(D00)`, `D1(D01)`, `D2(D10)`, `D3(D11)`, and `Y(Y)`.

12.3 Inside a Logic Synthesizer

The logic synthesizer parses the Verilog of Figure 12.1 and builds an internal data structure (usually a graph represented by linked lists). Such an abstract representation is not easy to visualize, so we shall use pictures instead. The first **Karnaugh map** in Figure 12.5(a) is a picture that represents the sel signal (labeled as the input to the three MUXes in the schematic of Figure 12.1) for the case when the inputs are such that a[2]b[2] = 00. The signal sel is responsible for steering the smallest input, a or b, to the output of the comparator/MUX. We insert a '1' in the Karnaugh map (which will select the input b to be the output) whenever b is smaller than a. When a = b we do not care whether we select a or b (since a and b are equal), so we insert an 'x', a don't care logic value, in the Karnaugh map of Figure 12.5(a). There are four Karnaugh maps for the signal sel, one each for the values a[2]b[2] = 00, a[2]b[2] = 01, a[2]b[2] = 10, and a[2]b[2] = 11.

Next, **logic minimization** tries to find a minimum **cover** for the Karnaugh maps—the smallest number of the largest possible circles to cover all the '1's. One possible cover is shown in Figure 12.5(b).

In order to understand the steps that follow we shall use some notation from the **Berkeley Logic Interchange Format (BLIF)** and from the Berkeley tools misII and sis. We shall use the logic operators (in decreasing order of their precedence): '!' (negation), '*' (AND), '+' (OR). We shall also abbreviate Verilog signal names; writing a[2] as a2, for example. We can write equations for sel and the output signals of the comparator/MUX in the format that is produced by sis, as follows (this is the same format as input file for the Berkeley tool eqntott):

```
sel = a1*!b1*!b2 + a0*!b1*!b2 + a0*a1*!b2 + a1*!b1*a2 + a0*!b1*a2 +
a0*a1*a2 + a2*!b2;                                                    [12.1]

outp2 = !sel*a2 + sel*b2;                                             [12.2]

outp1 = !sel*a1 + sel*b1;                                             [12.3]

outp0 = !sel*a0 + sel*b0;                                             [12.4]
```

Equations 12.1–12.4 describe the **synthesized network**. There are seven product terms in Eq. 12.1—the logic equation for sel (numbered and labeled in the drawing of the cover for sel in Figure 12.5). We shall keep track of the sel signal separately even though this is not exactly the way the logic synthesizer works—the synthesizer looks at all the signals at once.

Logic optimization uses a series of factoring, substitution, and elimination steps to simplify the equations that represent the synthesized network. A simple analogy would be the simplification of arithmetic expressions. Thus, for example, we can simplify $189/315$ to 0.6 by factoring the top and bottom lines and eliminating common factors as follows: $(3 \times 7 \times 9)/(5 \times 7 \times 9) = 3/5$. Boolean algebra is more complicated than ordinary algebra. To make logic optimization tractable, most tools use algorithms based on algebraic factors rather than Boolean factors.

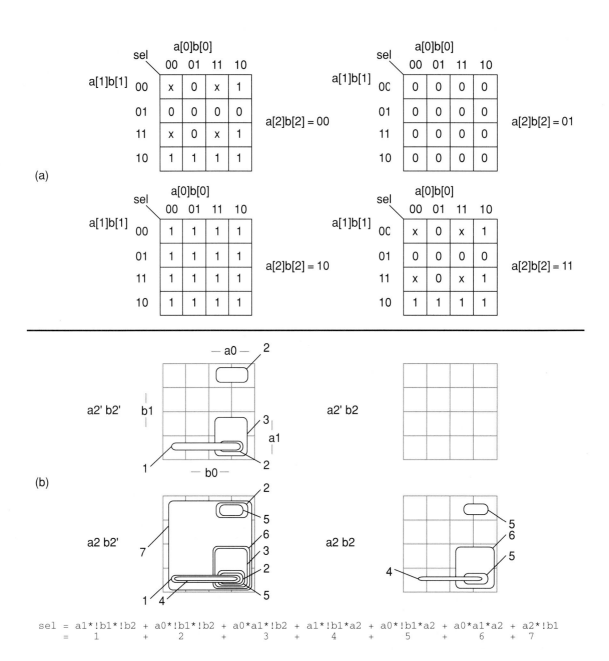

$$sel = a1*!b1*!b2 + a0*!b1*!b2 + a0*a1*!b2 + a1*!b1*a2 + a0*!b1*a2 + a0*a1*a2 + a2*!b1$$
$$\quad = \quad 1 \quad + \quad 2 \quad + \quad 3 \quad + \quad 4 \quad + \quad 5 \quad + \quad 6 \quad + \quad 7$$

FIGURE 12.5 Logic maps for the comparator/MUX. (a) If the input b is less than a, then sel is '1'. If a = b, then sel = 'x' (don't care). (b) A cover for sel.

Logic optimization attempts to simplify the equations in the hope that this will also minimize area and maximize speed. In the synthesis results presented in Table 12.3, we accepted the default optimization settings without setting any constraints. Thus only a minimum amount of logic optimization is attempted that did not alter the synthesized network in this case.

The **technology-decomposition** step builds a generic network from the optimized logic network. The generic network is usually simple NAND gates (sis uses either AND, or NOR gates, or both). This generic network is in a technology-independent form. To build this generic network involves creating intermediate nodes. The program sis labels these intermediate nodes [n], starting at n = 100.

```
sel = [100] * [101] * [102] ;                          [12.5]
[100] = !( !a2 * [103] );
[101] = !( b2 * [103] );
[102] = !( !a2 * b2 );
[103] = !( [104] * [105] * [106] );
[104] = !( !a1 * b1 );
[105] = !( b0 * [107] );
[106] = !( a0' * [107] );
[107] = !( a1 * !b1 );

outp2 = !( [108] * [109] );                            [12.6]
[108] = !( a2 * !sel );
[109] = !( sel * b2 );
```

There are two other sets of equations, similar to Eq. 12.6, for outp1 and outp0. Notice the polarity of the sel signal in Eq. 12.5 is correct and represents an AND gate (a consequence of labeling sel as the MUX select input in Table 12.1).

Next, the **technology-mapping** step (or **logic-mapping** step) implements the technology-independent network by matching pieces of the network with the logic cells that are available in a technology-dependent cell library (an FPGA or standard-cell library, for example). While performing the logic mapping, the algorithms attempt to minimize area (the default constraint) while meeting any other user constraints (timing or power constraints, for example).

Working backward from the outputs the logic mapper recognizes that each of the three output nodes (outp2, outp1, and outp0) may be mapped to a MUX. (We are using the term "node mapping to a logic cell" rather loosely here—an exact parallel is a compiler mapping patterns of source code to object code.) Here is the equation that shows the mapping for outp2:

```
outp2 = MUX(a, b, c) = ac + b!c                        [12.7]
a = b2 ; b = a2 ; c = sel
```

The equations for outp1 and outp0 are similar.

The node sel can be mapped to the three-input majority function as follows:

```
sel = MAJ3(w, x, y) = !(wx + wy + xy)                  [12.8]
w = !a2 ; x = b2 ; y = [103] ;
```

Next node `[103]` is mapped to an OAI22 cell,

```
[103] = OAI22(w, x, y, z) = ! ((w + x)(y + z)) =
(!w!x + !y!z)                                              [12.9]
w = a0 ; x = a1 ; y = !b1 z = [107] ;
```

Finally, node `[107]` is mapped to a two-input NOR with one inverted input,

```
[107] = !(b1 + !a1) ;                                     [12.10]
```

Putting Equations 12.7–12.10 together describes the following optimized logic network (corresponding to the structural netlist and schematic shown in Figure 12.3):

```
sel = !((( !a0 * !(a1&!b1) | (b1*!a1) ) * (!a2|b2) ) | (!a2*b2)) ;[12.11]

outp2 = !sel * a2 | sel * b2;
outp1 = !sel * a1 | sel * b1;
outp0 = !sel * a0 | sel * b0;
```

The comparator/MUX example illustrates how logic synthesis takes the behavioral model (the HDL input) and, in a series of steps, converts this to a structural model describing the connections of logic cells from a cell library.

When we write a C program we almost never think of the object code that will result. When we write HDL it is always necessary to consider the hardware. In C there is not much difference between $i*j$ and i/j. In an HDL, if i and j are 32-bit numbers, $i*j$ will take up a large amount of silicon. If j is a constant, equal to 2, then $i*j$ take up hardly any space at all. Most logic synthesizers cannot even produce logic to implement i/j. In the following sections we shall examine the Verilog and VHDL languages as a way to communicate with a logic synthesizer. Using one of these HDLs we have to tell the logic synthesizer what hardware we want—we **imply** A. The logic synthesizer then has to figure out what we want—it has to **infer** B. The problem is making sure that we write the HDL code such that A = B. As will become apparent, the more clearly we imply what we mean, the easier the logic synthesizer can infer what we want.

12.4   Synthesis of the Viterbi Decoder

In this section we return to the Viterbi decoder from Chapter 11. After an initial synthesis run that shows how logic synthesis works with a real example, we step back and study some of the issues and problems of using HDLs for logic synthesis.

12.4.1   ASIC I/O

Some logic synthesizers can include I/O cells automatically, but the designer may have to use directives to designate special pads (clock buffers, for example). It may also be necessary to use commands to set I/O cell features such as selection of pull-up resistor, slew rate, and so on. Unfortunately there are no standards in this area. Worse, there is currently no accepted way to set these parameters from an HDL. Designers may also use either generic technology-independent I/O models or instantiate I/O cells directly from an I/O cell library. Thus, for example, in the Compass tools the statement

```
asPadIn  #(3,"1,2,3") u0 (in0, padin0);
```

uses a generic I/O cell model, asPadIn. This statement will generate three input pads (with pin numbers "1", "2", and "3") if in0 is a 3-bit-wide bus.

The next example illustrates the use of generic I/O cells from a standard-component library. These components are technology independent (so they may equally well be used with a 0.6 µm or 0.35 µm technology).

```
module allPads(padTri, padOut, clkOut, padBidir, padIn, padClk);    //1
    output padTri, padOut, clkOut; inout padBidir;                  //2
    input [3:0] padIn; input padClk; wire [3:0] in;                //3
//compass dontTouch u*                                              //4
// asPadIn #(W, N, L, P) I (toCore, Pad) also asPadInInv           //5
// asPadOut #(W, N, L, P) I (Pad, frCore)                          //6
// asPadTri #(W, N, S, L, P) I (Pad, frCore, OEN)                  //7
// asPadBidir #(W, N, S, L, P) I (Pad, toCore, frCore, OEN)        //8
// asPadClk #(N, S, L) I (Clk, Pad) also asPadClkInv               //9
// asPadVxx #(N, subnet) I (Vxx)                                   //10
// W = width, integer (default=1)                                  //11
// N = pin number string, e.g. "1:3,5:8"                           //12
// S = strength = {2, 4, 8, 16} in mA drive                        //13
// L = level = {cmos, ttl, schmitt} (default = cmos)               //14
// P = pull-up resistor = {down, float, none, up}                  //15
// Vxx = {Vss, Vdd}                                                //16
// subnet = connect supply to {pad, core, both}                    //17
    asPadIn     #(4,"1:4","","none") u1 (in, padIn);               //18
    asPadOut    #(1,"5",13) u2 (padOut, d);                        //19
    asPadTri    #(1,"6",11) u3 (padTri, in[1], in[0]);             //20
    asPadBidir #(1,"7",2,"","") u4 (d, padBidir, in[3], in[2]);    //21
    asPadClk    #(8) u5 (clk, padClk);                             //22
    asPadOut    #(1, "9") u6 (clkOut, clk);                        //23
    asPadVdd    #("10:11","pads") u7 (vddr);                       //24
    asPadVss    #("12,13","pads") u8 (vssr);                       //25
    asPadVdd    #("14","core") u9 (vddc);                          //26
    asPadVss    #("15","core") u10 (vssc);                         //27
    asPadVdd    #("16","both") u11 (vddb);                         //28
    asPadVss    #("17","both") u12 (vssb);                         //29
endmodule                                                          //30
```

The following code is an example of the contents of a generic model for a three-state I/O cell (provided in a standard-component library or in an I/O cell library):

```
module PadTri (Pad, I, Oen); // active-low output enable        //1
parameter width = 1, pinNumbers = "", \strength = 1,            //2
   level = "CMOS", externalVdd = 5;                             //3
output [width-1:0] Pad; input  [width-1:0] I; input Oen;        //4
assign #1 Pad = (Oen ? {width{1'bz}} : I);                      //5
endmodule                                                       //6
```

The module `PadTri` can be used for simulation and as the basis for synthesizing an I/O cell. However, the synthesizer also has to be told to synthesize an I/O cell connected to a bonding pad and the outside world and not just an internal three-state buffer. There is currently no standard mechanism for doing this, and every tool and every ASIC company handles it differently.

The following model is a generic model for a bidirectional pad. We could use this model as a basis for input-only and output-only I/O cell models.

```
module PadBidir (C, Pad, I, Oen); // active-low output enable    //1
parameter width = 1, pinNumbers = "", \strength = 1,            //2
   level = "CMOS", pull = "none", externalVdd = 5;              //3
output [width-1:0] C; inout [width-1:0] Pad;                    //4
input [width-1:0] I; input Oen;                                 //5
assign #1 Pad = Oen ? {width{1'bz}} : I; assign #1 C = Pad;     //6
endmodule                                                       //7
```

In Chapter 8 we used the `halfgate` example to demonstrate an FPGA design flow—including I/O. If the synthesis tool is not capable of synthesizing I/O cells, then we may have to instantiate them by hand; the following code is a hand-instantiated version of lines 19–22 in module `allPads`:

```
pc5o05 u2_2 (.PAD(padOut), .I(d));
pc5t04r u3_2 (.PAD(padTri), .I(in[1]), .OEN(in[0]));
pc5b01r u4_3 (.PAD(padBidir), .I(in[3]), .CIN(d), .OEN(in[2]));
pc5d01r u5_in_1 (.PAD(padClk), .CIN(u5toClkBuf[0]));
```

The designer must find the names of the I/O cells (`pc5o05` and so on), and the names, positions, meanings, and defaults for the parameters from the cell-library documentation.

I/O cell models allow us to simulate the behavior of the synthesized logic inside an ASIC "all the way to the pads." To simulate "outside the pads" at a system level, we should use these same I/O cell models. This is important in ASIC design. For example, the designers forgot to put pull-up resistors on the outputs of some of the SparcStation ASICs. This was one of the very few errors in a complex project, but an error that could have been caught if a system-level simulation had included complete I/O cell models for the ASICs.

12.4.2   Flip-Flops

In Chapter 11 we used this D flip-flop model to simulate the Viterbi decoder:

```
module dff(D,Q,Clock,Reset); // N.B. reset is active-low          //1
output Q; input D,Clock,Reset;                                    //2
parameter CARDINALITY = 1; reg [CARDINALITY-1:0] Q;               //3
wire [CARDINALITY-1:0] D;                                         //4
always @(posedge Clock) if (Reset!==0) #1 Q=D;                    //5
always begin wait (Reset==0); Q=0; wait (Reset==1); end           //6
endmodule                                                         //7
```

Most simulators cannot synthesize this model because there are two `wait` statements in one `always` statement (line 6). We could change the code to use flip-flops from the synthesizer standard-component library by using the following code:

```
asDff ff1 (.Q(y), .D(x), .Clk(clk), .Rst(vdd));
```

Unfortunately we would have to change all the flip-flop models from 'dff' to 'asDff' and the code would become dependent on a particular synthesis tool. Instead, to maintain independence from vendors, we shall use the following D flip-flop model for synthesis and simulation:

```
module dff(D, Q, Clk, Rst); // new flip-flop for Viterbi decoder    //1
  parameter width = 1,  reset_value = 0; input [width - 1 : 0] D;   //2
  output [width - 1 : 0] Q; reg [width - 1 : 0] Q; input Clk, Rst;  //3
  initial Q <= {width{1'bx}};                                       //4
  always @ ( posedge Clk or negedge Rst )                           //5
    if ( Rst == 0 ) Q <= #1 reset_value; else Q <= #1 D;            //6
endmodule                                                           //7
```

12.4.3   The Top-Level Model

The following code models the top-level Viterbi decoder and instantiates (with instance name v_1) a copy of the Verilog module `viterbi` from Chapter 11. The model uses generic input, output, power, and clock I/O cells from the standard-component library supplied with the synthesis software. The synthesizer will take these generic I/O cells and map them to I/O cells from a technology-specific library. We do not need three-state I/O cells or bidirectional I/O cells for the Viterbi ASIC.

```
/* This is the top-level module, viterbi_ASIC.v */                 //1
module viterbi_ASIC                                                //2
(padin0, padin1, padin2, padin3, padin4, padin5, padin6, padin7,   //3
padOut, padClk, padRes, padError);                                 //4
input [2:0]    padin0, padin1, padin2, padin3,                     //5
               padin4, padin5, padin6, padin7;                     //6
input padRes, padClk; output padError; output [2:0] padOut;        //7
wire Error, Clk, Res; wire [2:0] Out; // core                      //8
wire padError, padClk, padRes; wire [2:0] padOut;                  //9
```

```
wire [2:0] in0,in1,in2,in3,in4,in5,in6,in7; // core        //10
wire [2:0]                                                  //11
   padin0, padin1,padin2,padin3,padin4,padin5,padin6,padin7; //12
// Do not let the software mess with the pads.              //13
//compass dontTouch u*                                      //14
   asPadIn      #(3,"1,2,3")      u0   (in0, padin0);       //15
   asPadIn      #(3,"4,5,6")      u1   (in1, padin1);       //16
   asPadIn      #(3,"7,8,9")      u2   (in2, padin2);       //17
   asPadIn      #(3,"10,11,12")   u3   (in3, padin3);       //18
   asPadIn      #(3,"13,14,15")   u4   (in4, padin4);       //19
   asPadIn      #(3,"16,17,18")   u5   (in5, padin5);       //20
   asPadIn      #(3,"19,20,21")   u6   (in6, padin6);       //21
   asPadIn      #(3,"22,23,24")   u7   (in7, padin7);       //22
   asPadVdd     #("25","both")    u25  (vddb);              //23
   asPadVss     #("26","both")    u26  (vssb);              //24
   asPadClk     #("27")           u27  (Clk, padClk);       //25
   asPadOut     #(1,"28")         u28  (padError, Error);   //26
   asPadin      #(1,"29")         u29  (Res, padRes);       //27
   asPadOut     #(3,"30,31,32")   u30  (padOut, Out);       //28
// Here is the core module:                                 //29
viterbi v_1                                                 //30
   (in0,in1,in2,in3,in4,in5,in6,in7,Out,Clk,Res,Error);    //31
endmodule                                                   //32
```

At this point we are ready to begin synthesis. In order to demonstrate how synthesis works, I am cheating here. The code that was presented in Chapter 11 has already been simulated and synthesized (requiring several iterations to produce error-free code). What I am doing is a little like the Galloping Gourmet's television presentation: "And then we put the soufflé in the oven ... and look at the soufflé that I prepared earlier." The synthesis results for the Viterbi decoder are shown in Table 12.6. Normally the worst thing we can do is prepare a large amount of code, put it in the synthesis oven, close the door, push the "synthesize and optimize" button, and wait. Unfortunately, it is easy to do. In our case it works (at least we may think so at this point) because this is a small ASIC by today's standards—only a few thousand gates. I made the bus widths small and chose this example so that the code was of a reasonable size. Modern ASICs may be over one million gates, hundreds of times more complicated than our Viterbi decoder example.

The derived schematic for the synthesized core logic is shown in Figure 12.6. There are eight boxes in Figure 12.6 that represent the eight modules in the Verilog code. The schematics for each of these eight blocks are too complex to be useful. With practice it is possible to "see" the synthesized logic from reports such as Table 12.6. First we check the following cells at the top level:

- pc5c01 is an I/O cell that drives the clock node into the logic core. ASIC designers also call an I/O cell a **pad cell**, and often refer to the pad cells (the bonding pads and associated logic) as just "the **pads**." From the library data

TABLE 12.6   Initial synthesis results of the Viterbi decoder ASIC.

Command	Synthesizer output[1, 2]					
> optimize		Num	Gate Count	Tot Gate	Width	Total
	Cell Name	Insts	Per Cell	Count	Per Cell	Width
	---------	-----	----------	--------	--------	--------
	pc5c01	1	315.4	315.4	100.8	100.8
	pc5d01r	26	315.4	8200.4	100.8	2620.8
	pc5o06	4	315.4	1261.6	100.8	403.2
	pv0f	1	315.4	315.4	100.8	100.8
	pvdf	1	315.4	315.4	100.8	100.8
	viterbi_p	1	1880.0	1880.0	18048.0	18048.0

[1]See footnote 1 in Table 12.3 for explanations of the abbreviations used in this table.
[2]I/O cell height (I/O cells have prefixes pc5 and pv) is approximately 650 µm in this cell library.

book we find this is a "core-driven, noninverting clock buffer capable of driving 125 pF." This is a large logic cell and does not have a bonding pad, but is placed in a pad site (a slot in the ring of pads around the perimeter of the die) as if it were an I/O cell with a bonding pad.

- pc5d01r is a 5V CMOS input-only I/O cell with a bus repeater. Twenty-four of these I/O cells are used for the 24 inputs (in0 to in7). Two more are used for Res and Clk. The I/O cell for Clk receives the clock signal from the bonding pad and drives the clock buffer cell (pc5c01). The pc5c01 cell then buffers and drives the clock back into the core. The power-hungry clock buffer is placed in the pad ring near the VDD and VSS pads.

- pc5o06 is a CMOS output-only I/O cell with 6X drive strength (6 mA AC drive and 4 mA DC drive). There are four output pads: three pads for the signal outputs, outp[2:0], and one pad for the output signal, error.

- pv0f is a power pad that connects all VSS power buses on the chip.

- pvdf is a power pad that connects all VDD power buses on the chip.

- viterbi_p is the core logic. This cell takes its name from the top-level Verilog module (viterbi). The software has appended a "_p" suffix (the default) to prevent input files being accidentally overwritten.

The software does not tell us any of this directly. We learn what is going on by looking at the names and number of the synthesized cells, reading the synthesis tool documentation, and from experience. We shall learn more about I/O pads and the layout of power supply buses in Chapter 16.

Next we examine the cells used in the logic core. Most synthesis tools can produce reports, such as that shown in Table 12.7, which lists all the synthesized cells. The most important types of cells to check are the sequential elements: flip-flops and

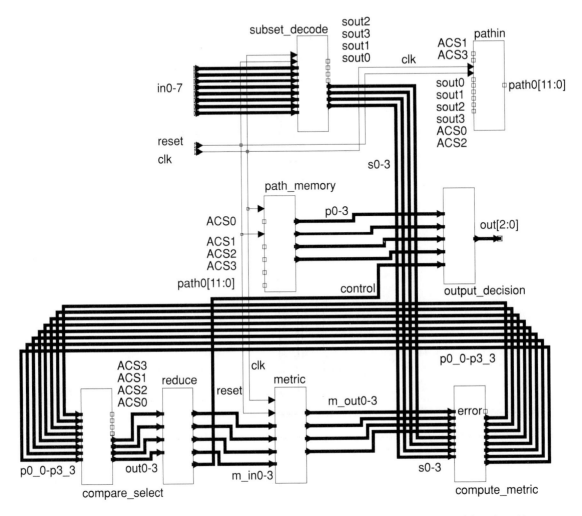

FIGURE 12.6 The core logic of the Viterbi decoder ASIC. Bus names are abbreviated in this figure for clarity. For example the label m_out0-3 denotes the four buses: m_out0, m_out1, m_out2, and m_out3.

latches (I have omitted all but the sequential logic cells in Table 12.7). One of the most common mistakes in synthesis is to accidentally leave variables unassigned in all situations in the HDL. Unassigned variables require memory and will generate unnecessary sequential logic. In the Viterbi decoder it is easy to identify the sequential logic cells that should be present in the synthesized logic because we used the module dff explicitly whenever we required a flip-flop. By scanning the code in

Chapter 11 and counting the references to the dff model, we can see that the only flip-flops that should be inferred are the following:

- 24 (3×8) D flip-flops in instance subset_decode
- 132 (11×12) D flip-flops in instance path_memory that contains 11 instances of path (12 D flip-flops in each instance of path)
- 12 D flip-flops in instance pathin
- 20 (5×4) D flip-flops in instance metric

The total is $24 + 132 + 12 + 20 = 188$ D flip-flops, which is the same as the number of dfctnb cell instances in Table 12.7.

TABLE 12.7   Number of synthesized flip-flops in the Viterbi ASIC.

Command	Synthesizer output[1]				
> report					
area -flat		Num	Gate Count	Tot Gate	Width	Total
	Cell Name	Insts	Per Cell	Count	Per Cell	Width
	---------	-----	----------	--------	--------	--------
	...					
	dfctnb	188	5.8	1081.0	55.2	10377.6
	...					
	---------	-----	----------	--------	--------	--------
	Totals:	1383		12716.5		25485.6

[1]See footnote 1 in Table 12.3 for explanations of the abbreviations used in this table. Logic cell dfctnb is a D flip-flop with clear in this standard-cell library.

Table 12.6 gives the total width of the standard cells in the logic core after logic optimization as 18,048 µm. Since the standard-cell height for this library is 72λ (21.6 µm), we can make a first estimate of the total logic cell area as

$$(18, 048 \ \mu m) \ (21.6 \ \mu m) \ = \ 390 \ k \ (\mu m^2) \approx \frac{390 \ k \ (\mu m^2)}{(25.4 \ \mu m)^2} \approx 600 \ mil^2 . \quad (12.12)$$

In the physical layout we shall need additional space for routing. The ratio of routing to logic cell area is called the **routing factor**. The routing factor depends primarily on whether we use two levels or three levels of metal. With two levels of metal the routing factor is typically between 1 and 2. With three levels of metal, where we may use over-the-cell routing, the routing factor is usually zero to 1. We thus expect a logic core area of 600–1000 mils^2 for the Viterbi decoder using this cell library.

From Table 12.6 we see the I/O cells in this library are 100.8 μm wide or approximately 4 mil (the width of a single pad site). From the I/O cell data book we find the I/O cell height is 650 μm (actually 648.825 μm) or approximately 26 mil. Each I/O cell thus occupies 104 mil². Our 33 pad sites will thus require approximately 3400 mil² which is larger than the estimated core logic area.

Let us go back and take a closer look at what it usually takes to get to this point. Remember we used an already prepared Verilog model for the Viterbi decoder.

12.5   Verilog and Logic Synthesis

A top-down design approach using Verilog begins with a single `module` at the top of the hierarchy to model the input and output response of the ASIC:

```
module MyChip_ASIC(); ... (code to model ASIC I/O) ... endmodule;
```

This top-level Verilog module is used to simulate the ASIC I/O connections and any bus I/O during the earliest stages of design. Often the reason that designs fail is lack of attention to the connection between the ASIC and the rest of the system.

As a designer, you proceed down through the hierarchy as you add lower-level modules to the top-level Verilog module. Initially the lower-level modules are just empty placeholders, or **stubs**, containing a minimum of code. For example, you might start by using inverters just to connect inputs directly to the outputs. You expand these stubs before moving down to the next level of modules.

```
module MyChip_ASIC()
  // behavioral "always", etc. ...
  SecondLevelStub1 port mapping
  SecondLevelStub2 port mapping
  ... endmodule
module SecondLevelStub1() ... assign Output1 = ~Input1; endmodule
module SecondLevelStub2() ... assign Output1 = ~Input1;
endmodule
```

Eventually the Verilog modules will correspond to the various component pieces of the ASIC.

12.5.1   Verilog Modeling

Before we could start synthesis of the Viterbi decoder we had to alter the model for the D flip-flop. This was because the original flip-flop model contained syntax (multiple `wait` statements in an `always` statement) that was acceptable to the simulation tool but not by the synthesis tool. This example was artificial because we had already prepared and tested the Verilog code so that it was acceptable to the synthesis software (we say we created **synthesizable** code). However, finding ourselves with nonsynthesizable code arises frequently in logic synthesis. The original OVI LRM included a **synthesis policy**, a set of guidelines that outline which parts of the Verilog language a synthesis tool should support and which parts are optional. Some EDA vendors call their synthesis policy a **modeling style**. There is no current standard on which parts of an HDL (either Verilog or VHDL) a synthesis tool should support.

It is essential that the structural model created by a synthesis tool is **functionally identical**, or **functionally equivalent**, to your behavioral model. Hopefully, we know this is true if the synthesis tool is working properly. In this case the logic is "correct by construction." If you use different HDL code for simulation and for synthesis, you have a problem. The process of **formal verification** can prove that two logic descriptions (perhaps structural and behavioral HDL descriptions) are identical in their behavior. We shall return to this issue in Chapter 13.

Next we shall examine Verilog and VHDL from the following viewpoint: "How do I write synthesizable code?"

12.5.2   Delays in Verilog

Synthesis tools ignore delay values. They must—how can a synthesis tool guarantee that logic will have a certain delay? For example, a synthesizer cannot generate hardware to implement the following Verilog code:

```
module Step_Time(clk, phase);                              //1
   input clk; output [2:0] phase; reg [2:0] phase;         //2
   always @(posedge clk) begin                             //3
     phase <=    4'b0000;                                  //4
     phase <= #1 4'b0001; phase <= #2 4'b0010;             //5
     phase <= #3 4'b0011; phase <= #4 4'b0100;             //6
   end                                                     //7
endmodule                                                  //8
```

We can avoid this type of timing problem by dividing a clock as follows:

```
module Step_Count (clk_5x, phase);                         //1
   input clk_5x; output [2:0] phase; reg [2:0] phase;      //2
   always@(posedge clk_5x)                                 //3
   case (phase)                                            //4
   0:phase = #1 1; 1:phase = #1 2; 2:phase = #1 3; 3:phase = #1 4;   //5
     default: phase  = #1 0;                               //6
   endcase                                                 //7
endmodule                                                  //8
```

12.5.3   Blocking and Nonblocking Assignments

There are some synthesis limitations that arise from the different types of Verilog assignment statements. Consider the following shift-register model:

```
module race(clk, q0); input clk, q0; reg q1, q2;
always @(posedge clk) q1 = #1 q0; always @(posedge clk) q2 = #1 q1;
endmodule
```

This example has a **race condition** (or a **race**) that occurs as follows. The synthesizer ignores delays and the two always statements are procedures that execute concurrently. So, do we update q1 first and then assign the new value of q1 to q2? or do we update q2 first (with the old value of q1), and then update q1? In real hardware two signals would be racing each other—and the winner is unclear. We must think like the hardware to guide the synthesis tool. Combining the assignment statements into a single always statement, as follows, is one way to solve this problem:

```
module no_race_1(clk, q0, q2); input clk, q0; output q2; reg q1, q2;
always @(posedge clk) begin q2 = q1; q1 = q0; end
endmodule
```

Evaluation is sequential within an always statement, and the order of the assignment statements now ensures q2 gets the old value of q1—before we update q1.

We can also avoid the problem if we use nonblocking assignment statements,

```
module no_race_2(clk, q0, q2); input clk, q0; output q2; reg q1, q2;
always @(posedge clk) q1 <= #1 q0; always @(posedge clk) q2 <= #1 q1;
endmodule
```

This code updates all the registers together, at the end of a time step, so q2 always gets the old value of q1.

12.5.4   Combinational Logic in Verilog

To model combinational logic, the sensitivity list of a Verilog always statement must contain only signals with no edges (no reference to keywords posedge or negedge). This is a **level-sensitive** sensitivity list—as in the following example that implies a two-input AND gate:

```
module And_Always(x, y, z); input x,y; output z; reg z;
always @(x or y) z <= x & y; // combinational logic method 1
endmodule
```

Continuous assignment statements also imply combinational logic (notice that z is now a wire rather than a reg),

```
module And_Assign(x, y, z); input x,y; output z; wire z;
assign z <= x & y; // combinational logic method 2 = method 1
endmodule
```

We may also use concatenation or bit reduction to synthesize combinational logic functions,

```
module And_Or (a,b,c,z); input a,b,c; output z; reg [1:0]z;
always @(a or b or c) begin z[1]<= &{a,b,c}; z[2]<= |{a,b,c}; end
endmodule
```

```
module Parity (BusIn, outp); input[7:0] BusIn; output outp; reg outp;
   always @(BusIn) if (^Busin == 0) outp = 1; else outp = 0;
endmodule
```

The number of inputs, the types, and the drive strengths of the synthesized combinational logic cells will depend on the speed, area, and load requirements that you set as constraints.

You must be careful if you reference a signal (`reg` or `wire`) in a level-sensitive `always` statement and do not include that signal in the sensitivity list. In the following example, signal b is missing from the sensitivity list, and so this code should be flagged with a warning or an error by the synthesis tool—even though the code is perfectly legal and acceptable to the Verilog simulator:

```
module And_Bad(a, b, c); input a, b; output c; reg c;
always@(a) c <= a & b; // b is missing from this sensitivity list
endmodule
```

It is easy to write Verilog code that will simulate, but that does not make sense to the synthesis software. You must think like the hardware. To avoid this type of problem with combinational logic inside an `always` statement you should either:

- include all variables in the event expression or
- assign to the variables before you use them

For example, consider the following two models:

```
module CL_good(a, b, c); input a, b; output c; reg c;
always@(a or b)
begin c = a + b; d = a & b; e = c + d; end // c, d: LHS before RHS
endmodule
```

```
module CL_bad(a, b, c); input a, b; output c; reg c;
always@(a or b)
begin e = c + d; c = a + b; d = a & b; end // c, d: RHS before LHS
endmodule
```

In `CL_bad`, the signals c and d are used on the right-hand side (RHS) of an assignment statement before they are defined on the left-hand side (LHS) of an assignment statement. If the logic synthesizer produces combinational logic for `CL_bad`, it should warn us that the synthesized logic may not match the simulation results.

When you are describing combinational logic you should be aware of the complexity of logic optimization. Some combinational logic functions are too difficult for the optimization algorithms to handle. The following module, `Achilles`, and large parity functions are examples of hard-to-synthesize functions. This is because most logic-optimization algorithms calculate the complement of the functions at some point. The complements of certain functions grow exponentially in the number of their product terms.

```
// The complement of this function is too big for synthesis.
module Achilles (out, in); output out; input [30:1] in;
assign out =     in[30]&in[29]&in[28]  | in[27]&in[26]&in[25]
              |  in[24]&in[23]&in[22]  | in[21]&in[20]&in[19]
              |  in[18]&in[17]&in[16]  | in[15]&in[14]&in[13]
              |  in[12]&in[11]&in[10]  | in[9] & in[8]&in[7]
              |  in[6] & in[5]&in[4]   | in[3] & in[2]&in[1];
endmodule
```

In a case like this you can isolate the problem function in a separate module. Then, after synthesis, you can use directives to tell the synthesizer not to try and optimize the problem function.

12.5.5   Multiplexers In Verilog

We imply a MUX using a case statement, as in the following example:

```
module Mux_21a(sel, a, b, z); input sel, a , b; output z; reg z;
always @(a or b or sel)
begin case(sel) 1'b0: z <= a; 1'b1: z <= b; end
endmodule
```

Be careful using 'x' in a case statement. Metalogical values (such as 'x') are not "real" and are only valid in simulation (and they are sometimes known as **simbits** for that reason). For example, a synthesizer cannot make logic to model the following and will usually issue a warning to that effect:

```
module Mux_x(sel, a, b, z); input sel, a, b; output z; reg z;
always @(a or b or sel)
begin case(sel) 1'b0: z <= 0; 1'b1: z <= 1; 1'bx: z <= 'x'; end
endmodule
```

For the same reason you should avoid using casex and casez statements.
An if statement can also be used to imply a MUX as follows:

```
module Mux_21b(sel, a, b, z); input sel, a, b; output z; reg z;
always @(a or b or sel) begin if (sel) z <= a else z <= b; end
endmodule
```

However, if you do not always assign to an output, as in the following code, you will get a latch:

```
module Mux_Latch(sel, a, b, z); input sel, a, b; output z; reg z;
always @(a or sel) begin if (sel) z <= a; end
endmodule
```

It is important to understand why this code implies a sequential latch and not a combinational MUX. Think like the hardware and you will see the problem. When `sel` is zero, you can pass through the `always` statement whenever a change occurs on the input a without updating the value of the output z. In this situation you need to "remember" the value of z when a changes. This implies sequential logic using a as the latch input, `sel` as the active-high latch enable, and z as the latch output.

The following code implies an 8:1 MUX with a three-state output:

```
module Mux_81(InBus, sel, OE, OutBit);              //1
input [7:0] InBus; input [2:0] Sel;                 //2
input OE; output OutBit; reg OutBit;                //3
always @(OE or sel or InBus)                        //4
  begin                                             //5
    if (OE == 1) OutBit = InBus[sel]; else OutBit = 1'bz;  //6
  end                                               //7
endmodule                                           //8
```

When you synthesize a large MUX the required speed and area, the output load, as well as the cells that are available in the cell library will determine whether the synthesizer uses a large MUX cell, several smaller MUX cells, or equivalent random logic cells. The synthesized logic may also use different logic cells depending on whether you want the fastest path from the select input to the MUX output or from the data inputs to the MUX output.

12.5.6 The Verilog Case Statement

Consider the following model:

```
module case8_oneHot(oneHot, a, b, c, z);           //1
input a, b, c; input [2:0] oneHot; output z; reg z; //2
always @(oneHot or a or b or c)                     //3
begin case(oneHot) //synopsys full_case             //4
  3'b001: z <= a; 3'b010: z <= b; 3'b100: z <= c;   //5
  default: z <= 1'bx; endcase                       //6
end                                                 //7
endmodule                                           //8
```

By including the `default` choice, the `case` statement is **exhaustive**. This means that every possible value of the select variable (`oneHot`) is accounted for in the arms of the `case` statement. In some synthesizers (Synopsys, for example) you may indicate the arms are exhaustive and imply a MUX by using a **compiler directive** or **synthesis directive**. A compiler directive is also called a **pseudocomment** if it uses the comment format (such as `//synopsys full_case`). The format of pseudocomments is very specific. Thus, for example, `//synopys` may be recognized but `// synopys` (with an extra space) or `//SynopSys` (uppercase) may not. The use of pseudocomments shows the problems of using an HDL for a purpose for which it was not intended. When we start "extending" the language we lose the advantages of a standard and sacrifice portability. A compiler directive in module `case8_oneHot` is unnecessary if the `default` choice is included. If you omit the `default` choice and you do not have the ability to use the `full_case` directive (or you use a different tool), the synthesizer will infer latches for the output z.

If the default in a `case` statement is `'x'` (signifying a **synthesis don't care value**), this gives the synthesizer flexibility in optimizing the logic. It does not mean that the synthesized logic output will be unknown when the default applies. The combinational logic that results from a `case` statement when a don't care (`'x'`) is included as a default may or may not include a MUX, depending on how the logic is optimized.

In `case8_oneHot` the choices in the arms of the `case` statement are exhaustive and also mutually exclusive. Consider the following alternative model:

```
module case8_priority(oneHot, a, b, c, z);                    //1
input a, b, c; input [2:0] oneHot; output z; reg z;           //2
always @(oneHot or a or b or c) begin                         //3
case(1'b1) //synopsys parallel_case                           //4
  oneHot[0]: z <= a;                                          //5
  oneHot[1]: z <= b;                                          //6
  oneHot[2]: z <= c;                                          //7
  default: z <= 1'bx; endcase                                 //8
end                                                           //9
endmodule                                                     //10
```

In this version of the `case` statement the choices are not necessarily mutually exclusive (`oneHot[0]` and `oneHot[2]` may both be equal to `1'b1`, for example). Thus the code implies a priority encoder. This may not be what you intended. Some logic synthesizers allow you to indicate mutually exclusive choices by using a directive (`//synopsys parallel_case`, for example). It is probably wiser not to use these "outside-the-language" directives if they can be avoided.

12.5.7   Decoders In Verilog

The following code models a 4:16 decoder with enable and three-state output:

```
module Decoder_4To16(enable, In_4, Out_16); // 4-to-16 decoder   //1
input enable; input [3:0] In_4; output [15:0] Out_16;            //2
reg [15:0] Out_16;                                               //3
always @(enable or In_4)                                         //4
  begin Out_16 = 16'hzzzz;                                       //5
  if (enable == 1)                                               //6
    begin Out_16 = 16'h0000; Out_16[In_4] = 1; end               //7
```

```
    end                                                                 //8
endmodule                                                               //9
```

In line 7 the binary-encoded 4-bit input sets the corresponding bit of the 16-bit output to `'1'`. The synthesizer infers a three-state buffer from the assignment in line 5. Using the equality operator, `'=='`, rather than the case equality operator, `'==='`, makes sense in line 6, because the synthesizer cannot generate logic that will check for enable being `'x'` or `'z'`. So, for example, do not write the following (though some synthesis tools will still accept it):

```
if (enable === 1) // can't make logic to check for enable = x or z
```

12.5.8   Priority Encoder in Verilog

The following Verilog code models a priority encoder with three-state output:

```
module Pri_Encoder32 (InBus, Clk, OE, OutBus);                         //1
input [31:0]InBus; input OE, Clk; output [4:0]OutBus;                  //2
reg j; reg [4:0]OutBus;                                                //3
    always@(posedge Clk)                                              //4
    begin                                                             //5
    if (OE == 0) OutBus = 5'bz ;                                      //6
    else                                                             //7
      begin OutBus = 0;                                              //8
      for (j = 31; j >= 0; j = j - 1)                                //9
        begin if (InBus[j] == 1) OutBus = j; end                     //10
      end                                                             //11
    end                                                               //12
endmodule                                                             //13
```

In lines 9–11 the binary-encoded output is set to the position of the lowest-indexed `'1'` in the input bus. The logic synthesizer must be able to unroll the loop in a `for` statement. Normally the synthesizer will check for fixed (or static) bounds on the loop limits, as in line 9 above.

12.5.9   Arithmetic in Verilog

You need to make room for the carry bit when you add two numbers in Verilog. You may do this using concatenation on the LHS of an assignment as follows:

```
module Adder_8 (A, B, Z, Cin, Cout);                                   //1
input [7:0] A, B; input Cin; output [7:0] Z; output Cout;             //2
assign {Cout, Z} = A + B + Cin;                                        //3
endmodule                                                             //4
```

In the following example, the synthesizer should recognize `'1'` as a carry-in bit of an adder and should synthesize one adder and not two:

```
module Adder_16 (A, B, Sum, Cout);                                     //1
input [15:0] A, B; output [15:0] Sum; output Cout;                    //2
```

```
reg [15:0] Sum; reg Cout;                                       //3
always @(A or B) {Cout, Sum} = A + B + 1;                       //4
endmodule                                                       //5
```

It is always possible to synthesize adders (and other arithmetic functions) using random logic, but they may not be as efficient as using datapath synthesis (see Section 12.5.12).

A logic sythesizer may infer two adders from the following description rather than shaping a single adder.

```
module Add_A (sel, a, b, c, d, y);                              //1
input a, b, c, d, sel; output y; reg y;                         //2
always@(sel or a or b or c or d)                                //3
  begin if (sel == 0) y <= a + b; else y <= c + d; end          //4
endmodule                                                       //5
```

To imply the presence of a MUX before a single adder we can use temporary variables. For example, the synthesizer should use only one adder for the following code:

```
module Add_B (sel, a, b, c, d, y);                              //1
input a, b, c, d, sel; output y; reg t1, t2, y;                 //2
always@(sel or a or b or c or d) begin                          //3
  if (sel == 0)     begin t1 = a; t2 = b; end // Temporary      //4
  else              begin t1 = c; t2 = d; end // variables.     //5
  y = t1 + t2; end                                              //6
endmodule                                                       //7
```

If a synthesis tool is capable of performing **resource allocation** and **resource sharing** in these situations, the coding style may not matter. However we may want to use a different tool, which may not be as advanced, at a later date—so it is better to use Add_B rather than Add_A if we wish to conserve area. This example shows that the simplest code (Add_A) does not always result in the simplest logic (Add_B).

Multiplication in Verilog assumes nets are unsigned numbers:

```
module Multiply_unsigned (A, B, Z);                             //1
input [1:0] A, B; output [3:0] Z;                               //2
assign Z <= A * B;                                              //3
endmodule                                                       //4
```

To multiply signed numbers we need to extend the multiplicands with their sign bits as follows (some simulators have trouble with the concatenation '{}' structures, in which case we have to write them out "long hand"):

```
module Multiply_signed (A, B, Z);                               //1
input [1:0] A, B; output [3:0] Z;                               //2
// 00 -> 00_00  01 -> 00_01  10 -> 11_10  11 -> 11_11           //3
assign Z = { { 2{A[1]} }, A} * { { 2{B[1]} }, B};               //4
endmodule                                                       //5
```

How the logic synthesizer implements the multiplication depends on the software.

12.5.10 Sequential Logic in Verilog

The following statement implies a positive-edge–triggered D flip-flop:

```
always@(posedge clock) Q_flipflop = D; // A flip-flop.
```

When you use edges (posedge or negedge) in the sensitivity list of an always statement, you imply a clocked storage element. However, an always statement does not have to be edge-sensitive to imply sequential logic. As another example of sequential logic, the following statement implies a level-sensitive transparent latch:

```
always@(clock or D) if (clock) Q_latch = D; // A latch.
```

On the negative edge of the clock the always statement is executed, but no assignment is made to Q_latch. These last two code examples concisely illustrate the difference between a flip-flop and a latch.

Any sequential logic cell or memory element must be initialized. Although you could use an initial statement to simulate power-up, generating logic to mimic an initial statement is hard. Instead use a reset as follows:

```
always@(posedge clock or negedge reset)
```

A problem now arises. When we use two edges, the synthesizer must infer which edge is the clock, and which is the reset. Synthesis tools cannot read any significance into the names we have chosen. For example, we could have written

```
always@(posedge day or negedge year)
```

—but which is the clock and which is the reset in this case?

For most synthesis tools you must solve this problem by writing HDL code in a certain format or pattern so that the logic synthesizer may correctly infer the clock and reset signals. The following examples show one possible pattern or **template**. These templates and their use are usually described in a **synthesis style guide** that is part of the synthesis software documentation.

```
always@(posedge clk or negedge reset) begin    // template for reset:
   if (reset == 0) Q = 0;                       // initialize,
   else Q = D;                                  // normal clocking
end

module Counter_With_Reset (count, clock, reset);                //1
input clock, reset; output count; reg [7:0] count;              //2
always @ (posedge clock or negedge reset)                       //3
   if (reset == 0) count = 0; else count = count + 1;           //4
endmodule                                                       //5

module DFF_MasterSlave (D, clock, reset, Q); // D type flip-flop   //1
input D, clock, reset; output Q; reg Q, latch;                    //2
always @(posedge clock or posedge reset)                          //3
   if (reset == 1) latch = 0; else latch = D; // the master.      //4
```

```
always @(latch) Q = latch; // the slave.                      //5
endmodule                                                     //6
```

The synthesis tool can now infer that, in these templates, the signal that is tested in the `if` statement is the reset, and that the other signal must therefore be the clock.

12.5.11 Component Instantiation in Verilog

When we give an HDL description to a synthesis tool, it will synthesize a netlist that contains generic logic gates. By generic we mean the logic is technology-independent (it could be CMOS standard cell, FPGA, TTL, GaAs, or something else—we have not decided yet). Only after logic optimization and mapping to a specific ASIC cell library do the speed or area constraints determine the cell choices from a cell library: NAND gates, OAI gates, and so on.

The only way to ensure that the synthesizer uses a particular cell, `'special'` for example, from a specific library is to write structural Verilog and instantiate the cell, `'special'`, in the Verilog. We call this **hand instantiation**. We must then decide whether to allow logic optimization to replace or change `'special'`. If we insist on using logic cell `'special'` and do not want it changed, we flag the cell with a synthesizer command. Most logic synthesizers currently use a pseudocomment statement or set an attribute to do this.

For example, we might include the following statement to tell the Compass synthesizer—"Do not change cell instance `my_inv_8x`." This is not a standard construct, and it is not portable from tool to tool either.

```
//Compass dontTouch my_inv_8x or // synopsys dont_touch
INVD8 my_inv_8x(.I(a), .ZN(b) );
```

(some compiler directives are trademarks). Notice, in this example, instantiation involves declaring the instance name and defining a structural port mapping.

There is no standard name for technology-independent models or components—we shall call them **soft models** or **standard components**. We can use the standard components for synthesis or for behavioral Verilog simulation. Here is an example of using standard components for flip-flops (remember there are no primitive Verilog flip-flop models—only primitives for the elementary logic cells):

```
module Count4(clk, reset, Q0, Q1, Q2, Q3);                    //1
input clk, reset; output Q0, Q1, Q2, Q3; wire Q0, Q1, Q2, Q3; //2
//          Q , D , clk, reset                                //3
asDff dff0( Q0,  ~Q0, clk, reset); // The asDff is a          //4
asDff dff1( Q1,  ~Q1, Q0,  reset); // standard component,     //5
asDff dff2( Q2,  ~Q2, Q1,  reset); // unique to one set of tools. //6
asDff dff3( Q3,  ~Q3, Q2,  reset);                            //7
endmodule                                                     //8
```

The `asDff` and other standard components are provided with the synthesis tool. The standard components have specific names and interfaces that are part of the software documentation. When we use a standard component such as `asDff` we are saying: "I want a D flip-flop, but I do not know which ASIC technology I want to use—give me a generic version. I do not want to write a Verilog model for the D flip-flop myself because I do not want to bother to synthesize each and every instance of a flip-flop. When the time comes, just map this generic flip-flop to whatever is available in the technology-dependent (vendor-specific) library."

If we try and simulate `Count4` we will get an error,

```
:Count4.v: L5: error: Module 'asDff' not defined
```

(and three more like this) because `asDff` is not a primitive Verilog model. The synthesis tool should provide us with a model for the standard component. For example, the following code models the behavior of the standard component, `asDff`:

```
module asDff (D, Q, Clk, Rst);                                   //1
parameter width = 1, reset_value = 0;                           //2
input [width-1:0] D; output [width-1:0] Q; reg [width-1:0] Q;    //3
input Clk,Rst; initial Q = {width{1'bx}};                       //4
   always @ ( posedge Clk or negedge Rst )                      //5
     if ( Rst==0 ) Q <= #1 reset_value; else Q <= #1 D;         //6
endmodule                                                        //7
```

When the synthesizer compiles the HDL code in `Count4`, it does not parse the `asDff` model. The software recognizes `asDff` and says "I see you want a flip-flop." The first steps that the synthesis software and the simulation software take are often referred to as compilation, but the two steps are different for each of these tools.

Synopsys has an extensive set of libraries, called **DesignWare**, that contains standard components not only for flip-flops but for arithmetic and other complex logic elements. These standard components are kept protected from optimization until it is time to map to a vendor technology. ASIC or EDA companies that produce design software and cell libraries can tune the synthesizer to the silicon and achieve a more efficient mapping. Even though we call them standard components, there are no standards that cover their names, use, interfaces, or models.

12.5.12 Datapath Synthesis in Verilog

Datapath synthesis is used for bus-wide arithmetic and other bus-wide operations. For example, synthesis of a 32-bit multiplier in random logic is much less efficient than using datapath synthesis. There are several approaches to datapath synthesis:

- Synopsys VHDL DesignWare. This models generic arithmetic and other large functions (counters, shift registers, and so on) using standard components. We can either let the synthesis tool map operators (such as '+') to VHDL DesignWare components, or we can hand instantiate them in the code. Many ASIC vendors support the DesignWare libraries. Thus, for example, we can instantiate a DesignWare counter in VHDL and map that to a cell predesigned and preoptimized by Actel for an Actel FPGA.

- Compiler directives. This approach uses synthesis directives in the code to steer the mapping of datapath operators either to specific components (a two-port RAM or a register file, for example) or flags certain operators to be implemented using a certain style ('+' to be implemented using a ripple-carry adder or a carry-lookahead adder, for example).

- X-BLOX is a system from Xilinx that allows us to keep the logic of certain functions (counters, arithmetic elements) together. This is so that the layout tool does not splatter the synthesized CLBs all over your FPGA, reducing the performance of the logic.

- LPM (library of parameterized modules) and RPM (relationally placed modules) are other techniques used principally by FPGA companies to keep logic that operates on related data close together. This approach is based on the use of the EDIF language to describe the modules.

In all cases the disadvantage is that the code becomes specific to a certain piece of software. Here are two examples of datapath synthesis directives:

```
module DP_csum(A1,B1,Z1); input [3:0] A1,B1; output Z1; reg [3:0] Z1;
always@(A1 or B1) Z1 <= A1 + B1;//Compass adder_arch cond_sum_add
endmodule
```

```
module DP_ripp(A2,B2,Z2); input [3:0] A2,B2; output Z2; reg [3:0] Z2;
always@(A2 or B2) Z2 <= A2 + B2;//Compass adder_arch ripple_add
endmodule
```

These directives steer the synthesis of a conditional-sum adder (usually the fastest adder implementation) or a ripple-carry adder (small but slow).

There are some limitations to datapath synthesis. Sometimes, complex operations are not synthesized as we might expect. For example, a datapath library may contain a subtracter that has a carry input; however, the following code may synthesize to random logic, because the synthesizer may not be able to infer that the signal CarryIn is a subtracter carry:

```
module DP_sub_A(A,B,OutBus,CarryIn);                              //1
input [3:0] A, B ; input CarryIn ;                               //2
output OutBus ; reg [3:0] OutBus ;                               //3
always@(A or B  or CarryIn) OutBus <= A - B - CarryIn ;          //4
endmodule                                                        //5
```

If we rewrite the code and subtract the carry as a constant, the synthesizer can more easily infer that it should use the carry-in of a datapath subtracter:

```
module DP_sub_B (A, B, CarryIn, Z) ;                             //1
input [3:0] A, B, CarryIn ; output [3:0] Z; reg [3:0] Z;         //2
always@(A or B or CarryIn) begin                                //3
   case (CarryIn)                                                //4
```

```
      1'b1 :        Z <= A - B - 1'b1;                          //5
      default :     Z <= A - B - 1'b0; endcase                 //6
end                                                            //7
endmodule                                                     //8
```

This is another example of thinking like the hardware in order to help the synthesis tool infer what we are trying to imply.

12.6   VHDL and Logic Synthesis

Most logic synthesizers insist we follow a set of rules when we use a logic system to ensure that what we synthesize matches the behavioral description. Here is a typical set of rules for use with the IEEE VHDL nine-value system:

- You can use logic values corresponding to states `'1'`, `'H'`, `'0'`, and `'L'` in any manner.
- Some synthesis tools do not accept the uninitialized logic state `'U'`.
- You can use logic states `'Z'`, `'X'`, `'W'`, and `'-'` in signal and variable assignments in any manner. `'Z'` is synthesized to three-state logic.
- The states `'X'`, `'W'`, and `'-'` are treated as unknown or don't care values.

The values `'Z'`, `'X'`, `'W'`, and `'-'` may be used in conditional clauses such as the comparison in an `if` or `case` statement. However, some synthesis tools will ignore them and only match surrounding `'1'` and `'0'` bits. Consequently, a synthesized design may behave differently from the simulation if a stimulus uses `'Z'`, `'X'`, `'W'` or `'-'`. The IEEE synthesis packages provide the `STD_MATCH` function for comparisons.

12.6.1   Initialization and Reset

You can use a VHDL `process` with a sensitivity list to synthesize clocked logic with a reset, as in the following code:

```
process (signal_1, signal_2) begin
  if (signal_2'EVENT and signal_2 = '0')
    then -- Insert initialization and reset statements.
    elsif (signal_1'EVENT and signal_1 = '1')
    then -- Insert clocking statements.
  end if;
end process;
```

Using a specific pattern the synthesizer can infer that you are implying a positive-edge clock (`signal_1`) and a negative-edge reset (`signal_2`). In order to be able to recognize sequential logic in this way, most synthesizers restrict you to using a maximum of two edges in a sensitivity list.

12.6.2 Combinational Logic Synthesis in VHDL

In VHDL a **level-sensitive process** is a process statement that has a sensitivity list with signals that are not tested for event attributes ('EVENT or 'STABLE, for example) within the process. To synthesize combinational logic we use a VHDL level-sensitive process or a concurrent assignment statement. Some synthesizers do not allow reference to a signal inside a level-sensitive process unless that signal is in the sensitivity list. In this example, signal b is missing from the sensitivity list:

```
entity And_Bad is port (a, b: in BIT; c: out BIT); end And_Bad;

architecture Synthesis_Bad of And_Bad is
  begin process (a) -- this should be process (a, b)
    begin c <= a and b;
  end process;
end Synthesis_Bad;
```

This situation is similar but not exactly the same as omitting a variable from an event control in a Verilog always statement. Some logic synthesizers accept the VHDL version of And_Bad but not the Verilog version or vice versa. To ensure that the VHDL simulation will match the behavior of the synthesized logic, the logic synthesizer usually checks the sensitivity list of a level-sensitive process and issues a warning if signals seem to be missing.

12.6.3 Multiplexers in VHDL

Multiplexers can be synthesized using a case statement (avoiding the VHDL reserved word 'select'), as the following example illustrates:

```
entity Mux4 is port
(i: BIT_VECTOR(3 downto 0); sel: BIT_VECTOR(1 downto 0); s: out BIT);
end Mux4;

architecture Synthesis_1 of Mux4 is
  begin process(sel, i) begin
    case sel is
    when "00" => s <= i(0); when "01" => s <= i(1);
    when "10" => s <= i(2); when "11" => s <= i(3);
    end case;
  end process;
end Synthesis_1;
```

The following code, using a concurrent signal assignment is equivalent:

```
architecture Synthesis_2 of Mux4 is
  begin with sel select s <=
    i(0) when "00", i(1) when "01", i(2) when "10", i(3) when "11";
end Synthesis_2;
```

In VHDL the `case` statement must be exhaustive in either form, so there is no question of any priority in the choices as there may be in Verilog.

For larger MUXes we can use an array, as in the following example:

```
library IEEE; use  ieee.std_logic_1164.all;
entity Mux8 is port
    (InBus : in STD_LOGIC_VECTOR(7 downto 0);
    Sel : in INTEGER range 0 to 7;
    OutBit : out STD_LOGIC);
end Mux8;

architecture Synthesis_1 of Mux8 is
    begin process(InBus, Sel)
    variable TmpBus : STD_LOGIC_VECTOR (7 downto 0);
    begin OutBit <= InBus(Sel);
    end process;
end Synthesis_1;
```

Most synthesis tools can infer that, in this case, `Sel` requires three bits. If not, you have to declare the signal as a `STD_LOGIC_VECTOR`,

```
Sel : in STD_LOGIC_VECTOR(2 downto 0);
```

and use a conversion routine from the `STD_NUMERIC` package like this:

```
OutBit <= InBus(TO_INTEGER ( UNSIGNED (Sel) ) ) ;
```

At some point you have to convert from an `INTEGER` to `BIT` logic anyway, since you cannot connect an `INTEGER` to the input of a chip! The VHDL `case`, `if`, and `select` statements produce similar results. Assigning don't care bits (`'x'`) in these statements will make it easier for the synthesizer to optimize the logic.

12.6.4   Decoders in VHDL

The following code implies a decoder:

```
library IEEE;                                               --1
use IEEE.STD_LOGIC_1164.all; use IEEE.NUMERIC_STD.all;      --2

entity Decoder is port (enable : in BIT;                    --3
    Din: STD_LOGIC_VECTOR (2 downto 0);                     --4
    Dout: out STD_LOGIC_VECTOR (7 downto 0));               --5
end Decoder;                                                --6

architecture Synthesis_1 of Decoder is                      --7
    begin                                                   --8
    with enable select Dout <=                              --9
    STD_LOGIC_VECTOR                                        --10
    (UNSIGNED'                                              --11
        (shift_left                                         --12
            ("00000001", TO_INTEGER (UNSIGNED(Din))         --13
            )                                               --14
```

```
     )                                                                 --15
   )                                                                   --16
   when '1',                                                           --17
   "11111111" when '0', "00000000" when others;                        --18
end Synthesis_1;                                                       --19
```

There are reasons for this seemingly complex code:

- Line 1 declares the IEEE library. The synthesizer does not parse the VHDL code inside the library packages, but the synthesis company should be able to guarantee that the logic will behave exactly the same way as a simulation that uses the IEEE libraries and does parse the code.

- Line 2 declares the STD_LOGIC_1164 package, for STD_LOGIC types, and the NUMERIC_STD package for conversion and shift functions. The shift *operators* (sll and so on–the infix operators) were introduced in VHDL-93, they are not defined for STD_LOGIC types in the 1164 standard. The shift *functions* defined in NUMERIC_STD are not operators and are called shift_left and so on. Some synthesis tools support NUMERIC_STD, but not VHDL-93.

- Line 10 performs a type conversion to STD_LOGIC_VECTOR from UNSIGNED.

- Line 11 is a type qualification to tell the software that the argument to the type conversion function is type UNSIGNED.

- Line 12 is the shift function, shift_left, from the NUMERIC_STD package.

- Line 13 converts the STD_LOGIC_VECTOR, Din, to UNSIGNED before converting to INTEGER. We cannot convert directly from STD_LOGIC_VECTOR to INTEGER.

- The others clause in line 18 is required by the logic synthesizer even though type BIT may only be '0' or '1'.

If we model a decoder using a process, we can use a case statement inside the process. A MUX model may be used as a decoder if the input bits are set at '1' (active-high decoder) or at '0' (active-low decoder), as in the following example:

```
library IEEE;                                                         --1
use IEEE.NUMERIC_STD.all; use IEEE.STD_LOGIC_1164.all;                --2

entity Concurrent_Decoder is port (                                   --3
   enable : in BIT;                                                   --4
   Din : in STD_LOGIC_VECTOR (2 downto 0);                            --5
   Dout : out STD_LOGIC_VECTOR (7 downto 0));                         --6
end Concurrent_Decoder;                                               --7

architecture Synthesis_1 of Concurrent_Decoder is                     --8
begin process (Din, enable)                                           --9
   variable T : STD_LOGIC_VECTOR(7 downto 0);                         --10
   begin                                                              --11
   if (enable = '1') then                                             --12
```

```
     T := "00000000"; T( TO_INTEGER (UNSIGNED(Din))) := '1';          --13
       Dout <= T ;                                                     --14
   else Dout <= (others => 'Z');                                      --15
   end if;                                                            --16
end process;                                                          --17
end Synthesis_1;                                                      --18
```

Notice that T must be a variable for proper timing of the update to the output. The else clause in the if statement is necessary to avoid inferring latches.

12.6.5 Adders in VHDL

To add two *n*-bit numbers and keep the overflow bit, we need to assign to a signal with more bits, as follows:

```
library IEEE;                                                         --1
use IEEE.NUMERIC_STD.all; use IEEE.STD_LOGIC_1164.all;               --2

entity Adder_1 is                                                     --3
port (A, B: in UNSIGNED(3 downto 0); C: out UNSIGNED(4 downto 0));   --4
end Adder_1;                                                          --5

architecture Synthesis_1 of Adder_1 is                              --6
  begin C <= ('0' & A) + ('0' & B);                                  --7
end Synthesis_1;                                                     --8
```

Notice that both A and B have to be SIGNED or UNSIGNED as we cannot add STD_LOGIC_VECTOR types directly using the IEEE packages. You will get an error if a result is a different length from the target of an assignment, as in the following example (in which the arguments are not resized):

```
adder_1:          begin C <= A + B;
Error: Width mis-match: right expression is 4 bits wide, c is 5 bits
wide
```

The following code may generate three adders stacked three deep:

```
z <= a + b + c + d;
```

Depending on how the expression is parsed, the first adder may perform $x = a + b$, a second adder $y = x + c$, and a third adder $z = y + d$. The following code should generate faster logic with three adders stacked only two deep:

```
z <= (a + b) + (c + d);
```

12.6.6 Sequential Logic in VHDL

Sensitivity to an edge implies sequential logic in VHDL. A synthesis tool can locate edges in VHDL by finding a process statement that has either:

- no sensitivity list with a wait until statement
- a sensitivity list and test for 'EVENT plus a specific level

Any signal assigned in an edge-sensitive process statement should also be reset—but be careful to distinguish between asynchronous and synchronous resets. The following example illustrates these points:

```
library IEEE; use IEEE.STD_LOGIC_1164.all; entity DFF_With_Reset is
    port(D, Clk, Reset : in STD_LOGIC; Q : out STD_LOGIC);
end DFF_With_Reset;

architecture Synthesis_1 of DFF_With_Reset is
    begin process(Clk, Reset) begin
        if (Reset = '0') then Q <= '0'; -- asynchronous reset
            elsif rising_edge(Clk) then Q <= D;
        end if;
    end process;
end Synthesis_1;

architecture Synthesis_2 of DFF_With_Reset is
    begin process begin
        wait until rising_edge(Clk);
-- This reset is gated with the clock and is synchronous:
        if (Reset = '0') then Q <= '0'; else Q <= D; end if;
    end process;
end Synthesis_2;
```

Sequential logic results when we have to "remember" something between successive executions of a process. This occurs when a process contains one or more of the following situations:

- A signal is read but is not in the sensitivity list of a process.
- A signal or variable is read before it is updated.
- A signal is not always updated.
- There are multiple wait statements.

Not all of the models that we could write using the above constructs will be synthesizable. Any models that do use one or more of these constructs and that are synthesizable will result in sequential logic.

12.6.7   Instantiation in VHDL

The easiest way to find out how to hand instantiate a component is to generate a structural netlist from a simple HDL input—for example, the following Verilog behavioral description (VHDL could have been used, but the Verilog is shorter):

```
`timescale 1ns/1ns                                              //1
module halfgate (myInput, myOutput);                            //2
input myInput; output myOutput; wire myOutput;                 //3
    assign myOutput = ~myInput;                                 //4
endmodule                                                       //5
```

We synthesize this module and generate the following VHDL structural netlist:

```
library IEEE; use IEEE.STD_LOGIC_1164.all;                     --1
library COMPASS_LIB; use COMPASS_LIB.COMPASS.all;              --2
--compass compile_off -- synopsys etc.                          --3
use COMPASS_LIB.COMPASS_ETC.all;                               --4
--compass compile_on -- synopsys etc.                           --5
entity halfgate_u is                                           --6
--compass compile_off -- synopsys etc.                          --7
generic (                                                      --8
  myOutput_cap : Real := 0.01;                                 --9
  INSTANCE_NAME : string := "halfgate_u" );                  --10
--compass compile_on -- synopsys etc.                         --11
port ( myInput : in Std_Logic := 'U';                         --12
myOutput : out Std_Logic := 'U' );                           --13
end halfgate_u;                                               --14

architecture halfgate_u of halfgate_u is                     --15
component in01d0                                              --16
port ( I : in Std_Logic; ZN : out Std_Logic ); end component; --17
begin                                                        --18
u2: in01d0 port map ( I => myInput, ZN => myOutput );        --19
end halfgate_u;                                              --20

--compass compile_off -- synopsys etc.                       --21
library cb60hd230d;                                          --22
configuration halfgate_u_CON of halfgate_u is               --23
  for halfgate_u                                             --24
    for u2 : in01d0 use configuration cb60hd230d.in01d0_CON  --25
    generic map (                                            --26
      ZN_cap => 0.0100 + myOutput_cap,                       --27
      INSTANCE_NAME => INSTANCE_NAME&"/u2" )                 --28
    port map ( I => I, ZN => ZN);                            --29
    end for;                                                 --30
  end for;                                                   --31
end halfgate_u_CON;                                          --32
--compass compile_on -- synopsys etc.                        --33
```

This gives a template to follow when hand instantiating logic cells. Instantiating a standard component requires the name of the component and its parameters:

```
component ASDFF
  generic (WIDTH : POSITIVE := 1;
    RESET_VALUE : STD_LOGIC_VECTOR := "0" );
  port    (Q    : out STD_LOGIC_VECTOR (WIDTH-1 downto 0);
           D    : in  STD_LOGIC_VECTOR (WIDTH-1 downto 0);
           CLK  : in  STD_LOGIC;
```

```
            RST  :  in  STD_LOGIC );
end component;
```

Now you have enough information to be able to instantiate both logic cells from a cell library and standard components. The following model illustrates instantiation:

```
library IEEE, COMPASS_LIB;                                          --1
use IEEE.STD_LOGIC_1164.all; use COMPASS_LIB.STDCOMP.all;          --2
entity Ripple_4 is                                                 --3
   port (Trig, Reset: STD_LOGIC; QN0_5x: out STD_LOGIC;            --4
    Q : inout STD_LOGIC_VECTOR(0 to 3));                           --5
end Ripple_4;                                                      --6
architecture structure of Ripple_4 is                             --7
   signal QN : STD_LOGIC_VECTOR(0 to 3);                           --8
component in01d1                                                   --9
port ( I : in Std_Logic; ZN : out Std_Logic ); end component;     --10
component in01d5                                                   --11
port ( I : in Std_Logic; ZN : out Std_Logic ); end component;     --12
begin                                                             --13
--compass dontTouch inv5x -- synopsys dont_touch etc.             --14
-- Named association for hand-instantiated library cells:         --15
   inv5x: IN01D5 port map( I=>Q(0), ZN=>QN0_5x );                 --16
   inv0 : IN01D1 port map( I=>Q(0), ZN=>QN(0) );                  --17
   inv1 : IN01D1 port map( I=>Q(1), ZN=>QN(1) );                  --18
   inv2 : IN01D1 port map( I=>Q(2), ZN=>QN(2) );                  --19
   inv3 : IN01D1 port map( I=>Q(3), ZN=>QN(3) );                  --20
-- Positional association for standard components:                --21
--                        Q        D       Clk    Rst             --22
   d0: asDFF  port map(Q (0 to 0), QN(0 to 0), Trig,  Reset);     --23
   d1: asDFF  port map(Q (1 to 1), QN(1 to 1), Q(0),  Reset);     --24
   d2: asDFF  port map(Q (2 to 2), QN(2 to 2), Q(1),  Reset);     --25
   d3: asDFF  port map(Q (3 to 3), QN(3 to 3), Q(2),  Reset);     --26
end structure;                                                    --27
```

- Lines 5 and 8. Type STD_LOGIC_VECTOR must be used for standard component ports, because the standard components are defined using this type.

- Line 5. Mode inout has to be used for Q since it has to be read/write and this is a structural model. You cannot use mode buffer since the formal outputs of the standard components are declared to be of mode out.

- Line 14. This synthesis directive prevents the synthesis tool from removing the 5X drive strength inverter inv5x. This statement ties the code to a particular synthesis tool.

- Lines 16–20. Named association for the hand-instantiated library cells. The names (IN01D5 and IN01D1) and port names (I and ZN) come from the cell library data book or from a template (such as the one created for the IN01D1 logic cell). These statements tie the code to a particular cell library.

- Lines 23–26. Positional port mapping of the standard components. The port locations are from the synthesis standard component library documentation. These `asDFF` standard components will be mapped to D flip-flop library cells. These statements tie the code to a particular synthesis tool.

You would receive the following warning from the logic synthesizer when it synthesizes this input code (entity `Ripple_4`):

```
Warning: Net has more than one driver: d3_Q[0]; connected to:
ripple_4_p.q[3], inv3.I, d3.Q
```

There is potentially more than one driver on a net because Q was declared as `inout`. There are a total of four warnings of this type for each of the flip-flop outputs. You can check the output netlist to make sure that you have the logic you expected as follows (the Verilog netlist is shorter and easier to read):

```
`timescale 1ns / 10ps                                          //1
module ripple_4_u (trig, reset, qn0_5x, q);                    //2
input  trig; input  reset; output qn0_5x; inout  [3:0] q;      //3
wire  [3:0] qn; supply1 VDD; supply0 VSS;                      //4
in01d5 inv5x (.I(q[0]),.ZN(qn0_5x));                           //5
in01d1 inv0 (.I(q[0]),.ZN(qn[0]));                             //6
in01d1 inv1 (.I(q[1]),.ZN(qn[1]));                             //7
in01d1 inv2 (.I(q[2]),.ZN(qn[2]));                             //8
in01d1 inv3 (.I(q[3]),.ZN(qn[3]));                             //9
dfctnb d0(.D(qn[0]),.CP(trig),.CDN(reset),.Q(q[0]),.QN(\d0.QN )); //10
dfctnb d1(.D(qn[1]),.CP(q[0]),.CDN(reset),.Q(q[1]),.QN(\d1.QN )); //11
dfctnb d2(.D(qn[2]),.CP(q[1]),.CDN(reset),.Q(q[2]),.QN(\d2.QN )); //12
dfctnb d3(.D(qn[3]),.CP(q[2]),.CDN(reset),.Q(q[3]),.QN(\d3.QN )); //13
endmodule                                                      //14
```

12.6.8   Shift Registers and Clocking in VHDL

The following code implies a serial-in/parallel-out (SIPO) shift register:

```
library IEEE;                                                  --1
use IEEE.STD_LOGIC_1164.all; use IEEE.NUMERIC_STD.all;         --2

entity SIPO_1 is port (                                        --3
  Clk :  in        STD_LOGIC;                                  --4
  SI :   in        STD_LOGIC;                    -- serial in   --5
  PO :   buffer    STD_LOGIC_VECTOR(3 downto 0)); -- parallel out --6
end SIPO_1;                                                    --7

architecture Synthesis_1 of SIPO_1 is                         --8
  begin process (Clk) begin                                   --9
    if (Clk = '1') then PO <= SI & PO(3 downto 1); end if;    --10
  end process;                                                --11
end Synthesis_1;                                              --12
```

Here is the Verilog structural netlist that results (dfntnb is a positive-edge–triggered D flip-flop without clear or reset):

```
module sipo_1_u (clk, si, po);                                      //1
input  clk; input  si; output [3:0] po;                            //2
supply1 VDD; supply0 VSS;                                          //3
dfntnb po_ff_b0 (.D(po[1]),.CP(clk),.Q(po[0]),.QN(\po_ff_b0.QN)); //4
dfntnb po_ff_b1 (.D(po[2]),.CP(clk),.Q(po[1]),.QN(\po_ff_b1.QN)); //5
dfntnb po_ff_b2 (.D(po[3]),.CP(clk),.Q(po[2]),.QN(\po_ff_b2.QN)); //6
dfntnb po_ff_b3 (.D(si),.CP(clk),.Q(po[3]),.QN(\po_ff_b3.QN )); //7
endmodule                                                          //8
```

The synthesized design consists of four flip-flops. Notice that (line 6 in the VHDL input) signal PO is of mode buffer because we cannot read a signal of mode out inside a process. This is acceptable for synthesis but not usually a good idea for simulation models. We can modify the code to eliminate the buffer port and at the same time we shall include a reset signal, as follows:

```
library IEEE;                                                      --1
use IEEE.STD_LOGIC_1164.all; use IEEE.NUMERIC_STD.all;            --2
entity SIPO_R is port (                                           --3
  clk : in STD_LOGIC ; res : in STD_LOGIC ;                       --4
  SI : in STD_LOGIC ; PO : out STD_LOGIC_VECTOR(3 downto 0));     --5
end;                                                              --6
architecture Synthesis_1 of SIPO_R is                            --7
  signal PO_t : STD_LOGIC_VECTOR(3 downto 0);                    --8
  begin                                                          --9
  process (PO_t) begin PO <= PO_t; end process;                 --10
  process (clk, res) begin                                      --11
    if (res = '0') then PO_t <= (others => '0');                --12
    elsif (rising_edge(clk)) then PO_t <= SI & PO_t(3 downto 1); --13
    end if;                                                     --14
  end process;                                                  --15
end Synthesis_1;                                               --16
```

Notice the following:

- Line 10 uses a temporary signal, PO_t, to avoid using a port of mode buffer for the output signal PO. We could have used a variable instead of a signal and the variable would consume less overhead during simulation. However, we must complete an assignment to a variable inside the clocked process (not in a separate process as we can for the signal). Assignment between a variable and a signal inside a single process creates its own set of problems.

- Line 11 is sensitive to the clock, clk, and the reset, res. It is not sensitive to PO_t or SI and this is what indicates the sequential logic.

- Line 13 uses the rising_edge function from the STD_LOGIC_1164 package.

The software synthesizes four positive-edge–triggered D flip-flops for design entity SIPO_R(Synthesis_1) as it did for design entity SIPO_1(Synthesis_1). The difference is that the synthesized flip-flops in SIPO_R have active-low resets. However, the simulation behavior of these two design entities will be different. In SIPO_R, the function rising_edge only evaluates to TRUE for a transition from '0' or 'L' to '1' or 'H'. In SIPO_1 we only tested for Clk = '1'. Since nearly all synthesis tools now accept rising_edge and falling_edge, it is probably wiser to use these functions consistently.

12.6.9   Adders and Arithmetic Functions

If you wish to perform BIT_VECTOR or STD_LOGIC_VECTOR arithmetic you have three choices:

- Use a vendor-supplied package (there are no standard vendor packages—even if a company puts its own package in the IEEE library).
- Convert to SIGNED (or UNSIGNED) and use the IEEE standard synthesis packages (IEEE Std 1076.3-1997).
- Use overloaded functions in packages or functions that you define yourself.

Here is an example of addition using a ripple-carry architecture:

```
library IEEE;                                               --1
use IEEE.STD_LOGIC_1164.all; use IEEE.NUMERIC_STD.all;      --2

entity Adder4 is port (                                     --3
  in1, in2 : in     BIT_VECTOR(3 downto 0) ;                --4
  mySum : out       BIT_VECTOR(3 downto 0) ) ;              --5
end Adder4;                                                 --6
architecture Behave_A of Adder4 is                          --7
  function DIY(L,R: BIT_VECTOR(3 downto 0)) return BIT_VECTOR is  --8
  variable sum:BIT_VECTOR(3 downto 0);variable lt,rt,st,cry: BIT; --9
    begin cry := '0';                                       --10
    for i in L'REVERSE_RANGE loop                           --11
    lt := L(i); rt := R(i); st := lt xor rt;                --12
    sum(i):= st xor cry; cry:= (lt and rt) or (st and cry); --13
    end loop;                                               --14
    return sum;                                             --15
  end;                                                      --16
  begin mySum <= DIY (in1, in2); -- do it yourself (DIY) add --17
end Behave_A;                                               --18
```

This model results in random logic.

An alternative is to use UNSIGNED or UNSIGNED from the IEEE NUMERIC_STD or NUMERIC_BIT packages as in the following example:

```
library IEEE;                                               --1
use IEEE.STD_LOGIC_1164.all; use IEEE.NUMERIC_STD.all;      --2
```

```
entity Adder4 is port (                                  --3
  in1, in2 : in      UNSIGNED(3 downto 0) ;              --4
  mySum : out        UNSIGNED(3 downto 0) ) ;            --5
end Adder4;                                              --6

architecture Behave_B of Adder4 is                       --7
  begin mySum <= in1 + in2; -- This uses an overloaded '+'. --8
end Behave_B;                                            --9
```

In this case, the synthesized logic will depend on the logic synthesizer.

12.6.10 Adder/Subtracter and Don't Cares

The following code models a 16-bit sequential adder and subtracter. The input signal, xin, is added to output signal, result, when signal addsub is high; otherwise result is subtracted from xin. The internal signal addout temporarily stores the result until the next rising edge of the clock:

```
library IEEE;                                            --1
use IEEE.STD_LOGIC_1164.all; use IEEE.NUMERIC_STD.all;  --2
entity Adder_Subtracter is port (                        --3
  xin : in               UNSIGNED(15 downto 0);          --4
  clk, addsub, clr: in     STD_LOGIC;                    --5
  result : out           UNSIGNED(15 downto 0));         --6
end Adder_Subtracter;                                    --7

architecture Behave_A of Adder_Subtracter is             --8
  signal addout, result_t: UNSIGNED(15 downto 0);        --9
  begin                                                  --10
    result <= result_t;                                  --11
    with addsub select                                   --12
    addout <=    (xin + result_t)    when '1',           --13
                 (xin - result_t)    when '0',           --14
                 (others => '-')     when others;        --15
      process (clr, clk) begin                           --16
        if (clr = '0') then result_t <= (others => '0'); --17
        elsif rising_edge(clk) then result_t <= addout;  --18
        end if;                                          --19
      end process;                                       --20
end Behave_A;                                            --21
```

Notice the following:

- Line 11 is a concurrent assignment to avoid using a port of mode buffer.
- Lines 12–15 define an exhaustive list of choices for the selected signal assignment statement. The default choice sets the result to '-' (don't care) to allow the synthesizer to optimize the logic.

Line 18 includes a reference to signal `addout` that could be eliminated by moving the selected signal assignment statement inside the clocked process as follows:

```
architecture Behave_B of Adder_Subtracter is          --1
  signal result_t: UNSIGNED(15 downto 0);             --2
    begin                                             --3
    result <= result_t;                               --4
      process (clr, clk) begin                        --5
      if (clr = '0') then result_t <= (others => '0');--6
      elsif rising_edge(clk) then                     --7
          case addsub is                              --8
            when '1'      => result_t <= (xin + result_t); --9
            when '0'      => result_t <= (xin - result_t); --10
            when others   => result_t <= (others => '-'); --11
          end case;                                   --12
      end if;                                         --13
    end process;                                      --14
end Behave_B;                                         --15
```

This code is simpler than architecture `Behave_A`, but the synthesized logic should be identical for both architectures. Since the logic that results is an adder/subtracter followed by a register (bank of flip-flops) the `Behave_A` `model` more clearly reflects the hardware.

12.7 Finite-State Machine Synthesis

There are three ways to synthesize a **finite-state machine** (**FSM**):

1. Omit any special synthesis directives and let the logic synthesizer operate on the state machine as though it were random logic. This will prevent any reassignment of states or state machine optimization. It is the easiest method and independent of any particular synthesis tool, but is the most inefficient approach in terms of area and performance.

2. Use directives to guide the logic synthesis tool to improve or modify state assignment. This approach is dependent on the software that you use.

3. Use a special state-machine compiler, separate from the logic synthesizer, to optimize the state machine. You then merge the resulting state machine with the rest of your logic. This method leads to the best results but is harder to use and ties your code to a particular set of software tools, not just the logic synthesizer.

Most synthesis tools require that you write a state machine using a certain style—a special format or template. Synthesis tools may also require that you declare an FSM, the encoding, and the state register using a synthesis directive or special software command. Common FSM encoding options are:

- **Adjacent encoding** assigns states by the minimum logic difference in the state transition graph. This normally reduces the amount of logic needed to decode each state. The minimum number of bits in the state register for an FSM with *n* states is log 2*n*. In some tools you may increase the state register width up to *n* to generate encoding based on Gray codes.

- **One-hot encoding** sets one bit in the state register for each state. This technique seems wasteful. For example, an FSM with 16 states requires 16 flip-flops for one-hot encoding but only four if you use a binary encoding. However, one-hot encoding simplifies the logic and also the interconnect between the logic. One-hot encoding often results in smaller and faster FSMs. This is especially true in programmable ASICs with large amounts of sequential logic relative to combinational logic resources.

- **Random encoding** assigns a random code for each state.

- **User-specified encoding** keeps the explicit state assignment from the HDL.

- **Moore encoding** is useful for FSMs that require fast outputs. A Moore state machine has outputs that depend only on the current state (Mealy state machine outputs depend on the current state and the inputs).

You need to consider how the reset of the state register will be handled in the synthesized hardware. In a programmable ASIC there are often limitations on the polarity of the flip-flop resets. For example, in some FPGAs all flip-flop resets must all be of the same polarity (and this restriction may or may not be present or different for the internal flip-flops and the flip-flops in the I/O cells). Thus, for example, if you try to assign the reset state as '0101', it may not be possible to set two flip-flops to '0' and two flip-flops to '1' at the same time in an FPGA. This may be handled by assigning the reset state, resSt, to '0000' or '1111' and inverting the appropriate two bits of the state register wherever they are used.

You also need to consider the initial value of the state register in the synthesized hardware. In some reprogrammable FPGAs, after programming is complete the flip-flops may all be initialized to a value that may not correspond to the reset state. Thus if the flip-flops are all set to '1' at start-up and the reset state is '0000', the initial state is '1111' and not the reset state. For this reason, and also to ensure fail-safe behavior, it is important that the behavior of the FSM is defined for every possible value of the state register.

12.7.1   FSM Synthesis in Verilog

The following FSM model uses **paired processes**. The first process synthesizes to sequential logic and the second process synthesizes to combinational logic:

```
`define resSt 0                                                   //1
`define S1 1                                                      //2
`define S2 2                                                      //3
`define S3 3                                                      //4

module StateMachine_1 (reset, clk, yOutReg);                     //5
  input reset, clk; output yOutReg;                              //6
  reg yOutReg, yOut; reg [1:0] curSt, nextSt;                    //7
  always @(posedge clk or posedge reset)                         //8
  begin:Seq //Compass statemachine oneHot curSt                  //9
    if (reset == 1)                                              //10
      begin yOut = 0; yOutReg = yOut; curSt = `resSt; end        //11
    else begin                                                   //12
      case (curSt)                                               //13
        `resSt:yOut = 0;`S1:yOut = 1;`S2:yOut = 1;`S3:yOut = 1;  //14
        default:yOut = 0;                                        //15
      endcase                                                    //16
      yOutReg = yOut; curSt = nextSt; // ... update the state.   //17
    end                                                          //18
  end                                                            //19
  always @(curSt or yOut) // Assign the next state:              //20
  begin:Comb                                                     //21
    case (curSt)                                                 //22
      `resSt:nextSt = `S3;        `S1:nextSt = `S2;              //23
      `S2:nextSt = `S1;           `S3:nextSt = `S1;              //24
      default:nextSt = `resSt;                                   //25
    endcase                                                      //26
  end                                                            //27
endmodule                                                        //28
```

Synopsys uses separate pseudocomments to define the states and state vector as in the following example:

```
module StateMachine_2 (reset, clk, yOutReg);                     //1
  input reset, clk; output yOutReg; reg yOutReg, yOut;           //2
  parameter [1:0] //synopsys enum states                         //3
    resSt = 2'b00, S1 = 2'b01, S2 = 2'b10, S3 = 2'b11;           //4
  reg [1:0] /* synopsys enum states */ curSt, nextSt;            //5
//synopsys state_vector curSt                                    //6
always @(posedge clk or posedge reset) begin                     //7
  if (reset == 1)                                                //8
    begin yOut = 0; yOutReg = yOut; curSt = resSt; end           //9
  else begin                                                     //10
    case (curSt) resSt:yOut = 0;S1:yOut = 1;S2:yOut = 1;S3:yOut = 1; //11
```

```
      default:yOut = 0; endcase                          //12
    yOutReg = yOut; curSt = nextSt; end                  //13
end                                                      //14
always @(curSt or yOut) begin                            //15
  case (curSt)                                           //16
  resSt:nextSt = S3; S1:nextSt = S2; S2:nextSt = S1; S3:nextSt = S1; //17
  default:nextSt = S1; endcase                           //18
end                                                      //19
endmodule                                                //20
```

To change encoding we can assign states explicitly by altering lines 3–4 to the following, for example:

```
parameter [3:0] //synopsys enum states
  resSt = 4'b0000, S1 = 4'b0010, S2 = 4'b0100, S3 = 4'b1000;
```

12.7.2   FSM Synthesis in VHDL

The first architecture that follows is a template for a Moore state machine:

```
library IEEE; use IEEE.STD_LOGIC_1164.all;               --1
entity SM1 is                                            --2
    port (aIn, clk : in Std_logic; yOut: out Std_logic); --3
end SM1;                                                 --4

architecture Moore of SM1 is                             --5
    type state is (s1, s2, s3, s4);                      --6
    signal pS, nS : state;                               --7
    begin                                                --8
    process (aIn, pS) begin                              --9
      case pS is                                         --10
      when s1 => yOut <= '0'; nS <= s4;                  --11
      when s2 => yOut <= '1'; nS <= s3;                  --12
      when s3 => yOut <= '1'; nS <= s1;                  --13
      when s4 => yOut <= '1'; nS <= s2;                  --14
      end case;                                          --15
    end process;                                         --16
    process begin                                        --17
      -- synopsys etc.                                   --18
      --compass Statemachine adj pS                      --19
      wait until clk = '1'; pS <= nS;                    --20
    end process;                                         --21
end Moore;                                               --22
```

An example input, aIn, is included but not used in the next state assignments. A reset is also omitted to further simplify this example.

An FSM compiler **extracts** the state machine. Some companies use FSM compilers that are separate from the logic synthesizers (and priced separately) because the algorithms for FSM optimization are different from those for optimizing combinational logic. We can see what is happening by asking the Compass synthesizer to write out intermediate results. The synthesizer extracts the FSM and produces the following output in a state-machine language used by the tools:

```
sm sm1_ps_sm;
inputs; outputs yout_smo; clock clk;
STATE S1 { let yout_smo=0 ; } --> S4;
STATE S2 { let yout_smo=1 ; } --> S3;
STATE S3 { let yout_smo=1 ; } --> S1;
STATE S4 { let yout_smo=1 ; } --> S2;
end
```

You can use this language to modify the FSM and then use this modified code as an input to the synthesizer if you wish. In our case, it serves as documentation that explains the FSM behavior.

Using one-hot encoding generates the following structural Verilog netlist (dfntnb is positive-edge-triggered D flip-flop, and nd03d0 is a three-input NAND):

```
dfntnb sm_ps4(.D(sm_ps1_Q),.CP(clk),.Q(sm_ps4_Q),.QN(sm_ps4_QN));
dfntnb sm_ps3(.D(sm_ps2_Q),.CP(clk),.Q(sm_ps3_Q),.QN(sm_ps3_QN));
dfntnb sm_ps2(.D(sm_ps4_Q),.CP(clk),.Q(sm_ps2_Q),.QN(sm_ps2_QN));
dfntnb sm_ps1(.D(sm_ps3_Q),.CP(clk),.Q(sm_ps1_Q),.QN(\sm_ps1.QN ));
nd03d0 i_6(.A1(sm_ps4_QN),.A2(sm_ps3_QN),.A3(sm_ps2_QN), .ZN(yout_smo));
```

(Each example shows only the logic cells and their interconnection in the Verilog structural netlists.) The synthesizer has assigned one flip-flop to each of the four states to form a 4-bit state register. The FSM output (renamed from yOut to yout_smo by the software) is taken from the output of the three-input NAND gate that decodes the outputs from the flip-flops in the state register.

Using adjacent encoding gives a simpler result,

```
dfntnb sm_ps2(.D(i_4_ZN),.CP(clk), .Q(\sm_ps2.Q ),.QN(sm_ps2_QN));
dfntnb sm_ps1(.D(sm_ps1_QN),.CP(clk),.Q(\sm_ps1.Q ),.QN(sm_ps1_QN));
oa04d1 i_4(.A1(sm_ps1_QN),.A2(sm_ps2_QN),.B(yout_smo),.ZN(i_4_ZN));
nd02d0 i_5(.A1(sm_ps2_QN), .A2(sm_ps1_QN), .ZN(yout_smo));
```

(oa04d1 is an OAI21 logic cell, nd02d0 is a two-input NAND). In this case binary encoding for the four states uses only two flip-flops. The two-input NAND gate decodes the states to produce the output. The OAI21 logic cell implements the logic that determines the next state. The combinational logic in this example is only slightly more complex than that for the one-hot encoding, but, in general, combinational logic for one-hot encoding is simpler than the other forms of encoding.

Using the option 'moore' for Moore encoding, we receive the following message from the FSM compiler:

```
The states were assigned these codes:
0?? : S1        100 : S2        101 : S3        110 : S4
```

The FSM compiler has assigned three bits to the state register. The first bit in the state register is used as the output. We can see more clearly what has happened by looking at the Verilog structural netlist:

```
dfntnb sm_ps3(.D(i_6_ZN),.CP(clk),.Q(yout_smo),.QN(sm_ps3_QN));
dfntnb sm_ps2(.D(sm_ps3_QN),.CP(clk),.Q(sm_ps2_Q),.QN(\sm_ps2.QN ));
dfntnb sm_ps1(.D(i_5_ZN),.CP(clk),.Q(sm_ps1_Q),.QN(\sm_ps1.QN ));
nr02d0 i_5(.A1(sm_ps3_QN),.A2(sm_ps2_Q),.ZN(i_5_ZN));
nd02d0 i_6(.A1(sm_ps1_Q),.A2(yout_smo),.ZN(i_6_ZN));
```

The output, yout_smo, is now taken directly from a flip-flop. This means that the output appears after the clock edge with no combinational logic delay (only the clock-to-Q delay). This is useful for FSMs that are required to produce outputs as soon as possible after the active clock edge (in PCI bus controllers, for example).

The following code is a template for a Mealy state machine:

```
library IEEE; use IEEE.STD_LOGIC_1164.all;                       --1
entity SM2 is                                                    --2
   port (aIn, clk : in Std_logic; yOut: out Std_logic);          --3
end SM2;                                                          --4

architecture Mealy of SM2 is                                     --1
   type state is (s1, s2, s3, s4);                               --2
   signal pS, nS : state;                                        --3
   begin                                                         --4
   process(aIn, pS) begin                                        --5
   case pS is                                                    --6
   when s1 => if (aIn = '1')                                     --7
      then yOut <= '0'; nS <= s4;                                --8
      else yOut <= '1'; nS <= s3;                                --9
      end if;                                                    --10
   when s2 => yOut <= '1'; nS <= s3;                             --11
   when s3 => yOut <= '1'; nS <= s1;                             --12
   when s4 => if (aIn = '1')                                     --13
      then yOut <= '1'; nS <= s2;                                --14
      else yOut <= '0'; nS <= s1;                                --15
      end if;                                                    --16
   end case;                                                     --17
   end process;                                                  --18
   process begin                                                 --19
   wait until clk = '1' ;                                        --20
   --Compass Statemachine oneHot pS                              --21
   pS <= nS;                                                     --22
```

```
   end process;                                                  --23
end Mealy;                                                       --24
```

12.8 Memory Synthesis

There are several approaches to memory synthesis:

1. Random logic using flip-flops or latches

2. Register files in datapaths

3. RAM standard components

4. RAM compilers

The first approach uses large vectors or arrays in the HDL code. The synthesizer will map these elements to arrays of flip-flops or latches depending on how the timing of the assignments is handled. This approach is independent of any software or type of ASIC and is the easiest to use but inefficient in terms of area. A flip-flop may take up 10 to 20 times the area of a six-transistor static RAM cell.

The second approach uses a synthesis directive or hand instantiation to synthesize a memory to a datapath component. Usually the datapath components are constructed from latches in a regular array. These are slightly more efficient than a random arrangement of logic cells, but the way we create the memory then depends on the software and the ASIC technology we are using.

The third approach uses standard components supplied by an ASIC vendor. For example, we can instantiate a small RAM using CLBs in a Xilinx FPGA. This approach is very dependent on the technology. For example, we could not easily transfer a design that uses Xilinx CLBs as SRAM to an Actel FPGA.

The last approach, using a custom RAM compiler, is the most area-efficient approach. It depends on having the capability to call a compiler from within the synthesis tool or to instantiate a component that has already been compiled.

12.8.1 Memory Synthesis in Verilog

Most synthesizers implement a Verilog memory array, such as the one shown in the following code, as an array of latches or flip-flops.

```
reg [31:0] MyMemory [3:0]; // a 4 x 32-bit register
```

For example, the following code models a small RAM, and the synthesizer maps the memory array to sequential logic:

```
module RAM_1(A, CEB, WEB, OEB, INN, OUTT);                       //1
   input [6:0] A; input CEB,WEB,OEB; input [4:0]INN;             //2
   output [4:0] OUTT;                                            //3
   reg [4:0] OUTT; reg [4:0] int_bus; reg [4:0] memory [127:0];  //4
always@(negedge CEB) begin                                       //5
   if (CEB == 0) begin                                           //6
```

```
          if (WEB == 1) int_bus = memory[A];                    //7
          else if (WEB == 0) begin memory[A] = INN; int_bus = INN; end  //8
          else int_bus = 5'bxxxxx;                              //9
      end                                                       //10
  end                                                           //11
always@(OEB or int_bus) begin                                   //12
    case (OEB) 0 : OUTT = int_bus;                              //13
      default : OUTT = 5'bzzzzz; endcase                        //14
  end                                                           //15
endmodule                                                       //16
```

Memory synthesis using random control logic and transparent latches for each bit is reasonable only for small, fast register files, or for local RAM on an MGA or CBIC. For large RAMs synthesized memory becomes very expensive and instead you should normally use a dedicated RAM compiler.

Typically there will be restrictions on synthesizing RAM with multiple read/writes:

- If you write to the same memory in two different processes, be careful to avoid address contention.

- You need a multiport RAM if you read or write to multiple locations simultaneously.

- If you write and read the same memory location, you have to be very careful. To mimic hardware you need to read before you write so that you read the old memory value. If you attempt to write before reading, the difference between blocking and nonblocking assignments can lead to trouble.

You cannot make a memory access that depends on another memory access in the same clock cycle. For example, you cannot do this:

```
memory[i + 1] = memory[i]; // needs two clock cycles
```

or this:

```
pointer = memory[memory[i]]; // needs two clock cycles
```

For the same reason (but less obviously) we cannot do this:

```
pc = memory[addr1]; memory[addr2] = pc + 1; // not on the same cycle
```

12.8.2   Memory Synthesis in VHDL

VHDL allows multidimensional arrays so that we can synthesize a memory as an array of latches by declaring a two-dimensional array as follows:

```
type memStor is array(3 downto 0) of integer; -- This is OK.

subtype MemReg is STD_LOGIC_VECTOR(15 downto 0); -- So is this.
type memStor is array(3 downto 0) of MemReg;
-- other code...
signal Mem1 : memStor;
```

As an example, the following code models a standard-cell RAM:

```
library IEEE;                                                    --1
use IEEE.STD_LOGIC_1164.all;                                     --2
package RAM_package is                                           --3
constant numOut : INTEGER := 8;                                  --4
constant wordDepth: INTEGER := 8;                                --5
constant numAddr : INTEGER := 3;                                 --6
subtype MEMV is STD_LOGIC_VECTOR(numOut-1 downto 0);            --7
type MEM is array (wordDepth-1 downto 0) of MEMV;               --8
end RAM_package;                                                 --9

library IEEE;                                                    --10
use IEEE.STD_LOGIC_1164.all; use IEEE.NUMERIC_STD.all;          --11
use work.RAM_package.all;                                        --12
entity RAM_1 is                                                  --13
   port (signal A : in STD_LOGIC_VECTOR(numAddr-1 downto 0);    --14
   signal CEB, WEB, OEB : in STD_LOGIC;                         --15
   signal INN : in  MEMV;                                       --16
   signal OUTT : out MEMV);                                     --17
end RAM_1;                                                       --18

architecture Synthesis_1 of RAM_1 is                            --19
   signal i_bus : MEMV; -- RAM internal data latch             --20
   signal mem : MEM;   -- RAM data                             --21
   begin                                                        --22
   process begin                                                --23
     wait until CEB = '0';                                      --24
       if WEB = '1' then i_bus <= mem(TO_INTEGER(UNSIGNED(A))); --25
       elsif WEB = '0' then                                     --26
         mem(TO_INTEGER(UNSIGNED(A))) <= INN;                   --27
         i_bus <= INN;                                          --28
       else i_bus <= (others => 'X');                           --29
       end if;                                                  --30
   end process;                                                 --31

   process(OEB, int_bus) begin -- control output drivers:      --32
     case (OEB) is                                              --33
     when '0'      => OUTT <= i_bus;                            --34
     when '1'      => OUTT <= (others => 'Z');                  --35
     when others => OUTT <= (others => 'X');                   --36
     end case;                                                  --37
   end process;                                                 --38
end Synthesis_1;                                                --39
```

12.9 The Multiplier

This section looks at the messages that result from attempting to synthesize the VHDL code from Section 10.2, "A 4-bit Multiplier." The following examples use the line numbers that were assigned in the comments at the end of each line of code in Tables 10.1–10.9. The first problem arises in the following code (line 7 of the full adder in Table 10.1):

```
Sum  <= X xor Y xor Cin after TS;
```

Warning: AFTER clause in a waveform element is not supported

This is not a serious problem if you are using a synchronous design style. If you are, then your logic will work whatever the delays (it may run slowly but it will work).

The next problem is from lines 3–4 of the 8-bit MUX in Table 10.5,

```
port (A, B : in BIT_VECTOR (7 downto 0); Sel : in BIT := '0'; Y : out
BIT_VECTOR (7 downto 0));
```

Warning: Default values on interface signals are not supported

The synthesis tool cannot mimic the behavior of a default value on a port in the software model. The default value is the value given to an input if nothing is connected ('open' in VHDL). In hardware either an input is connected or it is not. If it is connected, there will be a voltage on the wire. If it is not connected, the node will be floating. Default values are useful in VHDL—without a default value on an input port, an entity–architecture pair will not compile. The default value may be omitted in this model because this input port is connected at the next higher level of hierarchy.

The next problem illustrates what happens when a designer fails to think like the hardware (from line 3 of the zero-detector in Table 10.6),

```
port (X:BIT_VECTOR; F:out BIT );
```

Error: An index range must be specified for this data type

This code has the advantage of being flexible, but the synthesizer needs to know exactly how wide the bus will be. There are two other similar errors in shiftn, the variable-width shift register (from lines 4–5 in Table 10.7). There are also three more errors generated by the same problem in the component statement for Allzero (from lines 4–5 of package Mult_Components) and the component statement for shiftn (from lines 10–11 of package Mult_Components).

All of these index range problems may be fixed by sacrificing the flexible nature of the code and specifying an index range explicitly, as in the following example:

```
port (X:BIT_VECTOR(7 downto 0); F:out BIT );
```

Table 12.8 shows the synthesizable version of the shift-register model. The constrained index ranges in lines 6, 7, 11, 18, 22, and 23 fix the problem, but are rather ugly. It would be better to use generic parameters for the input and output bus widths. However, a shift register with different input and output widths is not that common so, for now, we will leave the code as it is.

TABLE 12.8   A synthesizable version of the shift register shown in Table 10.7.

```
entity ShiftN is                                          --1
  generic (TCQ:TIME := 0.3 ns; TLQ:TIME := 0.5 ns;       --2
    TSQ:TIME := 0.7 ns);                                  --3
  port(                                                   --4
    CLK, CLR, LD, SH, DIR: in BIT;                        --5
    D: in BIT_VECTOR(3 downto 0);                         --6
    Q: out BIT_VECTOR(7 downto 0) );                      --7
end ShiftN;                                               --8
architecture Behave of ShiftN is                          --9
  begin Shift: process (CLR, CLK)                         --10
  variable St: BIT_VECTOR(7 downto 0);                    --11
  begin                                                   --12
    if CLR = '1' then                                     --13
      St := (others => '0'); Q <= St after TCQ;           --14
    elsif CLK'EVENT and CLK='1' then                      --15
      if LD = '1' then                                    --16
        St := (others => '0');                            --17
        St(3 downto 0) := D;                              --18
        Q <= St after TLQ;                                --19
      elsif SH = '1' then                                 --20
        case DIR is                                       --21
        when '0'=>St:='0' & St(7 downto 1);               --22
        when '1'=>St:=St(6 downto 0) & '0';               --23
        end case;                                         --24
        Q <= St after TSQ;                                --25
      end if;                                             --26
    end if;                                               --27
  end process;                                            --28
end;                                                      --29
```

CLK	Clock
CLR	Clear, active high
LD	Load, active high
SH	Shift, active high
DIR	Direction, 1=left
D	Data in
Q	Data out

Shift register. Input width = 4. Output width = 8. Output is left-shifted or right-shifted under control of DIR. Unused MSBs are zero-padded during load. Clear is asynchronous. Load is synchronous.

Timing:
TCQ (CLR to Q) = 0.3 ns
TLQ (LD to Q) = 0.5 ns
TSQ (SH to Q) =0. 7 ns

The next problem occurs because VHDL is not a synthesis language (from lines 6–7 of the variable-width shift register in Table 10.7),

```
begin assert (D'LENGTH <= Q'LENGTH)
  report "D wider than output Q" severity Failure;
```

Warning: Assertion statements are ignored
Error: Statements in entity declarations are not supported

The synthesis tool warns us it does not know how to generate hardware that writes to our screen to implement an assertion statement. The error occurs because a synthesis tool cannot support any of the passive statements (no assignments to signals, for example) that VHDL allows in an entity declaration. Synthesis software usually provides a way around these problems by providing switches to turn the synthesizer on and off. For example, we might be able to write the following:

```
//Compass compile_off
begin assert (D'LENGTH <= Q'LENGTH)
  report "D wider than output Q" severity Failure;
//Compass compile_on
```

The disadvantage of this approach is that the code now becomes tied to a particular synthesis tool. The alternative is to move the statement to the architecture to eliminate the error, and ignore the warning.

The next error message is, at first sight, confusing (from lines 15–16 of the variable-width shift register in Table 10.7),

```
if CLR = '1' then St := (others => '0'); Q <= St after TCQ;
```

Error: Illegal use of aggregate with the choice "others": the derived subtype of an array aggregate that has a choice "others" must be a constrained array subtype

This error message is precise and uses the terminology of the LRM but does not reveal the source of the problem. To discover the problem we work backward through the model. We declared variable St as follows (lines 12–13 of Table 10.7):

```
subtype OutB is NATURAL range Q'LENGTH-1 downto 0;
  variable St: BIT_VECTOR(OutB);
```

(to keep the model flexible). Continuing backward we see Q is declared as type BIT_VECTOR with no index range as follows (lines 4–5 of Table 10.7):

```
port(CLK, CLR, LD, SH, DIR: in BIT;
    D: in BIT_VECTOR; Q: out BIT_VECTOR);
```

The error is thus linked to the previous problem (undeclared bus widths) in this entity/architecture. Because the synthesizer does not know the width of Q, it does not know how many '0's to put in St when it has to implement St := (others => '0'). There is one more error like this one in the second assignment to St (line 19 in Table 10.7). Again the problem may be solved by sacrificing flexibility and constraining the width of Q to be a fixed value.

The next warning involves names (line 5 in Table 10.9),

```
signal SRA, SRB, ADDout, MUXout, REGout: BIT_VECTOR(7 downto 0);
```

Warning: Name is reserved word in VHDL-93: sra

This problem can be fixed by (a) changing the signal name, (b) using an escaped name, or (c) accepting that this code will not work in a VHDL-93 environment.

Finally, there is the following warning (line 6 in Table 10.9):

```
signal Zero, Init, Shift, Add, Low: BIT := '0'; signal High: BIT := '1';
```

Warning: Initial values on signals are only for simulation and setting the value of undriven signals in synthesis. A synthesized circuit can not be guaranteed to be in any known state when the power is turned on.

Signals Low and High are used to tie inputs to a logic '0' and to a logic '1', respectively. This is because VHDL-87 does not allow '1' or '0', which are literals, as actual parameters. Thus one way to solve this problem is to change to a VHDL-93 environment, where this restriction was lifted. Some synthesis systems handle VDD and GND nets in a specific fashion. For example, VDD and GND may be declared as constants in a synthesis package. It does not really matter how inputs are connected to VDD and GND as long as they are connected in the synthesized logic.

12.9.1   Messages During Synthesis

After fixing the error and warning messages, we can synthesize the multiplier. During synthesis we see these messages:

```
These unused instances are being removed: in full_adder_p_dup8: u5, u2,
u3, u4
```

```
These unused instances are being removed: in dffclr_p_dup1: u2
```

and seven more similar to this for dffclr_p_dup2: u2 to dffclr_p_dup8: u2. We are suspicious because we did not include any redundant or unused logic in our input code. Let us dig deeper.

Turning to the second set of messages first, we need to discover the locations of dffclr_p_dup1: u2 and the other seven similarly named unused instances. We can ask the synthesizer to produce the following hierarchy map of the design:

```
************  Hierarchy of cell "mult8_p"  ************
    mult8_p
        adder8_p
        |  full_adder_p [x8]
        allzero_p
        mux8_p
        register8_p
        |  dffclr_p [x8]
```

```
                       shiftn_p [x2]
                       sm_1_p
```

The eight unused instances in question are inside the 8-bit shift register, register8_p. The only models in this shift register are eight copies of the D flip-flop model, DFFClr. Let us look more closely at the following code:

```
architecture Behave of DFFClr is                              --1
signal Qi : BIT;                                              --2
begin QB <= not Qi; Q <= Qi;                                 --3
process (CLR, CLK) begin                                      --4
   if CLR = '1' then Qi <= '0' after TRQ;                    --5
   elsif CLK'EVENT and CLK = '1' then Qi <= D after TCQ;     --6
   end if;                                                    --7
end process;                                                  --8
end;                                                          --9
```

The synthesizer infers an inverter from the first statement in line 3 (QB <= **not** Qi). What we meant to imply (A) was: "I am trying to describe the function of a D flip-flop and it has two outputs; one output is the complement of the other." What the synthesizer inferred (B) was: "You described a D flip-flop with an inverter connected to Q." Unfortunately A does not equal B.

Why were four cell instances (u5, u2, u3, u4) removed from inside a cell with instance name full_adder_p_dup8? The top-level cell mult8_p contains cell adder8_p, which in turn contains full_adder_p [x8]. This last entry in the hierarchy map represents eight occurrences or instances of cell full_adder_p. The logic synthesizer appends the suffix '_p' by default to the names of the design units to avoid overwriting any existing netlists (it also converts all names to lowercase). The synthesizer has then added the suffix 'dup8' to create the instance name full_adder_p_dup8 for the eighth copy of cell full_adder_p.

What is so special about the eighth instance of full_adder_p inside cell adder8_p? The following (line 13 in Table 10.9) instantiates Adder8:

```
A1:Adder8 port map(A=>SRB,B=>REGout,Cin=>Low,Cout=>OFL,Sum=>ADDout);
```

The signal OFL is declared but not used. This means that the formal port name Cout for the entity Adder8 in Table 10.2 is unconnected in the instance full_adder_p_dup8. Since the carry-out bit is unused, the synthesizer deletes some logic. Before dismissing this message as harmless, let us look a little closer. In the architecture for entity Adder8 we wrote:

```
Cout <= (X and Y) or (X and Cin) or (Y and Cin) after TC;
```

In one of the instances of Adder8, named full_adder_p_dup8, this statement is redundant since we never use Cout in that particular cell instance. If we look at the synthesized netlist for full_adder_p_dup8 before optimization, we find four

NAND cells that produce the signal Cout. During logic optimization the synthesizer removes these four instances. Their instance names are `full_adder_p_dup8:u2`, `u3`, `u4`, `u5`.

12.10 The Engine Controller

This section returns to the example from Section 10.16, "An Engine Controller." This ASIC gathers sampled temperature measurements from sensors, converts the temperature values from Fahrenheit to Centigrade, averages them, and stores them in a FIFO before passing the values to a microprocessor on a three-state bus. We receive the following message from the logic synthesizer when we use the FIFO-controller code shown in Table 10.25:

```
Warning: Made latches to store values on: net d(4), d(5), d(6), d(7),
d(8), d(9), d(10), d(11), in module fifo_control
```

This message often indicates that we forgot to initialize a variable.

Here is the part of the code from Table 10.25 that assigns to the vector D (the error message for d is in lowercase—remember VHDL is case insensitive):

```
case sel is
   when "01" =>   D <= D_1 after TPD; r1 <= '1' after TPD;
   when "10" =>   D <= D_2 after TPD; r2 <= '1' after TPD;
   when "00" =>   D(3) <= f1 after TPD; D(2) <= f2 after TPD;
                  D(1) <= e1 after TPD; D(0) <= e2 after TPD;
   when others => D <= "ZZZZZZZZZZZZ" after TPD;
   end case;
```

When sel = "00", there is no assignment to D(4) through D(11). This did not matter in the simulation, but to reproduce the exact behavior of the HDL code the logic synthesizer generates latches to remember the values of D(4) through D(11).

This problem may be corrected by replacing the "00" choice with the following:

```
   when "00" =>   D(3) <= f1 after TPD; D(2) <= f2 after TPD;
                  D(1) <= e1 after TPD; D(0) <= e2 after TPD;
                  D(11 downto 4) <= "ZZZZZZZZ" after TPD;
```

The synthesizer recognizes the assignment of the high-impedance logic value 'Z' to a signal as an indication to implement a three-state buffer. However, there are two kinds of three-state buffers: core logic three-state buffers and three-state I/O cells. We want a three-state I/O cell containing a bonding pad and not a three-state buffer located in the core logic. If we synthesize the code in Table 10.25, we get a three-state buffer in the core. Table 12.9 shows the modified code that will synthesize to three-state I/O cells. The signal OE_b drives the output enable (active-low) of the three-state buffers. Table 12.10 shows the top-level code including all the I/O cells.

TABLE 12.9   A modified version of the FIFO controller to drive three-state I/O cells.

```
library IEEE;use IEEE.STD_LOGIC_1164.all;use IEEE.NUMERIC_STD.all;        --1
entity fifo_control is generic TPD:TIME := 1 ns;                          --2
  port(D_1, D_2: in UNSIGNED(11 downto 0);                                --3
  sel : in UNSIGNED(1 downto 0) ;                                         --4
  read , f1, f2, e1, e2 : in STD_LOGIC;                                   --5
  r1, r2, w12:out STD_LOGIC; D: out UNSIGNED(11 downto 0);                --6
  OE:out STD_LOGIC ) ;                                                    --7
end;                                                                      --8
architecture rtl of fifo_control is                                       --9
  begin process (read, sel, D_1, D_2, f1, f2, e1, e2)                     --10
  begin                                                                   --11
  r1 <= '0' after TPD; r2 <= '0' after TPD; OE_b <= '0' after TPD;        --12
  if (read = '1') then                                                    --13
    w12 <= '0' after TPD;                                                 --14
    case sel is                                                           --15
    when "01" =>   D <= D_1 after TPD; r1 <= '1' after TPD;               --16
    when "10" =>   D <= D_2 after TPD; r2 <= '1' after TPD;               --17
    when "00" =>   D(3) <= f1 after TPD; D(2) <= f2 after TPD;            --18
                   D(1) <= e1 after TPD; D(0) <= e2 after TPD;            --19
                   D(11 downto 4) <= "00000000" after TPD;                --20
    when others => OE_b <= '1' after TPD;                                 --21
    end case;                                                             --22
  elsif (read = '0') then                                                 --23
    OE_b <= '0' after TPD; w12 <= '1' after TPD;                          --24
  else OE_b <= '0' after TPD;                                             --25
  end if;                                                                 --26
  end process;                                                            --27
end rtl;                                                                  --28
```

12.11 Performance-Driven Synthesis

Many logic synthesizers allow the use of directives. The pseudocomment in the following code directs the logic synthesizer to minimize the delay of an addition:

```
module add_directive (a, b, z); input [3:0] a, b; output [3:0] z;
    //compass maxDelay 2 ns
    //synopsys and so on.
    assign z = a + b;
endmodule
```

TABLE 12.10   The top-level VHDL code for the engine controller ASIC.

```
library COMPASS_LIB, IEEE ;                                              --1
use IEEE.STD.all; use IEEE.NUMERIC_STD.all;                             --2
use COMPASS_LIB.STDCOMP.all; use COMPASS_LIB.COMPASS.all;               --3
                                                                        --4
entity t_control_ASIC is port(                                          --5
   PadTri : out                      STD_LOGIC_VECTOR (11 downto 0) ;   --6
   PadClk, PadInreset, PadInreadv : in   STD_LOGIC_VECTOR ( 0 downto 0) ; --7
   PadInp1, PadInp2 : in             STD_LOGIC_VECTOR (11 downto 0) ;   --8
   PadInSens : in                    STD_LOGIC_VECTOR ( 1 downto 0) ) ; --9
end t_control_ASIC ;                                                    --10
                                                                        --11
architecture structure of t_control_ASIC is                            --12
for all : asPadIn      use entity COMPASS_LIB.aspadIn(aspadIn) ;        --13
for all : asPadClk     use entity COMPASS_LIB.aspadClk(aspadClk);       --14
for all : asPadTri     use entity COMPASS_LIB.aspadTri(aspadTri) ;      --15
for all : asPadVdd     use entity COMPASS_LIB.aspadVdd(aspadVdd) ;      --16
for all : asPadVss     use entity COMPASS_LIB.aspadVss(aspadVss) ;      --17
component pc3c01 port ( cclk : in STD_LOGIC; cp : out STD_LOGIC ); end component; --18
component t_control port(T_in1, T_in2 : in UNSIGNED(11 downto 0);       --19
   SENSOR: in UNSIGNED( 1 downto 0) ; clk, rd, rst : in STD_LOGIC;      --20
   D : out UNSIGNED(11 downto 0); oe_b : out STD_LOGIC ); end component ; --21
signal T_in1_sv, T_in2_sv :       STD_LOGIC_VECTOR(11 downto 0) ;       --22
signal T_in1_un, T_in2_un :       UNSIGNED(11 downto 0) ;               --23
signal sensor_sv :                STD_LOGIC_VECTOR(1 downto 0) ;        --24
signal sensor_un :                UNSIGNED(1 downto 0) ;                --25
signal clk_sv, rd_fifo_sv, reset_sv :  STD_LOGIC_VECTOR (0 downto 0)  ; --26
signal clk_core, oe_b :           STD_LOGIC ;                           --27
signal D_un : UNSIGNED(11 downto 0) ; signal D_sv : STD_LOGIC_VECTOR(11 downto 0) ; --28
begin --compass dontTouch u* -- synopsys dont_touch etc.                --29
u1 : asPadIn generic map(12,"2:13")      port map(t_in1_sv,PadInp1) ;   --30
u2 : asPadIn generic map(12,"14:25")     port map(t_in2_sv,PadInp2) ;   --31
u3 : asPadIn generic map(2,"26:27")      port map(sensor_sv, PadInSens ) ; --32
u4 : asPadIn generic map(1,"29")         port map(rd_fifo_sv, PadInReadv ) ; --33
u5 : asPadIn generic map(1,"30")         port map(reset_sv, PadInreset ) ; --34
u6 : asPadIn generic map(1,"32")         port map(clk_sv, PadClk) ;     --35
u7 : pc3c01                              port map(clk_sv(0), clk_core) ; --36
u8 : asPadTri generic map(12,"35:38,41:44,47:50") port map(PadTri,D_sv,oe_b); --37
u9 : asPadVdd generic map("1,31,34,40,45,52") port map(Vdd) ;           --38
u10: asPadVss generic map("28,33,39,46,51,53") port map(Vss) ;          --39
T_in1_un <= UNSIGNED(T_in1_sv) ; T_in2_un <= UNSIGNED(T_in2_sv) ;       --40
sensor_un <= UNSIGNED(sensor_sv) ; D_sv <= STD_LOGIC_VECTOR(D_un) ;     --41
v_1 : t_control port map                                                --42
   (T_in1_un,T_in2_un,sensor_un, Clk_core, rd_fifo_sv(0), reset_sv(0),D_un, oe_b) ; --43
end;                                                                    --44
```

These directives become complicated when we need to describe complex timing constraints. Figure 12.7(a) shows an example of a more flexible method to measure and specify delay using **timing arcs** (or timing paths). Suppose we wish to improve the performance of the comparator/MUX example from Section 12.2. First we define a **pathcluster** (a group of circuit nodes—see Figure 12.7b). Next, we specify the **required time** for a signal to reach the output nodes (the **end set**) as 2 ns. Finally, we specify the **arrival time** of the signals at all the inputs as 0 ns. We have thus constrained the delay of the comparator/MUX to be 2 ns—measured between any input and any output. The logic-optimization step will simplify the logic network and then map it to a cell library while attempting to meet the timing constraints.

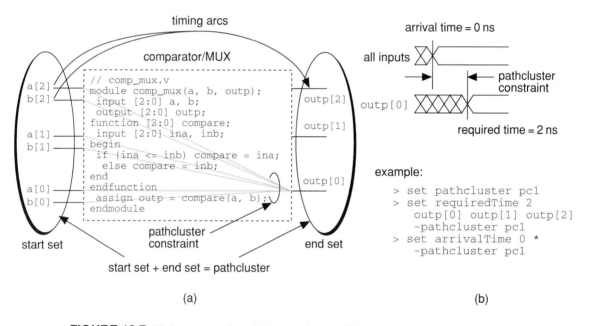

FIGURE 12.7 Timing constraints. (a) A pathcluster. (b) Defining constraints.

Table 12.11 shows the results of a timing-driven logic optimization for the comparator/MUX. Comparing these results with the default optimization results shown in Table 12.3 reveals that the timing has dramatically improved (critical path delay was 2.43 ns with default optimization settings, and the delay varies between 0.31 ns and 1.64 ns for the timing-driven optimization).

Figure 12.8 shows that timing-driven optimization and the subsequent mapping have simplified the logic considerably. For example, the logic for outp[2] has been

TABLE 12.11   Timing-driven synthesis reports for the comparator/MUX example of Section 12.2.

Command	Synthesizer output[1]					
> set pathcluster pc1						
> set requiredTime 2 outp[0] outp[1] outp[2] -pathcluster pc1						
> set arrivalTime 0 * -pathcluster pc1						
> optimize		Num	Gate Count	Tot Gate	Width	Total
	Cell Name	Insts	Per Cell	Count	Per Cell	Width
	---------	-----	----------	--------	--------	--------
	an02d1	1	1.3	1.3	12.0	12.0
	in01d0	2	.8	1.5	7.2	14.4
	mx21d1	2	2.2	4.5	21.6	43.2
	nd02d0	2	1.0	2.0	9.6	19.2
	oa03d1	1	1.8	1.8	16.8	16.8
	oa04d1	1	1.3	1.3	12.0	12.0
	---------	-----	----------	--------	--------	--------
	Totals:	9		12.2		117.6
> report timing -allpaths	path cluster name: pc1					
	path type: maximum					
	---					
	end node			current	required	slack
	---					
	outp[1]			1.64	2.00	.36 MET
	outp[0]			1.64	2.00	.36 MET
	outp[2]			.31	2.00	1.69 MET

[1]See footnote 1 in Table 12.3 for explanations of the abbreviations used in this table.

reduced to a two-input AND gate. Using sis reveals how optimization works in this case. Table 12.12 shows the equations for the intermediate signal sel and the three comparator/MUX outputs in the BLIF. Thus, for example, the following line of the BLIF code in Table 12.12 (the first line following .names a0 b0 a1 b1 a2 b2 sel) includes the term a0·b0'·a1'·b1'·a2'·b2' in the equation for sel:

`100000 1`

There are six similar lines that describe the six other product terms for sel. These seven product terms form a cover for sel in the Karnaugh maps of Figure 12.5.

In addition sis must be informed of the don't care values (called the **external don't care set**) in these Karnaugh maps. This is the function of the PLA-format input that follows the .exdc line. Now sis can simplify the equations including the don't care values using a standard script, rugged.script, that contains a sequence

```
`timescale 1ns / 10ps
module comp_mux_o (a, b, outp);
input  [2:0] a; input  [2:0] b;
output [2:0] outp;
supply1 VDD; supply0 VSS;

mx21d1 B1_i1 (.I0(a[0]),
.I1(b[0]), .S(B1_i6_ZN),
.Z(outp[0]));
oa03d1 B1_i2 (.A1(B1_i9_ZN),
.A2(a[2]), .B1(a[0]), .B2(a[1]),
.C(B1_i4_ZN), .ZN(B1_i2_ZN));
nd02d0 B1_i3 (.A1(a[1]),
.A2(a[0]), .ZN(B1_i3_ZN));
nd02d0 B1_i4 (.A1(b[1]),
.A2(B1_i3_ZN), .ZN(B1_i4_ZN));
mx21d1 B1_i5 (.I0(a[1]),
.I1(b[1]), .S(B1_i6_ZN),
.Z(outp[1]));
oa04d1 B1_i6 (.A1(b[2]),
.A2(B1_i7_ZN), .B(B1_i2_ZN),
.ZN(B1_i6_ZN));
in01d0 B1_i7 (.I(a[2]),
.ZN(B1_i7_ZN));
an02d1 B1_i8 (.A1(b[2]),
.A2(a[2]), .Z(outp[2]));
in01d0 B1_i9 (.I(b[2]),
.ZN(B1_i9_ZN));

endmodule
```

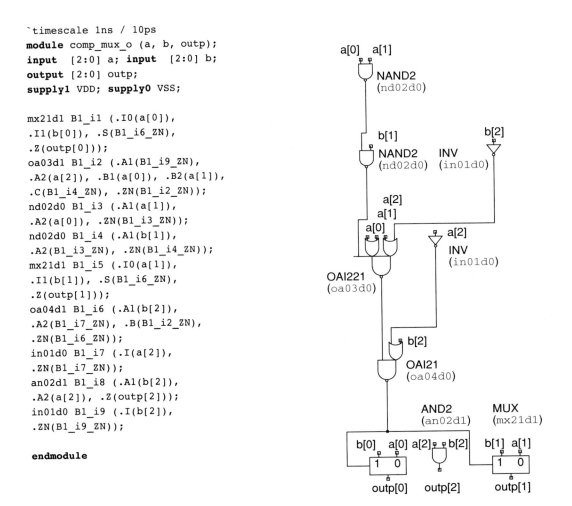

FIGURE 12.8 The comparator/MUX example of Section 12.2 after logic optimization with timing constraints. The figure shows the structural netlist, comp_mux_o2.v, and its derived schematic. Compare this with Figures 12.2 and 12.3.

of sis commands. This particular script uses a series of factoring and substitution steps. The output (Table 12.12) reveals that sis finds the same equation for outp[2] (named outp2 in the sis equations):

{outp2} = a2 b2

The other logic equations in Table 12.12 that sis produces are also equivalent to the logic in Figure 12.8. The technology-mapping step hides the exact details of the conversion between the internal representation and the optimized logic.

TABLE 12.12   Optimizing the comparator/MUX equations using sis.

sis **input file (BLIF)**	sis **results**
.model comp_mux	</usr/user1/msmith/sis> sis
.inputs a0 b0 a1 b1 a2 b2	UC Berkeley, SIS Development Version
.outputs outp0 outp1 outp2	(compiled 11-Oct-95 at 11:50 AM)
.names a0 b0 a1 b1 a2 b2 sel	sis> read_blif comp_mux.blif
100000 1	sis> print
101100 1	{outp0} = a0 sel' + b0 sel
--1000 1	{outp1} = a1 sel' + b1 sel
----10 1	{outp2} = a2 sel' + b2 sel
100011 1	sel = a0 a1 a2 b0' b1 b2
101111 1	+ a0 a1 a2' b0' b1 b2'
--1011 1	+ a0 a1' a2 b0' b1' b2
.names sel a0 b0 outp0	+ a0 a1' a2' b0' b1' b2'
1-1 1	+ a1 a2 b1' b2
01- 1	+ a1 a2' b1' b2'
.names sel a1 b1 outp1	+ a2 b2'
1-1 1	sis> source script.rugged
01- 1	sis> print
.names sel a2 b2 outp2	{outp0} = a0 sel' + b0 sel
1-1 1	{outp1} = a1 sel' + b1 sel
01- 1	{outp2} = a2 b2
.exdc	sel = [9] a2 b0'
.names a0 b0 a1 b1 a2 b2 sel	+ [9] b0' b2'
000000 1	+ a1 a2 b1'
110000 1	+ a1 b1' b2'
001100 1	+ a2 b2'
111100 1	[9] = a1 + b1'
000011 1	sis> quit
110011 1	</usr/user1/msmith/sis>
001111 1	
111111 1	
.end	

12.12 Optimization of the Viterbi Decoder

Returning to the Viterbi decoder example (from Section 12.4), we first set the
environment for the design using the following worst-case conditions: a die temperature of 25°C (fastest logic) to 120°C (slowest logic); a power supply voltage of
$V_{DD} = 5.5$ V (fastest logic) to $V_{DD} = 4.5$ V (slowest logic); and worst process (slowest
logic) to best process (fastest logic). Assume that this ASIC should run at a clock frequency of at least 33 MHz (clock period of 30 ns). An initial synthesis run gives a criti-

cal path delay at nominal conditions (the default setting) of about 25 ns and nearly 35 ns under worst-case conditions using a high-density 0.6 μm standard-cell target library.

Estimates (using simulation and calculation) show that data arrives at the input pins 5 ns (worst-case) after the rising edge of the clock. The reset signal arrives 10 ns (worst-case) after the rising edge of the clock. The outputs of the Viterbi decoder must be stable at least 4 ns before the rising edge of the clock. This allows these signals to be driven to another ASIC in time to be clocked. These timing constraints are particularly devastating. Together they effectively reduce the clock period that is available for use by 9 ns. However, these figures are typical for board-level delays.

The initial synthesis runs reveal the critical path is through the following six modules:

```
subset_decode -> compute_metric ->
compare_select -> reduce -> metric -> output_decision
```

The logic synthesizer can do little or no optimization across these module boundaries. The next step, then, is to rearrange the design hierarchy for synthesis. **Flattening** (merging or ungrouping) the six modules into a new cell, called `critical`, allows the synthesizer to reduce the critical path delay by optimizing one large module.

At present the last module in the critical path is `output_decision`. This combinational logic adds 2–3 ns to the output delay requirement of 4 ns (this means the outputs of the module `metric` must be stable 6–7 ns before the rising clock edge). Registering the output reduces this overhead and removes the module `output_decision` from the critical path. The disadvantage is an increase in latency by one clock cycle, but the latency is already 12 clock cycles in this design. If registering the output decreases the critical path delay by more than a factor of 12 / 13, performance will still improve.

To register the output, alter the code (on pages 575–576) as follows:

```
module viterbi_ASIC
...
wire [2:0] Out, Out_r; // Change: add Out_r.
...
    asPadOut    #(3,"30,31,32") u30 (padOut, Out_r); // Change: Out_r.
    Outreg o_1 (Out, Out_r, Clk, Res); // Change: add output register.
    ...

endmodule

module Outreg (Out, Out_r, Clk, Res); // Change: add this module.
input [2:0] Out; input Clk, Rst; output [2:0] Out_r;
    dff #(3) reg1(Out, Out_r, Clk, Res);
endmodule
```

These changes move the performance closer to the target. Prelayout estimates indicate the die perimeter required for the I/O pads will allow more than enough area to hold the core logic. Since there is unused area in the core, it makes sense to switch to a high-performance standard-cell library with a slightly larger cell height (96λ versus 72λ). This cell library is less dense, but faster.

Typically, at this point, the design is improved by altering the HDL, the hierarchy, and the synthesis controls in an iterative manner until the desired performance is achieved. However, remember there is still no information from the layout. The best that can be done is to estimate the contribution of the interconnect using wire-load models. As soon as possible the netlist should be passed to the floorplanner (or the place-and-route software in the absence of a floorplanner) to generate better estimates of interconnect delays.

TABLE 12.13   Critical-path timing report for the Viterbi decoder.

Instance name	Delay information[1]						
v_1.u100	inPin --> outPin	incr	arrival	trs	rampDel	cap(pF)	cell
u1.subout5.Q_ff_b0	CP --> QN	1.65	1.65	F	.20	.10	dfctnb
B1_i67	A1 --> ZN	.63	2.27	R	.14	.08	ao01d1
B1_i66	B --> ZN	.84	3.12	F	.15	.08	ao04d1
B1_i64	B2 --> ZN	.91	4.03	F	.35	.17	fn03d1
B1_i68	I --> ZN	.39	4.43	R	.23	.12	in01d1
B1_i316	S --> Z	.91	5.33	F	.34	.17	mx21d1
u3.add_rip1.u4	B0 --> CO	2.20	7.54	F	.24	.14	ad02d1
	... 28 other cell instances omitted ...						
u5.sub_rip1.u6	B0 --> CO	2.25	23.17	F	.23	.13	ad02d1
u5.sub_rip1.u8	CI --> CO	.53	23.70	F	.21	.09	ad01d1
B1_i301	A1 --> Z	.69	24.39	R	.19	.07	xo02d1
u2.metric3.Q_ff_b4	setup: D --> CP	.17	24.56	R	.00	.00	dfctnb
	slack: MET		.44				

[1]See the text for explanations of the column headings.

Table 12.13 is a timing report for the Viterbi decoder, which shows the critical path starts at a sequential logic cell (a D flip-flop in the present example), ends at a sequential logic cell (another D flip-flop), with 37 other combinational logic cells in-between. The first delay is the clock-to-Q delay of the first flip-flop. The last delay is the setup time of the last flip-flop. The critical path delay is 24.56 ns, which gives a **slack** of 0.44 ns from the constraint of 25 ns (reduced from 30 ns to give an extra margin). We have **met** the timing constraint (otherwise we say it is **violated**).

In Table 12.13 all instances in the critical path are inside instance v_1.u100. Instance name u100 is the new cell (cell name critical) formed by merging six blocks in module viterbi (instance name v_1).

The second column in Table 12.13 shows the timing arc of the cell involved on the critical path. For example, CP --> QN represents the path from the clock pin, CP, to the flip-flop output pin, QN, of a D flip-flop (cell name dfctnb). The pin names and their functions come from the library data book. Each company adopts a different naming convention (in this case CP represents a positive clock edge, for example). The conventions are not always explicitly shown in the data books but are normally easy to discover by looking at examples. As another example, B0 --> CO represents the path from the B input to the carry output of a 2-bit full adder (cell name ad02d1).

The third column (incr) represents the incremental delay contribution of the logic cell to the critical path.

The fourth column (arrival) shows the arrival time of the signal at the output pin of the logic cell. This is the cumulative delay to that point on the critical path.

The fifth column (trs) describes whether the transition at the output node is rising (R) or falling (F). The timing analyzer examines each possible combination of rising and falling delays to find the critical path.

The sixth column (rampDel) is a measure of the input slope (ramp delay, or slew rate). In submicron ASIC design this is an important contribution to delay.

The seventh column (Cap) is the capacitance at the output node of the logic cell. This determines the logic cell delay and also the signal slew rate at the node.

The last column (cell) is the cell name (from the cell-library data book). In this library suffix 'd1' represents normal drive strength with 'd0', 'd2', and 'd5' being the other available strengths.

12.13 Summary

A logic synthesizer may contain over 500,000 lines of code. With such a complex system, complex inputs, and little feedback at the output there is a danger of the "garbage in, garbage out" syndrome. Ask yourself "What do I expect to see at the output?" and "Does the output make sense?" If you cannot answer these questions, you should simplify the input (reduce the width of the buses, simplify or partition the code, and so on). The worst thing you can do is write and simulate a huge amount of code, read it into the synthesis tool, and try and optimize it all at once with the default settings.

With experience it is possible to recognize what the logic synthesizer is doing by looking at the number of cells, their types, and the drive strengths. For example, if there are many minimum drive strength cells on the critical path it is usually an indication that the synthesizer has room to increase speed by substituting cells with stronger drive. This is not always true, sometimes a higher-drive cell may actually slow down the circuit. This is because adding the larger cell increases load capacitance, but not enough drive to make up for it. This is why logical effort is a useful measure.

Because interconnect delay is increasingly dominant, it is important to begin the physical design steps as early as possible. Ideally floorplanning and logic synthesis should be completed at the same time. This ensures that the estimated interconnect delays are close to the actual delays after routing is complete.

12.14 Problems

* = Difficult, ** = Very difficult, *** = Extremely difficult

12.1 (Comparator/MUX)

a. (30 min.) Build a DesignWorks (or use another tool) model for the schematic in Figure 12.1 and simulate the operation of this circuit to check that it performs the same function as the Verilog code. *Hint:* You could also use VeriWell to simulate the Verilog netlist.

b. (30 min.) Simulate the schematic (or the Verilog netlist) shown in Figure 12.2 and check that it performs the comparator/MUX function correctly.

c. (30 min.) Simulate the schematic (or the Verilog netlist) of Figure 12.3. If you have access to a logic synthesizer and cell library, you might resynthesize the comparator/MUX and compare the results with those shown in Figures 12.2 and 12.3.

d. (20 min.) Build a schematic (or Verilog model) for macro cm8 in Figure 12.4.

e. (30 min.) Simulate the schematic (or Verilog netlist) shown in in Figure 12.4.

12.2 (*Verilog assignments, 15 min.) Simulate and test the following model paying attention to initialization. Attempt to synthesize it. Explain your results.

```
module dff (D, Q, Clk, Rst);
  parameter width = 1,  reset_value = 0; input [width - 1 : 0] D;
  output [width - 1 : 0] Q; reg [width - 1 : 0] Q; input Clk,Rst;
  initial Q = {width{1'bx}};
  always @ ( posedge Clk or negedge Rst )
    if ( Rst == 0 ) Q <= #1 reset_value; else Q <= #1 D;
endmodule
```

12.3 (Digital filter) (30 min.) Write HDL code to model the following filter:

```
y0 <= c(0)*x(0)+c(1)*x(1)+b(2)*x(2) ;
```

Use $c(0) = -4$, $c(0) = +5$, $c(0) = -3$, but make your code flexible so that these coefficients may be changed. (120 min.) Simulate, test, and synthesize your model. *Hint:* You should use the transfer equation in your code (Verilog or VHDL).

12.4 (Hand design, 60 min.) Use hand calculation and gate delay values obtained from a data book to estimate the critical path of the comparator/MUX shown in Figure 12.1. Assume the critical path (the one with the longest delay) is from the a[2] input (the input with the largest load) -> XOR -> inverter -> four-input NAND -> three-input OR -> select input of two-input MUX (the symbol -> means "through the"). You will need to find the t_{PHL} (falling) and t_{PLH} (rising) propagation delays for each gate used in the critical path. Do not adjust the delays for the loading (fanout) at the output of each gate on the critical path, assume a loading equal to one input of a two-input NAND gate. Change the AND–NOR gate combination to a NAND–NAND gate combination and recalculate the critical path delay.

12.5 (Critical path, 30 min.) Enter the schematic shown in Figure 12.1 and, using a gate-level simulator or a timing analyzer, obtain the delays from the a and b inputs to the outputs. What is the critical path?

12.6 (Verilog sensitivity list, 30 min.) Simulate the following Verilog module with the test pattern shown and explain your results.

```
module and2_bad(a, b, c); input a, b; output c; reg c;
// test pattern: (a b) = (1 1) (0 1) (0 0) (1 0) (1 1)
always@(a) c <= a & b;
endmodule
```

Can you synthesize this module as it is? What is the error message if you get one? If you can synthesize this module as it is, simulate the synthesized logic and compare the output with the Verilog simulation.

12.7 (Verilog decoder, 30 min.) Synthesize the following Verilog module with minimum-area constraint and then with maximum-speed constraint. Compare the resulting logic in each case.

```
module Decoder4_to_16(Enable, In_4, Out_16);
input Enable; input [3:0] In_4; output [15:0] Out_16;
reg [15:0] Out_16;
always @(Enable or In_4)
  begin
  Out_16 = 16'hzzzz;
  if (Enable == 1) begin Out_16 = 16'h0000; Out_16[In_4] = 1; end
  end
endmodule
```

What happens if you change the if statement to if (Enable === 1)?

12.8 (Verilog eight-input MUX, 20 min.) Synthesize the following code with maximum-speed constraint and then minimum-area constraint. Compare the results.

```
module Mux8_to_1(InBus, Select, OutEnable, OutBit);
input [7:0] InBus; input [2:0] Select; input OutEnable;
output OutBit; reg OutBit;
always @(OutEnable or Select or InBus)
  begin
```

```
      if (OutEnable == 1) OutBit = InBus[Select]; else OutBit = 1'bz;
    end
endmodule
```

12.9 (Verilog parity generator, 30 min.) Synthesize the following code with maximum-speed constraint and then minimum-area constraint. Compare the results.

```
module Parity (BusIn, ParityB);
    input[8:0] BusIn; output ParityB; reg ParityB;
    always @(BusIn) if (^Busin == 0 ) ParityB = 1; else ParityB = 0;
endmodule
```

12.10 (Verilog edges and levels, 30 min.) What is the function of the following model? List the cells produced by a logic synthesizer, their function, and an explanation of why they were synthesized.

```
module DD(D, C, R, Q, QB); input D, C, R; output Q, QB; reg Q, QB, L;
always @(posedge C or posedge R) if (R == 1) L = 0; else L = D;
always @(L) begin Q = L; QB = ~L; end
endmodule
```

12.11 (Verilog adders, 120 min.) Synthesize the following code with maximum-speed constraint and then minimum-area constraint. What type of adder architecture does the synthesis tool produce in each case (ripple-carry, lookahead, etc.)? Show exactly how you reached your conclusion. If you can, use either synthesis tool directives, shell commands, or standard components (Synopsys DesignWare or Xilinx X-BLOX, for example) to direct the synthesis tool to a specific adder implementation. Check that when you optimize the synthesized logic the adder architecture is not broken up. Next, if you can, find a way to make the synthesis tool break up the adder and reoptimize the logic. Does anything change?

```
module adder1(a, a, outp);
    input [3:0] a; input [3:0] b; output [3:0] outp; reg [3:0] outp;
// if you can, change the next line to drive your synthesis tool
// pragma|compass|synopsys|whatever max_delay constraint
    begin
        outp <= a + b; // Map me to DesignWare, X-Blox etc., if you can.
    end
endmodule
```

12.12 (Elementary gates in Verilog, 60 min.) Synthesize and optimize the following (you will have to write some more code to go around these statements):

```
And3 = &{In1,In2,In3}; Or3 = |{In1,In2,In3}; Xor3 = ^{In1,In2,In3};
```

This should produce three-input AND, OR, and XOR gates. Now synthesize and optimize eight-input AND, OR, and XOR gates in the same way with minimum-area constraint and then maximum-speed constraint. Compare your results. How and why do the synthesis results and your answers change if you place a large capacitive load on the outputs. *Hint:* Try a load equivalent to 16 minimum-size inverters. Can you explain these results using logical effort?

12.13 (Synthesizable VHDL, 20 min.) Complete the following code fragment and try to synthesize the VHDL:

```
process begin
    wait until Clk = '1';
    Phase <= "0" after 0 ns; Phase <= "1" after 10 ns;
end process;
```

What is the error message? Synthesize this code, and explain the results:

```
process begin
  wait until Clk_x_2 = '1';
    case (Phase) is
    when '0' => Phase <= '1'; when others => Phase <= '0';
    end case;
end process;
```

12.14 (VHDL and process sensitivity list, 15 min.) Simulate the following code with the test input vectors shown:

```
entity AND2 is port (a, b in : BIT; c out : BIT); end AND2;

architecture Bad_behavior of AND2 is begin
  test inputs: (a b) = (1 1) (0 1) (0 0) (1 0) (1 1)
    process (a) begin c <= a and b; end process;
end;
```

Now try to synthesize this code. Do you get an error message? If not, try simulating the synthesized logic and compare with your earlier simulation results.

12.15 (MUX logic, 20 min.) Synthesize the following VHDL:

```
entity MuxLogic is
  port (InBus : in BIT_VECTOR(3 downto 0);
  Sel : in BIT_VECTOR(1 downto 0);
  OutBit : out BIT);
end MuxLogic;

architecture Synthesis_1 of MuxLogic is
  begin process (Sel, InBus)
  begin
    case Sel is
    when "00" => OutBit <= not(InBus(0));
    when "01" => OutBit <= InBus(1) and InBus(2);
    when "10" => OutBit <= InBus(2) or InBus(1);
    when "11" => OutBit <= InBus(3) xor InBus(0);
    end case;
  end process;
end Synthesis_1;
```

Does the synthesizer implement the case statement using a MUX? Explain your answer carefully by using the synthesis reports and the synthesized netlist. Try synthesizing again with minimum-area constraint and then maximum-speed constraint. Does this alter the implementation chosen by the synthesis tool? Explain.

12.16 (Arithmetic overflow in VHDL) Synthesize the following model (you will need arithmetic packages):

```
entity Adder1 is port (InBusA,
   InBusB : in  Std_logic_vector(3 downto 0);
   OutBus : out Std_logic_vector(3 downto 0));
end Adder1;

architecture Behavior of Adder1 is begin OutBus <= InBusA + InBusB;
end Behavior;
```

Repeat the synthesis with the following modification and explain the difference:

```
OutBus : out Std_logic_vector(4 downto 0));
```

Finally, make the following additional modification and explain all your results:

```
OutBus <= ( "0" & InBusA) + ("0" &  InBusB) ;
```

12.17 (Verilog integers, 30 min.) Consider the following Verilog module:

```
module TestIntegers (clk, out)
   integer i; reg [1:0] out; input clk; output out;
   always @(posedge clk) begin i = i + 1; out = i; end
endmodule
```

Write a test module for `TestIntegers` and simulate the behavior. Try to synthesize `TestIntegers` and explain what happens.

12.18 (Verilog shift register, 30 min.) Consider this code for a shift register:

```
module Shift1 (clk, q0, q1, q2)
   input clk, q0; output q2, q1; reg q2, q1;
   always (@ posedge clk) q1 = q0; always (@ posedge clk) q2 = q1;
endmodule
```

Write a module `Test` to exercise this module. Does it simulate correctly? Can you synthesize your code for `Shift1` as it is? Change the body of the code as follows (call this module `Shift2`):

```
always (@ posedge clk) q1 = #1 q0; always (@ posedge clk) q2 = #1 q1;
```

Does this simulate correctly? Now change the code as follows (`Shift3`):

```
always (@ posedge clk) begin q1 = q0; q2 = q1; end
```

Does this simulate correctly? Can you synthesize `Shift3`? Finally, change the code to the following (`Shift4`):

```
always (@ posedge clk) q1 <= q0; always (@ posedge clk) q2 <= q1
```

Does this simulate correctly? Can you synthesize `Shift4`?

12.19 (Reset, 20 min.) Use simulation results to explain the difference between:

```
always (@posedge clk) if(clr) Q = 0;
always (@posedge clk) if(rst) Q = 1;
```

and

```
always (@ posedge clk) begin if (clr) Q = 0; if (rst) Q = 1; end
```

12.20 (Verilog assignments, 30 min.) Consider the following Verilog module:

```
module TestAssign1(sel) input sel; reg outp;
   always @sel begin outp <= 1; if (sel) outp <= 0; end
endmodule
```

Write a module to drive `TestAssign1` and simulate your code. Now consider the following modification (call this `TestAssign2`):

```
if (sel) outp <= 0; else outp <= 1;
```

Simulate `TestAssign2` and compare your results. Try to synthesize `TestAssign1` and `TestAssign2`. Comment on any problems you have and how you resolved them. Compare the behavior of the synthesized logic with the simulations.

12.21 (VHDL sequential logic, 60 min.) Consider the following processes:

```
S1: process (clk) begin
if clk'EVENT and clk = '1' then count <= count + inc; end if;
end process;

S2: process (clk) begin
   if rst = '1' then count <= 0;
   elsif clk'EVENT and clk = '1' then count <= count + inc;
end if;
end process;

S3: process (clk, rst) begin
   if rst = '1' then count <= 0; elsif clk'EVENT and clk = '1' then
     count <= count + inc; sum <= count + sum;
   end if;
end process;

S4: process (clk) begin
if clk'EVENT and clk = '1' then if rst = '1' then count <= 0;
   else count <= count + inc; end if;
end if;
end process;

S5: process (clk, rst) begin
if rst = '1' then count <= 0;
elsif clk'EVENT and clk = '1' then count <= count + inc;
else count <= count + 1;
```

```
end if;
end process;

S6: process (clk, rst) begin
   if rst = '1' then count <= 0;
   elsif clk'EVENT and clk = '1' then count <= count + inc;
   end if; inc <= not dec;
end process;
```

Write code to drive each of these processes and simulate them. Explain any errors or problems you encounter. Try to synthesize your code and check that the results behave correctly and match the simulation results. Explain any differences in behavior or any problems you encounter.

12.22 (Verilog signed multiplication, 30 min.) Show, by simulation, that the following code performs signed multiplication. Synthesize the code and compare the results with the simulation.

```
module Smpy (in1, in2, out); input [2:0] in1, in2; output [5:0] out;
assign out = {{3{in1[2]}},in1}*{{3{in2[2]}},in2};
endmodule
```

12.23 (Verilog arithmetic, 30 min.) Synthesize the following code and explain in detail the implementation that results:

```
module Arithmetic (in_4, out_2, out_3, out_7, out_14);
input [3:0] in_4; output [7:0] out_2, out_3, out_7, out_14;
assign out_2 = in_4*2; assign out_3 = in_4*3; assign out_7 = in_4*7;
assign out_14 = in_4 * 4'b1110;
endmodule
```

12.24 (Verilog overflow bit, 15 min.) Synthesize the following code and explain the implementation that results:

```
module Overflow (a, b, sum, cout);
input [7:0] a, b; output [7:0] sum; output cout;
assign {cout, sum} = a + b;
endmodule
```

12.25 (*VHDL latches, 60 min.) Consider the following two architectures:

```
entity latch1 is port(data: in BIT_VECTOR(1 to 4);
   reset: in BIT; delay: out BIT_VECTOR(1 to 4));
end latch1;

architecture Synthesis_1 of latch1 is
begin S1: process (data, reset) variable hold : BIT_VECTOR (1 to 4);
begin
   if reset = '1' then hold := "0000"; end if;
   delay <= hold; hold := data;
```

```
end process;
end Synthesis_1;

architecture Synthesis_2 of latch1 is
begin S2: process (data, enable, reset)
variable hold : BIT_VECTOR (1 to 4);
begin
if enable = '1' then hold := data; end if;
delay <= hold;
if reset = '0' then hold := "0000";
end process;
end Synthesis_2;
```

Try to synthesize both versions. Does the synthesizer accept the code? *Hint:* It should not. Explain any problems that you encounter, and how to correct them. Resynthesize your working code.

12.26 (*VHDL data slip, 60 min.) Consider the following process, a shift register core:

```
S1: process (data, enable) begin
if enable = '1' then Q <= Q(7 downto 0) & data; end if;
end process;
```

Complete the VHDL code and simulate to ensure your model operates correctly. Try to synthesize your code and compare the operation of the resulting implementation with the simulation results. Explain any problems you encounter.

12.27 (**Synchronous logic, hours) Investigate the following alternative ways to synthesize synchronous logic in VHDL. *Hint:* A few of these methods are illegal in both VHDL-87 and VHDL-93, some methods are only illegal in VHDL-87. Create a table for Q1–Q17 that summarizes your results. Assume all signals are STD_LOGIC. Can you create any more methods (positive-edge only)?

```
-- Let me count the ways to count.
-- Using wait statement:
process begin wait on clk; Q1 <= D; end process; -- 2 edges
process begin wait on clk until clk = '1'; Q2 <= D; end process;
process begin wait until clk = '1'; Q3 <= D; end process;
process begin wait until clk = '1' and clk'EVENT; Q4 <= D;
end process;
-- Using process and sensitivity list:
process(clk) begin if clk'EVENT and clk = '1' then Q5 <= D; end if;
end process;
process(clk) begin if not clk'STABLE and clk = '1' then Q6 <= D;
end if; end process;
process(clk) begin
if clk'LAST_VALUE = '0' and clk = '1' then Q7 <= D; end if;
end process;
-- Using rising_edge function from STD_LOGIC_1164:
process(clk) begin if rising_edge(clk) then Q8 <= D; end if;
```

```
end process;
process begin wait until rising_edge(clk); Q9 <= D; end process;
process begin wait on rising_edge(clk); Q10 <= D; end process;
-- rising_edge expanded:
process(clk) begin
if clk'EVENT and To_X01(clk) = '1'
   and To_X01(clk'LAST_VALUE) = '0' then Q11 <= D; end if;
end process;
-- Using concurrent signal assignments:
Q12 <= D when clk'EVENT and clk = '1'; -- VHDL-93 only (...else)
Q13 <= D when clk'EVENT and clk = '1' else Q13; -- need buffer
Q14 <= D when clk'EVENT and clk = '1' else unaffected; -- VHDL-93
Q15 <= D when clk'EVENT and clk = '1'
   else Q15'DRIVING_VALUE; -- VHDL-93
-- Using blocks:
F1:block(not clk'STABLE and clk = '1')
     begin Q16 <= guarded D;end block;
F2:block(clk'EVENT and clk = '1')
     begin Q17 <= guarded D;end block;
-- The bizarre and variations using '0', 'L', 'H', and '1':
process(clk) begin
if clk'LAST_VALUE = 'L' and clk = 'H' or clk = '1' then Q18 <= D;
   end if; end process;
process begin wait until clk = 'H' or clk = '1';
Q19 <= D; end process;
-- More?
```

12.28 (*State assignment, 30 min) If we have a state machine with r states and S_0 variables, how many different state assignments are there, for $S_0 = 1$ and $r = 2$? List the different state assignments with $S_0 = 2$, $r = 3$ and for $S_0 = 2$, $r = 4$. How many of these are distinct? For five states and three state variables there are 6720 different state assignments, of which 140 are distinct. For nine states and four state variables there are over 4×10^9 different possible state assignments and nearly 11 million of these are distinct. This makes the task of performing sequential logic synthesis by exhaustively considering all possible state assignments virtually impossible. *Hint:* McCluskey's book discusses the problem of state assignment [1965, pp. 266–267].

12.29 (*Synthesis scripts, hours) Write and document a script to synthesize the Viterbi decoder using a logic synthesizer of your choice.

12.30 (*Floorplanning, hours) Write and document a script to perform timing-driven synthesis and floorplanning for the Viterbi decoder.

12.31 (***Patents, 120 min.) Obtain a copy of U.S. Patent 5,530,841 "Method for converting a hardware independent user description of a logic circuit into hardware components." This patent caused controversy during the approval of the IEEE synthesis packages. Research this topic (including a visit to the Web site of the synthesis package working group and checking other synthesis patents). Do you feel (as an engineer) that the IEEE should be concerned?

12.15 Bibliography

One way to learn more about logic synthesis is to obtain a copy of misII or sis (or their newest derivatives) from the University of California at Berkeley (UCB). These tools form the basis of most commercially available logic-synthesis software. Included with the sis distribution is a PostScript copy of a tutorial paper (available also as ERL Memorandum UCB/ERL M92/41) on logic synthesis by the UCB synthesis group. The internal help in sis explains the theory and purpose of each command. In addition each logic-synthesis step is available separately so it is possible to see the logic being synthesized, optimized, and mapped.

Programmable ASIC vendors, Xilinx, Altera, and Actel have each produced reports explaining how to use Synopsys, Mentor, Cadence, and other synthesis tools with their products. These are available on these companies' Web sites.

Brayton [1984] describes the detailed operation of espresso, one of the first logic-minimization programs, and the foundation of most modern commercial logic-synthesis tools. Edited books by Birtwistle and Subrahmanyam [1988] and Dutton [1991] contain a collection of papers on logic synthesis. The book by Thomas et al. [1990] describes an early logic-synthesis system. A tutorial paper by Brayton, Hachtel, and Sangiovanni-Vincentelli [1990] is an advanced description of multilevel logic optimization. In this chapter we have focused on RTL synthesis; the edited books by Camposano and Wolf [1991]; Walker and Camposano [1991]; and Michel, Lauther, and Duzy [1992] contain papers on higher-level, or behavioral-level synthesis. Edwards provides an overview of synthesis including references to earlier work [1992]. Gebotys and Elmasry [1992] cover system-level synthesis. Sasao [1993] is a selection of papers from a conference on logic synthesis. Kurup and Abbasi [1995] describe the Synopsys logic-synthesis tools. The book by Murgai et al. [1995] focuses on logic synthesis for FPGAs. De Micheli's book [1994] is a detailed work on logic-synthesis algorithms. Ashar et al. [1992] and Lavagno and Sangiovanni-Vincentelli [1993] cover sequential logic synthesis in their books. The book by Airiau, Berge, and Olive [1994] covers VHDL-93 from the perspective of logic synthesis. A book by Knapp [1996], describing the Synopsys behavioral compiler, is the closest to this book's treatment of logic synthesis, and includes several practical examples.

I have included references for a number of books (some not yet published) that I was unable to obtain before this book went to press including titles by Rushton [1995] on logic synthesis using VHDL; Saucier [1995] on architectural synthesis; Hachtel and Somenzi [1996] on verification; Romdhane, Madisetti, and Hines [1996] on behavioral synthesis; and Villa et al. [1997] on FSM synthesis. I have included as much information as possible for these references including the LOC catalog information (it is possible to obtain an ISBN before publication).

12.16 References

Airiau, R., J.-M. Berge, and V. Olive. 1994. *Circuit Synthesis with VHDL*. Boston, 221 p. ISBN 0792394291. TK7885.7.A37.

Ashar, P. et al. 1992. *Sequential Logic Synthesis*. Norwell, MA: Kluwer, 225 p. ISBN 0-7923-9187-X. TK7868.L6.A84.

Birtwistle, G., and P. A. Subrahmanyam (Ed.). 1988. *VLSI Specification, Verification, and Synthesis*. Boston: Kluwer, 404 p. ISBN 0898382467. TK7874.V564. A collection of papers presented at a workshop held in Calgary, Canada, Jan. 1987.

Brayton, R. K. 1984. *Logic Minimization Algorithms for VLSI Synthesis*. Boston: Kluwer, 193 p. ISBN 0-89838-164-9. TK7868.L6L626. Includes an extensive bibliography. A complete description of espresso, the basis of virtually all commercial logic-synthesis tools. Difficult to read at first, but an excellent and clear description of the development of the algorithms used for two-level logic minimization.

Brayton, R. K., G. D. Hachtel, and A. L. Sangiovanni-Vincentelli. 1990. "Multilevel logic synthesis." *Proceedings of the IEEE*, Vol. 78, no. 2, pp. 264–300.

Camposano, R., and W. Wolf (Ed.). 1991. *High-level VLSI Synthesis*. Boston: Kluwer, 390 p. ISBN 0792391594. TK7874.H5243.

De Micheli, G. 1994. *Synthesis and Optimization of Digital Circuits*. New York: McGraw-Hill, 579 p. ISBN 0070163332. TK7874.65.D4.

Dutton, R. W. (Ed.). 1991. *VLSI Logic Synthesis and Design*. IOS Press. ISBN 905199046-4.

Edwards, M. D. 1992. *Automated Logic Synthesis Techniques for Digital Systems*. New York: McGraw-Hill, 186 p. ISBN 0-07-019417-3. TK7874.6.E34. Also Macmillan Press, Basingstoke, England, 1992. Includes an introduction to logic minimization and synthesis, and the topic of synthesis and testing.

Gebotys, C. H., and M. I. Elmasry. 1992. *Optimal VLSI Architectural Synthesis: Area, Performance, and Testability*. Boston, 289 p. ISBN 079239223X. QA76.9.A73.G42.

Hachtel, G. D., and F. Somenzi. 1996. *Logic Synthesis and Verification Algorithms*. Boston: Kluwer, 564 p. ISBN 0792397460. TK7874.75.H33.16 pages of references.

Knapp, D. W. 1996. *Behavioral Synthesis: Digital System Design using the Synopsys Behavioral Compiler*. Upper Saddle River, NJ: Prentice-Hall, 231 p. ISBN 0-13-569252-0. A description of the Synopsys software. Includes the following code examples: FIR and IIR filters; Inverse Discrete Cosine Transform; random logic for a Data Encryption Standard (DES) ASIC; and a packet router. Appendix A contains a description of the details of creating DesignWare components. Appendix B describes the subsets of VHDL and Verilog that are understood by the Synopsys compiler. Includes a diskette containing the code from the book.

Kurup, P., and T. Abbasi. 1995. *Logic Synthesis Using Synopsys*. Boston: Kluwer, 304 p. ISBN 0-7923-9582-4. TK7874.6.K87. Hints, tips, and problems with Synopsys synthesis tools. Synopsys has a technical support site on the World Wide Web for registered users of their tools. See also 2nd ed., 1997 ISBN 079239786X.

Lavagno, L., and A. Sangiovanni-Vincentelli. 1993. *Algorithms for Synthesis and Testing of Asynchronous Circuits*. Boston: Kluwer, 339 p. ISBN 0792393643. TK7888.4 .L38.

McCluskey, E. J. 1965. *Introduction to the Theory of Switching Circuits.* New York: McGraw-Hill, 318 p. TK7888.3.M25.

Michel, P., U. Lauther, and P. Duzy (Ed.). 1992. *The Synthesis Approach to Digital System Design.* Norwell: Kluwer, 415 p. ISBN 0792391993. TK7868.D5.S96. Includes 30 pages of references.

Murgai, R., et al. 1995. *Logic Synthesis for Field-Programmable Gate Arrays.* Boston: Kluwer, 427 p. ISBN 0-7923-9596-4. TK7895.G36M87.

Romdhane, M. S. B., V. K. Madisetti, and J. W. Hines. 1996. *Quick-Turnaround ASIC Design in VHDL: Core-Based Behavioral Synthesis.* Boston: Kluwer, 180 p. ISBN 0792397444. TK7874.6.R66. Includes 6 pages of references.

Rushton, A. 1995. *VHDL for Logic Synthesis: An Introductory Guide for Achieving Design Requirements.* New York: McGraw-Hill, 254 p. ISBN 0077090926. TK7885.7.R87.

Sasao, T. (Ed.). 1993. *Logic Synthesis and Optimization.* Boston: Kluwer. ISBN 0-7923-9308-2. TK7868.L6 L627. Papers from the International Symposium on Logic Synthesis and Microprocessor Architecture, Iizuka, Japan, July 1992.

Saucier, G. 1995. Logic and Architecture Synthesis. New York: Chapman & Hall. ISBN 0412726904. Not cataloged by the Library of Congress at the time of this book's publication.

Thomas, D. E., et al. 1990. *Algorithmic and Register-Transfer Level Synthesis: The System Architect's Workbench.* Boston: Kluwer. ISBN 0792390539. TK7874.A418.

Villa, T., et al. 1997. *Synthesis of Finite State Machines: Logic Optimization.* Boston: Kluwer. ISBN 0792398920. TK7868.L6.S944. In Library of Congress catalog, but was not available at the time of this book's publication.

Walker, R. A., and R. Camposano (Ed.). 1991. *A Survey of High-Level Synthesis Systems.* Boston: Kluwer, 182 p. ISBN 0792391586. TK7874.S857.

SIMULATION

13.1   Types of Simulation

13.2   The Comparator/MUX Example

13.3   Logic Systems

13.4   How Logic Simulation Works

13.5   Cell Models

13.6   Delay Models

13.7   Static Timing Analysis

13.8   Formal Verification

13.9   Switch-Level Simulation

13.10   Transistor-Level Simulation

13.11   Summary

13.12   Problems

13.13   Bibliography

13.14   References

Engineers used to prototype systems to check their designs, often using a breadboard with connector holes, allowing them to plug in ICs and wires. Breadboarding was feasible when it was possible to construct systems from a few off-the-shelf TTL parts. It is impractical for prototyping an ASIC. Instead most ASIC design engineers turn to **simulation** as the modern equivalent of breadboarding.

13.1 Types of Simulation

Simulators are usually divided into the following categories or **simulation modes**:

- Behavioral simulation
- Functional simulation
- Static timing analysis
- Gate-level simulation
- Switch-level simulation
- Transistor-level or circuit-level simulation

This list is ordered from high-level to low-level simulation (high-level being more abstract, and low-level being more detailed). Proceeding from high-level to low-level simulation, the simulations become more accurate, but they also become progressively more complex and take longer to run. While it is just possible to perform a behavioral-level simulation of a complete system, it is impossible to perform a circuit-level simulation of more than a few hundred transistors.

There are several ways to create an imaginary simulation model of a system. One method models large pieces of a system as black boxes with inputs and outputs. This type of simulation (often using VHDL or Verilog) is called **behavioral simulation**. **Functional simulation** ignores timing and includes **unit-delay simulation**, which sets delays to a fixed value (for example, 1 ns). Once a behavioral or functional simulation predicts that a system works correctly, the next step is to check the timing performance. At this point a system is partitioned into ASICs and a **timing simulation** is performed for each ASIC separately (otherwise the simulation run times become too long). One class of timing simulators employs **timing analysis** that analyzes logic in a static manner, computing the delay times for each path. This is called **static timing analysis** because it does not require the creation of a set of test (or stimulus) vectors (an enormous job for a large ASIC). Timing analysis works best with synchronous systems whose maximum operating frequency is determined by the longest path delay between successive flip-flops. The path with the longest delay is the **critical path**.

Logic simulation or **gate-level simulation** can also be used to check the timing performance of an ASIC. In a gate-level simulator a logic gate or logic cell (NAND, NOR, and so on) is treated as a black box modeled by a function whose variables are the input signals. The function may also model the delay through the logic cell. Setting all the delays to unit value is the equivalent of functional simulation. If the timing simulation provided by a black box model of a logic gate is not accurate enough, the next, more detailed, level of simulation is **switch-level simulation** which models transistors as switches—on or off. Switch-level simulation can provide more accurate timing predictions than gate-level simulation, but without the ability to use logic-cell delays as parameters of the models. The most accurate, but also the most complex and time-consuming, form of simulation is **transistor-level simulation**. A transistor-level simulator requires models of transistors, describing their nonlinear voltage and current characteristics.

Each type of simulation normally uses a different software tool. A **mixed-mode simulator** permits different parts of an ASIC simulation to use different simulation modes. For example, a critical part of an ASIC might be simulated at the transistor level while another part is simulated at the functional level. Be careful not to confuse mixed-level simulation with a mixed analog/digital simulator, these are **mixed-level simulators**.

Simulation is used at many stages during ASIC design. Initial **prelayout simulations** include logic cell delays but no interconnect delays. Estimates of capacitance may be included after completing logic synthesis, but only after physical design is it possible to perform an accurate **postlayout simulation**.

13.2   The Comparator/MUX Example

As an example we borrow the model from Section 12.2, "A Comparator/MUX,"

```
// comp_mux.v                                                      //1
module comp_mux(a, b, outp); input [2:0] a, b; output [2:0] outp;  //2
function [2:0] compare; input [2:0] ina, inb;                      //3
begin if (ina <= inb) compare = ina; else compare = inb; end       //4
endfunction                                                        //5
assign outp = compare(a, b);                                       //6
endmodule                                                          //7
```

We can use the following testbench to generate a sequence of input values (we call these **input vectors**) that test or **exercise** the behavioral model, comp_mux.v:

```
// testbench.v                                             //1
module comp_mux_testbench;                                 //2
integer i, j;                                              //3
reg [2:0] x, y, smaller; wire [2:0] z;                     //4
always @(x) $display("t    x y actual calculated");        //5
initial $monitor("%4g",$time,,x,,y,,z,,,,,,,smaller);      //6
initial $dumpvars; initial #1000 $finish;                  //7
initial                                                    //8
begin                                                      //9
  for (i = 0; i <= 7; i = i + 1)                           //10
  begin                                                    //11
    for (j = 0; j <= 7; j = j + 1)                         //12
    begin                                                  //13
      x = i; y = j; smaller = (x <= y) ? x : y;            //14
      #1 if (z  != smaller) $display("error");             //15
    end                                                    //16
  end                                                      //17
end                                                        //18
comp_mux v_1 (x, y, z);                                    //19
endmodule                                                  //20
```

The results from the behavioral simulation are as follows:

```
t    x y actual calculated
  0 0 0 0      0
  1 0 1 0      0
... 60 lines omitted...
 62 7 6 6      6
 63 7 7 7      7
```

We included a delay of one Verilog time unit in line 15 of the testbench model (allowing time to progress), but we did not specify the units—they could be nanoseconds or days. Thus, behavioral simulation can only tell us if our design does not work; it cannot tell us that real hardware will work.

13.2.1 Structural Simulation

We use logic synthesis to produce a structural model from a behavioral model. The following comparator/MUX model is adapted from the example in Section 12.11, "Performance-Driven Synthesis" (optimized for a 0.6 µm standard-cell library):

```
`timescale 1ns / 10ps // comp_mux_o2.v                          //1
module comp_mux_o (a, b, outp);                                 //2
input  [2:0] a; input  [2:0] b;                                //3
output [2:0] outp;                                             //4
supply1 VDD; supply0 VSS;                                      //5
mx21d1 b1_i1 (.i0(a[0]), .i1(b[0]), .s(b1_i6_zn), .z(outp[0]));//6
oa03d1 b1_i2 (.a1(b1_i9_zn), .a2(a[2]), .b1(a[0]), .b2(a[1]), //7
  .c(b1_i4_zn), .zn(b1_i2_zn));                                //8
nd02d0 b1_i3 (.a1(a[1]), .a2(a[0]), .zn(b1_i3_zn));           //9
nd02d0 b1_i4 (.a1(b[1]), .a2(b1_i3_zn), .zn(b1_i4_zn));       //10
mx21d1 b1_i5 (.i0(a[1]), .i1(b[1]), .s(b1_i6_zn), .z(outp[1]));//11
oa04d1 b1_i6 (.a1(b[2]), .a2(b1_i7_zn), .b(b1_i2_zn),        //12
  .zn(b1_i6_zn));                                              //13
in01d0 b1_i7 (.i(a[2]), .zn(b1_i7_zn));                      //14
an02d1 b1_i8 (.a1(b[2]), .a2(a[2]), .z(outp[2]));            //15
in01d0 b1_i9 (.i(b[2]), .zn(b1_i9_zn));                      //16
endmodule                                                     //17
```

Logic simulation requires Verilog models for the following six logic cells: `mx21d1` (2:1 MUX), `oa03d1` (OAI221), `nd02d0` (two-input NAND), `oa04d1` (OAI21), `in01d0` (inverter), and `an02d1` (two-input AND). These models are part of an ASIC library (often encoded so that they cannot be seen) and thus, from this point on, the designer is dependent on a particular ASIC library company. As an example of this dependence, notice that some of the names in the preceding code have changed from uppercase (in Figure 12.8 on p. 624) to lowercase. Verilog is case sensitive and we are using a cell library that uses lowercase. Most unfortunately, there are no standards for names, cell functions, or the use of case in ASIC libraries.

The following code (a simplified model from a 0.8 µm standard-cell library) models a 2:1 MUX and uses fixed delays:

```
`timescale 1 ns / 10 ps                                        //1
module mx21d1 (z, i0, i1, s); input i0, i1, s; output z;      //2
  not G3(N3, s);                                               //3
  and G4(N4, i0, N3), G5(N5, s, i1), G6(N6, i0, i1);          //4
  or G7(z, N4, N5, N6);                                        //5
specify                                                        //6
  (i0*>z) = (0.279:0.504:0.900, 0.276:0.498:0.890);           //7
  (i1*>z) = (0.248:0.448:0.800, 0.264:0.476:0.850);           //8
  (s*>z)  = (0.285:0.515:0.920, 0.298:0.538:0.960);           //9
```

```
endspecify                                                          //10
endmodule                                                           //11
```

This code uses Verilog primitive models (not, and, or) to describe the behavior of a MUX, but this is not how the logic cell is implemented.

To simulate the optimized structural model, module comp_mux_o2.v, we use the library cell models (module mx21d1 and the other five that are not shown here) together with the following new testbench model:

```
`timescale 1 ps / 1 ps // comp_mux_testbench2.v                     //1
module comp_mux_testbench2;                                         //2
integer i, j; integer error;                                       //3
reg [2:0] x, y, smaller; wire [2:0] z, ref;                        //4
always @(x) $display("t        x y derived reference");            //5
// initial $monitor("%8.2f",$time/1e3,,x,,y,,z,,,,,,,,ref);         //6
initial $dumpvars;                                                 //7
initial begin                                                      //8
  error = 0; #1e6 $display("%4g", error, " errors");               //9
  $finish;                                                         //10
end                                                                //11
initial begin                                                      //12
  for (i = 0; i <= 7; i = i + 1) begin                             //13
    for (j = 0; j <= 7; j = j + 1) begin                           //14
    x = i; y = j; #10e3;                                           //15
    $display("%8.2f",$time/1e3,,x,,y,,z,,,,,,,,ref);               //16
    if (z != ref)                                                  //17
    begin $display("error"); error = error + 1; end                //18
    end                                                            //19
  end                                                              //20
end                                                                //21
comp_mux_o v_1 (x, y, z); // comp_mux_o2.v                          //22
reference v_2 (x, y, ref);                                         //23
endmodule                                                          //24
```

```
// reference.v                                                      //1
module reference(a, b, outp);                                      //2
input [2:0] a, b;output [2:0] outp;                                //3
  assign outp = (a <= b) ? a : b; // different from comp_mux       //4
endmodule                                                          //5
```

In this testbench we have instantiated two models: a *reference model* (module reference) and a *derived model* (module comp_mux_o, the optimized structural model). The high-level behavioral model that represents the initial system specification (module reference) may be different from the model that we use as input to the logic-synthesis tool (module comp_mux). Which is the real reference model? We postpone this question until we discuss *formal verification* in Section 13.8. For the moment, we shall simply perform simulations to check the reference model against the derived model. The simulation results are as follows:

```
t           x y derived reference
   10.00 0 0 0        0
   20.00 0 1 0        0
... 60 lines omitted...
   630.00 7 6 6       6
   640.00 7 7 7       7
   0 errors
```

(A summary is printed at the end of the simulation to catch any errors.) The next step is to examine the timing of the structural model (by switching the leading '//' from line 6 to 16 in module comp_mux_testbench2). It is important to simulate using the worst-case delays by using a command-line **switch** as follows: verilog +maxdelays. We can then find the longest path delay by searching through the simulator output, part of which follows:

```
t           x y derived reference
... lines omitted...
   260.00 3 2 1       2
   260.80 3 2 3       2
   260.85 3 2 2       2
   270.00 3 3 2       3
   270.80 3 3 3       3
   280.00 3 4 3       3
   280.85 3 4 0       3
   283.17 3 4 3       3
... lines omitted...
```

At time 280 ns, the input vectors, x and y, switch from (x = 3, y = 3) to (x = 3, y = 4). The output of the derived model (which should be equal to the smaller of x and y) is the same for both of these input vectors and should remain unchanged. In fact there is a glitch at the output of the derived model, as it changes from 3 to 0 and back to 3 again, taking 3.17 ns to settle to its final value (this is the longest delay that occurs using this testbench). The glitch occurs because one of the input vectors (input y) changes from '011' (3 in decimal) to '100' (decimal 4). Changing several input bits simultaneously causes the output to vacillate.

Notice that the nominal and worst-case simulations will not necessarily give the same longest path delay. In addition the longest path delay found using this testbench is not necessarily the critical path delay. For example, the longest, and therefore critical, path delay might result from a transition from x = 3, y = 4 to x = 4, y = 3 (to choose a random but possible candidate set of input vectors). This testbench does not include tests with such transitions. To find the critical path using logic simulation requires simulating all possible input transitions ($64 \times 64 = 4096$) and then sifting through the output to find the critical path.

Vector-based simulation (or **dynamic simulation**) can show us that our design functions correctly—hence the name functional simulation. However, functional simulation does not work well if we wish to find the critical path. For this we turn to a different type of simulation—static simulation or static timing analysis.

TABLE 13.1 Timing analysis of the comparator/MUX structural model, `comp_mux_o2.v`, from Figure 12.8.

Command	Timing analyzer/logic synthesizer output[1]						
> report	instance name						
timing	inPin --> outPin	incr	arrival	trs	rampDel	cap	cell
		(ns)	(ns)		(ns)	(pf)	
	a[0]	.00	.00	R	.00	.12	comp_m...
	b1_i3						
	A2 --> ZN	.31	.31	F	.23	.08	nd02d0
	b1_i4						
	A2 --> ZN	.41	.72	R	.26	.07	nd02d0
	b1_i2						
	C --> ZN	1.36	2.08	F	.13	.07	oa03d1
	b1_i6						
	B --> ZN	.94	3.01	R	.24	.14	oa04d1
	b1_i5						
	S --> Z	1.04	4.06	F	.08	.04	mx21d1
	outp[0]	.00	4.06	F	.00	.00	comp_m...

[1]Using a 0.8 µm standard-cell library, VLSI Technology vsc450. Worst-case environment: worst-case process, $V_{DD} = 4.75$ V, and $T = 70$ °C. No wire capacitance, no input or output capacitance, prop–ramp timing model. The structural model was synthesized and optimized using a 0.6 µm library, but this timing analysis was performed using the 0.8 µm library. This is because the library models are simpler for the 0.8 µm library and thus easier to explain in the text.

13.2.2   Static Timing Analysis

A timing analyzer answers the question: "What is the longest delay in my circuit?" Table 13.1 shows the timing analysis of the comparator/MUX structural model, module `comp_mux_o2.v`. The longest or critical path delay is 4.06 ns under the following worst-case operating conditions: worst-case process, $V_{DD} = 4.75$ V, and $T = 70$°C (the same conditions as used for the library data book delay values). The timing analyzer gives us only the critical path and its delay. A timing analyzer does not give us the input vectors that will activate the critical path. In fact input vectors may not exist to activate the critical path. For example, it may be that the decimal values of the input vectors to the comparator/MUX may never differ by more than four, but the timing-analysis tool cannot use this information. Future timing-analysis tools may consider such factors, called **Boolean relations**, but at present they do not.

Section 13.2.1 explained why dynamic functional simulation does not necessarily find the critical path delay. Nevertheless, the difference between the longest path delay found using functional simulation, 3.17 ns, and the critical path delay reported by the static timing-analysis tool, 4.06 ns, is surprising. This difference occurs because the timing analysis accounts for the loading of each logic cell by the input capacitance of the logic cells that follow, but the simplified Verilog models used for functional simulation in Section 13.2.1 did not include the effects of capacitive loading. For example, in the model for the logic cell mx21d1, the (rising) delay from the i0 input to the output z, was fixed at 0.900 ns worst case (the maximum delay value is the third number in the first triplet in line 7 of module mx21d1). Normally library models include another portion that adjusts the timing of each logic cell—this portion was removed to simplify the model mx21d1 shown in Section 13.2.1.

Most timing analyzers do not consider the function of the logic when they search for the critical path. Thus, for example, the following code models z = NAND(a, NOT(a)), which means that the output, z, is always '1'.

```
module check_critical_path_1 (a, z);                              //1
input a; output z; supply1 VDD; supply0 VSS;                      //2
nd02d0 b1_i3 (.a1(a), .a2(b), .zn(z)); // 2-input NAND            //3
in01d0 b1_i7 (.i(a), .zn(b)); // inverter                        //4
endmodule                                                         //5
```

A timing-analyzer report for this model might show the following critical path:

```
inPin --> outPin      incr    arrival  trs  rampDel  cap   cell
                      (ns)     (ns)          (ns)     (pf)
---------------------------------------------------------------------
a                      .00      .00     R     .00      .08   check_...
b1_i7
I --> ZN               .38      .38     F     .30      .07   in01d0
b1_i3
A2 --> ZN              .28      .66     R     .13      .04   nd02d0
z                      .00      .66     R     .00      .00   check_...
```

Paths such as this, which are impossible to activate, are known as **false paths**. Timing analysis is essential to ASIC design but has limitations. A timing-analysis tool is more logic calculator than logic simulator.

13.2.3   Gate-Level Simulation

To illustrate the differences between functional simulation, timing analysis, and gate-level simulation, we shall simulate the comparator/MUX critical path (the path is shown in Table 13.1). We start by trying to find vectors that activate this critical path by working forward from the beginning of the critical path, the input a[0], toward the end of the critical path, output outp[0], as follows:

1. Input a[0] to the two-input NAND, nd02d0, cell instance b1_i3, changes from a '0' to a '1'. We know this because there is an 'R' (for rising) under

the `trs` (for transition) heading on the first line of the critical path timing analysis report in Table 13.1.

2. Input a[1] to the two-input NAND, nd02d0, cell instance b1_i3, must be a '1'. This allows the change on a[0] to propagate toward the output, outp[0].

3. Similarly, input b[1] to the two-input NAND, cell instance b1_i4, must be a '1'.

4. We skip over the required inputs to cells b1_i2 and b1_i6 for the moment.

5. From the last line of Table 13.1 we know the output of MUX, mx21d1, cell instance b1_i5, changes from '1' to a '0'. From the previous line in Table 13.1 we know that the select input of this MUX changes from '0' to a '1'. This means that the final value of input b[0] (the i1 input, selected when the select input is '1') must be '0' (since this is the final value that must appear at the MUX output). Similarly, the initial value of a[0] must be a '1'.

We have now contradicted ourselves. In step 1 we saw that the initial value of a[0] must be a '0'. The critical path is thus a false path. Nevertheless we shall proceed. We set the initial input vector to (a = '110', b = '111') and then to (a = '111', b = '110'). These vectors allow the change on a[0] to propagate to the select signal of the MUX, mx21d1, cell instance b1_i5. In decimal we are changing a from 6 to 7, and b from 7 to 6; the output should remain unchanged at 6. The simulation results from the gate-level simulator we shall use (CompassSim) can be displayed graphically or in the text form that follows:

```
...
# The calibration was done at Vdd=4.65V, Vss=0.1V, T=70 degrees C
Time = 0:0    [0 ns]
                          a   =   'D6   [0]   (input)(display)
                          b   =   'D7   [0]   (input)(display)
                   outp   =   'Buuu   ('Du)   [0]   (display)
                   outp -->  'B1uu   ('Du)   [.47]
                   outp -->  'B11u   ('Du)   [.97]
                   outp -->  'D6    [4.08]
                      a -->  'D7    [10]
                      b -->  'D6    [10]
                   outp -->  'D7    [10.97]
                   outp -->  'D6    [14.15]
    Time = 0:0 +20ns    [20 ns]
```

The code 'Buuu denotes that the output is initially, at $t = 0$ ns, a binary vector of three unknown or **unsettled** signals. The output bits become valid as follows: outp[2] at 0.47 ns, outp[1] at 0.97 ns, and outp[0] at 4.08 ns. The output is stable at 'D6 (decimal 6) or '110' at $t = 10$ ns when the input vectors are changed in an attempt to activate the critical path. The output glitches from 'D6 ('110') to 'D7 ('111') at t = 10.97 ns and back to 'D6 again at $t = 14.15$ ns. Thus, the output bit, outp[0], takes a total of 4.15 ns to settle.

Can we explain this behavior? The data book entry for the `mx21d1` logic cell gives the following equation for the rising delay as a function of `Cld` (the load capacitance, excluding the output capacitance of the logic cell itself, expressed in picofarads):

$$\texttt{tIOZ (IO->Z)} = 0.90 + 0.07 + (1.76 \times \texttt{Cld}) \text{ ns} \qquad (13.1)$$

The capacitance, `Cld`, at the output of each MUX is zero (because nothing is connected to the outputs). From Eq. 13.1, the path delay from the input, `a[0]`, to the output, `outp[0]`, is thus 0.97 ns. This explains why the output, `outp[0]`, changes from `'0'` to `'1'` at $t = 10.97$ ns, 0.97 ns after a change occurs on `a[0]`.

The gate-level simulation predicts that the input, `a[0]`, to the MUX will change before the changes on the inputs have time to propagate to the MUX select. Finally, at $t = 14.15$ ns, the MUX select will change and switch the output, `outp[0]`, back to `'0'` again. The total delay for this input vector stimulus is thus 4.15 ns. Even though this path is a false path (as far as timing analysis is concerned), it is a critical path. It is indeed necessary to wait for 4.15 ns before using the output signal of this circuit. A timing analyzer can only offer us a guarantee that there is no other path that is slower than the critical path.

13.2.4   Net Capacitance

The timing analyzer predicted a critical path delay of 4.06 ns compared to the gate-level simulation prediction of 4.15 ns. We can check our results by using another gate-level simulator (QSim) which uses a slightly different algorithm. Here is the output (with the same input vectors as before):

```
@nodes
a R10 W1; a[2] a[1] a[0]
b R10 W1; b[2] b[1] b[0]
outp R10 W1; outp[2] outp[1] outp[0]
@data
            .00                 a -> 'D6
            .00                 b -> 'D7
            .00              outp -> 'Du
            .53              outp -> 'Du
            .93              outp -> 'Du
           4.42              outp -> 'D6
          10.00                 a -> 'D7
          10.00                 b -> 'D6
          11.03              outp -> 'D7
          14.43              outp -> 'D6
### END OF SIMULATION TIME = 20   ns
@end
```

The output is similar but gives yet another value, 4.43 ns, for the path delay. Can this be explained? The simulator prints the following messages as a clue:

```
defCapacitance            = .1E-01  pF
incCapacitance            = .1E-01  pF/pin
```

The simulator is adding capacitance to the outputs of each of the logic cells to model the parasitic **net capacitance** (interconnect capacitance or wire capacitance) that will be present in the physical layout. The simulator adds 0.01 pF (defCapacitance) on each node and another 0.01 pF (incCapacitance) for each pin (logic cell input) attached to a node. The model that predicts these values is known as a **wire-load model**, **wire-delay model**, or **interconnect model**. Changing the wire-load model parameters to zero and repeating the simulation changes the critical-path delay to 4.06 ns, which agrees exactly with the logic-synthesizer timing analysis. This emphasizes that the net capacitance may contribute a significant delay.

The library data book (VLSI Technology, vsc450) lists the cell input and output capacitances. For example, the values for the nd02d0 logic cell are as follows:

$$\text{Cin (inputs, a1 and a2)} = 0.042 \text{ pF} \quad \text{Cout (output, zn)} = 0.038 \text{ pF} \tag{13.2}$$

Armed with this information, let us return to the timing analysis report of Table 13.1 on page 647 (the part of this table we shall focus on follows) and examine how a timing analyzer handles net capacitance.

inPin --> outPin	incr (ns)	arrival (ns)	trs	rampDel (ns)	cap (pf)	cell
a[0]	.00	.00	R	.00	.12	comp_m...
b1_i3						
A2 --> ZN	.31	.31	F	.23	.08	nd02d0
...						

The total capacitance at the output node of logic cell instance b1_i3 is 0.08 pF. This figure is the sum of the logic cell (nd02d0) output capacitance of cell instance b1_i3 (equal to 0.038 pF) and Cld, the input capacitance of the next cell, b1_i2 (also an nd02d0), equal to 0.042 pF.

The capacitance at the input node, a[0], is equal to the sum of the input capacitances of the logic cells connected to that node. These capacitances (and their sources) are as follows:

1. 0.042 pF (the a2 input of the two-input NAND, instance b1_i3, cell nd02d0)

2. 0.038 pF (the i0 input of the 2:1 MUX, instance b1_i1, cell mx21d1)

3. 0.038 pF (the b1 input of the OAI221, instance b1_i2, cell oa03d1)

The sum of these capacitances is the 0.12 pF shown in the timing-analysis report.

Having explained the capacitance figures in the timing-analysis report, let us turn to the delay figures. The fall-time delay equation for a `nd02d0` logic cell (again from the vsc450 library data book) is as follows:

$$tD(AX->ZN) = 0.08 + 0.11 + (2.89 \times Cld) \text{ ns} \qquad (13.3)$$

Notice $0.11 \text{ ns} = 2.89 \text{ nspF}^{-1} \times 0.038 \text{ pF}$, and this figure in Eq. 13.3 is the part of the cell delay attributed to the cell output capacitance. The ramp delay in the timing analysis (under the heading `rampDel` in Table 13.1) is the sum of the last two terms in Eq. 13.3. Thus, the ramp delay is $0.11 + (2.89 \times 0.042) = 0.231$ ns (since `Cld` is 0.042 pF). The total delay (under `incr` in Table 13.1) is $0.08 + 0.231 = 0.31$ ns.

There are thus the following four figures for the critical path delay:

1. 4.06 ns from a static timing analysis using the logic-synthesizer timing engine (worst-case process, $V_{DD} = 4.50$ V, and $T = 70°C$). No wire capacitance.

2. 4.15 ns from a gate-level functional simulation (worst-case process, $V_{SS} = 0.1$ V, $V_{DD} = 4.65$ V, and $T = 70°C$). No wire capacitance.

3. 4.43 ns from a gate-level functional simulation. Default wire-capacitance model $(0.01 \text{ pF} + 0.01 \text{ pF} / \text{pin})$.

4. 4.06 ns from a gate-level functional simulation. No wire capacitance.

Normally we do not check our simulation results this thoroughly. However, we can only trust the tools if we understand what they are doing, how they work, their limitations, and we are able to check that the results are reasonable.

13.3 Logic Systems

Digital signals are actually analog voltage (or current) levels that vary continuously as they change. **Digital simulation** assumes that digital signals may only take on a set of **logic values** (or **logic states**—here we will consider the two terms equivalent) from a **logic system**. A logic system must be chosen carefully. Too many values will make the simulation complicated and slow. With too few values the simulation may not accurately reflect the hardware performance.

A **two-value logic system** (or two-state logic system) has a logic value '0' corresponding to a **logic level** 'zero' and a logic value '1' corresponding to a logic level 'one'. However, when the power to a system is initially turned on, we do not immediately know whether the logic value of a flip-flop output is '1' or '0' (it will be one or the other, but we do not know which). To model this situation we introduce a logic value 'X', with an unknown logic level, or **unknown**. An unknown can **propagate** through a circuit. For example, if the inputs to a two-input NAND gate are logic values '1' and 'X', the output is logic value 'X' or unknown. Next, in order to model a three-state bus, we need a **high-impedance state**. A high-impedance state may have a logic level of 'zero' or 'one', but it is not being driven—we say it is floating. This will occur if none of the gates connected to a three-state bus is driving the bus. A **four-value logic system** is shown in Table 13.2.

TABLE 13.2   A four-value logic system.

Logic state	Logic level	Logic value
0	zero	zero
1	one	one
X	zero or one	unknown
Z	zero, one, or neither	high impedance

13.3.1   Signal Resolution

What happens if multiple drivers try to drive different logic values onto a bus? Table 13.3 shows a **signal-resolution function** for a four-value logic system that will predict the result.

TABLE 13.3   A resolution function R{A, B} that predicts the result of two drivers simultaneously attempting to drive signals with values A and B onto a bus.

R{A, B}	B = 0	B = 1	B = X	B = Z
A = 0	0	X	X	0
A = 1	X	1	X	1
A = X	X	X	X	X
A = Z	0	1	X	Z

A resolution function, $R\{A, B\}$, must be **commutative** and **associative**. That is,

$$R\{A, B\} = R\{B, A\} \quad \text{and} \quad R\{R\{A, B\}, C\} = R\{A, R\{B, C\}\}. \tag{13.4}$$

Equation 13.4 ensures that, if we have three (or more) signals to resolve, it does not matter in which order we resolve them. Suppose we have four drivers on a bus driving values '0', '1', 'X', and 'Z'. If we use Table 13.3 three times to resolve these signals, the answer is always 'X' whatever order we use.

13.3.2   Logic Strength

In CMOS logic we use n-channel transistors to produce a logic level 'zero' (with a forcing strength) and we use p-channel transistors to force a logic level 'one'. An *n*-channel transistor provides a weak logic level 'one'. This is a new logic value, a **resistive 'one'**, which has a logic level of 'one', but with **resistive strength**. Similarly, a *p*-channel transistor produces a **resistive 'zero'**. A resistive strength is not as strong as a forcing strength. At a high-impedance node there is nothing to keep the node at any logic level. We say that the logic strength is **high impedance**. A high-impedance strength is the weakest strength and we can treat it as either a very high-resistance connection to a power supply or no connection at all.

TABLE 13.4   A 12-state logic system.

| Logic strength | Logic level | | |
	zero	unknown	one
strong	S0	SX	S1
weak	W0	WX	W1
high impedance	Z0	ZX	Z1
unknown	U0	UX	U1

With the introduction of logic strength, a logic value may now have two properties: level and strength. Suppose we were to measure a voltage at a node N with a digital voltmeter (with a very high input impedance). Suppose the measured voltage at node N was 4.98 V (and the measured positive supply, $V_{DD} = 5.00$ V). We can say that node N is a logic level 'one', but we do not know the logic strength. Now suppose you connect one end of a 1 kΩ resistor to node N, the other to GND, and the voltage at N changes to 4.95 V. Now we can say that whatever is driving node N has a strong forcing strength. In fact, we know that whatever is driving N is capable of supplying a current of at least 4.95 V / 1 kΩ ≈ 5 mA. Depending on the logic-value system we are using, we can assign a logic value to N. If we allow all possible combinations of logic level with logic strength, we end up with a matrix of logic values and logic states. Table 13.4 shows the 12 states that result with three logic levels (zero, one, unknown) and four logic strengths (strong, weak, high-impedance, and unknown). In this logic system, node N has logic value S1—a logic level of 'one' with a logic strength of 'strong '.

The **Verilog logic system** has three logic levels that are called '1', '0', and 'x'; and the eight logic strengths shown in Table 13.5. The designer does not normally see the logic values that result—only the three logic levels.

The IEEE Std 1164-1993 logic system defines a variable type, std_ulogic, with the nine logic values shown in Table 13.6. When we wish to simulate logic cells using this logic system, we must define the primitive-gate operations. We also

TABLE 13.5 Verilog logic strengths.

Logic strength	Strength number	Models	Abbreviation	
supply drive	7	power supply	supply	Su
strong drive	6	default gate and assign output strength	strong	St
pull drive	5	gate and assign output strength	pull	Pu
large capacitor	4	size of trireg net capacitor	large	La
weak drive	3	gate and assign output strength	weak	We
medium capacitor	2	size of trireg net capacitor	medium	Me
small capacitor	1	size of trireg net capacitor	small	Sm
high impedance	0	not applicable	highz	Hi

TABLE 13.6 The nine-value logic system, IEEE Std 1164-1993.

Logic state	Logic value	Logic state	Logic value
'0'	strong low	'X'	strong unknown
'1'	strong high	'W'	weak unknown
'L'	weak low	'Z'	high impedance
'H'	weak high	'-'	don't care
		'U'	uninitialized

need to define the process of **VHDL signal resolution** using **VHDL signal-resolution functions**. For example, the function in the IEEE Std_Logic_1164 package that defines the and operation is as follows[1]:

```
function "and"(l,r : std_ulogic_vector) return std_ulogic_vector is   --1
  alias lv : std_ulogic_vector (1 to l'LENGTH ) is l;                  --2
  alias rv : std_ulogic_vector (1 to r'LENGTH ) is r;                  --3
variable result : std_ulogic_vector (1 to l'LENGTH );                  --4
constant and_table : stdlogic_table := (                               --5
-------------------------------------------------------                --6
--|  U    X    0    1    Z    W    L    H    -       |  |              --7
-------------------------------------------------------                --8
  ( 'U', 'U', '0', 'U', 'U', 'U', '0', 'U', 'U' ), -- | U |            --9
  ( 'U', 'X', '0', 'X', 'X', 'X', '0', 'X', 'X' ), -- | X |            --10
  ( '0', '0', '0', '0', '0', '0', '0', 'U', '0' ), -- | 0 |            --11
```

```
    ( 'U', 'X', '0', '1', 'X', 'X', '0', '1', 'X' ), --  | 1 |        --12
    ( 'U', 'X', '0', 'X', 'X', 'X', '0', 'X', 'X' ), --  | Z |        --13
    ( 'U', 'X', '0', 'X', 'X', 'X', '0', 'X', 'X' ), --  | W |        --14
    ( '0', '0', '0', '0', '0', '0', '0', '0', '0' ), --  | L |        --15
    ( 'U', 'X', '0', '1', 'X', 'X', '0', '1', 'X' ), --  | H |        --16
    ( 'U', 'X', '0', 'X', 'X', 'X', '0', 'X', 'X' ), --  | - |);      --17
begin                                                                 --18
   if (l'LENGTH /= r'LENGTH) then assert false report                 --19
"arguments of overloaded 'and' operator are not of the same          --20
length"                                                               --21
      severity failure;                                               --22
   else                                                               --23
     for i in result'RANGE loop                                       --24
       result(i) := and_table ( lv(i), rv(i) );                       --25
     end loop;                                                        --26
   end if;                                                            --27
   return result;                                                     --28
end "and";                                                            --29
```

If a = 'X' and b = '0', then (a and b) is '0' no matter whether a is, in fact, '0' or '1'.

13.4 How Logic Simulation Works

The most common type of digital simulator is an **event-driven simulator**. When a circuit node changes in value the time, the node, and the new value are collectively known as an **event**. The event is scheduled by putting it in an **event queue** or **event list**. When the specified time is reached, the logic value of the node is changed. The change affects logic cells that have this node as an input. All of the affected logic cells must be **evaluated**, which may add more events to the event list. The simulator keeps track of the current time, the current **time step**, and the event list that holds future events. For each circuit node the simulator keeps a record of the logic state and the strength of the source or sources driving the node. When a node changes logic state, whether as an input or as an output of a logic cell, this causes an event.

An **interpreted-code simulator** uses the HDL model as data, compiling an executable model as part of the simulator structure, and then executes the model. This type of simulator usually has a short compile time but a longer execution time compared to other types of simulator. An example is Verilog-XL. A **compiled-code simulator** converts the HDL model to an intermediate form (usually C) and then uses a separate compiler to create executable binary code (an executable). This results in a longer compile time but shorter execution time than an interpreted-code simulator. A **native-code simulator** converts the HDL directly to an executable and offers the shortest execution time.

The logic cells for each of these types of event-driven simulator are modeled using a primitive modeling language (primitive in the sense of "fundamental"). There are no standards for this primitive modeling language. For example, the following code is a primitive model of a two-input NAND logic cell:

```
model nd01d1 (a, b, zn)
function (a, b) !(a & b); function end
model end
```

The model has three ports: a, b, and zn. These ports are connected to nodes when a NAND gate is instantiated in an input structural netlist,

```
nand nd01d1(a2, b3, r7)
```

An event occurs when one of the circuit nodes a2 or b3 changes, and the function defined in the primitive model is called. For example, when a2 changes, it affects the port a of the model. The function will be called to set zn to the logical NAND of a and b. The implementation of the primitive functions is unique to each simulator and carefully coded to reduce execution time.

The data associated with an event consists of the affected node, a new logic value for the node, a time for the change to take effect, and the node that caused the event. Written in C, the data structure for an event might look like the following:

```
struct Event {
    event_ptr fwd_link, back_link;    /* event list */
    event_ptr node_link;              /* list of node events */
    node_ptr event_node;              /* node for the event */
    node_ptr cause;                   /* node causing event */
    port_ptr port;                    /* port which caused this event */
    long event_time;                  /* event time, in units of delta */
    char new_value;                   /* new value: '1' '0' etc. */
};
```

The event list keeps track of logic cells whose outputs are changing and the new values for each output. The **evaluation list** keeps track of logic cells whose inputs have changed. Using separate event and evaluation lists avoids any dependence on the order in which events are processed, since the evaluations occur only after all nodes have been updated. The sequence of event-list processing followed by the evaluation-list processing is called a **simulation cycle**, or an **event–evaluation cycle** (or event–eval cycle for short).

Delays are tracked using a **time wheel** divided into ticks or slots, with each slot representing a unit of time. A software pointer marks the current time on the timing wheel. As simulation progresses, the pointer moves forward by one slot for each time step. The event list tracks the events pending and, as the pointer moves, the simulator processes the event list for the current time.

13.4.1 VHDL Simulation Cycle

We shall use VHDL as an example to illustrate the steps in a **simulation cycle** (which is precisely defined in the LRM). In VHDL, before simulation begins, the design hierarchy is first **elaborated**. This means all the pieces of the model code (entities, architectures, and configurations) are put together. Then the nets in the model are initialized just before simulation starts. The simulation cycle is then continuously repeated during which processes are executed and signals are updated. A VHDL simulation cycle consists of the following steps:

1. The current time, t_c is set equal to t_n.
2. Each active signal in the model is updated and events may occur as a result.
3. For each process P, if P is currently sensitive to a signal S, and an event has occurred on signal S in this simulation cycle, then process P resumes.
4. Each resumed process is executed until it suspends.
5. The time of the next simulation cycle, t_n, is set to the earliest of:
   a. the next time at which a driver becomes active or
   b. the next time at which a process resumes
6. If $t_n = t_c$, then the next simulation cycle is a **delta cycle**.

Simulation is complete when we run out of time ($t_n = $ TIME'HIGH) and there are no active drivers or process resumptions at t_n (there are some slight modifications to these rules involving postponed processes—which we rarely use in ASIC design).

Time in an event-driven simulator has two dimensions. A **delta cycle** takes **delta time**, which does not result in a change in real time. Each event that occurs at the same **time step** executes in delta time. Only when all events have been completed and signals updated does real time advance to the next time step.

13.4.2 Delay

In VHDL you may assign a **delay mechanism** to an assignment statement. **Transport delay** is characteristic of wires and transmission lines that exhibit nearly infinite frequency response and will transmit any pulse, no matter how short. **Inertial delay** more closely models the real behavior of logic cells. Typically, a logic cell will not transmit a pulse that is shorter than the switching time of the circuit, and this is the default **pulse-rejection limit**. If we explicitly specify a pulse-rejection limit, the assignment will not transmit a pulse shorter than the limit. As an example, the following three assignments are equivalent to each other:

```
Op <= Ip after 10 ns;                              --1
Op <= inertial Ip after 10 ns;                     --2
Op <= reject 10 ns inertial Ip after 10 ns;        --3
```

Every assignment that uses transport delay can be written using inertial delay with a pulse-rejection limit, as the following examples illustrate.

```
--  Assignments using transport delay:                      --1
Op <= transport Ip after 10 ns;                             --2
Op <= transport Ip after 10 ns, not Ip after 20 ns;        --3
--  Their equivalent assignments:                           --4
Op <= reject 0 ns inertial Ip after 10 ns;                 --5
Op <= reject 0 ns inertial Ip after 10 ns, not Ip after 10 ns;  --6
```

13.5 Cell Models

There are several different kinds of logic cell models:

- Primitive models, which are produced by the ASIC library company and describe the function and properties of each logic cell (NAND, D flip-flop, and so on) using primitive functions.

- Verilog and VHDL models that are produced by an ASIC library company from the primitive models.

- Proprietary models produced by library companies that describe either small logic cells or larger functions such as microprocessors.

A logic cell model is different from the cell **delay model,** which is used to calculate the delay of the logic cell, from the **power model,** which is used to calculate power dissipation of the logic cell, and from the interconnect **timing model**, which is used to calculate the delays between logic cells (we return to these in Section 13.6).

13.5.1 Primitive Models

The following is an example of a **primitive model** from an ASIC library company (Compass Design Automation). This particular model (for a two-input NAND cell) is complex because it is intended for a $0.35\,\mu m$ process and has some advanced delay modeling features. The contents are not important to an ASIC designer, but almost all of the information about a logic cell is derived from the primitive model. The designer does not normally see this primitive model; it may only be used by an ASIC library company to generate other models—Verilog or VHDL, for example.

```
Function
(timingModel = oneOf("ism","pr");  powerModel = oneOf("pin");  )
Rec
Logic = Function (A1;  A2;  )Rec ZN = not (A1 AND A2);  End; End;
miscInfo = Rec Title = "2-Input NAND, 1X Drive"; freq_fact = 0.5;
tml = "nd02d1 nand 2 * zn a1 a2";
MaxParallel = 1; Transistors = 4; power = 0.179018;
Width = 4.2; Height = 12.6; productName = "stdcell35"; libraryName =
"cb35sc"; End;
```

```
Pin = Rec
A1 = Rec input;   cap = 0.010;   doc = "Data Input";   End;
A2 = Rec input;   cap = 0.010;   doc = "Data Input";   End;
ZN = Rec output;  cap = 0.009;   doc = "Data Output";  End; End;
Symbol = Select
timingModel
On pr Do Rec
tA1D_fr = |( Rec prop = 0.078;   ramp = 2.749;   End);
tA1D_rf = |( Rec prop = 0.047;   ramp = 2.506;   End);
tA2D_fr = |( Rec prop = 0.063;   ramp = 2.750;   End);
tA2D_rf = |( Rec prop = 0.052;   ramp = 2.507;   End); End
On ism Do Rec
tA1D_fr = |( Rec A0 = 0.0015; dA = 0.0789; D0 = -0.2828;
dD = 4.6642; B = 0.6879; Z = 0.5630; End );
tA1D_rf = |( Rec A0 = 0.0185; dA = 0.0477; D0 = -0.1380;
dD = 4.0678; B = 0.5329; Z = 0.3785; End );
tA2D_fr = |( Rec A0 = 0.0079; dA = 0.0462; D0 = -0.2819;
dD = 4.6646; B = 0.6856; Z = 0.5282; End );
tA2D_rf = |( Rec A0 = 0.0060; dA = 0.0464; D0 = -0.1408;
dD = 4.0731; B = 0.6152; Z = 0.4064; End ); End; End;
Delay = |( Rec from = pin.A1; to = pin.ZN;
edges = Rec fr = Symbol.tA1D_fr;  rf = Symbol.tA1D_rf;  End; End, Rec
from = pin.A2; to = pin.ZN; edges = Rec fr = Symbol.tA2D_fr;  rf =
Symbol.tA2D_rf;  End; End );
MaxRampTime = |( Rec check = pin.A1;  riseTime = 3.000;  fallTime =
3.000;  End, Rec check = pin.A2;  riseTime = 3.000;  fallTime = 3.000;
End, Rec check = pin.ZN;  riseTime = 3.000;  fallTime = 3.000;  End );
DynamicPower = |( Rec rise = { ZN };  val = 0.003;  End); End; End
```

This primitive model contains the following information:

- The logic cell name, the logic cell function expressed using primitive functions, and port names.
- A list of supported delay models (ism stands for input-slope delay model, and pr for prop–ramp delay model—see Section 13.6).
- Miscellaneous data on the logic cell size, the number of transistors and so on—primarily for use by logic-synthesis tools and for data book generation.
- Information for power dissipation models and timing analysis.

13.5.2 Synopsys Models

The ASIC library company may provide **vendor models** in formats unique to each CAD tool company. The following is an example of a Synopsys model derived from a primitive model similar to the example in Section 13.5.1. In a Synopsys library, each logic cell is part of a large file that also contains wire-load models and other characterization information for the cell library.

```
cell (nd02d1) {
/* title : 2-Input NAND, 1X Drive */
/* pmd checksum : 'HBA7EB26C */
area : 1;
  pin(a1) { direction : input; capacitance : 0.088;
    fanout_load : 0.088; }
  pin(a2) { direction : input; capacitance : 0.087;
    fanout_load : 0.087; }
  pin(zn) { direction : output; max_fanout : 1.786;
  max_transition : 3; function : "(a1 a2)'";
  timing() {
    timing_sense : "negative_unate"
    intrinsic_rise : 0.24 intrinsic_fall : 0.17
    rise_resistance : 1.68 fall_resistance : 1.13
    related_pin : "a1" }
  timing() { timing_sense : "negative_unate"
    intrinsic_rise : 0.32 intrinsic_fall : 0.18
    rise_resistance : 1.68 fall_resistance : 1.13
    related_pin : "a2"
} } } /* end of cell */
```

This file contains the only information the Synopsys logic synthesizer, simulator, and other design tools use. If the information is not in this model, the tools cannot produce it. You can see that not all of the information from a primitive model is necessarily present in a vendor model.

13.5.3   Verilog Models

The following is a Verilog model for an inverter (derived from a primitive model):

```
`celldefine                                                   //1
`delay_mode_path                                              //2
`suppress_faults                                              //3
`enable_portfaults                                            //4
`timescale 1 ns / 1 ps                                        //5
module in01d1 (zn, i); input i; output zn; not G2(zn, i);     //6
specify specparam                                             //7
InCap$i = 0.060, OutCap$zn = 0.038, MaxLoad$zn = 1.538,       //8
R_Ramp$i$zn = 0.542:0.980:1.750, F_Ramp$i$zn = 0.605:1.092:1.950;  //9
specparam cell_count = 1.000000; specparam Transistors = 4 ;  //10
specparam Power = 1.400000; specparam MaxLoadedRamp = 3 ;     //11
   (i => zn) = (0.031:0.056:0.100, 0.028:0.050:0.090);        //12
endspecify                                                    //13
endmodule                                                     //14
`nosuppress_faults                                            //15
```

```
`disable_portfaults                                                    //16
`endcelldefine                                                         //17
```

This is very similar in form to the model for the MUX of Section 13.2.1, except that this model includes additional timing parameters (at the beginning of the specify block). These timing parameters were omitted to simplify the model of Section 13.2.1 (see Section 13.6 for an explanation of their function).

There are no standards on writing Verilog logic cell models. In the Verilog model, in01d1, fixed delays (corresponding to zero load capacitance) are embedded in a specify block. The parameters describing the delay equations for the timing model and other logic cell parameters (area, power-model parameters, and so on) are specified using the Verilog specparam feature. Writing the model in this way allows the model information to be accessed using the Verilog PLI routines. It also allows us to back-annotate timing information by overriding the data in the specify block.

The following Verilog code tests the model for logic cell in01d1:

```
`timescale 1 ns / 1 ps                                                //1
module SDF_b; reg A; in01d1 i1 (B, A);                                //2
initial begin A = 0; #5; A = 1; #5; A = 0; end                        //3
initial $monitor("T=%6g",$realtime," A=",A," B=",B);                  //4
endmodule                                                             //5
```

```
T=      0 A=0 B=x
T= 0.056 A=0 B=1
T=      5 A=1 B=1
T=   5.05 A=1 B=0
T=     10 A=0 B=0
T=10.056 A=0 B=1
```

In this case the simulator has used the fixed, typical timing delays (0.056 ns for the rising delay, and 0.05 ns for the falling delay—both from line 12 in module in01d1). Here is an example SDF file (filename SDF_b.sdf) containing back-annotation timing delays:

```
(DELAYFILE
  (SDFVERSION "3.0") (DESIGN "SDF.v") (DATE "Aug-13-96")
  (VENDOR "MJSS") (PROGRAM "MJSS") (VERSION "v0")
  (DIVIDER .) (TIMESCALE 1 ns)
  (CELL (CELLTYPE "in01d1")
    (INSTANCE SDF_b.i1)
    (DELAY (ABSOLUTE
      (IOPATH i zn (1.151:1.151:1.151) (1.363:1.363:1.363))
    ))
  )
)
```

(Notice that since Verilog is case sensitive, the instance names and node names in the SDF file are also case sensitive.) This SDF file describes the path delay between input (pin i) and output (pin zn) as 1.151 ns (rising delay—minimum, typical, and maximum are identical in this simple example) and 1.363 ns (falling delay). These delays are calculated by a **delay calculator**. The delay calculator may be a stand-alone tool or part of the simulator. This tool calculates the delay values by using the delay parameters in the logic cell model (lines 8–9 in module in01d1).

We call a system task, $sdf_annotate, to perform back-annotation,

```
`timescale 1 ns / 1 ps                                               //1
module SDF_b; reg A; in01d1 i1 (B, A);                               //2
initial begin                                                       //3
$sdf_annotate ( "SDF_b.sdf", SDF_b, , "sdf_b.log", "minimum", , );  //4
A = 0; #5; A = 1; #5; A = 0; end                                    //5
initial $monitor("T=%6g",$realtime," A=",A," B=",B);               //6
endmodule                                                           //7
```

Here is the output (from MTI V-System/Plus) including back-annotated timing:

```
T=       0 A=0 B=x
T= 1.151 A=0 B=1
T=       5 A=1 B=1
T= 6.363 A=1 B=0
T=      10 A=0 B=0
T=11.151 A=0 B=1
```

The delay information from the SDF file has been passed to the simulator.

Back-annotation is not part of the IEEE 1364 Verilog standard, although many Verilog-compatible simulators do support the $sdf_annotate system task. Many ASIC vendors require the use of Verilog to complete a back-annotated timing simulation before they will accept a design for manufacture. Used in this way Verilog is referred to as a **golden simulator**, since an ASIC vendor uses Verilog to judge whether an ASIC design fabricated using its process will work.

13.5.4 VHDL Models

Initially VHDL did not offer a standard way to perform back-annotation. Here is an example of a VHDL model for an inverter used to perform a back-annotated timing simulation using an Altera programmable ASIC:

```
library IEEE; use IEEE.STD_LOGIC_1164.all;
library COMPASS_LIB; use COMPASS_LIB.COMPASS_ETC.all;
entity bknot is
   generic (derating : REAL := 1.0; Z1_cap : REAL := 0.000;
     INSTANCE_NAME : STRING := "bknot");
   port (Z2 : in Std_Logic; Z1 : out STD_LOGIC);
end bknot;
architecture bknot of bknot is
constant tplh_Z2_Z1 : TIME := (1.00 ns + (0.01 ns * Z1_Cap)) * derating;
constant tphl_Z2_Z1 : TIME := (1.00 ns + (0.01 ns * Z1_Cap)) * derating;
begin
   process(Z2)
```

```
      variable int_Z1 : Std_Logic := 'U';
      variable tplh_Z1, tphl_Z1, Z1_delay : time := 0 ns;
      variable CHANGED : BOOLEAN;
   begin
   int_Z1 := not (Z2);
   if Z2'EVENT then
      tplh_Z1 := tplh_Z2_Z1; tphl_Z1 := tphl_Z2_Z1;
   end if;
   Z1_delay := F_Delay(int_Z1, tplh_Z1, tphl_Z1);
   Z1 <= int_Z1 after Z1_delay;
   end process;
end bknot;
configuration bknot_CON of bknot is for bknot end for;
end bknot_CON;
```

This model accepts two generic parameters: load capacitance, `Z1_cap`, and a derating factor, `derating`, used to adjust postlayout timing delays. The proliferation of different VHDL back-annotation techniques drove the VHDL community to develop a standard method to complete back-annotation—VITAL.

13.5.5   VITAL Models

VITAL is the VHDL Initiative Toward ASIC Libraries, IEEE Std 1076.4 [1995].[2] VITAL allows the use of sign-off quality ASIC libraries with VHDL simulators. **Sign-off** is the transfer of a design from a customer to an ASIC vendor. If the customer has completed simulation of a design using **sign-off quality** models from an approved cell library and a golden simulator, the customer and ASIC vendor will sign off the design (by signing a contract) and the vendor guarantees that the silicon will match the simulation.

VITAL models, like Verilog models, may be generated from primitive models. Here is an example of a VITAL-compliant model for an inverter,

```
library IEEE; use IEEE.STD_LOGIC_1164.all;                       --1
use IEEE.VITAL_timing.all; use IEEE.VITAL_primitives.all;        --2
entity IN01D1 is                                                 --3
   generic (                                                     --4
   tipd_I            : VitalDelayType01   := (0 ns, 0 ns);       --5
   tpd_I_ZN          : VitalDelayType01   := (0 ns, 0 ns) );     --6
   port (                                                        --7
   I                 : in STD_LOGIC := 'U';                      --8
   ZN                : out STD_LOGIC := 'U' );                   --9
attribute VITAL_LEVEL0 of IN01D1 : entity is TRUE;               --10
end IN01D1;                                                      --11
architecture IN01D1 of IN01D1 is                                --12
attribute VITAL_LEVEL1 of IN01D1 : architecture is TRUE;        --13
signal I_ipd   : STD_LOGIC := 'X';                              --14
begin                                                           --15
```

_____

[2]IEEE Std 1076.4-1995, © 1995 IEEE. All rights reserved.

```
WIREDELAY:block                                               --16
   begin VitalWireDelay(I_ipd, I, tipd_I); end block;         --17
VITALbehavior : process (I_ipd)                               --18
variable ZN_zd              : STD_LOGIC;                       --19
variable ZN_GlitchData      : VitalGlitchDataType;            --20
begin                                                         --21
ZN_zd := VitalINV(I_ipd);                                     --22
VitalPathDelay01(                                             --23
   OutSignal         => ZN,                                   --24
   OutSignalName     => "ZN",                                 --25
   OutTemp           => ZN_zd,                                --26
   Paths             => (0 => (I_ipd'LAST_EVENT, tpd_I_ZN, TRUE)),  --27
   GlitchData        => ZN_GlitchData,                        --28
   DefaultDelay      => VitalZeroDelay01,                     --29
   Mode              => OnEvent,                              --30
   MsgOn             => FALSE,                                --31
   XOn               => TRUE,                                 --32
   MsgSeverity       => ERROR);                               --33
   end process;                                               --34
end IN01D1;                                                   --35
```

The following testbench, SDF_testbench, contains an entity, SDF, that in turn instantiates a copy of an inverter, in01d1:

```
library IEEE; use IEEE.STD_LOGIC_1164.all;                    --1
entity SDF is port ( A : in STD_LOGIC; B : out STD_LOGIC );   --2
end SDF;                                                      --3
architecture SDF of SDF is                                    --4
component in01d1 port ( I : in STD_LOGIC; ZN : out STD_LOGIC );  --5
end component;                                                --6
   begin i1: in01d1 port map ( I => A, ZN => B);              --7
end SDF;                                                      --8

library STD; use STD.TEXTIO.all;                              --1
library IEEE; use IEEE.STD_LOGIC_1164.all;                    --2
entity SDF_testbench is end SDF_testbench;                    --3
architecture SDF_testbench of SDF_testbench is                --4
component SDF port ( A : in STD_LOGIC; B : out STD_LOGIC );   --5
end component;                                                --6
signal A, B : STD_LOGIC := '0';                               --7
begin                                                        --8
   SDF_b : SDF port map ( A => A, B => B);                    --9
   process begin                                             --10
     A <= '0'; wait for 5 ns; A <= '1';                      --11
     wait for 5 ns; A <= '0'; wait;                          --12
   end process;                                              --13
   process (A, B) variable L: LINE; begin                    --14
     write(L, now, right, 10, TIME'(ps));                    --15
     write(L, STRING'(" A=")); write(L, TO_BIT(A));          --16
     write(L, STRING'(" B=")); write(L, TO_BIT(B));          --17
```

```
            writeline(output, L);                                    --18
        end process;                                                 --19
    end SDF_testbench;                                               --20
```

Here is an SDF file (`SDF_b.sdf`) that contains back-annotation timing information (min/typ/max timing values are identical in this example):

```
(DELAYFILE
    (SDFVERSION "3.0") (DESIGN "SDF.vhd") (DATE "Aug-13-96")
    (VENDOR "MJSS") (PROGRAM "MJSS") (VERSION "v0")
    (DIVIDER .) (TIMESCALE 1 ns)
    (CELL (CELLTYPE "in01d1")
        (INSTANCE i1)
        (DELAY (ABSOLUTE
            (IOPATH i zn (1.151:1.151:1.151) (1.363:1.363:1.363))
            (PORT i (0.021:0.021:0.021) (0.025:0.025:0.025))
        ))
    )
)
```

(VHDL is case insensitive, but to allow the use of an SDF file with both Verilog and
VHDL we must maintain case.) As in the Verilog example in Section 13.5.3 the
logic cell delay (from the input pin of the inverter, `i`, to the output pin, `zn`) follows
the `IOPATH` keyword. In this example there is also an interconnect delay that follows
the `PORT` keyword. The interconnect delay has been placed, or lumped, at the input
of the inverter. In order to include back-annotation timing using the SDF file,
`SDF_b.sdf`, we use a command-line switch to the simulator. In the case of MTI
V-System/Plus the command is as follows:

```
<msmith/MTI/vital> vsim -c -sdfmax /sdf_b=SDF_b.sdf sdf_testbench
...
#        0 ps A=0 B=0
#        0 ps A=0 B=0
#     1176 ps A=0 B=1
#     5000 ps A=1 B=1
#     6384 ps A=1 B=0
#    10000 ps A=0 B=0
#    11176 ps A=0 B=1
```

We have to explain to the simulator where in the design hierarchy to apply the
timing information in the SDF file. The situation is like giving someone directions
"Go North on the M1 and turn left at the third intersection," but where do we start?
London or Birmingham? VHDL needs much more precise directions. Using VITAL
we say we back-annotate to a **region**. The switch `/sdf_b=SDF_b.sdf` specifies that
all instance names in the SDF file, `SDF_b.sdf`, are relative to the region `/sdf_b`.
The region refers to instance name `sdf_b` (line 9 in entity `SDF_testbench`),
which is an instance of component `SDF`. Component `SDF` in turn contains an instance

of a component, in01d1, with instance name i1 (line 7 in architecture SDF). Through this rather (for us) difficult-to-follow set of directions, the simulator knows that

```
... (CELL (CELLTYPE "in01d1") (INSTANCE i1) ...
```

refers to (SDF) cell or (VHDL) component in01d1 with instance name i1 in instance SDF_b of the compiled model sdf_testbench.

Notice that we cannot use an SDF file of the following form (as we did for the Verilog version of this example):

```
... (CELL (CELLTYPE "in01d1") (INSTANCE SDF_b.i1) ...
```

There is no instance in the VHDL model "higher" than instance name SDF_b that we can use as a starting point for VITAL back-annotation. In the Verilog SDF file we can refer to the name of the top-level module (SDF_b in line 2 in module SDF_b). We cannot do this in VHDL; we must name an instance. The result is that, unless you are careful in constructing the hierarchy of your VHDL design, you may not be able to use the same SDF file for back-annotating both VHDL and Verilog.

13.5.6 SDF in Simulation

SDF was developed to handle back-annotation, but it is also used to describe forward-annotation of timing constraints from logic synthesis. Here is an example of an SDF file that contains the timing information for the halfgate ASIC design:

```
(DELAYFILE
  (SDFVERSION "1.0")
  (DESIGN "halfgate_ASIC_u")
  (DATE "Aug-13-96")
  (VENDOR "Compass")
  (PROGRAM "HDL Asst")
  (VERSION "v9r1.2")
  (DIVIDER .)
  (TIMESCALE 1 ns)
  (CELL (CELLTYPE "in01d0")
    (INSTANCE v_1.B1_i1)
    (DELAY (ABSOLUTE
      (IOPATH I ZN (1.151:1.151:1.151) (1.363:1.363:1.363))
    ))
  )
  (CELL (CELLTYPE "pc5o06")
    (INSTANCE u1_2)
    (DELAY (ABSOLUTE
      (IOPATH I PAD (1.216:1.216:1.216) (1.249:1.249:1.249))
    ))
  )
  (CELL (CELLTYPE "pc5d01r")
    (INSTANCE u0_2)
```

```
        (DELAY (ABSOLUTE
          (IOPATH PAD CIN (.169:.169:.169) (.199:.199:.199))
        ))
      )
)
```

This SDF file describes the delay due to the input pad (cell pc5d01r, instance name u0_2), our inverter (cell in01d0, instance name v_1.B1_i1), and the output pad (cell pc5o06, instance name u1_2). Since this SDF file was produced before any physical layout, there are no estimates for interconnect delay. The following partial SDF file illustrates how interconnect delay can be specified in SDF.

```
(DELAYFILE
  ...
  (PROCESS "FAST-FAST")
  (TEMPERATURE 0:55:100)
  (TIMESCALE 100ps)
(CELL (CELLTYPE "CHIP")
  (INSTANCE TOP)
  (DELAY (ABSOLUTE
    (INTERCONNECT A.INV8.OUT B.DFF1.Q (:0.6:) (:0.6:))
)))
```

This SDF file specifies an interconnect delay (using the keyword INTERCONNECT) of 60 ps (0.6 units with a timescale of 100 ps per unit) between the output port of an inverter with instance name A.INV8 (note that '.' is the hierarchy divider) in block A and the Q input port of a D flip-flop (instance name B.DFF1) in block B.

The triplet notation (min : typ : max) in SDF corresponds to minimum, typical, and maximum values of a parameter. Specifying two triplets corresponds to rising (the first triplet) and falling delays. A single triplet corresponds to both. A third triplet corresponds to turn-off delay (transitions to or from 'z'). You can also specify six triplets (rising, falling, '0' to 'z', 'z' to '1', '1' to 'z', and 'z' to '0'). When only the typical value is specified, the minimum and maximum are set equal to the typical value.

Logic cell delays can use several models in SDF. Here is one example:

```
(INSTANCE B.DFF1)
(DELAY (ABSOLUTE
  (IOPATH (POSEDGE CLK) Q (12:14:15) (11:13:15))))
```

The IOPATH construct specifies a delay between the input pin and the output pin of a cell. In this example the delay is between the positive edge of the clock (input port) and the flip-flop output.

The following example SDF file is for an AO221 logic cell:

```
(DELAYFILE
(DESIGN "MYDESIGN")
(DATE "26 AUG 1996")
  (VENDOR "ASICS_INC")
```

```
   (PROGRAM "SDF_GEN")
(VERSION "3.0")
   (DIVIDER .)
   (VOLTAGE 3.6:3.3:3.0)
   (PROCESS "-3.0:0.0:3.0")
   (TEMPERATURE 0.0:25.0:115.0)
(TIMESCALE )
(CELL
   (CELLTYPE "AOI221")
   (INSTANCE X0)
   (DELAY (ABSOLUTE
   (IOPATH A1 Y (1.11:1.42:2.47) (1.39:1.78:3.19))
   (IOPATH A2 Y (0.97:1.30:2.34) (1.53:1.94:3.50))
   (IOPATH B1 Y (1.26:1.59:2.72) (1.52:2.01:3.79))
   (IOPATH B2 Y (1.10:1.45:2.56) (1.66:2.18:4.10))
   (IOPATH C1 Y (0.79:1.04:1.91) (1.36:1.62:2.61))
))))
```

13.6 Delay Models

We shall use the term *timing model* to describe delays outside logic cells and the term *delay model* to describe delays inside logic cells. These terms are not standard and often people use them interchangeably. There are also different terms for various types of delay:

- A **pin-to-pin delay** is a delay between an input pin and an output pin of a logic cell. This usually represents the delay of the logic cell excluding any delay contributed by interconnect.

- A **pin delay** is a delay lumped to a certain pin of a logic cell (usually an input). This usually represents the delay of the interconnect, but may also represent the delay of the logic cell.

- A **net delay** or **wire delay** is a delay outside a logic cell. This always represents the delay of interconnect.

In this section we shall focus on delay models and logic cell delays. In Chapter 3 we modeled logic cell delay as follows (Eq. 3.10):

$$t_{PD} = R\,(C_{out} + C_p) + t_q \qquad\qquad (13.5)$$

A linear delay model is also known as a **prop–ramp delay model**, because the delay comprises a fixed propagation delay (the intrinsic delay) and a ramp delay (the extrinsic delay). As an example, the data book entry for the inverter, cell in01d0, in a 0.8 μm standard-cell library gives the following delay information (with delay measured in nanoseconds and capacitance in picofarads):

$$\text{RISE} = 0.10 + 0.07 + (1.75 \times \text{Cld}) \quad \text{FALL} = 0.09 + 0.07 + (1.95 \times \text{Cld}) \quad (13.6)$$

The first two terms in each of these equations represents the intrinsic delay, with the last term in each equation representing the extrinsic delay. We see that the Cld corresponds to C_{out}, $R_{pu} = 1.75\,\text{k}\Omega$, and $R_{pd} = 1.95\,\text{k}\Omega$ (R_{pu} is the pull-up resistance and R_{pd} is the pull-down resistance).

From the data book the pin capacitances for this logic cell are as follows:

$$\text{pin I (input)} = 0.060\,\text{pF} \quad \text{pin ZN (output)} = 0.038\,\text{pF} \quad (13.7)$$

Thus, $C_p = 0.038$ pF and we can calculate the component of the intrinsic delay due to the output pin capacitance as follows:

$$C_p \times R_{pu} = 0.038 \times 1.75 = 0.0665\,\text{ns} \quad \text{and} \quad C_p \times R_{pd} = 0.038 \times 1.95 = 0.0741\,\text{ns} \,(13.8)$$

Suppose t_{qr} and t_{qf} are the parasitic delays for the rising and falling waveforms respectively. By comparing the data book equations for the rise and fall delays with Eq. 13.5 and 13.8, we can identify $t_{qr} = 0.10$ ns and $t_{qf} = 0.09$ ns.

Now we can explain the timing section of the in01d0 model (Section 13.5.3),

```
specify specparam                                                      //1
InCap$i = 0.060, OutCap$zn = 0.038, MaxLoad$zn = 1.538,                 //2
R_Ramp$i$zn = 0.542:0.980:1.750, F_Ramp$i$zn = 0.605:1.092:1.950;       //3
specparam cell_count = 1.000000; specparam Transistors = 4 ;            //4
specparam Power = 1.400000; specparam MaxLoadedRamp = 3 ;               //5
  (i=>zn)=(0.031:0.056:0.100, 0.028:0.050:0.090);                       //6
```

The parameter OutCap$zn is C_p. The maximum value of the parameter R_Ramp$i$zn is R_{pu}, and the maximum value of parameter F_Ramp$i$zn is R_{pd}. Finally, the maximum values of the fixed-delay triplets correspond to t_{qr} and t_{qf}.

13.6.1 Using a Library Data Book

ASIC library data books typically contain two types of information for each cell in the library—capacitance loading and delay. Table 13.7 shows the input capacitances for the inverter family for both an **area-optimized library** (small) and a **performance-optimized library** (fast).

From Table 13.7, the input capacitance of the small library version of the inv1 (a 1X inverter gate) is 0.034 pF. Any logic cell that is driving an inv1 from the small library sees this as a load capacitance. This capacitance consists of the gate capacitance of a p-channel transistor, the gate capacitance of an n-channel transistor, and the internal cell routing. Similarly, 0.145 pF is the input capacitance of a fast inv1. We can deduce that the transistors in the fast library are approximately $0.145 / 0.034 \approx 4$ times larger than those in the small version. The small library and fast library may not have the same cell height (they usually do not), so that we cannot mix cells from different libraries in the same standard-cell area.

TABLE 13.7   Input capacitances for an inverter family (pF).[1]

Library	inv1	invh	invs	inv8	inv12
Area	0.034	0.067	0.133	0.265	0.397
Performance	0.145	0.292	0.584	1.169	1.753

[1]Suffix '1' denotes normal drive strength, suffix 'h' denotes high-power drive strength (approximately $\times 2$) , suffix 's' denotes superpower drive strength (approximately $\times 4$), and a suffix 'm' (m=8 or 12) denotes inverter blocks containing m inverters.

The delay table for a 2:1 MUX is shown in Table 13.8. For example, D0/ to Z/, indicates the path delay from the D0 input rising to the Z output rising. Rising delay is denoted by ' / ' and falling delay by ' \ '.

TABLE 13.8   Delay information for a 2:1 MUX.

		Propagation delay			
		Area		Performance	
From input	To output	Extrinsic/ nspF^{-1}	Intrinsic / ns	Extrinsic / ns	Intrinsic / ns
D0\	Z\	2.10	1.42	0.5	0.8
D0/	Z/	3.66	1.23	0.68	0.70
D1\	Z\	2.10	1.42	0.50	0.80
D1/	Z/	3.66	1.23	0.68	0.70
SD\	Z\	2.10	1.42	0.50	0.80
SD\	Z/	3.66	1.09	0.70	0.73
SD/	Z\	2.10	2.09	0.5	1.09
SD/	Z/	3.66	1.23	0.68	0.70

/ = rising and \ = falling.

Both intrinsic delay and extrinsic delay values are given in Table 13.8. For example, the delay t_{PD} (from DO\ to Z\) of a 2:1 MUX from the small library is

$$t_{PD} = 1.42 \text{ ns} + (2.10 \text{ ns/pF}) \times C_L \text{ (pF)}. \tag{13.9}$$

ASIC cell libraries may be characterized and the delay information presented in several ways in a data book. Some manufacturers simulate under worst-case slow conditions (4.5 V, 100°C, and slow process conditions, for example) and then derate each delay value to convert delays to nominal conditions (5.0 V, 25°C, and nominal process). This allows nominal delays to be used in the data book while maintaining accurate predictions for worst-case behavior. Other manufacturers characterize using nominal conditions and include worst-case values in the data book. In either case, we always design with worst-case values. Data books normally include process, voltage, and temperature derating factors as tables or graphs such as those shown in Tables 13.9 and 13.10.

For example, suppose we are measuring the performance of an ASIC on the bench and the lab temperature (25 °C) and the power supply voltage (5 V) correspond to nominal operating conditions. We shall assume, in the absence of other information, that we have an ASIC from a nominal process lot. We have data book values given as worst case (worst-case temperature, 100 °C; worst-case voltage, 4.5 V; slow process) and we wish to find nominal values for delay to compare them with our measured results. From Table 13.9 the derating factor from nominal process to slow process is 1.31. From Table 13.10 the derating factor from 100 °C and 4.5 V to nominal (25 °C and 5 V) is 1.60. The derating factor from nominal to worst-case (data book values) is thus:

$$\text{worst-case} = \text{nominal} \times 1.31 \text{ (slow process)} \times 1.60 \text{ (4.5 V, 100 °C)}. \tag{13.10}$$

To get from the data book values to nominal operating conditions we use the following equation:

$$\text{nominal} = \text{worst-case}/(1.31 \times 1.60) = 0.477 \times \text{worst-case}. \tag{13.11}$$

13.6.2 Input-Slope Delay Model

It is increasingly important for submicron technologies to account for the effects of the rise (and fall) time of the input waveforms to a logic cell. The nonlinear delay model described in this section was developed by Mike Misheloff at VLSI Technology and then at Compass. There are, however, no standards in this area—each ASIC company has its own, often proprietary, model.

We begin with some definitions:

- D_{t0} is the time from the beginning of the input to beginning of the output.
- D_{t1} is the time from the beginning of the input to the end of the output.
- I_R is the time from the beginning to the end of the input ramp.

TABLE 13.9 Process derating factors.

Process	Derating factor
Slow	1.31
Nominal	1.0
Fast	0.75

TABLE 13.10 Temperature and voltage derating factors.

Temperature/°C	Supply voltage				
	4.5V	4.75V	5.00V	5.25V	5.50V
−40	0.77	0.73	0.68	0.64	0.61
0	1.00	0.93	0.87	0.82	0.78
25	1.14	1.07	1.00	0.94	0.90
85	1.50	1.40	1.33	1.26	1.20
100	1.60	1.49	1.41	1.34	1.28
125	1.76	1.65	1.56	1.47	1.41

In these definitions "beginning" and "end" refer to the projected intersections of the input waveform or the output waveform with V_{DD} and V_{SS} as appropriate. Then we can calculate the delay, D (measured with 0.5 trip points at input and output), and output ramp, O_R, as follows:

$$D = (D_{t1} + D_{t0} - I_R)/2 \tag{13.12}$$

$$\text{and} \quad O_R = D_{t1} - D_{t0}. \tag{13.13}$$

Experimentally we find that the times, D_{t0} and D_{t1}, are accurately modeled by the following equations:

$$D_{t0} = A_0 + D_0 C_L + B \times \min(I_R, C_R) + Z \times \max(0, I_R - C_R) \tag{13.14}$$

and

$$D_{t1} = A_1 + B I_R + D_1 C_L. \tag{13.15}$$

C_R is the critical ramp that separates two regions of operation, we call these slow ramp and fast ramp. A sensible definition for C_R is the point at which the end of the input ramp occurs at the same time the output reaches the 0.5 trip point. This leads to the following equation for C_R:

$$C_R = \frac{A_0 + A_1 + (D_0 + D_1) C_L}{2(1 - B)}. \tag{13.16}$$

It is convenient to define two more parameters:

$$d_A = A_1 - A_0 \quad \text{and} \quad d_D = D_1 - D_0. \tag{13.17}$$

In the region that $C_R > I_R$, we can simplify Eqs. 13.14 and by using the definitions in Eq. 13.17, as follows:

$$D = (D_{t1} + D_{t0} - I_R)/2 = A_0 + D_0 C_L + d_A/2 + d_D C_L/2 \qquad (13.18)$$

$$\text{and} \quad O_R = D_{t1} - D_{t0} = d_A + d_D C_L. \qquad (13.19)$$

Now we can understand the timing parameters in the primitive model in Section 13.5.1. For example, the following parameter, `tA1D_fr`, models the falling input to rising output waveform delay for the logic cell (the units are a consistent set: all times are measured in nanoseconds and capacitances in picofarads):

```
A0 = 0.0015;dA = 0.0789;D0 = -0.2828;dD = 4.6642;B = 0.6879;Z = 0.5630;
```

The input-slope model predicts delay in the fast-ramp region, $D_{ISM}(50\%, \text{FR})$, as follows (0.5 trip points):

$$D_{ISM}(50\%, \text{FR}) = A_0 + D_0 C_L + 0.5 O_R = A_0 + D_0 C_L + d_A/2 + d_D C_L/2$$

$$= 0.0015 + 0.5 \times 0.0789 + (-0.2828 + 0.5 \times 4.6642) C_L$$

$$= 0.041 + 2.05 C_L. \qquad (13.20)$$

We can adjust this delay to 0.35/0.65 trip points as follows:

$$D_{ISM}(65\%, \text{FR}) = A_0 + D_0 C_L + 0.65 O_R$$

$$= 0.0015 + 0.65 \times 0.0789 + (-0.2828 C_L + 0.65 \times 4.6642) C_L$$

$$= 0.053 + 2.749 C_L. \qquad (13.21)$$

We can now compare Eq. 13.21 with the prop–ramp model. The prop–ramp parameters for this logic cell (from the primitive model in Section 13.5.1) are:

```
tA1D_fr = |( Rec prop = 0.078;   ramp = 2.749;   End);
```

These parameters predict the following prop–ramp delay (0.35/0.65 trip points):

$$D_{PR}(65\%) = 0.078 + 2.749 C_L. \qquad (13.22)$$

The input-slope delay model and the prop–ramp delay model predict similar delays in the fast-ramp region, but for slower inputs the differences can become significant.

13.6.3   Limitations of Logic Simulation

Table 13.11 shows the switching characteristics of a two-input NAND gate (1X drive) from a commercial 1 μm gate-array family. The difference in propagation delay (with FO = 0) between the inputs A and B is

$$(0.25 - 0.17) \times 2 / (0.25 + 0.17) = 38\%.$$

This difference is taken into account only by a pin-to-pin delay model.

TABLE 13.11   Switching characteristics of a two-input NAND gate.

		Fanout					
		FO = 0	FO = 1	FO = 2	FO = 4	FO = 8	K
Symbol	Parameter	/ns	/ns	/ns	/ns	/ns	/nspF^{-1}
t_{PLH}	Propagation delay, A to X	0.25	0.35	0.45	0.65	1.05	1.25
t_{PHL}	Propagation delay, B to X	0.17	0.24	0.30	0.42	0.68	0.79
t_R	Output rise time, X	1.01	1.28	1.56	2.10	3.19	3.40
t_f	Output fall time, X	0.54	0.69	0.84	1.13	1.71	1.83

FO = fanout in standard loads (one standard load = 0.08 pF). Nominal conditions: $V_{DD} = 5$ V, $T_A = 25$ °C.

Timing information for most gate-level simulators is calculated once, before simulation, using a delay calculator. This works as long as the logic cell delays and signal ramps do not change. There are some cases in which this is not true. Table 13.12 shows the switching characteristics of a half adder. In addition to pin-to-pin timing differences there is a timing difference depending on state. For example, the pin-to-pin timing from input pin A to the output pin S depends on the state of the input pin B. Depending on whether B = '0' or B = '1' the difference in propagation delay (at FO = 0) is

$$(0.93 - 0.58) \times 2 / (0.93 + 0.58) = 46\,\%.$$

This **state-dependent timing** is not taken into account by simple pin-to-pin delay models and is not accounted for by most gate-level simulators.

13.7 Static Timing Analysis

We return to the comparator/MUX example to see how timing analysis is applied to sequential logic. We shall use the same input code (comp_mux.v in Section 13.2), but this time we shall target the design to an Actel FPGA.

Before routing we obtain the following static timing analysis:

```
Instance name       in pin-->out pin    tr      total   incr    cell
-------------------------------------------------------------------
END_OF_PATH
outp_2_                                  R       27.26
OUT1                : D--->PAD           R       27.26   7.55    OUTBUF
I_1_CM8             : S11--->Y           R       19.71   4.40    CM8
I_2_CM8             : S11--->Y           R       15.31   5.20    CM8
I_3_CM8             : S11--->Y           R       10.11   4.80    CM8
```

TABLE 13.12   Switching characteristics of a half adder.

		Fanout					
Symbol	Parameter	FO = 0 /ns	FO = 1 /ns	FO = 2 /ns	FO = 4 /ns	FO = 8 /ns	K /nspF^{-1}
t_{PLH}	Delay, A to S (B = '0')	0.58	0.68	0.78	0.98	1.38	1.25
t_{PHL}	Delay, A to S (B = '1')	0.93	0.97	1.00	1.08	1.24	0.48
t_{PLH}	Delay, B to S (B = '0')	0.89	0.99	1.09	1.29	1.69	1.25
t_{PHL}	Delay, B to S (B = '1')	1.00	1.04	1.08	1.15	1.31	0.48
t_{PLH}	Delay, A to CO	0.43	0.53	0.63	0.83	1.23	1.25
t_{PHL}	Delay, A to CO	0.59	0.63	0.67	0.75	0.90	0.48
t_r	Output rise time, X	1.01	1.28	1.56	2.10	3.19	3.40
t_f	Output fall time, X	0.54	0.69	0.84	1.13	1.71	1.83

FO = fanout in standard loads (one standard load = 0.08 pF). Nominal conditions: $V_{DD} = 5$ V, $T_A = 25$ °C.

```
IN1                     : PAD--->Y          R       5.32    5.32    INBUF
a_2_                                         R       0.00    0.00
BEGIN_OF_PATH
```

The estimated prelayout critical path delay is nearly 30 ns including the I/O-cell delays (ACT 3, worst-case, standard speed grade). This limits the operating frequency to 33 MHz (assuming we can get the signals to and from the chip pins with no further delays—highly unlikely). The operating frequency can be increased by pipelining the design as follows (by including three register stages: at the inputs, the outputs, and between the comparison and the select functions):

```
// comp_mux_rrr.v                                               //1
module comp_mux_rrr(a, b, clock, outp);                         //2
input [2:0] a, b; output [2:0] outp; input clock;               //3
reg [2:0] a_r, a_rr, b_r, b_rr, outp; reg sel_r;                //4
wire sel = ( a_r <= b_r ) ? 0 : 1;                              //5
always @ (posedge clock) begin a_r <= a; b_r <= b; end          //6
always @ (posedge clock) begin a_rr <= a_r; b_rr <= b_r; end    //7
always @ (posedge clock) outp <= sel_r ? b_rr : a_rr;           //8
always @ (posedge clock) sel_r <= sel;                          //9
endmodule                                                       //10
```

Following synthesis we optimize module comp_mux_rrr for maximum speed. Static timing analysis gives the following preroute critical paths:

```
---------------------INPAD to SETUP longest path---------------------
Rise delay, Worst case
```

Instance name	in pin-->out pin	tr	total	incr	cell
END_OF_PATH					
D.a_r_ff_b2		R	4.52	0.00	DF1
INBUF_24	: PAD--->Y	R	4.52	4.52	INBUF
a_2_		R	0.00	0.00	
BEGIN_OF_PATH					

```
--------------------CLOCK to SETUP longest path--------------------
```
Rise delay, Worst case

Instance name	in pin-->out pin	tr	total	incr	cell
END_OF_PATH					
D.sel_r_ff		R	9.99	0.00	DF1
I_1_CM8	: S10--->Y	R	9.99	0.00	CM8
I_3_CM8	: S00--->Y	R	9.99	4.40	CM8
a_r_ff_b1	: CLK--->Q	R	5.60	5.60	DF1
BEGIN_OF_PATH					

```
--------------------CLOCK to OUTPAD longest path--------------------
```
Rise delay, Worst case

Instance name	in pin-->out pin	tr	total	incr	cell
END_OF_PATH					
outp_2_		R	11.95		
OUTBUF_31	: D--->PAD	R	11.95	7.55	OUTBUF
outp_ff_b2	: CLK--->Q	R	4.40	4.40	DF1
BEGIN_OF_PATH					

The timing analyzer has examined the following:

1. Paths that start at an input pad and end on the data input of a sequential logic cell (the D input to a D flip-flop, for example). We might call this an **entry path** (or input-to-D path) to a pipelined design. The longest **entry delay** (or input-to-setup delay) is 4.52 ns.

2. Paths that start at a clock input to a sequential logic cell and end at the data input of a sequential logic cell. This is a **stage path** (register-to-register path or clock-to-D path) in a pipeline stage. The longest **stage delay** (clock-to-D delay) is 9.99 ns.

3. Paths that start at a sequential logic cell output and end at an output pad. This is an **exit path** (clock-to-output path) from the pipeline. The longest **exit delay** (clock-to-output delay) is 11.95 ns.

By pipelining the design we added three clock periods of latency, but we increased the estimated operating speed. The longest prelayout critical path is now an exit delay, approximately 12 ns—more than doubling the maximum operating frequency. Next, we route the registered version of the design. The Actel software informs us that the postroute maximum stage delay is 11.3 ns (close to the preroute estimate of 9.99 ns). To check this figure we can perform another timing analysis. This time we shall measure the stage delays (the start points are all clock pins, and the end points are all inputs to sequential cells, in our case the D input to a D flip-flop). We need to define the **sets** of nodes at which to start and end the timing analysis (similar to the path clusters we used to specify timing constraints in logic synthesis). In the Actel timing analyzer we can use predefined sets 'clock' (flip-flop clock pins) and 'gated' (flip-flop inputs) as follows:

```
timer> startset clock
timer> endset gated
timer> longest
 1st  longest path to all endpins
Rank Total Start pin       First Net    End Net      End pin
   0  11.3 a_r_ff_b2:CLK   a_r_2_       block_0_OUT1 sel_r_ff:D
   1   6.6 sel_r_ff:CLK    sel_r        DEF_NET_50   outp_ff_b0:D
... 8 similar lines omitted ...
```

We could try to reduce the long stage delay (11.3 ns), but we have already seen from the preroute timing estimates that an exit delay may be the critical path. Next, we check some other important timing parameters.

13.7.1   Hold Time

Hold-time problems can occur if there is clock skew between adjacent flip-flops, for example. We first need to check for the shortest exit delays using the same sets that we used to check stage delays,

```
timer> shortest
 1st shortest path to all endpins
Rank Total Start pin       First Net    End Net      End pin
   0   4.0 b_rr_ff_b1:CLK  b_rr_1_      DEF_NET_48   outp_ff_b1:D
   1   4.1 a_rr_ff_b2:CLK  a_rr_2_      DEF_NET_46   outp_ff_b2:D
... 8 similar lines omitted ...
```

The shortest path delay, 4 ns, is between the clock input of a D flip-flop with instance name b_rr_ff_b1 (call this X) and the D input of flip-flop instance name outp_ff_b1 (Y). Due to clock skew, the clock signal may not arrive at both flip-flops simultaneously. Suppose the clock arrives at flip-flop Y 3 ns earlier than at flip-flop X. The D input to flip-flop Y is only stable for $(4-3) = 1$ ns after the clock edge. To check for hold-time violations we thus need to find the clock skew corresponding to each clock-to-D path. This is tedious and normally timing-analysis tools check hold-time requirements automatically, but we shall show the steps to illustrate the process.

13.7.2   Entry Delay

Before we can measure clock skew, we need to analyze the entry delays, including the clock tree. The synthesis tools automatically add I/O pads and the clock cells. This means that extra nodes are automatically added to the netlist with automatically generated names. The EDIF conversion tools may then modify these names. Before we can perform an analysis of entry delays and the clock network delay, we need to find the input node names. By looking for the EDIF 'rename' construct in the EDIF netlist we can associate the input and output node names in the behavioral Verilog model, comp_mux_rrr, and the EDIF names,

```
piron% grep rename comp_mux_rrr_o.edn
        (port (rename a_2_ "a[2]")  (direction INPUT))
... 8 similar lines renaming ports omitted ...
        (net (rename a_rr_0_ "a_rr[0]")  (joined
... 9 similar lines renaming nets omitted ...
piron%
```

Thus, for example, the EDIF conversion program has renamed input port a[2] to a_2_ because the design tools do not like the Verilog bus notation using square brackets. Next we find the connections between the ports and the added I/O cells by looking for 'PAD' in the Actel format netlist, which indicates a connection to a pad and the pins of the chip, as follows:

```
piron% grep PAD comp_mux_rrr_o.adl
NET DEF_NET_148;  outp_2_, OUTBUF_31:PAD.
NET DEF_NET_151;  outp_1_, OUTBUF_32:PAD.
NET DEF_NET_154;  outp_0_, OUTBUF_33:PAD.
NET DEF_NET_127;  a_2_, INBUF_24:PAD.
NET DEF_NET_130;  a_1_, INBUF_25:PAD.
NET DEF_NET_133;  a_0_, INBUF_26:PAD.
NET DEF_NET_136;  b_2_, INBUF_27:PAD.
NET DEF_NET_139;  b_1_, INBUF_28:PAD.
NET DEF_NET_142;  b_0_, INBUF_29:PAD.
NET DEF_NET_145;  clock, CLKBUF_30:PAD.
piron%
```

This tells us, for example, that the node we called clock in our behavioral model has been joined to a node (with automatically generated name) called CLKBUF_30:PAD, using a net (connection) named DEF_NET_145 (again automatically generated). This net is the connection between the node clock that is dangling in the behavioral model and the clock-buffer pad cell that the synthesis tools automatically added.

13.7.3   Exit Delay

We now know that the clock-pad input is CLKBUF_30:PAD, so we can find the exit delays (the longest path between clock-pad input and an output) as follows (using the clock-pad input as the start set):

```
timer> startset clockpad
Working startset 'clockpad' contains 0 pins.

timer> addstart CLKBUF_30:PAD
Working startset 'clockpad' contains 2 pins.
```

I shall explain why this set contains two pins and not just one presently. Next, we define the end set and trace the longest exit paths as follows:

```
timer> endset outpad
Working endset 'outpad' contains 3 pins.

timer> longest
 1st  longest path to all endpins
Rank Total Start pin       First Net     End Net       End pin
   0   16.1 CLKBUF_30/U0:PAD DEF_NET_144   DEF_NET_154   OUTBUF_33:PAD
   1   16.0 CLKBUF_30/U0:PAD DEF_NET_144   DEF_NET_151   OUTBUF_32:PAD
   2   16.0 CLKBUF_30/U0:PAD DEF_NET_144   DEF_NET_148   OUTBUF_31:PAD
3 pins
```

This tells us we have three paths from the clock-pad input to the three output pins (outp[0], outp[1], and outp[2]). We can examine the longest exit delay in more detail as follows:

```
timer> expand 0
 1st longest path to OUTBUF_33:PAD (rising) (Rank: 0)
Total Delay Typ Load Macro      Start pin       Net name
  16.1   3.7 Tpd   0  OUTBUF     OUTBUF_33:D     DEF_NET_154
  12.4   4.5 Tpd   1  DF1        outp_ff_b0:CLK  DEF_NET_1530
   7.9   7.9 Tpd  16  CLKEXT_0   CLKBUF_30/U0:PAD DEF_NET_144
```

The input-to-clock delay, t_{IC}, due to the clock-buffer cell (or macro) CLKEXT_0, instance name CLKBUF_30/U0, is 7.9 ns. The clock-to-Q delay, t_{CQ}, of flip-flop cell DF1, instance name outp_ff_b0, is 4.5 ns. The delay, t_{QO}, due to the output buffer cell OUTBUF, instance name OUTBUF_33, is 3.7 ns. The longest path between clock-pad input and the output, t_{CO}, is thus

$$t_{CO} = t_{IC} + t_{CQ} + t_{QO} = 16.1 \text{ ns} . \tag{13.23}$$

This is the critical path and limits the operating frequency to $(1 / 16.1 \text{ ns}) \approx 62 \text{ MHz}$.

When we created a start set using CLKBUF_30:PAD, the timing analyzer told us that this set consisted of two pins. We can list the names of the two pins as follows:

```
timer> showset clockpad
Pin name                    Net name              Macro name
CLKBUF_30/U0:PAD            <no net>              CLKEXT_0
CLKBUF_30/U1:PAD            DEF_NET_145           CLKTRI_0
2 pins
```

The clock-buffer instance name, CLKBUF_30/U0, is hierarchical (with a ' / ' hierarchy separator). This indicates that there is more than one instance inside the clock-buffer cell, CLKBUF_30. Instance CLKBUF_30/U0 is the input driver, instance CLKBUF_30/U1 is the output driver (which is disabled and unused in this case).

13.7.4   External Setup Time

Each of the six chip data inputs must satisfy the following set-up equation:

$$t_{SU} \text{ (external)} > t_{SU} \text{ (internal)} - \text{(clock delay)} + \text{(data delay)} \qquad (13.24)$$

(where both clock and data delays end at the same flip-flop instance). We find the clock delays in Eq. 13.24 using the clock input pin as the start set and the end set 'clock'. The timing analyzer tells us all 16 clock path delays are the same at 7.9 ns in our design, and the clock skew is thus zero. Actel's clock distribution system minimizes clock skew, but clock skew will not always be zero. From the discussion in Section 13.7.1, we see there is no possibility of internal hold-time violations with a clock skew of zero.

Next, we find the data delays in Eq, 13.24 using a start set of all input pads and an end set of 'gated',

```
timer> longest
... lines omitted ...
 1st  longest path to all endpins
Rank Total Start pin      First Net      End Net      End pin
 10   10.0 INBUF_26:PAD   DEF_NET_1320   DEF_NET_1320 a_r_ff_b0:D
 11    9.7 INBUF_28:PAD   DEF_NET_1380   DEF_NET_1380 b_r_ff_b1:D
 12    9.4 INBUF_25:PAD   DEF_NET_1290   DEF_NET_1290 a_r_ff_b1:D
 13    9.3 INBUF_27:PAD   DEF_NET_1350   DEF_NET_1350 b_r_ff_b2:D
 14    9.2 INBUF_29:PAD   DEF_NET_1410   DEF_NET_1410 b_r_ff_b0:D
 15    9.1 INBUF_24:PAD   DEF_NET_1260   DEF_NET_1260 a_r_ff_b2:D
16 pins
```

We are only interested in the last six paths of this analysis (rank 10–15) that describe the delays from each data input pad (a[0], a[1], a[2], b[0], b[1], b[2]) to the D input of a flip-flop. The maximum data delay, 10 ns, occurs on input buffer instance name INBUF_26 (pad 26); pin INBUF_26:PAD is node a_0_ in the EDIF file or input a[0] in our behavioral model. The six t_{SU} (external) equations corresponding to Eq, 13.24 may be reduced to the following worst-case relation:

$$t_{SU} (external)_{max} > t_{SU} (internal) - 7.9 \text{ ns} + \max (9.1 \text{ ns}, 10.0 \text{ ns})$$

$$> t_{SU} (internal) + 2.1 \text{ ns} \tag{13.25}$$

We calculated the clock and data delay terms in Eq. 13.24 separately, but timing analyzers can normally perform a single analysis as follows:

$$t_{SU} (external)_{max} > t_{SU} (internal) - (clock \ delay - data \ delay)_{min}. \tag{13.26}$$

Finally, we check that there is no external hold-time requirement. That is to say, we must check that t_{SU} (external) is never negative or

$$t_{SU} (external)_{min} > t_{SU} (internal) - (clock \ delay - data \ delay)_{max} > 0$$

$$> t_{SU} (internal) + 1.2 \text{ ns} > 0. \tag{13.27}$$

Since t_{SU} (internal) is always positive on Actel FPGAs, t_{SU} (external)$_{min}$ is always positive for this design. In large ASICs, with large clock delays, it is possible to have external hold-time requirements on inputs. This is the reason that some FPGAs (Xilinx, for example) have programmable delay elements that deliberately increase the data delay and eliminate irksome external hold-time requirements.

13.8   Formal Verification

Using logic synthesis we move from a behavioral model to a structural model. How are we to know (other than by trusting the logic synthesizer) that the two representations are the same? We have already seen that we may have to alter the original reference model because the HDL acceptable to a synthesis tool is a subset of HDL acceptable to simulators. **Formal verification** can prove, in the mathematical sense, that two representations are equivalent. If they are not, the software can tell us why and how two representations differ.

13.8.1   An Example

We shall use the following VHDL entity with two architectures as an example:[3]

```
entity Alarm is                                              --1
  port(Clock, Key, Trip : in bit; Ring : out bit);           --2
end Alarm;                                                    --3
```

---

[3]By one of the architects of the Compass VFormal software, Erich Marschner.

The following behavioral architecture is the **reference model**:

```
architecture RTL of Alarm is                                    --1
   type States is (Armed, Off, Ringing); signal State : States; --2
begin                                                           --3
   process (Clock) begin                                        --4
   if Clock = '1' and Clock'EVENT then                          --5
      case State is                                             --6
         when Off => if Key = '1' then State <= Armed; end if;  --7
         when Armed => if Key = '0' then State <= Off;          --8
                       elsif Trip = '1' then State <= Ringing;  --9
                       end if;                                  --10
         when Ringing => if Key = '0' then State <= Off; end if; --11
      end case;                                                 --12
   end if;                                                      --13
   end process;                                                 --14
   Ring <= '1' when State = Ringing else '0';                   --15
end RTL;                                                        --16
```

The following synthesized structural architecture is the **derived model**:

```
library cells; use cells.all; // ...contains logic cell models  --1
architecture Gates of Alarm is                                  --2
component Inverter port(i : in BIT;z : out BIT) ; end component; --3
component NAnd2 port(a,b : in BIT;z : out BIT) ; end component;  --4
component NAnd3 port(a,b,c : in BIT;z : out BIT) ; end component; --5
component DFF port(d,c : in BIT; q,qn : out BIT) ; end component; --6
signal State, NextState : BIT_VECTOR(1 downto 0 );              --7
signal s0, s1, s2, s3 : BIT;                                    --8
begin                                                           --9
   g2: Inverter port map ( i => State(0), z => s1 );            --10
   g3: NAnd2 port map ( a => s1, b => State(1), z => s2 );      --11
   g4: Inverter port map ( i => s2, z => Ring );                --12
   g5: NAnd2 port map ( a => State(1), b => Key, z => s0 );     --13
   g6: NAnd3 port map ( a => Trip, b => s1, c => Key, z => s3 ); --14
   g7: NAnd2 port map ( a => s0, b => s3, z => NextState(1) );  --15
   g8: Inverter port map ( i => Key, z => NextState(0) );       --16
   state_ff_b0: DFF port map                                    --17
   ( d => NextState(0), c => Clock, q => State(0), qn => open ); --18
   state_ff_b1: DFF port map                                    --19
   ( d => NextState(1), c => Clock, q => State(1), qn => open ); --20
end Gates;                                                      --21
```

To compare the reference and the derived models (two representations), formal verification performs the following steps: (1) the HDL is parsed, (2) a **finite-state machine compiler** extracts the states present in any sequential logic, (3) a **proof generator** automatically generates formulas to be proved, (4) the **theorem prover** attempts to prove the formulas. The results from the last step are as follows:

```
formulas to be proved:    8
formulas proved VALID:    8
```

By constructing and then proving formulas the software tells us that architecture RTL *implies* architecture Gates (implication is the default proof mechanism—we could also have asked if the architectures are exactly equivalent). Next, we shall explore what this means and how formal verification works.

13.8.2   Understanding Formal Verification

The **formulas** to be proved are generated in a separate file of **proof statements**:

```
# axioms                                                    //1
Let Axiom_ref = Axioms Of alarm-rtl                         //2
Let Axiom_der = Axioms Of alarm-gates                       //3
ProveNotAlwaysFalse (Axiom_ref)                             //4
Prove (Axiom_ref => Axiom_der)                              //5
# assertions                                                //6
Let Assert_ref = Asserts Of alarm-rtl                       //7
Let Assert_der = Asserts Of alarm-gates                     //8
Prove (Axiom_ref => (Assert_ref => Assert_der))             //9
# clocks                                                    //10
Let ClockEvents_ref = Clocks Of alarm-rtl                   //11
Let ClockEvents_der = Clocks Of alarm-gates                 //12
Let Master__clock_event_ref =                               //13
  Value (master__clock'event Of alarm-rtl)                  //14
Prove (Axiom_ref => (ClockEvents_ref <=> ClockEvents_der))  //15
# next state of memories                                    //16
Prove ((Axiom_ref And Master__clock_event_ref) =>          //17
(Transition (state(1) Of alarm-rtl) <=>                     //18
Transition (state_ff_b1.t Of alarm-gates)))                //19
Prove ((Axiom_ref And Master__clock_event_ref) =>          //20
(Transition (state(0) Of alarm-rtl) <=>                     //21
Transition (state_ff_b0.t Of alarm-gates)))                //22
# validity value of outbuses                                //23
Prove (Axiom_ref => (Domain (ring Of alarm-rtl) <=>        //24
Domain (ring Of alarm-gates)))                              //25
Prove (Axiom_ref => (Domain (ring Of alarm-rtl) =>         //26
(Value (ring Of alarm-rtl) <=>                              //27
Value (ring Of alarm-gates))))                              //28
```

Formal verification makes strict use of the terms *axiom* and *assertion*. An **axiom** is an explicit or implicit fact. For example, if a VHDL signal is declared to be type BIT, an implicit axiom is that this signal may only take the logic values '0' and '1'. An **assertion** is derived from a statement placed in the HDL code. For example, the following VHDL statement is an assertion:

```
assert Key /= '1' or Trip /= '1' or NextState = Ringing
  report "Alarm on and tripped but not ringing";
```

A VHDL assert statement prints only if the condition is FALSE. We know from de Morgan's theorem that (A+B+C)'=A'B'C'. Thus, this statement checks for a burglar alarm that does not ring when it is on and we are burgled.

In the proof statements the symbol '=>' means **implies**. In logic calculus we write $A \Rightarrow B$ to mean A implies B. The symbol '<=>' means **equivalence**, and this is stricter than implication. We write $A \Leftrightarrow B$ to mean: A is equivalent to B. Table 13.13 show the truth tables for these two logic operators.

TABLE 13.13   Implication and equivalence.

A	B	A => B	A <=> B
F	F	T	T
F	T	T	F
T	F	F	F
T	T	T	T

13.8.3   Adding an Assertion

If we include the assert statement from the previous section in architecture RTL and repeat formal verification, we get the following message from the FSM compiler:

```
<E>  Assertion may be violated
SEVERITY: ERROR
REPORT: Alarm on and tripped but not ringing
FILE: .../alarm-rtl3.vhdl
FSM: alarm-rtl3
STATEMENT or DECLARATION: line8
.../alarm-rtl3.vhdl (line 8)
Context of the message is:
(key And trip And memoryofdriver__state(0))
```

This message tells us that the assert statement that we included may be triggered under a certain condition: (key And trip And state(0)). The prefix 'memoryofdriver__' is used by the theorem prover to refer to the memory element used for `state(0)`. The state `'off'` in the reference model corresponds to `state(0)` in the encoding that the finite-state machine compiler has used (and also to `state(0)` in the derived model). From this message we can isolate the problem to the following `case` statement (the line numbers follow the original code in `architecture RTL`):

```
case State is                                          --6
  when Off => if Key = '1' then State <= Armed; end if;    --7
  when Armed => if Key = '0' then State <= Off;            --8
                elsif Trip = '1' then State <= Ringing;    --9
                end if;                                     --10
  when Ringing => if Key = '0' then State <= Off; end if;  --11
end case;                                                   --12
```

When we start in state `Off` and the two inputs are `Trip = '1'` and `Key = '1'`, we go to state `Armed`, and not to state `Ringing`. On the subsequent clock cycle we will go state `Ringing`, but only if `Trip` does not change. Since we have all seen "Mission Impossible" and the burglar who exits the top-secret computer room at the Pentagon at the exact moment the alarm is set, we know this is perfectly possible and the software is warning us of this fact. Continuing on, we get the following results from the theorem prover:

```
Prove (Axiom_ref => (Assert_ref => Assert_der))
Formula is NOT VALID
But is VALID under Assert Context of alarm-rtl3
```

We included the `assert` statement in the reference model (`architecture RTL`) but not in the derived model (`architecture Gates`). Now we are really mixed up: The `assertion` statement in the reference model says one thing, but the `case` statement in the reference model describes another. The theorem prover retorts: "The axioms of the reference model do not imply that the assertions of the reference model imply the assertions of the derived model." Translation: "These two architectures differ in some way." However, if we assume that the assertion is true (despite what the `case` statement says) then the formula is true. The prover is also saying: "Make up your mind, you cannot have it both ways." The prover goes on to explain the differences between the two representations:

```
***Difference is:
(Not state(1) And key And state(0) And trip)
There are 1 cubes and 4 literals in the complete equation

***Local Variable Assert_der is:
Not key Or Not state(0) Or Not trip
There are 3 cubes and 3 literals in the complete equation

***Local Variable Assert_ref is: 1

***Local Variable Axiom_ref is:
Not state(1) Or Not state(0)
```

There are 2 cubes and 2 literals in the complete equation

```
formulas to be proved:      8
formulas proved VALID:      7
formulas VALID under assert context of der.model:     1
```

Study these messages hard and you will see that the differences between the two models are consistent with our explanation.

13.8.4 Completing a Proof

To fix the problem we change the code as follows:

```
...
case State is
   when Off =>      if Key = '1' then
                       if Trip = '1' then NextState <= Ringing;
                       else NextState <= Armed;
                       end if;
                    end if;
   when Armed => if Key = '0' then NextState <= Off;
                    elsif Trip = '1' then NextState <= Ringing;
                    end if;
   when Ringing => if Key = '0' then NextState <= Off; end if;
end case;
...
```

This results in a minor change in the synthesized netlist,

```
g2: Inverter port map ( i => State(0), z => s1 );
g3: NAnd2    port map ( a => s1, b => State(1), z => s2 );
g4: Inverter port map ( i => s2, z => Ring );
g5: NAnd2    port map ( a => State(1), b => Key, z => s0 );
g6: NAnd3    port map ( a => Trip, b => s1, c => Key, z => s3 );
g7: NAnd2    port map ( a => s0, b => s3, z => NextState(1) );
g8: Inverter port map ( i => Key, z => NextState(0) );
state_ff_b0: DFF port map ( d => NextState(0), c => Clock, q =>
State(0), qn => open );
state_ff_b1: DFF port map ( d => NextState(1), c => Clock, q =>
State(1), qn => open );
```

Repeating the formal verification confirms and formally proves that the derived model will operate correctly. Strictly, we say that the operation of the derived model is implied by the reference model.

13.9 Switch-Level Simulation

The **switch-level simulator** is a more detailed level of simulation than we have discussed so far. Figure 13.1 shows the circuit schematic of a **true single-phase flip-flop** using **true single-phase clocking** (**TSPC**). TSPC has been used in some full-custom ICs to attempt to save area and power.

(a)   (b)

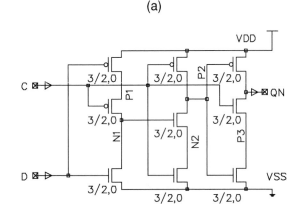

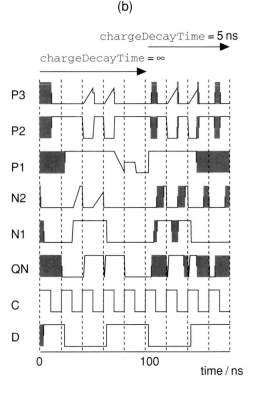

FIGURE 13.1 A TSPC (true single-phase clock) flip-flop. (a) The schematic (all devices are W/L = 3/2) created using a Compass schematic-entry tool. (b) The switch-level simulation results (Compass MixSim). The parameter `chargeDecayTime` sets the time after which the simulator sets an undriven node to an invalid logic level (shown shaded).

In a CMOS logic cell every node is driven to a strong '1' or a strong '0'. This is not true in TSPC, some nodes are left floating, so we ask the switch-level simulator to model charge leakage or charge decay (normally we need not worry about this low-level device issue). Figure 13.1 shows the waveform results. After five clock cycles, or 100 ns, we set the charge decay time to 5 ns. We notice two things. First, some of the node waveforms have values that are between logic '0' and '1'. Second, there are shaded areas on some node waveforms that represent the fact that, during the period of time marked, the logic value of the node is unknown. We can see that initially, before $t = 100$ ns (while we neglect the effects of charge decay), the circuit functions as a flip-flop. After $t = 100$ ns (when we begin including the effects of charge decay), the simulator tells us that this circuit may not function correctly. It is unlikely that all the charge would leak from a node in 5 ns, but we could not stop the clock in a design that uses a TSPC flip-flop. In ASIC design we do not use dangerous techniques such as TSPC and therefore do not normally need to use switch-level simulation.

A switch-level simulator keeps track of voltage levels as well as logic levels, and it may do this in several ways. The simulator may use a large possible set of discrete values or the value of a node may be allowed to vary continuously.

13.10 Transistor-Level Simulation

Sometimes we need to simulate a logic circuit with more accuracy than provided by switch-level simulation. In this case we turn to simulators that can solve circuit equations exactly, given models for the nonlinear transistors, and predict the analog behavior of the node voltages and currents in continuous time. This type of **transistor-level simulation** or **circuit-level simulation** is costly in computer time. It is impossible to simulate more than a few hundred logic cells using a circuit-level simulator. Virtually all circuit-level simulators used for ASIC design are commercial versions of the **SPICE** (or **Spice**, **Simulation Program with Integrated Circuit Emphasis**) developed at UC Berkeley.

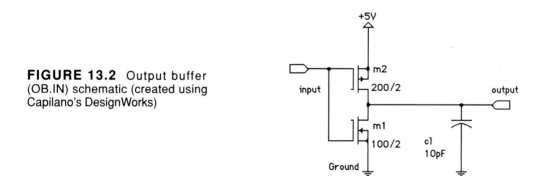

FIGURE 13.2 Output buffer (OB.IN) schematic (created using Capilano's DesignWorks)

13.10.1 A PSpice Example

Figure 13.2 shows the schematic for the output section of a CMOS I/O buffer driving a 10 pF output capacitor representing an off-chip load. The **PSpice** input file that follows is called a **deck** (from the days of punched cards):

```
OB September 5, 1996 17:27
.TRAN/OP 1ns 20ns
.PROBE
 cl  output  Ground  10pF
```

```
VIN   input   Ground    PWL(0us 5V 10ns 5V 12ns 0V 20ns 0V)
VGround   0   Ground    DC 0V
Vdd   +5V   0    DC 5V
m1   output   input   Ground Ground NMOS W=100u L=2u
m2   output   input   +5V +5V PMOS W=200u L=2u
.model nmos nmos level=2 vto=0.78 tox=400e-10 nsub=8.0e15 xj=-0.15e-6
+ ld=0.20e-6 uo=650 ucrit=0.62e5 uexp=0.125 vmax=5.1e4 neff=4.0
+ delta=1.4 rsh=37 cgso=2.95e-10 cgdo=2.95e-10 cj=195e-6 cjsw=500e-12
+ mj=0.76 mjsw=0.30 pb=0.80
.model pmos pmos level=2 vto=-0.8 tox=400e-10 nsub=6.0e15 xj=-0.05e-6
+ ld=0.20e-6 uo=255 ucrit=0.86e5 uexp=0.29 vmax=3.0e4 neff=2.65
+ delta=1 rsh=125 cgso=2.65e-10 cgdo=2.65e-10 cj=250e-6 cjsw=350e-12
+ mj=0.535 mjsw=0.34 pb=0.80
.end
```

Figure 13.3 shows the input and output waveforms as well as the current flowing in the devices. We can quickly check our circuit simulation results as follows. The total charge transferred to the 10 pF load capacitor as it charges from 0 V to 5 V is 50 pC (equal to $5 \, V \times 10 \, pF$). This total charge should be very nearly equal to the integral of the drain current of the pull-up (p-channel) transistor I_L(m2). We can get a quick estimate of the integral of the current by approximating the area under the waveform for id(m2) in Figure 13.3 as a triangle—half the base (about 12 ns) multiplied by the height (about 8 mA), so that

$$\int_{10\text{ns}}^{22\text{ns}} I_L(m2) \, dt = 0.5\,(8\text{mA})\,(12\text{ns}) \approx 50\text{pC} = 5\,(10\text{pF}) \,. \tag{13.28}$$

Notice that the two estimates for the transferred charge are equal.

Next, we can check the time derivative of the pull-up current. (We can also do this by using the Probe program and requesting a plot of did(m2); the symbol dn represents the time derivative of quantity n for Probe. The symbol id(m2) requests Probe to plot the drain current of m2.) The maximum derivative should be roughly equal to the maximum change of the drain current ($\Delta I_L(m2) = 8$ mA) divided by the time taken for that change (about $\Delta t = 2$ ns from Figure 13.3) or

$$\frac{|\Delta I_L(m2)|}{\Delta t} = \frac{8\text{mA}}{2\text{ns}} = 4 \times 10^6 \text{As}^{-1} \,. \tag{13.29}$$

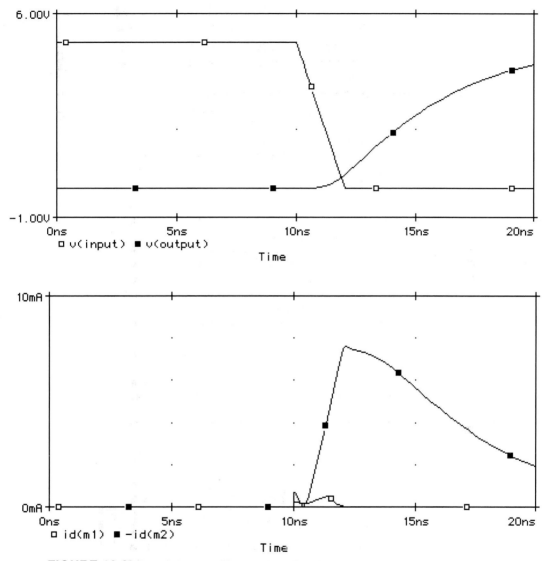

FIGURE 13.3 Output Buffer (OB.IN). (Top) The input and output voltage waveforms. (Bottom) The current flowing in the drains of the output devices.

The large time derivative of the device current, here $4 \, \mathrm{MAs}^{-1}$, causes problems in high-speed CMOS I/O. This sharp change in current must flow in the supply leads to the chip, and through the inductance associated with the bonding wires to the chip which may be of the order of 10 nanohenrys. An electromotive force (emf), V_P, will be generated in the inductance as follows,

$$V_P = -L\frac{dI}{dt} = -10\text{nH}\,(4{\times}10^6)\,\text{As}^{-1} = -40\text{ mV}\,. \tag{13.30}$$

The result is a glitch in the power supply voltage during the buffer output transient. This is known as **supply bounce** or **ground bounce**. To limit the amount of bounce we may do one of two things:

1. Limit the power supply lead inductance (minimize L)

2. Reduce the current pulse (minimize dI/dt)

We can work on the first solution by careful design of the packages and by using parallel bonding wires (inductors add in series, reduce in parallel).

13.10.2 SPICE Models

Table 13.14 shows the SPICE parameters for the typical 0.5 µm CMOS process (0.6 µm drawn gate length), G5, that we used in Section 2.1. These LEVEL = 3 parameters may be used with Spice3, PSpice, and HSPICE (see also Table 2.1 and Figure 2.4).

There are several levels of the SPICE MOSFET models, the following is a simplified overview (a huge number of confusing variations, fixes, and options have been added to these models—see Meta Software's HSPICE User's Manual, Vol. II, for a comprehensive description [1996]):

1. LEVEL = 1 (**Schichman–Hodges model**) uses the simple square-law I_{DS}–V_{DS} relation we derived in Section 2.1 (Eqs. 2.9 and 2.12).

2. LEVEL = 2 (**Grove–Frohman model**) uses the 3/2 power equations that result if we include the variation of threshold voltage across the channel.

3. LEVEL = 3 (**empirical model**) uses empirical equations.

4. The UCB **BSIM1** model (~1984, PSpice LEVEL = 4, HSPICE LEVEL = 13) focuses on modeling observed device data rather than on device physics. A commercial derivative (HSPICE LEVEL = 28) is widely used by ASIC vendors.

5. The UCB **BSIM2** model (~1991, the commercial derivative is HSPICE LEVEL = 39) improves modeling of subthreshold conduction.

6. The UCB **BSIM3** model (~1995, the commercial derivative is HSPICE LEVEL = 49) corrects potential nonphysical behavior of earlier models.

Table 13.15 shows the BSIM1 parameters (in the PSpice LEVEL = 4 format) for the G5 process. The **Berkeley short-channel IGFET model (BSIM)** family models capacitance in terms of charge. In Sections 2.1 and 3.2 we treated the gate–drain

TABLE 13.14 SPICE transistor model parameters (LEVEL = 3).

SPICE parameter	n-channel value	p-channel value (if different)	Units	Explanation
CGBO	4.0E-10	3.8E-10	Fm^{-1}	Gate–bulk overlap capacitance (CGBoh, not CGBzero)
CGDO	3.0E-10	2.4E-10	Fm^{-1}	Gate–drain overlap capacitance (CGDoh, not CGDzero)
CGSO	3.0E-10	2.4E-10	Fm^{-1}	Gate–source overlap capacitance (CGSoh, not CGSzero)
CJ	5.6E-4	9.3E-4	Fm^{-2}	Junction area capacitance
CJSW	5E-11	2.9E-10	Fm^{-1}	Junction sidewall capacitance
DELTA	0.7	0.29	m	Narrow-width factor for adjusting threshold voltage
ETA	3.7E-2	2.45E-2	1	Static-feedback factor for adjusting threshold voltage
GAMMA	0.6	0.47	V$^{0.5}$	Body-effect factor
KAPPA	2.9E-2	8	V^{-1}	Saturation-field factor (channel-length modulation)
KP	2E-4	4.9E-5	AV^{-2}	Intrinsic transconductance (μC_{ox}, not $0.5\mu C_{ox}$)
LD	5E-8	3.5E-8	m	Lateral diffusion into channel
LEVEL	3		none	Empirical model
MJ	0.56	0.47	1	Junction area exponent
MJSW	0.52	0.50	1	Junction sidewall exponent
NFS	6E11	6.5E11	cm^{-2}V^{-1}	Fast surface-state density
NSUB	1.4E17	8.5E16	cm^{-3}	Bulk surface doping
PB	1	1	V	Junction area contact potential
PHI	0.7		V	Surface inversion potential
RSH	2		Ω/ square	Sheet resistance of source and drain
THETA	0.27	0.29	V^{-1}	Mobility-degradation factor
TOX	1E-8		m	Gate-oxide thickness
TPG	1	-1	none	Type of polysilicon gate
U0	550	135	cm^{2}V^{-1}s^{-1}	Low-field bulk carrier mobility (Uzero, not Uoh)
XJ	0.2E-6		m	Junction depth
VMAX	2E5	2.5E5	ms^{-1}	Saturated carrier velocity
VTO	0.65	-0.92	V	Zero-bias threshold voltage (VTzero, not VToh)

Meta Software's HSPICE User's Manual [1996], p. 15-36 and pp.16-13 to 16-15, explains these parameters. Note that m or M both represent milli or 10^{-3} in SPICE, not mega or 10^6 (u or U = micro or 10^{-6} and so on).

TABLE 13.15   PSpice parameters for process G5 (PSpice LEVEL = 4).

```
.MODEL NM1 NMOS LEVEL=4                      .MODEL PM1 PMOS LEVEL=4
+ VFB=-0.7, LVFB=-4E-2, WVFB=5E-2            + VFB=-0.2, LVFB=4E-2, WVFB=-0.1
+ PHI=0.84, LPHI=0, WPHI=0                   + PHI=0.83, LPHI=0, WPHI=0
+ K1=0.78, LK1=-8E-4, WK1=-5E-2             + K1=0.35, LK1=-7E-02, WK1=0.2
+ K2=2.7E-2, LK2=5E-2, WK2=-3E-2            + K2=-4.5E-2, LK2=9E-3, WK2=4E-2
+ ETA=-2E-3, LETA=2E-02, WETA=-5E-3         + ETA=-1E-2, LETA=2E-2, WETA=-4E-4
+ MUZ=600, DL=0.2, DW=0.5                    + MUZ=140, DL=0.2, DW=0.5
+ U0=0.33, LU0=0.1, WU0=-0.1                 + U0=0.2, LU0=6E-2, WU0=-6E-2
+ U1=3.3E-2, LU1=3E-2, WU1=-1E-2            + U1=1E-2, LU1=1E-2, WU1=7E-4
+ X2MZ=9.7, LX2MZ=-6, WX2MZ=7               + X2MZ=7, LX2MZ=-2, WX2MZ=1
+ X2E=4.4E-4, LX2E=-3E-3, WX2E=9E-4         + X2E= 5E-5, LX2E=-1E-3, WX2E=-2E-4
+ X3E=-5E-5, LX3E=-2E-3, WX3E=-1E-3         + X3E=8E-4, LX3E=-2E-4, WX3E=-1E-3
+ X2U0=-1E-2, LX2U0=-1E-3, WX2U0=5E-3       + X2U0=9E-3, LX2U0=-2E-3, WX2U0=2E-3
+ X2U1=-1E-3, LX2U1=1E-3, WX2U1=-7E-4       + X2U1=6E-4, LX2U1=5E-4, WX2U1=3E-4
+ MUS=700, LMUS=-50, WMUS=7                  + MUS=150, LMUS=10, WMUS=4
+ X2MS=-6E-2, LX2MS=1, WX2MS=4              + X2MS=6, LX2MS=-0.7, WX2MS=2
+ X3MS=9, LX3MS=2, WX3MS=-6                 + X3MS=-1E-2, LX3MS=2, WX3MS=1
+ X3U1=9E-3, LX3U1=2E-4, WX3U1=-5E-3        + X3U1=-1E-3, LX3U1=-5E-4, WX3U1=1E-3
+ TOX=1E-2, TEMP=25, VDD=5                   + TOX=1E-2, TEMP=25, VDD=5
+ CGDO=3E-10, CGSO=3E-10, CGBO=4E-10        + CGDO=2.4E-10, CGSO=2.4E-10, CGBO=3.8E-10
+ XPART=1                                    + XPART=1
+ N0=1, LN0=0, WN0=0                         + N0=1, LN0=0, WN0=0
+ NB=0, LNB=0, WNB=0                         + NB=0, LNB=0, WNB=0
+ ND=0, LND=0, WND=0                         + ND=0, LND=0, WND=0
* n+ diffusion                              * p+ diffusion
+ RSH=2.1, CJ=3.5E-4, CJSW=2.9E-10          + RSH=2, CJ=9.5E-4, CJSW=2.5E-10
+ JS=1E-8, PB=0.8, PBSW=0.8                  + JS=1E-8, PB=0.85, PBSW=0.85
+ MJ=0.44, MJSW=0.26, WDF=0                  + MJ=0.44, MJSW=0.24, WDF=0
*, DS=0                                      *, DS=0
```

PSpice LEVEL = 4 is almost exactly equivalent to the UCB BSIM1 model, and closely equivalent to the HSPICE LEVEL = 13 model (see Table 14-1 and pp. 16–86 to 16–89 in Meta Software's HSPICE User's Manual [1996].

capacitance, C_{GD}, for example, as if it were a **reciprocal capacitance**, and could be written assuming there was charge associated with the gate, Q_G, and the drain, Q_D, as follows:

$$C_{GD} = -\frac{\delta Q_G}{\delta V_D} = C_{DG} = -\frac{\delta Q_D}{\delta V_G}. \tag{13.31}$$

Equation 13.31 (the **Meyer model**) would be true if the gate and drain formed a parallel plate capacitor and $Q_G = -Q_D$, but they do not. In general, $Q_G \neq -Q_D$ and Eq. 13.31 is not true. In an MOS transistor we have four regions of charge: Q_G

(gate), Q_D (channel charge associated with the drain), Q_S (channel charge associated with the drain), and Q_B (charge in the bulk depletion region). These charges are not independent, since

$$Q_G + Q_D + Q_S + Q_B = 0. \tag{13.32}$$

We can form a 4×4 matrix, **M**, whose entries are $\delta Q_i / \delta V_j$, where $V_j = V_G$, V_S, V_D, and V_B. Then $C_{ii} = M_{ii}$ are the terminal capacitances; and $C_{ij} = -M_{ij}$, where $i \neq j$, is a **transcapacitance**. Equation 13.32 forces the sum of each column of **M** to be zero. Since the charges depend on voltage differences, there are only three independent voltages (V_{GB}, V_{DB}, and V_{SB}, for example) and each row of **M** must sum to zero. Thus, we have nine (=16 – 7) independent entries in the matrix **M**. In general, C_{ij} is not necessarily equal to C_{ji}. For example, using PSpice and a LEVEL = 4 BSIM model, there are nine independent partial derivatives, printed as follows:

```
Derivatives of gate (dQg/dVxy) and bulk (dQb/dVxy) charges
DQGDVGB      1.04E-14
DQGDVDB     -1.99E-15
DQGDVSB     -7.33E-15
DQDDVGB     -1.99E-15
DQDDVDB      1.99E-15
DQDDVSB      0.00E+00
DQBDVGB     -7.51E-16
DQBDVDB      0.00E+00
DQBDVSB     -2.72E-15
```

From these derivatives we may compute six **nonreciprocal capacitances**:

$$
\begin{aligned}
C_{GB} &= \delta Q_G / \delta V_{GB} + \delta Q_G / \delta V_{DB} + \delta Q_G / \delta V_{SB} \\
C_{BG} &= -\delta Q_B / \delta V_{GB} \\
C_{GS} &= -\delta Q_G / \delta V_{SB} \\
C_{SG} &= \delta Q_G / \delta V_{GB} + \delta Q_B / \delta V_{GB} + \delta Q_D / \delta V_{GB} \\
C_{GD} &= -\delta Q_G / \delta V_{DB} \\
C_{DG} &= -\delta Q_D / \delta V_{GB}
\end{aligned}
\tag{13.33}
$$

and three terminal capacitances:

$$
\begin{aligned}
C_{GG} &= \delta Q_G / \delta V_{GB} \\
C_{DD} &= \delta Q_D / \delta V_{DB} \\
C_{SS} &= -(\delta Q_G / \delta V_{SB} + \delta Q_B / \delta V_{SB} + \delta Q_D / \delta V_{SB})
\end{aligned}
\tag{13.34}
$$

Nonreciprocal transistor capacitances cast a cloud over our analysis of gate capacitance in Section 3.2, but the error we made in neglecting this effect is small compared to the approximations we made in the sections that followed. Even though we now find the theoretical analysis was simplified, the conclusions in our treatment of logical effort and delay modeling are still sound. Sections 7.3 and 9.2 in the book on transistor modeling by Tsividis [1987] describe nonreciprocal capacitance in detail. Pages 15-42 to 15-44 in Vol. II of Meta Software's HSPICE User Manual [1996] also gives an explanation of transcapacitance.

13.11 Summary

We discussed the following types of simulation (from high level to low level):

- Behavioral simulation includes no timing information and can tell you only if your design will not work.

- Prelayout simulation of a structural model can give you estimates of performance, but finding a critical path is difficult because you need to construct input vectors to exercise the model.

- Static timing analysis is the most widely used form of simulation. It is convenient because you do not need to create input vectors. Its limitations are that it can produce false paths—critical paths that may never be activated.

- Formal verification is a powerful adjunct to simulation to compare two different representations and formally prove if they are equal. It cannot prove your design will work.

- Switch-level simulation is required to check the behavior of circuits that may not always have nodes that are driven or that use logic that is not complementary.

- Transistor-level simulation is used when you need to know the analog, rather than the digital, behavior of circuit voltages.

There is a trade-off in accuracy against run time. The high-level simulators are fast but are less accurate.

13.12 Problems

* = Difficult, ** = Very difficult, *** = Extremely difficult

13.1 (Errors, 30 min.) Change `a <= b` to `a >= b` in line 4 in module `reference` in Section 13.2.1. Simulate the testbench (write models for the five logic cell models not shown in Section 13.2.1). How many errors are there, and why? Answer: 56.

13.2 (False paths, 15 min.) The following code forces an output pin to a constant value. Perform a timing analysis on this model and comment on the results.

```
module check_critical_path_2 (a, z);                        //1
input a; output z; supply1 VDD; supply0 VSS;                //2
nd02d0 b1_i3 (.a1(a), .a2(VSS), .zn(z)); // 2-input NAND    //3
endmodule                                                   //4
```

13.3 (Timing loops, 30 min.) The following code models a set–reset latch with feedback to implement a memory element. Perform a timing analysis on this model and comment on the results.

```
module check_critical_path_3 (s, r, q, qn);                //1
input s, r; output q, qn; supply1 VDD; supply0 VSS;        //2
nr02d0 b1_i1 (.a1(s), .a2(qn), .zn(q)); // 2-input NOR     //3
nr02d0 b1_i2 (.a1(r), .a2(q), .zn(qn)); // 2-input NOR     //4
endmodule                                                   //5
```

13.4 (Simulation script, 30 min.) Perform a gate-level simulation of the comparator/MUX in Section 13.2.3. Write a script to set input values and so on.

13.5 (Verilog loops, 30 min.) Change the index from `integer` to `reg` (width three) in each loop in `testbench.v` from Section 13.2. Explain the simulation result.

13.6 (Verilog time, 30 min.) Remove `'#1'` from line 15 in `testbench.v` from Section 13.2. Explain carefully the simulation result.

13.7 (Infinite loops, 30 min.) Construct an HDL program that loops infinitely on a UNIX machine (with no output file!) and explain how the following helps:

```
<293> ps
  PID TT STAT  TIME COMMAND
...
28920 p1 R     0:30 verilog infinite_loop.v
...
<294> kill -9 28920
```

13.8 (Verilog graphics, 30 min.) Experiment with graphical waveform dumps from Verilog. For example, in VeriWell you need to include the following statement:

```
initial $dumpvars;
```

The file Dump file `veriwell.dmp` should appear. Next, select `File...`, then `Convert Dumpvar...` Write a cheat sheet on how to use and display simulation results from a hierarchical model.

13.9 (Unknowns, 30 min.) Explain, using truth tables, the function of primitive G6 in module mx21d1 from Section 13.2.1. *Hint:* Consider unknown propagation. Eliminate primitive G6 as follows and use simulation to compare the two models:

```
not G3(N3,s); and G4(N4,i0,N3), G5(N5,s,i1); or G7(z,N4,N5);
```

13.10 (Data books, 10 min.) Explain carefully what you safely can and cannot deduce from the data book figures in Table 13.16.

TABLE 13.16   Input capacitances—AOIabcd family (Problem 13.10).

	1X drive	2X drive	4X drive
Area	0.034 pF	0.069 pF	0.138 pF
Performance	0.145 pF	0.294 pF	0.588 pF

13.11 (Synthesis, 30 min.) Synthesize `comp_mux_rrr.v` in Section 13.7. What type and how many sequential elements result? *Answer:* 16.

13.12 (Place and route, 60 min.) Route both `comp_mux.v` (Section 13.2) and `comp_mux_rrr.v` (Section 13.7) using an FPGA. What fraction of the chip is used? *Answer:* For an Actel 1415 FPGA, `comp_mux_rrr.v` uses about 10 percent of the available logic.

13.13 (Timing analysis, 60 min.) Perform timing analysis on a routed version of `comp_mux.v` from Section 13.2. Use worst-case commercial conditions.

13.14 (***NAND gate delay, 120 min.) The following example of a six-input NAND gate illustrates the difference between transistor-level and other levels of simulation. A designer once needed a delay element (do not ask why!). Looking at the data book they found a six-input NAND gate had the right delay, but they did not know what to do with the other five inputs. So they tied all six inputs together. This is a horrendous error, but why? *Hint:* You might have to simulate a structural model using both digital simulation and a circuit-level simulation in order to explain.

13.15 (Logic systems, 30 min.) Compare the 12 value system of Table 13.5 with the IEEE 1164 standard and explain: Which logic values are equivalent in both systems, which logic values have no equivalents, and why there is a difference in the number of values (12 versus 9) when both systems have the same number of logic levels and logic strengths?

13.16 (VHDL overloaded functions, 30 min.) Write a definition for the type `stdlogic_table` used in the and function in Section 13.3.2,

```
constant and_table:stdlogic_table
```

Compile, simulate, and test the and function.

13.17 (**Scheduling transactions in VHDL, 60 min.) (From an example in the VHDL LRM.) Consider this assignment to an integer S in a VHDL process:

```
S <= reject 15 ns inertial 12 after 20 ns, 18 after 41 ns;
```

Assume that at the time this signal assignment is executed, the driver for s in the process has the following contents (the first entry is the current driving value):

1	2	2	12	5	8
now	+3ns	+12ns	+13ns	+20ns	+42ns

This is called the **projected output waveform** (times are relative to the current time). The LRM states the rule for updating a projected output waveform consists of the deletion of zero or more previously computed transactions (called old transactions) from the projected output waveform, and the addition of the new transactions, as follows:

1. All old transactions that are projected to occur at or after the time at which the earliest new transaction is projected to occur are deleted from the projected output waveform.

2. The new transactions are then appended to the projected output waveform in the order of their projected occurrence.

If the initial delay is inertial delay, the projected output waveform is further modified as follows:

1. All of the new transactions are marked.

2. An old transaction is marked if the time at which it is projected to occur is less than the time at which the first new transaction is projected to occur minus the pulse rejection limit.

3. For each remaining unmarked, old transaction, the old transaction is marked if it immediately precedes a marked transaction and its value component is the same as that of the marked transaction.

4. The transaction that determines the current value of the driver is marked.

5. All unmarked transactions (all of which are old transactions) are deleted from the projected output waveform.

For the purposes of marking transactions, any two successive null transactions in a projected output waveform are considered to have the same value component. Using these rules compute the new projected output waveform.

13.18 (***awk, 120 min.) Write an awk program with the following specification to compare two simulations:

```
# program to check two files with the format:
#    time signal value
# to check agreement within time tolerance delta (by default 0.1)
#
# Use: check file1 file2 [delta]
```

13.19 (VITAL, 60 min.) Simulate the model, sdf_testbench, shown in Section 13.5.5, with and without back-annotation timing information in SDF_b.sdf.

13.20 (Formal verification, 60 min.) Write a cheat sheet explaining how to run your formal verification tool. Repeat the example in Section 13.8.1.

13.21 (***Beetle problem) (Based on a problem by Seitz.) A planet has many geological gem mazes: A maze covers a square km or so, on a 10 mm grid; a maze cell is 10 mm by 10 mm and gems lie at cell centers; there is a path from every maze cell to every other; on average one in 64 cells has an overhead opening; on average one in seven cells has a single gem; there are no gems under overhead openings.

You are to design a gem-mining beetle ASIC with the following inputs: a nominal 1 MHz single-phase clock, CLK; wall sensors: WL, WR, WF, WB (wall to left/right/forward/behind); light sensors: LL, LR, LF, LB (light left/right/forward/behind); low-battery indicator: BLOW; gem sensor: GEM (directly over a gem); opening sensor: OPEN (when under an opening).

All signals are active high and the light sensor outputs are mutually exclusive. The beetle ASIC must produce the following (mutually exclusive) signals: move forward, MF; move backward, MB; turn 90 degrees clockwise, TC; turn 90 degrees anticlockwise, TA; pick up a gem, PICKUP; throw gem up and out of overhead opening, THROWUP; jump up to surface and shut down, SHUTUP.

The beetle specifications and limitations are as follows: Beetles are dropped into the maze to find the gems; beetles must find gems and carry them to an opening; beetles can eject gems through openings; beetles can carry only one gem at a time.

A beetle move is one of the following: taking one step (moving to an adjacent cell), turning 90 degrees, picking up a gem, ejecting a gem, jumping out of opening—all take the same time and energy. A battery can provide energy for about 200 moves before the low-battery signal comes on. After the low-battery warning is signaled the battery has energy for 50 moves to find an overhead opening, and the beetle must then eject itself for recharging. The cost of the beetle determines that we would like the probability of losing a beetle be below 0.01.

The following describes a state machine to drive a beetle. Jim Rowson used a state machine language that he developed—along with the first CAD tool that could automatically create state machines:

```
# Jim Rowson's beetle
sm smbtl;
clock clk;
reset res                        --> resetState;
inputs WL WL WR WB GEM LF LL LR LB OPEN BLOW;
outputs MF=0 MB=0 TC=0 TA=0 PICKUP=0 THROWUP=0 SHUTUP=0;
outputs haveAgem SHUTUP;
let getout = (BLOW|haveAgem) & (LL|LF|LR|LB);

state resetState                 --> searchState haveAgem=0 SHUTUP=0;
state searchState
    BLOW & OPEN                  --> jumpState,
    haveAgem & OPEN              --> ejectstate,
```

```
      getout & LL             --> turnLstate,
      getout & LF             --> goFwdState,
      getout & LR             --> turnRstate,
      getout & LB             --> turnAroundState,
      !haveAgem & GEM         --> getGemState,
      !WL                     --> turnLstate,
      !WF                     --> goFwdState,
      !WR                     --> turnRstate,
      !WB                     --> turnAroundState;
state goFwdState              --> MF searchState;
state turnLState             --> TA goFwdState;
state turnRState             --> TC goFwdState;
state turnAroundState        --> TC turnAgainState;
state ejectState             --> THROWUP !haveAgem searchState;
state jumpState              --> SHUTUP shutdownState;
state getGemState            --> PICKUP haveAgem searchState;
state shutDownState          --> SHUTUP shutDownState;
state turnAgainState         --> TC searchState;
end
```

a. (120 min.) Draw Jim's state machine diagram and translate it to an HDL.

b. (120 min.) Build a model for the maze that will work with Jim's design.

c. (120 min.) Simulate the operation of Jim's beetle using your maze model.

d. (Hours) Can you do better than Jim?

13.22 (Switch-level simulation, 120 min.) Perform the switch-level simulation shown in Section 13.9.

13.23 (**Simulation, 60 min.) (From a question posed by Ray Ryan to the VITAL timing group.) Suppose we have a two-input NAND gate (inputs I1 and I2, and output Q) with separate path delays from I1 to Q and from I2 to Q with delays as follows:

```
tpd_I1_Q =>
( tr01 => 10 ns, -- falling I1 -> rising  Q
  tr10 => 7 ns ) -- rising  I1 -> falling Q
tpd_I2_Q =>
( tr01 => 5 ns, -- falling I2 -> rising  Q
  tr10 => 3 ns ) -- rising  I1 -> falling Q
```

a. For inputs: (I1:0->1, 9 ns; I2:0->1, 10 ns), should Q fall at:

12 ns, 13 ns, 16 ns, 17 ns or other?

b. For inputs: (I2:0->1, 9 ns; I1:0->1, 10 ns), should Q fall at:

12 ns, 13 ns, 16 ns, 17 ns or other?

c. For inputs: (I2:0->1, 10 ns; I1:0->1, 10 ns), should Q fall at:

13 ns, 15 ns, 17 ns, 20 ns or other?

d. For inputs: (I1:1->0, 9 ns; I2:1->0, 10 ns), should Q rise at:

14 ns, 15 ns, 19 ns, 20 ns or other?

e. For inputs: (I2:1->0, 9 ns; I1:1->0, 10 ns), should Q rise at:

14 ns, 15 ns, 19 ns, 20 ns or other?

f. For inputs: (I1:0->1, 10 ns; I2:0->1, 10 ns), should Q fall at:

13 ns, 15 ns, 17 ns, 20 ns or other?

In each case explain your answer using actual simulation results to help you.

13.24 (VHDL trace, 30 min.) Write a simple testbench and trace through the following VHDL behavioral simulation.

```
library IEEE;                                               --1
use IEEE.std_logic_1164.all; use IEEE.NUMERIC_STD.all;      --2

entity comp_mux is                                          --3
  generic (TPD : TIME := 1 ns);                             --4
  port (A, B : in STD_LOGIC_VECTOR (2 downto 0);            --5
  Y : out STD_LOGIC_VECTOR (2 downto 0));                   --6
end;                                                        --7

architecture Behave of comp_mux is                          --8
begin                                                       --9
  Y <= A after TPD when (A <= B) else B after TPD;          --10
end;                                                        --11
```

13.25 (VHDL simulator, 30 min.) Explain the steps in using your VHDL simulator. Are there separate compile, analyze, elaborate, initialization, and simulate phases. Where and when do they occur. How do you know?

13.26 (Debugging VHDL, 60 min.) Correct the errors in the following code:

```
entity counter8 is port (
  rset, updn, clock : in bit; carry : out bit; count : buffer integer
range 0 to 255 );
end counter8;

architecture behave of counter8 is
begin process
  begin
  wait until clock'event and clock = '1';
  if (rset = '1') then count <= 0; carry <= '0';
  else case updn
    when '1' => count <= count + 1;
    if (count = 255) then carry <= '1'; else carry <= '0'; end if;
    when '0' => count <= count - 1;
    if (count = 0) then carry <= 1; else carry <= 0; end if;
    end case;
  end if;
end process;
end behave;
```

13.27 (***VITAL flip-flop) The following VITAL code models a D flip-flop:

```
LIBRARY ieee; USE ieee.Std_Logic_1164.all;                    --1
USE ieee.Vital_Timing.all; USE ieee.Vital_Primitives.all;     --2
ENTITY dff IS                                                  --3
  GENERIC (                                                    --4
  TimingChecksOn : BOOLEAN := TRUE;                            --5
  XGenerationOn : BOOLEAN := TRUE;                             --6
  InstancePath : STRING := "*";                                --7
  tipd_Clock :  DelayType01 := (0 ns, 0 ns);                   --8
  tipd_Data :  DelayType01 := (0 ns, 0 ns);                    --9
  tsetup_Data_Clock : DelayType01 := (0 ns, 0 ns);            --10
  thold_Data_Clock : DelayType01 := (0 ns, 0 ns);            --11
  tpd_Clock_Q : DelayType01 := (0 ns, 0 ns);                 --12
  tpd_Clock_Qbar : DelayType01 := (0 ns, 0 ns));             --13
  PORT (Clock, Data: Std_Logic; Q,Qbar:OUT Std_Logic);      --14
END dff;                                                      --15

ARCHITECTURE Gate OF dff IS                                    --1
  ATTRIBUTE Vital_Level1 of gate : ARCHITECTURE IS TRUE;       --2
  SIGNAL Clock_ipd : Std_Logic := 'X';                         --3
  SIGNAL Data_ipd  : Std_Logic := 'X';                         --4
BEGIN                                                          --5
Wire_Delay:BLOCK BEGIN --   INPUT PATH DELAYs                  --6
  VitalPropagateWireDelay                                      --7
    (Clock_ipd, Clock, VitalExtendToFillDelay(tipd_Clock));    --8
  VitalPropagateWireDelay                                      --9
    (Data_ipd, Data, VitalExtendToFillDelay(tipd_Data));      --10
END BLOCK;                                                    --11
VitalBehavior : PROCESS (Clock_ipd, Data_ipd)                --12
  CONSTANT Dff_tab:VitalStateTableType:= (                   --13
--Vio  CLOCK DATA  IQ    Q    QBAR                            --14
( 'X',  '-',  '-',  '-',  'X',  'X' ), -- Timing Violation    --15
( '-',  '\',  '0',  '-',  '0',  '1' ), -- Active Clock Edge   --16
( '-',  '\',  '1',  '-',  '1',  '0' ),                        --17
( '-',  '\',  'X',  '-',  'X',  'X' ),                        --18
( '-',  '-',  '0',  '0',  '0',  '1' ), -- X Reduction         --19
( '-',  '-',  '1',  '1',  '1',  '0' ),                        --20
( '-',  'D',  '-',  '-',  'X',  'X' ), -- X Generation        --21
( '-',  'B',  '-',  '-',  'S',  'S' ), -- Non-Active Clock Edge --22
( '-',  'X',  '-',  '-',  'S',  'S' ));                       --23
-- Anything else generates X on Q and QBAR                    --24
-- Timing Check Results                                       --25
  VARIABLE Tviol_Data_Clock : X01 := '0';                    --26
  VARIABLE Tmkr_Data_Clock  : TimeMarkerType;                --27
-- Functionality Results                                      --28
  VARIABLE Violation:X01:='0';                               --29
  VARIABLE PrevData:Std_Logic_Vector(1 to 3):=(OTHERS=>'X'); --30
```

```
        VARIABLE Results:Std_Logic_Vector(1 to 2):=(OTHERS =>'X');    --31
        ALIAS Q_zd:Std_Logic IS Results(1);                           --32
        ALIAS Qbar_zd:Std_Logic IS Results(2);                        --33
    -- Output Glitch Detection Variables                              --34
        VARIABLE Q_GlitchData : GlitchDataType;                       --35
        VARIABLE Qbar_GlitchData : GlitchDataType;                    --36
    BEGIN --   Timing Check Section                                   --37
        IF (TimingChecksOn) THEN                                      --38
        VitalTimingCheck (                                            --39
        Data_ipd, "Data", Clock_ipd, "Clock",                        --40
        t_setup_hi => tsetup_Data_Clock(tr01),                       --41
        t_setup_lo => tsetup_Data_Clock(tr10),                       --42
        t_hold_hi => thold_Data_Clock(tr01),                         --43
        t_hold_lo => thold_Data_Clock(tr10),                         --44
        CheckEnabled  => TRUE,                                        --45
        RefTransition => (Clock_ipd = '0'),                          --46
        HeaderMsg => InstancePath & "/DFF",                          --47
        TimeMarker => Tmkr_Data_Clock,                               --48
        Violation => Tviol_Data_Clock);                              --49
        END IF;                                                       --50
    --   Functionality Section                                       --51
        Violation := Tviol_Data_Clock ;                              --52
        VitalStateTable(StateTable => Dff_tab,                       --53
        DataIn => (Violation, Clock_ipd, Data_ipd),                 --54
        NumStates  => 1,                                             --55
        Result => Results,                                           --56
        PreviousDataIn => PrevData);                                 --57
    --   Path Delay Section                                          --58
        VitalPropagatePathDelay (Q, "Q", Q_zd,                      --59
        Paths => (0 => (Clock_ipd'LAST_EVENT,                       --60
        VitalExtendToFillDelay(tpd_Clock_Q), TRUE),                 --61
          1 => (Clock_ipd'LAST_EVENT,                               --62
        VitalExtendToFillDelay(tpd_Clock_Q), TRUE)),                --63
          GlitchData => Q_GlitchData,                               --64
          GlitchMode => MessagePlusX,                               --65
          GlitchKind => OnEvent );                                  --66
        VitalPropagatePathDelay ( Qbar, "Qbar", Qbar_zd,           --67
          Paths => (0 => (Clock_ipd'LAST_EVENT,                     --68
        VitalExtendToFillDelay(tpd_Clock_Qbar), TRUE),             --69
          1 => (Clock_ipd'LAST_EVENT,                               --70
        VitalExtendToFillDelay(tpd_Clock_Qbar), TRUE)),           --71
          GlitchData => Qbar_GlitchData,                           --72
          GlitchMode => MessagePlusX,                              --73
          GlitchKind => OnEvent );                                 --74
        END PROCESS;                                                --75
    END Gate;                                                        --76
```

a. (120 min.) Build a testbench for this model.

b. (30 min.) Simulate and check the model using your testbench.

c. (60 min.) Explain the function of each line.

d. (60 min.) Explain the glitch detection.

e. (120 min.) Explain the unknown propagation behavior.

13.28 (VCD, 30 min.) Verilog can create a **value change dump** (**VCD**) file:

```
module waves; reg clock; integer count;
initial begin clock = 0; count = 0; $dumpvars; #340 $finish; end
always #10 clock = ~ clock;
always begin @ (negedge clock); if (count == 7) count = 0;
    else count = count + 1; end
endmodule
```

A VCD file contains header information, variable definitions, and the value changes for variables [Verilog LRM 15]. Try and explain the format of the file that results.

13.29 (*Formal verification, 60 min.) (Based on an example by Browne, Clarke, Dill, and Mishra.) A designer needs to fold an 8-bit ripple-carry adder into a small space on an ASIC and check the circuit extracted from the layout. With two 8-bit inputs, A and B, and a 1-bit carry Cin, exhaustively testing all possible inputs requires 2^{17} or over 128,000 input vectors. Instead the designer selects a subset of tests. The three tests in Table 13.17 check that all the bits of the output can be '0' or '1'. The two tests in Table 13.18 make sure that the carry propagates through the

TABLE 13.17 Test to check for output toggling (Problem 13.29).

A	00000000	00000000	01010101
B	00000000	11111111	10101010
Cin	0	0	0
Sum	000000000	011111111	011111111

TABLE 13.18 Test to check for carry propagation (Problem 13.29).

A	00000001	11111111
B	11111111	11111111
Cin	0	0
Sum	100000000	111111110

adder, and that the adder can handle the largest numbers. The designer then repeats all of these five tests with the carry-in Cin set to '1' instead of '0'. Next the designer performs a series of 24 tests using the three patterns shown in Table 13.19, with all eight possible combinations of '0' and '1' for x, y, and z. These patterns test each full adder in isolation for all possible sum inputs (A and B) and carry input (Cin). These tests appear comprehensive and reduce the number of vectors required from over 128,000 to 34. Confident, the designer releases the chip for fabrication. Unfortunately, the chip does not work. Which connections between adders did the designer's tests fail to check?

TABLE 13.19   Test with all possible combinations of ' 0 ' and ' 1 ' for x, y, and z (Problem 13.29).

A	xz0xz0xz	z0xz0xz0	0xz0xz0x
B	yz0yz0yz	z0yz0yz0	0yz0yz0y
C	0	z	z
Sum	cs0cs0cs0	z0cs0cs0z	0cs0cs0cs

13.30 (*BSIM1 parameters, 120 min.) SPICE models are tangled webs. For example, there are two formats for the 69 UCB BSIM1 transistor parameters: (1) using parameter names (Table 13.15); and (2) without parameter names (Table 13.20). MOSIS uses format (2). The first 58 parameters starting with VFB (19 rows of 3 parameters plus one, XPART) are the same order in format (1) and (2). Format (2) uses two dummy parameters (zero) following XPART. The final nine parameters (NO to WND) are the same order in both formats. There are 10 additional parameters that follow the *n*- and *p*-channel transistor parameters that model the *n*- and *p*-diffusion, respectively (in the same order in both formats). To complicate things further: (i) HSPICE, SPICE, and PSpice use different names for some parameters (for example PSpice uses VFB, HSPICE uses VFB0); (ii) HSPICE accepts names for the dummy parameters (DUM1 and DUM2), but PSpice does not; (iii) HSPICE accepts the final parameter DS (though it is ignored), but PSpice does not (DS models mask bias and can be neglected without too much fear).

Convert the models shown in Table 13.20 to format (2) for your chosen simulator (PSpice LEVEL = 4, HSPICE LEVEL = 13). Compare the resulting I_{DS}–V_{DS} characteristics with the LEVEL = 3 parameters (Table 13.14) and the (PSpice) LEVEL = 4 parameters (Table 13.15) for the G5 process. MOSIS has stored the results of its process runs in the format shown in Table 13.20.

13.31 (**Nonreciprocal capacitance, 120 min.)

a. Starting from the equation for transient current flowing into the gate,

$$i_G = \frac{\delta Q_G}{\delta V_D}\frac{dV_D}{dt} + \frac{\delta Q_G}{\delta V_G}\frac{dV_G}{dt} + \frac{\delta Q_G}{\delta V_S}\frac{dV_S}{dt} + \frac{\delta Q_G}{\delta V_B}\frac{dV_B}{dt}, \tag{13.35}$$

(where $\delta Q_i/\delta V_j$ are elements of matrix **M**), show

$$i_G = -C_{GD}\frac{dV_D}{dt} + C_{GG}\frac{dV_G}{dt} - C_{GS}\frac{dV_S}{dt} - C_{GB}\frac{dV_B}{dt} \tag{13.36}$$

and thus that the rows of **M** sum to zero by showing that

$$C_{GG} = C_{GD} + C_{GS} + C_{GB} \tag{13.37}$$

TABLE 13.20   MOSIS SPICE parameters (Problem 13.30).

*NMOS PARAMETERS			*PMOS PARAMETERS		
-7.05628E-01,	-3.86432E-02,	4.98790E-02	-2.02610E-01,	3.59493E-02,	-1.10651E-01
8.41845E-01,	0.00000E+00,	0.00000E+00	8.25364E-01,	0.00000E+00,	0.00000E+00
7.76570E-01,	-7.65089E-04,	-4.83494E-02	3.54162E-01,	-6.88193E-02,	1.52476E-01
2.66993E-02,	4.57480E-02,	-2.58917E-02	-4.51065E-02,	9.41324E-03,	3.52243E-02
-1.94480E-03,	1.74351E-02,	-5.08914E-03	-1.07507E-02,	1.96344E-02,	-3.51067E-04
5.75297E+02,	1.70587E-001,	4.75746E-001	1.37992E+02,	1.92169E-001,	4.68470E-001
3.30513E-01,	9.75110E-02,	-8.58678E-02	1.89331E-01,	6.30898E-02,	-6.38388E-02
3.26384E-02,	2.94349E-02,	-1.38002E-02	1.31710E-02,	1.44096E-02,	6.92372E-04
9.73293E+00,	-5.62944E+00,	6.55955E+00	6.57709E+00,	-1.56096E+00,	1.13564E+00
4.37180E-04,	-3.07010E-03,	8.94355E-04	4.68478E-05,	-1.09352E-03,	-1.53111E-04
-5.05012E-05,	-1.68530E-03,	-1.42701E-03	7.76679E-04,	-1.97213E-04,	-1.12034E-03
-1.11542E-02,	-9.58423E-04,	4.61645E-03	8.71439E-03,	-1.92306E-03,	1.86243E-03
-1.04401E-03,	1.29001E-03,	-7.10095E-04	5.98941E-04,	4.54922E-04,	3.11794E-04
6.92716E+02,	-5.21760E+01,	7.00912E+00	1.49460E+02,	1.36152E+01,	3.55246E+00
-6.41307E-02,	1.37809E+00,	4.15455E+00	6.37235E+00,	-6.63305E-01,	2.25929E+00
8.86387E+00,	2.06021E+00,	-6.19817E+00	-1.21135E-02,	1.92973E+00,	1.00182E+00
9.02467E-03,	2.06380E-04,	-5.20218E-03	-1.16599E-03,	-5.08278E-04,	9.56791E-04
9.60000E-003,	2.70000E+01,	5.00000E+00	9.60000E-003,	2.70000E+01,	5.00000E+00
3.60204E-010,	3.60204E-010,	4.37925E-010	4.18427E-010,	4.18427E-010,	4.33943E-010
1.00000E+000,	0.00000E+000,	0.00000E+000	1.00000E+000,	0.00000E+000,	0.00000E+000
1.00000E+000,	0.00000E+000,	0.00000E+000	1.00000E+000,	0.00000E+000,	0.00000E+000
0.00000E+000,	0.00000E+000,	0.00000E+000	0.00000E+000,	0.00000E+000,	0.00000E+000
0.00000E+000,	0.00000E+000,	0.00000E+000	0.00000E+000,	0.00000E+000,	0.00000E+000
*N+ diffusion::			*P+ diffusion::		
2.1, 3.5e-04, 2.9e-10, 1e-08, 0.8			2, 9.4529e-04, 2.4583e-10, 1e-08, 0.85		
0.8, 0.44, 0.26, 0, 0			0.85, 0.439735, 0.237251, 0, 0		

Source: MOSIS, process = HP-NID, technology = scn05h, run = n5bo, wafer = 42, date = 1-Feb-1996.

---

and three other similar equations for C_{DD}, C_{SS}, and C_{BB}.

b. Show

$$i_G = -C_{GD}\frac{dV_{DB}}{dt} + C_{GG}\frac{dV_{GB}}{dt} - C_{GS}\frac{dV_{SB}}{dt} \tag{13.38}$$

and derive similar equations for the transient currents i_S, i_D, and i_B.

c. Using the fact that $i_G + i_S + i_D + i_B = 0$, show

$$C_{GG} = C_{DG} + C_{SG} + C_{BG} \tag{13.39}$$

and, by deriving similar expressions for C_{DD}, C_{SS}, and C_{BB}, show that the columns of **M** sum to zero.

13.13 Bibliography

Capilano Computing produces books (including software) that explain its schematic editor and logic simulators, LogicWorks and DesignWorks, for PC and Macintosh platforms [1995], as well as its Verilog interface [1997]. The book by Ciccarelli [1995] includes a circuit simulator, BreadBoard, with a schematic-entry program.

Miczo [1994] covers digital simulation in general. Arora [1993] covers MOS models in detail. Carey et al. [1996] cover the mathematical aspects of circuit and device modeling. Cheng and Agrawal [1989] cover vector generation from the perspective of testing. Hëorbst's edited book contains papers on simulation [1986]. Hill and Coelho [1987] cover mixed-level or multilevel simulation. Tuinenga [1988], Banzhaf [1989], Morris [1991], Fenical [1992], Conant [1993], Nilsson and Riedel [1993], Kielkowski [1994], and Lamey [1995] are all introductory books on simulation using the SPICE or PSpice. The book by Al-Hashimi [1995] on PSpice covers both digital and analog simulation. Massobrio and Antognetti [1993] cover the internal details of the SPICE and PSpice models. Meta Software's HSPICE User Manual is very detailed and an essential companion for serious users of any flavor of the SPICE [1996]. McCalla [1988] covers the mathematical principles of circuit simulation. Ogrodzki [1994] covers simulation algorithms. Pillage et al. [1994] cover newer circuit and system simulation methods as alternatives to the SPICE including **asymptotic waveform evaluation** (AWE). Rao et al. [1989] cover switch-level simulation. White and Sangiovanni-Vincentelli [1987] cover **waveform relaxation** simulation. Zukowski [1986] is an advanced text on bounding approach to simulation. Divekar [1988] covers device modeling. Fjeldly, Ytterdal, and Shur [1997] cover device modeling and simulation. Two books by Tsividis cover device modeling: the first [1987] is an advanced treatment of the MOS transistor; the second [1996] includes an introduction to the problems of device modeling.

13.14 References

Al-Hashimi, B. 1995. *The Art of Simulation Using PSpice: Analog and Digital.* Boca Raton, FL: CRC Press, 249 p. ISBN 0849378958. TK454.A454.

Arora, N. 1993. *MOSFET Models for VLSI Circuit Simulation: Theory and Practice.* New York: Springer-Verlag, 605 p. ISBN 321182395-6, ISBN 0-387-82395-6. TK7871.95.A76.

Banzhaf, W. 1989. *Computer-Aided Circuit Analysis Using SPICE.* Englewood Cliffs, NJ: Prentice-Hall. ISBN 0131625799. TK454.B33.

Capilano Computing. 1995. *LogicWorks 3.0 for Windows and the Macintosh.* Menlo Park, CA: Addison-Wesley, 454 p. ISBN 0-8053-1319-2. TK7874.65.L65.

Capilano Computing. 1997. *LogicWorks Verilog Modeler: Interactive Circuit Simulation Software for Windows and Macintosh.* Menlo Park, CA: Capilano Computing, 102 p. ISBN 0201895854. TK7888.4.L64.

Carey, G. F., et al. 1996. *Circuit, Device, and Process Simulation: Mathematical and Numerical Aspects.* New York: Wiley, 425 p. ISBN 0471960195. TK7867.C4973. 31 pages of references.

Cheng, K.-T., and V. D. Agrawal. 1989. *Unified Methods for VLSI Simulation and Test Generation.* Norwell, MA: Kluwer, 148 p. ISBN 0-7923-9025-3. TK7874.C525. 377 references. The first three chapters give a good introduction to fault simulation and test-vector generation.

Ciccarelli, F. A. 1995. *Circuit Modeling: Exercises and Software.* 3rd ed. Englewood Cliffs: Prentice-Hall, 190 p. ISBN 0023224738. TK454.C59. Includes BreadBoard, an IBM-PC compatible circuit analysis computer program.

Conant, R. 1993. *Engineering Circuit Analysis with PSpice and Probe: Macintosh Version.* New York: McGraw-Hill, 176 p. ISBN 0079116795. TK454.C674.

Divekar, D. 1988. *FET Modeling for Circuit Simulation.* Boston: Kluwer, 183 p. ISBN 0898382645. TK7871.95.D58. 12 pages of references.

Fenical, L. H. 1992. *PSpice: A Tutorial.* Englewood Cliffs, NJ: Prentice-Hall, 344 p. ISBN 0136811493. TK454.F46.

Fjeldly, T. A., T. Ytterdal, and M. Shur. 1997. *Introduction to Device Modeling and Circuit Simulation.* New York: Wiley, ISBN 0471157783. TK7871.85.F593.

Hëorbst, E. (Ed.). 1986. *Logic Design and Simulation.* New York: Elsevier Science. ISBN 0-444-87892-0. TK7868.L6L624.

Hill, D. D., and D. R. Coelho. 1987. *Multi-Level Simulation for VLSI Design.* Boston: Kluwer, 206 p. ISBN 0-89838-184-3. TK7874.H525.

IEEE 1076.4-1995. *IEEE Standard VITAL Application-Specific Integrated Circuit (ASIC) Modeling Specification.* 96p. ISBN 1-55937-691-0. IEEE Ref. SH94382-NYF. The Institute of Electrical and Electronics Engineers. Available from The IEEE, 345 East 47th Street, New York, NY 10017 USA. [cited on p. 664 of this chapter]

Kielkowski, R. M. 1994. *Inside SPICE: Overcoming the Obstacles of Circuit Simulation.* New York: McGraw-Hill, 188 p. ISBN 0-07-911525-X. TK454.K48.

Lamey, R. 1995. *The Illustrated Guide to PSpice.* Albany, NY: Delmar, 219 p. ISBN 0827365241. TK454.L35.

Massobrio, G., and P. Antognetti. 1993. *Semiconductor Device Modeling with SPICE.* New York: McGraw-Hill, 479 p. ISBN 0-07-002469-3. TK7871.85.S4454. Contains a more detailed analysis of the SPICE models than other introductory texts.

McCalla, W. J. 1988. *Fundamentals of Computer-Aided Circuit Simulation.* Boston: Kluwer, 175 p. ISBN 0-89838-248-3. TK7874.M355.

Meta Software. 1996. *HSPICE User's Manual.* No catalog information. Available from Customer Service, 1300 White Oaks Road, Campbell, CA 95008, cs@metasw.com. This is a three-volume paperback set that is available separately from the HSPICE program. Volume I, Simulation and Analysis, explains the operation of the HSPICE program. Volume II, Elements and Device Models, contains a comprehensive description of all device models used in HSPICE. Volume III, Analysis and Methods, details input control, types of analysis, output format, optimization, filter and system design, statistical and worst-case analysis, characterization, behavioral applications, and signal integrity (packaging). [cited on p. 692, p. 693, p. 694, p. 696 of this chapter]

Miczo, A. 1994. *Digital Logic Testing and Simulation.* New York: Harper & Row, 414 p. ISBN 0-06-044444-4. TK7868.D5M49.

Morris, J. F. 1991. *Introduction to PSpice with Student Exercise Disk.* Boston: Houghton Mifflin, 145 p. ISBN 0395571073. TK454.M66. To accompany text, Basic Circuit Analysis, Cunningham and Stuller.

Nilsson, J. W., and S. A. Riedel. 1993. *Introduction to PSpice.* Reading, MA: Addison-Wesley, 154 p. ISBN 0201513188. TK454.N54. This is a supplement to the book Electric Circuits, fourth edition, but is also very useful as a stand-alone text.

Ogrodzki, J. 1994. *Circuit Simulation Methods and Algorithms.* Boca Raton, FL: CRC Press, 465 p. ISBN 0-8493-7894-X. TK7867.O33.

Pillage, L., et al. 1994. *Electronic Circuit and System Simulation Methods.* New York: McGraw-Hill, 392 p. ISBN 0-07-050169-6. TK7874.P52.

Rao, V. B., et al. 1989. *Switch-Level Timing Simulation of MOS VLSI Circuits.* Boston: Kluwer, 209 p. ISBN 0-89838-302-1. TK7874.S87. Fairly mathematical treatment of network partitioning techniques for switch-level simulators.

Tsividis, Y. P. 1987. *Operation and Modeling of the MOS Transistor.* New York: McGraw-Hill, 505 p. ISBN 0-07-065381-X. TK7871.99.M44.T77. [cited on p. 696 of this chapter]

Tsividis, Y. P. 1996. *Mixed Analog-Digital VLSI Devices and Technology: An Introduction.* New York: McGraw-Hill, 284 p. ISBN 0-07-065402-6. TK7874.75.T78.

Tuinenga, P. W. 1988. *SPICE: A Guide to Circuit Simulation and Analysis using PSpice.* Englewood Cliffs, NJ: Prentice-Hall, 200 p. ISBN 0-13-834607-0. TK454.T85.

White, J. K., and A. Sangiovanni-Vincentelli. 1987. *Relaxation Techniques for the Simulation of VLSI Circuits.* Boston: Kluwer, 202 p. ISBN 0-89838-186-X. TK7874.W48. Contents: Introduction; The Circuit Simulation Problem; Numerical Techniques; Waveform Relaxation; The Implementation of WR.

Zukowski, C. A. 1986. *The Bounding Approach to VLSI Circuit Simulation.* Norwell, MA: Kluwer, 220 p. ISBN 0-89838-176-2. TK7874.Z85. Based on an MIT Ph.D. thesis. Uses bounds on transient response of RC-networks to simplify circuit simulation. Contents: Introduction, VLSI Circuit Simulation; Simulation with Bounds; The VLSI Circuit Model; Bound Relaxation; Algorithms and Experimental Results; Conclusion.

TEST

ASICs are tested at two stages during manufacture using **production tests**. First, the silicon die are tested after fabrication is complete at **wafer test** or **wafer sort**. Each wafer is tested, one die at a time, using an array of probes on a **probe card** that descend onto the bonding pads of a single die. The **production tester** applies signals generated by a **test program** and measures the ASIC **test response**. A test program often generates hundreds of thousands of different **test vectors** applied at a frequency of several megahertz over several hundred milliseconds. Chips that fail are automatically marked with an ink spot. Production testers are large machines that take up their own room and are very expensive (typically well over $1 million). Either the customer, or the ASIC manufacturer, or both, develops the test program.

A diamond saw separates the die, and the good die are bonded to a lead carrier and packaged. A second, **final test** is carried out on the packaged ASIC (usually with the same test vectors used at wafer sort) before the ASIC is shipped to the customer. The customer may apply a **goods-inward test** to incoming ASICs if the customer has the resources and the product volume is large enough. Normally, though, parts are directly assembled onto a bare **printed-circuit board** (**PCB** or **board**) and then the board is tested. If the board test shows that an ASIC is bad at this point, it is difficult to replace a surface-mounted component soldered on the board, for example. If there are several board failures due to a particular ASIC, the board manufacturer typically ships the defective chips back to the ASIC vendor. ASIC vendors have sophisticated **failure analysis** departments that take packaged ASICs apart and can often determine the failure mechanism. If the ASIC production tests are adequate, failures are often due to the soldering process, electrostatic damage during handling, or other problems that can occur between the part being shipped and board test. If the problem is traced to defective ASIC fabrication, this indicates that the test program may be inadequate. As we shall see, failure and diagnosis at the board level is very expensive. Finally, ASICs may be tested and replaced (usually by swapping boards) either by a customer who buys the final product or by servicing—this is **field repair**. Such system-level diagnosis and repair is even more expensive.

Programmable ASICs (including FPGAs) are a special case. Each programmable ASIC is tested to the point that the manufacturer can guarantee with a high degree of confidence that if your design works, and if you program the FPGA correctly, then your ASIC will work. Production testing is easier for some programmable ASIC architectures than others. In a reprogrammable technology the manufacturer can test the programming features. This cannot be done for a one-time programmable antifuse technology, for example. A programmable ASIC is still tested in a similar fashion to any other ASIC and you are still paying for test development and design. Programmable ASICs also have similar test, defect, and manufacturing problems to other members of the ASIC family. Finally, once a programmable ASIC is soldered to a board and part of a system, it looks just like any other ASIC. As you will see in the next section, considering board-level and system-level testing is a very important part of ASIC design.

14.1   The Importance of Test

One measure of **product quality** is the **defect level**. If the ABC Company sells 100,000 copies of a product and 10 of these are defective, then we say the defect level is 0.1 percent or 100 ppm. The **average quality level** (**AQL**) is equal to one minus the defect level (ABC's AQL is thus 99.9 percent).

Suppose the semiconductor division of ABC makes an ASIC, the bASIC, for the PC division. The PC division buys 100,000 bASICs, tested by the semiconductor division, at $10 each. The PC division includes one surface-mounted bASIC on each PC motherboard it assembles for the aPC computer division. The aPC division tests the finished motherboards. Rejected boards due to defective bASICs incur an average $200 board repair cost. The board repair cost as a function of the ASIC defect level is shown in Table 14.1. A defect level of 5 percent in bASICs costs $1 million dollars in board repair costs (the same as the total ASIC part cost). Things are even worse at the system level, however.

TABLE 14.1   Defect levels in printed-circuit boards (PCB).[1]

ASIC defect level	Defective ASICs	Total PCB repair cost
5%	5000	$1 million
1%	1000	$200,000
0.1%	100	$20,000
0.01%	10	$2,000

[1]Assumptions: The number of parts shipped is 100,000; part price is $10; total part cost is $1 million; the cost of a fault in an assembled PCB is $200.

Suppose the ABC Company sells its aPC computers for $5,000, with a profit of $500 on each. Unfortunately the aPC division also has a defect level. Suppose that 10 percent of the motherboards that contain defective bASICs that passed the chip test also manage to pass the board tests (10 percent may seem high, but chips that have hard-to-test faults at the chip level may be very hard to find at the board level—catching 90 percent of these rogue chips would be considered good). The system-level repair cost as a function of the bASIC defect level is shown in Table 14.2. In this example a 5 percent defect level in a $10 bASIC part now results in a $5 million cost at the system level. From Table 14.2 we can see it would be worth spending $4 million (i.e., $5 million – $1 million) to reduce the bASIC defect density from 5 percent to 1 percent.

TABLE 14.2   Defect levels in systems.[1]

ASIC defect level	Defective ASICs	Defective boards	Total repair cost at system level
5%	5000	500	$5 million
1%	1000	100	$1 million
0.1%	100	10	$100,000
0.01%	10	1	$10,000

[1]Assumptions: The number of systems shipped is 100,000; system cost is $5,000; total cost of systems shipped is $500 million; the cost of repairing or replacing a system due to failure is $10,000; profit on 100,000 systems is $50 million.

14.2 Boundary-Scan Test

It is possible to test ICs in dual-in-line packages (DIPs) with 0.1 inch (2.5 mm) lead spacing on low-density boards using a **bed-of-nails tester** with probes that contact test points underneath the board. Mechanical testing becomes difficult with board trace widths and separations below 0.1 mm or 100 µm, package-pin separations of 0.3 mm or less, packages with 200 or more pins, surface-mount packages on both sides of the board, and multilayer boards [Scheiber, 1995].

In 1985 a group of European manufacturers formed the **Joint European Test Action Group (JETAG)** to study board testing. With the addition of North American companies, JETAG became the **Joint Test Action Group (JTAG)** in 1986. The JTAG 2.0 test standard formed the basis of the **IEEE Standard 1149.1 Test Port and Boundary-Scan Architecture** [IEEE 1149.1b, 1994], approved in February 1990 and also approved as a standard by the American National Standards Institute (ANSI) in August 1990 [Bleeker, v. d. Eijnden, and de Jong, 1993; Maunder and Tulloss, 1990; Parker, 1992]. The IEEE standard is still often referred to as JTAG, although there are important differences between the last JTAG specification (version 2.0) and the IEEE 1149.1 standard.

Boundary-scan test (BST) is a method for testing boards using a four-wire interface (five wires with an optional master reset signal). A good analogy would be the RS-232 interface for PCs. The BST standard interface was designed to test boards, but it is also useful to test ASICs. The BST interface provides a standard means of communicating with test circuits on-board an ASIC. We do need to include extra circuits on an ASIC in order to use BST. This is an example of increasing the cost and complexity (as well as potentially reducing the performance) of an ASIC to reduce the cost of testing the ASIC and the system.

Figure 14.1(a) illustrates failures that may occur on a PCB due to shorts or opens in the copper traces on the board. Less frequently, failures in the ASIC package may also arise from shorts and opens in the wire bonds between the die and the package frame (Figure 14.1b). Failures in an ASIC package that occur during ASIC fabrication are caught by the ASIC production test, but stress during automated handling and board assembly may cause package failures. Figure 14.1(c) shows how a group of ASICs are linked together in boundary-scan testing. To detect the failures shown in Figure 14.1(a) or (b) manufacturers use boundary scan to test every connection between ASICs on a board. During boundary scan, test data is loaded into each ASIC and then driven onto the board traces. Each ASIC monitors its inputs, captures the data received, and then shifts the captured data out. Any defects in the board or ASIC connections will show up as a discrepancy between expected and actual measured continuity data.

In order to include BST on an ASIC, we add a special logic cell to each ASIC I/O pad. These cells are joined together to form a chain and create a boundary-scan shift register that extends around each ASIC. The input to a boundary-scan shift register is the **test-data input (TDI)**. The output of a boundary-scan shift register is

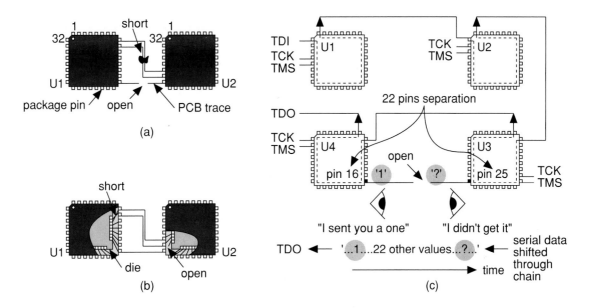

FIGURE 14.1 IEEE 1149.1 boundary scan. (a) Boundary scan is intended to check for shorts or opens between ICs mounted on a board. (b) Shorts and opens may also occur inside the IC package. (c) The boundary-scan architecture is a long chain of shift registers allowing data to be sent over all the connections between the ICs on a board.

the **test-data output** (**TDO**). These boundary-scan shift registers are then linked in a serial fashion with the boundary-scan shift registers on other ASICs to form one long boundary-scan shift register. The boundary-scan shift register in each ASIC is one of several **test-data registers** (**TDR**) that may be included in each ASIC. All the TDRs in an ASIC are connected directly between the TDI and TDO ports. A special register that decodes instructions provides a way to select a particular TDR and control operation of the boundary-scan test process.

Controlling all of the operations involved in selecting registers, loading data, performing a test, and shifting out results are the **test clock** (**TCK**) and **test-mode select** (**TMS**). The boundary-scan standard specifies a four-wire test interface using the four signals: TDI, TDO, TCK, and TMS. These four dedicated signals, the **test-access port** (**TAP**), are connected to the TAP controller inside each ASIC. The TAP controller is a state machine clocked on the rising edge of TCK, and with state transitions controlled by the TMS signal. The **test-reset input signal** (**TRST***, **nTRST**, or **TRST**—always an active-low signal) is an optional (fifth) dedicated interface pin to reset the TAP controller.

Normally the boundary-scan shift-register cells at each ASIC I/O pad are transparent, allowing signals to pass between the I/O pad and the core logic. When an ASIC is put into boundary-scan test mode, we first tell the TAP controller which

TDR to select. The TAP controller then tells each boundary-scan shift register in the appropriate TDR either to capture input data, to shift data to the neighboring cell, or to output data.

There are many acronyms in the IEEE 1149.1 standard (referred to as "**dot one**"); Table 14.3 provides a list of the most common terms.

TABLE 14.3   Boundary-scan terminology.

Acronym	Meaning	Explanation
BR	Bypass register	A TDR, directly connects TDI and TDO, bypassing BSR
BSC	Boundary-scan cell	Each I/O pad has a BSC to monitor signals
BSR	Boundary-scan register	A TDR, a shift register formed from a chain of BSCs
BST	Boundary-scan test	Not to be confused with BIST (built-in self-test)
IDCODE	Device-identification register	Optional TDR, contains manufacturer and part number
IR	Instruction register	Holds a BST instruction, provides control signals
JTAG	Joint Test Action Group	The organization that developed boundary scan
TAP	Test-access port	Four- (or five-)wire test interface to an ASIC
TCK	Test clock	A TAP wire, the clock that controls BST operation
TDI	Test-data input	A TAP wire, the input to the IR and TDRs
TDO	Test-data output	A TAP wire, the output from the IR and TDRs
TDR	Test-data register	Group of BST registers: IDCODE, BR, BSR
TMS	Test-mode select	A TAP wire, together with TCK controls the BST state
TRST* or nTRST	Test-reset input signal	Optional TAP wire, resets the TAP controller (active-low)

14.2.1   BST Cells

Figure 14.2 shows a **data-register cell** (**DR cell**) that may be used to implement any of the TDRs. The most common DR cell is a **boundary-scan cell** (**BS cell**, or **BSC**), or **boundary-register cell** (this last name is not abbreviated to BR cell, since this term is reserved for another type of cell) [IEEE 1149.1b-1994, p. 10-18, Fig. 10-16].

A BSC contains two sequential elements. The **capture flip-flop** or **capture register** is part of a shift register formed by series connection of BSCs. The **update flip-flop**, or **update latch**, is normally drawn as an edge-triggered D flip-flop, though it may be a transparent latch. The inputs to a BSC are: **scan in** (serial in or **SI**); **data in** (parallel in or **PI**); and a control signal, **mode** (also called **test/normal**). The BSC outputs are: **scan out** (serial out or **SO**); **data out** (parallel out or **PO**). The BSC in Figure 14.2 is **reversible** and can be used for both chip inputs and outputs. Thus data_in may be connected to a pad and data_out to the core logic or vice versa.

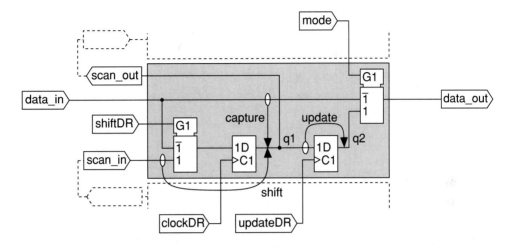

```
entity DR_cell is port (mode, data_in, shiftDR, scan_in, clockDR, updateDR: BIT;     --1
   data_out, scan_out: out BIT ); end DR_cell;                                        --2

architecture behave of DR_cell is signal q1, q2 : BIT; begin                          --3
CAP : process(clockDR) begin if clockDR = '1' then                                    --4
   if shiftDR = '0' then q1 <= data_in; else q1 <= scan_in; end if; end if;           --5
end process;                                                                          --6
UPD : process(updateDR) begin if updateDR = '1' then q2 <= q1; end if; end process;   --7
data_out <= data_in when mode = '0' else q2; scan_out <= q1;                          --8
end behave;                                                                           --9
```

FIGURE 14.2 A DR (data register) cell. The most common use of this cell is as a boundary-scan cell (BSC).

The IEEE 1149.1 standard shows the sequential logic in a BSC controlled by the gated clocks: clockDR (whose positive edge occurs at the positive edge of TCK) and updateDR (whose positive edge occurs at the negative edge of TCK). The IEEE 1149.1 schematics illustrate the standard but do not define how circuits should be implemented. The function of the circuit in Figure 14.2 (and its model) follows the IEEE 1149.1 standard and many other published schematics, but this is not necessarily the best, or even a safe, implementation. For example, as drawn here, signals clockDR and updateDR are gated clocks—normally to be avoided if possible. The update sequential element is shown as an edge-triggered D flip-flop but may be implemented using a latch.

Figure 14.3 [IEEE 1149.1b-1994, Chapter 9] shows a **bypass-register cell** (**BR cell**). The BR inputs and outputs, scan in (serial in, SI) and scan out (serial out, SO), have the same names as the DR cell ports, but DR cells and BR cells are not directly connected.

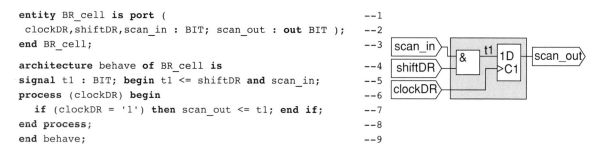

```
entity BR_cell is port (                                --1
 clockDR,shiftDR,scan_in : BIT; scan_out : out BIT );   --2
end BR_cell;                                            --3

architecture behave of BR_cell is                       --4
signal t1 : BIT; begin t1 <= shiftDR and scan_in;       --5
process (clockDR) begin                                 --6
   if (clockDR = '1') then scan_out <= t1; end if;      --7
end process;                                            --8
end behave;                                             --9
```

FIGURE 14.3 A BR (bypass register) cell.

Figure 14.4 shows an **instruction-register cell** (**IR cell**) [IEEE 1149.1b-1994, Chapter 6]. The IR cell inputs are: scan_in, data_in; as well as clock, shift, and update signals (with names and functions similar to those of the corresponding signals in the BSC). The reset signals are nTRST and reset_bar (active-low signals often use an asterisk, reset* for example, but this is not a legal VHDL name). The two LSBs of data_in must permanently be set to '01' (this helps in checking the integrity of the scan chain during testing). The remaining data_in bits are status bits under the control of the designer. The update sequential element (sometimes called the **shadow register**) in each IR cell may be set or reset (depending on reset_value). The IR cell outputs are: data_out (the instruction bit passed to the instruction decoder) and scan_out (the data passed to the next IR cell in the IR).

14.2.2   BST Registers

Figure 14.5 shows a **boundary-scan register** (**BSR**), which consists of a series connection, or chain, of BSCs. The BSR surrounds the ASIC core logic and is connected to the I/O pad cells. The BSR monitors (and optionally controls) the inputs and outputs of an ASIC. The direction of information flow is shown by an arrow on each of the BSCs in Figure 14.5. The control signal, mode, is decoded from the IR. Signal mode is drawn as common to all cells for the BSR in Figure 14.5, but that is not always the case.

Figure 14.6 shows an **instruction register** (**IR**), which consists of at least two IR cells connected in series. The IEEE 1149.1 standard specifies that the IR cell is reset to '00...01' (the optional IDCODE instruction). If there is no IDCODE TDR, then the IDCODE instruction defaults to the BYPASS instruction.

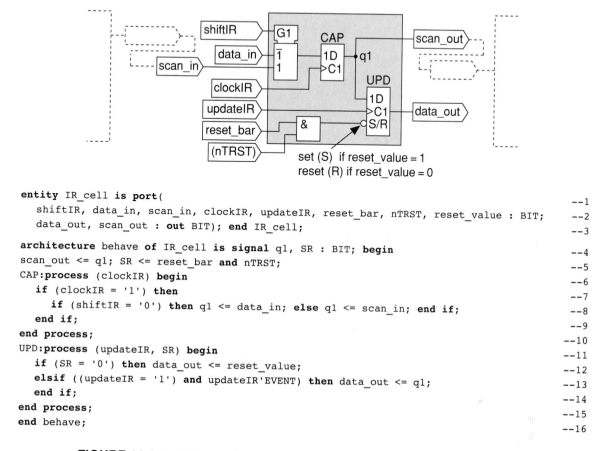

FIGURE 14.4 An IR (instruction register) cell.

```
entity IR_cell is port(                                                              --1
   shiftIR, data_in, scan_in, clockIR, updateIR, reset_bar, nTRST, reset_value : BIT; --2
   data_out, scan_out : out BIT); end IR_cell;                                        --3

architecture behave of IR_cell is signal q1, SR : BIT; begin                          --4
scan_out <= q1; SR <= reset_bar and nTRST;                                            --5
CAP:process (clockIR) begin                                                           --6
   if (clockIR = '1') then                                                            --7
     if (shiftIR = '0') then q1 <= data_in; else q1 <= scan_in; end if;               --8
   end if;                                                                            --9
end process;                                                                          --10
UPD:process (updateIR, SR) begin                                                      --11
   if (SR = '0') then data_out <= reset_value;                                        --12
   elsif ((updateIR = '1') and updateIR'EVENT) then data_out <= q1;                   --13
   end if;                                                                            --14
end process;                                                                          --15
end behave;                                                                           --16
```

14.2.3 Instruction Decoder

Table 14.4 on page 722 shows an **instruction decoder**. This model is capable of decoding the following minimum set of boundary-scan instructions:

1. EXTEST, external test. Drives a known value onto each output pin to test connections between ASICs.

2. SAMPLE/PRELOAD (often abbreviated to SAMPLE). Performs two functions: first sampling the present input value from input pad during capture; and then preloading the BSC update register output during update (in preparation for an EXTEST instruction, for example).

3. IDCODE. An optional instruction that allows the **device-identification register** (IDCODE) to be shifted out. The IDCODE TDR is an optional register that

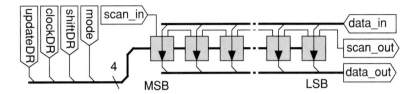

```
entity BSR is                                                            --1
generic (width : INTEGER := 3);                                          --2
port (shiftDR, clockDR, updateDR, mode, scan_in : BIT;                   --3
  scan_out : out BIT;                                                    --4
  data_in : BIT_VECTOR(width-1 downto 0);                               --5
  data_out : out BIT_VECTOR(width-1 downto 0));                         --6
end BSR;                                                                 --7

architecture structure of BSR is                                        --8
component DR_cell port (                                                 --9
  mode, data_in, shiftDR, scan_in, clockDR, updateDR : BIT;             --10
  data_out, scan_out : out BIT);                                        --11
end component;                                                           --12
for all : DR_cell use entity WORK.DR_cell(behave);                      --13
signal int_scan : BIT_VECTOR (data_in'RANGE);                           --14
begin                                                                    --15
BSR : for i in data_in'LOW to data_in'HIGH generate                     --16
  RIGHT : if (i = 0) generate                                           --17
  BSR_LSB : DR_cell port map (mode, data_in(i), shiftDR,                --18
  int_scan(i), clockDR, updateDR, data_out(i), scan_out);              --19
  end generate;                                                         --20
  MIDDLE : if ((i > 0) and (i < data_in'HIGH)) generate                 --21
  BSR_i : DR_cell port map (mode, data_in(i), shiftDR,                  --22
  int_scan(i), clockDR, updateDR, data_out(i), int_scan(i-1));         --23
  end generate;                                                         --24
  LFET : if (i = data_in'HIGH) generate                                 --25
  BSR_MSB : DR_cell port map (mode, data_in(i), shiftDR,                --26
  scan_in, clockDR, updateDR, data_out(i), int_scan(i-1));             --27
  end generate;                                                         --28
end generate;                                                           --29
end structure;                                                          --30
```

FIGURE 14.5 A BSR (boundary-scan register). An example of the component data-register (DR) cells (used as boundary-scan cells) is shown in Figure 14.2.

allows the tester to query the ASIC for the manufacturer's name, part number, and other data that is shifted out on TDO. IDCODE defaults to the BYPASS instruction if there is no IDCODE TDR.

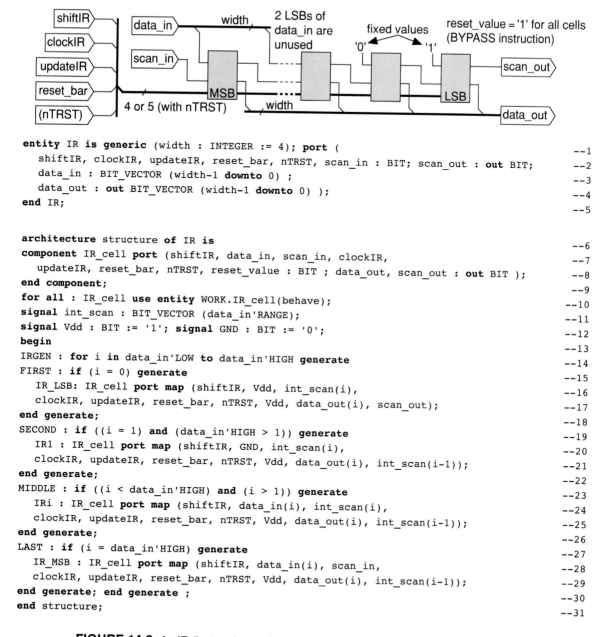

```
entity IR is generic (width : INTEGER := 4); port (                              --1
  shiftIR, clockIR, updateIR, reset_bar, nTRST, scan_in : BIT; scan_out : out BIT;  --2
  data_in : BIT_VECTOR (width-1 downto 0) ;                                       --3
  data_out : out BIT_VECTOR (width-1 downto 0) );                                --4
end IR;                                                                           --5


architecture structure of IR is                                                  --6
component IR_cell port (shiftIR, data_in, scan_in, clockIR,                       --7
  updateIR, reset_bar, nTRST, reset_value : BIT ; data_out, scan_out : out BIT ); --8
end component;                                                                    --9
for all : IR_cell use entity WORK.IR_cell(behave);                               --10
signal int_scan : BIT_VECTOR (data_in'RANGE);                                    --11
signal Vdd : BIT := '1'; signal GND : BIT := '0';                               --12
begin                                                                           --13
IRGEN : for i in data_in'LOW to data_in'HIGH generate                           --14
FIRST : if (i = 0) generate                                                     --15
  IR_LSB: IR_cell port map (shiftIR, Vdd, int_scan(i),                          --16
  clockIR, updateIR, reset_bar, nTRST, Vdd, data_out(i), scan_out);             --17
end generate;                                                                   --18
SECOND : if ((i = 1) and (data_in'HIGH > 1)) generate                           --19
  IR1 : IR_cell port map (shiftIR, GND, int_scan(i),                            --20
  clockIR, updateIR, reset_bar, nTRST, Vdd, data_out(i), int_scan(i-1));        --21
end generate;                                                                   --22
MIDDLE : if ((i < data_in'HIGH) and (i > 1)) generate                           --23
  IRi : IR_cell port map (shiftIR, data_in(i), int_scan(i),                     --24
  clockIR, updateIR, reset_bar, nTRST, Vdd, data_out(i), int_scan(i-1));        --25
end generate;                                                                   --26
LAST : if (i = data_in'HIGH) generate                                           --27
  IR_MSB : IR_cell port map (shiftIR, data_in(i), scan_in,                      --28
  clockIR, updateIR, reset_bar, nTRST, Vdd, data_out(i), int_scan(i-1));        --29
end generate; end generate ;                                                    --30
end structure;                                                                   --31
```

FIGURE 14.6 An IR (instruction register).

4. BYPASS. Selects the single-cell bypass register (instead of the BSR) and allows data to be quickly shifted between ASICs.

The IEEE 1149.1 standard predefines additional optional instructions and also defines the implementation of custom instructions that may use additional TDRs.

TABLE 14.4   An IR (instruction register) decoder.

```
entity IR_decoder is generic (width : INTEGER := 4); port (            --1
  shiftDR, clockDR, updateDR : BIT; IR_PO : BIT_VECTOR (width-1 downto 0) ;   --2
  test_mode, selectBR, shiftBR, clockBR, shiftBSR, clockBSR, updateBSR : out BIT );   --3
end IR_decoder;                                                       --4

architecture behave of IR_decoder is                                 --5
type INSTRUCTION is (EXTEST, SAMPLE_PRELOAD, IDCODE, BYPASS);         --6
signal I : INSTRUCTION;                                               --7
begin process (IR_PO) begin case BIT_VECTOR'( IR_PO(1), IR_PO(0) ) is --8
  when "00" => I <= EXTEST; when "01" => I <= SAMPLE_PRELOAD;         --9
  when "10" => I <= IDCODE; when "11" => I <= BYPASS;                 --10
end case; end process;                                               --11
test_mode <= '1' when I = EXTEST else '0';                           --12
selectBR  <= '1' when (I = BYPASS or I = IDCODE) else '0';           --13
shiftBR <= shiftDR;                                                  --14
clockBR <= clockDR when (I = BYPASS or I = IDCODE) else '1';         --15
shiftBSR <= shiftDR;                                                 --16
clockBSR <= clockDR when (I = EXTEST or I = SAMPLE_PRELOAD) else '1'; --17
updateBSR <= updateDR when (I = EXTEST or I = SAMPLE_PRELOAD) else '0'; --18
end behave;                                                          --19
```

14.2.4   TAP Controller

Figure 14.7 shows the TAP controller finite-state machine. The 16-state diagram contains some symmetry: states with suffix '_DR' operate on the data registers and those with suffix '_IR' apply to the instruction register. All transitions between states are determined by the TMS (test mode select) signal and occur at the rising edge of TCK, the boundary-scan clock. An optional active-low reset signal, nTRST or TRST*, resets the state machine to the initial state, Reset. If the dedicated nTRST is not used, there must be a power-on reset signal (POR)—not an existing system reset signal.

The outputs of the TAP controller are not shown in Figure 14.7, but are derived from each TAP controller state. The TAP controller operates rather like a four-button digital watch that cycles through several states (alarm, stopwatch, 12 hr / 24 hr, countdown timer, and so on) as you press the buttons. Only the shaded states in Figure 14.7 affect the ASIC core logic; the other states are intermediate steps. The pause states let the controller jog in place while the tester reloads its memory with a new set of test vectors, for example.

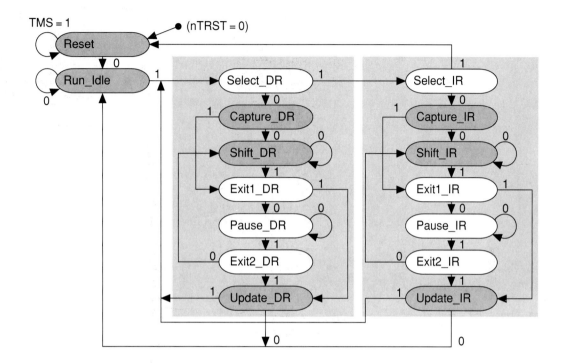

```
use work.TAP.all; entity TAP_sm_states is                                    --1
  port (TMS, TCK, nTRST : in BIT; S : out TAP_STATE); end TAP_sm_states;      --2

architecture behave of TAP_sm_states is                                      --3
type STATE_ARRAY is array (TAP_STATE, 0 to 1) of TAP_STATE;                  --4
constant T : STATE_ARRAY := ( (Run_Idle, Reset),                            --5
(Run_Idle, Select_DR), (Capture_DR, Select_IR), (Shift_DR, Exit1_DR),        --6
(Shift_DR, Exit1_DR), (Pause_DR, Update_DR), (Pause_DR, Exit2_DR),           --7
(Shift_DR, Update_DR), (Run_Idle, Select_DR), (Capture_IR, Reset),           --8
(Shift_IR, Exit1_IR), (Shift_IR, Exit1_IR), (Pause_IR, Update_IR),           --9
(Pause_IR, Exit2_IR), (Shift_IR, Update_IR), (Run_idle, Select_DR) );        --10
begin process (TCK, nTRST) variable S_i: TAP_STATE; begin                   --11
  if ( nTRST = '0' ) then S_i := Reset;                                      --12
  elsif ( TCK = '1' and TCK'EVENT ) then -- transition on +VE clock edge     --13
    if ( TMS = '1' ) then S_i := T(S_i, 1); else S_i := T(S_i, 0); end if;    --14
  end if; S <= S_i; -- update signal with already updated internal variable  --15
end process;                                                                 --16
end behave;                                                                  --17
```

FIGURE 14.7 The TAP (test-access port) controller state machine.

Table 14.5 shows the output control signals generated by the TAP state machine. I have taken the unusual step of writing separate entities for the state machine and its outputs. Normally this is bad practice because it makes it difficult for synthesis tools to extract and optimize the logic, for example. This separation of functions reflects the fact that the operation of the TAP controller state machine is precisely defined by the IEEE 1149.1 standard—independent of the implementation of the register cells and number of instructions supported. The model in Table 14.5 contains the following combinational, registered, and gated output signals and will change with different implementations:

- `reset_bar`. Resets the IR to IDCODE (or BYPASS in absence of IDCODE TDR).
- `selectIR`. Connects a register, the IR or a TDR, to TDO.
- `enableTDO`. Enables the three-state buffer that drives TDO. This allows data to be shifted out of the ASIC on TDO, either from the IR or from the DR, in states `shift_IR` or `shift_DR` respectively.
- `shiftIR`. Selects the serial input to the capture flip-flop in the IR cells.
- `clockIR`. Causes data at the input of the IR to be captured or the contents of the IR to be shifted toward TDO (depending on `shiftIR`) on the *negative* edge of TCK following the *entry* to the states `shift_IR` or `capture_IR`. This is a dirty signal.
- `updateIR`. Clocks the update sequential element on the *positive* edge of TCK at the same time as the *exit* from state `update_IR`. This is a dirty signal.
- `shiftDR`, `clockDR`, and `updateDR`. Same functions as corresponding IR signals applied to the TDRs. These signals may be gated to the appropriate TDR by the instruction decoder.

The signals `reset_bar`, `enableTDO`, `shiftIR`, and `shiftDR` are registered or clocked by TCK (on the positive edge of TCK). We say these signals are **clean** (as opposed to being dirty gated clocks).

14.2.5 Boundary-Scan Controller

Figure 14.8 shows a boundary-scan controller. It contains the following four parts:

1. Bypass register.
2. TDO output circuit. The data to be shifted out of the ASIC on TDO is selected from the serial outputs of bypass register (`BR_SO`), instruction register (`IR_SO`), or boundary-scan register (`BSR_SO`). Notice the registered output means that data appears on TDO at the *negative* edge of TCK. This prevents race conditions between ASICs.
3. Instruction register and instruction decoder.
4. TAP controller.

TABLE 14.5 The TAP (test-access port) control.[1]

State / Output	Reset	Run_Idle	Select_DR	Capture_DR	Shift_DR	Exit1_DR	Pause_DR	Exit2_DR	Update_DR	Select_IR	Capture_IR	Shift_IR	Exit1_IR	Pause_IR	Exit2_IR	Update_IR
reset_bar	0R															
selectIR	1	1								1	1	1	1	1	1	1
enableTDO					1R							1R				
shiftIR												1R				
clockIR											0G	0G				
updateIR																1G
shiftDR					1R											
clockDR				0G	0G											
updateDR									1G							

```
use work.TAP.all; entity TAP_sm_output is                                    --1
port (TCK : in BIT; S : in TAP_STATE; reset_bar, selectIR, enableTDO, shiftIR, --2
   clockIR, updateIR, shiftDR, clockDR, updateDR : out BIT);                  --3
end TAP_sm_output;                                                            --4

architecture behave_1 of TAP_sm_output is begin -- registered outputs         --5
process (TCK) begin if ( (TCK = '0') and TCK'EVENT ) then                     --6
   if S = Reset then reset_bar <= '0'; else reset_bar <= '1'; end if;         --7
   if S = Shift_IR or S = Shift_DR then enableTDO <= '1'; else enableTDO <= '0'; end if; --8
   if S = Shift_IR then ShiftIR <= '1'; else shiftIR <= '0'; end if;          --9
   if S = Shift_DR then ShiftDR <= '1'; else shiftDR <= '0'; end if;          --10
end if;                                                                       --11
end process;                                                                  --12
process (TCK) begin -- dirty outputs gated with not(TCK)                      --13
if (TCK = '0' and (S = Capture_IR or S = Shift_IR))                           --14
   then clockIR <= '0'; else clockIR <= '1'; end if;                          --15
if (TCK = '0' and (S = Capture_DR or S = Shift_DR))                           --16
   then clockDR <= '0'; else clockDR <= '1'; end if;                          --17
if TCK = '0' and S=Update_IR then updateIR <= '1'; else updateIR <= '0'; end if; --18
if TCK = '0' and S=Update_DR then updateDR <= '1'; else updateDR <= '0'; end if; --19
end process;                                                                  --20
selectIR <= '1' when (S = Reset or S = Run_Idle or S = Capture_IR or S = Shift_IR --21
   or S = Exit1_IR or S = Pause_IR or S = Exit2_IR or S = Update_IR) else '0'; --22
end behave_1;                                                                 --23
```

[1]Outputs: G = gated with −TCK, R = registered on falling edge of TCK. Only active levels are shown in the table.

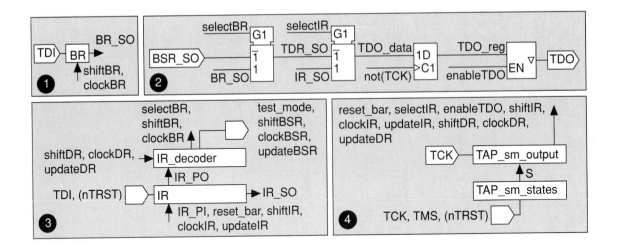

```
library IEEE; use IEEE.std_logic_1164.all; use work.TAP.all;                    --1
entity Control is generic (width : INTEGER := 2); port (TMS, TCK, TDI, nTRST : BIT;   --2
    TDO: out STD_LOGIC; BSR_SO : BIT; BSR_PO : BIT_VECTOR (width-1 downto 0);    --3
    shiftBSR, clockBSR, updateBSR, test_mode : out BIT); end Control;            --4


architecture mixed of Control is use work.BST_components.all;                    --5
signal reset_bar, selectIR, enableTDO, shiftIR, clockIR, updateIR, shiftDR,      --6
    clockDR, updateDR, IR_SO, BR_SO, TDO_reg, TDO_data, TDR_SO, selectBR,        --7
    clockBR, shiftBR : BIT;                                                      --8
signal IR_PI, IR_PO : BIT_VECTOR (1 downto 0); signal S : TAP_STATE;             --9
begin                                                                           --10
IR_PI <= "01";                                                                  --11
TDO <= TO_STDULOGIC(TDO_reg) when enableTDO = '1' else 'Z';                      --12
R1 : process (TCK) begin if (TCK='0') then TDO_reg <= TDO_data; end if; end process;  --13
TDO_data <= IR_SO when selectIR = '1' else TDR_SO;                               --14
TDR_SO <= BR_SO when selectBR = '1' else BSR_SO;                                 --15
TC1 : TAP_sm_states port map (TMS, TCK, nTRST, S);                              --16
TC2 : TAP_sm_output port map (TCK, S, reset_bar, selectIR, enableTDO,            --17
    shiftIR, clockIR, updateIR, shiftDR, clockDR, updateDR);                     --18
IR1 : IR generic map (width => 2) port map (shiftIR, clockIR, updateIR,          --19
    reset_bar, nTRST, TDI, IR_SO, IR_PI, IR_PO);                                 --20
DEC1 : IR_decoder generic map (width => 2) port map (shiftDR, clockDR, updateDR, --21
    IR_PO, test_mode, selectBR, shiftBR, clockBR, shiftBSR, clockBSR, updateBSR);--22
BR1 : BR_cell port map (clockBR, shiftBR, TDI, BR_SO);                          --23
end mixed;                                                                       --24
```

FIGURE 14.8 A boundary-scan controller.

The BSR (and other optional TDRs) are connected to the ASIC core logic outside the BST controller.

14.2.6   A Simple Boundary-Scan Example

Figure 14.9 shows an example of a simple ASIC (our comparator/MUX example) containing boundary scan. The following two packages define the TAP states and the components (these are not essential to understanding what follows, but are included so that the code presented here forms a complete BST model):

```
package TAP is                                                --1
type TAP_STATE is (reset, run_idle, select_DR, capture_DR,    --2
  shift_DR, exit1_DR, pause_DR, exit2_DR, update_DR, select_IR, --3
  capture_IR, shift_IR, exit1_IR, pause_IR, exit2_IR, update_IR); --4
end TAP;                                                       --5

use work.TAP.all; library IEEE; use IEEE.std_logic_1164.all;  --1
package BST_Components is                                      --2

component DR_cell port (                                       --3
  mode, data_in, shiftDR, scan_in, clockDR, updateDR: BIT;     --4
  data_out, scan_out : out BIT );                              --5
end component;                                                 --6

component IR_cell port (                                       --7
  shiftIR, data_in, scan_in, clockIR, updateIR, reset_bar,     --8
  nTRST, reset_value : BIT; data_out, scan_out : out BIT);     --9
end component;                                                 --10

component BR_cell port (                                       --11
  clockDR,shiftDR,scan_in : BIT; scan_out: out BIT );          --12
end component;                                                 --13

component BSR                                                  --14
  generic (width : INTEGER := 5); port (                       --15
  shiftDR, clockDR, updateDR, mode, scan_in : BIT;             --16
  scan_out : out BIT;                                          --17
  data_in : BIT_VECTOR(width-1 downto 0);                      --18
  data_out : out BIT_VECTOR(width-1 downto 0));                --19
end component;                                                 --20

component IR generic (width : INTEGER := 4); port (            --21
  shiftIR, clockIR, updateIR, reset_bar, nTRST,                --22
  scan_in : BIT; scan_out : out BIT;                           --23
  data_in : BIT_VECTOR (width-1 downto 0) ;                    --24
  data_out : out BIT_VECTOR (width-1 downto 0) );              --25
end component;                                                 --26

component IR_decoder generic (width : INTEGER := 4); port (    --27
  shiftDR, clockDR, updateDR : BIT;                            --28
  IR_PO : BIT_VECTOR (width-1 downto 0);                       --29
```

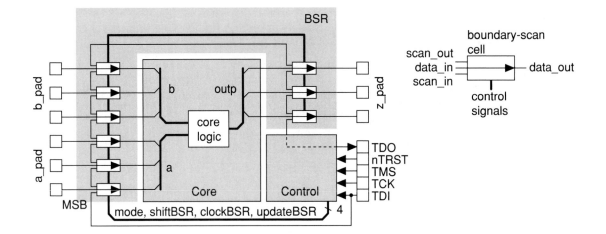

```
entity Core is port (a, b : BIT_VECTOR (2 downto 0);                          --1
  outp : out BIT_VECTOR (2 downto 0)); end Core;                              --2
architecture behave of Core is begin outp <= a when a < b else b;            --3
end behave;                                                                   --4

library IEEE; use IEEE.std_logic_1164.all;                                    --5
entity BST_ASIC is port (TMS, TCK, TDI, nTRST : BIT; TDO : out STD_LOGIC;    --6
  a_PAD, b_PAD : BIT_VECTOR (2 downto 0); z_PAD : out BIT_VECTOR (2 downto 0)); --7
end BST_ASIC;                                                                 --8

architecture structure of BST_ASIC is use work.BST_components.all;           --9
component Core port (a, b: BIT_VECTOR (2 downto 0);                          --10
  outp: out BIT_VECTOR (2 downto 0)); end component;                        --11
for all : Core use entity work.Core(behave);                                --12
constant BSR_width : INTEGER := 9;                                          --13
signal BSR_SO, test_mode, shiftBSR, clockBSR, updateBSR : BIT;              --14
signal BSR_PI, BSR_PO : BIT_VECTOR (BSR_width-1 downto 0);                  --15
signal a, b, z : BIT_VECTOR (2 downto 0);                                   --16
begin BSR_PI <= a_PAD & b_PAD & z ;                                         --17
  a <= BSR_PO(8 downto 6); b <= BSR_PO(5 downto 3); z_pad <= BSR_PO(2 downto 0); --18
CORE1 : Core port map (a, b, z);                                            --19
C1 : Control generic map (width => BSR_width) port map (TMS, TCK, TDI, nTRST, --20
TDO, BSR_SO, BSR_PO, shiftBSR, clockBSR, updateBSR, test_mode);             --21
BSR1 : BSR generic map (width => BSR_width) port map (shiftBSR, clockBSR,   --22
  updateBSR, test_mode, TDI, BSR_SO, BSR_PI, BSR_PO);                       --23
end structure;                                                              --24
```

FIGURE 14.9 A boundary-scan example.

```
  test_mode, selectBR, shiftBR, clockBR, shiftBSR, clockBSR,        --30
  updateBSR: out BIT );                                             --31
end component;                                                      --32

component TAP_sm_states port (                                      --33
  TMS, TCK, nTRST : in BIT; S : out TAP_STATE); end component;      --34

component TAP_sm_output port (                                      --35
  TCK: BIT; S : TAP_STATE; reset_bar, selectIR,                     --36
  enableTDO, shiftIR, clockIR, updateIR, shiftDR, clockDR,          --37
  updateDR : out BIT);                                              --38
end component;                                                      --39

component Control generic (width : INTEGER := 2); port (            --40
  TMS, TCK, TDI, nTRST : BIT; TDO : out STD_LOGIC;                  --41
  BSR_SO : BIT; BSR_PO : BIT_VECTOR (width-1 downto 0);             --42
  shiftBSR, clockBSR, updateBSR, test_mode : out BIT);              --43
end component;                                                      --44

component BST_ASIC port (                                           --45
  TMS, TCK, TDI : BIT; TDO : out STD_LOGIC;                         --46
  a_PAD, b_PAD : BIT_VECTOR (2 downto 0);                           --47
  z_PAD : out BIT_VECTOR (2 downto 0));                             --48
end component;                                                      --49

end;                                                                --50
```

The following testbench, Test_BST, performs these functions:

1. Resets the TAP controller at $t = 10$ ns using nTRST.

2. Continuously clocks the BST clock, TCK, at a frequency of 10 MHz. Rising edges of TCK occur at 100 ns, 200 ns, and so on.

3. Drives a series of values onto the TAP inputs TDI and TMS. The sequence shifts in instruction code '01'(SAMPLE/PRELOAD), followed by '00'(EXTEST).

```
library IEEE; use IEEE.std_logic_1164.all;                         --1
library STD; use STD.TEXTIO.all;                                    --2
entity Test_BST is end;                                            --3
architecture behave of Test_BST is                                 --4
component BST_ASIC port (TMS, TCK, TDI, nTRST: BIT;                 --5
  TDO : out STD_LOGIC; a_PAD, b_PAD : BIT_VECTOR (2 downto 0);      --6
  z_PAD : out BIT_VECTOR (2 downto 0));                             --7
end component;                                                      --8
for all : BST_ASIC use entity work.BST_ASIC(behave);               --9
signal TMS, TCK, TDI, nTRST : BIT; signal TDO : STD_LOGIC;          --10
signal TDI_TMS : BIT_VECTOR (1 downto 0);                           --11
signal a_PAD, b_PAD, z_PAD : BIT_VECTOR (2 downto 0);               --12
begin                                                              --13
TDI <= TDI_TMS(1) ; TMS <= TDI_TMS(0) ;                             --14
ASIC1 : BST_ASIC port map                                          --15
```

```
       (TMS, TCK, TDI, nTRST, TDO, a_PAD, b_PAD, z_PAD);          --16
nTRST_DRIVE : process begin                                        --17
   nTRST <= '1', '0' after 10 ns, '1' after 20 ns; wait;          --18
PAD_DRIVE : process begin                                          --19
   a_PAD <= ('0', '1', '0'); b_PAD <= ('0', '1', '1'); wait;      --20
end process;                                                       --21
end process;                                                       --22
TCK_DRIVE : process begin -- rising edge at 100 ns                 --23
   TCK <= '0' after 50 ns, '1' after 100 ns; wait for 100 ns;     --24
   if (now > 3000 ns) then wait; end if;                          --25
end process;                                                       --26
BST_DRIVE : process begin   TDI_TMS <=                             --27
                            -- State after +VE edge:               --28
   ('0', '1') after 0 ns,      -- Reset                            --29
   ('0', '0') after 101 ns,    -- Run_Idle                         --30
   ('0', '1') after 201 ns,    -- Select_DR                        --31
   ('0', '1') after 301 ns,    -- Select_IR                        --32
   ('0', '0') after 401 ns,    -- Capture_IR                       --33
   ('0', '0') after 501 ns,    -- Shift_IR                         --34
   ('1', '0') after 601 ns,    -- Shift_IR                         --35
   ('0', '1') after 701 ns,    -- Exit1_IR                         --36
   ('0', '1') after 801 ns,    -- Update_IR, 01 = SAMPLE/PRELOAD   --37
   ('0', '1') after 901 ns,    -- Select_DR                        --38
   ('0', '0') after 1001 ns,   -- Capture_DR                       --39
   ('0', '0') after 1101 ns,   -- Shift_DR                         --40
-- shift 111111101 into BSR, TDI(time) = 101111111 starting now    --41
   ('1', '0') after 1201 ns,   -- Shift_DR                         --42
   ('0', '0') after 1301 ns,   -- Shift_DR                         --43
   ('1', '0') after 1401 ns,   -- Shift_DR -- shift 4 more 1's     --44
   ('1', '0') after 1901 ns,   -- Shift_DR -- in-between           --45
   ('1', '1') after 2001 ns,   -- Exit1_DR                         --46
   ('0', '1') after 2101 ns,   -- Update_DR                        --47
   ('0', '1') after 2201 ns,   -- Select_DR                        --48
   ('0', '1') after 2301 ns,   -- Select_IR                        --49
   ('0', '0') after 2401 ns,   -- Capture_IR                       --50
   ('0', '0') after 2501 ns,   -- Shift_IR                         --51
   ('0', '0') after 2601 ns,   -- Shift_IR                         --52
   ('0', '1') after 2701 ns,   -- Exit1_IR                         --53
   ('0', '1') after 2801 ns,   -- Update_IR, 00=EXTEST             --54
   ('0', '0') after 2901 ns;   -- Run_Idle                         --55
   wait;                                                           --56
end process;                                                       --57
process (TDO, a_pad, b_pad, z_pad) variable L : LINE; begin        --58
   write (L, now, RIGHT, 10); write (L, STRING'(" TDO="));         --59
   if TDO = 'Z' then write (L, STRING'("Z")) ;                     --60
      else write (L, TO_BIT(TDO)); end if;                         --61
   write (L, STRING'(" PADS=")); write (L, a_pad & b_pad & z_pad); --62
   writeline (output, L);                                          --63
```

end process;   --64
end behave;   --65

Here is the output from this testbench:

```
#          0 ns  TDO=0  PADS=000000000
#          0 ns  TDO=Z  PADS=010011000
#          0 ns  TDO=Z  PADS=010011010
#        650 ns  TDO=1  PADS=010011010
#        750 ns  TDO=0  PADS=010011010
#        850 ns  TDO=Z  PADS=010011010
#       1250 ns  TDO=0  PADS=010011010
#       1350 ns  TDO=1  PADS=010011010
#       1450 ns  TDO=0  PADS=010011010
#       1550 ns  TDO=1  PADS=010011010
#       1750 ns  TDO=0  PADS=010011010
#       1950 ns  TDO=1  PADS=010011010
#       2050 ns  TDO=0  PADS=010011010
#       2150 ns  TDO=Z  PADS=010011010
#       2650 ns  TDO=1  PADS=010011010
#       2750 ns  TDO=0  PADS=010011010
#       2850 ns  TDO=Z  PADS=010011010
#       2950 ns  TDO=Z  PADS=010011101
```

This trace shows the following activities:

- All changes to TDO and at the pads occur at the negative edge of TCK.

- The core logic output is z_pad = '010' and appears at the I/O pads at $t = 0$ ns. This is the smaller of the two inputs, a_pad = '010' and b_pad = '011', and the correct output when the pads are connected to the core logic.

- At $t = 650$ ns the IDCODE instruction '01' is shifted out on TDO (with '1' appearing first). If we had multiple ASICs in the boundary-scan chain, this would show us that the chain was intact.

- At $t = 850$ ns the TDO output is floated (to 'Z') as we exit the shift_IR state.

- At $t = 1200$ ns the TAP controller begins shifting the serial data input from TDI ('111111101') into the BSR.

- At $t = 1250$ ns the BSR data starts shifting out. This is data that was captured during the SAMPLE/PRELOAD instruction from the device input pins, a_pad and b_pad, as well as the driver of the output pins, z_pad. The data appears as the pattern '010011010'. This pattern consists of a_pad = '010', b_pad = '011', followed by z_pad = '010' (notice that TDO does not change at $t = 1650$ ns or 1850 ns).

- At $t = 2150$ ns, TDO is floated after we exit the shift_DR state.

- At $t = 2650$ ns the IDCODE instruction '01' (loaded into the IR as we passed through capture_IR the second time) is again shifted out as we shift the EXTEST instruction from TDI into the IR.

- At $t = 2650$ ns the TDO output is floated after we exit the shift_IR state.
- At $t = 2950$ ns the output, z_pad, is driven with '101'. The inputs a_pad and b_pad remain unchanged since they are driven from outside the chip. The change on z_pad occurs on the negative edge of TCK because the IR is loaded with the instruction EXTEST on the negative edge of TCK. When this instruction is decoded, the signal mode changes (this signal controls the MUX at the output of the BSCs).

Figure 14.10 shows a signal trace from the MTI simulator for the last four negative edges of TCK. Notice that we shifted in the test pattern on TDI in the order '101111111'. The output z_pad (3 bits wide) is last in the BSR (nearest TDO) and thus is driven with the first 3 bits of this pattern, '101'. Forcing '101' onto the ASIC output pins would allow us to check that this pattern is correctly received at inputs of other connected ASICs through the bonding wires and board traces. In a later test cycle we can force '010' onto z_pad to check that both logic levels can be transmitted and received. We may also capture other signals (which are similarly being forced onto the outputs of neighboring ASICs) at the inputs.

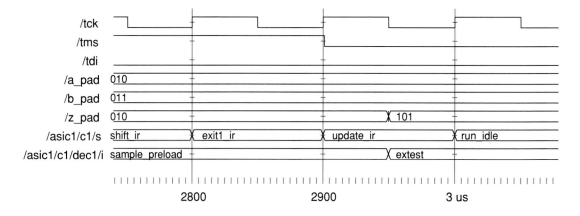

FIGURE 14.10 Results from the MTI simulator for the boundary-scan testbench.

14.2.7 BSDL

The **boundary-scan description language (BSDL)** is an extension of IEEE 1149.1 but without any overlap. BSDL uses a subset of VHDL. The BSDL for an ASIC is part of an imaginary data sheet; it is not intended for simulation and does not include models for any boundary-scan components. BSDL is a standard way to describe the features and behavior of an ASIC that includes IEEE 1149.1 boundary scan and a standard way to pass information to test-generation software. Using BSDL, test software can also check that the BST features are correct. As an example, test software can use the BSDL to check that the ASIC uses the correct boundary-scan cells for the instructions that claim to be supported. BSDL cannot prove that an implementation works, however.

The following example BSDL description corresponds to our halfgate ASIC example with BST (this code was generated automatically by the Compass tools):

```
entity asic_p is                                               --1
generic (PHYSICAL_PIN_MAP : STRING := "DUMMY_PACKAGE");        --2
port (                                                         --3
    pad_a:in BIT_VECTOR (0 to 0);                              --4
    pad_z:buffer BIT_VECTOR (0 to 0);                          --5
    TCK:in BIT;                                                --6
    TDI:in BIT;                                                --7
    TDO:out BIT;                                               --8
    TMS:in BIT;                                                --9
    TRST:in BIT);                                              --10
use STD_1149_1_1994.all;                                       --11
attribute PIN_MAP of asic_p : entity is PHYSICAL_PIN_MAP;      --12
-- CUSTOMIZE package pin mapping.                              --13
constant DUMMY_PACKAGE : PIN_MAP_STRING :=                     --14
    "pad_a:(1)," &                                             --15
    "pad_z:(2)," &                                             --16
    "TCK:3," &                                                 --17
    "TDI:4," &                                                 --18
    "TDO:5," &                                                 --19
    "TMS:6," &                                                 --20
    "TRST:7";                                                  --21
attribute TAP_SCAN_IN of TDI : signal is TRUE;                 --22
attribute TAP_SCAN_MODE of TMS : signal is TRUE;               --23
attribute TAP_SCAN_OUT of TDO : signal is TRUE;                --24
attribute TAP_SCAN_RESET of TRST : signal is TRUE;             --25
-- CUSTOMIZE TCK max freq and safe stop state.                 --26
attribute TAP_SCAN_CLOCK of TCK : signal is (20.0e6, BOTH);    --27
attribute INSTRUCTION_LENGTH of asic_p : entity is 3;          --28
attribute INSTRUCTION_OPCODE of asic_p : entity is             --29
    "IDCODE   (001)," &                                        --30
    "STCTEST  (101)," &                                        --31
    "INTEST   (100)," &                                        --32
    "BYPASS   (111)," &                                        --33
    "SAMPLE   (010)," &                                        --34
    "EXTEST   (000)";                                          --35
attribute INSTRUCTION_CAPTURE of asic_p : entity is "001";     --36
-- attribute INSTRUCTION_DISABLE of asic_p : entity is " "     --37
-- attribute INSTRUCTION_GUARD of asic_p : entity is " "       --38
-- attribute INSTRUCTION_PRIVATE of asic_p : entity is " "     --39
attribute IDCODE_REGISTER of asic_p : entity is               --40
    "0000" &                -- 4-bit version                   --41
    "0000000000000000" &    -- 16-bit part number              --42
```

```
          "00000101011" &          -- 11-bit manufacturer          --43
          "1";                     -- mandatory LSB                 --44
-- attribute USERCODE_REGISTER of asic_p : entity is " "           --45
attribute REGISTER_ACCESS of asic_p : entity is                    --46
     "BOUNDARY (STCTEST)";                                          --47
attribute BOUNDARY_CELLS of asic_p : entity is                     --48
     "BC_1, BC_2";                                                 --49
attribute BOUNDARY_LENGTH of asic_p : entity is 2;                 --50
attribute BOUNDARY_REGISTER of asic_p : entity is                  --51
   -- num   cell     port    function  safe [ccell disval rslt]    --52
   "    1 ( BC_2, pad_a(0),     input,   X)," &                    --53
   "    0 ( BC_1, pad_z(0),   output2,   X)";                      --54
   -- " 98 ( BC_1, OE, input, X), " &                              --55
   -- " 98 ( BC_1, *, control, 0), " &                             --56
   -- " 99 ( BC_1, myport(0), output3, X, 98, 0, Z);               --57
end asic_p;                                                         --58
```

The functions of the lines of this BSDL description are as follows:

- Line 2 refers to the ASIC package. We can have the same part (with identical pad numbers on the silicon die) in different ASIC packages. We include the name of the ASIC package in line 2 and the pin mapping between bonding pads and ASIC package pins in lines 14–21.

- Lines 3–10 describe the signal names of inputs and outputs, the TAP pins, and the optional fifth TAP reset signal. The BST signals do not have to be given the names used in the standard: TCK, TDI, and so on.

- Line 11 refers to the VHDL package, STD_1149_1_1994. This is a small VHDL package (just over 100 lines) that contains definitions of the constants, types, and attributes used in a BSDL description. It does not contain any models for simulation.

- Lines 22–25 attach signal names to the required TAP pins and the optional fifth TAP reset signal.

- Lines 26–27 refer to the maximum test clock frequency in hertz, and whether the clock may be stopped in both states or just the low state (just the high state is not valid).

- Line 28 describes a 3-bit IR (in the comparator/MUX example we used a 2-bit IR). Length must be greater than or equal to 2.

- Lines 29–35 describe the three required instruction opcodes and mnemonics (BYPASS, SAMPLE, EXTEST) and three optional instructions: IDCODE, STCTEST (which is a scan test mode), and INTEST (which supports internal testing in the same fashion as EXTEST supports external testing). EXTEST must be all ones; BYPASS must be all zeros. A mnemonic may have more than one opcode (and opcodes may be specified using 'x'). Other instructions that may appear here include CLAMP and HIGHZ, both optional instructions that were added to 1149.1 (see Supplement A, 1149.1a). String concatenation is used in BSDL to avoid line-break problems.

- Lines 37–39 include instruction attributes INSTRUCTION_DISABLE (for HIGHZ), INSTRUCTION_GUARD (for CLAMP), as well as INSTRUCTION_PRIVATE (for user-defined instructions) that are not used in this example.

- Lines 40–44 describe the IDCODE TDR. The 11-bit manufacturer number is determined from codes assigned by JEDEC Publication 106-A.

- Line 45 describes the USERCODE TDR in a similar fashion to IDCODE, but is not used here.

- Lines 46–47 describe the TDRs for user-defined instructions. In this case the existing BOUNDARY TDR is inserted between TDI and TDO during STCTEST. User-defined instructions listed here may use the other existing IDCODE and BYPASS TDRs or define new TDRs.

- Lines 48–49 list the boundary-scan cells used in the ASIC. These may be any of the following cells defined in the 1149.1 standard and defined in the VHDL package, STD_1149_1_1994: BC_1 (Figs. 10-18, 10-29, 10-31c, 10-31d, and 10-33c), BC_2 (Figs. 10-14, 10-30, 10-32c, 10-32d, 10-35c), BC_3 (Fig. 10-15), BC_4 (Figs. 10-16, 10-17), BC_5 (Fig. 10-41c), BC_6 (Fig. 10-34d). The figure numbers in parentheses here refer to the IEEE 1149.1 standard [IEEE 1149.1b-1994]. Alternatively the cells may be user-defined (and must then be declared in a package).

- Line 50 must be an integer greater than zero and match the number defined by following register description.

- Lines 51–54 are an array of records, numbered by cell, with seven fields: four required and three that only appear for certain cells. Field 1 specifies the scan cell name as defined in the STD_1149_1_1994 or user-defined package. Field 2 is the port name, with a subscript if the type is BIT_VECTOR. An '*' denotes no connection. Field 3 is one of the following cell functions (with figure or page numbers from the IEEE standard [IEEE 1149.1b-1994]): input (Fig. 10-18), clock (Fig. 10-17), output2 (two-state output, Fig. 10-29), output3 (three-state, Fig. 10-31d), internal (p. 33, 1149.1b), control (Fig. 10-31c), controlr (Fig. 10-33c), bidir_in (a reversible cell acting as an input, Fig. 10-34d), bidir_out (a reversible cell acting as an output, Fig. 10-34d). Field 4, safe, contains the safe value to be loaded into the update flip-flop when otherwise unspecified, with 'X' as a don't care value.

- Lines 55–57 illustrate the use of the optional three fields. Field 5, ccell or control cell, refers to the cell number (98 in this example) of the cell that controls an output or bidirectional cell. The control cell number 98 is a merged cell in this example with an input cell, input signal name OE, also labeled as cell number 98. The ASIC input OE (for output enable) thus directly controls (enables) the ASIC three-state output, myport(0).

The boundary-scan standard may seem like a complicated way to test the connections *outside* an ASIC. However, the IEEE 1149.1 standard also gives us a method to communicate with test circuits *inside* an ASIC. Next, we turn our attention from problems at the board level to problems that may occur within the ASIC.

14.3 Faults

Fabrication of an ASIC is a complicated process requiring hundreds of processing steps. Problems may introduce a **defect** that in turn may introduce a **fault** (Sabnis [1990] describes **defect mechanisms**). Any problem during fabrication may prevent a transistor from working and may break or join interconnections. Two common types of defects occur in metallization [Rao, 1993]: either underetching the metal (a problem between long, closely spaced lines), which results in a **bridge** or short circuit (**shorts**) between adjacent lines, or overetching the metal and causing **breaks** or open circuits (**opens**). Defects may also arise after chip fabrication is complete—while testing the wafer, cutting the die from the wafer, or mounting the die in a package. Wafer probing, wafer saw, die attach, wire bonding, and the intermediate handling steps each have their own defect and failure mechanisms. Many different materials are involved in the packaging process that have different mechanical, electrical, and thermal properties, and these differences can cause defects due to corrosion, stress, adhesion failure, cracking, and peeling. Yield loss also occurs from human error—using the wrong mask, incorrectly setting the implant dose—as well as from physical sources: contaminated chemicals, dirty etch sinks, or a troublesome process step. It is possible to repeat or **rework** some of the reversible steps (a lithography step, for example—but not etching) if there are problems. However, reliance on rework indicates a poorly controlled process.

14.3.1 Reliability

It is possible for defects to be nonfatal but to cause failures early in the life of a product. We call this **infant mortality**. Most products follow the same kinds of trend for failures as a function of life. Failure rates decrease rapidly to a low value that remains steady until the end of life when failure rates increase again; this is called a **bathtub curve**. The end of a product lifetime is determined by various **wearout mechanisms** (usually these are controlled by an exponential energy process). Some of the most important wearout mechanisms in ASICs are hot-electron wearout, electromigration, and the failure of antifuses in FPGAs.

We can catch some of the products that are susceptible to early failure using **burn-in**. Many failure mechanisms have a failure rate proportional to $\exp(-E_a/kT)$. This is the **Arrhenius equation**, where E_a is a known **activation energy** (k is Boltzmann's constant, $8.62 \times 10^{-5}\,\mathrm{eVK^{-1}}$, and T the absolute temperature). Operating an ASIC at an elevated temperature accelerates this type of failure mechanism. Depending on the physics of the failure mechanism, additional stresses, such as elevated current or voltage, may also accelerate failures. The longer and harsher the burn-in conditions, the more likely we are to find problems, but the more costly the process and the more costly the parts.

We can measure the overall **reliability** of any product using the **mean time between failures (MTBF)** for a repairable product or **mean time to failure (MTTF)** for a fatal failure. We also use **failures in time (FITs)** where 1 FIT equals a single failure in 10^9 hours. We can sum the FITs for all the components in a product to determine an overall measure for the product reliability. Suppose we have a system with the following components:

- Microprocessor (standard part) 5 FITs
- 100 TTL parts, 50 parts at 10 FITs, 50 parts at 15 FITs
- 100 RAM chips, 6 FITs

The overall failure rate for this system is $5 + 50 \times 10 + 50 \times 15 + 100 \times 6 = 1855$ FITs. Suppose we could reduce the component count using ASICs to the following:

- Microprocessor (custom) 7 FITs
- 9 ASICs, 10 FITs
- 5 SIMMs, 15 FITs

The failure rate is now $10 + 9 \times 10 + 5 \times 15 = 175$ FITs, or about an order of magnitude lower. This is the rationale behind the Sun SparcStation 1 design described in Section 1.3, "Case Study."

14.3.2 Fault Models

Table 14.6 shows some of the causes of faults. The first column shows the **fault level**—whether the fault occurs in the logic gates on the chip or in the package. The second column describes the **physical fault**. There are too many of these and we need a way to reduce and simplify their effects—by using a fault model.

There are several types of **fault model**. First, we simplify things by mapping from a physical fault to a **logical fault**. Next, we distinguish between those logical faults that degrade the ASIC performance and those faults that are fatal and stop the ASIC from working at all. There are three kinds of logical faults in Table 14.6: a degradation fault, an open-circuit fault, and a short-circuit fault.

A **degradation fault** may be a **parametric fault** or **delay fault** (**timing fault**). A parametric fault might lead to an incorrect switching threshold in a TTL/CMOS level converter at an input, for example. We can test for parametric faults using a production tester. A **delay fault** might lead to a critical path being slower than specification. Delay faults are much harder to test in production. An **open-circuit fault** results from physical faults such as a bad contact, a piece of metal that is missing or overetched, or a break in a polysilicon line. These physical faults all result in failure to transmit a logic level from one part of a circuit to another—an open circuit. A **short-circuit fault** results from such physical faults as: underetching of metal; spiking, pinholes or shorts across the gate oxide; and diffusion shorts. These faults result

TABLE 14.6   Mapping physical faults to logical faults.

Fault level	Physical fault	Logical fault		
		Degradation fault	Open-circuit fault	Short-circuit fault
Chip				
	Leakage or short between package leads	•		•
	Broken, misaligned, or poor wire bonding		•	
	Surface contamination, moisture	•		
	Metal migration, stress, peeling		•	•
	Metallization (open or short)		•	•
Gate				
	Contact opens		•	
	Gate to S/D junction short	•		•
	Field-oxide parasitic device	•		•
	Gate-oxide imperfection, spiking	•		•
	Mask misalignment	•		•

in a circuit being accidentally connected—a short circuit. Most short-circuit faults occur in interconnect; often we call these **bridging faults** (BF). A BF usually results from **metal coverage** problems that lead to shorts. You may see reference to **feedback bridging faults** and **nonfeedback bridging faults**, a useful distinction when trying to predict the results of faults on logic operation. Bridging faults are a frequent problem in CMOS ICs.

14.3.3   Physical Faults

Figure 14.11 shows the following examples of physical faults in a logic cell:

- F1 is a short between m1 lines and connects node n1 to VSS.
- F2 is an open on the poly layer and disconnects the gate of transistor t1 from the rest of the circuit.
- F3 is an open on the poly layer and disconnects the gate of transistor t3 from the rest of the circuit.
- F4 is a short on the poly layer and connects the gate of transistor t4 to the gate of transistor t5.
- F5 is an open on m1 and disconnects node n4 from the output Z1.
- F6 is a short on m1 and connects nodes p5 and p6.
- F7 is a nonfatal defect that causes necking on m1.

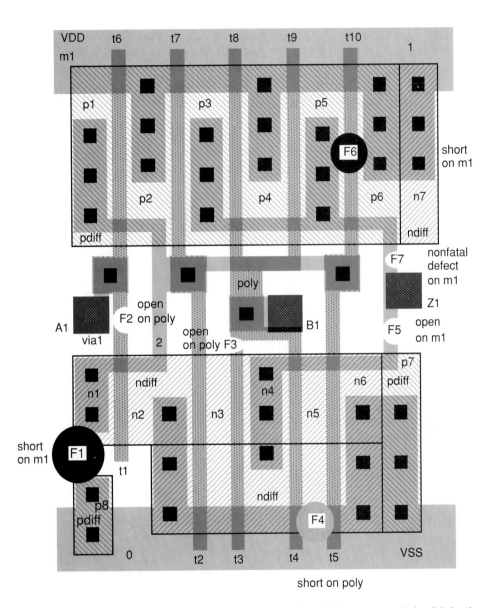

FIGURE 14.11 Defects and physical faults. Many types of defects occur during fabrication. Defects can be of any size and on any layer. Only a few small sample defects are shown here using a typical standard cell as an example. Defect density for a modern CMOS process is of the order of 1 cm^{-2} or less across a whole wafer. The logic cell shown here is approximately 64 × 32 λ^2, or 250 μm^2 for a λ = 0.25 μm process. We would thus have to examine approximately 1 cm^{-2}/250 μm^2 or 400,000 such logic cells to find a single defect.

Once we have reduced the large number of physical faults to fewer logical faults, we need a model to predict their effect. The most common model is the **stuck-at fault model**.

14.3.4   Stuck-at Fault Model

The **single stuck-at fault** (SSF) model assumes that there is just one fault in the logic we are testing. We use a single stuck-at fault model because a **multiple stuck-at fault model** that could handle several faults in the logic at the same time is too complicated to implement. We hope that any multiple faults are caught by single stuck-at fault tests [Agarwal and Fung, 1981; Hughes and McCluskey, 1986]. In practice this seems to be true.

There are other fault models. For example, we can assume that faults are located in the transistors using a **stuck-on fault** and **stuck-open fault** (or **stuck-off fault**). Fault models such as these are more realistic in that they more closely model the actual physical faults. However, in practice the simple SSF model has been found to work—and work well. We shall concentrate on the SSF model.

In the SSF model we further assume that the effect of the physical fault (whatever it may be) is to create only two kinds of logical fault. The two types of logical faults or **stuck-at faults** are: a **stuck-at-1 fault** (abbreviated to SA1 or s@1) and a **stuck-at-0 fault** (SA0 or s@0). We say that we **place faults** (**inject faults**, **seed faults**, or **apply faults**) on a node (or net), on an input of a circuit, or on an output of a circuit. The location at which we place the fault is the **fault origin**.

A **net fault** forces all the logic cell inputs that the net drives to a logic '1' or '0'. An **input fault** attached to a logic cell input forces the logic cell input to a '1' or '0', but does not affect other logic cell inputs on the same net. An **output fault** attached to the output of a logic cell can have different strengths. If an output fault is a **supply-strength fault** (or **rail-strength** fault) the logic-cell output node and every other node on that net is forced to a '1' or '0'—as if all these nodes were connected to one of the supply rails. An alternative assigns the same strength to the output fault as the drive strength of the logic cell. This allows contention between outputs on a net driving the same node. There is no standard method of handling **output-fault strength**, and no standard for using types of stuck-at faults. Usually we do not inject net faults; instead we inject only input faults and output faults. Some people use the term **node fault**—but in different ways to mean either a net fault, input fault, or output fault.

We usually inject stuck-at faults to the inputs and outputs, the pins, of logic cells (AND gates, OR gates, flip-flops, and so on). We do not inject faults to the internal nodes of a flip-flop, for example. We call this a **pin-fault model** and say the fault level is at the **structural level**, gate level, or cell level. We could apply faults to the internal logic of a logic cell (such as a flip-flop) and (the fault level would then be at the transistor level or switch level. We do not use transistor-level or switch-level fault models because there is often no need. From experience, but not from any theoretical reason, it turns out that using a fault model that applies faults at the logic-cell level is sufficient to catch the bad chips in a production test.

When a fault changes the circuit behavior, the change is called the **fault effect**. Fault effects travel through the circuit to other logic cells causing other fault effects. This phenomenon is **fault propagation**. If the fault level is at the structural level, the phenomenon is **structural fault propagation**. If we have one or more large functional blocks in a design, we want to apply faults to the functional blocks only at the inputs and outputs of the blocks. We do not want to place (or cannot place) faults inside the blocks, but we do want faults to propagate through the blocks. This is **behavioral fault propagation**.

Designers adjust the fault level to the appropriate level at which they think there may be faults. Suppose we are performing a fault simulation on a board and we have already tested the chips. Then we might set the fault level to the chip level, placing faults only at the chip pins. For ASICs we use the logic-cell level. You have to be careful, though, if you mix behavioral level and structural level models in a **mixed-level fault simulation**. You need to be sure that the behavioral models propagates faults correctly. In particular, if the behavioral model responds to faults on its inputs by propagating too many unknown 'X' values to its outputs, this will decrease the fault coverage, because the model is hiding the logic beyond it.

14.3.5 Logical Faults

Figure 14.12 and the following list show how the defects and physical faults of Figure 14.11 translate to logical faults (not all physical faults translate to logical faults—most do not):

- F1 translates to node n1 being stuck at 0, equivalent to A1 being stuck at 1.

- F2 will probably result in node n1 remaining high, equivalent to A1 being stuck-at-0.

- F3 will affect half of the n-channel pull-down stack and may result in a degradation fault, depending on what happens to the floating gate of T3. The cell will still work, but the fall time at the output will approximately double. A fault such as this in the middle of a chain of logic is extremely hard to detect.

- F4 is a bridging fault whose effect depends on the relative strength of the transistors driving this node. The fault effect is not well modeled by a stuck-at fault model.

- F5 completely disables half of the n-channel pulldown stack and will result in a degradation fault.

- F6 shorts the output node to VDD and is equivalent to Z1 stuck at 1.

- Fault F7 could result in infant mortality. If this line did break due to electromigration the cell could no longer pull Z1 up to VDD. This would translate to a Z1 stuck at 0. This fault would probably be fatal and stop the ASIC working.

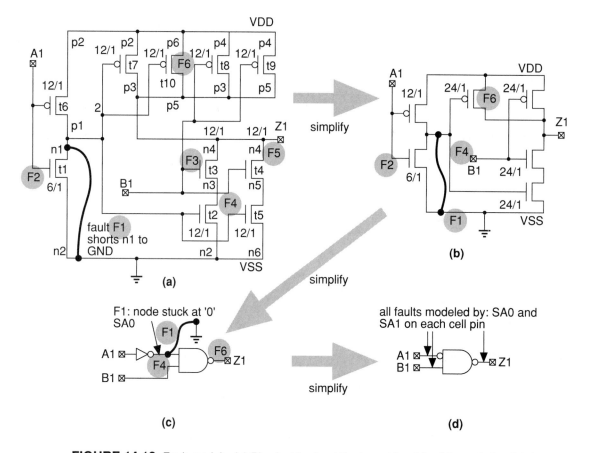

FIGURE 14.12 Fault models. (a) Physical faults at the layout level (problems during fabrication) shown in Figure 14.11 translate to electrical problems on the detailed circuit schematic. The location and effect of fault F1 is shown. The locations of the other fault examples from Figure 14.11 (F2–F6) are shown, but not their effect. (b) We can translate some of these faults to the simplified transistor schematic. (c) Only a few of the physical faults still remain in a gate-level fault model of the logic cell. (d) Finally at the functional-level fault model of a logic cell, we abandon the connection between physical and logical faults and model all faults by stuck-at faults. This a very poor model of the physical reality, but it works well in practice.

14.3.6   IDDQ Test

When they receive a prototype ASIC, experienced designers measure the resistance between VDD and GND pins. Providing there is not a short between VDD and GND, they connect the power supplies and measure the power-supply current. From experience they know that a supply current of more than a few milliamperes indicates a bad chip. This is exactly what we want in production test: Find the bad chips quickly, get them off the tester, and save expensive tester time. An **IDDQ** (IDD stands for the supply current, and Q stands for quiescent) test is one of the first production tests applied to a chip on the tester, after the chip logic has been initialized [Gulati and Hawkins, 1993; Rajsuman, 1994]. High supply current can result from bridging faults that we described in Section 14.3.2. For example, the bridging fault F4 in Figure 14.11 and Figure 14.12 would cause excessive IDDQ if node n1 and input B1 are being driven to opposite values.

14.3.7   Fault Collapsing

Figure 14.13(a) shows a test for a stuck-at-1 output of a two-input NAND gate. Figure 14.13(b) shows tests for other stuck-at faults. We assume that the NAND gate still works correctly in the **bad circuit** (also called the **faulty circuit** or **faulty machine**) even if we have an input fault. The input fault on a logic cell is presumed to arise either from a fault from a preceding logic cell or a fault on the connection to the input.

Stuck-at faults attached to different points in a circuit may produce identical fault effects. Using **fault collapsing** we can group these **equivalent faults** (or **indistinguishable faults**) into a **fault-equivalence class**. To save time we need only consider one fault, called the **prime fault** or **representative fault**, from a fault-equivalence class. For example, Figure 14.13(a) and (b) show that a stuck-at-0 input and a stuck-at-1 output are equivalent faults for a two-input NAND gate. We only need to check for one fault, Z1 (output stuck at 1), to catch any of the equivalent faults.

Suppose that any of the tests that detect a fault B also detects fault A, but only some of the tests for fault A also detect fault B. W say A is a **dominant fault**, or that fault A dominates fault B (this the definition of fault dominance that we shall use, some texts say fault B dominates fault A in this situation). Clearly to reduce the number of tests using **dominant fault collapsing** we will pick the test for fault B. For example, Figure 14.13(c) shows that the output stuck at 0 dominates either input stuck at 1 for a two-input NAND. By testing for fault A1, we automatically detect the fault Z1. Confusion over dominance arises because of the difference between focusing on faults (Figure 14.13d) or test vectors (Figure 14.13e).

Figure 14.13(f) shows the six stuck-at faults for a two-input NAND gate. We can place SA1 or SA0 on each of the two input pins (four faults in total) and SA1 or SA0 on the output pins. Using fault equivalence (Figure 14.13g) we can collapse six faults to four: SA1 on each input, and SA1 or SA0 on the output. Using fault dominance (Figure 14.13h) we can collapse six faults to three. There is no way to tell the difference between equivalent faults, but if we use dominant fault collapsing we may lose information about the fault location.

14.3.8   Fault-Collapsing Example

Figure 14.14 shows an example of fault collapsing. Using the properties of logic cells to reduce the number of faults that we need to consider is called **gate collapsing**. We can also use **node collapsing** by examining the effect of faults on the same

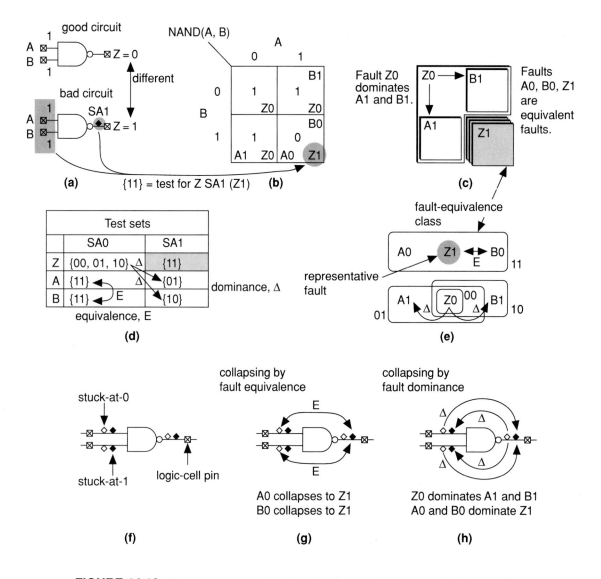

FIGURE 14.13 Fault dominance and fault equivalence. (a) We can test for fault Z0 (Z stuck at 0) by applying a test vector that makes the bad (faulty) circuit produce a different output than the good circuit. (b) Some test vectors provide tests for more than one fault. (c) A test for A stuck at 1 (A1) will also test for Z stuck at 0; 0 dominates A1. The fault effects of faults: A0, B0 and Z1 are the same. These faults are equivalent. (d) There are six sets of input vectors that test for the six stuck-at faults. (e) We only need to choose a subset of all test vectors that test for all faults. (f) The six stuck-at faults for a two-input NAND logic cell. (g) Using fault equivalence we can collapse six faults to four. (h) Using fault dominance we can collapse six faults to three.

node. Consider two inverters in series. An output fault on the first inverter collapses with the node fault on the net connecting the inverters. We can collapse the node fault in turn with the input fault of the second inverter. The details of fault collapsing depends on whether the simulator uses net or pin faults, the fanin and fanout of nodes, and the output fault-strength model used.

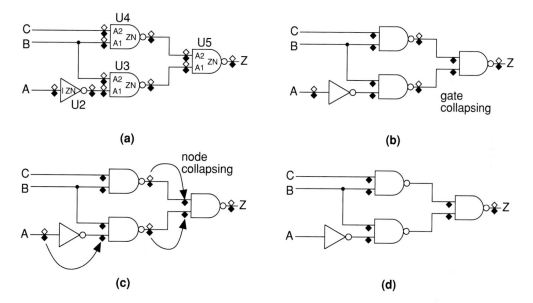

(a)

(b)

(c)

(d)

FIGURE 14.14 Fault collapsing for A'B + BC. (a) A pin-fault model. Each pin has stuck-at-0 and stuck-at-1 faults. (b) Using fault equivalence the pin faults at the input pins and output pins of logic cells are collapsed. This is gate collapsing. (c) We can reduce the number of faults we need to consider further by collapsing equivalent faults on nodes and between logic cells. This is node collapsing. (d) The final circuit has eight stuck-at faults (reduced from the 22 original faults). If we wished to use fault dominance we could also eliminate the stuck-at-0 fault on Z. Notice that in a pin-fault model we cannot collapse the faults U4.A1.SA1 and U3.A2.SA1 even though they are on the same net.

14.4   Fault Simulation

We use **fault simulation** after we have completed logic simulation to see what happens in a design when we deliberately introduce faults. In a production test we only have access to the package pins—the **primary inputs (PIs)** and **primary outputs (POs)**. To test an ASIC we must devise a series of sets of input patterns that will detect any faults. A **stimulus** is the application of one such set of inputs (a **test**

vector) to the PIs of an ASIC. A typical ASIC may have several hundred PIs and therefore each test vector is several hundred bits long. A **test program** consists of a set of test vectors. Typical ASIC test programs require tens of thousands and sometimes hundreds of thousands of test vectors.

The **test-cycle time** is the period of time the tester requires to apply the stimulus, sense the POs, and check that the actual output is equal to the expected output. Suppose the test cycle time is 100 ns (corresponding to a test frequency of 10 MHz), in which case we might **sense** (or **strobe**) the POs at 90 ns after the beginning of each test cycle. Using fault simulation we mimic the behavior of the production test. The fault simulator deliberately introduces all possible faults into our ASIC, one at a time, to see if the test program will find them. For the moment we dodge the problem of how to create the thousands of test vectors required in a typical test program and focus on fault simulation.

As each fault is inserted, the fault simulator runs our test program. If the fault simulation shows that the POs of the faulty circuit are different than the PIs of the good circuit at any strobe time, then we have a **detected fault**; otherwise we have an **undetected fault**. The list of **fault origins** is collected in a file and as the faults are inserted and simulated, the results are recorded and the faults are marked according to the result. At the end of fault simulation we can find the **fault coverage**,

$$\text{fault coverage} = \text{detected faults} \,/\, \text{detectable faults.} \tag{14.1}$$

Detected faults and detectable faults will be defined in Section 14.4.5, after the description of fault simulation. For now assume that we wish to achieve close to 100 percent fault coverage. How does fault coverage relate to the ASIC defect level?

Table 14.7 shows the results of a typical experiment to measure the relationship between single stuck-at fault coverage and AQL. Table 14.7 completes a circle with test and repair costs in Table 14.1 and defect levels in Table 14.2. These experimental results are the only justification (but a good one) for our assumptions in adopting the SSF model. We are not quite sure why this model works so well, but, being engineers, as long as it continues to work we do not worry too much.

TABLE 14.7   Average quality level as a function of single stuck-at fault coverage.

Fault coverage	Average defect level	Average quality level (AQL)
50%	7%	93 %
90%	3%	97 %
95%	1%	99 %
99%	0.1%	99.9 %
99.9%	0.01%	99.99 %

There are several algorithms for fault simulation: serial fault-simulation, parallel fault-simulation, and concurrent fault-simulation. Next, we shall discuss each of these types of fault simulation in turn.

14.4.1 Serial Fault Simulation

Serial fault simulation is the simplest fault-simulation algorithm. We simulate two copies of the circuit, the first copy is a good circuit. We then pick a fault and insert it into the faulty circuit. In test terminology, the circuits are called **machines**, so the two copies are a **good machine** and a **faulty machine**. We shall continue to use the term *circuit* here to show the similarity between logic and fault simulation (the simulators are often the same program used in different modes). We then repeat the process, simulating one faulty circuit at a time. Serial simulation is slow and is impractical for large ASICs.

14.4.2 Parallel Fault Simulation

Parallel fault simulation takes advantage of multiple bits of the words in computer memory. In the simplest case we need only one bit to represent either a '1' or '0' for each node in the circuit. In a computer that uses a 32-bit word memory we can simulate a set of 32 copies of the circuit at the same time. One copy is the good circuit, and we insert different faults into the other copies. When we need to perform a logic operation, to model an AND gate for example, we can perform the operation across all bits in the word simultaneously. In this case, using one bit per node on a 32-bit machine, we would expect parallel fault simulation to be about 32 times faster than serial simulation. The number of bits per node that we need in order to simulate each circuit depends on the number of states in the logic system we are using. Thus, if we use a four-state system with '1', '0', 'X' (unknown), and 'Z' (high-impedance) states, we need two bits per node.

Parallel fault simulation is not quite as fast as our simple prediction because we have to simulate all the circuits in parallel until the last fault in the current set is detected. If we use serial simulation we can stop as soon as a fault is detected and then start another fault simulation. Parallel fault simulation is faster than serial fault simulation but not as fast as concurrent fault simulation. It is also difficult to include behavioral models using parallel fault simulation.

14.4.3 Concurrent Fault Simulation

Concurrent fault simulation is the most widely used fault-simulation algorithm and takes advantage of the fact that a fault does not affect the whole circuit. Thus we do not need to simulate the whole circuit for each new fault. In concurrent simulation we first completely simulate the good circuit. We then inject a fault and resimulate a copy of only that part of the circuit that behaves differently (this is the **diverged circuit**). For example, if the fault is in an inverter that is at a primary output, only the inverter needs to be simulated—we can remove everything preceding the inverter.

Keeping track of exactly which parts of the circuit need to be diverged for each new fault is complicated, but the savings in memory and processing that result allow hundreds of faults to be simulated concurrently. Concurrent simulation is split into several chunks, you can usually control how many faults (usually around 100) are simulated in each chunk or **pass**. Each pass thus consists of a series of test cycles. Every circuit has a unique **fault-activity signature** that governs the divergence that occurs with different test vectors. Thus every circuit has a different optimum setting for **faults per pass**. Too few faults per pass will not use resources efficiently. Too many faults per pass will overflow the memory.

14.4.4   Nondeterministic Fault Simulation

Serial, parallel, and concurrent fault-simulation algorithms are forms of **deterministic fault simulation**. In each of these algorithms we use a set of test vectors to simulate a circuit and discover which faults we can detect. If the fault coverage is inadequate, we modify the test vectors and repeat the fault simulation. This is a very time-consuming process.

As an alternative we give up trying to simulate every possible fault and instead, using **probabilistic fault simulation**, we simulate a subset or sample of the faults and extrapolate fault coverage from the sample.

In **statistical fault simulation** we perform a fault-free simulation and use the results to predict fault coverage. This is done by computing measures of observability and controllability at every node.

We know that a node is not stuck if we can make the node toggle—that is, change from a '0' to '1' or vice versa. A **toggle test** checks which nodes toggle as a result of applying test vectors and gives a statistical estimate of **vector quality**, a measure of faults detected per test vector. There is a strong correlation between high-quality test vectors, the vectors that will detect most faults, and the test vectors that have the highest **toggle coverage**. Testing for nodes toggling simply requires a single logic simulation that is much faster than complete fault simulation.

We can obtain a considerable improvement in fault simulation speed by putting the high-quality test vectors at the beginning of the simulation. The sooner we can detect faults and eliminate them from having to be considered in each simulation, the faster the simulation will progress. We take the same approach when running a production test and initially order the test vectors by their contribution to fault coverage. This assumes that all faults are equally likely. Test engineers can then modify the test program if they discover vectors late in the test program that are efficient in detecting faulty chips.

14.4.5   Fault-Simulation Results

The output of a fault simulator separates faults into several **fault categories**. If we can detect a fault at a location, it is a **testable fault**. A testable fault must be placed on a **controllable net**, so that we can change the logic level at that location from '0' to '1' and from '1' to '0'. A testable fault must also be on an **observable net**, so that we can see the effect of the fault at a PO. This means that **uncontrollable nets** and **unobservable nets** result in faults we cannot detect. We call these faults **untested faults, untestable faults,** or **impossible faults**.

If a PO of the good circuit is the opposite to that of the faulty circuit, we have a detected fault (sometimes called a **hard-detected fault** or a **definitely detected fault**). If the POs of the good circuit and faulty circuit are identical, we have an **undetected fault**. If a PO of the good circuit is a '1' or a '0' but the corresponding PO of the faulty circuit is an 'X' (unknown, either '0' or '1'), we have a **possibly detected fault** (also called a **possible-detected fault, potential fault,** or **potentially detected fault**).

If the PO of the good circuit changes between a '1' and a '0' while the faulty circuit remains at 'X', then we have a **soft-detected fault**. Soft-detected faults are a subset of possibly detected faults. Some simulators keep track of these soft-detected faults separately. Soft-detected faults are likely to be detected on a real tester if this sequence occurs often. Most fault simulators allow you to set a **fault-drop threshold** so that the simulator will remove faults from further consideration after soft-detecting or possibly detecting them a specified number of times. This is called **fault dropping** (or **fault discarding**). The more often a fault is possibly detected, the more likely it is to be detected on a real tester.

A **redundant fault** is a fault that makes no difference to the circuit operation. A combinational circuit with no such faults is **irredundant**. There are close links between logic-synthesis algorithms and redundancy. Logic-synthesis algorithms can produce combinational logic that is irredundant and 100 % testable for single stuck-at faults by removing redundant logic as part of logic minimization.

If a fault causes a circuit to oscillate, it is an **oscillatory fault**. Oscillation can occur within feedback loops in combinational circuits with zero-delay models. A fault that affects a larger than normal portion of the circuit is a **hyperactive fault**. Fault simulators have settings to prevent such faults from using excessive amounts of computation time. It is very annoying to run a fault simulation for several days only to discover that the entire time was taken up by simulating a single fault in a RS flip-flop or on the clock net, for example. Figure 14.15 shows some examples of fault categories.

14.4.6 Fault-Simulator Logic Systems

In addition to the way the fault simulator counts faults in various fault categories, the number of detected faults during fault simulation also depends on the logic system used by the fault simulator. As an example, Cadence's VeriFault concurrent fault simulator uses a logic system with the six logic values: '0', '1', 'Z', 'L', 'H', 'X'. Table 14.8 shows the results of comparing the faulty and the good circuit simulations.

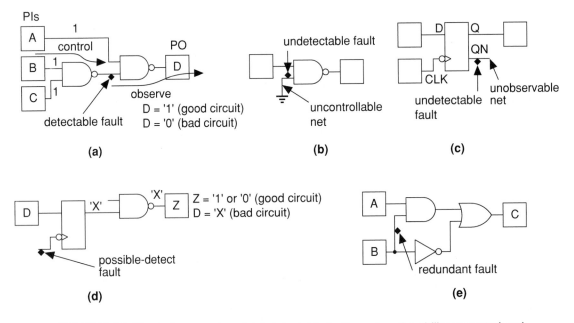

FIGURE 14.15 Fault categories. (a) A detectable fault requires the ability to control and observe the fault origin. (b) A net that is fixed in value is uncontrollable and therefore will produce one undetected fault. (c) Any net that is unconnected is unobservable and will produce undetected faults. (d) A net that produces an unknown 'X' in the faulty circuit and a '1' or a '0' in the good circuit may be detected (depending on whether the 'X' is in fact a '0' or '1'), but we cannot say for sure. At some point this type of fault is likely to produce a discrepancy between good and bad circuits and will eventually be detected. (e) A redundant fault does not affect the operation of the good circuit. In this case the AND gate is redundant since AB + B' = A + B'.

From Table 14.8 we can deduce that, in this logic system:

- Fault detection is possible only if the good circuit and the bad circuit both produce either a '1' or a '0'.

- If the good circuit produces a 'z' at a three-state output, no faults can be detected (not even a fault on the three-state output).

- If the good circuit produces anything other than a '1' or '0', no faults can be detected.

A fault simulator assigns faults to each of the categories we have described. We define the fault coverage as:

$$\text{fault coverage} = \text{detected faults} / \text{detectable faults}. \qquad (14.2)$$

The number of detectable faults excludes any undetectable fault categories (untestable or redundant faults). Thus,

$$\text{detectable faults} = \text{faults} - \text{undetectable faults}, \tag{14.3}$$

$$\text{undetectable faults} = \text{untested faults} + \text{redundant faults}. \tag{14.4}$$

The fault simulator may also produce an analysis of **fault grading**. This is a graph, histogram, or tabular listing showing the cumulative fault coverage as a function of the number of test vectors. This information is useful to remove **dead test cycles**, which contain vectors that do not add to fault coverage. If you reinitialize the circuit at regular intervals, you can remove vectors up to an initialization without altering the function of any vectors after the initialization. The list of faults that the simulator inserted is the **fault list.** In addition to the fault list, a **fault dictionary** lists the faults with their corresponding primary outputs (the **faulty output vector**). The set of input vectors and faulty output vectors that uniquely identify a fault is the **fault signature**. This information can be useful to test engineers, allowing them to work backward from production test results and pinpoint the cause of a problem if several ASICs fail on the tester for the same reasons.

TABLE 14.8   The VeriFault concurrent fault simulator logic system.[1]

		Faulty circuit					
		0	1	Z	L	H	X
Good circuit	0	U	D	P	P	P	P
	1	D	U	P	P	P	P
	Z	U	U	U	U	U	U
	L	U	U	U	U	U	U
	H	U	U	U	U	U	U
	X	U	U	U	U	U	U

[1] L = 0 or Z; H = 1 or Z; Z = high impedance; X = unknown; D = detected; P = potentially detected; U = undetected.

14.4.7 Hardware Acceleration

Simulation engines or **hardware accelerators** use computer architectures that are tuned to fault-simulation algorithms. These special computers allow you to add multiple simulation boards in one chassis. Since each board is essentially a workstation produced in relatively low volume and there are between 2 and 10 boards in one accelerator, these machines are between one and two orders of magnitude more expensive than a workstation. There are two ways to use multiple boards for fault simulation. One method runs good circuits on each board in parallel with the same stimulus and generates faulty circuits concurrently with other boards. The acceleration factor is less than the number of boards because of overhead. This method is usually faster than distributing a good circuit across multiple boards. Some fault simulators allow you to use multiple circuits across multiple machines on a network in **distributed fault simulation**.

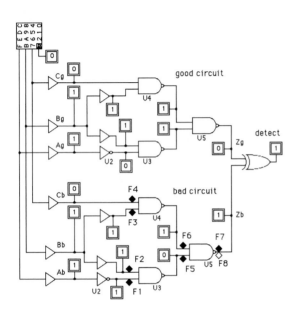

Fault	Type	[1]Vectors (hex)	Good output	Bad output
F1	SA1	**3**	0	1
F2	SA1	0, 4	0, 0	1, 1
F3	SA1	4, 5	0, 0	1, 1
F4	SA1	3	0	1
F5	SA1	2	1	0
F6	SA1	7	1	0
F7	SA1	0, 1, 3, 4, 5	0, 0, 0, 0, 0	1, 1, 1, 1, 1
F8	SA0	2, 6, 7	1, 1, 1	0, 0, 0

[1]Test vector format:
$\quad$ **3** = 011, so that CBA = 011: C = '0', B = '1', A = '1'

FIGURE 14.16 Fault simulation of A'B + BC. The simulation results for fault F1 (U2 output stuck at 1) with test vector value hex **3** (shown in bold in the table) are shown on the LogicWorks schematic. Notice that the output of U2 is 0 in the good circuit and stuck at 1 in the bad circuit.

14.4.8 A Fault-Simulation Example

Figure 14.16 illustrates fault simulation using the circuit of Figure 14.14. We have used all possible inputs as a test vector set in the following order: {000, 001, 010, 011, 100, 101, 110, 111}. There are eight collapsed SSFs in this circuit, F1–F8. Since the good circuit is irredundant, we have 100 percent fault coverage. The following fault-simulation results were derived from a logic simulator rather than a fault simulator, but are presented in the same format as output from an automated test system.

```
Total number of faults: 22
Number of faults in collapsed fault list: 8
```

Test Vector	Faults detected	Coverage/%	Cumulative/%
000	F2, F7	25.0	25.0
001	F7	12.5	25.0

010	F5, F8	25.0	62.5
011	F1, F4, F7	37.5	75.0
100	F2, F3, F7	37.5	87.5
101	F3, F7	25.0	87.5
110	F8	12.5	100.0
111	F6, F8	25.0	100.0

```
Total number of vectors    : 8
                        Noncollapsed        Collapsed
Fault counts:
Detected                        16              8
Untested                         0              0
                            ------          ------
Detectable                      16              8

Redundant                        0              0
Tied                             0              0
FAULT COVERAGE           100.00 %        100.00 %
```

Fault simulation tells us that we need to apply seven test vectors in order to achieve full fault coverage. The highest-quality test vectors are {011} and {100}. For example, test vector {011} detects three faults (F1, F4, and F7) out of eight. This means if we were to reduce the test set to just {011} the fault coverage would be 3/8, or 37 percent. Proceeding in this fashion we reorder the test vectors in terms of their contribution to cumulative test coverage as follows: {011, 100, 010, 111, 000, 001, 101, 110}. This is a hard problem for large numbers of test vectors because of the interdependencies between the faults detected by the different vectors. Repeating the fault simulation gives the following fault grading:

Test Vector	Faults detected	Coverage/%	Cumulative/%
011	F1, F4, F7	37.5	37.5
100	F2, F3, F7	37.5	62.5
010	F5, F8	25.0	87.5
111	F6, F8	25.0	100.0
000	F2, F7	25.0	100.0
001	F7	12.5	100.0
101	F3, F7	25.0	100.0
110	F8	12.5	100.0

Now, instead of using seven test vectors, we need only apply the first four vectors from this set to achieve 100 percent fault coverage, cutting the expensive production test time nearly in half. Reducing the number of test vectors in this fashion is called **test-vector compression** or **test-vector compaction**.

The fault signatures for faults F1–F8 for the last test sequence, {011, 100, 010, 111, 000, 001, 101, 110}, are as follows:

```
#  fail      good      bad
-- --------  --------  --------
F1 10000000  00110001  10110001
F2 01001000  00110001  01111001
F3 01000010  00110001  01110011
F4 10000000  00110001  10110001
F5 00100000  00110001  00010001
F6 00010000  00110001  00100001
F7 11001110  00110001  11111111
F8 00110001  00110001  00000000
```

The first pattern for each fault indicates which test vectors will fail on the tester (we say a test vector fails when it successfully detects a faulty circuit during a production test). Thus, for fault F1, pattern '10000000' indicates that only the first test vector will fail if fault F1 is present. The second and third patterns for each fault are the POs of the good and bad circuits for each test vector. Since we only have one PO in our simple example, these patterns do not help further distinguish between faults. Notice, that as far as an external view is concerned, faults F1 and F4 have identical fault signatures and are therefore indistinguishable. Faults F1 and F4 are said to be **structurally equivalent**. In general, we cannot detect structural equivalence by looking at the circuit. If we apply only the first four test vectors, then faults F2 and F3 also have identical fault signatures. Fault signatures are only useful in diagnosing fault locations if we have one, or a very few faults.

Not all fault simulators give all the information we have described. Most fault simulators drop hard-detected faults from consideration once they are detected to increase the speed of simulation. With dropped hard-detected faults we cannot independently grade each vector and we cannot construct a fault dictionary. This is the reason we used a logic simulator to generate the preceding results.

14.4.9   Fault Simulation in an ASIC Design Flow

At the beginning of this section we dodged the issue of test-vector generation. It is possible to automatically generate test vectors and test programs (with certain restrictions), and we shall discuss these methods in Section 14.5. A by-product of some of these automated systems is a measure of fault coverage. However, fault simulation is still used for the following reasons:

- Test-generation software is expensive, and many designers still create test programs manually and then grade the test vectors using fault simulation.

- Automatic test programs are not yet at the stage where fault simulation can be completely omitted in an ASIC design flow. Usually we need fault simulation to add some vectors to test logic not covered automatically, to check that test logic has been inserted correctly, or to understand and correct fault coverage problems.

- It is far too expensive to use a production tester to debug a production test. One use of a fault simulator is to perform this function off line.

- The reuse and automatic generation of large cells is essential to decrease the complexity of large ASIC designs. Megacells and embedded blocks (an embedded microcontroller, for example) are normally provided with **canned test vectors** that have already been fault simulated and fault graded. The megacell has to be isolated during test to apply these vectors and measure the response. Cell compilers for RAM, ROM, multipliers, and other regular structures may also generate test vectors. Fault simulation is one way to check that the various embedded blocks and their vectors have been correctly glued together with the rest of the ASIC to produce a complete set of test vectors and a test program.

- Production testers are very expensive. There is a trend away from the use of test vectors to include more of the test function on an ASIC. Some internal test logic structures generate test vectors in a random or pseudorandom fashion. For these structures there is no known way to generate the fault coverage. For these types of test structures we will need some type of fault simulation to measure fault coverage and estimate defect levels.

14.5   Automatic Test-Pattern Generation

In this section we shall describe a widely used algorithm, PODEM, for **automatic test-pattern generation** (**ATPG**) or **automatic test-vector generation** (**ATVG**). Before we can explain the PODEM algorithm we need to develop a shorthand notation and explain some terms and definitions using a simpler ATPG algorithm.

14.5.1   The D-Calculus

Figure 14.17(a) and (b) shows a shorthand notation, the **D-calculus**, for tracing faults. The D-calculus was developed by Roth [1966] together with an ATPG algorithm, the **D-algorithm**. The symbol D (for detect) indicates the value of a node is a logic '0' in the good circuit and a logic '1' in the bad circuit. We can also write this as $D = 0/1$. In general we write g/b, a **composite logic value**, to indicate a node value in the good circuit is g and b in the bad circuit (by convention we always write the good circuit value first and the faulty circuit value second). The complement of D is $\overline{D} = 1/0$ ($\overline{D}$ is rarely written as D' since $\overline{D}$ is a logic value just like '1' and '0'). Notice that $\overline{D}$ does not mean *not* detected, but simply that we see a '0' in the good circuit and a '1' in the bad circuit. We can apply Boolean algebra to the composite logic values D and $\overline{D}$ as shown in Figure 14.17(c). The composite values 1/1 and 0/0 are equivalent to '1' and '0' respectively. We use the unknown logic value 'X' to

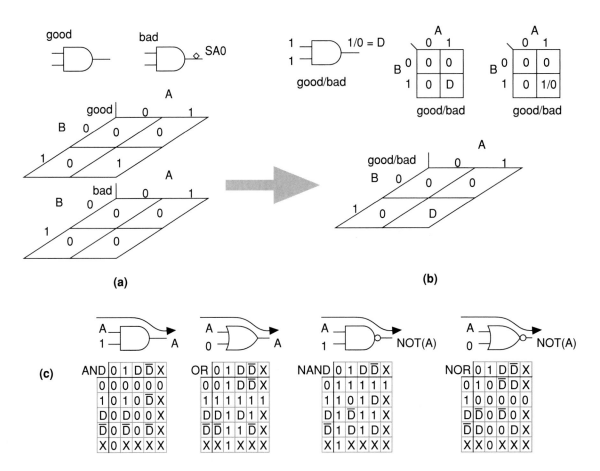

FIGURE 14.17 The D-calculus. (a) We need a way to represent the behavior of the good circuit and the bad circuit at the same time. (b) The composite logic value D (for detect) represents a logic '1' in the good circuit and a logic '0' in the bad circuit. We can also write this as D = 1/0. (c) The logic behavior of simple logic cells using the D-calculus. Composite logic values can propagate through simple logic gates if the other inputs are set to their enabling values.

represent a logic value that is one of '0', '1', D, or $\overline{D}$, but we do not know or care which.

If we wish to **propagate** a signal from one or more inputs of a logic cell to the logic cell output, we set the remaining inputs of that logic cell to what we call the **enabling value**. The enabling value is '1' for AND and NAND gates and '0' for OR and NOR gates. Figure 14.17(c) illustrates the use of enabling values. In contrast, setting at least one input of a logic gate to the **controlling value**, the opposite of the enabling value for that gate, forces or **justifies** the output node of that logic gate to a fixed value. The controlling value of '0' for an AND gate justifies the output to '0' and for a NAND gate justifies the output to '1'. The controlling values of '1' justifies the output of an OR gate to '1' and justifies the output of a NOR gate to '0'. To find controlling and enabling values for more complex logic cells, such as AOI and OAI logic cells, we can use their simpler AND, OR, NAND, and NOR gate representations.

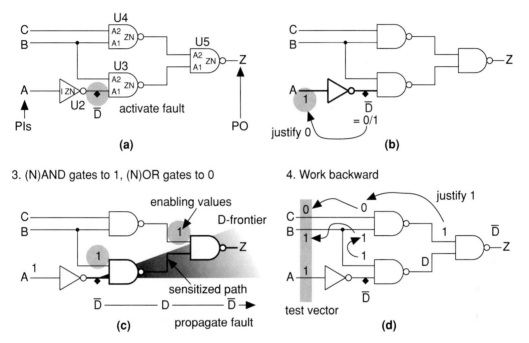

FIGURE 14.18 A basic ATPG (automatic test-pattern generation) algorithm for A'B + BC. (a) We activate a fault, U2.ZN stuck at 1, by setting the pin or node to '0', the opposite value of the fault. (b) We work backward from the fault origin to the PIs (primary inputs) by recursively justifying signals at the output of logic cells. (c) We then work forward from the fault origin to a PO (primary output), setting inputs to gates on a sensitized path to their enabling values. We propagate the fault until the D-frontier reaches a PO. (d) We then work backward from the PO to the PIs recursively justifying outputs to generate the sensitized path. This simple algorithm always works, providing signals do not branch out and then rejoin again.

14.5.2 A Basic ATPG Algorithm

A basic algorithm to generate test vectors automatically is shown in Figure 14.18. We detect a fault by first **activating** (or **exciting** the fault). To do this we must drive the faulty node to the opposite value of the fault. Figure 14.18(a) shows a stuck-at-1 fault at the output pin, ZN, of the inverter U2 (we call this fault U2.ZN.SA1). To create a test for U2.ZN.SA1 we have to find the values of the PIs that will justify node U2.ZN to '0'. We work backward from node U2.ZN justifying each logic gate output until we reach a PI. In this case we only have to justify U2.ZN to "0", and this is easily done by setting the PI A = '0'. Next we work forward from the fault origin and **sensitize** a path to a PO (there is only one PO in this example). This propagates the fault effect to the PO so that it may be **observed**. To propagate the fault effect to the PO Z, we set U3.A2 = '1' and then U5.A2 = '1'.

We can visualize fault propagation by supposing that we set all nodes in a circuit to unknown, 'X'. Then, as we successively propagate the fault effect toward the POs, we can imagine a wave of D's and $\overline{D}$'s, called the **D-frontier**, that propagates from the fault origin toward the POs. As a value of D or $\overline{D}$ reaches the inputs of a logic cell whose other inputs are 'X', we add that logic cell to the D-frontier. Then we find values for the other inputs to propagate the D-frontier through the logic cell to continue the process.

This basic algorithm of justifying and then propagating a fault works when we can justify nodes without interference from other nodes. This algorithm breaks down when we have **reconvergent fanout**. Figure 14.19(a) shows another example of justifying and propagating a fault in a circuit with reconvergent fanout. For direct comparison Figure 14.19(b) shows an irredundant circuit, similar to part (a), except the fault signal, B stuck at 1, branches and then reconverges at the inputs to gate U5. The reconvergent fanout in this new circuit breaks our basic algorithm. We now have two sensitized paths that propagate the fault effect to U5. These paths combine to produce a constant '1' at Z, the PO. We have a **multipath sensitization** problem.

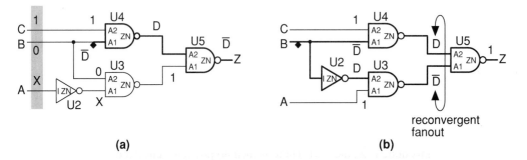

(a)   (b)

FIGURE 14.19 Reconvergent fanout. (a) Signal B branches and then reconverges at logic gate U5, but the fault U4.A1 stuck at 1 can still be excited and a path sensitized using the basic algorithm of Figure 14.18. (b) Fault B stuck-at-1 branches and then reconverges at gate U5. When we enable the inputs to both gates U3 and U4 we create two sensitized paths that prevent the fault from propagating to the PO (primary output). We can solve this problem by changing A to '0', but this breaks the rules of the algorithm illustrated in Figure 14.18. The PODEM algorithm solves this problem.

14.5.3 The PODEM Algorithm

The **path-oriented decision making** (**PODEM**) algorithm solves the problem of reconvergent fanout and allows multipath sensitization [Goel, 1981]. The method is similar to the basic algorithm we have already described except PODEM will retry a step, reversing an incorrect decision. There are four basic steps that we label: objective, backtrace, implication, and D-frontier. These steps are as follows:

1. Pick an *objective* to set a node to a value. Start with the fault origin as an objective and all other nodes set to 'X'.

2. *Backtrace* to a PI and set it to a value that will help meet the objective.

3. Simulate the network to calculate the effect of fixing the value of the PI (this step is called *implication*). If there is no possibility of sensitizing a path to a PO, then retry by reversing the value of the PI that was set in step 2 and simulate again.

4. Update the *D-frontier* and return to step 1. Stop if the D-frontier reaches a PO.

Figure 14.20 shows an example that uses the following iterations of the four steps in the PODEM algorithm:

1. We start with activation of the fault as our objective, U3.A2 = '0'. We backtrace to J. We set J = '1'. Since K is still 'X', implication gives us no further information. We have no D-frontier to update.

2. The objective is unchanged, but this time we backtrace to K. We set K = '1'. Implication gives us U2.ZN = '1' (since now J = '1' and K = '1') and therefore U7.ZN = '1'. We still have no D-frontier to update.

3. We set U3.A1 = '1' as our objective in order to propagate the fault through U3. We backtrace to M. We set M = '1'. Implication gives us U2.ZN = '1' and U3.ZN = D. We update the D-frontier to reflect that U4.A2 = D and U6.A1 = D, so the D-frontier is U4 and U6.

4. We pick U6.A2 = '1' as an objective in order to propagate the fault through U6. We backtrace to N. We set N = '1'. Implication gives us U6.ZN = $\overline{\text{D}}$. We update the D-frontier to reflect that U4.A2 = D and U8.A1 = $\overline{\text{D}}$, so the D-frontier is U4 and U8.

5. We pick U8.A1 = '1' as an objective in order to propagate the fault through U8. We backtrace to L. We set L = '0'. Implication gives us U5.ZN = '0' and therefore U8.ZN = '0' (this node is Z, the PO). There is then no possible sensitized path to the PO Z. We must have made an incorrect decision, we retry and set L = '1'. Implication now gives us U8.ZN = D and we have propagated the D-frontier to a PO.

We can see that the PODEM algorithm proceeds in two phases. In the first phase, iterations 1 and 2 in Figure 14.20, the objective is fixed in order to activate the fault. In the second phase, iterations 3–5, the objective changes in order to prop-

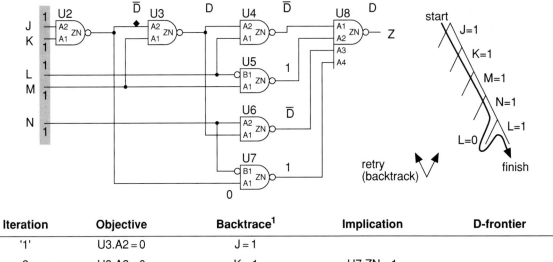

Iteration	Objective	Backtrace[1]	Implication	D-frontier
'1'	U3.A2 = 0	J = 1		
2	U3.A2 = 0	K = 1	U7.ZN = 1	
3	U3.A1 = 1	M = 1	U3.ZN = D	U4, U6
4	U6.A2 = 1	N = 1	U6.ZN = $\overline{D}$	U4, U8
5a	U8.A1 = 1	L = 0	U8.ZN = 1	U4, U8
5b	Retry	L = 1	U8.ZN = D	A

[1]Backtrace is not the same as retry or backtrack.

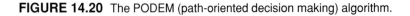

FIGURE 14.20 The PODEM (path-oriented decision making) algorithm.

agate the fault. In step 3 of the PODEM algorithm there must be at least one path containing unknown values between the gates of the D-frontier and a PO in order to be able to complete a sensitized path to a PO. This is called the **X-path check**.

You may wonder why there has been no explanation of the backtrace mechanism or how to decide a value for a PI in step 2 of the PODEM algorithm. The decision tree shown in Figure 14.20 shows that it does not matter. PODEM conducts an implicit binary search over all the PIs. If we make an incorrect decision and assign the wrong value to a PI at some step, we will simply need to retry that step. Texts, programs, and articles use the term *backtrace* as we have described it, but then most use the term **backtrack** to describe what we have called a retry, which can be confusing. I also did not explain how to choose the objective in step 1 of the PODEM algorithm. The initial objective is to activate the fault. Subsequently we select a logic gate from the D-frontier and set one of its inputs to the enabling value in an attempt to propagate the fault.

We can use intelligent procedures, based on *controllability* and *observability*, to guide PODEM and reduce the number of incorrect decisions. PODEM is a development of the D-algorithm, and there are several other ATPG algorithms that are developments of PODEM. One of these is **FAN (fanout-oriented test generation)** that removes the need to backtrace all the way to a PI, reducing the search time [Fujiwara and Shimono, 1983; Schulz, Trischler, and Sarfert, 1988]. Algorithms based on the D-algorithm, PODEM, and FAN are the basis of many commercial ATPG systems.

14.5.4   Controllability and Observability

In order for an ATPG system to provide a test for a fault on a node it must be possible to both control and observe the behavior of the node. There are both theoretical and practical issues involved in making sure that a design does not contain buried circuits that are impossible to observe and control. A software program that measures the **controllability** (with three 1's) and **observability** of nodes in a circuit is useful in conjunction with ATPG software.

There are several different measures for controllability and observability [Butler and Mercer, 1992]. We shall describe one of the first such systems called **SCOAP** (**Sandia Controllability/Observability Analysis Program**) [Goldstein, 1979]. These measures are also used by ATPG algorithms.

Combinational controllability is defined separately from **sequential controllability**. We also separate **zero-controllability** and **one-controllability**. For example, the **combinational zero-controllability** for a two-input AND gate, $Y = \text{AND}(X_1, X_2)$, is recursively defined in terms of the input controllability values as follows:

$$\text{CC0}(Y) = \min\{\text{CC0}(X_1), \text{CC0}(X_2)\} + 1. \qquad (14.5)$$

We choose the minimum value of the two-input controllability values to reflect the fact that we can justify the output of an AND gate to '0' by setting any input to the control value of '0'. We then add 1 to this value to reflect the fact that we have passed through an additional level of logic. Incrementing the controllability measures for each level of logic represents a measure of the **logic distance** between two nodes.

We define the **combinational one-controllability** for a two-input AND gate as

$$\text{CC1}(Y) = \text{CC1}(X_1) + \text{CC1}(X_2) + 1. \qquad (14.6)$$

This equation reflects the fact that we need to set all inputs of an AND gate to the enabling value of '1' to justify a '1' at the output. Figure 14.21(a) illustrates these definitions.

An inverter, $Y = \text{NOT}(X)$, reverses the controllability values:

$$\text{CC1}(Y) = \text{CC0}(X) + 1 \quad \text{and} \quad \text{CC0}(Y) = \text{CC1}(X) + 1. \quad (14.7)$$

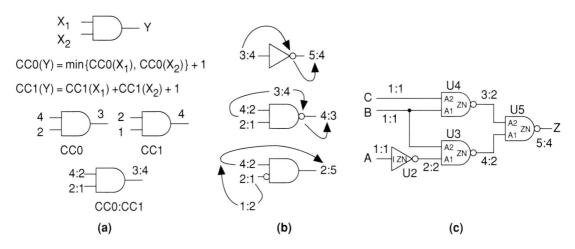

FIGURE 14.21 Controllability measures. (a) Definition of combinational zero-controllability, CC0, and combinational one-controllability, CC1, for a two-input AND gate. (b) Examples of controllability calculations for simple gates, showing intermediate steps. (c) Controllability in a combinational circuit.

Since we can construct all other logic cells from combinations of two-input AND gates and inverters we can use Eqs. 14.5–14.7 to derive their controllability equations. When we do this we only increment the controllability by one for each primitive gate. Thus for a three-input NAND with an inverting input, $Y = \text{NAND}(X_1, X_2, \text{NOT}(X_3))$:

$$\text{CC0}(Y) = \text{CC1}(X_1) + \text{CC1}(X_2) + \text{CC0}(X_3) + 1,$$

$$\text{CC1}(Y) = \min\{\text{CC0}(X_1), \text{CC0}(X_2), \text{CC1}(X_3)\} + 1. \qquad (14.8)$$

For a two-input NOR, $Y = \text{NOR}(X_1, X_2) = \text{NOT}(\text{AND}(\text{NOT}(X_1), \text{NOT}(X_2)))$:

$$\text{CC1}(Y) = \min\{\text{CC1}(X_1), \text{CC1}(X_2)\} + 1,$$

$$\text{CC0}(Y) = \text{CC0}(X_1) + \text{CC0}(X_2) + 1. \qquad (14.9)$$

Figure 14.21(b) shows examples of controllability calculations. A bubble on a logic gate at the input or output swaps the values of CC1 and CC0. Figure 14.21(c) shows how controllability values for a combinational circuit are calculated by working forward from each PI that is defined to have a controllability of one.

We define observability in terms of the controllability measures. The **combinational observability**, OC (X_1), of input X_1 of a two-input AND gate can be expressed in terms of the controllability of the other input CC1 (X_2) and the combinational observability of the output, OC (Y):

$$OC(X_1) = CC1(X_2) + OC(Y) + 1. \qquad (14.10)$$

If a node X_1 branches (has fanout) to nodes X_2 and X_3 we choose the most observable of the branches:

$$OC(X_1) = \min\{ O(X_2) + O(X_3) \}. \qquad (14.11)$$

Figure 14.22(a) and (b) show the definitions of observability. Figure 14.22(c) illustrates calculation of observability at a three-input NAND; notice we sum the CC1 values for the other inputs (since the enabling value for a NAND gate is one, the same as for an AND gate). Figure 14.22(d) shows the calculation of observability working back from the PO which, by definition, has an observability of zero.

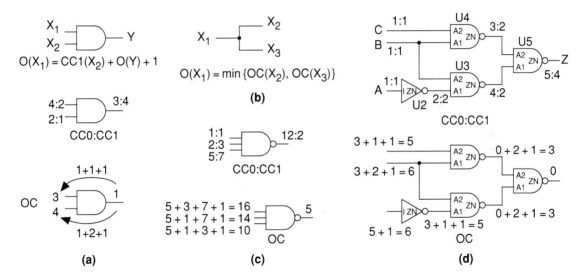

FIGURE 14.22 Observability measures. (a) The combinational observability, OC(X_1), of an input, X_1, to a two-input AND gate defined in terms of the controllability of the other input and the observability of the output. (b) The observability of a fanout node is equal to the observability of the most observable branch. (c) Example of an observability calculation at a three-input NAND gate. (d) The observability of a combinational network can be calculated from the controllability measures, CC0:CC1. The observability of a PO (primary output) is defined to be zero.

Sequential controllability and observability can be measured using similar equations to the combinational measures except that in the sequential measures (SC1, SC0, and OS) we measure logic distance in terms of the layers of sequential logic, not the layers of combinational logic.

14.6 Scan Test

Sequential logic poses a very difficult ATPG problem. Consider the example of a 32-bit counter with a final carry. If the designer included a reset, we have to clock the counter 2^{32} (approximately 4×10^9) times to check the carry logic. Using a 1 MHz tester clock this requires 4×10^3 seconds, 1 hour, or (at approximately $0.25 per second) $1,000 of tester time. Consider a 16-bit state machine implemented using a one-hot state register with 16 D flip-flops. If the designer did not include a reset we have a very complicated initialization problem. A sequential ATPG algorithm must consider over 2000 states when constructing sequential test vectors. In an ad hoc approach to testing we could construct special reset circuits or create manual test vectors to deal with these special situations, one at a time, as they arise. Instead we can take a **structured test** approach (also called **design for test**, though this term covers a wider field).

We can automatically generate test vectors for combinational logic, but ATPG is much harder for sequential logic. Therefore the most common sequential structured test approach converts sequential logic to combinational logic. In full-scan design we replace every sequential element with a scan flip-flop. The result is an internal form of boundary scan and, if we wish, we can use the IEEE 1149.1 TAP to access (and the boundary-scan controller to control) an internal-scan chain.

Table 14.9 shows a VHDL model and schematic symbols for a scan flip-flop. There is an area and performance penalty to pay for scan design. The scan MUX adds the delay of a 2:1 MUX to the setup time of the flip-flop; this will directly subtract from the critical path delay. The 2:1 MUX and any separate driver for the scan output also adds approximately 10 percent to the area of the flip-flop (depending on the features present in the original flip-flop). The scan chain must also be routed, and this complicates physical design and adds to the interconnect area. In ASIC design the benefits of eliminating complex sequential ATPG and the addition of observability and controllability usually outweigh these disadvantages.

The highly structured nature of full scan allows test software (usually called a **test compiler**) to perform automatic **scan insertion**. Using scan design we turn the output of each flip-flop into a **pseudoprimary input** and the input to each flip-flop into a **pseudoprimary output**. ATPG software can then generate test vectors for the combinational logic between scan flip-flops.

There are other approaches to scan design. In **partial scan** we replace a subset of the sequential elements with scan flip-flops. We can choose this subset using heuristic procedures to allow the remaining sequential logic to be tested using sequen-

TABLE 14.9 Scan flip-flop.

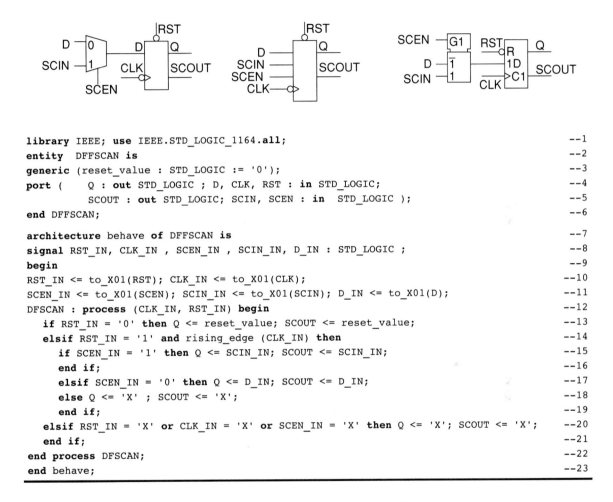

```
library IEEE; use IEEE.STD_LOGIC_1164.all;                              --1
entity  DFFSCAN is                                                      --2
generic (reset_value : STD_LOGIC := '0');                              --3
port (    Q : out STD_LOGIC ; D, CLK, RST : in STD_LOGIC;              --4
          SCOUT : out STD_LOGIC; SCIN, SCEN : in  STD_LOGIC );          --5
end DFFSCAN;                                                            --6

architecture behave of DFFSCAN is                                      --7
signal RST_IN, CLK_IN , SCEN_IN , SCIN_IN, D_IN : STD_LOGIC ;          --8
begin                                                                  --9
RST_IN <= to_X01(RST); CLK_IN <= to_X01(CLK);                          --10
SCEN_IN <= to_X01(SCEN); SCIN_IN <= to_X01(SCIN); D_IN <= to_X01(D);   --11
DFSCAN : process (CLK_IN, RST_IN) begin                                --12
  if RST_IN = '0' then Q <= reset_value; SCOUT <= reset_value;         --13
  elsif RST_IN = '1' and rising_edge (CLK_IN) then                     --14
    if SCEN_IN = '1' then Q <= SCIN_IN; SCOUT <= SCIN_IN;              --15
    end if;                                                            --16
    elsif SCEN_IN = '0' then Q <= D_IN; SCOUT <= D_IN;                 --17
    else Q <= 'X' ; SCOUT <= 'X';                                      --18
    end if;                                                            --19
  elsif RST_IN = 'X' or CLK_IN = 'X' or SCEN_IN = 'X' then Q <= 'X'; SCOUT <= 'X'; --20
  end if;                                                              --21
end process DFSCAN;                                                    --22
end behave;                                                            --23
```

tial ATPG techniques. In **destructive scan** we remove the values at the outputs of the flip-flops during the scan process (this is the usual form of scan design). In **nondestructive scan** we keep the flip-flop outputs intact so that we can shift out the scan chain and then resume where we left off. **Level-sensitive scan design** (LSSD) is a form of scan design developed at IBM that uses separate clock phases to drive scan elements.

We shall describe scan design, automated scan insertion, and test-program generation with several examples. First, though, we describe another important structured-test technique.

14.7 Built-in Self-test

The trend to include more test logic on an ASIC has already been mentioned. **Built-in self-test** (**BIST**) is a set of structured-test techniques for combinational and sequential logic, memories, multipliers, and other embedded logic blocks. In each case the principle is to generate test vectors, apply them to the **circuit under test** (**CUT**) or **device under test** (**DUT**), and then check the response.

14.7.1 LFSR

Figure 14.23 shows a **linear feedback shift register** (**LFSR**). The exclusive-OR gates and shift register act to produce a **pseudorandom binary sequence** (**PRBS**) at each of the flip-flop outputs. By correctly choosing the points at which we take the feedback from an n-bit shift register (see Section 14.7.5), we can produce a PRBS of length $2^n - 1$, a **maximal-length sequence** that includes all possible patterns (or vectors) of n bits, excluding the all-zeros pattern.

FIGURE 14.23 A linear feedback shift register (LFSR). A 3-bit maximal-length LFSR produces a repeating string of seven pseudorandom binary numbers: 7, 3, 1, 4, 2, 5, 6.

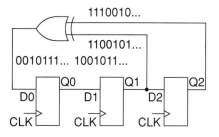

Table 14.10 shows the maximal-length sequence, with length $2^3 - 1 = 7$, for the 3-bit LFSR shown in Figure 14.23. Notice that the first (clock tick 1) and last rows (clock tick 8) are identical. Rows following the seventh row repeat rows 1–7, so that the length of this 3-bit LFSR sequence is $7 = 2^3 - 1$, the maximal length. The shaded regions show how bits are shifted from one clock cycle to the next. We assume the register is initialized to the all-ones state, but any initial state will work and produce the same PRBS, as long as the initial state is not all zeros (in which case the LFSR will stay stuck at all zeros).

14.7.2 Signature Analysis

Figure 14.24 shows the LFSR of Figure 14.23 with an additional XOR gate used in the first stage of the shift register. If we apply a binary input sequence to IN, the shift register will perform **data compaction** (or **compression**) on the input sequence. At the end of the input sequence the shift-register contents, Q0Q1Q2, will form a pattern that we call a **signature**. If the input sequence and the **serial-input**

TABLE 14.10 LFSR example of Figure 14.23.

Clock tick, t =	$Q0_{t+1} = Q1_t \oplus Q2_t$	$Q1_{t+1} = Q0_t$	$Q2_{t+1} = Q1_t$	Q0Q1Q2
1	1	1	1	7
2	0	1	1	3
3	0	0	1	1
4	1	0	0	4
5	0	1	0	2
6	1	0	1	5
7	1	1	0	6
8	1	1	1	7

signature register (**SISR**) are long enough, it is unlikely (though possible) that two different input sequences will produce the same signature. If the input sequence comes from logic that we wish to test, a fault in the logic will cause the input sequence to change. This causes the signature to change from a known good value and we shall then know that the circuit under test is bad. This technique, called **signature analysis**, was developed by Hewlett-Packard to test equipment in the field in the late 1970s.

FIGURE 14.24 A 3-bit serial-input signature register (SISR) using an LFSR (linear feedback shift register). The LFSR is initialized to Q1Q2Q3 = '000' using the common RES (reset) signal. The signature, Q1Q2Q3, is formed from shift-and-add operations on the sequence of input bits (IN).

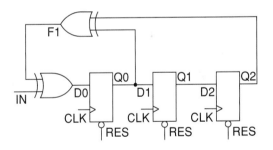

14.7.3 A Simple BIST Example

We can combine the PRBS generator of Figure 14.23 together with the signature register of Figure 14.24 to form the simple BIST structure shown in Figure 14.25(a). LFSR1 generates a maximal-length ($2^3 - 1 = 7$ cycles) PRBS. LFSR2 computes the signature ('011' for the good circuit) of the CUT. LFSR1 is initialized to '100' (Q0 = 1, Q1 = 0, Q2 = 0) and LFSR2 is initialized to '000'. The schematic in Figure 14.25(a) shows the bit sequences in the circuit, both for a good circuit and for a bad circuit with a stuck-at-1 fault, F1. Figure 14.25(b) shows how the bit sequences are calculated in the good circuit. The signature is formed as R0R1R2 seven clock edges (on the eighth clock cycle) after the active-low reset is taken high. Figure 14.26 shows the waveforms in the good and bad circuit. The bad circuit signature, '000', differs from the good circuit and the signature can either be compared with the known good signature on-chip or the signature may be shifted out and compared off-chip (both approaches are used in practice).

14.7.4   Aliasing

In Figure 14.26 the good and bad circuits produced different signatures. There is a small probability that the signature of a bad circuit will be the same as a good circuit. This problem is known as **aliasing** or **error masking**. For the example in Figure 14.25, the bit stream input to the signature analysis register is 7 bits long. There are 2^7 or 128 possible 7-bit-long bit-stream patterns. We assume that each of these 128 bit-stream patterns is equally likely to produce any of the eight (all-zeros is an allowed pattern in a signature register) possible 3-bit signatures. It turns out that this is a good assumption. Thus there are $128/8$ or 16 bit-streams that produce the good signature, one of these belongs to the good circuit, the remaining 15 cause aliasing. Since there are a total of $128 - 1 = 127$ bit-streams due to bad circuits, the fraction of bad-circuit bit-streams that cause aliasing is $15/127$, or 0.118. If all bad circuit bit-streams are equally likely (and this is a poor assumption) then 0.118 is also the probability of aliasing.

In general, if the length of the test sequence is L and the length of the signature register is R the probability p of aliasing (not detecting an error) is

$$p = \frac{2^{L-R} - 1}{2^L - 1}.$$ (14.12)

Thus, for the example in Figure 14.25, $L = 7$ and $R = 3$, and the probability of aliasing is $p = (2^{(7-3)} - 1)/(2^7 - 1) = 15/127 = 0.118$, as we have just calculated. This is a very high probability of error and we would not use such a short test sequence and such a short signature register in practice.

For $L \gg R$ the error probability is

$$p \approx 2^{-R}.$$ (14.13)

For example, if $R = 16$, $p \approx 0.0000152$ corresponding to an **error coverage** $(1 - p)$ of approximately 99.9984 percent. Unfortunately, these equations for error coverage are rather meaningless since there is no easy way to relate the error coverage to fault coverage. The problem lies in our assumption that all bad-circuit bit-streams are equally likely, and this is not true in practice (for example, bit-stream outputs of all ones or all zeros are more likely to occur as a result of faults). Nevertheless signature analysis with high error-coverage rates is found to produce high fault coverage.

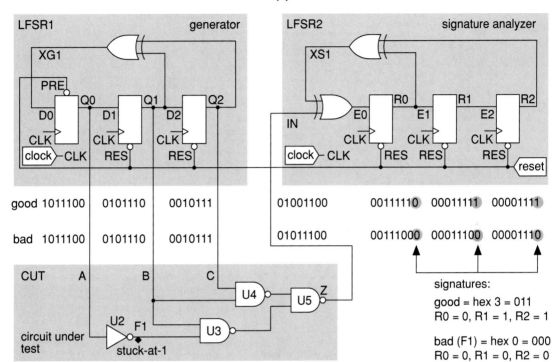

FIGURE 14.25 BIST example. (a) A simple BIST structure showing bit sequences for both good and bad circuits. (b) Bit sequence calculations for the good circuit. The signature appears on the eighth clock cycle (after seven positive clock edges) and is R0 = '0', R1 = '1', R2 = '1'; with R2 as the MSB this is '011' or hex 3.

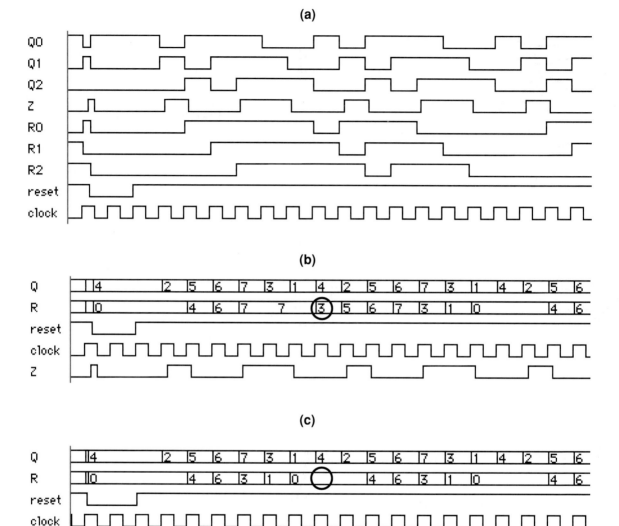

FIGURE 14.26 The waveforms of the BIST circuit of Figure 14.25. (a) The good-circuit response. The waveforms Q1 and Q2, as well as R1 and R2, are delayed by one clock cycle as they move through each stage of the shift registers. (b) The same good-circuit response with the register outputs Q0–Q2 and R0–R2 grouped and their values displayed in hexadecimal (Q0 and R0 are the MSBs). The signature hex 3 or '011' (R0 = 0, R1 = 1, R2 = 1) in R appears seven positive clock edges after the reset signal is taken high. This is one clock cycle after the generator completes its first sequence (hex pattern 4, 2, 5, 6, 7, 3, 1). (b) The response of the bad circuit with fault F1 and fault signature hex 0 (circled).

14.7.5   LFSR Theory

The operation of LFSRs is related to the mathematics of polynomials and Galois-field theory. The properties and behavior of these polynomials are well known and they are also used extensively in coding theory. Every LFSR has a **characteristic polynomial** that describes its behavior. The characteristic polynomials that cause an LFSR to generate a maximum-length PRBS are called **primitive polynomials.** Consider the primitive polynomial

$$P(x) = 1 \oplus x^1 \oplus x^3 , \tag{14.14}$$

where $a \oplus b$ represents the exclusive-OR of a and b. The order of this polynomial is three, and the corresponding LFSR will generate a PRBS of length $2^3 - 1 = 7$. For a primitive polynomial of order n, the length of the PRBS is $2^n - 1$. Figure 14.27 shows the nonzero coefficients of some primitive polynomials [Golomb et al., 1982].

n	s	Octal	Binary
1	0, 1	3	11
2	0, 1, 2	7	111
3	0, 1, 3	13	1011
4	0, 1, 4	3	10011
5	0, 2, 5	45	100101
6	0, 1, 6	103	1000011
7	0, 1, 7	211	10001001
8	0, 1, 5, 6, 8	435	100011101
9	0, 4, 9	1021	1000010001
10	0, 3, 10	2011	10000001001

For $n = 3$ and $s = 0, 1, 3$: $c_0 = 1$, $c_1 = 1$, $c_2 = 0$, $c_3 = 1$

$$P(x) = 1 \oplus c_1 x \oplus \ldots \oplus c_{n-1} x^{n-1} \oplus x^n$$

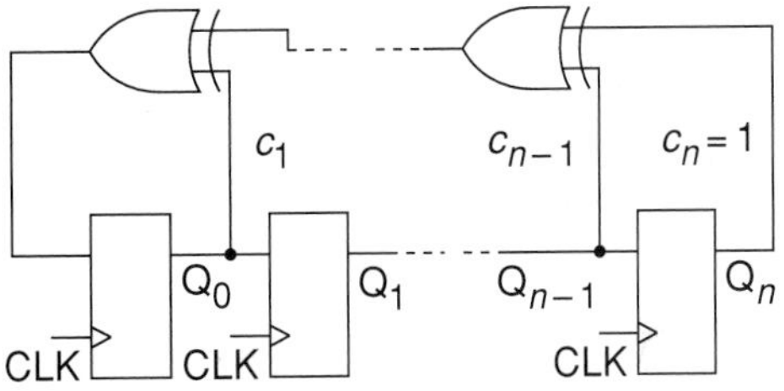

or $P^*(x) = 1 \oplus c_{n-1} x \oplus \ldots \oplus c_1 x^{n-1} \oplus x^n$

FIGURE 14.27 Primitive polynomial coefficients for LFSRs (linear feedback shift registers) that generate a maximal-length PRBS (pseudorandom binary sequence). A schematic for a type 1 LFSR is shown.

Any primitive polynomial can be written as

$$P(x) = c_0 \oplus c_1 x^1 \oplus \ldots \oplus c_n x^n , \tag{14.15}$$

where c_0 and c_n are always one. Thus for example, from Figure 14.27 for $n = 3$, we see $s = 0, 1, 3$; and thus the nonzero coefficients are c_0, c_1, and c_3. This corresponds to the primitive polynomial $P(x) = 1 \oplus x^1 \oplus x^3$. There is no easy way to determine the coefficients of primitive polynomials, especially for large n. There are many primitive polynomials for each n, but Figure 14.27 lists the one with the fewest nonzero coefficients.

The schematic in Figure 14.27 shows how the feedback taps on a LFSR correspond to the nonzero coefficients of the primitive polynomial. If the ith coefficient c_i is 1, then we include a feedback connection and an XOR gate in that position. If c_i is zero, there is no feedback connection and no XOR gate in that position.

The reciprocal of a primitive polynomial, $P^*(x)$, is also primitive, where

$$P^*(x) = x^n P(x^{-1}) . \tag{14.16}$$

For example, by taking the reciprocal of the primitive polynomial $P(x) = 1 \oplus x^1 \oplus x^3$ from Eq. 14.17, we can form

$$P^*(x) = 1 \oplus x^3 \oplus x^4, \tag{14.17}$$

which is also a primitive polynomial.

This means that there are two possible LFSR implementations for every $P(x)$. Or, looked at another way, for every LFSR implementation, the characteristic polynomial can be written in terms of two primitive polynomials, $P(x)$ and $P^*(x)$, that are reciprocals of each other.

We may also implement an LFSR by using XOR gates in series with each flip-flop output rather than external to the shift register. The **external-XOR LFSR** is called a **type 1 LFSR** and the **internal-XOR LFSR** is called a **type 2 LFSR** (this is a nomenclature that most follow). Figure 14.28 shows the four different LFSRs that may be constructed for each primitive polynomial, $P(x)$.

There are differences between the four different LFSRs for each polynomial. Each gives a different output sequence. The outputs for the type 1 LFSRs, taken from the Q outputs of each flip-flop, are identical, but delayed by one clock cycle from the previous output. This is a problem when we use the parallel output from an LFSR to test logic because of the strong correlation between the test signals. The type 2 LFSRs do not have this problem. The type 2 LFSRs also are capable of higher-frequency operation since there are fewer series XOR gates in the signal path than in the corresponding type 1 LFSR. For these reasons, the type 2 LFSRs are usually used in BIST structures. The type 1 LFSR does have the advantage that it can be more easily constructed using register structures that already exist on an ASIC.

Table 14.11 shows primitive polynomial coefficients for higher values of n than Figure 14.27. Test length grows quickly with the size of the LFSR. For example, a 32-bit generator will produce a sequence with $2^{32} = 4{,}294{,}967{,}296 \approx 4.3 \times 10^9$ bits. With a 100 MHz clock (with 10 ns cycle time), the test time of 43 seconds would be impractical.

There is confusion over naming, labeling, and drawing of LFSRs in texts and test programs. Looking at the schematic in Figure 14.27, we can draw the LFSR with signals flowing from left to right or vice versa (two ways), we can name the leftmost flip-flop output Q_0 or Q_n (two more ways), and we can name the coefficient that goes with Q_0 either c_0 or c_{n-1} (two more ways). There are thus at least $2^3 \times 4$

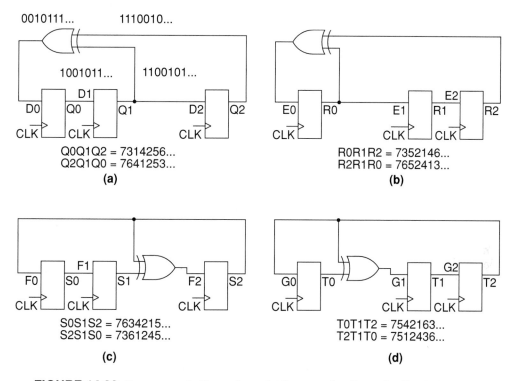

FIGURE 14.28 For every primitive polynomial there are four linear feedback shift registers (LFSRs). There are two types of LFSR; one type uses external XOR gates (type 1) and the other type uses internal XOR gates (type 2). For each type the feedback taps can be constructed either from the polynomial P(x) or from its reciprocal, P*(x). The LFSRs in this figure correspond to $P(x) = 1 \oplus x \oplus x^3$ and $P^*(x) = 1 \oplus x^2 \oplus x^3$. Each LFSR produces a different pseudorandom sequence, as shown. The binary values of the LFSR seen as a register, with the bit labeled as zero being the MSB, are shown in hexadecimal. The sequences shown are for each register initialized to '111', hex 7. (a) Type 1, P*(x). (b) Type 1, P(x). (c) Type 2, P(x). (d) Type 1, P*(x).

different ways to draw an LFSR for a given polynomial. Four of these are distinct. You can connect the LFSR feedback in the reverse order and the LFSR will still work—you will, however, get a different sequence. Usually this does not matter.

14.7.6   LFSR Example

We can use a cell compiler to produce LFSR and signature register BIST structures. For example, we might complete a property sheet as follows:

TABLE 14.11   Nonzero coefficients of primitive polynomials for LFSRs (linear feedback shift registers) that generate a maximal-length PRBS (pseudorandom binary sequence).

n	s	n	s	n	s	n	s
1	0, 1	11	0, 2, 11	21	0, 2, 21	31	0, 3, 31
2	0, 1, 2	12	0, 3, 4, 7, 12	22	0, 1, 22	32	0, 1, 27, 28, 32
3	0, 1, 3	13	0, 1, 3, 4, 13	23	0, 5, 23	40	0, 2, 19, 21, 40
4	0, 1, 4	14	0, 1, 11, 12, 14	24	0, 1, 3, 4, 24	50	0, 1, 26, 27, 50
5	0, 2, 5	15	0, 1, 15	25	0, 3, 25	60	0, 1, 60
6	0, 1, 6	16	0, 2, 3, 5, 16	26	0, 1, 7, 26	70	0, 1, 15, 16, 70
7	0, 1, 7	17	0, 3, 17	27	0, 1, 7, 27	80	0, 1, 37, 38, 80
8	0, 1, 5, 6, 8	18	0, 7, 18	28	0, 3, 28	90	0, 1, 18, 19, 90
9	0, 4, 9	19	0, 1, 5, 6, 19	29	0, 2, 29	100	0, 37, 100
10	0, 3, 10	20	0, 3, 20	30	0, 1, 15, 16, 30	256	0, 1, 3, 16, 256

```
property name            value      property name            value
------------------       -----      ------------------       -----
LFSR_is_bilbo            false      LFSR_configuration       generator
LFSR_length             3          LFSR_init_hex_value       4
LFSR_scan               false      LFSR_mux_data            false
LFSR_mux_output         false      LFSR_xor_hex_function     max_length
LFSR_zero_state         false      LFSR_signature_inputs     1
```

The Verilog structural netlist for the compiled type 2 LFSR generator is shown in Table 14.12. According to our notation and the primitive polynomials in Figure 14.27, the corresponding primitive polynomial is $P^*(x) = 1 \oplus x^2 \oplus x^3$. The LFSR has both serial and parallel outputs (taken from the inverted flip-flop outputs with inverting buffers, cell names in02d1). The clock and reset inputs are buffered (with noninverting buffers, cell names ni01d1) since these inputs would normally have to drive a load of more than 3 bits. Looking in the cell data book we find that the flip-flop corresponding to the MSB, instance FF0 with cell name dfptnb, has an active-low set input SDN. The remaining flip-flops, cell name dfctnb, have active-low clears, CDN. This gives us the initial value '100'.

Table 14.13 shows the serial-input signature register compiled using the reciprocal polynomial. Again the compiler has included buffers. All the flip-flops, cell names dfctnb, have active-low clear so that the initial content of the register is '000'.

TABLE 14.12   Compiled LFSR generator, using $P^*(x) = 1 \oplus x^2 \oplus x^3$.

```
module lfsr_generator (OUT, SERIAL_OUT, INITN, CP);
output [2:0] OUT; output SERIAL_OUT; input   INITN, CP;
    dfptnb FF2 (.D(FF0_Q), .CP(u4_Z), .SDN(u2_Z), .Q(FF2_Q), .QN(FF2_QN));
    dfctnb FF1 (.D(XOR0_Z), .CP(u4_Z), .CDN(u2_Z), .Q(FF1_Q), .QN(FF1_QN));
    dfctnb FF0 (.D(FF1_Q), .CP(u4_Z), .CDN(u2_Z), .Q(FF0_Q), .QN(FF0_QN));
    ni01d1 u2 (.I(u3_Z), .Z(u2_Z)); ni01d1 u3 (.I(INITN), .Z(u3_Z));
    ni01d1 u4 (.I(u5_Z), .Z(u4_Z)); ni01d1 u5 (.I(CP), .Z(u5_Z));
    xo02d1 XOR0 (.A1(FF2_Q), .A2(FF0_Q), .Z(XOR0_Z));
    in02d1 INV2X0 (.I(FF0_QN), .ZN(OUT[0]));
    in02d1 INV2X1 (.I(FF1_QN), .ZN(OUT[1]));
    in02d1 INV2X2 (.I(FF2_QN), .ZN(OUT[2]));
    in02d1 INV2X3 (.I(FF0_QN), .ZN(SERIAL_OUT));
endmodule
```

TABLE 14.13   Compiled serial-input signature register, using $P(x) = 1 \oplus x \oplus x^3$.

```
module lfsr_signature (OUT, SERIAL_OUT, INITN, CP, IN);
output [2:0] OUT; output SERIAL_OUT; input   INITN, CP; input  [0:0] IN;
    dfctnb FF2 (.D(XOR1_Z), .CP(u4_Z), .CDN(u2_Z), .Q(FF2_Q), .QN(FF2_QN));
    dfctnb FF1 (.D(FF2_Q), .CP(u4_Z), .CDN(u2_Z), .Q(FF1_Q), .QN(FF1_QN));
    dfctnb FF0 (.D(XOR0_Z), .CP(u4_Z), .CDN(u2_Z), .Q(FF0_Q), .QN(FF0_QN));
    ni01d1 u2 (.I(u3_Z), .Z(u2_Z)); ni01d1 u3 (.I(INITN), .Z(u3_Z));
    ni01d1 u4 (.I(u5_Z), .Z(u4_Z)); ni01d1 u5 (.I(CP), .Z(u5_Z));
    xo02d1 XOR1 (.A1(IN[0]), .A2(FF0_Q), .Z(XOR1_Z));
    xo02d1 XOR0 (.A1(FF1_Q), .A2(FF0_Q), .Z(XOR0_Z));
    in02d1 INV2X1 (.I(FF1_QN), .ZN(OUT[1]));
    in02d1 INV2X2 (.I(FF2_QN), .ZN(OUT[2]));
    in02d1 INV2X3 (.I(FF0_QN), .ZN(SERIAL_OUT));
    in02d1 INV2X0 (.I(FF0_QN), .ZN(OUT[0]));
endmodule
```

14.7.7 MISR

A serial-input signature register can only be used to test logic with a single output. We can extend the idea of a serial-input signature register to the **multiple-input signature register** (**MISR**) shown in Figure 14.29. There are several ways to connect the inputs to both types (type 1 and type 2) of LFSRs to form an MISR. Since the XOR operation is linear and associative, so that $(A \oplus B) \oplus C = A \oplus (B \oplus C)$, as long as the result of the additions are the same then the different representations are equivalent. If we have an n-bit long MISR we can accommodate up to n inputs to form the signature. If we use $m < n$ inputs we do not need the extra XOR gates in the last $n - m$ positions of the MISR.

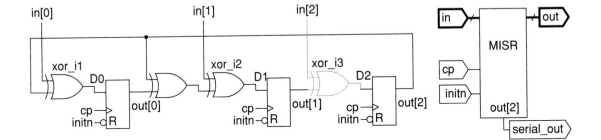

FIGURE 14.29 Multiple-input signature register (MISR). This MISR is formed from the type 2 LFSR (with $P^*(x) = 1 \oplus x^2 \oplus x^3$) shown in Figure 14.28(d) by adding XOR gates xor_i1, xor_i2, and xor_i3. This 3-bit MISR can form a signature from logic with three outputs. If we only need to test two outputs then we do not need XOR gate, xor_i3, corresponding to input in[2].

There are several types of BIST architecture based on the MISR. By including extra logic we can reconfigure an MISR to be an LFSR or a signature register; this is called a **built-in logic block observer** (**BILBO**). By including the logic that we wish to test in the feedback path of an MISR, we can construct circular BIST structures. One of these is known as the **circular self-test path** (**CSTP**).

We can test compiled blocks including RAM, ROM, and datapath elements using an LFSR generator and a MISR. To generate all 2^n address values for a RAM or ROM we can modify the LFSR feedback path to force entrance and exit from the all-zeros state. This is known as a **complete LFSR**. The pattern generator does not have to be an LFSR or exhaustive.

For example, if we were to apply an exhaustive test to a 4-bit by 4-bit multiplier this would require 2^8 or 256 vectors. An 8-bit by 8-bit multiplier requires 65,536 vectors and, if it were possible to test a 32-bit by 32-bit multiplier exhaustively, it would require 1.8×10^{19} vectors. Table 14.14 shows two sets of nonexhaustive test patterns, {SA} and {SAE}, if A and B are both 4 bits wide. The test sequences {SA} and {SAE} consist of nested sequences of **walking 1's** and **walking 0's** (S1 and S1B), **walking pairs** (S2 and S2B), and triplets (S3, S3B). The sequences are extended for larger inputs, so that, for example, {S2} is a sequence of seven vectors for an 8-bit input and so on. Intermediate sequences {SX} and {SXB} are concatenated from S1, S2, and S3; and from S1B, S2B, and S3B respectively. These sequences are chosen to exercise as many of the add-and-carry functions within the multiplier as possible.

TABLE 14.14   Multiplier test patterns.[1]

Sequence {SX}	Sequence {SXB}	Sequence {SA}	Sequence {SAE}
S1={1000 0100 0010 0001}	S1B={0111 1011 1101 0111}	{	{ { AB={S1, SX} }
S2={1100 0110 0011}	S2B={0011 1001 1100}	AB={S1, SX}	{ AB={S1B, SXB} }
S3={1110 0111}	S3B={0001 1000}	}	{ AB={S2, SX} }
			{ AB={S2B, SXB} }
SX={ {S1} {S2} {S3}}	SXB={ {S1B} {S2B} {S3B} }		{ AB={S3, SX} }
			{ AB={S3B, SXB} }
			}
Total =3(X−1)=9, X=4	Total =3(X−1)=9, X=4	Total=4×9 = 3A(B−1)=36	Total=3(2A−1)(3B−2) =3×7×10=210

[1]{AB={S1, SB} } means for each value of A in the sequence {S1} set B equal to all the values in {SB}.

The sequence length of {SA} is 3A (B − 1), and 3(2A − 1)(3B − 2) for {SAE}, where A and B are the sizes of the multiplier inputs. For example, {SA} is 168 vectors for A = B = 8 and 2976 vectors for A = B = 32; {SAE} is 990 vectors (A = B = 8) and 17,766 vectors (A = B = 32). From fault simulation, the stuck-at fault coverage is 93 percent for sequence {SA} and 97 percent for sequence {SAE}.

Figure 14.30 shows an MISR with a scan chain. We can now include the BIST logic as part of a boundary-scan chain, this approach is called **scanBIST**.

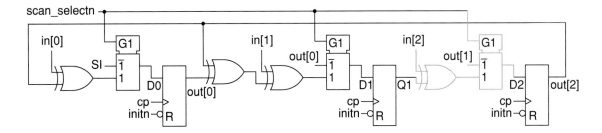

FIGURE 14.30 Multiple-input signature register (MISR) with scan generated from the MISR of Figure 14.29.

14.8 A Simple Test Example

As an example, we will describe automatic test generation using boundary scan together with internal scan. We shall use the function $Z = A'B + BC$ for the core logic and register the three inputs using three flip-flops. We shall test the resulting sequential logic using a scan chain. The simple logic will allow us to see how the test vectors are generated.

14.8.1 Test-Logic Insertion

Figure 14.31 shows a structural Verilog model of the logic core. The three flip-flops (cell name dfctnb) implement the input register. The combinational logic implements the function, outp = a_r[0]'.a_r[1] + a_r[1].a_r[2]. This is the same function as Figure 14.14 and Figure 14.16.

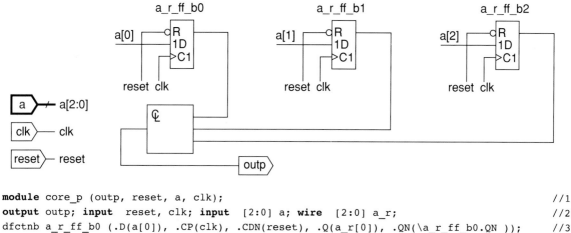

```
module core_p (outp, reset, a, clk);                                            //1
output outp; input  reset, clk; input  [2:0] a; wire  [2:0] a_r;                //2
dfctnb a_r_ff_b0 (.D(a[0]), .CP(clk), .CDN(reset), .Q(a_r[0]), .QN(\a_r_ff_b0.QN ));   //3
dfctnb a_r_ff_b1 (.D(a[1]), .CP(clk), .CDN(reset), .Q(a_r[1]), .QN(\a_r_ff_b1.QN ));   //4
dfctnb a_r_ff_b2 (.D(a[2]), .CP(clk), .CDN(reset), .Q(a_r[2]), .QN(\a_r_ff_b2.QN ));   //5
in01d0 u2 (.I(a_r[0]),    .ZN(u2_ZN));                                          //6
nd02d0 u3 (.A1(u2_ZN),    .A2(a_r[1]),    .ZN(u3_ZN));                          //7
nd02d0 u4 (.A1(a_r[1]),   .A2(a_r[2]),    .ZN(u4_ZN));                          //8
nd02d0 u5 (.A1(u3_ZN),    .A2(u4_ZN),     .ZN(outp));                           //9
endmodule                                                                       //10
```

FIGURE 14.31 Core of the Threegates ASIC.

Table 14.15 shows the structural Verilog for the top-level logic of the Three-gates ASIC including the I/O pads. There are nine pad cells. Three instances (up1_b0, up1_b1, and up1_b2) are the data-input pads, and one instance, up2_1, is the output pad. These were vectorized pads (even for the output that had a range of 1), so the synthesizer has added suffixes ('_1' and so on) to the pad instance names. Two pads are for power, one each for ground and the positive supply, instances up11 and up12. One pad, instance up3_1, is for the reset signal. There are two pad cells for the clock. Instance up4_1 is the clock input pad attached to the package pin and instance up6 is the clock input buffer.

The next step is to insert the boundary-scan logic and the internal-scan logic. Some synthesis tools can create test logic as they synthesize, but for most tools we need to perform **test-logic insertion** as a separate step. Normally we complete a parameter sheet specifying the type of test logic (boundary scan with internal scan in this case), as well as the ordering of the scan chain. In our example, we shall include all of the sequential cells in the boundary-scan register and order the boundary-scan cells using the pad numbers (in the original behavioral input). Figure 14.32 shows the modified core logic. The test software has changed all the flip-flops (cell names dfctnb) to scan flip-flops (with the same instance names, but the cell names are changed to mfctnb). The test software also adds a noninverting buffer to drive the scan-select signal to all the scan flip-flops.

The test software also adds logic to the top level. We do not need a detailed understanding of the automatically generated logic, but later in the design flow we will need to understand what has been done. Figure 14.33 shows a high-level view of the Threegates ASIC before and after test-logic insertion.

TABLE 14.15   The top level of the Threegates ASIC before test-logic insertion.

```
module asic_p (pad_outp, pad_a, pad_reset, pad_clk);
output [0:0] pad_outp; input  [2:0] pad_a; input [0:0] pad_reset, pad_clk;
wire [0:0] reset_sv, clk_sv, outp_sv; wire [2:0] a_sv; supply1 VDD; supply0 VSS;
core_p uc1 (.outp(outp_sv[0]), .reset(reset_sv[0]), .a(a_sv[2:0]), .clk(clk_bit));
pc3o07    up2_1      (.PAD(pad_outp[0]),    .I(outp_sv[0]));
pc3c01    up6        (.CCLK(clk_sv[0]),     .CP(clk_bit));
pc3d01r   up3_1      (.PAD(pad_reset[0]),   .CIN(reset_sv[0]));
pc3d01r   up4_1      (.PAD(pad_clk[0]),     .CIN(clk_sv[0]));
pc3d01r   up1_b0     (.PAD(pad_a[0]),       .CIN(a_sv[0]));
pc3d01r   up1_b1     (.PAD(pad_a[1]),       .CIN(a_sv[1]));
pc3d01r   up1_b2     (.PAD(pad_a[2]),       .CIN(a_sv[2]));
pv0f      up11       (.VSS(VSS));
pvdf      up12       (.VDD(VDD));
endmodule
```

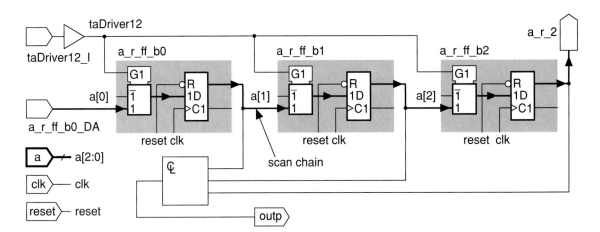

```
module core_p_ta (a_r_2, outp, a_r_ff_b0_DA, taDriver12_I, a, clk, reset);    //1
output a_r_2, outp; input a_r_ff_b0_DA, taDriver12_I;                          //2
input [2:0] a; input clk, reset; wire [1:0] a_r; supply1 VDD; supply0 VSS;     //3
ni01d5 taDriver12 (.I(taDriver12_I), .Z(taDriver12_Z));                        //4
mfctnb a_r_ff_b0 (.DA(a_r_ff_b0_DA), .DB(a[0]), .SA(taDriver12_Z), .CP(clk),   //5
  .CDN(reset), .Q(a_r[0]), .QN(\a_r_ff_b0.QN ));                               //6
mfctnb a_r_ff_b1 (.DA(a_r[0]), .DB(a[1]), .SA(taDriver12_Z), .CP(clk), .CDN(reset),  //7
  .Q(a_r[1]), .QN(\a_r_ff_b1.QN ));                                            //8
mfctnb a_r_ff_b2 (.DA(a_r[1]), .DB(a[2]), .SA(taDriver12_Z), .CP(clk), .CDN(reset),  //9
  .Q(a_r_2), .QN(\a_r_ff_b2.QN ));                                             //10
in01d0 u2 (.I(a_r[0]),    .ZN(u2_ZN));                                         //11
nd02d0 u3 (.A1(u2_ZN),    .A2(a_r[1]),    .ZN(u3_ZN));                         //12
nd02d0 u4 (.A1(a_r[1]),   .A2(a_r_2),     .ZN(u4_ZN));                         //13
nd02d0 u5 (.A1(u3_ZN),    .A2(u4_ZN),     .ZN(outp));                          //14
endmodule                                                                     //15
```

FIGURE 14.32 The core of the Threegates ASIC after test-logic insertion.

14.8.2   How the Test Software Works

The structural Verilog for the Threegates ASIC is lengthy, so Figure 14.34 shows only the essential parts. The following main blocks are labeled in Figure 14.34:

  A. This block is the logic core shown in Figure 14.32. The Verilog module header shows the "local" and "formal" port names. Arrows indicate whether each signal is an input or an output.

  B. This is the main body of logic added by the test software. It includes the boundary-scan controller and clock control.

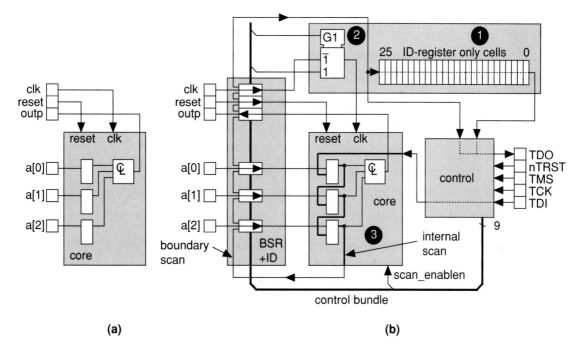

FIGURE 14.33 The Threegates ASIC. (a) Before test-logic insertion. (b) After test-logic insertion.

C. This block groups together the buffers that the test software has added at the top level to drive the control signals throughout the boundary-scan logic.

D. This block is the first boundary-scan cell in the BSR. There are six boundary-scan cells: three input cells for the data inputs, one output cell for the data output, one input cell for the reset, and one input cell for the clock. Only the first (the boundary-scan input cell for a[0]) and the last boundary-scan cells are shown. The others are similar.

E. This is the last boundary-scan cell in the BSR, the output cell for the clock.

F. This is the clock pad (with input connected to the ASIC package pin). The cell itself is unchanged by the test software, but the connections have been altered.

G. This is the clock-buffer cell that has not been changed.

H. The test software adds five I/O pads for the TAP. Four are input pad cells for TCK, TMS, TDO, and TRST. One is a three-state output pad cell for TDO.

I. The power pad cells remain unchanged.

J. The remaining I/O pad cells for the three data inputs, the data output, and reset remain unchanged, but the connections to the core logic are broken and the boundary-scan cells inserted.

The numbers in Figure 14.34 link the signals in each block to the following explanations:

1. The control signals for the input BSCs are `C_0`, `C_1`, `C_2`, and `C_4` and these are all buffered, together with the test clock TCK. The single output BSC also requires the control signal `C_3` and this is driven from the BST controller.

2. The clock enters the ASIC package through the clock pad as `.PAD(clk[0])` and exits the clock pad cell as `.CIN(up_4_1_CIN1)`. The test software routes this to the data input of the last boundary-scan cell as `.PI(up_4_1_CIN1)` and the clock exits as `.PO(up_4_1_cin)`. The clock then passes through the clock buffer, as before.

3. The serial input of the first boundary-scan cell comes from the controller as `.bst_control_BST_SI(test_logic_bst_control_BST_SI)`.

4. The serial output of the last boundary-scan cell goes to the controller as `.bst_control_BST(up4_1_bst_SO)`.

5. The beginning of the BSR is the first scan flip-flop in the core, which is connected to the TDI input as `.a_r_ff_b0_DA(ta_TDI_CIN)`.

6. The end of the scan chain leaves the core as `.a_r_2(uc1_a_r_2)` and enters the controller as `.bst_control_scan_SO(uc1_a_r_2)`.

7. The scan-enable signal `.bst_control_C_9(test_logic_bst_control_C_9)` is generated by the boundary-scan controller, and connects to the core as `.taDriver12_I(test_logic_bst_control_C_9)`.

The added test logic is shown in Figure 14.35. The blocks are as follows:

A. This is the module declaration for the test logic in the rest of the diagram, it corresponds to block B in Table 14.34.

B. This block contains buffers and clock control logic.

C. This is the boundary-scan controller.

D. This is the first of 26 IDR cells. In this implementation the IDCODE register is combined with the BSR. Since there are only six BSR cells we need $(32-6)$ or 26 IDR cells to complete the 32-bit IDR.

E. This is the last IDR cell.

The numbers in Figure 14.35 refer to the following explanations:

1. The system clock (CLK, not the test clock TCK) from the top level (after passing through the boundary-scan cell) is fed through a MUX so that CLK may be controlled during scan.

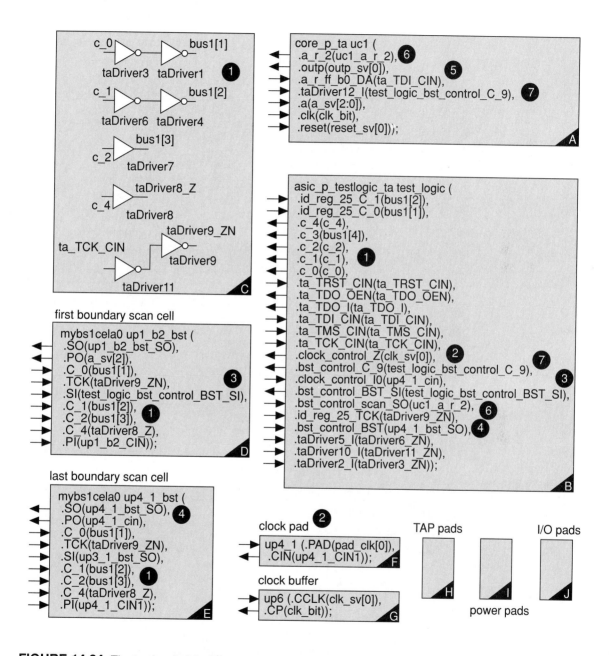

FIGURE 14.34 The top level of the Threegates ASIC after test-logic insertion.

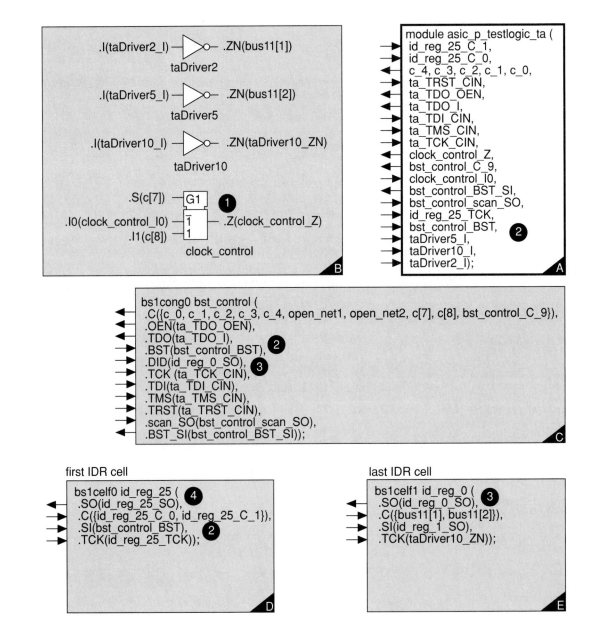

FIGURE 14.35 Test logic inserted in the Threegate ASIC.

TABLE 14.16   The TAP (test-access port) control.[1]

TAP state	C_0	C_1	C_2	C_3	C_4	C_5	C_6	C_7	C_8[2]	C_9
Reset	x	x	xxxx0xx	xxxx0xx	xxxx0xx	xxxx0xx	xxxx1xx	xxxx0xx	xxxx0xx	xxxx0xx
Run_Idle	00x0xxx	11x1xxx	0	1001011	0001011	0000010	1	0000001	0000000	0000000
Select_DR	00x0xxx	11x1xxx	0	1001011	0001011	0000010	1	0000001	0000000	0000000
Capture_DR	00x01xx	00x00xx	0	1001011	0001011	0000010	1	0000001	000000T	0000000
Shift_DR	11x11xx	11x11xx	0	1001011	0001011	0000010	1111101	0000001	000000T	0000001
Exit1_DR	00x00xx	11x11xx	0	1001011	0001011	0000010	1	0000001	0000000	0000000
Pause_DR	00x00xx	11x11xx	0	1001011	0001011	0000010	1	0000001	0000000	0000000
Exit2_DR	00x00xx	11x11xx	0	1001011	0001011	0000010	1	0000001	0000000	0000000
Update_DR	00x0xxx	11x1xxx	110100	1001011	0001011	0	1111101	0000001	0000000	0000000
Select_IR	x	x	0	1001011	0001011	00000x0	11111x1	0000001	0000000	0000000
Capture_IR	x	x	0	1001011	0001011	00000x0	11111x1	0000001	0000000	0000000
Shift_IR	x	x	0	1001011	0001011	00000x0	11111x1	0000001	0000000	0000000
Exit1_IR	x	x	0	1001011	0001011	00000x0	11111x1	0000001	0000000	0000000
Pause_IR	x	x	0	1001011	0001011	00000x0	11111x1	0000001	0000000	0000000
Exit2_IR	x	x	0	1001011	0001011	00000x0	11111x1	0000001	0000000	0000000
Update_IR	x	x	0	1001011	0001011	00000x0	1111101	0000001	0000000	0000000

[1]Outputs are specified for each instruction as 0123456, where: 0 = EXTEST, 1 = SAMPLE, 2 = BYPASS, 3 = INTEST, 4 = IDCODE, 5 = RUNBIST, 6 = SCANM.
[2]T denotes gated clock TCK.

2. The signal `bst_control_BST` is the end (output) of the boundary-scan cells and the start (input) to the ID register only cells.

3. The signal `id_reg_0_SO` is the end (output) of the ID register.

4. The signal `bst_control_BST_SI` is the start of the boundary-scan chain.

The job of the boundary-scan controller is to produce the control signals (`C_1` through `C_9`) for each of the 16 TAP controller states (`reset` through `update_IR`) for each different instruction. In this BST implementation there are seven instructions: the required `EXTEST`, `SAMPLE`, and `BYPASS`; `IDCODE`; `INTEST` (which is the equivalent of `EXTEST`, but for internal test); `RUNBIST` (which allows on-chip test structures to operate); and `SCANM` (which controls the internal-scan chains). The boundary-scan controller outputs are shown in Table 14.16.

There are two very important differences between this controller and the one described in Table 14.5. The first, and most obvious, is that the control signals now depend on the instruction. This is primarily because INTEST requires the control signal at the output of the BSCs to be in different states for the input and output cells. The second difference is that the logic for the boundary-scan cell control signals is now purely combinational—we have removed the gated clocks. For example, Figure 14.36 shows the input boundary-scan cell. The clock for the shift flip-flop is now TCK and not a gated clock as it was in Table 14.5. We can do this because the output of the flip-flop, SO, the scan output, is added as input to the MUX that feeds the flip-flop data input. Thus, when we wish to hold the state of the flip-flop, the control signals select SO to be connected from the output to the input. This is called a **polarity-hold flip-flop**. Unfortunately, we have little choice but to gate the system clock if we make the scan chain part of the BSR. We cannot have one clock for part of the BSR and another for the rest. The costly alternative is to change every scan flip-flop to a scanned polarity-hold flip-flop.

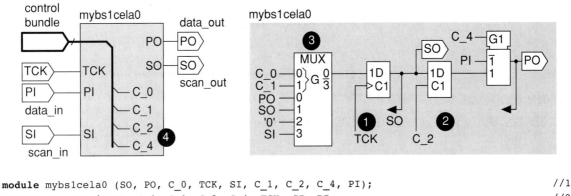

```
module mybs1cela0 (SO, PO, C_0, TCK, SI, C_1, C_2, C_4, PI);                          //1
output SO, PO; input  C_0, C_1, C_2, C_4, TCK, SI, PI;                               //2
in01d1 inv_0      (.I(C_0), .ZN(iv0_ZN));                                            //3
in01d1 inv_1      (.I(C_1), .ZN(iv1_ZN));                                            //4
oa03d1 oai221_1   (.A1(C_0), .A2(SO), .B1(iv0_ZN), .B2(SI), .C(C_1), .ZN(oa1_ZN));   //5
nd02d1 nand2_1    (.A1(na2_ZN), .A2(oa1_ZN), .ZN(na1_ZN));                           //6
nd03d1 nand3_1    (.A1(PO), .A2(iv0_ZN), .A3(iv1_ZN), .ZN(na2_ZN));                  //7
mx21d1 mux21_1    (.I0(PI), .I1(upo), .S(C_4), .Z(PO));                              //8
dfntnb dff_1      (.D(na1_ZN), .CP(TCK), .Q(SO), .QN(\so.QN ));                      //9
lantnb latch_1    (.E(C_2), .D(SO), .Q(upo), .QN(\upo.QN ));                         //10
endmodule                                                                            //11
```

FIGURE 14.36 Input boundary-scan cell (BSC) for the Threegates ASIC. Compare this to the generic data-register (DR) cell (used as a BSC) shown in Figure 14.2.

14.8.3   ATVG and Fault Simulation

Table 14.17 shows the results of running the Compass ATVG software on the Three-gates ASIC. We might ask: Why so many faults? and why is the fault coverage so poor? First we look at the details of the test software output. We notice the following:

- Line 2. The backtrace limit is 30. We do not have any deep complex combinational logic so that this should not cause a problem.

- Lines 4–6. An uncollapsed fault count of 184 indicates the test software has inserted faults on approximately 100 nodes, or at most 50 gates assuming a fanout of 1, less gates with any realistic fanout. Clearly this is less than all of the test logic that we have inserted.

To discover why the fault coverage is 68.5 percent we must examine each of the fault categories. First, Table 14.18 shows the undetected faults.

The ATVG program is generating tests for the core using internal scan. We cannot test the BST logic itself, for example. During the production test we shall test the BST logic first, separately from the core—this is often called a **flush test**. Thus we can ignore any faults from the BST logic for the purposes of internal-scan testing.

Next we find two redundant faults: TA_TDO.1.I sa0 and sa1. Since TDO is three-stated during the test, it makes no difference to the function of the logic if this node is tied high or low—hence these faults are redundant. Again we should ensure these faults will be caught during the flush test. Finally, Table 14.19 shows the tied faults.

Now that we can explain all of the undetectable faults, we examine the detected faults. Table 14.20 shows only the detected faults in the core logic. Faults F1–F8 in the first part of Table 14.20 correspond to the faults in Figure 14.16. The fault list in the second part of Table 14.20 shows each fault in the core and whether it was detected (D) or collapsed and detected as an equivalent fault (CD). There are no undetected faults (U) in the logic core.

14.8.4   Test Vectors

Next we generate the test vectors for the Threegates ASIC. There are three types of vectors in scan testing. **Serial vectors** are the bit patterns that we shift into the scan chain. We have three flip-flops in the scan chain plus six boundary-scan cells, so each serial vector is 9 bits long. There are serial input vectors that we apply as a stimulus and serial output vectors that we expect as a response. **Parallel vectors** are applied to the pads before we shift the serial vectors into the scan chain. We have nine input pads (three core data, one core clock, one core reset, and four input TAP pads—TMS, TCK, TRST, and TDI) and two outputs (one core data output and TDO). Each parallel vector is thus 11 bits long and contains 9 bits of stimulus and 2 bits of response. A test program consists of applying the stimulus bits from one parallel vector to the nine input pins for one test cycle. In the next nine test cycles we shift a 9-bit stimulus from a serial vector into the scan chain (and receive a 9-bit

TABLE 14.17   ATVG (automatic test-vector generation) report for the Threegates ASIC.

```
CREATE: Output vector database cell defaulted to [svf]asic_p_ta          --1
CREATE: Backtrack limit defaulted to 30                                  --2
CREATE: Minimal compression effort: 10 (default)                         --3
Fault list generation/collapsing                                         --4
Total number of faults: 184                                              --5
Number of faults in collapsed fault list: 80                             --6
Vector generation                                                        --7
#                                                                        --8
# VECTORS   FAULTS    FAULT COVER                                        --9
#         processed                                                      --10
#                                                                        --11
#    5       184      60.54%                                             --12
#                                                                        --13
# Total number of backtracks: 0                                          --14
# Highest backtrack      : 0                                             --15
# Total number of vectors   : 5                                          --16
#                                                                        --17
# STAR RESULTS summary                                                   --18
#                       Noncollapsed      Collapsed                      --19
# Fault counts:                                                          --20
#    Aborted                0                0                           --21
#    Detected               89               43                          --22
#    Untested               58               20                          --23
#                         ------           ------                        --24
#    Total of detectable    147              63                          --25
#                                                                        --26
#    Redundant              6                2                           --27
#    Tied                   31               15                          --28
#                                                                        --29
# FAULT COVERAGE          60.54 %          68.25 %                       --30
#                                                                        --31
# Fault coverage = nb of detected faults / nb of detectable faults       --32
Vector/fault list database [svf]asic_p_ta created.                      --33
```

response, the result of the previous tests, from the scan chain). We can generate the serial and parallel vectors separately, or we can merge the vectors to give a set of **broadside vectors**. Each broadside vector corresponds to one test cycle and can be used for simulation. Some testers require broadside vectors; others can generate them from the serial and parallel vectors.

Table 14.21 shows the serial test vectors for the Threegates ASIC. The third serial test vector is '110111010'. This test vector is shifted into the BSR, so that the first three bits in this vector end up in the first three bits of the BSR. The first three bits of the BSR, nearest TDI, are the scan flip-flops, the other six bits are

TABLE 14.18   Untested faults (not observable) for the Threegates ASIC.

Faults	Explanation
TADRIVER4.ZN sa0	Internal driver for BST control bundle (seven more faults like this).
TA_TRST.1.CIN sa0	BST reset TRST is active-low and tied high during test.
TDI.O sa0 sa1	TDI is BST serial input.
UP1_B0.1.CIN sa0 sa1	Data input pad (two more faults like this one).
UP3_1.1.CIN sa0	System reset is active-low and tied high during test.
UP4_1.1.CIN sa0 sa1	System clock input pad.
# Total number: 20	

TABLE 14.19   Tied faults.

Fault(s)	Explanation
TADRIVER1.ZN sa0	Internal BST buffer (seven more faults like this one).
TA_TMS.1.CIN sa0	TMS input tied low.
TA_TRST.1.CIN sa1	TRST input tied high.
TEST_LOGIC.BST_CONTROL.U1.ZN sa1	Internal BST logic.
UP1_B0_BST.U1.A2 sa0	Input pad (two more faults like this).
UP3_1.1.CIN sa1	Reset input pad tied high.
# Total number: 15	

boundary-scan cells). Since UC1.A_R_FF_B0.Q is a_r[0] and so on, the third test vector will set a_r = 011 where a_r[2] = 0. This is the vector we require to test the function a_r[0]'.a_r[1] + a_r[1].a_r[2] for fault UC1.U2.ZN sa1 in the Threegates ASIC. From Figure 14.31 we see that this is a stuck-at-1 fault on the output of the inverter whose input is connected to a_r[0]. This fault corresponds to fault F1 in the circuit of Figure 14.16. The fault simulation we performed earlier told us the vector ABC = 011 is a test for fault F1 for the function A'B + BC.

14.8.5   Production Tester Vector Formats

The final step in test-program generation is to format the test vectors for the production tester. As an example the following shows the Sentry tester file format for testing a D flip-flop. For an average ASIC there would be thousands of vectors in this file.

```
# Pin declaration: pin names are separated by semi-colons (all pins
# on a bus must be listed and separated by commas)
pre_; clr_; d; clk; q; q_;
```

TABLE 14.20   Detected core-logic faults in the Threegates ASIC.

Fault(s)	Explanation
`UC1.U2.ZN sa1`	F1
`UC1.U3.A2 sa1`	F2
`UC1.U3.ZN sa1`	F5
`UC1.U4.A1 sa1`	F3
`UC1.U4.ZN sa1`	F6
`UC1.U5.ZN sa0`	F8
`UC1.U5.ZN sa1`	F7
`UC1.A_R_FF_B2.Q.O sa1`	F4
`Fault list`	
`UC1.A_R_FF_B0.Q: (O) CD CD`	SA0 and SA1 collapsed to U3.A1
`UC1.A_R_FF_B1.Q: (O) D D`	SA0 and SA1 detected.
`UC1.A_R_FF_B2.Q: (O) CD D`	SA0 collapsed to U2. SA1 is F4.
`UC1.U2: (I) CD CD (ZN) CD D`	I.SA1/0 collapsed to O.SA1/0. O. SA1 is F1.
`UC1.U3: (A1) CD CD (A2) CD D (ZN) CD D`	A1.SA1 collapsed to U2.ZN.SA1.
`UC1.U4: (A1) CD D (A2) CD CD (ZN) CD D`	A2.SA1 collapsed to A_R_FF_B2.Q.SA1.
`UC1.U5: (A1) CD CD (A2) CD CD (ZN) D D`	A1.SA1 collapsed to U3.ZN.SA1

TABLE 14.21   Serial test vectors

			Serial-input scan data					
#1	1	1	1	0	1	0	1	1	0
#2	1	0	1	1	0	1	0	0	1
#3	<u>1</u>	<u>1</u>	<u>0</u>	1	1	1	0	1	0
#4	0	0	0	1	0	0	0	0	0
#5	0	1	0	0	1	1	1	0	1

```
^UC1.A_R_FF_B0.Q      ^UP1_B2_BST.SO.Q      ^UP2_1_BST.SO.Q
     ^UC1.A_R_FF_B1.Q      ^UP1_B1_BST.SO.Q      ^UP3_1_BST.SO.Q
          ^UC1.A_R_FF_B2.Q      ^UP1_B0_BST.SO.Q      ^UP4_1_BST.SO.Q
```

Fault	Fault number	Vector number	Core input
`UC1.U2.ZN sa1`	**F1**	**3**	**011**
`UC1.U3.A2 sa1`	F2	4	000
`UC1.U3.ZN sa1`	F5	5	010
`UC1.U4.A1 sa1`	F3	2	101
`UC1.U4.ZN sa1`	F6	1	111
`UC1.U5.ZN sa0`	F8	1	111
`UC1.U5.ZN sa1`	F7	2	101
`UC1.A_R_FF_B2.Q.O sa1`	F4	2	101

```
# Pin declarations are separated from test vectors by $
$
# The first number on each line is the time since start in ns,
# followed by space or a tab.
# The symbols following the time are the test vectors
# (in the same order as the pin declaration)
# an "=" means don't do anything
# an "s" means sense the pin at the beginning of this time point
# (before the input changes at this time point have any effect)
#
#  pcdcqq
#  rlal _
#  ertk
#   _a
00 1010== # clear the flip-flop
10 1110ss # d=1, clock=0
20 1111ss # d=1, clock=1
30 1110ss # d=1, clock=0
40 1100ss # d=0, clock=0
50 1101ss # d=0, clock=1
60 1100ss # d=0, clock=0
70 ====ss
```

14.8.6 Test Flow

Normally we leave test-vector generation and the production-test program generation until the very last step in ASIC design after physical design is complete. All of
the steps have been described before the discussion of physical design, because it is
still important to consider test very early in the design flow. Next, as an example of
considering test as part of logical design, we shall return to our Viterbi decoder
example.

14.9 The Viterbi Decoder Example

Table 14.22 shows the timing analysis for the Viterbi decoder before and after test
insertion. The Compass test software inserts internal scan and boundary scan exactly
as in the Threegates example. The timing analysis is in the form of histograms
showing the distributions of the timing delays for all paths. In this analysis we set an
aggressive constraint of 20 ns (50 MHz) for the clock. The critical path before test
insertion is 21.75 ns (the slack is thus negative at −1.75 ns). The path starts at
u1.subout6.Q_ff_b0 and ends at u2.metric0.Q_ff_b4, both flip-flops inside
the flattened block, v_1.u100, that we created during synthesis in an attempt to
improve speed. The first flip-flop in the path is a dfctnb; the last flip-flop is a
dfctnh. The suffix 'b' denotes 1X drive and suffix 'h' denotes 2X drive.

TABLE 14.22   Timing effects of test-logic insertion for the Viterbi decoder.

Timing of critical paths before test-logic insertion

```
#   Slack(ns)   Num Paths
#    -3.3826     1        *
#    -1.7536     18       *******
#     -.1245     4        **
#     1.5045     1        *
#     3.1336     0        *
#     4.7626     0        *
#     6.3916     134      ******************************************
#     8.0207     6        ***
#     9.6497     3        **
#    11.2787     0        *
#    12.9078     24       ********
```

```
# instance name
# inPin --> outPin       incr    arrival   trs   rampDel   cap    cell
#                        (ns)     (ns)            (ns)      (pf)

# v_1.u100.u1.subout6.Q_ff_b0
# CP --> QN               1.73     1.73     R     .20       .10    dfctnb
...
# v_1.u100.u2.metric0.Q_ff_b4
# setup: D --> CP          .16    21.75     F     .00       .00    dfctnh
```

After test-logic insertion

```
#    -4.0034     1        *
#    -1.9835     18       *****
#      .0365     4        **
#     2.0565     1        *
#     4.0764     0        *
#     6.0964     138      ******************************
#     8.1164     2        *
#    10.1363     3        **
#    12.1563     24       ******
#    14.1763     0        *
#    16.1963     187      ******************************************
```

```
# v_1.u100.u1.subout7.Q_ff_b1
# CP --> Q                1.40     1.40     R     .28       .13    mfctnb
...
# v_1.u100.u2.metric0.Q_ff_b4
# setup: DB --> CP         .39    21.98     F     .00       .00    mfctnh
```

After test insertion the critical path is 21.98 ns. The end point is identical, but the start point is now subout7.Q_ff_b1. This is not too surprising. What is happening is that there are a set of paths of nearly equal length. Changing the flip-flops to their scan versions (mfctnb and mfctnh) increases the delay slightly. The exact delay depends on the capacitive load at the output, the path (clock-to-Q, clock-to-QN, or setup), and the input signal rise time.

Adding test logic has not increased the critical path delay substantially. Almost as important is that the distribution of delays has not changed substantially. Also very important is the fact that the distributions show that there are only approxi-

---

TABLE 14.23   Fault coverage for the Viterbi decoder.

```
Fault list generation/collapsing
Total number of faults: 8846
Number of faults in collapsed fault list: 3869
Vector generation
#
# VECTORS   FAULTS    FAULT COVER
#          processed
#
#    20      7515      82.92%
#    40      8087      89.39%
#    60      8313      91.74%
#    80      8632      95.29%
#    87      8846      96.06%


# Total number of backtracks: 3000
# Highest backtrack       : 30
# Total number of vectors : 87

# STAR RESULTS summary
#                        Noncollapsed        Collapsed
# Fault counts:
#    Aborted                 178                85
#    Detected                8427              3680
#    Untested                168                60
#                          ------            ------
#    Total of detectable     8773              3825
#
#    Redundant               10                 6
#    Tied                    63                38
#
# FAULT COVERAGE           96.06 %            96.21 %
```

mately 20 paths with delays close to the critical path delay. This means that we should be able to constrain these paths during physical design and achieve a performance after routing that is close to our preroute predictions.

Next we check the logic for fault coverage. Table 14.23 shows that the ATPG software has inserted nearly 9000 faults, which is reasonable for the size of our design. Fault coverage is 96 percent. Most of the untested and tied faults arise from the BST logic exactly as we have already described in the Threegates example. If we had not completed this small test case first, we might not have noticed this. The aborted faults are almost all within the large flattened block, v_1.u100. If we assume the approximately 60 faults due to the BST logic are covered by a flush test, our fault coverage increases to 3740/3825 or 98 percent. To improve upon this figure, some, but not all, of the aborted faults can be detected by substantially increasing the backtrack limit from the default value of 30. To discover the reasons for the remaining aborted faults, we could use a controllability/observability program. If we wish to increase the fault coverage even further, we either need to change our test approach or change the design architecture. In our case we believe that we can probably obtain close to 99 percent stuck-at fault coverage with the existing architecture and thus we are ready to move on to physical design.

14.10 Summary

The primary reason to consider test early during ASIC design is that it can become very expensive if we do not. The important points we covered in this chapter are:

- Boundary scan
- Single stuck-at fault model
- Controllability and observability
- ATPG using test vectors
- BIST with no test vectors

14.11 Problems

* = Difficult, ** = Very difficult, *** = Extremely difficult

14.1 (Acronyms, 10 min.) Translate the following excerpt from a MOSIS report: "Chip description: DLX RISC ASIC with DFT, IEEE 1149 BST, and BIST using PRBS LFSR and MISR. Test results: compaction shorted words."

14.2 (Economics of defect levels, 15 min.) You are the product manager for a new workstation. You use 10 similar ASICs as the key component in a computer that sells for $10,000 with a profit margin of 20 percent. You buy the ASICs for $10 each, and the shipping defect level is certified to be 0.1 percent by the ASIC vendor. You are having a problem with a large number of field failures, which you have traced to one of the ASICs. In the first nine months of shipment you have sold 49,500 computers, but 51 have failed in the field, 26 due to the ASIC. Finance estimates that all the field failures have cost at least $1 million in revenue and goodwill. You do not have the time, money, or capability to improve your incoming inspection or assembly tests. You estimate the product lifetime is another 18 months, in which time you will sell another 50,000 units at roughly the same price and profit margin. At an emergency meeting, the ASIC vendor's test engineer proposes to reduce the ASIC defect level to 0.01 percent immediately by improving the test program, but at a cost. You suggest a coffee break. With the information that you have, you have 15 minutes to estimate just how much extra you are prepared to pay for each ASIC.

14.3 (Defect level, 10 min.) In a series of experiments a customer of Zycad, which makes hardware fault-simulation accelerators, tested 10,000 parts from a lot with 30 percent yield. Each experiment used a different fraction of the test vector set. Fit the data in Table 14.24 to a model.

TABLE 14.24   Defect level as a function of fault coverage (Problem 14.3).

Fault coverage/%	Rejects	Defective parts	Defect level/%
50	6773	227	7
90	6877	133	3
99	6910	90	1
99.99	6997	3	0.01

14.4 (Test cost, 5 min.) Suppose, in the example of Section 14.1, reducing the bASIC defect level to 0.1 percent added an extra cost of $1 to each part. Now what is the best way to build the system?

14.5 (Defects, 5 min.) Finding defects in an ASIC is a hard problem. The average defect density for a submicron process is 1 cm^{-2} or less.

a. On average how many defects are there on a 1 cm chip?

b. If the average defect is $1\lambda^2$, and $\lambda = 0.25\ \mu\text{m}$, what is defect area/chip area?

c. Estimate the ratio of needle volume to haystack volume and comment.

14.6 (Faults and nodes, 10 min.)

a. How many faults are there in a circuit with n nodes?

b. Considering fanout how many collapsed faults are there?

c. Estimate how many test cycles a fault simulator needs to find these faults.

d. With a 10 MHz clock, how long is a 100 k-gate test (with your estimates)?

e. Using a 100 MHz computer, how long does this fault simulation take? (Assume simulation time is four orders of magnitude slower than real time.)

14.7 (PRBS, 10 min.) What are the first three patterns for a 4-bit maximal-length LFSR, given a seed of '0001'? *Hint:* Is there more than one answer?

14.8 (Test time, 10 min.)

a. How long does a 16-bit shift-register test take at a clock speed of 1 MHz?

b. Estimate how long it takes to test a 64 k-bit static RAM using a walking 1's (or marching 1's) pattern.

14.9 (Test time, 10 min.) A modern production tester costs $5–10 million. This cost is depreciated over the life of the tester (usually five years in the United States due to Internal Revenue Service guidelines).

a. If the tester is in use 24 hours a day, 365 days a year, how much does 1 second of test time cost?

b. If, due to down time (maintenance, operator sick time and so on) a $10 million tester is actually in use 50 percent of the time for chip testing and test time is 2 seconds, how much does test add to the cost of an ASIC?

c. Suppose the ASIC die is 300 mils on a side, is fabricated on a 6-inch wafer whose fabrication cost is $1750, and the yield is 68 percent. What is the fraction of test cost to total die cost (fabrication plus test costs)? Assume that the number of die per wafer is equal to wafer area divided by chip area.

14.10 (Fault collapsing, 10 min.) Draw up tables to show how input and output faults collapse using gate collapsing for the following primitive logic gates: AND, OR, NAND, NOR, and EXOR (assume two-input logic cells in each case with inputs A, B and output F); a two-input MUX (inputs S0, S1, and SEL0; output F).

14.11 (Fault simulation, 15 min.) Mentor Graphic Corporation's QuickFault concurrent fault simulator uses a 12-state logic system with three logic values ('0', '1', 'X') and four strengths (strong = S, resistive = R, high impedance = Z, I = indeterminate). Complete Table 14.25 using D = detected fault, P = possibly detected fault, and '–' = undetected fault. Give two values, 1/2, for each cell: The first value is for the default fault model in which a tester cannot tell the difference between Z/S/R; the second value is for testers that can differentiate between Z and S/R. *Hint:* One line of the table has been completed as an example.

14.12 (Finding faults, 30 min.)

a. List all the possible stuck-at faults for the circuit in Figure 14.37 using node faults.

b. Find all of the equivalent fault classes using node collapsing.

c. List the prime faults.

d. List all possible stuck-at faults using input and output faults (use A1.B and A2.B to distinguish between different inputs and outputs on the same net).

TABLE 14.25 The logic system used by Mentor Graphic Corporation's fault simulator, QuickFault (Problem 14.11).[1]

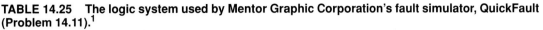

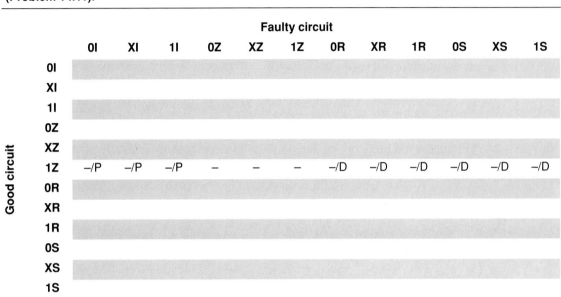

		Faulty circuit										
		0I	XI	1I	0Z	XZ	1Z	0R	XR	1R	0S	XS	1S
Good circuit	0I												
	XI												
	1I												
	0Z												
	XZ												
	1Z	–/P	–/P	–/P	–	–	–	–/D	–/D	–/D	–/D	–/D	–/D
	0R												
	XR												
	1R												
	0S												
	XS												
	1S												

[1] D=detected; P=possibly detected; '–'=undetected; x/y means x is the result of the default detection mechanism and y is the result when three-state detection is enabled (allowing the detection of the difference between Z and R/S strength).

FIGURE 14.37 An example circuit for fault collapsing (Problem 14.12).

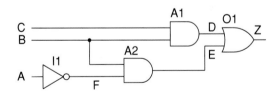

e. List the fault-equivalence classes using gate collapsing.

f. List the prime faults.

14.13 (Blind faith, 10 min.) Consider the following code: a = b && f(c). Verilog stops executing an expression as soon as it determines that the expression is false, whereas VeriFault does not. What effect does this have?

14.14 (Fault collapsing, 10 min.) Draw the Karnaugh maps including stuck-at faults for four-input NAND, AND, OR, and NOR gates.

14.15 (Fault dominance, 10 min.) If T_x is the set of test vectors that test for fault x and $T_b \subseteq T_a$, what can you say about faults a and b?

14.16 (*Fault dominance, 10 min.) Consider the network $C = AND(A, B)$, $D = NOT(B)$. List the PIs, POs, and faults under a pin-fault model. For each fault, state whether it is an equivalent fault, dominant fault, or dominated fault. Now consider this more formal definition of fault dominance: Fault a dominates b if and only if a and b are equivalent under the set of tests T for b. Two faults are equivalent under a test T if and only if the circuit response of the two faulty circuits is identical. *Hint:* Consider the fault at the input of the inverter very carefully.

14.17 (Japanese TVs, 20 min.) As an experiment a Japanese manufacturer decided not to perform any testing of its TVs before turning them on at the end of the production line. They achieved over a 90 percent turn-on rate. Build a cost model for this approach to testing. Make a one-page list of its advantages and disadvantages.

14.18 (Test costs, 20 min.) The CEO of an ASIC vendor called a meeting and asked the production manager to bring all wafers queued for rework. The CEO produced a hammer and smashed the several hundred wafers on the boardroom table. Construct a model around the following assumptions: 2 percent of wafers-in-process currently require rework after each of the 12 photo steps in the process, wafer cost is $2,000, 30 percent of the wafer costs are in the photo steps; current process yield is 85 percent, 30 percent of the reworked wafers have to be scrapped. Explain why you were not as shocked by this episode as the production manager and how it helped you to explain to the CEO the need to add time to your ASIC design schedule to include design for test.

14.19 (ZyCAD RP, 10 min.) The ZyCAD Paradigm RP rapid prototyping system consists of a set of emulation boards. Each emulation board contains 18 Xilinx 3090 chips and 16 Xilinx 4010 chips. The Xilinx 4010 chips are mounted on eight daughterboards, and the 3090 chips are mounted directly on the motherboard. The Xilinx 4010 chips are used for logic block emulation and the Xilinx 3090 chips are used for crossbar routing. Each daughterboard has 288 I/O pins that are available to the crossbar chips for routing. Each Xilinx 4010 device has the capability to interface with any other 4010 device on the emulation board. The Xilinx 4010 devices have 400 Configurable Logic Blocks (CLBs) per device and 160 programmable I/O1s. Estimate the size of an ASIC that you could prototype with this system.

14.20 (IDDQ testing, 10 min.) In the **six-shorts-per-transistor fault model** for IDDQ testing we model six shorts per transistor. What are they?

14.21 (PRBS) Consider Table 14.26.

a. (15 min.) What is the autocorrelation function for a maximal-length pseudorandom binary sequence?

b. ** (30 min.) Suppose we apply a pseudorandom sequence to a linear system. What is its response?

c. *** (60 min.) Suppose we correlate this response with the original pseudorandom sequence delayed by n cycles. What is this correlation function?

TABLE 14.26   Autocorrelation of pseudorandom binary sequences (Problem 14.21).

	Delay (clock ticks)						
	0	1	2	3	4	5	6
	$Q2_t$	$Q2_{t-1}$	$Q2_{t-2}$	$Q2_{t-3}$	$Q2_{t-4}$	$Q2_{t-5}$	$Q2_{t-6}$
	1	0	1	0	0	1	1
	1	1	0	1	0	0	1
	1	1	1	0	1	0	0
	0	1	1	1	0	1	0
	0	0	1	1	1	0	1
	1	0	0	1	1	1	0
	0	1	0	0	1	1	1
Correlation with $Q2_t$	4	2	2	2	2	2	2

14.22 (Sentry, 20 min.) Write a Sentry test file to check the preset of a D flip-flop.

14.23 (Synthesis, 20 min.) Consider the following equations:

```
f1 = x1'x2' + y3; f2 = x1x2' + x1'x2 = y2; f3 = x1x2y2' + x1'x2' = y3
```

How many untestable stuck-at faults are there in this network? Suppose we simplify the logic to the following:

```
f1* = y2'; f2* = x1x2' + x1'x2
```

How many untestable stuck-at faults are there? *Hint:* If you are stuck, see [Bartlett et al., 1988; Brayton, Hachtel, and Sangiovanni-Vincentelli, 1990].

14.24 (Threegates, 30 min.) Recreate the Threegates example.

14.25 (LFSR) Determine the pattern sequence generated by the 4-bit LFSR shown in Figure 14.38. Use the same format as Table 14.10.

14.26 (BIST, 15 min.) Find the signature if the CUT of Figure 14.25 is $Z = A'B + AC$.

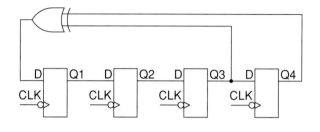

FIGURE 14.38 A 4-bit linear feedback shift register (LFSR) (Problem 14.25).

14.12 Bibliography

Books by Feugate and McIntyre [1988], Cheng and Agrawal [1989], and Fritzemeier, Nagle, and Hawkins [1989] contain explanations of basic testing terms and techniques. The book by Abramovici, Breuer, and Friedman [1990] is an advanced undergraduate and graduate-level review of test techniques. Needham's [1991] book reviews wafer and package testing. The text by Russell and Sayers [1989] is an undergraduate-level text with explanations of test algorithms. Turino's [1990] book covers a wide range of testing topics.

There are a number of books with collections of research papers on test, including works by Eichelberger, Lindblom, Waicukauski, and Williams [1991]; Lombardi and Sami [1987]; Williams [1986]; and Zobrist [1993]. Tsui's book contains a review of scan test and a large bibliography [1987]. The book by Ghosh, Devadas, and Newton [1992] describes test-generation algorithms for state machines at a level intended for CAD researchers. Bardell, McAnney, and Savir [1987] focus on pseudorandom BIST. A book by Yarmolik [1990] covers BIST and signature analysis; a second book by Yarmolik and Kachan [1993] concentrates on self-test. Books by Lavagno and Sangiovanni-Vincentelli [1993] and by Lee [1997] are advanced works on the integration of test synthesis and logic synthesis. The text by Jha and Kundu [1990] covers reliability in design. The book by Bhattacharya and Hayes [1990] covers modeling for testing (and includes a good description of the D and PODEM algorithms). There are alternative ASIC test techniques that we have not covered. For example, Chandra's paper describes the **CrossCheck** architecture for gate arrays [1993]. A book by Chakradhar, Agrawal, and Bushnell [1991] covers neural models for testing.

The major conferences in the area of test are the International Test Conference, known as the ITC (TK7874.I593, ISSN 0743-1686), the International Test Symposium (TK7874.I3274, ISBN depends on year), and the European Design and Test Conference (TK7888.4.E968, 1994: ISBN 0-8186-5410-4). The IEEE International Workshop on Memory Technology, Design, and Testing (TK7895.M4.I334) is a conference on memory testing. US DoD standard procedure

5012 of Mil-Std-883 sets requirements for simulation algorithms, fault collapsing, undetectable faults, potential detection, and detection strobing (see also *IEEE Design & Test Magazine*, Sept. 1993, pp. 68–79).

The IEEE has published a series of tutorials on test: *VLSI Support Technologies: Computer-Aided Design, Testing, and Packaging,* TK7874.T886, 1982; *VLSI Testing & Validation Techniques,* ISBN 0818606681, TK7874.T8855, 1985; *Test Generation for VLSI Chips,* ISBN 081868786X, TK7874.T8857, 1988.

The **Waveform and Vector Exchange Specification** (WAVES), IEEE Std 1029.1-1991 [IEEE 1029.1-1991], is a standard representation for digital stimulus and response for both design and test and allows digital stimulus and response information to be exchanged between different simulation and test tools. The syntax of WAVES is a subset of VHDL. WAVES was developed by the WAVES Analysis and Standardization Group (WASG). The WASG was jointly sponsored by the Automatic Test Program Generation (ATPG) subcommittee of the Standards Coordination Committee 20 (SCC20) and the Design Automation Standards Subcommittee (DASS) of the Computer Society.

14.13 References

Page numbers in brackets after the reference indicate the location in the chapter body.

Abramovici, M., M. A. Breuer, and A. D. Friedman. 1990. *Digital Systems Testing and Testable Design.* New York: W. H. Freeman, 653 p. ISBN 0-7167-8179-4. TK7874.A23. Introduction to testing and BIST. See also Breuer, M. A., and A. D. Friedman, 1976. *Diagnosis and Reliable Design of Digital Systems.* 2nd ed. Potomac, MD: Computer Science Press, ISBN 0-914894-57-9. TK7868.D5B73. [p. 800]

Agarwal, V. K., and A. S. F. Fung. 1981. "Multiple fault testing of large circuits by single fault test sets." *IEEE Transactions on Computing,* Vol. C-30, no. 11, pp. 855–865. [p. 740]

Bardell, P. H., W. H. McAnney, and J. Savir. 1987. *Built-In Test for VLSI: Pseudorandom Techniques.* New York: Wiley, 354 p. ISBN 0-471-62463-2. TK7874.B374. [p. 800]

Bartlett, K., et al. 1988. "Multilevel logic minimization using implicit don't cares,"*IEEE Transactions on Computer-Aided Design,* Vol. CAD-7, no. 6, pp. 723–740. [p. 799]

Bhattacharya, D., and J. P. Hayes. 1990. *Hierarchical Modeling for VLSI Circuit Testing.* Boston: Kluwer, 159 p. ISBN 079239058X. TK7874.B484. Contains a good description of the D and PODEM algorithms. [p. 800]

Bleeker, H., P. v. d. Eijnden, and F. de Jong. 1993. *Boundary-Scan Test: A Practical Approach.* Boston: Kluwer, 225 p. ISBN 0-7923-9296-5. [p. 714]

Brayton, R. K., G. D. Hachtel, and A. L. Sangiovanni-Vincentelli. 1990. "Multilevel logic synthesis." *Proceedings of the IEEE,* Vol. 78, no. 2, pp. 264–300. [p. 799]

Butler, K. M., and M. R. Mercer. 1992. *Assessing Fault Model and Test Quality.* Norwell, MA: Kluwer, 125 p. ISBN 0-7923-9222-1. TK7874.B85. Introductory level discussion of test terminology, fault models and their limitations. Research-level discussion of the use of BDDs, ATPG, and controllability/observability. [p. 761]

Chandra, S., et al. 1993. "CrossCheck: an innovative testability solution."*IEEE Design & Test of Computers,* Vol. 10, no. 2, pp. 56–68. Describes a gate-array test architecture used by Sony, for example. [p. 800]

Chakradhar, S. T., V. D. Agrawal, and M. L. Bushnell. 1991. *Neural Models and Algorithms for Digital Testing.* Boston: Kluwer, 184 p. ISBN 0792391659. TK7868.L6.C44. [p. 800]

Cheng, K.-T., and V. D. Agrawal. 1989. *Unified Methods for VLSI Simulation and Test Generation.* Norwell, MA: Kluwer, 148 p. ISBN 0-7923-9025-3. TK7874.C525. 377 references. The first three chapters give a good introduction to fault simulation and test vector generation. [p. 800]

Eichelberger, E. B., E. Lindblom, J. A. Waicukauski, and T. W. Williams. 1991. *Structured Logic Testing.* Englewood Cliffs, NJ: Prentice-Hall, 183 p. ISBN 0-13-8536805. TK7868.L6S78. Includes material printed in 19 articles by the authors from 1987 to 1989. [p. 800]

Feugate Jr., R. J., and S. M. McIntyre. 1988. *Introduction to VLSI Testing.* Englewood Cliffs, NJ: Prentice-Hall, 226 p. ISBN 0134988663. TK7874 .F48. Chapters on: Automated Testing Overview; IC Fabrication and Device Specifications; Testing Integrated Circuits: Parametric Tests; Functional Tests; Example of a Functional Test Program; Characterization testing; Developing Test Patterns; Special Testing Problems: Memories; Special Testing Problems: Microcontrollers; Design for Testability; LSTL Language Summary; Example of a Production Test program; The D-Algorithm. [p. 800]

Fujiwara, H., and T. Shimono. 1983. "On the acceleration of test generation algorithms." *IEEE Transactions on Computers,* Vol. C-32, no. 12, pp. 1137–1144. Describes the FAN ATPG algorithm. [p. 761]

Fritzemeier, R. R., H. T. Nagle, and C. F. Hawkins. 1989. "Fundamentals of testability—a tutorial." *IEEE Transactions on Industrial Electronics,* Vol. 36, no. 2, pp. 117–128. 54 refs. A review of testing, failure mechanisms, fault models, fault simulation, testability analysis, and test-generation methods for CMOS VLSI circuits. [p. 800]

Ghosh, A., S. Devadas, and A. R. Newton. 1992. *Sequential Logic Testing and Verification.* Norwell, MA: Kluwer, 214 p. ISBN 0-7923-91888. TK7868.L6G47. Describes test generation algorithms for state machines at a level intended for CAD researchers. [p. 800]

Goel, P. 1981. "An implicit enumeration algorithm to generate tests for combinational logic circuits." *IEEE Transactions on Computers,* Vol. C-30, no. 3, pp. 215–222. [p. 759]

Goldstein, L. H. 1979. "Controllability/observability analysis of digital circuits." *IEEE Transactions on Circuits and Systems,* Vol. CAS-26, no. 9, pp. 685–693. Describes SCOAP measures. [p. 761]

Golomb, S. W., et al. 1982. *Shift Register Sequences.* 2nd ed. Laguna Hills, CA: Aegean Park Press, 247 p. ISBN 0-89412-048-4. QA267.5.S4 G6. See also: Golomb, S. W., *Shift Register Sequences* (with portions co-authored by L. R. Welch, R. M. Goldstein and A. W. Hales). San Francisco: Holden-Day (1967), 224 p. QA267.5.S4 G6. The second edition has a long bibliography. [p. 771]

Gulati, R. K., and C. F. Hawkins. (Ed.). 1993. *IDDQ Testing of VLSI Circuits.* Boston: Kluwer, 120 p. ISBN 0792393155. TK7874.I3223. [p. 743]

Hughes, J. L. A., and E. J. McCluskey. 1986. "Multiple stuck-at fault coverage of single stuck-at fault test sets." In *Proceedings of the IEEE International Test Conference,* pp. 368–374. [p. 740]

IEEE 1029.1. 1991. IEEE Standard for Waveform and Vector Exchange (WAVES) (ANSI). 96 p. IEEE reference numbers: [1-55937-195-1] [SH15032-NYF]. [p. 801]

IEEE 1149.1b. 1994. IEEE Std 1149.1-1990 Access Port and Boundary-Scan Architecture. 176 p. The first part of this updated standard includes supplement 1149.1a-1993. IEEE reference numbers: [1-55937-350-4] [SH16626-NYK] The second part of this standard is includes 1149.1b-1994 Supplement to IEEE Std 1149.1-1990, IEEE Standard Test Access Port and Boundary-Scan Architecture (ANSI) (available separately). 80 p. IEEE reference numbers: [1-55937-497-7] [SH94256-NYK]. [p. 714, p. 716, p. 718, p. 718, p. 735, p. 735]

Jha, N. K., and S. Kundu. 1990. *Testing and Reliable Design of CMOS Circuits*. Boston: Kluwer, 231 p. ISBN 0792390563. TK7871.99.M44.J49. [p. 800]

Lavagno, L., and A. Sangiovanni-Vincentelli. 1993. *Algorithms for Synthesis and Testing of Asynchronous Circuits*. Boston: Kluwer, 339 p. ISBN 0792393643. TK7888.4.L38. [p. 800]

Lee, M. T.-C. 1997. *High-Level Test Synthesis of Digital VLSI Circuits*. Boston: Artech House, ISBN 0890069077. TK7874.75.L44. [p. 800]

Lombardi, F., and M. Sami (Ed.). 1987. *Testing and Diagnosis of VLSI and ULSI*. Norwell, MA: Kluwer, 533 p. ISBN 90-247-3794-X. TK7874.N345. A series of 20 research-level papers presented at a NATO advanced Study Institute. Contents: Trends in Design for Testability; Statistical Testing; Fault Models; Fault Detection and Design for Testability of CMOS Logic Circuits; Parallel Computer Systems Testing and Integration; Analog Fault Diagnosis; Spectral Techniques for Digital Testing; Logic Verification, Testing and Their Relationships to Logic Synthesis; Proving the Next Stage from Simulation; Petri Nets and Their Relation to Design Validation and Testing; Functional Test of ASICs and Boards; Fault Simulation Techniques — Theory and Practical Examples; Threshold-Value Simulation and Test Generation; Behavioral Testing of Programmable Systems; Testing of Processing Arrays; Old and New Approaches for the Repair of Redundant Memories; Reconfiguration of Orthogonal Arrays by Front Deletion; Device Testing and SEM Testing Tools; Advances in Electron Beam Testing. [p. 800]

Maunder, C. M., and R. E. Tulloss (Ed.). 1990. *The Test Access Port and Boundary-Scan Architecture*. Washington, DC: IEEE Computer Society Press. ISBN 0-8186-9070-4. TK867.T39. [p. 714]

Needham, W. M. 1991. *Designer's Guide to Testable ASIC Devices*. New York: Van Nostrand Reinhold, 284 p. ISBN 0-442-00221-1. TK7874.N385. Practical review of wafer and package testing. Includes summary of features and test file formats used by logic testers. [p. 800]

Parker, K. P. 1992. *The Boundary-Scan Handbook*. Norwell, MA: Kluwer, 262 p. ISBN 0-7923-9270-1. TK7868.P7 P3. Describes BSDL. [p. 714]

Rajsuman, R. 1994. *Iddq Testing for CMOS VLSI*. Boston: Artech House, 193 p. ISBN 0-89006-726-0. TK7871.99.M44R35. [p. 743]

Rao, G. K. 1993. *Multilevel Interconnect Technology*. New York: McGraw-Hill. ISBN 0-07-051224-8. Covers the design of a multilevel interconnect process, and manufacturing and reliability issues. [p. 736]

Roth, J. P. 1966. "Diagnosis of automata failures: A calculus and a method." *IBM Journal of Research and Development*, Vol. 10, no. 4, pp. 278–291. Describes the D-calculus and the D-algorithm. [p. 755]

Russell, G., and I. L. Sayers. 1989. *Advanced Simulation and Test Methodologies for VLSI Design*. London: Van Nostrand Reinhold (International), 378 p. ISBN 0-7476-0001-5. TK7874.R89. Good explanations with a simple example of the D-algorithm. [p. 800]

Sabnis, A. G. (Ed.). 1990. *VLSI Reliability*. San Diego: Academic Press. ISBN 0-12-234122-8. Covers ESD, electromigration, packaging issues, quality assurance, failure analysis, radiation damage. [p. 736]

Scheiber, S. F. 1995. *Building a Successful Board-Test Strategy*. Boston: Butterworth–Heineman, 286 p. ISBN 0-7506-9432-7. TK7868.P7S33. Practical description from a management point of view of board-level testing. [p. 714]

Schulz, M. H., E. Trischler, and T. M. Sarfert. 1988. "SOCRATES: a highly efficient automatic test pattern generation system." *IEEE Transactions on Computer-Aided Design*, Vol. 7, no. 1, pp. 126–137. [p. 761]

Turino, J. 1990. *Design to Test—A Definitive Guide for Electronic Design, Manufacture and Service*. 2nd ed. New York: Van Nostrand Reinhold, 368 p. ISBN 0-442-00170-3. TK7874.T83. A small encyclopedia of testing. Includes a general introduction to testability, and guidelines for: system-level, analog, and general circuit testing; board-level guidelines, boundary scan, built-in test, testability buses, mechanical issues, surface-mount technology, test software, documentation, implementation, ad-hoc test techniques and strategies, testability checklists, and a testability rating system. [p. 800]

Tsui, F. F. 1987. *LSI/VLSI Testability Design*. New York: McGraw-Hill, 700 p. ISBN 0-07-065341-0. TK7874.T78. Extensive review of scan-test techniques. Approximately 100-page bibliography of papers published on test from 1962–1986. [p. 800]

Williams, T. W. (Ed.). 1986. *VLSI Testing*. Amsterdam: Elsevier Science, 275 p. ISBN 0-444-87895-5 (part of set 0-444-87890-4). TK7874.V5666. Seven papers on fault modeling, test generation, and fault simulation, testable PLA designs, design for testability, memory testing, semiconductor test equipment, and board level test equipment. [p. 800]

Yarmolik, V. N. 1990. *Fault Diagnosis of Digital Circuits*. New York: Wiley. Translated from Russian text. Covers D-algorithm, LSSD, random and pseudorandom testing and analysis, and signature analysis. [p. 800]

Yarmolik, V. N., and I. V. Kachan. 1993. *Self-Testing VLSI Design*. New York: Elsevier, 345 p. ISBN 0-444-89640-6. TK7874.I16. Extensive reference on pseudorandom testing techniques. Includes description of pseudorandom sequence generators and polynomials. [p. 800]

Zobrist, G.W. (Ed.). 1993. *VLSI Fault Modeling and Testing Techniques*. Norwood, NJ: Ablex, 199 p. ISBN 0-89391-781-8. TK7874.V5625. Includes six research-level papers on physical fault modeling, testing of CMOS open faults, testing bridging faults, BIST for PLAs, design for testability, and synthesis methods for testable circuits. [p. 800]

ASIC CONSTRUCTION

A town planner works out the number, types, and sizes of buildings in a development project. An architect designs each building, including the arrangement of the rooms in each building. Then a builder carries out the construction according to the architect's drawings. Electrical wiring is one of the last steps in the construction of each building. The physical design of ASICs is normally divided into *system partitioning, floorplanning, placement,* and *routing.* A microelectronic system is the town and the ASICs are the buildings. System partitioning corresponds to town planning, ASIC floorplanning is the architect's job, placement is done by the builder, and the routing is done by the electrician. We shall design most, but not all, ASICs using these design steps.

15.1 Physical Design

Figure 15.1 shows part of the design flow, the physical design steps, for an ASIC (omitting simulation, test, and other logical design steps that have already been covered). Some of the steps in Figure 15.1 might be performed in a different order from that shown. For example, we might, depending on the size of the system, perform system partitioning before we do any design entry or synthesis. There may be some iteration between the different steps too.

FIGURE 15.1   Part of an ASIC design flow showing the system partitioning, floorplanning, placement, and routing steps. These steps may be performed in a slightly different order, iterated or omitted depending on the type and size of the system and its ASICs. As the focus shifts from logic to interconnect, floorplanning assumes an increasingly important role. Each of the steps shown in the figure must be performed and each depends on the previous step. However, the trend is toward completing these steps in a parallel fashion and iterating, rather than in a sequential manner.

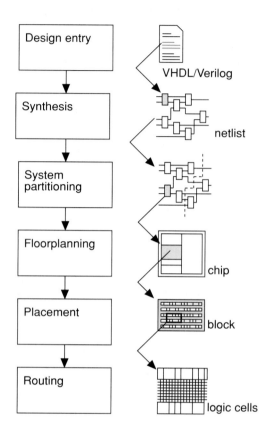

We must first apply **system partitioning** to divide a microelectronics system into separate ASICs. In **floorplanning** we estimate sizes and set the initial relative locations of the various blocks in our ASIC (sometimes we also call this **chip planning**). At the same time we allocate space for clock and power wiring and decide on the location of the I/O and power pads. **Placement** defines the location of the logic cells within the flexible blocks and sets aside space for the interconnect to each logic cell. Placement for a gate-array or standard-cell design assigns each logic cell to a position in a row. For an FPGA, placement chooses which of the fixed logic resources on the chip are used for which logic cells. Floorplanning and placement are closely related and are sometimes combined in a single CAD tool. **Routing** makes the connections between logic cells. Routing is a hard problem by itself and is normally split into two distinct steps, called global and local routing. **Global routing** determines where the interconnections between the placed logic cells and blocks will be situated. Only the routes to be used by the interconnections are decided in this step, not the actual locations of the interconnections within the wiring areas. Global routing is sometimes called **loose routing** for this reason. **Local routing** joins the logic cells with interconnections. Information on which interconnection areas to use comes from the global router. Only at this stage of layout do we finally decide on the width, mask layer, and exact location of the interconnections. Local routing is also known as **detailed routing**.

15.2   CAD Tools

In order to develop a CAD tool it is necessary to convert each of the physical design steps to a problem with well-defined goals and objectives. The **goals** for each physical design step are the things we must achieve. The **objectives** for each step are things we would like to meet on the way to achieving the goals. Some examples of goals and objectives for each of the ASIC physical design steps are as follows:

System partitioning:

- Goal. Partition a system into a number of ASICs.
- Objective. Minimize the number of external connections between the ASICs. Keep each ASIC smaller than a maximum size.

Floorplanning:

- Goal. Calculate the sizes of all the blocks and assign them locations.
- Objective. Keep the highly connected blocks physically close to each other.

Placement:

- Goal. Assign the interconnect areas and the location of all the logic cells within the flexible blocks.
- Objectives. Minimize the ASIC area and the interconnect density.

Global routing:

- Goal. Determine the location of all the interconnect.
- Objective. Minimize the total interconnect area used.

Detailed routing:

- Goal. Completely route all the interconnect on the chip.
- Objective. Minimize the total interconnect length used.

There is no magic recipe involved in the choice of the ASIC physical design steps. These steps have been chosen simply because, as tools and techniques have developed historically, these steps proved to be the easiest way to split up the larger problem of ASIC physical design. The boundaries between the steps are not cast in stone. For example, floorplanning and placement are often thought of as one step and in some tools placement and routing are performed together.

15.2.1   Methods and Algorithms

A CAD tool needs **methods** or **algorithms** to generate a solution to each problem using a reasonable amount of computer time. Often there is no best solution possible to a particular problem, and the tools must use **heuristic algorithms**, or rules of thumb, to try and find a good solution. The term *algorithm* is usually reserved for a method that always gives a solution.

We need to know how practical any algorithm is. We say the **complexity** of an algorithm is $O(f(n))$ (read as **order $f(n)$**) if there are constants k and n_0 so that the running time of the algorithm $T(n)$ is less than $kf(n)$ for all $n > n_0$ [Sedgewick, 1988]. Here n is a measure of the size of the problem (number of transistors, number of wires, and so on). In ASIC design n is usually very large. We have to be careful, though. The notation does not specify the units of time. An algorithm that is $O(n^2)$ nanoseconds might be better than an algorithm that is $O(n)$ seconds, for quite large values of n. The notation $O(n)$ refers to an upper limit on the running time of the algorithm. A practical example may take less running time—it is just that we cannot prove it. We also have to be careful of the constants k and n_0. They can hide overhead present in the implementation and may be large enough to mask the dependence on n, up to large values of n. The function $f(n)$ is usually one of the following kinds:

- $f(n)$ = constant. The algorithm is **constant in time**. In this case, steps of the algorithm are repeated once or just a few times. It would be nice if our algorithms had this property, but it does not usually happen in ASIC design.

- $f(n)$ = log n. The algorithm is **logarithmic in time**. This usually happens when a big problem is (possibly recursively) transformed into a smaller one.

- $f(n)$ = n. The algorithm is **linear in time**. This is a good situation for an ASIC algorithm that works with n objects.

- $f(n)$ = n log n. This type of algorithm arises when a large problem is split into a number of smaller problems, each solved independently.

- $f(n)$ = n^2. The algorithm is **quadratic in time** and usually only practical for small ASIC problems.

If the time it takes to solve a problem increases with the size of the problem at a rate that is polynomial but faster than quadratic (or worse in an exponential fashion), it is usually not appropriate for ASIC design. Even after subdividing the ASIC physical design problem into smaller steps, each of the steps still results in problems that are hard to solve automatically. In fact, each of the ASIC physical design steps, in general, belongs to a class of mathematical problems known as **NP-complete** problems. This means that it is unlikely we can find an algorithm to solve the problem exactly in polynomial time.

Suppose we find a practical method to solve our problem, even if we can find a solution we now have a dilemma. How shall we know if we have a good solution if, because the problem is NP-complete, we cannot find the optimum or best solution to which to compare it? We need to know how close we are to the optimum solution to a problem, even if that optimum solution cannot be found exactly. We need to make a quantitative **measurement** of the quality of the solution that we are able to find. Often we combine several parameters or **metrics** that measure our goals and objectives into a **measurement function** or **objective function**. If we are minimizing the measurement function, it is a **cost function**. If we are maximizing the measurement function, we call the function a **gain function** (sometimes just **gain**).

Now we are ready to solve each of the ASIC physical design steps with the following items in hand: a set of goals and objectives, a way to measure the goals and objectives, and an algorithm or method to find a solution that meets the goals and objectives. As designers attempt to achieve a desired ASIC performance they make a continuous trade-off between speed, area, power, and several other factors. Presently CAD tools are not smart enough to be able to do this alone. In fact, current CAD tools are only capable of finding a solution subject to a few, very simple, objectives.

15.3 System Partitioning

Microelectronic systems typically consist of many functional blocks. If a functional block is too large to fit in one ASIC, we may have to split, or **partition**, the function into pieces using goals and objectives that we need to specify. For example, we might want to minimize the number of pins for each ASIC to minimize package cost. We can use CAD tools to help us with this type of system partitioning.

Figure 15.2 shows the system diagram of the Sun Microsystems SPARCstation 1. The system is partitioned as follows; the numbers refer to the labels in Figure 15.2. (See Section 1.3, "Case Study" for the sources of infomation in this section.)

- Nine custom ASICs (1–9)
- Memory subsystems (SIMMs, single-in-line memory modules): CPU cache (10), RAM (11), memory cache (12, 13)
- Six ASSPs (application-specific standard products) for I/O (14–19)
- An ASSP for time of day (20)
- An EPROM (21)
- Video memory subsystem (22)
- One analog/digital ASSP DAC (digital-to-analog converter) (23)

Table 15.1 shows the details of the nine custom ASICs used in the SPARCstation 1. Some of the partitioning of the system shown in Figure 15.2 is determined by whether to use ASSPs or custom ASICs. Some of these design decisions are based on intangible issues: time to market, previous experience with a technology, the ability to reuse part of a design from a previous product. No CAD tools can help with such decisions. The goals and objectives are too poorly defined and finding a way to measure these factors is very difficult. CAD tools cannot

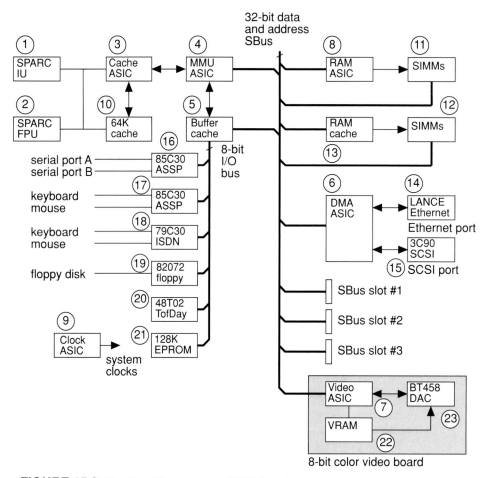

FIGURE 15.2 The Sun Microsystems SPARCstation 1 system block diagram. The acronyms for the various ASICs are listed in Table 15.1.

answer a question such as: "What is the cheapest way to build my system?" but can help the designer answer the question: "How do I split this circuit into pieces that will fit on a chip?" Table 15.2 shows the partitioning of the SPARCstation 10 so you can compare it to the SPARCstation 1. Notice that the gate counts of nearly all of the SPARCstation 10 ASICs have increased by a factor of 10, but the pin counts have increased by a smaller factor.

TABLE 15.1   System partitioning for the Sun Microsystems SPARCstation 1.

	SPARCstation 1 ASIC	Gates /k-gate	Pins	Package	Type
1	SPARC IU (integer unit)	20	179	PGA	CBIC
2	SPARC FPU (floating-point unit)	50	144	PGA	FC
3	Cache controller	9	160	PQFP	GA
4	MMU (memory-management unit)	5	120	PQFP	GA
5	Data buffer	3	120	PQFP	GA
6	DMA (direct memory access) controller	9	120	PQFP	GA
7	Video controller/data buffer	4	120	PQFP	GA
8	RAM controller	1	100	PQFP	GA
9	Clock generator	1	44	PLCC	GA

Abbreviations:

PGA = pin-grid array   CBIC = LSI Logic cell-based ASIC

PQFP = plastic quad flat pack   GA = LSI Logic channelless gate array

PLCC = plastic leaded chip carrier   FC = full custom

15.4   Estimating ASIC Size

Table 15.3 shows some useful numbers for estimating ASIC die size. Suppose we wish to estimate the die size of a 40 k-gate ASIC in a 0.35 μm gate array, three-level metal process with 166 I/O pads. For this ASIC the minimum feature size is 0.35 μm. Thus λ (one-half the minimum feature size) = 0.35 μm/2 = 0.175 μm. Using our data and Table 15.3, we can derive the following information. We know that 0.35 μm standard-cell density is roughly 5×10^{-4} gate/λ^2. From this we can calculate the gate density for a 0.35 μm gate array:

$$\text{gate density} = 0.35 \, \mu\text{m standard-cell density} \times (0.8 \text{ to } 0.9)$$

$$= 4 \times 10^{-4} \text{ to } 4.5 \times 10^{-4} \, \text{gate}/\lambda^2. \qquad (15.1)$$

This gives the core size (logic and routing only) as

$$(4 \times 10^4 \text{ gates/gate density}) \times \text{routing factor} \times (1/\text{gate-array utilization})$$

$$= 4 \times 10^4/(4 \times 10^{-4} \text{ to } 4.5 \times 10^{-4}) \times (1 \text{ to } 2) \times 1/(0.8 \text{ to } 0.9) = 10^8 \text{ to } 2.5 \times 10^8 \, \lambda^2$$

$$= 4840 \text{ to } 11{,}900 \, \text{mil}^2. \qquad (15.2)$$

TABLE 15.2 System partitioning for the Sun Microsystems SPARCstation 10.

	SPARCstation 10 ASIC	Gates	Pins	Package	Type
1	SuperSPARC Superscalar SPARC	3 M-transistors	293	PGA	FC
2	SuperCache cache controller	2 M-transistors	369	PGA	FC
3	EMC memory control	40 k-gate	299	PGA	GA
4	MSI MBus–SBus interface	40 k-gate	223	PGA	GA
5	DMA2 Ethernet, SCSI, parallel port	30 k-gate	160	PQFP	GA
6	SEC SBus to 8-bit bus	20 k-gate	160	PQFP	GA
7	DBRI dual ISDN interface	72 k-gate	132	PQFP	GA
8	MMCodec stereo codec	32 k-gate	44	PLCC	FC

Abbreviations:

PGA = pin-grid array   GA = channelless gate array

PQFP = plastic quad flat pack   FC = full custom

PLCC = plastic leaded chip carrier

We shall need to add $(0.175/0.5) \times 2 \times (15 \text{ to } 20) = 10.5$ to 21 mil (per side) for the pad heights (we included the effects of scaling in this calculation). With a pad pitch of 5 mil and roughly $166/4 = 42$ I/Os per side (not counting any power pads), we need a die at least $5 \times 42 = 210$ mil on a side for the I/Os. Thus the die size must be at least $210 \times 210 = 4.4 \times 10^4 \text{ mil}^2$ to fit 166 I/Os. Of this die area only $1.19 \times 10^4/(4.4 \times 10^4) = 27\%$ (at most) is used by the core logic. This is a severely pad-limited design and we need to rethink the partitioning of this system.

Table 15.4 shows some typical areas for datapath elements. You would use many of these datapath elements in floating-point arithmetic (these elements are large—you should not use floating-point arithmetic unless you have to):

- A leading-one detector with barrel shifter normalizes a mantissa.
- A priority encoder corrects exponents due to mantissa normalization.
- A denormalizing barrel shifter aligns mantissas.
- A normalizing barrel shifter with a leading-one detector normalizes mantissa subtraction.

Most datapath elements have an area per bit that depends on the number of bits in the datapath (the datapath width). Sometimes this dependency is linear (for the multipliers and the barrel shifter, for example); in other elements it depends on the logarithm (to base 2) of the datapath width (the leading one, all ones, and zero detectors, for example). In some elements you might expect there to be a dependency on datapath width, but it is small (the comparators are an example).

TABLE 15.3   Some useful numbers for ASIC estimates, normalized to a 1μm technology unless noted.

Parameter	Typical value	Comment[1]	Scaling
Lambda, λ	0.5 μm = 0.5 (minimum feature size)	In a 1 μm technology, λ ≈ 0.5 μm.	NA
CAD pitch	1 micron = 10^{-6} m = 1 μm = minimum feature size	Not to be confused with minimum CAD grid size (which is usually less than 0.01 μm).	λ
Effective gate length	0.25 to 1.0 μm	Less than drawn gate length, usually by about 10 percent.	λ
I/O-pad width (pitch)	5 to 10 mil = 125 to 250 μm	For a 1 μm technology, 2LM (λ = 0.5 μm). Scales less than linearly with λ.	λ
I/O-pad height	15 to 20 mil = 375 to 500 μm	For a 1 μm technology, 2LM (λ = 0.5 μm). Scales approximately linearly with λ.	λ
Large die	1000 mil/side, 10^6 mil²	Approximately constant	1
Small die	100 mil/side, 10^4 mil²	Approximately constant	1
Standard-cell density	1.5×10^{-3} gate/μm² = 1.0 gate/mil²	For 1μm, 2LM, library = 4×10^{-4} gate/λ² (independent of scaling).	$1/\lambda^2$
Standard-cell density	8×10^{-3} gate/μm² = 5.0 gate/mil²	For 0.5 μm, 3LM, library = 5×10^{-4} gate/λ² (independent of scaling).	$1/\lambda^2$
Gate-array utilization	60 to 80 %	For 2LM, approximately constant	1
	80 to 90 %	For 3LM, approximately constant	1
Gate-array density	(0.8 to 0.9) × standard cell density	For the same process as standard cells	1
Standard-cell routing factor = (cell area + route area)/cell area	1.5 to 2.5 (2LM) 1.0 to 2.0 (3LM)	Approximately constant	1
Package cost	$0.01/pin, "penny per pin"	Varies widely, figure is for low-cost plastic package, approximately constant	1
Wafer cost	$1k to $5k average $2k	Varies widely, figure is for a mature, 2LM CMOS process, approximately constant	1

[1] 2LM = two-level metal; 3LM = three-level metal.

The area estimates given in Table 15.4 can be misleading. The exact size of an adder, for example, depends on the architecture: carry-save, carry-select, carry-lookahead, or ripple-carry (which depends on the speed you require). These area figures also exclude the routing between datapath elements, which is difficult to predict—it will depend on the number and size of the datapath elements, their type, and how much logic is random and how much is datapath.

TABLE 15.4 Area estimates for datapath functions.[1]

Datapath function	Area per bit/λ^2	Area/λ^2 (32-bit)	Area/λ^2 (64-bit)
High-speed comparator (4–32 bit)	24,000	7.7E + 05	1.5E + 06
High-speed comparator (32–128 bit)	28,800	9.2E + 05	1.8E + 06
Leading-one detector (n-bit)	7200 $\log_2 n$	1.2E + 06	2.8E + 06
All-ones detector (n-bit)	6000 + 800 $\log_2 n$	3.2E + 05	6.9E + 05
Priority encoder (n-bit)	19,000 + 1400 $\log_2 (n-2)$	8.4E + 05	1.8E + 06
Zero detector (n-bit)	5500 + 800 $\log_2 n$	3.0E + 05	6.6E + 05
Barrel shifter/rotator (n- by m-bit)	19,000 + 1000n + 1600 m	3.4E + 06	1.2E + 07
Carry-save adder	24,000	7.7E + 05	1.5E + 06
Digital delay line (n delay stages, t output taps)	12,000 + 6000n + 8400 t	1.5E + 07	6.0E + 07
Synchronous FIFO (n-bit)	34,000 + 9600n	1.1E + 07	4.1E + 07
Multiplier-accumulator (n-bit)	190,000 + 18,000n	2.4E + 07	8.5E + 07
Unsigned multiplier (n- by m-bit)	54,000 + 18,000 $(n-2)$	1.9E + 07	7.4E + 07
2:1 MUX	7200	2.3E + 05	4.6E + 05
8:1 MUX	29,000	9.2E + 05	1.8E + 06
Low-speed adder	28,000	8.8E + 05	1.8E + 06
2901 ALU	41,000	1.3E + 06	2.6E + 06
Low-speed adder/subtracter	30,000	9.6E + 05	1.9E + 06
Sync. up–down counter with sync. load and clear	43,000	1.4E + 06	2.8E + 06
Low-speed decrementer	14,000	4.6E + 05	9.2E + 05
Low-speed incrementer	14,000	4.6E + 05	9.2E + 05
Low-speed incrementer/decrementer	20,000	6.5E + 05	1.3E + 06

[1]Area estimates are for a two-level metal (2 LM) process. Areas for a three-level metal (3LM) process are approximately 0.75 to 1.0 times these figures.

Figure 15.3(a) shows the typical size of SRAM constructed on an ASIC. These figures are based on the use of a RAM compiler (as opposed to building memory from flip-flops or latches) using a standard CMOS ASIC process, typically using a six-transistor cell. The actual size of a memory will depend on (1) the required access time, (2) the use of synchronous or asynchronous read or write, (3) the number and type of ports (read–write), (4) the use of special design rules, (5) the number of interconnect layers available, (6) the RAM architecture (number of devices in RAM cell), and (7) the process technology (active pull-up devices or pull-up resistors).

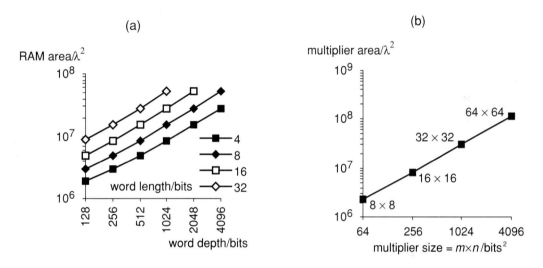

FIGURE 15.3 (a) ASIC memory size. These figures are for static RAM constructed using compilers in a 2LM ASIC process, but with no special memory design rules. The actual area of a RAM will depend on the speed and number of read–write ports. (b) Multiplier size for a 2LM process. The actual area will depend on the multiplier architecture and speed.

The maximum size of SRAM in Figure 15.3(a) is 32 k-bit, which occupies approximately $6.0 \times 10^7 \lambda^2$. In a 0.5 µm process (with $\lambda = 0.25$ µm), the area of a 32 k-bit SRAM is $6.0 \times 10^7 \times 0.25 \times 0.25 = 3.75 \times 10^6$ µm^2 (or about 2 mm on a side—a large piece of silicon). If you need an SRAM that is larger than this, you probably need to consult with your ASIC vendor to determine the best way to implement a large on-chip memory. Figure 15.3(b) shows the typical sizes for multipliers. Again the actual multiplier size will depend on the architecture (Booth encoding, Wallace tree, and so on), the process technology, and design rules. Table 15.5 shows some estimated gate counts for medium-size functions corresponding to some popular ASSP devices.

TABLE 15.5   Gate size estimates for popular ASSP functions.

ASSP device	Function	Gate estimate
8251A	Universal synchronous/asynchronous receiver/transmitter (USART)	2900
8253	Programmable interval timer	5680
8255A	Programmable peripheral interface	784–1403
8259	Programmable interrupt controller	2205
8237	Programmable DMA controller	5100
8284	Clock generator/driver	99
8288	Bus controller	250
8254	Programmable interval timer	3500
6845	CRT controller	2843
87030	SCSI controller	3600
87012	Ethernet controller	3900
2901	4 bit ALU	917
2902	Carry-lookahead ALU	33
2904	Status and shift control	500
2910	12-bit microprogram controller	1100

Source: Fujitsu channelless gate-array data book, AU and CG21 series.

15.5   Power Dissipation

Power dissipation in CMOS logic arises from the following sources:

- Dynamic power dissipation due to **switching current** from charging and discharging parasitic capacitance.
- Dynamic power dissipation due to **short-circuit current** when both n-channel and p-channel transistors are momentarily on at the same time.
- Static power dissipation due to **leakage current** and **subthreshold current**.

15.5.1   Switching Current

When the p-channel transistor in an inverter is charging a capacitance, C, at a frequency, f, the current through the transistor is $C(dV/dt)$. The power dissipation is thus $CV(dV/dt)$ for one-half the period of the input, $t = 1/(2f)$. The power dissipated in the p-channel transistor is thus

$$\int_{0}^{1/(2f)} CV \left(\frac{dV}{dt} \right) dt = \int_{0}^{V_{DD}} CV \, dV = \frac{1}{2} CV_{DD}^2 . \tag{15.3}$$

When the *n*-channel transistor discharges the capacitor, the power dissipation is equal, making the total power dissipation

$$P_1 = fCV_{DD}^2 . \tag{15.4}$$

Most of the power dissipation in a CMOS ASIC arises from this source—the switching current. The best way to reduce power is to reduce V_{DD} (because it appears as a squared term in Eq. 15.4), and to reduce C, the amount of capacitance we have to switch. A rough estimate is that 20 percent of the nodes switch (or **toggle**) in a circuit per clock cycle. To determine more accurately the power dissipation due to switching, we need to find out how many nodes toggle during typical circuit operation using a dynamic logic simulator. This requires input vectors that correspond to typical operation, which can be difficult to produce. Using a digital simulator also will not take into account the effect of glitches, which can be significant. Power simulators are usually a hybrid between SPICE transistor-level simulators and digital event-driven simulators [Najm, 1994].

15.5.2 Short-Circuit Current

The short-circuit current or **crowbar current** can be particularly important for output drivers and large clock buffers. For a CMOS inverter (see Problem 15.17) the power dissipation due to the crowbar current is

$$P_2 = \frac{\beta f t_{rf}}{12} (V_{DD} - 2V_{tn})^3 , \tag{15.5}$$

where we assume the following: We ratio the *p*-channel and *n*-channel transistor sizes so that $\beta = (W/L)\mu C_{ox}$ is the same for both *p*- and *n*-channel transistors, the magnitude of the threshold voltages $|V_{tn}|$ are assumed equal for both transistor types, and t_{rf} is the rise and fall time (assumed equal) of the input signal [Veendrick, 1984]. For example, consider an output buffer that is capable of sinking 12 mA at an output voltage of 0.5 V. From Eq. 2.9 we can derive the transistor gain factor that we need as follows:

$$\beta = \frac{I_{DS}}{\left[(V_{GS} - V_{tn}) - \frac{1}{2}V_{DS} \right] V_{DS}} = \frac{12 \times 10^{-3}}{[(3.3 - 0.65) - (0.5)(0.5)](0.5)}$$

$$= \frac{12 \times 10^{-3}}{[(3.3 - 0.65) - (0.5)(0.5)](0.5)} \tag{15.6}$$

$$= 0.01 \, \text{AV}^{-1} .$$

If the output buffer is switching at 100 MHz and the input rise time to the buffer is 2 ns, we can calculate the power dissipation due to short-circuit current as

$$
\begin{aligned}
P_2 &= \frac{\beta f t_{rf}}{12} (V_{DD} - 2V_{tn})^3 \\
&= \frac{(0.01)\,(100 \times 10^6)\,(2 \times 10^{-9})}{12} (3.3 - (2)\,(0.65))^3 \\
&= 0.00133333\,\text{W} \quad \text{or about 1 mW.}
\end{aligned}
\tag{15.7}
$$

If the output load is 10 pF, the dissipation due to switching current is

$$
P_1 = f C V_{DD}^2 = (100 \times 10^6)\,(10 \times 10^{-12})\,(3.3)^2 = 0.01089\ \text{W} \quad \text{or about 10 mW.}
$$

As a general rule, if we adjust the transistor sizes so that the rise times and fall times through a chain of logic are approximately equal (as they should be), the short-circuit current is typically less than 20 percent of the switching current.

For the example output buffer, we can make a rough estimate of the output-node switching time by assuming the buffer output drive current is constant at 12 mA. This current will cause the voltage on the output load capacitance to change between 3.3 V and 0 V at a constant slew rate dV/dt for a time

$$
\Delta t = \frac{C \Delta V}{I} = \frac{(10 \times 10^{-12})\,(3.3)}{(12 \times 10^{-3})} = 2.75\ \text{ns.}
\tag{15.8}
$$

This is close to the input rise time of 2 ns. So our estimate of the short-circuit current being less than 20 percent of the switching current assuming equal input rise time and output rise time is valid in this case.

15.5.3   Subthreshold and Leakage Current

Despite the claim made in Section 2.1, a CMOS transistor is never completely *off*. For example, a typical specification for a 0.5 μm process for the **subthreshold current** (per micron of gate width for $V_{GS} = 0\,\text{V}$) is less than 5 pAμm^{-1}, but not zero. With 10 million transistors on a large chip and with each transistor 10 μm wide, we will have a total subthreshold current of 0.1 mA; high, but reasonable. The problem is that the subthreshold current does not scale with process technology.

When the gate-to-source voltage, V_{GS}, of an MOS transistor is less than the threshold voltage, V_t, the transistor conducts a very small subthreshold current in the **subthreshold region**

$$
I_{DS} = I_0 \exp\!\left(\frac{q V_{GS}}{nkT} - 1\right),
\tag{15.9}
$$

where I_0 is a constant, and the constant, n, is normally between 1 and 2.

The slope, S, of the transistor current in the subthreshold region is

$$S = \frac{-nkT}{q}\log_{10}e = 2.3\frac{nkT}{q} \text{ V/decade.} \tag{15.10}$$

For example, at a junction temperature, $T = 125\,°C$ ($\approx 400\,K$) and assuming $n \approx 1.5$, $S = 120\,mV/decade$ ($q = 1.6 \times 10^{-19}\,Fm^{-1}$, $k = 1.38 \times 10^{-23}\,JK^{-1}$), which does not scale. The constant value of $S = 120\,mV/decade$ means it takes 120 mV to reduce the subthreshold current by a factor of 10 in any process. If we reduce the threshold voltages to 0.36 V in a deep-submicron process, for example, this means at $V_{GS} = 0$ V we can only reduce I_{DS} to 0.001 times its value at $V_{GS} = V_t$. This problem can lead to large static currents.

Transistor leakage is caused by the fact that a reverse-biased diode conducts a very small **leakage current**. The sources and drains of every transistor, as well as the junctions between the wells and substrate, form parasitic diodes. The parasitic-diode leakage currents are strongly dependent on the type and quality of the process as well as temperature. The parasitic diodes have two components in parallel: an area diode and a perimeter diode. The ideal parasitic diode currents are given by the following equation:

$$I = I_s \exp\left(\frac{qV_D}{nkT} - 1\right). \tag{15.11}$$

Table 15.6 shows specified maximum leakage currents of junction parasitic diodes as well as the leakage currents of the **field transistors** (the parasitic MOS transistors formed when poly crosses over the thick oxide, or field oxide) in a typical $0.5\,\mu m$ process.

TABLE 15.6   Diffusion leakage currents (at 25 °C) for a typical 0.5 μm ($\lambda = 0.25\,\mu m$) CMOS process.

Junction	Diode type	Leakage (max.)	Unit
n-diffusion/*p*-substrate	area	0.6	$fA\mu m^{-2}V^{-1}$
n-diffusion/*p*-substrate	perimeter	2.0	$fA\mu m^{-1}V^{-1}$
p-diffusion/*n*-well	area	0.6	$fA\mu m^{-2}V^{-1}$
p-diff/*n*-well	perimeter	3.0	$fA\mu m^{-1}V^{-1}$
n-well/*p*-substrate	area	1.0	$fA\mu m^{-2}V^{-1}$
Field NMOS transistor		100	$fA\mu m^{-1}$
Field PMOS transistor		30	$fA\mu m^{-1}$

For example, if we have an n-diffusion region at a potential of 3.3 V that is 10 µm by 4 µm in size, the parasitic leakage current due to the area diode would be

$$40 \; \mu m^2 \times 3.3 V \times 0.6 fA \; \mu m^{-2} V^{-1} \; = \; (40) \; (3.3) \; (0.6 \times 10^{-15}) \; = \; 7.92 \times 10^{-14} A,$$

or approximately 80 fA.

The perimeter of this drain region is 28 µm, so that the leakage current due to the perimeter diode is

$$28 \; \mu m \times 3.3 V \times 2.0 \; fA \; \mu m^{-1} V^{-1} \; = \; (28) \; (3.3) \; (2.0 \times 10^{-15}) \; = \; 1.848 \times 10^{-13} A,$$

or approximately 0.2 pA, over twice as large as the area diode leakage current.

As a very rough estimate, if we have 100,000 transistors each with a source and a drain 10 µm by 4 µm, and half of them are biased at 3.3 V, then the total leakage current would be

$$(100 \times 10^5) \; (2) \; (0.5) \; (280 \times 10^{-15}) \; = \; 2.8 \times 10^{-6} A, \tag{15.12}$$

or approximately 3 µA. This is the same order of magnitude (a few microamperes) as the **quiescent leakage current**, I_{DDQ}, that we expect to measure when we test an ASIC with power applied, but with no signal activity. A measurement of more current than this in a nonactive CMOS ASIC indicates a problem with the chip manufacture or the design. We use this measurement to test an ASIC using an **IDDQ test**.

15.6   FPGA Partitioning

In Section 15.3 we saw how many different issues have to be considered when partitioning a complex system into custom ASICs. There are no commercial tools that can help us with all of these issues—a spreadsheet is the best tool in this case. Things are a little easier if we limit ourselves to partitioning a group of logic cells into FPGAs—and restrict the FPGAs to be all of the same type.

15.6.1   ATM Simulator

In this section we shall examine a hardware simulator for **Asynchronous Transfer Mode** (**ATM**). ATM is a signaling protocol for many different types of traffic including constant bit rates (voice signals) as well as variable bit rates (compressed video). The ATM Connection Simulator is a card that is connected to a computer. Under computer control the card monitors and corrupts the ATM signals to simulate the effects of real networks. An example would be to test different video compression algorithms. Compressed video is very bursty (brief periods of very high activity), has very strict delay constraints, and is susceptible to errors. ATM is based on ATM cells (packets). Each ATM cell has 53 bytes: a 5-byte header and a 48-byte payload; Figure 15.4 shows the format of the ATM packet. The ATM Connection Simulator looks at the entire header as an address.

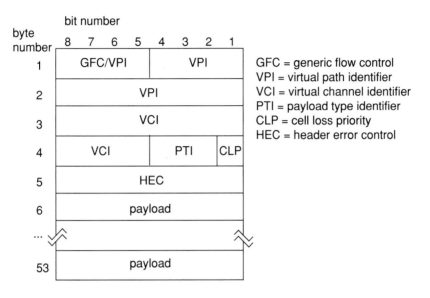

FIGURE 15.4 The asynchronous transfer mode (ATM) cell format. The ATM protocol uses 53-byte cells or packets of information with a data payload and header information for routing and error control.

Figure 15.5 shows the system block diagram of the ATM simulator designed by Craig Fujikami at the University of Hawaii. Now produced by AdTech, the simulator emulates the characteristics of a single connection in an ATM network and models ATM traffic policing, ATM cell delays, and ATM cell errors. The simulator is partitioned into the three major blocks, shown in Figure 15.5, and connected to an IBM-compatible PC through an Intel 80186 controller board together with an interface board. These three blocks are

- The traffic policer, which regulates the input to the simulator.
- The delay generator, which delays ATM cells, reorders ATM cells, and inserts ATM cells with valid ATM cell headers.
- The error generator, which produces bit errors and four random variables that are needed by the other two blocks.

The error generator performs the following operations on ATM cells:

1. Payload bit error ratio generation. The user specifies the Bernoulli probability, p_{BER}, of the payload bit error ratio.

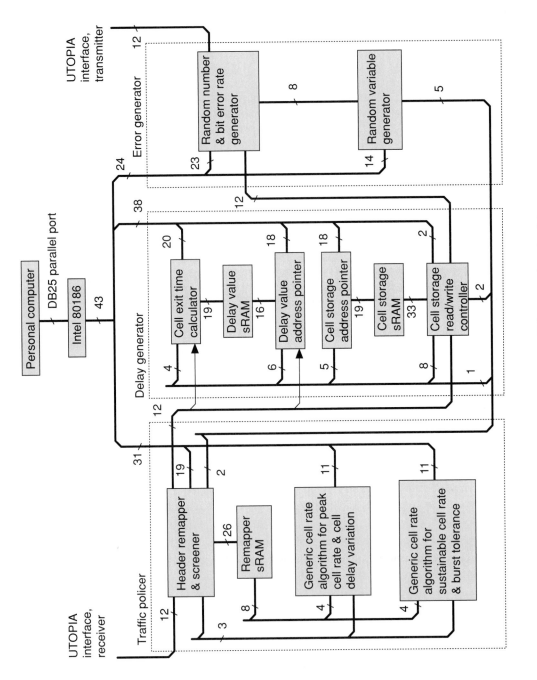

FIGURE 15.5 An asynchronous transfer mode (ATM) connection simulator.

2. Random-variable generation for ATM cell loss, misinsertion, reordering, and deletion.

The delay generator delays, misinserts, and reorders the target ATM cells. Finally, the traffic policer performs the following operations:

3. Performs header screening and remapping.

4. Checks ATM cell conformance.

5. Deletes selected ATM cells.

Table 15.7 shows the partitioning of the ATM board into 12 Lattice Logic FPGAs (ispLSI 1048) corresponding to the 12 blocks shown in Figure 15.5. The Lattice Logic ispLSI 1048 has 48 GLBs (generic logic blocks) on each chip. This system was partitioned by hand—with difficulty. Tools for automatic partitioning of systems like this will become increasingly important. In Section 15.6.2 we shall briefly look at some examples of such tools, before examining the partitioning methods that are used in Section 15.7.

TABLE 15.7 Partitioning of the ATM board using Lattice Logic ispLSI 1048 FPGAs. Each FPGA contains 48 generic logic blocks (GLBs).

Chip #	Size	Chip #	Size
1	42 GLBs	7	36 GLBs
2	64k-bit × 8 SRAM	8	22 GLBs
3	38 GLBs	9	256k-bit × 16 SRAM
4	38 GLBs	10	43 GLBs
5	42 GLBs	11	40 GLBs
6	64k-bit × 16 SRAM	12	30 GLBs

15.6.2 Automatic Partitioning with FPGAs

Some vendors of programmable ASICs provide partitioning software. For example, Altera uses its own software system for design. You can perform design entry using an HDL, schematic entry, or using the Altera hardware design language (AHDL)—similar to PALASM or ABEL. In AHDL you can direct the partitioner to automatically partition logic into chips within the same family, using the AUTO keyword:

```
DEVICE top_level IS AUTO; % the partitioner assign logic
```

You can use the CLIQUE keyword to keep logic together (this is not quite the same as a clique in a graph—more on this in Section 15.7.3):

```
CLIQUE fast_logic
BEGIN
```

```
|shift_register: MACRO; % keep this in one device
END;
```

An additional option, to reserve space on a device, is very useful for making last minute additions or changes.

15.7 Partitioning Methods

System partitioning requires goals and objectives, methods and algorithms to find solutions, and ways to evaluate these solutions. We start with measuring connectivity, proceed to an example that illustrates the concepts of system partitioning and then to the algorithms for partitioning.

Assume that we have decided which parts of the system will use ASICs. The goal of partitioning is to divide this part of the system so that each partition is a single ASIC. To do this we may need to take into account any or all of the following objectives:

- A maximum size for each ASIC
- A maximum number of ASICs
- A maximum number of connections for each ASIC
- A maximum number of total connections between all ASICs

We know how to measure the first two objectives. Next we shall explain ways to measure the last two.

15.7.1 Measuring Connectivity

To measure connectivity we need some help from the mathematics of graph theory. It turns out that the terms, definitions, and ideas of graph theory are central to ASIC construction, and they are often used in manuals and books that describe the knobs and dials of ASIC design tools.

Figure 15.6(a) shows a circuit schematic, netlist, or **network**. The network consists of **circuit modules** A–F. Equivalent terms for a circuit module are a cell, logic cell, macro, or a block. A cell or logic cell usually refers to a small logic gate (NAND etc.), but can also be a collection of other cells; macro refers to gate-array cells; a block is usually a collection of gates or cells. We shall use the term *logic cell* in this chapter to cover all of these.

Each logic cell has electrical connections between the **terminals** (**connectors** or **pins**). The network can be represented as the mathematical **graph** shown in Figure 15.6(b). A graph is like a spider's web: it contains **vertexes** (or **vertices**) A–F (also known as graph **nodes** or **points**) that are connected by **edges**. A graph **vertex** corresponds to a logic cell. An electrical **connection** (a **net** or a **signal**) between two logic cells corresponds to a graph **edge**.

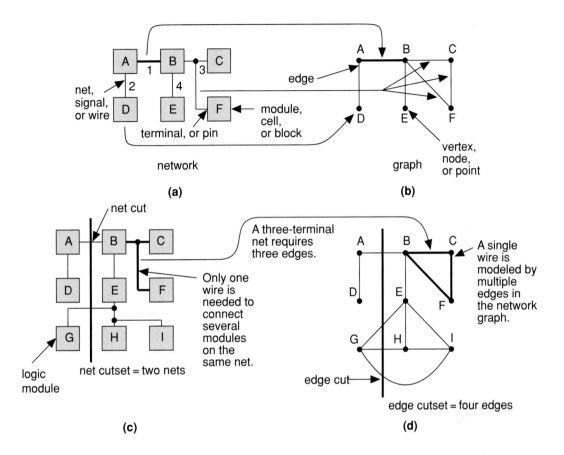

FIGURE 15.6 Networks, graphs, and partitioning. (a) A network containing circuit logic cells and nets. (b) The equivalent graph with vertexes and edges. For example: logic cell D maps to node D in the graph; net 1 maps to the edge (A, B) in the graph. Net 3 (with three connections) maps to three edges in the graph: (B, C), (B, F), and (C, F). (c) Partitioning a network and its graph. A network with a net cut that cuts two nets. (d) The network graph showing the corresponding edge cut. The net cutset in c contains two nets, but the corresponding edge cutset in d contains four edges. This means a graph is not an exact model of a network for partitioning purposes.

Figure 15.6(c) shows a network with nine logic cells A–I. A connection, for example between logic cells A and B in Figure 15.6(c), is written as net (A, B). Net (A, B) is represented by the single edge (A, B) in the network graph, shown in Figure 15.6(d). A net with three terminals, for example net (B, C, F), must be modeled with three edges in the network graph: edges (B, C), (B, F), and (C, F). A net with four terminals requires six edges and so on. Figure 15.6 illustrates the differences between the nets of a network and the edges in the network graphs. Notice that a net can have more than two terminals, but a terminal has only one net.

If we divide, or partition, the network shown in Figure 15.6(c) into two parts, corresponding to creating two ASICs, we can divide the network's graph in the same way. Figure 15.6(d) shows a possible division, called a **cutset**. We say that there is a **net cutset** (for the network) and an **edge cutset** (for the graph). The connections between the two ASICs are **external connections**, the connections inside each ASIC are **internal connections**.

Notice that the number of external connections is not modeled correctly by the network graph. When we divide the network into two by drawing a line across connections, we make **net cuts**. The resulting set of net cuts is the net cutset. The number of net cuts we make corresponds to the number of external connections between the two partitions. When we divide the network graph into the same partitions we make **edge cuts** and we create the edge cutset. We have already shown that nets and graph edges are not equivalent when a net has more than two terminals. Thus the number of edge cuts made when we partition a graph into two is not necessarily equal to the number of net cuts in the network. As we shall see presently the differences between nets and graph edges is important when we consider partitioning a network by partitioning its graph [Schweikert and Kernighan, 1979].

15.7.2 A Simple Partitioning Example

Figure 15.7(a) shows a simple network we need to partition [Goto and Matsud, 1986]. There are 12 logic cells, labeled A–L, connected by 12 nets (labeled 1–12). At this level, each logic cell is a large circuit block and might be RAM, ROM, an ALU, and so on. Each net might also be a bus, but, for the moment, we assume that each net is a single connection and all nets are weighted equally. The goal is to partition our simple network into ASICs. Our objectives are the following:

- Use no more than three ASICs.
- Each ASIC is to contain no more than four logic cells.
- Use the minimum number of external connections for each ASIC.
- Use the minimum total number of external connections.

Figure 15.7(b) shows a partitioning with five external connections; two of the ASICs have three pins; the third has four pins. We might be able to find this arrangement by hand, but for larger systems we need help.

Splitting a network into several pieces is a **network partitioning problem**. In the following sections we shall examine two types of algorithms to solve this problem and describe how they are used in system partitioning. Section 15.7.3 describes **constructive partitioning**, which uses a set of rules to find a solution. Section 15.7.4 describes **iterative partitioning improvement** (or **iterative partitioning refinement**), which takes an existing solution and tries to improve it.

(a)

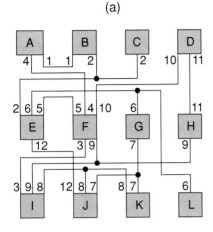

(b)

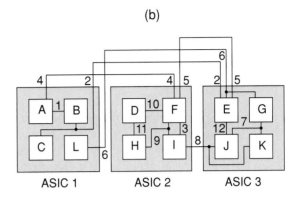

(c)

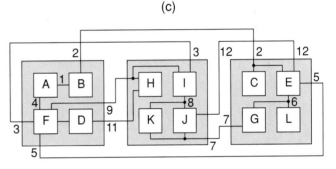

FIGURE 15.7 Partitioning example. (a) We wish to partition this network into three ASICs with no more than four logic cells per ASIC. (b) A partitioning with five external connections (nets 2, 4, 5, 6, and 8)—the minimum number. (c) A constructed partition using logic cell C as a seed. It is difficult to get from this local minimum, with seven external connections (2, 3, 5, 7, 9,11,12), to the optimum solution of b.

Often we apply iterative improvement to a constructive partitioning. We also use many of these partitioning algorithms in solving floorplanning and placement problems that we shall discuss in Chapter 16.

15.7.3 Constructive Partitioning

The most common constructive partitioning algorithms use **seed growth** or **cluster growth**. A simple seed-growth algorithm for constructive partitioning consists of the following steps:

1. Start a new partition with a seed logic cell.

2. Consider all the logic cells that are not yet in a partition. Select each of these logic cells in turn.

3. Calculate a gain function, $g(m)$, that measures the benefit of adding logic cell m to the current partition. One measure of gain is the number of connections between logic cell m and the current partition.

4. Add the logic cell with the highest gain $g(m)$ to the current partition.

5. Repeat the process from step 2. If you reach the limit of logic cells in a partition, start again at step 1.

We may choose different gain functions according to our objectives (but we have to be careful to distinguish between connections and nets). The algorithm starts with the choice of a **seed logic cell** (**seed module**, or just **seed**). The logic cell with the most nets is a good choice as the seed logic cell. You can also use a set of seed logic cells known as a **cluster**. Some people also use the term *clique*—borrowed from graph theory. A **clique** of a graph is a subset of nodes where each pair of nodes is connected by an edge—like your group of friends at school where everyone knows everyone else in your clique . In some tools you can use schematic pages (at the leaf or lowest hierarchical level) as a starting point for partitioning. If you use a high-level design language, you can use a Verilog module (different from a circuit module) or VHDL entity/architecture as seeds (again at the leaf level).

15.7.4 Iterative Partitioning Improvement

The most common iterative improvement algorithms are based on **interchange** and **group migration**. The process of interchanging (swapping) logic cells in an effort to improve the partition is an **interchange method**. If the swap improves the partition, we accept the trial interchange; otherwise we select a new set of logic cells to swap.

There is a limit to what we can achieve with a partitioning algorithm based on simple interchange. For example, Figure 15.7(c) shows a partitioning of the network of part a using a constructed partitioning algorithm with logic cell C as the seed. To get from the solution shown in part c to the solution of part b, which has a minimum number of external connections, requires a complicated swap. The three pairs: D and F, J and K, C and L need to be swapped—all at the same time. It would take a very long time to consider all possible swaps of this complexity. A simple interchange algorithm considers only one change and rejects it immediately if it is not an improvement. Algorithms of this type are **greedy algorithms** in the sense that they will accept a move only if it provides immediate benefit. Such shortsightedness leads an algorithm to a **local minimum** from which it cannot escape. Stuck in a valley, a greedy algorithm is not prepared to walk over a hill to see if there is a better solution in the next valley. This type of problem occurs repeatedly in CAD algorithms.

Group migration consists of swapping groups of logic cells between partitions. The **group migration algorithms** are better than simple interchange methods at improving a solution but are more complex. Almost all group migration methods are based on the powerful and general **Kernighan–Lin algorithm** (**K–L algorithm**) that partitions a graph [Kernighan and Lin, 1970]. The problem of dividing a graph into two pieces, minimizing the nets that are cut, is the **min-cut problem**—a very important one in VLSI design. As the next section shows, the K–L algorithm can be applied to many different problems in ASIC design. We shall examine the algorithm next and then see how to apply it to system partitioning.

15.7.5   The Kernighan–Lin Algorithm

Figure 15.8 illustrates some of the terms and definitions needed to describe the K–L algorithm. External edges cross between partitions; internal edges are contained inside a partition. Consider a network with $2m$ nodes (where m is an integer) each of equal size. If we assign a cost to each edge of the network graph, we can define a **cost matrix** $C = c_{ij}$, where $c_{ij} = c_{ji}$ and $c_{ii} = 0$. If all connections are equal in importance, the elements of the cost matrix are 1 or 0, and in this special case we usually call the matrix the **connectivity matrix**. Costs higher than 1 could represent the number of wires in a bus, multiple connections to a single logic cell, or nets that we need to keep close for timing reasons.

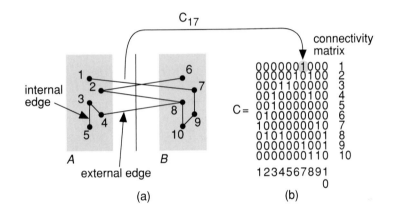

FIGURE 15.8 Terms used by the Kernighan–Lin partitioning algorithm. (a) An example network graph. (b) The connectivity matrix, C; the column and rows are labeled to help you see how the matrix entries correspond to the node numbers in the graph. For example, C_{17} (column 1, row 7) equals 1 because nodes 1 and 7 are connected. In this example all edges have an equal weight of 1, but in general the edges may have different weights.

Suppose we already have split a network into two partitions, A and B, each with m nodes (perhaps using a constructed partitioning). Our goal now is to swap nodes between A and B with the objective of minimizing the number of external edges connecting the two partitions. Each external edge may be weighted by a cost, and our objective corresponds to minimizing a cost function that we shall call the total external cost, **cut cost**, or **cut weight**, W:

$$W = \sum_{a \in A, b \in B} c_{ab} .$$ (15.13)

In Figure 15.8(a) the cut weight is 4 (all the edges have weights of 1).

In order to simplify the measurement of the change in cut weight when we interchange nodes, we need some more definitions. First, for any node a in partition A, we define an **external edge cost,** which measures the connections from node a to B,

$$E_a = \sum_{y \in B} c_{ay}. \tag{15.14}$$

For example, in Figure 15.8(a) $E_1 = 1$, and $E_3 = 0$. Second, we define the **internal edge cost** to measure the internal connections to a,

$$I_a = \sum_{z \in A} c_{az}. \tag{15.15}$$

So, in Figure 15.8(a), $I_1 = 0$, and $I_3 = 2$. We define the edge costs for partition B in a similar way (so $E_8 = 2$, and $I_8 = 1$). The cost difference is the difference between external edge costs and internal edge costs,

$$D_x = E_x - I_x. \tag{15.16}$$

Thus, in Figure 15.8(a) $D_1 = 1$, $D_3 = -2$, and $D_8 = 1$. Now pick any node in A, and any node in B. If we swap these nodes, a and b, we need to measure the reduction in cut weight, which we call the gain, g. We can express g in terms of the edge costs as follows:

$$g = D_a + D_b - 2c_{ab}. \tag{15.17}$$

The last term accounts for the fact that a and b may be connected. So, in Figure 15.8(a), if we swap nodes 1 and 6, then $g = D_1 + D_6 - 2c_{16} = 1 + 1$. If we swap nodes 2 and 8, then $g = D_2 + D_8 - 2c_{28} = 1 + 2 - 2$.

The K–L algorithm finds a group of node pairs to swap that increases the gain even though swapping individual node pairs from that group might decrease the gain. First we pretend to swap all of the nodes a pair at a time. Pretend swaps are like studying chess games when you make a series of trial moves in your head.

This is the algorithm:

1. Find two nodes, a_i from A, and b_i from B, so that the gain from swapping them is a maximum. The gain is

$$g_i = D_{a_i} + D_{b_i} - 2c_{a_i b_i}. \tag{15.18}$$

2. Next pretend swap a_i and b_i even if the gain g_i is zero or negative, and do not consider a_i and b_i eligible for being swapped again.

3. Repeat steps 1 and 2 a total of m times until all the nodes of A and B have been pretend swapped. We are back where we started, but we have ordered pairs of nodes in A and B according to the gain from interchanging those pairs.

4. Now we can choose which nodes we shall actually swap. Suppose we only swap the first n pairs of nodes that we found in the preceding process. In other words we swap nodes $X = a_1, a_2,..., a_n$ from A with nodes $Y = b_1, b_2,..., b_n$ from B. The total gain would be

$$G_n = \sum_{i=1}^{n} g_i. \tag{15.19}$$

5. We now choose n corresponding to the maximum value of G_n.

If the maximum value of $G_n > 0$, then we swap the sets of nodes X and Y and thus reduce the cut weight by G_n. We use this new partitioning to start the process again at the first step. If the maximum value of $G_n = 0$, then we cannot improve the current partitioning and we stop. We have found a locally optimum solution.

Figure 15.9 shows an example of partitioning a graph using the K–L algorithm. Each completion of steps 1 through 5 is a pass through the algorithm. Kernighan and Lin found that typically 2–4 passes were required to reach a solution. The most important feature of the K–L algorithm is that we are prepared to consider moves even though they seem to make things worse. This is like unraveling a tangled ball of string or solving a Rubik's cube puzzle. Sometimes you need to make things worse so they can get better later. The K–L algorithm works well for partitioning graphs. However, there are the following problems that we need to address before we can apply the algorithm to network partitioning:

- It minimizes the number of *edges* cut, not the number of *nets* cut.
- It does not allow logic cells to be different sizes.
- It is expensive in computation time.
- It does not allow partitions to be unequal or find the optimum partition size.
- It does not allow for selected logic cells to be fixed in place.
- The results are random.
- It does not directly allow for more than two partitions.

To implement a **net-cut partitioning** rather than an **edge-cut partitioning**, we can just keep track of the nets rather than the edges [Schweikert and Kernighan, 1979]. We can no longer use a connectivity or cost matrix to represent connections, though. Fortunately, several people have found efficient data structures to handle the bookkeeping tasks. One example is the Fiduccia–Mattheyses algorithm to be described shortly.

To represent nets with multiple terminals in a network accurately, we can extend the definition of a network graph. Figure 15.10 shows how a **hypergraph** with a special type of vertex, a **star**, and a **hyperedge**, represents a net with more than two terminals in a network.

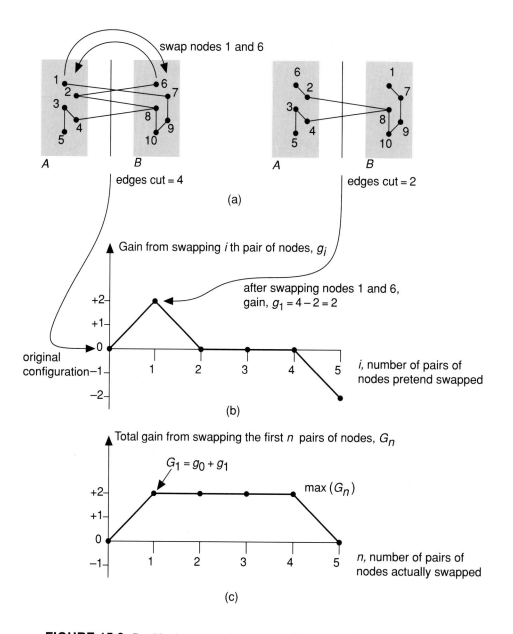

(a)

(b)

(c)

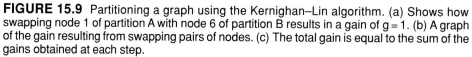

FIGURE 15.9 Partitioning a graph using the Kernighan–Lin algorithm. (a) Shows how swapping node 1 of partition A with node 6 of partition B results in a gain of $g = 1$. (b) A graph of the gain resulting from swapping pairs of nodes. (c) The total gain is equal to the sum of the gains obtained at each step.

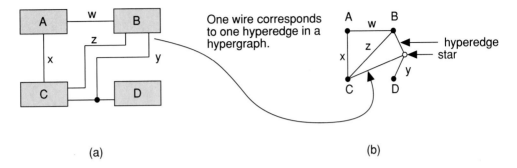

FIGURE 15.10 A hypergraph. (a) The network contains a net y with three terminals. (b) In the network hypergraph we can model net y by a single hyperedge (B, C, D) and a star node. Now there is a direct correspondence between wires or nets in the network and hyperedges in the graph.

In the K–L algorithm, the internal and external edge costs have to be calculated for all the nodes before we can select the nodes to be swapped. Then we have to find the pair of nodes that give the largest gain when swapped. This requires an amount of computer time that grows as $n^2 \log n$ for a graph with $2n$ nodes. This n^2 dependency is a major problem for partitioning large networks. The **Fiduccia–Mattheyses algorithm** (the **F–M algorithm**) is an extension to the K–L algorithm that addresses the differences between nets and edges and also reduces the computational effort [Fiduccia and Mattheyses, 1982]. The key features of this algorithm are the following:

- Only one logic cell, the **base logic cell**, moves at a time. In order to stop the algorithm from moving all the logic cells to one large partition, the base logic cell is chosen to maintain **balance** between partitions. The balance is the ratio of total logic cell size in one partition to the total logic cell size in the other. Altering the balance allows us to vary the sizes of the partitions.

- Critical nets are used to simplify the gain calculations. A net is a **critical net** if it has an attached logic cell that, when swapped, changes the number of nets cut. It is only necessary to recalculate the gains of logic cells on critical nets that are attached to the base logic cell.

- The logic cells that are free to move are stored in a doubly linked list. The lists are sorted according to gain. This allows the logic cells with maximum gain to be found quickly.

These techniques reduce the computation time so that it increases only slightly more than linearly with the number of logic cells in the network, a very important improvement [Fiduccia and Mattheyses, 1982].

Kernighan and Lin suggested simulating logic cells of different sizes by clumping s logic cells together with highly weighted nets to simulate a logic cell of size s. The F–M algorithm takes logic cell size into account as it selects a logic cell to swap based on maintaining the balance between the total logic cell size of each of the partitions. To generate unequal partitions using the K–L algorithm, we can introduce dummy logic cells with no connections into one of the partitions. The F–M algorithm adjusts the partition size according to the balance parameter.

Often we need to fix logic cells in place during partitioning. This may be because we need to keep logic cells together or apart for reasons other than connectivity, perhaps due to timing, power, or noise constraints. Another reason to fix logic cells would be to improve a partitioning that you have already partially completed. The F–M algorithm allows you to fix logic cells by removing them from consideration as the base logic cells you move. Methods based on the K–L algorithm find locally optimum solutions in a random fashion. There are two reasons for this. The first reason is the random starting partition. The second reason is that the choice of nodes to swap is based on the gain. The choice between moves that have equal gain is arbitrary. Extensions to the K–L algorithm address both of these problems. Finding nodes that are naturally grouped or clustered and assigning them to one of the initial partitions improves the results of the K–L algorithm. Although these are constructive partitioning methods, they are covered here because they are closely linked with the K–L iterative improvement algorithm.

15.7.6   The Ratio-Cut Algorithm

The **ratio-cut algorithm** removes the restriction of constant partition sizes. The cut weight W for a cut that divides a network into two partitions, A and B, is given by

$$W = \sum_{a \in A, b \in B} c_{ab}. \tag{15.20}$$

The K–L algorithm minimizes W while keeping partitions A and B the same size. The **ratio** of a cut is defined as

$$R = \frac{W}{|A||B|}. \tag{15.21}$$

In this equation $|A|$ and $|B|$ are the sizes of partitions A and B. The size of a partition is equal to the number of nodes it contains (also known as the **set cardinality**). The cut that minimizes R is called the **ratio cut**. The original description of the ratio-cut algorithm uses ratio cuts to partition a network into small, highly connected groups. Then you form a reduced network from these groups—each small group of logic cells forms a node in the reduced network. Finally, you use the F–M algorithm to improve the reduced network [Cheng and Wei, 1991].

15.7.7 The Look-ahead Algorithm

Both the K–L and F–M algorithms consider only the immediate gain to be made by moving a node. When there is a tie between nodes with equal gain (as often happens), there is no mechanism to make the best choice. This is like playing chess looking only one move ahead. Figure 15.11 shows an example of two nodes that have equal gains, but moving one of the nodes will allow a move that has a higher gain later.

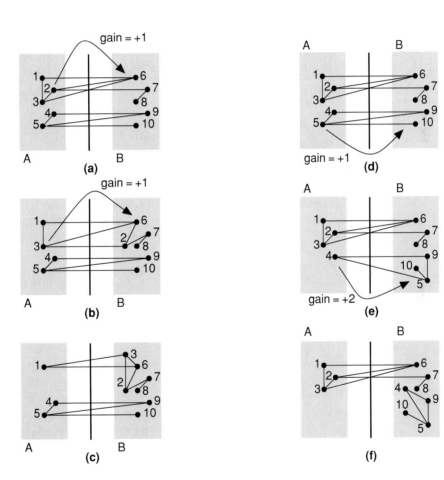

FIGURE 15.11 An example of network partitioning that shows the need to look ahead when selecting logic cells to be moved between partitions. Partitionings (a), (b), and (c) show one sequence of moves, partitionings (d), (e), and (f) show a second sequence. The partitioning in (a) can be improved by moving node 2 from A to B with a gain of 1. The result of this move is shown in (b). This partitioning can be improved by moving node 3 to B, again with a gain of 1. The partitioning shown in (d) is the same as (a). We can move node 5 to B with a gain of 1 as shown in (e), but now we can move node 4 to B with a gain of 2.

We call the gain for the initial move the first-level gain. Gains from subsequent moves are then second-level and higher gains. We can define a **gain vector** that contains these gains. Figure 15.11 shows how the first-level and second-level gains are calculated. Using the gain vector allows us to use a **look-ahead algorithm** in the choice of nodes to be swapped. This reduces both the mean and variation in the number of cuts in the resulting partitions.

We have described algorithms that are efficient at dividing a network into two pieces. Normally we wish to divide a system into more than two pieces. We can do this by recursively applying the algorithms. For example, if we wish to divide a system network into three pieces, we could apply the F–M algorithm first, using a balance of 2:1, to generate two partitions, with one twice as large as the other. Then we apply the algorithm again to the larger of the two partitions, with a balance of 1:1, which will give us three partitions of roughly the same size.

15.7.8   Simulated Annealing

A different approach to solving large graph problems (and other types of problems) that arise in VLSI layout, including system partitioning, uses the **simulated-annealing algorithm** [Kirkpatrick et al., 1983]. Simulated annealing takes an existing solution and then makes successive changes in a series of random moves. Each move is accepted or rejected based on an **energy function**, calculated for each new trial configuration. The minimums of the energy function correspond to possible solutions. The best solution is the **global minimum**.

So far the description of simulated annealing is similar to the interchange algorithms, but there is an important difference. In an interchange strategy we accept the new trial configuration only if the energy function decreases, which means the new configuration is an improvement. However, in the simulated-annealing algorithm, we accept the new configuration even if the energy function increases for the new configuration—which means things are getting worse. The probability of accepting a worse configuration is controlled by the exponential expression $\exp(-\Delta E/T)$, where ΔE is the resulting increase in the energy function. The parameter T is a variable that we control and corresponds to the temperature in the annealing of a metal cooling (this is why the process is called simulated annealing).

We accept moves that seemingly take us away from a desirable solution to allow the system to escape from a local minimum and find other, better, solutions. The name for this strategy is **hill climbing**. As the temperature is slowly decreased, we decrease the probability of making moves that increase the energy function. Finally, as the temperature approaches zero, we refuse to make any moves that increase the energy of the system and the system falls and comes to rest at the nearest local minimum. Hopefully, the solution that corresponds to the minimum we have found is a good one.

The critical parameter governing the behavior of the simulated-annealing algorithm is the rate at which the temperature T is reduced. This rate is known as the **cooling schedule**. Often we set a parameter α that relates the temperatures, T_i and T_{i+1}, at the ith and $i+1$th iteration:

$$T_{i+1} = \alpha T_i . \tag{15.22}$$

To find a good solution, a local minimum close to the global minimum, requires a high initial temperature and a slow cooling schedule. This results in many trial moves and very long computer run times [Rose, Klebsch, and Wolf, 1990]. If we are prepared to wait a long time (forever in the worst case), simulated annealing is useful because we can guarantee that we can find the optimum solution. Simulated annealing is useful in several of the ASIC construction steps and we shall return to it in Section 16.2.7.

15.7.9 Other Partitioning Objectives

In partitioning a real system we need to weight each logic cell according to its area in order to control the total areas of each ASIC. This can be done if the area of each logic cell can either be calculated or estimated. This is usually done as part of floorplanning, so we may need to return to partitioning after floorplanning.

There will be many objectives or constraints that we need to take into account during partitioning. For example, certain logic cells in a system may need to be located on the same ASIC in order to avoid adding the delay of any external interconnections. These **timing constraints** can be implemented by adding weights to nets to make them more important than others. Some logic cells may consume more power than others and you may need to add **power constraints** to avoid exceeding the power-handling capability of a single ASIC. It is difficult, though, to assign more than rough estimates of power consumption for each logic cell at the system planning stage, before any simulation has been completed. Certain logic cells may only be available in a certain technology—if you want to include memory on an ASIC, for example. In this case, **technology constraints** will keep together logic cells requiring similar technologies. We probably want to impose **cost constraints** to implement certain logic cells in the lowest cost technology available or to keep ASICs below a certain size in order to use a low-cost package. The type of test strategy you adopt will also affect the partitioning of logic. Large RAM blocks may require BIST circuitry; large amounts of sequential logic may require scan testing, possibly with a boundary-scan interface. One of the objects of testability is to maintain controllability and observability of logic inside each ASIC. In order to do this, **test constraints** may require that we force certain connections to be external. No automated partitioning tools can take into account all of these constraints. The best CAD tool to help you with these decisions is a spreadsheet.

15.8 Summary

The construction or physical design of ASICs in a microelectronics system is a very large and complex problem. To solve the problem we divide it into several steps: system partitioning, floorplanning, placement, and routing. To solve each of these smaller problems we need goals and objectives, measurement metrics, as well as algorithms and methods.

System partitioning is the first step in ASIC assembly. An example of the SPARCstation 1 illustrated the various issues involved in partitioning. Presently commercial CAD tools are able to automatically partition systems and chips only at a low level, at the level of a network or netlist. Partitioning for FPGAs is currently the most advanced. Next we discussed the methods to use for system partitioning. We saw how to represent networks as graphs, containing nets and edges, and how the mathematics of graph theory is useful in system partitioning and the other steps of ASIC assembly. We covered methods and algorithms for partitioning and explained that most are based on the Kernighan–Lin min-cut algorithm.

The important points in this chapter are

- The goals and objectives of partitioning
- Partitioning as an art not a science
- The simple nature of the algorithms necessary for VLSI-sized problems
- The random nature of the algorithms we use
- The controls for the algorithms used in ASIC design

15.9 Problems

*=Difficult, **=Very difficult, ***=Extremely difficult

15.1 (Complexity, 10 min.) Suppose the workstations we use to design ASICs increase in power (measured in MIPS—a million instructions per second) by a factor of 2 every year. If we want to keep the length of time to solve an ASIC design problem fixed, calculate how much larger chips can get each year if constrained by an algorithm with the following complexities:

    a. $O(k)$.

    b. $O(n)$.

    c. $O(\log n)$.

    d. $O(n \log n)$.

    e. $O(n^2)$.

15.2 (Complexity, 10 min.) In a film the main character looks 12 moves ahead to win a chess championship.

a. Estimate (stating your assumptions) the number of possible chess moves looking 12 moves ahead.

b. How long would it take to evaluate all these moves on a modern workstation?

15.3 (Chips and towns, 20 min.) This problem is adapted from an analogy credited to Chuck Seitz. Complete the entries in Table 15.8, which shows the progression of integrated circuit complexity using the analogy of town and city planning. If λ is half the minimum feature size, assume that a transistor is a square 2λ on a side and is equivalent to a city block (which we estimate at 200 m on a side).

TABLE 15.8 Complexity of ASICs (Problems 15.3 and 15.4).

Year	$\lambda/\mu m$	Chip size (mm on a side)	Transistor size (μm on a side)	Transistors = city blocks	City size (km on a side, 1 block = 200m)	Example
1970	50	5	200	25 x 25 = 625	5	Palo Alto
1980	5	10	20	500 x 500 = 25×10^3		
1990	0.5	20	1	1,000 x 1,000 = 1×10^6		
2000	0.05	40	0.2	20,000 x 20,000 = 400×10^6		

15.4 (Polygons, 10 min.) Estimate (stating and explaining all your assumptions) how many polygons there are on the layouts for each of the chips in Table 15.8.

15.5 (Algorithm complexity, 10 min.) I think of a number between 1 and 100. You guess the number and I shall tell you whether you are high or low. We then repeat the process. If you were to write a computer program to play this game, what would be the complexity of your algorithm?

15.6 (Algorithms, 60 min.) For each of these problems write or find (stating your source) an algorithm to solve the problem:

a. An algorithm to sort n numbers.

b. An algorithm to discover whether a number n is prime.

c. An algorithm to generate a random number between 1 and n.

List the algorithm using a sequence of steps, pseudocode, or a flow chart. What is the complexity of each algorithm?

15.7 (Measurement, 30 min.) The traveling-salesman problem is a well-known example of an NP-complete problem (you have a list of cities and their locations and you have to find the shortest route between them, visiting each only once). Propose a simple measure to estimate the length of the solution. If I had to visit the 50 capitals of the United States, what is your estimate of my frequent-flyer mileage?

15.8 (Construction, 30 min.) Try and make a quantitative comparison (stating and explaining all your assumptions) of the difficulty and complexity of construction (for example, how many components in each?) for each of the following: a Boeing 747 jumbo jet, the space shuttle, and an Intel Pentium microprocessor. Which, in your estimation, is the most complex and why? Smailagic [1995] proposes measures of design and construction complexity in a description of the wearable computer project at Carnegie-Mellon University.

15.9 (Productivity, 20 min.). If I have six months to design an ASIC:

a. What is the productivity (in transistors/day) required for each of the chips in Table 15.8?

b. What does this translate to in terms of a productivity increase (measured in percent increase in productivity per month)?

c. Moore's Law says that chip sizes double every 18 months. What does this correspond to in terms of a percentage increase per month?

d. Comment on your answers.

15.10 (Graphs and edges, 30 min.) We know a net with two connections requires a single edge in the network graph, a net with three connections requires three edges, and a net with four connections requires six edges.

a. Can you guess a formula for the number of edges in the network graph corresponding to a net with n connections?

b. Can you prove the formula you guessed in part a? *Hint:* How many edges are there from one node to $n - 1$ other nodes?

c. Large nets cause problems for partitioning algorithms based on a connectivity matrix (edges rather than wires). Suppose we have a 50-net connection that is no more critical for timing than any other net. Suggest a way to fool the partitioning algorithm so this net does not drag all its logic cells into one partition.

Most CAD programs treat large nets (like the clock, reset, or power nets) separately, but the nets are required to have special names and you only can have a limited number of them. The average net in an ASIC has between two and four connections and as a rule of thumb 80 percent of nets have a fanout of 4 or less (a fanout of 4 means a gate drives four others, making a total of five connections on the net).

15.11 (PC partitioning, 60 min.) Open an IBM-compatible PC, Apple Macintosh, or PowerPC that has a motherboard that you can see easily. Make a list of the chips (manufacturer and type), their packages, and pin counts. Make intelligent guesses as to the function of most of the chips. Obviously manufacturer's logos and chip identification markings help—perhaps they are in a data book. Identify the types of packages (pin-grid array, quad flat pack). Look for nearby components that may give a hint—crystals for clock generators or the video subsystem. Where are the chips located on the board—are they near the connectors for the floppy disk subsystem, the modem or serial port, or video output? To help you, Table 15.9 shows an example—a list of the first row of chips on an old H-P Vectra ES/12 motherboard. Use the same format for your list.

TABLE 15.9 A list of the chips on the first row of an HP Vectra PC (Problem 15.11).

Manufacturer	Chip	Package	Function	Comment
HP	87411AAE	24-pin DIP		
Intel	L7220048	40-pin DIP	EPROM (9/3/87)	Boot commands
Chips	7014-0093	80-pin quad flat pack	Custom ASIC	
Intel	80286-12	68-pin package	Microprocessor	CPU
TI	AS00	14-pin DIP	Quad 2-input NAND gate	Addressing
	S74F08D	14-pin DIP	Quad 2-input AND gate	Addressing
	F74F51	14-pin DIP	AOI gate	Addressing

15.12 (Estimates, 60 min.) System partitioning is not exact science. Estimate:

a. The power developed by a grasshopper, in watts (from a Cambridge University entrance exam).

b. The number of doors in New York City.

c. The number of grains of sand on Hawaii's beaches.

d. The total length of the roads in the continental United States in kilometers.

In each case: (i) Provide an equation that depends on parameters and symbols that you define. (ii) List the parameters in your equation, and the values that you assume with their uncertainty. (iii) Give the answer as a number (with units where necessary). (iv) Include a numerical estimate of the uncertainty in your answer.

15.13 (Pad-limited and core-limited die, 10 min.) As the number of I/O pads increases, an ASIC can become **pad-limited**. The spacing between I/O pads is determined by mechanical limitations of the equipment used for bonding—usually 2–5 mil (a mil is a thousandth of an inch). In a pad-limited design the number of pads around the outer edge of the die determines the die size, not the number of gates (see Figure 15.12). For the pad-limited design, shown in Figure 15.12(a), the price per I/O pad is more important than the price per gate. When we have a lot of logic but few I/O pads, we have a **core-limited** design—the opposite of a pad-limited ASIC—as shown in Figure 15.12(b). For a given number of I/O pads and a pad-limited design, all the different ASIC types will have the same die size, determined by a graph such as the one shown in Figure 15.12(c). If I/O pad spacing is 5 mil and gate density is $1.0 \, \text{gate/mil}^2$, when does an ASIC becomes pad-limited? Express your answer as a function of the number of gates, G, and the number of I/Os, I.

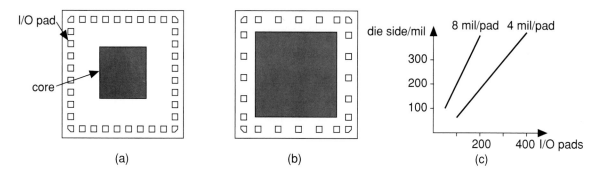

FIGURE 15.12 Die size. (a) A pad-limited die, the die size is determined by the number of I/O pads. (b) A core-limited die, the die size is limited by the amount of logic in the core. (c) For a given pad spacing we can determine the die size for a pad-limited die.

15.14 (Estimating ASIC size, 120 min.) Let us pretend we are going to build a laptop SPARCstation. We need to drastically reduce the number of chips used in the desktop system. Focus on the I/O subsystems in Figure 15.2 (chip labels are shown in parentheses): LANCE Ethernet controller (14), 3C90 SCSI controller (15), 85C30 serial port controller (16, 17), 79C30 ISDN interface (18), and 82072 floppy-disk controller (19). Consider combining these functions into a single custom ASIC.

a. Collect as much data as you can on the ASSP chips (14–19) that are currently used in the SPARCstation 1, similar to that presented in Table 15.5. National Semiconductor, Texas Instruments, AMD, Intel, and Motorola produce these or similar chips. You will need one or more of their ASSP data books. Try to find the pin count, power dissipation, and gate count for each chip. If you can't find one of these parameters, make an estimate and explain your assumptions.

b. Using your data, make an estimate of the size, power dissipation, and pin count of the ASIC to replace chips 14–19 in Figure 15.2.

c. As a sanity check compare your results with the DMA2 Ethernet, SCSI, and parallel port chip in the SPARCstation 10 (see Table 15.2). This is a 30 k-gate array in a 160-pin quad flat pack.

15.15 (Power dissipation, 20 min.) If a Pentium microprocessor dissipates 5 W and, on average, 20 percent of the circuit nodes toggle every clock cycle

a. Calculate the total capacitance of all the circuit nodes in picofarads if the clock frequency is 100 MHz and $V_{DD} = 5$ V.

b. If half of this is due to interconnect capacitance at 2 pFcm^{-1}, what is the total length of interconnect?

c. If there are 100 I/Os driving an average of 20 pF load off-chip at an average frequency of 50 MHz, what is the power dissipation in the I/Os?

d. A Pentium chip contains about 3×10^6 transistors. How many gates is this?

e. How many gates are switching on average every clock cycle?

15.16 (Parasitic power dissipation, 20 min.) Consider the following arguments: The energy stored in a capacitor is $1/2(CV^2)$ (measured in joules). Suppose we charge and discharge a capacitance C between zero and V volts at a frequency f. We have to replace this energy f times per second and we shall dissipate a power (measured in watts) equal to

$$P = \frac{1}{2}fCV^2 . \tag{15.23}$$

When the p-channel transistor in an inverter is charging a capacitance, C, at a frequency, f, the current through the transistor is $C(dV/dt)$, the power dissipation is $CV(dV/dt)$ for one-half the period of the input, $t = 1/(2f)$. The power dissipated in the p-channel transistor is thus

$$P = \int_0^{1/(2f)} CV \left(\frac{dV}{dt} \right) dt = \frac{1}{2}fCV^2 . \tag{15.24}$$

During the second half-period of the input signal the p-channel transistor is off, so that there can be no power dissipation in the power supply. The power dissipation that occurs in the n-channel transistor must come from the stored energy in the capacitor—which is accounted for in the equation. In both cases the total power dissipation should be $1/2(fCV^2)$, not (fCV^2) as we have stated in Eq. 15.4. Point out the errors in both of these arguments. (If you are interested in situations in which these equations do hold, you can search for the term **adiabatic logic**.)

15.17 (Short-circuit power dissipation, 30 min.) Prove Eq. 15.5 as follows: The input to a CMOS inverter is a linear ramp with rise time t_{rf}. Calculate the n-channel transistor current as a function of the input voltage, V_{in}, assuming the n-channel transistor turns on when $V_{in} = V_{tn}$ and the current reaches a maximum when $V_{in} = V_{DD}/2$ at $t = t_{rf}/2$.

The transistor current is given by Eq. 2.9. Assume $\beta = (W/L)\mu C_{ox}$ is the same for both p- and n-channel transistors, the magnitude of the threshold voltages $|V_{tn}|$ are assumed equal for both transistor types, and τ is the rise time and fall time (assumed equal) of the input signal.

Show that for a CMOS inverter (Eq. 15.5):

$$P_2 = \frac{\beta f \tau}{12} (V_{DD} - 2V_{tn})^3 , \tag{15.25}$$

where $\beta = (W/L)\mu C_{ox}$ is the same for both p- and n-channel transistors, the magnitude of the threshold voltages $|V_t|$ are assumed equal for both transistors, and τ is the rise time and fall time (assumed equal) of the input signal [Veendrick, 1984].

15.18 (Connectivity matrix, 10 min.) Find the connectivity matrix for the ATM Connection Simulator shown in Figure 15.5. Use the following scheme to number the blocks and ordering of the matrix rows and columns: 1 = Personal Computer, 2 = Intel 80186, 3 = UTOPIA receiver, 4 = UTOPIA transmitter, 5 = Header remapper and screener, 6 = Remapper SRAM, . . . 15 = Random-number and bit error rate generator, 16 = Random-variable generator. All buses are labeled with their width except for two single connections (the arrows).

15.19 (K–L algorithm, 15 min.)

a. Draw the network graph for the following connectivity matrix:

$$\mathbf{C} \;=\; \begin{bmatrix} 0 & 0 & 0 & 0 & 0 & 0 & 1 & 0 & 0 & 0 \\ 0 & 0 & 0 & 0 & 0 & 1 & 0 & 1 & 0 & 0 \\ 0 & 0 & 0 & 1 & 0 & 0 & 0 & 1 & 0 & 0 \\ 0 & 0 & 1 & 0 & 1 & 0 & 0 & 0 & 1 & 0 \\ 0 & 0 & 0 & 1 & 0 & 0 & 0 & 0 & 0 & 0 \\ 0 & 1 & 0 & 0 & 0 & 0 & 0 & 0 & 1 & 0 \\ 1 & 0 & 0 & 0 & 0 & 0 & 0 & 0 & 1 & 0 \\ 0 & 1 & 1 & 0 & 0 & 0 & 0 & 0 & 1 & 0 \\ 0 & 0 & 0 & 1 & 0 & 0 & 1 & 1 & 0 & 1 \\ 0 & 0 & 0 & 0 & 0 & 0 & 0 & 0 & 1 & 0 \end{bmatrix} \tag{15.26}$$

b. Draw the partitioned network graph for **C** with nodes 1–5 in partition A and nodes 6–10 in partition B. What is the cut weight?

c. Improve the initial partitioning using the K–L algorithm. Show the gains at each stage. What problems did you find in following the algorithm and how do you resolve them?

15.20 (The gain graph in the K–L algorithm, 20 min.). Continue with the K–L algorithm for the network that we started to partition in Figure 15.9(a).

a. Show that choices of logic cells to swap and the gains correspond to the graph of Figure 15.9(b).

b. Notice that $G_5 = 0$. In fact G_m (where there are $2m$ nodes to be partitioned) will always be zero. Can you explain why?

15.21 (Look-ahead gain in the K–L algorithm, 20 min.) In the K–L algorithm we have to compute the gain each time we consider swapping one pair of nodes:

$$g_I \;=\; D_a + D_b - 2c_{ab}. \tag{15.27}$$

If we swap two pairs of nodes (a_1 and b_1 followed by a_2 and b_2), show that the gain is

$$g_{II} \;=\; D_{a_2} + D_{b_2} - 2c_{a_2 b_2} + 2c_{a_2 a_1} - 2c_{a_2 b_1} - 2c_{b_2 a_1} + 2c_{b_2 b_1}. \tag{15.28}$$

15.22 (FPGA partitioning, 30 min.) Table 15.10 shows some data on FPGAs from company Z.

TABLE 15.10 FPGAs from company Z (Problem 15.22).

FPGA size	Die area/cm^2	Average gate count	Package pins	Cost
S	0.26	1500	68	$26
M	0.36	2300	44	$35
L	0.46	2800	84	$50
XL	0.64	4700	84	$90
XXL	0.84	6200	84	$130

a. Notice that the FPGAs come in different package sizes. To eliminate the effect of package price, multiply the price for the S chip by 106 percent, and the M chip by 113 percent. Now all prices are normalized for an 84-pin plastic package. All the chips are the same speed grade; if they were not, we could normalize for this too (a little harder to justify though).

b. Plot the normalized chip prices vs. gate count. What is the cost per gate?

c. The part cost ought to be related to the yield, which is directly related to die area. If the cost of a 6-inch-diameter wafer is fixed (approximately $1000), calculate the cost per die, assuming a yield Y (in percent), as a function of the die area, A (in cm^2). Assume you completely fill the wafer and you can have fractional die (i.e., do not worry about packing square die into a circular wafer).

d. There are many models for the yield of a process, Y. Two common models are

$$Y = \exp\left(-\sqrt{AD}\right) \qquad (15.29)$$

and

$$Y = \left(\frac{1 - \exp(-AD)}{AD}\right)^2. \qquad (15.30)$$

Parameter A is the die area in cm^2 and D is the spot defect density in defects/cm^2 and is usually around 1.0 defects/cm^2 for a good submicron CMOS process (above 5.0 defects/cm^2 is unusual). The most important thing is the yield; anything below about 50 percent good die per wafer is usually bad news for an ASIC foundry. Does the FPGA cost data fit either model?

e. Now disregard the current pricing strategy of company Z. If you had to bet that physics would determine the true price of the chip, how much worse or better off are you using two small FPGAs rather than one larger FPGA (assume the larger die is exactly twice the area of the smaller one) under these two yield models?

f. What assumptions are inherent in the calculation you made in part e? How much do you think they might affect your answer, and what else would affect your judgment?

g. Give some reasons why you might select two smaller FPGAs rather than a larger FPGA, even if the larger FPGA is a cheaper solution.

h. Give some reasons why you would select a larger FPGA rather than two smaller FPGAs, even if the smaller FPGAs were a cheaper solution.

15.23 (Constructive partitioning, 30 min.) We shall use the simple network with 12 blocks shown in Figure 15.7 to experiment with constructive partitioning. This example is topologically equivalent to that used in [Goto and Matsud, 1986].

a. We shall use a gain function, $g(m)$, calculated as follows: Sum the number of the *nets* (not *connections*) from the selected logic cell, m, that connect to the current partition—call this $P(m)$. Now calculate the number of *nets* that connect logic cell m to logic cells which are not yet in partitions—call this $N(m)$. Then $g(m) = P(m) - N(m)$ is the gain of adding the logic cell m to the partition currently being filled.

b. Partition the network using the seed growth algorithm with logic cell C as the seed. Show how this choice of seed can lead to the partitioning shown in Figure 15.7(c). Use a table like Table 15.11 as a bookkeeping aid (a spreadsheet will help too). Each row corresponds to a pass through the algorithm. Fill in the measures, $P(m) - N(m)$, equal to the gain, $g(m)$. Once a logic cell is assigned to a partition, fill in the name of the partition (X, Y, or Z) in that column. The first row shows you how logic cell L is selected; proceed from there. What problems do you encounter while completing the algorithm, and how do you resolve them?

c. Now partition using logic cell F as the seed instead—the logic cell with the highest number of nets. When you have a tie between logic cells with the same gain, or you are starting a new partition, pick the logic cell with the largest $P(m)$. Use a copy of Table 15.12 as a bookkeeping aid. How does your partition compare with those we have already made (summarized in Table 15.13)?

d. Comment on your results.

Table 15.14 will help in constructing the gain function at each step of the algorithm.

15.24 (Simulated annealing, 15 min.) If you have a fixed amount of time to solve a partitioning problem, comment on the following alternatives and choose one:

    i. Run a single simulated annealing cycle using a slow cooling schedule.

TABLE 15.11 Bookkeeping table for Problem 15.23 (b).

Pass	Gain	A	B	C	D	E	F	G	H	I	J	K	L
1	P−N	0−2	1−2	X	0−2	1−4	0−5	0−2	0−2	0−3	0−3	0−2	0−1
	= g	= −2	= −1		= −2	= −3	= −5	= −2	= −2	= −3	= −3	= −2	= −1
2				X							X		X

TABLE 15.12 Bookkeeping table for Problem 15.23 (c).

Pass	Gain	A	B	C	D	E	F	G	H	I	J	K	L
1	P−N	1−2	0−2	1−1	1−1	1−3	X	0−2	1−2	2−2	0−3	0−2	0−1
	= g	= −1	= −2	= 0	= 0	= −2		= −2	= −1	= 0	= −3	= −2	= −1
2							X			X			

TABLE 15.13 Different partitions for the network shown in Figure 15.7 (Problem 15.23 c).

Partitioning	Total external connections	Partition contents X, Y, Z	Connections to each partition
Figure 15.7(b)	5	X = (A, B, C, L)	3
	(2, 4, 5, 6, 8)	Y = (D, F, H, I)	3
		Z = (E, G, J, K)	4
Figure 15.7(c)	7	X = (A, B, F, D)	5
	(2, 3, 5, 7, 9, 11, 12)	Y = (H, I, J, K)	5
		Z = (C, E, G, L)	4

ii. Run several (faster) min-cut based partitionings, using different seeds, and pick the best one.

iii. Run several simulated annealing cycles using a faster cooling schedule, and pick the best result.

15.25 (Net weights, 15 min.) Figure 15.13 shows a small part of a system and will help illustrate some potential problems when you weight nets for partitioning. Nets s1–s3 are critical, nets c1–c4 are not. Assume that all nets are weighted by a cost of one unless the special net weight symbol is attached.

a. Explain the problem with the net weights as shown in Figure 15.13(a).

b. Figure 15.13(b) shows a different way to assign weights. What problems might this cause in the rest of the system?

TABLE 15.14   An aid to calculating the gains for Problem 15.23.

Logic cell	Connects to:	Number of nets	Number of connections
A	B, F	2	2
B	A, (C, E)	2	3
C	(B, E)	1	2
D	F, H	2	2
E	(B, C), F, (G, L), J	4	6
F	A, D, E, (H, I_1), I_2	5	6
G	(E, L), (J, K)	2	4
H	D, (F, I)	2	3
I	F_1, (F_2, H), (J, K)	3	5
J	E, (G, K_1), (I, K_2)	3	5
K	(G, J_1), (I, J_2)	2	4
L	(E, G)	1	2

c. Figure 15.13(c) shows another possible solution. Discuss the advantages of this approach.

d. Can you think of another way to solve the problem?

This situation represents a very real problem with using net weights and tools that use min-cut algorithms. As soon as you get one critical net right, the tool makes several other nets too long and they become critical. The problem is worse during system partitioning when the blocks are big and there are many different nets with differing importance attached to each block—but it can happen during floorplanning and placement also.

15.26 (Cost, 60 min.) You have three chip sizes available for your part of project "DreamOn" (a new video game): S, M, and L. The L chip has twice the logic of the M chip. The M chip has twice the logic of the S chip. The L chip costs $16, which is 4 times as much as the M chip and 16 times as much as the S chip. There are two speed grades available: fast (F) and turbocharged (T). The T chip costs twice as much as the F version. Using a partitioning program, you find you need the equivalent of 1.8 of the L chips, but only a third of your logic needs a T chip.

a. What is the cheapest way to build "DreamOn"?

b. During prototyping you find you can use 90 percent of the S and M type chips, but for reliable routing you can only count on a maximum utilization of 85 percent for the L chip. You also find that, to maximize performance, you need to keep all of the logic that requires the turbo speed on one chip.

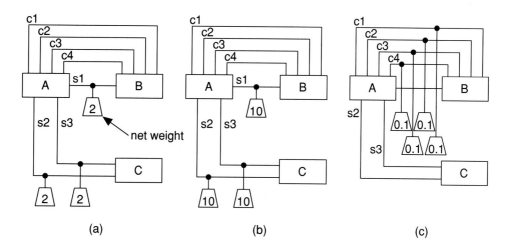

FIGURE 15.13 (For Problem 15.25.) An example of a problem in weighting nets. The symbols attached to the nets apply a weight or cost to that net during partitioning. Nets c1–c4 are control lines—they are not critical for timing purposes. Nets s1–s3 are signal lines that are critical—they must be kept short. The figure shows three different ways to handle this using net weights.

Our ASIC vendor, Xactera, promises us that the chip prices will fall by the time we go into production in one year. The estimates are that the prices will be almost proportional to chip size: The L chip will cost 2.2 times the M chip and 4.4 times whatever is the cost of the S chip by then (but Xactera will not commit to a future price for the S chip, only the present price). You predict the price of the S chip will fall 20 percent in one year (this is about average for the annual rate of price decrease for semiconductors). Xactera says the turbocharged speed grade will stay about twice the cost of the fast grade. How does this information affect your decision?

c. Some time later, as you are ready to go on vacation, the production department tells you that the board cost is about the same as the chip cost! The board area does not make much difference to the price, but there is an extra charge per package pin to reflow solder the surface-mount chips. We only need each chip to have the minimum size package—a 44-pin quad plastic package. Production has two price quotes: Boards-R-Us charges $5 per board plus $0.01 per pin, and PCB Inc. quotes at $0.05 per pin. What should we do? The CEO needs a recommendation today.

d. You come back from holiday and find out from your e-mail that we went with your recommendation on the board vendor but now we have other problems. The test company is charging per chip pin on the board since we are using an old style bed-of-nails tester. The cost is about $0.01 per chip pin. You can go back and add a test interface to all the chips, which is the equivalent of adding 10 percent of a small chip (type S) on each chip (S, M, or L). This would eliminate the bed-of-nails test, and reduce board test cost to $1 per board. Xactera also just lowered their prices: L chips are now $4, M chips are $2, and S chips are $0.95. There is also a new Xactera XL chip that has twice the capacity of the L chips and costs $8 (but you do not know what utilization to expect). These prices are for the fast speed grades, the turbo versions are now 2.5 times more expensive.

e. There are some serious consequences to making any design changes now (including schedule slips). We have an emergency meeting with production, finance, marketing, and the CEO this afternoon in the boardroom. I have to prepare a presentation outlining our past decisions and the advantages and disadvantages of each of our options (with quantitative estimates of their effect). Can you prepare four foils for me, and a one-page spreadsheet that will allow us to make some rapid "what-if" decisions in the meeting? Print the foils and the one-page spreadsheet.

f. A year later we are in full production and all is well. We are reviewing your performance on project "DreamOn." What did you learn from this project and how would you do things differently next time? (You only have room for 100 words on your review form.)

15.10 Bibliography

Many of the references in the bibliography in Chapter 1 are also sources for information on the physical design of ASICs. The European Conference on Design Automation is known as EuroDAC (TK7867.E93, ISBN and cataloging varies with year). Another European conference, EuroASIC, was absorbed by EuroDAC (TK7874.6.E88, ISSN 1066-1409 and ISSN 1064-5322, cataloging varies).

Preas and Lorenzetti's book [1988] contains an overview chapter on partitioning and placement. To dig a little deeper see the review article by Goto and Matsud [1986]. If you want to explore further the detailed workings of partitioning algorithms, Sherwani's book [1993] catalogs physical design algorithms, including those for partitioning. To learn more about simulated annealing see Sechen's book [1988]. Partitioning is an important part of high-level synthesis, and the book by Gajski et al. [1992] contains a chapter on partitioning for allocation and scheduling as well as system partitioning—including a description of clustering methods, which are not well covered elsewhere.This book describes SpecSyn, a tool that allows you to enter a design using a behavioral description with a graphical tool. SpecSyn can then partition the design given area, timing, and cost specifications. System partitioning at the behavioral level (**architectural partitioning**) is an area of current research (see [Lagnese and Thomas, 1991] for a description of the APARTY system). This means we partition a design based on a hardware design language rather than a schematic or other physical description. Papers published in the *Proceedings of the Design Automation Conference* (DAC) and articles in the *IEEE Transactions on Computer-Aided Design of Integrated Circuits and Systems* form a point at which to start working back through the recent research literature on system partitioning, an example is [Kucukcakar and Parker, 1991].

The *Proceedings of the 32nd Design Automation Conference* (1995) describe a special session on the design of the Sun Microsystems UltraSPARC-I (albeit from more of a systems perspective), which forms an interesting comparison to the SPARCstation 1 and SPARCstation 10 designs.

15.11 References

Page numbers in brackets after the reference indicate the location in the chapter body.

Cheng, C.-K., and Y.-C. A. Wei. 1991. "An improved two-way partitioning algorithm with stable performance." *IEEE Transactions on Computer-Aided Design of Integrated Circuits and Systems,* Vol. 10, no. 12, pp. 1502–1511. Describes the ratio-cut algorithm. [p. 834]

Fiduccia, C. M., and R. M. Mattheyses. 1982. "A linear-time heuristic for improving network partitions." In *Proceedings of the 19th Design Automation Conference,* pp. 175–181. Describes modification to Kernighan-Lin algorithm to reduce computation time. [p. 833]

Gajski, D. D., N. D. Dutt, A. C.-H. Wu, and S. Y.-L. Lin. 1992. *High-Level Synthesis: Introduction to Chip and System Design.* Norwell, MA: Kluwer. ISBN 0-7923-9194-2. TK7874.H52422. Chapter 6, Partitioning, is an introduction to system-level partitioning algorithms. It also includes a description of the system partitioning features of SpecSyn, a research tool developed at UC-Irvine. [p. 850]

Goto, S., and T. Matsud. 1986. "Partitioning, assignment and placement." In *Layout Design and Verification.* Vol. 4 of *Advances in CAD for VLSI* (T. Ohtsuki, Ed.) pp. 55–97, New York: Elsevier. [p. 826]

Kernighan, B. W., and S. Lin. 1970. "An efficient heuristic procedure for partitioning graphs." *Bell Systems Technical Journal,* Vol. 49, no. 2, February, pp. 291–307. The original description of the Kernighan–Lin partitioning algorithm. [p. 828]

Kirkpatrick, S., et al. 1983. "Optimization by simulated annealing." *Science,* Vol. 220, no. 4598, pp. 671–680. [p. 836]

Kucukcakar, K., and A. C. Parker, 1991. "CHOP: A constraint-driven system-level partitioner." In *Proceedings of the 28th Design Automation Conference*, pp. 514–519. [p. 851]

Lagnese, E., and D. Thomas. 1991. "Architectural partitioning for system level synthesis of integrated circuits." *IEEE Transactions on Computer-Aided Design of Integrated Circuits and Systems,* Vol. 10, no. 7, pp. 847–860. [p. 850]

Najm, F. N. 1994. "A survey of power estimation techniques in VLSI circuits." *IEEE Transactions on Very Large Scale Integration (VLSI) Systems,* Vol. 2, no. 4, pp. 446–455. 43 refs. [p. 817]

Preas, B. T., and P. G. Karger, 1988. "Placement, assignment and floorplanning." In *Physical Design Automation of VLSI Systems* (B. T. Preas and M. J. Lorenzetti, Eds.), pp. 87–155. Menlo Park, CA: Benjamin-Cummings. ISBN 0-8053-0412-9. TK7874.P47. [p. 850]

Rose, J., W. Klebsch, and J. Wolf, 1990. "Temperature measurement and equilibrium dynamics of simulated annealing placements." *IEEE Transactions on Computer-Aided Design of Integrated Circuits and Systems,* Vol. 9, no. 3, pp. 253–259. Discusses ways to speed up simulated annealing. [p. 837]

Schweikert, D. G., and B. W. Kernighan. 1979. "A proper model for the partitioning of electrical circuits." In *Proceedings of the 9th Design Automation Workshop.* Points out the difference between nets and edges. [pp. 831, 831]

Sechen, C. 1988. *VLSI Placement and Global Routing Using Simulated Annealing.* New York: Kluwer. Introduction; The Simulated Annealing Algorithm; Placement and Global Routing of Standard Cell Integrated Circuits; Macro/Custom Cell Chip-Planning, Placement, and Global Routing; Average Interconnection Length Estimation; Interconnect-Area Estimation for Macro Cell Placements; An Edge-Based Channel Definition Algorithm for Rectilinear Cells; A Graph-Based Global Router Algorithm; Conclusion; Island-Style Gate Array Placement. [p. 850]

Sedgewick, R. 1988. *Algorithms.* Reading, MA: Addison-Wesley. ISBN 0-201-06673-4. QA76.6.S435. Reference for basic sorting and graph-searching algorithms. [p. 808]

Sherwani, N. A. 1993. *Algorithms for VLSI Physical Design Automation.* Norwell, MA: Kluwer. ISBN 0-7923-9294-9. TK874.S455. [p. 850]

Smailagic, A., et al. 1995. "Benchmarking an interdisciplinary concurrent design methodology for electronic/mechanical systems." In *Proceedings of the 32nd Design Automation Conference.* San Francisco. Describes the evolution of the VuMan wearable computer. Includes some interesting measures of the complexity of system design. [p. 840]

Veendrick, H. J. M. 1984. "Short-circuit dissipation of static CMOS circuitry and its impact on the design of buffer circuits." *IEEE Journal of Solid-State Circuits,* Vol. SC-19, no. 4, pp. 468–473. [pp. 817, 843]

FLOORPLANNING AND PLACEMENT

16

16.1   Floorplanning

16.2   Placement

16.3   Physical Design Flow

16.4   Information Formats

16.5   Summary

16.6   Problems

16.7   Bibliography

16.8   References

The input to the floorplanning step is the output of system partitioning and design entry—a netlist. Floorplanning precedes placement, but we shall cover them together. The output of the placement step is a set of directions for the routing tools.

At the start of floorplanning we have a netlist describing circuit blocks, the logic cells within the blocks, and their connections. For example, Figure 16.1 shows the Viterbi decoder example as a collection of standard cells with no room set aside yet for routing. We can think of the standard cells as a hod of bricks to be made into a wall. What we have to do now is set aside spaces (we call these spaces the **channels**) for interconnect, the mortar, and arrange the cells. Figure 16.2 shows a finished wall—after floorplanning and placement steps are complete. We still have not completed any routing at this point—that comes later—all we have done is placed the logic cells in a fashion that we hope will minimize the total interconnect length, for example.

16.1 Floorplanning

Figure 16.3 shows that both interconnect delay and gate delay decrease as we scale down feature sizes—but at different rates. This is because interconnect capacitance tends to a limit of about $2\,\mathrm{pFcm}^{-1}$ for a minimum-width wire while gate delay continues to decrease (see Section 17.4, "Circuit Extraction and DRC"). Floorplanning allows us to predict this interconnect delay by estimating interconnect length.

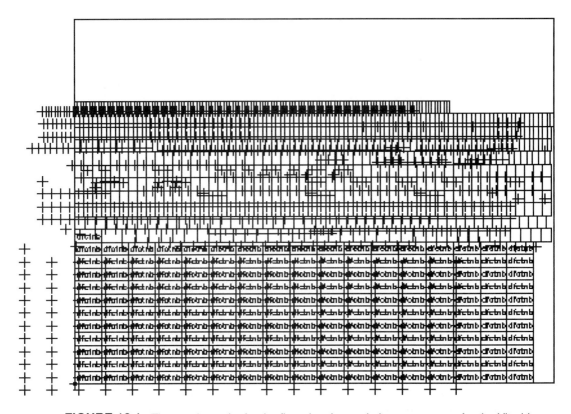

FIGURE 16.1 The starting point for the floorplanning and placement steps for the Viterbi decoder (containing only standard cells). This is the initial display of the floorplanning and placement tool. The small boxes that look like bricks are the outlines of the standard cells. The largest standard cells, at the bottom of the display (labeled dfctnb) are 188 D flip-flops. The '+' symbols represent the drawing origins of the standard cells—for the D flip-flops they are shifted to the left and below the logic cell bottom left-hand corner. The large box surrounding all the logic cells represents the estimated chip size. (This is a screen shot from Cadence Cell Ensemble.)

16.1.1 Floorplanning Goals and Objectives

The input to a floorplanning tool is a hierarchical netlist that describes the interconnection of the **blocks** (RAM, ROM, ALU, cache controller, and so on); the logic cells (NAND, NOR, D flip-flop, and so on) within the blocks; and the logic cell connectors (the terms *terminals, pins,* or *ports* mean the same thing as *connectors*). The netlist is a logical description of the ASIC; the floorplan is a physical description of an ASIC. Floorplanning is thus a mapping between the logical description (the netlist) and the physical description (the floorplan).

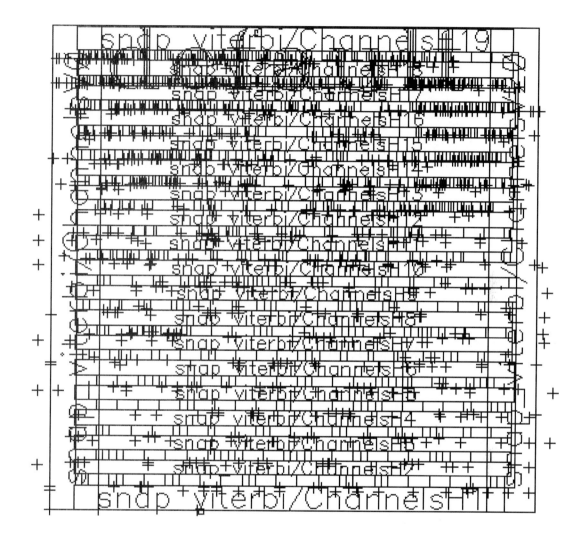

FIGURE 16.2 The Viterbi Decoder (from Figure 16.1) after floorplanning and placement. There are 18 rows of standard cells separated by 17 horizontal channels (labeled 2–18). The channels are routed as numbered. In this example, the I/O pads are omitted to show the cell placement more clearly. Figure 17.1 shows the same placement without the channel labels. (A screen shot from Cadence Cell Ensemble.)

The goals of floorplanning are to:

- arrange the blocks on a chip,
- decide the location of the I/O pads,
- decide the location and number of the power pads,

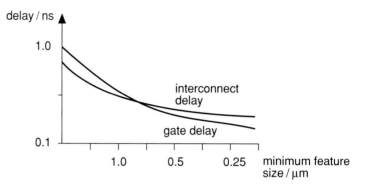

FIGURE 16.3 Interconnect and gate delays. As feature sizes decrease, both average interconnect delay and average gate delay decrease—but at different rates. This is because interconnect capacitance tends to a limit that is independent of scaling. Interconnect delay now dominates gate delay.

- decide the type of power distribution, and

- decide the location and type of clock distribution.

The objectives of floorplanning are to minimize the chip area and minimize delay. Measuring area is straightforward, but measuring delay is more difficult and we shall explore this next.

16.1.2   Measurement of Delay in Floorplanning

Throughout the ASIC design process we need to predict the performance of the final layout. In floorplanning we wish to predict the interconnect delay before we complete any routing. Imagine trying to predict how long it takes to get from Russia to China without knowing where in Russia we are or where our destination is in China. Actually it is worse, because in floorplanning we may move Russia or China.

To predict delay we need to know the **parasitics** associated with interconnect: the **interconnect capacitance** (**wiring capacitance** or **routing capacitance**) as well as the interconnect resistance. At the floorplanning stage we know only the **fanout** (**FO**) of a net (the number of gates driven by a net) and the size of the block that the net belongs to. We cannot predict the resistance of the various pieces of the interconnect path since we do not yet know the shape of the interconnect for a net. However, we can estimate the total length of the interconnect and thus estimate the total capacitance. We estimate interconnect length by collecting statistics from previously routed chips and analyzing the results. From these statistics we create tables that predict the interconnect capacitance as a function of net fanout and block size. A floorplanning tool can then use these **predicted-capacitance tables** (also known as **interconnect-load tables** or **wire-load tables**). Figure 16.4 shows how we derive and use wire-load tables and illustrates the following facts:

- Typically between 60 and 70 percent of nets have a FO = 1.

- The distribution for a FO = 1 has a very long tail, stretching to interconnects that run from corner to corner of the chip.

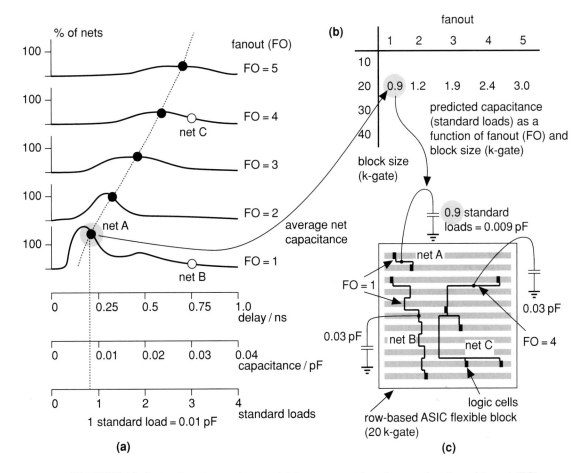

FIGURE 16.4 Predicted capacitance. (a) Interconnect lengths as a function of fanout (FO) and circuit-block size. (b) Wire-load table. There is only one capacitance value for each fanout (typically the average value). (c) The wire-load table predicts the capacitance and delay of a net (with a considerable error). Net A and net B both have a fanout of 1, both have the same predicted net delay, but net B in fact has a much greater delay than net A in the actual layout (of course we shall not know what the actual layout is until much later in the design process).

- The distribution for a FO = 1 often has two peaks, corresponding to a distribution for close neighbors in subgroups within a block, superimposed on a distribution corresponding to routing between subgroups.

- We often see a twin-peaked distribution at the chip level also, corresponding to separate distributions for **interblock routing** (inside blocks) and **intrablock routing** (between blocks).

- The distributions for FO > 1 are more symmetrical and flatter than for FO = 1.
- The wire-load tables can only contain one number, for example the average net capacitance, for any one distribution. Many tools take a worst-case approach and use the 80- or 90-percentile point instead of the average. Thus a tool may use a predicted capacitance for which we know 90 percent of the nets will have less than the estimated capacitance.
- We need to repeat the statistical analysis for blocks with different sizes. For example, a net with a FO = 1 in a 25 k-gate block will have a different (larger) average length than if the net were in a 5 k-gate block.
- The statistics depend on the shape (aspect ratio) of the block (usually the statistics are only calculated for square blocks).
- The statistics will also depend on the type of netlist. For example, the distributions will be different for a netlist generated by setting a constraint for minimum logic delay during synthesis—which tends to generate large numbers of two-input NAND gates—than for netlists generated using minimum-area constraints.

There are no standards for the wire-load tables themselves, but there are some standards for their use and for presenting the extracted loads (see Section 16.4). Wire-load tables often present loads in terms of a **standard load** that is usually the input capacitance of a two-input NAND gate with a 1X (default) drive strength.

TABLE 16.1   A wire-load table showing average interconnect lengths (mm).[1]

| Array (available gates) | Chip size (mm) | Fanout | | |
		1	2	4
3 k	3.45	0.56	0.85	1.46
11 k	5.11	0.84	1.34	2.25
105 k	12.50	1.75	2.70	4.92

[1] Interconnect lengths are derived from interconnect capacitance data. Interconnect capacitance is $2\,\mathrm{pFcm^{-1}}$.

Table 16.1 shows the estimated metal interconnect lengths, as a function of die size and fanout, for a series of three-level metal gate arrays. In this case the interconnect capacitance is about $2\,\mathrm{pFcm^{-1}}$, a typical figure.

Figure 16.5 shows that, because we do not decrease chip size as we scale down feature size, the worst-case interconnect delay increases. One way to measure the worst-case delay uses an interconnect that completely crosses the chip, a **coast-to-coast interconnect**. In certain cases the worst-case delay of a $0.25\,\mu m$ process may be worse than a $0.35\,\mu m$ process, for example.

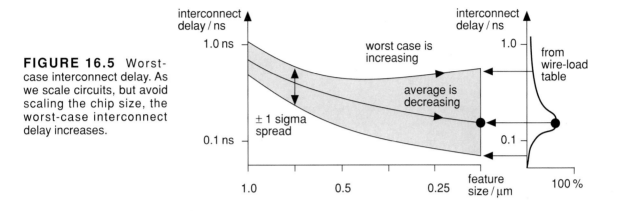

FIGURE 16.5 Worst-case interconnect delay. As we scale circuits, but avoid scaling the chip size, the worst-case interconnect delay increases.

16.1.3 Floorplanning Tools

Figure 16.6(a) shows an initial **random floorplan** generated by a floorplanning tool. Two of the blocks, A and C in this example, are standard-cell areas (the chip shown in Figure 16.1 is one large standard-cell area). These are **flexible blocks** (or **variable blocks**) because, although their total area is fixed, their shape (aspect ratio) and connector locations may be adjusted during the placement step. The dimensions and connector locations of the other **fixed blocks** (perhaps RAM, ROM, compiled cells, or megacells) can only be modified when they are created. We may force logic cells to be in selected flexible blocks by **seeding**. We choose **seed cells** by name. For example, ram_control* would select all logic cells whose names started with ram_control to be placed in one flexible block. The special symbol, usually '*', is a **wildcard symbol**. Seeding may be hard or soft. A **hard seed** is fixed and not allowed to move during the remaining floorplanning and placement steps. A **soft seed** is an initial suggestion only and can be altered if necessary by the floorplanner. We may also use **seed connectors** within flexible blocks—forcing certain nets to appear in a specified order, or location at the boundary of a flexible block.

The floorplanner can complete an estimated placement to determine the positions of connectors at the boundaries of the flexible blocks. Figure 16.6(b) illustrates a **rat's nest** display of the connections between blocks. Connections are shown as **bundles** between the centers of blocks or as **flight lines** between connectors. Figure 16.6(c) and (d) show how we can move the blocks in a floorplanning tool to minimize routing **congestion**.

We need to control the **aspect ratio** of our floorplan because we have to fit our chip into the **die cavity** (a fixed-size hole, usually square) inside a package. Figure 16.7(a)–(c) show how we can rearrange our chip to achieve a square aspect ratio. Figure 16.7(c) also shows a **congestion map**, another form of **routability** display. There is no standard measure of routability. Generally the **interconnect channels**, (or wiring channels—I shall call them channels from now on) have a cer-

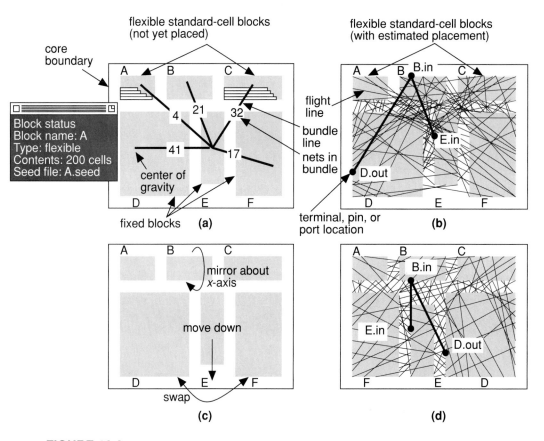

FIGURE 16.6 Floorplanning a cell-based ASIC. (a) Initial floorplan generated by the floor-planning tool. Two of the blocks are flexible (A and C) and contain rows of standard cells (unplaced). A pop-up window shows the status of block A. (b) An estimated placement for flexible blocks A and C. The connector positions are known and a rat's nest display shows the heavy congestion below block B. (c) Moving blocks to improve the floorplan. (d) The updated display shows the reduced congestion after the changes.

tain **channel capacity**; that is, they can handle only a fixed number of interconnects. One measure of congestion is the difference between the number of interconnects that we actually need, called the **channel density**, and the channel capacity. Another measure, shown in Figure 16.7(c), uses the ratio of channel density to the channel capacity. With practice, we can create a good initial placement by floorplanning and a pictorial display. This is one area where the human ability to recognize patterns and spatial relations is currently superior to a computer program's ability.

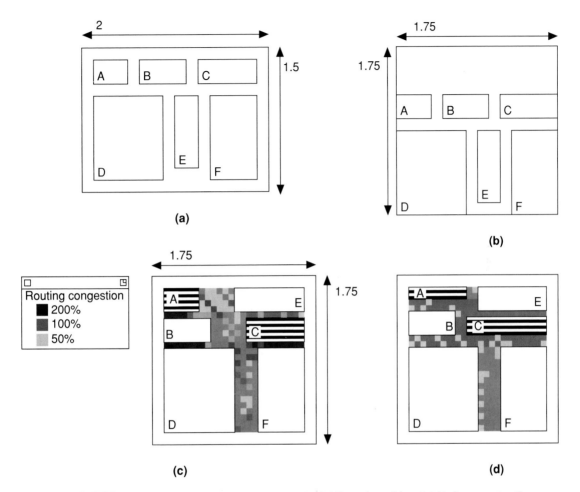

FIGURE 16.7 Congestion analysis. (a) The initial floorplan with a 2:1.5 die aspect ratio. (b) Altering the floorplan to give a 1:1 chip aspect ratio. (c) A trial floorplan with a congestion map. Blocks A and C have been placed so that we know the terminal positions in the channels. Shading indicates the ratio of channel density to the channel capacity. Dark areas show regions that cannot be routed because the channel congestion exceeds the estimated capacity. (d) Resizing flexible blocks A and C alleviates congestion.

16.1.4 Channel Definition

During the floorplanning step we assign the areas between blocks that are to be used for interconnect. This process is known as **channel definition** or **channel allocation**. Figure 16.8 shows a T-shaped junction between two rectangular channels

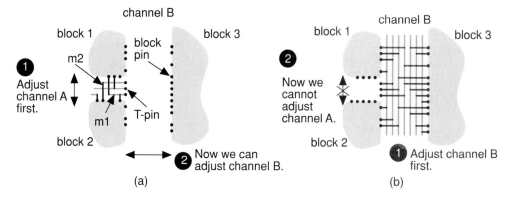

FIGURE 16.8 Routing a T-junction between two channels in two-level metal. The dots represent logic cell pins. (a) Routing channel A (the stem of the T) first allows us to adjust the width of channel B. (b) If we route channel B first (the top of the T), this fixes the width of channel A. We have to route the stem of a T-junction before we route the top.

and illustrates why we must route the stem (vertical) of the T before the bar. The general problem of choosing the order of rectangular channels to route is **channel ordering**.

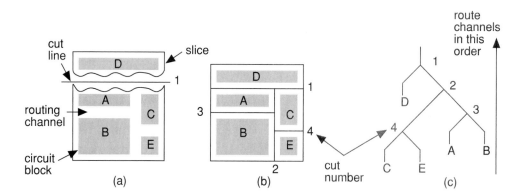

FIGURE 16.9 Defining the channel routing order for a slicing floorplan using a slicing tree. (a) Make a cut all the way across the chip between circuit blocks. Continue slicing until each piece contains just one circuit block. Each cut divides a piece into two without cutting through a circuit block. (b) A sequence of cuts: 1, 2, 3, and 4 that successively slices the chip until only circuit blocks are left. (c) The slicing tree corresponding to the sequence of cuts gives the order in which to route the channels: 4, 3, 2, and finally 1.

Figure 16.9 shows a floorplan of a chip containing several blocks. Suppose we cut along the block boundaries slicing the chip into two pieces (Figure 16.9a). Then suppose we can slice each of these pieces into two. If we can continue in this fashion until all the blocks are separated, then we have a **slicing floorplan** (Figure 16.9b). Figure 16.9(c) shows how the sequence we use to slice the chip defines a hierarchy of the blocks. Reversing the slicing order ensures that we route the stems of all the channel T-junctions first.

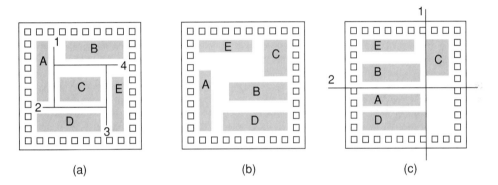

FIGURE 16.10 Cyclic constraints. (a) A nonslicing floorplan with a cyclic constraint that prevents channel routing. (b) In this case it is difficult to find a slicing floorplan without increasing the chip area. (c) This floorplan may be sliced (with initial cuts 1 or 2) and has no cyclic constraints, but it is inefficient in area use and will be very difficult to route.

Figure 16.10 shows a floorplan that is not a slicing structure. We cannot cut the chip all the way across with a knife without chopping a circuit block in two. This means we cannot route any of the channels in this floorplan without routing all of the other channels first. We say there is a **cyclic constraint** in this floorplan. There are two solutions to this problem. One solution is to move the blocks until we obtain a slicing floorplan. The other solution is to allow the use of L-shaped, rather than rectangular, channels (or areas with fixed connectors on all sides—a **switch box**). We need an area-based router rather than a channel router to route L-shaped regions or switch boxes (see Section 17.2.6, "Area-Routing Algorithms").

Figure 16.11(a) displays the floorplan of the ASIC shown in Figure 16.7. We can remove the cyclic constraint by moving the blocks again, but this increases the chip size. Figure 16.11(b) shows an alternative solution. We **merge** the flexible standard cell areas A and C. We can do this by **selective flattening** of the netlist. Sometimes flattening can reduce the routing area because routing between blocks is usually less efficient than routing inside the row-based blocks. Figure 16.11(b) shows the channel definition and **routing order** for our chip.

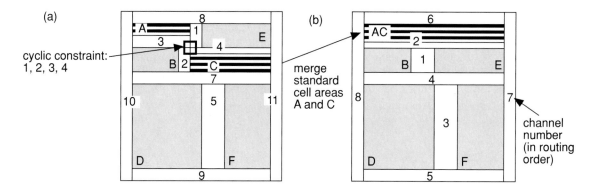

FIGURE 16.11 Channel definition and ordering. (a) We can eliminate the cyclic constraint by merging the blocks A and C. (b) A slicing structure.

16.1.5   I/O and Power Planning

Every chip communicates with the outside world. Signals flow onto and off the chip and we need to supply power. We need to consider the I/O and power constraints early in the floorplanning process. A silicon chip or **die** (plural die, dies, or dice) is mounted on a **chip carrier** inside a chip **package**. Connections are made by **bonding** the chip **pads** to fingers on a metal **lead frame** that is part of the package. The metal lead-frame fingers connect to the **package pins**. A die consists of a logic **core** inside a **pad ring**. Figure 16.12(a) shows a **pad-limited die** and Figure 16.12(b) shows a **core-limited die**. On a pad-limited die we use tall, thin **pad-limited pads**, which maximize the number of pads we can fit around the outside of the chip. On a core-limited die we use short, wide **core-limited pads**. Figure 16.12(c) shows how we can use both types of pad to change the aspect ratio of a die to be different from that of the core.

Special **power pads** are used for the positive supply, or VDD, **power buses** (or **power rails**) and the ground or negative supply, VSS or GND. Usually one set of VDD/VSS pads supplies one **power ring** that runs around the pad ring and supplies power to the I/O pads only. Another set of VDD/VSS pads connects to a second power ring that supplies the logic core. We sometimes call the I/O power **dirty power** since it has to supply large transient currents to the output transistors. We keep dirty power separate to avoid injecting noise into the internal-logic power (the **clean power**). I/O pads also contain special circuits to protect against **electrostatic discharge** (**ESD**). These circuits can withstand very short high-voltage (several kilovolt) pulses that can be generated during human or machine handling.

Depending on the type of package and how the foundry attaches the silicon die to the **chip cavity** in the chip carrier, there may be an electrical connection between the chip carrier and the die substrate. Usually the die is cemented in the chip cavity with a conductive epoxy, making an electrical connection between substrate and the

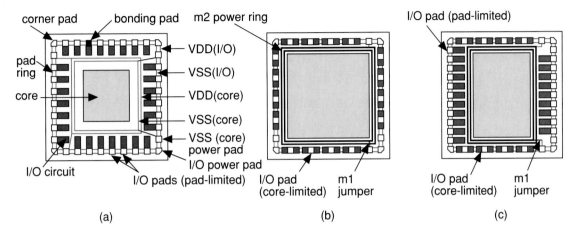

FIGURE 16.12 Pad-limited and core-limited die. (a) A pad-limited die. The number of pads determines the die size. (b) A core-limited die: The core logic determines the die size. (c) Using both pad-limited pads and core-limited pads for a square die.

package cavity in the chip carrier. If we make an electrical connection between the substrate and a chip pad, or to a package pin, it must be to VDD (*n*-type substrate) or VSS (*p*-type substrate). This **substrate connection** (for the whole chip) employs a **down bond** (or drop bond) to the carrier. We have several options:

- We can dedicate one (or more) chip pad(s) to down bond to the chip carrier.
- We can make a connection from a chip pad to the lead frame and down bond from the chip pad to the chip carrier.
- We can make a connection from a chip pad to the lead frame and down bond from the lead frame.
- We can down bond from the lead frame without using a chip pad.
- We can leave the substrate and/or chip carrier unconnected.

Depending on the package design, the type and positioning of down bonds may be fixed. This means we need to fix the position of the chip pad for down bonding using a **pad seed**.

A **double bond** connects two pads to one chip-carrier finger and one package pin. We can do this to save package pins or reduce the series inductance of bond wires (typically a few nanohenries) by parallel connection of the pads. A **multiple-signal pad** or pad group is a set of pads. For example, an **oscillator pad** usually comprises a set of two adjacent pads that we connect to an external crystal. The oscillator circuit and the two signal pads form a single logic cell. Another common example is a **clock pad**. Some foundries allow a special form of **corner pad** (normal pads are **edge pads**) that squeezes two pads into the area at the corners of a chip using a special **two-pad corner cell**, to help meet **bond-wire angle design rules** (see also Figure 16.13b and c).

To reduce the series resistive and inductive impedance of power supply networks, it is normal to use multiple VDD and VSS pads. This is particularly important with the **simultaneously switching outputs** (**SSOs**) that occur when driving buses off-chip [Wada, Eino, and Anami, 1990]. The output pads can easily consume most of the power on a CMOS ASIC, because the load on a pad (usually tens of picofarads) is much larger than typical on-chip capacitive loads. Depending on the technology it may be necessary to provide dedicated VDD and VSS pads for every few SSOs. Design rules set how many SSOs can be used per VDD/VSS pad pair. These dedicated VDD/VSS pads must "follow" groups of output pads as they are seeded or planned on the floorplan. With some chip packages this can become difficult because design rules limit the location of package pins that may be used for supplies (due to the differing series inductance of each pin).

Using a **pad mapping** we translate the **logical pad** in a netlist to a **physical pad** from a **pad library**. We might control pad seeding and mapping in the floorplanner. The handling of I/O pads can become quite complex; there are several nonobvious factors that must be considered when generating a pad ring:

- Ideally we would only need to design library pad cells for one orientation. For example, an edge pad for the south side of the chip, and a corner pad for the southeast corner. We could then generate other orientations by rotation and flipping (mirroring). Some ASIC vendors will not allow rotation or mirroring of logic cells in the mask file. To avoid these problems we may need to have separate horizontal, vertical, left-handed, and right-handed pad cells in the library with appropriate logical to physical pad mappings.

- If we mix pad-limited and core-limited edge pads in the same pad ring, this complicates the design of corner pads. Usually the two types of edge pad cannot abut. In this case a corner pad also becomes a **pad-format changer**, or **hybrid corner pad**.

- In single-supply chips we have one VDD net and one VSS net, both **global power nets**. It is also possible to use **mixed power supplies** (for example, 3.3 V and 5 V) or **multiple power supplies** (digital VDD, analog VDD).

Figure 16.13(a) and (b) are magnified views of the southeast corner of our example chip and show the different types of I/O cells. Figure 16.13(c) shows a **stagger-bond** arrangement using two rows of I/O pads. In this case the design rules for bond wires (the spacing and the angle at which the bond wires leave the pads) become very important.

Figure 16.13(d) shows an **area-bump** bonding arrangement (also known as flip-chip, solder-bump or C4, terms coined by IBM who developed this technology [Masleid, 1991]) used, for example, with **ball-grid array** (**BGA**) packages. Even

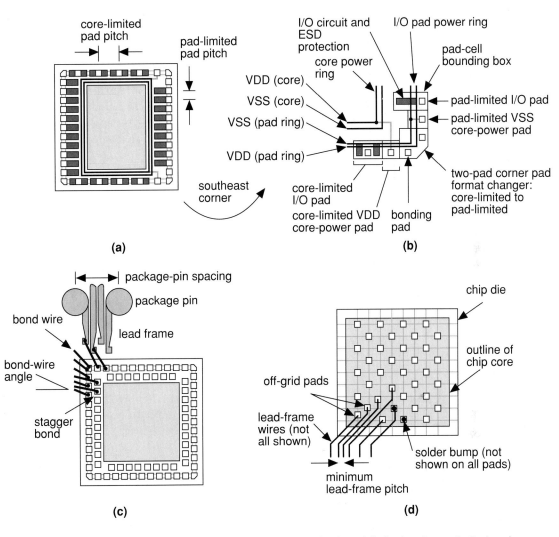

FIGURE 16.13 Bonding pads. (a) This chip uses both pad-limited and core-limited pads. (b) A hybrid corner pad. (c) A chip with stagger-bonded pads. (d) An area-bump bonded chip (or flip-chip). The chip is turned upside down and solder bumps connect the pads to the lead frame.

though the bonding pads are located in the center of the chip, the I/O circuits are still often located at the edges of the chip because of difficulties in power supply distribution and integrating I/O circuits together with logic in the center of the die.

In an MGA the pad spacing and I/O-cell spacing is fixed—each pad occupies a fixed **pad slot** (or **pad site**). This means that the properties of the pad I/O are also fixed but, if we need to, we can parallel adjacent output cells to increase the drive. To increase flexibility further the I/O cells can use a separation, the **I/O-cell pitch**, that is smaller than the **pad pitch**. For example, three 4 mA driver cells can occupy two pad slots. Then we can use two 4 mA output cells in parallel to drive one pad, forming an 8 mA output pad as shown in Figure 16.14. This arrangement also means the I/O pad cells can be changed without changing the base array. This is useful as bonding techniques improve and the pads can be moved closer together.

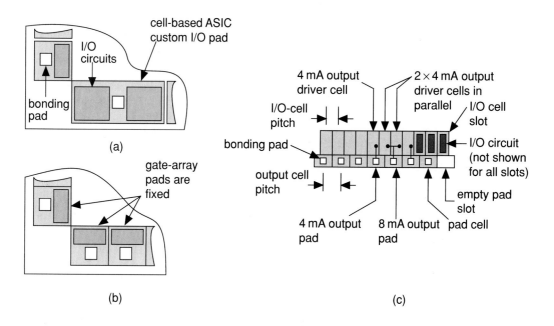

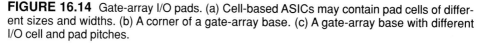

FIGURE 16.14 Gate-array I/O pads. (a) Cell-based ASICs may contain pad cells of different sizes and widths. (b) A corner of a gate-array base. (c) A gate-array base with different I/O cell and pad pitches.

Figure 16.15 shows two possible power distribution schemes. The long direction of a rectangular channel is the **channel spine**. Some automatic routers may require that metal lines parallel to a channel spine use a **preferred layer** (either m1, m2, or m3). Alternatively we say that a particular metal layer runs in a **preferred direction**. Since we can have both horizontal and vertical channels, we may have the situation shown in Figure 16.15, where we have to decide whether to use a preferred layer or the preferred direction for some channels. This may or may not be handled automatically by the routing software.

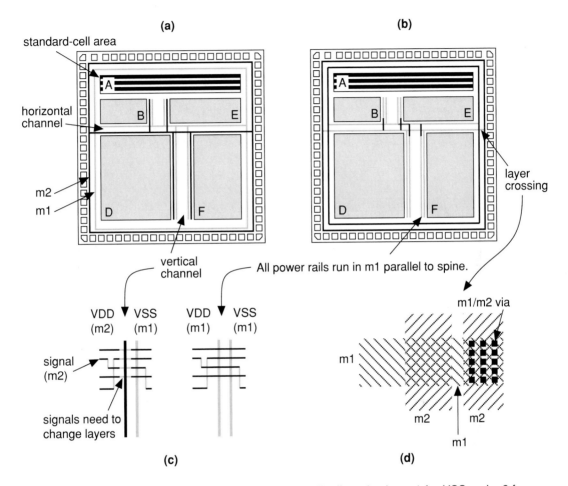

FIGURE 16.15 Power distribution. (a) Power distributed using m1 for VSS and m2 for VDD. This helps minimize the number of vias and layer crossings needed but causes problems in the routing channels. (b) In this floorplan m1 is run parallel to the longest side of all channels, the channel spine. This can make automatic routing easier but may increase the number of vias and layer crossings. (c) An expanded view of part of a channel (interconnect is shown as lines). If power runs on different layers along the spine of a channel, this forces signals to change layers. (d) A closeup of VDD and VSS buses as they cross. Changing layers requires a large number of via contacts to reduce resistance.

16.1.6 Clock Planning

Figure 16.16(a) shows a **clock spine** (not to be confused with a channel spine) routing scheme with all clock pins driven directly from the clock driver. MGAs and FPGAs often use this fish bone type of clock distribution scheme. Figure 16.16(b)

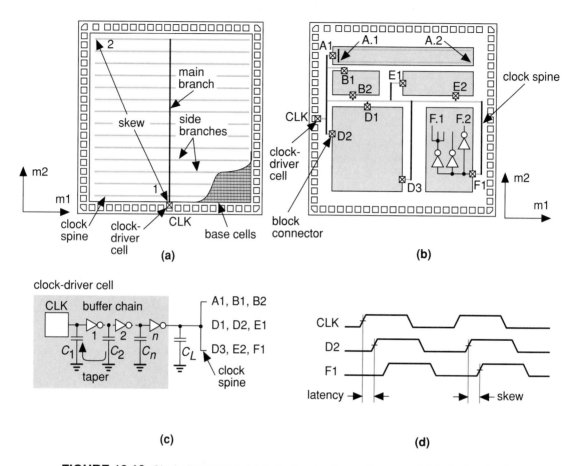

FIGURE 16.16 Clock distribution. (a) A clock spine for a gate array. (b) A clock spine for a cell-based ASIC (typical chips have thousands of clock nets). (c) A clock spine is usually driven from one or more clock-driver cells. Delay in the driver cell is a function of the number of stages and the ratio of output to input capacitance for each stage (taper). (d) Clock latency and clock skew. We would like to minimize both latency and skew.

shows a clock spine for a cell-based ASIC. Figure 16.16(c) shows the clock-driver cell, often part of a special clock-pad cell. Figure 16.16(d) illustrates **clock skew** and **clock latency**. Since all clocked elements are driven from one net with a clock spine, skew is caused by differing interconnect lengths and loads. If the clock-driver delay is much larger than the interconnect delays, a clock spine achieves minimum skew but with long latency.

Clock skew represents a fraction of the clock period that we cannot use for computation. A clock skew of 500 ps with a 200 MHz clock means that we waste 500 ps of every 5 ns clock cycle, or 10 percent of performance. Latency can cause a similar loss of performance at the system level when we need to resynchronize our output signals with a master system clock.

Figure 16.16(c) illustrates the construction of a clock-driver cell. The delay through a chain of CMOS gates is minimized when the ratio between the input capacitance C_1 and the output (load) capacitance C_2 is about 3 (exactly e $\approx$ 2.7, an exponential ratio, if we neglect the effect of parasitics). This means that the fastest way to drive a large load is to use a chain of buffers with their input and output loads chosen to maintain this ratio, or **taper** (we use this as a noun and a verb). This is not necessarily the smallest or lowest-power method, though.

Suppose we have an ASIC with the following specifications:

- 40,000 flip-flops
- Input capacitance of the clock input to each flip-flop is 0.025 pF
- Clock frequency is 200 MHz
- $V_{DD} = 3.3$ V
- Chip size is 20 mm on a side
- Clock spine consists of 200 lines across the chip
- Interconnect capacitance is 2 pFcm^{-1}

In this case the clock-spine capacitance $C_L = 200 \times 2$ cm $\times 2$ pFcm$^{-1} = 800$ pF. If we drive the clock spine with a chain of buffers with taper equal to e $\approx$ 2.7, and with a first-stage input capacitance of 0.025 pF (a reasonable value for a 0.5 μm process), we will need

$$\log \frac{800 \times 10^{-12}}{0.025 \times 10^{-12}} = 10.4 , \quad \text{or 11 stages.} \qquad (16.1)$$

The power dissipated charging the input capacitance of the flip-flop clock is $fC V^2$ or

$$P_1^1 = (4 \times 10^4) \, (200 \text{ MHz}) \, (0.025 \text{ pF}) \, (3.3 \text{ V})^2 = 2.178 \text{ W}, \qquad (16.2)$$

or approximately 2 W. This is only a little larger than the power dissipated driving the 800 pF clock-spine interconnect that we can calculate as follows:

$$P_1^2 = (200) \, (200 \text{ MHz}) \, (20 \text{ mm}) \, (2 \text{ pFcm}^{-1}) \, (3.3 \text{ V})^2 = 1.7424 \text{ W}. \qquad (16.3)$$

All of this power is dissipated in the clock-driver cell. The worst problem, however, is the enormous peak current in the final inverter stage. If we assume the needed rise time is 0.1 ns (with a 200 MHz clock whose period is 5 ns), the peak current would have to approach

$$I = \frac{(800 \text{ pF}) \ (3.3 \text{ V})}{0.1 \text{ ns}} = 25 \text{ A}. \tag{16.4}$$

Clearly such a current is not possible without extraordinary design techniques. Clock spines are used to drive loads of 100–200 pF but, as is apparent from the power dissipation problems of this example, it would be better to find a way to spread the power dissipation more evenly across the chip.

We can design a tree of clock buffers so that the taper of each stage is e ≈ 2.7 by using a fanout of three at each node, as shown in Figure 16.17(a) and (b). The **clock tree**, shown in Figure 16.17(c), uses the same number of stages as a clock spine, but with a lower peak current for the inverter buffers. Figure 16.17(c) illustrates that we now have another problem—we need to balance the delays through the tree carefully to minimize clock skew (see Section 17.3.1, "Clock Routing").

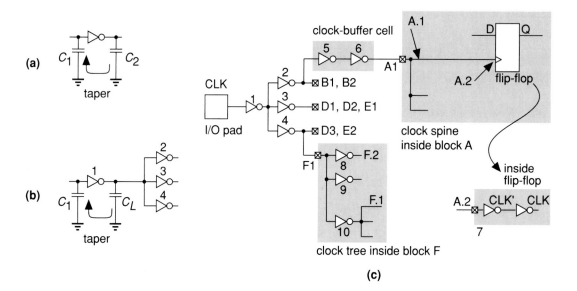

FIGURE 16.17 A clock tree. (a) Minimum delay is achieved when the taper of successive stages is about 3. (b) Using a fanout of three at successive nodes. (c) A clock tree for the cell-based ASIC of Figure 16.16b. We have to balance the clock arrival times at all of the leaf nodes to minimize clock skew.

Designing a clock tree that balances the rise and fall times at the leaf nodes has the beneficial side-effect of minimizing the effect of **hot-electron wearout**. This problem occurs when an electron gains enough energy to become "hot" and jump out of the channel into the gate oxide (the problem is worse for electrons in n-channel devices because electrons are more mobile than holes). The trapped electrons change the threshold voltage of the device and this alters the delay of the buffers. As the buffer delays change with time, this introduces unpredictable skew. The problem is worst when the n-channel device is carrying maximum current with a high voltage across the channel—this occurs during the rise-and fall-time transitions. Balancing the rise and fall times in each buffer means that they all wear out at the same rate, minimizing any additional skew.

A **phase-locked loop** (PLL) is an electronic flywheel that locks in frequency to an input clock signal. The input and output frequencies may differ in phase, however. This means that we can, for example, drive a clock network with a PLL in such a way that the output of the clock network is locked in phase to the incoming clock, thus eliminating the latency of the clock network. A PLL can also help to reduce random variation of the input clock frequency, known as **jitter**, which, since it is unpredictable, must also be discounted from the time available for computation in each clock cycle. Actel was one of the first FPGA vendors to incorporate PLLs, and Actel's online product literature explains their use in ASIC design.

16.2 Placement

After completing a floorplan we can begin placement of the logic cells within the flexible blocks. Placement is much more suited to automation than floorplanning. Thus we shall need measurement techniques and algorithms. After we complete floorplanning and placement, we can predict both intrablock and interblock capacitances. This allows us to return to logic synthesis with more accurate estimates of the capacitive loads that each logic cell must drive.

16.2.1 Placement Terms and Definitions

CBIC, MGA, and FPGA architectures all have rows of logic cells separated by the interconnect—these are **row-based ASICs**. Figure 16.18 shows an example of the interconnect structure for a CBIC. Interconnect runs in horizontal and vertical directions in the channels and in the vertical direction by crossing through the logic cells. Figure 16.18(c) illustrates the fact that it is possible to use **over-the-cell routing** (**OTC** routing) in areas that are not blocked. However, OTC routing is complicated by the fact that the logic cells themselves may contain metal on the routing layers. We shall return to this topic in Section 17.2.7, "Multilevel Routing." Figure 16.19 shows the interconnect structure of a two-level metal MGA.

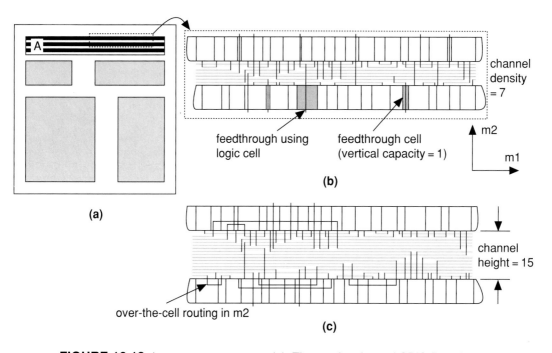

FIGURE 16.18 Interconnect structure. (a) The two-level metal CBIC floorplan shown in Figure 16.11b. (b) A channel from the flexible block A. This channel has a channel height equal to the maximum channel density of 7 (there is room for seven interconnects to run horizontally in m1). (c) A channel that uses OTC (over-the-cell) routing in m2.

Most ASICs currently use two or three levels of metal for signal routing. With two layers of metal, we route within the rectangular channels using the first metal layer for horizontal routing, parallel to the channel spine, and the second metal layer for the vertical direction (if there is a third metal layer it will normally run in the horizontal direction again). The maximum number of horizontal interconnects that can be placed side by side, parallel to the channel spine, is the **channel capacity**.

Vertical interconnect uses **feedthroughs** (or **feedthrus** in the United States) to cross the logic cells. Here are some commonly used terms with explanations (there are no generally accepted definitions):

- An unused **vertical track** (or just **track**) in a logic cell is called an **uncommitted feedthrough** (also **built-in feedthrough**, **implicit feedthrough**, or **jumper**).

- A vertical strip of metal that runs from the top to bottom of a cell (for **double-entry cells**), but has no connections inside the cell, is also called a feedthrough or jumper.

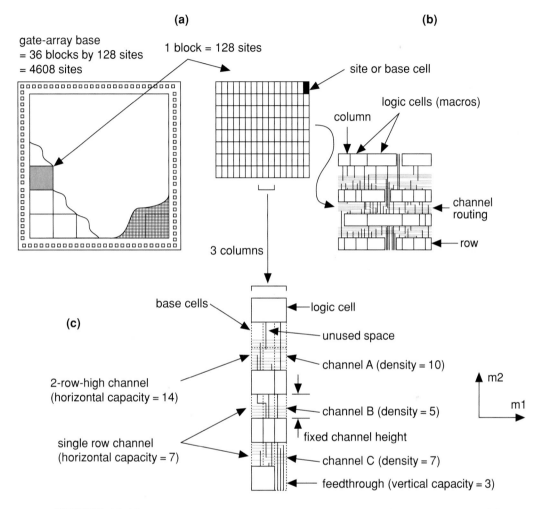

FIGURE 16.19 Gate-array interconnect. (a) A small two-level metal gate array (about 4.6 k-gate). (b) Routing in a block. (c) Channel routing showing channel density and channel capacity. The channel height on a gate array may only be increased in increments of a row. If the interconnect does not use up all of the channel, the rest of the space is wasted. The interconnect in the channel runs in m1 in the horizontal direction with m2 in the vertical direction.

- Two connectors for the same physical net are **electrically equivalent connectors** (or **equipotential connectors**). For double-entry cells these are usually at the top and bottom of the logic cell.
- A dedicated **feedthrough cell** (or **crosser cell**) is an empty cell (with no logic) that can hold one or more vertical interconnects. These are used if there are no other feedthroughs available.

- A **feedthrough pin** or **feedthrough terminal** is an input or output that has connections at both the top and bottom of the standard cell.

- A **spacer cell** (usually the same as a feedthrough cell) is used to fill space in rows so that the ends of all rows in a flexible block may be aligned to connect to power buses, for example.

There is no standard terminology for connectors and the terms can be very confusing. There is a difference between connectors that are joined inside the logic cell using a high-resistance material such as polysilicon and connectors that are joined by low-resistance metal. The high-resistance kind are really two separate **alternative connectors** (that cannot be used as a feedthrough), whereas the low-resistance kind are electrically equivalent connectors. There may be two or more connectors to a logic cell, which are not joined inside the cell, and which must be joined by the router (**must-join connectors**).

There are also **logically equivalent connectors** (or functionally equivalent connectors, sometimes also called just equivalent connectors—which is very confusing). The two inputs of a two-input NAND gate may be logically equivalent connectors. The placement tool can swap these without altering the logic (but the two inputs may have different delay properties, so it is not always a good idea to swap them). There can also be **logically equivalent connector groups**. For example, in an OAI22 (OR-AND-INVERT) gate there are four inputs: A1, A2 are inputs to one OR gate (gate A), and B1, B2 are inputs to the second OR gate (gate B). Then group A = (A1, A2) is logically equivalent to group B = (B1, B2)—if we swap one input (A1 or A2) from gate A to gate B, we must swap the other input in the group (A2 or A1).

In the case of channeled gate arrays and FPGAs, the horizontal interconnect areas—the channels, usually on m1—have a fixed capacity (sometimes they are called **fixed-resource ASICs** for this reason). The channel capacity of CBICs and channelless MGAs can be expanded to hold as many interconnects as are needed. Normally we choose, as an objective, to minimize the number of interconnects that use each channel. In the vertical interconnect direction, usually m2, FPGAs still have fixed resources. In contrast the placement tool can always add vertical feedthroughs to a channeled MGA, channelless MGA, or CBIC. These problems become less important as we move to three and more levels of interconnect.

16.2.2   Placement Goals and Objectives

The goal of a placement tool is to arrange all the logic cells within the flexible blocks on a chip. Ideally, the objectives of the placement step are to

- Guarantee the router can complete the routing step
- Minimize all the critical net delays
- Make the chip as dense as possible

We may also have the following additional objectives:

- Minimize power dissipation
- Minimize cross talk between signals

Objectives such as these are difficult to define in a way that can be solved with an algorithm and even harder to actually meet. Current placement tools use more specific and achievable criteria. The most commonly used placement objectives are one or more of the following:

- Minimize the total estimated interconnect length
- Meet the timing requirements for critical nets
- Minimize the interconnect congestion

Each of these objectives in some way represents a compromise.

16.2.3 Measurement of Placement Goals and Objectives

In order to determine the quality of a placement, we need to be able to measure it. We need an approximate measure of interconnect length, closely correlated with the final interconnect length, that is easy to calculate.

The graph structures that correspond to making all the connections for a net are known as **trees on graphs** (or just **trees**). Special classes of trees—**Steiner trees**—minimize the total length of interconnect and they are central to ASIC routing algorithms. Figure 16.20 shows a minimum Steiner tree. This type of tree uses diagonal connections—we want to solve a restricted version of this problem, using interconnects on a rectangular grid. This is called **rectilinear routing** or **Manhattan routing** (because of the east–west and north–south grid of streets in Manhattan). We say that the **Euclidean distance** between two points is the straight-line distance ("as the crow flies"). The **Manhattan distance** (or rectangular distance) between two points is the distance we would have to walk in New York.

The **minimum rectilinear Steiner tree** (MRST) is the shortest interconnect using a rectangular grid. The determination of the MRST is in general an NP-complete problem—which means it is hard to solve. For small numbers of terminals heuristic algorithms do exist, but they are expensive to compute. Fortunately we only need to estimate the length of the interconnect. Two approximations to the MRST are shown in Figure 16.21.

The **complete graph** has connections from each terminal to every other terminal [Hanan, Wolff, and Agule, 1973]. The **complete-graph measure** adds all the interconnect lengths of the complete-graph connection together and then divides by $n/2$, where n is the number of terminals. We can justify this since, in a graph with n terminals, $(n-1)$ interconnects will emanate from each terminal to join the other $(n-1)$ terminals in a complete graph connection. That makes $n(n-1)$ interconnects in total. However, we have then made each connection twice. So there are one-half

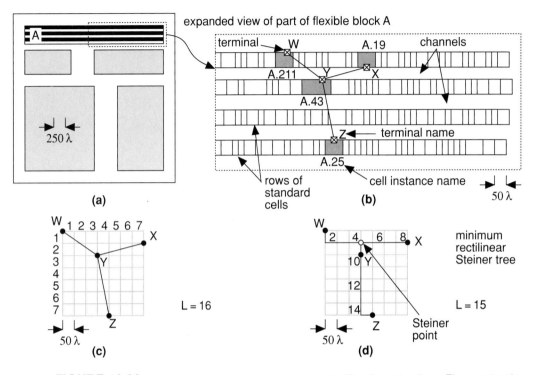

FIGURE 16.20 Placement using trees on graphs. (a) The floorplan from Figure 16.11b. (b) An expanded view of the flexible block A showing four rows of standard cells for placement (typical blocks may contain thousands or tens of thousands of logic cells). We want to find the length of the net shown with four terminals, W through Z, given the placement of four logic cells (labeled: A.211, A.19, A.43, A.25). (c) The problem for net (W, X, Y, Z) drawn as a graph. The shortest connection is the minimum Steiner tree. (d) The minimum rectilinear Steiner tree using Manhattan routing. The rectangular (Manhattan) interconnect-length measures are shown for each tree.

this many, or $n(n-1)/2$, interconnects needed for a complete graph connection. Now we actually only need $(n-1)$ interconnects to join n terminals, so we have $n/2$ times as many interconnects as we really need. Hence we divide the total net length of the complete graph connection by $n/2$ to obtain a more reasonable estimate of minimum interconnect length. Figure 16.21(a) shows an example of the complete-graph measure.

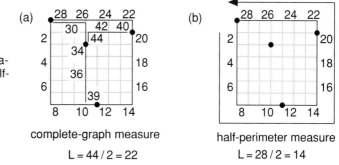

FIGURE 16.21 Interconnect-length measures. (a) Complete-graph measure. (b) Half-perimeter measure.

complete-graph measure

$$L = 44 / 2 = 22$$

half-perimeter measure

$$L = 28 / 2 = 14$$

The **bounding box** is the smallest rectangle that encloses all the terminals (not to be confused with a logic cell bounding box, which encloses all the layout in a logic cell). The **half-perimeter measure** (or bounding-box measure) is one-half the perimeter of the bounding box (Figure 16.21b) [Schweikert, 1976]. For nets with two or three terminals (corresponding to a fanout of one or two, which usually includes over 50 percent of all nets on a chip), the half-perimeter measure is the same as the minimum Steiner tree. For nets with four or five terminals, the minimum Steiner tree is between one and two times the half-perimeter measure [Hanan, 1966]. For a circuit with m nets, using the half-perimeter measure corresponds to minimizing the cost function,

$$f = \frac{1}{2} \sum_{i=1}^{m} h_i \, , \tag{16.5}$$

where h_i is the half-perimeter measure for net i.

It does not really matter if our approximations are inaccurate if there is a good correlation between actual interconnect lengths (after routing) and our approximations. Figure 16.22 shows that we can adjust the complete-graph and half-perimeter measures using correction factors [Goto and Matsuda, 1986]. Now our wiring length approximations are functions, not just of the terminal positions, but also of the number of terminals, and the size of the bounding box. One practical example adjusts a Steiner-tree approximation using the number of terminals [Chao, Nequist, and Vuong, 1990]. This technique is used in the Cadence Gate Ensemble placement tool, for example.

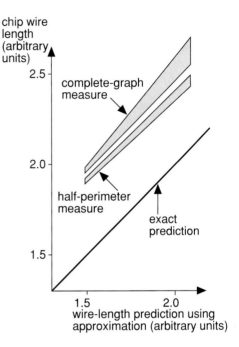

FIGURE 16.22 Correlation between total length of chip interconnect and the half-perimeter and complete-graph measures.

One problem with the measurements we have described is that the MRST may only approximate the interconnect that will be completed by the detailed router. Some programs have a **meander factor** that specifies, on average, the ratio of the interconnect created by the routing tool to the interconnect-length estimate used by the placement tool. Another problem is that we have concentrated on finding estimates to the MRST, but the MRST that minimizes total net length may not minimize net delay (see Section 16.2.8).

There is no point in minimizing the interconnect length if we create a placement that is too congested to route. If we use minimum **interconnect congestion** as an additional placement objective, we need some way of measuring it. What we are trying to measure is interconnect density. Unfortunately we always use the term *density* to mean channel density (which we shall discuss in Section 17.2.2, "Measurement of Channel Density"). In this chapter, while we are discussing placement, we shall try to use the term *congestion*, instead of density, to avoid any confusion.

One measure of interconnect congestion uses the **maximum cut line**. Imagine a horizontal or vertical line drawn anywhere across a chip or block, as shown in Figure 16.23. The number of interconnects that must cross this line is the **cut size** (the number of interconnects we cut). The maximum cut line has the highest cut size.

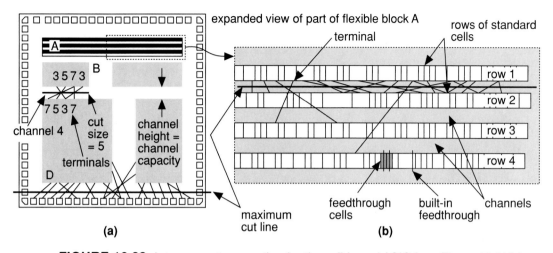

FIGURE 16.23 Interconnect congestion for the cell-based ASIC from Figure 16.11(b). (a) Measurement of congestion. (b) An expanded view of flexible block A shows a maximum cut line.

Many placement tools minimize estimated interconnect length or interconnect congestion as objectives. The problem with this approach is that a logic cell may be placed a long way from another logic cell to which it has just one connection. This logic cell with one connection is less important as far as the total wire length is concerned than other logic cells, to which there are many connections. However, the one long connection may be critical as far as timing delay is concerned. As technology is scaled, interconnection delays become larger relative to circuit delays and this problem gets worse.

In **timing-driven placement** we must estimate delay for every net for every trial placement, possibly for hundreds of thousands of gates. We cannot afford to use anything other than the very simplest estimates of net delay. Unfortunately, the minimum-length Steiner tree does not necessarily correspond to the interconnect path that minimizes delay. To construct a minimum-delay path we may have to route with non-Steiner trees. In the placement phase typically we take a simple interconnect-length approximation to this minimum-delay path (typically the half-perimeter measure). Even when we can estimate the length of the interconnect, we do not yet have information on which layers and how many vias the interconnect will use or how wide it will be. Some tools allow us to include estimates for these parameters. Often we can specify **metal usage**, the percentage of routing on the different layers to expect from the router. This allows the placement tool to estimate RC values and delays—and thus minimize delay.

16.2.4   Placement Algorithms

There are two classes of placement algorithms commonly used in commercial CAD tools: constructive placement and iterative placement improvement. A **constructive placement method** uses a set of rules to arrive at a constructed placement. The most commonly used methods are variations on the **min-cut algorithm**. The other commonly used constructive placement algorithm is the **eigenvalue method**. As in system partitioning, placement usually starts with a constructed solution and then improves it using an iterative algorithm. In most tools we can specify the locations and relative placements of certain critical logic cells as **seed placements**.

The **min-cut placement** method uses successive application of partitioning [Breuer, 1977]. The following steps are shown in Figure 16.24:

1. Cut the placement area into two pieces.

2. Swap the logic cells to minimize the cut cost.

3. Repeat the process from step 1, cutting smaller pieces until all the logic cells are placed.

Usually we divide the placement area into **bins**. The size of a bin can vary, from a bin size equal to the base cell (for a gate array) to a bin size that would hold several logic cells. We can start with a large bin size, to get a rough placement, and then reduce the bin size to get a final placement.

The **eigenvalue placement algorithm** uses the cost matrix or weighted **connectivity matrix** (eigenvalue methods are also known as **spectral methods**) [Hall, 1970]. The measure we use is a cost function f that we shall minimize, given by

$$f = \frac{1}{2} \sum_{i,j=1}^{n} c_{ij} \, d_{ij}^{\,2} \, , \tag{16.6}$$

where $\mathbf{C} = [c_{ij}]$ is the (possibly weighted) connectivity matrix, and d_{ij} is the Euclidean distance between the centers of logic cell i and logic cell j. Since we are going to minimize a cost function that is the square of the distance between logic cells, these methods are also known as **quadratic placement** methods. This type of cost function leads to a simple mathematical solution. We can rewrite the cost function f in matrix form:

$$f = \frac{1}{2} \sum_{i,j=1}^{n} c_{ij} (x_i - x_j)^2 + (y_i - y_j)^2 = \mathbf{x}^T \mathbf{B} \mathbf{x} + \mathbf{y}^T \mathbf{B} \mathbf{y} \, , \tag{16.7}$$

In Eq. 16.7, $\mathbf{B}$ is a symmetric matrix, the **disconnection matrix** (also called the Laplacian).

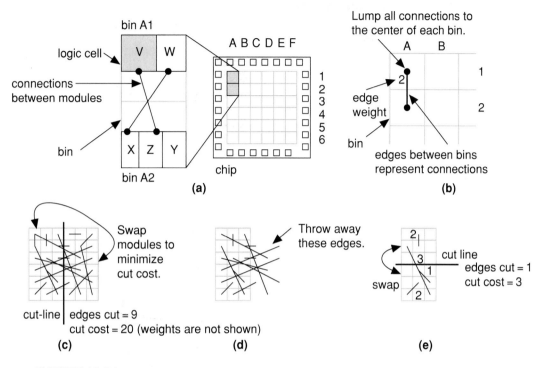

FIGURE 16.24 Min-cut placement. (a) Divide the chip into bins using a grid. (b) Merge all connections to the center of each bin. (c) Make a cut and swap logic cells between bins to minimize the cost of the cut. (d) Take the cut pieces and throw out all the edges that are not inside the piece. (e) Repeat the process with a new cut and continue until we reach the individual bins.

We may express the Laplacian **B** in terms of the connectivity matrix **C**; and **D**, a diagonal matrix (known as the degree matrix), defined as follows:

$$\mathbf{B} = \mathbf{D} - \mathbf{C}; \; d_{ii} = \sum_{j=1}^{n} c_{ij}, \; i = 1, \ldots, n; \; d_{ij} = 0, \; i \neq j. \tag{16.8}$$

We can simplify the problem by noticing that it is symmetric in the x- and y-coordinates. Let us solve the simpler problem of minimizing the cost function for the placement of logic cells along just the x-axis first. We can then apply this solution to the more general two-dimensional placement problem. Before we solve this simpler problem, we introduce a constraint that the coordinates of the logic cells must correspond to valid positions (the cells do not overlap and they are placed on-grid). We make another simplifying assumption that all logic cells are the same size and we must place them in fixed positions. We can define a vector **p** consisting of the valid positions:

$$\mathbf{p} = [p_1, ..., p_n] \,. \tag{16.9}$$

For a valid placement the x-coordinates of the logic cells,

$$\mathbf{x} = [x_1, ..., x_n] \,, \tag{16.10}$$

must be a permutation of the fixed positions, **p**. We can show that requiring the logic cells to be in fixed positions in this way leads to a series of n equations restricting the values of the logic cell coordinates [Cheng and Kuh, 1984]. If we impose all of these constraint equations the problem becomes very complex. Instead we choose just one of the equations:

$$\sum_{i=1}^{n} x_i^2 = \sum_{i=1}^{n} p_i^2 \,. \tag{16.11}$$

Simplifying the problem in this way will lead to an approximate solution to the placement problem. We can write this single constraint on the x-coordinates in matrix form:

$$\mathbf{x}^T \mathbf{x} = P; \qquad P = \sum_{i=1}^{n} p_i^2 \,, \tag{16.12}$$

where P is a constant. We can now summarize the formulation of the problem, with the simplifications that we have made, for a one-dimensional solution. We must minimize a cost function, g (analogous to the cost function f that we defined for the two-dimensional problem in Eq. 16.7), where

$$g = \mathbf{x}^T \mathbf{B} \mathbf{x} \tag{16.13}$$

subject to the constraint:

$$\mathbf{x}^T \mathbf{x} = P \,. \tag{16.14}$$

This is a standard problem that we can solve using a Lagrangian multiplier:

$$\Lambda = \mathbf{x}^T \mathbf{B} \mathbf{x} - \lambda [\mathbf{x}^T \mathbf{x} - P] \,. \tag{16.15}$$

To find the value of **x** that minimizes g we differentiate Λ partially with respect to **x** and set the result equal to zero. We get the following equation:

$$[\mathbf{B} - \lambda \mathbf{I}] \mathbf{x} = \mathbf{0} \,. \tag{16.16}$$

This last equation is called the **characteristic equation** for the disconnection matrix **B** and occurs frequently in matrix algebra (this λ has nothing to do with scaling). The solutions to this equation are the **eigenvectors** and **eigenvalues** of **B**. Multiplying Eq. 16.16 by $\mathbf{x}^T$ we get:

$$\lambda \mathbf{x}^T \mathbf{x} = \mathbf{x}^T \mathbf{B} \mathbf{x} .$$ (16.17)

However, since we imposed the constraint $\mathbf{x}^T \mathbf{x} = P$ and $\mathbf{x}^T \mathbf{B} \mathbf{x} = g$, then

$$\lambda = \frac{g}{P} .$$ (16.18)

The eigenvectors of the disconnection matrix **B** are the solutions to our placement problem. It turns out that (because something called the rank of matrix **B** is $n-1$) there is a degenerate solution with all x-coordinates equal ($\lambda = 0$)—this makes some sense because putting all the logic cells on top of one another certainly minimizes the interconnect. The smallest, nonzero, eigenvalue and the corresponding eigenvector provides the solution that we want. In the two-dimensional placement problem, the x- and y-coordinates are given by the eigenvectors corresponding to the two smallest, nonzero, eigenvalues. (In the next section a simple example illustrates this mathematical derivation.)

16.2.5   Eigenvalue Placement Example

Consider the following connectivity matrix **C** and its disconnection matrix **B**, calculated from Eq. 16.8 [Hall, 1970]:

$$\mathbf{C} = \begin{bmatrix} 0 & 0 & 0 & 1 \\ 0 & 0 & 1 & 1 \\ 0 & 1 & 0 & 0 \\ 1 & 1 & 0 & 0 \end{bmatrix}; \ \mathbf{B} = \begin{bmatrix} 1 & 0 & 0 & 0 \\ 0 & 2 & 0 & 0 \\ 0 & 0 & 1 & 0 \\ 0 & 0 & 0 & 2 \end{bmatrix} - \begin{bmatrix} 0 & 0 & 0 & 1 \\ 0 & 0 & 1 & 1 \\ 0 & 1 & 0 & 0 \\ 1 & 1 & 0 & 0 \end{bmatrix} = \begin{bmatrix} 1 & 0 & 0 & -1 \\ 0 & 2 & -1 & -1 \\ 0 & -1 & 1 & 0 \\ -1 & -1 & 0 & 2 \end{bmatrix} .$$ (16.19)

Figure 16.25(a) shows the corresponding network with four logic cells (1–4) and three nets (A-C). Here is a MatLab script to find the eigenvalues and eigenvectors of **B**:

```
C=[0 0 0 1; 0 0 1 1; 0 1 0 0; 1 1 0 0]
D=[1 0 0 0; 0 2 0 0; 0 0 1 0; 0 0 0 2]
B=D-C
[X,D] = eig(B)
```

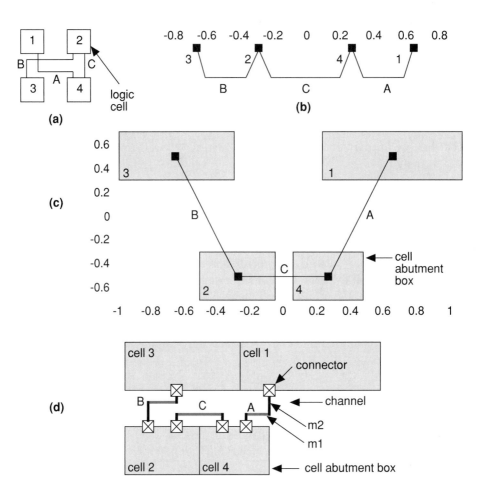

FIGURE 16.25 Eigenvalue placement. (a) An example network. (b) The one-dimensional placement.The small black squares represent the centers of the logic cells. (c) The two-dimensional placement. The eigenvalue method takes no account of the logic cell sizes or actual location of logic cell connectors. (d) A complete layout. We snap the logic cells to valid locations, leaving room for the routing in the channel.

Running this script, we find the eigenvalues of **B** are 0.5858, 0.0, 2.0, and 3.4142. The corresponding eigenvectors of **B** are

$$
\begin{bmatrix}
0.6533 & 0.5000 & 0.5000 & -0.2706 \\
-0.2706 & 0.5000 & -0.5000 & -0.6533 \\
-0.6533 & 0.5000 & 0.5000 & 0.2706 \\
0.2706 & 0.5000 & -0.5000 & 0.6533
\end{bmatrix} .
\tag{16.20}
$$

For a one-dimensional placement (Figure 16.25b), we use the eigenvector (0.6533, –0.2706, –0.6533, –0.2706) corresponding to the smallest nonzero eigenvalue (which is 0.5858) to place the logic cells along the x-axis. The two-dimensional placement (Figure 16.25c) uses these same values for the x-coordinates and the eigenvector (0.5, –0.5, 0.5, –0.5) that corresponds to the next largest eigenvalue (which is 2.0) for the y-coordinates. Notice that the placement shown in Figure 16.25(c), which shows logic-cell outlines (the logic-cell abutment boxes), takes no account of the cell sizes, and cells may even overlap at this stage. This is because, in Eq. 16.11, we discarded all but one of the constraints necessary to ensure valid solutions. Often we use the approximate eigenvalue solution as an initial placement for one of the iterative improvement algorithms that we shall discuss in Section 16.2.6.

16.2.6 Iterative Placement Improvement

An **iterative placement improvement** algorithm takes an existing placement and tries to improve it by moving the logic cells. There are two parts to the algorithm:

- The selection criteria that decides which logic cells to try moving.
- The measurement criteria that decides whether to move the selected cells.

There are several **interchange** or **iterative exchange** methods that differ in their selection and measurement criteria:

- pairwise interchange,
- force-directed interchange,
- force-directed relaxation, and
- force-directed pairwise relaxation.

All of these methods usually consider only pairs of logic cells to be exchanged. A source logic cell is picked for trial exchange with a destination logic cell. We have already discussed the use of interchange methods applied to the system partitioning step. The most widely used methods use group migration, especially the Kernighan–Lin algorithm. The **pairwise-interchange algorithm** is similar to the interchange algorithm used for iterative improvement in the system partitioning step:

1. Select the source logic cell at random.
2. Try all the other logic cells in turn as the destination logic cell.
3. Use any of the measurement methods we have discussed to decide on whether to accept the interchange.
4. The process repeats from step 1, selecting each logic cell in turn as a source logic cell.

Figure 16.26(a) and (b) show how we can extend pairwise interchange to swap more than two logic cells at a time. If we swap λ logic cells at a time and find a locally optimum solution, we say that solution is λ-**optimum**. The **neighborhood exchange algorithm** is a modification to pairwise interchange that considers only

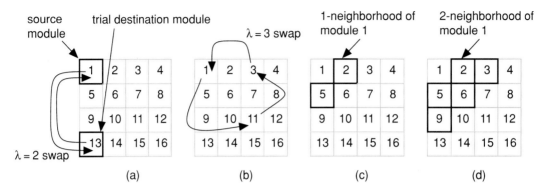

FIGURE 16.26 Interchange. (a) Swapping the source logic cell with a destination logic cell in pairwise interchange. (b) Sometimes we have to swap more than two logic cells at a time to reach an optimum placement, but this is expensive in computation time. Limiting the search to neighborhoods reduces the search time. Logic cells within a distance ε of a logic cell form an ε-neighborhood. (c) A one-neighborhood. (d) A two-neighborhood.

destination logic cells in a **neighborhood**—cells within a certain distance, ε, of the source logic cell. Limiting the search area for the destination logic cell to the **ε-neighborhood** reduces the search time. Figure 16.26(c) and (d) show the one- and two-neighborhoods (based on Manhattan distance) for a logic cell.

Neighborhoods are also used in some of the **force-directed placement methods**. Imagine identical springs connecting all the logic cells we wish to place. The number of springs is equal to the number of connections between logic cells. The effect of the springs is to pull connected logic cells together. The more highly connected the logic cells, the stronger the pull of the springs. The force on a logic cell i due to logic cell j is given by **Hooke's law**, which says the force of a spring is proportional to its extension:

$$F_{ij} = -c_{ij}x_{ij} \tag{16.21}$$

The vector component x_{ij} is directed from the center of logic cell i to the center of logic cell j. The vector magnitude is calculated as either the Euclidean or Manhattan distance between the logic cell centers. The c_{ij} form the connectivity or cost matrix (the matrix element c_{ij} is the number of connections between logic cell i and logic cell j). If we want, we can also weight the c_{ij} to denote critical connections. Figure 16.27 illustrates the force-directed placement algorithm.

In the definition of connectivity (Section 15.7.1, "Measuring Connectivity") it was pointed out that the network graph does not accurately model connections for nets with more than two terminals. Nets such as clock nets, power nets, and global reset lines have a huge number of terminals. The force-directed placement algorithms usually make special allowances for these situations to prevent the largest

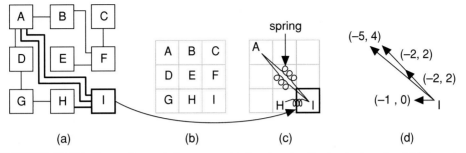

FIGURE 16.27 Force-directed placement. (a) A network with nine logic cells. (b) We make a grid (one logic cell per bin). (c) Forces are calculated as if springs were attached to the centers of each logic cell for each connection. The two nets connecting logic cells A and I correspond to two springs. (d) The forces are proportional to the spring extensions.

nets from snapping all the logic cells together. In fact, without external forces to counteract the pull of the springs between logic cells, the network will collapse to a single point as it settles. An important part of force-directed placement is fixing some of the logic cells in position. Normally ASIC designers use the I/O pads or other external connections to act as anchor points or fixed seeds.

Figure 16.28 illustrates the different kinds of force-directed placement algorithms. The **force-directed interchange** algorithm uses the force vector to select a

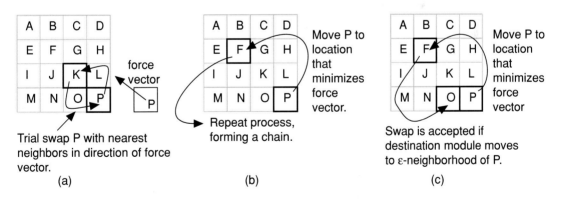

FIGURE 16.28 Force-directed iterative placement improvement. (a) Force-directed interchange. (b) Force-directed relaxation. (c) Force-directed pairwise relaxation.

pair of logic cells to swap. In **force-directed relaxation** a chain of logic cells is moved. The **force-directed pairwise relaxation** algorithm swaps one pair of logic cells at a time.

We reach a force-directed solution when we minimize the energy of the system, corresponding to minimizing the sum of the squares of the distances separating logic cells. Force-directed placement algorithms thus also use a quadratic cost function.

16.2.7   Placement Using Simulated Annealing

The principles of simulated annealing were explained in Section 15.7.8, "Simulated Annealing." Because simulated annealing requires so many iterations, it is critical that the placement objectives be easy and fast to calculate. The optimum connection pattern, the MRST, is difficult to calculate. Using the half-perimeter measure (Section 16.2.3) corresponds to minimizing the total interconnect length. Applying simulated annealing to placement, the algorithm is as follows:

1. Select logic cells for a trial interchange, usually at random.

2. Evaluate the objective function E for the new placement.

3. If ΔE is negative or zero, then exchange the logic cells. If ΔE is positive, then exchange the logic cells with a probability of $\exp(-\Delta E/T)$.

4. Go back to step 1 for a fixed number of times, and then lower the temperature T according to a cooling schedule: $T_{n+1} = 0.9 T_n$, for example.

Kirkpatrick, Gerlatt, and Vecchi first described the use of simulated annealing applied to VLSI problems [1983]. Experience since that time has shown that simulated annealing normally requires the use of a slow cooling schedule and this means long CPU run times [Sechen, 1988; Wong, Leong, and Liu, 1988]. As a general rule, experiments show that simple min-cut based constructive placement is faster than simulated annealing but that simulated annealing is capable of giving better results at the expense of long computer run times. The iterative improvement methods that we described earlier are capable of giving results as good as simulated annealing, but they use more complex algorithms.

While I am making wild generalizations, I will digress to discuss **benchmarks** of placement algorithms (or any CAD algorithm that is random). It is important to remember that the results of random methods are themselves random. Suppose the results from two random algorithms, A and B, can each vary by ±10 percent for any chip placement, but both algorithms have the same average performance. If we compare single chip placements by both algorithms, they could falsely show algorithm A to be better than B by up to 20 percent or vice versa. Put another way, if we run enough test cases we will eventually find some for which A is better than B by 20 percent—a trick that Ph.D. students and marketing managers both know well. Even single run evaluations over multiple chips is hardly a fair comparison. The only way to obtain meaningful results is to compare a statistically meaningful number of runs for a statistically meaningful number of chips for each algorithm. This same caution applies to any VLSI algorithm that is random. There was a Design Automation Conference panel session whose theme was "Enough of algorithms claiming improvements of 5 %."

16.2.8   Timing-Driven Placement Methods

Minimizing delay is becoming more and more important as a placement objective. There are two main approaches: net based and path based. We know that we can use net weights in our algorithms. The problem is to calculate the weights. One method finds the *n* most critical paths (using a timing-analysis engine, possibly in the synthesis tool). The net weights might then be the number of times each net appears in this list. The problem with this approach is that as soon as we fix (for example) the first 100 critical nets, suddenly another 200 become critical. This is rather like trying to put worms in a can—as soon as we open the lid to put one in, two more pop out.

Another method to find the net weights uses the **zero-slack algorithm** [Hauge et al., 1987]. Figure 16.29 shows how this works (all times are in nanoseconds). Figure 16.29(a) shows a circuit with **primary inputs** at which we know the **arrival times** (this is the original definition, some people use the term **actual times**) of each signal. We also know the **required times** for the **primary outputs**—the points in time at which we want the signals to be valid. We can work forward from the primary inputs and backward from the primary outputs to determine arrival and required times at each input pin for each net. The difference between the required and arrival times at each input pin is the **slack time** (the time we have to spare). The zero-slack algorithm adds delay to each net until the slacks are zero, as shown in Figure 16.29(b). The net delays can then be converted to weights or constraints in the placement. Notice that we have assumed that all the gates on a net switch at the same time so that the net delay can be placed at the output of the gate driving the net—a rather poor timing model but the best we can use without any routing information.

An important point to remember is that adjusting the net weight, even for every net on a chip, does not theoretically make the placement algorithms any more complex—we have to deal with the numbers anyway. It does not matter whether the net weight is 1 or 6.6, for example. The practical problem, however, is getting the weight information for each net (usually in the form of timing constraints) from a synthesis tool or timing verifier. These files can easily be hundreds of megabytes in size (see Section 16.4).

With the zero-slack algorithm we simplify but overconstrain the problem. For example, we might be able to do a better job by making some nets a little longer than the slack indicates if we can tighten up other nets. What we would really like to do is deal with *paths* such as the critical path shown in Figure 16.29(a) and not just *nets*. Path-based algorithms have been proposed to do this, but they are complex and not all commercial tools have this capability (see, for example, [Youssef, Lin, and Shragowitz, 1992]).

There is still the question of how to predict path delays between gates with only placement information. Usually we still do not compute a routing tree but use simple approximations to the total net length (such as the half-perimeter measure) and then use this to estimate a net delay (the same to each pin on a net). It is not until the routing step that we can make accurate estimates of the actual interconnect delays.

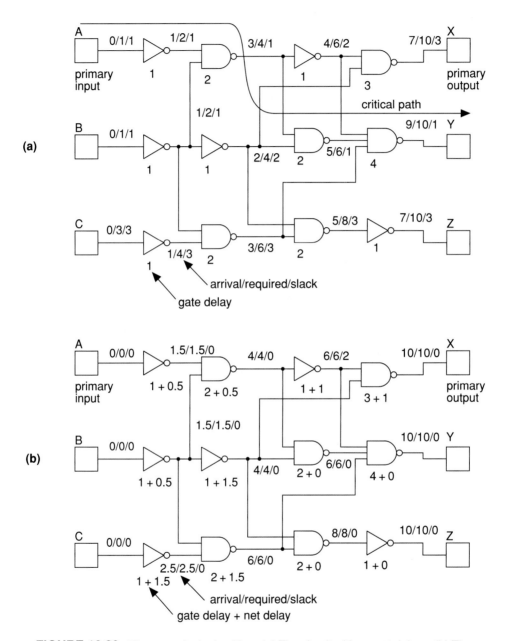

FIGURE 16.29 The zero-slack algorithm. (a) The circuit with no net delays. (b) The zero-slack algorithm adds net delays (at the outputs of each gate, equivalent to increasing the gate delay) to reduce the slack times to zero.

16.2.9   A Simple Placement Example

Figure 16.30 shows an example network and placements to illustrate the measures

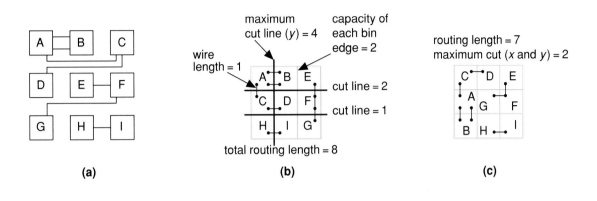

(a)   (b)   (c)

FIGURE 16.30 Placement example.
(a) An example network. (b) In this placement, the bin size is equal to the logic cell size
and all the logic cells are assumed equal size.
(c) An alternative placement with a lower total
routing length. (d) A layout that might result
from the placement shown in b. The channel
densities correspond to the cut-line sizes.
Notice that the logic cells are not all the same
size (which means there are errors in the
interconnect-length estimates we made during placement).

(d)

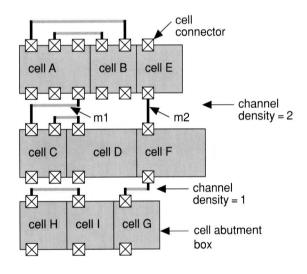

for interconnect length and interconnect congestion. Figure 16.30(b) and (c) illustrate the meaning of total routing length, the maximum cut line in the x-direction, the
maximum cut line in the y-direction, and the maximum density. In this example we
have assumed that the logic cells are all the same size, connections can be made to
terminals on any side, and the routing channels between each adjacent logic cell have
a capacity of 2. Figure 16.30(d) shows what the completed layout might look like.

16.3   Physical Design Flow

Historically placement was included with routing as a single tool (the term P&R is often used for place and route). Because interconnect delay now dominates gate delay, the trend is to include placement within a floorplanning tool and use a separate router. Figure 16.31 shows a design flow using synthesis and a floorplanning tool that includes placement. This flow consists of the following steps:

1. *Design entry.* The input is a logical description with no physical information.

2. *Synthesis.* The initial synthesis contains little or no information on any interconnect loading. The output of the synthesis tool (typically an EDIF netlist) is the input to the floorplanner.

3. *Initial floorplan.* From the initial floorplan interblock capacitances are input to the synthesis tool as load constraints and intrablock capacitances are input as wire-load tables.

4. *Synthesis with load constraints.* At this point the synthesis tool is able to resynthesize the logic based on estimates of the interconnect capacitance each

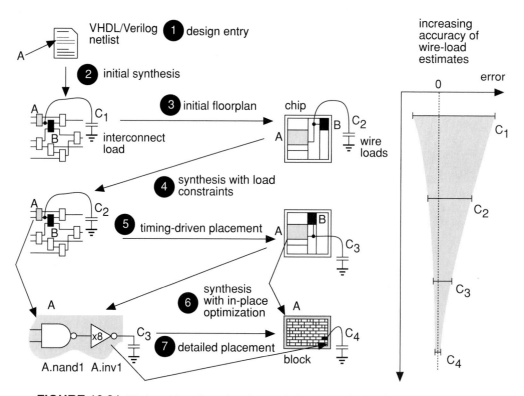

FIGURE 16.31 Timing-driven floorplanning and placement design flow. Compare with Figure 15.1 on p. 806.

gate is driving. The synthesis tool produces a forward annotation file to constrain path delays in the placement step.

5. *Timing-driven placement.* After placement using constraints from the synthesis tool, the location of every logic cell on the chip is fixed and accurate estimates of interconnect delay can be passed back to the synthesis tool.

6. *Synthesis* with **in-place optimization** (**IPO**). The synthesis tool changes the drive strength of gates based on the accurate interconnect delay estimates from the floorplanner without altering the netlist structure.

7. *Detailed placement.* The placement information is ready to be input to the routing step.

In Figure 16.31 we iterate between floorplanning and synthesis, continuously improving our estimate for the interconnect delay as we do so.

16.4   Information Formats

With the increasing importance of interconnect a great deal of information needs to flow between design tools. There are some de facto standards that we shall look at next. Some of the companies involved are working toward releasing these formats as IEEE standards.

16.4.1   SDF for Floorplanning and Placement

In Section 13.5.6, "SDF in Simulation," we discussed the structure and use of the standard delay format (SDF) to describe gate delay and interconnect delay. We may also use SDF with floorplanning and synthesis tools to **back-annotate** an interconnect delay. A synthesis tool can use this information to improve the logic structure. Here is a fragment of SDF:

```
(INSTANCE B) (DELAY (ABSOLUTE
    (INTERCONNECT A.INV8.OUT B.DFF1.Q (:0.6:) (:0.6:))))
```

In this example the rising and falling delay is 60 ps (equal to 0.6 units multiplied by the time scale of 100 ps per unit specified in a TIMESCALE construct that is not shown). The delay is specified between the output port of an inverter with instance name A.INV8 in block A and the Q input port of a D flip-flop (instance name B.DFF1) in block B. A '.' (period or fullstop) is set to be the hierarchy divider in another construct that is not shown.

There is another way of specifying interconnect delay using NETDELAY (a short form of the INTERCONNECT construct) as follows:

```
(TIMESCALE 100ps) (INSTANCE B) (DELAY (ABSOLUTE
(NETDELAY net1 (0.6)))
```

In this case all delays from an output port to, possibly multiple, input ports have the same value (we can also specify the output port name instead of the net name to identify the net). Alternatively we can lump interconnect delay at an input port:

```
(TIMESCALE 100ps) (INSTANCE B.DFF1) (DELAY (ABSOLUTE
    (PORT CLR (16:18:22) (17:20:25))))
```

This PORT construct specifies an interconnect delay placed at the input port of a logic cell (in this case the CLR pin of a flip-flop). We do not need to specify the start of a path (as we do for INTERCONNECT).

We can also use SDF to **forward-annotate** path delays using **timing constraints** (there may be hundreds or thousands of these in a file). A synthesis tool can pass this information to the floorplanning and placement steps to allow them to create better layout. SDF describes timing checks using a range of TIMINGCHECK constructs. Here is an example of a single path constraint:

```
(TIMESCALE 100ps) (INSTANCE B) (TIMINGCHECK
    (PATHCONSTRAINT A.AOI22_1.O B.ND02_34.O (0.8) (0.8)))
```

This describes a constraint (keyword PATHCONSTRAINT) for the rising and falling delays between two ports at each end of a path (which may consist of several nets) to be less than 80 ps. Using the SUM construct we can constrain the sum of path delays to be less than a specific value as follows:

```
(TIMESCALE 100ps) (INSTANCE B) (TIMINGCHECK
    (SUM (AOI22_1.O ND02_34.I1) (ND02_34.O ND02_35.I1) (0.8)))
```

We can also constrain skew between two paths (in this case to be less than 10 ps) using the DIFF construct:

```
(TIMESCALE 100ps) (INSTANCE B) (TIMINGCHECK
    (DIFF (A.I_1.O B.ND02_1.I1) (A.I_1.O.O B.ND02_2.I1) (0.1)))
```

In addition we can constrain the skew between a reference signal (normally the clock) and all other ports in an instance (again in this case to be less than 10 ps) using the SKEWCONSTRAINT construct:

```
(TIMESCALE 100ps) (INSTANCE B) (TIMINGCHECK
    (SKEWCONSTRAINT (posedge clk) (0.1)))
```

At present there is no easy way in SDF to constrain the skew between a reference signal and other signals to be greater than a specified amount.

16.4.2   PDEF

The **physical design exchange format** (**PDEF**) is a proprietary file format used by Synopsys to describe placement information and the clustering of logic cells. Here is a simple, but complete PDEF file:

```
(CLUSTERFILE
    (PDEVERSION "1.0")
```

```
(DESIGN "myDesign")
(DATE "THU AUG 6 12:00 1995")
(VENDOR "ASICS_R_US")
(PROGRAM "PDEF_GEN")
(VERSION "V2.2")
(DIVIDER .)
(CLUSTER (NAME "ROOT")
  (WIRE_LOAD "10mm x 10mm")
  (UTILIZATION 50.0)
  (MAX_UTILIZATION 60.0)
  (X_BOUNDS 100 1000)
  (Y_BOUNDS 100 1000)
    (CLUSTER (NAME "LEAF_1")
      (WIRE_LOAD "50k gates")
      (UTILIZATION 50.0)
      (MAX_UTILIZATION 60.0)
      (X_BOUNDS 100 500)
      (Y_BOUNDS 100 200)
      (CELL (NAME L1.RAM01)
      (CELL (NAME L1.ALU01)
      )
  )
)
```

This file describes two clusters:

- ROOT, which is the top-level (the whole chip). The file describes the size (*x*- and *y*-bounds), current and maximum area utilization (i.e., leaving space for interconnect), and the name of the wire-load table, '10mm x 10mm', to use for this block, chosen because the chip is expected to be about 10 mm on a side.

- LEAF_1, a block below the top level in the hierarchy. This block is to use predicted capacitances from a wire-load table named '50k gates' (chosen because we know there are roughly 50 k-gate in this block). The LEAF_1 block contains two logic cells: L1.RAM01 and L1.ALU01.

16.4.3 LEF and DEF

The **library exchange format** (**LEF**) and **design exchange format** (**DEF**) are both proprietary formats originated by Tangent in the TanCell and TanGate place-and-route tools which were bought by Cadence and now known as Cell3 Ensemble and Gate Ensemble respectively. These tools, and their derivatives, are so widely used that these formats have become a de facto standard. LEF is used to define an IC process and a logic cell library. For example, you would use LEF to describe a gate array: the base cells, the legal sites for base cells, the logic macros with their size and connectivity information, the interconnect layers and other information to set up the database that the physical design tools need. You would use DEF to describe all the physical aspects of a particular chip design including the netlist and physical location of cells on the chip. For example, if you had a complete placement from a floorplanning tool and wanted to exchange this information with Cadence Gate Ensemble or Cell3 Ensemble, you would use DEF.

16.5 Summary

Floorplanning follows the system partitioning step and is the first step in arranging circuit blocks on an ASIC. There are many factors to be considered during floorplanning: minimizing connection length and signal delay between blocks; arranging fixed blocks and reshaping flexible blocks to occupy the minimum die area; organizing the interconnect areas between blocks; planning the power, clock, and I/O distribution. The handling of some of these factors may be automated using CAD tools, but many still need to be dealt with by hand. Placement follows the floorplanning step and is more automated. It consists of organizing an array of logic cells within a flexible block. The criterion for optimization may be minimum interconnect area, minimum total interconnect length, or performance. There are two main types of placement algorithms: based on min-cut or eigenvector methods. Because interconnect delay in a submicron CMOS process dominates logic cell delay, planning of interconnect will become more and more important. Instead of completing synthesis before starting floorplanning and placement, we will have to use synthesis and floorplanning/placement tools together to achieve an accurate estimate of timing.

The key points of this chapter are:

- Interconnect delay now dominates gate delay.
- Floorplanning is a mapping between logical and physical design.
- Floorplanning is the center of ASIC design operations for all types of ASIC.
- Timing-driven floorplanning is becoming an essential ASIC design tool.
- Placement is now an automated function.

16.6 Problems

* = Difficult, ** = Very difficult, *** = Extremely difficult

16.1 (Wire loads, 30 min.) Table 16.2 shows a wire-load table. Since you might expect the interconnect load to be a monotonic increasing function of fanout and block area, it seems as though some of the data in Table 16.2 may be in error; these figures are shown preceded by an asterisk, '*' (this table is from an ASIC vendor data book). Using a spreadsheet, analyze the data in Table 16.2.

  a. By graphing the data, indicate any figures in Table 16.2 that you think might be in error. If you think that there is an error, predict the correct values—either by interpolation (for values in error in the body of the table), or by fitting the linear model parameters, the slope and the intercept (for any values in error in the last two columns of the table).

b. Including any corrections, how accurate is the model that predicts load as a linear function of fanout for a given block size? (Use the maximum error of the linear model expressed as a percentage of the table value.)

c. Can you fit a simple function to the (possibly corrected) figures in the last column of the table and explain its form?

d. What did you learn about wire-load tables from this problem?

TABLE 16.2   Wire- load table. Predicted interconnect loads (measured in standard loads) as a function of block size and fanout (Problem 16.1).

Size (/mm²)	Fanout											Slope	Intercept
	1	2	3	4	5	6	7	8	16	32	64		
0.5×0.5	0.65	0.95	1.25	1.54	1.84	2.14	2.44	2.74	5.13	9.91	19.47	0.299	0.349
1×1	0.80	1.20	1.59	1.99	2.39	2.79	3.19	3.59	6.77	13.15	25.9	0.398	0.398
2×2	0.96	1.48	1.99	2.51	3.02	3.54	4.05	4.57	8.68	16.92	33.38	0.515	0.448
3×3	1.20	1.83	2.46	3.09	3.72	4.35	4.98	5.61	10.66	20.75	40.94	0.631	0.564
4×4	1.41	2.11	2.81	3.50	4.20	4.90	5.59	6.29	11.87	23.02	45.33	0.697	0.714
5×5	1.51	2.24	2.97	3.70	4.43	5.16	5.89	6.62	12.47	24.15	47.53	0.730	0.780
6×6	1.56	2.31	3.05	3.80	4.55	5.30	6.04	6.79	12.77	24.72	48.62	0.747	0.813
7×7	1.83	2.62	3.42	4.22	5.01	5.81	6.61	7.40	13.78	26.53	52.02	0.797	*1.029
8×8	1.88	2.74	3.6	4.47	5.33	6.19	7.06	7.92	14.82	26.64	56.26	0.863	1.013
9×9	2.01	2.94	3.87	4.80	5.73	6.66	7.59	8.52	15.95	30.83	60.57	0.930	1.079
10×10	2.01	2.98	3.94	4.90	5.86	6.83	7.79	8.75	16.45	31.86	62.67	0.963	*1.050
11×11	2.46	3.46	4.45	5.45	6.44	7.44	8.44	9.43	17.4	33.33	65.20	0.996	1.465
12×12	3.04	4.1	5.17	6.23	7.3	8.35	9.42	10.48	18.8	36.03	70.00	1.063	1.964

16.2 (Trees, 20 min.) For the network graph shown in Figure 16.32(f), draw the following trees and calculate their Manhattan lengths:

a. The minimum Steiner tree.

b. The **chain connection**.

c. The minimum rectilinear Steiner tree.

d. The **minimum rectilinear spanning tree** [Hwang, 1976].

e. The minimum single-trunk rectilinear Steiner tree (with a horizontal or vertical trunk).

f. The **minimum rectilinear chain connection** (easy to compute).

g. The **minimum source-to-sink connection**.

Calculate:

h. The complete-graph measure and the half-perimeter measure.

Figure 16.32 parts (a–e) illustrate the definitions of these trees. There is no known solution to the minimum Steiner-tree problem for nets with more than five terminals.

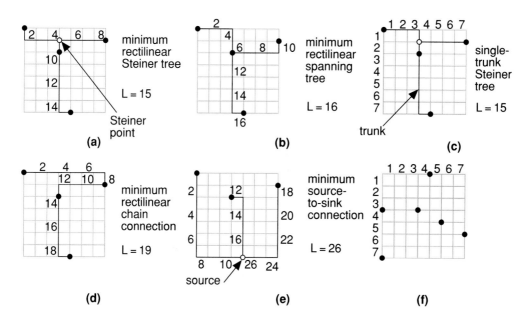

FIGURE 16.32 Tree routing. (a) The minimum rectilinear Steiner tree (MRST). (b) The minimum rectilinear spanning tree. (c) The minimum single-trunk rectilinear Steiner tree (1-MRST). (d) The minimum rectilinear chain connection. (e) The minimum source-to-sink connection. (f) Example net for Problem 16.2.

16.3 (Eigenvalue placement constraints, 10 min. [Cheng and Kuh, 1984]) Consider the one-dimensional placement problem with a vector list of valid positions for the logic cells $\mathbf{p} = [p_i]$ and a vector list of x-coordinates for the logic cells $\mathbf{x} = [x_i]$.

Show that for a valid placement $\mathbf{x}$ (where the vector elements x_i are some permutation of the vector elements p_i), the following equations hold:

$$\sum_{i=1}^{n} x_i = \sum_{i=1}^{n} p_i \qquad \sum_{i=1}^{n} x_i^2 = \sum_{i=1}^{n} p_i^2 \qquad \cdots \qquad \sum_{i=1}^{n} x_i^n = \sum_{i=1}^{n} p_i^n \quad (16.22)$$

(*Hint:* Consider the polynomial $(x + x_i)^n$. In our simplification to the problem, we chose to impose only the second equation of these constraints.)

16.4 (*Eigenvalue placement, 30 min.) You will need MatLab, Mathematica, or a similar mathematical calculus program for this problem.

a. Find the eigenvalues and eigenvectors for the disconnection matrix corresponding to the following connection matrix:

```
C=
[ 0 1 1 0 0 0 1 0 0;
  1 0 0 0 0 0 0 0 0;
  1 0 0 1 0 0 0 1 0;
  0 0 1 0 0 1 0 0 0;
  0 0 0 0 0 1 0 0 1;
  0 0 0 1 1 0 1 0 0;
  1 0 0 0 0 1 0 0 0;
  0 0 1 0 0 0 0 0 1;
  0 0 0 0 1 0 0 1 0;]
```

(*Hint:* Check your answer. The smallest, nonzero, eigenvalue should be 0.5045.)

b. Use your results to place the logic cells. Plot the placement and show the connections between logic cells (this is easy to do using an X-Y plot in an Excel spreadsheet).

c. Check that the following equation holds:

$$\lambda = \frac{g}{P}.$$

16.5 (Die size, 10 min.) Suppose the minimum spacing between pad centers is W mil (1 mil = 10^{-3} inch), there are N I/O pads on a chip, and the die area (assume a square die) is A mil^2:

a. Derive a relationship between W, N, and A that corresponds to the point at which the die changes from being pad-limited to core-limited.

b. Plot this relationship with N (ranging from 50 to 500 pads) on the x-axis, A on the y-axis (for dies ranging in size from 1 mm to 20 mm on a side), and W as a parameter (for W = 1, 2, 3, and 4 mil).

16.6 (Power buses, 20 min.) Assume aluminum metal interconnect has a resistance of about 30 mΩ/square (a low value). Consider a power ring for the I/O pads. Suppose you have a high-power chip that dissipates 5 W at V_{DD} = 5 V, and assume that half of the supply current (0.5 A) is due to I/O. Suppose the square die is L mil on a side, and that the I/O current is equally distributed among the N VDD pads that are on the chip. In the worst case, you want no more than 100 mV drop between any VDD pad and the I/O circuits drawing power (notice that there will be an equal drop on the VSS side; just consider the VDD drop).

a. Model the power distribution as a ring of N equally spaced pads. Each pad is connected by a resistor equal to the aluminum VDD power-bus resistance between two pads. Assume the I/O circuits associated with each pad can be considered to connect to just one point on the resistors between each pad. If the resistance between each pad is R, what is the worst-case resistance between the I/O circuits and the supply?

b. Plot a graph showing L (in mil) on the x-axis, W (the required power-bus width in microns) on the y-axis, with N as a parameter (with $N = 1, 2, 5, 10$).

c. Comment on your results.

d. An upper limit on current density for aluminum metallization is about $50 \, \text{kAcm}^{-2}$; at current densities higher than this, failure due to electromigration (which we shall cover in Section 17.3.2, "Power Routing") is a problem. Assume the metallization is $0.5 \, \mu\text{m}$ thick. Calculate the current density in the VDD power bus for this chip in terms of the power-bus width and the number of pads. Comment on your answer.

16.7 (Interconnect length approximation, 10 min.) Figure 16.22 shows the correlation between actual interconnect length and two approximations. Use this graph to derive a correction function (together with an estimation of the error) for the complete graph measure and the half-perimeter measure.

16.8 (Half-perimeter measure, 10 min.) Draw a tree on a rectangular grid for which the MRST is equal to the half-perimeter measure. Draw a tree on a rectangular grid for which the MRST is twice the half-perimeter measure.

16.9 (***Min-cut, 120 min.) Many floorplanning and placement tools use min-cut methods and allow you to alter the type and sequence of bisection cuts. Research and describe the difference between: quadrature min-cut placement, bisection min-cut placement, and slice/bisection min-cut placement.

16.10 (***Terminal propagation, 120 min.) There is a problem with the min-cut algorithm in the way connectivity is measured. Figure 16.33 shows a situation in which logic cells G and H are connected to other logic cells (A and F) outside the area R_1 that is currently being partitioned. The min-cut algorithm ignores connections outside the area to be divided. Thus logic cells G and H may be placed in partition R_3 rather than partition R_2. Suggest solutions to this problem. *Hint:* See Dunlop [1983]; Hartoog [1986]; or the Barnes-Hut galaxy model.

16.11 (Benchmarks and statistics, 30 min.) Your boss asks you to compare two placement programs from companies ABC and XYZ. You run five test cases for both on a single netlist, P1. You get results (measured in arbitrary units) of 9, 8, 9, 7, 11 for ABC; 6, 9, 10, 13, 8 for XYZ.

a. Calculate the mean and standard deviations for these results.

b. What confidence (in the statistical sense) do you have in these figures?

c. What can you say about the relative performance of ABC and XYZ?

On average each test case takes about 0.5 hours (wall clock) for both ABC and XYZ. Next you run six test cases on another netlist, P2 with the following results: 4, 6, 7, 8, 5, 7 for ABC, and 4, 5, 3, 6, 4, 3 for XYZ. These test cases take about 0.75 hours (wall clock) each.

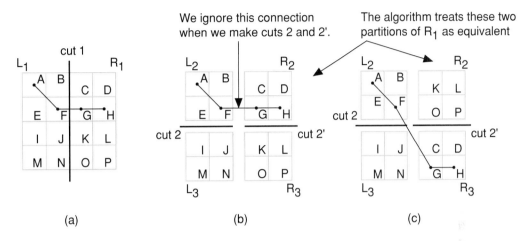

We ignore this connection when we make cuts 2 and 2'.

The algorithm treats these two partitions of R_1 as equivalent

(a)   (b)   (c)

FIGURE 16.33 (For Problem 16.10.) A problem with the min-cut algorithm is that it ignores connections to logic cells outside the area being partitioned. (a) We perform a vertical cut 1 producing the areas R_1 and R_2. (b) Next we make a horizontal cut 2, producing L_2 and L_3, and a cut 2', producing R_2 and R_3. (c) The min-cut algorithm ignores the connection from L_2 and is equally likely to produce the arrangement shown here when we make cut 2'.

d. What can you say about the P2 results?

e. Given the P1 and P2 results together, what can you say about ABC and XYZ?

f. How many P1 test cases should you run to get a result so that you can say ABC is better or worse than XYZ with 90 percent confidence (i.e., you make the right decision 9 out of 10 times)? How long would this take?

g. Find the same figures for the P2 netlist. Comment on your answers.

h. Suppose you had more netlists and information about the variation of results from each netlist, together with the average time to run each netlist. How would you use this information to get the most meaningful result in the shortest time?

16.12 (Linear and quadratic placement, 20 min.) [Sigl, Doll, and Johannes, 1991] Figure 16.34(a) shows a simple network that we will place. Figure 16.34(b) shows the problem. The logic cells are all the same size: 1 grid unit wide by 1 grid unit high. Logic cells 1 and 3 are fixed at the locations shown. Logic cell 2 is movable and placed at coordinates (for the lower-left corner) of (x_2, y_2). The lower-left corners of logic cells should be placed at grid locations and should not overlap.

a. What is the connection matrix c_{ij} for this network?

b. Calculate and draw (showing the logic cell coordinates) the placement that minimizes the linear cost function (or objective function) f_L,

$$f_L = \frac{1}{2} \sum_{i,\, j \,=\, 1}^{n} c_{ij} d_{ij} \tag{16.23}$$

where d_{ij} is the distance between logic cells i and j.

c. Calculate and draw (showing coordinates) the placement that minimizes the quadratic cost function f_Q,

$$f_Q = \frac{1}{2} \sum_{i,\, j \,=\, 1}^{n} c_{ij} d_{ij}^2 . \tag{16.24}$$

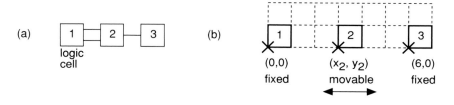

FIGURE 16.34   Problem 16.12 illustrates placement objectives. (a) An example network for placement. (b) The placement restrictions. Logic cells 1 and 3 are fixed in position, the placement problem is to optimize the position of logic cell 2 under different placement objectives.

16.13 (Placement interconnect lengths, 45 min.) Figure 16.30(d) shows the actual routing corresponding to a placement with an estimated routing length of 8 units (Figure 16.30b).

a. Draw the layout (with routing) corresponding to the placement of Figure 16.30(c), which has a lower estimated total routing length of 7 units.

b. Compare the actual total routing length for both layouts and explain why they are different from the estimated lengths and describe the sources of the errors.

c. Consider flipping both logic cells A and B about the y-axis in the layout shown in Figure 16.30(d). How much does this shorten the total interconnect length? Some placement algorithms consider such moves.

16.14 (Zero-slack algorithm, 60 min.) For the circuit of Figure 16.35:

a. Find all of the arrival, required, and slack times (all delays are in nanoseconds).

b. What is the critical path?

c. If the gate delay of A2 is increased to 5 ns, what is the new critical path?

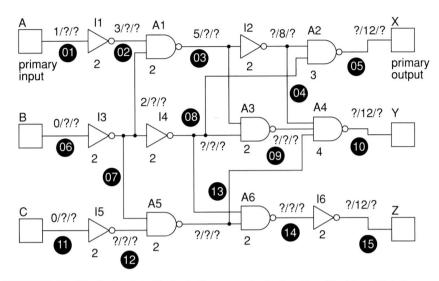

FIGURE 16.35 A circuit to illustrate the zero-slack algorithm (Problem 16.14).

d. ** Using your answer to part a find the upper bounds on net delays by means of the zero-slack algorithm as follows:

  i. Find arrival, required, and slack times on all nets.

  ii. Find an input pin p with the least nonzero slack S_p on a net which has not already been selected. If there are none go to step 6.

  ii. Find the path through p (may include several gates) on which all pins have slack S_p.

  iv. Distribute a delay equal to the slack S_p along the path assigning a fraction to each net at the output pins of the gates on the path.

  v. Work backward from p updating all the required times as necessary and forward from p updating all the arrival times.

  vi. Convert net delays to net lengths.

Hint: You can consult the original description of the zero-slack algorithm if this is not clear [Hauge et al., 1987].

16.15 (World planning, 60 min.) The seven continents are (with areas in millions of square miles): Europe—strictly a peninsula of Asia (4.1), Asia (17.2), North America (9.4), South America (6.9), Australia (3.0), Africa (11.7), and Antarctica (5.1). Assume the continents are flexible blocks whose aspect ratio may be adjusted.

  a. Create a slicing floorplan of the world with a square aspect ratio.

  b. Draw a world connectivity graph with seven nodes and whose edges are labeled with the distances between Moscow, Beijing, Chicago, Rio de Janeiro, Sydney, Nairobi, and the South Pole.

c. Suppose you want to floorplan the world so that the difference in distances between the centers of the continental blocks and the corresponding edges in the world connectivity graph is minimized. How would you measure the differences in distance? Suggest a method to minimize your measure.

d. Use an eigenvalue method to floorplan the world. Draw the result with coordinates for each block and explain your approach.

16.7   Bibliography

There are no recent monographs or review articles on floorplanning modern ASICs with interconnect delay dominating gate delay. Placement is a much more developed topic. Perhaps the simplest place to dig deeper is the book by Preas and Lorenzetti that contains a chapter titled "Placement, assignment, and floorplanning" [Preas and Karger, 1988]. The collection edited by Ohtsuki [1986] contains a review paper by Yoshida titled "Partitioning, assignment, and placement." Sangiovanni-Vincentelli's review article [1986] complements Ohtsuki's edited book, but both are now dated. Sechen's book [1988] describes simulated annealing and its application to placement and chip-planning for standard cell and gate array ASICs. Part III of the IEEE Press book edited by Hu and Kuh [1983] is a collection of papers on wireability, partitioning, and placement covering some of the earlier and fundamental work in this area. For a more recent and detailed look at the inner workings of floorplanning and placement tools, Lengauer's [1990] book on algorithms contains a chapter on graph algorithms and a chapter on placement, assignment, and floorplanning. Most of these earlier book references deal with placement before the use of timing as an additional objective. The tutorial paper by Benkoski and Strojwas [1991] contains a number of references on performance-driven placement. Luk's book [1991] describes methods for estimating net delay during placement.

Papers and tutorials on all aspects of floorplanning and placement (with an emphasis on algorithms) are published in *IEEE Transactions on Computer-Aided Design*. The newest developments in floorplanning and placement appear every year in the *Proceedings of the ACM/IEEE Design Automation Conference* (DAC) and *Proceedings of the IEEE International Conference on Computer-Aided Design* (ICCAD).

16.8   References

Page numbers in brackets after a reference indicate its location in the chapter body.

Benkoski, J., and A. J. Strojwas. 1991. "The role of timing verification in layout synthesis." In *Proceedings of the 28th ACM/IEEE Design Automation Conference,* San Francisco, pp. 612–619. Tutorial paper with 60 references. This was an introduction to a session on Placement for Performance Optimization containing five other papers on this topic. [p. 906]

Breuer, M. A. 1977. "Min-cut placement." *Journal of Design Automation and Fault Tolerant Computing,* Vol. 1, no. 4, pp. 343–362. [p. 882]

Chao, A. H., E. M. Nequist, and T. D. Vuong. 1990. "Direct solution of performance constraints during placement." In *Proceedings of the IEEE Custom Integrated Circuits Conference.* Describes algorithms used in Cadence Gate Ensemble for performance-driven placement. Wiring estimate is based on single trunk Steiner tree with corrections for bounding rectangle aspect ratio and pin count. [p. 879]

Cheng, C.-K., and E. S. Kuh. 1984. "Module placement based on resistive network optimization." *IEEE Transactions on Computer-Aided Design for Integrated-Circuits and Systems,* Vol. CAD-3, pp. 218–225. [pp. 884, 900]

Dunlop, A. E., and B. W. Kernighan. 1983. "A placement procedure for polycell VLSI circuits." In *Proceedings of the IEEE International Conference on Computer Aided Design,* Santa Clara, CA, September 13–15. Describes the terminal propagation algorithm. [p. 902]

Goto, S. and T. Matsuda. 1986. "Partitioning, assignment and placement." In *Layout Design and Verification,* T. Ohtsuki (Ed.), Vol. 4, pp. 55–97. New York: Elsevier. ISBN 0444878947. TK 7874. L318. [p. 879]

Hall, K. M. 1970. "An r-dimensional quadratic placement algorithm." *Management Science,* Vol. 17, no. 3, pp. 219–229. [p. 885]

Hanan, M. 1966. "On Steiner's problem with rectilinear distance." *Journal SIAM Applied Mathematics,* Vol. 14, no. 2, pp. 255–265. [p. 879]

Hanan, M., P. K. Wolff Sr., and B. J. Agule. 1973. "Some experimental results on placement techniques." In *Proceedings of the 13th Design Automation Conference.* Reference to complete graph wire measure. [p. 877]

Hartoog, M. R., 1986. "Analysis of placement procedures for VLSI standard cell layout." In *Proceedings of the 23rd Design Automation Conference.* [p. 902]

Hauge, P. S., et al. 1987. "Circuit placement for predictable performance." In *Proceedings of the IEEE International Conference on Computer Aided Design,* pp. 88–91. Describes the zero-slack algorithm. *See also:* Nair, R., C. L. Berman, P. S. Hauge, and E. J. Yoffa, "Generation of performance constraints for layout," *IEEE Transactions on Computer Aided Design,* Vol. 8, no. 8, pp. 860–874, August 1989; and Burstein, M. and M. N. Housewife, "Timing influenced layout design," in *Proceedings of the 22nd Design Automation Conference,* 1985. Defines required, actual, and slack times. Describes application of timing-driven restrictions to placement using F–M algorithm and hierarchical global routing. [p. 905]

Hu, T. C., and E. S. Kuh (Eds.). 1983. *VLSI Circuit Layout: Theory and Design.* New York: IEEE Press. Contains 26 papers divided into six parts; Part 1: Overview; Part II: General; Part III: Wireability, Partitioning and Placement; Part IV: Routing; Part V: Layout Systems; Part VI: Module Generation. ISBN 0879421932. TK7874. V5573. [p. 906]

Hwang, F. K. 1976. "On Steiner minimal trees with rectilinear distance." *SIAM Journal of Applied Mathematics,* Vol. 30, pp. 104–114. *See also:* Hwang, F. K., "An O(n log n) Algorithm for Suboptimal Rectilinear Steiner Trees," *IEEE Transactions on Circuits and Systems,* Vol. CAS-26, no. 1, pp. 75–77, January 1979. Describes an algorithm to improve the rectilinear minimum spanning tree (RMST) approximation to the minimal rectilinear Steiner tree (minimal RST). The approximation is at most 1.5 times longer than the minimal RST, since the RMST is at worst 1.5 times the length of the minimal RST. [p. 899]

Kirkpatrick, S., C. D. Gerlatt Jr., and M. P. Vecchi. 1983. "Optimization by simulated annealing," *Science,* Vol. 220, no. 4598, pp. 671–680. [p. 890]

Lengauer, T. 1990. *Combinatorial Algorithms for Integrated Circuit Layout.* Chichester, England: Wiley. ISBN 0-471-92838-0. TK7874.L36. Contains chapters on circuit layout; optimization problems; graph algorithms; operations research and statistics; combinatorial layout problems; circuit partitioning; placement; assignment; floorplanning; global routing and area routing; detailed routing; and compaction. 484 references. [p. 906]

Luk, W. K. 1991. "A fast physical constraint generator for timing driven layout." In *Proceedings of the 28th ACM/IEEE Design Automation Conference.* Introduction to timing-driven placement and net- and path-based approaches. Describes some different methods to estimate interconnect delay during placement. ISBN 0-89791-395-7. [p. 906].

Masleid, R. P. 1991. "High-density central I/O circuits for CMOS." *IEEE Journal of Solid-State Circuits,* Vol. 26, no. 3, pp. 431–435. An I/O circuit design that reduces the percentage of chip area occupied by I/O circuits from roughly 22 percent to under 3 percent for a 256 I/O chip. Uses IBM C4 technology that allows package connections to be located over chip circuitry. 10 references. [p. 866]

Ohtsuki, T. (Ed.). 1986. *Layout Design and Verification.* New York: Elsevier. Includes nine papers on CAD tools and algorithms: "Layout strategy, standardisation, and CAD tools," Ueda, Kasai and Sudo; "Layout compaction," Mylynski and Sung; "Layout verification," Yoshida; "Partitioning, assignment and placement," Goto and Matsuda; "Computational complexity of layout problems," Shing and Hu; "Computational and geometry algorithms," Asano, Sato and Ohtsuki; an excellent survey and tutorial paper by M. Burstein: "Channel routing"; "Maze-running and line-search algorithms" an easily-readable paper on detailed routing by Ohtsuki; and a mathematical paper, "Global routing," by Kuh and Marek-Sadowska. ISBN 0444878947. TK7874. L318. [p. 906]

Preas, B. T., and P. G. Karger. 1988. "Placement, assignment and floorplanning." In *Physical Design Automation of VLSI Systems,* B. T. Preas and M. J. Lorenzetti (Eds.), pp. 87–155. Menlo Park, CA: Benjamin-Cummings. ISBN 0-8053-0412-9. TK7874.P47. [p. 906]

Sangiovanni-Vincentelli, A. 1986. "Automatic layout of integrated circuits." In *Nato Advanced Study on "Logic Synthesis and Silicon Compilers for VLSI Design",* G. De Micheli, A. Sangiovanni-Vincentelli, and A. Paolo (Eds.). Norwell, MA: Kluwer. ISBN 90-247-2689-1, 90-247-3561-0. TK7874.N338. [p. 906]

Schweikert, D. G., 1976. "A 2-dimensional placement algorithm for the layout of electrical circuits." In *Proceedings of the 9th Design Automation Conference.* Description of half-perimeter wire measure. [p. 879]

Sechen, C. 1988. *VLSI Placement and Global Routing Using Simulated Annealing.* Norwell, MA: Kluwer. Contains chapters on the simulated annealing algorithm; placement and global routing; floorplanning; average interconnection length estimation; interconnect-area estimation; a channel definition algorithm; and a global router algorithm. ISBN 0898382815. TK7874. S38. [p. 890]

Sigl, G., K. Doll, and F. M. Johannes. 1991. "Analytical placement: a linear or quadratic objective function?" In *Proceedings of the 28th ACM/IEEE Design Automation Conference.* Compares quadratic and linear cost function for placement algorithms. Explains the Gordian place-and-route system from the Technical University of Munich. ISBN 0-89791-395-7. [p. 903].

Wada, T., M. Eino, and K. Anami. 1990. "Simple noise model and low-noise data-output buffer for ultrahigh-speed memories." *IEEE Journal of Solid-State Circuits,* Vol. 25, no. 6, pp. 1586–1588. An analytic noise model for voltage bounce on internal VDD/VSS lines. [p. 866]

Wong, D. F., H. W. Leong, and C. L. Liu. 1988. *Simulated Annealing for VLSI Design.* Norwell, MA: Kluwer. Introduction; Placement; Floorplan Design; Channel Routing; Permutation Channel Routing; PLA Folding; Gate Matrix Layout; Array Optimization. ISBN 0898382564. TK7874. W65. [p. 890]

Youssef, H., R.-B. Lin, and E. Shragowitz. 1992. "Bounds on net delays for VLSI circuits." *IEEE Transactions on Circuits and Systems II: Analog and Digital Signal Processing,* Vol. 39, no. 11, pp. 315–324. An alternative to the weight-based approach is development of delay bounds on all nets. 21 references. [p. 891].

ROUTING

17

Once the designer has floorplanned a chip and the logic cells within the flexible blocks have been placed, it is time to make the connections by routing the chip. This is still a hard problem that is made easier by dividing it into smaller problems. Routing is usually split into **global routing** followed by **detailed routing**.

Suppose the ASIC is North America and some travelers in California need advice on how to drive from Stanford (near San Francisco) to Caltech (near Los Angeles). The floorplanner has decided that California is on the left (west) side of the ASIC and the placement tool has put Stanford in Northern California and Caltech in Southern California. Floorplanning and placement have defined the roads and freeways. There are two ways to go: the coastal route (using Highway 101) or the inland route (using Interstate I5, which is usually faster). The global router specifies the coastal route because the travelers are not in a hurry and I5 is congested (the global router knows this because it has already routed onto I5 many other travelers that are in a hurry today). Next, the detailed router looks at a map and gives indications from Stanford onto Highway 101 south through San Jose, Monterey, and Santa Barbara to Los Angeles and then off the freeway to Caltech in Pasadena.

Figure 17.1 shows the core of the Viterbi decoder after the placement step. This implementation consists entirely of standard cells (18 rows). The I/O pads are not included in this example—we can route the I/O pads after we route the core (though this is not always a good idea). Figure 17.2 shows the Viterbi decoder chip after global and detailed routing. The routing runs in the channels between the rows of logic cells, but the individual interconnections are too small to see.

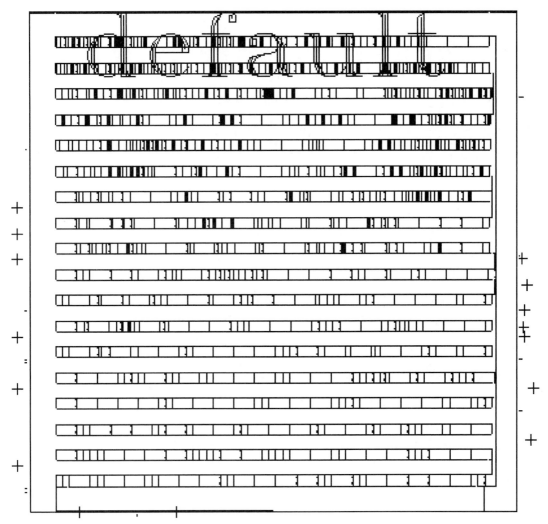

FIGURE 17.1 The core of the Viterbi decoder chip after placement (a screen shot from Cadence Cell Ensemble). This is the same placement as shown in Figure 16.2, but without the channel labels. You can see the rows of standard cells; the widest cells are the D flip-flops.

17.1 Global Routing

The details of global routing differ slightly between cell-based ASICs, gate arrays, and FPGAs, but the principles are the same in each case. A global router does not make any connections, it just plans them. We typically global route the whole chip

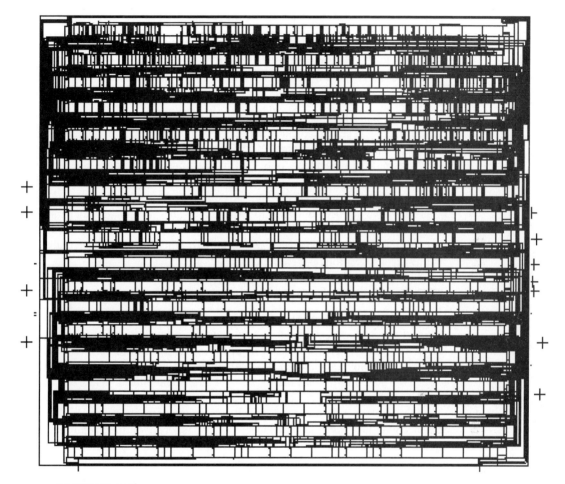

FIGURE 17.2 The core of the Viterbi decoder chip after the completion of global and detailed routing (a screen shot from Cadence Cell Ensemble). This chip uses two-level metal. Although you cannot see the difference, m1 runs in the horizontal direction and m2 in the vertical direction.

(or large pieces if it is a large chip) before detail routing the whole chip (or the pieces). There are two types of areas to global route: inside the flexible blocks and between blocks (the Viterbi decoder, although a cell-based ASIC, only involved the global routing of one large flexible block).

17.1.1   Goals and Objectives

The input to the global router is a floorplan that includes the locations of all the fixed and flexible blocks; the placement information for flexible blocks; and the locations of all the logic cells. The goal of global routing is to provide complete instructions to the detailed router on where to route every net. The objectives of global routing are one or more of the following:

- Minimize the total interconnect length.
- Maximize the probability that the detailed router can complete the routing.
- Minimize the critical path delay.

In both floorplanning and placement, with minimum interconnect length as an objective, it is necessary to find the shortest total path length connecting a set of *terminals*. This path is the MRST, which is hard to find. The alternative, for both floorplanning and placement, is to use simple approximations to the length of the MRST (usually the half-perimeter measure). Floorplanning and placement both assume that interconnect may be put anywhere on a rectangular grid, since at this point nets have not been assigned to the channels, but the global router must use the wiring channels and find the actual path. Often the global router needs to find a path that minimizes the delay between two terminals—this is not necessarily the same as finding the shortest total path length for a set of terminals.

17.1.2 Measurement of Interconnect Delay

Floorplanning and placement need a fast and easy way to estimate the interconnect delay in order to evaluate each trial placement; often this is a predefined look-up table. After placement, the logic cell positions are fixed and the global router can afford to use better estimates of the interconnect delay. To illustrate one method, we shall use the Elmore constant to estimate the interconnect delay for the circuit shown in Figure 17.3.

The problem is to find the voltages at the inputs to logic cells B and C taking into account the parasitic resistance and capacitance of the metal interconnect. Figure 17.3(c) models logic cell A as an ideal switch with a pull-down resistance equal to R_{pd} and models the metal interconnect using resistors and capacitors for each segment of the interconnect.

The Elmore constant for node 4 (labeled V_4) in the network shown in Figure 17.3(c) is

$$\tau_{D4} = \sum_{k=1}^{4} R_{k4} C_k = R_{14} C_1 + R_{24} C_2 + R_{34} C_3 + R_{44} C_4, \qquad (17.1)$$

where,

$$
\begin{aligned}
R_{14} &= R_{pd} + R_1 & R_{24} &= R_{pd} + R_1 \\
R_{34} &= R_{pd} + R_1 + R_3 & R_{44} &= R_{pd} + R_1 + R_3 + R_4
\end{aligned}
\qquad (17.2)
$$

In Eq. 17.2 notice that $R_{24} = R_{pd} + R_1$ (and not $R_{pd} + R_1 + R_2$) because R_1 is the resistance to V_0 (ground) shared by node 2 and node 4.

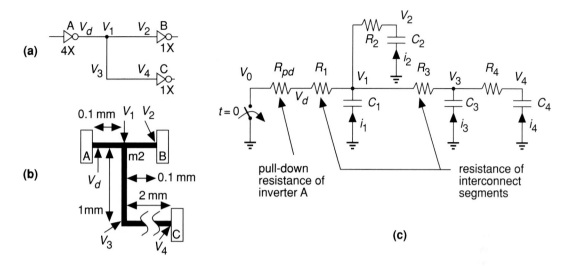

FIGURE 17.3 Measuring the delay of a net. (a) A simple circuit with an inverter A driving a net with a fanout of two. Voltages V_1, V_2, V_3, and V_4 are the voltages at intermediate points along the net. (b) The layout showing the net segments (pieces of interconnect). (c) The RC model with each segment replaced by a capacitance and resistance. The ideal switch and pull-down resistance R_{pd} model the inverter A.

Suppose we have the following parameters (from the generic 0.5 µm CMOS process, G5) for the layout shown in Figure 17.3(b):

- m2 resistance is 50 mΩ/square.
- m2 capacitance (for a minimum-width line) is 0.2 pFmm^{-1}.
- 4X inverter delay is 0.02 ns + 0.5C_L ns (C_L is in picofarads).
- Delay is measured using 0.35/0.65 output trip points.
- m2 minimum width is 3λ = 0.9 µm.
- 1X inverter input capacitance is 0.02 pF (a standard load).

First we need to find the pull-down resistance, R_{pd}, of the 4X inverter. If we model the gate with a linear pull-down resistor, R_{pd}, driving a load C_L, the output waveform is $\exp -t/(C_L R_{pd})$ (normalized to 1V). The output reaches 63 percent of its final value when $t = C_L R_{pd}$, because $\exp(-1) = 0.63$. Then, because the delay is measured with a 0.65 trip point, the constant 0.5 nspF^{-1} = 0.5 kΩ is very close to the equivalent pull-down resistance. Thus, $R_{pd} \approx 500\,\Omega$.

From the given data, we can calculate the R's and C's:

$$R_1 = R_2 = \frac{(0.1 \text{ mm}) (50 \times 10^{-3} \Omega)}{0.9 \text{ }\mu\text{m}} = 6 \text{ }\Omega$$

$$R_3 = \frac{(1 \text{ mm}) (50 \times 10^{-3} \Omega)}{0.9 \text{ }\mu\text{m}} = 56 \text{ }\Omega \tag{17.3}$$

$$R_4 = \frac{(2 \text{ mm}) (50 \times 10^{-3} \Omega)}{0.9 \text{ }\mu\text{m}} = 112 \text{ }\Omega$$

$$C_1 = (0.1 \text{mm}) (0.2 \text{ pFmm}^{-1}) = 0.02 \text{ pF}$$

$$C_2 = (0.1 \text{ mm}) (0.2 \text{ pFmm}^{-1}) + 0.02 \text{ pF} = 0.04 \text{ pF}$$

$$C_3 = (1 \text{ mm}) (0.2 \text{ pFmm}^{-1}) = 0.2 \text{ pF} \tag{17.4}$$

$$C_4 = (2 \text{ mm}) (0.2 \text{ pFmm}^{-1}) + 0.02 \text{ pF} = 0.42 \text{ pF}$$

Now we can calculate the path resistance, R_{ki}, values (notice that $R_{ki} = R_{ik}$):

$$R_{14} = 500 \text{ }\Omega + 6 \text{ }\Omega = 506 \text{ }\Omega$$

$$R_{24} = 500 \text{ }\Omega + 6 \text{ }\Omega = 506 \text{ }\Omega$$

$$R_{34} = 500 \text{ }\Omega + 6 \text{ }\Omega + 56 \text{ }\Omega = 562 \text{ }\Omega \tag{17.5}$$

$$R_{44} = 500 \text{ }\Omega + 6 \text{ }\Omega + 56 \text{ }\Omega + 112 \text{ }\Omega = 674 \text{ }\Omega$$

Finally, we can calculate Elmore's constants for node 4 and node 2 as follows:

$$
\begin{aligned}
\tau_{D4} &= R_{14}C_1 + R_{24}C_2 + R_{34}C_3 + R_{44}C_4 \\
&= (506) (0.02) + (506) (0.04) + (562) (0.2) + (674) (0.42) \\
&= 425 \text{ ps,}
\end{aligned}
\tag{17.6}
$$

$$
\begin{aligned}
\tau_{D2} &= R_{12}C_1 + R_{22}C_2 + R_{32}C_3 + R_{42}C_4 \\
&= (R_{pd} + R_1 + R_2) C_2 + (R_{pd} + R_1) (C_1 + C_3 + C_4) \\
&= (500 + 6 + 6) (0.04) + (500 + 6) (0.02 + 0.2 + 0.42) \\
&= 344 \text{ ps,}
\end{aligned}
\tag{17.7}
$$

and $\tau_{D4} - \tau_{D2} = (425 - 344) = 81 \text{ ps.}$

A **lumped-delay model** neglects the effects of interconnect resistance and simply sums all the node capacitances (the **lumped capacitance**) as follows:

$$
\begin{aligned}
t_D &= R_{pd}(C_1 + C_2 + C_3 + C_4) \\
&= (500)\,(0.02 + 0.04 + 0.2 + 0.42) \\
&= 340 \text{ ps}.
\end{aligned}
\tag{17.8}
$$

Comparing Eqs. 17.6–17.8, we can see that the delay of the inverter can be assigned as follows: 20 ps (the intrinsic delay, 0.2 ns, due to the cell output capacitance), 340 ps (due to the pull-down resistance and the output capacitance), 4 ps (due to the interconnect from A to B), and 65 ps (due to the interconnect from A to C). We can see that the error from neglecting interconnect resistance can be important.

Even using the Elmore constant we still made the following assumptions in estimating the path delays:

- A step-function waveform drives the net.

- The delay is measured from when the gate input changes.

- The delay is equal to the time constant of an exponential waveform that approximates the actual output waveform.

- The interconnect is modeled by discrete resistance and capacitance elements.

The global router could use more sophisticated estimates that remove some of these assumptions, but there is a limit to the accuracy with which delay can be estimated during global routing. For example, the global router does not know how much of the routing is on which of the layers, or how many vias will be used and of which type, or how wide the metal lines will be. It may be possible to estimate how much interconnect will be horizontal and how much is vertical. Unfortunately, this knowledge does not help much if horizontal interconnect may be completed in either m1 or m3 and there is a large difference in parasitic capacitance between m1 and m3, for example.

When the global router attempts to minimize interconnect delay, there is an important difference between a path and a net. The path that minimizes the delay between two terminals on a net is not necessarily the same as the path that minimizes the total path length of the net. For example, to minimize the path delay (using the Elmore constant as a measure) from the output of inverter A in Figure 17.3(a) to the input of inverter B requires a rather complicated algorithm to construct the best path. We shall return to this problem in Section 17.1.6.

17.1.3 Global Routing Methods

Global routing cannot use the interconnect-length approximations, such as the half-perimeter measure, that were used in placement. What is needed now is the actual path and not an approximation to the path length. However, many of the methods used in global routing are still based on the solutions to the tree on a graph problem.

One approach to global routing takes each net in turn and calculates the shortest path using tree on graph algorithms—with the added restriction of using the available channels. This process is known as **sequential routing**. As a sequential routing algorithm proceeds, some channels will become more congested since they hold more interconnects than others. In the case of FPGAs and channeled gate arrays, the channels have a fixed channel capacity and can only hold a certain number of interconnects. There are two different ways that a global router normally handles this problem. Using **order-independent routing**, a global router proceeds by routing each net, ignoring how crowded the channels are. Whether a particular net is processed first or last does not matter, the channel assignment will be the same. In order-independent routing, after all the interconnects are assigned to channels, the global router returns to those channels that are the most crowded and reassigns some interconnects to other, less crowded, channels. Alternatively, a global router can consider the number of interconnects already placed in various channels as it proceeds. In this case the global routing is **order dependent**—the routing is still sequential, but now the order of processing the nets will affect the results. Iterative improvement or simulated annealing may be applied to the solutions found from both order-dependent and order-independent algorithms. This is implemented in the same way as for system partitioning and placement: A constructed solution is successively changed, one interconnect path at a time, in a series of random moves.

In contrast to sequential global-routing methods, which handle nets one at a time, **hierarchical routing** handles all nets at a particular level at once. Rather than handling all of the nets on the chip at the same time, the global-routing problem is made more tractable by dividing the chip area into levels of hierarchy. By considering only one level of hierarchy at a time the size of the problem is reduced at each level. There are two ways to traverse the levels of hierarchy. Starting at the whole chip, or highest level, and proceeding down to the logic cells is the top-down approach. The bottom-up approach starts at the lowest level of hierarchy and globally routes the smallest areas first.

17.1.4   Global Routing Between Blocks

Figure 17.4 illustrates the global-routing problem for a cell-based ASIC. Each edge in the **channel-intersection graph** in Figure 17.4(c) represents a channel. The global router is restricted to using these channels. The weight of each edge in the graph corresponds to the length of the channel. The global router plans a path for each interconnect using this graph.

Figure 17.5 shows an example of global routing for a net with five terminals, labeled A1 through F1, for the cell-based ASIC shown in Figure 17.4. If a designer wishes to use minimum total interconnect path length as an objective, the global router finds the minimum-length tree shown in Figure 17.5(b). This tree determines the channels the interconnects will use. For example, the shortest connection from A1 to B1 uses channels 2, 1, and 5 (in that order). This is the information the global router passes to the detailed router. Figure 17.5(c) shows that minimizing the total path length may not correspond to minimizing the path delay between two points.

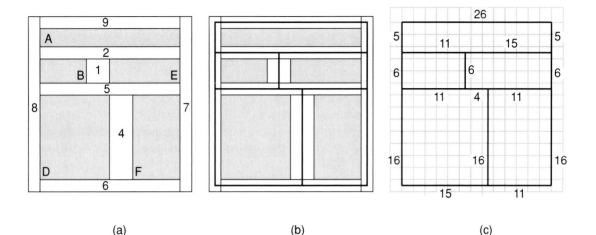

(a) (b) (c)

FIGURE 17.4 Global routing for a cell-based ASIC formulated as a graph problem. (a) A cell-based ASIC with numbered channels. (b) The channels form the edges of a graph. (c) The channel-intersection graph. Each channel corresponds to an edge on a graph whose weight corresponds to the channel length.

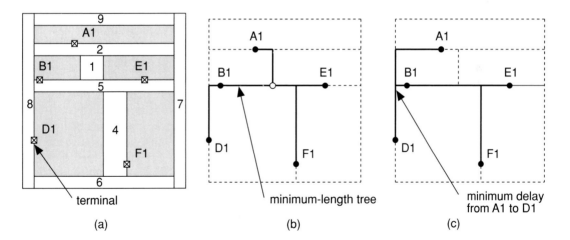

(a) (b) (c)

FIGURE 17.5 Finding paths in global routing. (a) A cell-based ASIC (from Figure 17.4) showing a single net with a fanout of four (five terminals). We have to order the numbered channels to complete the interconnect path for terminals A1 through F1. (b) The terminals are projected to the center of the nearest channel, forming a graph. A minimum-length tree for the net that uses the channels and takes into account the channel capacities. (c) The minimum-length tree does not necessarily correspond to minimum delay. If we wish to minimize the delay from terminal A1 to D1, a different tree might be better.

Global routing is very similar for cell-based ASICs and gate arrays, but there is a very important difference between the types of channels in these ASICs. The size of the channels in sea-of-gates arrays, channelless gate arrays, and cell-based ASICs can be varied to make sure there is enough space to complete the wiring. In channeled gate-arrays and FPGAs the size, number, and location of channels are fixed. The good news is that the global router can allocate as many interconnects to each channel as it likes, since that space is committed anyway. The bad news is that there is a maximum number of interconnects that each channel can hold. If the global router needs more room, even in just one channel on the whole chip, the designer has to repeat the placement-and-routing steps and try again (or use a bigger chip).

17.1.5 Global Routing Inside Flexible Blocks

We shall illustrate global routing using a gate array. Figure 17.6(a) shows the routing resources on a sea-of-gates or channelless gate array. The gate array base cells are arranged in 36 blocks, each block containing an array of 8 by 16 gate-array base cells, making a total of 4068 base cells.

The horizontal interconnect resources are the routing channels that are formed from unused rows of the gate-array base cells, as shown in Figure 17.6(b) and (c). The vertical resources are feedthroughs. For example, the logic cell shown in Figure 17.6(d) is an inverter that contains two types of feedthrough. The inverter logic cell uses a single gate-array base cell with terminals (or *connectors*) located at the top and bottom of the logic cell. The inverter input pin has two electrically equivalent terminals that the global router can use as a feedthrough. The output of the inverter is connected to only one terminal. The remaining vertical **track** is unused by the inverter logic cell, so this track forms an uncommitted feedthrough.

You may see any of the terms **landing pad** (because we say that we "drop" a via to a landing pad), **pick-up point**, **connector**, **terminal**, **pin**, or **port** used for the connection to a logic cell. The term *pick-up point* refers to the physical pieces of metal (or sometimes polysilicon) in the logic cell to which the router connects. In a three-level metal process, the global router may be able to connect to anywhere in an area—an **area pick-up point**. In this book we use the term *connector* to refer to the physical pick-up point. The term *pin* more often refers to the connection on a logic schematic icon (a dot, square box, or whatever symbol is used), rather than layout. Thus the difference between a pin and a connector is that we can have multiple connectors for one pin. *Terminal* is often used when we talk about routing. The term *port* is used when we are using text (EDIF netlists or HDLs, for example) to describe circuits.

In a gate array the channel capacity must be a multiple of the number of **horizontal tracks** in the gate-array base cell. Figure 17.6(e) shows a gate-array base cell with seven horizontal tracks (see Section 17.2 for the factors that determine the track width and track spacing). Thus, in this gate array, we can have a channel with a capacity of 7, 14, 21, ... horizontal tracks—but not between these values.

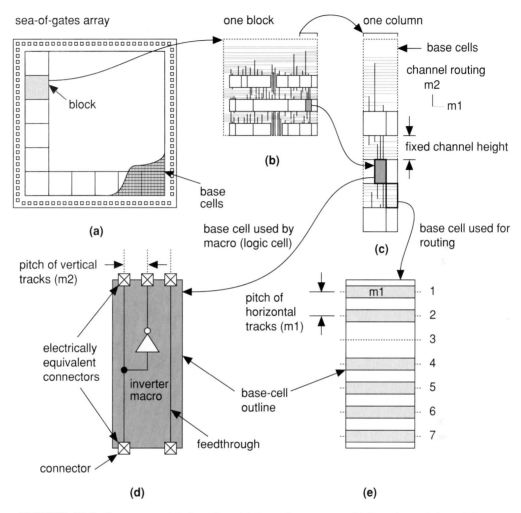

sea-of-gates array

one block

one column

base cells

channel routing
m2

m1

fixed channel height

block

base
cells

(b)

(a)

base cell used by
macro (logic cell)

base cell used for
routing

(c)

pitch of vertical
tracks (m2)

pitch of
horizontal
tracks (m1)

m1   1

2

3

electrically
equivalent
connectors

inverter
macro

base-cell
outline

4

5

6

feedthrough

7

connector

(d)

(e)

FIGURE 17.6   Gate-array global routing. (a) A small gate array. (b) An enlarged view of the routing. The top channel uses three rows of gate-array base cells; the other channels use only one. (c) A further enlarged view showing how the routing in the channels connects to the logic cells. (d) One of the logic cells, an inverter. (e) There are seven horizontal wiring tracks available in one row of gate-array base cells—the channel capacity is thus 7.

Figure 17.7 shows the inverter macro for the sea-of-gates array shown in Figure 17.6. Figure 17.7(a) shows the base cell. Figure 17.7(b) shows how the internal inverter wiring on m1 leaves one vertical track free as a feedthrough in a two-level metal process (connectors placed at the top and bottom of the cell). In a three-level metal process the connectors may be placed inside the cell abutment box (Figure 17.7c). Figure 17.8 shows the global routing for the sea-of-gates array. We

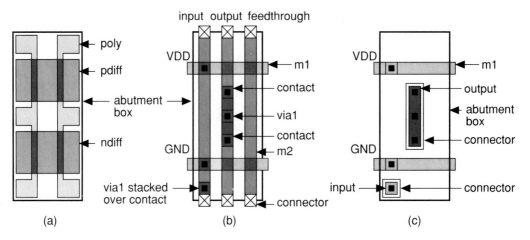

FIGURE 17.7 The gate-array inverter from Figure 17.6d. (a) An oxide-isolated gate-array base cell, showing the diffusion and polysilicon layers. (b) The metal and contact layers for the inverter in a 2LM (two-level metal) process. (c) The router's view of the cell in a 3LM process.

divide the array into nonoverlapping **routing bins** (or just **bins**, also called **global routing cells** or **GRCs**), each containing a number of gate-array base cells.

We need an aside to discuss our use of the term *cell*. Be careful not to confuse the global routing cells with gate-array base cells (the smallest element of a gate array, consisting of a small number of *n*-type and *p*-type transistors), or with logic cells (which are NAND gates, NOR gates, and so on).

A large routing bin reduces the size of the routing problem, and a small routing bin allows the router to calculate the wiring capacities more accurately. Some tools permit routing bins of different size in different areas of the chip (with smaller routing bins helping in areas of dense routing). Figure 17.8(a) shows a routing bin that is 2 by 4 gate-array base cells. The logic cells occupy the lower half of the routing bin. The upper half of the routing bin is the channel area, reserved for wiring. The global router calculates the edge capacities for this routing bin, including the vertical feedthroughs. The global router then determines the shortest path for each net considering these edge capacities. An example of a global-routing calculation is shown in Figure 17.8(b). The path, described by a series of adjacent routing bins, is passed to the detailed router.

17.1.6   Timing-Driven Methods

Minimizing the total pathlength using a Steiner tree does not necessarily minimize the interconnect delay of a path. Alternative tree algorithms apply in this situation, most using the Elmore constant as a method to estimate the delay of a path (Section 17.1.2). As in timing-driven placement, there are two main approaches to

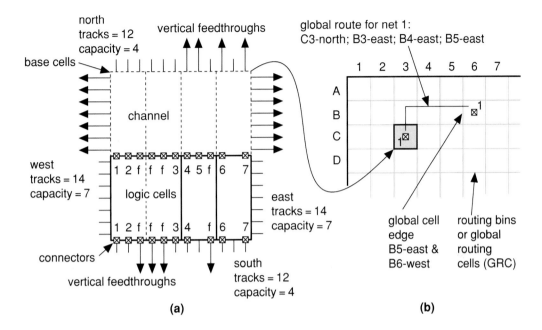

FIGURE 17.8 Global routing a gate array. (a) A single global-routing cell (GRC or routing bin) containing 2 by 4 gate-array base cells. For this choice of routing bin the maximum horizontal track capacity is 14, the maximum vertical track capacity is 12. The routing bin labeled C3 contains three logic cells, two of which have feedthroughs marked 'f'. This results in the edge capacities shown. (b) A view of the top left-hand corner of the gate array showing 28 routing bins. The global router uses the edge capacities to find a sequence of routing bins to connect the nets.

timing-driven routing: net-based and path-based. Path-based methods are more sophisticated. For example, if there is a critical path from logic cell A to B to C, the global router may increase the delay due to the interconnect between logic cells A and B if it can reduce the delay between logic cells B and C. Placement and global routing tools may or may not use the same algorithm to estimate net delay. If these tools are from different companies, the algorithms are probably different. The algorithms must be compatible, however. There is no use performing placement to minimize predicted delay if the global router uses completely different measurement methods. Companies that produce floorplanning and placement tools make sure that the output is compatible with different routing tools—often to the extent of using different algorithms to target different routers.

17.1.7 Back-annotation

After global routing is complete it is possible to accurately predict what the length of each interconnect in every net will be after detailed routing, probably to within 5 percent. The global router can give us not just an estimate of the total net length (which was all we knew at the placement stage), but the resistance and capacitance of each path in each net. This **RC information** is used to calculate net delays. We can back-annotate this net delay information to the synthesis tool for in-place optimization or to a timing verifier to make sure there are no timing surprises. Differences in timing predictions at this point arise due to the different ways in which the placement algorithms estimate the paths and the way the global router actually builds the paths.

17.2 Detailed Routing

The global routing step determines the channels to be used for each interconnect. Using this information the detailed router decides the exact location and layers for each interconnect. Figure 17.9(a) shows typical metal rules. These rules determine the m1 **routing pitch** (**track pitch**, **track spacing**, or just **pitch**). We can set the m1 pitch to one of three values:

1. **via-to-via** (**VTV**) pitch (or spacing),
2. **via-to-line** (**VTL** or **line-to-via**) pitch, or
3. **line-to-line** (**LTL**) pitch.

The same choices apply to the m2 and other metal layers if they are present. Via-to-via spacing allows the router to place vias adjacent to each other. Via-to-line spacing is hard to use in practice because it restricts the router to nonadjacent vias. Using line-to-line spacing prevents the router from placing a via at all without using jogs and is rarely used. Via-to-via spacing is the easiest for a router to use and the most common. Using either via-to-line or line-to-line spacing means that the routing pitch is larger than the minimum metal pitch.

Sometimes people draw a distinction between a cut and a via when they talk about large connections such as shown in Figure 17.10(a). We split or **stitch** a large via into identically sized cuts (sometimes called a **waffle via**). Because of the profile of the metal in a contact and the way current flows into a contact, often the total resistance of several small cuts is less than that of one large cut. Using identically sized cuts also means the processing conditions during contact etching, which may vary with the area and perimeter of a contact, are the same for every cut on the chip.

In a **stacked via** the contact cuts all overlap in a layout plot and it is impossible to tell just how many vias on which layers are present. Figure 17.10(b–f) show an alternative way to draw contacts and vias. Though this is not a standard, using the diagonal box convention makes it possible to recognize stacked vias and contacts on a layout (in any orientation). I shall use these conventions when it is necessary.

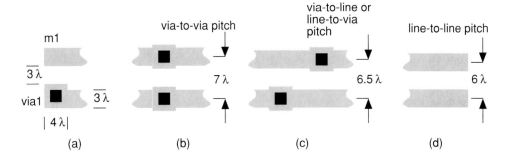

FIGURE 17.9 The metal routing pitch. (a) An example of λ-based metal design rules for m1 and via1 (m1/m2 via). (b) Via-to-via pitch for adjacent vias. (c) Via-to-line (or line-to-via) pitch for nonadjacent vias. (d) Line-to-line pitch with no vias.

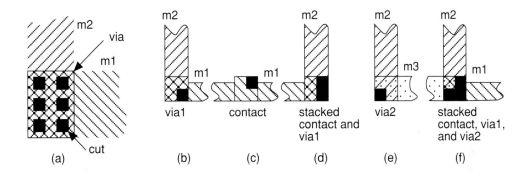

FIGURE 17.10 (a) A large m1 to m2 via. The black squares represent the holes (or cuts) that are etched in the insulating material between the m1 and 2 layers. (b) A m1 to m2 via (a via1). (c) A contact from m1 to diffusion or polysilicon (a contact). (d) A via1 placed over (or stacked over) a contact. (e) A m2 to m3 via (a via2) (f) A via2 stacked over a via1 stacked over a contact. Notice that the black square in parts b–c do *not* represent the actual location of the cuts. The black squares are offset so you can recognize stacked vias and contacts.

In a two-level metal CMOS ASIC technology we complete the wiring using the two different metal layers for the horizontal and vertical directions, one layer for each direction. This is **Manhattan routing**, because the results look similar to the rectangular north-south and east-west layout of streets in New York City. Thus, for example, if terminals are on the m2 layer, then we route the horizontal branches in a channel using m2 and the vertical trunks using m1. Figure 17.11 shows that, although we may choose a **preferred direction** for each metal layer (for example, m1 for horizontal routing and m2 for vertical routing), this may lead to problems in cases that have both horizontal and vertical channels. In these cases we define a **preferred metal layer** in the direction of the channel spine. In Figure 17.11, because the logic cell connectors are on m2, any vertical channel has to use vias at every logic cell location. By changing the orientation of the metal directions in vertical channels, we can avoid this, and instead we only need to place vias at the intersection of horizontal and vertical channels.

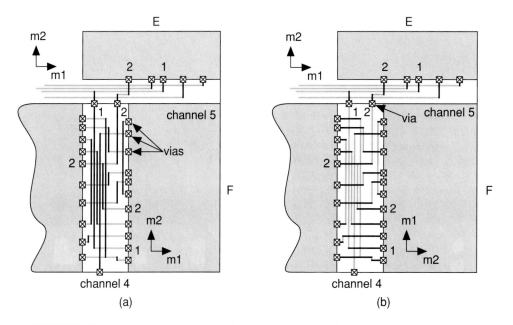

FIGURE 17.11 An expanded view of part of a cell-based ASIC. (a) Both channel 4 and channel 5 use m1 in the horizontal direction and m2 in the vertical direction. If the logic cell connectors are on m2 this requires vias to be placed at every logic cell connector in channel 4. (b) Channel 4 and 5 are routed with m1 along the direction of the channel spine (the long direction of the channel). Now vias are required only for nets 1 and 2, at the intersection of the channels.

Figure 17.12 shows an imaginary logic cell with connectors. Double-entry logic cells intended for two-level metal routing have connectors at the top and bottom of the logic cell, usually in m2. Logic cells intended for processes with three or more levels of metal have connectors in the center of the cell, again usually on m2. Logic cells may use both m1 and m2 internally, but the use of m2 is usually minimized. The router normally uses a simplified view of the logic cell called a **phantom**. The phantom contains only the logic cell information that the router needs: the connector locations, types, and names; the abutment and bounding boxes; enough layer information to be able to place cells without violating design rules; and a **blockage map**—the locations of any metal inside the cell that blocks routing.

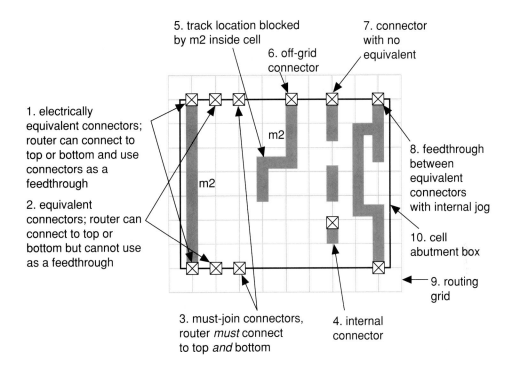

5. track location blocked by m2 inside cell

6. off-grid connector

7. connector with no equivalent

1. electrically equivalent connectors; router can connect to top or bottom and use connectors as a feedthrough

2. equivalent connectors; router can connect to top or bottom but cannot use as a feedthrough

m2

m2

8. feedthrough between equivalent connectors with internal jog

10. cell abutment box

9. routing grid

3. must-join connectors, router *must* connect to top *and* bottom

4. internal connector

FIGURE 17.12 The different types of connections that can be made to a cell. This cell has connectors at the top and bottom of the cell (normal for cells intended for use with a two-level metal process) and internal connectors (normal for logic cells intended for use with a three-level metal process). The interconnect and connections are drawn to scale.

Figure 17.13 illustrates some terms used in the detailed routing of a channel. The channel spine in Figure 17.13 is horizontal with terminals at the top and the bottom, but a channel can also be vertical. In either case terminals are spaced along the longest edges of the channel at given, fixed locations. Terminals are usually located on a grid defined by the routing pitch on that layer (we say terminals are either **on-grid** or **off-grid**). We make connections between terminals using interconnects that consist of one or more **trunks** running parallel to the length of the channel and **branches** that connect the trunk to the terminals. If more than one trunk is used, the trunks are connected by **doglegs**. Connections exit the channel at **pseudoterminals**.

The trunk and branch connections run in **tracks** (equispaced, like railway tracks). If the trunk connections use m1, the **horizontal track spacing** (usually just called the **track spacing** for channel routing) is equal to the m1 routing pitch. The maximum number of interconnects we need in a channel multiplied by the horizontal track spacing gives the minimum height of a channel (see Section 17.2.2 on how to determine

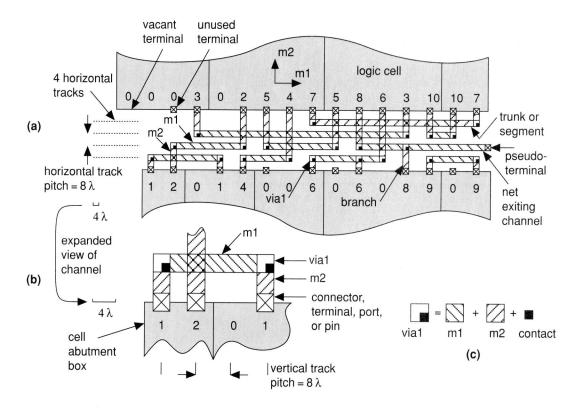

FIGURE 17.13 Terms used in channel routing. (a) A channel with four horizontal tracks. (b) An expanded view of the left-hand portion of the channel showing (approximately to scale) how the m1 and m2 layers connect to the logic cells on either side of the channel. (c) The construction of a via1 (m1/m2 via).

the maximum number of interconnects needed). Each terminal occupies a **column**. If the branches use m2, the **column spacing** (or **vertical track-spacing**) is equal to the m2 routing pitch.

17.2.1   Goals and Objectives

The goal of detailed routing is to complete all the connections between logic cells. The most common objective is to minimize one or more of the following:

- The total interconnect length and area
- The number of layer changes that the connections have to make
- The delay of critical paths

Minimizing the number of layer changes corresponds to minimizing the number of vias that add parasitic resistance and capacitance to a connection.

In some cases the detailed router may not be able to complete the routing in the area provided. In the case of a cell-based ASIC or sea-of-gates array, it is possible to increase the channel size and try the routing steps again. A channeled gate array or FPGA has fixed routing resources and in these cases we must start all over again with floorplanning and placement, or use a larger chip.

17.2.2 Measurement of Channel Density

We can describe a channel-routing problem by specifying two lists of nets: one for the top edge of the channel and one for the bottom edge. The position of the net number in the list gives the column position. The net number zero represents a vacant or unused terminal. Figure 17.14 shows a channel with the numbered terminals to be connected along the top and the bottom of the channel.

We call the number of nets that cross a line drawn vertically anywhere in a channel the **local density**. We call the maximum local density of the channel the **global density** or sometimes just **channel density**. Figure 17.14 has a channel density of 4. Channel density is an important measure in routing—it tells a router the absolute fewest number of horizontal interconnects that it needs at the point where the local density is highest. In two-level routing (all the horizontal interconnects run on one routing layer) the channel density determines the minimum height of the channel. The channel capacity is the maximum number of interconnects that a channel can hold. If the channel density is greater than the channel capacity, that channel definitely cannot be routed (to learn how channel density is calculated, see Section 17.2.5).

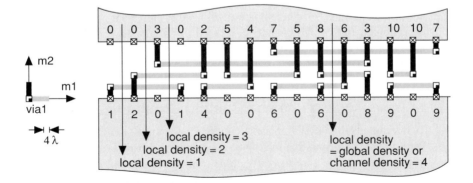

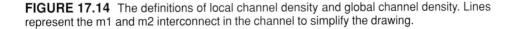

FIGURE 17.14 The definitions of local channel density and global channel density. Lines represent the m1 and m2 interconnect in the channel to simplify the drawing.

17.2.3 Algorithms

We start discussion of routing methods by simplifying the general channel-routing problem. The **restricted channel-routing problem** limits each net in a channel to use only one horizontal segment. In other words the channel router uses only one trunk for each net. This restriction has the effect of minimizing the number of connections between the routing layers. This is equivalent to minimizing the number of vias used by the channel router in a two-layer metal technology. Minimizing the number of vias is an important objective in routing a channel, but it is not always practical. Sometimes constraints will force a channel router to use jogs or other methods to complete the routing (see Section 17.2.5). Next, though, we shall study an algorithm that solves the restricted channel-routing problem.

17.2.4 Left-Edge Algorithm

The **left-edge algorithm** (**LEA**) is the basis for several routing algorithms [Hashimoto and Stevens, 1971]. The LEA applies to two-layer channel routing, using one layer for the trunks and the other layer for the branches. For example, m1 may be used in the horizontal direction and m2 in the vertical direction. The LEA proceeds as follows:

1. Sort the nets according to the leftmost edges of the net's horizontal segment.
2. Assign the first net on the list to the first free track.
3. Assign the next net on the list, which will fit, to the track.
4. Repeat this process from step 3 until no more nets will fit in the current track.
5. Repeat steps 2–4 until all nets have been assigned to tracks.
6. Connect the net segments to the top and bottom of the channel.

Figure 17.15 illustrates the LEA. The algorithm works as long as none of the branches touch—which may occur if there are terminals in the same column belonging to different nets. In this situation we have to make sure that the trunk that connects to the top of the channel is placed above the lower trunk. Otherwise two branches will overlap and short the nets together. In the next section we shall examine this situation more closely.

17.2.5 Constraints and Routing Graphs

Two terminals that are in the same column in a channel create a **vertical constraint**. We say that the terminal at the top of the column imposes a vertical constraint on the lower terminal. We can draw a graph showing the vertical constraints imposed by terminals. The nodes in a **vertical-constraint graph** represent terminals. A vertical constraint between two terminals is shown by an edge of the graph connecting the two terminals. A graph that contains information in the direction of an edge is a **directed graph**. The arrow on the graph edge shows the direction of the con-

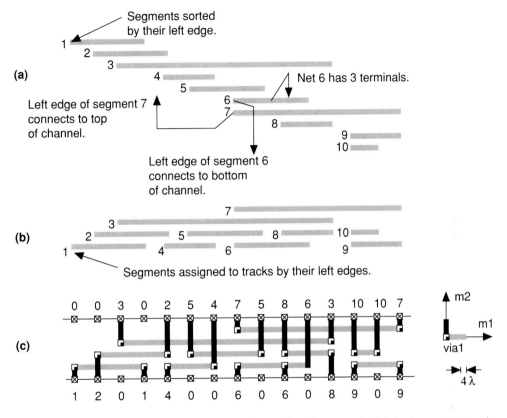

FIGURE 17.15 Left-edge algorithm. (a) Sorted list of segments. (b) Assignment to tracks. (c) Completed channel route (with m1 and m2 interconnect represented by lines).

straint—pointing to the lower terminal, which is constrained. Figure 17.16(a) shows an example of a channel, and Figure 17.16(b) shows its vertical constraint graph.

We can also define a **horizontal constraint** and a corresponding **horizontal-constraint graph**. If the trunk for net 1 overlaps the trunk of net 2, then we say there is a horizontal constraint between net 1 and net 2. Unlike a vertical constraint, a horizontal constraint has no direction. Figure 17.16(c) shows an example of a horizontal constraint graph and shows a group of 4 terminals (numbered 3, 5, 6, and 7) that must all overlap. Since this is the largest such group, the global channel density is 4.

If there are no vertical constraints at all in a channel, we can guarantee that the LEA will find the minimum number of routing tracks. The addition of vertical constraints transforms the restricted routing problem into an NP-complete problem. There is also an arrangement of vertical constraints that none of the algorithms based on the LEA can cope with. In Figure 17.17(a) net 1 is above net 2 in the first

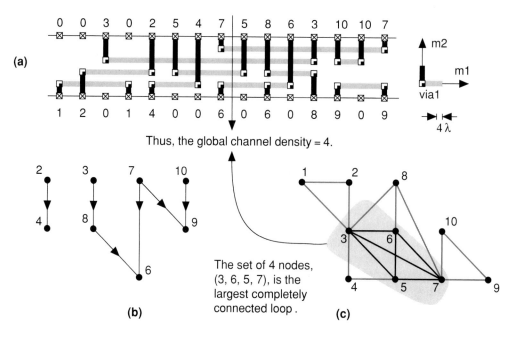

FIGURE 17.16 Routing graphs. (a) Channel with a global density of 4. (b) The vertical constraint graph. If two nets occupy the same column, the net at the top of the channel imposes a vertical constraint on the net at the bottom. For example, net 2 imposes a vertical constraint on net 4. Thus the interconnect for net 4 must use a track above net 2. (c) Horizontal-constraint graph. If the segments of two nets overlap, they are connected in the horizontal-constraint graph. This graph determines the global channel density.

column of the channel. Thus net 1 imposes a vertical constraint on net 2. Net 2 is above net 1 in the last column of the channel. Then net 2 also imposes a vertical constraint on net 1. It is impossible to route this arrangement using two routing layers with the restriction of using only one trunk for each net. If we construct the vertical-constraint graph for this situation, shown in Figure 17.17(b), there is a loop or cycle between nets 1 and 2. If there is any such **vertical-constraint cycle** (or **cyclic constraint**) between two or more nets, the LEA will fail. A **dogleg router** removes the restriction that each net can use only one track or trunk. Figure 17.17(c) shows how adding a dogleg permits a channel with a cyclic constraint to be routed.

The channel-routing algorithms we have described so far do not allow interconnects on one layer to run on top of other interconnects on a different layer. These algorithms allow interconnects to cross at right angles to each other on different layers, but not to **overlap**. When we remove the restriction that horizontal and vertical routing must use different layers, the density of a channel is no longer the lower bound for the number of tracks required. For two routing layers the ultimate lower

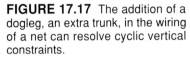

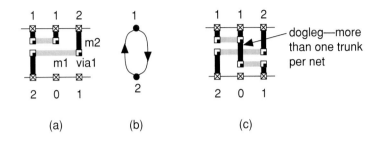

FIGURE 17.17 The addition of a dogleg, an extra trunk, in the wiring of a net can resolve cyclic vertical constraints.

bound becomes half of the channel density. The practical reasoning for restricting overlap is the parasitic **overlap capacitance** between signal interconnects. As the dimensions of the metal interconnect are reduced, the capacitance between adjacent interconnects on the same layer (**coupling capacitance**) is comparable to the capacitance of interconnects that overlap on different layers (**overlap capacitance**). Thus, allowing a short overlap between interconnects on different layers may not be as bad as allowing two interconnects to run adjacent to each other for a long distance on the same layer. Some routers allow you to specify that two interconnects must not run adjacent to each other for more than a specified length.

The channel height is fixed for channeled gate arrays; it is variable in discrete steps for channelless gate arrays; it is continuously variable for cell-based ASICs. However, for all these types of ASICs, the channel wiring is fully customized and so may be compacted or compressed after a channel router has completed the interconnect. The use of **channel-routing compaction** for a two-layer channel can reduce the channel height by 15 percent to 20 percent [Cheng et al., 1992].

Modern channel routers are capable of routing a channel at or near the theoretical minimum density. We can thus consider channel routing a solved problem. Most of the difficulty in detailed routing now comes from the need to route more than two layers and to route arbitrary shaped regions. These problems are best handled by area routers.

17.2.6 Area-Routing Algorithms

There are many algorithms used for the detailed routing of general-shaped areas (see the paper by Ohtsuki in [Ohtsuki, 1986]). Many of these were originally developed for PCB wiring. The first group we shall cover and the earliest to be used historically are the **grid-expansion** or **maze-running** algorithms. A second group of methods, which are more efficient, are the **line-search** algorithms.

Figure 17.18 illustrates the **Lee maze-running algorithm**. The goal is to find a path from X to Y—i.e., from the start (or source) to the finish (or target)—avoiding any obstacles. The algorithm is often called **wave propagation** because it sends out waves, which spread out like those created by dropping a stone into a pond.

5	4	3	2	3	4			
4	3	2	1	2	3	4		
3	2	1	X	1	2	3	4	4
4	3					4	4	
	4					4	3	
						3	2	
				4	3	2	1	Y
					4	3	2	1

FIGURE 17.18 The Lee maze-running algorithm. The algorithm finds a path from source (X) to target (Y) by emitting a wave from both the source and the target at the same time. Successive outward moves are marked in each bin. Once the target is reached, the path is found by backtracking (if there is a choice of bins with equal labeled values, we choose the bin that avoids changing direction). (The original form of the Lee algorithm uses a single wave.)

Algorithms that use lines rather than waves to search for connections are more efficient than algorithms based on the Lee algorithm. Figure 17.19 illustrates the **Hightower algorithm**—a **line-search algorithm** (or **line-probe algorithm**):

1. Extend lines from both the source and target toward each other.

2. When an extended line, known as an **escape line**, meets an obstacle, choose a point on the escape line from which to project another escape line at right angles to the old one. This point is the **escape point**.

3. Place an escape point on the line so that the next escape line just misses the edge of the obstacle. Escape lines emanating from the source and target intersect to form the path.

FIGURE 17.19 Hightower area-routing algorithm. (a) Escape lines are constructed from source (X) and target (Y) toward each other until they hit obstacles. (b) An escape point is found on the escape line so that the next escape line perpendicular to the original misses the next obstacle. The path is complete when escape lines from source and target meet.

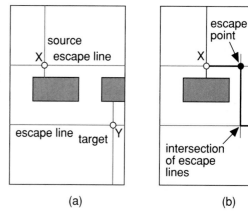

(a)   (b)

The Hightower algorithm is faster and requires less memory than methods based on the Lee algorithm.

17.2.7   Multilevel Routing

Using **two-layer routing**, if the logic cells do not contain any m2, it is possible to complete some routing in m2 using over-the-cell (OTC) routing. Sometimes poly is used for short connections in the channel in a two-level metal technology; this is known as **2.5-layer routing**. Using a third level of metal in **three-layer routing**, there is a choice of approaches. **Reserved-layer routing** restricts all the interconnect on each layer to flow in one direction in a given routing area (for example, in a channel, either parallel or perpendicular to the channel spine). **Unreserved-layer routing** moves in both horizontal and vertical directions on a given layer. Most routers use reserved routing. Reserved three-level metal routing offers another choice: Either use m1 and m3 for horizontal routing (parallel to the channel spine), with m2 for vertical routing (**HVH routing**) or use **VHV routing**. Since the logic cell interconnect usually blocks most of the area on the m1 layer, HVH routing is normally used. It is also important to consider the pitch of the layers when routing in the same direction on two different layers. Using HVH routing it is preferable for the m3 pitch to be a simple multiple of the m1 pitch (ideally they are the same). Some processes have more than three levels of metal. Sometimes the upper one or two metal layers have a coarser pitch than the lower layers and are used in **multilevel routing** for power and clock lines rather than for signal interconnect.

Figure 17.20 shows an example of three-layer channel routing. The logic cells are 64 λ high, the m1 routing pitch is 8 λ, and the m2 and m3 routing pitch is 16 λ. The channel in Figure 17.20 is the same as the channel using two-layer metal shown in Figure 17.13, but using three-level metal reduces the channel height from 40 λ ($=5 \times 8\,\lambda$) to 16 λ. Submicron processes try to use the same metal pitch on all metal layers. This makes routing easier but processing more difficult.

With three or more levels of metal routing it is possible to reduce the channel height in a row-based ASIC to zero. All of the interconnect is then completed over the cell. If all of the channels are eliminated, the core area (logic cells plus routing) is determined solely by the logic-cell area. The point at which this happens depends on not only the number of metal layers and channel density, but also the routing resources (the blockages and feedthroughs) in the logic cell. This the **cell porosity**. Designing porous cells that help to minimize routing area is an art. For example, it is quite common to be able to produce a smaller chip using larger logic cells if the larger cells have more routing resources.

17.2.8   Timing-Driven Detailed Routing

In detailed routing the global router has already set the path the interconnect will follow. At this point little can be done to improve timing except to reduce the number of vias, alter the interconnect width to optimize delay, and minimize overlap

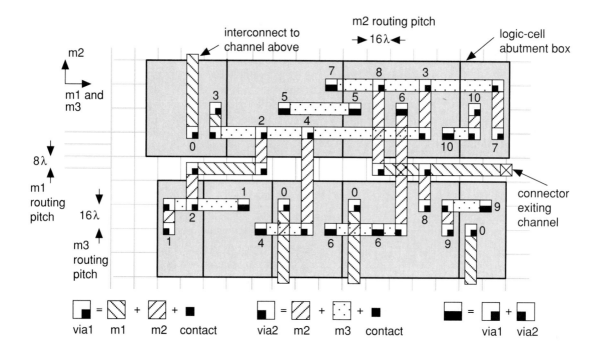

FIGURE 17.20 Three-level channel routing. In this diagram the m2 and m3 routing pitch is set to twice the m1 routing pitch. Routing density can be increased further if all the routing pitches can be made equal—a difficult process challenge.

capacitance. The gains here are relatively small, but for very long branching nets even small gains may be important. For high-frequency clock nets it may be important to shape and **chamfer** (round) the interconnect to match impedances at branches and control reflections at corners.

17.2.9 Final Routing Steps

If the algorithms to estimate congestion in the floorplanning tool accurately perfectly reflected the algorithms used by the global router and detailed router, routing completion should be guaranteed. Often, however, the detailed router will not be able to completely route all the nets. These problematical nets are known as **unroutes**. Routers handle this situation in one of two ways. The first method leaves the problematical nets unconnected. The second method completes all interconnects anyway but with some design-rule violations (the problematical nets may be shorted to other nets, for example). Some tools flag these problems as a warning (in fact there can be no more serious error).

If there are many unroutes the designer needs to discover the reason and return to the floorplanner and change channel sizes (for a cell-based ASIC) or increase the base-array size (for a gate array). Returning to the global router and changing bin sizes or adjusting the algorithms may also help. In drastic cases it may be necessary to change the floorplan. If just a handful of difficult nets remain to be routed, some tools allow the designer to perform hand edits using a **rip-up and reroute** router (sometimes this is done automatically by the detailed router as a last phase in the routing procedure anyway). This capability also permits **engineering change orders** (**ECO**)—corresponding to the little yellow wires on a PCB. One of the last steps in routing is **via removal**—the detailed router looks to see if it can eliminate any vias (which can contribute a significant amount to the interconnect resistance) by changing layers or making other modifications to the completed routing. **Routing compaction** can then be performed as the final step.

17.3 Special Routing

The routing of nets that require special attention, clock and power nets for example, is normally done before detailed routing of signal nets. The architecture and structure of these nets is performed as part of floorplanning, but the sizing and topology of these nets is finalized as part of the routing step.

17.3.1 Clock Routing

Gate arrays normally use a clock spine (a regular grid), eliminating the need for special routing (see Section 16.1.6, "Clock Planning"). The clock distribution grid is designed at the same time as the gate-array base to ensure a minimum clock skew and minimum clock latency—given power dissipation and clock buffer area limitations. Cell-based ASICs may use either a clock spine, a clock tree, or a hybrid approach. Figure 17.21 shows how a clock router may minimize clock skew in a clock spine by making the path lengths, and thus net delays, to every leaf node equal—using jogs in the interconnect paths if necessary. More sophisticated clock routers perform **clock-tree synthesis** (automatically choosing the depth and structure of the clock tree) and **clock-buffer insertion** (equalizing the delay to the leaf nodes by balancing interconnect delays and buffer delays).

The clock tree may contain multiply-driven nodes (more than one active element driving a net). The net delay models that we have used break down in this case and we may have to extract the clock network and perform circuit simulation, followed by back-annotation of the clock delays to the netlist (for circuit extraction, see Section 17.4) and the bus currents to the clock router. The sizes of the clock buses depend on the current they must carry. The limits are set by reliability issues to be discussed next.

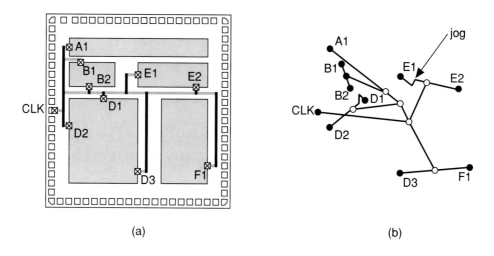

(a)   (b)

FIGURE 17.21 Clock routing. (a) A clock network for the cell-based ASIC from Figure 16.11. (b) Equalizing the interconnect segments between CLK and all destinations (by including jogs if necessary) minimizes clock skew.

Clock skew induced by hot-electron wearout was mentioned in Section 16.1.6, "Clock Planning." Another factor contributing to unpredictable clock skew is changes in clock-buffer delays with variations in power-supply voltage due to data-dependent activity. This **activity-induced clock skew** can easily be larger than the skew achievable using a clock router. For example, there is little point in using software capable of reducing clock skew to less than 100 ps if, due to fluctuations in power-supply voltage when part of the chip becomes active, the clock-network delays change by 200 ps.

The power buses supplying the buffers driving the clock spine carry direct current (unidirectional current or DC), but the clock spine itself carries alternating current (bidirectional current or AC). The difference between *electromigration* failure rates due to AC and DC leads to different rules for sizing clock buses. As we explained in Section 16.1.6, "Clock Planning," the fastest way to drive a large load in CMOS is to taper successive stages by approximately $e \approx 3$. This is not necessarily the smallest-area or lowest-power approach, however [Veendrick, 1984].

17.3.2   Power Routing

Each of the power buses has to be **sized** according to the current it will carry. Too much current in a power bus can lead to a failure through a mechanism known as **electromigration** [Young and Christou, 1994]. The required power-bus widths can be estimated automatically from library information, from a separate **power simulation** tool, or by entering the power-bus widths to the routing software by hand.

Many routers use a default power-bus width so that it is quite easy to complete routing of an ASIC without even knowing about this problem.

For a direct current (DC) the **mean time to failure** (MTTF) due to electromigration is experimentally found to obey the following equation:

$$\text{MTTF} = AJ^{-2}\exp\frac{-E}{\text{k}T}, \tag{17.9}$$

where J is the current density; E is approximately 0.5 eV; k, Boltzmann's constant, is 8.62×10^{-5} eVK; and T is absolute temperature in kelvins.

There are a number of different approaches to model the effect of an AC component. A typical expression is

$$\text{MTTF} = \frac{A\exp\dfrac{-E}{\text{k}T}}{\bar{J}\overline{|J|} + \text{k}_{\text{AC/DC}}\overline{|J|}^2}, \tag{17.10}$$

where $\bar{J}$ is the average of $J(t)$, and $\overline{|J|}$ is the average of $|J|$. The constant $\text{k}_{\text{AC/DC}}$ relates the relative effects of AC and DC and is typically between 0.01 and 0.0001. Electromigration problems become serious with a MTTF of less than 10^5 hours (approximately 10 years) for current densities (DC) greater than 0.5 GAm^{-2} at temperatures above 150 °C.

Table 17.1 lists example **metallization reliability rules**—limits for the current you can pass through a metal layer, contact, or via—for the typical 0.5 µm three-level metal CMOS process, G5. The limit of 1 mA of current per square micron of metal cross section is a good rule-of-thumb to follow for current density in aluminum-based interconnect.

Some CMOS processes also have **maximum metal-width rules** (or **fat-metal rules**). This is because stress (especially at the corners of the die, which occurs during **die attach**—mounting the die on the chip carrier) can cause large metal areas to lift. A solution to this problem is to place slots in the wide metal lines. These rules are dependent on the ASIC vendor's level of experience.

To determine the power-bus widths we need to determine the bus currents. The largest problem is emulating the system's operating conditions. Input vectors to test the system are not necessarily representative of actual system operation. Clock-bus sizing depends strongly on the parameter $\text{k}_{\text{AC/DC}}$ in Eq. 17.10, since the clock spine carries alternating current. (For the sources of power dissipation in CMOS, see Section 15.5, "Power Dissipation.")

Gate arrays normally use a regular **power grid** as part of the gate-array base. The gate-array logic cells contain two fixed-width power buses inside the cell, running horizontally on m1. The horizontal m1 power buses are then strapped in a vertical direction by m2 buses, which run vertically across the chip. The resistance of the power grid is extracted and simulated with SPICE during the base-array design to model the effects of IR drops under worst-case conditions.

TABLE 17.1   Metallization reliability rules for a typical 0.5 micron ($\lambda = 0.25\mu m$) CMOS process.

Layer/contact/via	Current limit[1]	Metal thickness[2]	Resistance[3]
m1	$1\,mA\,\mu m^{-1}$	7000 Å	95 mΩ/square
m2	$1\,mA\,\mu m^{-1}$	7000 Å	95 mΩ/square
m3	$2\,mA\,\mu m^{-1}$	12,000 Å	48 mΩ/square
0.8 μm square m1 contact to diffusion	0.7 mA		11 Ω
0.8 μm square m1 contact to poly	0.7 mA		16 Ω
0.8 μm square m1/m2 via (via1)	0.7 mA		3.6 Ω
0.8 μm square m2/m3 via (via2)	0.7 mA		3.6 Ω

[1] At 125 °C for unidirectional current. Limits for 110 °C are × 1.5 higher. Limits for 85 °C are × 3 higher. Current limits for bidirectional current are × 1.5 higher than the unidirectional limits.
[2] 10,000 Å (ten thousand angstroms) = 1 μm.
[3] Worst case at 110 °C.

Standard cells are constructed in a similar fashion to gate-array cells, with power buses running horizontally in m1 at the top and bottom of each cell. A row of standard cells uses **end-cap cells** that connect to the VDD and VSS power buses placed by the power router. Power routing of cell-based ASICs may include the option to include vertical m2 straps at a specified intervals. Alternatively the number of standard cells that can be placed in a row may be limited during placement. The power router forms an interdigitated comb structure, minimizing the number of times a VDD or VSS power bus needs to change layers. This is achieved by routing with a **routing bias** on preferred layers. For example, VDD may be routed with a left-and-down bias on m1, with VSS routed using right-and-up bias on m2.

Three-level metal processes either use a m3 with a thickness and pitch that is comparable to m1 and m2 (which usually have approximately the same thickness and pitch) or they use metal that is much thicker (up to twice as thick as m1 and m2) with a coarser pitch (up to twice as wide as m1 and m2). The factor that determines the m3/4/5 properties is normally the sophistication of the fabrication process.

In a three-level metal process, power routing is similar to two-level metal ASICs. Power buses inside the logic cells are still normally run on m1. Using HVH routing it would be possible to run the power buses on m3 and drop vias all the way down to m1 when power is required in the cells. The problem with this approach is that it creates pillars of blockage across all three layers.

Using three or more layers of metal for routing, it is possible to eliminate some of the channels completely. In these cases we complete all the routing in m2 and m3 on top of the logic cells using connectors placed in the center of the cells on m1. If we can eliminate the channels between cell rows, we can flip rows about a horizontal axis and abut adjacent rows together (a technique known as **flip and abut**). If the power buses are at the top (VDD) and bottom (VSS) of the cells in m1 we can abut or overlap the power buses (joining VDD to VDD and VSS to VSS in alternate rows).

Power distribution schemes are also a function of process and packaging technology. Recall that flip-chip technology allows pads to be placed anywhere on a chip (see Section 16.1.5, "I/O and Power Planning," especially Figure 16.13d). Four-level metal and aggressive stacked-via rules allow I/O pad circuits to be placed in the core. The problems with this approach include placing the ESD and latch-up protection circuits required in the I/O pads (normally kept widely separated from core logic) adjacent to the logic cells in the core.

17.4 Circuit Extraction and DRC

After detailed routing is complete, the exact length and position of each interconnect for every net is known. Now the parasitic capacitance and resistance associated with each interconnect, via, and contact can be calculated. This data is generated by a **circuit-extraction** tool in one of the formats described next. It is important to extract the parasitic values that will be on the silicon wafer. The mask data or CIF widths and dimensions that are drawn in the logic cells are not necessarily the same as the final silicon dimensions. Normally mask dimensions are altered from drawn values to allow for process bias or other effects that occur during the transfer of the pattern from mask to silicon. Since this is a problem that is dealt with by the ASIC vendor and not the design software vendor, ASIC designers normally have to ask very carefully about the details of this problem.

Table 17.2 shows values for the parasitic capacitances for a typical $1\,\mu m$ CMOS process. Notice that the fringing capacitance is greater than the parallel-plate (area) capacitance for all layers except poly. Next, we shall describe how the parasitic information is passed between tools.

17.4.1 SPF, RSPF, and DSPF

The **standard parasitic format** (SPF) (developed by Cadence [1990], now in the hands of OVI) describes interconnect delay and loading due to parasitic resistance and capacitance. There are three different forms of SPF: two of them (**regular SPF** and **reduced SPF**) contain the same information, but in different formats, and model the behavior of interconnect; the third form of SPF (**detailed SPF**) describes the actual parasitic resistance and capacitance components of a net. Figure 17.22 shows the different types of simplified models that regular and reduced SPF support. The load at the output of gate A is represented by one of three models: lumped-C, lumped-RC, or PI segment. The pin-to-pin delays are modeled by RC delays. You can represent the pin-to-pin interconnect delay by an ideal voltage source, V(A_1) in this case, driving an RC network attached to each input pin. The actual pin-to-pin delays may not be calculated this way, however.

TABLE 17.2   Parasitic capacitances for a typical 1 μm ($\lambda = 0.5$ μm) three-level metal CMOS process.[1]

Element	Area/fFμm^{-2}	Fringing/fFμm^{-1}
poly (over gate oxide) to substrate	1.73	NA[2]
poly (over field oxide) to substrate	0.058	0.043
m1 to diffusion or poly	0.055	0.049
m1 to substrate	0.031	0.044
m2 to diffusion	0.019	0.038
m2 to substrate	0.015	0.035
m2 to poly	0.022	0.040
m2 to m1	0.035	0.046
m3 to diffusion	0.011	0.034
m3 to substrate	0.010	0.033
m3 to poly	0.012	0.034
m3 to m1	0.016	0.039
m3 to m2	0.035	0.049
$n+$ junction (at 0V bias)	0.36	NA
$p+$ junction (at 0V bias)	0.46	NA

[1]Fringing capacitances are per isolated line. Closely spaced lines will have reduced fringing capacitance and increased interline capacitance, with increased total capacitance.
[2]NA = not applicable.

The key features of regular and reduced SPF are as follows:

- The loading effect of a net as seen by the driving gate is represented by choosing one of three different RC networks: lumped-C, lumped-RC, or PI segment (selected when generating the SPF) [O'Brien and Savarino, 1989].

- The pin-to-pin delays of each path in the net are modeled by a simple RC delay (one for each path). This can be the Elmore constant for each path (see Section 17.1.2), but it need not be.

Here is an example regular SPF file for just one net that uses the PI segment model shown in Figure 17.22(e):

```
#Design Name : EXAMPLE1
#Date : 6 August 1995
#Time : 12:00:00
#Resistance Units : 1 ohms
#Capacitance Units : 1 pico farads
```

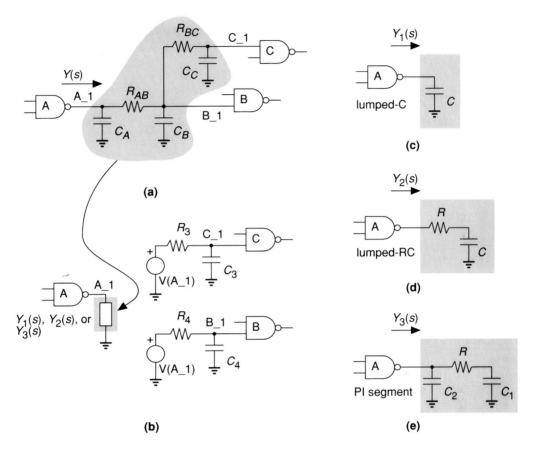

FIGURE 17.22 The regular and reduced standard parasitic format (SPF) models for interconnect. (a) An example of an interconnect network with fanout. The driving-point admittance of the interconnect network is $Y(s)$. (b) The SPF model of the interconnect. (c) The lumped-capacitance interconnect model. (d) The lumped-RC interconnect model. (e) The PI segment interconnect model (notice the capacitor nearest the output node is labeled C_2 rather than C_1). The values of C, R, C_1, and C_2 are calculated so that $Y_1(s)$, $Y_2(s)$, and $Y_3(s)$ are the first-, second-, and third-order Taylor-series approximations to $Y(s)$.

```
#Syntax :
#N <netName>
#C <capVal>
# F <from CompName> <fromPinName>
# GC <conductance>
# |
# REQ <res>
# GRC <conductance>
```

```
# T <toCompName> <toPinName> RC <rcConstant> A <value>
# |
# RPI <res>
# C1 <cap>
# C2 <cap>
# GPI <conductance>
# T <toCompName> <toPinName> RC <rcConstant> A <value>
# TIMING.ADMITTANCE.MODEL = PI
# TIMING.CAPACITANCE.MODEL = PP
N CLOCK
C 3.66
   F ROOT Z
   RPI 8.85
   C1 2.49
   C2 1.17
   GPI = 0.0
   T DF1 G RC 22.20
   T DF2 G RC 13.05
```

This file describes the following:

- The preamble contains the file format.

- This representation uses the PI segment model (Figure 17.22e).

- This net uses pin-to-pin timing.

- The driving gate of this net is ROOT and the output pin name is Z.

- The PI segment elements have values: C1 = 2.49 pF, C2 = 1.17 pF, RPI = 8.85 Ω. Notice the order of C1 and C2 in Figure 17.22(e). The element GPI is not normally used in SPF files.

- The delay from output pin Z of ROOT to input pin G of DF1 is 22.20 ns.

- The delay from pin Z of ROOT to pin G of DF2 is 13.05 ns.

The **reduced SPF** (RSPF) contains the same information as regular SPF, but uses the SPICE format. Here is an example RSPF file that corresponds to the previous regular SPF example:

```
* Design Name : EXAMPLE1
* Date : 6 August 1995
* Time : 12:00:00
* Resistance Units : 1 ohms
* Capacitance Units : 1 pico farads
*| RSPF 1.0
*| DELIMITER "_"
.SUBCKT EXAMPLE1 OUT IN
*| GROUND_NET VSS
* TIMING.CAPACITANCE.MODEL = PP
*|NET CLOCK 3.66PF
*|DRIVER ROOT_Z ROOT Z
```

```
*|S (ROOT_Z_OUTP1 0.0 0.0)
R2 ROOT_Z ROOT_Z_OUTP1 8.85
C1 ROOT_Z_OUTP1 VSS 2.49PF
C2 ROOT_Z VSS 1.17PF
*|LOAD DF2_G DF1 G
*|S (DF1_G_INP1 0.0 0.0)
E1 DF1_G_INP1 VSS ROOT_Z VSS 1.0
R3 DF1_G_INP1 DF1_G 22.20
C3 DF1_G VSS 1.0PF
*|LOAD DF2_G DF2 G
*|S (DF2_G_INP1 0.0 0.0)
E2 DF2_G_INP1 VSS ROOT_Z VSS 1.0
R4 DF2_G_INP1 DF2_G 13.05
C4 DF2_G VSS 1.0PF
*Instance Section
XDF1 DF1_Q DF1_QN DF1_D DF1_G DF1_CD DF1_VDD DF1_VSS DFF3
XDF2 DF2_Q DF2_QN DF2_D DF2_G DF2_CD DF2_VDD DF2_VSS DFF3
XROOT ROOT_Z ROOT_A ROOT_VDD ROOT_VSS BUF
.ENDS
.END
```

This file has the following features:

- The PI segment elements (C1, C2, and R2) have the same values as the previous example.

- The pin-to-pin delays are modeled at each of the gate inputs with a capacitor of value 1 pF (C3 and C4 here) and a resistor (R3 and R4) adjusted to give the correct RC delay. Since the load on the output gate is modeled by the PI segment it does not matter what value of capacitance is chosen here.

- The RC elements at the gate inputs are driven by ideal voltage sources (E1 and E2) that are equal to the voltage at the output of the driving gate.

The **detailed SPF** (DSPF) shows the resistance and capacitance of each segment in a net, again in a SPICE format. There are no models or assumptions on calculating the net delays in this format. Here is an example DSPF file that describes the interconnect shown in Figure 17.23(a):

```
.SUBCKT BUFFER OUT IN
* Net Section
*|GROUND_NET VSS
*|NET IN 3.8E-01PF
*|P (IN I 0.0 0.0 5.0)
*|I (INV1:A INV A I 0.0 10.0 5.0)
C1 IN VSS 1.1E-01PF
C2 INV1:A VSS 2.7E-01PF
R1 IN INV1:A 1.7E00
*|NET OUT 1.54E-01PF
*|S (OUT:1 30.0 10.0)
```

```
*|P (OUT O 0.0 30.0 0.0)
*|I (INV:OUT INV1 OUT O 0.0 20.0 10.0)
C3 INV1:OUT VSS 1.4E-01PF
C4 OUT:1 VSS 6.3E-03PF
C5 OUT VSS 7.7E-03PF
R2 INV1:OUT OUT:1 3.11E00
R3 OUT:1 OUT 3.03E00
*Instance Section
XINV1 INV:A INV1:OUT INV
.ENDS
```

The nonstandard SPICE statements in DSPF are comments that start with '`*|`' and have the following formats:

```
*|I(InstancePinName InstanceName PinName PinType PinCap X Y)
*|P(PinName PinType PinCap X Y)
*|NET NetName NetCap
*|S(SubNodeName X Y)
*|GROUND_NET NetName
```

Figure 17.23(b) illustrates the meanings of the DSPF terms: `InstancePinName`, `InstanceName`, `PinName`, `NetName`, and `SubNodeName`. The `PinType` is `I` (for IN) or `O` (the letter 'O', not zero, for OUT). The `NetCap` is the total capacitance on each net. Thus for net IN, the net capacitance is

$$0.38 \, \text{pF} = C1 + C2 = 0.11 \text{ pF} + 0.27 \text{ pF}.$$

This particular file does not use the pin capacitances, `PinCap`. Since the DSPF represents every interconnect segment, DSPF files can be very large in size (hundreds of megabytes).

17.4.2   Design Checks

ASIC designers perform two major checks before fabrication. The first check is a **design-rule check** (**DRC**) to ensure that nothing has gone wrong in the process of assembling the logic cells and routing. The DRC may be performed at two levels. Since the detailed router normally works with logic cell phantoms, the first level of DRC is a **phantom-level DRC**, which checks for shorts, spacing violations, or other design-rule problems between logic cells. This is principally a check of the detailed router. If we have access to the real library-cell layouts (sometimes called **hard layout**), we can instantiate the phantom cells and perform a second-level DRC at the transistor level. This is principally a check of the correctness of the library cells. Normally the ASIC vendor will perform this check using its own software as a type of incoming inspection. The Cadence Dracula software is one de facto standard in this area, and you will often hear reference to a **Dracula deck** that consists of the Dracula code describing an ASIC vendor's design rules. Sometimes ASIC vendors will give their Dracula decks to customers so that the customers can perform the DRCs themselves.

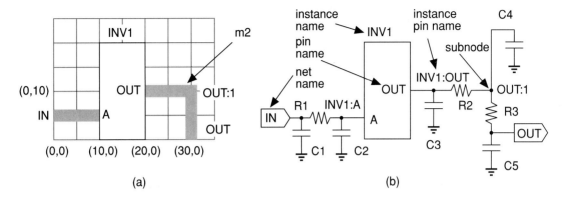

FIGURE 17.23 The detailed standard parasitic format (DSPF) for interconnect representation. (a) An example network with two m2 paths connected to a logic cell, INV1. The grid shows the coordinates. (b) The equivalent DSPF circuit corresponding to the DSPF file in the text.

The other check is a **layout versus schematic** (**LVS**) check to ensure that what is about to be committed to silicon is what is really wanted. An electrical schematic is extracted from the physical layout and compared to the netlist. This closes a loop between the logical and physical design processes and ensures that both are the same. The LVS check is not as straightforward as it may sound, however.

The first problem with an LVS check is that the transistor-level netlist for a large ASIC forms an enormous graph. LVS software essentially has to match this graph against a reference graph that describes the design. Ensuring that every node corresponds exactly to a corresponding element in the schematic (or HDL code) is a very difficult task. The first step is normally to match certain key nodes (such as the power supplies, inputs, and outputs), but the process can very quickly become bogged down in the thousands of mismatch errors that are inevitably generated initially.

The second problem with an LVS check is creating a true reference. The starting point may be HDL code or a schematic. However, logic synthesis, test insertion, clock-tree synthesis, logical-to-physical pad mapping, and several other design steps each modify the netlist. The reference netlist may not be what we wish to fabricate. In this case designers increasingly resort to formal verification that extracts a Boolean description of the function of the layout and compare that to a known good HDL description.

17.4.3 Mask Preparation

Final preparation for the ASIC artwork includes the addition of a **maskwork symbol** (M inside a circle), copyright symbol (C inside a circle), and company logos on each mask layer. A bonding editor creates a bonding diagram that will show the connection of pads to the lead carrier as well as checking that there are no design-rule violations (bond wires that are too close to each other or that leave the chip at extreme angles). We also add the **kerf** (which contains alignment marks, mask identification, and other artifacts required in fabrication), the **scribe lines** (the area where the die will be separated from each other by a diamond saw), and any special hermetic **edge-seal structures** (usually metal).

The final output of the design process is normally a magnetic tape written in **Caltech Intermediate Format** (**CIF**, a public domain text format) or **GDSII Stream** (formerly also called Calma Stream, now Cadence Stream), which is a proprietary binary format. The tape is processed by the ASIC vendor or foundry (the **fab**) before being transferred to the **mask shop**.

If the layout contains drawn *n*-diffusion and *p*-diffusion regions, then the fab generates the active (thin-oxide), *p*-type implant, and *n*-type implant layers. The fab then runs another polygon-level DRC to check polygon spacing and overlap for all mask levels. A **grace value** (typically 0.01 μm) is included to prevent false errors stemming from rounding problems and so on. The fab will then adjust the mask dimensions for fabrication either by bloating (expanding), shrinking, and merging shapes in a procedure called **sizing** or **mask tooling**. The exact procedures are described in a **tooling specification**. A **mask bias** is an amount added to a drawn polygon to allow for a difference between the mask size and the feature as it will eventually appear in silicon. The most common adjustment is to the active mask to allow for the **bird's beak effect**, which causes an active area to be several tenths of a micron smaller on silicon than on the mask.

The mask shop will use e-beam mask equipment to generate metal (usually chromium) on glass masks or **reticles**. The e-beam **spot size** determines the resolution of the mask-making equipment and is usually 0.05 μm or 0.025 μm (the smaller the spot size, the more expensive is the mask). The spot size is significant when we break the integer-lambda scaling rules in a deep-submicron process. For example, for a 0.35 μm process ($\lambda = 0.175$ μm), a 1.5λ separation is 0.525 μm, which requires more expensive mask-making equipment with a 0.025 μm spot size. For **critical layers** (usually the polysilicon mask) the mask shop may use **optical proximity correction** (**OPC**), which adjusts the position of the mask edges to allow for light diffraction and reflection (the deep-UV light used for printing mask images on the wafer has a wavelength comparable to the minimum feature sizes).

17.5 Summary

The completion of routing finishes the ASIC physical design process. Routing is a complicated problem best divided into two steps: global and detailed routing. Global routing plans the wiring by finding the channels to be used for each path. There are differences between global routing for different types of ASICs, but the algorithms to find the shortest path are similar. Two main approaches to global routing are: one net at a time, or all nets at once. With the inclusion of timing-driven routing objectives, the routing problem becomes much harder and requires understanding the differences between finding the shortest net and finding the net with the shortest delay. Different types of detail routing include channel routing and area-based or maze routing. Detailed routing with two layers of metal is a fairly well understood problem.

The most important points in this chapter are:

- Routing is divided into global and detailed routing.
- Routing algorithms should match the placement algorithms.
- Routing is not complete if there are unroutes.
- Clock and power nets are handled as special cases.
- Clock-net widths and power-bus widths must usually be set by hand.
- DRC and LVS checks are needed before a design is complete.

17.6 Problems

* = Difficult, ** = Very difficult, *** = Extremely difficult

17.1 (Routing measures, 20 min.). Channel density is a useful measure, but with the availability of more than two layers of metal, area-based maze routers are becoming more common. Lyle Smith, in his 1983 Stanford Ph.D. thesis, defines the **Manhattan area measure** (MAM) as:

$$\text{MAM} = \text{area needed} / \text{area available}, \qquad (17.11)$$

where you calculate the area needed by assuming routing on a single layer and ignore any interconnect overlaps. Calculate the MAM for Figure 17.14. Once the MAM reaches 0.5, most two-layer routers have difficulty.

17.2 (*Benchmarking routers, 30 min.) Your design team needs a new router to complete your ASIC project. Your boss puts you in charge of benchmarking. She wants a list of the items you will test, and a description of how you will test them.

17.3 (Timing-driven routing) **(a)** Calculate the delay from A to C in Figure 17.3(b) if the wire between V_3 and V_4 is increased to 5 mm. **(b)** If you want to measure the delay to the 90 percent point, what is the skew in signal arrival time between inverters B and C? **(c)** If you use the Elmore constant to characterize the delay between inverter A and inverter C as an RC element, what is the delay (measured to the 50 percent trip point) if you replace the step function at the output of inverter A with a linear ramp with a fall time of 0.1 ns?

17.4 (Elmore delay, 30 min.) Recalculate τ_{D4}, τ_{D2}, and $\tau_{D4} - \tau_{D2}$ for the example in Section 17.1.2 neglecting the pull-down resistance R_{pd} and comment on your answers.

17.5 (Clock routing, 30 min.) Design a clock distribution system with minimum latency given the following specifications: The clocked elements are distributed randomly, but uniformly across the chip. The chip is 400 mil per side. There are 16,000 flip-flops to clock; each flip-flop clock input presents a load of 0.02 pF (one standard load). There are four different types of inverting buffer available (typical for a 0.5 μm process):

1X buffer: $T_D = 0.1 + 1.5 \, C_L$ ns; 4X buffer: $T_D = 0.3 + 0.55 \, C_L$ ns;

8X buffer: $T_D = 0.5 + 0.25 \, C_L$ ns; 32X buffer: $T_D = 2 + 0.004 \, C_L$ ns.

In these equations T_D is the buffer delay (assume rise and fall times are approximately equal) and C_L is the buffer load expressed in standard loads. Electromigration limits require a limit of 1 mA (DC) per micron metal width or 10 mA per micron for AC signals with no DC component. No metal bus may be wider than 100 μm. The m2 line capacitance is 0.015 f Fμm^{-2} (area) and 0.035 f Fμm^{-1} (fringing).

17.6 (Power and ground routing, 10 min.) Calculate the parallel-plate capacitance between a VDD power ring routed on m2 and an identical VSS ring routed on m1 directly underneath. The chip is 500 mil on a side; assume the power ring runs around the edge of the chip. The VDD and VSS bus are capable of carrying 0.5 A and are both 500 μm wide. Assume that m1 and m2 are separated by a SiO$_2$ dielectric 10,000 Å thick. This capacitance can actually be used for decoupling supplies.

17.7 (Overlap capacitance, 10 min.) Consider two interconnects, both of width W, separated by a layer of SiO$_2$ of thickness T, and that overlap for a distance L.

a. What is the overlap capacitance, assuming there are no fringing effects?

b. Calculate the overlap capacitance if $W = 1$ μm, $T = 0.5$ μm, for $L = 1$, 10, and 100 μm.

c. Calculate the gate capacitance of an n-channel transistor with transistor size $W/L = 2/1$ (that is, $W = 2$ μm, $L = 1$ μm), with a gate oxide thickness of 200 Å (again assuming no fringing).

d. Comment on your answers.

17.8 (Standard load, 10 min.) Calculate the size of a standard load for the 1 μm process with the parasitic capacitance values shown in Table 17.2. Assume the n-channel and p-channel devices in a two-input NAND gate are all 10/1 with minimum length.

17.9 (Fringing capacitance, 45 min) You can calculate the capacitance per unit length (including fringing capacitance) of an interconnect with rectangular cross section (width W, thickness T, and a distance H above a ground plane) from the approximate formula (from [Barke, 1988]—the equation was originally proposed by van der Meijs and Fokkema):

$$C = \varepsilon\left(\frac{W}{H} + 1.064\sqrt{\frac{W}{H}} + 1.06\sqrt{\frac{T}{H}} + 0.77\right), \tag{17.12}$$

where $\varepsilon = \varepsilon_r \varepsilon_0$ is the dielectric constant of the insulator surrounding the interconnect. The relative permittivity of a SiO_2 dielectric $\varepsilon_r = 3.9$, and the permittivity of free space $\varepsilon_0 = 3.45 \times 10^{-11} \ \text{Fm}^{-1}$.

a. Calculate C for $W = T = H = 1 \ \mu\text{m}$.

b. Compare this value with the parallel-plate value (assuming no fringing capacitance).

c. Assume that the interconnect cross-sectional area (i.e., WH) is kept constant as technology scales, in order to keep the resistance per unit length of the interconnect constant. Assume that the width scales as sW, the height as sH, and the thickness as T/s, where s is a scaling factor from one to 0.1. Use a spreadsheet to calculate values for different scaling factors, assuming that for $s = 1$: $W = T = H = 1 \ \mu\text{m}$.

d. Plot your results (with C on the y-axis vs. s on the x-axis).

17.10 (Coupling capacitance, 30 min.) One of the reasons to follow quasi-ideal scaling for the physical dimensions of the interconnect is to try and reduce the parasitic area capacitance as we scale. (The other reason is to try and keep interconnect resistance constant.) Area capacitance scales as $1/s$ by following ideal scaling rules, but scales as $1/s^{1.5}$ by using quasi-ideal scaling. Using quasi-ideal scaling means reducing the widths and horizontal spacing of the interconnect by $1/s$ and the height of the lines and their vertical separation from other layers by only $1/s^{0.5}$. The effect is rather like turning the interconnects on their sides. As a result we must consider parasitic capacitances other than just the parallel-plate capacitance between two layers. The parasitic capacitance between neighboring interconnects is called **coupling capacitance**. **Fringing capacitance** results from the fact that the electric field lines spill out from the edges of a conductor. This means the total parasitic capacitance is greater than if we just considered the capacitance to be formed by two parallel plates.

The following equation is an approximate expression for the capacitance per unit length of an isolated conductor of width W and thickness T, separated by a distance H from a conducting plane, and surrounded by a medium of permittivity ε [Sakurai and Tamaru, 1983]:

$$\frac{C_1}{\varepsilon} = 1.15 \left(\frac{W}{H} \right) + 2.80 \left(\frac{T}{H} \right)^{0.222} . \tag{17.13}$$

This equation is of the form,

$$C_1 = C_a + C_b , \tag{17.14}$$

where C_a represents the contribution from two parallel plates and C_b is the fringing capacitance (for both edges). The following equation then takes into account the coupling capacitance to a neighbor conductor separated horizontally by a gap G between the edges of the conductors:

$$\frac{C_2}{\varepsilon} = \frac{C_1}{\varepsilon} + \left[0.03\left(\frac{W}{H}\right) + 0.83\left(\frac{T}{H}\right) - 0.07\left(\frac{T}{H}\right)^{0.222}\right]\left(\frac{G}{H}\right)^{-1.34}. \quad (17.15)$$

This equation is of the form,

$$C_2 = C_1 + C_c, \quad (17.16)$$

where C_c is the coupling capacitance from the conductor to one neighbor. For a conductor having two neighbors (one on each side), the total capacitance will be

$$C_2 = C_1 + 2C_c. \quad (17.17)$$

Table 17.3 shows the result of evaluating these equations for different values of T/H, W/H, and S/H for $\lambda = 0.5$ μm.

a. Calculate the corresponding values for $\lambda = 0.125$ μm assuming quasi-ideal scaling.

Table 17.4 shows the predicted fringing and coupling capacitance for a $\lambda = 0.5$ μm process expressed in pFcm^{-1}.

b. Complete the corresponding values for $\lambda = 0.125$ μm, again assuming quasi-ideal scaling.

c. Comment on the difference between $\lambda = 0.5$ μm and $\lambda = 0.125$ μm.

17.11 (**Routing algorithms, 60 min.) "The Lee algorithm is guaranteed to find a path if it exists, but not necessarily the shortest path." Do you agree with this statement? Can you prove or disprove it?

"The Hightower algorithm is not guaranteed to find a path, even if one exists." Do you agree with this statement? Can you prove or disprove it? *Hint:* The problems occur not with routing any one net but with routing a sequence of nets.

17.12 (Constraint graphs, 10 min.) Draw the horizontal and vertical constraint graphs for the channel shown in Figure 17.13(a). Explain how to handle the net that exits the channel and its pseudoterminal.

17.13 (**Electromigration, 60 min.) You just received the first prototype of your new ASIC. The first thing you do is measure the resistance between VDD and VSS and find they are shorted. Horrified, you find that you added your initials on m1 instead of m2 and shorted the supplies, next to the power pads. Your initials are only 10 μm wide, but about 200 μm high! Fortunately only the first capital "I" is actually shorting the supplies. The power-supply rails are approximately 100 μm wide at that

TABLE 17.3   Calculated fringing capacitance (per unit length and normalized by permittivity) using quasi-ideal scaling and the Sakurai–Tamaru equations. Problem 17.10 completes this table.

Parameter	$\lambda = 0.5\,\mu m$	$\lambda = 0.125\,\mu m$
$T\,(\mu m)$	0.5	
$W\,(\mu m)$	1.5	
$S\,(\mu m)$	1.5	
$H\,(\mu m)$	0.5	
T/H	1	
$W/H, S/H$	3	
$C_1 = C_a + C_b$	6.25	
$C_2 = C_1 + C_c$	6.44	
$C_3 = C_1 + 2\,C_c$	6.63	
$C_a = $ parallel plate	3.45	
$C_b = $ fringe (two edges)	2.80	
$C_c = $ coupling (one neighbor)	0.19	
C_c/C_a	6%	
C_a/C_3	52%	
C_b/C_3	42%	
C_c/C_3	3%	

TABLE 17.4   Predicted line capacitance including fringing and coupling capacitance ($pF cm^{-1}$) for $\lambda = 0.125\,\mu m$ and using quasi-ideal scaling and the Sakurai equations. Problem 17.10 completes this table.

Parameter	$\lambda = 0.5\,\mu m$	$\lambda = 0.125\,\mu m$	Comment
$C_1 = C_a + C$	2.16		C_1 is capacitance of line to ground.
$C_2 = C_1 + C_c$	2.22		C_2 is capacitance including one neighbor.
$C_3 = C_1 + 2C_c$	2.29		C_3 is capacitance including two neighbors.
$C_a = $ plate	1.19		C_a is parallel-plate capacitance.
$C_b = $ fringe	0.97		C_b is fringe for both edges.
$C_c = $ coupling	0.07		C_c is coupling to one neighbor only.

point. A thought occurs to you—maybe you can electromigrate your initial away. You remember that electromigration obeys an equation of the form:

$$\text{MTTF} = \frac{A \exp \dfrac{-E}{kT}}{J^2} \tag{17.18}$$

where MTTF is the mean time to failure, A is a constant, J is the current density, E is an activation energy, k is Boltzmann's constant, and T is absolute temperature. You also remember the rule that you can have about 1 mA of current for every λ of metal width for a reasonable time to failure of more than 10 years. Since this chip is in 0.5 μm CMOS ($\lambda = 0.25$ μm), you guess that the metal is about 0.5 μm thick, and the resistance is at least 50 mΩ/square.

a. How much current do you estimate you need to make your initials fail so that you can test the chip before your boss gets back in a week's time?

b. What else could you do to speed things up?

c. How are you going to do this? (P.S. This sometimes actually works.)

17.14 (**Routing problems, 20 min.) We have finished the third iteration on the new game chip and are having yield problems in production. This is what we know:

1. We changed the routing on v3 by using an ECO mechanism in the detailed router from Shortem. We just ripped up a few nets and rerouted them without changing anything else.

2. The ASIC vendor, Meltem, is having yield problems due to long metal lines shorting—but only in one place. It looks as though they are the metal lines we changed in v3. Meltem blames the mask vendor—Smokem.

3. To save money we changed mask vendors after completing the prototype version v1, so that v2 and v3 uses the new mask vendor (Smokem). Smokem confirms there is a problem with the v3 mask—the lines we changed are shifted very slightly toward others and have a design rule violation. However, the v2 mask was virtually identical to v3 and there are no problems with that one, so Smokem blames the router from Shortem.

4. Shortem checks the CIF files for us, claims the mask data is correct, and they suggest we blame Meltem.

We do not care (yet) who is to blame, we just need the problem fixed. We need suggestions for the source of the problem (however crazy), some possible fixes, and some ideas to test them. Can you help?

17.15 (*Coupling capacitance, 30 min.) Suppose we have three interconnect lines running parallel to each other on a bus. Consider the following situations (VDD = 5 V, VSS = 0 V):

a. The center line switches from VSS to VDD. The neighbor lines are at VSS.

b. The center line switches from VSS to VDD. At the same time the neighbor lines switch from VDD to VSS.

c. The center line switches from VSS to VDD. At the same time the neighbor lines also switch from VDD to VSS.

How do you define capacitance in these cases? In each case what is the effective capacitance from the center to the neighboring lines using your definition?

17.16 (**2LM and 3LM routing, 10 min.) How would you attempt to measure the difference in die area obtained by using the same standard-cell library with two-level and three-level routing?

17.17 (***SPF, 60 min)

a. Write a regular SPF file for the circuit shown in Figure 17.3(b), using the lumped-C model and the Elmore constant for the pin-to-pin timings.

b. Write the equivalent RSPF file.

c. Write a DSPF file for the same circuit.

d. Calculate the PI segment parameters for the circuit shown in Figure 17.3(b). *Hint:* You may need to consult [O'Brien and Savarino, 1989] if you need help.

17.18 (***Standard-cell aspect ratio, 30 min.) How would you decide the optimum value for the logic cell height of a standard-cell library?

17.19 (Electromigration, 20 min.)

a. What is the current density in a 1 μm wide wire that is 1 μm thick and carries a current of 1 mA?

b. Using Eq. 17.9, can you explain the temperature behavior of the parameters in Table 17.1?

c. Using Eq. 17.10, can you explain the dependence on current direction?

17.20 (***SPF parameters, 120 min.). *Hint:* You may need help from [O'Brien and Savarino, 1989] for this question.

a. Find an expression for $Y(s)$, where $s = j\omega$, the driving-point admittance (the reciprocal of the driving-point impedance), for the interconnect network shown in Figure 17.22(a), in terms of C_A, C_B, C_C, R_{AB}, and R_{BC}.

b. Find the first three terms of the Taylor-series expansion for $Y(s)$.

c. Derive expressions for $Y_1(s)$, $Y_2(s)$, and $Y_3(s)$ for the lumped-C, the lumped-RC, and the PI segment network models (Figure 17.22b–d).

d. Comparing your answers to parts b and c, derive the values of the parameters of the lumped-C, the lumped-RC, and the PI segment network models in terms of C_A, C_B, C_C, R_{AB}, and R_{BC}.

17.21 (**Distributed-delay routing, 120 min. [Kahng and Robins, 1995]) The Elmore constant is one measure of net delay,

$$\tau_{Di} = \sum_k R_{ki} C_k \,. \qquad\qquad (17.19)$$

The **distributed delay**, defined as follows, is another measure of delay in a network:

$$\tau_P = \sum_k R_{kk} C_k \,.$$ (17.20)

We can write this equation in terms of network components as follows:

$$\tau_P = \sum_{\text{nodes } k} (R_0 L_{kn} + R_d)(C_0 + C_n) \,.$$ (17.21)

In this equation there are two types of capacitors: those due to the interconnect, C_0, and those due to the gate loads at each sink, C_n. R_d is the driving resistance of the driving gate (the pull-up or pull-down resistance); R_0 is the resistance of a one-grid-long piece of interconnect; and C_0 is the capacitance of a one-grid-long piece of interconnect. Thus,

$$C_k = C_0 + C_n \quad \text{and} \quad R_{kn} = R_0 L_{kn} + R_d \,,$$ (17.22)

since every path to ground must pass through R_d. L_{kn} is the path length (in routing-grid units) between a node k and one of the n sink nodes.

With these definitions we can expand Eq. 17.21 to the following:

$$\tau_P = \sum_{\text{nodes } k} C_0 R_0 L_{kn} + \sum_{\text{nodes } k} C_n R_0 L_{kn} + R_d C_0 + R_d C_n \,.$$ (17.23)

Figure 17.24 shows examples of three different types of trees. The MRST minimizes the rectilinear path length. The **shortest-path tree** (**SPT**) minimizes the sum of path lengths to all sinks. The **quadratic minimum Steiner tree** (**QMST**) minimizes the sum of path lengths to all nodes (every grid-point on the tree).

a. Find the measures for the MRST, SPT, and QMST for each of the three different tree types shown in Figure 17.24.

b. Explain how to apply these trees to Eq. 17.23.

c. Compare Eqs. 17.19 and 17.20 for the purposes of timing-driven routing.

17.22 (**Elmore delay, 120 min.) Figure 17.25 shows an RC tree. The mth moment of the impulse response for node i in an RC tree network with n nodes is

$$\mu_1(i) = \sum_{k=1}^{n} R_{ki} C_k$$

$$\mu_{m+1}(i) = (m+1) \sum_{k=1}^{n} R_{ki} C_k \mu_m(k) \,.$$ (17.24)

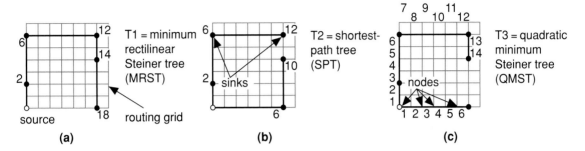

FIGURE 17.24 Examples of trees for timing-driven layout. (a) The MRST. (b) The shortest-path tree (SPT). (c) The quadratic minimum Steiner tree (QMST). (Problem 17.21)

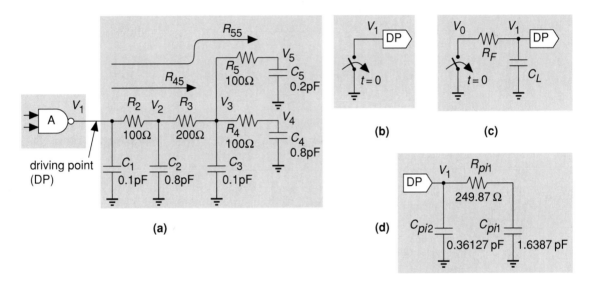

FIGURE 17.25 Standard parasitic format (SPF) (Problem 17.22). (a) An RC interconnect tree driven by a NAND gate. (b) The NAND gate modeled by an ideal switch. (c) The NAND gate modeled with a pull-down resistance, R_F, and output capacitance, C_L. (d) The PI segment model for the RC tree (the order of C_{pi1}—last—and C_{pi2} is correct).

The Elmore constant is the first moment of the impulse response. We calculate the weighted-capacitance values in Eq. 17.24 as follows:

$$k_0 = \sum_{k=1}^{n} C_k,$$

$$k_m = \frac{1}{m!} \sum_{k=1}^{n} C_k \mu_m(k). \tag{17.25}$$

We derive the PI segment parameters used in SPF from the k_i as follows:

$$C_{pi1} = k_1^2/k_2; \quad R_{pi1} = k_2^2/k_1^3; \quad C_{pi2} = k_0 - C_{pi1}.$$

a. Calculate Elmore's constant for the RC tree in Figure 17.25(a).

b. Derive the PI segment model shown in Figure 17.25(d).

c. What is the difference between using the model of Figure 17.25(b) and the model of Figure 17.25(c) for the NAND gate?

17.7   Bibliography

The *IEEE Transactions on Computer-Aided Design* (TK7874.I327, ISSN 0278-0070) contains papers and tutorials on routing (with an emphasis on algorithms). The *Proceedings of the ACM/IEEE Design Automation Conference* (DAC, TA174.D46a, ISSN 0146-7123, catalogued under various titles) and the *Proceedings of the IEEE International Conference on Computer-Aided Design* (ICCAD, TK7874.I3235a, ISSN 1063-6757 and 1092-3152) document the two conferences at which new ideas on routing are often presented.

The edited book by Preas and Lorenzetti [1988] is the best place to learn more about routing. Books by Sarrafzadeh and Wong [1996] and Sait and Youssef [1995] are more recent introductions to physical design including routing. The book Hu and Kuh [1983] edited for IEEE Press contains early papers on routing, including an introductory paper with many references. Ohtsuki's [1986] edited book on layout contains tutorials on routing, including reviews of channel routing by Burstein and area routing by Ohtsuki; a more recent edited book by Zobrist [1994] also contains papers on routing. A good introduction to routing is Joobanni's thesis published as a book [1986]. New routing techniques are becoming important for FPGAs, a recent paper describes some of these [Roy, 1993]. Books by Lengauer [1990] and Sherwani [1993] describe algorithms for both the global and detailed routing problems. A book by Sherwani et al. [1995] covers two-level and three-level routing. Kahng and Robins [1995] cover timing-driven detailed routing in their book; Sapatnekar and Kang [1993] cover timing-driven physical design in general. The book by Pillage et al. [1994] includes a chapter on bounding and asymptotic approximations that are related to the models used in SPF. Nakhla and Zhang [1994] and Goel [1994] cover modeling of interconnect. The IEEE Press book edited by Friedman [1995] covers clock distribution. Routing is often performed in parallel on several machines; books by Banerjee [1994] and Ravikumar [1996] describe parallel algorithms for physical design. Taylor and Russell [1992] review knowledge-based physical design in an edited book.

Najm's review paper covers power estimation [1994]. Books by Shenai [1991] and Murarka [1993] cover all aspects of metallization. To learn more about the causes of electromigration in particular, see D'Heurle's [1971] classic paper and a paper by Black [1969]. The edited book by Gildenblat and Schwartz [1991] covers metallization reliability. A tutorial paper by Young and Christou [1994] reviews current theories of the causes of electromigration. To learn more about masks and microlithography in VLSI, see the handbook by Glendinning and Helbert [1991].

17.8   References

Page numbers in brackets after a reference indicate its location in the chapter body.

Banerjee, P. 1994. *Parallel Algorithms for VLSI Computer-Aided Design Applications.* Englewood Cliffs, NJ: Prentice-Hall, 699 p. ISBN 0130158356. TK7874.75.B36. [p. 956]

Barke, E. 1988. "Line-to-ground capacitance calculation for VLSI: A comparison." *IEEE Transactions on Computer-Aided Design,* Vol. 7, no. 2, pp. 295–298. Compares various equations for line to ground capacitance and finds the van der Meijs and Fokkema equation the most accurate. [p. 948]

Black, J. R. 1969. "Electromigration failure modes in aluminum metallization for semiconductor devices." *Proceedings of the IEEE,* Vol. 57, no. 9, pp. 1587–1594. Describes mechanism and theory of electromigration. Two failure modes are discussed: dissolution of silicon into aluminum, and condensation of aluminum vacancies to form voids. Electromigration failures in aluminum become important (less than 10 year lifetime) at current densities greater than 50 kA/sq.cm and temperatures greater than 150 °C. [p. 956]

Cadence. 1990. "Gate Ensemble User Guide." Product Release 2.0. Describes gate-array place-and-route software. The algorithms for timing-driven placement are described in A. H. Chao, E. M. Nequist, and T. D. Vuong, "Direct solution of performance constraints during placement," in *Proceedings of the IEEE Custom Integrated Circuits Conference,* 1990. The delay models for timing analysis are described in "Modeling the driving-point characteristic of resistive interconnect for accurate delay estimation," in P. R. O'Brien and T. L. Savarino, in *Proceedings of the International Conference on Computer-Aided Design,* 1989. [p. 939]

Cheng, C.-K., et al. 1992. "Geometric compaction on channel routing." *IEEE Transactions on Computer-Aided Design,* Vol. 11, no. 1, pp. 115–127. [p. 931]

Chowdhury, S., and J. S. Barkatullah. 1988. "Current estimation in MOS IC logic circuits." In *Proceedings of the International Conference on Computer-Aided Design.* Compares estimates for transient current flow for CMOS logic gates. Algebraic models give results close to SPICE simulations. The rest of the paper discusses the calculation of static current flow for nMOS logic gates. A model for static current for CMOS gates is developed in terms of the nMOS models.

D'Heurle, F. M. 1971. "Electromigration and failure in electronics: an introduction." *Proceedings of the IEEE,* Vol. 59, no. 10, pp. 1409–1417. Describes the theory behind electromigration in bulk and thin-film metals. Includes some experimental results and reviews work by others. Describes the beneficial effects of adding copper to aluminum metallization. [p. 956]

Friedman, E. G. (Ed.). 1995. *Clock Distribution Networks in VLSI Circuits and Systems.* New York: IEEE Press, ISBN 0780310586. TK7874.75.C58. [p. 956]

Gildenblat, G. S., and G. P. Schwartz (Eds.). 1991. *Metallization: Performance and Reliability Issues for VLSI and ULSI.* Bellingham, WA: SPIE, the International Society for Optical Engineering, 159 p. ISBN 0819407275. TK7874.M437. [p. 956]

Glendinning, W. B., and J. N. Helbert, (Eds.). 1991. *Handbook of VLSI Microlithography : Principles, Technology, and Applications.* Park Ridge, NJ: Noyes Publications, 649 p. ISBN 0815512813. TK7874.H3494. [p. 957]

Goel, A. K. 1994. *High Speed VLSI Interconnections: Modeling, Analysis, and Simulation.* New York: Wiley-Interscience, 622 p. ISBN 0471571229. TK7874.7.G63. 21 pages of references. [p. 956]

Hashimoto, A., and J. Stevens. 1971. "Wire routing by optimal channel assignment within large apertures." In *Proceedings of the 8th Design Automation Workshop,* pp. 155–169. [p. 928]

Hu, T. C., and E. S. Kuh (Eds.). 1983. *VLSI Circuit Layout: Theory and Design.* New York: IEEE Press. ISBN 0879421932. TK7874 .V5573. Contains 26 papers divided into six chapters; Part 1: Overview (a paper written for this book with 167 references on layout and routing); Part II: General; Part III: Wireability, Partitioning and Placement; Part IV: Routing; Part V: Layout Systems; Part VI: Module Generation. [p. 956]

Joobbani, R. 1986. *An Artificial Intelligence Approach to VLSI Routing.* Hingham, MA: Kluwer. ISBN 0-89838-205-X. TK7874.J663. Ph.D thesis on the development and testing of an intelligent router including an overview of the detailed routing problem and the Lee and "greedy" algorithms. [p. 956]

Kahng, A. B., and G. Robins. 1995. *On Optimal Interconnections for VLSI.* Norwell, MA: Kluwer. ISBN 0-7923-9483-6. TK7874.75.K34. Extensive reference work on timing-driven detailed routing. [pp. 953, 956]

Lengauer, T. 1990. *Combinatorial Algorithms for Integrated Circuit Layout.* Chichester, England: Wiley. ISBN 0-471-92838-0. TK7874.L36. Background: Introduction to circuit layout; Optimization problems; Graph algorithms; Operations research and statistics. Combinatorial layout problems: The layout problem; Circuit partitioning; Placement, assignment, and floorplanning; Global routing and area routing; Detailed routing; Compaction. 484 references. [p. 956]

Nakhla, M. S., and Q. J. Zhang (Eds.). 1994. *Modeling and Simulation of High Speed VLSI Interconnects.* Boston: Kluwer, 106 p. ISBN 0792394410. TK7874.75.M64. [p. 956]

Murarka, S. P. 1993. *Metallization: Theory and Practice for VLSI and ULSI.* Stoneham, MA: Butterworth-Heinemann, 250 p. ISBN 0-7506-9001-1. TK7874.M868. Includes chapters on metal properties; crystal structure; electrical and mechanical properties; diffusion and reaction in thin metallic films; deposition method and techniques; pattern definition; packaging applications; reliability. [p. 956]

Najm, F. N. 1994. "A survey of power estimation techniques in VLSI circuits." *IEEE Transactions on Very Large Scale Integration (VLSI) Systems,* Vol. 2, no. 4, pp. 446–55. 43 references. [p. 956]

O'Brien, P. R., and T. L. Savarino. 1989. "Modeling the driving-point characteristic of resistive interconnect for accurate delay estimation." In *Proceedings of the International Conference on Computer-Aided Design,* pp. 512–515. Describes SPF PI segment model. [pp. 940, 953].

Ohtsuki, T. (Ed.). 1986. *Layout Design and Verification.* New York: Elsevier Science, ISBN 0444878947. TK7874.L318. Includes nine papers on CAD tools and algorithms: "Layout strategy, standardisation, and CAD tools," Ueda, Kasai, and Sudo; "Layout compaction," Mylynski and Sung; "Layout verification," Yoshida; "Partitioning, assignment and placement," Goto and Matsuda; "Computational complexity of layout problems," Shing and Hu; "Computational and geometry algorithms," Asano, Sato, and Ohtsuki; an excellent survey and tutorial paper by M. Burstein — "Channel routing;" "Maze-running and line-search algorithms," a good, easily readable paper on detailed routing by Ohtsuki; and a more mathematical paper, "Global routing," by Kuh and Marek-Sadowska. [pp. 932, 957]

Pillage, L., et al. 1994. *Electronic Circuit and System Simulation Methods.* New York: McGraw-Hill, 392 p. ISBN 0-07-050169-6. TK7874.P52. [p. 956]

Preas, B. T., and M. J. Lorenzetti. 1988. *Physical Design Automation of VLSI Systems.* Menlo Park, CA: Benjamin-Cummings, 510 p. ISBN 0805304129. TK7874.P47. Chapters on: physical design automation; interconnection analysis, logic partitioning; placement, assignment and floorplanning; routing; symbolic layout and compaction; module generation and silicon compilation; layout analysis and verification; knowledge-based physical design automation; combinatatorial complexity of layout problems. [p. 956]

Ravikumar, C. P. 1996. *Parallel Methods for VLSI Layout Design.* Norwood, NJ: Ablex, 195 p. ISBN 0893918288. TK7874.R39. [p. 956]

Roy, K. 1993. "A bounded search algorithm for segmented channel routing for FPGA's and associated channel architecture issues." *IEEE Transactions on Computer-Aided Design*, Vol. 12, no. 11, pp. 1695–1704. [p. 956].

Sait, S. M., and H. Youssef. 1995. *VLSI Physical Design Automation, Theory and Practice.* New York: IEEE Press/McGraw-Hill copublication, 426 p. ISBN 0-07-707742-3. TK7874.75.S24. Covers floorplanning, placement, and routing. [p. 956]

Sakurai, T., and K. Tamaru. 1983. "Simple formulas for two- and three-dimensional capacitances." *IEEE Transactions on Electron Devices.* Vol. 30, no. 2. [p. 949]

Sapatnekar, S. S., and S.-M. Kang. 1993. *Design Automation for Timing-Driven Layout Synthesis.* Boston: Kluwer, 269 p. ISBN 0792392817. TK7871.99.M44.S37. 19 pages of references. [p. 956]

Sarrafzadeh, M., and C. K. Wong. 1996. *An Introduction to VLSI Physical Design.* New York: McGraw-Hill, 334 p. ISBN 0070571945. TK7874.75.S27. 17 pages of references. [p. 956]

Shenai, K. (Ed.). 1991. *VLSI Metallization: Physics and Technologies.* Boston: Artech House, 529 p. ISBN 0890065012. TK7872.C68.V58. [p. 956]

Sherwani, N. A. 1993. *Algorithms for VLSI Physical Design Automation.* 2nd ed. Norwell, MA: Kluwer, 538 p. ISBN 0-7923-9294-9. TK874.S455. See also the first edition. [p. 956]

Sherwani, N. A., et al. 1995. *Routing in the Third Dimension: From VLSI Chips to MCMs.* New York: IEEE Press. ISBN 0-7803-1089-6. TK7874.75.R68. Reviews two-layer and multilayer routing algorithms. Contains chapters on: graphs and basic algorithms; channel routing; routing models; routing algorithms for two- and three-layer processes and MCMs. [p. 956]

Taylor, G., and G. Russell. (Eds.). 1992. *Algorithmic and Knowledge Based CAD for VLSI.* London: P. Peregrinus, 273 p. ISBN 086341267X. TK7874.A416. [p. 956]

Veendrick, H. J. M. 1984. "Short-circuit dissipation of static CMOS circuitry and its impact on the design of buffer circuits." *IEEE Journal of Solid-State Circuits,* Vol. 19, no. 4, pp. 468–473. [p. 936]

Young, D., and A. Christou. 1994. "Failure mechanism models for electromigration." *IEEE Transactions on Reliability,* Vol. 43, no. 2, pp. 186–192. A tutorial on electromigration and its relation to microstructure. [pp. 936, 957]

Zobrist, G. W. (Ed.). 1994. *Routing, Placement, and Partitioning.* Norwood, NJ: Ablex, 293 p. ISBN 0893917842. TK7874.R677. [p. 956]

VHDL RESOURCES

The definitive reference for VHDL is the VHDL **language reference manual** (**LRM**), currently IEEE Std 1076-1993.[1] References here such as [93LRM 1.1], for example, refer to Section 1.1 of the VHDL-93 LRM [IEEE 1076-1993]. According to IEEE bylaws all standards are updated (reaffirmed, reballoted, or dropped) every five years, and thus VHDL-87 (the original standard) is superceded by VHDL-93. However, some software systems (and some IEEE standards, notably VITAL) are based on VHDL-87 [IEEE 1076-1987]. Both VHDL-93 and VHDL-87 are covered in this Appendix.

A.1 BNF

Appendix A of the LRM describes the syntax of VHDL using **keywords** (or **reserved words**) and characters in a shorthand notation called the **BNF** (**Backus–Naur form**). As an example, the BNF definition given in Appendix A of the LRM for the syntax of the `wait` statement is

```
wait_statement ::=
  [label : ] wait [ sensitivity_clause ] [ condition_clause ]
    [ timeout_clause ] ;
```

This definition means: "The `wait` statement consists of the keyword, `wait`, followed by three optional parts: a sensitivity clause, a condition clause, and a timeout clause."

You treat the BNF as a series of equations. The left-hand side is called a **production** or **construct**, the symbol `::=` (two colons and an equal sign) represents **equivalence**, the right-hand side contains the **parts** that comprise the production. Parts may be keywords (in bold here). Parts may be other productions contained in square brackets `[ ]`. This signifies that the part is optional. Parts may also have curly brackets or

---

[1]IEEE Std 1076-1993, © Copyright 1995 IEEE. All rights reserved. The BNF in this appendix is derived from the IEEE copyright material with permission.

braces {}. This indicates that the part is optional and may be repeated. The BNF is hierarchical; for example, the `wait` statement is defined in terms of other constructs. We can expand the `wait` statement definition, by substituting the BNF for `sensitivity_clause`, `condition_clause`, and `timeout_clause`:

```
wait_statement ::=
   [label : ] wait
      [ on signal_name { , signal_name } ]
      [ until boolean_expression ]
      [ for time_expression ] ;
```

Expanding the BNF makes it easier to see the structure of the `wait` statement. The expanded BNF shows that the following are valid `wait` statements (as far as syntax is concerned):

```
wait;
wait on a;
wait on a, b, c until count = 0 for 1 + 1 ns;
```

A disadvantage of expanding the BNF is that we lose the names and the definitions of the intermediate constructs (`sensitivity_clause`, `condition_clause`, and `timeout_clause`). The VHDL-93 LRM uses 238 production rules; the following section contains the same definitions in BNF, but in expanded form (using 94 rules).

There is one other disadvantage of expanding the BNF syntax definitions. Expanding the definition of a loop statement illustrates this problem:

```
loop_statement ::=
     [ loop_label : ]
   [ iteration_scheme ] loop
   sequence_of_statements
   end loop [ loop_label ] ;
```

The definition of `sequence_of_statements` is

```
sequence_of_statements ::= {sequential_statement}
```

The definition of `iteration_scheme` is

```
iteration_scheme ::= while condition | for loop_parameter_specification
```

The definitions of `condition` and `parameter_specification` are

```
condition ::= boolean_expression
parameter_specification ::= identifier in discrete_range
```

The definition of `discrete_range` is

```
discrete_range ::= discrete_subtype_indication | range
```

If we stop expanding at this level, we can write out what we have so far in our expanded definition of a loop statement:

```
loop_statement ::=
[ loop_label : ]
[ while boolean_expression
```

```
     | for identifier in discrete_range ]
loop
     {sequential_statement}
end loop [ loop_label ] ;
```

There is (theoretically) some ambiguity in this definition as far as the choices either side of the | symbol are concerned. Does this definition mean that we choose between **while** *boolean*_expression and **for** identifier **in** discrete_range? If we were in a contrary mood, we could also interpret the BNF as indicating a choice between *boolean*_expression and **for**. Notice that this ambiguity is also present in the definition of iteration_scheme.

Adding angle brackets around the clauses, < **while** ... > | < **for** ... >, makes the grouping of choices clear:

```
loop_statement ::=
[ loop_label : ]
[ < while boolean_expression >
   | < for identifier in discrete_range > ]
loop
   { sequential_statement }
end loop [ loop_label ] ;
```

Unfortunately the symbols < and > are already valid lexical elements in VHDL. In fact, since {} and [ ] are already used, and ( ) are part of the language too, there are no brackets left to use. We live with this inconvenience. The BNF (here or in the LRM) does not define VHDL, but helps us understand it.

A.2 VHDL Syntax

In the rules that follow an underline (<u>like this</u>) indicates syntax that is present in VHDL-93, but not in VHDL-87. A strikethrough (~~like this~~) indicates syntax that is present in VHDL-87, but not in VHDL-93; this occurs only in the rule for file_declaration (rule 38 on p. 968). This means that any VHDL-87 code that contains keywords **in** or **out** in a file declaration will not compile in a VHDL-93 environment. Except for this one exception, VHDL-93 is a superset of VHDL-87.

The VHDL productions are in alphabetical order. The highest-level production is the definition for design_file; this is where you start to traverse the tree starting at the top level. The following parts (indicated by the use of uppercase in the BNF) are the lowest-level constructions: UPPER_CASE_LETTER (A–Z plus accented uppercase letters), LOWER_CASE_LETTER (a–z and accented lowercase letters, é, and so on), LETTER (either uppercase or lowercase letters, a–z, and all accented letters), DIGIT (0–9), SPACE_CHARACTER (' ' and nonbreaking space), UNDERLINE ('_'), SPECIAL_CHARACTER (" # & ' ( ) * + , - . / : ; < = > [ ] _ |), and OTHER_SPECIAL_CHARACTER (all remaining characters such as ! $ % @ ? and so on, but not including format effectors). Format effectors are the ISO (and ASCII) characters called horizontal tabulation, vertical tabulation, carriage return, line feed, and form feed.

Keywords are shown in bold. Notice that the terms *label, literal,* and *range* are keywords (**label, literal, range**) and are also used as the name of a part (label, literal, range), as they are in the LRM. Construct names that commence with italics, such as *time*_expression, are intended to make the syntax definitions easier to read. The italic part of the construct is treated as a comment. You look up the definition for *time*_expression under `'e'` for expression, not `'t'` for time. There are no formal definitions of the italic modifiers; if you are not sure exactly what is meant, you must look up the semantics in the body of the LRM.

```
actual_part ::= [93LRM 4.3.2.2]                                              [1]
    expression
    | signal_name | variable_name | file_name | open
    | function_name (expression | signal_name | variable_name | file_name | open)
    | type_mark ( expression | signal_name | variable_name | file_name | open)
```

```
aggregate ::= [93LRM 7.3.2]                                                  [2]
    ( [ choice { | choice } => ] expression {, [ choice { | choice } => ] expression } )
```

```
alias_declaration ::= [93LRM 4.3.3]                                         [3]
    alias identifier | ' graphic_character ' | " { graphic_character } "
    [ : subtype_indication ] is name [ signature ] ;
```

```
architecture_body ::= [93LRM 1.2]                                           [4]
    architecture identifier of entity_name is
        { block_declarative_item }
    begin
        { concurrent_statement }
    end [ architecture ] [architecture_identifier ];
```

```
assertion ::= [93LRM 8.2]                                                   [5]
    assert boolean_expression [ report expression ] [ severity expression ]
```

```
association_list ::= [93LRM 4.3.2.2]                                        [6]
    [ formal_part => ] actual_part {, [ formal_part => ] actual_part }
```

```
attribute_declaration ::= [93LRM 4.4] attribute identifier : type_mark ;    [7]
```

```
attribute_name ::= [93LRM 6.6] prefix [ signature ] ' attribute_identifier  [8]
    [ ( expression ) ]
```

```
attribute_specification ::= [93LRM 5.1]                                     [9]
    attribute attribute_identifier of entity_name_list : entity_class is expression ;
```

```
based_literal ::= [93LRM 13.4.2]                                           [10]
    integer # DIGIT | LETTER { [ UNDERLINE ] DIGIT | LETTER }
    [ . DIGIT | LETTER { [ UNDERLINE ] DIGIT | LETTER } ]
    # [ E [ + ] integer | E − integer ]
```

```
basic_graphic_character ::= [93LRM 13.1]                                   [11]
    UPPER_CASE_LETTER | DIGIT | SPECIAL_CHARACTER | SPACE_CHARACTER
```

```
bit_string_literal ::= [93LRM 13.7]                                        [12]
    B | O | X " [DIGIT | LETTER { [ UNDERLINE ] DIGIT | LETTER } ]"
```

```
block_configuration ::= [93LRM 1.3.1]                                      [13]
    for architecture_name
    | block_statement_label
```

```
     | generate_statement_label
       [ ( discrete_subtype_indication | range | static_expression ) ]
     { use prefix.suffix {, prefix.suffix } ; }
     { block_configuration | component_configuration }
     end for ;

block_declarative_item ::= [93LRM 1.2.1]                                        [14]
     subprogram_specification; | subprogram_body | type_declaration
     | subtype_declaration | constant_declaration | signal_declaration
     | shared variable_declaration
     | file_declaration | alias_declaration
     | component_declaration | attribute_declaration
     | attribute_specification | configuration_specification
     | disconnection_specification | use_clause
     | group_template_declaration | group_declaration

block_statement ::= [93LRM 9.1]                                                [15]
     block_label :
     block [ ( guard_expression ) ] [ is ]
       [ generic ( generic_interface_list );
       [ generic map (generic_association_list ) ; ] ]
       [ port (port_interface_list );
       [ port map (port_association_list ) ; ] ]
         { block_declarative_item }
         begin
         { concurrent_statement }
     end block [ block_label ] ;

case_statement ::= [93LRM 8.8]                                                 [16]
     [ case_label : ] case expression is
       when choice { | choice } => { sequential_statement }
       { when choice { | choice } => { sequential_statement } }
     end case [ case_label ] ;

choice ::= [93LRM 7.3.2]                                                       [17]
     simple_expression | discrete_range | element_identifier | others

component_configuration ::= [93LRM 1.3.2]                                      [18]
     for
       instantiation_label { , instantiation_label } : component_name
       | others : component_name
       | all : component_name
         [ [ use
           entity entity_name [ ( architecture_identifier ) ]
           | configuration configuration_name
           | open ]
         [ generic map (generic_association_list ) ]
         [ port map ( port_association_list ) ] ; ]
       [ block_configuration ]
     end for ;
```

```
component_declaration ::= [93LRM 4.5]                                              [19]
   component identifier [ is ]
      [ generic (local_generic_interface_list ) ; ]
      [ port (local_port_interface_list ) ; ]
   end component [ component_identifier ] ;

component_instantiation_statement ::= [93LRM 9.6]                                  [20]
   instantiation_label : [ component ] component_name
      | entity entity_name [ ( architecture_identifier ) ]
      | configuration configuration_name
   [ generic map ( generic_association_list )]
   [ port map ( port_association_list ) ] ;

concurrent_statement ::= [93LRM 9]                                                 [21]
   block_statement
   | process_statement
   | [ label : ] [ postponed ] procedure_call ;
   | [ label : ] [ postponed ] assertion ;
   | [ label : ] [ postponed ] conditional_signal_assignment
   | [ label : ] [ postponed ] selected_signal_assignment
   | component_instantiation_statement
   | generate_statement

conditional_signal_assignment ::= [93LRM 9.5.1]                                   [22]
   name | aggregate <= [ guarded ] [ transport | [ reject time_expression ] inertial ]
   { waveform when boolean_expression else }
   waveform [ when boolean_expression ] ;

configuration_declaration ::= [93LRM 1.3]                                         [23]
   configuration identifier of entity_name is
      { use prefix.suffix { , prefix.suffix } ;
      | attribute_specification
      | group_declaration }
      block_configuration
   end [ configuration ] [ configuration_identifier ] ;

configuration_specification ::= [93LRM 5.2]                                       [24]
   for
      instantiation_label { ,instantiation_label } : component_name
      | others : component_name
      | all : component_name
   [ use
      entity entity_name [ ( architecture_identifier ) ]
      | configuration configuration_name
      | open ]
   [ generic map ( generic_association_list ) ]
   [ port map ( port_association_list ) ] ;

constant_declaration ::= [93LRM 4.3.1.1]                                          [25]
   constant identifier { , identifier } : subtype_indication [ := expression ] ;
```

```
constraint ::= range_constraint | index_constraint [93LRM 4.2]                [26]

decimal_literal ::= [93LRM 13.4.1]                                            [27]
   integer [ . integer ] [ E [ + ] integer | E - integer ]

design_file ::= [93LRM 11.1]                                                  [28]
   { library_clause | use_clause } library_unit
   { { library_clause | use_clause } library_unit }

disconnection_specification ::= [93LRM 5.3]                                   [29]
   disconnect guarded_signal_list : type_mark after time_expression ;

discrete_range ::= [93LRM 3.2.1] discrete_subtype_indication | range          [30]

entity_class ::= [93LRM 5.1]                                                  [31]
   entity
   | architecture    | configuration   | procedure    | function
   | package         | type            | subtype      | constant
   | signal          | variable        | component    | label
   | literal         | units           | group        | file

entity_declaration ::= [93LRM 1.1]                                           [32]
   entity identifier is
      [ generic ( formal_generic_interface_list ) ; ]
      [ port ( formal_port_interface_list ) ; ]
      { subprogram_specification ;      | subprogram_body
      | subtype_declaration             | constant_declaration
      | signal_declaration              | file_declaration
      | alias_declaration               | attribute_declaration
      | attribute_specification         | type_declaration
      | disconnection_specification     | use_clause
      | shared variable_declaration
      | group_template_declaration      | group_declaration }
   [ begin
      { [ label : ] [ postponed ] assertion ;
      | [ label : ] [ postponed ] passive_procedure_call ;
      | passive_process_statement } ]
   end [ entity ] [entity_identifier ] ;

entity_name_list ::= [93LRM 5.1]                                             [33]
   identifier | " { graphic_character } " | ' graphic_character ' [ signature ]
   { , identifier | " { graphic_character } " | ' graphic_character ' [ signature ] }
   | others
   | all

enumeration_literal ::= [93LRM 3.1.1] identifier | ' graphic_character '      [34]

exit_statement ::= [93LRM 8.11]                                             [35]
[label:] exit [ loop_label ] [ when boolean_expression ] ;

expression ::= [93LRM 7.1]                                                   [36]
   relation { and relation }
```

```
    | relation { or relation }
    | relation { xor relation }
    | relation [ nand relation ]
    | relation [ nor relation ]
    | relation { xnor relation }
```

factor ::= [93LRM 7.1] primary [** primary] | **abs** primary | **not** primary   [37]

file_declaration ::= [93LRM 4.3.1.4]   [38]
   file identifier { , identifier } : subtype_indication
   [[**open** *file_open_kind*_expression] **is** ~~[in | out]~~ *string*_expression] ;

formal_part ::= [93LRM 4.3.2.2]   [39]
   *generic*_name | *port*_name | *parameter*_name
   | *function*_name (*generic*_name | *port*_name | *parameter*_name)
   | type_mark (*generic*_name | *port*_name | *parameter*_name)

function_call ::= [93LRM 7.3.3] *function*_name [(*parameter*_association_list)]   [40]

generate_statement ::= [93LRM 9.7]   [41]
   *generate*_label:
   for identifier **in**
      *discrete*_subtype_indication | range
   | **if** *boolean*_expression
   generate
   [{ block_declarative_item } **begin**]
     { concurrent_statement }
   end generate [*generate*_label] ;

graphic_character ::= [93LRM 13.1]   [42]
   basic_graphic_character | LOWER_CASE_LETTER | OTHER_SPECIAL_CHARACTER

group_declaration ::= [93LRM 4.7]   [43]
   group identifier : *group_template*_name
   (name | ' graphic_character '
     { , name | ' graphic_character ' }) ;

group_template_declaration ::= [93LRM 4.6]   [44]
   group identifier **is** (entity_class [<>] { , entity_class [<>] }) ;

identifier ::= [93LRM 13.3]   [45]
   LETTER { [UNDERLINE] LETTER | DIGIT }
   | \ graphic_character { graphic_character } \

if_statement ::= [93LRM 8.7]   [46]
   [*if*_label :] **if** *boolean*_expression **then** { sequential_statement }
    { **elsif** *boolean*_expression **then** { sequential_statement } }
    [**else** { sequential_statement }]
   end if [*if*_label] ;

index_constraint ::= [93LRM 3.2.1] (discrete_range { , discrete_range })   [47]

integer ::= [§ 13.4.1] DIGIT { [UNDERLINE] DIGIT }   [48]

```
interface_list ::= [93LRM 4.3.2.1] interface_declaration {; interface_declaration}    [49]

interface_declaration ::= [93LRM 4.3.2]                                               [50]
   [constant] identifier { , identifier }
      : [ in ] subtype_indication [ := static_expression ]
   | [ signal ] identifier { , identifier }
      : [ in | out | inout | buffer | linkage ]
      subtype_indication [ bus ] [ := static_expression ]
   | [ variable ] identifier { , identifier}
      : [in | out | inout | buffer | linkage ] subtype_indication [ := static_expression]
   | file identifier { , identifier } : subtype_indication

label ::=  identifier [93LRM 9.7]                                                     [51]

library_clause ::= [93LRM 11.2] library identifier {, identifier} ;                   [52]

library_unit ::= [93LRM 11.1]                                                         [53]
   entity_declaration | configuration_declaration | package_declaration
   | architecture_body | package_body

literal ::= [93LRM 7.3.1]                                                             [54]
   decimal_literal        | based_literal      | physical_literal
   | enumeration_literal   | string_literal     | bit_string_literal | null

loop_statement ::= [93LRM 8.9]                                                        [55]
   [ loop_label : ]
   [ while boolean_expression | for identifier in discrete_range ]
      loop
         { sequential_statement }
      end loop [ loop_label ] ;

name ::= [93LRM 6.1]                                                                  [56]
   identifier
   | " { graphic_character } "
   | prefix.suffix
   | prefix ( expression { , expression } )
   | prefix ( discrete_range )
   | attribute_name

next_statement ::= [93LRM 8.10]                                                       [57]
   [ label : ] next [ loop_label ] [ when boolean_expression ] ;

null_statement ::= [93LRM 8.13] [ label : ] null ;                                    [58]

package_body ::= [93LRM 2.6]                                                          [59]
   package body package_identifier is
   { subprogram_specification ; | subprogram_body | type_declaration
   | subtype_declaration | constant_declaration | file_declaration
   | alias_declaration | use_clause
   | shared variable_declaration
   | group_template_declaration | group_declaration }
   end [ package body ] [ package_identifier ] ;
```

```
package_declaration ::= [93LRM 2.5]                                           [60]
   package identifier is
   { subprogram_specification ; | type_declaration | subtype_declaration
   | constant_declaration | signal_declaration | file_declaration
   | alias_declaration | component_declaration
   | attribute_declaration | attribute_specification
   | disconnection_specification | use_clause
   | shared variable_declaration
   | group_template_declaration | group_declaration }
   end [ package ] [ package_identifier ] ;
```

```
physical_literal ::= [93LRM 3.1.3] [ decimal_literal | based_literal ] unit_name   [61]
```

```
physical_type_definition ::= [93LRM 3.1.3]                                    [62]
   range_constraint
      units identifier ;
      { identifier = physical_literal ; }
      end units [ physical_type_identifier ]
```

```
prefix ::= [93LRM 6.1] name | function_call                                   [63]
```

```
primary ::= [93LRM 7.1]                                                       [64]
   name | literal | aggregate | function_call
   | type_mark ' ( expression ) | type_mark ' aggregate | type_mark ( expression )
   | ( expression )
   | new subtype_indication | new type_mark ' (expression) | new type_mark ' aggregate
```

```
procedure_call ::= [93LRM 8.6] procedure_name [ ( parameter_association_list ) ]   [65]
```

```
process_statement ::= [93LRM 9.2 ]                                            [66]
   [ process_label : ]
   [ postponed ] process [ ( signal_name { , signal_name } ) ] [ is ]
      { subprogram_specification; | subprogram_body
      | type_declaration
      | subtype_declaration | constant_declaration
      | variable_declaration
      | file_declaration | alias_declaration | attribute_declaration
      | attribute_specification | use_clause
      | group_template_declaration | group_declaration }
   begin
      { sequential_statement }
   end [ postponed ] process [ process_label ] ;
```

```
range ::= [93LRM 3.1]                                                         [67]
   range_attribute_name
   | simple_expression to | downto simple_expression
```

```
range_constraint ::= [93LRM 3.1] range range                                 [68]
```

```
record_type_definition ::= [93LRM 3.2.2]                                      [69]
   record
      identifier {, identifier} : subtype_indication ;
```

```
        { identifier {, identifier} : subtype_indication ; }
      end record [ record_type_identifier ]
```

relation ::= [93LRM 7.1]   [70]
```
    simple_expression [ sll | srl | sla | sra | rol | ror simple_expression ]
    [ = | /= | < | <= | > | >=
    simple_expression [ sll | srl | sla | sra | rol | ror simple_expression ] ]
```

report_statement ::= [93LRM 8.3]   [71]
```
    [ label : ] report expression [ severity expression ] ;
```

return_statement ::= [93LRM 8.12] [label :] return [expression] ;   [72]

selected_signal_assignment ::= [93LRM 9.5.2]   [73]
```
    with expression select
      name | aggregate <= [ guarded ]
    [ transport | [ reject time_expression ] inertial ]
      waveform when choice { | choice }
        { , waveform when choice { | choice } } ;
```

sequential_statement ::= [93LRM 8]   [74]
```
    wait_statement
    | [ label : ] assertion ;
    | report_statement
    | signal_assignment_statement
    | variable_assignment_statement
    | [ label : ] procedure_call ;
    | if_statement
    | case_statement
    | loop_statement
    | next_statement
    | exit_statement
    | return_statement
    | null_statement
```

signal_assignment_statement ::= [93LRM 8.4]   [75]
```
    [ label : ] name | aggregate <=
    [ transport | [ reject time_expression ] inertial ] waveform ;
```

signal_declaration ::= [93LRM 4.3.1.2]   [76]
```
    signal identifier {, identifier } : subtype_indication
      [register | bus] [ := expression] ;
```

signal_list ::= [93LRM 5.3] signal_name { , signal_name } | others | all   [77]

signature ::= [93LRM 2.3.2]   [78]
```
    [ [ type_mark { , type_mark } ] [ return type_mark ] ]
```

simple_expression ::= [93LRM 7.1] [+ | -] term { + | - | & term }   [79]

string_literal ::= [93LRM 13.6] " { graphic_character } "   [80]

```
subprogram_body ::= [93LRM 2.2]                                              [81]
   subprogram_specification is
   { subprogram_specification ;
   | subprogram_body
   | type_declaration
   | subtype_declaration
   | constant_declaration
   | variable_declaration
   | file_declaration
   | alias_declaration
   | attribute_declaration
   | attribute_specification
   | use_clause
   | group_template_declaration
   | group_declaration }
   begin
      { sequential_statement }
   end [ procedure | function ]
      [ identifier | " { graphic_character } " ] ;

subprogram_specification ::= [93LRM 2.1]                                     [82]
   procedure identifier | " { graphic_character } "
      [ ( parameter_interface_list ) ]
   | [ pure | impure ] function identifier | " { graphic_character } "
      [ ( parameter_interface_list ) ]
   return type_mark

subtype_declaration ::= [93LRM 4.2]                                          [83]
   subtype identifier is
   [ resolution_function_name ] type_mark [ constraint ] ;

subtype_indication ::= [93LRM 4.2]                                           [84]
   [ resolution_function_name ] type_mark [ constraint ]

suffix ::= [93LRM 6.3]                                                       [85]
   identifier
   | ' graphic_character '
   | " { graphic_character } "
   | all

term ::= [93LRM 7.1] factor { * | / | mod | rem factor }                     [86]

type_declaration ::= [93LRM 4.1]                                             [87]
   type identifier ;
   | type identifier is
      ( identifier | ' graphic_character '
        { , identifier | ' graphic_character ' } ) ;
      | range_constraint ;
      | physical_type_definition ;
      | record_type_definition ;
```

```
        |  access subtype_indication ;
        |  file of type_mark ;
        |  array index_constraint of element_subtype_indication ;
        |  array ( type_mark range <> { , type_mark range <> } ) of
           element_subtype_indication ;
```

type_mark ::= [93LRM 4.2] *type*_name | *subtype*_name   [88]

use_clause ::= [93LRM 10.4] **use** prefix.suffix {, prefix.suffix} ;   [89]

variable_assignment_statement ::= [93LRM 8.5]   [90]
  [label :] name | aggregate := expression ;

variable_declaration ::= [93LRM 4.3.1.3]   [91]
  [**shared**] **variable** identifier {, identifier} : subtype_indication
  [:= expression] ;

wait_statement ::= [93LRM 8.1]   [92]
  [label :] **wait**
    [**on** *signal*_name { , *signal*_name }]
    [**until** *boolean*_expression]
    [**for** *time*_expression] ;

waveform ::= [93LRM 8.4] waveform_element { , waveform_element } | **unaffected**   [93]

waveform_element ::= [93LRM 8.4.1]   [94]
  *value*_expression [**after** *time*_expression] | **null** [**after** *time*_expression]

A.3 BNF Index

Table A.1 is an index to the VHDL BNF productions. For example, to find the legal positions for a pro-cess statement you would locate production rules 21 and 32 opposite process_statement in Table A.1. These rule numbers correspond to the productions for concurrent_statement (21) and entity_declaration (32). Next, turning to rule 32 for entity_declaration on page 967, you will find that only a *passive*_process_statement is allowed in an entity declaration. Table A.2 is a list of VHDL keywords and an index to rules that reference a keyword.

A.4 Bibliography

The book by Ashenden [1995] covers VHDL-93 in detail. Other books on VHDL include: Coelho [1989]; Lipsett, Schaefer, and Ussery [1989]; Armstrong [1989]; Augustin et al. [1991]; Perry [1991]; Mazor and Langstraat [1992]; three books by Bhasker [1992, 1995, 1996]; Armstrong and Gray [1993]; Baker [1993]; Navabi [1993]; Ott and Wilderotter [1994]; Airiau, Bergé, and Olive [1994]; two books by Cohen [1995, 1997]; Pick [1996]; Jerraya et al. [1997]; Pellerin and Taylor [1997]; Sjoholm and Lindh [1997]; and Chang [1997]. Of these, the book by Armstrong and Gray and Perry's books (two editions) are easy-to-read

TABLE A.1   Index to VHDL BNF rules (list of rules that reference a rule).

[1] 13, 15, 16, 18, 20, 21, 24, 31, 32, 35, 41, 46, 55, 57, 66, 71, 72, 74, 75, 90, 92
[2] 1, 3, 4, 13, 18, 20, 22, 23, 24, 39, 40, 43, 61, 63, 64, 65, 66, 73, 75, 77, 83, 84, 88, 90, 92
[3] 1,2, 5, 8, 9, 13, 15, 16, 17, 22, 25, 29, 35, 39, 41, 46, 50, 55, 56, 57, 64, 67, 70, 71, 72, 73, 75, 76, 79, 90, 91, 92, 94
[4] 3, 13, 25, 30, 38, 41, 50, 64, 69, 76, 87, 91
[5] 3, 4, 7, 8, 9, 17, 18, 18, 20, 23, 24, 25, 32, 33, 34, 38, 41, 43, 44, 50, 51, 52, 55, 56, 59, 60, 61, 62, 69, 76, 81, 82, 83, 85, 87, 91

TABLE A.2   VHDL keywords and index (list of rules that reference a keyword).[1]

abs 37	disconnect 29	inout 50	package 31, 59,60	sra 70
access 87	downto 67	is 3, 4, 9, 15, 16, 19,	port 15, 18, 19, 20,	srl 70
after 29, 94	else 22, 46	23, 32, 38, 44, 59,	24, 32	subtype 31, 83
alias 3	elsif 46	60, 66, 81, 83, 87	postponed 21, 32,	then 46
all 18, 24, 77, 85	end 4, 13, 15, 16, 18,	label 31	66	to 67
and 36	19, 23, 32, 41, 46,	library 52	procedure 31, 81,	transport 22, 73,
architecture 4,	55, 59, 60, 62, 66,	linkage 50	82	75
31	69, 81	literal 31	process 66	type 31, 87
array 87	entity 18, 20, 24,	loop 55	pure 82	unaffected 93
assert 5	31, 32	map 15, 18, 20, 24	range 68	units 31, 62
attribute 7, 9	exit 35	mod 86	record 69	until 92
begin 4, 15, 32, 41,	file 31, 38, 87	nand 36	register 76	use 13, 18, 23, 24, 89
66, 81	for 13, 18, 24, 41,	new 64	reject 22, 73, 75	variable 31, 50, 91
block 15	55, 92	next 57	rem 86	wait 92
body 59	function 31, 81, 82	nor 36	report 5, 71	when 16, 22, 35, 57,
buffer 50	generate 41	not 37	return 72, 78, 82	73
bus 50, 76	generic 15, 18, 19,	null 54, 58, 94	rol 70	while 55
case 16	20, 24, 32	of 4, 9, 23, 87	ror 70	with 73
component 19, 20,	group 31, 43, 44	on 92	select 73	xnor 36
31	guarded 22, 73	open 1, 18, 24, 38	severity 5, 71	xor 36
configuration	if 41, 46	or 36	signal 31, 50, 76	
18, 20, 23, 24, 31	impure 82	others 17, 18, 24,	shared 91	
constant 25, 31,	in[2] 41, 50, 55	33, 77	sla 70	
50	inertial 22, 73, 75	out[3] 50	sll 70	

[1]Underlines denote VHDL-93 keywords that are not VHDL-87 keywords.
[2]Excluding VHDL-87 file_declaration.
[3]Excluding VHDL-87 file_declaration.

introductions. The following books describe example VHDL models for ASICs: Leung and Shanblatt [1989], Skahill [1996], Smith [1996]. Edited books by Bergé et al. [1992, 1993]; Harr and Stanculescu [1991]; Mermet [1992]; and Schoen et al. [1991] contain papers on more advanced aspects of VHDL.

There are some issues and interpretations of VHDL that are covered in a separate IEEE document [IEEE 1076-1991]; also relevant are the IEEE standard logic system for VHDL [IEEE 1164-1993], the WAVES standard [IEEE 1029.1-1991], and the VITAL standard [IEEE 1076.4-1995]. The IEEE has produced a VHDL interactive tutorial on CD-ROM [IEEE 1164-1997]. Hanna et al. [1997] cover the IEEE WAVES standard.

Updates and extensions to VHDL are controlled by the IEEE working groups (WG). These include study and WGs on: Object Oriented VHDL, Open Modeling Forum, Simulation Control Language (SimCL), System Design & Description Language, VHDL Analog Extensions (PAR 1076.1), VHDL Math Package (PAR 1076.2), VHDL Synthesis Package (PAR 1076.3), Utility (PAR 1076.5), VHDL Shared Variables (PAR 1076; mod a), VHDL Analysis and Standards Group (VASG) Issues Screening and Analysis Committee (ISAC), VHDL Library, VHDL Parallel Simulation, and VHDL Test. Links to the activities of these groups, as well as an explanation of a Project Authorization Request (PAR) and the standards process, may be found at `http://ieee.org` and `http://stdsbbs.ieee.org`.

A.5   References

Page numbers in brackets after a reference indicate its location in the chapter body.

The current IEEE standards and material listed here are published by The Institute of Electrical and Electronics Engineers, Inc., 345 East 47th Street, New York, NY 10017 USA. Inside the United States, IEEE standards may be ordered at 1-800-678-4333. See also `http://ieee.org` and `http://stdsbbs.ieee.org`.

Airiau, R., J.-M. Bergé, and V. Olive. 1994. *Circuit Synthesis with VHDL.* Boston: Kluwer, 221 p. ISBN 0792394291. TK7885.7.A37. Introduction to VHDL aimed at ASIC designers.

Armstrong, J. R. 1989. *Chip-Level Modeling with VHDL.* Englewood Cliffs, NJ: Prentice-Hall, 148 p. ISBN 0131331906. TK7874.A75 1989.

Armstrong, J. R., and F. G. Gray. 1993. *Structured Logic Design with VHDL.* Englewood Cliffs, NJ: Prentice-Hall, 482 p. ISBN 0138552061. TK7885.7.A76. 20 pages of references.

Ashenden, P. J. 1995. *The Designer's Guide to VHDL.* San Francisco: Morgan Kaufmann, 688 p. ISBN 1-55860-270-4. TK7888.3.A863. A complete reference to VHDL from a system design perspective.

Augustin, L. M., et al. 1991. *Hardware Design and Simulation in VAL/VHDL.* Boston: Kluwer, 322 p. ISBN 0792390873. TK7885.7.H38. Two pages of references.

Baker, L. 1993. *VHDL Programming with Advanced Topics.* New York: Wiley, 365 p. ISBN 0471574643. TK7885.7.B35. Basic to intermediate level coverage of VHDL.

Bergé, J.-M., et al. (Eds.). 1992. *VHDL Designer's Reference.* Boston: Kluwer, 455 p. ISBN 0792317564. TK7885.7.V47. Two pages of references.

Bergé, J.-M., et al. (Eds.). 1993. *VHDL '92.* Boston: Kluwer, 214 p. ISBN 0792393562. TK7885.7.V46. Covers new constructs in VHDL-93.

Bhasker, J. 1992. *A VHDL Primer.* Englewood Cliffs, NJ: Prentice-Hall, 253 p. ISBN 013952987X. TK7885.7.B53. See also the revised edition, ISBN 0131814478, 1995. A basic introduction to VHDL.

Bhasker, J. 1995. *A Guide to VHDL Syntax: Based on the New IEEE Std 1076-1993.* Englewood Cliffs, NJ: Prentice-Hall, 268 p. ISBN 0133243516. TK7885.7.B52. Uses graphics to illustrate BNF syntax.

Bhasker, J. 1996. *A VHDL Synthesis Primer.* Allentown, PA: Star Galaxy, 238 p. ISBN 0965039102. TK7885.7.B534.

Chang, K. C. 1997. *Digital Design and Modeling with VHDL and Synthesis.* Los Alamitos, CA: IEEE Computer Society Press. ISBN 0818677163. TK7874.7.C47.

Coelho, D. R. 1989. *The VHDL Handbook.* Boston: Kluwer, 389 p. ISBN 0792390318. TK7874.C6. A description of VHDL models, including details of models for simple combinational and sequential logic devices and memory. Two pages of references.

Cohen, B. 1995. *VHDL Coding Styles and Methodologies.* Boston: Kluwer, 365 p. ISBN 0792395980. TK7885.7.C65.

Cohen, B. 1997. *VHDL Answers to Frequently Asked Questions.* Boston: Kluwer, 291 p. ISBN 0792397916. TK7885.7.C64.

Hanna, J. P., et al. 1997. *Using WAVES and VHDL for Effective Design and Testing.* Boston: Kluwer, 304 p. ISBN 0792397991. TK7874.7.U87.

Harr, R. E., and A. G. Stanculescu (Eds.). 1991. *Applications of VHDL to Circuit Design.* Boston: Kluwer, 232 p ISBN 0792391535. TK7867.A64.

IEEE 1076-1987. *IEEE Standard VHDL Language Reference Manual.* This version of the VHDL LRM is replaced by VHDL-93; however, some systems (and some IEEE Standards, notably VITAL) are based on VHDL-87. For instructions on how to obtain obsolete IEEE standards (known as archive standards), see http://stdsbbs.ieee.org. [cited on p. 961]

IEEE 1076-1991. *1076 Interpretations, 1991 IEEE Standards Interpretations: IEEE Std 1076-1987, IEEE Standard VHDL Language Reference Manual.* 208 p. ISBN 1-55937-181-1. TK7885.7.I58. IEEE Ref. SH14894-NYF.

IEEE 1029.1-1991. *IEEE Standard for Waveform and Vector Exchange (WAVES) (ANSI).* 96 p. ISBN 1-55937-195-1. IEEE Ref. SH15032-NYF.

IEEE 1164-1993. *IEEE Standard Multivalue Logic System for VHDL Model Interoperability (Std_logic_1164).* 24 p. ISBN 1-55937-299-0. IEEE Ref. SH16097-NYF.

IEEE 1076-1993. *IEEE Standard VHDL Language Reference Manual (ANSI).* 288 p. ISBN 1-55937-376-8. IEEE Ref. SH16840-NYF. [cited on p. 961]

IEEE 1076.4-1995. *IEEE Standard VITAL Application-Specific Integrated Circuit (ASIC) Modeling Specification.* 96 p. ISBN 1-55937-691-0. IEEE Ref. SH94382-NYF. Includes an MS-DOS diskette containing the ASCII code for the VITAL_Timing and VITAL_Primitives packages.

IEEE 1076-1997. *VHDL Interactive Tutorial.* This CD-ROM tutorial is available from IEEE by itself or with a printed version of the VHDL LRM. The CD-ROM is available in the following formats: IBM Windows (Windows 3.1 and Windows 95), Macintosh, Sun OS, and Sun Solaris.

Jerraya, A. A., et al. 1997. *Behavioral Synthesis and Component Reuse with VHDL.* Boston: Kluwer, 263 p. ISBN 0792398270. TK7874.75.B45. Eight pages of references.

Leung, S. S., and M. A. Shanblatt. 1989. *ASIC System Design with VHDL: A Paradigm.* Boston: Kluwer, 206 p. ISBN 0-7923-90932-6. TK7874.L396. Describes VHDL models for an ASIC intended for IKS (inverse kinematic solution) which converts cartesian space to the robot-joint space. Eight pages of references.

Lipsett, R., C. Schaefer, and C. Ussery. 1989. *VHDL: Hardware Description and Design.* Boston: Kluwer, 299 p. ISBN 079239030X. TK7887.5.L57. Intermediate guide to VHDL.

Mazor, S., and P. Langstraat. 1992. *A Guide to VHDL.* Boston: Kluwer. ISBN 0792392558. TK7885.7.M39. See also 2nd ed., ISBN 0792393872, 1993. Basic introduction to VHDL.

Mermet, J. (Ed.). 1992. *VHDL for Simulation, Synthesis, and Formal Proofs of Hardware.* Boston: Kluwer. ISBN 0792392531. TK7885.7.V48.

Navabi, Z. 1993. *VHDL: Analysis and Modeling of Digital Systems.* New York: McGraw-Hill, 375 p. ISBN 0070464723. TK7874.N36. Introduction to VHDL.

Ott, D. E., and T. J. Wilderotter. 1994. *A Designer's Guide to VHDL Synthesis.* Boston: Kluwer. ISBN 0792394720. TK7885.7.O89.

Pellerin, D., and D. Taylor. 1997. *VHDL Made Easy!* Upper Saddle River, NJ: Prentice-Hall, 419 p. ISBN 0136507638. TK7885.7.P46.

Perry, D. L. 1991. *VHDL.* New York: McGraw-Hill, 458 p. ISBN 0070494339. TK7885.7.P47. See also 2nd ed., ISBN 0070494347, 1994. Good introduction to VHDL.

Pick, J. 1996. *VHDL Techniques, Experiments, and Caveats.* New York: McGraw-Hill, 382 p. ISBN 0070499063. TK7885.7.P53. A series of intermediate to advanced examples that illustrate mistakes in VHDL.

Schoen, J. M., et al. (Eds.). 1991. *Performance and Fault Modeling with VHDL.* Englewood Cliffs, NJ: Prentice-Hall, 406 p ISBN 0136588166. TK7888.4.P47.

Sjoholm, S., and L. Lindh. 1997. *VHDL for Designers.* Englewood Cliffs, NJ: Prentice-Hall. ISBN 0134734149. TK7885.7.S54.

Skahill, K. 1996. *VHDL for Programmable Logic.* Menlo Park, CA: Addison-Wesley, 593 p. ISBN 0-201-89573-0. TK7885.7.S55. Covers VHDL design for PLDs using Cypress Warp.

Smith, D. J. 1996. *HDL Chip Design: A Practical Guide for Designing, Synthesizing, and Simulating ASICs and FPGAs using VHDL or Verilog.* Madison, AL: Doone Publications, 448 p. ISBN 0965193438. TK7874.6.S62.

VERILOG HDL RESOURCES

The definitive reference for the Verilog HDL is IEEE Std 1364-1995. This standard is known as the **IEEE Verilog**® **HDL language reference manual** (**LRM**) and the 1995 version is referred to here as the 95 LRM [IEEE 1364-1995].[1] Verilog is a registered trademark of Cadence Design Systems and Verilog-XL is a commercial simulator.

B.1   Explanation of the Verilog HDL BNF

Annex A of the Verilog HDL LRM describes syntax using the BNF (Backus–Naur form). The Verilog HDL BNF is slightly different from that employed in the VHDL LRM (see Appendix A, Section A.1, "BNF"). The BNF syntax in the Verilog LRM is **normative**, which means that the syntax is part of the definition of the language (and the complete BNF description is contained in an **annex**). The BNF syntax in the VHDL LRM is **informative**, which means the BNF is not part of the standard defining the language (and the complete BNF description is contained in an **appendix**). The following items summarize the Verilog HDL BNF syntax:

- name (in lowercase) is a **syntax construct item** (**term**, or **syntactic category**) defined by other syntax construct token items (**items**, **parts**, or **tokens**) or by lexical token items.
- NAME (in uppercase) is a **lexical token item**, the leaves in a tree of definitions.
- [name] is an **optional item**.
- { name } is one or more items.
- The symbol ::= gives a syntax definition (**definition**, **rule**, **construct**, or **production**) for an item (i.e., the symbol ::= means *is equivalent to*).
- | introduces an alternative syntax definition (i.e., the symbol | means *or*).
- Braces and brackets, { } and [ ], that are required by the syntax are set in bold, { } [ ], in the 95 LRM, but are difficult to distinguish from the plain versions. Here they are set in outline, like this: { } [ ].

- The vertical bar, |, that represents an alternative definition is set in bold, |, in the 95 LRM, but is difficult to distinguish from the plain version. Here it is set in outline, like this: ⫾.
- All other characters that are set in bold (as they are in Annex A of the 95 LRM) are literals required by the syntax (for example, a plus sign '+').
- Italic prefixes, for example, *rising_mintypmax* are comments.
- Keywords are printed in `bold`, as they are in Annex A of the 95 LRM.
- Definitions here are in alphabetical order (Annex A of the 95 LRM groups definitions by function). The highest-level definition is `source_text`; this is where you start. The lowest-level items are in uppercase; these are where you end.
- The BNF is reproduced *exactly* as it appears in Annex A of the 95 LRM. Footnotes explain a number of typographical issues.
- References in brackets immediately following the ::= symbol form backward-pointing links to the constructs that reference a particular item. Thus, for example, `always_construct` ::= [94] indicates that construct number 94 (`module_item`) references the item `always_construct` (see also Table B.1 on p. 995, which collects all these links together, and Table B.2 on p. 996, which is a keyword index).
- References in brackets following the construct links refer to the 95 LRM. Thus, for example, `always_construct` ::= [94] [95LRM 9.9.2], indicates that section 9.9.2 of the 95 LRM contains the definition for `always_construct`.

B.2   Verilog HDL Syntax

```
always_construct ::= [94] [95LRM 9.9.2] always statement                      [1]

binary_base ::= [4] [95LRM 2.5.1] 'b | 'B                                      [2]

binary_digit ::= [4] [95LRM 2.5.1] x | X | z | Z | 0 | 1                       [3]

binary_number ::= [114] [95LRM 2.5.1]                                          [4]
  [ size ] binary_base binary_digit { _ | binary_digit }

binary_operator ::= [19, 52] [95LRM 4.1.2]                                     [5]
   + | - | * | / | % | == | != | === | !== | && | ||
   | < | <= | > | >= | & | | | ^ | ^~ | ~^ | >> | <<

blocking assignment² ::= [181] [95LRM 9.2.1]                                   [6]
  reg_lvalue = [ delay_or_event_control ] expression

block_item_declaration ::= [57, 133, 166, 190] [95LRM 9.8.1]                   [7]
   parameter_declaration | reg_declaration
```

---

²The term `blocking(space)assignment` is referenced as `blocking(underscore)assignment`.

```
        | integer_declaration | real_declaration | time_declaration
        | realtime_declaration | event_declaration
```

case_item ::= [9] [95LRM 9.5] expression { , expression } : statement_or_null   [8]
    | **default** [:] statement_or_null

case_statement ::= [181] [95LRM 9.5]   [9]
    | **case** (expression) case_item { case_item } **endcase**
    | **casez** (expression) case_item { case_item } **endcase**
    | **casex** (expression) case_item { case_item } **endcase**

charge_strength ::= [107] [95LRM 3.4.1] (**small**) | (**medium**) | (**large**)   [10]

cmos_switchtype ::= [58] [95LRM 7.7] **cmos** | **rcmos**   [11]

cmos_switch_instance ::= [58] [95LRM 7.1] [name_of_gate_instance]   [12]
    (output_terminal , input_terminal ,
        ncontrol_terminal , pcontrol_terminal)

combinational_body ::= [198] [95LRM 8.1.4]   [13]
    table combinational_entry { combinational_entry } **endtable**

combinational_entry ::= [13] [95LRM 8.1.4] level_input_list : output_symbol ;   [14]

comment ::= [—] [95LRM 2.3] short_comment | long_comment   [15]

comment_text ::= [88, 168] [95LRM 2.3] { Any_ASCII_character }   [16]

concatenation ::= [21, 109, 146, 161] [95LRM 4.1.14] { expression { , expression } }   [17]

conditional_statement ::= [181] [95LRM 9.4]   [18]
    | **if** (expression) statement_or_null [**else** statement_or_null]

constant_expression ::= [see Table B.1] [95LRM 4.1] constant_primary   [19]
    | unary_operator constant_primary
    | constant_expression binary_operator constant_expression
    | constant_expression ? constant_expression : constant_expression
    | string

constant_mintypmax_expression ::= [34, 74, 139] [95LRM 4.3] constant_expression   [20]
    | constant_expression : constant_expression : constant_expression

constant_primary ::= [19] [95LRM 4.1] number | *parameter*_identifier   [21]
    | *constant*_concatenation | *constant*_multiple_concatenation

continuous_assign ::= [94] [95LRM 6.1]   [22]
    assign [drive_strength] [delay3] list_of_net_assignments ;

controlled_timing_check_event ::= [189] [95LRM 14.5.11]   [23]
    timing_check_event_control
        specify_terminal_descriptor [**&&&** timing_check_condition]

current_state ::= [165] [95LRM 8.1] level_symbol   [24]

```
data_source_expression ::= [53, 127] [95LRM 13.3.3] expression                      [25]

decimal_base ::= [28] [95LRM 2.5.1] 'd | 'D                                         [26]

decimal_digit ::= [206] [95LRM 2.5.1] 0 | 1 | 2 | 3 | 4 | 5 | 6 | 7 | 8 | 9 | 0     [27]

decimal_number ::= [114] [95LRM 2.5.1] [ sign ] unsigned_number                     [28]
   | [ size ] decimal_base unsigned_number

delay2 ::= [58, 202] [95LRM 7.1, 7.15]                                              [29]
   # delay_value | # ( delay_value [ , delay_value ] )

delay3 ::= [22, 58, 107] [95LRM 7.1, 7.15]                                          [30]
    # delay_value | # ( delay_value [ , delay_value [ , delay_value ] ] )

delay_control ::= [32] [95LRM 9.7, 9.7.1]                                           [31]
   # delay_value | # ( mintypmax_expression )

delay_or_event_control ::= [6, 112, 148] [95LRM 9.7]                                [32]
   delay_control | event_control | repeat ( expression ) event_control

delay_value ::= [29, 30, 31] [95LRM 7.1.3, 7.15]                                    [33]
   unsigned_number | parameter_identifier | constant_mintypmax_expression

description ::= [173] [95LRM 8.1, 12.1] module_declaration | udp_declaration        [34]

disable_statement³ ::= [181] [95LRM 11]                                             [35]
   | disable task_identifier ; | disable block_identifier ;

drive_strength ::= [22, 58, 107, 202] [95LRM 3.2.1, 3.4.2, 6.1.4]                   [36]
   ( strength0 , strength1 ) | ( strength1 , strength0 )
   | ( strength0 , highz1 ) | ( strength1 , highz0 )
   | ( highz1 , strength0 ) | ( highz0 , strength1 )

edge_control_specifier⁴ ::= [196] [95LRM 14.5.9] edge                               [37]
   [ edge_descriptor [ , edge_descriptor ] ]

edge_descriptor ::= [37] [95LRM 14.5.9] 01 | 10 | 0x | x1 | 1x | x0                 [38]

edge_identifier ::= [53, 127] [95LRM 14.5.9] posedge | negedge                      [39]

edge_indicator ::= [41] [95LRM 8.1, 8.1.6, 8.4]                                     [40]
   ( level_symbol level_symbol ) | edge_symbol

edge_input_list ::= [167] [95LRM 8.1, 8.1.6, 8.4]                                   [41]
   { level_symbol } edge_indicator { level_symbol }

edge_sensitive_path_declaration ::= [138, 183] [95LRM 13.3.3]                       [42]
   parallel_edge_sensitive_path_description = path_delay_value
   | full_edge_sensitive_path_description = path_delay_value
```

---

[3]The construct for disable_statement has a leading vertical bar, |, in Annex A of the 95 LRM.

[4]The outer brackets in term edge_control_specifier are lexical elements; the inner brackets are an optional item.

The BNF syntax on this page is from IEEE Std 1364-1995, Copyright © 1995. IEEE. All rights reserved.

```
edge_symbol ::= [40] [95LRM 8.1.6] r | R | f | F | p | P | n | N | *          [43]

enable_gatetype ::= [58] [95LRM 7.1] bufif0 | bufif1 | notif0 | notif1        [44]

enable_gate_instance ::= [58] [95LRM 7.1] [ name_of_gate_instance ]           [45]
   ( output_terminal , input_terminal , enable_terminal )

enable_terminal ::= [ 45, 98, 134] [95LRM 7.1] scalar_expression              [46]

escaped_identifier ::= [63] [95LRM 2.7.1]                                     [47]
   \ {Any_ASCII_character_except_white_space} white_space

event_control ::= [32] [95LRM 9.7] @ event_identifier | @ ( event_expression ) [48]

event_declaration ::= [7, 95] [95LRM 9.7.3]                                   [49]
   event event_identifier { , event_identifier } ;

event_expression ::= [48, 50] [95LRM 9.7] expression | event_identifier       [50]
   | posedge expression | negedge expression
   | event_expression or event_expression

event_trigger⁵ ::= [181] [95LRM 9.7.3] | -> event_identifier ;               [51]

expression ::= [see Table B.1] [95LRM 4] primary | unary_operator primary     [52]
   | expression binary_operator expression | expression ? expression : expression
   | string

full_edge_sensitive_path_description⁶ ::= [42] [95LRM 13.3.2]                 [53]
   ( [ edge_identifier ] list_of_path_inputs *>
      list_of_path_outputs
        [ polarity_operator ] : data_source_expression ) )

full_path_description ::= [171] [95LRM 13.3.2, 13.3.5]                         [54]
   ( list_of_path_inputs [ polarity_operator ] *> list_of_path_outputs )

function_call ::= [146] [95LRM 10.3.3]                                        [55]
   function_identifier ( expression { , expression} )
   | name_of_system_function [ ( expression { , expression} ) ]

function_declaration ::= [95] [95LRM 10.3.1]                                  [56]
   function [ range_or_type ] function_identifier ;
   function_item_declaration { function_item_declaration }
   statement
   endfunction

function_item_declaration ::= [56] [95LRM 10.3.1]                             [57]
   block_item_declaration | input_declaration
```

---

[5]The construct for `event_trigger` has a leading vertical bar, |, in Annex A of the 95 LRM.

[6]The term `full_edge_sensitive_path_description` contains an unmatched right parenthesis in Annex A and Section 13.3.3 of the 95 LRM. The examples in Section 13.3.3 of the 95 LRM do not include the final trailing right parenthesis.

```
gate_instantiation⁷ ::= [94] [95LRM 7.1] n_input_gatetype [ drive_strength ]        [58]
   [delay2] n_input_gate_instance { , n_input_gate_instance } ;
   | n_output_gatetype [ drive_strength ] [ delay2 ]
     n_output_gate_instance { , n_output_gate_instance } ;
   | enable_gatetype [ drive_strength ] [ delay3 ]
     enable_gate_instance { , enable_gate_instance} ;
   | mos_switchtype [ delay3 ]
     mos_switch_instance { , mos_switch_instance } ;
   | pass_switchtype pass_switch_instance { , pass_switch_instance } ;
   | pass_en_switchtype [ delay3 ]
     pass_en_switch_instance { , pass_en_switch_instance } ;
   | cmos_switchtype [ delay3 ]
     cmos_switch_instance { , cmos_switch_instance } ;
   | pullup [ pullup_strength ]
     pull_gate_instance { , pull_gate_instance } ;
   | pulldown [ pulldown_strength ]
     pull_gate_instance { , pull_gate_instance } ;

hex_base ::= [61] [95LRM 2.5.1] 'h | 'H                                             [59]

hex_digit ::= [61] [95LRM 2.5.1]                                                    [60]
   x | X | z | Z | 0 | 1 | 2 | 3 | 4 | 5 | 6 | 7 | 8 | 9
   | a | b | c | d | e | f | A | B | C | D | E | F

hex_number ::= [114] [95LRM 2.5.1] [ size ] hex_base hex_digit { _ | hex_digit }    [61]

identifier ::= [see Table B.1] [95LRM 2.7] IDENTIFIER [ { . IDENTIFIER } ]          [62]
   The period in identifier may not be preceded or followed by a space.

IDENTIFIER ::= [62] [95LRM 2.7] simple_identifier | escaped_identifier              [63]

initial_construct ::= [94] [95LRM 9.9.1] initial statement                          [64]

init_val ::= [200] [95LRM 8.1, 8.5]                                                 [65]
   1'b0 | 1'b1 | 1'bx | 1'bX | 1'B0 | 1'B1 | 1'Bx | 1'BX | 1 | 0

inout_declaration ::= [95, 190] [95LRM 12.3.2]                                      [66]
   inout [ range ] list_of_port_identifiers ;

inout_terminal ::= [134, 137] [95LRM 7.1]                                           [67]
   terminal_identifier | terminal_identifier [ constant_expression ]

input_declaration ::= [57, 95, 203] [95LRM 12.3.2]                                  [68]
   input [ range ] list_of_port_identifiers ;

input_identifier ::= [175] [95LRM 13.3.2]                                           [69]
   input_port_identifier | inout_port_identifier

input_terminal ::= [12, 45, 98, 116, 118] [95LRM 7.1] scalar_expression             [70]
```

---

⁷The term pass_en_switch_instance is defined as pass_enable_switch_instance.

```
integer_declaration ::= [7, 95] [95LRM 3.9] integer list_of_register_identifiers ;        [71]

level_input_list ::= [14, 167] [95LRM 8.1, 8.1.6] level_symbol { level_symbol }           [72]

level_symbol ::= [24, 40, 41, 72] [95LRM 8.1, 8.1.6] 0 | 1 | x | X | ? | b | B             [73]

limit_value ::= [152] [95LRM 13.7] constant_mintypmax_expression                           [74]

list_of_module_connections ::= [92] [95LRM 12.1.2, 12.3.3, 12.3.4]                          [75]
    ordered_port_connection { , ordered_port_connection }
  | named_port_connection { , named_port_connection }

list_of_net_assignments ::= [22] [95LRM 3.10] net_assignment { , net_assignment }          [76]

list_of_net_decl_assignments ::= [107] [95LRM 3.2.1]                                        [77]
    net_decl_assignment { , net_decl_assignment }

list_of_net_identifiers ::= [107] [95LRM 2.7] net_identifier { , net_identifier }          [78]

list_of_param_assignments ::= [129, 130] [95LRM 3.10]                                       [79]
    param_assignment { , param_assignment }

list_of_path_delay_expressions ::= [140] [95LRM 13.4]                                       [80]
    t_path_delay_expression
  | trise_path_delay_expression, tfall_path_delay_expression
  | trise_path_delay_expression, tfall_path_delay_expression, tz_path_delay_expression
  | t01_path_delay_expression, t10_path_delay_expression, t0z_path_delay_expression,
    tz1_path_delay_expression, t1z_path_delay_expression, tz0_path_delay_expression
  | t01_path_delay_expression, t10_path_delay_expression, t0z_path_delay_expression,
    tz1_path_delay_expression, t1z_path_delay_expression, tz0_path_delay_expression,
    t0x_path_delay_expression, tx1_path_delay_expression, t1x_path_delay_expression,
    tx0_path_delay_expression, txz_path_delay_expression, tzx_path_delay_expression

list_of_path_inputs ::= [53, 54] [95LRM 13.3.2]                                             [81]
    specify_input_terminal_descriptor { , specify_input_terminal_descriptor }

list_of_path_outputs ::= [53, 54] [95LRM 13.3.2]                                            [82]
    specify_output_terminal_descriptor { , specify_output_terminal_descriptor }

list_of_ports ::= [91] [95LRM 12] ( port { , port } )                                       [83]

list_of_port_identifiers ::= [66, 68, 123] [95LRM 12.3.2]                                   [84]
    port_identifier { , port_identifier }

list_of_real_identifiers ::= [155, 156] [95LRM 2.7]                                         [85]
    real_identifier { , real_identifier }

list_of_register_identifiers ::= [71, 160, 193] [95LRM 3.2.2]                               [86]
    register_name { , register_name }

list_of_specparam_assignments ::= [180] [95LRM 13.2]                                        [87]
    specparam_assignment { , specparam_assignment }

long_comment ::= [15] [95LRM 2.3] /* comment_text */                                        [88]
```

```
loop_statement ::= [181] [95LRM 9.6]                                        [89]
   | forever statement
   | repeat ( expression ) statement
   | while ( expression ) statement
   | for ( reg_assignment ; expression ; reg_assignment ) statement

mintypmax_expression ::= [31, 146] [95LRM 4.3] expression                   [90]
   | expression : expression : expression

module_declaration ::= [34] [95LRM 12.1] module_keyword module_identifier   [91]
   [ list_of_ports ] ; {module_item } endmodule

module_instance ::= [93] [95LRM 12.1, 12.1.2]                               [92]
   name_of_instance ( [ list_of_module_connections ] )

module_instantiation ::= [94] [95LRM 12.1.2]                               [93]
   module_identifier [ parameter_value_assignment ]
   module_instance { , module_instance } ;

module_item ::= [91] [95LRM 12.1]                                          [94]
   module_item_declaration | parameter_override
   | continuous_assign | gate_instantiation | udp_instantiation
   | module_instantiation | specify_block | initial_construct
   | always_construct

module_item_declaration ::= [94] [95LRM 12.1]                              [95]
   parameter_declaration | input_declaration
   | output_declaration | inout_declaration | net_declaration
   | reg_declaration | integer_declaration | real_declaration
   | time_declaration | realtime_declaration | event_declaration
   | task_declaration | function_declaration

module_keyword ::= [91] [95LRM 12.1] module | macromodule                  [96]

mos_switchtype ::= [58] [95LRM 7.1, 7.5] nmos | pmos | rnmos | rpmos        [97]

mos_switch_instance ::= [58] [95LRM 7.1]                                   [98]
   [ name_of_gate_instance ] ( output_terminal , input_terminal , enable_terminal )

multiple_concatenation⁸ ::= [21, 146] [95LRM 4.1.14]                       [99]
   { expression { expression { , expression } } }

named_port_connection ::= [75] [95LRM 12.1.2, 12.3.4]                      [100]
   . port_identifier ( [ expression ] )

name_of_gate_instance ::= [12, 45, 98, 116, 118, 134, 137, 151] [95LRM 7.1] [101]
   gate_instance_identifier [ range ]
```

---

[8]The two sets of outer braces (four) in the term multiple_concatenation are lexical elements; the inner braces (two) indicate an optional item.

```
name_of_instance ::= [92] [95LRM 12.1.2] module_instance_identifier [ range ]        [102]

name_of_system_function ::= [55] [95LRM 14] $identifier                              [103]
    Note: the $ in name_of_system_function may not be followed by a space.

name_of_udp_instance ::= [201] [95LRM 8.6] udp_instance_identifier [ range ]         [104]

ncontrol_terminal ::= [12] [95LRM 7.1] scalar_expression                             [105]

net_assignment ::= [76, 147] [95LRM 6.1, 9.3] net_lvalue = expression                [106]

net_declaration ::= [95] [95LRM 3.2.1]                                               [107]
    net_type [ vectored | scalared ] [ range ] [ delay3 ] list_of_net_identifiers ;
   | trireg [ vectored | scalared ]
     [ charge_strength ] [ range ] [ delay3 ] list_of_net_identifiers ;
   | net_type [ vectored | scalared ]
     [drive_strength] [range] [delay3] list_of_net_decl_assignments ;

net_decl_assignment ::= [77] [95LRM 3.2.1] net_identifier = expression               [108]

net_lvalue ::= [106, 147] [95LRM 6.1]                                                [109]
    net_identifier | net_identifier [ expression ]
   | net_identifier [ msb_constant_expression : lsb_constant_expression ]
   | net_concatenation

net_type ::= [107] [95LRM 3.2.1]                                                     [110]
    wire | tri | tri1 | supply0 | wand | triand | tri0 | supply1 | wor | trior

next_state ::= [165] [95LRM 8.1, 8.1.6] output_symbol | -                            [111]

non-blocking assignment⁹ ::= [181] [95LRM 9.2.2]                                     [112]
    reg_lvalue <= [ delay_or_event_control ] expression

notify_register ::= [189] [95LRM 14.5.10] register_identifier                        [113]

number ::= [21, 146] [95LRM 2.5]                                                     [114]
    decimal_number | octal_number | binary_number | hex_number | real_number

n_input_gatetype ::= [58] [95LRM 7.1] and | nand | or | nor | xor | xnor             [115]

n_input_gate_instance ::= [58] [95LRM 7.1]                                           [116]
    [ name_of_gate_instance ] ( output_terminal , input_terminal { , input_terminal } )

n_output_gatetype ::= [58] [95LRM 7.1] buf | not                                     [117]

n_output_gate_instance ::= [58] [95LRM 7.1]                                          [118]
    [ name_of_gate_instance ] ( output_terminal { , output_terminal } , input_terminal )

octal_base ::= [121] [95LRM 2.5.1] 'o | 'O                                           [119]

octal_digit ::= [121] [95LRM 2.5.1]                                                  [120]
    x | X | z | Z | 0 | 1 | 2 | 3 | 4 | 5 | 6 | 7
```

---

⁹The term, non(hyphen)blocking(space)assignment, is referenced as non(underscore)blocking(space)assign-ment.

```
octal_number ::= [114] [95LRM 2.5.1]                                        [121]
    [ size ] octal_base octal_digit { _ | octal_digit}

ordered_port_connection ::= [75] [95LRM 12.1.2, 12.3.3] [ expression ]       [122]

output_declaration ::= [95, 190, 203] [95LRM 12.3.2]                         [123]
    output [ range ] list_of_port_identifiers ;

output_identifier ::= [177] [95LRM 13.3.2]                                   [124]
    output_port_identifier | inout_port_identifier

output_symbol ::= [14, 111] [95LRM 8.1, 8.1.6] 0 | 1 | x | X                 [125]

output_terminal ::= [12, 45, 98, 116, 118, 151] [95LRM 7.1]                  [126]
    terminal_identifier | terminal_identifier [ constant_expression ]
```

parallel_edge_sensitive_path_description[10] ::= [42] [95LRM 13.3.2]   [127]
```
    ( [ edge_identifier ] specify_input_terminal_descriptor =>
    specify_output_terminal_descriptor
      [ polarity_operator ] : data_source_expression ) )

parallel_path_description ::= [171] [95LRM 13.3.2]                           [128]
    ( specify_input_terminal_descriptor
      [ polarity_operator ] => specify_output_terminal_descriptor )

parameter_declaration ::= [7, 95] [95LRM 3.10]                              [129]
    parameter list_of_param_assignments ;

parameter_override ::= [94] [95LRM 12.2] defparam list_of_param_assignments ; [130]

parameter_value_assignment ::= [93] [95LRM 12.1.2]                          [131]
    # ( expression { , expression } )

param_assignment ::= [79] [95LRM 3.10] parameter_identifier = constant_expression [132]

par_block ::= [181] [95LRM 9.8.2]                                           [133]
    fork [ : block_identifier { block_item_declaration } ] { statement } join
```

pass_enable_switch_instance[11] ::= [58] [95LRM 7.1]   [134]
```
    [ name_of_gate_instance ] ( inout_terminal , inout_terminal , enable_terminal )

pass_en_switchtype ::= [58] [95LRM 7.1]                                     [135]
    tranif0 | tranif1 | rtranif1 | rtranif0

pass_switchtype ::= [58] [95LRM 7.1] tran | rtran                           [136]

pass_switch_instance ::= [58] [95LRM 7.1]                                   [137]
    [ name_of_gate_instance ] ( inout_terminal , inout_terminal )
```

---

[10]The term `parallel_edge_sensitive_path_description` has an unmatched right parenthesis in Annex A and Section 13.3.3 of the 95 LRM. The examples in Section 13.3.3 do not include the final trailing right parenthesis.

[11]The term `pass_enable_switch_instance` is referenced as `pass_en_switch_instance`.

```
path_declaration¹² ::= [176] [95LRM 13.3] simple_path_declaration ;          [138]
    | edge_sensitive_path_declaration ; | state-dependent_path_declaration ;

path_delay_expression ::= [80] [95LRM 13.4] constant_mintypmax_expression    [139]

path_delay_value ::= [42, 171] [95LRM 13.4]                                  [140]
    list_of_path_delay_expressions | ( list_of_path_delay_expressions )

pcontrol_terminal ::= [12] [95LRM 7.1] scalar_expression                     [141]

polarity_operator ::= [53, 54, 127, 128] [95LRM 13.3.2] + | -               [142]

port ::= [83] [95LRM 12.3.1]                                                 [143]
    [ port_expression ] | . port_identifier ( [ port_expression ] )

port_expression ::= [143] [95LRM 12.3.1]                                     [144]
    port_reference | { port_reference { , port_reference } }

port_reference ::= [144] [95LRM 12.3.1] port_identifier                      [145]
    | port_identifier [ constant_expression ]
    | port_identifier [ msb_constant_expression : lsb_constant_expression ]

primary ::= [52] [95LRM 4] number | identifier | identifier [ expression ]   [146]
    | identifier [ msb_constant_expression : lsb_constant_expression ]
    | concatenation | multiple_concatenation | function_call
    | ( mintypmax_expression )

procedural_continuous_assignment¹³ ::= [181] [95LRM 9.3]                     [147]
    | assign reg_assignment ;
    | deassign reg_lvalue ; | force reg_assignment ;
    | force net_assignment ; | release reg_lvalue ;
    | release net_lvalue ;

procedural_timing_control_statement ::= [181] [95LRM 9.7]                    [148]
    delay_or_event_control statement_or_null

pulldown_strength ::= [58] [95LRM 7.1] ( strength0 , strength1 )             [149]
    | ( strength1 , strength0 ) | ( strength0 )

pullup_strength ::= [58] [95LRM 7.1] ( strength0 , strength1 )               [150]
    | ( strength1 , strength0 ) | ( strength1 )

pull_gate_instance ::= [58] [95LRM 7.1] [ name_of_gate_instance ] ( output_terminal )  [151]

pulse_control_specparam¹⁴ ::= [179] [95LRM 13.7]                            [152]
    PATHPULSE$ = ( reject_limit_value [ , error_limit_value ] ) ;
```

---

[12] The term state-dependent_path_declaration is defined as state_dependent_path_declaration.

[13] The construct for procedural_continuous_assignment has a leading vertical bar, |, in Annex A of the 95 LRM.

[14] The specparam PATHPULSE$ is shown in bold in the 95 LRM but is not a keyword.

```
     | PATHPULSE$specify_input_terminal_descriptor$specify_output_terminal_descriptor
       = ( reject_limit_value [ , error_limit_value ] ) ;
```

```
range ::= [66, 68, 101, 102, 104, 107, 123, 154, 160] [95LRM 7.1.5]                [153]
    [ msb_constant_expression : lsb_constant_expression ]
```

```
range_or_type ::= [56] [95LRM 10.3.1]                                              [154]
    range | integer | real | realtime | time
```

```
realtime_declaration ::= [7, 95] [95LRM 3.9] realtime list_of_real_identifiers ;   [155]
```

```
real_declaration ::= [7, 95] [95LRM 3.9] real list_of_real_identifiers ;           [156]
```

```
real_number15 ::= [114] [95LRM 2.5.1]                                              [157]
    [ sign ] unsigned_number . unsigned_number
    | [ sign ] unsigned_number [ . unsigned_number] e [ sign ] unsigned_number
    | [ sign ] unsigned_number [ . unsigned_number] e [ sign ] unsigned_number
```

```
register_name ::= [86] [95LRM 3.2.2] register_identifier                           [158]
    | memory_identifier [ upper_limit_constant_expression :
      lower_limit_constant_expression ]
```

```
reg_assignment ::= [89, 147] [95LRM 9.3] reg_lvalue = expression                   [159]
```

```
reg_declaration ::= [7, 95, 203] [95LRM 3.2.2]                                     [160]
    reg [ range ] list_of_register_identifiers ;
```

```
reg_lvalue ::= [6, 112, 147, 159] [95LRM 9.2.1]                                    [161]
    reg_identifier | reg_identifier [ expression ]
    | reg_identifier [ msb_constant_expression : lsb_constant_expression ]
    | reg_concatenation
```

```
scalar_constant ::= [163] [95LRM 2.5.1]                                            [162]
    1'b0 | 1'b1 | 1'B0 | 1'B1 | 'b0 | 'b1 | 'B0 | 'B1 | 1 | 0
```

```
scalar_timing_check_condition ::= [194] [95LRM 14.5.11] expression                 [163]
    | ~ expression | expression == scalar_constant
    | expression === scalar_constant
    | expression != scalar_constant
    | expression !== scalar_constant
```

```
sequential_body ::= [198] [95LRM 8.1, 8.1.4] [ udp_initial_statement ]             [164]
    table sequential_entry { sequential_entry } endtable
```

```
sequential_entry ::= [164] [95LRM 8.1, 8.3, 8.4]                                   [165]
    seq_input_list : current_state : next_state ;
```

```
seq_block ::= [181] [95LRM 9.8.1] begin [ : block_identifier                       [166]
    { block_item_declaration } ] { statement } end
```

---

[15]The term real_number has identical entries for the two forms of scientific notation in Annex A of the 95 LRM. In Section 2.5 of the 95 LRM the last alternative uses E (uppercase) instead of e (lowercase).

seq_input_list ::= [165] [95LRM 8.1] level_input_list | edge_input_list   [167]

short_comment ::= [15] [95LRM 2.3] **//** comment_text **\n**   [168]

sign ::= [28, 157] [95LRM 2.5.1] **+** | **-**   [169]

simple_identifier ::= [63] [95LRM 2.7] [a-zA-Z][a-zA-Z_$]   [170]

simple_path_declaration ::= [138, 183] [95LRM 13.3.2]   [171]
    parallel_path_description = path_delay_value
  | full_path_description = path_delay_value

size ::= [4, 28, 61, 121] [95LRM 2.5.1] unsigned_number   [172]

source_text ::= [−] [95LRM 2.1] { description }   [173]

specify_block ::= [94] [95LRM 13.1] **specify** [specify_item] **endspecify** [174]

specify_input_terminal_descriptor ::= [81, 127, 128, 152, 178] [95LRM 13.3.2]   [175]
    input_identifier
  | input_identifier [constant_expression]
  | input_identifier [*msb*_constant_expression : *lsb*_constant_expression]

specify_item ::= [174] [95LRM 13.1]   [176]
    specparam_declaration | path_declaration | system_timing_check

specify_output_terminal_descriptor ::= [82, 127, 128, 152, 178] [95LRM 13.3.2] [177]
    output_identifier
  | output_identifier [constant_expression]
  | output_identifier [*msb*_constant_expression : *lsb*_constant_expression]

specify_terminal_descriptor ::= [23, 195] [95LRM 13.3.2]   [178]
    specify_input_terminal_descriptor
  | specify_output_terminal_descriptor

specparam_assignment ::= [87] [95LRM 13.2]   [179]
    *specparam*_identifier **=** constant_expression | pulse_control_specparam

specparam_declaration ::= [176] [95LRM 13.2]   [180]
    specparam list_of_specparam_assignments ;

statement[16] ::= [1, 56, 64, 89, 133, 166, 182] [95LRM 9.1]   [181]
    blocking_assignment ; | non_blocking assignment ;
  | procedural_continuous_assignments ;
  | procedural_timing_control_statement | conditional_statement
  | case_statement | loop_statement | wait_statement
  | disable_statement | event_trigger | seq_block | par_block
  | task_enable | system_task_enable

---

[16]The term blocking(underscore)assignment is defined as blocking(space)assignment. The term non(underscore)blocking(space)assignment is a single term defined as non(hyphen)blocking(space)assignment. The term procedural_continuous_assignments (plural) is defined as procedural_continuous_assignment (singular).

```
statement_or_null¹⁷ ::= [8, 18, 148, 191, 207] [95LRM 9.1]              [182]
   statement | ;

state_dependent_path_declaration¹⁸ ::= [138] [95LRM 13.3.4]            [183]
     if ( conditional_expression ) simple_path_declaration
   | if ( conditional_expression ) edge_sensitive_path_declaration
   | ifnone simple_path_declaration

strength0 ::= [36, 149, 150] [95LRM 7.10]                              [184]
   supply0 | strong0 | pull0 | weak0

strength1 ::= [36, 149, 150] [95LRM 7.10]                              [185]
   supply1 | strong1 | pull1 | weak1

string ::= [19] [95LRM 2.6] " { Any_ASCII_Characters_except_new_line } "   [186]

system_task_enable ::= [181] [95LRM 2.7.3]                            [187]
   system_task_name [ ( expression { , expression } ) ] ;

system_task_name ::= [187] [95LRM 2.7.3] $identifier                  [188]
   Note: The $ may not be followed by a space.

system_timing_check¹⁹ ::= [176] [95LRM 14.5]                          [189]
   $setup ( timing_check_event , timing_check_event ,
     timing_check_limit [ , notify_register ] ) ;
   | $hold ( timing_check_event , timing_check_event ,
     timing_check_limit [ , notify_register ] ) ;
   | $period ( controlled_timing_check_event , timing_check_limit
     [ , notify_register ] ) ;
   | $width ( controlled_timing_check_event , timing_check_limit ,
     constant_expression [ , notify_register ] ) ;
   | $skew ( timing_check_event , timing_check_event ,
     timing_check_limit [ , notify_register ] ) ;
   | $recovery ( controlled_timing_check_event , timing_check_event ,
     timing_check_limit [ , notify_register ] ) ;
   | $setuphold ( timing_check_event , timing_check_event ,
     timing_check_limit , timing_check_limit [ , notify_register ] ) ;

task_argument_declaration²⁰ ::= [191?] [95LRM 10.2.1]                 [190]
   block_item_declaration | output_declaration | inout_declaration
```

---

[17]The term `statement_or_null` is equivalent to a statement term (which, when expanded, will be terminated by a semicolon) or the combination of nothing (null) followed by a semicolon.

[18]The term `state_dependent_path_declaration` is referenced as `state-dependent_path_declaration`.

[19]The names of the system timing check tasks are shown in bold in the 95 LRM but are not keywords.

[20]Annex A of the 95 LRM defines `task_argument_declaration`, which is not referenced in Annex A; see the footnote for the term `task_declaration`.

```
task_declaration²¹ ::= [95] [95LRM 10.2.1]                                           [191]
   task task_identifier ; {task_item_declaration} statement_or_null endtask

task_enable ::= [181] [95LRM 10.2.2]                                                 [192]
   task_identifier [ ( expression { , expression } ) ] ;

time_declaration ::= [7, 95] [95LRM 3.9] time list_of_register_identifiers ;         [193]

timing_check_condition ::= [23, 195] [95LRM 14.5.11]                                 [194]
   scalar_timing_check_condition | ( scalar_timing_check_condition )

timing_check_event ::= [189] [95LRM 14.5]                                            [195]
   [ timing_check_event_control ]
   specify_terminal_descriptor [ &&& timing_check_condition ]

timing_check_event_control ::= [23, 195] [95LRM 14.5]                                [196]
   posedge | negedge | edge_control_specifier

timing_check_limit ::= [189] [95LRM 14.5] expression                                 [197]

udp_body ::= [199] [95LRM 8.1] combinational_body | sequential_body                  [198]

udp_declaration ::= [34] [95LRM 8.1, 8.1.1]                                          [199]
   primitive udp_identifier ( udp_port_list ) ;
      udp_port_declaration { udp_port_declaration } udp_body
   endprimitive

udp_initial_statement ::= [164] [95LRM 8.1, 8.5]                                     [200]
   initial udp_output_port_identifier = init_val ;

udp_instance ::= [202] [95LRM 8.6]                                                   [201]
   [ name_of_udp_instance ]
   ( output_port_connection , input_port_connection { , input_port_connection } )

udp_instantiation ::= [94] [95LRM 8.6]                                               [202]
   udp_identifier [ drive_strength ] [ delay2 ] udp_instance { , udp_instance } ;

udp_port_declaration ::= [199] [95LRM 8.1]                                           [203]
   output_declaration | input_declaration | reg_declaration

udp_port_list ::= [199] [95LRM 8.1, 8.1.2]                                           [204]
   output_port_identifier , input_port_identifier { , input_port_identifier }

unary_operator ::= [19, 52] [95LRM 4.1]                                              [205]
   + | - | ! | ~ | & | ~& | | | ~| | ^ | ~^ | ^~

unsigned_number ::= [28, 33, 157, 172] [95LRM 2.5.1]                                 [206]
   decimal_digit { _ | decimal_digit }
```

---

[21]Annex A and Section 10.2.1 of the 95 LRM define task_declaration using the term task_item_declaration, which is not defined in Annex A. Section 10.2.1 defines task_item_declaration similarly to the Annex A definition of task_argument_declaration, but with the addition of the alternative term input_declaration.

wait_statement[22] ::= [181] [95LRM 9.7.5]   [207]
  | **wait** (expression) statement_or_null

white_space ::= [47] [95LRM 2.2] space | tab | newline   [208]

B.3   BNF Index

Table B.1 is an index to the 208 Verilog HDL BNF productions, as defined in Annex A of the 95 LRM. For example, to find the legal positions of wait_statement (rule 207) we look up 207 in Table B.1 and find rule 181 (statement), which is in turn referenced by rules 1, 56, 64, 89, 133, 166, and 182. Thus we know a wait statement is legal in the following places: always_construct (1), function_declaration (56), initial_construct (64), loop_statement (89), par_block (a parallel block, 133), seq_block (a sequential block, 166), and anywhere statement_or_null (182) is legal. Turning again to Table B.1 (or using the backward-pointing links in rule 182), we find statement_or_null (rule 182) is legal in the following places: 8 (case_item), 18 (conditional_statement), 148 (procedural_timing_control_statement), 191 (task_declaration), and 207 (wait_statement).

Table B.2 is a list of the 102 Verilog HDL keywords in the 95 LRM and an index to the rules that reference these keywords. Note the spelling of the keyword scalared (not scalered). For example, to find out how to use the keyword parameter to define a constant, we look up *parameter* in Table B.2 to find rule 129 (parameter_declaration), which includes a reference to section 3.10 of the 95 LRM. The index in this book will also help (the entry for *parameter* points you to examples in Section 11.2.4, "Numbers," in this case).

There are many Verilog tools currently available that use many versions of the Verilog language. Most tool vendors explain which of the Verilog constructs are supported; many use the 95 LRM BNF syntax in this explanation.

B.4   Verilog HDL LRM

An important feature of Verilog is the ability to extend tools by writing your own code and integrating it with a Verilog-based tool. For example, the following code calls a user-written system task, $hello:

```
initial $hello(a_reg);
```

Here is the C program, hello.c, that prints the full hierarchical name of the instance in which the Verilog code containing the call to $hello is located:

```
#include "veriuser.h"
#include "acc_user.h"
int hello()
```

---

[22]The construct for wait_statement has a leading vertical bar, |, in Annex A of the 95 LRM.

  The BNF syntax on this page is from IEEE Std 1364-1995, Copyright © 1995. IEEE. All rights reserved.

TABLE B.1   Index to Verilog HDL BNF rules (list of rules that reference a rule).

1	94	43	40	85	155, 156	127	42	169	28, 157
2	4	44	58	86	71, 160, 193	128	171	170	63
3	4	45	58	87	180	129	7, 95	171	138, 183
4	114	46	45, 98, 134	88	15	130	94	172	4, 28, 61, 121
5	19, 52	47	63	89	181	131	93	173	Highest-level
6	181	48	32	90	31, 146	132	79	174	94
7	57, 133, 166, 190	49	7, 95	91	34	133	181	175	81, 127, 128, 152, 178
8	9	50	48, 50	92	93	134	58	176	174
9	181	51	181	93	94	135	58	177	82, 127, 128, 152, 178
10	107	52	See below	94	91	136	58	178	23, 195
11	58	53	42	95	94	137	58	179	87
12	58	54	171	96	91	138	176	180	176
13	198	55	146	97	58	139	80	181	See below
14	13	56	95	98	58	140	42, 171	182	8, 18, 148, 191, 207
15	Not referenced	57	56	99	21, 146	141	12	183	138
16	88, 168	58	94	100	75	142	53, 54, 127, 128	184	36, 149, 150
17	21, 109, 146, 161	59	61	101	See below	143	83	185	36, 149, 150
18	181	60	61	102	92	144	143	186	19
19	See below	61	114	103	55	145	144	187	181
20	33, 74, 139	62	See below	104	201	146	52	188	187
21	19	63	62	105	12	147	181	189	176
22	94	64	94	106	76, 147	148	181	190	191 (See BNF footnote)
23	189	65	200	107	95	149	58	191	95
24	165	66	95, 190	108	77	150	58	192	181
25	53, 127	67	134, 137	109	106, 147	151	58	193	7, 95
26	28	68	57, 95, 203	110	107	152	179	194	23, 195
27	206	69	175	111	165	153	See below	195	189
28	114	70	See below	112	181	154	56	196	23, 195
29	58, 202	71	7, 95	113	189	155	7, 95	197	189
30	22, 58, 107	72	14, 167	114	21, 146	156	7, 95	198	199
31	32	73	24, 40, 41, 72	115	58	157	114	199	34
32	6, 112, 148	74	152	116	58	158	86	200	164
33	29, 30, 31	75	92	117	58	159	89, 147	201	202
34	173	76	22	118	58	160	7, 95, 203	202	94
35	181	77	107	119	121	161	6, 112, 147, 159	203	199
36	22, 58, 107, 202	78	107	120	121	162	163	204	199
37	196	79	129, 130	121	114	163	194	205	19, 52
38	37	80	140	122	75	164	198	206	28, 33, 157, 172
39	53, 127	81	53, 54	123	95, 190, 203	165	164	207	181
40	41	82	53, 54	124	177	166	181	208	47
41	167	83	91	125	14, 111	167	165		
42	138, 183	84	66, 68, 123	126	See below	168	15		

19	19, 20, 67, 109, 126, 132, 145, 146, 153, 158, 161, 175, 177, 179, 189
52	6, 8, 9, 17, 18, 25, 32, 50, 52, 55, 89, 90, 99, 100, 106, 108, 109, 112, 122, 131, 146, 159, 161, 163, 187, 192, 197, 207
62	21, 35, 48, 49, 50, 51, 55, 56, 67, 69, 78, 84, 85, 91, 93, 100, 101, 102, 103, 104, 108, 109, 113, 124, 126, 132, 133, 143, 145, 146, 158, 161, 166, 179, 188, 191, 192, 199, 200, 202, 204
70	12, 45, 98, 116, 118
101	12, 45, 98, 116, 118, 134, 137, 151
126	12, 45, 98, 116, 118, 151
153	66, 68, 101, 102, 104, 107, 123, 154, 160
181	1, 56, 64, 89, 133, 166, 182

TABLE B.2   Verilog HDL keywords and index (list of rules that reference a keyword).

```
{ handle mod_handle; char *full_name; acc_initialize();
mod_handle = acc_handle_tfarg(1);
io_printf("Hello from: %s\n", acc_fetch_fullname(mod_handle));
acc_close(); }
```

The details of how to compile and link your program with the Verilog executable depend on the particular tool; the names, functions, and parameters of ACC routines, the header files, `veriuser.h` and `acc_user.h` (most companies include these with their Verilog products), as well as older TF routines and the newer VPI routines are described in detail in Sections 17–23 of the 95 LRM.

Annex F of the 95 LRM describes widely used Verilog system tasks and functions that are not required to be supported as part of IEEE Std 1364-1995. Table B.3 summarizes these tasks and functions. Annex G of the 95 LRM describes additional compiler directives that are not part of IEEE Std 1364-1995 and are not often used by ASIC designers. Two directives, `default_decay_time` and `default_trireg_strength`, are used to model charge decay and the strength of high-impedance `trireg` nets. Four more compiler directives: `delay_mode_distributed`, `delay_mode_path`, `delay_mode_unit`, and `delay_mode_zero` are used to specify the delay mode for modules.

TABLE B.3   System tasks and functions (not required in IEEE Std 1364-1995).

`$countdrivers ( net, [ net_is_forced, number_of_01x_drivers, number_of_0_drivers,`
`           number_of_1_drivers, number_of_x_drivers ] ) ;`
Returns a 0 if there is no more than one driver on the net and returns a 1 otherwise (indicating contention).

`$getpattern ( mem_element ) ; // Drive a pattern from an indexed memory.`
Example: **assign** `{i1, i2, i3, i4} = $getpattern ( mem [ index ] )`

`$input ("filename"); // Allows input from file rather than terminal.`
`$key [ ( "filename" ) ] ; $nokey ; // Enable/disable key file in interactive mode.`
`$list [ ( hierarchical_name ) ] ; // List current or specified object.`
`$log [ ( "filename" ) ] ; $nolog ; // Enable/disable log file for standard output.`

`$reset [ ( stop_value [ , reset_value , [ diagnostics_value ] ] ) ] ; // Reset time.`
`$reset_count ; // Count the number of resets.`
`$reset_value ; // Pass information prior to reset to simulation after reset.`

`$save ( "file_name" ) ; // Save simulation for later restart.`
`$restart ( "file_name" ) ; // Restart simulation from saved file.`
`$incsave ( "incremental_file_name" ) ; // Save only changes since last $save`

`$scale ( hierarchical_name ) ; // Convert to time units of invoking module.`
`$scope ( hierarchical_name ) ; // Sets the specified level of hierarchy as current scope.`
`$showscopes [ ( n ) ]; // Show scope (n = none or zero) else show all items below scope.`
`$showvars [ ( list_of_variables ) ] ; // Show status of scope or specified variables.`

`$sreadmemb ( mem_name , start_address , finish_address , string { , string } ) ;`
`$sreadmemh ( mem_name , start_address , finish_address , string { , string } ) ;`
Load data into `mem_name` from character string (same format as `$readmemb/h`).

B.5   Bibliography

There are fewer books available on Verilog than on VHDL. The best reference book is the IEEE Verilog HDL LRM [IEEE 1364-1995]; it is detailed as well as containing many examples. In addition to the references given in Chapter 11, the following books concentrate on Verilog: Sternheim, Singh, and Trivedi [1990] (Yatin Trivedi was the technical editor for the 95 LRM); Thomas and Moorby [1991]; Smith [1996]; and Golze and Blinzer [1996]. Capilano Computing Systems has produced a book to accompany its Verilog Modeler product [Capilano, 1997].

Sandstrom compiled an interesting cross-reference between Verilog and VHDL (a 2.5 page table listing the correspondence between major constructs in both languages) in a pull-out supplement to *Integrated System Design Magazine*. An electronic version of this article is at http://www.isdmag.com (the article is labeled January 1996, but filed under October 1995). Other online articles related to Verilog at www.isdmag.com, include case studies of Sun Microsystems' ULTRASparc-1 (June 1996) and Hewlett–Packard's PA-8000 (January, February, and March 1997); both CPUs were designed with Verilog behavioral models. The March 1997 issue also contains an article on the recent history and the future plans of Open Verilog International (OVI). OVI helped create IEEE Std 1364-1995 and sponsored the annual *International Verilog HDL Conference* (IVC). In 1997 the IVC merged with the VHDL International Users' Forum (VIUF) to form the *IVC/VIUF Conference* (see http://www.hdlcon.org).

In January of 1995 OVI reactivated the Technical Coordinating Committee (TCC) to recommend updates and changes to Verilog HDL. The TCC comprises technical subcommittees (TSC), which are developing a delay calculator standard (LM-TSC), analog extensions to Verilog HDL (VA-TSC), an ASIC library modeling standard (PS-TSC), cycle-based simulation standard (VC-TSC), timing-constraint formats (VS-TSC), as well as Verilog language enhancements and extensions (VD-TSC). Links and information about OVI are available at http://www.avanticorp.com and http://www.chronologic.com. The OVI web site is http://www.verilog.org/ovi. Information on the activities of the OVI committees is available at the Meta-Software site, ftp://ftp.metasw.com/pub.

The work of the OVI and IEEE groups is related. For example, the IEEE Design Automation Standards Committee (DASC) contains the Verilog Working Group (PAR 1364), the Circuit Delay and Power Calculation (DPC) System Study Group (P1481), as well as the VHDL and other WGs. Thus, the OVI DC-TSC directory contains the Standard Delay Calculation System (DCS) Specification (v1.0) approved by OVI/CFI and currently being studied by the IEEE DPC Study Group. DCS provides a standard system for designers to calculate chip delay and power using the following methods: Delay Calculation Language (DCL) from IBM and CFI, Detailed Standard Parasitic Format (DSPF) and Reduced Standard Parasitic Format (RSPF) from Cadence Design Systems (combined into a new Standard Parasitics Exchange Format, SPEF), and Physical Design Exchange Format (PDEF) from Synopsys. The current IEEE standardization work is expanding the scope to add power calculation. Thus, useful information relating to Verilog may be found at the VHDL site, VIUF Internet Services (VIIS at http://www.vhdl.org), as well as the OVI site.

Two usenet newsgroups are related to Verilog: comp.lang.verilog and comp.cad.synthesis. In January of 1997 the Verilog news archive was lost due to a disk problem. While attempts are made to restore the archive, the Verilog Frequently Asked Questions (FAQ) list is still available at http://www.lib.ox.ac.uk/internet/news/faq/archive/verilog-faq.html. A list of CAD-related newsgroups (including comp.lang.verilog) is maintained at Sun Microsystems' DACafe (http://www.ibsystems.com/DACafe/TECHNICAL/Resources/NewsGps.html. Sun (~/DACafe/USERSGROUPS) also maintains the following user groups that often discuss Verilog: Cadence, Mentor Graphics, Synopsys, VeriBest, and Viewlogic. A number of tools and resources are available on the World Wide Web, including Verilog modes for the emacs editor; Verilog preprocessors in Perl and C (which allow the use of `define and `ifdef with logic synthesis tools, for example); and demonstration versions of the following simulators: Viper from InterHDL (http://www.interhdl.com) and VeriWell from Wellspring Solutions (http://www.wellspring.com). VeriWell now supports the Verilog PLI, including the acc and tf routines in IEEE Std 1364-1995 (requiring Visual C++ 4.0 or newer for the Windows version, Code Warrior 9 or newer for the Macintosh, and GNU C 2.7.0 or newer for the Linux and Sparc versions).

Several personal Web pages focus on Verilog HDL; these change frequently but can be found by searching. Actel has placed a number of Verilog examples (including synthesizable code for a FIFO and a RAM) at its site: `http://wwwtest.actel.com/HLD/verimain.html`. Many universities maintain Web pages for Verilog-related classes. Examples are the Web site for the ee282 class at Stanford (`http://lummi.Stanford.EDU/class/ee282`), which contains Verilog models for the DLX processor in the second edition of Hennessy and Patterson's "Computer Architecture: A Quantitative Approach"; and course material for 18-360, "Introduction to Computer-Aided Digital Design," by Prof. Don Thomas at `http://www.ece.cmu.edu`.

B.6 References

Page numbers in brackets after a reference indicate its location in the chapter body.

Capilano. 1997. *LogicWorks Verilog Modeler: Interactive Circuit Simulation Software for Windows and Macintosh*. Menlo Park, CA: Capilano Computing, 102 p. ISBN 0201895854. TK7888.4.L64 (as cataloged by the LOC). Addison-Wesley also gives the following additional ISBN numbers for this work: ISBN 0-201-49885-5 (Windows book and software), ISBN 0-201-49884-7 (Macintosh book and software); also available bundled with LogicWorks 3: ISBN 0-201-87436-9 (Macintosh), ISBN 0-201-87437-7 (Windows).

Golze, U., and P. Blinzer. 1996. *VLSI Chip Design with the Hardware Description Language VERILOG: An Introduction Based on a Large RISC Processor Design*. New York: Springer, 358 p. ISBN 3540600329. TK7874.75.G65. Four pages of references. Includes a version of VeriWell from Wellsprings Solutions.

IEEE 1364-1995. *IEEE Standard Description Language Based on the Verilog® Hardware Description Language*. 688 p. ISBN 1-55937-727-5. IEEE Ref. SH94418-NYF. Published by The IEEE, Inc., 345 East 47th Street, New York, NY 10017, USA. Inside the United States, IEEE standards may be ordered at 1-800-678-4333. See also `http://www.ieee.org` and `http://stdsbbs.ieee.org`. This standard was approved by the IEEE on 12 December, 1995; and approved by ANSI on 1 August, 1996 (and thus these two organizations have different publication dates). Contents: overview (4 pages); lexical conventions (8 pages); data types (13 pages); expressions (18 pages); scheduling semantics (5 pages); assignments (4 pages); gate and switch level modeling (31 pages); user-defined primitives (11 pages); behavioral modeling (26 pages); tasks and functions (6 pages); disabling of named blocks and tasks (1 page); hierarchical structures (16 pages); specify blocks (18 pages); system tasks and functions (35 pages); value change dump file (11 pages); compiler directives (8 pages); PLI TF and ACC interface mechanism (6 pages); using ACC routines (36 pages); ACC routine definitions (178 pages); using TF routines (5 pages); TF routine definitions (76 pages); using VPI routines (6 pages); VPI routine definitions (25 pages); formal syntax definition; list of keywords; system tasks and functions; compiler directives; `acc_user.h`; `veriuser.h`; `vpi_user.h`. [p. 979]

Smith, D. J. 1996. *HDL Chip Design: A Practical Guide for Designing, Synthesizing, and Simulating ASICs and FPGAs using VHDL or Verilog*. Madison, AL: Doone Publications, 448 p. ISBN 0965193438. TK7874.6.S62.

Sternheim, E., R. Singh, and Y. Trivedi. 1990. *Digital Design with Verilog HDL*. Cupertino, CA: Automata Publishing, 215 p. ISBN 0962748803. TK7885.7.S74.

Thomas, D. E., and P. Moorby. 1991. *The Verilog Hardware Description Language*. Boston, MA: Kluwer, 223 p. ISBN 0-7923-9126-8, TK7885.7.T48 (1st ed.). ISBN 0-7923-9523-9 (2nd ed.). ISBN 0792397231 (3rd ed.).

GLOSSARY OF SYMBOLS AND ACRONYMS

Symbols

A_0, parameter in input-slope delay model 673
A_1, parameter in input-slope delay model 673
A_D, transistor drain area 124
A_S, transistor source area 124
β_n, transistor gain factor 44
C, transistor gate capacitance 43
C_{BD}, bulk-to-drain capacitance 123
C_{BDJ}, bulk-to-drain junction area capacitance 123
C_{BDSW}, bulk-to-drain junction sidewall capacitance 123
C_{BS}, bulk-to-source capacitance 123
C_{BSJ}, bulk-to-source junction area capacitance 123
$C_{BDJGATE}$, bulk-to-drain channel-edge capacitance 123
$C_{BSJGATE}$, bulk-to-drain channel-edge capacitance 123
C_{BSSW}, bulk-to-source junction sidewall capacitance 123
C_{GB}, gate-to-bulk capacitance 123
C_{GBOV}, gate-to-bulk overlap capacitance 123
C_{GD}, gate-to-drain variable capacitance 123
C_{GDOV}, gate-to-drain overlap capacitance 123
C_{GS}, gate-to-source capacitance 123
C_{GSOV}, gate-to-source overlap capacitance 123
C_{inv}, input capacitance of minimum-size inverter 131
C_{JGATE}, channel edge capacitance 124
C_L, output load capacitance 138
C_O, transistor gate capacitance (calculated using effective gate width and effective gate length) 126
C_{out}, extrinsic output capacitance 118
C_{ox}, gate capacitance per unit area 43
C_p, intrinsic output capacitance 118
C_R, critical ramp delay in input-slope model 673
C_S, transistor channel–bulk depletion capacitance 126
D, delay in input-slope model 673
D, path delay in logical effort model 136
D_0, experimentally determined factor in input-slope delay model 673
D_0, parameter in input-slope delay model 673
D_1, parameter in input-slope delay model 673

d_A, parameter in input-slope delay model 673
d_D, parameter in input-slope delay model 673
D_{t0}, time from the beginning of the input to the beginning of the output (input-slope delay model) 672
D_{t1}, time from the beginning of the input to the end of the output (input-slope delay model) 672
E, electric field (vector) 42
ε_0, vacuum permittivity 104
ε_r, relative permittivity of silicon 104
ε_{Si}, permittivity of silicon 104
ε_{ox}, permittivity of silicon dioxide 43
E_x, horizontal component of electric field in a transistor 42
F, path effort 139
f, effort delay 131
ϕ_0, surface potential 104
G, path logical effort 138
γ, back-gate bias coefficient 104
g, logical effort 131
H, path electrical effort 139
h, electrical effort 131
h_i, stage electrical effort 139
$I_{DS(sat)}$, transistor drain–source saturation current 44
I_{DSn}, transistor drain–source current 42
I_R, time from the beginning to the end of the input ramp (input-slope delay model) 672
k'_n, process transconductance parameter 44
L, transistor length 43
L_D, lateral diffusion 123
L_{eff}, transistor effective gate length 45
μ_n, electron mobility 42
μ_p, hole mobility 42
N, number of inverters in an inverter chain 140
n, number of inputs to a logic cell 133
O_R, output ramp delay in input-slope model 673
P, path parasitic delay 139
p, parasitic delay 132
P_D, transistor drain perimeter (excluding channel edge) 124
P_S, transistor source perimeter (excluding channel edge) 124
Q, path nonideal delay 139

D

DAC, Design Automation Conference 851
DASC, Design Automation Standards Committee 998
DASS, Design Automation Standards Subcommittee 801
DC, direct current 937
DCL, Delay Calculation Language 998
DCS, Delay Calculation System 998
DEF, design-exchange format 897
DEL, delete 400
DELTA, SPICE parameter 693
DES, data encryption standard 639
DIP, dual-in-line package 714
DMA, direct memory access 18
DoD, (U.S.) Department of Defense 379
DP, datapath 9
DPC, Delay and Power Calculation 998
DRAM, dynamic random-access memory 3
DRC, design-rule check 944
DS, SPICE parameter 706
DSPF, detailed SPF (standard parasitic format) 943
DUM1, SPICE parameter 706
DUT, device under test 766

E

E2W3, Electrical Engineering on the World Wide Web 37
ECL, emitter-coupled logic 2
EDA, electronic design automation 21
EDAC, Electronic Design Automation Companies 37
EEPROM, electrically erasable PROM 15
EIA, Electronic Industries Association 37
emf, electromotive force 691
EOS, electrical overstress 101
EPLD, erasable PLD 15
EPROM, electrically programmable read-only memory 15
ESD, electrostatic discharge 100, 864
ETA, SPICE parameter 693
EXOR, exclusive-OR 69

F

FA, full adder 75
FAMOS, floating-gate avalanche MOS 175
FAN, fanout-oriented test generation 761
FAQ, frequently asked questions 321
FEOL, front end of the line 60
FF, form feed 391, 400
FIFO, first-in first-out register 98
FIT, failures in time 737
FO, fanout 856

FOX, field oxide 52
FPU, floating-point unit 18
FS, ASCII control character (FSP in VHDL) 400
FSB, functional system block 7
FSM, finite-state machine 605

G

GA, gate array 11
GaAs, gallium arsenide 36
GAMMA, SPICE parameter 693
GB, gain–bandwidth product 251
GDS, small-signal drain–source conductance, SPICE output parameter 122
GM, small-signal transconductance, SPICE output parameter 122
GMB, small-signal back-gate transconductance, SPICE output parameter 122
GND, negative supply voltage 40
GRC, global-routing cell 920
GS, ASCII control character (GSP in VHDL) 400
GTL, Gunning transistor logic 242

H

HBM, human-body model 101
HDL, hardware description language 300
HT, horizontal tabulation 391
HTTP, HyperText Transfer Protocol 37
HVH, horizontal-vertical-horizontal 933

I

ICCAD, International Conference on Computer-Aided Design 956
ICCD, International Conference on Computer Design 114
IDCODE, device identification register 716
IDD, supply current 743
IDDQ, quiescent supply current (IDD) 743
IEC, International Electrotechnical Committee 101
IEEE, Institute of Electrical and Electronics Engineers 3
ILD, inter-level dielectric 58
IMO, inter-metal oxide 58
IOB, input/output block 258
IOC, I/O Control Block 261
IOE, I/O Element 261
IR, instruction register 716
IRE, Institute of Radio Engineers 114
ISAC, VHDL Issues Screening and Analysis Committee 976
ISBN, International Standard Book Number vii
ISI, Information Sciences Institute 37
ISP, in-system programming 172

W

X

INDEX

Page references in bold refer to principal entries. For acronyms see the glossary.

Symbols

(ab), *, or ?, in a Verilog UDP table 511
?, use of, in Verilog 507
\
    use of, in Verilog 482
    use of, in VHDL 392
{ }
    use of, in Verilog BNF 979
    use of, in VHDL BNF 962
See also characters; symbol

Numerics

1076, IEEE VHDL standard 380
1164, IEEE VHDL logic system 654
2.5-layer routing 933
22V10, programmable logic device 211
2-bit, or (7, 3), full adder 93
2LM, 2-layer metal 58
3 to 2 compressor 90
3LM, 3-layer metal 58
74AS4374, metastable-hardened TTL flip-flop 253
74LS74, TTL flip-flop metastability 253
87 LRM (VHDL) 380, 961
93 LRM (VHDL) 380
95 LRM (Verilog HDL) 479, 979
95 LRM (VHDL) 961

A

ABEL hardware design language 300, 346
absolute value operator, VHDL 431
abstract literals, in VHDL 393
AC supply, for I/O circuits 100
access routines (ACC), Verilog 541, **996**
    acc_close 994
    acc_fetch_fullname 994
    acc_handle_tfarg 994
    acc_initialize 994
    acc_user.h 996
access types, in VHDL 412

accumulator, description of 98, 383
activation
    energy, in the Arrhenius equation 736
    of a fault 757
'ACTIVE, VHDL attribute 421
active
    clock edge, of a flip-flop 73
    extension, in design rules 61
    mask layer 52
activity-induced clock skew 936
actual times, in zero-slack algorithm 891
actuals, VHDL
    and locals, in a port map 407
    as ports 395
    declaration as parameters 416
    used as subprogram parameters 426
ad hoc test methods 764
adder 75–86
    addend 78
    adder/subtracter 97
    augend 78
    Brent–Kung 83
    carry bypass 81
    carry completion 86
    carry lookahead 83
    carry propagate 81
    carry save 80
    carry select 83
    carry skip 82
    conditional sum **83**, 112
    delete signal 79
    full adder 75
    generate signal 79
    kill signal 79
    Manchester carry chain 81
    overflow signals, in a datapath 77
    overflow, in Verilog (exercise) 635
    parallel 86
    propagate signal 79
    ripple carry **75**, 603
    serial 86, 604
    See also arithmetic; multiplier; subtracter
adding operators, VHDL 430
addition
    in Verilog **493**, 588, 592, 620, 631, 633

    in Verilog (exercise) 544, 550
    in VHDL 381, 431, **432**, 434, 444, 449, 597, 603
address contention, in RAM 102, 612
adiabatic logic (exercise) 843
adjacent encoding, for FSM synthesis 606
aggregate notation, VHDL 413, 471, 616
algorithms, in design automation 808
alias declaration, in VHDL 418
aliased
    error patterns, in testing 768
    nets, in schematic entry 341
all-ones detector, description of 98
all-zeros detector, description of 98
Alta Frequenza, as a source of information on computer-arithmetic architectures 114
alternative connectors, in a logic cell 876
ambient temperature, in specifications 201, 672
Analog Extensions, VHDL, IEEE working group 975
analog VDD 866
analysis phase
    in logic synthesis 564
    in simulation 380
AND plane, in a PLA or PAL 15, **211**
AND-OR-INVERT logic cells 60
angstrom, unit of measure 50
annex, in Verilog LRM 979
anonymous subtype, in VHDL 413
ANSI A–E, schematic sheet sizes 328
antifuse
    as an FPGA technology 170
    oxide–nitride–oxide dielectric 170
    resistance 170, 172, 283
AOI logic-cell family 63
appendix, in VHDL LRM 979
application, of faults 740
application-specific IC (ASIC)
    core limited 841
    definition of 1
    foundry 28
    NASA design guide 37
    package limited 32
    pad limited 841
    vendor 27